Feature Extraction and Image Processing for Computer Vision

Feature Extraction and Image Processing for Computer Vision

Fourth Edition

Mark S. Nixon Electronics and Computer Science, University of Southampton

Alberto S. Aguado Foundry, London

Academic Press is an imprint of Elsevier
125 London Wall, London EC2Y 5AS, United Kingdom
525 B Street, Suite 1650, San Diego, CA 92101, United States
50 Hampshire Street, 5th Floor, Cambridge, MA 02139, United States
The Boulevard, Langford Lane, Kidlington, Oxford OX5 1GB, United Kingdom

Library of Congress Cataloging-in-Publication Data
A catalog record for this book is available from the Library of Congress

British Library Cataloguing-in-Publication Data
A catalogue record for this book is available from the British Library

ISBN: 978-0-12-814976-8

For information on all Academic Press publications visit our website at https://www.elsevier.com/books-and-journals

Publisher: Mara Conner
Acquisition Editor: Tim Pitts
Editorial Project Manager: Joanna M. Collett
Production Project Manager: Anitha Sivaraj
Cover Designer: Alan Studholme

Typeset by TNQ Technologies

We would like to dedicate this book to our parents. To Gloria and to Joaquin Aguado, and to the late Brenda and Ian Nixon.

Contents

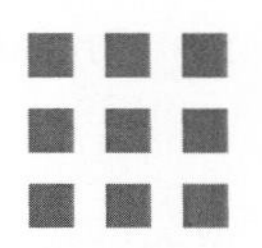

Preface

What is new in the fourth edition?

Society makes increasing use of image processing and computer vision: manufacturing systems, medical image analysis, robotic cars, and biometrics are splendid examples of where society benefits from this technology. To achieve this there has been, and continues to be, much research and development. The research develops into books, and so the books need updating. We have always been interested to note that our book contains stock image processing and computer vision techniques which are yet to be found in other regular textbooks (OK, some are to be found in specialist books, though these rarely include much tutorial material). This was true of the previous editions and certainly occurs here.

A big change in the Fourth Edition is the move to Python and Matlab, to replace the earlier use of Mathcad and Matlab. We have reordered much of the material and added new material where appropriate. There continue to be many new techniques for feature extraction and description. There has been quite a revolution in image processing and computer vision whilst the Fourth Edition was in process, namely the emergence of deep learning. This is noted throughout, and a new chapter is added on this topic. As well as deep learning, other additions include filtering techniques (non-local means and bilateral filtering), keypoint detectors, saliency operators, optical flow techniques, feature descriptions (Krawtchouk moments), region-based analysis (watershed, MSER and superpixels), space–time interest points and more distance measures (histogram intersection, Chi^2 (χ^2) and the earth mover's distance). We do not include statistical pattern recognition approaches, and for that it is best to look elsewhere (this book would otherwise be enormous). Our interest here is in the implementation and usage of feature extraction. As such, this book—IOHO—remains the most up-to-date text in feature extraction and image processing in computer vision.

As there are four editions now, it is appropriate to have a recap on the previous additions. Each edition corrected the previous production errors, some of which we must confess are our own, and included more tutorial material where appropriate. (If you find an error, there is a promise of free beer in the next section.) The completely new material in the Third Edition was on moving object detection, tracking and description. We also extended the book to use colour, and more modern techniques for object extraction and description especially those capitalising on wavelets and on scale space. The Second Edition updated and extended with new material on smoothing, geometric active contours, keypoint detection and moments. Some material has been filtered out at each stage to retain consistency. Our apologies if your favourite, or your own, technique has been omitted. Feature extraction and image processing is as large as it is enjoyable.

Why did we write this book?

We always expected to be asked: 'why on earth write a new book on computer vision?', and we have been. Fair question: there are already many good books on computer vision already out in the bookshops, as you will find referenced later, so why add to them. Part of the answer is that any textbook is a snapshot of material that exists prior to it. Computer vision, the art of processing images stored within a computer, has seen a considerable amount of research by highly qualified people, and the volume of research would appear even to have increased in recent years. That means many new techniques have been developed, and many of the more recent approaches have yet to migrate to textbooks. It is not just the new research: part of the speedy advance in computer vision technique has left some areas covered only in scanty detail. By the nature of research, one cannot publish material on technique that is seen more to fill historical gaps, rather than to advance knowledge. This is again where a new text can contribute.

Finally, the technology itself continues to advance. This means that there is new hardware, new programming languages and new programming environments. In particular for computer vision, the advance of technology means that computing power and memory are now relatively cheap. It is certainly considerably cheaper than when computer vision was starting as a research field. One of the authors here notes that his phone has more considerably more memory, is faster, has bigger disk space and better graphics than the computer that served the entire university of his student days. And he is not that old! One of the more advantageous recent changes brought by progress has been the development of mathematical programming systems. These allow us to concentrate on mathematical technique itself, rather than on implementation detail. There are several sophisticated flavours of which Matlab, one of the chosen vehicles here, is (arguably) the most popular. We have been using these techniques in research and in teaching, they have been of considerable benefit there. In research, they help us to develop technique faster and to evaluate its final implementation. For teaching, the power of a modern laptop and a mathematical system combines to show students, in lectures and in study, not only how techniques are implemented but also how and why they work with an explicit relation to conventional teaching material.

We wrote this book for these reasons. There is a host of material we could have included but chose to omit; the taxonomy and structure we use to expose the subject is of our own construction. By virtue of the enormous breadth of the subject of image processing and computer vision, we restricted the focus to feature extraction and image processing in computer vision for this has not only been the focus of our research, and it is also where the attention of established textbooks, with some exceptions, can be rather sparse. It is, however, one of the prime targets of applied computer vision, so would benefit from better attention. We have aimed to clarify some of its origins and development, whilst also exposing implementation using mathematical systems. As such, we have written this text with our original aims in mind and maintained the approach through the later editions.

The book and its support

Each chapter of this book presents a package of information concerning feature extraction in image processing and computer vision. Each package is developed from its origins and later referenced to material that is more recent. Naturally, there is often theoretical development prior to implementation. We provide working implementations of most of the major techniques we describe, and applied them to process a selection of imagery. Though the focus of our own work has been more in analysing medical imagery or in biometrics (the science of recognising people by behavioural or physiological characteristics, like face recognition), the techniques are general and can migrate to other application domains.

You will find a host of further supporting information at the book's website: https://www.southampton.ac.uk/~msn/book/. First, you will find the Matlab and Python implementations that support the text so that you can study the techniques described herein. The website will be kept up-to-date as possible, for it also contains links to other material such as websites devoted to techniques and to applications, as well as to available software and on-line literature. Finally, any errata will be reported there. It is our regret and our responsibility that these will exist, and our inducement for their reporting concerns a pint of beer. If you find an error that we do not know about (not typos like spelling, grammar and layout) then use the mailto on the website and we shall send you a pint of good English beer, free!

There is a certain amount of mathematics in this book. The target audience is third or fourth year students in BSc/BEng/MEng/MSc in electrical or electronic engineering, software engineering and computer science, or in mathematics or physics, and this is the level of mathematical analysis here. Computer vision can be thought of as a branch of applied mathematics, though this does not really apply to some areas within its remit, and certainly applies to the material herein. The mathematics essentially concerns mainly calculus and geometry though some of it is rather more detailed than the constraints of a conventional lecture course might allow. Certainly, not all the material here is covered in detail in undergraduate courses at Southampton.

The book starts with an overview of computer vision hardware, software and established material, with reference to the most sophisticated vision system yet 'developed': the human vision system. Though the precise details of the nature of processing that allows us to see have yet to be determined, there is a considerable range of hardware and software that allows us to give a computer system the capability to acquire, process and reason with imagery, the function of 'sight'. The first chapter also provides a comprehensive bibliography of material you can find on the subject, not only including textbooks, and also available software and other material. As this will no doubt be subject to change, it might well be worth consulting the website for more up-to-date information. The preferences for journal references are those which are likely to be found in local university libraries or on the web, *IEEE Transactions* in particular. These are often subscribed to as they are relatively low cost and are often of very high quality.

The next chapter concerns the basics of signal processing theory for use in computer vision. It introduces the Fourier transform that allows you to look at a signal in a new way, in terms of its frequency content. It also allows us to work out the minimum size of a picture to conserve information, to analyse the content in terms of frequency and even helps to speed up some of the later vision algorithms. It does involve a few equations, but it is a new way of looking at data and at signals and proves to be a rewarding topic of study in its own right. It extends to wavelets, which are a popular analysis tool in image processing.

We then start to look at basic image processing techniques, where image points are mapped into a new value first by considering a single point in an original image and then by considering groups of points. Not only do we see common operations to make a picture's appearance better, especially for human vision, but also see how to reduce the effects of different types of commonly encountered image noise. We shall see some of the modern ways to remove noise and thus clean images, and we shall look at techniques which process an image using notions of shape, rather than mapping processes.

The following chapter concerns low-level features that are the techniques that describe the content of an image, at the level of a whole image rather than in distinct regions of it. One of the most important processes we shall meet is called edge detection. Essentially, this reduces an image to a form of a caricaturist's sketch, though without a caricaturist's exaggerations. The major techniques are presented in detail, together with descriptions of their implementation. Other image properties we can derive include measures of curvature, which developed into modern methods of feature extraction, and measures of movement. The newer techniques are keypoints that localise image information and feature point detection in particular. There are other image properties that can also be used for low-level feature extraction such as phase congruency and saliency. Together, many techniques can be used to describe the content of an image.

The edges, the keypoints, the curvature or the motion need to be grouped in some way so that we can find shapes in an image. Using basic thresholding rarely suffices for shape extraction. One of the approaches is to group low-level features to find an object—in a way this is object extraction without shape. Another approach to shape extraction concerns analysing the match of low-level information to a known template of a target shape. As this can be computationally very cumbersome, we then progress to a technique that improves computational performance, whilst maintaining an optimal performance. The technique is known as the Hough transform, and it has long been a popular target for researchers in computer vision who have sought to clarify its basis, improve its speed and increase its accuracy and robustness. Essentially, by the Hough transform we estimate the parameters that govern a shape's appearance, where the shapes range from lines to ellipses and even to unknown shapes.

Some applications of shape extraction require determination of rather more than the parameters that control appearance, and require to be able to deform or flex to match the image template. For this reason, the chapter on shape extraction by matching is followed by one on flexible shape analysis. This leads to interactive segmentation via snakes (active contours). The later material on the formulation by level-set methods brought new power to deformable shape extraction techniques. Further, we shall see how we can describe a shape by its skeleton though with practical difficulty which can be alleviated by symmetry (though this can be slow to compute) and also how global constraints concerning the statistics of a shape's appearance can be used to guide final extraction.

Up to this point, we have not considered techniques that can be used to describe the shape found in an image. We shall find that the two major approaches concern techniques that describe a shape's perimeter and those that describe its area. Some of the perimeter description techniques, the Fourier descriptors, are even couched using Fourier transform theory that allows analysis of their frequency content. One of the major approaches to area description, statistical moments, also has a form of access to frequency components, though it is of a very different nature to the Fourier analysis. We now include new formulations that are phrased in discrete terms, rather than as approximations to discrete. One advantage is that insight into descriptive ability can be achieved by reconstruction which should get back to the original shape.

We then move on to region-based analysis. This includes some classic computer vision approaches for segmentation and description, especially superpixels which are a grouping process reflecting structure and reduced resolution. Then we move to texture which describes patterns with no known analytical description and has been the target of considerable research in computer vision and image processing.

Much computer vision, for computational reasons, concerns spatial images only, and here we describe spatiotemporal techniques detecting and analysing moving objects from within sequences of images. Moving objects are detected by separating the foreground from the background, known as background subtraction. Having separated the moving components, one approach is then to follow or track the object as it moves within a sequence of image frames. The moving object can be described and recognised from the tracking information or by collecting together the sequence of frames to derive moving object descriptions.

We include material that is germane to the text, such as camera models and co-ordinate geometry and on methods of colour description. These are aimed to be short introductions and are germane to much of the material throughout but not needed directly to cover it.

We then describe how to learn and discriminate between objects and patterns. There is also introductory material on how to classify these patterns against known data, with a selection of the distance measures that can be used within that, and this is a window on a much larger area, to which appropriate pointers are given. This book is not about machine learning, and there are plenty of excellent texts that describe that. We have to address deep learning, since it is a combination of feature extraction and learning. Taking the challenge directly, we address deep learning and its particular relation with feature extraction and classification. This is a new way of processing images which has great power and can be very fast. We show the relationship between the new deep learning approaches and classic feature extraction techniques.

An underlying premise throughout the text is that there is never a panacea in engineering, it is invariably about compromise. There is material not contained in the book, and some of this and other related material is referenced throughout the text, especially on-line material.

In this way, the text covers all major areas of feature extraction and image processing in computer vision. There is considerably more material in the subject than is presented here: for example, there is an enormous volume of material in 3D computer vision and in 2D signal processing which is only alluded to here. Topics that are specifically not included are 3D processing, watermarking, image coding, statistical pattern recognition and machine learning. To include all that would lead to a monstrous book that no one could afford, or even pick up. So we admit we give a snapshot, and we hope more that it is considered to open another window on a fascinating and rewarding subject.

In gratitude

We are immensely grateful to the input of our colleagues, in particular to Prof Steve Gunn, Dr John Carter, Dr Sasan Mahmoodi, Dr Kate Farrahi and to Dr Jon Hare. The family who put up with it are Maria Eugenia and Caz and the nippers. We are also very grateful to past and present researchers in computer vision at the Vision Learning and Control (VLC) research group under (or who have survived?) Mark's supervision at the Electronics and Computer Science, University of Southampton. As well as Alberto and Steve, these include Dr Hani Muammar, Prof Xiaoguang Jia, Prof Yan Qiu Chen, Dr Adrian Evans, Dr Colin Davies, Dr Mark Jones, Dr David Cunado, Dr Jason Nash, Dr Ping Huang, Dr Liang Ng, Dr David Benn, Dr Douglas Bradshaw, Dr David Hurley, Dr John Manslow, Dr Mike Grant, Bob Roddis, Prof Andrew Tatem, Dr Karl Sharman, Dr Jamie Shutler, Dr Jun Chen, Dr Andy Tatem, Dr Chew-Yean Yam, Dr James Hayfron-Acquah, Dr Yalin Zheng, Dr Jeff Foster, Dr Peter Myerscough, Dr David Wagg, Dr Ahmad Al-Mazeed, Dr Jang-Hee Yoo, Dr Nick Spencer, Dr Stuart Mowbray, Dr Stuart Prismall, Prof Peter Gething, Dr Mike Jewell, Dr David Wagg, Dr Alex Bazin, Hidayah Rahmalan, Dr Xin Liu, Dr Imed Bouchrika, Dr Banafshe Arbab-Zavar, Dr Dan Thorpe, Dr Cem Direkoglu, Dr Sina Samangooei, Dr John Bustard, D. Richard Seely, Dr Alastair Cummings, Dr Muayed Al-Huseiny, Dr Mina Ibrahim, Dr Darko Matovski, Dr Gunawan Ariyanto, Dr Sung-Uk Jung, Dr Richard Lowe, Dr Dan Reid, Dr George Cushen, Dr Ben Waller, Dr Nick Udell, Dr Anas Abuzaina, Dr Thamer Alathari, Dr Musab Sahrim, Dr Ah Reum Oh, Dr Tim Matthews, Dr Emad Jaha, Dr Peter Forrest, Dr Jaime Lomeli, Dr Dan Martinho-Corbishley, Dr Bingchen Guo, Dr Jung Sun, Dr Nawaf Almudhahka, Di Meng, Moneera Alamnakani, and John Evans (for the great hippo photo). There has been much input from Mark's postdocs too, omitting those already mentioned, these include Dr Hugh Lewis, Dr Richard Evans, Dr Lee Middleton, Dr Galina Veres, Dr Baofeng Guo,

Dr Michaela Goffredo and Dr Wenshu Zhang. We are also very grateful to other past Southampton students of BEng and MEng Electronic Engineering, MEng Information Engineering, BEng and MEng Computer Engineering, MEng Software Engineering and BSc Computer Science who have pointed our earlier mistakes (and enjoyed the beer), have noted areas for clarification and in some cases volunteered some of the material herein. Beyond Southampton, we remain grateful to the reviewers and to those who have written in and made many helpful suggestions, and to Prof Daniel Cremers, Dr Timor Kadir, Prof Tim Cootes, Prof Larry Davis, Dr Pedro Felzenszwalb, Prof Luc van Gool, Prof Aaron Bobick, Prof Phil Torr, Dr Long Tran-Thanh, Dr Tiago de Freitas, Dr Seth Nixon, for observations on and improvements to the text and/or for permission to use images. Naturally we are very grateful to the Elsevier editorial team who helped us reach this point, particularly Joanna Collett and Tim Pitts, and especially to Anitha Sivaraj for her help with the final text. To all of you, our very grateful thanks.

Final message

We ourselves have already benefited much by writing this book. As we already know, previous students have also benefited and contributed to it as well. It remains our hope that it does inspire people to join in this fascinating and rewarding subject that has proved to be such a source of pleasure and inspiration to its many workers.

Mark S. Nixon
Electronics and Computer Science, University of Southampton

Alberto S. Aguado
Foundry, London
Nov 2019
Feature Extraction and Image Processing in Computer Vision

Introduction

1.1 Overview

This is where we start, by looking at the human visual system to investigate what is meant by vision, how a computer can be made to sense pictorial data and how we can process an image. The overview of this chapter is shown in Table 1.1; you will find a similar overview at the start of each chapter. References/citations are collected at the end of each chapter.

1.2 Human and computer vision

A computer vision system processes images acquired from an electronic camera, which is like the human vision system where the brain processes images derived from the eye. Computer vision is a rich and rewarding topic for study and research for electronic engineers, computer scientists and many others. Now that cameras are cheap and widely available and computer power and memory are vast, computer vision is found in many places. There are now many vision systems in routine industrial use: cameras inspect mechanical parts to check size, food is inspected for quality and images used in astronomy benefit from computer vision techniques. Forensic studies and biometrics (ways to recognise people) using computer vision include automatic face recognition

Table 1.1 Overview of chapter 1.

Main topics	Subtopics	Main points
Human vision system	How the eye works, how visual information is processed and how it can fail.	*Sight*, *vision*, lens, retina, image, colour, monochrome, processing, brain, visual illusions.
Computer vision systems	How electronic images are formed, how video is fed into a computer and how we can process the information using a computer.	*Picture elements*, *pixels*, *video* standard, *camera* technologies, pixel technology, performance effects, specialist cameras, video conversion.
Processing images	How we can process images using the Python computer language and mathematical packages; introduction to Python and to Matlab.	*Programming* and processing images, visualisation of results, availability, use.
Literature	Other textbooks and other places to find information on image processing, computer vision and feature extraction.	*Journals*, *textbooks*, websites and this book's website.

Feature Extraction and Image Processing for Computer Vision. https://doi.org/10.1016/B978-0-12-814976-8.00001-4

and recognising people by the 'texture' of their irises. These studies are paralleled by biologists and psychologists who continue to study how our human vision system works and how we see and recognise objects (and people).

A selection of (computer) images is given in Fig. 1.1, these images comprise a set of points or *picture elements* (usually concatenated to *pixels*) stored as an array of numbers in a computer. To recognise faces, based on an image such as Fig. 1.1A, we need to be able to analyse constituent shapes, such as the shape of the nose, the eyes and the eyebrows, to make some measurements to describe and then recognise a face. Fig. 1.1B is an ultrasound image of the carotid artery (which is near the side of the neck and supplies blood to the brain and the face), taken as a cross-section through it. The top region of the image is near the skin; the bottom is inside the neck. The image arises from combinations of the reflections of the ultrasound radiation by tissue. This image comes from a study aimed to produce three-dimensional models of arteries, to aid vascular surgery. Note that the image is very noisy, and this obscures the shape of the (elliptical) artery. Remotely sensed images are often analysed by their texture content. The perceived texture is different between the road junction and the different types of foliage seen in Fig. 1.1C. Finally, Fig. 1.1D is a magnetic resonance image (MRI) of a cross section near the middle of a human body. The chest is at the top of the image, and the lungs and blood vessels are the dark areas, the internal organs and the fat appear grey. MRI images are in routine medical use nowadays, owing to their ability to provide high-quality images.

There are many different image sources. In medical studies, MRI is good for imaging soft tissue but does not reveal the bone structure (the spine cannot be seen in Fig. 1.1D); this can be achieved by using computerised tomography which is better at imaging bone, as opposed to soft tissue. Remotely sensed images can be derived from infrared (thermal) sensors or synthetic-aperture radar, rather than by cameras, as in Fig. 1.1C. Spatial information can be provided by two-dimensional arrays of sensors, including sonar arrays. There are perhaps more varieties of sources of spatial data in medical studies than in any other area. But computer vision techniques are used to analyse any form of data, not just the images from cameras.

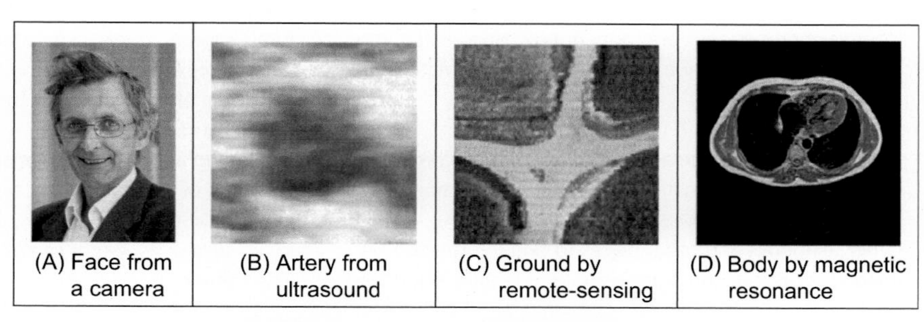

(A) Face from a camera
(B) Artery from ultrasound
(C) Ground by remote-sensing
(D) Body by magnetic resonance

FIGURE 1.1 Real images from different sources.

Synthesised images are good for evaluating techniques and finding out how they work, and some of the bounds on performance. Two synthetic images are shown in Fig. 1.2. Fig. 1.2A is an image of circles that were specified mathematically. The image is an ideal case: the circles are perfectly defined and the brightness levels have been specified to be constant. This type of synthetic image is good for evaluating techniques which find the borders of the shape (its edges), the shape itself and even for making a description of the shape. Fig. 1.2B is a synthetic image made up of sections of real image data. The borders between the regions of image data are exact, again specified by a program. The image data come from a well-known texture database, the Brodatz album of textures. This was scanned and stored as a computer image. This image can be used to analyse how well computer vision algorithms can identify regions of differing texture.

This chapter will show you how basic computer vision systems work, in the context of the human vision system. It covers the main elements of human vision showing you how your eyes work (and how they can be deceived!). For computer vision, this chapter covers the hardware and the software used for image analysis, giving an introduction to Python and Matlab®, the software and mathematical packages, respectively, used throughout this text to implement computer vision algorithms. Finally, a selection of pointers to other material is provided, especially those for more detail on the topics covered in this chapter.

1.3 The human vision system

Human vision is a sophisticated system that senses and acts on visual stimuli. It has evolved for millions of years, primarily for defence or survival. Intuitively, computer and human vision appear to have the same function. The purpose of both systems is to interpret spatial data, data that are indexed by more than one dimension. Even though computer and human vision are functionally similar, you cannot expect a computer vision system to exactly replicate the function of the human eye. This is partly because we do not understand fully how the vision system of the eye and brain works, as we shall

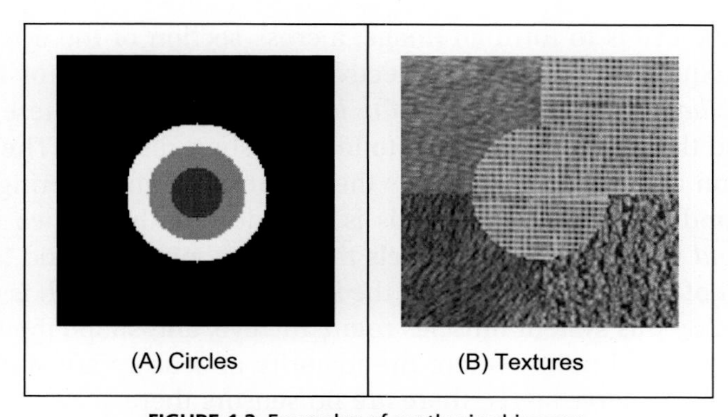

FIGURE 1.2 Examples of synthesised images.

see in this section. Accordingly, we cannot design a system to exactly replicate its function. In fact, some of the properties of the human eye are useful when developing computer vision techniques, whereas others are actually undesirable in a computer vision system. But we shall see computer vision techniques which can to some extent, replicate -and in some cases even improve upon -the human vision system.

You might ponder this, so put one of the fingers from each of your hands in front of your face and try to estimate the distance between them. This is difficult, and we are sure you would agree that your measurement would not be very accurate. Now put your fingers very close together. You can still tell that they are apart even when the distance between them is tiny. So human vision can distinguish relative distance well, but is poor for absolute distance. Computer vision is the other way around: it is good for estimating absolute difference, but with relatively poor resolution for relative difference. The number of pixels in the image imposes the accuracy of the computer vision system, but that does not come until the next chapter. Let us start at the beginning, by seeing how the human vision system works.

In human vision, the sensing element is the eye from which images are transmitted via the optic nerve to the brain, for further processing. The optic nerve has insufficient bandwidth to carry all the information sensed by the eye. Accordingly, there must be some pre-processing before the image is transmitted down the optic nerve. The human vision system can be modelled in three parts:

1. the eye – this is a physical model since much of its function can be determined by pathology;
2. a processing system – this is an experimental model since the function can be modelled, but not determined precisely; and
3. analysis by the brain – this is a psychological model since we cannot access or model such processing directly, but only determine behaviour by experiment and inference.

1.3.1 The eye

The function of the eye is to form an image; a cross-section of the eye is illustrated in Fig. 1.3. Vision requires an ability to selectively focus on objects of interest. This is achieved by the *ciliary muscles* that hold the *lens*. In old age, it is these muscles which become slack, and the eye loses its ability to focus at short distance. The *iris*, or pupil, is like an aperture on a camera and controls the amount of light entering the eye. It is a delicate system and needs protection, this is provided by the cornea (sclera). This is outside the *choroid* which has blood vessels that supply nutrition and is opaque to cut down the amount of light. The *retina* is on the inside of the eye, which is where light falls to form an image. By this system muscles rotate the eye, and shape the lens, to form an image on the *fovea* (focal point) where the majority of sensors are situated. The *blind spot* is where the optic nerve starts, there are no sensors there.

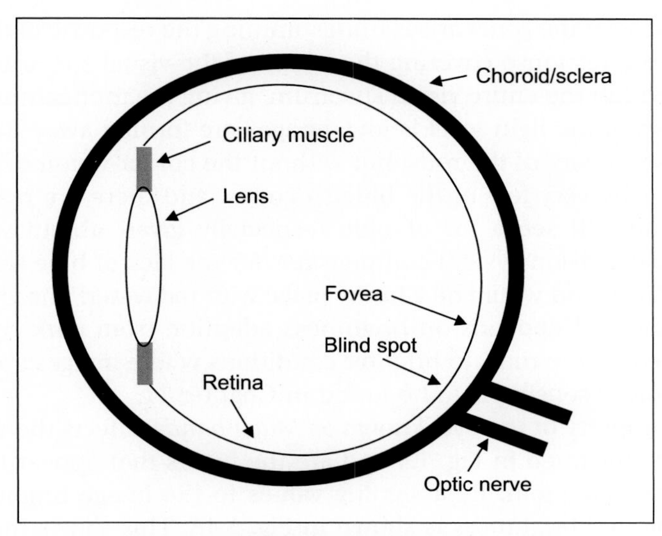

FIGURE 1.3 Human eye.

Focussing involves shaping the lens, rather than positioning it as in a camera. The lens is shaped to refract close images greatly, and distant objects little, essentially by 'stretching' it. The distance of the focal centre of the lens varies from approximately 14 mm to around 17 mm depending on the lens shape. This implies that a world scene is translated into an area of about 2 mm^2. Good vision has high *acuity* (sharpness), which implies that there must be very many sensors in the area where the image is formed.

There are actually nearly 100 million sensors dispersed around the retina. Light falls on these sensors to stimulate photochemical transmissions, which results in nerve impulses that are collected to form the signal transmitted by the eye. There are two types of sensor: firstly, the *rods* – these are used for black and white (*scotopic*) vision; and secondly, the *cones* – these are used for colour (*photopic*) vision. There are approximately 10 million cones and nearly all are found within 5 degrees of the fovea. The remaining 100 million rods are distributed around the retina, with the majority between 20 and 5 degrees of the fovea. Acuity is actually expressed in terms of spatial resolution (sharpness) and brightness/colour resolution and is greatest within 1 degree of the fovea.

There is only one type of rod, but there are three types of cones. These types are the following:

1. S – short wavelength: these sense light towards the blue end of the visual spectrum;
2. M – medium wavelength: these sense light around green; and
3. L – long wavelength: these sense light towards the red region of the spectrum.

The total response of the *cones* arises from summing the response of these three types of cones, this gives a response covering the whole of the visual spectrum. The rods are sensitive to light within the entire visual spectrum, giving the monochrome capability of scotopic vision. When the light level is low, images are formed away from the fovea to use the superior sensitivity of the rods, but without the colour vision of the cones. Note that there are actually very few of the blueish cones, and there are many more of the others. But we can still see a lot of blue (especially given ubiquitous denim!). So, somehow, the human vision system compensates for the lack of blue sensors, to enable us to perceive it. The world would be a funny place with red water! The vision response is actually logarithmic and depends on brightness adaption from dark conditions where the image is formed on the rods, to brighter conditions where images are formed on the cones. More on colour sensing is to be found in Chapter 11.

One inherent property of the eye, known as *Mach bands*, affects the way we perceive images. These are illustrated in Fig. 1.4 and are the bands that appear to be where two stripes of constant shade join. By assigning values to the image brightness levels, the cross-section of plotted brightness is shown in Fig. 1.4A. This shows that the picture is formed from stripes of constant brightness. Human vision perceives an image for which

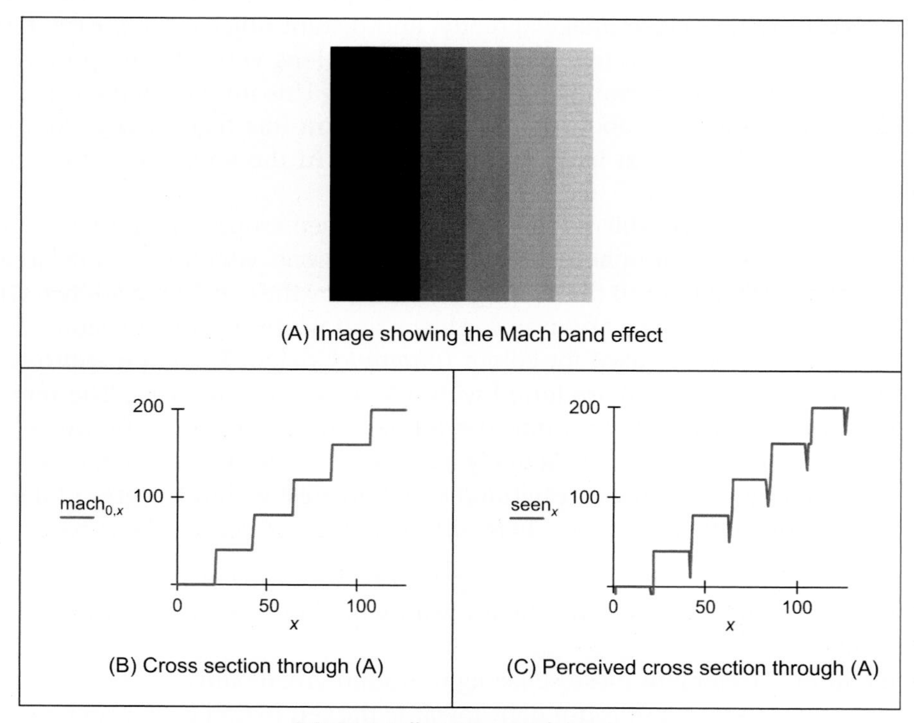

FIGURE 1.4 Illustrating mach bands.

the cross-section is as plotted in Fig. 1.4C. These Mach bands do not really exist, but are introduced by your eye. The bands arise from overshoot in the eyes' response at boundaries of regions of different intensity (this aids us to differentiate between objects in our field of view). The real cross-section is illustrated in Fig. 1.4B. Note also that a human eye can distinguish only relatively few grey levels. It actually has a capability to discriminate between 32 levels (equivalent to 5 bits), whereas the image of Fig. 1.4A could have many more brightness levels. This is why your perception finds it more difficult to discriminate between the low-intensity bands on the left of Fig. 1.4A. (Note that Mach bands cannot be seen in the earlier image of circles, Fig. 1.2A, due to the arrangement of grey levels.) This is the limit of our studies of the first level of human vision; for those who are interested, [Cornsweet70] provides many more details concerning visual perception.

So we have already identified two properties associated with the eye that it would be difficult to include, and would often be unwanted, in a computer vision system: Mach bands and sensitivity to unsensed phenomena. These properties are integral to human vision. At present, human vision is far more sophisticated than we can hope to achieve with a computer vision system. Infrared-guided missile vision systems can actually have difficulty in distinguishing between a bird at 100 m and a plane at 10 km. Poor birds! (Lucky plane?). Human vision can handle this with ease.

1.3.2 The neural system

Neural signals provided by the eye are essentially the transformed response of the wavelength dependent receptors, the cones and the rods. One model is to combine these transformed signals by addition, as illustrated in Fig. 1.5. The response is transformed by a logarithmic function, mirroring the known response of the eye. This is then multiplied by a weighting factor that controls the contribution of a particular sensor. This can be arranged to allow combination of responses from a particular region. The weighting factors can be chosen to afford particular filtering properties. For example, in *lateral inhibition*, the weights for the centre sensors are much greater than the weights for those at the extreme. This allows the response of the centre sensors to dominate the combined response given by addition. If the weights in one half are chosen to be negative, whilst those in the other half are positive, then the output will show detection of contrast (change in brightness), given by the differencing action of the weighting functions.

The signals from the cones can be combined in a manner that reflects *chrominance* (colour) and *luminance* (brightness). This can be achieved by subtraction of logarithmic functions, which is then equivalent to taking the logarithm of their ratio. This allows measures of chrominance to be obtained. In this manner, the signals derived from the sensors are combined prior to transmission through the optic nerve. This is an experimental model, since there are many ways possible to combine the different signals together.

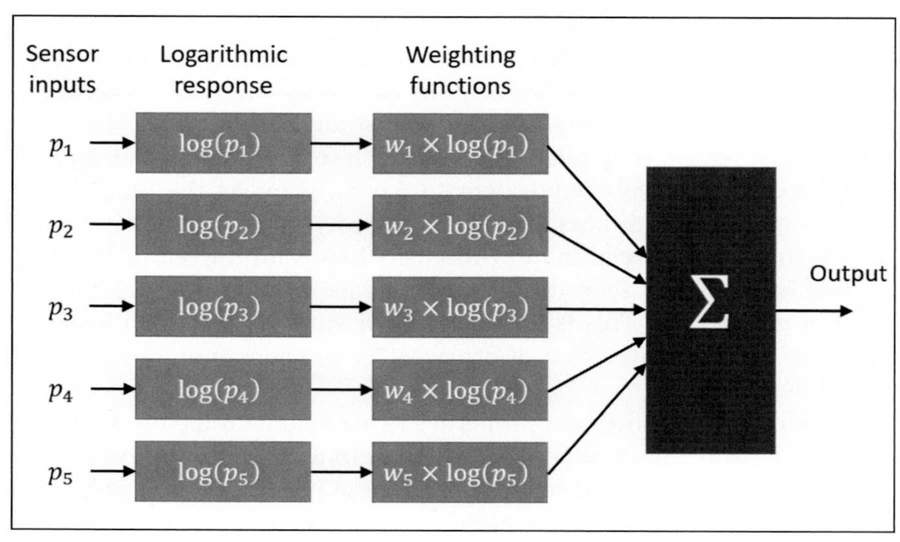

FIGURE 1.5 Neural processing.

Visual information is then sent back to arrive at the *lateral geniculate nucleus* (LGN) which is in the thalamus and is the primary processor of visual information. This is a layered structure containing different types of cells, with differing functions. The axons from the LGN pass information on to the visual cortex. The function of the LGN is largely unknown, though it has been shown to play a part in coding the signals that are transmitted. It is also considered to help the visual system focus its attention, such as on sources of sound. For further information on retinal neural networks, see [Ratliff65]; an alternative study of neural processing can be found in [Overington92].

1.3.3 Processing

The neural signals are then transmitted to two areas of the brain for further processing. These areas are the *associative cortex*, where links between objects are made, and the *occipital cortex*, where patterns are processed. It is naturally difficult to determine precisely what happens in this region of the brain. To date, there have been no volunteers for detailed study of their brain's function (though progress with new imaging modalities such as positive emission tomography or electrical impedance tomography will doubtless help). For this reason, there are only psychological models to suggest how this region of the brain operates.

It is well known that one function of the human vision system is to use edges, or boundaries, of objects. We can easily read the word in Fig. 1.6A, this is achieved by filling in the missing boundaries in the knowledge that the pattern most likely represents a printed word. But we can infer more about this image; there is a suggestion of illumination, causing shadows to appear in unlit areas. If the light source is bright, then the

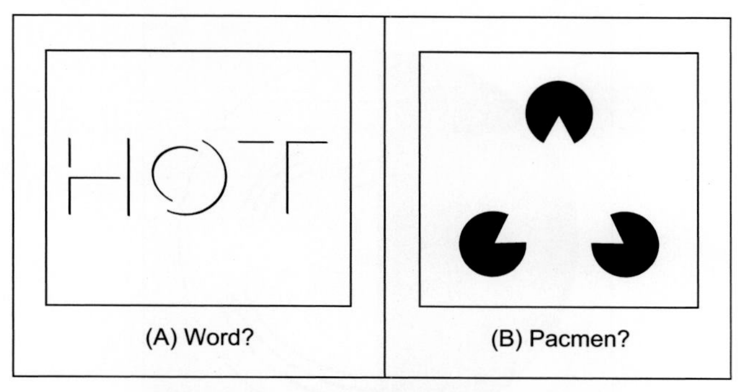

FIGURE 1.6 How human vision uses edges.

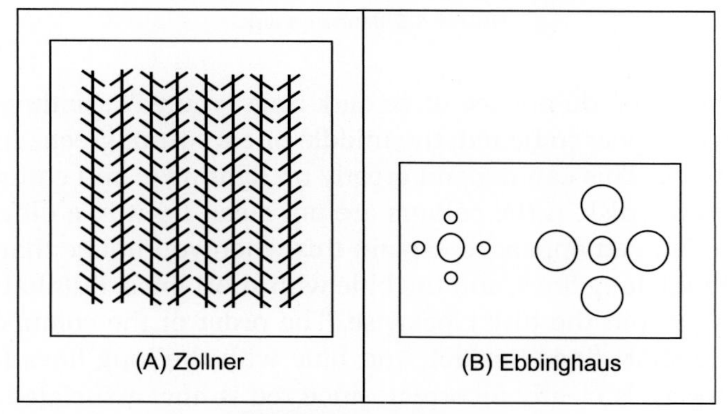

FIGURE 1.7 Static illusions.

image will be washed out, causing the disappearance of the boundaries which are interpolated by our eyes. So there is more than just physical response, there is also knowledge, including prior knowledge of solid geometry. This situation is illustrated in Fig. 1.6B that could represent three 'pacmen' about to collide, or a white triangle placed on top of three black circles. Either situation is possible.

It is also possible to deceive human vision, primarily by imposing a scene that it has not been trained to handle. In the famous *Zollner illusion*, Fig. 1.7A, the bars appear to be slanted, whereas in reality they are vertical (check this by placing a pen between the lines): the small crossbars mislead your eye into perceiving the vertical bars as slanting. In the *Ebbinghaus illusion*, Fig. 1.7B, the inner circle appears to be larger when surrounded by small circles, than it is when surrounded by larger circles.

There are dynamic illusions too: you can always impress children with the 'see my wobbly pencil' trick. Just hold the pencil loosely between your fingers then, to whoops of childish glee, when the pencil is shaken up and down, the solid pencil will appear to bend. *Benham's disk*, Fig. 1.8, shows how hard it is to model vision accurately. If you make up a version of this disk into a spinner (push a matchstick through the centre) and

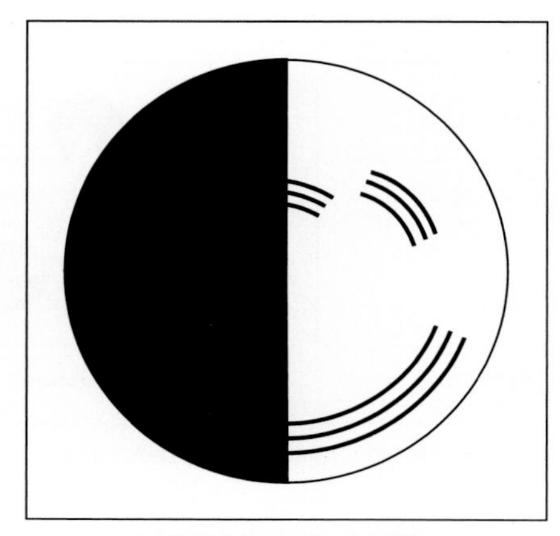

FIGURE 1.8 Benham's disk.

spin it anti-clockwise, you do not see three dark rings, you will see three coloured ones. The outside one will appear to be red, the middle one a sort of green, and the inner one will appear deep blue. (This can depend greatly on lighting – and contrast between the black and white on the disk. If the colours are not clear, try it in a different place, with different lighting.) You can appear to explain this when you notice that the red colours are associated with the long lines, and the blue with short lines. But that is from physics, not psychology. Now spin the disk clockwise. The order of the colours reverses: red is associated with the short lines (inside), and blue with the long lines (outside). So the argument from physics is clearly incorrect, since red is now associated with short lines not long ones, revealing the need for psychological explanation of the eyes' function. This is not colour perception, see [Armstrong91] for an interesting (and interactive!) study of colour theory and perception.

Naturally, there are many texts on human vision – one popular text on human visual perception (and its relationship with visual art) is by Livingstone [Livingstone14]; there is an online book: *The Joy of Vision* (http://www.yorku.ca/eye/thejoy.htm) – useful, despite its title! Marr's seminal text [Marr82] is a computational investigation into human vision and visual perception, investigating it from a computer vision viewpoint. For further details on pattern processing in human vision, see [Bruce90]; for more illusions see [Rosenfeld82] and an excellent – and dynamic – collection at https://michaelbach.de/ot. Many of the properties of human vision are hard to include in a computer vision system, but let us now look at the basic components that are used to make computers see.

1.4 Computer vision systems

Given the progress in computer technology and domestic photography, computer vision hardware is now relatively inexpensive; a basic computer vision system requires a camera, a camera interface and a computer. These days, many personal computers offer the capability for a basic vision system, by including a camera and its interface within the system. There are specialised systems for computer vision, offering high performance in more than one aspect. These can be expensive, as any specialist system is.

1.4.1 Cameras

A *camera* is the basic sensing element. In simple terms, most cameras rely on the property of light to cause hole–electron pairs (the charge carriers in electronics) in a conducting material. When a potential is applied (to attract the charge carriers), this charge can be sensed as current. By Ohm's law, the voltage across a resistance is proportional to the current through it, so the current can be turned in to a voltage by passing it through a resistor. The number of hole–electron pairs is proportional to the amount of incident light. Accordingly, greater charge (and hence greater voltage and current) is caused by an increase in brightness. In this manner, cameras can provide as output, a voltage which is proportional to the brightness of the points imaged by the camera.

There are three main types of camera: *vidicons, charge-coupled devices* (CCDs) and, later, *CMOS* cameras (complementary metal oxide silicon – now the dominant technology for logic circuit implementation). Vidicons are the old (analogue) technology, which though cheap (mainly by virtue of longevity in production) have largely been replaced by the newer CCD and CMOS digital technologies. The digital technologies now dominate much of the camera market because they are lightweight and cheap (with other advantages) and are therefore used in the domestic video market.

Vidicons operate in a manner akin to an old television in reverse. The image is formed on a screen, and then sensed by an electron beam that is scanned across the screen. This produces an output which is continuous, the output voltage is proportional to the brightness of points in the scanned line, and is a continuous signal, a voltage which varies continuously with time. On the other hand, CCDs and CMOS cameras use an array of sensors; these are regions where charge is collected, which is proportional to the light incident on that region. This is then available in discrete, or sampled, form as opposed to the continuous sensing of a vidicon. This is similar to human vision with its array of cones and rods, but digital cameras use a rectangular regularly spaced lattice, whereas human vision uses a hexagonal lattice with irregular spacing.

Two main types of semiconductor pixel sensors are illustrated in Fig. 1.9. In the *passive sensor*, the charge generated by incident light is presented to a bus through a pass transistor. When the signal Tx is activated, the pass transistor is enabled and the sensor provides a capacitance to the bus, one that is proportional to the incident light. An *active pixel* includes an amplifier circuit that can compensate for limited fill factor of the photodiode. The select signal again controls presentation of the sensor's information to the bus. A further reset signal allows the charge site to be cleared when the image is rescanned.

The basis of a CCD sensor is illustrated in Fig. 1.10. The number of charge sites gives the resolution of the CCD sensor; the contents of the charge sites (or buckets) need to be

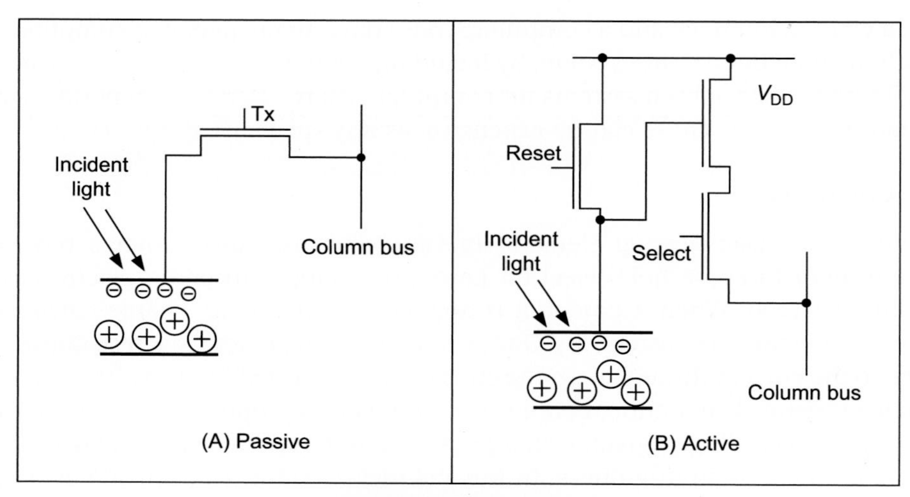

FIGURE 1.9 Pixel sensors.

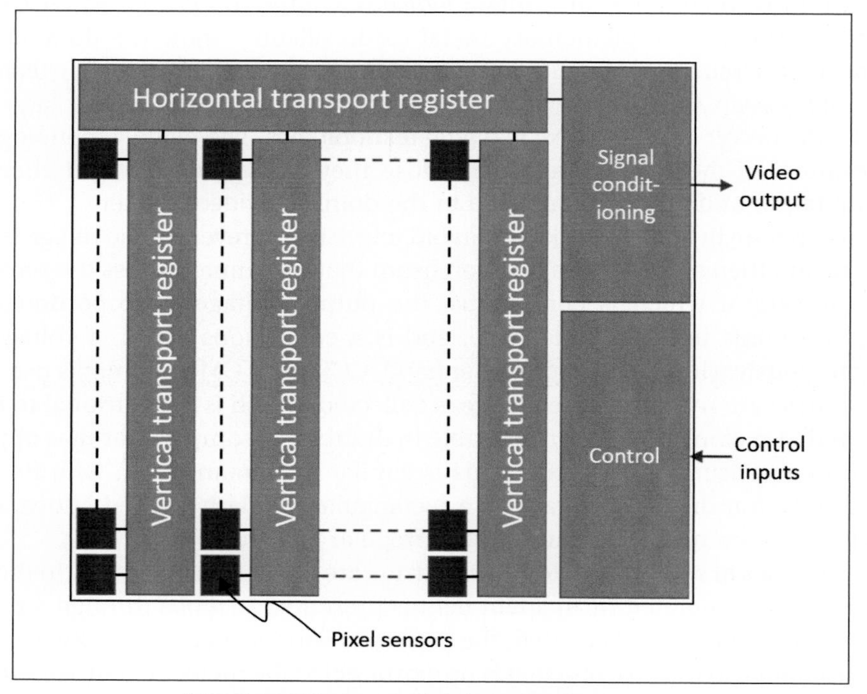

FIGURE 1.10 Charge-coupled device sensing element.

converted to an output (voltage) signal. In simple terms, the contents of the buckets are emptied into vertical transport registers which are shift registers moving information towards the horizontal transport registers. This is the column bus supplied by the pixel sensors. The horizontal transport registers empty the information row by row (point by point) into a signal conditioning unit which transforms the sensed charge into a voltage which is proportional to the charge in a bucket, and hence proportional to the brightness of the corresponding point in the scene imaged by the camera. CMOS cameras are like a form of memory: the charge incident on a particular site in a two-dimensional lattice is proportional to the brightness at a point. The charge is then read like computer memory. (In fact, a computer memory RAM chip can act as a rudimentary form of camera when the circuit – the one buried in the chip – is exposed to light.)

There are many more varieties of vidicon (Chalnicon, etc.) than there are of CCD technology (charge injection device, etc.), perhaps due to the greater age of basic vidicon technology. Vidicons are cheap but have a number of intrinsic performance problems. The scanning process essentially relies on 'moving parts'. As such, the camera performance will change with time, as parts wear; this is known as *ageing*. Also, it is possible to *burn* an image into the scanned screen by using high incident light levels; vidicons can also suffer *lag* that is a delay in response to moving objects in a scene. On the other hand, the digital technologies are dependent on the physical arrangement of charge sites and as such do not suffer from ageing, but can suffer from irregularity in the charge sites' (silicon) material. The underlying technology also makes CCD and CMOS cameras less sensitive to lag and burn, but the signals associated with the CCD transport registers can give rise to *readout effects*. CCDs actually only came to dominate camera technology when technological difficulty associated with *quantum efficiency* (the magnitude of response to incident light) for the shorter, blue, wavelengths was solved. One of the major problems in CCD cameras is *blooming* where bright (incident) light causes a bright spot to grow and disperse in the image (this used to happen in the analogue technologies too). This happens much less in CMOS cameras because the charge sites can be much better defined and reading their data is equivalent to reading memory sites as opposed to shuffling charge between sites. Also, CMOS cameras have now overcome the problem of *fixed pattern noise* that plagued earlier MOS cameras. CMOS cameras are actually much more recent than CCDs. This begs a question as to which is best: CMOS or CCD? An early view was that CCD could provide higher-quality images, whereas CMOS is a cheaper technology and because it lends itself directly to intelligent cameras with on-board processing. The feature size of points (pixels) in a CCD sensor is limited to be about 4 μm so that enough light is collected. In contrast, the feature size in CMOS technology is considerably smaller. It is then possible to integrate signal processing within the camera chip, and thus it is perhaps possible that CMOS cameras will eventually replace CCD technologies for many applications. However, modern CCDs' process technology is more mature, so the debate will doubtless continue!

Finally, there are specialist cameras, which include high-resolution devices (giving pictures with many points), low-light level cameras which can operate in very dark conditions and *infrared* cameras which sense heat to provide thermal images; *hyperspectral* cameras have more sensing bands. For more detail concerning modern camera practicalities and imaging systems, see [Nakamura05] and more recently [Kuroda14]. For more details on sensor development, particularly CMOS, [Fossum97] is still well worth a look. For more detail on images, see [Phillips18] with a particular focus on quality (hey – there is even mosquito noise!).

A *light field* – or *plenoptic* – camera is one that can sense depth as well as brightness [Adelson05]. The light field is essentially a two-dimensional set of spatial images, thus giving a four-dimensional array of pixels. The light field can be captured in a number of ways, by moving cameras, or multiple cameras. The aim is to capture the plenoptic function that describes the light as a function of position, angle, wavelength and time [Wu17]. These days, commercially available cameras use lenses to derive the light field. These can be used to render an image into full depth of plane focus (imagine an image of an object taken at close distance where only the object is in focus combined with an image where the background is in focus to give an image where both the object and the background are in focus). A surveillance operation could focus on what is behind an object which would show in a normal camera image. This gives an alternative approach to 3D object analysis, by sensing the object in 3D. Wherever there are applications, industry will follow, and that has proved to be the case.

There are new *dynamic vision sensors* which sense motion [Lichtsteiner08, Son17] and are much closer to the starting grid than the light field cameras. Clearly, the resolution and speed continue to improve, and there are applications emerging that use these sensors. We shall find in Chapters 4 and 9 it is possible to estimate motion from sequences of images. These sensors are different, since they specifically target motion. As the target application is security (much security video is dull stuff indeed, with little motion) allowing recording only of material of likely interest.

1.4.2 Computer interfaces

Though digital cameras continue to advance, there are still some legacies from the older analogue systems to be found in the some digital systems. There is also some older technology in deployed systems. As such, we shall cover the main points of the two approaches. Essentially, the image sensor converts light into a signal which is expressed either as a continuous signal, or in sampled (digital) form. Some (older) systems expressed the camera signal as an analogue continuous signal, according to a standard, and this was converted at the computer (and still is in some cases, using a frame grabber). Modern digital systems convert the sensor information into digital information with on-chip circuitry and then provide the digital information according to a specified standard. The older systems, such as surveillance systems, supplied (or supply) video whereas the newer systems are digital. Video implies delivering the moving image as a sequence of *frames* of which one format is *digital video* (DV).

An analogue continuous camera signal is transformed into digital (discrete) format using an analogue to digital (A/D) converter. *Flash converters* are usually used due to the high speed required for conversion (say 11 MHz that cannot be met by any other conversion technology). Usually, 8-bit A/D converters are used; at 6dB/bit, this gives 48 dB

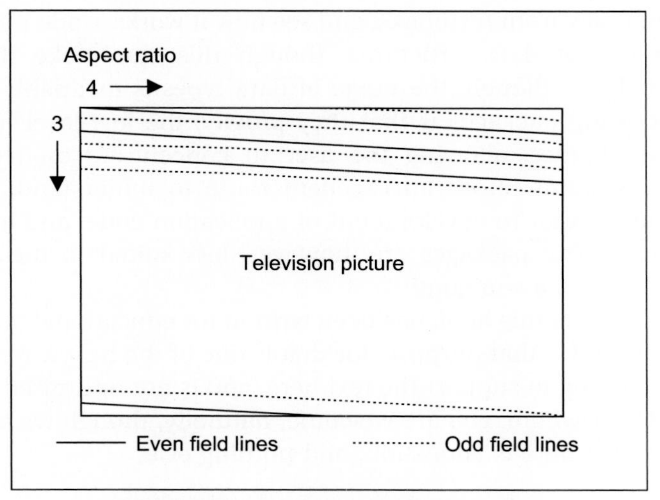

FIGURE 1.11 Interlacing in television pictures.

which just satisfies the CCIR stated *bandwidth* of approximately 45 dB. The outputs of the A/D converter are then stored. Note that there are aspects of the sampling process which are of considerable interest in computer vision; these are covered in Chapter 2.

In digital camera systems, this processing is usually performed on the camera chip, and the camera eventually supplies digital information, often in coded form. Currently, Thunderbolt is the hardware interface that dominates the high end of the market and USB is used at the lower end. There was a system called Firewire, but it has now faded. Images are constructed from a set of lines, those lines scanned by a camera. In the older analogue systems, in order to reduce requirements on transmission (and for viewing), the 625 lines (in the *PAL* system, *NTSC* is of lower resolution) were transmitted in two *interlaced fields*, each of 312.5 lines, as illustrated in Fig. 1.11. These were the odd and the even fields. Modern televisions are *progressive scan*, which is like reading a book: the picture is constructed line by line. There is also an *aspect ratio* in picture transmission: pictures are arranged to be longer than they are high. These factors are chosen to make television images attractive to human vision. Nowadays, *digital video cameras* can provide digital output, in progressive scan delivering sequences of images that are readily processed. There are Gigabit Ethernet cameras which transmit high-speed video and control information over Ethernet networks. Or there are *webcams*, or just *digital camera systems* that deliver images straight to the computer. Life just gets easier!

1.5 Processing images

We shall be using software and packages to process computer images. There are many programming languages, and we have chosen Python as perhaps the most popular language at the time of writing. Several *mathematical systems* allow you to transpose mathematics more easily from textbooks, and see how it works. Code functionality is not obscured by the use of data structures, though this can make the code appear cumbersome (to balance though, the range of data types is invariably small). A major advantage of processing packages is that they provide the low-level functionality and data visualisation schemes, allowing the user to concentrate on techniques alone. Accordingly, these systems afford an excellent route to understand, and appreciate, mathematical systems prior to development of application code, and to check the final code works correctly. The packages are, however, less suited to the development of application code. Chacun à son gout!

The code that supports this book has been written for educational purposes only. We encourage you to use it for that purpose, for that is one of the best ways of learning. It is written for clarity, aiming to support the text here, and is not optimised in any way. You might use the code elsewhere: you are welcome, naturally, though we admit no liability of any form. Our target here is education, and nothing else.

1.5.1 Processing

Most image processing and computer vision techniques are implemented in computer software. Often, only the simplest techniques migrate to hardware; though coding techniques to maximise efficiency in image transmission are of sufficient commercial interest that they have warranted extensive, and very sophisticated, hardware development. The systems include the *Joint Photographic Expert Group* (JPEG) and the *Moving Picture Expert Group* (MPEG) image coding formats. C, C++, Python and Java are by now the most popular languages for vision system implementation because of strengths in integrating high- and low-level functions, and the availability of good compilers. As systems become more complex, C++, Python and Java become more attractive when encapsulation and polymorphism may be exploited. Many people use Python and JAVA as a development language partly due to platform independence but also due to ease in implementation (though some claim that speed/efficiency is better in C/C++). Python is currently a language of choice, not for any specific reasons. Some are up and coming, so there are advocates for JULIA too. There are some textbooks that offer image processing systems implemented in these languages. Also, there are many commercial packages available, though these are often limited to basic techniques, and do not include the more sophisticated shape extraction techniques – and the underlying implementation can be hard to check. Some popular texts present working algorithms, such as [O'Gorman08], [Parker10] and [Solem12].

In terms of software packages, the most popular is OpenCV (Open Source Computer Vision) whose philosophy is to 'aid commercial uses of computer vision in human–computer interface, robotics, monitoring, biometrics and security by providing a free and open infrastructure where the distributed efforts of the vision community can be consolidated and performance optimized'. This contains a wealth of technique and (optimised) implementation – there's a Wikipedia entry and a discussion website

Table 1.2 Software packages for computer vision.

OpenCV	(Originally intel)	opencv.org/
VXL	Many international contributors	vxl.github.io/
CImg	Many international contributors	sourceforge.net/projects/cimg/
VLFeat	Oxford and UCLA	vlfeat.org/
OpenIMAJ	Southampton	openimaj.org

supporting it. The system has now moved to OpenCV 4. That means there were versions 1, 2 and 3, and unfortunately the systems are not compatible. The first textbook describing its use [Bradski08] had/has excellent descriptions of how to use the code (and some great diagrams) but omitted much of the (mathematical) background and analysis so it largely describes usage rather than construction. There are more recent texts for OpenCV, but the reviews are mixed: the web is a better source of reference for implementation material and systems that are constantly updated.

Then there are the VXL libraries (the vision-*something*-libraries, groan). This is 'a collection of C++ libraries designed for computer vision research and implementation'. The CImg Library (another duff acronym: it derives from Cool Image) is a system aimed to be easy to use, efficient, and a generic base for image processing algorithms. VLFeat is 'a cross-platform open source collection of vision algorithms with a special focus on visual features'. Finally, there is Southampton's OpenIMAJ which has lots of functional capabilities and is supported by tutorials and user data (as are all the other packages). Note that these packages are open source, and there are licences and conditions on use and exploitation. Web links are shown in Table 1.2.

1.5.2 Hello Python, hello images!

We shall be using *Python* as our main vehicle for processing images. It is now a dominant language, and it is quite mature. Mark first encountered it a long time ago when we used it to arrange the conference proceedings of the British Machine Vision Conference (BMVC) 1998 and that was Python 1 (we also used Adobe 3.1). It has clearly moved from strength to strength, part by virtue of simplicity and part by virtue of some excellent engineering. This is not a textbook on programming in Python and for that you would best look elsewhere, e.g. [Lutz13] is a well-proven text. Here we are using Python as a vehicle to show how algorithms can be made to work. For that reason, it is not a style guide either.

Python is a scripting programming language that was developed to provide clear and simple code. It is also very general, it runs on many platforms, and it has comprehensive standard libraries. Here, we use Python to show how the maths behind machine vision techniques can be translated into working algorithms. In general, there are several levels at which you can understand a technique. It is possible to understand the basic ideas by studying the meaning and aims of a method that your program calls from a library. You can also understand a more formal definition by studying the mathematics that support the ideas. Alternatively, you can understand a technique as a series of steps that define an algorithm that processes some data. In this book, we discuss the formal ideas with mathematical terms and then present a more practical approach by including algorithms derived from the mathematical formulation.

However, presenting working algorithms is not straightforward, and we have puzzled on how to code without ending up with a lot of wrapper material that can obscure functionality or whether to go to the other extreme and just end up calling a function from a package. There again, one could argue that it is best to accommodate complex code in the support material, and show its operations in the book. However, that could limit functionality, performance and complexity. Today's implementations of machine vision algorithms include concepts like multi-threading and GPU processing. Implementations follow object-oriented, functional or procedural definitions that organize computations in complex and efficient data structures. They also include specific code to improve robustness. In order to keep the scope manageable and for clarity, the code in this book is limited to the main steps of algorithms. However, you should be able to understand and develop more complex implementations once you have the knowledge of the basic approach.

If you want to execute the presented code, you will need to set up Python, install some Python packages and set up the book's scripts. There are several ways to set up a Python environment, and we provide setup instructions on the book's website. The scripts presented in this book do not call Python packages directly, but through two utility scripts (`ImageSupport` and `PlotSupport`) that wrap the basic image manipulations and drawing functionalities. The main idea is to present the code independently of software for drawing and loading images. You can either execute the scripts using the `ImageSupport` and `PlotSupport` definitions provided or you can implement similar utilities by using alternative Python libraries.

`ImageSupport` implements functions for reading, showing or creating images. `PlotSupport` implements functions for drawing surfaces, curves and histograms. The scripts in this book contain imports from these two utility files. In our implementation, `ImageSupport` uses pillow (a 'friendly' Python Imaging Library fork no less) for loading and saving images and `Numpy` to define arrays for image data. `PlotSupport` uses `Numpy` since it requires image data, and it also uses `Matplotlib` for drawing. Thus, if you use the support utilities, you need to install `PIL`, `Numpy` and `Matplot` and set your environment path such that scripts can access `ImageSupport` and `PlotSupport` utilities.

In addition to image and plot support, scripts also import functions from other utility files. This is done in the code in this book to show all the steps in an implementation algorithm whilst avoiding repetition. For example, a technique such as edge detection will be shown as a script with all the steps of the algorithm. When edge detection is used in more complex algorithms such as corner detection, the corner detection algorithm will just call a function to perform the edge detection steps. Thus, you will find the edge detection code as a script in an algorithm or as a utility function. The algorithm functions are organized by chapter, so `FourierTransformUtilities` defines functions for the scripts explained in Chapter 2 and `FeatureExtractionUtilities` for functions in Chapter 4. The code in the utilities is similar to the code explained in other parts of the book.

Code 1.1 shows our first example of a Python script. This script is used to visualize an image in different forms. It loads and displays an image, it prints the pixels' values and it shows the image as a surface. To run this code (from, say, the directory `c:\imagebook\` with the images stored in `c:\imagebook\input\`) then in the command line type

```
# Feature Extraction and Image Processing
# Mark S. Nixon & Alberto S. Aguado
# Code1_1_Imagedisplay.py: Loads, inverts and displays an image.
# Shows image as a surface and prints pixel data

# Set utility folder
import sys
sys.path.insert(0, '../Utilities/')

# Set utility functions
from ImageSupport import imageReadL, showImageL, printImageRangeL, createImageF
from PlotSupport import plot3DColorHistogram

'''
Parameters:
    pathToDir = Input image directory
    imageName = Input image name
'''
pathToDir = "Input/"
imageName = "Square.png"

# Read image into array
inputImage, width, height = imageReadL(pathToDir + imageName)

# Show input image
showImageL(inputImage)

# Print pixel's values in an image range
printImageRangeL(inputImage, [0, width-1], [0, height-1])

# Create an image to store the z values for surface
outputZ = createImageF(width, height)

# Three float arrays to store colours of the surface
colorsRGB = createImageF(width, height, 3)

# Set surface and colour values
for x in range(0, width):
    for y in range(0, height):
        pixelValue = float(inputImage[y,x])
        outputZ[y,x] = pixelValue
        pointColour = float(inputImage[y,x])/255.0
        colorsRGB[y,x] = [pointColour, pointColour, pointColour]

# Plot histogram to show image
plot3DColorHistogram(outputZ, colorsRGB, [0,400])
```

CODE 1.1 Load, invert and display an image.

Python Code1_1_Imagedisplay.py, and it will run and produce images. The first lines of the script set the path to the directory of the utilities. Scripts in other chapters will omit these lines, but you need to set the environment in your system to access the utility files. The next part of the script imports the functions that we use for image handling and plotting. Then, we set the variables that define the parameters of the algorithm. In this case, the file name of the image we want to display. The utility function imageReadL reads an image and stores the data in an array (a matrix) of grey level values. The storage of image pixel data is first covered in the next Chapter, Section 2.2. The function returns an array containing a single grey level value uint8 (8-bit unsigned integer) per pixel and the size of the image. The function showImageL displays an image on the screen as shown in Fig. 1.12A. In this example, the image is very small (12 × 12 pixels), so we can see the pixels as squares. The script uses the utility function printImageRangeL to display the values of the pixels in matrix form as shown in Fig. 1.12B. Note that the outer rows and columns are black with some slight variation – this variation cannot be perceived in the displayed image.

In order to display images as surfaces, the script in Code 1.1 creates two images that store the height and the colour for each surface sample. The function createImageF creates an array of floats (floating point numbers), and its last parameter defines the

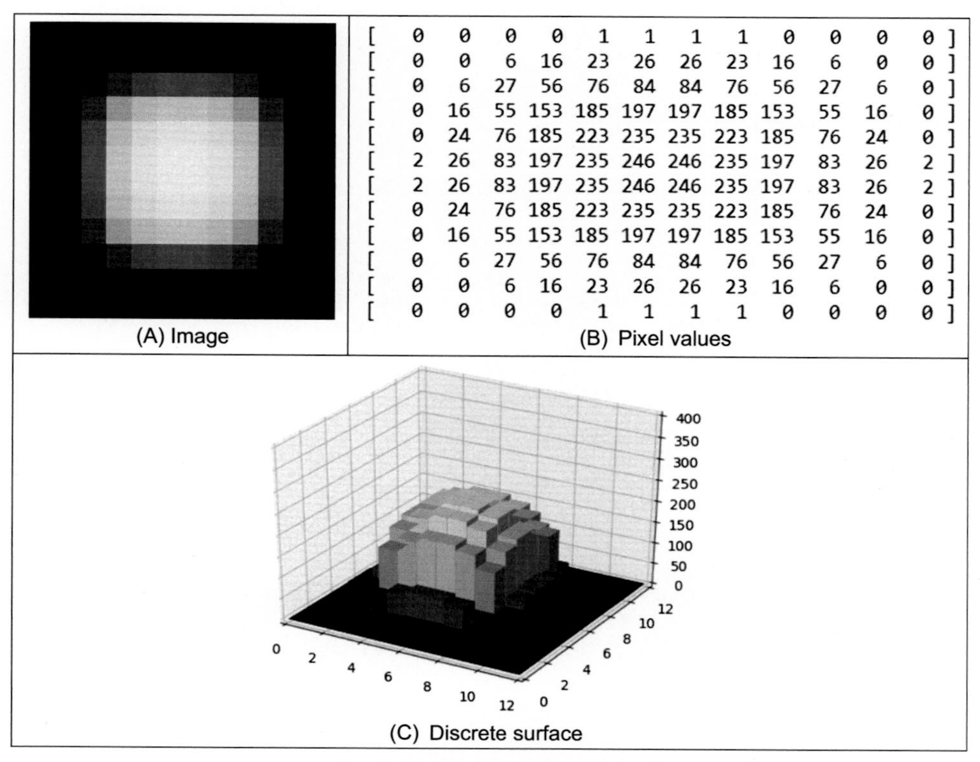

FIGURE 1.12 Python image visualization.

number of floats per pixel. In this example, we create an array to store the height value of the surface and an array to store the colour. The arrays are filled by using the data in the input image in two nested loops. Notice that indentation is used to define the scope of each loop and that image data are accessed in [row][column] format. In a grey level image, the maximum value is 255 which corresponds to white. Colour is a complex topic studied next in Section 2.2 and later in detail in Chapter 11 – we need colour here to show the images. We set the height to be larger for brighter pixels. The colour array gives the same value to the red, green and blue components, so it defines values of grey that correspond to the pixel grey value. The script uses the utility function `plot3DColorHistogram` to draw a discrete surface as shown in Fig. 1.12C.

The script in Code 1.2 illustrates the way data in an image array is processed. The script uses the function `createImageL` to create a grey level image that contains the processed data. In addition to the name of the image, the script has two variables that are used as parameters. `brightDelta` defines an amount that is added to the input pixel to produce an output pixel, and `printRange` defines a range of pixels that are printed out. Similar to Code 1.1, the script iterates through all the values of the input image by addressing the columns from 0 to width, and the rows from 0 to height. However, Code 1.2 defines the two nested loops in a single line by using the function `itertools.product` imported from `timeit`. Both the iterative and the nested loops have the same functionality. This book uses the iterator to perform nested loops to reduce indentation and keep the code clearer. Inside the loop, the output pixels $q(x,y)$ result from adding Δ_{bright} to the input pixels $p(x,y)$ as

$$q(x,y) = p(x,y) + \Delta_{bright} \tag{1.1}$$

In code, this is computed as the value of the input pixel plus the value of `brightDelta`. There is some jacketing software which prevents values exceeding 255—if the result of addition exceeds this then the value stops at 255. This is one large difference between describing algorithms as maths and as code—some of the code never appears in the maths but is necessary to make the maths work correctly. Fig. 1.13 shows the result of the script. The figure shows the input and the resulting image as well as some of the pixel values in matrix form.

1.5.3 Mathematical tools

Mathematica, Maple and Matlab are amongst the most popular of current mathematical systems, and Mathcad was used in earlier editions of this book. There have been surveys that compare their efficacy, but it is difficult to ensure precise comparison due to the impressive speed of development of techniques. Most systems have their protagonists and detractors, as in any commercial system. There are many books which use these packages for particular subjects, and there are often handbooks as addenda to the packages. We shall use Matlab throughout this text, aiming to expose the range of systems that are available. Matlab dominates this market these days, especially in image

```
# Feature Extraction and Image Processing
# Mark S. Nixon & Alberto S. Aguado
# Chapter 1: Image brightening

# Set utility folder
import sys
sys.path.insert(0, '../Utilities/')

# Iteration
from timeit import itertools

# Set utility functions
from ImageSupport import imageReadL, showImageL, printImageRangeL, createImageL

'''
Parameters:
    pathToDir = Input image directory
    imageName = Input image name
    brightDelta = Increase brightness
    printRange = Image range to print
'''
pathToDir = "Input/"
imageName = "Zebra.png"
brightDelta = 80;
printRange = [0, 10]

# Read image into array and create and output image
inputImage, width, height = imageReadL(pathToDir + imageName)
outputImage = createImageL(width, height)

# Set the pixels in the output image
for x,y in itertools.product(range(0, width), range(0, height)):
    outValue = int(inputImage[y,x]) + brightDelta
    if outValue < 255:
        outputImage[y,x] = outValue
    else:
        outputImage[y,x] = 255

# Show images
showImageL(inputImage)
showImageL(outputImage)

# Print image range
printImageRangeL(inputImage, printRange, printRange)
printImageRangeL(outputImage, printRange, printRange)
```

CODE 1.2 Image brightening.

processing and computer vision, and its growth rate has been enormous; older versions of this text used Mathcad which was more sophisticated (and WYSWYG) but had a more chequered commercial history. Note that there is an open source compatible system for Matlab called Octave. This is of course free. Most universities have a site licence for Matlab and without that it can be rather (too) expensive for many. The web links for the main mathematical packages are given in Table 1.3.

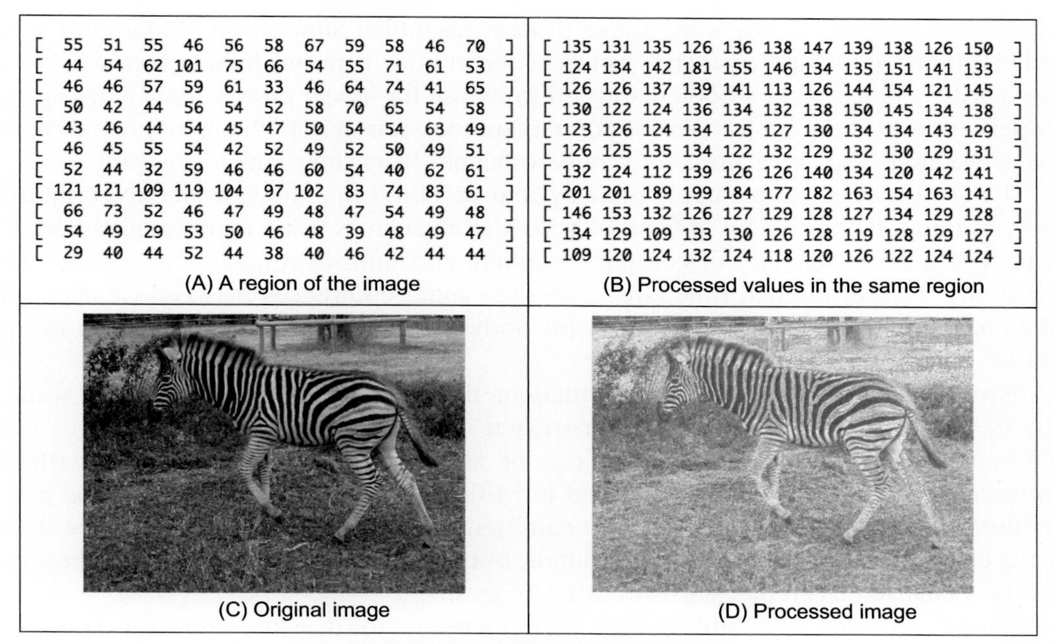

[55 51 55 46 56 58 67 59 58 46 70]
[44 54 62 101 75 66 54 55 71 61 53]
[46 46 57 59 61 33 46 64 74 41 65]
[50 42 44 56 54 52 58 70 65 54 58]
[43 46 44 54 45 47 50 54 54 63 49]
[46 45 55 54 42 52 49 52 50 49 51]
[52 44 32 59 46 46 60 54 40 62 61]
[121 121 109 119 104 97 102 83 74 83 61]
[66 73 52 46 47 49 48 47 54 49 48]
[54 49 29 53 50 46 48 39 48 49 47]
[29 40 44 52 44 38 40 46 42 44 44]
[135 131 135 126 136 138 147 139 138 126 150]
[124 134 142 181 155 146 134 135 151 141 133]
[126 126 137 139 141 113 126 144 154 121 145]
[130 122 124 136 134 132 138 150 145 134 138]
[123 126 124 134 125 127 130 134 134 143 129]
[126 125 135 134 122 132 129 132 130 129 131]
[132 124 112 139 126 126 140 134 120 142 141]
[201 201 189 199 184 177 182 163 154 163 141]
[146 153 132 126 127 129 128 127 134 129 128]
[134 129 109 133 130 126 128 119 128 129 127]
[109 120 124 132 124 118 120 126 122 124 124]

(A) A region of the image

(B) Processed values in the same region

(C) Original image

(D) Processed image

FIGURE 1.13 Processing an image in Python.

Table 1.3 Mathematical package websites.

General		
Guide to available Mathematical Software	NIST	gams.nist.gov/
Vendors		
Mathcad	Parametric Technology Corp.	ptc.com/en/products/Mathcad
Mathematica	Wolfram Research	wolfram.com/
Matlab	Mathworks	mathworks.com/
Maple	Maplesoft	maplesoft.com/
Matlab compatible		
Octave	Gnu (Free Software Foundation)	gnu.org/software/octave/

1.5.4 Hello Matlab

For those who are less enamoured with programming, we shall use the *Matlab* package to accompany Python. Matlab offers a set of mathematical tools and visualisation capabilities in a manner arranged to be very similar to conventional computer programs. The system was originally developed for matrix functions, hence the 'Mat' in the name. There are a number of advantages to Matlab, not least the potential speed advantage in computation and the facility for debugging, together with a considerable amount of established support. There is an image processing toolkit supporting Matlab, but it is rather limited compared with the range of techniques exposed in this text. Matlab's popularity is reflected in a book dedicated to its use for image processing [Gonzalez09] by perhaps one of the subject's most popular authors. It is of note that many researchers make available Matlab versions for others to benefit from their new techniques.

The Octave open source compatible system was built mainly with Matlab compatibility in mind. It shares a lot of features with Matlab such as using matrices as the basic data type, with availability of complex numbers and built-in functions as well as the capability for user-defined functions. There are some differences between Octave and Matlab, and there is extensive support for both. We shall refer to both systems using Matlab as a general term.

Essentially, Matlab is the set of instructions that process the data stored in a workspace, which can be extended by user-written commands. The workspace stores the different lists of data and these data can be stored in a MAT file; the user-written commands are functions that are stored in M-files (files with extension .M). The procedure operates by instructions at the command line to process the workspace data using either one of Matlab's own commands, or using your own commands. The results can be visualised as graphs, surfaces or as images.

Matlab provides powerful matrix manipulations to develop and test complex implementations. In this book, we avoid matrix implementations in favour of a more C++ algorithmic form. Thus, matrix expressions are transformed into loop sequences. This helps students without experience in matrix algebra to understand and implement the techniques without dependency on matrix manipulation software libraries. Implementations in this book only serve to gain understanding of the techniques' performance and correctness, and favour clarity rather than speed.

Matlab processes images, so we need to know what an image represents. Images are spatial data, which are indexed by two spatial co-ordinates. The camera senses the brightness at a point with co-ordinates x,y. Usually, x and y refer to the horizontal and vertical axes, respectively. Throughout this text we shall work in orthographic projection, ignoring perspective, where real-world co-ordinates map directly to x and y co-ordinates in an image. The homogeneous co-ordinate system is a popular and proven method for handling three-dimensional co-ordinate systems (x, y and z where z is depth), though it will not be used here as we shall process two-dimensional images only. The brightness sensed by a camera is transformed to a signal which is stored as a value within the computer, referenced to the co-ordinates x,y in the image. Accordingly, a computer image is a matrix of points. For a greyscale image, the value of each point is proportional to the brightness of the corresponding point in the scene viewed by the camera. These points are the picture elements, or pixels.

Consider, for example, the set of pixel values in Fig. 1.14A. These values were derived from the image of a bright peak on a dark background. The peak is brighter where the pixels have a larger value (here over 200 brightness levels); the background is dark and those pixels have a smaller value (near 0 brightness levels). (We shall consider how many

0	0	0	0	1	2	2	1	0	0	0	0
0	0	6	16	23	26	26	23	16	6	0	0
0	24	76	185	223	235	235	223	185	76	24	0
0	24	76	185	223	235	235	223	185	76	24	0
0	24	76	185	223	235	235	223	185	76	24	0
2	26	83	197	235	246	246	235	197	83	26	2
2	26	83	197	235	246	246	235	197	83	26	2
0	24	76	185	223	235	235	223	185	76	24	0
0	24	76	185	223	235	235	223	185	76	24	0
0	24	76	185	223	235	235	223	185	76	24	0
0	0	6	16	23	26	26	23	16	6	0	0
0	0	0	0	1	2	2	1	0	0	0	0

(A) Set of pixel values

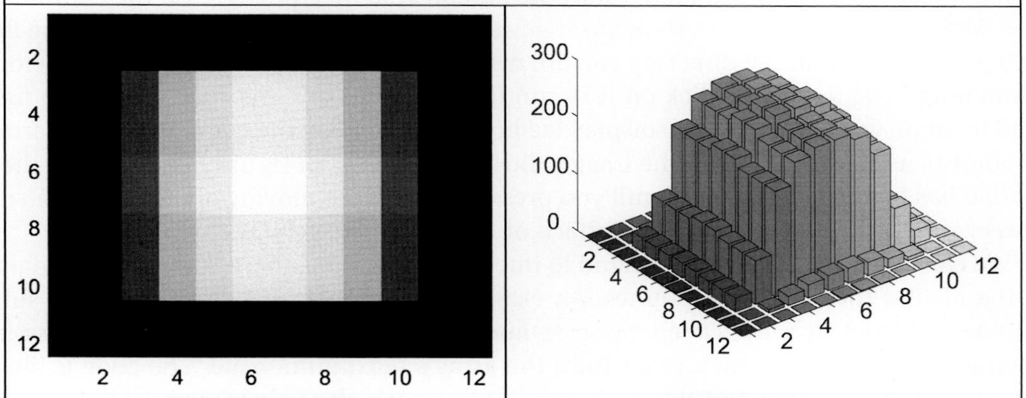

(B) Matlab image

(C) Matlab surface plot

FIGURE 1.14 Matlab image visualization.

points we need in an image and the possible range of values for pixels in Chapter 2.) The peak can be viewed as an image in Fig. 1.14B, or as a surface in Fig. 1.14C.

As in the Python code, there are considerably more sophisticated systems and usage than this version of Matlab code. Like Python in Section 1.5.2, our aim here is not to show people how to use Matlab and all its wonderful functionality. We are using the simplest versions with default settings so that people can process images quickly and conveniently. The Matlab code might appear clearer than the Python code. It is, but that is at the cost of access to data, and Python has much greater freedom there. One can get

```
%read in an image
a=imread('Input\Square.png');
%view image
imagesc(a);
%view it in black and white
disp ('We shall  display the data as a grey level image')
colormap(gray);
% Let's hold so we can view it
disp ('When you are ready to move on, press RETURN')
pause;
disp ('Now we shall display the data as a surface')
bar3(a);
```

CODE 1.3 Example Matlab script.

to Manchester from London using a Mini or a Rolls Royce: the style is different (and the effect on the environment is different....), but the result is the same. That is how we shall use Python and Matlab in this textbook.

Matlab runs on Unix/Linux, Windows and Macintosh systems; a student version is available. We shall use a script, to develop our approaches, which is the simplest type of M-file, as illustrated in Code 1.3. To start the Matlab system, type `Matlab` at the command line. At the `Matlab` prompt `(>>)`type `chapter1` to load and run the script (given that the file `Code_1_3.m` is saved in the directory you are working in). Alternatively, open the directory containing `Code_1_3.m` and click on it to run it. Comments are preceded by a `%`; we first read in an image. Having set the display facility to black and white, we can view the array of points `a` as a surface. When the image, illustrated in Fig. 1.14B has been plotted, then Matlab has been made to `pause` until you press `Return` before moving on. Here, when you press `Return`, you will next see the surface of the array, Fig. 1.14C.

We can use Matlab's own command to interrogate the data: these commands find use in the M-files that store subroutines. An example routine is called after this. This subroutine is stored in a file called `invert.m` and is a function that inverts brightness by subtracting the value of each point from the array's maximum value. The code is illustrated in Code 1.4. Note that this code uses for loops which are best avoided to improve speed, using Matlab's vectorised operations. The whole procedure can actually be implemented by the command `inverted =max(max(pic))-pic`. In fact, one of Matlab's assets is a 'profiler' which allows you to determine exactly how much time is spend on different parts of your programs. Naturally, there is facility for importing graphics files, which is quite extensive (i.e., it accepts a wide range of file formats). When images are used we find that Matlab has a range of data types. We must move from the unsigned integer data type, used for images, to the double-precision data type to allow processing as a set of real numbers. (Matlab does make this rather easy and can handle complex numbers with ease too.) In these ways Matlab can, and will, be used to process images throughout this book, with the caveat that this is not a book about Matlab (or Python). Note that the translation to application code is perhaps easier via Matlab than for other

```
function inverted = invert(image)

% Subtract image point brightness from maximum
% Usage: new image = invert(old image)
% Parameters: image      - array of points

[rows,cols]=size(image); % get dimensions

maxi = max(max(image)); % find the maximum

% subtract image points from maximum
for x = 1:cols %address all columns
  for y = 1:rows %address all rows
    inverted(y,x)=maxi-image(y,x);
  end
end
```

CODE 1.4 Matlab function `invert.m` to invert an Image.

systems, and it offers direct compilation of the code. There are Matlab scripts available at the book's website (https://www.southampton.ac.uk/~msn/book/) for online tutorial support of the material in this book. As with the caveat earlier, these are provided for educational purposes only. There are many other implementations of techniques available on the web in Matlab. The edits required to make the Matlab worksheets run in Octave are described in the file readme.txt in the downloaded zip.

1.6 Associated literature

1.6.1 Journals, magazines and conferences

As in any academic subject, there are many sources of literature and when used within this text the cited references are to be found at the end of each chapter. The professional magazines include those that are more systems oriented, like *Vision Systems Design*. These provide more general articles and are often a good source of information about new computer vision products. For example, they survey available equipment, such as cameras and monitors, and provide listings of those available, including some of the factors by which you might choose to purchase them.

There is a wide selection of research journals – probably more than you can find in your nearest library unless it is particularly well stocked. These journals have different merits: some are targeted at short papers only, whereas some have short and long papers; some are more dedicated to the development of new theory, whereas others are more pragmatic and focus more on practical, working, image processing systems. But it is rather naive to classify journals in this way, since all journals welcome good research, with new ideas, which has been demonstrated to satisfy promising objectives.

The main research journals include *IEEE Transactions on Pattern Analysis and Machine Intelligence* (in later references this will be abbreviated to *IEEE Trans. on PAMI*); *Image Processing* (*IP*); *Systems, Man and Cybernetics* (*SMC*); and on *Medical Imaging* (there are many more IEEE transactions, e.g., the *IEEE Transactions on Biometrics, Behavior and Identity Science,* which sometimes publish papers of interest in, or application of, image processing and computer vision). The *IEEE Transactions* are usually found in (university) libraries since they are available at comparatively low cost; they are online to subscribers at the IEEE Explore site (ieeexplore.ieee.org/) and include conferences. *Computer Vision and Image Understanding* and *Graphical Models and Image Processing* arose from the splitting of one of the subject's earlier journals, *Computer Vision, Graphics and Image Processing* (*CVGIP*), into two parts. Do not confuse *Pattern Recognition* (*Pattern Recog.*) with *Pattern Recognition Letters* (*Pattern Recog. Lett.*), published under the aegis of the Pattern Recognition Society and the International Association of Pattern Recognition, respectively, since the latter contains shorter papers only. The *International Journal of Computer Vision* and *Image and Vision Computing* are well established journals too. Finally, do not miss out on the *IET Computer Vision* and other journals.

Most journals are now online, but usually to subscribers only; some go back a long way. Academic Press titles include *Computer Vision and Image Understanding, Graphical Models and Image Processing* and *Real-Time Image Processing.*

There are plenty of *conferences* too: the proceedings of IEEE conferences are also held on the Explore site and two of the top conferences are *Computer Vision and Pattern Recognition* (*CVPR*) which is held annually in the United States, the *International Conference on Computer Vision* (*ICCV*) is biennial and moves internationally. The IEEE also hosts specialist conferences, e.g., on biometrics or on computational photography. *Lecture Notes in Computer Science* are hosted by Springer (springer.com) and are usually the proceedings of conferences. Some conferences such as the *British Machine Vision Conference* series maintain their own site (bmva.org). The excellent Computer Vision Conferences page conferences.visionbib.com/Iris-Conferences.html is brought to us by Keith Price and lists conferences in Computer Vision, Image Processing and Pattern Recognition.

1.6.2 Textbooks

There are many *textbooks* in this area. Increasingly, there are web versions, or web support, as summarised in Table 1.4. The difficulty is of access as you need a subscription to be able to access the online book (and sometimes even to see that it is available online), though there are also Kindle versions. For example, this book is available online to those subscribing to Referex in Engineering Village (engineeringvillage.org). The site given in Table 1.4 for this book is the support site which includes demonstrations, worksheets, errata and other information. The site given next, at Edinburgh University, the UK, is part of the excellent CVOnline site (many thanks to

Table 1.4 Web textbooks and homepages.

This book's homepage	Southampton University	https://www.southampton.ac.uk/~msn/book/
CVOnline – online book compendium	Edinburgh University	homepages.inf.ed.ac.uk/rbf/CVonline/books.htm
World of Mathematics	Wolfram Research	mathworld.wolfram.com
Numerical Recipes	Cambridge University Press	numerical.recipes
Digital signal Processing	Steven W. Smith	dspguide.com
The Joy of Visual Perception	York University	https://www.yorku.ca/eye/

Bob Fisher there) and it lists current books as well pdfs of which are more dated, but still excellent (e.g., [Ballard82]). There is also continuing debate on appropriate education in image processing and computer vision, for which review material is available [Bebis03].

For support material, the *World of Mathematics* comes from Wolfram research (the distributors of Mathematica) and gives an excellent web-based reference for mathematics. *Numerical Recipes* [Press07] is one of the best established texts in signal processing. It is beautifully written, with examples and implementation and is on the web too. *Digital Signal Processing* is an online site with focus on the more theoretical aspects which will be covered in Chapter 2. *The Joy of Visual Perception* is an online site on how the human vision system works. We have not noted *Wikipedia* – computer vision is there too.

By way of context, for comparison with other textbooks, this text aims to start at the foundation of computer vision, and to reach current research. Its content specifically addresses techniques for image analysis, considering feature extraction and shape analysis in particular. Matlab and Python are used as vehicles to demonstrate implementation. There are of course other texts, and these can help you to develop your interest in other areas of computer vision.

Some of the main textbooks are now out of print, but pdfs can be found at the CVOnline site. There are more than given here, some of which will be referred to in later chapters; each offers a particular view or insight into computer vision and image processing. Some of the main textbooks include *Vision* [Marr82] which concerns vision and visual perception (as previously mentioned); *Fundamentals of Computer Vision* [Jain89] which is stacked with theory and technique, but omits implementation and some image analysis, as does *Robot Vision* [Horn86]; *Machine Vision* [Jain95] offers concise coverage of 3D and motion; *Digital Image Processing* [Gonzalez17] has more tutorial elements than many of the basically theoretical texts and has a fantastic reputation for introducing people to the field; *Digital Picture Processing* [Rosenfeld82] is very dated now, but is a well-proven text for much of the basic material; and *Digital Image Processing* [Pratt01], which was originally one of the earliest books on image processing, and like *Digital Picture Processing*, is a well-proven text for much of the basic material, particularly image transforms. Despite its name, *Active Contours* [Blake98] concentrates rather more on models of motion and deformation and probabilistic treatment of shape and motion than on the active contours which we shall find here. As such it is a more research text, reviewing many of the advanced techniques to describe shapes and their motion. *Image Processing – The Fundamentals* [Petrou10] (by two Petrous!) surveys the subject (as its title implies) from an image processing viewpoint. *Computer Vision* [Shapiro01] includes chapters on image databases and on virtual and augmented reality. *Computer Vision: A Modern Approach* [Forsyth11] offers much new – and needed – insight into this continually developing subject. One text [Brunelli09] focusses on object recognition techniques 'employing the idea of projection to match image patterns' which is a class of approaches to be found later in this text. A much newer text *Computer Vision: Algorithms and Applications* [Szeliski11] is naturally much more up to date than older texts, and has an online (earlier) electronic version available too. An excellent (and popular) text *Computer Vision Models, Learning, and Inference* [Prince12] – electronic version available – is based on models and learning. One of the bases of the book is 'to organize our knowledge ... what is most critical is the model itself – the statistical relationship between the world and the measurements' and thus covers many of the learning aspects of computer vision which complement and extend this book's focus on feature extraction. Finally, very recently there has been a condensed coverage of Image Processing and Analysis [Gimel'farb18].

Also, Kasturi, R., and Jain, R. C. eds: *Computer Vision: Principles* [Kasturi91a] and *Computer Vision: Advances and Applications* [Kasturi91b] present a collection of seminal papers in computer vision, many of which are cited in their original form (rather than in this volume) in later chapters. There are other interesting edited collections [Chellappa92], one edition [Bowyer96] honours Azriel Rosenfeld's many contributions.

Section 1.5 describes some of the image processing software packages available and their textbook descriptions. Of the texts with a more practical flavour *Image Processing and Computer Vision* [Parker10] includes description of software rather at the expense of lacking range of technique. There is excellent coverage of practicality in *Practical Algorithms for Image Analysis* [O'Gorman08]. One JAVA text, *The Art of Image Processing with Java,* [Hunt11] emphasises software engineering more than feature extraction (giving basic methods only).

Other textbooks include the long-standing *The Image Processing Handbook* [Russ17] which contains many basic techniques with excellent visual support, but without any supporting theory; *Computer Vision: Principles, Algorithms, Applications, Learning* [Davies17] which is targeted primarily at (industrial) machine vision systems but covers much basic techniques, with pseudocode to describe their implementation; and the *Handbook of Pattern Recognition and Computer Vision* [Cheng16] covers much technique. There are specialist texts too and they usually concern particular sections of this book, and they will be mentioned there. Last but by no means least, there is even a (illustrated) dictionary [Fisher13] to guide you through the terms that are used.

1.6.3 The web

This book's homepage (https://www.southampton.ac.uk/~msn/book/) details much of the support material, including worksheets, code and demonstrations, and any errata we regret have occurred (and been found). The Computer Vision Online (CVOnline) homepage homepages.inf.ed.ac.uk/rbf/CVonline/ has been brought to us by Bob Fisher from the University of Edinburgh. There's a host of materials, including its description. If you have access to the web-based indexes of published papers, the Web of Science covers a lot and includes INSPEC which has papers more related to engineering, together with papers in conferences. Explore is for the IEEE – with paper access for subscribers; many researchers turn to Google Scholar as this is freely available with ability to retrieve the papers as well as to see where they have been used. Many use Scholar since it also allows you to see the collection (and metrics) of papers in authors' pages. The availability of papers within these systems has been changing with the new Open Access systems, which at the time of writing are still in some flux.

1.7 Conclusions

This chapter has covered most of the pre-requisites for feature extraction in image processing and computer vision. We need to know how we see, in some form, where we can find information and how to process data. More importantly, we need an image, or some form of spatial data. This is to be stored in a computer and processed by our new techniques. As it consists of data points stored in a computer, these data are sampled or discrete. Extra material on image formation, camera models and image geometry is to be found in Chapter 10, but we shall be considering images as a planar array of points hereon. We need to know some of the bounds on the sampling process, on how the image is formed. These are the subjects of the next chapter which also introduces a new way of looking at the data, how it is interpreted (and processed) in terms of frequency.

References

[Adelson05] Adelson, E. H. and Wang, J. Y. A., 1992. Single Lens Stereo With a Plenoptic Camera, IEEE Trans. on PAMI, (2), pp 99-106.

[Armstrong91] Armstrong, T., *Colour Perception – A Practical Approach to Colour Theory*, Tarquin Publications, Diss UK, 1991.

[Ballard82] Ballard, D. H., Brown, C. M., *Computer Vision*, Prentice-Hall Inc New Jersey USA, 1982.

[Bebis03] Bebis, G., Egbert, D., and Shah, M., Review of Computer Vision Education, IEEE Transactions on Education, 46(1), pp. 2-21, 2003.

[Blake98] Blake, A., and Isard, M., *Active Contours*, Springer-Verlag London Limited, London UK, 1998.

[Bowyer96] Bowyer, K., and Ahuja, N., Eds., Advances in Image Understanding, A Festschrift for Azriel Rosenfeld, IEEE Computer Society Press, Los Alamitos, CA USA, 1996.

[Bradski08] Bradski, G., and Kaehler, A., *Learning OpenCV: Computer Vision With the OpenCV Library*, O'Reilly Media, Inc, Sebastopol, CA USA, 2008.

[Bruce90] Bruce, V., and Green, P., *Visual Perception: Physiology, Psychology and Ecology*, 2nd Edition, Lawrence Erlbaum Associates, Hove UK, 1990.

[Chellappa92] Chellappa, R., *Digital Image Processing*, 2nd Edition, IEEE Computer Society Press, Los Alamitos, CA USA, 1992.

[Cheng16] Cheng, C. H., and Wang, P. S. P., *Handbook of Pattern Recognition and Computer Vision*, 5th Edition, World Scientific, Singapore, 2016.

[Cornsweet70] Cornsweet, T. N., *Visual Perception*, Academic Press Inc., N.Y. USA, 1970.

[Davies17] Davies, E. R., *Computer Vision: Principles, Algorithms, Applications, Learning*, Academic Press, 5th Edition, 2017.

[Fisher13] Fisher, R. B., Breckon, T. P., Dawson-Howe, K., Fitzgibbon, A., and Robertson, C., Trucco, E., and Williams C. K. I., *Dictionary of Computer Vision and Image Processing*, Wiley, Chichester UK, 2nd Ed 2013.

[Forsyth11] Forsyth, D., and Ponce, J., *Computer Vision: A Modern Approach*, Prentice Hall, N.J. USA, 2nd Edition 2011.

[Fossum97] Fossum, E. R., CMOS Image Sensors: Electronic Camera-On-A-Chip, IEEE Transactions on Electron Devices, 44(10), pp1689-1698, 1997.

[Gimel'farb18] Gimel'farb, G., Patrice, D., *Image Processing and Analysis: A Primer*, World Scientific Europe Ltd, London UK, 2018.

[Gonzalez17] Gonzalez, R. C., and Woods, R. E., *Digital Image Processing*, 4th Edition, Pearson Education, 2017.

[Gonzalez09] Gonzalez, R. C., Woods, R. E., and Eddins, S. L., *Digital Image Processing Using MATLAB*, Prentice Hall, 2nd Edition, 2009.

[Horn86] Horn, B. K. P., *Robot Vision*, MIT Press, Boston USA, 1986.

[Hunt11] Hunt, K. A., *The Art of Image Processing with Java*, CRC Press (A. K. Peters Ltd), Natick MA USA, 2011.

[Jain89] Jain A. K., *Fundamentals of Computer Vision*, Prentice Hall International (UK) Ltd, Hemel Hempstead UK, 1989.

[Jain95] Jain, R. C., Kasturi, R., and Schunk, B. G., *Machine Vision*, McGraw-Hill Book Co., Singapore, 1995.

[Kasturi91a] Kasturi, R., and Jain, R. C., *Computer Vision: Principles*, IEEE Computer Society Press, Los Alamitos CA USA, 1991.

[Kasturi91b] Kasturi, R., and Jain, R. C., *Computer Vision: Advances and Applications*, IEEE Computer Society Press, Los Alamitos CA USA, 1991.

[Kuroda14] Kuroda, T., *Essential Principles of Image Sensors*, CRC Press, Boca Raton FL USA, 2014.

[Lichtsteiner08] Lichtsteiner, P., Posch, C., and Delbruck, T., A 128×128 120 Db 15μs Latency Asynchronous Temporal Contrast Vision Sensor. IEEE Journal of Solid-State Circuits, 43(2), pp 566–576, 2008.

[Livingstone14] Livingstone, M. S., *Vision and Art* (Updated and Expanded Edition), Harry N. Abrams, New York USA, 2nd Edition 2014.

[Lutz13] Lutz, M., *Learning Python*, O'Reilly Media, Sebastopol CA USA, 5th Edition 2013.

[Marr82] Marr, D., *Vision*, W. H. Freeman and Co., N.Y. USA, 1982.

[Nakamura05] Nakamura, J., *Image Sensors and Signal Processing for Digital Still Cameras,* CRC Press, Boca Raton FL USA, 2005.

[O'Gorman08] O'Gorman, L., and Sammon, M. J., Seul, M., *Practical Algorithms for Image Analysis,* 2nd Edition, Cambridge University Press, Cambridge UK, 2008.

[Overington92] Overington, I., *Computer Vision – A Unified, Biologically-Inspired Approach,* Elsevier Science Press, Holland, 1992.

[Parker10] Parker, J. R., *Algorithms for Image Processing and Computer Vision,* Wiley, Indianapolis IN USA, 2nd Edition 2010.

[Petrou10] Petrou, M., and Petrou, C., *Image Processing – the Fundamentals,* Wiley-Blackwell, London UK, 2nd Edition, 2010.

[Phillips18] Phillips J. B., and Eliasson, H., *Camera Image Quality Benchmarking,* Wiley, Hoboken NJ USA, 2018.

[Pratt01] Pratt, W. K., *Digital Image Processing: PIKS inside,* Wiley, 3rd Edition, 2001.

[Press07] Press, W. H., Teukolsky, S. A., Vetterling, W. T., and Flannery, B. P., *Numerical Recipes 3rd Edition: The Art of Scientific Computing,* 3rd Edition, Cambridge University Press, Cambridge UK, 2007.

[Prince12] Prince, S. J. D., *Computer Vision Models, Learning, and Inference,* Cambridge University Press, Cambridge UK, 2012.

[Ratliff65] Ratliff, F., *Mach Bands: Quantitative Studies on Neural Networks in the Retina,* Holden-Day Inc., San Francisco USA, 1965.

[Rosenfeld82] Rosenfeld, A., and Kak, A. C., Digital Picture Processing, 2nd Edition, vols 1 and 2, Academic Press Inc., Orlando FL USA, 1982.

[Russ17] Russ, J. C., *The Image Processing Handbook,* 7th Edition, CRC Press (Taylor & Francis), Boca Raton FL USA, 2017.

[Shapiro01] Shapiro, L. G., and Stockman, G. C., *Computer Vision,* Prentice Hall, 2001.

[Solem12] Solem, JE, *Programming Computer Vision with Python: Tools and Algorithms for Analyzing Images,* O'Reilly Media Newton Mass. USA, 2012.

[Son17] Son, B., Suh, Y., Kim, S., Jung, H., Kim, J.S., Shin, C., Park, K., Lee, K., Park, J., Woo, J. and Roh, Y., A 640×480 Dynamic Vision Sensor with a 9μm Pixel and 300Meps Address-Event Representation. Proc. 2017 IEEE Int.l Solid-State Circuits Conf. (ISSCC). pp 66-67. 2017.

[Szeliski11] Szeliski, R., *Computer Vision: Algorithms and Applications,* Springer Verlag, London UK, 2011.

[Wu17] Wu, G., Masia, B., Jarabo, A., Zhang, Y., Wang, L., Dai, Q., Chai, T. and Liu, Y., Light Field Image Processing: an Overview. IEEE J. of Selected Topics in Signal Processing, 11(7), pp 926-954, 2017.

2

Images, sampling and frequency domain processing

2.1 Overview

In this chapter, we shall look at the basic theory which underlies image formation and processing. We shall start by investigating what makes up a picture and look at the consequences of having a different number of points in the image. We shall also look at images in a different representation, known as the frequency domain. In this, as the name implies, we consider an image as a collection of frequency components. We can actually operate on images in the frequency domain and we shall also consider different transformation processes. These allow us different insights into images and image processing which will be used in later chapters not only as a means to develop techniques but also to give faster (computer) processing (Table 2.1).

2.2 Image formation

A computer image is a matrix (a two-dimensional (2D) array) of *pixels*. The value of each pixel is proportional to the brightness of the corresponding point in the scene; its value is, of course, usually derived from the output of an A/D converter. We can define a square image as $N \times N$ m-bit pixels, where N is the number of points and m controls the

Table 2.1 Overview of chapter 2.

Main topic	Subtopics	Main points
Images	Effects of differing numbers of points and of number range for those points.	*Greyscale*, *colour*, *resolution*, dynamic range, storage.
Fourier transform theory	What is meant by the frequency domain, how it applies to discrete (sampled) images, how it allows us to interpret images and the sampling resolution (number of points).	*Continuous Fourier transform* and properties, sampling criterion, *discrete Fourier transform* and properties, image transformation, transform duals, *inverse Fourier transform,* importance of *magnitude* and *phase*.
Consequences of transform approach	Basic properties of Fourier transforms, other transforms, frequency domain operations.	*Translation* (shift), *rotation* and *scaling; principle of superposition* and linearity; *Walsh*, *Hartley*, *discrete cosine* and *wavelet transforms; filtering* and other operations.

Feature Extraction and Image Processing for Computer Vision. https://doi.org/10.1016/B978-0-12-814976-8.00002-6

number of brightness values. Using m bits gives a range of 2^m values, ranging from 0 to 2^m-1. If m is 8, this gives brightness levels ranging between 0 and 255, which are usually displayed as black and white, respectively, with shades of grey in between, as they are for the *greyscale image* of a scene in Fig. 2.1A. Smaller values of m give fewer available levels reducing the available contrast in an image. We are concerned with images here, not their formation; imaging geometry (pinhole cameras etc.) is to be found in Chapter 10.

The ideal value of m is actually related to the *signal to noise ratio* (*dynamic range*) of the camera. This is stated as approximately 45 dB for an analog camera and since there are 6 dB per bit, then 8 bits will cover the available range. Choosing 8-bit pixels has further advantages in that it is very convenient to store pixel values as bytes, and 8-bit A/D converters are cheaper than those with a higher resolution. For these reasons images are nearly always stored as 8-bit bytes, though some applications use a different

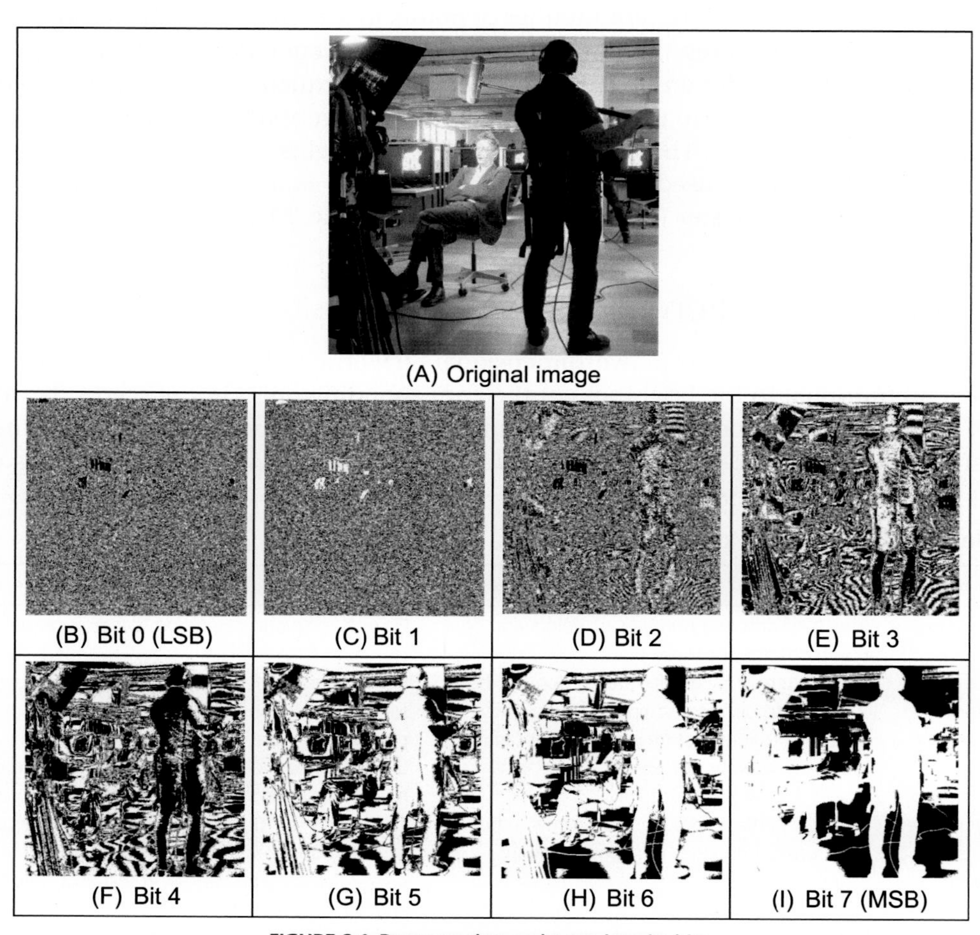

FIGURE 2.1 Decomposing an image into its bits.

range. These are the 8-bit numbers encountered in Section 1.5.2, stored as unsigned 8-bit bytes (`uint8`). The relative influence of the 8 bits is shown in the image of the subjects in Fig. 2.1. Here, the least significant bit, bit 0 (Fig. 2.1B), carries the least information (it changes most rapidly) and is largely noise. As the order of the bits increases, they change less rapidly and carry more information. The most information is carried by the most significant bit, bit 7 (Fig. 2.1I). Clearly, the fact that there are people in the original image can be recognised much better from the high order bits, much more reliably than it can from the other bits (also notice the odd effects which would appear to come from lighting in the middle order bits). The variation in lighting is hardly perceived by human vision.

Colour images (also mentioned in Section 1.5.2) follow a similar storage strategy to specify pixels' intensities. However, instead of using just one image plane, colour images are represented by three intensity components. These components generally correspond to red, green and blue (the RGB model) although there are other colour schemes. For example, the CMYK colour model is defined by the components cyan, magenta, yellow and black. In any colour mode, the pixel's colour can be specified in two main ways. First, you can associate an integer value, with each pixel, that can be used as an index to a table that stores the intensity of each colour component. The index is used to recover the actual colour from the table when the pixel is going to be displayed, or processed. In this scheme, the table is known as the image's palette and the display is said to be performed by colour mapping. The main reason for using this colour representation is to reduce memory requirements. That is, we only store a single image plane (i.e. the indices) and the palette. This is less than storing the red, green and blue components separately and so makes the hardware cheaper, and it can have other advantages, for example, when the image is transmitted. The main disadvantage is that the quality of the image is reduced since only a reduced collection of colours is actually used. An alternative to represent colour is to use several image planes to store the colour components of each pixel. This scheme is known as true colour, and it represents an image more accurately, essentially by considering more colours. The most common format uses 8 bits for each of the three RGB components. These images are known as 24-bit true colour, and they can contain 16,777,216 different colours simultaneously. In spite of requiring significantly more memory, the image quality and the continuing reduction in cost of computer memory make this format a good alternative, even for storing the image frames from a video sequence. Of course, a good compression algorithm is always helpful in these cases, particularly, if images need to be transmitted on a network. Here we will consider the processing of grey level images only since they contain enough information to perform feature extraction and image analysis; greater depth on colour analysis/parameterisation is to be found in Chapter 11. Should the image be originally in colour, we will consider processing its luminance only, often computed in a standard way. In any case, the amount of memory used is always related to the image size.

Choosing an appropriate value for the image size, N, is far more complicated. We want N to be sufficiently large to resolve the required level of spatial detail in the image.

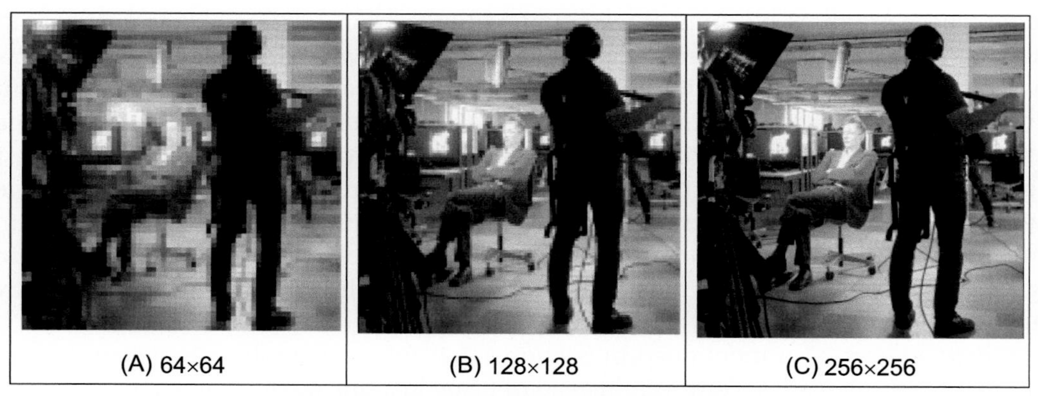

FIGURE 2.2 Effects of differing image resolution.

If N is too small, the image will be coarsely *quantised*: lines will appear to be very 'blocky' and some of the details will be lost. Larger values of N give more detail, but need more storage space, and the images will take longer to process, since there are more pixels. For example, with reference to the image in Fig. 2.1A, Fig 2.2 shows the effect of taking the image at different resolutions. Fig. 2.2A is a 64 × 64 image, which shows only the broad structure. It is impossible to see any detail in the sitting subject's face, or anywhere else. Fig. 2.2B is a 128 × 128 image, which is starting to show more of the detail, but it would be hard to determine the subject's identity. The original image, repeated in Fig. 2.2C, is a 256×256 image which shows a much greater level of detail, and the subject can be recognised from the image. Note that the images in Fig. 2.2 have been scaled to be the same size. As such, the pixels in Fig. 2.2A are much larger than those in Fig. 2.2C which emphasises its blocky structure. Common choices are for 512 × 512 or 1024 × 1024 8-bit images which require 256 KB and 1 MB of storage, respectively. If we take a sequence of, say, 20 images for motion analysis, we will need more than 5 MB to store 20 512 × 512 images. Even though memory continues to become cheaper, this can still impose high cost. But it is not just cost which motivates an investigation of the appropriate image size, the appropriate value for N. The main question is: are there theoretical guidelines for choosing it? The short answer is 'yes'; the long answer is to look at digital signal processing theory.

The choice of sampling frequency is dictated by the *sampling criterion*. Presenting the sampling criterion requires understanding of how we interpret signals in the *frequency domain*. The way in is to look at the Fourier transform. This is a highly theoretical topic, but do not let that put you off (it leads to image coding, like the JPEG format, so it is very useful indeed). The Fourier transform has found many uses in image processing and understanding; it might appear to be a complex topic (that is actually a horrible pun!), but it is a very rewarding one to study. The particular concern is number of points per unit area or the appropriate sampling frequency of (essentially, the value for N), or the rate at which pixel values are taken from, a camera's video signal.

2.3 The Fourier Transform

The *Fourier transform* is a way of mapping a signal into its component frequencies. *Frequency* measures in Hertz (Hz), the rate of repetition with time, measured in seconds (s); time is the reciprocal of frequency and vice versa (Hertz = 1/seconds; s = 1/Hz).

Consider a music centre: the sound comes from a computer, a CD player (or a tape, whatever) and is played on the speakers after it has been processed by the amplifier. On the amplifier, you can change the bass or the treble (or the loudness which is a combination of bass and treble). Bass covers the low-frequency components and treble covers the high-frequency ones. The Fourier transform is a way of mapping the signal, which is a signal varying continuously with time, into its frequency components. When we have transformed the signal, we know which frequencies made up the original sound.

So why do we do this? We have not changed the signal, only its representation. We can now visualise it in terms of its frequencies, rather than as a voltage which changes with time. However, we can now change the frequencies (because we can see them clearly), and this will change the sound. If, say, there is hiss on the original signal, then since hiss is a high-frequency component, it will show up as a high-frequency component in the Fourier transform. So we can see how to remove it by looking at the Fourier transform. If you have ever used a graphic equaliser, you have done this before. The graphic equaliser is a way of changing a signal by interpreting its frequency domain representation; you can selectively control the frequency content by changing the positions of the controls of the graphic equaliser. The equation which defines the *Fourier transform*, Fp, of a signal p, is given by a complex integral

$$Fp(\omega) = \Im(p(t)) = \int_{-\infty}^{\infty} p(t)e^{-j\omega t}dt \tag{2.1}$$

where $Fp(\omega)$ is the Fourier transform and $\Im$ denotes the Fourier transform process; ω is the angular frequency, $\omega = 2\pi f$ measured in radians/s (where the frequency f is the reciprocal of time t, $f = 1/t$); j is the complex variable $j = \sqrt{-1}$ (electronic engineers prefer j to i since they cannot confuse it with the symbol for current; perhaps they do not want to be mistaken for mathematicians who use $i = \sqrt{-1}$), $p(t)$ is a *continuous signal* (varying continuously with time); and $e^{-j\omega t} = \cos(\omega t) - j\sin(\omega t)$ gives the frequency components in $p(t)$.

We can derive the Fourier transform by applying Eq. (2.1) to the signal of interest. We can see how it works by constraining our analysis to simple signals. (We can then say that complicated signals are just made up by adding up lots of simple signals.) If we take a pulse which is of amplitude (size) A between when it starts at time $t = -T/2$ and it ends at $t = T/2$, and zero elsewhere, the *pulse* is

$$p(t) = \begin{vmatrix} A & \text{if} \quad -T/2 \le t \le T/2 \\ 0 & \text{otherwise} \end{vmatrix} \tag{2.2}$$

To obtain the Fourier transform, we substitute for $p(t)$ in Eq. (2.1). $p(t) = A$ only for a specified time so we choose the limits on the integral to be the start and end points of our pulse (it is zero elsewhere) and set $p(t) = A$, its value in this time interval. The Fourier transform of this pulse is the result of computing

$$Fp(\omega) = \int_{-T/2}^{T/2} Ae^{-j\omega t}dt \tag{2.3}$$

When we solve this we obtain an expression for $Fp(\omega)$

$$Fp(\omega) = -\frac{Ae^{-j\omega T/2} - Ae^{j\omega T/2}}{j\omega} \tag{2.4}$$

By simplification, using the relation $\sin(\theta) = (e^{j\theta} - e^{-j\theta})/2j$, then the Fourier transform of the pulse is

$$Fp(\omega) = \begin{vmatrix} \frac{2A}{\omega}\sin\left(\frac{\omega T}{2}\right) & \text{if} \quad \omega \neq 0 \\ AT \quad \text{if} \quad \omega = 0 \end{vmatrix} \tag{2.5}$$

This is a version of the *sinc* function, $\text{sinc}(x) = \sin(x)/x$. The original pulse and its transform are illustrated in Fig. 2.3. Eq. (2.5) (as plotted in Fig. 2.3B) suggests that a pulse is made up of a lot of low frequencies (the main body of the pulse) and a few higher frequencies (which give us the edges of the pulse). (The range of frequencies is symmetrical around zero frequency; negative frequency is a necessary mathematical abstraction.) The plot of the Fourier transform is actually called the *spectrum* of the signal, which can be considered akin with the spectrum of light.

So what actually is this Fourier transform? It tells us what frequencies make up a time domain signal. The magnitude of the transform at a particular frequency is the amount of that frequency in the original signal. If we collect together sinusoidal signals in amounts specified by the Fourier transform, we should obtain the originally transformed signal. This process is illustrated in Fig. 2.4 for the signal and transform illustrated in Fig. 2.3. Note that since the Fourier transform is actually a complex number it has real and imaginary parts, and we only plot the real part here. A low frequency, that for $\omega = 1$,

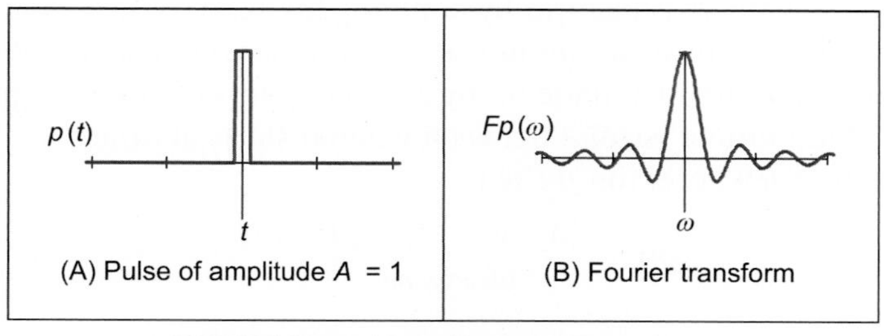

FIGURE 2.3 A pulse and its Fourier transform.

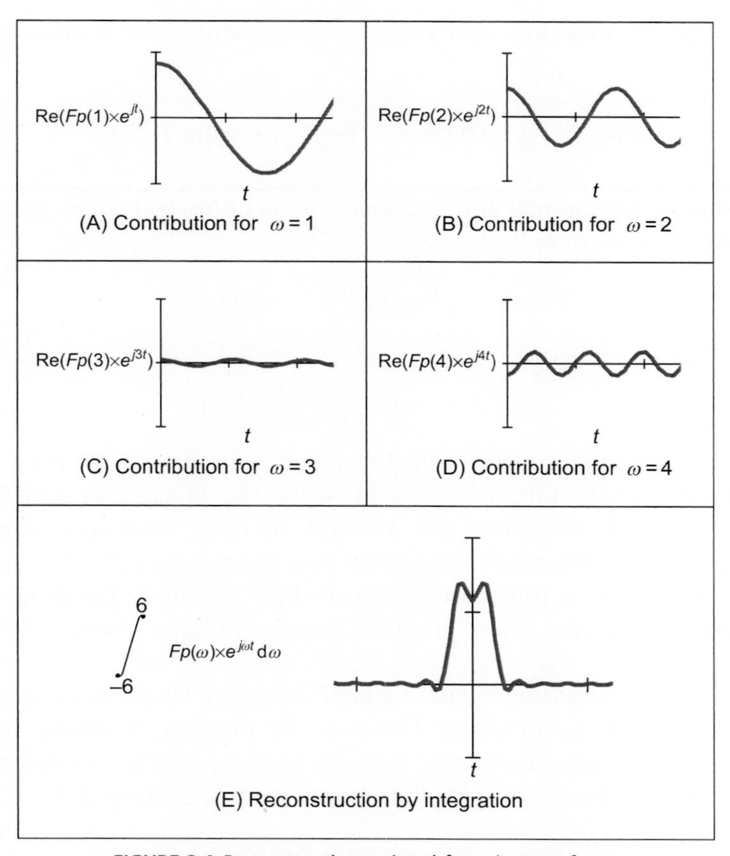

FIGURE 2.4 Reconstructing a signal from its transform.

in Fig. 2.4A contributes a large component of the original signal; a higher frequency, that for $\omega = 2$, contributes less as in Fig. 2.4B. This is because the transform coefficient is less for $\omega = 2$ than it is for $\omega = 1$. There is a very small contribution for $\omega = 3$, Fig. 2.4C, though there is more for $\omega = 4$, Fig. 2.4D. This is because there are frequencies for which there is no contribution, where the transform is zero. When these signals are integrated together, we achieve a signal that looks similar to our original pulse, Fig. 2.4E. Here we have only considered frequencies from $\omega = -6$ to $\omega = 6$. If the frequency range in integration was larger, more high frequencies would be included, leading to a more faithful reconstruction of the original pulse.

The result of the Fourier transform is actually a complex number: each value $Fp(w)$ is represented by a pair of numbers that represent its real and imaginary parts. Rather than use the real and imaginary parts, the values are usually represented in terms of *magnitude* (or size, or modulus) and *phase* (or argument). The transform can be represented as

$$Fp(\omega) = \int_{-\infty}^{\infty} p(t)e^{-j\omega t}dt = \mathrm{Re}(Fp(\omega)) + j\mathrm{Im}(Fp(\omega)) \tag{2.6}$$

where Re( ) and Im( ) are the real and imaginary parts of the transform, respectively. The magnitude of the transform is then

$$|Fp(\omega)| = \sqrt{\mathrm{Re}(Fp(\omega))^2 + \mathrm{Im}(Fp(\omega))^2} \tag{2.7}$$

and the phase is

$$\arg(Fp(\omega)) = \tan^{-1}\left(\frac{\mathrm{Im}(Fp(\omega))}{\mathrm{Re}(Fp(\omega))}\right) \tag{2.8}$$

where the signs of the real and the imaginary components can be used to determine which quadrant the phase (argument) is in, since the phase can vary from 0 to 2π radians. The magnitude describes the amount of each frequency component, the phase describes timing, when the frequency components occur. The magnitude and phase of the transform of a pulse are shown in Fig. 2.5 where the magnitude returns a positive transform, and the phase is either 0 or 2π radians (consistent with the sine function).

In order to return to the time domain signal, from the frequency domain signal, we require the *inverse Fourier transform*. This was the process illustrated in Fig. 2.4, the process by which we reconstructed the pulse from its transform components. The inverse FT calculates $p(t)$ from $Fp(\omega)$ by the inverse transformation $\Im^{-1}$

$$p(t) = \Im^{-1}(Fp(\omega)) = \frac{1}{2\pi}\int_{-\infty}^{\infty} Fp(\omega)e^{j\omega t}\, d\omega \tag{2.9}$$

Together, Eqs. (2.1) and (2.9) form a relationship known as a *transform pair* that allows us to transform into the frequency domain, and back again. By this process, we can perform operations in the frequency domain or in the time domain, since we have a way of changing between them. One important process is known as *convolution*. The

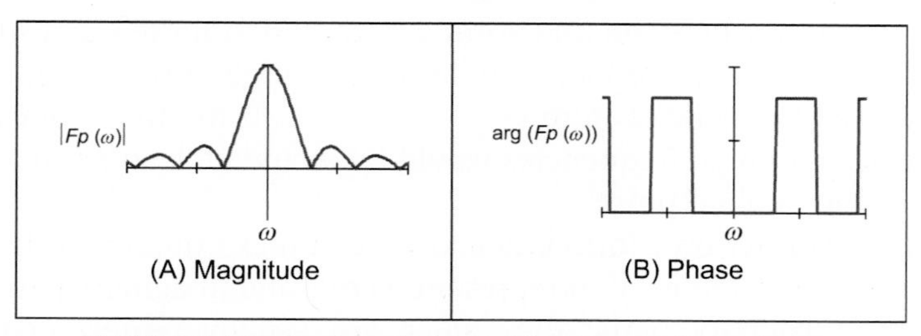

FIGURE 2.5 Magnitude and phase of Fourier transform of pulse.

convolution of one signal $p_1(t)$ with another signal $p_2(t)$, where the convolution process denoted by $*$ is given by the integral

$$p_1(t) * p_2(t) = \int_{-\infty}^{\infty} p_1(\tau)p_2(t-\tau)d\tau \tag{2.10}$$

This is actually the basis of systems theory where the output of a system is the convolution of a stimulus, say p_1, and a system's response, p_2. By inverting the time axis of the system response, to give $p_2(t-\tau)$, we obtain a memory function. The convolution process then sums the effect of a stimulus multiplied by the memory function: the current output of the system is the cumulative response to a stimulus. By taking the Fourier transform of Eq. (2.10), the Fourier transform of the convolution of two signals is

$$\begin{aligned} \Im[p_1(t) * p_2(t)] &= \int_{-\infty}^{\infty} \left\{ \int_{-\infty}^{\infty} p_1(\tau)p_2(t-\tau)d\tau \right\} e^{-j\omega t}dt \\ &= \int_{-\infty}^{\infty} \left\{ \int_{-\infty}^{\infty} p_2(t-\tau)e^{-j\omega t}dt \right\} p_1(\tau)d\tau \end{aligned} \tag{2.11}$$

Now since $\Im[p_2(t-\tau)] = e^{-j\omega\tau}Fp_2(\omega)$ (to be considered later in Section 2.6.1), then

$$\begin{aligned} \Im[p_1(t) * p_2(t)] &= \int_{-\infty}^{\infty} Fp_2(\omega)p_1(\tau)e^{-j\omega\tau}d\tau \\ &= Fp_2(\omega) \int_{-\infty}^{\infty} p_1(\tau)e^{-j\omega\tau}d\tau \\ &= Fp_2(\omega) \times Fp_1(\omega) \end{aligned} \tag{2.12}$$

As such, the frequency domain dual of convolution is multiplication; the convolution integral can be performed by *inverse Fourier transformation* of the product of the transforms of the two signals. A frequency domain representation essentially presents signals in a different way, but it also provides a different way of processing signals. Later, we shall use the duality of convolution to speed up the computation of vision algorithms considerably.

Further, *correlation* is defined to be

$$p_1(t) \otimes p_2(t) = \int_{-\infty}^{\infty} p_1(\tau)p_2(t+\tau)d\tau \tag{2.13}$$

where $\otimes$ denotes correlation ($\odot$ is another symbol which is used sometimes, but there is not much consensus on this symbol – if comfort is needed: 'in esoteric astrology $\odot$ represents the creative spark of divine consciousness' no less!). Correlation gives a measure of the match between the two signals $p_2(\omega)$ and $p_1(\omega)$. When $p_2(\omega) = p_1(\omega)$ we are correlating a signal with itself, and the process is known as *autocorrelation*. We shall be using correlation later to find things in images.

Before proceeding further, we also need to define the *delta function*, which can be considered to be a function occurring at a particular time interval

$$delta(t-\tau) = \begin{vmatrix} 1 & \text{if} \quad t=\tau \\ 0 & \text{otherwise} \end{vmatrix} \tag{2.14}$$

The relationship between a signal's time domain representation and its frequency domain version is also known as a *transform pair*: the transform of a pulse (in the time domain) is a sinc function in the frequency domain. Since the transform is symmetrical, the Fourier transform of a sinc function is a pulse.

There are other Fourier transform pairs, as illustrated in Fig. 2.6. First, Figs. 2.6A and B show that the Fourier transform of a cosine function is two points in the frequency domain (at the same value for positive and negative frequency) – we expect this since there is only one frequency in the cosine function, the frequency shown by its transform. Figs. 2.6C and D show that the transform of the *Gaussian function* is another Gaussian function, this illustrates linearity (for linear systems it is Gaussian in, Gaussian out which is another version of GIGO). Fig. 2.6E is a single point (the delta function) which has a transform that is an infinite set of frequencies, Fig. 2.6F, an alternative interpretation is that a delta function contains an equal amount of all frequencies. This can be explained by using Eq. (2.5), where if the pulse is of shorter duration (T tends to zero), the sinc function is wider; as the pulse becomes infinitely thin, the spectrum becomes infinitely flat.

Finally, Figs. 2.6G and H shows that the transform of a set of uniformly spaced delta functions is another set of uniformly spaced delta functions, but with a different spacing. The spacing in the frequency domain is the reciprocal of the spacing in the time domain. By way of a (nonmathematical) explanation, let us consider that the Gaussian function in Fig. 2.6C is actually made up by summing a set of closely spaced (and very thin) Gaussian functions. Then, since the spectrum for a delta function is infinite, as the Gaussian function is stretched in the time domain (eventually to be a set of pulses of uniform height) we obtain a set of pulses in the frequency domain, but spaced by the reciprocal of the time domain spacing. This transform pair is actually the basis of sampling theory (which we aim to use to find a criterion which guides us to an appropriate choice for the image size).

2.4 The sampling criterion

The *sampling criterion* specifies the condition for the correct choice of sampling frequency. *Sampling* concerns taking instantaneous values of a continuous signal, physically these are the outputs of an A/D converter sampling a camera signal. Clearly, the samples are the values of the signal at sampling instants. This is illustrated in Fig. 2.7, where Fig. 2.7A concerns taking samples at a high frequency (the spacing between samples is low), compared with the amount of change seen in the signal of which the samples are taken. Here, the samples are taken sufficiently fast to notice the slight dip in

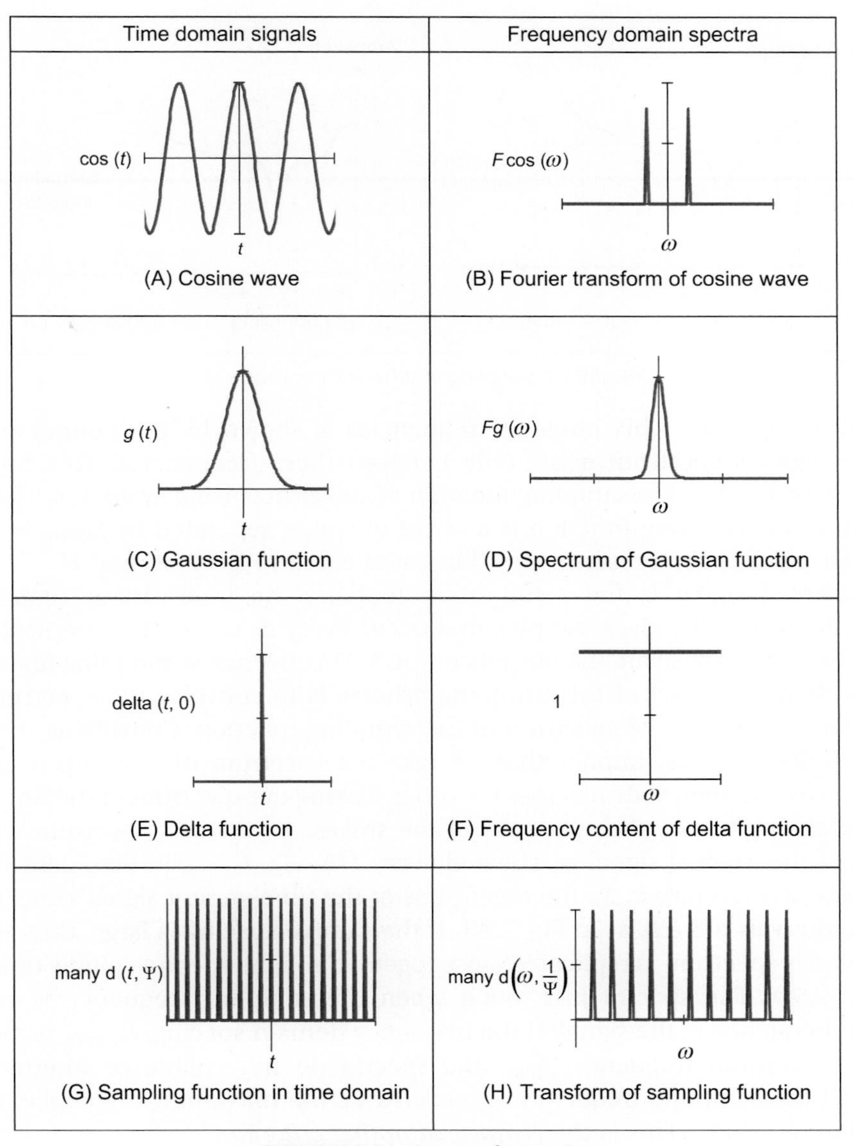

FIGURE 2.6 Fourier transform pairs.

the sampled signal. Fig. 2.7B concerns taking samples at a low frequency, compared with the rate of change of (the maximum frequency in) the sampled signal. Here, the slight dip in the sampled signal is not seen in the samples taken from it.

We can understand the process better in the frequency domain. Let us consider a time-variant signal which has a range of frequencies between $-f_{max}$ and f_{max} as

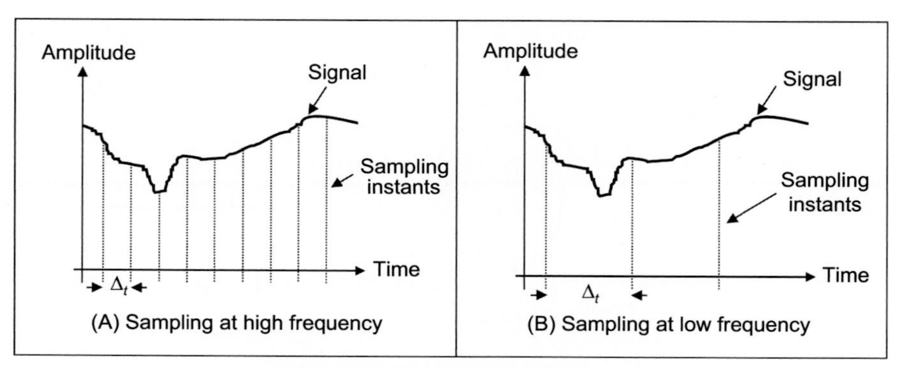

FIGURE 2.7 Sampling at different frequencies.

illustrated in Fig. 2.9B. This range of frequencies is shown by the Fourier transform where the signal's spectrum exists only between these frequencies. This function is sampled every Δ_t s: this is a sampling function of spikes occurring every Δ_t s. The Fourier transform of the sampling function is a series of spikes separated by $f_{sample} = 1/\Delta_t$ Hz. The Fourier pair of this transform was illustrated earlier, Figs. 2.6G and H.

The sampled signal is the result of multiplying the time-variant signal by the sequence of spikes, this gives samples that occur every Δ_t s, and the sampled signal is shown in Fig. 2.9A. These are the outputs of the A/D converter at sampling instants. The frequency domain analog of this sampling process is to convolve the spectrum of the time-variant signal with the spectrum of the sampling function. Convolving the signals, the convolution process, implies that we take the spectrum of one, flip it along the horizontal axis and then slide it across the other. Taking the spectrum of the time-variant signal and sliding it over the spectrum of the spikes, results in a spectrum where the spectrum of the original signal is repeated every $1/\Delta_t$ Hz, f_{sample} in Figs. 2.9B–D. If the spacing between samples is Δ_t, the repetitions of the time-variant signal's spectrum are spaced at intervals of $1/\Delta_t$, as in Fig. 2.9B. If the sample spacing is large, then the time-variant signal's spectrum is replicated close together and the spectra collide, or interfere, as in Fig. 2.9D. The spectra just touch when the sampling frequency is twice the maximum frequency in the signal. If the frequency domain spacing, f_{sample}, is more than twice the maximum frequency, $f_{\max}$, the spectra do not collide or interfere, as in Fig. 2.9C. If the sampling frequency exceeds twice the maximum frequency, then the spectra cannot collide. This is the *Nyquist sampling criterion*:

In order to reconstruct a signal from its samples, the sampling frequency must be at least twice the highest frequency of the sampled signal.

If we do not obey Nyquist's sampling theorem the spectra collide. When we inspect the sampled signal, whose spectrum is within $-f_{\max}$ to $f_{\max}$, wherein the spectra collided, the corrupt spectrum implies that by virtue of sampling, we have ruined some of the

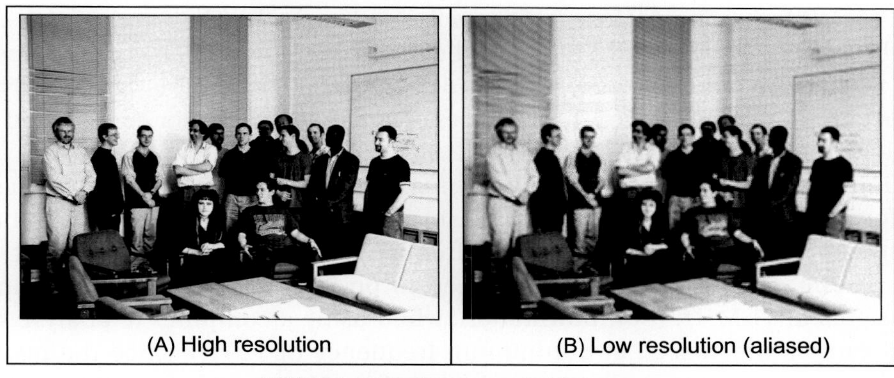

FIGURE 2.8 Aliasing in sampled imagery.

information. If we were to attempt to reconstruct a signal by inverse Fourier transformation of the sampled signal's spectrum, processing Fig. 2.9D would lead to the wrong signal, whereas inverse Fourier transformation of the frequencies between $-f_{max}$ and $f_{\max}$ in Figs. 2.9B and C would lead back to the original signal. This can be seen in computer images as illustrated in Fig. 2.8, which show an image of a group of people (the computer vision research team at Southampton) displayed at different spatial resolutions (the contrast has been increased to the same level in each subimage so that the effect we want to demonstrate should definitely show up in the print copy). Essentially, the people become less distinct in the lower resolution image, Fig. 2.8B. Now, look closely at the window blinds behind the people. At higher resolution, in Fig. 2.8A, these appear as normal window blinds. In Fig. 2.8B, which is sampled at a much lower resolution, a new pattern appears: the pattern appears to be curved, and if you consider the blinds' relative size the shapes actually appear to be much larger than normal window blinds. So by reducing the resolution, we are seeing something different, an alias of the true information – something that is not actually there at all, but appears to be there by result of sampling. This is the result of sampling at too low a frequency: if we sample at high frequency, the interpolated result matches the original signal; if we sample at too low a frequency we can get the wrong signal. (For these reasons people on television tend to wear non-chequered clothes – or should not!) Note that this effect can be seen, in the way described, in the printed version of this book. This is because the printing technology is very high resolution. If you were to print this page offline (and sometimes even to view it), e.g. from a Google Books sample, the nature of the effect of aliasing depends on the resolution of the printed image, and so the aliasing effect might also be seen in the high-resolution image as well as in the low-resolution version – which rather spoils the point.

In art, Dali's picture 'Gala Contemplating the Mediterranean Sea, which at 20 m becomes the portrait of Abraham Lincoln' (Homage to Rothko) is a classic illustration of sampling. At high resolution, you see a detailed surrealist image, with Mrs Dali as a central figure. Viewed from a distance – or for the shortsighted, without your spectacles on – the image becomes a (low-resolution) picture of Abraham Lincoln. For a more modern view of sampling [Unser00] is well worth a look. The *compressive sensing* approach [Donoho06] takes advantage of the fact that many signals have components that are significant, or nearly zero, leading to cameras which acquire significantly fewer elements to represent an image. This provides an alternative basis for compressed image acquisition without loss of resolution (Fig. 2.9).

Obtaining the wrong signal is called *aliasing*: our interpolated signal is an alias of its proper form. Clearly, we want to avoid aliasing, so according to the sampling theorem we must sample at twice the maximum frequency of the signal coming out of the camera. The maximum frequency is defined to be 5.5 MHz, so we must sample the camera signal at 11 MHz. (For information, when using a computer to analyse speech we must sample the speech at a minimum frequency of 12 kHz since the maximum speech frequency is 6 kHz.) Given the timing of a video signal, sampling at 11 MHz implies a minimum image resolution of 576×576 pixels. This is unfortunate: 576 is not an integer power of two which has poor implications for storage and processing. Accordingly, since some image processing systems have a maximum resolution of 512×512, they must anticipate aliasing. This is mitigated somewhat by the observations that:

1. globally, the lower frequencies carry more information, whereas locally the higher frequencies contain more information so the corruption of high-frequency information is of less importance and
2. there is limited depth of focus in imaging systems (reducing high-frequency content).

But aliasing can, and does, occur and we must remember this when interpreting images. A different form of this argument applies to the images derived from digital cameras. The basic argument that the precision of the estimates of the high-order frequency components is dictated by the relationship between the effective sampling frequency (the number of image points) and the imaged structure, naturally still applies.

The effects of sampling can often be seen in films, especially in the rotating wheels of cars, as illustrated in Fig. 2.10. This shows a wheel with a single spoke, for simplicity. The film is a sequence of frames starting on the left. The sequence of frames plotted in Fig. 2.10A is for a wheel which rotates by 20° between frames, as illustrated in Fig. 2.10B. If the wheel is rotating much faster, by 340° between frames, as in Fig. 2.10C and D, to a human viewer, the wheel will appear to rotate in the opposite direction. If the wheel rotates by 360° between frames, it will appear to be stationary. In order to perceive the wheel as rotating forwards, then the rotation between frames must be 180° at most. This is consistent with sampling at more than twice the maximum frequency. Our eye can resolve this in films (when watching a film, we bet you have not thrown a wobbly because the car's going forwards, whereas the wheels say it is going the other way) since we know that the direction of the car must be consistent with the motion of its wheels, and we expect to see the wheels appear to go the wrong way, sometimes.

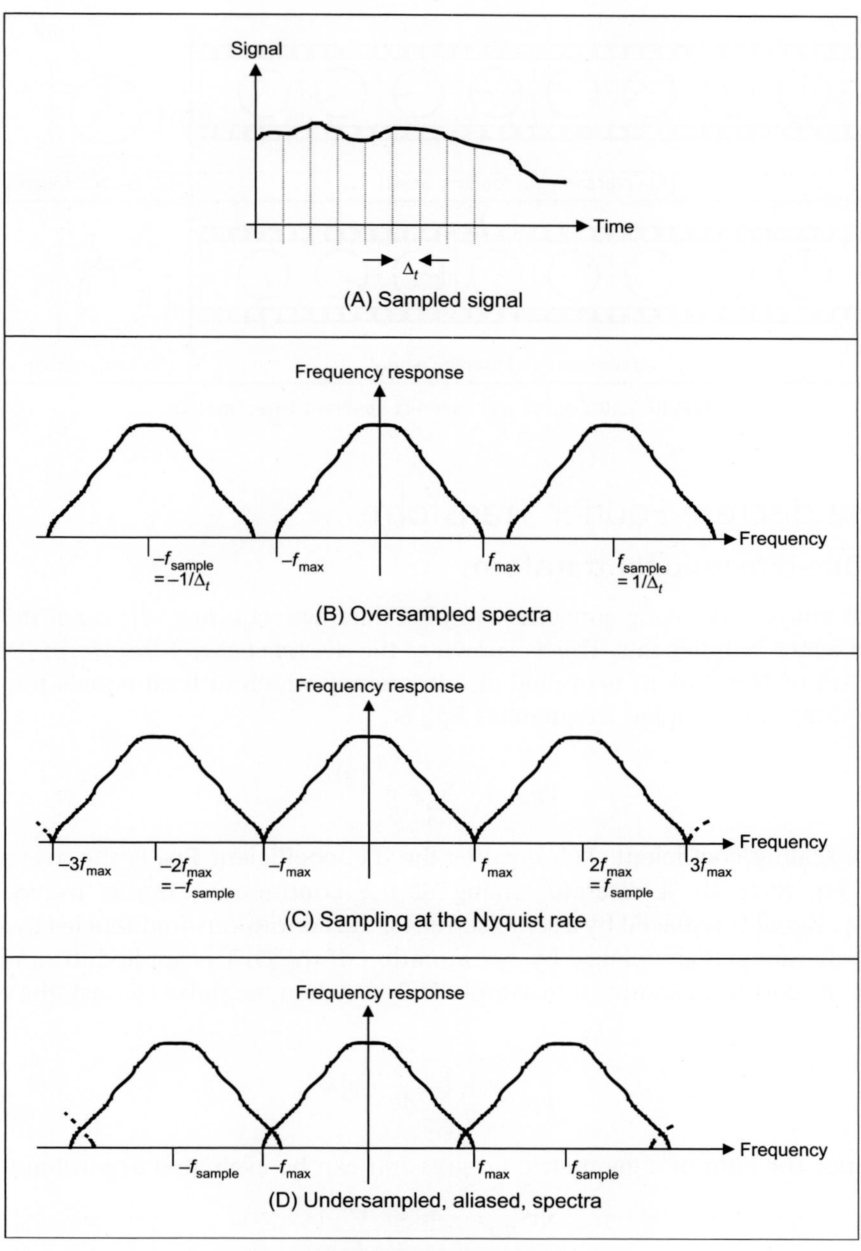

FIGURE 2.9 Sampled spectra.

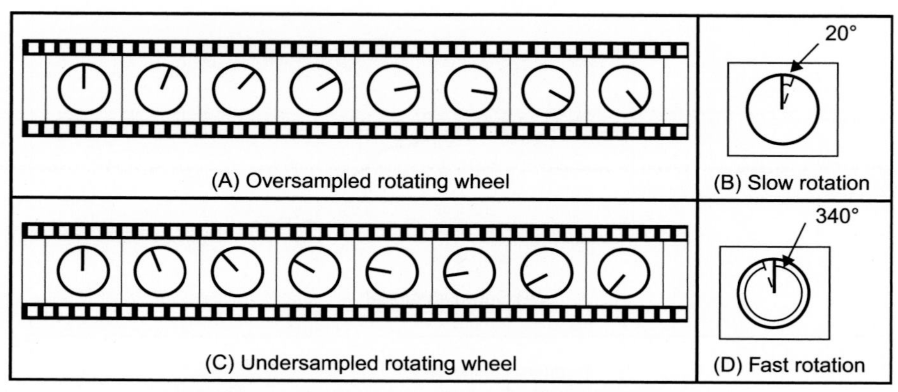

FIGURE 2.10 Correct and incorrect apparent wheel motion.

2.5 The discrete Fourier Transform

2.5.1 One-dimensional transform

Given that image processing concerns sampled data, we require a version of the Fourier transform which handles this. This is known as the *discrete Fourier transform* (DFT). The DFT of a set of N points $\mathbf{p}_x$ (sampled at a frequency which at least equals the Nyquist sampling rate) into sampled frequencies $\mathbf{Fp}_u$ is

$$\mathbf{Fp}_u = \frac{1}{N}\sum_{x=0}^{N-1} \mathbf{p}_x e^{-j\left(\frac{2\pi}{N}\right)xu} \tag{2.15}$$

where the scaling coefficient $1/N$ ensures the d.c. coefficient $\mathbf{Fp}_0$ is the average of all samples. Eq. (2.15) is a discrete analog of the continuous Fourier transform: the continuous signal is replaced by a set of samples, the continuous frequencies by sampled ones, and the integral is replaced by a summation. If the DFT is applied to samples of a pulse in a window from sample 0 to sample $N/2-1$ (when the pulse ceases), the equation becomes

$$\mathbf{Fp}_u = \frac{1}{N}\sum_{x=0}^{\frac{N}{2}-1} A e^{-j\left(\frac{2\pi}{N}\right)xu} \tag{2.16}$$

And since the sum of a geometric progression can be evaluated according to

$$\sum_{k=0}^{n} a_0 r^k = \frac{a_0(1-r^{n+1})}{1-r} \tag{2.17}$$

the discrete Fourier transform of a sampled pulse is given by

$$\mathbf{Fp}_u = \frac{A}{N}\left(\frac{1-e^{-j\left(\frac{2\pi}{N}\right)\left(\frac{N}{2}\right)u}}{1-e^{-j\left(\frac{2\pi}{N}\right)u}}\right) \tag{2.18}$$

By rearrangement, we obtain

$$\mathbf{Fp}_u = \frac{A}{N} e^{-j\left(\frac{\pi u}{2}\right)\left(1-\frac{2}{N}\right)} \frac{\sin(\pi u/2)}{\sin(\pi u/N)} \tag{2.19}$$

The modulus of the transform is

$$|\mathbf{Fp}_u| = \frac{A}{N}\left|\frac{\sin(\pi u/2)}{\sin(\pi u/N)}\right| \tag{2.20}$$

since the magnitude of the exponential function is 1. The original pulse is plotted in Fig. 2.11A, and the magnitude of the Fourier transform plotted against frequency is given in Fig. 2.11B.

This is clearly comparable with the result of the continuous Fourier transform of a pulse, Fig. 2.3, since the transform involves a similar, sinusoidal, signal. The spectrum is equivalent to a set of sampled frequencies; we can build up the sampled pulse by adding up the frequencies according to the Fourier description. Consider a signal such as that shown in Fig. 2.12A. This has no explicit analytic definition, as such it does not have a closed Fourier transform; the Fourier transform is generated by direct application of Eq. (2.15). The result is a set of samples of frequency, Fig. 2.12B.

The Fourier transform in Fig. 2.12B can be used to reconstruct the original signal in Fig. 2.12A, as illustrated in Fig. 2.13. Essentially, the coefficients of the Fourier transform tell us how much there is of each of a set of sine waves (at different frequencies), in the original signal. The lowest frequency component $\mathbf{Fp}_0$, for zero frequency, is called the d.c. component (it is constant and equivalent to a sine wave with no frequency), and it represents the average value of the samples. Adding the contribution of the first coefficient $\mathbf{Fp}_0$, Fig. 2.13B, to the contribution of the second coefficient $\mathbf{Fp}_1$, Fig. 2.13C, is shown in Fig. 2.13D. This shows how addition of the first two frequency components approaches the original sampled signal. The approximation improves when the contribution due to the fourth component, $\mathbf{Fp}_3$, is included, as shown in Fig. 2.13E. Finally, adding up all six frequency components gives a close approximation to the original signal, as shown in Fig. 2.13F.

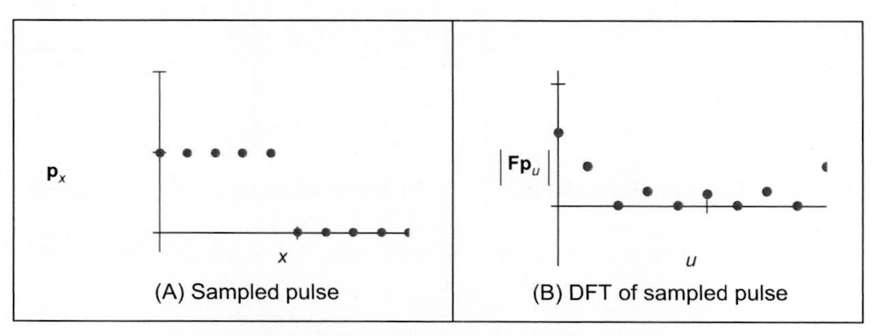

FIGURE 2.11 Transform pair for sampled pulse.

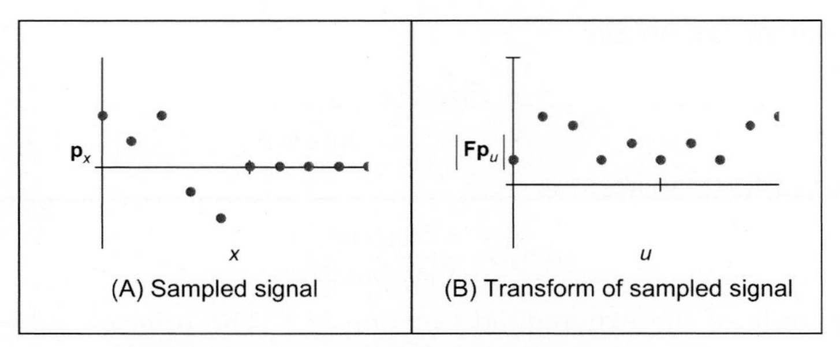

FIGURE 2.12 A sampled signal and its discrete transform.

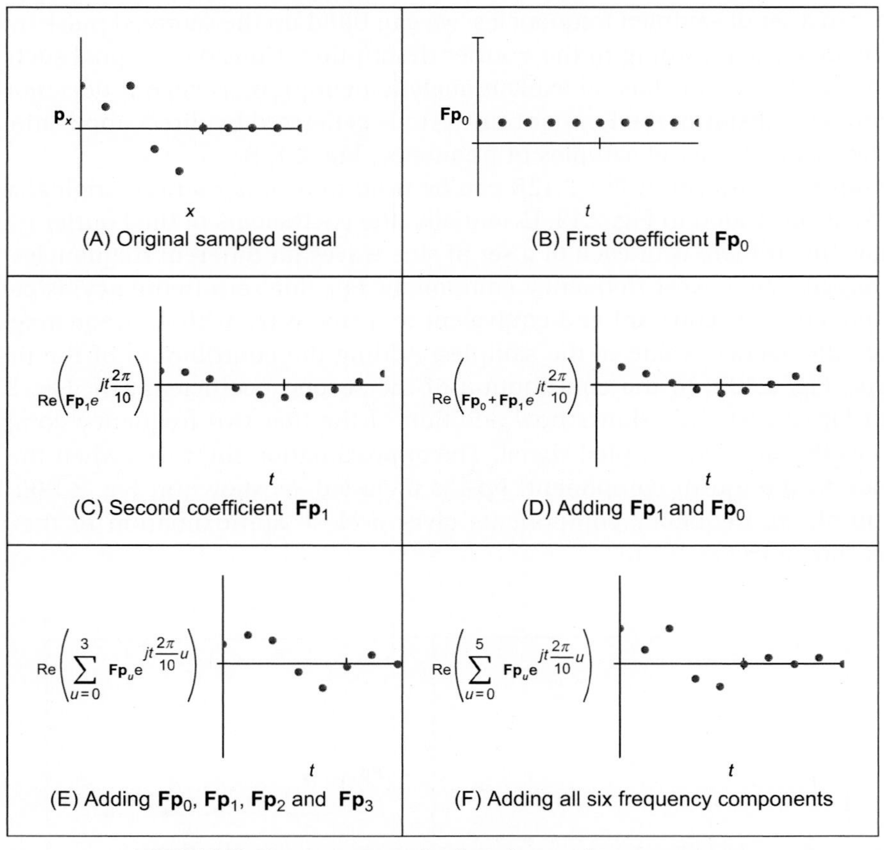

FIGURE 2.13 Signal reconstruction from its transform components.

This process is, of course, the *inverse DFT*. This can be used to reconstruct a sampled signal from its frequency components by

$$\mathbf{p}_x = \sum_{u=0}^{N-1} \mathbf{Fp}_u e^{j\left(\frac{2\pi}{N}\right)ux} \tag{2.21}$$

Note that there are several assumptions made prior to application of the DFT. The first is that the sampling criterion has been satisfied. The second is that the sampled function replicates to infinity. When generating the transform of a pulse, Fourier theory assumes that the pulse repeats outside the window of interest. (There are window operators that are designed specifically to handle difficulty at the ends of the sampling window.) Finally, the maximum frequency corresponds to half the sampling period. This is consistent with the assumption that the sampling criterion has not been violated, otherwise the high-frequency spectral estimates will be corrupted.

2.5.2 Two-dimensional transform

Eq. (2.15) gives the DFT of a one-dimensional signal. We need to generate Fourier transforms of images so we need a 2D DFT. This is a transform of pixels (sampled picture points) with a 2D spatial location indexed by coordinates x and y. This implies that we have two dimensions of frequency, u and v, which are the horizontal and vertical spatial frequencies, respectively. Given an image of a set of vertical lines, the Fourier transform will show only horizontal spatial frequency. The vertical spatial frequencies are zero since there is no vertical variation along the y axis. The 2D Fourier transform evaluates the frequency data, $\mathbf{FP}_{u,v}$, from the $N \times N$ pixels $\mathbf{P}_{x,y}$ as

$$\mathbf{FP}_{u,v} = \frac{1}{N^2} \sum_{x=0}^{N-1} \sum_{y=0}^{N-1} \mathbf{P}_{x,y}\, e^{-j\left(\frac{2\pi}{N}\right)(ux+vy)} \tag{2.22}$$

Where the scaling coefficient $1/N^2$ makes the d.c. coefficient $\mathbf{FP}_{0,0}$ equal the average of all points in the image (in Matlab® the scaling coefficient is 1.0). The Fourier transform of an image can actually be obtained *optically* by transmitting a laser through a photographic slide and forming an image using a lens. The Fourier transform of the image of the slide is formed in the front focal plane of the lens. This is still restricted to transmissive systems, whereas reflective formation would widen its application potential considerably (since optical computation is just slightly faster than its digital counterpart). The magnitude of the 2D DFT of an image of vertical bars (Fig. 2.14A) is shown in Fig. 2.14B. This shows that there are only horizontal spatial frequencies; the image is constant in the vertical axis and there are no vertical spatial frequencies.

The *2D inverse DFT* transforms from the frequency domain back to the image domain, to reconstruct the image. The 2D inverse DFT is given by

$$\mathbf{P}_{x,y} = \sum_{u=0}^{N-1} \sum_{v=0}^{N-1} \mathbf{FP}_{u,v} e^{j\left(\frac{2\pi}{N}\right)(ux+vy)} \tag{2.23}$$

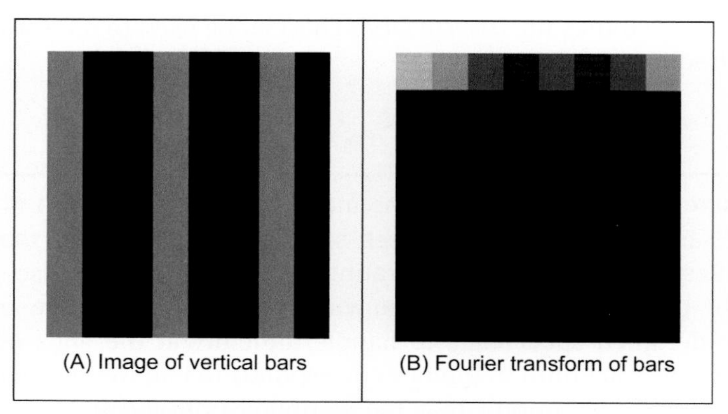

FIGURE 2.14 Applying the 2D discrete Fourier transform.

The contribution of different frequencies is illustrated in Fig. 2.15 where we have images showing in the first row (A)–(D) the position of the image transform components (presented as log[magnitude]), in the second row (F)–(I) the image constructed from that single component and in the third row (J)–(M) the reconstruction (by the inverse

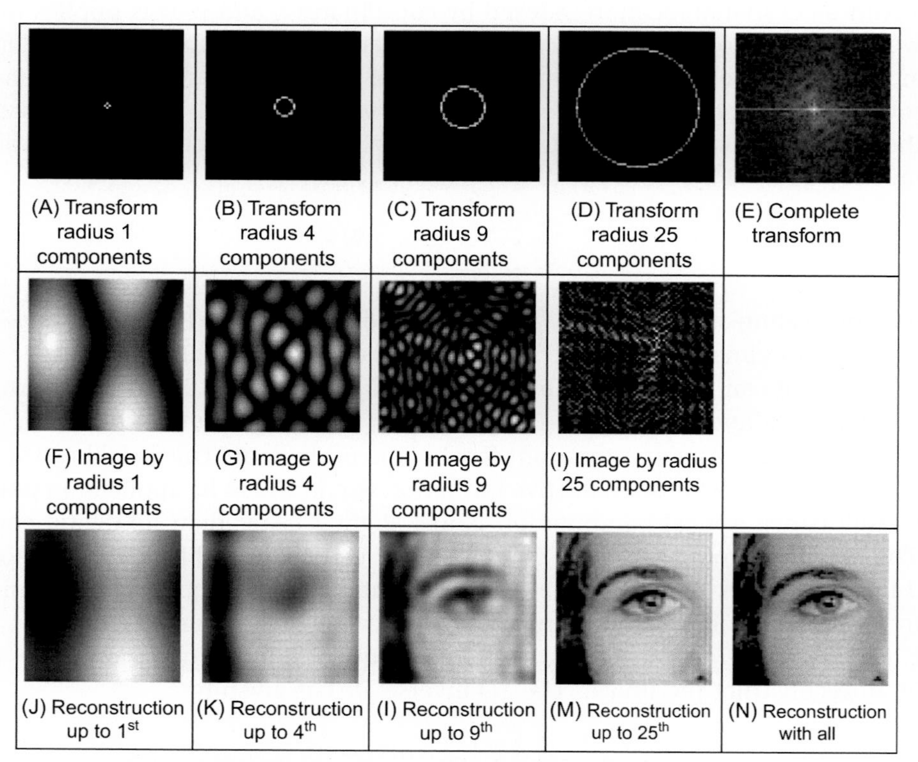

FIGURE 2.15 Image reconstruction and different frequency components.

FT) using frequencies up to and including that component. There is also the image of the magnitude of the Fourier transform, (E). We shall take the transform components from a circle centred at the middle of the transform image. In Fig. 2.15, the first column is the transform components at radius 1 (which are low-frequency components), the second column is the radius 4 components, the third column is at radius 9 and the fourth column is the radius 25 components (the higher frequency components). The last column has the complete Fourier transform image (E) and the reconstruction of the image from the transform (N). As we include more components, we include more detail; the lower order components carry the bulk of the shape, not the detail. In the bottom row, the first components plus the d.c. component give a very coarse approximation (Fig. 2.15J) when the components up to radius four are added we can see the shape of a face (Fig. 2.15K); the components up to radius 9 order allow us to see the face features (Fig. 2.15L), but they are not sharp; we can infer identity from the components up to radius 25 (Fig. 2.15M), noting that there are still some image artefacts on the right-hand side of the image; when all components are added (Fig. 2.15N), we return to the original image. This also illustrates *coding*, as the image can be encoded by retaining fewer of the components of the image than are in the complete transform. Fig. 2.15M is a good example of where an image of acceptable quality can be reconstructed, even when about half of the components are discarded. There are considerably better coding approaches than this, though we shall not consider coding in this text, and compression ratios can be considerably higher and still achieve acceptable quality. Note that it is common to use logarithms of magnitude to display Fourier transforms (Section 3.3.1) as otherwise the magnitude of the d.c. component can make the transform difficult to see.

One of the important properties of the FT is *replication* which implies that the transform repeats in frequency up to infinity, as indicated in Fig. 2.9 for 1D signals. To show this for 2D signals, we need to investigate the Fourier transform, originally given by $\mathbf{FP}_{u,v}$, at integer multiples of the number of sampled points $\mathbf{FP}_{u+mM,v+nN}$ (where m and n are integers). The Fourier transform $\mathbf{FP}_{u+mM,v+nN}$ is, by substitution in Eq. (2.22)

$$\mathbf{FP}_{u+mN,v+nN} = \frac{1}{N^2}\sum_{x=0}^{N-1}\sum_{y=0}^{N-1}\mathbf{P}_{x,y}e^{-j\left(\frac{2\pi}{N}\right)((u+mN)x+(v+nN)y)} \tag{2.24}$$

so,

$$\mathbf{FP}_{u+mN,v+nN} = \frac{1}{N^2}\sum_{x=0}^{N-1}\sum_{y=0}^{N-1}\mathbf{P}_{x,y}e^{-j\left(\frac{2\pi}{N}\right)(ux+vy)} \times e^{-j2\pi(mx+ny)} \tag{2.25}$$

and since $e^{-j2\pi(mx+ny)} = 1$ (since the term in brackets is always an integer and then the exponent is always an integer multiple of 2π) then

$$\mathbf{FP}_{u+mN,v+nN} = \mathbf{FP}_{u,v} \tag{2.26}$$

which shows that the replication property does hold for the Fourier transform. However, Eqs. (2.22) and (2.23) are very slow for large image sizes. They are usually implemented by using the *Fast Fourier transform* (FFT) which is a splendid rearrangement of the Fourier transform's computation which improves speed dramatically. The FFT algorithm is beyond the scope of this text but is also a rewarding topic of study (particularly for computer scientists or software engineers). The FFT can only be applied to square images whose size is an integer power of 2 (without special arrangement). Calculation actually involves the *separability* property of the Fourier transform. Separability means that the Fourier transform is calculated in two stages: the rows are first transformed using a 1D FFT, then these data are transformed in columns, again using a 1D FFT. This process can be achieved since the sinusoidal *basis functions* are orthogonal. Analytically, this implies that the 2D DFT can be decomposed as in Eq. (2.27)

$$\mathbf{FP}_{u,v} = \frac{1}{MN}\sum_{x=0}^{N-1}\sum_{y=0}^{M-1}\mathbf{P}_{x,y}e^{-j2\pi\left(\frac{ux}{M}+\frac{vy}{N}\right)} = \frac{1}{MN}\sum_{x=0}^{N-1}\left\{\sum_{y=0}^{M-1}\mathbf{P}_{x,y}e^{-j\left(\frac{2\pi}{N}\right)(vy)}\right\}e^{-j\left(\frac{2\pi}{M}\right)(ux)} \tag{2.27}$$

where M and N are the numbers of columns and rows, respectively. Eq. (2.27) shows how separability is achieved, since the inner term expresses transformation along one axis (the y axis), and the outer term transforms this along the other (the x axis).

Code 2.1 illustrates the implementation of Eq. (2.27) in Matlab. The implementation simply evaluates the complex exponent in the definition. Since the computational cost of a 1D FFT of N points is $O(N\log_2(N))$, the cost (by separability) for the 2D FFT is $O(N^2\log_2(N))$, whereas the computational cost of the 2D DFT is $O(N^3)$. This implies a considerable saving since it suggests that the FFT requires much less time, particularly for large image sizes (so for a 1024 × 1024 image, if the FFT takes seconds, the DFT will take minutes). The 2D FFT is available in Matlab using the `fft2` function which gives a

```
function [Fourier] = F_transform(image)

image=double(image);
[rows, cols] = size(image);
%we deploy equation 2.27, so that we can handle non square images
for u=1:cols % along the horizontal axis
    for v=1:rows % down the vertical axis
        sumx=0;
        for x=1:cols
            %first we transform the rows
            sumy=0;
            for y=1:rows %Eq 2.27 inner bracket
                sumy=sumy+image(y,x)*exp(-1j*2*pi*(v-1)*(y-1)/rows);
            end
            %then we do the columns Eq 2.27 outer
            sumx=sumx+sumy*exp(-1j*2*pi*(u-1)*(x-1)/cols);
        end %and finally normalise
        Fourier(v,u) = sumx/(rows*cols);
    end
end
```

CODE 2.1 Two-dimensional DFT, Exponential Form implementing Eq. (2.27).

result equivalent to Eq. (2.22) or (2.27). You can note the difference in time between executing the code in Code 2.1 (or our Python version) and Matlab's own FFT operator (note there is some difference due to compiled vs interpreted code; do not run the basic version on a large image as it will take very long time). The inverse 2D FFT, Eq. (2.23), can be implemented using the Matlab `ifft2` function. (The difference between many Fourier transform implementations essentially concerns the chosen scaling factor, though the order of the frequency components differs from the basic equations in the Matlab functions.) The direct Matlab implementation of the 2D DFT in Eq. (2.27) is given in Code 2.1. This is simply called using the command `b=F_Transform(a)`, and the routine enforces the change from an integer format to double precision, as needed when using complex numbers in Matlab. It is easier to work in double precision throughout when developing code; integer formats can be used to speed real implementations (with caution: an early ARIANE space rocket blew up given erroneous conversion of a 32-bit integer to a 16-bit version).

In general, Eq. (2.27) is difficult to compute since it requires evaluation of complex exponents. The result of a complex exponent is a complex number, thus the implementation requires representing functions, operations, and variables for storage and processing using complex numbers. Although operations with complex numbers are well supported in mathematical packages, this equation obscures the true interpretation of the Fourier definition. Fortunately, by algebraic manipulation we can rewrite Eq. (2.27) in a form that separates the imaginary and real parts. By recalling Euler's formula $e^{-jwt} = cos(wt) - jsin(wt)$, then Eq. (2.27) becomes

$$\mathbf{FP}_{u,v} = \frac{1}{MN}\sum_{x=0}^{N-1}\sum_{y=0}^{M-1}\mathbf{P}_{x,y}\left(cos\left(\frac{2\pi}{M}vy\right) - jsin\left(\frac{2\pi}{M}vy\right)\right)\left(cos\left(\frac{2\pi}{N}ux\right) - jsin\left(\frac{2\pi}{N}ux\right)\right) \tag{2.28}$$

By grouping terms, we have that

$$\begin{aligned}\mathbf{FP}_{u,v} = \frac{1}{MN}\sum_{x=0}^{N-1}\sum_{y=0}^{M-1}\mathbf{P}_{x,y}\Bigg(&\left(\cos\left(\frac{2\pi}{N}ux\right)\cos\left(\frac{2\pi}{M}vy\right) - \sin\left(\frac{2\pi}{N}ux\right)\sin\left(\frac{2\pi}{M}vy\right)\right)\\ &-j\left(\cos\left(\frac{2\pi}{N}ux\right)\sin\left(\frac{2\pi}{M}vy\right) + \sin\left(\frac{2\pi}{N}ux\right)\cos\left(\frac{2\pi}{M}vy\right)\right)\Bigg)\end{aligned} \tag{2.29}$$

Eqs. (2.27) and (2.28) represent the same transform, but Eq. (2.28) permits computation of the real and imaginary parts as trigonometric functions. More importantly, the trigonometric form shows how the values of u and v define the frequency used in the transform. This equation also shows the symmetry of the transform; since $\sin(-t) = -\sin(t)$ and $\cos(-t) = \cos(t)$, then the magnitude of the transform defined in Eq. (2.7) is symmetrical at the origin.

The implementation of the trigonometric form is shown in Code 2.2. To illustrate separability, the implementation computes the inner and outer summations in Eq. (2.28), though the same result would be obtained if the real and imaginary parts were computed by using Eq. (2.29). In any case, the implementation should perform the sum for the real and imaginary parts by evaluating sines and cosines at different frequencies. In the code, the array `sumY[0]` and `coeff[u,v][0]` store the real values and `sumY[1]` and

```
for u in range(-maxFreqW, maxFreqW + 1):
    entryW = u + maxFreqW

    for v in range(-maxFreqH, maxFreqH + 1):
        entryH = v + maxFreqH
        coeff[entryH, entryW] = [0, 0]

        for x in range(0, width):
            sumY = [0, 0]

            for y in range(0, height):
                sumY[0] += inputImage[y,x] * cos(y * wh * v)
                sumY[1] += inputImage[y,x] * sin(y * wh * v)
            coeff[entryH, entryW][0] += sumY[0]*cos(x*ww*u)-sumY[1]*sin(x*ww*u)
            coeff[entryH, entryW][1] -= cos(x*ww*u)*sumY[1]+sin(x * ww*u)* sumY[0]
```

CODE 2.2 Two-dimensional discrete Fourier transform in trigonometric form.

`coeff[u,v][1]` the imaginary values. Finally, the coefficients need to be scaled by $\frac{1}{MN}$ according to Eq. (2.28).

Fig. 2.16 shows two examples of the DFT obtained with Code 2.2. The results of the Fourier expansion are not presented by showing the imaginary and real values of $\mathbf{FP}_{u,v}$, but the complex values are shown as magnitude and phase (Eqs. 2.7 and 2.8). Note the symmetries in the magnitude and phase that result from the symmetries of the cosine and sine functions.

Eq. (2.29) reveals the nature of the Fourier transform as a description of an image using frequency; each value $\mathbf{FP}_{u,v}$ defines sine and cosine waves at a given frequency. The values of u and v produce waves with frequency that increases as these values increase. As such, the position of each component reflects its frequency: low-frequency

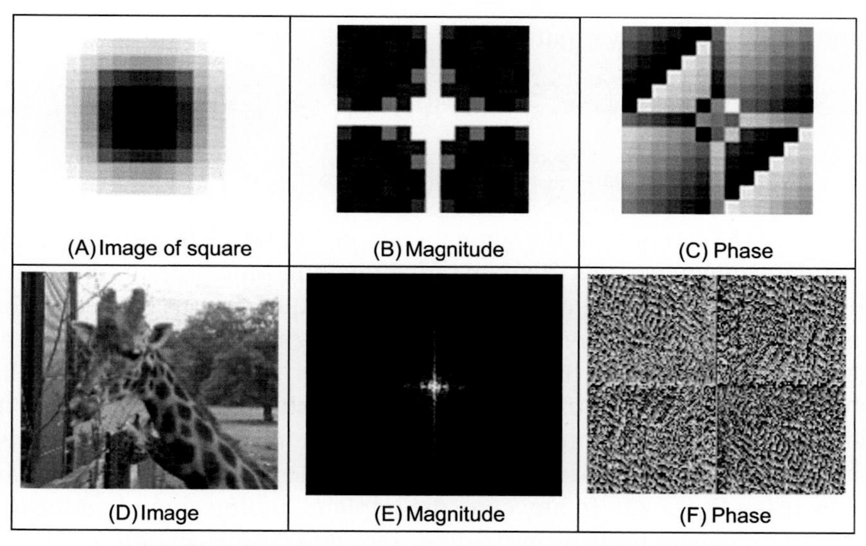

FIGURE 2.16 Two-dimensional discrete Fourier transform examples.

components are near the origin and high-frequency components are further away. Notice also that frequencies can be positive and negative and the lowest frequency component, for zero frequency – the d.c. component – represents the average value of the samples. In Code 2.2, we used this interpretation where u and v represent frequencies. As such, the loops in the implementation iterate over a frequency range. These ranges can be arbitrarily selected to obtain only the fine detail by just computing high frequencies or to obtain coarse features by choosing low frequencies. As we discussed in Section 2.4, the maximum frequency we can use is given by the half of image size (or the result will contain aliasing). In the implementation, the result of the summation for each pair u, v is stored in a cell in the output array `coeff`. The index to the cell is stored in the variables `entryW` and `entryH`. These values are set such that the zero frequency is stored in the centre of the output array, and the negative frequencies are to the left of and down from the centre position. This way to select the output cells is just a standard way to organise and visualise the frequencies. It is important to notice that the loops can be changed to iterate over the output array (since Eqs. (2.29) and (2.27) are the same transform), but iterating in frequency gives a clear meaning to the frequency content in the output.

Code 2.1 shows the origin of the transform (low-frequency components) at the corners of the transform. The image of the square in 2.17(A) produces the result for 2.17(B). A spatial transform is easier to visualise if the d.c. (zero frequency) component is in the centre, with frequency increasing towards the edge of the image. This can be arranged either by rotating each of the four quadrants in the Fourier transform by 180°. An alternative is to *reorder* the original image to give a transform which has been shifted to the centre. Both operations result in the image in 2.17(C) wherein the transform is much more easily seen. Note that this is aimed to improve visualisation and does not change any of the frequency domain information, only the standard way it is displayed.

To rearrange the image so that the d.c. component is in the centre, the frequency components need to be reordered. This can be achieved simply by multiplying each image point $\mathbf{P}_{x,y}$ by $-1^{(x+y)}$. Since $\cos(-\pi) = -1$, then $-1 = e^{-j\pi}$ (the minus sign is introduced just to keep the analysis neat) so we obtain the transform of the multiplied image as

$$\begin{aligned}
\frac{1}{N^2}\sum_{x=0}^{N-1}\sum_{y=0}^{N-1}\mathbf{P}_{x,y}\,e^{-j\left(\frac{2\pi}{N}\right)(ux+vy)} \times -1^{(x+y)} &= \frac{1}{N^2}\sum_{x=0}^{N-1}\sum_{y=0}^{N-1}\mathbf{P}_{x,y}\,e^{-j\left(\frac{2\pi}{N}\right)(ux+vy)} \times e^{-j\pi(x+y)} \\
&= \frac{1}{N^2}\sum_{x=0}^{N-1}\sum_{y=0}^{N-1}\mathbf{P}_{x,y}\,e^{-j\left(\frac{2\pi}{N}\right)\left(\left(u+\frac{N}{2}\right)x+\left(v+\frac{N}{2}\right)y\right)} \\
&= \mathbf{FP}_{u+\frac{N}{2},v+\frac{N}{2}}
\end{aligned} \tag{2.30}$$

```
function rearranged = rearrange(image)
%get dimensions
[rows,cols]=size(image);

%rearrange image
for x = 1:cols %address all columns
  for y = 1:rows %address all rows
    rearranged(y,x)=image(y,x)*((-1)^(y+x)); %Eq. 2.30
  end
end
```

CODE 2.3 Reordering for transform calculation.

According to Eq. (2.30), when pixel values are multiplied by $-1^{(x+y)}$, the Fourier transform becomes shifted along each axis by half the number of samples. According to the replication theorem, Eq. (2.26), the transform replicates along the frequency axes. This implies that the centre of a transform image will now be the d.c. component. (Another way of interpreting this is that rather than look at the frequencies centred on where the image is, our viewpoint has been shifted so as to be centred on one of its corners – thus invoking the replication property.) This brings equivalence between the trigonometric form (for the magnitude see Figs. 2.16B and D) and the exponential form (see Fig. 2.17B). The operator `Rearrange`, in Code 2.3, is used prior to transform calculation and leads to the image of Fig. 2.17C, and all later transform images.

The full effect of the Fourier transform is shown by application to an image of much higher resolution. Fig. 2.18A shows the image of a group of people and Fig. 2.18B shows its transform. The transform reveals that much of the information is carried in the lower frequencies since this is where most of the spectral components concentrate. This is because the image has many regions where the brightness does not change a lot, such as in the foliage. The high-frequency components reflect change in intensity. Accordingly, the higher frequency components arise from things that change fast and from the borders of objects.

As with the 1D Fourier transform, there are 2D Fourier transform pairs, illustrated in Fig. 2.19. The 2D Fourier transform of a 2D pulse, Fig. 2.19A, is a 2D sinc function, in

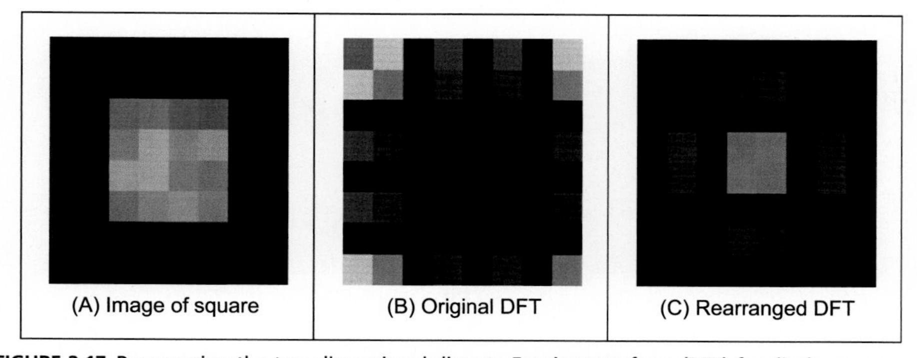
(A) Image of square (B) Original DFT (C) Rearranged DFT

FIGURE 2.17 Rearranging the two-dimensional discrete Fourier transform (DFT) for display purposes.

(A) Image of group
(B) Transform of image of group

FIGURE 2.18 Applying the Fourier transform to the image of a group of people.

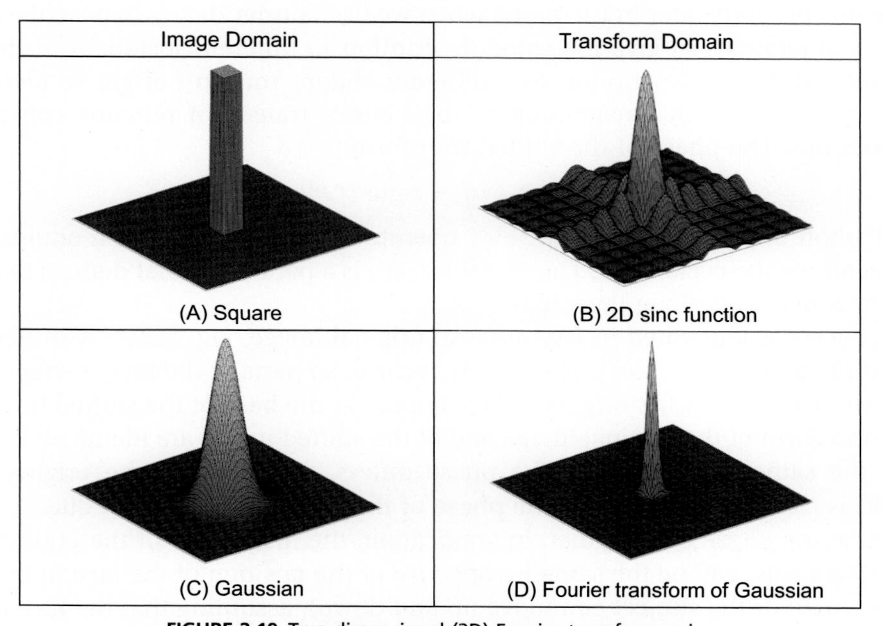

FIGURE 2.19 Two-dimensional (2D) Fourier transform pairs.

Fig. 2.19B. The 2D Fourier transform of a Gaussian function, Fig. 2.19C, is again a 2D Gaussian function in the frequency domain, Fig. 2.19D.

2.6 Properties of the Fourier Transform

2.6.1 Shift invariance

The decomposition into spatial frequency does not depend on the position of features within the image. If we shift all the features by a fixed amount, or acquire the image from a different position, the magnitude of its Fourier transform does not change. This property is known as *shift invariance*. By denoting the delayed version of $p(t)$ as $p(t-\tau)$, where τ is the delay, and the Fourier transform of the shifted version as $\Im[p(t-\tau)]$, we obtain the relationship between a time domain shift in the time and frequency domains as

$$\Im[p(t-\tau)] = e^{-j\omega\tau}P(\omega) \tag{2.31}$$

Accordingly, the magnitude of the Fourier transform is

$$|\Im[p(t-\tau)]| = \left|e^{-j\omega\tau}P(\omega)\right| = \left|e^{-j\omega\tau}\right||P(\omega)| = |P(\omega)| \tag{2.32}$$

and since the magnitude of the exponential function is 1.0 then the magnitude of the Fourier transform of the shifted image equals that of the original (unshifted) version. We shall use this property later in Chapter 7 when we use Fourier theory to describe shapes. There, it will allow us to give the same description to different instances of the same shape, but a different description to a different shape. You do not get something for nothing: even though the magnitude of the Fourier transform remains constant, its phase does not. The phase of the shifted transform is

$$\arg(\Im[p(t-\tau)]) = \arg\left(e^{-j\omega\tau}P(\omega)\right) \tag{2.33}$$

The Python implementation of a `shift` operator, Code 2.4, uses the modulus operation `%` to enforce the cyclic shift. The `shiftDistance` is a parameter that defines the length of the horizontal shift along the x axis.

This process is illustrated in Fig. 2.20. An original image, Fig. 2.20A, is shifted along the x and the y axes, Fig. 2.20D. The shift is cyclical, so parts of the image wrap around; those parts at the top of the original image appear at the base of the shifted image. The Fourier transform of the original image and of the shifted image are identical: Fig. 2.20B appears the same as Fig. 2.20E. The phase differs: the phase of the original image Fig. 2.20C is clearly different from the phase of the shifted image, Fig. 2.20F.

The differing phase implies that, in application, the magnitude of the Fourier transform of a face, say, will be the same irrespective of the position of the face in the image (i.e. the camera or the subject can move up and down), assuming that the face is much larger than its image version. This implies that if the magnitude of the Fourier transform is used to analyse an image of a human face or one of cloth, to describe it by its spatial frequency, we do not need to control the position of the camera, or the object, precisely.

2.6.2 Rotation

The Fourier transform of an image *rotates* when the source image rotates. This is to be expected since the decomposition into spatial frequency reflects the orientation of

```
for x,y in itertools.product(range(0, width), range(0, height)):
    xShift = (x - shiftDistance) % width
    shiftImage[y,x] = inputImage[y,xShift]
```

CODE 2.4 Shifting an image.

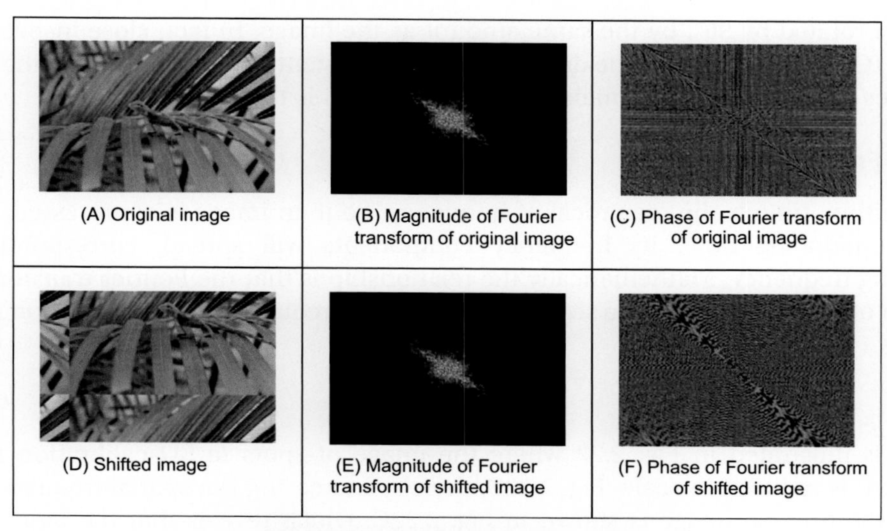

FIGURE 2.20 Illustrating shift invariance.

features within the image. As such, orientation dependency is built into the Fourier transform process.

This implies that if the frequency domain properties are to be used in image analysis, via the Fourier transform, the orientation of the original image needs to be known, or fixed. It is often possible to fix orientation, or to estimate its value when a feature's orientation cannot be fixed. Alternatively, there are techniques to impose invariance to rotation, say by translation to a polar representation, though this can prove to be complex.

The effect of rotation is illustrated in Fig. 2.21. An image, Fig. 2.21A, is rotated by 90° to give the image in Fig. 2.21B. Comparison of the transform of the original image, Fig. 2.21C, with the transform of the rotated image, Fig. 2.21D, shows that the transform

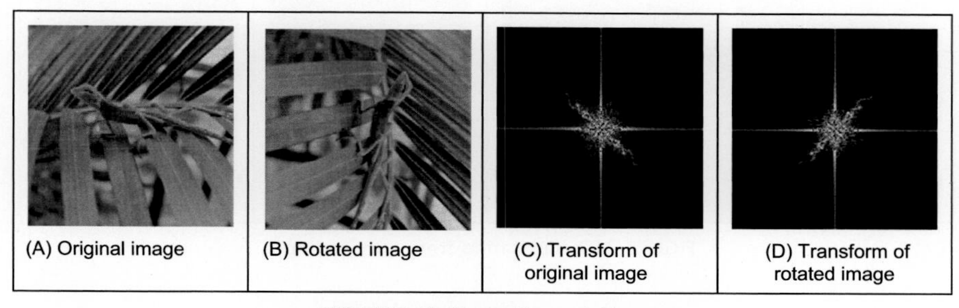

FIGURE 2.21 Illustrating rotation.

has been rotated by 90°, by the same amount as the image. In fact, close inspection of Figs. 2.21C and D shows that the diagonal axis is consistent with the normal to the axis of the leaves (where the change mainly occurs), and this is the axis that rotates.

2.6.3 Frequency scaling

By definition, time is the reciprocal of frequency. So if an image is compressed, equivalent to reducing time, its frequency components will spread, corresponding to increasing frequency. Mathematically the relationship is that the Fourier transform of a function of time multiplied by a scalar λ, $p(\lambda t)$, gives a frequency domain function $P(\omega/\lambda)$, so

$$\Im[p(\lambda t)] = \frac{1}{\lambda}P\left(\frac{\omega}{\lambda}\right) \tag{2.34}$$

This is illustrated in Fig. 2.22 where the image of spots (a 3D calibration target), Fig. 2.22A, is reduced in scale, Fig. 2.22B, thereby increasing the spatial frequency. The DFT of the original image is shown in Fig. 2.22C, which reveals that the large spatial frequencies in the original image are arranged in a star-like pattern. As a consequence of scaling the original image, the spectrum will spread from the origin consistent with the change in spatial frequency, as shown in Fig. 2.22D. This retains the star-like pattern, at a different scale.

The implications of this property are that if we reduce the scale of an image, say by imaging at a greater distance, we will alter the frequency components. The relationship is linear: the amount of reduction, say the proximity of the camera to the target, is directly proportional to the scaling in the frequency domain.

2.6.4 Superposition (linearity)

The *principle of superposition* is very important in systems analysis. Essentially, it states that a system is linear if its response to two combined signals equals the sum of the responses to the individual signals. Given an output O which is a function of two inputs

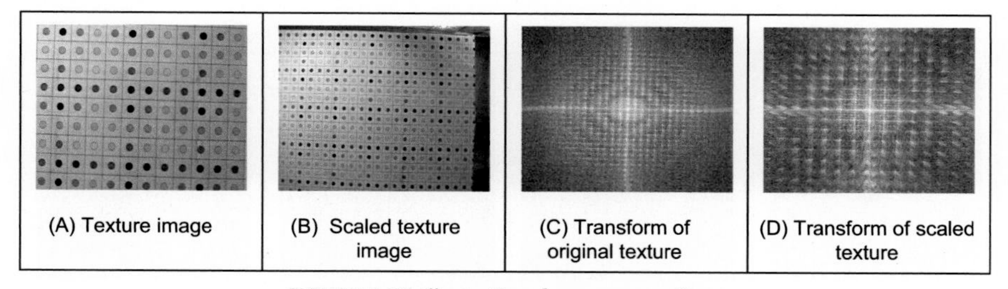

FIGURE 2.22 Illustrating frequency scaling.

I_1 and I_2, the response to signal I_1 is $O(I_1)$, that to signal I_2 is $O(I_2)$, and the response to I_1 and I_2, when applied together, is $O(I_1+I_2)$, the superposition principle states

$$O(I_1+I_2) = O(I_1) + O(I_2) \tag{2.35}$$

Any system which satisfies the principle of superposition is termed *linear*. The Fourier transform is a linear operation since, for two signals p_1 and p_2

$$\Im[p_1+p_2] = \Im[p_1] + \Im[p_2] \tag{2.36}$$

In application, this suggests that we can separate images by looking at their frequency domain components. This is illustrated for one-dimensional signals in Fig. 2.23. One signal is shown in Fig. 2.23A and a second is shown in Fig. 2.23C. The Fourier transforms of these signals are shown in Figs. 2.23B and D. The addition of these signals is shown in Fig. 2.23E, and its transform in Fig. 2.23F. The Fourier transform of the added signals differs little from the addition of their transforms, Fig. 2.23G. This is confirmed by subtraction of the two, Fig. 2.23H (some slight differences can be seen, but these are due to numerical error).

By way of example, given the image of a fingerprint in blood on cloth it is very difficult to separate the fingerprint from the cloth by analysing the combined image. However, by translation to the frequency domain, the Fourier transform of the combined image shows strong components due to the texture (this is the spatial frequency of the cloth's pattern) and weaker, more scattered, components due to the fingerprint. If we suppress the frequency components due to the cloth's texture, and invoke the inverse Fourier transform, then the cloth will be removed from the original image. The fingerprint can now be seen in the resulting image.

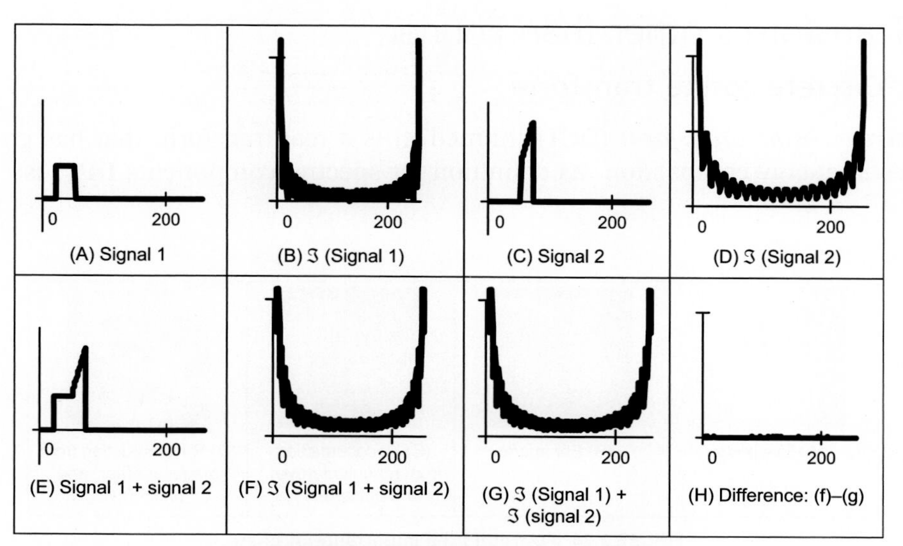

FIGURE 2.23 Illustrating superposition.

2.6.5 The importance of phase

You might reasonably ask: 'what is the importance of phase?'. It is actually a pretty reasonable question. *Phase* is about how signals are arranged (or add up), whereas magnitude is about how big the signals are. As such, one might intuitively think that the magnitude is more important than the phase. It is more complex than this: phase can actually be viewed to be more important (though you need both magnitude and phase to reconstruct a signal). To illustrate this we shall take two images, one of the eye and the other of an ear (OK, ears are rather ugly but they are unique to their owner) as shown in Fig. 2.24. Here we have reconstructed images by taking the magnitude of one image and the phase (the argument) of another. From Eq. (2.6) we have

$$\begin{aligned}\mathbf{Fp}(\omega) &= \mathrm{Re}(\mathbf{Fp}(\omega)) + j\mathrm{Im}(\mathbf{Fp}(\omega)) \\ &= \mathit{magnitude} \times \cos(\mathit{phase}) + j \times \mathit{magnitude} \times \sin(\mathit{phase})\end{aligned} \tag{2.37}$$

where magnitude and phase are calculated according to Eqs. (2.7) and (2.8), respectively. The rearranged Fourier transform is then

$$\mathbf{Fp}(\omega) = |\mathbf{Fp}(\text{image 1})| \times \cos(\mathit{arg}(\mathbf{Fp}(\text{image 2}))) + j \times |\mathbf{Fp}(\text{image 1})| \times \sin(\mathit{arg}(\mathbf{Fp}(\text{image 2})))$$

When image 1 is the eye and image 2 is the ear, then the reconstructed image (via the inverse FT) looks most like the image of the ear, Fig. 2.24C; when it is the other way found, the image is much closer to the eye, Fig. 2.24D. So it is the phase that is controlling the reconstruction in this case, not the magnitude (the bit represented by the magnitude hardly shows in the reconstructions here). Clearly the phase is very important in the representation of a signal.

2.7 Transforms other than Fourier

2.7.1 Discrete cosine transform

The *discrete cosine Transform* (DCT) [Ahmed74] is a real transform that has great advantages in energy compaction. Its definition for spectral components $\mathbf{DP}_{u,v}$ is:

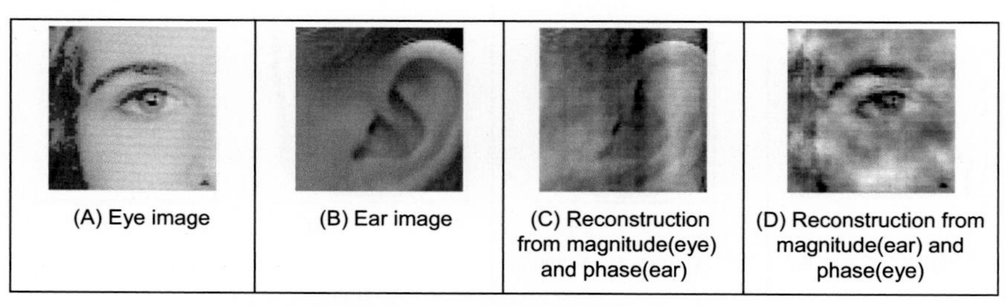

FIGURE 2.24 Illustrating the importance of phase.

$$\mathbf{DP}_{u,v} = \begin{cases} \dfrac{1}{N^2}\displaystyle\sum_{x=0}^{N-1}\sum_{y=0}^{N-1}\mathbf{P}_{x,y} & \text{if} \quad u=0 \quad \text{and} \quad v=0 \\ \dfrac{2}{N^2}\displaystyle\sum_{x=0}^{N-1}\sum_{y=0}^{N-1}\mathbf{P}_{x,y}\times\cos\left(\dfrac{(2x+1)u\pi}{2N}\right)\times\cos\left(\dfrac{(2y+1)v\pi}{2N}\right) & \text{otherwise} \end{cases} \tag{2.38}$$

There are many variants of the definition of the DCT, and we are concerned only with principles here. The inverse DCT is defined by

$$\mathbf{P}_{x,y} = \frac{1}{N^2}\sum_{u=0}^{N-1}\sum_{v=0}^{N-1}\mathbf{DP}_{u,v}\times\cos\left(\frac{(2x+1)u\pi}{2N}\right)\times\cos\left(\frac{(2y+1)v\pi}{2N}\right) \tag{2.39}$$

A fast version of the DCT is available, like the FFT, and calculation can be based on the FFT. Both implementations offer about the same speed. The Fourier transform is not actually optimal for *image coding* since the DCT can give a higher compression rate, for the same image quality. This is because the cosine basis functions can afford for high-energy compaction. This can be seen by comparison of Fig. 2.25B with Fig. 2.25A, which reveals that the DCT components are much more concentrated around the origin, than those for the Fourier transform. This is the compaction property associated with the DCT. The DCT has actually been considered as optimal for image coding, and this is why it is found in the JPEG and MPEG standards for coded image transmission.

The DCT is actually shift variant, due to its cosine basis functions. In other respects, its properties are very similar to the DFT, with one important exception: it has not yet proved possible to implement convolution with the DCT. It is actually possible to calculate the DCT via the FFT. This has been performed in Fig. 2.25B.

The Fourier transform essentially decomposes, or decimates, a signal into sine and cosine components, so the natural partner to the DCT is the *discrete sine transform* (DST). However, the DST transform has odd basis functions (sine) rather than the even ones in the DCT. This lends the DST transform some less desirable properties, and it finds much less application than the DCT.

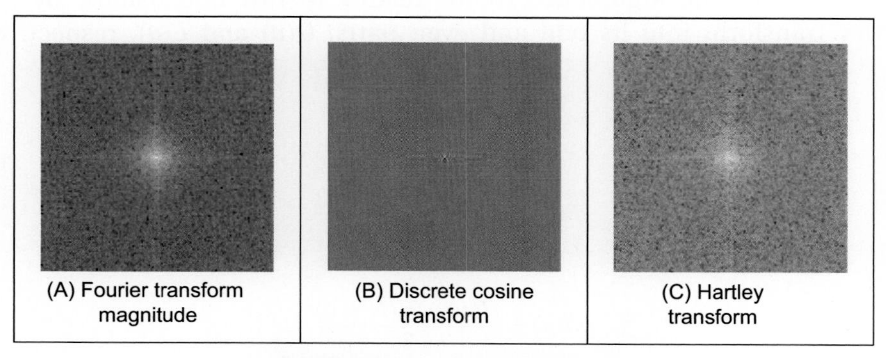

FIGURE 2.25 Comparing transforms.

2.7.2 Discrete Hartley Transform

The *Hartley transform* [Hartley42] is a form of the Fourier transform, but without complex arithmetic, with result for the face image shown in Fig. 2.25C. Oddly, though it sounds like a very rational development, the Hartley transform was first invented in 1942, but not rediscovered and then formulated in discrete form until 1983 [Bracewell83]. One advantage of the Hartley transform is that the forward and inverse transforms are the same operation; a disadvantage is that phase is built into the order of frequency components since it is not readily available as the argument of a complex number. The definition of the discrete Hartley transform (DHT) replaces the exponent basis by the cas function defined as

$$\text{cas}(t) = \cos(t) + \sin(t) \tag{2.40}$$

Thus the transform components $\mathbf{HP}_{u,v}$ are

$$\mathbf{HP}_{u,v} = \frac{1}{\sqrt{MN}} \sum_{x=0}^{N-1} \sum_{y=0}^{M-1} \mathbf{P}_{x,y} \left(\cos\left(\frac{2\pi}{M} vy\right) + \sin\left(\frac{2\pi}{M} vy\right) \right) \left(\cos\left(\frac{2\pi}{N} ux\right) + \sin\left(\frac{2\pi}{N} ux\right) \right) \tag{2.41}$$

For a square image, this can be written as

$$\mathbf{HP}_{u,v} = \frac{1}{N} \sum_{x=0}^{N-1} \sum_{y=0}^{N-1} \mathbf{P}_{x,y} \left(\sin\left(\frac{2\pi}{N}(ux + vy)\right) + \cos\left(\frac{2\pi}{N}(ux - vy)\right) \right) \tag{2.42}$$

The inverse Hartley transform is the same process, but applied to the transformed image.

$$\mathbf{P}_{x,y} = \frac{1}{N} \sum_{x=0}^{N-1} \sum_{y=0}^{N-1} \mathbf{HP}_{x,y} \left(\sin\left(\frac{2\pi}{N}(ux + vy)\right) + \cos\left(\frac{2\pi}{N}(ux - vy)\right) \right) \tag{2.43}$$

The implementation is then the same for both the forward and the inverse transforms. Again, a fast implementation is available – the *fast Hartley transform* [Bracewell84] (though some suggest that it should be called the Bracewell transform, eponymously). It is actually possible to calculate the DFT of a function, $F(u)$, from its Hartley transform, $H(u)$. The analysis here is based on one-dimensional data, but only for simplicity since the argument extends readily to two dimensions. By splitting the Hartley transform into its odd and even parts, $O(u)$ and $E(u)$, respectively, we obtain

$$H(u) = O(u) + E(u) \tag{2.44}$$

where

$$E(u) = \frac{H(u) + H(N-u)}{2} \tag{2.45}$$

and

$$O(u) = \frac{H(u) - H(N-u)}{2} \tag{2.46}$$

The DFT can then be calculated from the DHT simply by

$$F(u) = E(u) - j \times O(u) \tag{2.47}$$

Conversely, the Hartley transform can be calculated from the Fourier transform by

$$H(u) = \text{Re}[F(u)] - \text{Im}[F(u)] \tag{2.48}$$

where Re[ ] and Im[ ] denote the real and the imaginary parts, respectively. This emphasises the natural relationship between the Fourier and the Hartley transform. The image of Fig. 2.25C has been calculated via the 2D FFT using Eq. (2.48). Note that the transform in Fig. 2.25C is the complete transform whereas the Fourier transform in Fig. 2.25A shows magnitude only. Naturally, as with the DCT, the properties of the Hartley transform mirror those of the Fourier transform. Unfortunately, the Hartley transform does not have shift invariance but there are ways to handle this. Also, convolution requires manipulation of the odd and even parts.

Code 2.5 illustrates the computation of the Hartley transform in Eq. (2.28). Similar to Code 2.2 the values are defined for a range of frequencies and the result is processed such that the zero frequency is at the centre of the output array. Notice that this equation is also separable, so it is possible to follow a similar implementation of the Fourier transform by maintaining the first cosine and sine sum in one direction and then performing the multiplication with the terms in the other direction. In this implementation, the components are computed by combining the product of both directions.

Fig. 2.26 shows an example of the transform obtained using Code 2.5. Fig. 2.26A shows the input image, and Fig. 2.26B shows the result of the transform. The resulting components have positive and negative values, so to show the results in an image it is necessary to perform some normalisation. The image shown in Fig. 2.26B shows the log of the

```
for u in range(-maxFreqW, maxFreqW + 1):
    entryW = u + maxFreqW
    for v in range(-maxFreqH, maxFreqH + 1):
        entryH = v + maxFreqH
        for x,y in itertools.product(range(0, width), range(0, height)):
            coeff[entryH, entryW] += inputImage[y,x] *                          \
                        (cos(x*ww*u) + sin(x*ww*u)) * (cos(y*wh*v) + sin(y*wh*v))
```

CODE 2.5 Hartley transform.

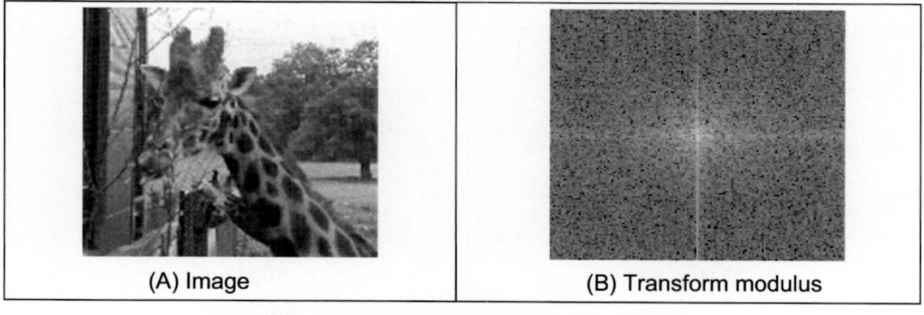

FIGURE 2.26 Applying the Hartley transform.

absolute value, so it is comparable to the Fourier magnitude. Notice that the transform is symmetrical, and it is rather similar to the results in Fig. 2.16E. This is because both the Fourier and Hartley transforms decompose the image into frequency components.

2.7.3 Introductory wavelets

2.7.3.1 Gabor Wavelet

Wavelets are more recent approach to signal processing than the Fourier transform, being introduced only in the nineties [Daubechies90]. Their main advantage is that they allow multiresolution analysis (analysis at different scales, or resolution). Furthermore, wavelets allow decimation in space and frequency, simultaneously. Earlier transforms actually allow decimation in frequency, in the forward transform, and in time (or position) in the inverse. In this way, the Fourier transform gives a measure of the frequency content of the whole image: the contribution of the image to a particular frequency component. Simultaneous decimation allows us to describe an image in terms of frequency which occurs at a position, as opposed to an ability to measure frequency content across the whole image. Clearly this gives us a greater descriptional power, which can be used to good effect.

First though, we need a basis function, so that we can decompose a signal. The basis functions in the Fourier transform are sinusoidal waveforms at different frequencies. The function of the Fourier transform is to convolve these sinusoids with a signal to determine how much of each is present. The *Gabor wavelet* is well suited to introductory purposes, since it is essentially a sine wave modulated by a Gaussian envelope. The Gabor wavelet *gw* is given by

$$gw(t, \omega_0, \sigma) = e^{-j\omega_0 t} e^{-\left(\frac{t-t_0}{\sigma}\right)^2} \tag{2.49}$$

where $\omega_0 = 2\pi f_0$ is the modulating frequency, t_0 dictates position and σ controls the width of the Gaussian envelope which embraces the oscillating signal. An example Gabor wavelet is shown in Fig. 2.27 which shows the real and the imaginary parts (the modulus

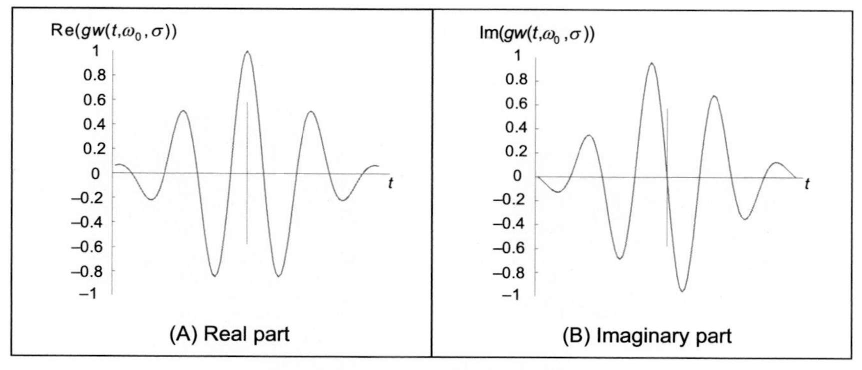

FIGURE 2.27 An example Gabor Wavelet.

is the Gaussian envelope). Increasing the value of ω_0 increases the frequency content within the envelope whereas increasing the value of σ spreads the envelope without affecting the frequency. So why does this allow simultaneous analysis of time and frequency? Given that this function is the one convolved with the test data, then we can compare it with the Fourier transform. In fact, if we remove the term on the right-hand side of Eq. (2.49), we return to the sinusoidal basis function of the Fourier transform, the exponential in Eq. (2.1). Accordingly, we can return to the Fourier transform by setting σ to be very large. Alternatively, setting f_0 to zero removes frequency information. Since we operate in between these extremes, we obtain position and frequency information simultaneously.

Actually, an infinite class of wavelets exists which can be used as an expansion basis in signal decimation. One approach [Daugman88] has generalised the Gabor function to a 2D form aimed to be optimal in terms of spatial and spectral resolution. These 2D Gabor wavelets are given by

$$gw2D(x, y, \omega_0, \sigma) = \frac{1}{\sigma\sqrt{\pi}} e^{-\left(\frac{(x-x_0)^2+(y-y_0)^2}{2\sigma^2}\right)} e^{-j\omega_0((x-x_0)\cos(\theta)+(y-y_0)\sin(\theta))} \tag{2.50}$$

where x_0 and y_0 control position, $\omega_0 = 2\pi f_0$ controls the frequency of modulation along either axis, and θ controls the direction (orientation) of the wavelet (as implicit in a 2D system). Naturally, the shape of the area imposed by the 2D Gaussian function could be elliptical if different variances were allowed along the x and y axes (the frequency can also be modulated differently along each axis). Fig. 2.28, of an example 2D Gabor wavelet, shows that the real and imaginary parts are even and odd functions, respectively; again, different values for f_0 and σ control the frequency and envelope's spread, respectively, the extra parameter θ controls rotation.

The function of the wavelet transform is to determine where and how each wavelet specified by the range of values for each of the free parameters occurs in the image. Clearly, there is a wide choice that depends on application. An example transform is given in Fig. 2.29. Here, the Gabor wavelet parameters have been chosen in such a way as to select face features: the eyes, nose and mouth have come out very well. These features are where

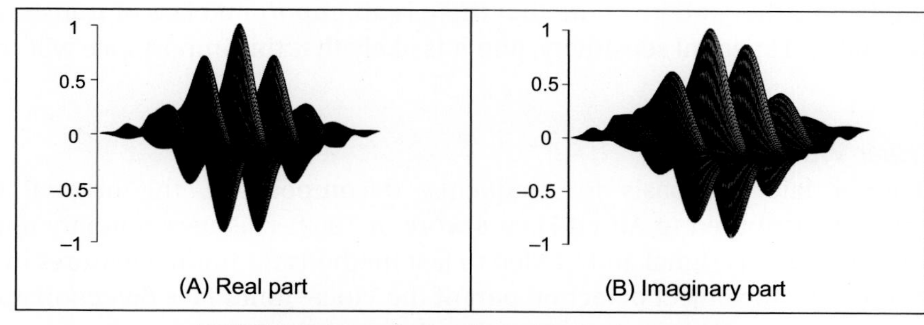

FIGURE 2.28 Example two-dimensional Gabor Wavelet.

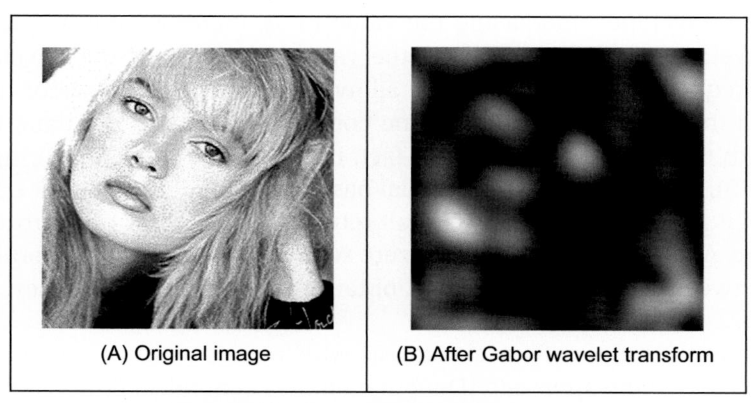

FIGURE 2.29 An example Gabor Wavelet transform.

there is local frequency content with orientation according to the head's inclination. Naturally, these are not the only features with these properties, the cuff of the sleeve is highlighted too! But this does show the Gabor wavelet's ability to select and analyse localised variation in image intensity.

However, the conditions under which a set of continuous Gabor wavelets will provide a complete representation of any image (i.e. that any image can be reconstructed) were developed later. However, the theory is naturally very powerful, since it accommodates frequency and position simultaneously, and further it facilitates multiresolution analysis – the analysis is then sensitive to scale which is advantageous since objects which are far from the camera appear smaller than those which are close. We shall find wavelets again, when processing images to find low-level features. Amongst applications of Gabor wavelets, we can find measurement of iris texture to give a very powerful security system [Daugman93] and face feature extraction for automatic face recognition [Lades93]. Wavelets continue to develop [Daubechies90] and have found applications in image texture analysis [Laine93], in coding [daSilva96] and in image restoration [Banham96]. Unfortunately, the discrete wavelet transform is not shift invariant, though there are approaches aimed to remedy this (see, for example, [Donoho95]). As such, we shall not study it further and just note that there is an important class of transforms that combine spatial and spectral sensitivity, and it is likely that this importance will continue to grow.

2.7.3.2 Haar Wavelet

Though Fourier laid the basis for frequency decomposition, the original wavelet approach is now attributed to Alfred Haar's work in 1909. This uses a binary approach, rather than a continuous signal and has led to fast methods for finding features in images [Oren97] (especially the object detection part of the Viola–Jones face detection approach

[Viola01]). Essentially, the binary functions can be considered to form averages over sets of points, thereby giving means for compression and for feature detection. If we are to form a new vector (at level $h+1$) by taking averages of pairs of elements (and retaining the integer representation) of the N points in the previous vector (at level h of the $log_2(N)$ levels) as

$$\mathbf{p}_i^{h+1} = \frac{\mathbf{p}_{2\times i}^h + \mathbf{p}_{2\times i+1}^h}{2} \quad i \in 0 \ldots \frac{N}{2} - 1; h \in 1, \ldots \log_2(N) \tag{2.51}$$

By way of example, consider a vector of points at level 0 as

$$\mathbf{p}^0 = [1 \quad 3 \quad 21 \quad 19 \quad 17 \quad 19 \quad 1 \quad -1] \tag{2.52}$$

then the first element in the new vector becomes $(1 + 3)/2 = 2$ and the next element is $(21 + 19)/2 = 20$ and so on, so the next level is

$$\mathbf{p}^1 = [2 \quad 20 \quad 18 \quad 0] \tag{2.53}$$

And is naturally half the number of points. If we also generate some detail, which is how we return to the original points, then we have a vector

$$\mathbf{d}^1 = [-1 \quad 1 \quad -1 \quad 1] \tag{2.54}$$

and when each element of the detail $\mathbf{d}^1$ is successively added and subtracted from the elements of $\mathbf{p}^1$ as $[\mathbf{p}_0^1 + \mathbf{d}_0^1 \quad \mathbf{p}_0^1 - \mathbf{d}_0^1 \quad \mathbf{p}_1^1 + \mathbf{d}_1^1 \quad \mathbf{p}_1^1 - \mathbf{d}_1^1 \quad \mathbf{p}_2^1 + \mathbf{d}_2^1 \quad \mathbf{p}_2^1 - \mathbf{d}_2^1 \quad \mathbf{p}_3^1 + \mathbf{d}_3^1 \ \mathbf{p}_3^1 - \mathbf{d}_3^1]$ by which we obtain

$$[2+(-1) \quad 2-(-1) \quad 20+1 \quad 20-1 \quad 18+(-1) \quad 18-(-1) \quad 0+1 \quad 0-1]$$

which returns us to the original vector $\mathbf{p}^0$ (Eq. 2.52). If we continue to similarly form a series of decompositions (averages of adjacent points), together with the detail at each point, we generate

$$\mathbf{p}^2 = [11 \quad 9]; \quad \mathbf{d}^2 = [-9 \quad 9] \tag{2.55}$$

$$\mathbf{p}^3 = [10]; \quad \mathbf{d}^3 = [1] \tag{2.56}$$

We can then store the image as a code

$$[\mathbf{p}^3 \quad \mathbf{d}^3 \quad \mathbf{d}^2 \quad \mathbf{d}^1] = [10 \quad 1 \quad -9 \quad 9 \quad -1 \quad 1 \quad -1 \quad 1] \tag{2.57}$$

The process is illustrated in Fig. 2.30 for a sine wave. Fig. 2.30A shows the original sine wave, (B) shows the decomposition to level 3, and it is a close but discrete representation, whereas (C) shows the decomposition to level 6, which is very coarse. The original signal can be reconstructed from the final code, and this is without error. If the signal is reconstructed by filtering the detail to reduce the amount of stored data, the reconstruction of the original signal (D) at level 0 is quite close to the original signal, and the reconstruction at the other levels is similarly close as expected. The reconstruction error is also shown in (D)–(F). Components of the detail (of magnitude less than one) were removed, achieving a compression ratio of approximately 50%. Naturally, a Fourier transform would encode the signal better, as the Fourier transform

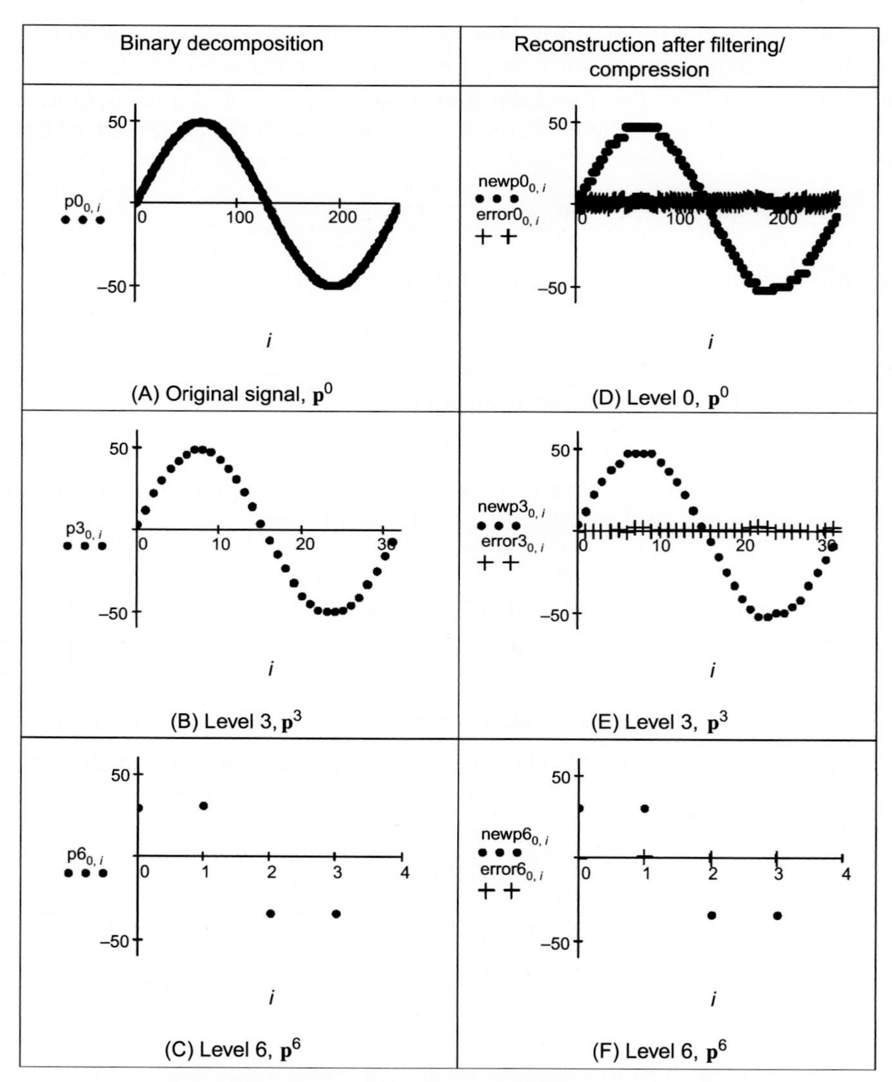

FIGURE 2.30 Binary signal decomposition and reconstruction.

is best suited to representing a sine wave. Like Fourier, this discrete approach can encode the signal, we can also reconstruct the original signal (reverse the process), and shows how the signal can be represented at different scales, since there are less points in the higher levels.

By Eq. (2.57), this gives a set of numbers of the same size as the original data, and is an alternative representation from which we can reconstruct the original data. There are two important differences:

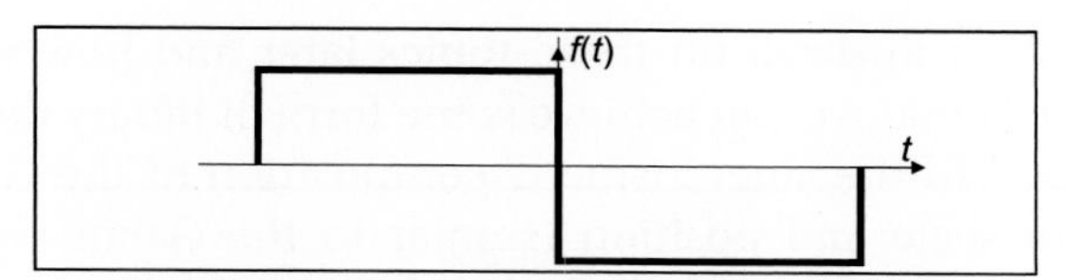

FIGURE 2.31 Example Haar Wavelet function.

(i) we have an idea of scale by virtue of the successive averaging ($\mathbf{p}^1$ is similar in structure to $\mathbf{p}^0$, but at a different scale) and

(ii) we can compress (or code) the image by removing the small numbers in the new representation (by setting them to zero, noting that there are efficient ways of encoding structures containing large numbers of zeros).

A process of successive averaging and differencing can be expressed as a function of the form in Fig. 2.31. This is a mother wavelet which can be applied at different scales, but retains the same shape at those scales. So we now have a binary decomposition rather than the sine waves of the Fourier transform.

To detect objects, these wavelets need to be arranged in two dimensions. These can be arranged to provide for object detection, by selecting the 2D arrangement of points. By defining a relationship which is a summation of the points in an image prior to a given point

$$\mathbf{sP}_{x,y} = \sum_{x'<x, y'<y} \mathbf{P}_{x',y'} \tag{2.58}$$

Then we can achieve wavelet type features which are derived by using these summations. Four of these wavelets are shown in Fig. 2.32. These are placed at selected positions in the image to which they are applied. There are white and black areas: the sum of the pixels under the white area(s) is subtracted from the sum of the pixels under the dark area(s), in a way similar to the earlier averaging operation in Eq. (2.52). The first template, Fig. 2.32A, will detect shapes which are brighter on one side than the other; the second (Fig 2.32B) will detect shapes which are brighter in a vertical sense; the third will detect a dark object which has brighter areas on either side. There is a family of these arrangements, and that can apply at selected levels of scale. By collecting the analysis, we can determine objects whatever their position, size (objects further away will appear

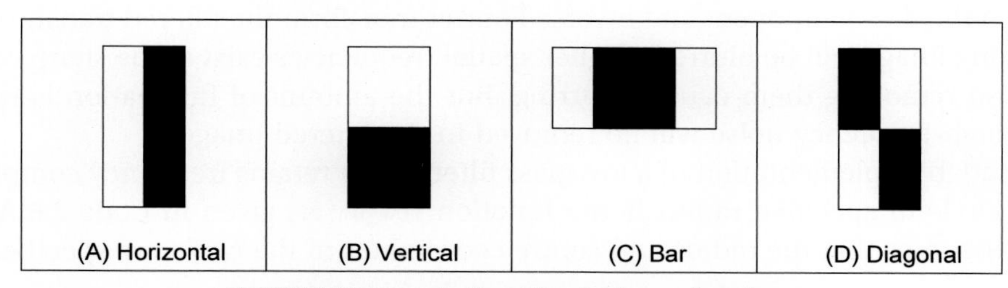

FIGURE 2.32 Example Haar Wavelet image functions.

smaller) or rotation. We will dwell on these topics later and how we find and classify shapes. The point here is that we can achieve some form of binary decomposition in two dimensions, as opposed to the sine/cosine decomposition of the Gabor wavelet whilst retaining selectivity to scale and position (similar to the Gabor wavelet). This is also simpler, so the binary functions can be processed more quickly.

2.7.4 Other transforms

Decomposing a signal into sinusoidal components was actually one of the first approaches to transform calculus, and this is why the Fourier transform is so important. The sinusoidal functions are actually called *basis functions*, the implicit assumption is that the basis functions map well to the signal components. As such, the Haar wavelets are binary basis functions. There is (theoretically) an infinite range of basis functions. Discrete signals can map better into collections of binary components rather than sinusoidal ones. These collections (or sequences) of binary data are called sequence components and form the basis of the *Walsh transform* [Walsh23], which is a global transform when compared with the Haar functions (like Fourier compared with Gabor). This has found wide application in the interpretation of digital signals, though it is less widely used in image processing (one disadvantage is the lack of shift invariance). The *Karhunen–Loéve* transform [Karhunen47] [Loéve48] (also called the *Hotelling* transform from which it was derived, or more popularly *Principal Component Analysis*) is a way of analysing (statistical) data to reduce it to those data which are informative, discarding those which are not.

2.8 Applications using frequency domain properties

Filtering is a major use of Fourier transforms, particularly because we can understand an image, and how to process it, much better in the frequency domain. An analogy is the use of a graphic equaliser to control the way music sounds. In images, if we want to remove high-frequency information (like the hiss on sound) then we can filter, or remove, it by inspecting the Fourier transform. If we retain low-frequency components, we implement a *low-pass filter*. The low-pass filter describes the area in which we retain spectral components, the size of the area dictates the range of frequencies retained and is known as the filter's bandwidth. If we retain components within a circular region centred on the d.c. component and inverse Fourier transform the filtered transform then the resulting image will be blurred. Higher spatial frequencies exist at the sharp edges of features, so removing them causes blurring. But the amount of fluctuation is reduced too; any high-frequency noise will be removed in the filtered image.

The Matlab implementation of a low-pass filter which retains frequency components within a circle of specified radius is the function `low_filter`, given in Code 2.6(A). This operator assumes that the radius and centre coordinates of the circle are specified prior

```
function output = low_filter(image,value)
%get dimensions
[rows,cols]=size(image);

%filter the transform
for x = 1:cols %address all columns
  for y = 1:rows %address all rows
    if (((y-(rows/2))^2)+((x-(cols/2))^2)-(value^2))>0
        output(y,x)=0; %discard components outside the circle
    else
        output(y,x)=image(y,x); %and keep the ones inside
    end
  end
end
```

(A) Matlab

```
for kw,kh in itertools.product(range(-maxFreqW, maxFreqW + 1),        \
                               range(-maxFreqH, maxFreqH + 1)):
    IndexW, indexH = kw + maxFreqW, kh + maxFreqH

    if sqrt(kw * kw + kh * kh) < cutFrequency:
        coeffLow[indexH, IndexW][0] = coeff[indexH, IndexW][0]
        coeffLow[indexH, IndexW][1] = coeff[indexH, IndexW][1]
    else:
        coeffHigh[indexH, IndexW][0] = coeff[indexH, IndexW][0]
                   coeffHigh[indexH, IndexW][1] = coeff[indexH, IndexW][1]
```

(B) Python

CODE 2.6 Implementing low-pass filtering.

to its use. Points within the circle remain unaltered, whereas those outside the circle are set to zero, black. The Python version is given in Code 2.6(B). The function uses Fourier coefficients in the array `coeff`. This array is computed in Code 2.2. The value `cutFrequency` is used to select frequencies and should be set to between the maximum and minimum frequency values in the image. The code iterates over all frequencies and it computes the distance to the zero frequency. If the distance is lower than `cutFrequency`, then the frequency is copied to the array `coeffLow`, otherwise it is copied to the `coeffHigh` array. That is, the code fills two arrays that contain the low and high frequencies in the image.

When applied to an image, we obtain a low-pass filtered version. In application to an image of a face, the low spatial frequencies are the ones which change slowly as reflected in the resulting, blurred image, Fig. 2.33A. The high-frequency components have been removed as shown in the transform, Fig. 2.33B. The radius of the circle controls how much of the original image is retained. In this case, the radius is 10 pixels (and the image resolution is 256×256). If a larger circle were to be used, more of the high-frequency detail would be retained (and the image would look more like its original version); if the circle was very small, an even more blurred image would result, since only the lowest spatial frequencies would be retained. This differs from the earlier Gabor wavelet approach that allows for localised spatial frequency analysis. Here, the analysis is global: we are filtering the frequency across the whole image.

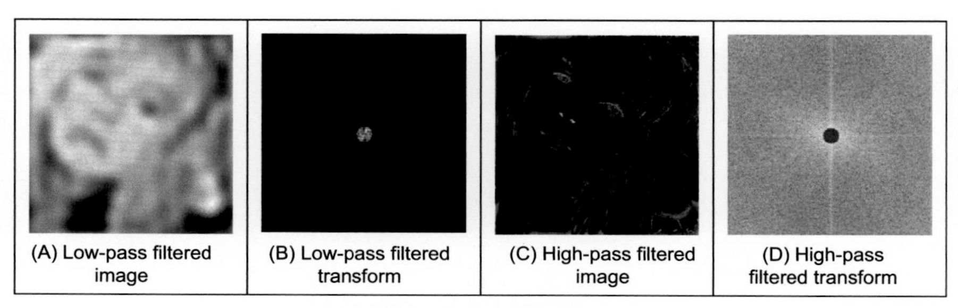

(A) Low-pass filtered image
(B) Low-pass filtered transform
(C) High-pass filtered image
(D) High-pass filtered transform

FIGURE 2.33 Illustrating low- and high-pass filtering.

Alternatively, we can retain high-frequency components and remove low-frequency ones. This is a *high-pass filter*. If we remove components near the d.c. component and retain all the others, the result of applying the inverse Fourier transform to the filtered image will be to emphasise the features that were removed in low-pass filtering. This can lead to a popular application of the high-pass filter: to 'crispen' an image by emphasising its high-frequency components. An implementation using a circular region merely requires selection of the set of points outside the circle, rather than inside as for the low-pass operator. The effect of high-pass filtering can be observed in Fig. 2.33C which shows removal of the low-frequency components: this emphasises the hair and the borders of a face's features since these are where brightness varies rapidly. The retained components are those which were removed in low-pass filtering, as illustrated in the transform, Fig. 2.33D.

It is also possible to retain a specified range of frequencies. This is known as *band-pass filtering*. It can be implemented by retaining frequency components within an annulus centred on the d.c. component. The width of the annulus represents the bandwidth of the band-pass filter.

This leads to digital signal processing theory. There are many considerations to be made in the way you select and the manner in which frequency components are retained or excluded. This is beyond a text on computer vision. For further study in this area, Rabiner and Gold [Rabiner75], or Oppenheim and Schafer [Oppenheim09], although published (in their original form) a long time ago now, remain as popular introductions to digital signal processing theory and applications.

It is actually possible to recognise the object within the low-pass filtered image. Intuitively, this implies that we could just store the frequency components selected from the transform data, rather than all the image points. In this manner a fraction of the information would be stored, and still provide a recognisable image, albeit slightly blurred. This concerns *image coding* which is a popular target for image processing techniques, for further information, see [Clarke85] or a newer text, like [Woods11] or [Sayood17]. Note that the JPEG coding approach uses frequency domain decomposition, and is arguably the most ubiquitous image coding technique used today.

2.9 Further reading

We shall meet the frequency domain throughout this book, since it allows for an alternative interpretation of operation, in the frequency domain as opposed to the time domain. This will occur in low- and high-level feature extraction and in shape description. Further, it actually allows for some of the operations we shall cover. Further, because of the availability of the FFT, it is also used to speed up algorithms.

Given these advantages, it is well worth looking more deeply. Mark's copy of Fourier's original book has a review 'Fourier's treatise is one of the very few scientific books which can never be rendered antiquated by the progress of science' – penned by James Clerk Maxwell no less. For introductory study, there is *Who is Fourier* [Lex12] which offers a lighthearted and completely digestible overview of the Fourier transform, it is simply excellent for a starter view of the topic. For further study (and entertaining study too!) of the Fourier transform, try *The Fourier Transform and Its Applications* by [Bracewell86], or a newer text [Nussbaumer12]. A number of the standard image processing texts include much coverage of transform calculus, such as [Jain89], [Gonzalez17], and [Pratt13]. There is a relatively new text concentrating on image processing using Python [Chityala15]. For more coverage of the DCT, try [Jain89]; for an excellent coverage of the Walsh transform, try Beauchamp's superb text [Beauchamp75]. On compressed sensing, [Eldar12] is worth a read. For wavelets, try the book by Wornell that introduces wavelets from a signal processing standpoint [Wornell96], there is Mallat's classic text [Mallat08] or a new text that includes images [Broughton18]. For general signal processing theory, there are introductory texts (see, for example, Meade and Dillon [Meade86], or Ifeachor's excellent book [Ifeachor02]), for more complete coverage try [Rabiner75] or [Oppenheim09] (as mentioned earlier). Finally, on the implementation side of the FFT (and for many other signal processing algorithms) *Numerical Recipes in C* [Press07] is an excellent book. It is extremely readable, full of practical detail – well worth a look. *Numerical Recipes* is on the web too, together with other signal processing sites, as listed in Table 1.4.

References

[Ahmed74] Ahmed, N., Natarajan, T. and Rao, K. R., Discrete Cosine Transform, *IEEE Trans. on Computers*, pp 90-93, 1974.

[Banham96] Banham, M. R., and Katsaggelos, K., Spatially Adaptive Wavelet-Based Multiscale Image Restoration, *IEEE Trans. on Image Processing*, 5(4), pp 619-634 , 1996.

[Beauchamp75] Beauchamp, K. G., *Walsh Functions and Their Applications*, Academic Press, London UK, 1975.

[Bracewell84] Bracewell, R. N., The Fast Hartley Transform, *Proceedings of the IEEE*, 72(8), pp 1010-1018, 1984.

[Bracewell83] Bracewell, R. N., The Discrete Hartley Transform, Journal of the Optical Society of America, 73(12), pp 1832-1835, 1984.

[Bracewell86] Bracewell, R. N., The Fourier Transform and its Applications, Revised 2nd Edition, McGraw-Hill, Book Co., Singapore, 1986.

[Broughton18] Broughton, S. A., Bryan, K., *Discrete Fourier Analysis and Wavelets: Applications to Signal and Image Processing*, Wiley, Chichester UK, 2nd Edition 2018.

[Chityala15] Chityala, R., and Pudipeddi, S., *Image Processing and Acquisition Using Python*, CRC Press, Boca Raton FL USA, 2015.

[Clarke85] Clarke, R. J., *Transform Coding of Images*, Addison Wesley, Reading MA USA, 1985.

[daSilva96] da Silva, E. A. B., and Ghanbari, M., On the Performance of Linear Phase Wavelet Transforms in Low Bit-Rate Image Coding, *IEEE Trans. on Image Processing*, 5(5), pp 689-704, 1996.

[Daubechies90] Daubechies, I., The Wavelet Transform, Time Frequency Localisation and Signal Analysis, *IEEE Trans. on Information Theory*, 36(5), pp 961-1004, 1990.

[Daugman88] Daugman, J. G., Complete Discrete 2D Gabor Transforms by Neural Networks for Image Analysis and Compression, *IEEE Trans. on Acoustics, Speech and Signal Processing*, 36(7), pp 1169-1179, 1988.

[Daugman93] Daugman, J. G., High Confidence Visual Recognition of Persons by a Test of Statistical Independence, *IEEE Trans. on PAMI*, 15(11), pp1148-1161, 1993.

[Donoho95] Donoho, D. L., Denoising by Soft Thresholding, *IEEE Trans. on Information Theory*, 41(3), pp 613-627, 1995.

[Donoho06] Donoho, D. L., Compressed Sensing, *IEEE Trans. on Information Theory*, 52(4), pp 1289—1306, 2006.

[Eldar12] Eldar, Y. C., and Kutyniok, G., Editors, *Compressed Sensing: Theory and Applications*, Cambridge University Press, Cambridge UK, 2012.

[Gonzalez17] Gonzalez, R. C., and Woods, R. E., *Digital Image Processing*, 4th Edition, Pearson Education, 2017.

[Hartley42] Hartley, R. L. V., A More Symmetrical Fourier Analysis Applied to Transmission Problems, *Proc. IRE*, 144, pp 144-150, 1942.

[Ifeachor02] Ifeachor, E. C., and Jervis, B. W., *Digital Signal Processing*, Prentice Hall, Hemel Hempstead UK, 2nd Edition 2002.

[Jain89] Jain A. K., *Fundamentals of Computer Vision*, Prentice Hall International (UK) Ltd., Hemel Hempstead UK, 1989.

[Karhunen47] Karhunen, K., Über Lineare Methoden in der Wahrscheinlich-Keitsrechnung, *Ann. Acad. Sci. Fennicae, Ser A.I.37*, 1947 (Translation in I. Selin, On Linear Methods in Probability Theory, Doc. T-131, The RAND Corp., Santa Monica CA, 1960.).

[Lades93] Lades, M., Vorbruggen, J. C., Buhmann, J., and Lange, J., Madsburg, C. V. D., Wurtz, R. P., and Konen, W., Distortion Invariant Object Recognition in the Dynamic Link Architecture, *IEEE Trans. on Computers*, 42, pp 300-311, 1993.

[Laine93] Laine, A., and Fan, J., Texture Classification by Wavelet Packet Signatures, *IEEE Trans. on PAMI*, 15, pp 1186-1191, 1993.

[Lex12] Lex, T. C. O. L. T. (!!), *Who Is Fourier, a Mathematical Adventure*, Language Research Foundation, Boston MA USA, 2nd Edition 2012.

[Loéve48] Loéve, M., Fonctions Alétoires de Seconde Ordre, in: P. Levy, Ed., *Processus Stochastiques et Mouvement Brownien, Hermann, Paris* 1948.

[Mallat08] Mallat, S., *A Wavelet Tour of Signal Processing*, 3rd Edition, Academic Press, Burlington MA USA, 2008.

[Meade86] Meade, M. L. and Dillon, C. R., *Signals and Systems, Models and Behaviour*, Van Nostrand Reinhold (UK) Co. Ltd., Wokingham UK, 1986.

[Nussbaumer12] Nussbaumer, H. J., *Fast Fourier Transform and Convolution Algorithms*, Springer Science and Business Media, 2nd Edition., Berlin Germany, 2012.

[Oppenheim09] Oppenheim, A. V., Schafer, R. W., and Buck, J. R. *Discrete-Time Signal Processing*, Prentice Hall International (UK) Ltd., Hemel Hempstead UK, 3rd Edition, 2009.

[Oren97] Oren, M., Papageorgiou, C., Sinha, P., Osuna, E., and Poggio, T., Pedestrian Detection Using Wavelet Templates, *Proc. IEEE Computer Society Conference on Computer Vision and Pattern Recognition (CVPR'97)*, pp193-199, 1997.

[Pratt13] Pratt, W. K., *Introduction to Digital Image Processing*, CRC Press, Boca Raton FL USA, 2013.

[Press07] Press, W. H., Teukolsky, S. A., Vetterling, W. T., and Flannery, B. P., *Numerical Recipes 3rd Edition: The Art of Scientific Computing*, Cambridge University Press, 3rd Edition, 2007.

[Rabiner75] Rabiner, L. R. and Gold, B., *Theory and Application of Digital Signal Processing*, Prentice Hall Inc., Englewood Cliffs NJ USA, 1975.

[Sayood17] Sayood, K., *Introduction to Data Compression*, Morgan Kaufmann, Cambridge MA USA, 5th Edition 2017.

[Unser00] Unser, M., Sampling - 50 Years after Shannon, *Proceedings of the IEEE*, 88(4), pp 569-587, 2000.

[Viola01] Viola, P., and Jones, M., Rapid Object Detection Using a Boosted Cascade of Simple Features, *Proc. IEEE Computer Society Conference on Computer Vision and Pattern Recognition (CVPR'01)*, 1, pp.511-519, 2001.

[Walsh23] Walsh, J. L., A Closed Set of Normal Orthogonal Functions, *American Journal of Mathematics*, 45(1), pp 5-24, 1923.

[Woods11] Woods, J. W., *Multidimensional Signal, Image, and Video Processing and Coding*, Academic Press, Wakham MA USA, 2nd Edition 2011.

[Wornell96] Wornell, G. W., *Signal Processing with Fractals, a Wavelet-Based Approach*, Prentice Hall Inc., Upper Saddle River NJ USA, 1996.

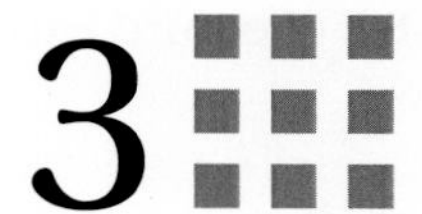

Image processing

3.1 Overview

We shall now start to process digital images. First, we shall describe the brightness variation in an image using its histogram. We shall then look at operations which manipulate the image so as to change the histogram, and at processes that shift and scale the result (making the image brighter or dimmer, in different ways). We shall also consider thresholding techniques that turn an image from grey level into binary. These are called single point operations. After, we shall move to group operations where the group is those points found inside a template. Some of the most common operations on the groups of points are statistical, providing images where each point is the result of, say, averaging the neighbourhood of each point in the original image. We shall see how the statistical operations can reduce noise in the image, which is of benefit to the feature extraction techniques to be considered later. As such, these basic operations are usually for preprocessing for later feature extraction or to improve display quality (Table 3.1).

Table 3.1 Overview of this chapter.

Main topic	Subtopics	Main points
Image description	Portray variation in image brightness content as a graph/histogram.	*Histograms*, image *contrast*.
Point operations	Calculate new image points as a function of the point at the same place in the original image. The functions can be mathematical, or can be computed from the image itself and will change the image's histogram. Finally, thresholding turns an image from grey level to a binary (black and white) representation.	*Histogram* manipulation; *intensity mapping*: addition, inversion, scaling, logarithm, exponent; *intensity normalisation*; *histogram equalisation; thresholding* and *optimal thresholding*.
Group operations	Calculate new image points as a function of the neighbourhood of the point at the same place in the original image. The functions can be statistical including mean (average); median; and mode. Advanced filtering techniques, including feature preservation.	*Template convolution* (including frequency domain implementation). *Statistical operators*: *direct averaging*, *median* filter, and *mode* filter. *Nonlocal means*, *anisotropic diffusion,* and *bilateral filter* for image smoothing. Other operators: *force field* and *image ray* transforms.
Image morphology and operators	Morphological operators that process an image according to shape, starting with binary and moving to grey level operations.	*Mathematical morphology*: *hit or miss transform*, *erosion*, *dilation* (including grey level operators) and *Minkowski* operators.

Feature Extraction and Image Processing for Computer Vision. https://doi.org/10.1016/B978-0-12-814976-8.00003-8

3.2 Histograms

The intensity *histogram* shows how individual brightness levels are occupied in an image; the *image contrast* is measured by the range of brightness levels. The histogram plots the number of pixels with a particular brightness level against the brightness level. For 8-bit pixels, the brightness ranges from zero (black) to 255 (white). Fig. 3.1 shows an image and its histogram. The histogram, Fig. 3.1B, shows that not all the grey levels are used and the lowest and highest intensity levels are far apart, reflecting good contrast. Note that the image contains many light grey pixels that produce the wide lower peak in the histogram. If the image was darker, overall, the histogram would be concentrated towards black. If the image was brighter, but with lower contrast, then the histogram would be thinner and concentrated near the whiter brightness levels.

This histogram shows us that we have not used all available grey levels. Accordingly, we can stretch the image to use them all, and the image would become clearer. This is essentially cosmetic attention to make the image's appearance better. Making the appearance better, especially in view of later processing, is the focus of many basic image processing operations, as will be covered in this chapter. The histogram can also reveal if there is much noise in the image, if the ideal histogram is known. We might want to remove this noise, not only to improve the appearance of the image but to ease the task of (and to present the target better for) later feature extraction techniques. This chapter concerns these basic operations which can improve the appearance and quality of images.

3.3 Point operators

3.3.1 Basic point operations

The most basic operations in image processing are *point operations* where each pixel value is replaced with a new value obtained from the old one. If we want to increase the brightness to stretch the contrast we can simply multiply all pixel values by a scalar, say by two to double the range. Conversely, to reduce the contrast (though this is not usual),

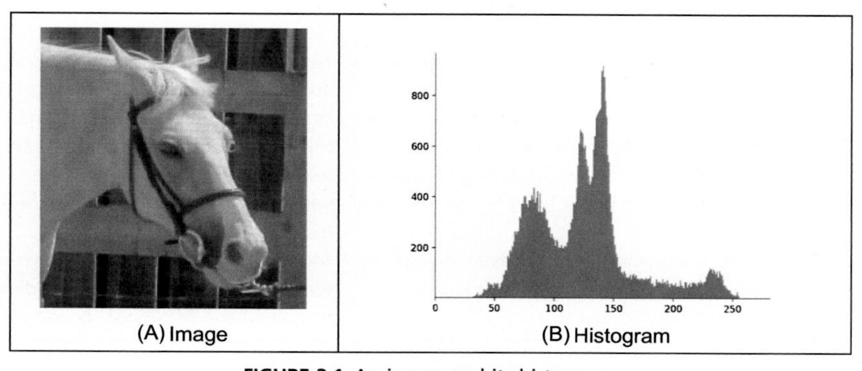

FIGURE 3.1 An image and its histogram.

we can divide all point values by a scalar. If the overall brightness is controlled by a *level*, l (e.g. the brightness of global light) and the range is controlled by a gain, k, the brightness of the points in a new picture, **N**, can be related to the brightness in old picture, **O**, by

$$\mathbf{N}_{x,y} = k \times \mathbf{O}_{x,y} + l \qquad \forall x, y \in 1, N \tag{3.1}$$

This is a point operator that replaces the brightness at points in the picture according to a linear brightness relation. The level controls overall brightness and is the minimum value of the output picture. The gain controls the contrast, or range, and if the gain is greater than unity, the output range will be increased, this process is illustrated in Fig. 3.2. So the image, processed by $k = 1.1$ and $l = -10$ will become brighter, Fig. 3.2A, and with better contrast, though in this case the brighter points are mostly set near to white (255). These factors can be seen in its histogram, Fig. 3.2B.

The basis of the implementation of point operators was given earlier, for inversion in Code 1.2. The stretching process can be displayed as a mapping between the input and output ranges, according to the specified relationship, as in Fig. 3.3. Fig. 3.3A is a mapping where the output is a direct copy of the input (this relationship is the dotted line in Fig. 3.3C and D); Fig. 3.3B is the mapping for *brightness inversion* where dark parts in an image become bright and vice versa. Fig. 3.3C is the mapping for *addition* and Fig. 3.3D is the mapping for *multiplication* (or *division*, if the slope was less than that of the input). In these mappings, if the mapping produces values that are smaller than the expected minimum (say negative when zero represents black), or larger than a specified maximum, then a *clipping* process can be used to set the output values to a chosen level. For example, if the relationship between input and output aims to produce output points with intensity values greater than 255, as used for white, the output value can be set to white for these points, as it is in Fig. 3.2.

Finally, rather than simple multiplication, we can use arithmetic functions such as the logarithm to reduce the range or the exponent to increase it. This can be used, say, to equalise the response of a camera, or to compress the range of displayed brightness levels. If the camera has a known exponential performance, and outputs a value for

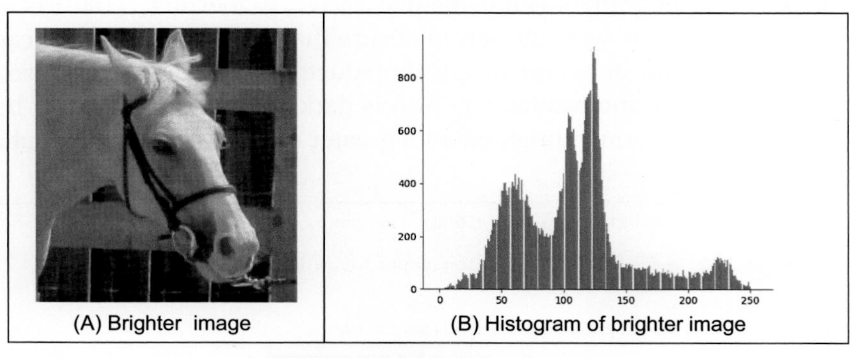

FIGURE 3.2 Brightening an image.

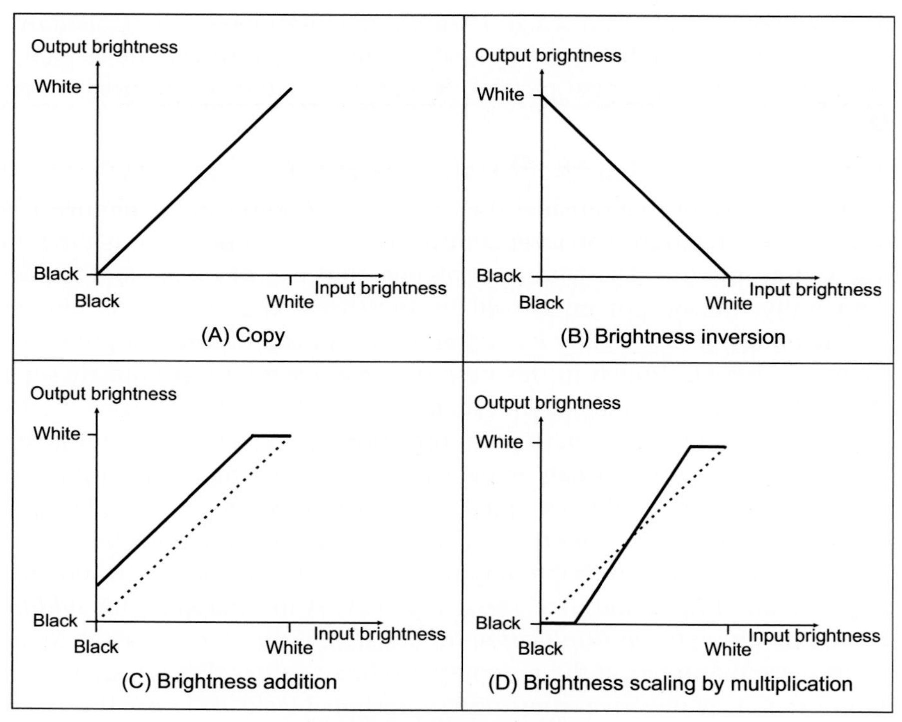

FIGURE 3.3 Intensity mappings.

brightness which is proportional to the exponential of the brightness of the corresponding point in the scene of view, the application of a *logarithmic point operator* will restore the original range of brightness levels. The implementation of point operators for arithmetic functions is illustrated in Code 3.1. This code simply computes the logarithm or exponential value of the value at each pixel position.

The effect of replacing a point's brightness by a scaled version of its natural logarithm (implemented as $N_{x,y} = 20\ln(100O_{x,y})$) is shown in Fig. 3.4A; the effect of a scaled version of the exponent of its brightness (implemented as $N_{x,y} = 20\exp(O_{x,y}/100)$) is shown in Fig. 3.4B. The scaling factors were chosen to ensure that the resulting image can be displayed since the logarithm or exponent greatly reduce or magnify, pixel values, respectively. This can be seen in the results: Fig. 3.4A is dark with a small range of brightness levels, whereas Fig. 3.4B is much brighter, with greater contrast. Naturally, application of

```
for x,y in itertools.product(range(0, width), range(0, height)):
    # Set the pixels in the Logarithmic
    outputLogarithmicImage[y,x] = 20 * log(inputImage[y,x] * 100.0)

    # Set the pixels in the Exponential image
    outputExponentialImage[y,x] = 20 * exp(inputImage[y,x] / 100.0)
```

CODE 3.1 Point operations.

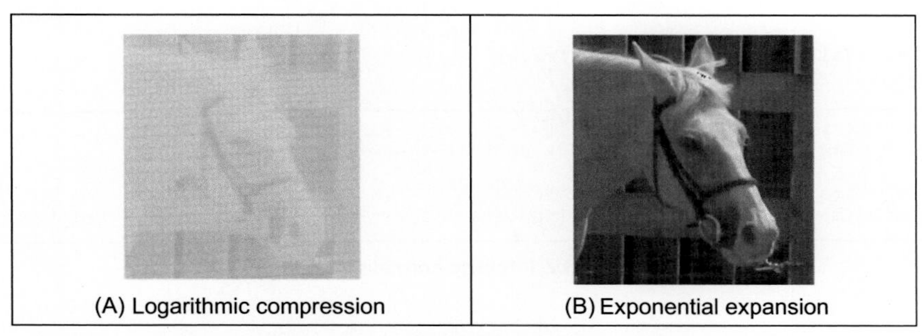

FIGURE 3.4 Applying exponential and logarithmic point operators.

the logarithmic point operator will change any multiplicative changes in brightness to become additive. As such, the logarithmic operator can find application in reducing the effects of multiplicative intensity change. The logarithm operator is often used to compress Fourier transforms for display purposes. This is because the d.c. component can be very large, or the contrast too large, to allow the other points to be seen.

In hardware, point operators can be implemented using *lookup tables* (LUTs). LUTs give an output that is programmed, and stored, in a table entry that corresponds to a particular input value. If the brightness response of the camera is known, it is possible to pre-program an LUT to make the camera response equivalent to a uniform or flat response across the range of brightness levels (in software, this can be implemented as an array or by using a map associative container).

3.3.2 Histogram normalisation

Popular techniques to stretch the range of intensities include *histogram* (*intensity*) *normalisation*. Here, the original histogram is stretched, and shifted, to cover all the 256 available levels. If the original histogram of an old picture **O** starts at **O***min* and extends up to **O***max* brightness levels, then we can scale up the image so that the pixels in the new picture **N** lie between a minimum output level **N***min* and a maximum level **N***max*, simply by scaling up the input intensity levels according to

$$\mathbf{N}_{x,y} = \frac{\mathbf{N}max - \mathbf{N}min}{\mathbf{O}max - \mathbf{O}min} \times (\mathbf{O}_{x,y} - \mathbf{O}min) + \mathbf{N}min \qquad \forall x, y \in 1, N \tag{3.2}$$

Code 3.2 gives an implementation of intensity normalisation. The code uses an output ranging from $\mathbf{N}min = 0$ to $\mathbf{N}max = 255$ that is the maximum range for images that use a byte per pixel. This is scaled by the input range that is determined from the maximum and minimum values are returned by the `imageMaxMin` function. Each point in the picture is then scaled as in Eq. (3.2). Note that Matlab's `imagesc` function appears to effect normalisation.

The normalisation process is illustrated in Fig. 3.5 and can be compared with the original image and histogram in Fig. 3.1. An intensity-normalised version of the image is

```
# Maximum and range
maxVal, miniVal = imageMaxMin(inputImage)
brightRange = float(maxVal - miniVal)

# Set the pixels in the output image
for x,y in itertools.product(range(0, width), range(0, height)):

    # Normalize the pixel value according to the range
    outputNormalizedImage[y,x] = ((inputImage[y,x] - miniVal) * 255.0 / brightRange)
```

CODE 3.2 Intensity normalisation.

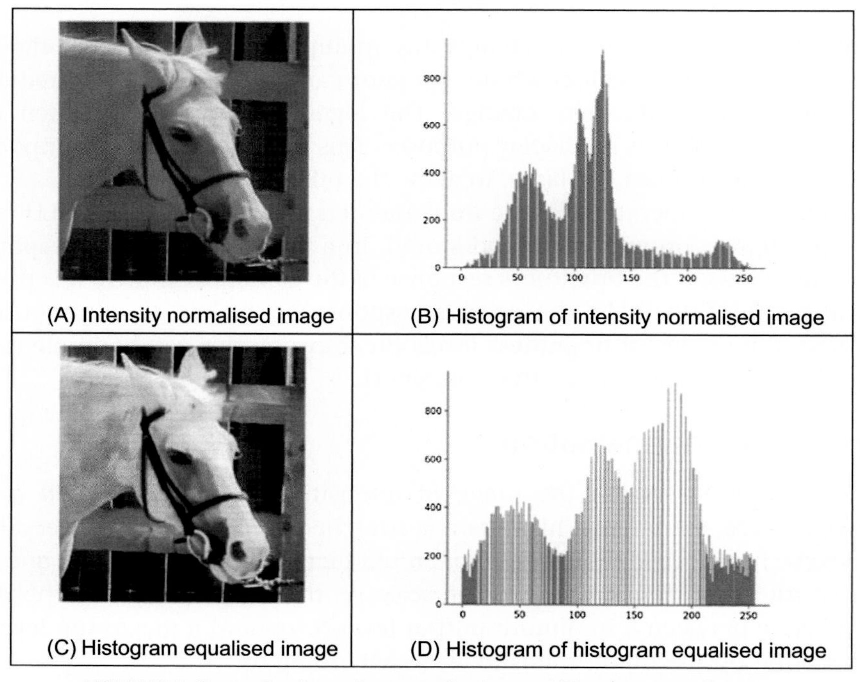

FIGURE 3.5 Illustrating intensity normalisation and histogram equalisation.

shown in Fig. 3.5A which now has better contrast and appears better to human vision. Its histogram, Fig. 3.5B, shows that the intensity now ranges across all available levels (there is actually one black pixel!).

3.3.3 Histogram equalisation

Histogram equalisation is a nonlinear process aimed to highlight image brightness in a way particularly suited to human visual analysis. Histogram equalisation aims to change a picture in such a way as to produce a picture with a flatter histogram, where all levels are equiprobable. In order to develop the operator, we can first inspect the histograms. For a range of M levels then the histogram plots the points per level against level. For the input (old) and the output (new) image, the number of points per level is denoted as $\mathbf{O}(l)$ and $\mathbf{N}(l)$ (for $0 < l < M$), respectively. For square images, there are N^2 points in the input and the output image, so the sum of points per level in each should be equal.

$$\sum_{l=0}^{M} \mathbf{O}(l) = \sum_{l=0}^{M} \mathbf{N}(l) \tag{3.3}$$

Also, this should be the same for an arbitrarily chosen level p, since we are aiming for an output picture with a uniformly flat histogram. So the cumulative histogram up to level p should be transformed to cover up to the level q in the new histogram

$$\sum_{l=0}^{p} \mathbf{O}(l) = \sum_{l=0}^{q} \mathbf{N}(l) \tag{3.4}$$

Since the output histogram is uniformly flat, the cumulative histogram up to level p should be a fraction of the overall sum. So the number of points per level in the output picture is the ratio of the number of points to the range of levels in the output image

$$\mathbf{N}(l) = \frac{N^2}{\mathbf{N}max - \mathbf{N}min} \tag{3.5}$$

So the cumulative histogram of the output picture is

$$\sum_{l=0}^{q} \mathbf{N}(l) = q \times \frac{N^2}{\mathbf{N}max - \mathbf{N}min} \tag{3.6}$$

By Eq. (3.4) this is equal to the cumulative histogram of the input image, so that

$$q \times \frac{N^2}{\mathbf{N}max - \mathbf{N}min} = \sum_{l=0}^{p} \mathbf{O}(l) \tag{3.7}$$

This gives a mapping for the output pixels at level q, from the input pixels at level p as

$$q = \frac{\mathbf{N}max - \mathbf{N}min}{N^2} \times \sum_{l=0}^{p} \mathbf{O}(l) \tag{3.8}$$

This gives a mapping function that provides an output image that has an approximately flat histogram. The mapping function is given by phrasing Eq. (3.8) as an equalising function (E) of the level (q) and the image ($\mathbf{O}$) as

$$E(q, \mathbf{O}) = \frac{\mathbf{N}max - \mathbf{N}min}{N^2} \times \sum_{l=0}^{p} \mathbf{O}(l) \tag{3.9}$$

The output image is then

$$\mathbf{N}_{x,y} = E(\mathbf{O}_{x,y}, \mathbf{O}) \tag{3.10}$$

The result of equalising an image is shown in Fig. 3.5C and D. The intensity equalised image, Fig. 3.5C, has much better defined features than in the original version (Fig. 3.1). The histogram, Fig. 3.5D, reveals the nonlinear mapping process whereby white and black are not assigned equal weight, as they were in intensity normalisation. Accordingly, more pixels are mapped into the darker region and the brighter intensities become better spread, consistent with the aims of histogram equalisation.

Its performance can be very convincing since it is well mapped to the properties of human vision. If a linear brightness transformation is applied to the original image, then the equalised histogram will be the same. If we replace pixel values with ones computed according to Eq. (3.1), the result of histogram equalisation will not change. An alternative interpretation is that if we equalise images (prior to further processing) then we need not to worry about any brightness transformation in the original image. This is to be expected, since the linear operation of the brightness change in Eq. (3.2) does not change the overall shape of the histogram, only its size and position. However, noise in the image acquisition process will affect the shape of the original histogram, and hence the equalised version. So the equalised histogram of a picture will not be the same as the equalised histogram of a picture with some noise added to it. You cannot avoid noise in electrical systems, however well you design a system to reduce its effect. Accordingly, histogram equalisation finds little use in generic image processing systems, except for display, though it can be potent in specialised applications. For these reasons, intensity normalisation is often preferred when a picture's histogram requires manipulation.

In implementation, the function `equalise` in Code 3.3, we shall use an output range where $\mathbf{N}min = 0$ and $\mathbf{N}max = 255$. The implementation first determines the cumulative histogram for each level of the brightness histogram. This is then used as an LUT for the new output brightness at that level. The LUT is used to speed implementation of Eq. (3.9), since it can be precomputed from the image to be equalised.

An alternative argument also against the use of histogram equalisation is that it is a nonlinear process and is irreversible. We cannot return to the original picture after equalisation, and we cannot separate the histogram of an unwanted picture. On the other hand, intensity normalisation is a linear process and we can return to the original image, should we need to, or separate pictures – if required. Note that there have been extensions to histogram equalisation, and *adaptive histogram equalisation* with some extensions [Pizer87] has proved particularly enduring.

3.3.4 Thresholding

The last point operator of major interest is called *thresholding*. This operator selects pixels which have a particular value, or are within a specified range. It can be used to find

```
function equalised = equalise(image)
%get dimensions
[rows,cols]=size(image);
%specify range of levels
range=255;
%and the number of points
number=cols*rows;

%initialise the image histogram
hist(1:256)=0;

%work out the histogram
for x = 1:cols %address all columns
  for y = 1:rows %address all rows
    hist(image(y,x)+1)=hist(image(y,x)+1)+1;
  end
end;

%evaluate the cumulative histogram
sum=0;
for i=1:256
  sum=sum+hist(i);
  cumhist(i)=floor(sum*range/number); %Eq. 3.9
end

%map using the cumulative histogram
for x = 1:cols %address all columns
  for y = 1:rows %address all rows
    equalised(y,x)=cumhist(image(y,x)); %Eq 3.10
  end
end
```

CODE 3.3 Histogram equalisation.

objects within a picture if their brightness level (or range) is known. This implies that the object's brightness must be known as well. There are two main forms: uniform and adaptive thresholding. In *uniform thresholding*, pixels above a specified level are set to white, those below the specified level are set to black.

$$\mathbf{N}_{x,y} = \begin{vmatrix} 255 & if \quad \mathbf{O}_{x,y} > threshold \\ 0 & otherwise \end{vmatrix} \tag{3.11}$$

As shown in Code 3.4, the implementation of thresholding sets the value of the output image by an `if` condition according to the threshold parameter.

Given the original eye image, Fig. 3.6 shows a thresholded image where all pixels above 160 brightness levels are set to white, and those below 160 brightness levels are set to black. By this process, the parts pertaining to the facial skin are separated from the

```
for x,y in itertools.product(range(0, width), range(0, height)):
    if inputImage[y,x] > threshold:
        outputImage[y,x] = 255
    else:
        outputImage[y,x] = 0
```

CODE 3.4 Image thresholding.

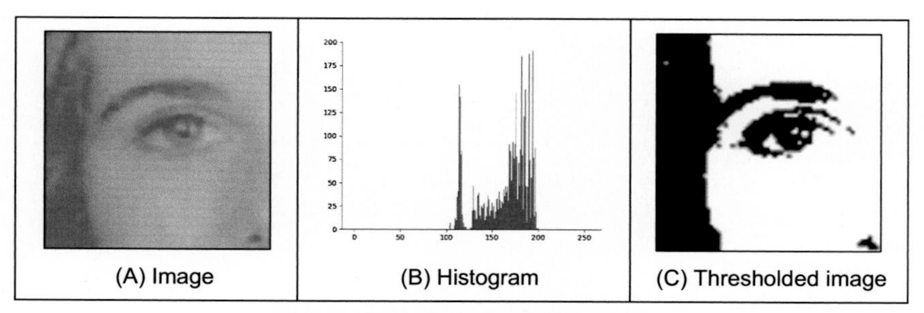

FIGURE 3.6 Thresholding the eye image.

background; the cheeks, forehead and other bright areas are separated from the hair and eyes. This can therefore provide a way of isolating points of interest.

Uniform thresholding clearly requires knowledge of the grey level, or the target features might not be selected in the thresholding process. If the level is not known, histogram equalisation or intensity normalisation can be used, but with the restrictions on performance stated earlier. This is, of course, a problem of image interpretation. These problems can only be solved by simple approaches, such as thresholding, for very special cases.

There are more advanced techniques, known as *optimal thresholding*. These usually seek to select a value for the threshold that separates an object from its background. This suggests that the object has a different range of intensities to the background, in order that an appropriate threshold can be chosen, as illustrated in Fig. 3.7. *Otsu's method* [Otsu79] is one of the most popular techniques of optimal thresholding; there have been surveys [Sahoo88, Lee90, Glasbey93] which compare the performance different methods can achieve. Essentially, Otsu's technique maximises the likelihood that the threshold is chosen so as to split the image between an object and its background. This is achieved by selecting a threshold that gives the best separation of classes, for all pixels in an image. The basis is use of the normalised histogram where the number of points at each level is

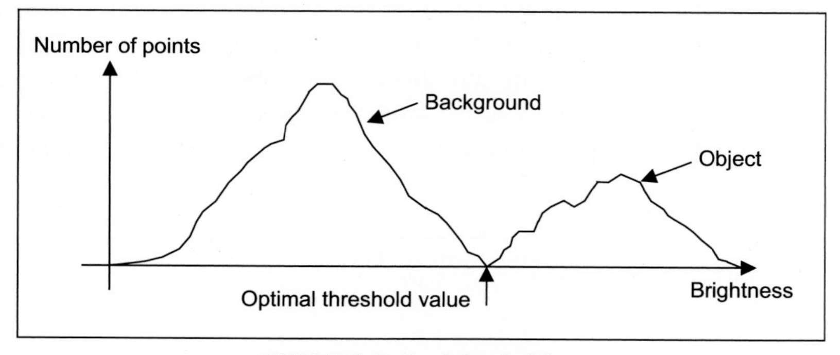

FIGURE 3.7 Optimal thresholding.

divided by the total number of points in the original image. As such, this represents a probability distribution for the intensity levels as

$$p(l) = \frac{\mathbf{O}(l)}{N^2} \tag{3.12}$$

This can be used to compute then zero- and first-order cumulative moments of the normalised histogram up to the kth level as

$$\omega(k) = \sum_{l=1}^{k} p(l) \tag{3.13}$$

and

$$\mu(k) = \sum_{l=1}^{k} l \cdot p(l) \tag{3.14}$$

The total mean level μ_T of the image is given by

$$\mu_{\text{T}} = \sum_{l=1}^{N\text{max}} l \cdot p(l) \tag{3.15}$$

The variance of the class separability (the similarity between the variables of the same class) is then the ratio

$$\sigma_B^2(k) = \frac{(\mu_{\text{T}} \cdot \omega(k) - \mu(k))^2}{\omega(k)(1 - \omega(k))} \qquad \forall\, k \in 1, N\text{max} \tag{3.16}$$

The optimal threshold is the level for which the variance of class separability is at its maximum, namely the optimal threshold T_{opt} is that for which the variance

$$\sigma_B^2(T_{\text{opt}}) = \max_{1 \leq k < N\text{max}} \left(\sigma_B^2(k)\right) \tag{3.17}$$

The implementation of the optimal thresholding is shown in Code 3.5. The code finds the optimum threshold in two stages. First, it uses the histogram of the input image to compute the moments in Eqs. (3.13) and (3.14). A second step computes the separability measure in Eq. (3.16). The code keeps all the separability values for display, but in practice, we only require to keep the maximum value.

Fig. 3.8 shows an example of optimal thresholding obtained with Code 3.5. Fig. 3.8A shows the separability computed for each potential threshold. Low values represent thresholds that produce two regions with high interclass variance and high values minimise the interclass variance. The threshold for the maximum value is used to produce the thresholded image in Fig. 3.8B. In this figure, the pixels are divided in two classes whose variance is minimum compared with any other possible threshold.

```
# Obtain histograms
normalization = 1.0 / float(width * height)
w[0] = normalization * inputHistogram[0]
for level in range(1, 256):
    w[level] = w[level-1] + normalization * inputHistogram[level]
    m[level] = m[level-1] + level * normalization * inputHistogram[level]

# Look for the maximum
maximumLevel = 0
for level in range(0, 256):
    if w[level] * (float(level) - w[level]) != 0:
        separability[level] = float(pow( ( m[255] * w[level] - m[level]), 2)      \
                                   / (w[level] * (float(level) - w[level])))

        if separability[level] > separability[maximumLevel]:
            maximumLevel = level
```

CODE 3.5 Optimal thresholding.

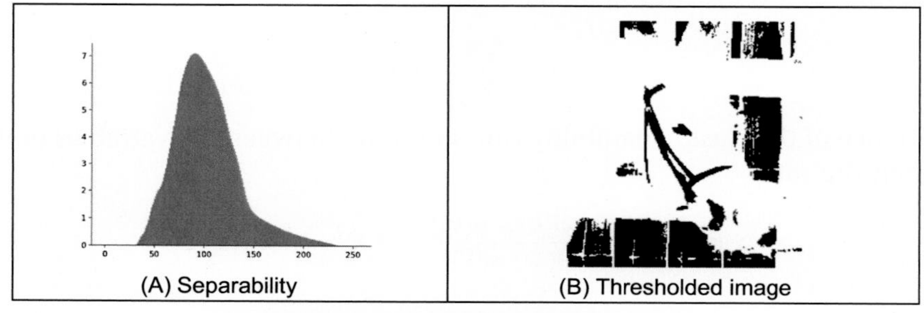

(A) Separability (B) Thresholded image

FIGURE 3.8 Optimal thresholding example.

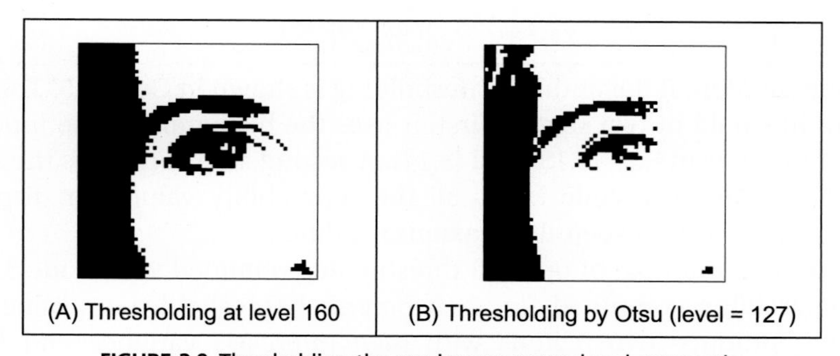

(A) Thresholding at level 160 (B) Thresholding by Otsu (level = 127)

FIGURE 3.9 Thresholding the eye image: manual and automatic.

A comparison of uniform thresholding with optimal thresholding is given in Fig. 3.9 for the eye image. The threshold selected by Otsu's operator is actually lower than the value selected manually, and so the thresholded image does omit some detail around the eye, especially in the eyelids. However, the selection by Otsu is automatic, as opposed to

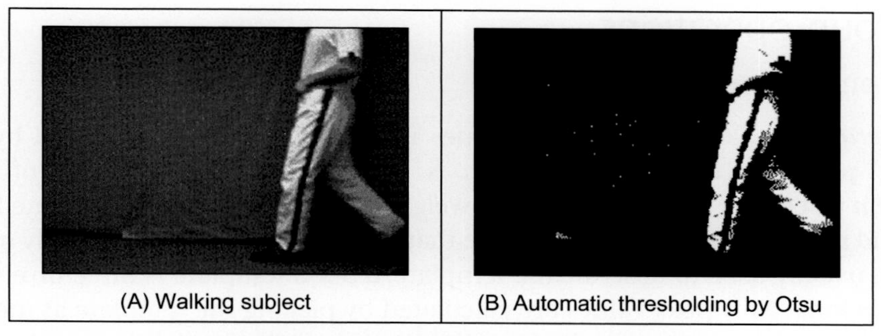

FIGURE 3.10 Thresholding an image of a walking subject.

manual, and this can be to application advantage in automated vision. Consider, for example, the need to isolate the human figure in Fig. 3.10A. This can be performed automatically by Otsu as shown in Fig. 3.10B. Note, however, that there are some extra points, due to illumination, which have appeared in the resulting image together with the human subject. It is easy to remove the isolated points, as we will see later, but more difficult to remove the connected ones. In this instance, the size of the human shape could be used as information to remove the extra points though you might like to suggest other factors that could lead to their removal.

Also, we have so far considered global techniques, methods that operate on the entire image. There are also locally adaptive techniques that are often used to binarise document images prior to character recognition. As mentioned before, surveys of thresholding are available, and one approach [Rosin01] targets thresholding of images whose histogram is unimodal (has a single peak). One survey [Trier95] compares global and local techniques with reference to document image analysis. These techniques are often used in statistical pattern recognition: the thresholded object is classified according to its statistical properties. However, these techniques find less use in image interpretation, where a common paradigm is that there is more than one object in the scene, such as Fig. 3.6 where the thresholding operator has selected many objects of potential interest. As such, only uniform thresholding is used in many vision applications, since objects are often occluded (hidden), and many objects have similar ranges of pixel intensity. Accordingly, more sophisticated metrics are required to separate them, by using the uniformly thresholded image, as discussed in later chapters. Further, the operation to process the thresholded image, say to fill in the holes in the silhouette or to remove the noise on its boundary or outside, is *morphology* which is covered later in Section 3.6. In general, it is often prudent to investigate the more sophisticated techniques of feature selection and extraction, to be covered later. Prior to that, we shall investigate group operators, which are a natural counterpart to point operators.

3.4 Group operations

3.4.1 Template convolution

Group operations calculate new pixel values from a pixel's neighbourhood by using a 'grouping' process. The group operation is usually expressed in terms of *template convolution* where the template is a set of weighting coefficients. The template is usually square, and its size is usually odd to ensure that the result positioned precisely on a pixel. The size is usually used to describe the template; a 3×3 template is three pixels wide by three pixels long. New pixel values are calculated by placing the template at the point of interest. Pixel values are multiplied by the corresponding weighting coefficient and added to an overall sum. The sum (usually) evaluates a new value for the centre pixel (where the template is centred), and this becomes the pixel in the output image. If the template's position has not yet reached the end of a line, the template is then moved horizontally by one pixel and the process repeats.

This is illustrated in Fig. 3.11, where a new image is calculated from an original one, by template convolution. The calculation obtained by template convolution at the centre pixel of the template in the original image becomes the point in the output result image. Since the template cannot extend beyond the original image, a new value cannot be computed for points at the border of the result image. When the template reaches the end of a line, it is repositioned to proceed from the start of the next line. The process is shown part way through the raster scan, the next pixel to be calculated would be derived

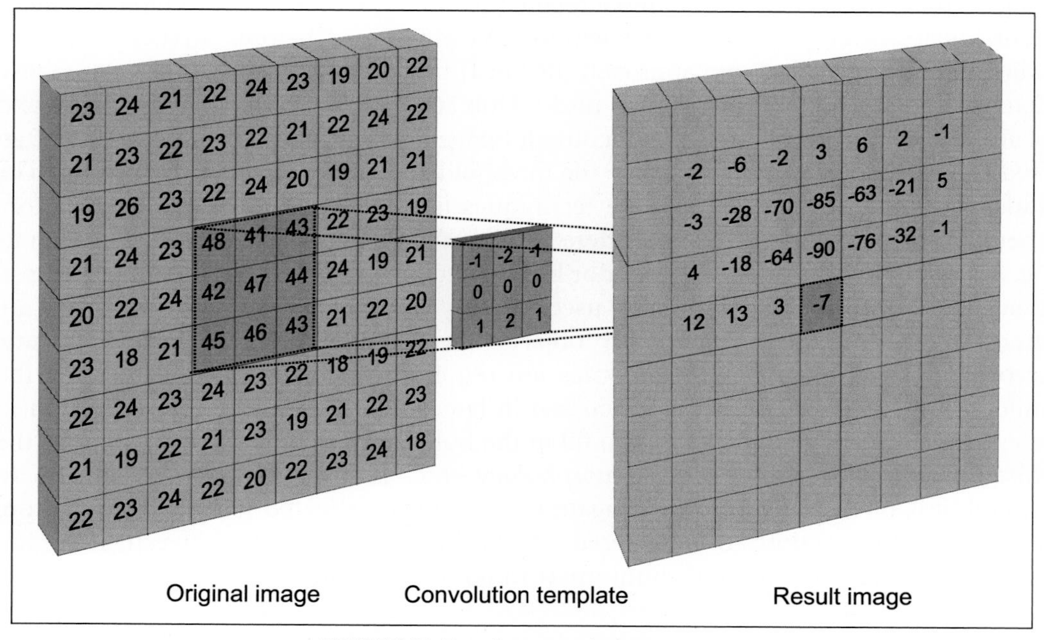

FIGURE 3.11 Template convolution process.

from the nine points to the right of the current position of the centre point of the template, and stored to the right of the point containing −7. For a 3 × 3 neighbourhood, Fig. 3.12, nine weighting coefficients w_t are applied to points in the original image to calculate a point in the new image. The position of the new point (at the centre) is shaded in the template.

To calculate the value in new image, **N**, at point with coordinates *x,y*, the template in Fig. 3.12 operates on an original image **O** according to

$$\mathbf{N}_{x,y} = \sum_{i \in \text{template}} \sum_{j \in \text{template}} w_{i,j} \times \mathbf{O}_{x(i),y(j)} \tag{3.18}$$

where the coordinates of the image point $x(i)$, $y(j)$ denote the position of the point that matches the weighting coefficient position. Note that we cannot ascribe values to the picture's *borders*. This is because when we place the template at the border, parts of the template fall outside the image and have no information from which to calculate the new pixel value. The width of the border equals half the size of the template. In Fig. 3.11 the single pixel border points have been left blank. To calculate values for the border pixels, we have three choices:

1. set the border to black (or deliver a smaller picture);
2. assume (as in Fourier) that the image replicates to infinity along both dimensions and calculate new values by cyclic shift from the far border; or
3. calculate the border pixel value from a smaller area.

None of these approaches is optimal. The results in this book use the first option and set border pixels to black. Note that in many applications the object of interest is imaged centrally or, at least, imaged within the picture. As such, the border information is of little consequence to the remainder of the process. Here, the border points are set to black, by starting functions with a zero function which sets all the points in the picture initially to black (0).

An alternative representation for this process is given by using the convolution notation as

$$\mathbf{N} = \mathbf{W} * \mathbf{O} \tag{3.19}$$

where **N** is the new image which results from convolving the template **W** (of weighting coefficients) with the image **O**.

w_0	w_1	w_2
w_3	w_4	w_5
w_6	w_7	w_8

FIGURE 3.12 3 × 3 template and weighting coefficients.

The Matlab® implementation of a template convolution operator `template_convolve` is given in Code 3.6. This function accepts, as arguments, the picture `image` and the template to be convolved with it, `template`. The result of template convolution is an image `convolved`. The operator first sets the resulting image to black (zero brightness levels). The widths `tc` and `tr` give the range of picture points to be processed in the outer `for` loops that give the coordinates of all points resulting from template convolution. The template is convolved at each picture point by generating a running summation of the pixel values within the template's window multiplied by the respective template weighting coefficient.

Note that according to Eq. (2.10), for convolution one of the signals is inverted along its principal axis. For images, convolution requires inversion along both axes, which is why the template's arguments are inverted in Code 3.6. We shall consider convolution again in the next section, via the frequency domain, and in Section 5.3.2.

Template convolution can of course be implemented in hardware and requires a two-line store, together with some further latches, for the (input) video data. The output is the result of template convolution, summing the result of multiplying weighting coefficients by pixel values. This is called pipelining, since the pixels essentially move along a pipeline of information. Note that two line stores can be used if the video fields only are processed. To process a full frame, one of the fields must be stored if it is presented in interlaced format. Processing can be analog, using operational amplifier circuits and charge-coupled device for storage along bucket brigade delay lines. Finally, an

```
function convolved = template_convolve(image,template)
%get image dimensions
[rows,cols]=size(image);
%get template dimensions
[trows,tcols]=size(template);

%half of template rows is
tr=floor(trows/2);
%half of template cols is
tc=floor(tcols/2);

%set an output as black
convolved(1:rows,1:cols)=0;

%then convolve the template
for x = tc+1:cols-tc %address all columns except border
    for y = tr+1:rows-tr %address all rows except border
        sum=0; %initialise the sum
        for iwin=1:tcols %address all points in the template
            for jwin=1:trows
                sum=sum+image(y+jwin-tr-1,x+iwin-tc-1)*... % sum, Eq. 3.18
                           template(trows-jwin+1,tcols-iwin+1);
            end
        end
        convolved(y,x)=sum; %store as new point
    end
end
```

CODE 3.6 Template convolution operator.

alternative implementation is to use a parallel architecture: for multiple instruction multiple data (MIMD) architectures, the picture can be split into blocks (spatial partitioning); single instruction multiple data (SIMD) architectures can implement template convolution as a combination of shift and add instructions.

3.4.2 Averaging operator

For an *averaging operator*, the template weighting functions are unity (or 1/9 to ensure that the result of averaging nine white pixels is white, not more than white!). The template for a 3×3 averaging operator, implementing Eq. (3.18), is given by the template in Fig. 3.13 where the location of the point of interest is again shaded. The averaging operator is then

$$\mathbf{N}_{x,y} = \frac{1}{MN} \sum_{i \in M} \sum_{j \in N} \mathbf{O}_{x(i),y(j)} \tag{3.20}$$

where $x(i)$, $y(j)$ are the coordinates of image points within the template and M, N are the numbers of columns and rows in the template. The result of averaging an image with a 9×9 operator is shown in Fig. 3.14. This shows that much of the detail has now disappeared revealing the broad image structure. In order to implement averaging by using the template convolution operator, we need to define a template and then convolve it with the image (note also that there is an averaging operator `mean` in Matlab that can be used for this purpose).

The effect of averaging is to reduce noise, this is its advantage. An associated disadvantage is that averaging causes blurring which reduces detail in an image. It is also a low-pass filter since its effect is to allow low spatial frequencies to be retained, and to suppress high-frequency components. A larger template, say 9×9 or 15×15, will remove more noise (high frequencies) but reduce the level of detail. The size of an averaging operator is then equivalent to the reciprocal of the bandwidth of a low-pass filter it implements.

3.4.3 On different template size

Templates can be larger than 3×3. Since they are usually centred on a point of interest, to produce a new output value at that point, they are usually of odd dimension. For reasons of speed, the most common sizes are 3×3, 5×5, and 7×7. Beyond this, say

1/9	1/9	1/9
1/9	1/9	1/9
1/9	1/9	1/9

FIGURE 3.13 3×3 averaging operator template coefficients.

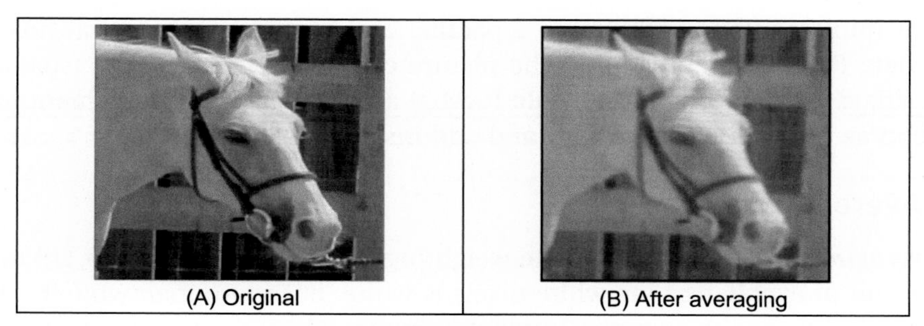

FIGURE 3.14 Applying direct averaging.

9 × 9, many template points are used to calculate a single value for a new point, and this imposes high computational cost, especially for large images. (For example, a 9 × 9 operator covers nine times more points than a 3 × 3 operator.) Square templates have the same properties along both image axes. Some implementations use vector templates (a line), either because their properties are desirable in a particular application, or for reasons of speed.

The effect of larger averaging operators is to smooth the image more, to remove more detail whilst giving greater emphasis to the large structures. This is illustrated in Fig. 3.15. A 5 × 5 operator, Fig. 3.15A, retains more detail than a 7 × 7 operator, Fig. 3.15B, and much more than a 9 × 9 operator, Fig. 3.15C. Conversely, the 9 × 9 operator retains only the largest structures such as the eye region (and virtually removing the iris), whereas this is retained more by the operators of smaller size. Note that the larger operators leave a larger border (since new values cannot be computed in that region), and this can be seen in the increase in border size for the larger operators, in Fig. 3.15B and C.

3.4.4 Template convolution via the Fourier transform

The Fourier transform actually gives an alternative method to implement template convolution and to speed it up, for larger templates. The question to be answered here is

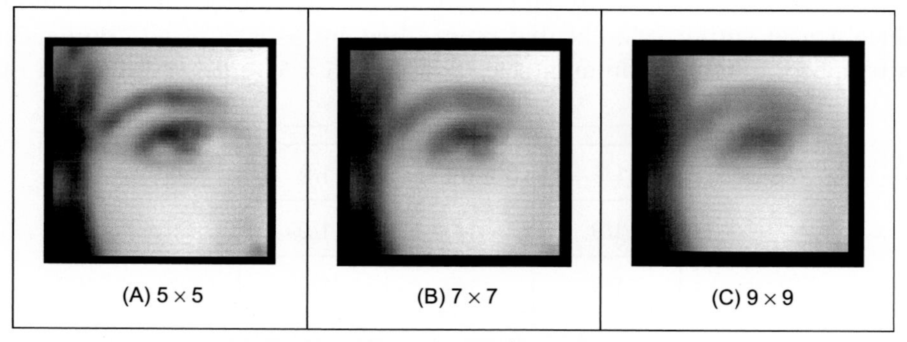

FIGURE 3.15 Illustrating the effect of window size.

'how big?'. In Fourier transforms, the process that is dual to *convolution* is multiplication (as in Section 2.3). So template convolution (denoted $*$) can be implemented by multiplying the Fourier transform of the template $\Im(\mathbf{T})$ with the Fourier transform of the picture $\Im(\mathbf{P})$, to which the template is to be applied. It is perhaps a bit confusing that we appear to be multiplying matrices, but the multiplication is point by point in that the result at each point is that of multiplying the (single) points at the same positions in the two matrices. The result needs to be inverse transformed to return to the picture domain.

$$\mathbf{P} * \mathbf{T} = \Im^{-1}(\Im(\mathbf{P}). \times \Im(\mathbf{T})) \tag{3.21}$$

The transform of the template and the picture need to be the same size before we can perform the point-by-point multiplication ($.\times$). Accordingly, the image containing the template is zero-padded prior to its transform which simply means that zeroes are added to the template which leads to a template of the same size as the image. The process is illustrated in Code 3.7(A) and starts by calculation of the transforms of the image and of the zero-padded template. Then, the transform of the template is multiplied by the transform of the picture point-by-point (using the `.*` operator). (Theoretical study of this

```
image_eye=imread('eye_orig.jpg');
image_eye=double(image_eye(:,:,1));
image_transform=fft2(image_eye);
template_transform=fft2(pad(image_eye, ave_template(7)));
inverted_transform=ifft2(rearrange(image_transform.*template_transform));
```

The transform based implementation of direct averaging can be combined as

```
averaged_image=ifft2(rearrange(fft2(eye).*fft2(pad(eye,ave_template(7)))));
```

(A) Matlab

```
# Padding
widthPad, heightPad = width+kernelSize-1, height+kernelSize-1

templatePadFlip = createImageF(widthPad, heightPad)
for x,y in itertools.product(range(0, kernelSize), range(0, kernelSize)):
    templatePadFlip[y, x] = kernelImage[kernelSize-y-1, kernelSize-x-1]

# Compute coefficients
imageCoeff, maxFrequencyW, maxFrequencyH = computeCoefficients(inputPad)
templateCoeff, _, _ = computeCoefficients(templatePadFlip)

# Frequency domain multiplication
for kw,kh in itertools.product(range(-maxFrequencyW, maxFrequencyW + 1),      \
                               range(-maxFrequencyH, maxFrequencyH + 1)):
    w = kw + maxFrequencyW
    h = kh + maxFrequencyH

    resultCoeff[h,w][0] = (imageCoeff[h,w][0] * templateCoeff[h,w][0] -       \
                           imageCoeff[h,w][1] * templateCoeff[h,w][1])
    resultCoeff[h,w][1] = (imageCoeff[h,w][1] * templateCoeff[h,w][0] +       \
                           imageCoeff[h,w][0] * templateCoeff[h,w][1])
```

(B) Python

CODE 3.7 Template convolution via the Fourier transform.

process is presented in Section 5.3.2 where we show how the same process can be used to find shapes in images.) Finally, the inverse Fourier transform is used to deliver the result. Code 3.7(B) shows an implementation in Python. This code computes the summation defining the Fourier transform by performing an iteration. First, the template is flipped and padded. Afterwards, the coefficients are obtained by performing the multiplication of the complex numbers of the image and of the template coefficients.

Code 3.7 is simply a different implementation of direct averaging. It achieves a similar result, but by transform domain calculus. The operation is shown in Fig. 3.16: an image of the eye (A) is transformed to give (D); the averaging template is padded to the same size as the image (B) and transformed (E); the multiplied transforms (F) are inverse transformed to give an averaged version of the eye (C). There is one major difference between the Fourier and the direct implementations: the borders of the images differ (where the *border* is of width equal to one half of the template's width). This is because for direct averaging the border points are set to zero, whereas in the Fourier implementation the image is assumed to replicate to infinity, as in Eq. (2.26). (The rearrange function, Eq. (2.30), is used since the padding function places the template at the centre of the image.) Note that the template transform is a 2D sinc function viewed as an image and that the *logarithm* of the magnitude (Section 3.3.1) has been used to display all transforms.

It can be faster to use the transform-based implementation (Code 3.7) rather than the direct implementation (Code 3.6), depending on the size of the template. For a square template with $N \times N$ points the computational cost of a 2D FFT is of the order of $2N^2\log_2(N)$. If the transform of the template is precomputed, there are two transforms

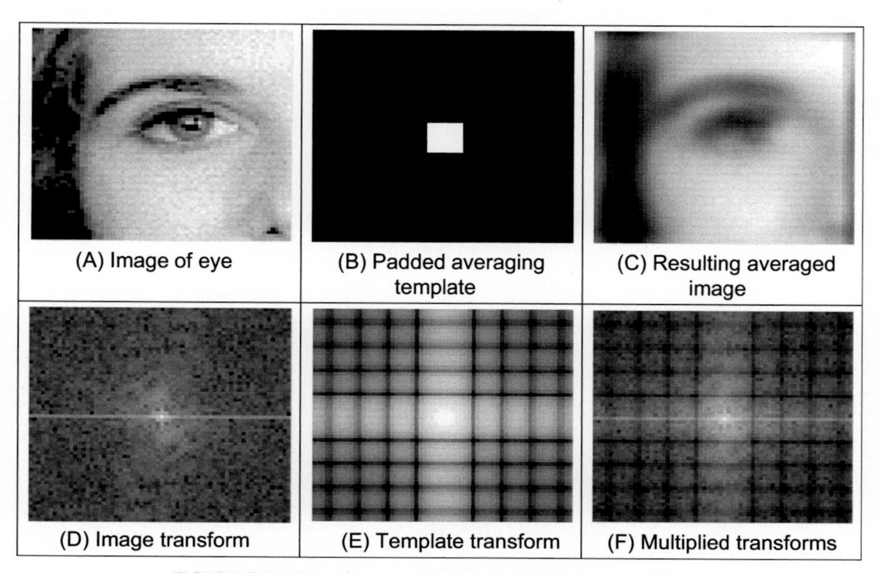

FIGURE 3.16 Template convolution via Fourier transform.

required and there is one multiplication for each of the N^2 transformed points. The total cost of the Fourier implementation of template convolution is then of the order of

$$C_{FFT} = 4N^2 \log(N) + N^2 \tag{3.22}$$

The cost of the direct implementation for an $m \times m$ template is then m^2 multiplications for each image point, so the cost of the direct implementation is of the order of

$$C_{dir} = N^2 m^2 \tag{3.23}$$

For $C_{dir} < C_{FFT}$, we require that

$$N^2 m^2 < 4N^2 \log(N) + N^2 \tag{3.24}$$

If the direct implementation of template matching is faster than its Fourier implementation, we need to choose m so that

$$m^2 < 4 \log(N) + 1 \tag{3.25}$$

This implies that, for a 256×256 image, a direct implementation is fastest for 3×3 and 5×5 templates, whereas a transform-based calculation is faster for larger ones. An alternative analysis [Campbell69] suggested that [Gonzalez17] 'if the number of nonzero terms in (the template) is less than 132 then a direct implementation .... is more efficient than using the FFT approach'. In OpenCV, for some versions the limit appears to 7×7 [OpenCV-TM] for using the FFT and for a kernel size of 5×5 or less a direct version is used. An 11×11 operator is a considerably larger template than our analysis suggests, whereas OpenCV has the same limit as the analysis here. This might be due to higher considerations of complexity than our analysis has included. There are, naturally, further considerations in the use of transform calculus, the most important being the use of windowing (such as Hamming or Hanning) operators to reduce variance in high-order spectral estimates. This implies that template convolution by transform calculus should be used when large templates are involved, and when speed is critical. If speed is indeed critical, it might be prudent to implement the operator in dedicated hardware, as described earlier.

3.4.5 Gaussian averaging operator

The *Gaussian averaging operator* has been considered to be optimal for image smoothing. The template for the Gaussian operator has values set by the Gaussian relationship. The *Gaussian function* g at coordinates x,y is controlled by the *variance* σ^2 according to

$$g(x, y, \sigma) = \frac{1}{2\pi\sigma^2} e^{\frac{-(x^2+y^2)}{2\sigma^2}} \tag{3.26}$$

Eq. (3.26) gives a way to calculate coefficients for a Gaussian template which is then convolved with an image. The effects of selection of Gaussian templates of differing size are shown in Fig. 3.17. The Gaussian function essentially removes the influence of points greater than 3σ in (radial) distance from the centre of the template. The 3×3 operator,

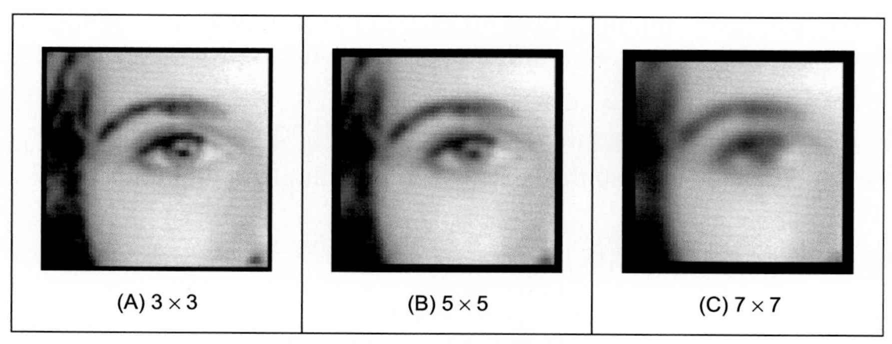

FIGURE 3.17 Applying Gaussian averaging.

Fig. 3.17A, retains many more of the features than those retained by direct averaging (Fig. 3.15). The effect of larger size is to remove more detail (and noise) at the expense of losing features. This is reflected in the loss of internal eye component by the 5×5 and the 7×7 operators in Fig. 3.17B and C, respectively.

A surface plot of the 2D Gaussian function of Eq. (3.26) has the famous bell shape, as shown in Fig. 3.18 (for a window size of 19×19 and standard deviation of 4.0). The values of the function at discrete points are the values of a Gaussian template. Convolving this template with an image gives Gaussian averaging: the point in the averaged picture is calculated from the sum of a region where the central parts of the picture are weighted to contribute more than the peripheral points. The size of the template essentially dictates appropriate choice of the variance. The variance is chosen to ensure that template coefficients drop to near zero at the template's edge. The template for size 5×5 with variance unity is shown in Fig. 3.19.

When a Gaussian template is convolved with an image, it produces Gaussian blurring. It is actually possible to give the Gaussian blurring function antisymmetric properties by scaling the x and y coordinates. This can find application when an object's shape, and orientation, is known prior to image analysis.

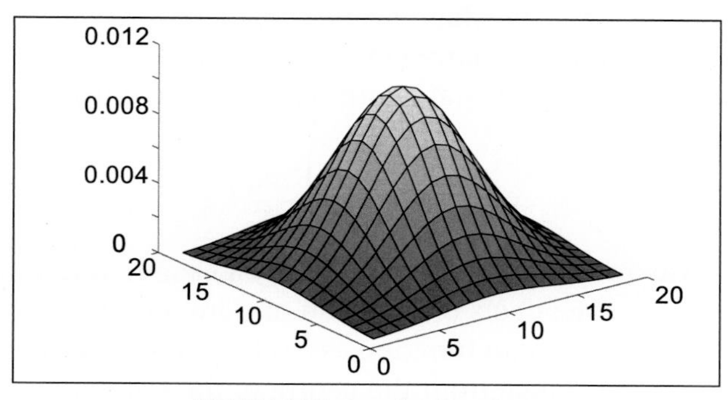

FIGURE 3.18 Gaussian function.

0.002	0.013	0.022	0.013	0.002
0.013	0.060	0.098	0.060	0.013
0.022	0.098	0.162	0.098	0.022
0.013	0.060	0.098	0.060	0.013
0.002	0.013	0.022	0.013	0.002

FIGURE 3.19 Template for the **5** $\times$ **5** Gaussian averaging operator ($\sigma = 1.0$).

By reference to Fig. 3.17, it is clear that the Gaussian filter can offer improved performance compared with direct averaging: more features are retained whilst the noise is removed. This can be understood by Fourier transform theory. In Section 2.5.2, we found that the Fourier transform of a square is a two-dimensional sinc function. This has a frequency response where the magnitude of the transform does not reduce in a smooth manner and has regions where it becomes negative, called sidelobes. These can have undesirable effects since there are high frequencies that contribute more than some lower ones, a bit paradoxical in low-pass filtering which aims to remove noise. In contrast, the Fourier transform of a Gaussian function is another Gaussian function, which decreases smoothly without these sidelobes. This can lead to better performance since the contributions of the frequency components reduce in a controlled manner.

In a software implementation of the Gaussian operator, we need a function implementing Eq. (3.26), the `Gaussian_template` function in Code 3.8. This is used to calculate the coefficients of a template to be centred on an image point. The two arguments are `winsize`, the (square) operator's size, and the standard deviation `sigma` that controls its width, as discussed earlier. The operator coefficients are normalised by the sum of template values, as before. This summation is stored in `sum`, which is initialised to zero. The centre of the square template is then evaluated as half the size of the operator. Then, all template coefficients are calculated by a version of Eq. (3.26) which specifies a weight relative to the centre coordinates. Finally, the normalised template coefficients are returned as the Gaussian template. The operator is used in template convolution, via `template_convolve` (Code 3.6) or by Fourier (Code 3.7).

```
centre = (kernelSize - 1) / 2
sumValues = 0
for x,y in itertools.product(range(0, kernelSize), range(0, kernelSize)):
    kernelImage[y,x] =  math.exp( -0.5 * (math.pow((x - centre)/sigma, 2.0) +     \
                                          math.pow((y - centre)/sigma, 2.0)) )
    sumValues += kernelImage[y,x]

# Normalisation
for x,y in itertools.product(range(0, kernelSize), range(0, kernelSize)):
    kernelImage[y,x] /= sumValues
```

CODE 3.8 Gaussian template specification.

3.4.6 More on averaging

There is more than could be discussed on basic smoothing, e.g. smoothing was earlier achieved by low-pass filtering via the Fourier transform (Section 2.8), but we shall move on to other operators. The averaging process is actually a statistical operator since it aims to estimate the mean of a local neighbourhood. The *error* in the process is naturally high, for a population of N samples, the statistical error is of the order of

$$error = \frac{mean}{\sqrt{N}} \tag{3.27}$$

Increasing the averaging operator's size improves the error in the estimate of the mean, but at the expense of fine detail in the image. The average is of course an estimate optimal for a signal corrupted by *additive Gaussian noise*. The estimate of the mean maximised the probability that the noise has its mean value, namely zero. According to the *central limit theorem*, the result of adding many noise sources together is a Gaussian distributed noise source. In images, noise arises in sampling, in quantisation, in transmission, and in processing. By the central limit theorem, the result of these (independent) noise sources is that image noise can be assumed to be Gaussian. In fact, image noise is not necessarily Gaussian-distributed, giving rise to more statistical operators. One of these is the median operator which has demonstrated capability to reduce noise whilst retaining feature boundaries (in contrast to smoothing which blurs both noise and the boundaries), and the mode operator which can be viewed as optimal for a number of noise sources, including *Rayleigh noise*, but is very difficult to determine for small, discrete, populations.

3.5 Other image processing operators

3.5.1 Median filter

The *median* is another frequently used statistic; the median is the centre of a rank-ordered distribution. The median is usually taken from a template centred on the point of interest. Given the arrangement of pixels in Fig. 3.20A, the pixel values are

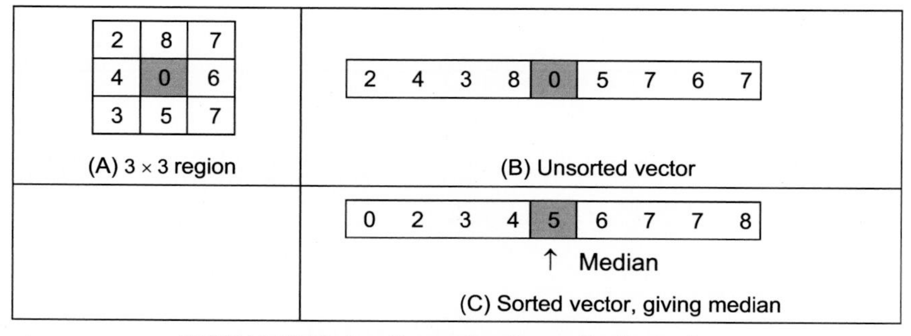

FIGURE 3.20 Finding the median from a **3** × **3** template.

arranged into a vector format, Fig. 3.20B. The vector is then sorted into ascending order, Fig. 3.20C. The median is the central component of the sorted vector, this is the fifth component since we have nine values.

The median can of course be taken from larger template sizes. The development here has aimed not only to demonstrate how the median operator works but also to provide a basis for further development. The rank ordering process is computationally demanding (slow) and motivates study into the deployment of fast algorithms, such as Quicksort (e.g. [Huang79] is an early approach), though other approaches abound [Weiss06]. The computational demand also has motivated use of template shapes, other than a square. A selection of alternative shapes is shown in Fig. 3.21. Common alternative shapes include a cross or a line (horizontal or vertical), centred on the point of interest, which can afford much faster operation since they cover fewer pixels. The basis of the arrangement presented here could be used for these alternative shapes, if required.

The median has a well-known ability to remove *salt and pepper noise*. This form of noise, arising from, say, decoding errors in picture transmission systems can cause isolated white and black points to appear within an image. It can also arise when rotating an image, when points remain unspecified by a standard rotation operator (Chapter 10), as in a texture image, rotated by 10° in Fig. 3.22A. When a median operator is applied, the salt and pepper noise points will appear at either end of the rank-ordered list and are removed by the median process, as shown in Fig. 3.22B. The median operator has practical advantage, due to its ability to retain edges (the boundaries of shapes in images) whilst suppressing the noise contamination. As such, like direct averaging, it

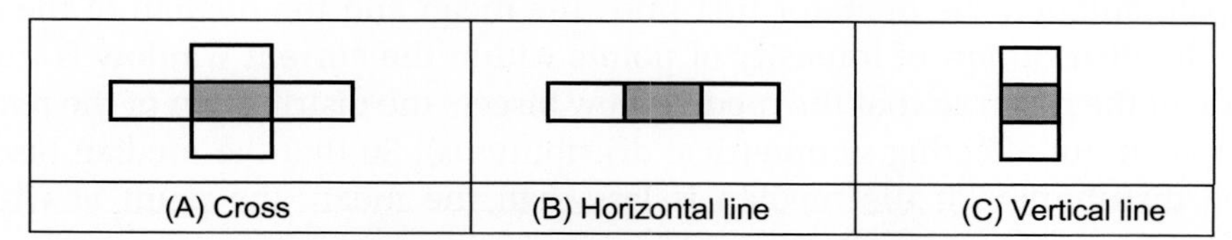

FIGURE 3.21 Alternative template shapes for median operator.

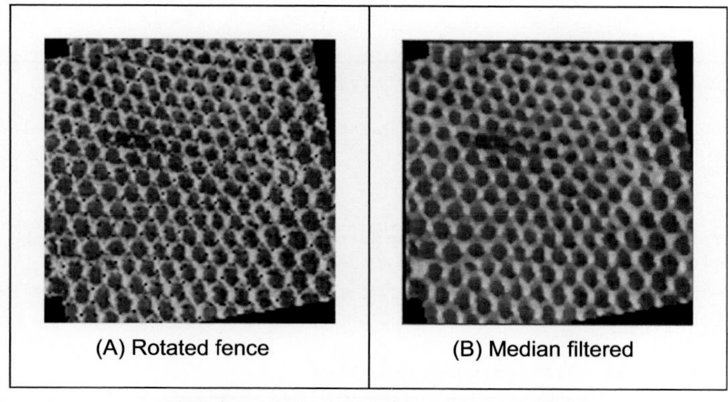

FIGURE 3.22 Illustrating median filtering.

remains a worthwhile member of the stock of standard image processing tools. For further details concerning properties and implementation, have a peep at [Hodgson85]. (Note that practical implementation of image rotation is a computer graphics issue and is usually by texture mapping; further details can be found in [Hearn97].)

Code 3.9 illustrates the process of applying a median filter to an image. Each pixel defines a list containing the values in a window region. The value of the pixel in the output image is obtained by finding the central element of the sorted list. The image in Fig. 3.22B was obtained using Code 3.9 with a kernel size parameter of 5.

3.5.2 Mode filter

The *mode* is the final statistic of interest, though there are more advanced filtering operators to come. The mode is of course very difficult to determine for small populations and theoretically does not even exist for a continuous distribution. Consider, for example, determining the mode of the pixels within a square 5×5 template. Naturally, it is possible for all 25 pixels to be different, so each could be considered to be the mode. As such we are forced to estimate the mode: the truncated median filter, as introduced by Davies [Davies88], aims to achieve this. The *truncated median filter* is based on the premise that for many non-Gaussian distributions, the order of the mean, the median and the mode is the same for many images, as illustrated in Fig. 3.23. Accordingly, if we truncate the distribution (i.e. remove part of it, where the part selected to be removed in Fig. 3.23 is from the region beyond the mean) then the median of the truncated distribution will approach the mode of the original distribution.

In implementation the operator first finds the mean and the median of the current window. The distribution of intensity of points within the current window is truncated on the side of the mean so that the median now bisects the distribution of the remaining points (as such not affecting symmetrical distributions). So that the median bisects the remaining distribution, if the median is less than the mean, the point at which the distribution is truncated, *upper*, is

```
for x,y in itertools.product(range(0, width), range(0, height)):
    region = [ ]
    for wx,wy in itertools.product(range(0, kernelSize), range(0, kernelSize)):

        posY = y + wy - kernelCentre
        posX = x + wx - kernelCentre

        if posY > -1 and posY <  height and  posX > -1 and posX <  width:
            region.append(inputImage[posY,posX])

    numPixels = len(region)
    if  numPixels > 0:
        region.sort()
        outputImage[y,x] = region[numPixels/2]
```

CODE 3.9 Median filtering.

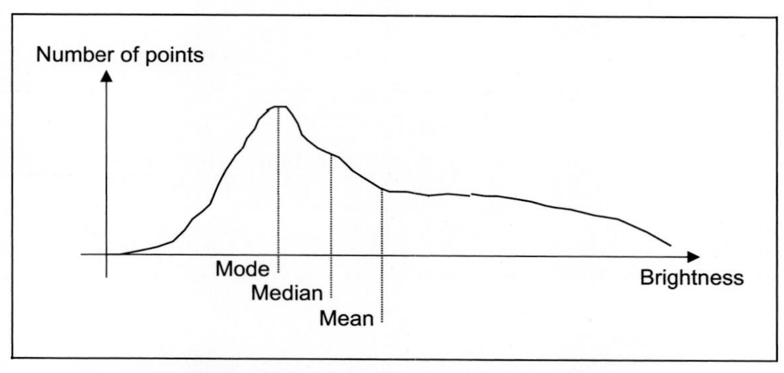

FIGURE 3.23 Arrangement of mode, median and mean.

$$\begin{aligned} upper &= median + (median - \min(distribution)) \\ &= 2 \cdot median - \min(distribution) \end{aligned} \tag{3.28}$$

If the median is greater than the mean, then we need to truncate at a lower point (before the mean), *lower*, given by

$$lower = 2 \cdot median - \max(distribution) \tag{3.29}$$

The median of the remaining distribution then approaches the mode. The truncation is performed by storing pixels values in a vector. The median of the truncated vector is then the output of the truncated median filter at that point. Naturally, the window is placed at each possible image point, as in template convolution. However, there can be several iterations at each position to ensure that the mode is approached. In practice, only few iterations are usually required for the median to converge to the mode. The window size is usually large, say 7 × 7 or 9 × 9 or even more.

Code 3.10 illustrates the implementation of the operator. The current window pixels are contained in the `region` list. The `mean` and `median` variables store statistics of the region, and they are used to compute the values of the `upper` and `lower` variables according to Eqs. (3.28) and (3.29). These values are used to create the list `truncatedRegion` that contains the truncated vector. Finally, the centre point of this vector is used to produce the output pixel value.

The action of the operator is illustrated in Fig. 3.24 when applied to a 128 × 128 part of the ultrasound image (Fig. 1.1B), from the centre of the image and containing a cross-sectional view of an artery. Ultrasound results in particularly noisy images, in part because the scanner is usually external to the body. The noise is actually multiplicative Rayleigh noise for which the mode is the optimal estimate. This noise obscures the artery which appears in cross-section in Fig. 3.24A; the artery is basically elliptical in shape. The action of the 9 × 9 truncated median operator, Fig. 3.24B is to remove noise whilst retaining feature boundaries whilst a larger operator shows better effect, Fig. 3.24C. An extra example is shown in Fig. 3.24D. This image contains added salt and pepper noise to highlight the usefulness of the filter. We can observe that a small kernel is enough to

```
kernelCentre = (kernelSize - 1) / 2
for x,y in itertools.product(range(0, width), range(0, height)):

    # Iterate Window to collect values to compute mean and median
    region = [ ]
    sumValues = 0
    for wx,wy in itertools.product(range(0, kernelSize), range(0, kernelSize)):
        posY, posX = y + wy - kernelCentre, x + wx - kernelCentre

        if posY > -1 and posY <  height and  posX > -1 and posX <  width:
            sumValues += inputImage[posY,posX]
            region.append(inputImage[posY,posX])

    # Compute mean and median of the window
    numPixels = len(region)
    if numPixels > 0:

        # Mean and median
        mean = sumValues / numPixels
        region.sort()
        median = region[numPixels/2]

        # Upper and low
        upper, lower = 2.0*median-region[0], 2.0*median-region[numPixels-1]

        # Create a list of truncated values
        truncatedRegion = [ ]
        for wx,wy in itertools.product(range(0, kernelSize), range(0, kernelSize)):
            posY, posX = y + wy - kernelCentre, x + wx - kernelCentre

            if posY > -1 and posY <  height and  posX > -1 and posX <  width:
                if (inputImage[posY,posX] < upper and median < mean) or          \
                   (inputImage[posY,posX] > lower and median > mean):
                    truncatedRegion.append(inputImage[posY,posX])

        # Compute median of truncated pixels
        numTruncatedPixels = len(truncatedRegion)
        if  numTruncatedPixels > 0:
            truncatedRegion.sort()
            outputImage[y,x] = truncatedRegion[numTruncatedPixels/2]
        else:
            outputImage[y,x] = median
```

CODE 3.10 Truncated median filtering.

remove such noise. However, edge definition is lost. This problem is more evident for larger kernels.

Close examination of the result of the truncated median filter is that a selection of boundaries are preserved which are not readily apparent in the original ultrasound image. This is one of the known properties of median filtering: an ability to reduce noise whilst retaining feature boundaries. Indeed, there have actually been many other approaches to speckle filtering; the most popular for ultrasound include direct averaging [Shankar86], median filtering, adaptive (weighted) median filtering [Loupas87] and with basis using nonlocal means [Coupé09] and anisotropic (coherent) diffusion [Abd-Elmoniem 2002] (the latter two to be covered next).

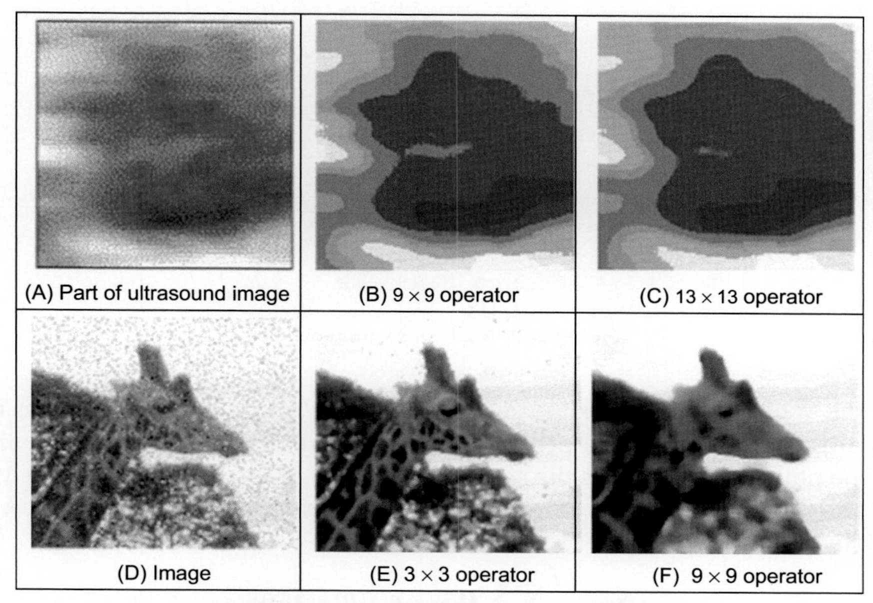

FIGURE 3.24 Applying truncated median filtering.

3.5.3 Nonlocal means

The *nonlocal means* operator [Buades05] is an extended version of the averaging operator. The basic function of the operator is to assign a point a value that is the mean of an area that is closest to the mean at the value of the point, rather than the mean at that point. As the original paper puts it 'the denoised value at x is a mean of the values of all points whose Gaussian neighbourhood looks like the neighbourhood of x'. As the former, this was rather hard to express and the latter is rather terse, it will be difficult to understand. So let us slow down a bit. By denoting the average (mean) at point p as $\overline{x}(p)$, for an $N \times N$ region, from Eq. (3.20)

$$\overline{x}(p) = \frac{1}{N^2}\sum_{i\in M}\sum_{j\in N}\mathbf{O}_{x(i),y(j)} \tag{3.30}$$

where $x(i)$, $y(j)$ are the coordinates of image points within the template. If this operation is performed over the whole image, we have applied the direct averaging operator. The parts of the process are shown in Fig. 3.25.

As averaging processes use a weighted sum if we use the Gaussian function, via Eq. (3.26), to calculate a weighting w between the average at point p and the average at point q

$$w(p,q) = g(\overline{x}(p) - \overline{x}(q)) = \frac{1}{2\pi\sigma^2}e^{\frac{-(\overline{x}(p)-\overline{x}(q))^2}{2\sigma^2}} \tag{3.31}$$

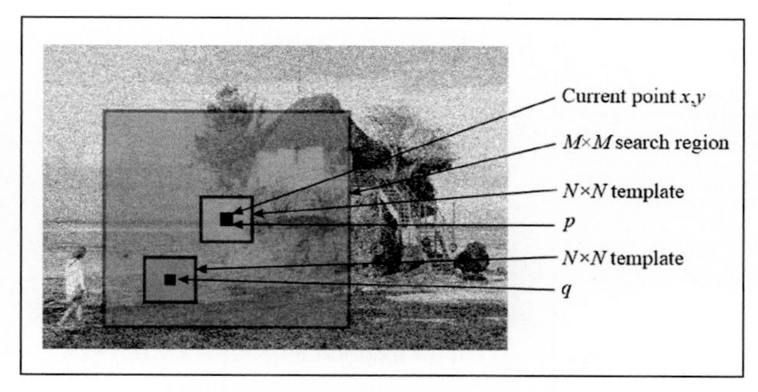

FIGURE 3.25 Nonlocal means process.

Then the weight will be maximum when $\overline{x}(p) = \overline{x}(q)$and much less when the two averages are very different. The product $\overline{x}(p) \times w(p,q)$ will be close to $\overline{x}(p)$ when the mean of the point of interest p is the same as the mean of the region at point q. We shall use an $M \times M$ search region. The nonlocal means operator is then a weighted summation

$$\begin{aligned} \mathbf{N}_{x,y} &= \frac{1}{k}\sum_{i\in M}\sum_{j\in M}\mathbf{O}_{x(i),y(j)}g(\overline{x}(p)-\overline{x}(q)) \\ &= \frac{1}{\sum_{i\in M}\sum_{j\in M}g(\overline{x}(p)-\overline{x}(q))}\sum_{i\in M}\sum_{j\in M}\mathbf{O}_{x(i),y(j)}g(\overline{x}(p)-\overline{x}(q)) \end{aligned} \tag{3.32}$$

where k is the normalising function $k = \sum_{i\in M}\sum_{j\in N}g(\overline{x}(p) - \overline{x}(q))$. The parameters that must be chosen are the window size of the averaging operator, N, the size of the search region, M, and the standard deviation. A Matlab implementation is given in Code 3.11 which follows the equations above. The border of the resulting image is set to half the window size of the larger of the averaging and range operators.

The effect of the nonlocal means operator compared with Gaussian averaging is shown in Fig. 3.26. The image here, Fig. 3.26A, is one to which synthetic noise has been added, and that is clearly seen to be removed by both operators. The function of the nonlocal means operator is to preserve regions of intensity and that is what is achieved (compare the wall of the hut in Fig. 3.26B to that in Fig. 3.26C). These images are not intended to be optimal, since optimisation depends on the application image and whether preservation of detail is more important than preservation of regions. This is implicit in the compromise between the choice of the size of the search region and the variance σ^2. A common choice for the window size, N, of the averaging operator is 7×7 or 9×9 to preserve local features and larger search sizes, M, to reduce noise. The concern on the selection of the range and its relationship with the noise has motivated approaches that adapt the range according to image content [Kervrann06]. The image here, Fig. 3.26A, is one to which synthetic noise has been added, and that is clearly seen to be removed by both operators. Note that the image would originally contain noise

```
function filtered = non_local_means(image,winsize,searchsize,st_dev)

%get image dimensions
[rows,cols]=size(image);

%set the output image to black
filtered(1:rows,1:cols)=0;
local_mean(1:rows,1:cols)=0;

%half of template is
halfwin=floor(winsize/2);
%and half of the search
halfsearch=floor(searchsize/2);

%process points according to largest window function
if winsize>searchsize
    border=halfwin; %normal case
else
    border=halfsearch; %which is possible, but daft
end

%%then form the local averages
local_mean=floor(ave(image,winsize));

%we start by looking at all image points except those in the border
for x = border+1:cols-border
  for y = border+1:rows-border
      %need to total up the weights (for later normalisation)
      weightsum=0;
      %need to total up the weighted points
      productsum=0;
      for iwin = 1:searchsize
        for jwin = 1:searchsize
            % Gaussian weight based on the intensity difference %Eq. 3.31
            weightp=exp(-(local_mean(y+jwin-halfsearch-1,x+iwin-halfsearch-1)-...
                                    local_mean(y,x))^2/(2*st_dev*st_dev));
            %and add a weighted amount of the image information
            productsum=productsum+weightp*... %Eq 3.32
                                    image(y+jwin-halfsearch-1,x+iwin-halfsearch-1);
            %and add up the weights
            weightsum=weightsum+weightp;
        end
      end
      filtered(y,x)=floor(productsum/weightsum);
  end
end
```

CODE 3.11 Nonlocal means operator.

without the addition of its synthesised form, but the results would be less easy to see. Performance analysis often depends on a chosen application.

Calling the operator nonlocal is actually rather misleading, as the originators later noted [Buades11] and a more appropriate name could have been semilocal means. Given that much of its popularity is due to performance, there is a natural interest in speeding the algorithm. One approach concentrates on implementation to improve speed [Dowson11] which, due to computational complexity, is needed when processing volumetric images.

FIGURE 3.26 Reducing noise by nonlocal means and gaussian operators.

3.5.4 Bilateral filtering

Bilateral filtering is a nonlinear filter introduced by Tomasi and Manduchi [Tomasi98]. The filter is based on Gaussian averaging and prevents blurring across feature boundaries by decreasing the filter weight when the intensity difference is too large. By denoting Gaussian averaging as the convolution of the template in Eq. (3.26) to form a new point $\mathbf{G}_{x,y}$ as a weighted sum of image points within a template

$$\begin{aligned}\mathbf{G}_{x,y} &= \frac{1}{ks}\sum_{i\in N}\sum_{j\in N}\mathbf{O}_{x(i),y(j)}g(i,j,\sigma_d) \\ &= \frac{1}{\sum\limits_{i\in N}\sum\limits_{j\in N}g(i,j,\sigma_d)}\sum_{i\in N}\sum_{j\in N}\mathbf{O}_{x(i),y(j)}e^{\frac{-\left((x(i)-x)^2+(y(j)-y)^2\right)}{2\sigma_d^2}}\end{aligned} \tag{3.33}$$

where σ_d is the standard deviation of this spatial (domain) operator, $x(i)$, $y(j)$ are again the coordinates of image points within the template, ks is the normalising coefficient and the template is of size $N\times N$. The bilateral filtering process introduces another weighting based on the difference of image intensities. Inevitably, this is formed as a Gaussian (range) function in the manner of Eq. (3.31)

$$g(p,q,\sigma_r)=\frac{1}{2\pi\sigma_r^2}e^{\frac{-(p-q)^2}{2\sigma_r^2}} \tag{3.34}$$

where p, q are point intensities and σ_r is the standard deviation, controlling width. When the intensity difference is small then this function is large, and the operator preserves feature boundaries, preventing blurring. This is one of the advantages of the median operator and a disadvantage of the Gaussian smoothing operator. The bilateral filter is given by the combination of spatial averaging with the Gaussian weighted difference in brightness as

$$\begin{aligned}\mathbf{N}_{x,y}&=\frac{1}{kb}\sum_{i\in M}\sum_{j\in M}\mathbf{G}_{x(i),y(j)}g\left(\mathbf{O}_{x,y},\mathbf{O}_{x(i),y(j)},\sigma_r\right)\\&=\frac{1}{kb}\sum_{i\in M}\sum_{j\in M}\mathbf{G}_{x(i),y(j)}e^{\frac{-\left(\mathbf{O}_{x,y}-\mathbf{O}_{x(i),y(j)}\right)^2}{2\sigma_r^2}}\end{aligned} \tag{3.35}$$

where kb is the sum of the template coefficients. The parameters that must be chosen are the window sizes and the two values for standard deviation. Note that the operator reverts to a Gaussian operator when σ_r is large, and a range filter when σ_d is large. The difference from nonlocal means is that both areas and feature boundaries are preserved, though we shall not show the result here, partly as performance is similar to that of anisotropic diffusion, the following smoothing operator. Optimised versions are available, which do not need parameter selection [Paris08, Weiss06]. Another method is based on the use of the frequency domain and uses linear filtering [Dabov07].

3.5.5 Anisotropic diffusion

Another form of smoothing that preserves the boundaries of the image features in the smoothing process [Perona90]. The process is called *anisotropic diffusion*, by virtue of its basis. Its result is illustrated in Fig. 3.27B where the feature boundaries (such as those of the eyebrows or the eyes) in the smoothed image are crisp and the skin is more matte in appearance. This implies that we are filtering within the features and not at their edges. By way of contrast, the Gaussian operator result in Fig. 3.27C smooths not just the skin but also the boundaries (the eyebrows in particular seem quite blurred) giving a less pleasing and less useful result. Since we shall later use the boundary information to interpret the image, its preservation is of much interest. The example in the second row in Fig. 3.27 illustrates how the filter is capable of maintaining fine structures. Notice how the branches of the trees in the background and the large-scale texture detail are all clear.

As ever, there are some parameters to select to control the operation, so we shall consider the technique's basis so as to guide their selection. Further, it is

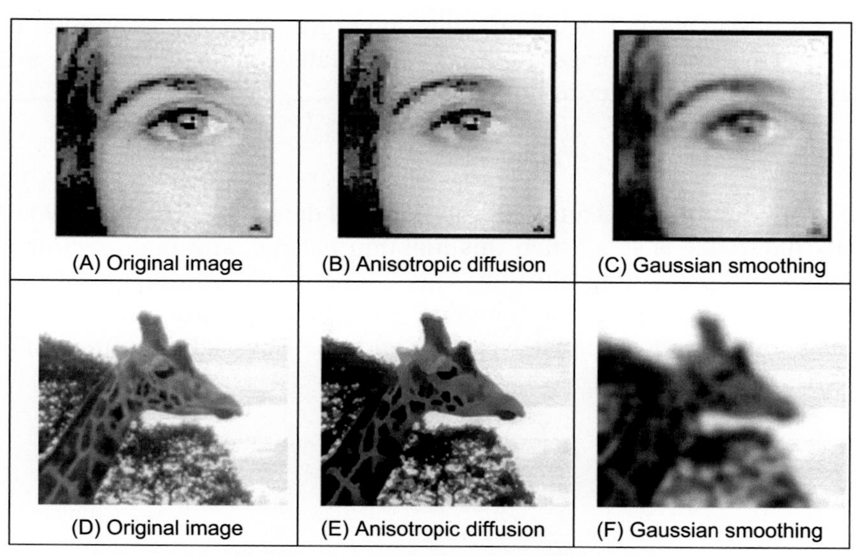

FIGURE 3.27 Filtering by anisotropic diffusion and the Gaussian operator.

computationally more complex than other filtering operators. The basis of anisotropic diffusion is, however, rather complex, especially here, and invokes concepts of low-level feature extraction which are covered in the next chapter. One strategy you might use is to mark this page, then go ahead and read Sections 4.1 and 4.2 and return here. Alternatively, you could just plough on, since that is exactly what we shall do. The complexity is because the process not only invokes low-level feature extraction (to preserve feature boundaries) but also as its basis actually invokes concepts of heat flow, as well as introducing the concept of scale-space. So it will certainly be a hard read for many, but comparison of Fig. 3.27B with Fig. 3.27C shows that it is well worth the effort.

The essential idea of scale-space is that there is a multiscale representation of images, from low resolution (a coarsely sampled image) to high resolution (a finely sampled image). This is inherent in the sampling process where the coarse image is the structure and the higher resolution increases the level of detail. As such, we can derive a scale-space set of images by convolving an original image with a Gaussian function,

$$\mathbf{P}_{x,y}(\sigma) = \mathbf{P}_{x,y}(0) * g(x, y, \sigma) \tag{3.36}$$

where $\mathbf{P}_{x,y}(0)$ is the original image, $g(x, y, \sigma)$ is the Gaussian template derived from Eq. (3.26) and $\mathbf{P}_{x,y}(\sigma)$ is the image at level σ. The coarser level corresponds to larger values of the standard deviation σ; conversely the finer detail is given by smaller values. (Scale-space will be considered again in Section 4.4.2 as it pervades the more modern operators.) We have already seen that the larger values of σ reduce the detail and are then equivalent to an image at a coarser scale, so this is a different view of the same process.

The difficult bit is that the family of images derived this way can equivalently be viewed as the solution of the heat equation

$$\partial \mathbf{P}/\partial t = \nabla \mathbf{P}_{x,y}(t) \tag{3.37}$$

where ∇ denotes del, the (directional) gradient operator from vector algebra and with the initial condition that $\mathbf{P}_0 = \mathbf{P}_{x,y}(0)$. The heat equation itself describes the temperature T changing with time t as a function of the thermal diffusivity (related to conduction) κ as

$$\partial T/\partial t = \kappa \nabla^2 T \tag{3.38}$$

and in one dimensional form this is

$$\partial T/\partial t = \kappa \frac{\partial^2 T}{\partial x^2} \tag{3.39}$$

so the temperature measured along a line is a function of time, distance, the initial and boundary conditions and the properties of a material. The direct relation of this with image processing is clearly an enormous ouch! There are clear similarities between Eq. (3.39) and Eq. (3.37). This is the same functional form and allows for insight, analysis and parameter selection. The heat equation, Eq. (3.37) is the anisotropic diffusion equation

$$\partial \mathbf{P}/\partial t = \nabla \cdot (c_{x,y}(t) \nabla \mathbf{P}_{x,y}(t)) \tag{3.40}$$

where $\nabla \cdot$ is the divergence operator (which essentially measures how the density within a region changes), with diffusion coefficient $c_{x,y}$. The diffusion coefficient applies to the local change in the image $\nabla \mathbf{P}_{x,y}(t)$ in different directions. If we have a lot of local change, we seek to retain it since the amount of change is the amount of boundary information. The diffusion coefficient indicates how much importance we give to local change: how much of it is retained. (The equation reduces to isotropic diffusion – Gaussian filtering – if the diffusivity is constant since $\nabla c = 0$.) There is no explicit solution to this equation. By approximating differentiation by differencing (this is explored more in Section 4.2) the rate of change of the image between time step t and time step $t+1$, we have

$$\partial \mathbf{P}/\partial t = \mathbf{P}(t+1) - \mathbf{P}(t) \tag{3.41}$$

This implies we have an iterative solution, and for later consistency we shall denote the image $\mathbf{P}$ at time step t+1 as $\mathbf{P}^{<t+1>} = \mathbf{P}(t+1)$, so we then have

$$\mathbf{P}^{<t+1>} - \mathbf{P}^{<t>} = \nabla \cdot \left(c_{x,y}(t) \nabla \mathbf{P}_{x,y}^{<t>} \right) \tag{3.42}$$

and again by approximation, using differences evaluated this time over the four compass directions north, south, east and west, we have

$$\nabla_N(\mathbf{P}_{x,y}) = \mathbf{P}_{x,y-1} - \mathbf{P}_{x,y} \tag{3.43}$$

$$\nabla_S(\mathbf{P}_{x,y}) = \mathbf{P}_{x,y+1} - \mathbf{P}_{x,y} \tag{3.44}$$

$$\nabla_E(\mathbf{P}_{x,y}) = \mathbf{P}_{x+1,y} - \mathbf{P}_{x,y} \tag{3.45}$$

$$\nabla_W(\mathbf{P}_{x,y}) = \mathbf{P}_{x-1,y} - \mathbf{P}_{x,y} \tag{3.46}$$

The template and weighting coefficients for these are shown in Fig. 3.28.

When we use these as an approximation to the right-hand side in Eq. (3.42), we then have $\nabla \cdot \left(c_{x,y}(t)\nabla\mathbf{P}_{x,y}^{<t>}\right) = \lambda(cN_{x,y}\nabla_N(\mathbf{P}) + cS_{x,y}\nabla_S(\mathbf{P}) + cE_{x,y}\nabla_E(\mathbf{P}) + cW_{x,y}\nabla_W(\mathbf{P}))$ which gives

$$\mathbf{P}^{<t+1>} - \mathbf{P}^{<t>} = \lambda\left(cN_{x,y}\nabla_N(\mathbf{P}) + cS_{x,y}\nabla_S(\mathbf{P}) + cE_{x,y}\nabla_E(\mathbf{P}) + cW_{x,y}\nabla_W(\mathbf{P})\right) \quad \Big| \mathbf{P} = \mathbf{P}_{x,y}^{<t>} \tag{3.47}$$

where $0 \leq \lambda \leq 1/4$ and where $cN_{x,y}$, $cS_{x,y}$, $cE_{x,y}$ and $cW_{x,y}$ denote the conduction coefficients in the four compass directions. By rearrangement of this, we obtain the equation we shall use for the anisotropic diffusion operator

$$\mathbf{P}^{<t+1>} = \mathbf{P}^{<t>} + \lambda\left(cN_{x,y}\nabla_N(\mathbf{P}) + cS_{x,y}\nabla_S(\mathbf{P}) + cE_{x,y}\nabla_E(\mathbf{P}) + cW_{x,y}\nabla_W(\mathbf{P})\right) \quad \Big| \mathbf{P} = \mathbf{P}_{x,y}^{<t>} \tag{3.48}$$

This shows that the solution is iterative: images at one time step (denoted by $^{<t+1>}$) are computed from images at the previous time step (denoted $^{<t>}$), given the initial condition that the first image is the original (noisy) image. Change (in time and in space) has been approximated as the difference between two adjacent points which gives the iterative equation and shows that the new image is formed by adding a controlled amount of the local change consistent with the main idea: that the smoothing process retains some of the boundary information.

We are not finished yet though, since we need to find values for $cN_{x,y}$, $cS_{x,y}$, $cE_{x,y}$ and $cW_{x,y}$. These are chosen to be a function of the difference along the compass directions, so that the boundary (edge) information is preserved. In this way we seek a function that tends to zero with increase in the difference (an edge or boundary with greater contrast) so that diffusion does not take place across the boundaries, keeping the edge information. As such we seek

$$\begin{aligned} cN_{x,y} &= g(\|\nabla_N(\mathbf{P})\|) \\ cS_{x,y} &= g(\|\nabla_S(\mathbf{P})\|) \\ cE_{x,y} &= g(\|\nabla_E(\mathbf{P})\|) \\ cW_{x,y} &= g(\|\nabla_W(\mathbf{P})\|) \end{aligned} \tag{3.49}$$

and one function that can achieve this is

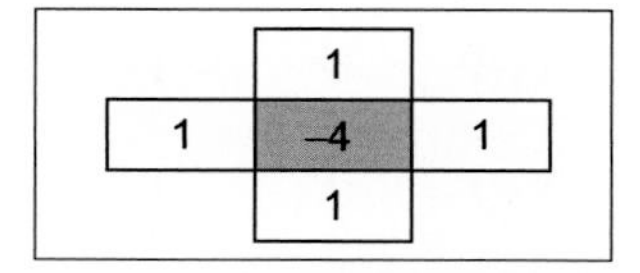

FIGURE 3.28 Approximations by spatial difference in anisotropic diffusion.

$$g(x,k) = e^{-x^2/k^2} \tag{3.50}$$

(There is potential confusion with using the same symbol as for the Gaussian function, Eq. (3.26), but we have followed the original authors' presentation.) This function clearly has the desired properties since when the values of the differences ∇ are large, the function g is very small, conversely when ∇ is small, then g tends to unity. k is another parameter whose value we have to choose: it controls the rate at which the conduction coefficient decreases with increasing difference magnitude. The effect of this parameter is shown in Fig. 3.29. Here, the solid line is for the smaller value of k and the dotted one is for a larger value. Evidently, a larger value of k means that the contribution of the difference reduces less than for a smaller value of k. In both cases, the resulting function is near unity for small differences and near zero for large differences, as required. An alternative to this is to use the function

$$g2(x,k) = \frac{1}{1 + x^2/k^2} \tag{3.51}$$

which has similar properties to the function in Eq. (3.50).

This all looks rather complicated, so let us recap. First, we want to filter an image by retaining boundary points. These are retained according to the value of k chosen in Eq. (3.50). This function is operated in the four compass directions, to weight the brightness difference in each direction, Eq. (3.49). These contribute to an iterative equation which calculates a new value for an image point by considering the contribution from its four neighbouring points, Eq. (3.48). This needs choice of one parameter λ. Further, we need to choose the number of iterations for which calculation proceeds. For information, Fig. 3.27B was calculated over 20 iterations, and we need to use sufficient iterations to ensure that convergence has been achieved. Fig. 3.30 shows how we approach this. Fig. 3.30A is after a single iteration, Fig. 3.30B after 2, Fig. 3.30C after 5 and Fig.

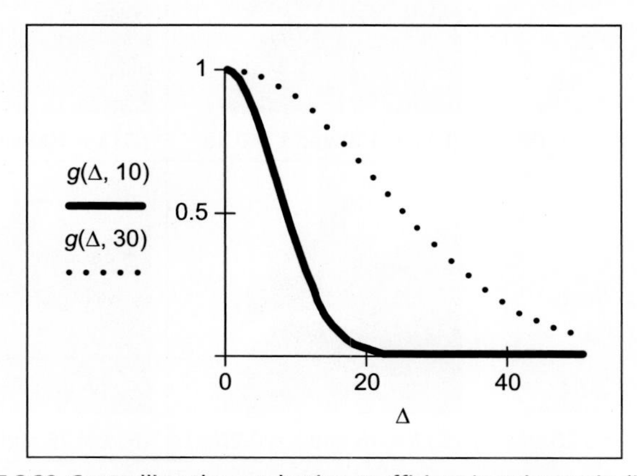

FIGURE 3.29 Controlling the conduction coefficient in anisotropic diffusion.

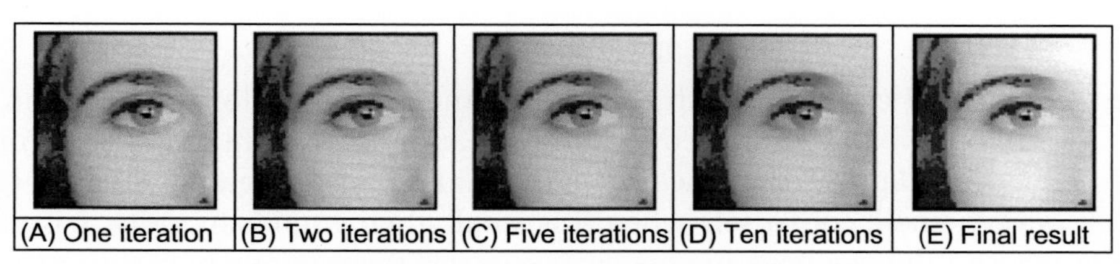

FIGURE 3.30 Iterations of anisotropic diffusion.

3.30D after 10 and Fig. 3.30E after 20. Manifestly we could choose to reduce the number of iterations, accepting a different result – or even go further.

We also need to choose values for k and λ. By analogy, k is the conduction coefficient and low values preserve edges and high values allow diffusion (conduction) to occur – how much smoothing can take place. The two parameters are naturally interrelated, though λ largely controls the amount of smoothing. Given that low values of either parameter means that no filtering effect is observed, we can investigate their effect by setting one parameter to a high value and varying the other. In Figs. 3.31A–C, we use a high value of k which means that edges are not preserved and we can observe that different values of λ control the amount of smoothing. (A discussion of how this Gaussian filtering process is achieved can be inferred from Section 3.4.5.) Conversely, we can see how different values for k control the level of edge preservation in Figs. 3.31D–F where some structures are not preserved for larger values of k.

By design, the result is akin with that of bilateral filtering (which it preceded) – indeed, the relationship has already been established [Barash02]. One of the major

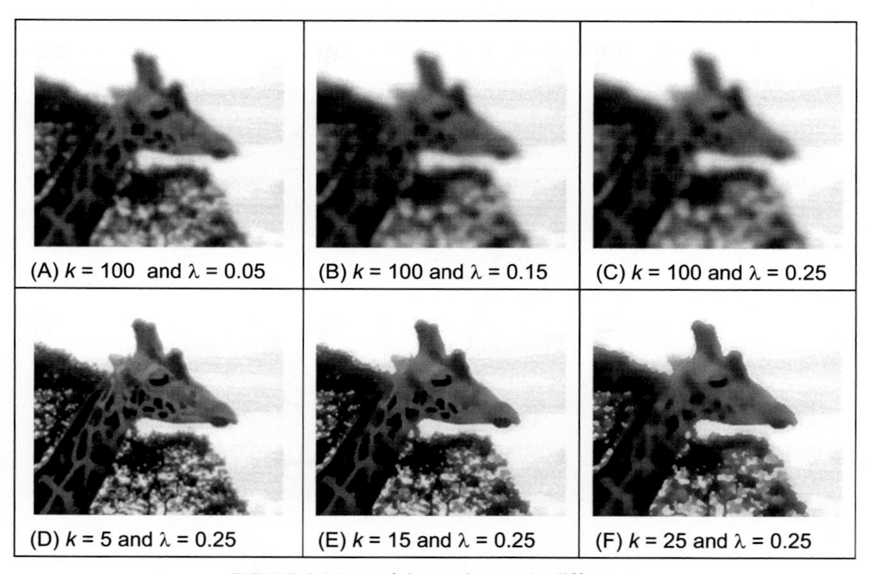

FIGURE 3.31 Applying anisotropic diffusion.

disadvantages is that anisotropic diffusion is an iterative process, the advantages include greater control of the filtering process. The original presentation of anisotropic diffusion [Perona90] is extremely lucid and well worth a read if you consider selecting this technique. Naturally, it has greater detail on formulation and on analysis of results, than space here allows for (and is suitable at this stage). Amongst other papers on this topic, one [Black98] studied the choice of conduction coefficient leading to a function which preserves sharper edges and improves automatic termination. A more recent study has considered parameter and function choice [Tsiotsios13]. As ever, with techniques that require much computation there have been approaches which speed implementation, or achieve similar performance faster (e.g. [Fischl99]).

Code 3.12 illustrates the implementation of the anisotropic process. The main loop contains the diffusion iterations. The iteration process uses a pair of images. The `outputImage` is the image computed in the previous iteration, and `image` is the image updated in the current iteration. Each pixel value is updated according to the region defined by `kernelSize`. The implementation computes a weight for each pixel in the window according to Eq. (3.50). This weight measures the differences in Eq. (3.43) and is inversely proportional to the gradient or changes around the pixel. That is, when the pixel is close to an edge this value is low; and it will produce less smoothing. The weight is multiplied by `lambda` that controls the global smoothing. Notice that the weights are used to compute a simple average. In a more complete implementation the average could be replaced by a Gaussian operator that models the diffusion process more accurately. The examples in Fig. 3.31 were obtained with this implementation.

```
for iteration in range(0, numIterations):
    for x,y in itertools.product(range(0, width), range(0, height)):
        image[y, x] = outputImage[y, x]

    for x,y in itertools.product(range(0, width), range(0, height)):
        sumWeights = 0;
        outputImage[y, x] = 0

        centrePixleValue = image[y, x]
        for wx,wy in itertools.product(range(0, kernelSize), range(0, kernelSize)):
            posY, posX = y + wy - kernelCentre, x + wx - kernelCentre

            if posY > -1 and posY <  height and  posX > -1 and posX <  width:
                # Weight according to gradient
                weight = exp(-pow((image[posY, posX]-centrePixleValue)/k, 2) );

                # Use lambda to weight the pixel value
                if posY != y and posX != x:
                    weight *= lamda

                sumWeights += weight
                outputImage[y, x] += weight * float(image[posY, posX])
        # Normalize
        if sumWeights > 0:
            outputImage[y, x] /= sumWeights
```

CODE 3.12 Anisotropic diffusion process.

3.5.6 Comparison of smoothing operators

A principled way to address performance is to add noise with known properties. This can be Gaussian noise for most operators, or black and white noise for the median operator. The results of some different image filtering operators are shown for comparison in Fig. 3.32. (This is a detail – actually a restaurant called The Rock – as it is hard to see advantages in a whole image, as in Fig. 3.26). The processed image is Fig. 3.24A corrupted by added Gaussian noise, Fig. 3.32B. All operators are 9×9 with parameters chosen for best performance. Naturally, 'best' is subjective: is it best to retain feature boundaries (e.g. the roof edge or the foliage) or to retain local structure (e.g. the roof's thatching) – or just the local average (e.g. the wall)? That invariably depends on application. Figs. 3.32C–H results from averaging (mean), Gaussian averaging, median, truncated median, anisotropic diffusion and nonlocal means, respectively. Each operator shows a different performance: the mean operator removes much noise but blurs feature boundaries; Gaussian averaging retains more features, but shows little advantage over

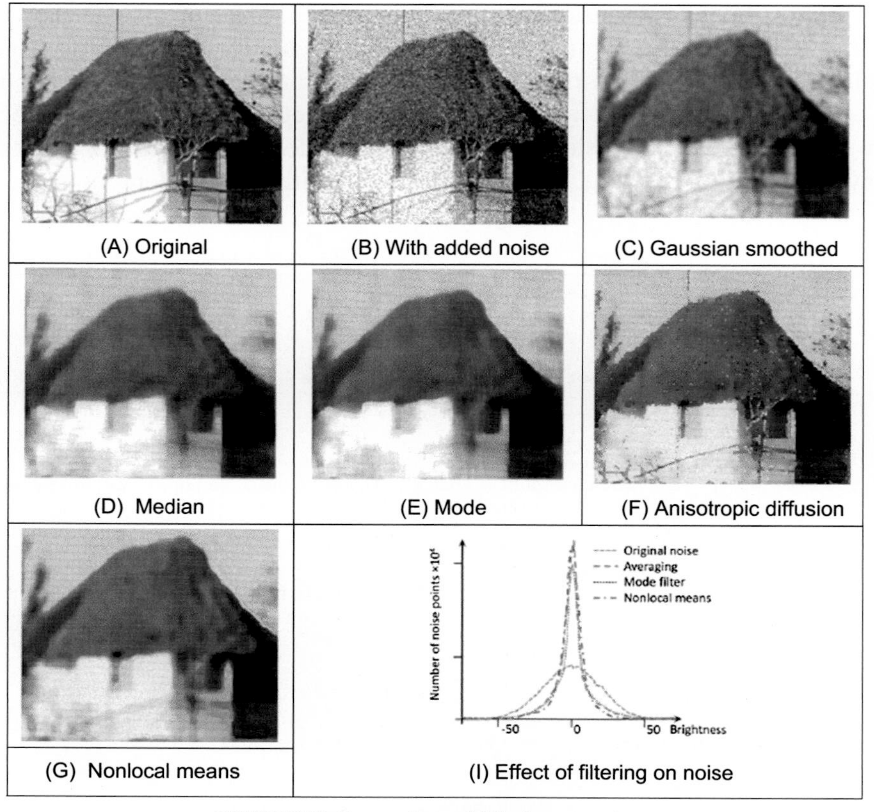

FIGURE 3.32 Comparison of filtering operators.

direct averaging; the median operator retains some noise but with clear feature boundaries; whereas the truncated median removes more noise, but along with picture detail. Clearly, the increased size of the truncated median template, by the results in Fig. 3.24B and C, can offer improved performance. This is to be expected since by increasing the size of the truncated median template, we are essentially increasing the size of the distribution from which the mode is found. The effect of filtering can be assessed by studying the distribution of noise in the resulting image. The noise remaining after filtering can be separated by differencing the original image (without the noise added) from the resulting filtered image. Some histograms are shown in Fig. 3.32 for the addition of noise, the effect of Gaussian averaging and nonlocal means. Clearly the noise is reduced (tends on average to zero), and such information can be helpful when optimising choice of the parameters used.

This performance evaluation has been for real images since that is more appealing, but when the noise is unknown we can only perform subjective analysis. Accordingly, better appraisal is based on the use of feature extraction. Boundaries are the low-level features studied in the next chapter; shape is a high-level feature studied in Chapter 5. Also, we shall later use the filtering operators as a basis for finding objects which move in sequences of images, in Chapter 9.

Naturally, comparing the operators begs the question: when will denoising approaches be developed which are at the performance limit? Manifestly, the volume of research following development of a particular operator, say nonlocal means, suggests that optimality is rarely achieved. One such study [Chatterjee10] concluded that 'despite the phenomenal recent progress in the quality of denoising algorithms, some room for improvement still remains for a wide class of general images'. A later study [Levin11] showed, by modelling natural image statistics, that for small windows the state-of-the-art denoising algorithms appeared to be approaching optimality with little room for improvement. A very recent approach concerns noise reduction and upsampling [Ham19]. There are now deep learning approaches for image quality improvement, e.g. [Zhang17] shows that discriminative model learning for image denoising has been attracting considerable attention due to its favourable performance. These will be introduced in Chapter 12. Denoising is not finished and perhaps may never be. However, having covered the major noise filtering operators, we shall finish with them and move on to operators that preserve selected features, since feature detection is the topic of the following chapter.

3.5.7 Force field transform

There are of course many more image filtering operators; we have so far covered those that are amongst the most popular. There are others which offer alternative insight, sometimes developed in the context of a specific application. By way of example, Hurley developed a transform called the *force field transform* [Hurley02, Hurley05] which uses an analogy to gravitational force. The transform pretends that each pixel exerts a force on its neighbours which is inversely proportional to the square of the distance between them. This generates a force field where the net force at each point is the aggregate of the forces exerted by all the other pixels on a 'unit test pixel' at that point. This very large-scale summation affords very powerful averaging which reduces the effect of noise. The approach was developed in the context of ear biometrics, recognising people by their ears, which has unique advantage as a biometric in that the shape of people's ears does not change with age, and of course – unlike a face – ears do not smile! The force field transform of an ear, Fig. 3.33A, is shown in Fig. 3.33B. Here, the averaging process is reflected in the reduction of the effects of hair. The transform itself has highlighted ear structures, especially the top of the ear and the lower 'keyhole' (the intertragic notch).

The image shown is actually the magnitude of the force field. The transform itself is a vector operation and includes direction [Hurley02]. The transform is expressed as the calculation of the force $\mathbf{F}$ between two points at positions $\mathbf{r}_i$ and $\mathbf{r}_j$ which is dependent on the value of a pixel at point $\mathbf{r}_i$ as

$$\mathbf{F}_i(\mathbf{r}_j) = \mathbf{P}(\mathbf{r}_i)\frac{\mathbf{r}_i - \mathbf{r}_j}{|\mathbf{r}_i - \mathbf{r}_j|^3} \tag{3.52}$$

which assumes that the point $\mathbf{r}_j$ is of unit 'mass'. This is a directional force (which is why the inverse square law is expressed as the ratio of the difference to its magnitude cubed), and the magnitude and directional information has been exploited to determine an ear 'signature' by which people can be recognised. In application, Eq. (3.52) can be used to define the coefficients of a template that are convolved with an image (implemented by the FFT to improve speed), as with many of the techniques that have been covered in this chapter; an implementation is also given [Hurley02]. Note that this transform actually exposes low-level features (the boundaries of the ears) which are the focus of the next chapter. How we can determine shapes is a higher level process, and how the processes by which we infer or recognise identity from the low- and the high-level features will be covered in Chapter 12.

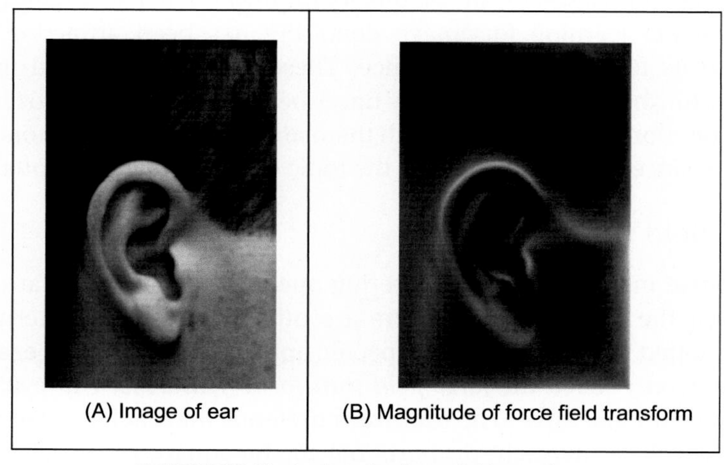

FIGURE 3.33 Illustrating the force field transform.

3.5.8 Image ray transform

The force field transform shows that there are other mathematical bases available for processing a whole image, as did the use of heat in the anisotropic diffusion operator. Another technique is called the *Image Ray Transform* (IRT) [Cummings11] and this uses an analogy to the propagation of light to transform an image to a new representation, with particular advantages.

As shown in Fig. 3.34A, the IRT operates in principle by initialising a torch in multiple positions and orientations and then tracing the path of the torch's beam. This analogises an image as a matrix of glass blocks, where the image brightness is proportional to the refractive index of each block. Essentially, the technique uses Snell's law which describes propagation of light. The angle of relection θ_r of a ray of light is calculated using Snell's law as

$$\frac{\sin\theta_i}{\sin\theta_r} = \frac{n_2}{n_1} \tag{3.53}$$

where θ_i is the angle of an incident ray, n_1 is the refractive index of the incident medium and n_2 is the refractive index of the exit medium. Whether or not a ray is refracted or reflected depends on the critical angle that is calculated from the ratio of the refractive indices. The refractive index is calculated from the image intensity i, given a chosen maximum refractive index $n_{\max}$, as

$$n_i = 1 + \left(\frac{i}{255}\right)(n_{\max} - 1) \tag{3.54}$$

There are many other refinements necessary for the technique, such as ray length, number of rays, and other parameters used in the refractive index calculation.

A result of the IRT on the retina image of Fig. 3.34A is shown in Fig. 3.34B. Essentially this shows the number of times beams crossed different points in the image. (It should be noted that diabetic retinopathy is of major interest in medicine, as it can show onset

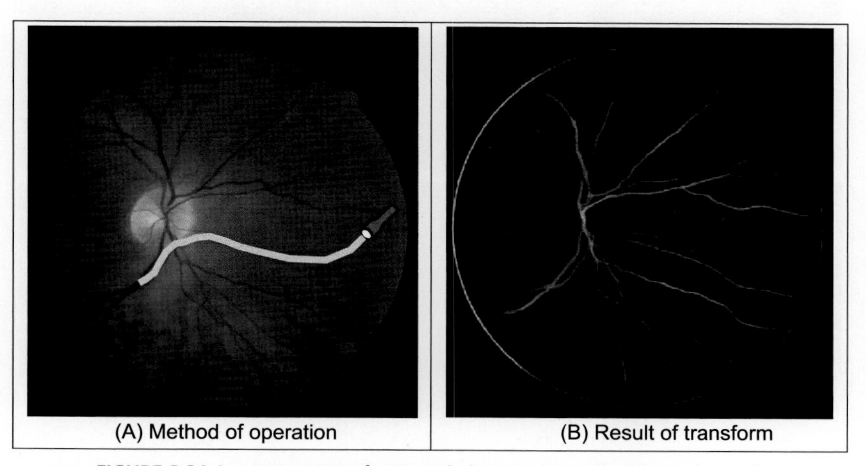

FIGURE 3.34 Image ray transform analysis in retinopathy [Cummings11].

of diabetes. This image derives from the DRIVE data set [Staal04] which is used within evaluation of techniques in this area.) In Fig. 3.34B, the transform has highlighted the vessels and not the optical disc (the bright part of the centre of the eye, where the vessels appear to converge). This changes the image representation in a way combining feature extraction with filtering.

By its nature, the IRT is suited to application in images that contain tubular or circular structures and the transform will emphasise (light is trapped in tubular structures, in a manner akin with optical fibres). This is shown in Figs. 3.35A and B as well as a poor result in Fig. 3.35C. The poor result arises from an image where the two circular structures could be expected to be emphasised, but the resolution of the image is poor with respect to these two structures and the shadow of the car produces a stronger tubular structure, directing rays away from the wheels.

No technique is a panacea, and that should never be expected. There is a wide variety of processing operators possible, many more than have been shown here and in application one chooses the most appropriate. We have described the major operators and compared their performance, though only for demonstration purposes on image quality improvement. We shall move to techniques that explicitly locate low-level image structures in the next chapter. Before that we shall move to a complementary approach to the image processing that has been presented so far.

3.6 Mathematical morphology

Mathematical morphology analyses images by using operators developed using set theory [Serra86, Soille13]. It was originally developed for binary images and was

FIGURE 3.35 Applying the image ray transform [Cummings11].

extended to include grey level data. The word morphology actually concerns shapes: in mathematical morphology, we process images according to shape, by treating both as sets of points. In this way, morphological operators define *local transformations* that change pixel values that are represented as *sets*. The ways pixel values are changed is formalised by the definition of the *hit or miss transformation*.

In the hit and miss transform, an object represented by a set X is examined through a structural element represented by a set B. Different structuring elements are used to change the operations on the set X. The hit or miss transformation is defined as the point operator:

$$X \otimes B = \{ \, x \,|\, B_x^1 \subset X \ \cap \ B_x^2 \subset X^c \} \tag{3.55}$$

In this equation, x represents one element of X that is a pixel in an image. The symbol X^c denotes the complement of X (the image pixels which are not in the set X) and the structuring element B is represented by two parts, B^1 and B^2, that are applied to the set X or to its complement X^c. The structuring element is a shape, and this is how mathematical morphology operations process images according to shape properties. The operation of B^1 on X is a *hit*; the operation of B^2 on X^c is a *miss*. The subindex x in the structural element indicates that it is moved to the position of the element x. That is, in a manner similar to other group operators, B defines a window that is moved through the image.

Fig. 3.36 illustrates a binary image and a structuring element. Image pixels are divided into those belonging to X and those belonging to its complement X^c. The figure shows a structural element and its decomposition into the two sets B^1 and B^2. Each subset is used to analyse the set X and its complement. Here, we use black for the elements of B^1 and white for B^2 to indicate that they are applied to X and X^c, respectively.

Eq. (3.55) defines a process that moves the structural element B to be placed at each pixel in the image, and it performs a pixel-by-pixel comparison against the template B. If the value of the image is the same as that of the structuring element, then the image's pixel forms part of the resulting set $X \otimes B$. An important feature of this process is that it is not invertible. That is, information is removed in order to suppress or enhance geometrical features in an image.

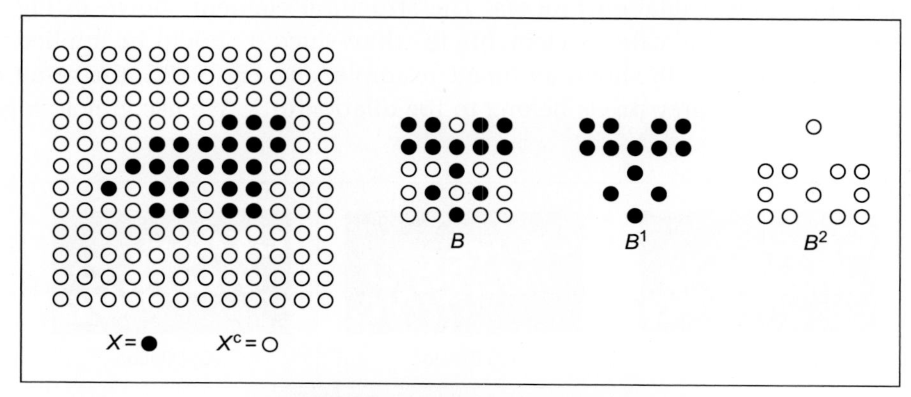

FIGURE 3.36 Image and structural element.

3.6.1 Morphological operators

The simplest form of morphological operators is defined when either B^1 or B^2 is empty. When B^1 is empty Eq. (3.55) defines an *erosion* (reduction), and when B^2 is empty it defines a *dilation* (increase). That is, an erosion operation is given by

$$X \Theta B = \{x \mid B_x^1 \subset X\} \tag{3.56}$$

and a dilation is given by

$$X \oplus B = \{x \mid B_x^2 \subset X^c\} \tag{3.57}$$

In the erosion operator, the hit or miss transformation establishes that a pixel x belongs to the eroded set if each point of the element B^1 translated to x is on X. Since all the points in B^1 need to be in X, this operator removes the pixels at the borders of objects in the set X. Thus, it actually erodes or shrinks the set. One of the most common applications of this is to remove noise in thresholded images. This is illustrated in Fig. 3.37 where in Fig. 3.37A we have a noisy binary image, the image is eroded in Fig. 3.37B removing noise but making the letters smaller, and this is corrected by opening in Fig. 3.37C. We shall show how we can use shape to improve this filtering process – put the morph into morphology.

Fig. 3.38 illustrates the operation of the erosion operator. Fig. 3.38A contains a 3 × 3 template that defines the structural element B^1. The centre pixel is the origin of the set. Fig. 3.38B shows an image containing a region of black pixels that defines the set X. Fig. 3.38C shows the result of the erosion. The eroded set is formed from black pixels only, and we use grey to highlight the pixels that were removed from X by the erosion operator. For example, when the structural element is moved to the position shown as a grid in Fig. 3.38C, the central pixel is removed since only five pixels of the structural element are in X.

The dilation operator defined in Eq. (3.57) establishes that a point belongs to the dilated set when all the points in B^2 are in the complement. This operator erodes or shrinks the complement and when the complement is eroded, the set X is dilated.

Fig. 3.39 illustrates a dilation process. The structural element shown in Fig. 3.39A defines the set B^2. We indicate its elements in white since it should be applied to the complement of X. Fig. 3.39B shows an image example, and Fig. 3.39C, the result of the dilation. The black and grey pixels belong to the dilation of X. We use grey to highlight

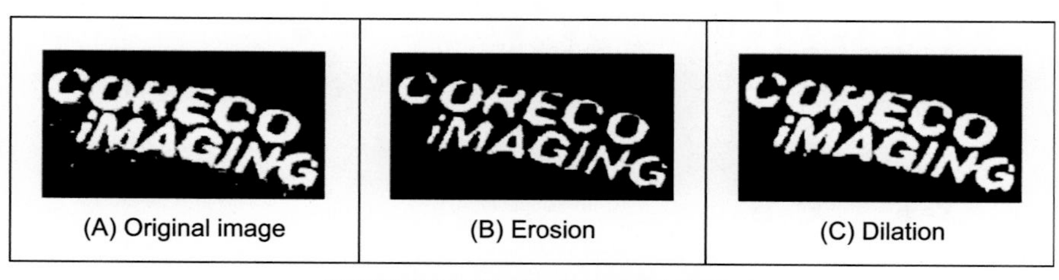

FIGURE 3.37 Filtering by morphology.

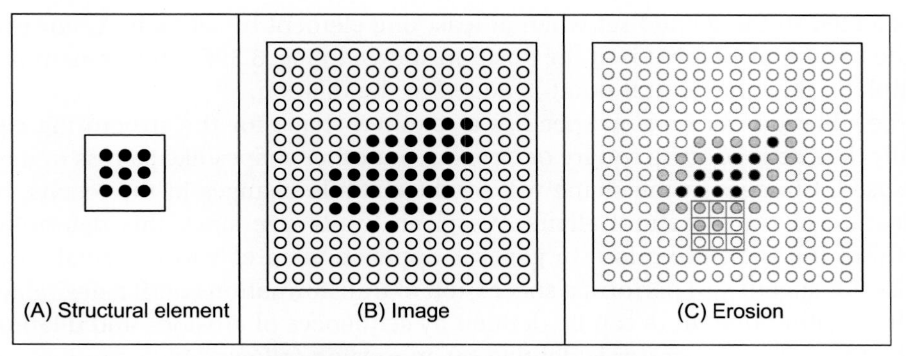

FIGURE 3.38 Example of the erosion operator.

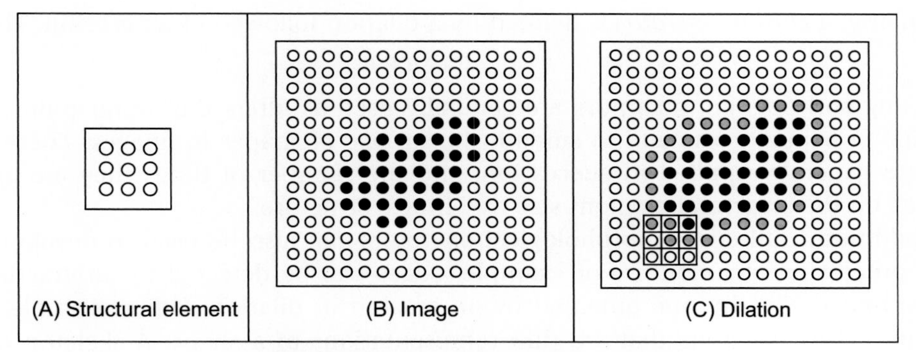

FIGURE 3.39 Example of the dilation operator.

the pixels that are added to the set. During the dilation, we place the structural element on each pixel in the complement. That is, the white pixels in Fig. 3.39B. When the structural element is not fully contained, it is removed form the complement, so it becomes part of *X*. For example, when the structural element is moved to the position shown as a grid in Fig. 3.39C, the central pixel is removed from the complement since one of the pixels in the template is in *X*.

There is an alternative formulation for the dilation operator that defines the transformation over the set *X* instead to its complement. This definition is obtained by observing that when all elements of B^2 are in X^c, is equivalent to none of the elements in the negation of B^2 are in *X*. That is, dilation can also be written as intersection of translated sets as

$$X \oplus B = \left\{ x \,\middle|\, x \in \neg B_x^2 \right\} \tag{3.58}$$

Here the symbol $\neg$ denotes negation, and it changes the structural element from being applied to the complement to the set. For example, the negation of the structural element in Fig. 3.39A is the set in Fig. 3.38A. Thus, Eq. (3.58) defines a process where a point is added to the dilated set when at least one element of $\neg B^2$ is in X. For example, when the structural element is at the position shown in Fig. 3.39C, one element in X is in the template, thus the central point is added to the dilation.

Neither dilation nor erosion specifies a required shape for the structuring element. Generally, it is defined to be square or circular, but other shapes like a cross or a triangle can be used. Changes in the shape will produce subtle changes in the results, but the main feature of the structural element is given by its size since this determines the 'strength' of the transformation. In general, applications prefer to use small structural elements (for speed) and perform a succession of transformations until a desirable result is obtained. Other operators can be defined by sequences of erosions and dilations. For example, the *opening operator* is defined by an erosion followed by a dilation. That is,

$$X \circ B = (X \Theta B) \oplus B \tag{3.59}$$

Similarly, a *closing operator* is defined by a dilation followed of an erosion. That is,

$$X \bullet B = (X \oplus B) \Theta B \tag{3.60}$$

Closing and opening operators are generally used as filters that remove dots characteristic of pepper noise and to smooth the surface of shapes in images. These operators are generally applied in succession, and the number of times they are applied depends on the structural element size and image structure.

In addition to filtering, morphological operators can also be used to develop other image processing techniques. For example, edges can be detected by subtracting the original image and the one obtained by an erosion or dilation. Other example is the computation of skeletons that are thin representations of a shape. A skeleton can be computed as the union of subtracting images obtained by applying erosions and openings with structural elements of increasing sizes.

3.6.2 Grey level morphology

In the definition in Eq. (3.55), pixels belong to either the set X or to its complement. Thus, it only applies to binary images. Grey level morphology extends Eq. (3.55) to represent functions as sets, thus morphology operators can be applied to grey level images. There are two alternative representations of functions as sets: the cross-section [Serra86, Soille13] and the umbra [Sternberg86]. The cross-section representation uses multiple thresholds to obtain a pile of binary images. Thus, the definition of Eq. (3.55) can be applied to grey level images by considering a collection of binary images as a stack of binary images formed at each threshold level. The formulation and implementation of this approach is cumbersome since it requires multiple structural elements and operators over the stack. The umbra approach is more intuitive, and it defines sets as the points contained below functions. The umbra of a function $f(x)$ consists of all points that satisfy $f(x)$. That is,

$$U(X) = \{ (x, z) | z < f(x) \} \tag{3.61}$$

Here, x represents a pixel and $f(x)$ its grey level. Thus, the space (x, z) is formed by the combination of all pixels and grey levels. For images, x is defined in 2D, thus all the points of the form (x, z) define a cube in 3D space. An umbra is a collection of points in this 3D space. Notice that morphological definitions are for discrete sets, thus the function is defined at discrete points and for discrete grey levels.

Fig. 3.40 illustrates the concept of an umbra. For simplicity, we show $f(x)$ as 1D function. In Fig. 3.40A, the umbra is drawn as a collection of points below the curve. The complement of the umbra is denoted as $U^c(X)$, and it is given by the points on and above the curve. The union of $U(X)$ and $U^c(X)$ defines all the image points and grey level values (x, z). In grey level morphology, images and structural elements are represented by umbrae. Fig. 3.40B illustrates the definition of two structural elements. The first example defines a structural element for the umbra, that is, B^1. Similar to an image function, the umbra of the structural elements is defined by the points under the curve. The second example in Fig. 3.40B defines a structural element for the complement, that is, B^2. Similar to the complement of the umbra, this operator defines the points on and over the curve.

The hit or miss transformation in Eq. (3.55) is extended to grey level functions by considering the inclusion operator in the umbrae. That is,

$$U(X \otimes B) = \left\{(x,z) \,\middle|\, U\left(B^1_{x,z}\right) \subset U(X) \;\cap\; U\left(B^2_{x,z}\right) \subset U^c(X)\right\} \tag{3.62}$$

Similar to the binary case, this equation defines a process that evaluates the inclusion of the translated structural element B. At difference of the binary definition, the structural element is translated along the pixels and grey level values. That is, to the points (x, z). Thus, a point (x, z) belongs to the umbra of the hit or miss transformation, if the umbrae of the elements B^1 and B^2 translated to (x, z) are included in the umbra and its complement, respectively. The inclusion operator is defined for the umbra and its complement in different ways. An umbra is contained in other umbra if corresponding values of its function are equal or lower. For the complement, an umbra is contained if corresponding values of its function are equal or greater.

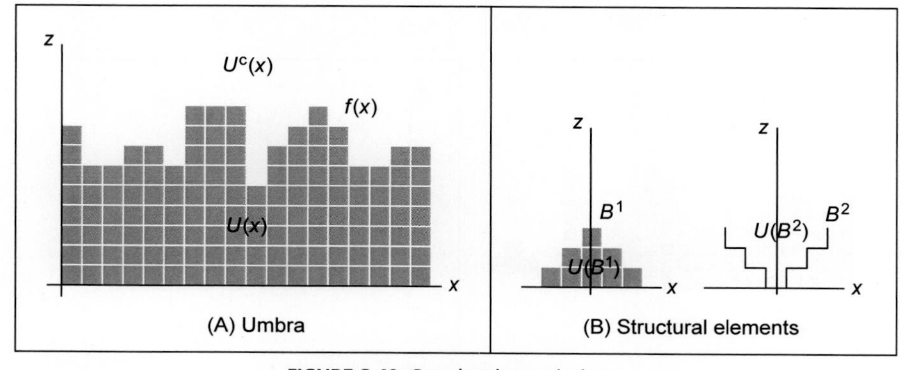

FIGURE 3.40 Grey level morphology.

We can visualise the process in Eq. (3.62) by translating the structural element in the example in Fig. 3.40. To know if a point (x, z) is in the transformed set, we move the structural element B^1 to the point and see if its umbra fully intersects $U(X)$. If that is the case, the umbra of the structural element is contained in the umbra of the function and $U\left(B^1_{x,t}\right) \subset U(X)$ is true. Similarly, to test for $U\left(B^2_{x,t}\right) \subset U^c(X)$, we move the structural element B^2 and see if it is contained in the upper region of the curve. If both conditions are true, then the point where the operator is translated belongs to the umbra of the hit or miss transformation.

3.6.3 Grey level erosion and dilation

Based on the generalisation in Eq. (3.62), it is possible to reformulate operators developed for binary morphology so they can be applied to grey level data. The *erosion* and *dilation* defined in Eqs. (3.56) and (3.57) are generalised to grey level morphology as

$$U(X \ominus B) = \left\{(x,z) \,\middle|\, U\left(B^1_{x,z}\right) \subset U(X)\right\} \tag{3.63}$$

and

$$U(X \oplus B) = \left\{(x,z) \,\middle|\, U\left(B^2_{x,z}\right) \subset U^c(X)\right\} \tag{3.64}$$

The erosion operator establishes that the point (x, z) belongs to the umbra of the eroded set if each point of the umbra of the element B^1 translated to the point (x, z) is under the umbra of X. A common way to visualise this process is to think that we move the structural element upwards in the grey level axis. The erosion border is the highest point we can reach without going out of the umbra. Similar to the binary case, this operator removes the borders of the set X by increasing the separation in holes. Thus, it actually erodes or shrinks the structures in an image. Fig. 3.41A illustrates the erosion operator for the image in Fig. 3.40A. Fig. 3.41A shows the result of the erosion for the structural element shown in the right. For clarity we have marked the origin of the structure element with a black spot. In the result, only the black pixels form the eroded set, and we use grey to highlight the pixels that were removed from the umbra of X. It is

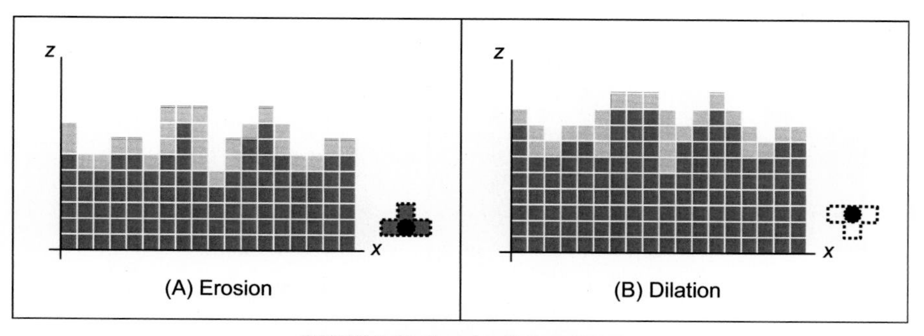

FIGURE 3.41 Grey level operators.

easy to see that when the structural element is translated to a point that is removed, its umbra intersects $U^c(X)$.

Analogous to binary morphology, the dilation operator can be seen as an erosion of the complement of the umbra of X. That is, a point belongs to the dilated set when all the points in the umbra of B^2 are in $U^c(X)$. This operator erodes or shrinks the set $U^c(X)$. When the complement is eroded, the umbra of X is dilated. The dilation operator fills holes decreasing the separation between prominent structures. This process is illustrated in Fig. 3.41B for the example in Fig. 3.41A. The structural element used is shown to the right in Fig. 3.41B. In the results, the black and grey pixels belong to the dilation. We use grey to highlight points that are added to the set. Points are removed from the complement and added to $U(X)$ by translating the structural element looking for points where the structural element is not fully included in $U^c(X)$. It is easy to see that when the structural element is translated to a point that is added to the dilation, its umbra intersects $U(X)$.

Similar to Eq. (3.58), dilation can be written as intersection of translated sets, thus it can be defined as an operator on the umbra of an image. That is,

$$U(X \oplus B) = \left\{(x,z) \,\middle|\, (x,z) \in U\left(\neg B^2_{x,z}\right)\right\} \tag{3.65}$$

The negation changes the structural element from being applied to the complement of the umbra to the umbra. That is, it changes the sign of the umbra to be defined below the curve. For the example in Fig. 3.41B, it is easy to see that if the structural element $\neg B^2$ is translated to any point added during the dilation, it intersects the umbra at least in one point.

3.6.4 Minkowski operators

Eqs. (3.63)–(3.65) require the computation of intersections of the pixels of a structural element that is translated to all the points in the image and for each grey level value. Thus, its computation involves significant processing. However, some simplifications can be made. For the erosion process in Eq. (3.63), the value of a pixel can be simply computed by comparing the grey level values of the structural element and corresponding image pixels'. The highest position that we can translate the structural element without intersecting the complement is given by the minimum value of the difference between the grey level of the image pixel and the corresponding pixel in the structural element. That is,

$$\Theta(x) = \min_i\{f(x-i) - B(i)\} \tag{3.66}$$

Here, $B(i)$ denotes the value of the ith pixel of the structural element. Fig. 3.42A illustrates a numerical example for this equation. The structural element has three pixels with values 0, 1, and 0, respectively. The subtractions for the position shown in Fig. 3.42A are $4-0=4$, $6-1=5$, and $7-0=7$. Thus, the minimum value is 4. As shown in Fig. 3.42A, this corresponds to the highest grey level value that we can move up to the structural element, and it is still fully contained in the umbra of the function.

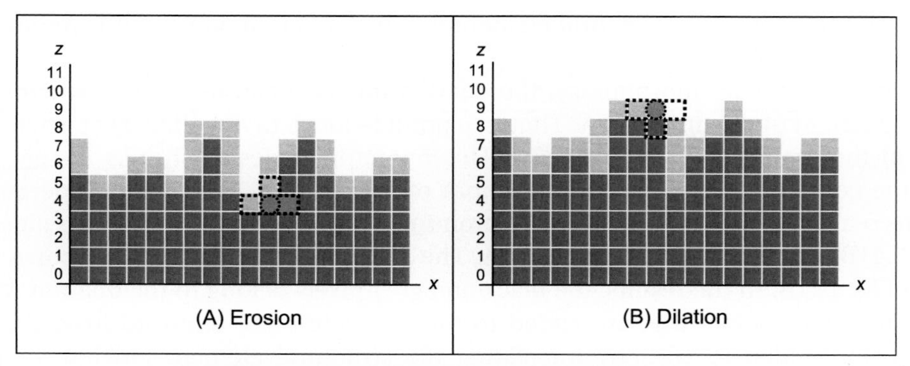

FIGURE 3.42 Example of Minkowski difference and addition.

Similar to Eq. (3.66), the dilation can be obtained by comparing the grey level values of the image and the structural element. For the dilation we have that

$$\oplus(x) = \max_i\{f(x-i) + B(i)\} \tag{3.67}$$

Fig. 3.42B illustrates a numerical example of this equation. For the position of the structural element in Fig. 3.42B, the summation gives the values $8 + 0 = 8$, $8 + 1 = 9$, and $4 + 0 = 4$. As shown in the figure, the maximum value of 9 corresponds to the point where the structural element still intersects the umbra, thus this point should be added to the dilation.

Eqs. (3.66) and (3.67) are known as the Minkowski operators, and they formalise set operations as summations and differences. Thus, they provide definitions very useful for computer implementations. Code 3.13 shows the implementation of the erosion operator based on Eq. (3.66). Similar to Code 3.6, the value pixels in the output image are obtained by translating the operator along the image pixels. The code subtracts the value of corresponding image and template pixels, and it sets the value of the pixel in the output image to the minima.

```
kernelCentre = (kernelSize - 1) / 2
for x,y in itertools.product(range(0, width), range(0, height)):

    minValue = 256;
    for wx,wy in itertools.product(range(0, kernelSize), range(0, kernelSize)):
        posY = y + wy - kernelCentre
        posX = x + wx - kernelCentre

        if posY > -1 and posY < height and  posX > -1 and posX <  width:
            sub = float(inputImage[posY,posX]) - kernelImage[wy, wx]

            if sub > 0 and sub < minValue:
                minValue = sub

    outputImage[y,x] = minValue
```

CODE 3.13 Erosion implementation.

```
kernelCentre = (kernelSize - 1) / 2
for x,y in itertools.product(range(0, width), range(0, height)):

    maxValue = 0;
    for wx,wy in itertools.product(range(0, kernelSize), range(0, kernelSize)):
        posY = y + wy - kernelCentre
        posX = x + wx - kernelCentre

        if posY > -1 and posY < height and  posX > -1 and posX <  width:
            sub = float(inputImage[posY,posX]) - kernelImage[wy, wx]

            if sub > 0 and sub > maxValue:
                maxValue = sub

    outputImage[y,x] = maxValue
```

CODE 3.14 Dilation implementation.

Code 3.14 shows the implementation of the dilation operator based on Eq. (3.67). This code is similar to Code 3.13, but corresponding values of the image and the structural element are added, and the maximum value is set as the result of the dilation.

Fig. 3.43 shows an example of the results obtained from the erosion and dilation using Codes 3.13 and 3.14. The original image shown in Fig. 3.43A has 256 × 144 pixels, and we used a flat structural element defined by an image with 5 × 5 pixels set to zero. For its simplicity, flat structural elements are very common in applications, and they are generally set to zero to avoid creating offsets in the grey levels. In Fig. 3.43, we can see that the erosion operation reduces the objects in the image whilst dilation expands white regions. We also used the erosion and dilation in succession to perform the opening show in Fig. 3.43D. The opening operation has a tendency to form regular regions of

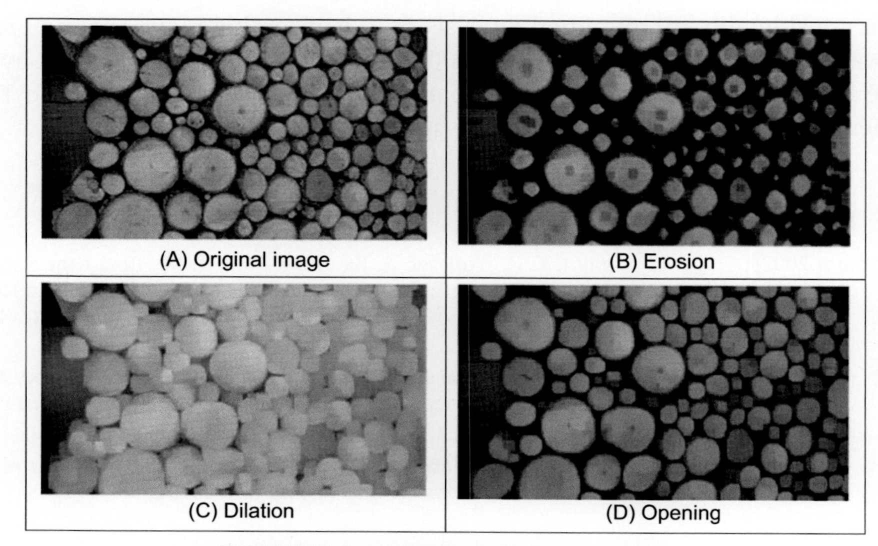

FIGURE 3.43 Examples of morphology operators.

similar size to the original image while removing peaks and small regions. The 'strength' of the operators is defined by the size of the structural elements. In these examples we use a fixed size, and we can see that it strongly modifies regions during dilation and erosion. Elaborate techniques have combined multiresolution structures and morphological operators to analyse an image with operators of different sizes [Montiel95]. We shall see the deployment of morphology later, to improve the results when finding moving objects in sequences of images, in Section 9.2.1.2.

3.7 Further reading

Many texts cover basic point and group operators in much detail, in particular some texts give many more examples, such as [Russ11], [Seul00] and there is a recent book intended to 'introduce students to image processing and analysis' [Russ 2017]. Much material here is well established so the texts here are rather dated now, but note that basics never change – and there is always room for new techniques which offer improved performance. There is a relatively new text concentrating on image processing using Python [Chityala15]. Some of the more advanced texts include more coverage of low-level operators, such as Rosenfeld and Kak [Rosenfeld82] and Castleman [Castleman96]. There is Matlab code for many of the low-level operations in this chapter in [Gonzalez09]. For study of the effect of the median operator on image data, see [Bovik87]. Some techniques receive little treatment in the established literature, except for [Chan05] (with extensive coverage of noise filtering too). The truncated median filter is covered again in Davies [Davies17]. Notwithstanding the discussion on more recent denoising operators at the end of Section 3.5.6, for further study of different statistical operators on ultrasound images, see [Evans96]. The concept of scale-space allows for considerably more refined analysis than is given here, and we shall revisit it later. It was originally introduced by Witkin [Witkin83] and further developed by others including Koenderink [Koenderink84] (who also considers the heat equation). There is even series of conferences devoted to scale-space and morphology.

References

[Abd-Elmoniem 2002] Abd-Elmoniem, K. Z., Youssef, A. B., and Kadah, Y. M., Real-time Speckle Reduction and Coherence Enhancement in Ultrasound Imaging via Nonlinear Anisotropic Diffusion, *IEEE Transactions on Biomedical Engineering*, **49**(9), pp 997-1014, 2002.

[Barash02] Barash, D., A Fundamental Relationship between Bilateral Filtering, Adaptive Smoothing and the Nonlinear Diffusion Equation, *IEEE Transactions on PAMI*, **24**(6), pp 844-849, 2002.

[Black98] Black, M. J., Sapiro, G., Marimont, D. H., and Meeger, D., Robust Anisotropic Diffusion, *IEEE Transactions on IP*, **7**(3), pp 421-432, 1998.

[Bovik87] Bovik A. C., Huang T. S., and Munson D. C., The Effect of Median Filtering on Edge Estimation and Detection, *IEEE Transactions on PAMI*, **9**(2), pp 181-194, 1987.

[Buades05] Buades, A., Coll, B., and Morel, J. M., A Non-local Algorithm for Image Denoising, *Proceedings of CVPR*, **2**, pp 60-65, 2005.

[Buades11] Buades, A., Coll, B., and Morel, J. M., Non-local Means Denoising. *Image Processing On Line*, **1**, pp 208-212, 2011.

[Campbell69] Campbell, J. D., *Edge Structure and the Representation of Pictures*, PhD Thesis, Univ. Missouri Columbia USA, 1969.

[Castleman96] Castleman, K. R., *Digital Image Processing*, Prentice Hall Inc., Englewood Cliffs N. J., USA, 1996.

[Chan05] Chan, T., and Shen, J., *Image Processing and Analysis: Variational, PDE, Wavelet, and Stochastic Methods*, Society for Industrial and Applied Mathematics, 2005.

[Chatterjee10] Chatterjee, P., and Milanfar, P., Is Denoising Dead? *IEEE Transactions on IP*, **19**(4), pp 895-911, 2010.

[Coupé09] Coupé, P., Hellier, P., Kervrann, C., and Barillot, C., Nonlocal Means-Based Speckle Filtering for Ultrasound Images. *IEEE Transactions on IP*, **18**(10), pp 2221-2229, 2009.

[Chityala15] Chityala, R., and Pudipeddi, S., *Image Processing and Acquisition Using Python*, CRC Press, Boca Raton, FL, USA, 2015.

[Cummings11] Cummings, A. H., Nixon, M. S., and Carter, J. N., The Image Ray Transform for Structural Feature Detection, *Pattern Recognition Letters*, **32**(15), pp 2053-2060, 2011.

[Dabov07] Dabov, K., Foi, A., Katkovnik, V., and Egiazarian, K., Image Denoising by Sparse 3-D Transform-Domain Collaborative Filtering, *IEEE Transactions on IP*, **16**(8), pp 2080-2095, 2007.

[Davies88] Davies, E. R., On the Noise Suppression Characteristics of the Median, Truncated Median and Mode Filters, *Pattern Recognition Letters*, **7**(2), pp 87-97, 1988.

[Davies17] Davies, E. R., *Computer Vision: Principles, Algorithms, Applications, Learning*, Academic Press, 5th Edition, 2017.

[Dowson11] Dowson, N., & Salvado, O. Hashed Nonlocal Means for Rapid Image Filtering. *IEEE Transactions on PAMI*, **33**(3), 485-499. 2011.

[Evans96] Evans, A. N., and Nixon M. S., Biased Motion-Adaptive Temporal Filtering for Speckle Reduction in Echocardiography, *IEEE Transactions on Medical Imaging*, **15**(1), pp 39-50, 1996.

[Fischl99] Fischl, B., and Schwartz, E. L., Adaptive Nonlocal Filtering: a Fast Alternative to Anisotropic Diffusion for Image Enhancement, *IEEE Transactions on PAMI*, **21**(1)pp 42-48, 1999.

[Glasbey93] Glasbey, C. A., An Analysis of Histogram-Based Thresholding Algorithms, *CVGIP: Graphical Models and Image Processing*, **55**(6), pp 532-537, 1993.

[Gonzalez17] Gonzalez, R. C., and Woods, R. E., *Digital Image Processing*, 4th Edition, Pearson Education, 2017.

[Gonzalez09] Gonzalez, R. C., Woods, R. E., and Eddins, S. L., *Digital Image Processing Using MATLAB*, 2nd Edition, Prentice Hall, 2009.

[Ham19] Ham, B., Cho, M., and Ponce, J., Robust Guided Image Filtering Using Nonconvex Potentials. *IEEE Transactions on PAMI*, **40**(1), pp 192-207, 2018.

[Hearn97] Hearn, D., and Baker, M. P., *Computer Graphics C Version*, 2nd Edition, Prentice Hall, Inc., Upper Saddle River, NJ, USA, 1997.

[Hodgson85] Hodgson, R. M., Bailey, D. G., Naylor, M. J., Ng A., and McNeill S. J., Properties, Implementations and Applications of Rank Filters, *Image and Vision Computing*, **3**(1), pp 3-14, 1985.

[Huang79] Huang, T., Yang, G., and Tang, G., A Fast Two-Dimensional Median Filtering Algorithm, *IEEE Transactions on ASSP*, **27**(1), pp 13-18, 1979.

[Hurley02] Hurley, D. J., Nixon, M. S. and Carter, J. N., Force Field Energy Functionals for Image Feature Extraction, *Image and Vision Computing*, **20**, pp 311-317, 2002.

[Hurley05] Hurley, D. J., Nixon, M. S. and Carter, J. N., Force Field Feature Extraction for Ear Biometrics, *Computer Vision and Image Understanding*, **98**(3), pp 491-512, 2005.

[Kervrann06] Kervrann, C., and Boulanger, J., Optimal Spatial Adaptation for Patch-Based Image Denoising. *IEEE Transactions on IP*, **15**(10), 2866-2878, 2006.

[Koenderink84] Koenderink, J., The Structure of Images, *Biological Cybernetics*, **50**, pp 363-370, 1984.

[Lee90] Lee, S. A., Chung, S. Y. and Park, R. H., A Comparative Performance Study of Several Global Thresholding Techniques for Segmentation, *CVGIP*, **52**, pp 171-190, 1990.

[Levin11] Levin, A., and Nadler, B., Natural Image Denoising: Optimality and Inherent Bounds, *Proceedings of CVPR*, 2011.

[Loupas87] Loupas, T., and McDicken, W. N., Noise Reduction in Ultrasound Images by Digital Filtering, *British Journal of Radiology*, **60**, pp 389-392, 1987.

[Montiel95] Montiel, M. E., Aguado, A. S., Garza, M., and Alarcón, J., Image Manipulation Using M-Filters in a Pyramidal Computer Model, *IEEE Transactions on PAMI*, **17**(11), pp 1110-1115, 1995.

[OpenCV-TM] OpenCV Template Operator https://github.com/opencv/opencv/blob/master/modules/imgproc/src/filter.cpp.

[Otsu79] Otsu, N., A Threshold Selection Method from Gray-Level Histograms, *IEEE Transactions on SMC*, **9**(1), pp 62-66, 1979.

[Paris08] Paris, S., and Durand, F., A Fast Approximation of the Bilateral Filter Using a Signal Processing Approach, *International Journal of Computer Vision*, **81**(1), pp 24 – 52, 2008.

[Perona90] Perona, P., and Malik, J., Scale-Space and Edge Detection Using Anisotropic Diffusion, *IEEE Transactions on PAMI*, **17**(7), pp 629-639, 1990.

[Pizer87] Pizer, S. M., Amburn, E. P., Austin, J. D., Cromartie, R., Geselowitz, A., Greer, T., ... and Zuiderveld, K., Adaptive Histogram Equalization and its Variations. *Computer Vision, Graphics, and Image Processing*, **39**(3), 355-368, 1987.

[Rosenfeld82] Rosenfeld, A and Kak A. C., Digital Picture Processing, 2nd Edition, vols. 1 and 2, Academic Press Inc., Orlando, FL, USA, 1982.

[Rosin01] Rosin, P. L., Unimodal Thresholding, *Pattern Recognition*, **34**(11), pp 2083-2096, 2001.

[Russ11] Russ, J. C., *The Image Processing Handbook*, 6th Edition, CRC Press (IEEE Press), Boca Raton, FL, USA, 2011.

[Russ17] Russ, J. C., and Russ, J. C., *Introduction to Image Processing and Analysis*, CRC Press, Boca Raton, FL, USA, 2017.

[Seul00] Seul, M., O'Gorman, L., and Sammon, M. J., *Practical Algorithms for Image Analysis: Descriptions, Examples, and Code*, Cambridge University Press, Cambridge, UK, 2000.

[Sahoo88] Sahoo, P. K., Soltani, S. Wong, A. K. C., and Chen, Y. C., Survey of Thresholding Techniques, *CVGIP*, **41**(2), pp 233-260, 1988.

[Serra86] Serra, J., Introduction to Mathematical Morphology, *Computer Vision, Graphics, and Image Processing*, **35**, pp 283-305, 1986.

[Soille13] Soille, P., *Morphological Image Analysis: Principles and Applications*, Springer Science & Business Media, Heidelberg, Germany, 2013.

[Shankar86] Shankar, P. M., Speckle Reduction in Ultrasound B Scans Using Weighted Averaging in Spatial Compounding, *IEEE Transactions on Ultrasonics, Ferroelectrics and Frequency Control*, **33**(6), pp754-758, 1986.

[Sternberg86] Sternberg, S. R., Gray Scale Morphology, *Computer Vision, Graphics, and Image Processing*, **35**, pp 333-355, 1986.

[Staal04] Staal, J., Abramoff, M. Niemeijer, M.,Viergever, M., van Ginneken, B., Ridge Based Vessel Segmentation in Color Images of the Retina, *IEEE Transactions on Medical Imaging*, **23**, pp 501-509, 2004.

[Tomasi98] C. Tomasi, and R. Manduchi, Bilateral Filtering for Gray and Color Images, *Proceedings of ICCV 1998*, pp 839-846, Bombay, India, 1998.

[Trier95] Trier, O. D., and Jain, A. K., Goal-Directed Evaluation of Image Binarisation Methods, *IEEE Transactions on PAMI*, **17**(12), pp 1191-1201, 1995.

[Tsiotsios13] Tsiotsios, C., and Petrou, M., On the Choice of the Parameters for Anisotropic Diffusion in Image Processing, *Pattern Recognition*, **46**(5), 1369-1381, 2013.

[Weiss06] Weiss, B., Fast Median and Bilateral Filtering, *Proceedings of ACM SIGGRAPH 2006*, pp 519-526, 2006.

[Witkin83] Witkin, A., Scale-Space Filtering: a New Approach to Multi-Scale Description, *Proceeding of International Joint Conference on Artificial Intelligence*, pp 1019-1021, 1983.

[Zhang17] Zhang, K., Zuo, K., Chen, Y., Meng, D., Beyond a Gaussian Denoiser: Residual Learning of Deep CNN for Image Denoising, *IEEE Transactions on IP*, **26**(7), pp 3142-3155, 2017.

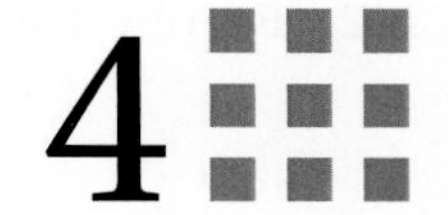

Low-level feature extraction (including edge detection)

4.1 Overview

We shall define *low-level features* to be those basic features that can be extracted automatically from an image without any shape information (information about spatial relationships). As such, thresholding is actually a form of low-level feature extraction performed as a point operation. Naturally, all of these approaches can be used in high-level feature extraction, where we find shapes in images. It is well known that we can recognise people from caricaturists' portraits. That is the first low-level feature we shall encounter. It is called *edge detection*, and it aims to produce a line drawing, like Fig 4.1B, something akin to a caricaturist's sketch though without the exaggeration a caricaturist would imbue. There are very basic techniques and more advanced ones, and we shall look at some of the most popular approaches. The first-order detectors are equivalent to first-order differentiation and, naturally, the second-order edge detection operators are equivalent to a one-higher level of differentiation. An alternative form of edge detection is called phase congruency, and we shall again see the frequency domain used to aid analysis, this time for low-level feature extraction.

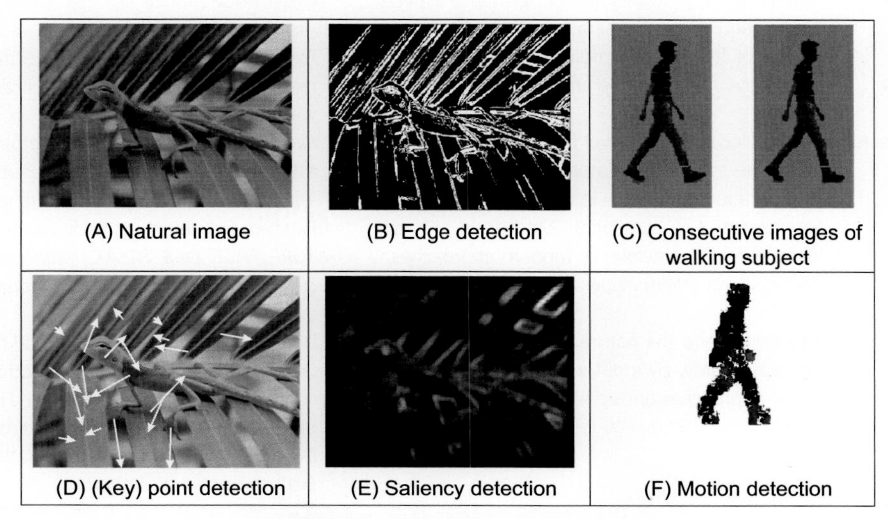

FIGURE 4.1 Low-level feature detection.

Feature Extraction and Image Processing for Computer Vision. https://doi.org/10.1016/B978-0-12-814976-8.00004-X

We shall also consider corner detection, Table 4.1, which can be thought of as detecting those points where lines bend very sharply with high curvature, such as the lizard's head in Figs. 4.1A and B. These are other low-level features that again can be extracted automatically from the image. These are largely techniques for localised feature extraction, in this case the curvature Fig. 4.1D, and the more modern approaches extend to the detection of localised regions or patches of interest, Fig. 4.1E. Finally, we shall investigate a technique that describes motion, called optical flow. This is illustrated in Figs. 4.1C and F with the optical flow from images of a walking man: the bits that are moving fastest are the brightest points, like the hands and the feet. All of these can provide a set of points, albeit points with different properties, but all are suitable for grouping for shape extraction. Consider a square box moving though a sequence of images. The edges are the perimeter of the box; the corners are the apices; the flow is how the box moves. All these can be collected together to find the moving box. We shall start with the edge detection techniques, with the first-order operators which accord with the chronology of development. The first-order techniques date back by more than 30 years.

Table 4.1 Overview of this chapter.

Main topic	Subtopics	Main points
First-order edge detection	What is an edge and how we detect it. The equivalence of operators to first-order differentiation and the insight this brings. The need for filtering and more sophisticated first-order operators.	Difference operation; *Roberts Cross*, smoothing, *Prewitt*, *Sobel*, *Canny*. Basis of the operators and frequency domain analysis.
Second-order edge detection	Relationship between first- and second-order differencing operations. The basis of a second-order operator. The need to include filtering and better operations.	Second-order differencing; *Laplacian*, *zero-crossing detection*; *Marr–Hildreth*, *Laplacian of Gaussian*, *difference of Gaussians*, *scale space*.
Other edge operators	Alternative approaches and performance aspects. Comparing different operators.	Other noise models: *Spacek*. Other edge models: *Petrou* and *Susan*.
Phase congruency	Phase for feature extraction; inverse Fourier transform; alternative form of edge and feature detection.	Frequency domain analysis; detecting a range of features; photometric invariance, wavelets.
Localised feature extraction	Finding localised low-level features; extension from curvature to patches. Nature of curvature and computation from edge information; by change in intensity; and by correlation. Motivation of patch detection and principles of modern approaches. Saliency and saliency operators.	*Planar curvature*; corners. Curvature estimation by change in *edge direction*; intensity change; *Harris* corner detector. Patch-based detectors; scale space. *SIFT*, *SURF*, *FAST*, *ORB*, *FREAK*, *brightness clustering*. *Saliency* operators. *Context aware saliency*.
Optical flow estimation	Movement and the nature of optical flow. Estimating the optical flow by a differential approach. Need for other approaches (including matching regions).	Detection by differencing. *Optical flow*; *velocity*; *aperture problem*; smoothness constraint. *Differential approach*; Horn and Schunk method; *correlation*. Extensions: *DeepFlow*; *EpicFlow* and *acceleration*. *Evaluation* of optical flow.

4.2 Edge detection

4.2.1 First-order edge detection operators

4.2.1.1 Basic operators

Many approaches to image interpretation are based on edges, since analysis based on edge detection is insensitive to change in the overall illumination level. *Edge detection* highlights *image contrast*. Detecting contrast, which is difference in intensity, can emphasise the boundaries of features within an image, since this is where image contrast occurs. This is, naturally, how human vision can perceive the perimeter of an object, since the object is of different intensity to its surroundings. Essentially, the boundary of an object is a step change in the intensity levels. The edge is at the position of the step change. To detect the edge position, we can use *first-order* differentiation since this emphasises change; first-order differentiation gives no response when applied to signals that do not change. The first edge detection operators to be studied here are group operators which aim to deliver an output which approximates the result of first-order differentiation.

A change in intensity can be revealed by differencing adjacent points. Differencing horizontally adjacent points will detect vertical changes in intensity and is often called a *horizontal edge detector* by virtue of its action. A horizontal operator will not show up horizontal changes in intensity since the difference is zero. (This is the form of edge detection used within the anisotropic diffusion smoothing operator in the previous chapter.) When applied to an image **P** the action of the horizontal edge detector forms the difference between two horizontally adjacent points, as such detecting the vertical edges, **Ex**, as

$$\mathbf{Ex}_{x,y} = \left|\mathbf{P}_{x,y} - \mathbf{P}_{x+1,y}\right| \qquad \forall x \in 1, N-1; y \in 1, N \tag{4.1}$$

In order to detect horizontal edges, we need a *vertical edge detector* which differences vertically adjacent points. This will determine horizontal intensity changes, but not vertical ones; so the vertical edge detector detects the horizontal edges, **Ey**, according to

$$\mathbf{Ey}_{x,y} = \left|\mathbf{P}_{x,y} - \mathbf{P}_{x,y+1}\right| \qquad \forall x \in 1, N; y \in 1, N-1 \tag{4.2}$$

Figs. 4.2B and C show the application of the vertical and horizontal operators to the synthesised image of the square in Fig. 4.2A. The left hand vertical edge in Fig. 4.2B appears to be beside the square by virtue of the forward differencing process. Likewise, the upper edge in Fig. 4.2C appears above the original square.

The combination of the horizontal and vertical detectors defines an operator **E** that can detect vertical and horizontal edges together. That is

$$\mathbf{E}_{x,y} = \left|\mathbf{P}_{x,y} - \mathbf{P}_{x+1,y} + \mathbf{P}_{x,y} - \mathbf{P}_{x,y+1}\right| \qquad \forall x, y \in 1, N-1 \tag{4.3}$$

which gives

$$\mathbf{E}_{x,y} = \left|2 \times \mathbf{P}_{x,y} - \mathbf{P}_{x+1,y} - \mathbf{P}_{x,y+1}\right| \qquad \forall x, y \in 1, N-1 \tag{4.4}$$

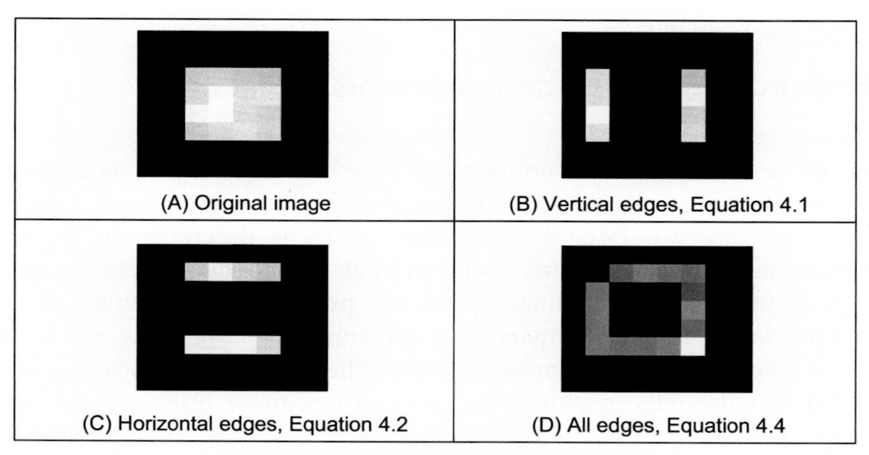

FIGURE 4.2 First-order edge detection.

Eq. (4.4) gives the coefficients of a differencing template which can be convolved with an image to detect all the edge points, such as those shown in Fig. 4.2D. As in the previous chapter, the current point of a template's operation (the position of the point we are computing a new value for) is shaded. The template shows only the weighting coefficients and not the modulus operation. Note that the bright point in the lower right corner of the edges of the square in Fig. 4.2D is much brighter than the other points. This is because it is the only point to be detected as an edge by both the vertical and the horizontal operators and is therefore much brighter than the other edge points. In contrast, the upper left corner point is detected by neither operator and so does not appear in the final image.

The template in Fig. 4.3 is convolved with the image to detect edges. The direct implementation of this operator, i.e. using Eq. (4.4) rather than template convolution, is given in Code 4.1. Naturally, template convolution could be used, but it is unnecessarily complex in this case.

Uniform thresholding (Section 3.3.4) can be used to select the brightest edge points. The threshold level controls the number of selected points; too high a level can select too few points, whereas too low a level can select too much noise. Often, the threshold level is chosen by experience or by experiment, but it can be determined automatically by considering edge data [Venkatesh95], or empirically [Haddon88]. For the moment, let us concentrate on the development of edge detection operators, rather than on their application.

2	−1
−1	0

FIGURE 4.3 Template for first-order difference.

```
function edge = basic_difference(image)

for x = 1:cols-2 %address all columns except border
  for y = 1:rows-2 %address all rows except border
    edge(y,x)=abs(2*image(y,x)-image(y+1,x)-image(y,x+1)); % Eq. 4.4
  end
end
```

CODE 4.1 First-order edge detection.

4.2.1.2 Analysis of the basic operators

Taylor series analysis reveals that differencing adjacent points provides an estimate of the first-order derivative at a point. If the difference is taken between points that are separated by Δx, then by Taylor expansion for $f(x+\Delta x)$ we obtain

$$f(x+\Delta x)=f(x)+\Delta x\times f'(x)+\frac{\Delta x^2}{2!}\times f''(x)+O(\Delta x^3) \tag{4.5}$$

By rearrangement, the first-order derivative $f'(x)$ is

$$f'(x)=\frac{f(x+\Delta x)-f(x)}{\Delta x}-O(\Delta x) \tag{4.6}$$

This shows that the difference between adjacent points is an estimate of the first-order derivative, with error $O(\Delta x)$. This error depends on the size of the interval Δx and on the complexity of the curve. When Δx is large, this error can be significant. The error is also large when the high-order derivatives take large values. In practice, the close sampling of image pixels and the reduced high frequency content make this approximation adequate. However, the error can be reduced by spacing the differenced points by one pixel. This is equivalent to computing the first-order difference delivered by Eq. (4.1) at two adjacent points, as a new horizontal difference **Exx** where

$$\mathbf{Exx}_{x,y}=\mathbf{Ex}_{x+1,y}+\mathbf{Ex}_{x,y}=\mathbf{P}_{x+1,y}-\mathbf{P}_{x,y}+\mathbf{P}_{x,y}-\mathbf{P}_{x-1,y}=\mathbf{P}_{x+1,y}-\mathbf{P}_{x-1,y} \tag{4.7}$$

This is equivalent to incorporating spacing to detect the edges **Exx** by

$$\mathbf{Exx}_{x,y}=\left|\mathbf{P}_{x+1,y}-\mathbf{P}_{x-1,y}\right| \qquad \forall x\in 2,N-1;y\in 1,N \tag{4.8}$$

To analyse this, again by Taylor series, we expand $f(x-\Delta x)$ as

$$f(x-\Delta x)=f(x)-\Delta x\times f'(x)+\frac{\Delta x^2}{2!}\times f''(x)-O(\Delta x^3) \tag{4.9}$$

By differencing Eq. (4.9) from Eq. (4.5), we obtain the first-order derivative as

$$f'(x)=\frac{f(x+\Delta x)-f(x-\Delta x)}{2\Delta x}-O(\Delta x^2) \tag{4.10}$$

Eq. (4.10) suggests that the estimate of the first-order difference is now the difference between points separated by one pixel, with error $O(\Delta x^2)$. If $\Delta x<1$, this error is clearly smaller than the error associated with differencing adjacent pixels, in Eq. (4.6). Again, averaging has reduced noise, or error. The template for a horizontal edge detection operator is given in Fig. 4.4A. This template gives the vertical edges detected at its centre

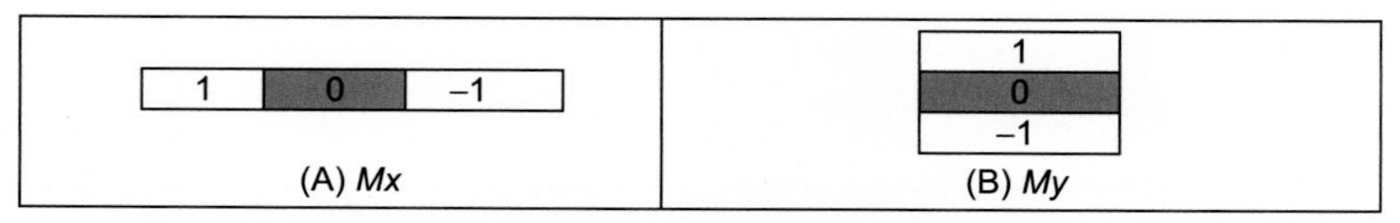

FIGURE 4.4 Templates for improved first-order difference.

pixel. A transposed version of the template gives a vertical edge detection operator, Fig. 4.4B.

The *Roberts cross operator* [Roberts65] was one of the earliest edge detection operators. It implements a version of basic first-order edge detection and uses two templates which difference pixel values in a diagonal manner, as opposed to along the axes' directions. The two templates are called M^+ and M^- and are given in Fig. 4.5.

In implementation, the maximum value delivered by application of these templates is stored as the value of the edge at that point. The edge point $\mathbf{E}_{x,y}$ is then the maximum of the two values derived by convolving the two templates at an image point $\mathbf{P}_{x,y}$:

$$\mathbf{E}_{x,y} = \max\{|M^+ * \mathbf{P}_{x,y}|, |M^- * \mathbf{P}_{x,y}|\} \qquad \forall x, y \in 1, N-1 \tag{4.11}$$

The application of the Roberts cross operator to the image of the square is shown in Fig. 4.6. The two templates provide the results in Figs. 4.6A and B, and the result delivered by the Roberts operator is shown in Fig. 4.6C. Note that the corners of the square now appear in the edge image, by virtue of the diagonal differencing action, whereas they were less apparent in Fig. 4.2D (where the top left corner did not appear).

An alternative to taking the maximum is to simply add the results of the two templates together to combine horizontal and vertical edges. There are of course more varieties of edges, and it is often better to consider the two templates as providing components of an *edge vector*: the strength of the edge along the horizontal and vertical axes. These give components of a vector and can be added in a vectorial manner (which is perhaps more usual for the Roberts operator). The *edge magnitude* is the length of the vector, the *edge direction* is the vector's orientation, as shown in Fig. 4.7.

4.2.1.3 Prewitt edge detection operator

Edge detection is akin to differentiation. Since it detects change, it is bound to respond to noise, as well as to step-like changes in image intensity (its frequency domain analogue is high-pass filtering as illustrated in Fig. 2.30C). It is therefore prudent to incorporate *averaging* within the edge detection process. We can then extend the vertical template, *Mx*, along three rows, and the horizontal template, *My*, along three columns. These give the *Prewitt edge detection* operator [Prewitt66] that consists of two templates, Fig. 4.8.

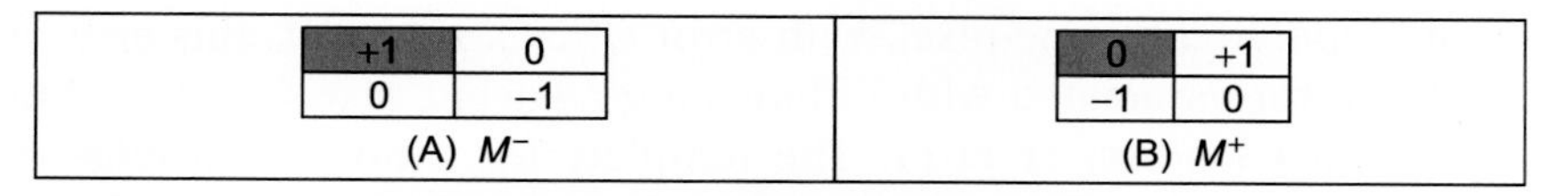

FIGURE 4.5 Templates for Roberts cross operator.

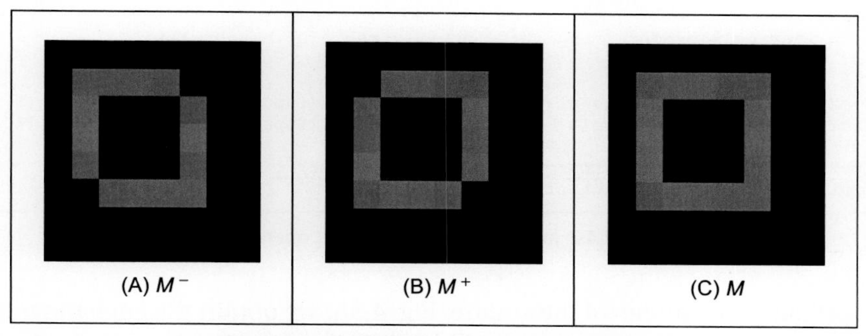

FIGURE 4.6 Applying the Roberts cross operator.

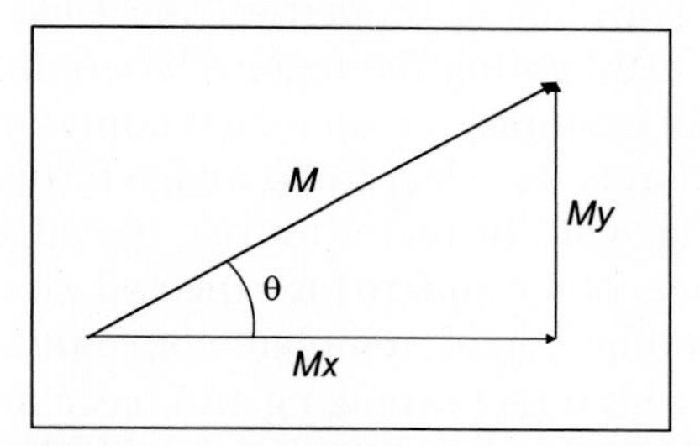

FIGURE 4.7 Edge detection in vectorial format.

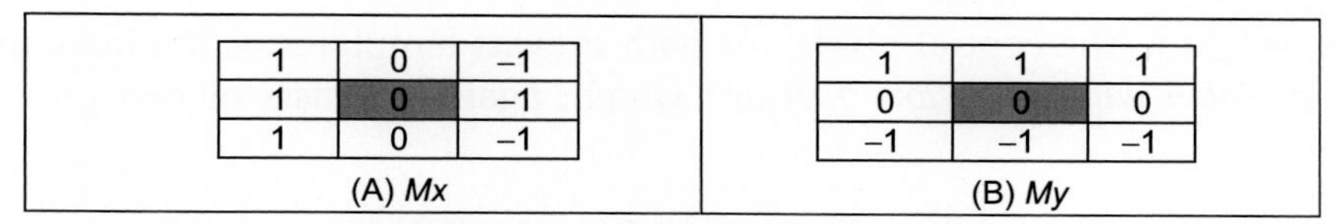

FIGURE 4.8 Templates for Prewitt operator.

This gives two results: the rate of change of brightness along each axis. As such, this is the vector illustrated in Fig. 4.7: the *edge magnitude, M,* is the length of the vector and the *edge direction,* θ, is the angle of the vector

$$M(x,y) = \sqrt{Mx(x,y)^2 + My(x,y)^2} \tag{4.12}$$

$$\theta(x,y) = \tan^{-1}\left(\frac{My(x,y)}{Mx(x,y)}\right) \tag{4.13}$$

The signs of *Mx* and *My* can be used to determine the appropriate quadrant for the edge direction. An implementation of the Prewitt operator is given in Code 4.2. In this code, both templates operate on a 3 × 3 region. Again, template convolution could be used to implement this operator, but (as with direct averaging and basic first-order edge detection) it is less suited to small templates.

```
for x,y in itertools.product(range(0, width-1), range(0, height-1)):
    mX,mY = 0.0, 0.0
    for c in range(-1, 2):
        mX += float(inputImage[y - 1, x + c]) - float(inputImage[y + 1, x + c])
        mY += float(inputImage[y + c, x - 1]) - float(inputImage[y + c, x + 1])

    outputMagnitude[y,x] = math.sqrt(mX * mX + mY * mY)
    outputDirection[y,x] = math.atan2(mY, mX)
```

CODE 4.2 Implementing the Prewitt operator.

When applied to the image of the square, Fig. 4.9A, we obtain the edge magnitude and direction, Figs. 4.9B and D, respectively. The edge direction in Fig. 4.9D is shown as an image as the numbers are rather uninformative. Though the regions of edge points are wider due to the operator's averaging properties, the edge data are clearer than the earlier first-order operator, highlighting the regions where intensity changed in a more reliable fashion (compare, for example, the upper left corner of the square which was not revealed earlier). The direction is less clear in an image format and is better exposed by Matlab's `quiver` format in Fig. 4.9C. In vector format, the edge direction data are clearly less well defined at the corners of the square (as expected, since the first-order derivative is discontinuous at these points). Again, template convolution could be used to implement this operator, but (as with direct averaging and basic first-order edge detection) it is less suited to small templates.

4.2.1.4 Sobel edge detection operator

When the weight at the central pixels, for both Prewitt templates, is doubled, this gives the famous *Sobel edge detection operator* which, again, consists of two templates to

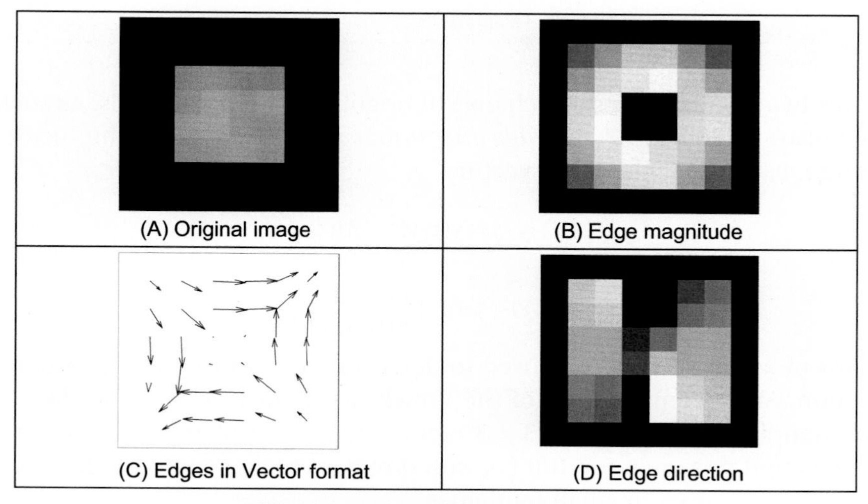

FIGURE 4.9 Applying the Prewitt operator.

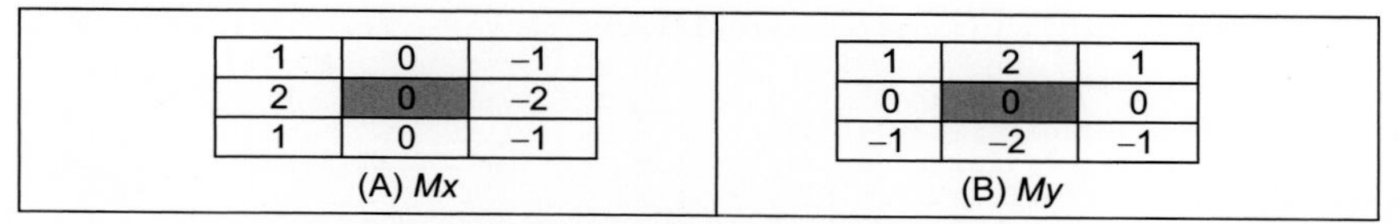

(A) *Mx*

1	0	−1
2	0	−2
1	0	−1

(B) *My*

1	2	1
0	0	0
−1	−2	−1

FIGURE 4.10 Templates for Sobel operator.

determine the edge in vector form. The Sobel operator was the most popular edge detection operator until the development of edge detection techniques with a theoretical basis. It proved popular because it gave, overall, a better performance than other contemporaneous edge detection operators, such as the Prewitt operator. The templates for the Sobel operator can be found in Fig. 4.10.

The implementation of these masks is very similar to the implementation of the Prewitt operator, Code 4.2, again operating on a 3×3 subpicture. However, all template-based techniques can be larger than 5×5, so, as with any group operator, there is a 7×7 Sobel and so on. The virtue of a larger edge detection template is that it involves more smoothing to reduce noise but edge blurring becomes a great problem. The estimate of edge direction can be improved with more smoothing since it is particularly sensitive to noise. So how do we form larger templates, say for 5×5 or 7×7? Few textbooks state the original Sobel derivation, but it has been attributed [Heath97] as originating from a PhD thesis [Sobel70]. Unfortunately a theoretical basis, that can be used to calculate the coefficients of larger templates, is rarely given. One approach to a theoretical basis is to consider the optimal forms of averaging and of differencing. Gaussian averaging has already been stated to give optimal averaging. The binomial expansion gives the integer coefficients of a series that, in the limit, approximates the normal distribution. Pascal's triangle gives sets of coefficients for a smoothing operator which, in the limit, approaches the coefficients of a Gaussian smoothing operator. Pascal's triangle is then:

Window size									
2				1		1			
3			1		2		1		
4		1		3		3		1	
5	1		4		6		4		1

This gives the (unnormalised) coefficients of an optimal discrete smoothing operator (it is essentially a Gaussian operator with integer coefficients). The rows give the coefficients for increasing template, or window, size. The coefficients of smoothing within the Sobel operator Fig. 4.10 are those for a window size of 3. In Python, the template coefficients can be calculated as shown in Code 4.3. The code uses the array `smooth` to store a pair of 2D templates that contain the coefficients in x and y directions.

```
for x,y in itertools.product(range(0, kernelSize), range(0, kernelSize)):

    # Smooth
    smooth[y,x,0] = factorial(kernelSize - 1) /                          \
                    (factorial(kernelSize - 1 - x) * factorial(x))
    smooth[y,x,1] = factorial(kernelSize - 1) /                          \
                    (factorial(kernelSize - 1 - y) * factorial(y))

    # Pascal
    if (kernelSize - 2 - x >= 0):
        pascal1[y,x,0] = factorial(kernelSize - 2) /                     \
                         (factorial(kernelSize - 2 - x) * factorial(x))

    if (kernelSize - 2 - y >= 0):
        pascal1[y,x,1] = factorial(kernelSize - 2) /                     \
                         (factorial(kernelSize - 2 - y) * factorial(y))

    # Pascal shift to the right
    xp = x - 1
    if (kernelSize - 2 - xp >= 0 and xp >= 0):
        pascal2[y,x,0] = factorial(kernelSize - 2) /                     \
                         (factorial(kernelSize - 2 - xp) * factorial(xp))

    yp = y - 1
    if (kernelSize - 2 - yp >= 0 and yp >= 0):
        pascal2[y,x,1] = factorial(kernelSize - 2) /                     \
                         (factorial(kernelSize - 2 - yp) * factorial(yp))

    # Sobel
    sobel[y,x,0] = smooth[y,x,1] * (pascal1[y,x,0] - pascal2[y,x,0])
    sobel[y,x,1] = smooth[y,x,0] * (pascal1[y,x,1] - pascal2[y,x,1])
```

CODE 4.3 Creating Sobel kernels.

The differencing coefficients are given by Pascal's triangle for subtraction:

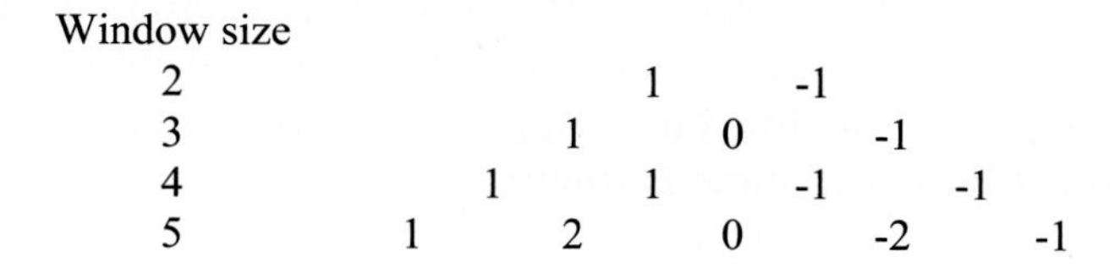

Window size								
2				1		-1		
3			1		0		-1	
4		1		1		-1		-1
5	1		2		0		-2		-1

This can be implemented by subtracting the templates derived from two adjacent Pascal expansions from a smaller window size. In Code 4.3, the arrays `pascal1` and `pascal2` have the expansions for the Pascal triangle and a shifted version. The code uses the factorial definition of the Pascal coefficients to compute both expansions, but the second one can be also computed by shifting the values of the first array. Note that each Pascal expansion has a template for vertical and horizontal direction. Fig. 4.11 shows the coefficients computed with the implementation for a 7x7 window size.

The differencing template is then given by the difference between two Pascal expansions, as shown in Code 4.3. The array `Sobel` stores the result of the difference between the two shifted templates. The result is multiplied by the smoothing array. Thus, the result gives the coefficients of optimal differencing and optimal smoothing. This

(A) Smooth 7×7	(B) Pascal 7×7	(C) Shift 7×7	(D) Sobel kernel 7×7
[1 6 15 20 15 6 1]	[1 5 10 10 5 1 0]	[0 1 5 10 10 5 1]	[1 4 5 0 -5 -4 -1]
[1 6 15 20 15 6 1]	[1 5 10 10 5 1 0]	[0 1 5 10 10 5 1]	[6 24 30 0 -30 -24 -6]
[1 6 15 20 15 6 1]	[1 5 10 10 5 1 0]	[0 1 5 10 10 5 1]	[15 60 75 0 -75 -60 -15]
[1 6 15 20 15 6 1]	[1 5 10 10 5 1 0]	[0 1 5 10 10 5 1]	[20 80 100 0 -100 -80 -20]
[1 6 15 20 15 6 1]	[1 5 10 10 5 1 0]	[0 1 5 10 10 5 1]	[15 60 75 0 -75 -60 -15]
[1 6 15 20 15 6 1]	[1 5 10 10 5 1 0]	[0 1 5 10 10 5 1]	[6 24 30 0 -30 -24 -6]
[1 6 15 20 15 6 1]	[1 5 10 10 5 1 0]	[0 1 5 10 10 5 1]	[1 4 5 0 -5 -4 -1]

FIGURE 4.11 Creating templates for the Sobel operator.

general form of the Sobel operator combines optimal smoothing along one axis, with optimal differencing along the other.

Fig. 4.11 shows the full process used to generate the 7×7 Sobel kernels. Each column shows the template computed with Code 4.3. Fig. 4.11A shows the smoothing template. Figs. 4.11B and C show the Pascal and shifted Pascal templates. Fig. 4.11D shows the final kernel.

The Sobel templates can be applied by operating on a matrix of dimension equal to the window size, from which edge magnitude and gradient are calculated. The implementation in Code 4.4 convolves the generalised Sobel templates (of size chosen to be `kernelize`) with the image supplied as argument, to give an output which contains the images of edge magnitude and direction. The kernel is created according to the implementation in Code 4.3.

The results of applying the 5×5 Sobel operator can be seen in Fig. 4.12. The original image Fig. 4.12A has many edges of the leaves and around the lizard's eye. This is shown in the edge magnitude image, Fig. 4.12B. When this is thresholded at a suitable value, many edge points are found, as shown in Fig. 4.12C. Note that in areas of the image where the brightness remains fairly constant, such as within the blades of the leaves,

```
# Create Kernel
sobelX, sobelY = createSobelKernel(kernelSize)

# The center of the kernel
kernelCentre = (kernelSize - 1) / 2

# Convolution with two kernels
for x,y in itertools.product(range(0, width), range(0, height)):
    mX, wX, mY, wY = 0.0, 0.0, 0.0, 0.0
    for wx,wy in itertools.product(range(0, kernelSize), range(0, kernelSize)):
        posY = y + wy - kernelCentre
        posX = x + wx - kernelCentre

        if posY > -1 and posY <  height and  posX > -1 and posX <  width:
            mX += float(inputImage[posY,posX]) * sobelX[wy, wx]
            wX += sobelX[wy, wx]

            mY += float(inputImage[posY,posX]) * sobelY[wy, wx]
            wY += sobelY[wy, wx]

    if wX > 0:  mX = mX / wX
    if wY > 0:  mY = mY / wY

    outputMagnitude[y,x] = math.sqrt(mX * mX + mY * mY)
    outputDirection[y,x] = math.atan2(mX, -mY)
```

CODE 4.4 Generalised Sobel operator.

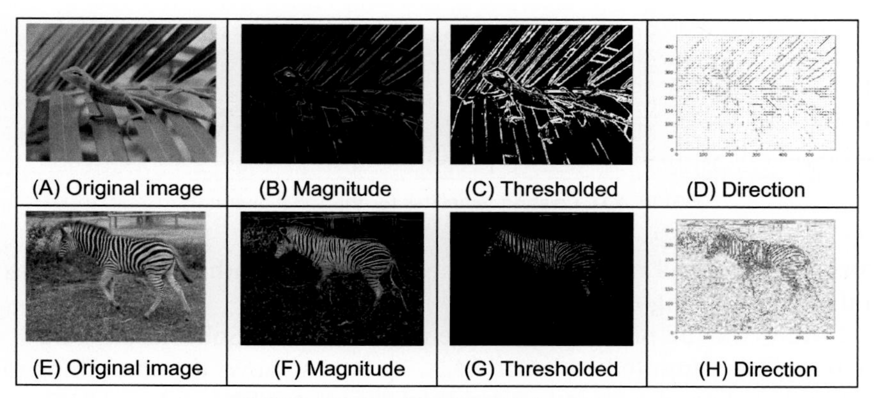

FIGURE 4.12 Applying the Sobel operator.

there is little change which is reflected by low edge magnitude and few points in the thresholded data. The example in the last row in Fig. 4.12 illustrates how edge magnitude and direction are well defined in image regions with high contrast.

The Sobel edge direction data can be arranged to point in different ways, as can the direction provided by the Prewitt operator. If the templates are inverted to be of the form shown in Fig. 4.13, the edge direction will be inverted around both axes. If only one of the templates is inverted, the measured edge direction will be inverted about the chosen axis.

This gives four possible directions for measurement of the *edge direction* provided by the Sobel operator, two of which (for the templates of Figs 4.10 and 4.13) are illustrated in Figs. 4.14A and B, respectively, where inverting the *Mx* template does not highlight discontinuity at the corners. (The edge magnitude of the Sobel applied to the square is not shown, but is similar to that derived by application of the Prewitt operator, Fig. 4.9B). By swapping the Sobel templates, the measured edge direction can be arranged to be normal to the edge itself (as opposed to tangential data along the edge). This is illustrated in Figs. 4.14C and D for swapped versions of the templates given in Figs 4.10 and 4.13, respectively. The rearrangement can lead to simplicity in algorithm construction when finding shapes, as to be shown later. Any algorithm which uses edge direction for finding shapes must know precisely which arrangement has been used, since the edge direction can be used to speed algorithm performance, but it must map precisely to the expected image data if used in that way.

−1	0	1
−2	0	2
−1	0	1

(A) −*Mx*

−1	−2	−1
0	0	0
1	2	1

(B) −*My*

FIGURE 4.13 Inverted templates for Sobel operator.

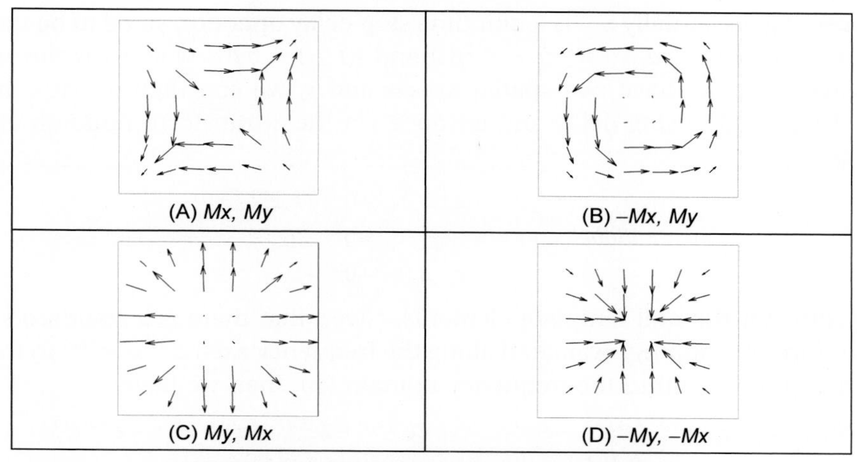

FIGURE 4.14 Alternative arrangements of edge direction.

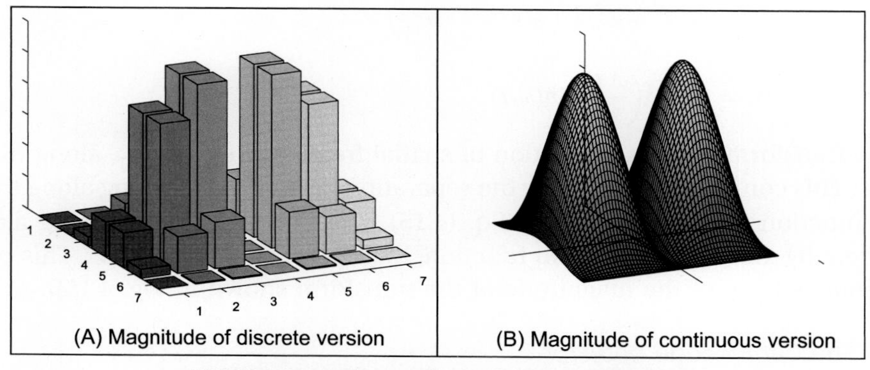

FIGURE 4.15 Fourier transform of the Sobel operator.

Detecting edges by *template convolution* again has a frequency domain interpretation. The magnitude of the *Fourier transform* of a 7 × 7 Sobel template of Fig. 4.11 is given in Fig. 4.15. The magnitude of the discrete Fourier transform is given in relief in Fig. 4.15A. The template is for horizontal differencing action, *Mx*, In Fig. 4.15A, the vertical frequencies are selected from a region near the origin (*low-pass* filtering – consistent with averaging over five lines), whereas the horizontal frequencies are selected away from the origin (*high-pass* – consistent with the differencing action). This highlights the action of the Sobel operator: to combine smoothing along one axis with differencing along the other. In Fig. 4.15A, the smoothing is of vertical spatial frequencies, whilst the differencing is of horizontal spatial frequencies.

An alternative frequency domain analysis of the Sobel can be derived via the *z-transform* operator. This is more the domain of signal processing courses in electronic and electrical engineering and is included here for completeness and for linkage with signal processing. Essentially z^{-1} is a unit time step delay operator, so z can be thought of a unit (time step) advance, so $f(t\text{-}\tau) = z^{-1}f(t)$ and $f(t+\tau) = z\,f(t)$ where τ is the sampling interval. Given that we have two spatial axes x and y, we can then express the Sobel operator of Fig. 4.13A using delay and advance via the z-transform notation along the two axes as

$$Sobel(x,y) = \begin{array}{lll} -z_x^{-1}z_y^{-1} & +0 & +z_x z_y^{-1} \\ -2z_x^{-1} & +0 & +2z_x \\ -z_x^{-1}z_y & +0 & +z_x z_y \end{array} \tag{4.14}$$

including zeros for the null template elements. Given that there is a standard substitution (by conformal mapping, evaluated along the frequency axis) $z^{-1} = e^{-j\omega t}$ to transform from the time (z) domain to the frequency domain (ω), then we have

$$\begin{aligned} Sobel(\omega_x, \omega_y) &= -e^{-j\omega_x t}e^{-j\omega_y t} + e^{j\omega_x t}e^{-j\omega_y t} - 2e^{-j\omega_x t} + 2e^{j\omega_x t} - e^{-j\omega_x t}e^{j\omega_y t} + e^{j\omega_x t}e^{j\omega_y t} \\ &= \left(e^{-j\omega_y t} + 2 + e^{j\omega_y t}\right)\left(-e^{-j\omega_x t} + e^{j\omega_x t}\right) \\ &= \left(e^{\frac{-j\omega_y t}{2}} + e^{\frac{j\omega_y t}{2}}\right)^2\left(-e^{-j\omega_x t} + e^{j\omega_x t}\right) \\ &= 8j\cos^2\left(\frac{\omega_y t}{2}\right)\sin(\omega_x t) \end{aligned} \tag{4.15}$$

where the transform *Sobel* is a function of spatial frequency ω_x and ω_y, along the x and the y axes. This confirms rather nicely the separation between smoothing along the y axis (the cos function in the first part of Eq. (4.15), low-pass) and differencing along the other – here by differencing (the sin function, high-pass) along the x axis. This provides the continuous form of the magnitude of the transform shown in Fig. 4.15B.

4.2.1.5 The Canny edge detector

The *Canny edge detection operator* [Canny86] is perhaps the most popular edge detection technique at present. It was formulated with three main objectives:

1. optimal detection with no spurious responses;
2. good localisation with minimal distance between detected and true edge position and
3. single response to eliminate multiple responses to a single edge.

The first requirement aims to reduce the response to noise. This can be effected by *optimal smoothing*; Canny was the first to demonstrate that Gaussian filtering is optimal for edge detection (within his criteria). The second criterion aims for accuracy: edges are to be detected, in the right place. This can be achieved by a process of *nonmaximum suppression* (which is equivalent to peak detection). Nonmaximum suppression retains only those points at the top of a ridge of edge data, whilst suppressing all others. This results in thinning: the output of nonmaximum suppression is thin lines of edge points, in the right place. The third constraint concerns location of a single-edge point in response to a change in brightness. This is because more than one edge can be denoted to be present, consistent with the output obtained by earlier edge operators.

Canny showed that the *Gaussian operator* was optimal for image smoothing. Recalling that the Gaussian operator $g(x,y,\sigma)$ is given by

$$g(x,y,\sigma) = e^{\frac{-(x^2+y^2)}{2\sigma^2}} \tag{4.16}$$

By differentiation, for unit vectors $U_x = [1,0]$ and $U_y = [0,1]$ along the co-ordinate axes, we obtain

$$\begin{aligned}\nabla g(x,y) &= \frac{\partial g(x,y,\sigma)}{\partial x}U_x + \frac{\partial g(x,y,\sigma)}{\partial y}U_y \\ &= -\frac{x}{\sigma^2}e^{\frac{-(x^2+y^2)}{2\sigma^2}}U_x - \frac{y}{\sigma^2}e^{\frac{-(x^2+y^2)}{2\sigma^2}}U_y\end{aligned} \tag{4.17}$$

Eq. (4.17) gives a way to calculate the coefficients of a *derivative of Gaussian* template that combines first-order differentiation with Gaussian smoothing. This is a smoothed image, and so the edge will be a ridge of data. In order to mark an edge at the correct point (and to reduce multiple responses), we can convolve an image with an operator which gives the first derivative in a direction normal to the edge. The maximum of this function should be the peak of the edge data, where the gradient in the original image is sharpest, and hence the location of the edge. Accordingly, we seek an operator, G_n, which is a first derivative of a Gaussian function g in the direction of the normal, $\mathbf{n}_\perp$

$$G_n = \frac{\partial g}{\partial \mathbf{n}_\perp} \tag{4.18}$$

where $\mathbf{n}_\perp$ can be estimated from the first-order derivative of the Gaussian function g convolved with the image $\mathbf{P}$, and scaled appropriately as

$$\mathbf{n}_\perp = \frac{\nabla(\mathbf{P} * g)}{|\nabla(\mathbf{P} * g)|} \tag{4.19}$$

The location of the true edge point is then at the maximum point of G_n convolved with the image. This maximum is when the differential (along $\mathbf{n}_\perp$) is zero

$$\frac{\partial(G_n * \mathbf{P})}{\partial \mathbf{n}_\perp} = 0 \tag{4.20}$$

By substitution of Eq. (4.18) in Eq. (4.20),

$$\frac{\partial^2(G * \mathbf{P})}{\partial \mathbf{n}_\perp^2} = 0 \tag{4.21}$$

Eq. (4.21) provides the basis for an operator which meets one of Canny's criteria, namely that edges should be detected in the correct place. This is nonmaximum suppression, which is equivalent to retaining peaks (and thus equivalent to differentiation perpendicular to the edge), which thins the response of the edge detection operator to give edge points which are in the right place, without multiple response and with

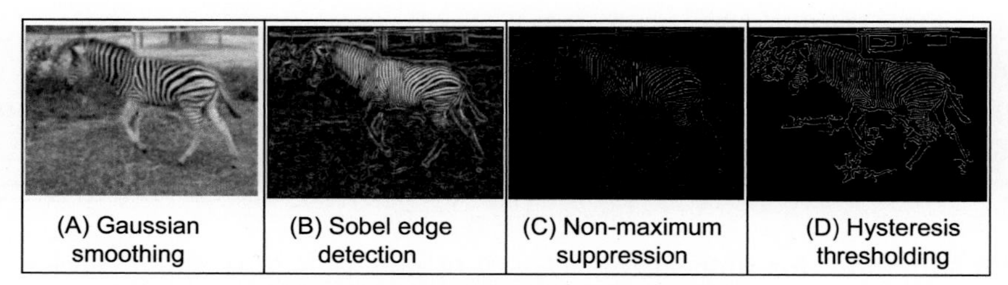

FIGURE 4.16 Stages in Canny edge detection.

minimal response to noise. However, it is virtually impossible to achieve an exact implementation of Canny given the requirement to estimate the normal direction.

A common approximation is as illustrated in Fig. 4.16:

1. use *Gaussian smoothing* (as in Section 3.4.5), Fig. 4.16A;
2. use the *Sobel operator*, Fig. 4.16B;
3. use *nonmaximum supp*ression, Fig. 4.16C and
4. threshold with *hysteresis* to connect edge points, Fig. 4.16D.

Note that the first two stages can be combined using a version of Eq. (4.17), but are separated here so that all stages in the edge detection process can be shown clearly. An alternative implementation of Canny's approach [Deriche87] used Canny's criteria to develop two-dimensional recursive filters, claiming performance and implementation advantage over the approximation here.

Nonmaximum suppression essentially locates the highest points in the edge magnitude data. This is performed by using edge direction information, to check that points are at the peak of a ridge. Given a 3 × 3 region, a point is at a maximum if the gradient at either side of it is less than the gradient at the point. This implies that we need values of gradient along a line which is normal to the edge at a point. This is illustrated in Fig. 4.17, which shows the neighbouring points to the point of interest, $\mathbf{P}_{x,y}$, the edge direction at $\mathbf{P}_{x,y}$ and the normal to the edge direction at $\mathbf{P}_{x,y}$. The point $\mathbf{P}_{x,y}$ is to be marked as maximum if its gradient, $M(x,y)$, exceeds the gradient at points 1 and 2, M_1 and M_2, respectively. Since we have a discrete neighbourhood, M_1 and M_2 need to be interpolated, First-order interpolation using Mx and My at $\mathbf{P}_{x,y}$, and the values of Mx and My for the neighbours gives

$$M_1 = \frac{My}{Mx} M(x+1, y-1) + \frac{Mx - My}{Mx} M(x, y-1) \tag{4.22}$$

and

$$M_2 = \frac{My}{Mx} M(x-1, y+1) + \frac{Mx - My}{Mx} M(x, y+1) \tag{4.23}$$

The point $\mathbf{P}_{x,y}$ is then marked as a maximum if $M(x,y)$ exceeds both M_1 and M_2., otherwise it is set to zero. In this manner the peaks of the ridges of edge magnitude data are retained, whilst those not at the peak are set to zero. Code 4.5 illustrates the implementation of nonmaximum suppression. It takes as inputs the images `magnitude` and `angle`

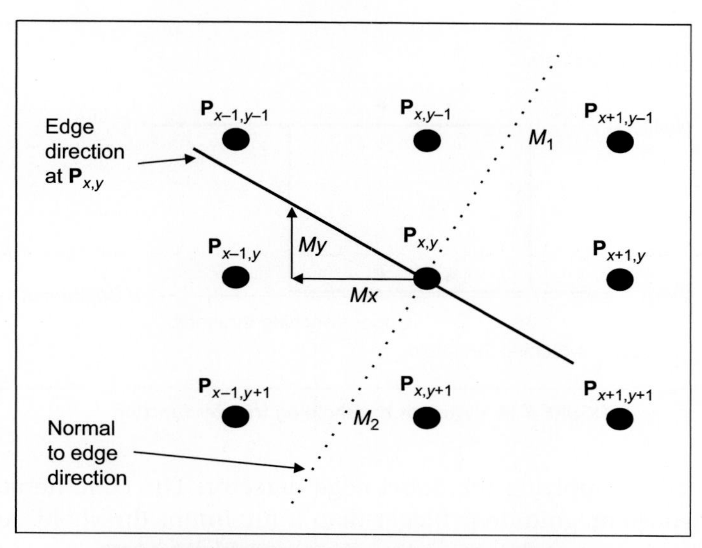

FIGURE 4.17 Interpolation in nonmaximum suppression.

```
for x,y in itertools.product(range(border, width-border),                    \
                             range(border, height-border)):
    # Only potential edges can be maximum
    if magnitude[y,x] > lowerT:
        # The normal angle is perpendicular to the edge angle
        normalAngle = angle[y,x] - pi / 2.0

        # Make sure the angle is between 0 and pi
        while normalAngle < 0:   normalAngle += pi
        while normalAngle > pi:  normalAngle -= pi

        # Angle defining the first point
        baseAngle = int( 4 * normalAngle / pi ) * (pi / 4.0)

        # Integer delta positions for interpolation
        # We use -y since the image origin is in top corner
        x1, y1 = int(round(cos(baseAngle))), -int(round(sin(baseAngle)))
        x2, y2 = int(round(cos(baseAngle + pi / 4.0))),                       \
                -int(round(sin(baseAngle + pi / 4.0)))

        # How far we are from (x1,y1).
        # Maximum difference is pi / 4.0, so we multiply by 2
        w = cos(2.0*(normalAngle - baseAngle))

        # Point to interpolate
        M1 = w * magnitude[y+y1,x+x1] + (1.0 - w) * magnitude[y+y2,x+x2]

        # Point to interpolate for pixels in the other side of the edge
        M2 = w * magnitude[y-y1,x-x1] + (1.0 - w) * magnitude[y-y2,x-x2]

        # Determine if it is a maximum. If so make sure it will be preserved
        if magnitude[y,x] > M1 and magnitude[y,x] > M2:
            maxImage[y,x] = magnitude[y,x]
```

CODE 4.5 Nonmaximum suppression.

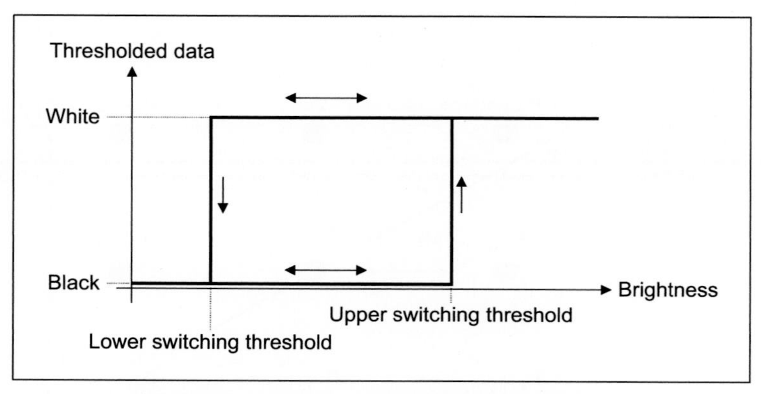

FIGURE 4.18 Hysteresis thresholding transfer function.

that were obtained by applying the Sobel edge detector. The code iterates for all pixel positions `(x,y)` whose magnitude is bigger than a minimum threshold. Any point lower than this threshold cannot be an edge. The variable `normalAngle` stores the angle perpendicular to the edge. This angle is used to obtain the two pixels defined by the variables `(x1,y1)` and `(x2,y2)`. These points are used to compute M_1 and M_2. If the magnitude in the point `(x,y)` is greater than these values, then we consider that the point is a maximum. The resulting `maxImage` will be zero if the point is not maximum and the value of the magnitude otherwise.

The result of nonmaximum suppression is used in the hysteresis thresholding process. As illustrated in Fig. 4.18, this process delineates the borders by choosing the maximum pixels. The transfer function associated with *hysteresis thresholding* is shown in Fig. 4.18. Points are set to white (edges) once the upper threshold is exceeded and set to black when the lower threshold is reached. The arrows reflect possible movement: there is only one way to change from black to white and vice versa.

The application of nonmaximum suppression and hysteresis thresholding is illustrated in Fig. 4.19. This contains a ridge of edge data, the edge magnitude. The action of nonmaximum suppression is to select the points along the top of the ridge. Given that

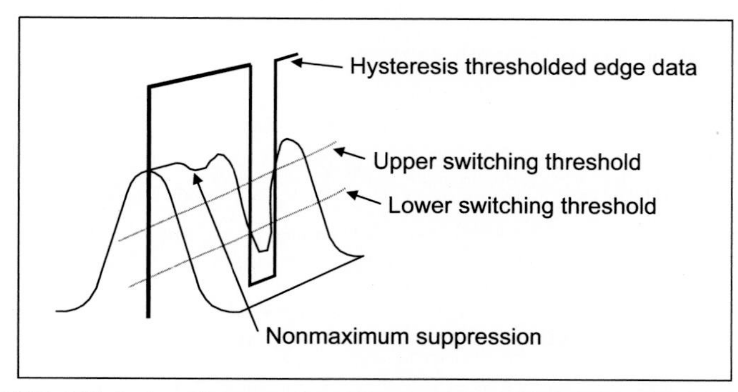

FIGURE 4.19 Action of nonmaximum suppression and hysteresis thresholding.

the top of the ridge initially exceeds the upper threshold, the thresholded output is set to white until the peak of the ridge falls beneath the lower threshold. The thresholded output is then set to black until the peak of the ridge exceeds the upper switching threshold.

Hysteresis thresholding requires two thresholds: an upper and a lower threshold. The process starts when an edge point from nonmaximum suppression is found to exceed the upper threshold. This is labelled as an edge point (usually white, with a value 255) and forms the first point of a line of edge points. The neighbours of the point are then searched to determine whether or not they exceed the lower threshold, as in Fig. 4.20. Any neighbour that exceeds the lower threshold is labelled as an edge point, and its neighbours are then searched to determine whether or not they exceed the lower threshold. In this manner, the first edge point found (the one that exceeded the upper threshold) becomes a seed point for a search. Its neighbours, in turn, become seed points if they exceed the lower threshold, and so the search extends, along branches arising from neighbours that exceeded the lower threshold. For each branch, the search terminates at points that have no neighbours above the lower threshold.

The implementation of *hysteresis thresholding* clearly requires recursion to delineate the edges by repeatedly selecting the neighbours of pixels that have been labelled as edges. Having found the initial seed point, it is set to white and its neighbours are searched. Code 4.6 illustrates an implementation of this process. First, the pixels in the `edge` image are labelled, according to the values of the two thresholds, as edges (with a value of 255), no edges (with a value of 0) or as points that may be edges (with a value of 128). The code visits all pixels to find initial seeds. For each seed found, the code looks for the neighbours that exceed the lower threshold. These neighbours are labelled as edges and stored in the list `potentialEdges`. Recursion is implemented by looking for edges in the neighbours of each element in the list. That is, the code uses the list to keep the edges grown from the seed.

A comparison between *uniform thresholding* and hysteresis thresholding is shown in Fig. 4.21. Fig. 4.21A shows the edges for dual thresholding of a Sobel edge detected image. This image shows edges with an upper threshold set to 0.4 and a lower threshold of 0.1 of the normalised edge magnitude. Edges larger than the lower threshold are shown in grey and edges larger than the upper threshold in white. This example shows that it is difficult to choose a single threshold that characterises adequately the edges in the image. Figs. 4.21B and C show the result of uniform thresholding with these two

≥ Lower	≥ Lower	≥ Lower
≥ Lower	Seed ≥ upper	≥ Lower
≥ Lower	≥ Lower	≥ Lower

FIGURE 4.20 Neighbourhood search for hysteresis thresholding.

```
# Divide pixels as edges, no edges and unassigned
for x,y in itertools.product(range(1, width-1), range(1, height-1)):
    # These are edges
    if maxImage[y,x] > upperT:    edges[y,x] = 255
    # These are pixels that we do not want as edges
    if maxImage[y,x] < lowerT:    edges[y,x] = 0
    # These may be edges
    if maxImage[y,x] > lowerT and maxImage[y,x] <= upperT:
        edges[y,x] = 128

# Show double threshold image
showImageF(edges)

# Resolve the potential edges
for x,y in itertools.product(range(1, width-1), range(1, height-1)):
    # For each edge
    if edges[y,x] == 255:

        # Examine neighbors
        potentialEdges = [ ]
        for wx,wy in itertools.product(range(-windowDelta, windowDelta+1),       \
                                       range(-windowDelta, windowDelta+1)):
            # It becomes an edge
            if edges[y+wy,x+wx] == 128:
                edges[y+wy,x+wx] = 255
                potentialEdges.append((y+wy,x+wx))

        # Look into new edges
        while len(potentialEdges) > 0:
            # Take element from potential edges
            y, x = (potentialEdges[0])[0],  (potentialEdges[0])[1]
            potentialEdges = potentialEdges[1:]

            # Examine neighbor
            for wx,wy in itertools.product(range(-windowDelta, windowDelta+1),     \
                                           range(-windowDelta, windowDelta+1)):
                # It becomes an edge
                if edges[y+wy,x+wx] == 128:
                    edges[y+wy,x+wx] = 255
                    potentialEdges.append((y+wy,x+wx))

# Clean up remaining potential edges
for x,y in itertools.product(range(1, width-1), range(1, height-1)):
    if edges[y,x] == 128:    edges[y,x] = 0
```

CODE 4.6 Hysteresis thresholding process.

thresholds. Notice that uniform thresholding can select too few points if the threshold is too high or too many if it is too low. Fig. 4.21D shows that hysteresis thresholding naturally selects all the points in Fig. 4.21B and some of those in Fig. 4.21C, those connected to the points in Fig. 4.21B. Hysteresis thresholding therefore has an ability to detect major features of interest in the edge image, in an improved manner to uniform thresholding.

The action of the Canny operator is shown in Fig. 4.22, in comparison with the result of the Sobel operator. Fig. 4.22A is the original image of a lizard, Fig. 4.22B is the result of the Canny operator (using a 5×5 Gaussian operator with $\sigma = 1.0$ and with upper and lower thresholds set appropriately) and Fig. 4.22C is the result of a 3×3 Sobel operator

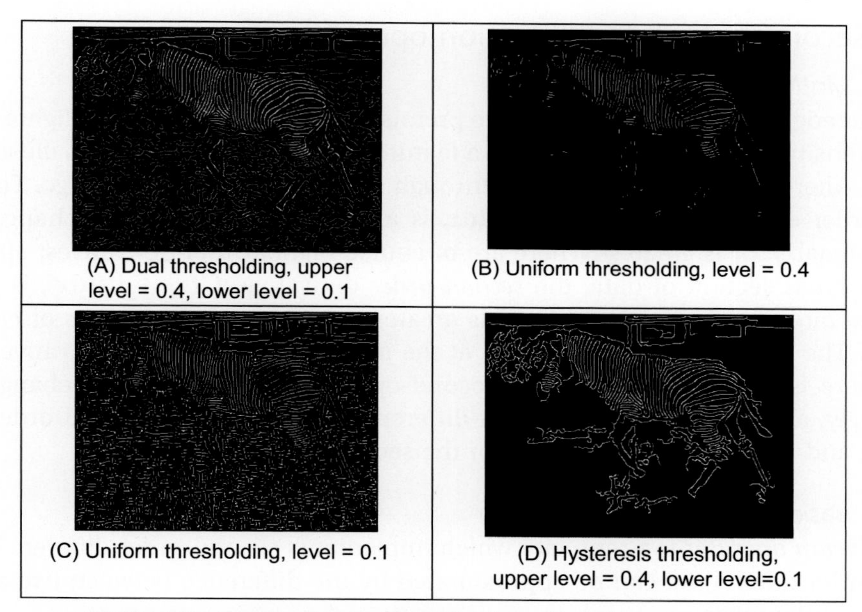

FIGURE 4.21 Comparing hysteresis thresholding with uniform thresholding.

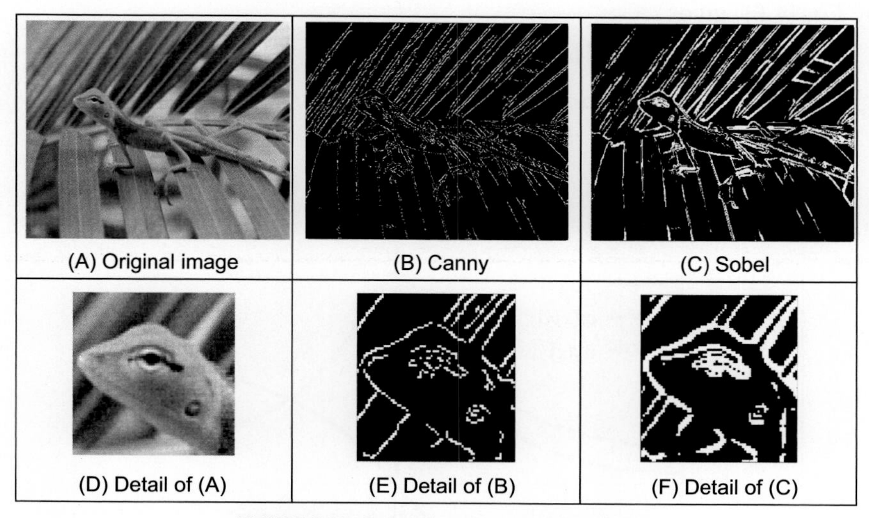

FIGURE 4.22 Comparing Canny with Sobel.

with uniform thresholding. The retention of major detail by the Canny operator is very clear; the edges are thin and complete in Fig. 4.22B, whereas they are blurred and less complete in Fig. 4.22C. Closer inspection of the lizard's eye shows greater detail too.

4.2.2 Second-order edge detection operators

4.2.2.1 Motivation

First-order edge detection is based on the premise that differentiation highlights change; image intensity changes in the region of a feature boundary. The process is illustrated in Fig. 4.23, where there is a cross section through image data which is an edge. The result of first-order edge detection, $f'(x) = \mathrm{d}f/\mathrm{d}x$, is a peak where the rate of change of the original signal, $f(x)$, is greatest. There are of course higher order derivatives; applied to the same cross section of data, the *second-order* derivative, $f''(x) = \mathrm{d}^2f/\mathrm{d}x^2$, is greatest where the rate of change of the signal is greatest and zero when the rate of change is constant. The rate of change is constant at the peak of the first-order derivative. This is where there is a *zero-crossing* in the second-order derivative, where it changes sign. Accordingly, an alternative to first-order differentiation is to apply second-order differentiation and then find zero-crossings in the second-order information.

4.2.2.2 Basic operators: The Laplacian

The *Laplacian operator* is a template which implements second-order differencing. The second-order differential can be approximated by the difference between two adjacent first-order differences

$$f''(x) \cong f'(x) - f'(x+1) \tag{4.24}$$

which, by Eq. (4.6), gives

$$f''(x+1) \cong -f(x) + 2f(x+1) - f(x+2) \tag{4.25}$$

This gives a horizontal second-order template as given in Fig. 4.24.

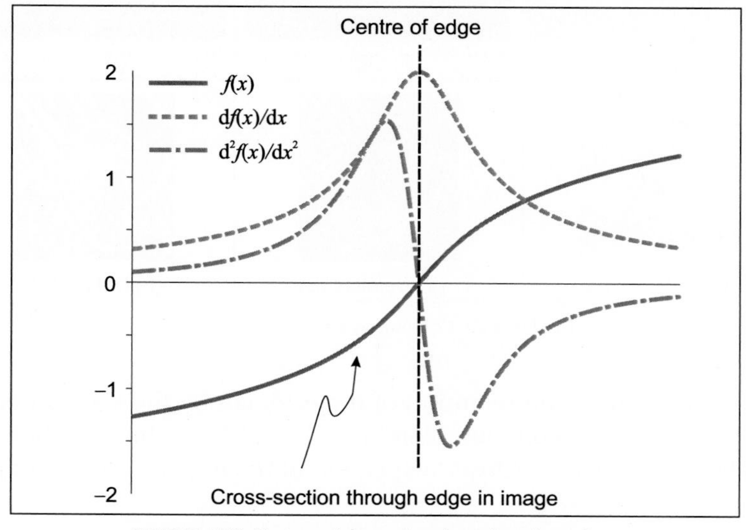

FIGURE 4.23 First- and second-order edge detection.

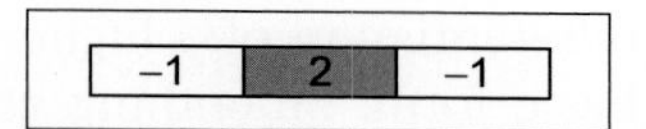

FIGURE 4.24 Horizontal second-order template.

0	–1	0
–1	4	–1
0	–1	0

FIGURE 4.25 Laplacian edge detection operator.

When the horizontal second-order operator is combined with a vertical second-order difference, we obtain the full Laplacian template, given in Fig. 4.25. Essentially, this computes the difference between a point and the average of its four direct neighbours. This was the operator used earlier in anisotropic diffusion, Section 3.5.5, where it is an approximate solution to the heat equation.

Application of the Laplacian operator to the image of the square is given in Fig. 4.26. The original image is provided in numeric form in Fig. 4.26A. The detected edges are the zero-crossings in Fig. 4.26B and can be seen to lie between the edge of the square and its background. The result highlights the boundary of the square in the original image, but there is also a slight problem: there is a small hole in the shape in the lower right. This is by virtue of second-order differentiation, which is inherently more susceptible to noise. Accordingly, to handle noise we need to introduce smoothing.

An alternative structure to the template in Fig. 4.25 is one where the central weighting is 8 and the neighbours are all weighted as -1. Naturally, this includes a different form of image information, so the effects are slightly different. (Essentially, this now computes the difference between a pixel and the average of its neighbouring points, including the corners.) In both structures, the central weighting can be negative and that of the four or the eight neighbours can be positive, without loss of generality. Actually, it is important to ensure that the sum of template coefficients is zero, so that edges are not detected in areas of uniform brightness. One advantage of the Laplacian operator is that it is isotropic (like the Gaussian operator): it has the same properties in each direction. However, as yet it contains no smoothing and will again respond to noise, more so than a

1	2	3	4	1	1	2	1
2	2	3	0	1	2	2	1
3	0	38	39	37	36	3	0
4	1	40	44	41	42	2	1
1	2	43	44	40	39	3	1
2	0	39	41	42	40	2	0
0	2	0	2	2	3	1	1
0	2	1	3	1	0	4	2

(A) Image data

0	0	0	0	0	0	0	0
0	1	-31	-47	-36	-32	0	0
0	-44	70	37	31	60	-28	0
0	-42	34	12	1	50	-41	0
0	-37	47	8	-6	31	-32	0
0	-45	72	37	45	74	-36	0
0	6	-44	-38	-40	-31	-6	0
0	0	0	0	0	0	0	0

(B) Result of the Laplacian operator

FIGURE 4.26 Edge Detection via the Laplacian operator.

first-order operator since it is differentiation of a higher order. As such, the Laplacian operator is rarely used in its basic form. Smoothing can use the averaging operator described earlier but a more optimal form is Gaussian smoothing. When this is incorporated within the Laplacian, we obtain a *Laplacian of Gaussian (LoG) operator* which is the basis of the *Marr–Hildreth* approach, to be considered next. A clear disadvantage with the Laplacian operator is that edge direction is not available. It does, however, impose low computational cost, which is its main advantage. Though interest in the Laplacian operator abated with rising interest in the Marr–Hildreth approach, a nonlinear Laplacian operator was developed [Vliet89] and shown to have good performance, especially in low-noise situations.

4.2.2.3 The Marr–Hildreth operator

The *Marr–Hildreth* approach [Marr80] again uses Gaussian filtering. In principle, we require an image which is the second differential ∇^2 of a Gaussian operator $g(x,y)$ convolved with an image $\mathbf{P}$. This convolution process can be separated as

$$\nabla^2(g(x,y) * \mathbf{P}) = \nabla^2(g(x,y)) * \mathbf{P} \tag{4.26}$$

Accordingly, we need to compute a template for $\nabla^2(g(x,y))$ and convolve this with the image. By further differentiation of Eq. (4.17), we achieve a *Laplacian of Gaussian* (LoG) operator

$$\begin{aligned}
\nabla^2 g(x,y) &= \frac{\partial^2 g(x,y,\sigma)}{\partial x^2}U_x + \frac{\partial^2 g(x,y,\sigma)}{\partial y^2}U_y \\
&= \frac{\partial \nabla g(x,y,\sigma)}{\partial x}U_x + \frac{\partial \nabla g(x,y,\sigma)}{\partial y}U_y \\
&= \left(\frac{x^2}{\sigma^2} - 1\right)\frac{e^{\frac{-(x^2+y^2)}{2\sigma^2}}}{\sigma^2} + \left(\frac{y^2}{\sigma^2} - 1\right)\frac{e^{\frac{-(x^2+y^2)}{2\sigma^2}}}{\sigma^2} \\
&= \frac{1}{\sigma^2}\left(\frac{(x^2+y^2)}{\sigma^2} - 2\right)e^{\frac{-(x^2+y^2)}{2\sigma^2}}
\end{aligned} \tag{4.27}$$

This is the basis of the Marr–Hildreth operator. Eq. (4.27) can be used to calculate the coefficients of a template which, when convolved with an image, combines *Gaussian smoothing* with second-order differentiation. The operator is sometimes called a 'Mexican hat' operator, since its surface plot is the shape of a sombrero, as illustrated in Fig. 4.27.

The calculation of the LoG can be approximated by the difference of Gaussians where the difference is formed from two Gaussian filters with differing variance [Marr82, Lindeberg94].

$$\sigma\nabla^2 g(x,y,\sigma) = \frac{\partial g}{\partial \sigma} = \lim_{k\to 1}\frac{g(x,y,k\sigma) - g(x,y,\sigma)}{k\sigma - \sigma} \tag{4.28}$$

where $g(x,y,\sigma)$ is the Gaussian function and k is a constant. Although similarly named, the derivative of Gaussian, Eq. (4.17), is a first-order operator including Gaussian smoothing, $\nabla g(x,y)$. It does actually seem counterintuitive that the difference of two

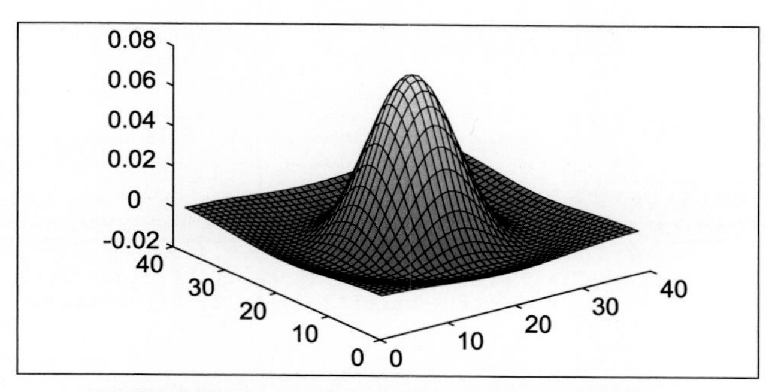

FIGURE 4.27 Shape of Laplacian of Gaussian operator.

smoothing operators should lead to second-order edge detection. The approximation is illustrated in Fig. 4.28 where in 1-D two Gaussian distributions of different variance are subtracted to form a 1-D operator whose cross section is similar to the shape of the LoG operator (a cross section of Fig. 4.27).

The implementation of Eq. (4.27) to calculate the template coefficients for the `LoG_template` operator is given in Code 4.7. The function includes a normalisation function which ensures that the sum of the template coefficients is unity, so that edges are not detected in area of uniform brightness. This is in contrast with the earlier Laplacian operator (where the template coefficients summed to zero) since the LoG operator includes smoothing within the differencing action, whereas the Laplacian is pure differencing. The template generated by this function can then be used within template convolution. The Gaussian operator again suppresses the influence of points away from the centre of the template, basing differentiation on those points nearer the centre; the standard deviation, `sigma`, is chosen to ensure this action. Again, it is isotropic consistent with Gaussian smoothing.

Determining the *zero-crossing* points is a major difficulty with this approach. There is a variety of techniques which can be used, including manual determination of zero-crossings or a least squares fit of a plane to local image data, which is followed by determination of the point at which the plane crosses zero, if it does. The former is too simplistic, whereas the latter is quite complex.

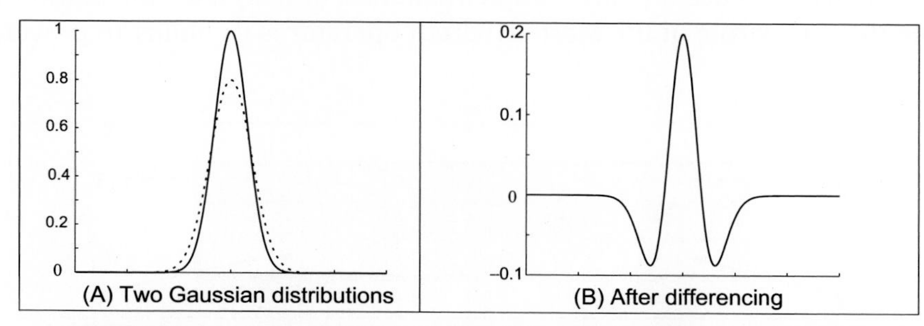

FIGURE 4.28 Approximating the Laplacian of Gaussian by difference of Gaussian.

```
function snd_order = LoG_template(winsize,sigma)

half=floor(winsize/2)+1;
snd_order(1:winsize,1:winsize)=0;

%then form the LoG template
sum=0;
for x = 1:winsize %address all columns
  for y = 1:winsize %address all rows except border, Eq. 4.27
    snd_order(y,x)= (1/(sigma^2))*((((x-half)^2+(y-half)^2)/sigma^2)-2)*...
                                 exp(-(((x-half)^2+(y-half)^2)/(2*sigma^2)));
    sum=sum+snd_order(y,x);
  end
end
snd_order=snd_order/sum;
end
```

CODE 4.7 Implementation of the Laplacian of Gaussian operator.

The approach here is much simpler: given a local 3 × 3 area of an image, this is split into quadrants. These are shown in Fig. 4.29 where each quadrant contains the centre pixel. The first quadrant contains the four points in the upper left corner, and the third quadrant contains the four points in the upper right. If the average of the points in any quadrant differs in sign from the average in any other quadrant, there must be a zero-crossing at the centre point. In `zero_cross`, Code 4.8, the total intensity in each quadrant is evaluated, giving four values `int(1)` to `int(4)`. If the maximum value of these points is positive, and the minimum value is negative, there must be a zero-crossing within the neighbourhood. If one exists, the output image at that point is marked as white, otherwise it is set to black.

The action of the Marr–Hildreth operator is given in Fig. 4.30, applied to the lizard image in Fig. 4.22A. The output of convolving the LoG operator is hard to interpret visually and is not shown here (remember that it is the zero-crossings which mark the edge points and it is hard to see them). The detected zero-crossings (for a 3 × 3 neighbourhood) are shown in Figs. 4.30B and C for LoG operators of size 9 × 9 with $\sigma = 1.4$ and 19 × 19 with $\sigma = 3.0$, respectively. These show that the selection of window size and variance can be used to provide edges at differing scales. Some of the smaller regions in Fig. 4.30B join to form larger regions in Fig. 4.30C. Given the size of these templates, it is usual to use a Fourier implementation of template convolution (Section 3.4.4). Note that one virtue of the Marr–Hildreth operator is its ability to provide closed

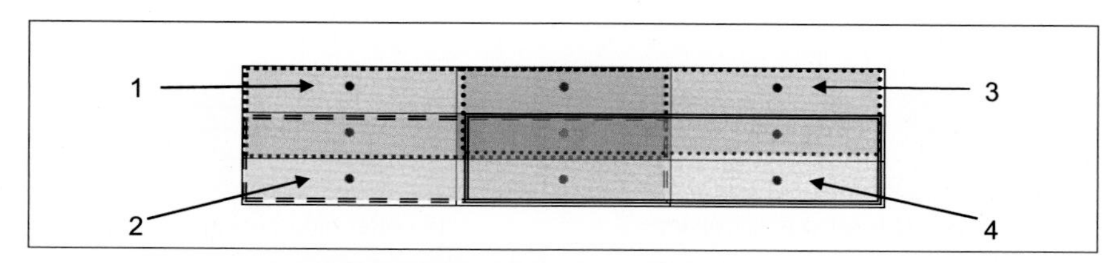

FIGURE 4.29 Regions for zero-crossing detection.

```
function zero_xing = zero_cross(image)
%New image shows zero crossing points

%get dimensions
[rows,cols]=size(image);

%set the output image to black (0)
zero_xing(1:rows,1:cols)=0;

%then form the four quadrant points
for x = 2:cols-1 %address all columns except border
  for y = 2:rows-1 %address all rows except border
    int(1)=image(y-1,x-1)+image(y-1,x)+image(y,x-1)+image(y,x);
    int(2)=image(y,x-1)+image(y,x)+image(y+1,x-1)+image(y+1,x);
    int(3)=image(y-1,x)+image(y-1,x+1)+image(y,x)+image(y,x+1);
    int(4)=image(y,x)+image(y,x+1)+image(y+1,x)+image(y+1,x+1);
    %now work out the max and min values
    maxval=max(int);
    minval=min(int);
    %and label it as zero crossing if there is one (!)
    if (maxval>0)&&(minval<0)
        zero_xing(y,x)=255;
    end
  end
end
```

CODE 4.8 Zero-crossing detector.

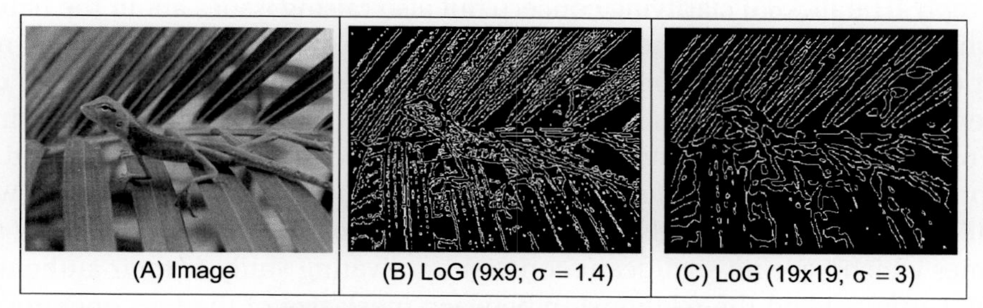

(A) Image	(B) LoG (9x9; σ = 1.4)	(C) LoG (19x19; σ = 3)

FIGURE 4.30 Marr–Hildreth edge detection.

edge borders which the Canny operator cannot. Another virtue is that it avoids the recursion associated with hysteresis thresholding that can require a massive stack size for large images.

The Fourier transform of a (large) LoG operator is shown in relief in Fig. 4.31A and as an image in Fig. 4.31B. The transform is circular symmetric, as expected. Since the transform reveals that the LoG operator omits low and high frequencies (those close to the origin and those far away from the origin), it is equivalent to a *band-pass filter*. Choice of the value of σ controls the spread of the operator in the spatial domain and the 'width' of the band in the frequency domain: setting σ to a high value gives *low-pass* filtering, as expected. This differs from first-order edge detection templates which offer a high-pass (differencing) filter along one axis with a low-pass (smoothing) action along the other axis.

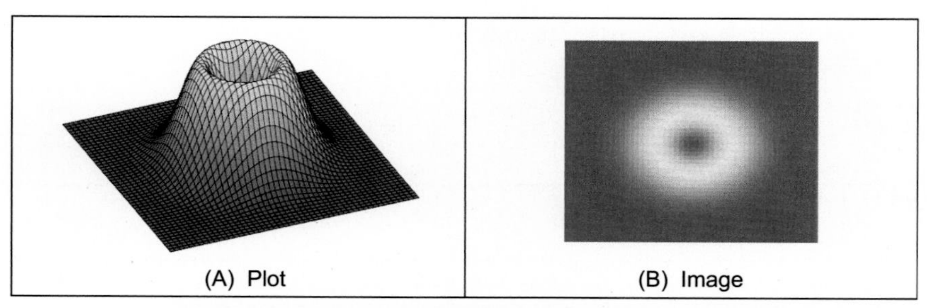

FIGURE 4.31 Fourier transform of Laplacian of Gaussian operator.

The Marr–Hildreth operator has stimulated much attention, perhaps in part because it has an appealing relationship to human vision, and its ability for multiresolution analysis (the ability to detect edges at differing scales). In fact, it has been suggested that the original image can be reconstructed from the zero-crossings at different scales. One early study [Haralick84] concluded that the Marr–Hildreth operator could give good performance. Unfortunately, the implementation appeared to be different from the original LoG operator (and has actually appeared in some texts in this form) as noted by one of the Marr–Hildreth study's originators [Grimson85]. This led to a somewhat spirited reply [Haralick85] clarifying concern but also raising issues about the nature and operation of edge detection schemes which remain relevant today. Given the requirement for convolution of large templates, attention quickly focused on frequency domain implementation [Huertas86], and speed improvement was later considered in some detail [Forshaw88]. Later, schemes were developed to refine the edges produced via the LoG approach [Ulupinar90]. Though speed and accuracy are major concerns with the Marr–Hildreth approach, it is also possible for zero-crossing detectors to mark as edge points ones which have no significant contrast, motivating study of their authentication [Clark89]. Gunn studied the relationship between mask size of the LoG operator and its error rate [Gunn99]. Essentially, an acceptable error rate defines a truncation error which in turn gives an appropriate mask size. Gunn also observed the paucity of studies on zero-crossing detection and offered a detector slightly more sophisticated than the one here (as it includes the case where a zero-crossing occurs at a boundary whereas the one here assumes that the zero-crossing can only occur at the centre). The similarity is not co-incidental: Mark developed the one here after conversations with Steve Gunn, who he works with!

4.2.3 Other edge detection operators

There have been many approaches to edge detection. This is not surprising since it is often the first stage in a vision process. The most popular operators are the Sobel, Canny and Marr–Hildreth operators. Clearly, in any implementation there is a compromise between (computational) cost and efficiency. In some cases, it is difficult to justify the extra complexity associated with the Canny and the Marr–Hildreth operators. This is in part due to the images: few images contain the adverse noisy situations that complex edge operators are designed to handle. Also, when finding shapes, it is often prudent to extract more than enough low-level information, and to let the more sophisticated shape detection process use, or discard, the information as appropriate. For these reasons we will study only three more edge detection approaches, and only briefly. Two of these operators are the *Spacek* and the *Petrou* operators: both are designed to be optimal and both have different properties and a different basis (the smoothing functional in particular) to the Canny and Marr–Hildreth approaches. The Spacek and Petrou operators are included by virtue of their optimality. Essentially, whilst Canny maximised the ratio of the signal-to-noise ratio with the localisation, Spacek [Spacek86] maximised the ratio of the product of the signal-to-noise ratio and the peak separation with the localisation. In Spacek's work, since the edge was again modelled as a step function, the ideal filter appeared to be of the same form as Canny's. Spacek's operator can give better performance than Canny's formulation [Jia95], as such challenging the optimality of the Gaussian operator for noise smoothing (in step edge detection), though such advantage should be explored in application.

Petrou questioned the validity of the step edge model for real images [Petrou91]. Given that the composite performance of an image acquisition system can be considered to be that of a low-pass filter, any step changes in the image will be smoothed to become a ramp. As such, a more plausible model of the edge is a ramp rather than a step. Since the process is based on ramp edges, and because of limits imposed by its formulation, the Petrou operator uses templates that are much wider in order to preserve optimal properties. As such, the operator can impose greater computational complexity but is a natural candidate for applications with the conditions for which its properties were formulated.

Of the other approaches, Korn developed a unifying operator for symbolic representation of grey level change [Korn88]. The *Susan* operator [Smith97] derives from an approach aimed to find more than just edges since it can also be used to derive *corners* (where feature boundaries change direction sharply, as in *curvature* detection in Section 4.4.1) and structure-preserving image noise reduction. Essentially, SUSAN derives from Smallest Univalue Segment Assimilating Nucleus which concerns aggregating the difference between elements in a (circular) template centred on the nucleus. The USAN is essentially the number of pixels within the circular mask which have similar brightness to the nucleus. The edge strength is then derived by subtracting the USAN size from a geometric threshold, which is say $^3/_4$ of the maximum USAN size. The method includes a way of calculating edge direction, which is essential if nonmaximum suppression is to be applied. The advantages are in simplicity (and hence speed), since it is based on simple operations, and the possibility of extension to find other feature types.

4.2.4 Comparison of edge detection operators

Naturally, the selection of an edge operator for a particular application depends on the application itself. As has been suggested, it is not usual to require the sophistication of the advanced operators in many applications. This is reflected in analysis of the performance of the edge operators on the images here. In order to provide a different basis for comparison, we shall consider the difficulty of low-level feature extraction in ultrasound images. As has been seen earlier (Section 3.5), ultrasound images are very noisy and require filtering prior to analysis. Fig. 4.32A is part of the ultrasound image which could have been filtered using the truncated median operator (Section 3.5.2). The image contains a feature called the pitus (it's the 'splodge' in the middle), and we shall see how different edge operators can be used to detect its perimeter, though without noise filtering. The median is a very popular filtering processes for general (i.e. non-ultrasound) applications. Accordingly, it is of interest that one study [Bovik87] has suggested that the known advantages of median filtering (the removal of noise with the preservation of edges, especially for salt and pepper noise) are shown to good effect if it is used as a prefilter to first- and second-order approaches, though naturally with the cost of the median filter. However, we will not consider median filtering here: its choice depends more on suitability to a particular application.

The results for all edge operators have been generated using hysteresis thresholding where the thresholds were selected manually for best performance. The basic first-order operator, Fig. 4.32B, responds rather nicely to the noise, and it is difficult to select a threshold which reveals a major part of the pitus border. Some is present in the Prewitt and Sobel operators' results, Figs. 4.32C and D, respectively, but there is still much noise in the processed image, though there is less in the Sobel – as expected. The Laplacian operator, Fig. 4.32E, gives very little information indeed, as to be expected with such

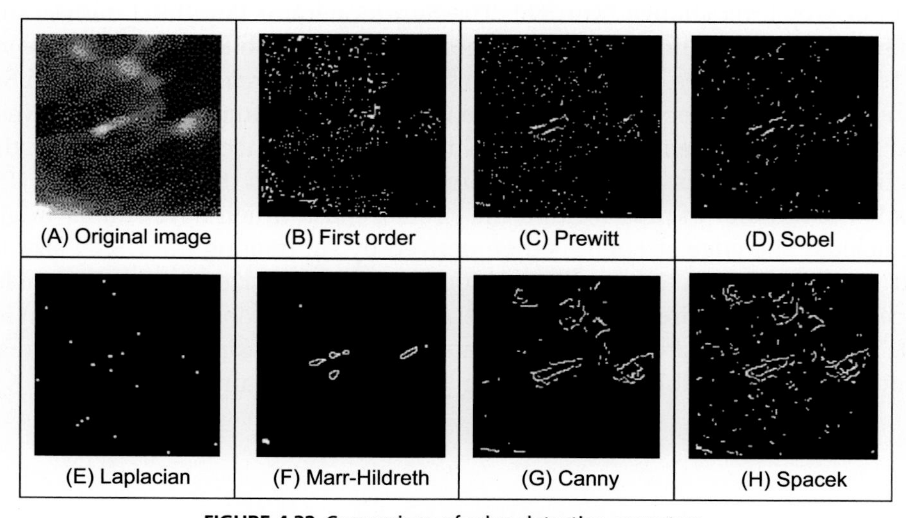

FIGURE 4.32 Comparison of edge detection operators.

noisy imagery. However, the more advanced operators can be used to good effect. The Marr–Hildreth approach improves matters, Fig. 4.32F, but suggests that it is difficult to choose a LoG operator of appropriate size to detect a feature of these dimensions in such noisy imagery – illustrating the compromise between the size of operator needed for noise filtering and the size needed for the target feature. However, the Canny and Spacek operators can be used to good effect, as shown in Figs. 4.32G and H, respectively. These reveal much of the required information, together with data away from the pitus itself. In an automated analysis system, for this application, the extra complexity of the more sophisticated operators would clearly be warranted.

4.2.5 Further reading on edge detection

Few computer vision and image processing texts omit detail concerning edge detection operators, though few give explicit details concerning implementation. Naturally, many of the earlier texts omit the bases of techniques. Further information can be found in journal papers; Petrou's excellent study of edge detection [Petrou94] highlights study of the performance factors involved in the optimality of the Canny, Spacek and Petrou operators with extensive tutorial support (though Petrou junior might have been embarrassed by the frequency his mugshot was used as his teeth showed up very well!). There have been a number of surveys of edge detection highlighting performance attributes in comparison. See, for example, [Torre86] that gives a theoretical study of edge detection and considers some popular edge detection techniques in light of this analysis. One survey, [Heath97] reviews many approaches, comparing them in particular with the Canny operator (and states where code for some of the techniques they compared can be found). This showed that best results can be achieved by tuning an edge detector for a particular application and highlighted good results by the Bergholm operator [Bergholm87]. Marr, [Marr82], considers the Marr–Hildreth approach to edge detection in the light of human vision (and its influence on perception), with particular reference to scale in edge detection. [Yitzhaky03] suggests 'a general tool to assist in practical implementations of parametric edge detectors where an automatic process is required' and uses statistical tests to evaluate edge detector performance. Since edge detection is one of the most important vision techniques, it continues to be a focus of research interest. In this regard: one recent paper used a patch-based approach aimed at accuracy and computational efficiency [Dollár15]; another has been aimed to improve edge direction accuracy [Kimia18]. More recently, as we shall find in Chapter 12, deep learning approaches can base information flow on oriented edge detectors through an analysis network [LeCun15]. Accordingly, it is always worth looking at recent papers to find new techniques, or perhaps more likely performance comparison or improvements that might help you solve a problem.

4.3 Phase congruency

The comparison of edge detectors highlights some of their innate problems: incomplete contours; the need for selective thresholding; and their response to noise. Further, the selection of a threshold is often inadequate for all the regions in an image since there are many changes in local illumination. We shall find that some of these problems can be handled at a higher level, when shape extraction can be arranged to accommodate partial data and to reject spurious information. There is though natural interest in refining the low-level feature extraction techniques further.

Phase congruency is a feature detector with two main advantages: it can detect a broad range of features; and it is invariant to local (and smooth) change in illumination. As the name suggests, it is derived by frequency domain considerations operating on the considerations of phase (a.k.a. time). It is illustrated detecting some one-dimensional features in Fig. 4.33 where the features are the solid lines: a (noisy) step function in Fig. 4.33A, and a peak (or impulse) in Fig. 4.33B. By Fourier transform analysis, any function is made up from the controlled addition of sine waves of differing frequencies. For the step function to occur (the solid line in Fig. 4.33A), the constituent frequencies (the dotted lines in Fig. 4.33A) must all change at the same time, so they add up to give the edge. Similarly, for the peak to occur, then the constituent frequencies must all peak at the same time; in Fig. 4.33B the solid line is the peak and the dotted lines are some of its constituent frequencies. This means that in order to find the feature we are interested in, we can determine points where events happen at the same time: this is phase congruency. By way of generalisation, a triangle wave is made of peaks and troughs: phase congruency implies that the peaks and troughs of the constituent signals should coincide.

In fact, the constituent sine waves plotted in Fig. 4.33A were derived by taking the Fourier transform and then determining the sine waves according to their magnitude

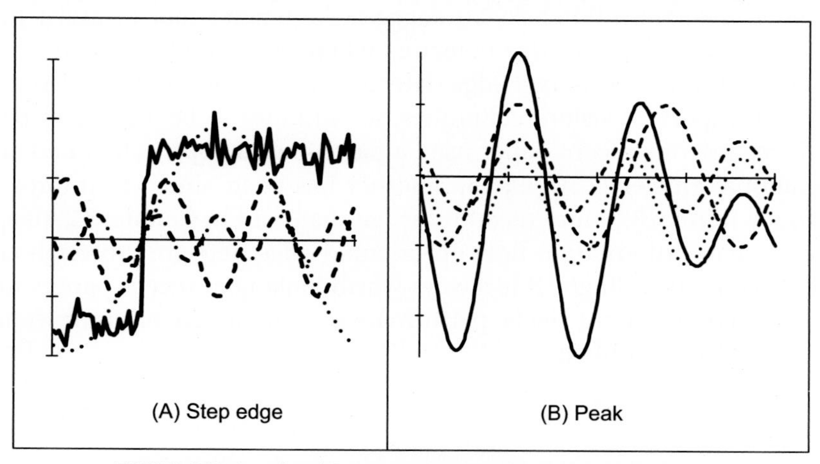

FIGURE 4.33 Low-level Feature extraction by phase congruency.

and phase. The Fourier transform in Eq. (2.15) delivers the complex Fourier components **Fp**. These can be used to show the constituent signals xc by

$$xc(t) = |\mathbf{Fp}_u| e^{j\left(\frac{2\pi}{N}ut + \phi(\mathbf{Fp}_u)\right)} \tag{4.29}$$

where $|\mathbf{Fp}_u|$ is again the magnitude of the uth Fourier component (Eq. (2.7)) and $\phi(\mathbf{Fp}_u) = \langle \mathbf{Fp}_u$ is the argument, the phase in Eq. (2.8). The (dotted) frequencies displayed in Fig. 4.33 are the first four odd components (the even components for this function are zero, as shown in the Fourier transform of the step in Fig. 2.11). The addition of these components is indeed the *inverse Fourier transform* which reconstructs the step feature.

The advantages are that detection of congruency is invariant with local contrast: the sine waves still add up so the changes are still in the same place, even if the magnitude of the step edge is much smaller. In images, this implies that we can change the contrast and still detect edges. This is illustrated in Fig. 4.34. Here a standard image processing image, the 'cameraman' image from the early UCSD dataset has been changed between the left and right side so the contrast changes in the two halves of the image, Fig. 4.34A. Edges detected by *Canny* are shown in Fig. 4.34B and by phase congruency in Fig. 4.34C. The basic structure of the edges detected by phase congruency is very similar to that structure detected by Canny, and the phase congruency edges appear somewhat cleaner (there is a single line associated with the tripod control in phase congruency); both detect the change in brightness between the two halves. There is a major difference though: the building in the lower right side of the image is barely detected in the Canny image, whereas it can clearly be seen by phase congruency. Its absence is due to the parameter settings used in the Canny operator. These can be changed, but if the contrast were to change again, then the parameters would need to be re-optimised for the new arrangement. This is not the case for phase congruency.

Naturally, such a change in brightness might appear unlikely in practical applications, but this is not the case with moving objects which interact with illumination or in fixed applications where illumination changes. In studies aimed to extract spinal

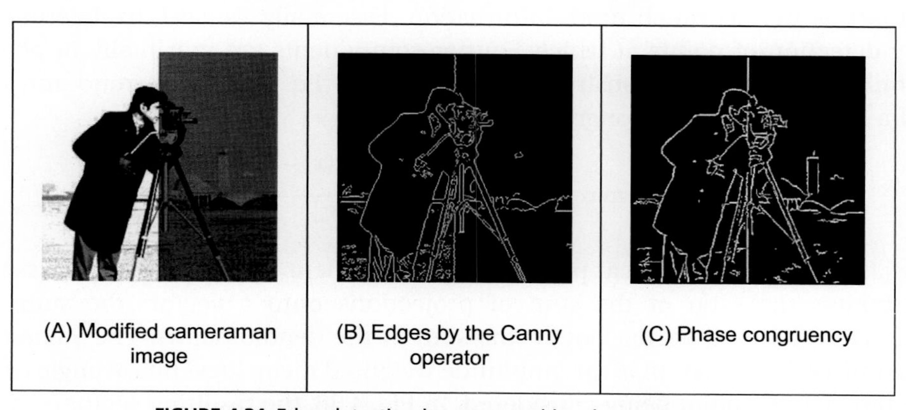

FIGURE 4.34 Edge detection by canny and by phase congruency.

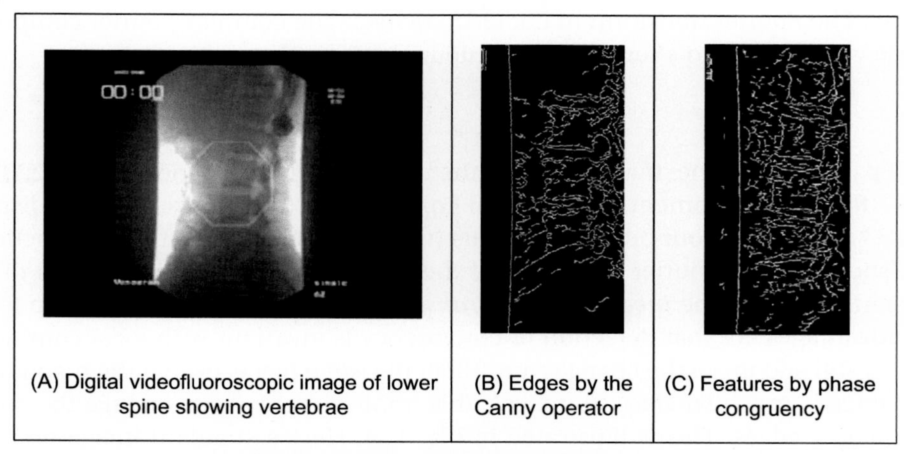

FIGURE 4.35 Spinal contour by phase congruency.

information from digital videofluoroscopic X-ray images in order to provide guidance for surgeons [Zheng04], phase congruency was found to be immune to the changes in contrast caused by slippage of the shield used to protect the patient while acquiring the image information. One such image is shown in Fig. 4.35. The lack of shielding is apparent in the bloom at the side of the images. This changes as the subject is moved so it proved difficult to optimise the parameters for Canny over the whole sequence, Fig. 4.35B, but the detail of a section of the phase congruency result, Fig. 4.35C, shows that the vertebrae information is readily available for later high-level feature extraction.

The original notions of phase congruency are the concepts of *local energy* [Morrone87], with links to the human visual system [Morrone88]. One of the most sophisticated implementations was by Kovesi [Kovesi99], with added advantage that his Matlab® implementation is available on the web (https://www.peterkovesi.com/matlabfns/) as well as much more information. Essentially we seek to determine features by detection of points at which Fourier components are maximally in phase. By extension of the Fourier reconstruction functions in Eq. (4.29), Morrone and Owens defined a measure of phase congruency PC as

$$PC(x) = \max_{\overline{\phi}(x)\in 0,2\pi}\left(\frac{\sum\limits_{u}|\mathbf{Fp}_u|\cos\left(\phi_u(x)-\overline{\phi}(x)\right)}{\sum\limits_{u}|\mathbf{Fp}_u|}\right) \tag{4.30}$$

where $\phi_u(x)$ represents the local phase of the component $\mathbf{Fp}_u$ at position x. Essentially this computes the ratio of the sum of projections onto a vector (the sum in the numerator) to the total vector length (the sum in the denominator). The value of $\phi(x)$ that maximises this equation is the amplitude weighted mean local phase angle of all the Fourier terms at the point being considered. In Fig. 4.36, the resulting vector is made up

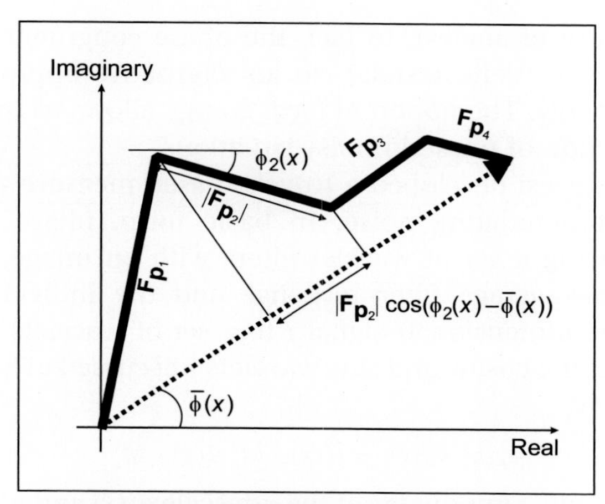

FIGURE 4.36 Summation in phase congruency.

of four components, highlighting the projection of the second onto the resulting vector. Clearly, the value of PC ranges from 0 to 1, the maximum occurring when all elements point along the resulting vector. As such, the resulting phase congruency is a dimensionless normalised measure which is thresholded for image analysis.

In this way, we have calculated the phase congruency for the step function in Fig. 4.37A which is shown in Fig. 4.37B. Here, the position of the step is at time step 40; this is the position of the peak in phase congruency, as required. Note that the noise can be seen to affect the result, though the phase congruency is largest at the right place.

One interpretation of the measure is that since for small angles, $\cos\theta = 1-\theta^2$, then Eq. (4.30) expresses the ratio of the magnitudes weighted by the variance of the difference to the summed magnitude of the components. There is certainly difficulty with this measure, apart from difficulty in implementation: it is sensitive to noise, as is any phase measure; it is not conditioned by the magnitude of a response (small responses are not discounted); and it is not well localised (the measure varies with the cosine of the difference in phase, not with the difference itself – though it does avoid discontinuity

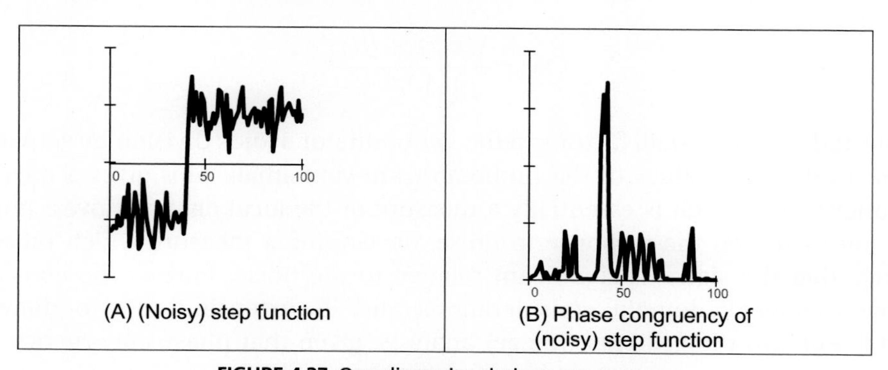

FIGURE 4.37 One-dimensional phase congruency.

problems with direct use of angles). In fact, the phase congruency is directly proportional to the local energy [Venkatesh89], so an alternative approach is to search for maxima in the local energy. The notion of local energy allows us to compensate for the sensitivity to the detection of phase in noisy situations.

For these reasons, Kovesi developed a *wavelet*-based measure which improved performance, whilst accommodating noise. In basic form, phase congruency can be determined by convolving a set of wavelet filters with an image, and calculating the difference between the average filter response and the individual filter responses. The response of a (one-dimensional) signal I to a set of wavelets at scale n is derived from the convolution of the cosine and sine wavelets (discussed in Section 2.7.3) denoted M_n^e and M_n^o, respectively,

$$[e_n(x), o_n(x)] = \left[I(x) * M_u^e, I(x) * M_u^o\right] \tag{4.31}$$

to deliver the even and odd components at the nth scale $e_n(x)$ and $o_n(x)$, respectively. The amplitude of the transform result at this scale is the local energy

$$A_n(x) = \sqrt{e_n(x)^2 + o_n(x)^2} \tag{4.32}$$

At each point x, we will have an array of vectors which correspond to each scale of the filter. Given that we are only interested in phase congruency that occurs over a wide range of frequencies (rather than just at a couple of scales), the set of wavelet filters needs to be designed so that adjacent components overlap. By summing the even and odd components we obtain

$$\begin{aligned} F(x) &= \sum_n e_n(x) \\ H(x) &= \sum_n o_n(x) \end{aligned} \tag{4.33}$$

and a measure of the total energy A as

$$\sum_n A_n(x) \approx \sum_n \sqrt{e_n(x)^2 + o_n(x)^2} \tag{4.34}$$

then a measure of phase congruency is

$$PC(x) = \frac{\sqrt{F(x)^2 + H(x)^2}}{\sum_n A_n(x) + \varepsilon} \tag{4.35}$$

where the addition of a small factor ε in the denominator avoids division by zero and any potential result when values of the numerator are very small. This gives a measure of phase congruency, which is essentially a measure of the local energy. Kovesi improved on this, improving on the response to noise, developing a measure which reflects the confidence that the signal is significant relative to the noise. Further, he considers in detail the frequency domain considerations and its extension to two dimensions [Kovesi99]. For two-dimensional (image) analysis, given that phase congruency can be determined by convolving a set of wavelet filters with an image, and calculating the difference between the average filter response and the individual filter responses. The filters are constructed in the frequency domain by using complementary spreading functions; the filters must be constructed in the Fourier domain because the log-Gabor function has a singularity at zero frequency. In order to construct a filter with appropriate properties, a filter is constructed in a manner similar to the Gabor wavelet, but here in the frequency domain and using different functions. Following Kovesi's implementation, the first filter is a low-pass filter, here a Gaussian filter g with L different orientations,

$$g(\theta, \theta_l) = \frac{1}{\sqrt{2\pi}\sigma_s} e^{-\frac{(\theta-\theta_l)^2}{2\sigma_s^2}} \tag{4.36}$$

where θ is the orientation, σ_s controls the spread about that orientation and θ_l is the angle of local orientation focus. The other spreading function is a band-pass filter, here a log-Gabor filter lg with M different scales.

$$lg(\omega, \omega_m) = \begin{cases} 0 & \omega = 0 \\ \frac{1}{\sqrt{2\pi}\sigma_\beta} e^{-\frac{\left(\log\left(\omega/\omega_m\right)\right)^2}{2(\log(\beta))^2}} & \omega \neq 0 \end{cases} \tag{4.37}$$

where ω is the scale, β controls bandwidth at that scale and ω is the centre frequency at that scale. The combination of these functions provides a two-dimensional filter $l2Dg$ which can act at different scales and orientations.

$$l2Dg(\omega, \omega_m, \theta, \theta_l) = g(\theta, \theta_l) \times lg(\omega, \omega_m) \tag{4.38}$$

One measure of phase congruency based on the convolution of this filter with the image $\mathbf{P}$ is derived by inverse Fourier transformation $\Im^{-1}$ of the filter $l2Dg$ (to yield a spatial domain operator) which is convolved as

$$S(m)_{x,y} = \Im^{-1}(l2Dg(\omega, \omega_m, \theta, \theta_l))_{x,y} * \mathbf{P}_{x,y} \tag{4.39}$$

to deliver the convolution result S at the mth scale. The measure of phase congruency over the M scales is then

$$PC_{x,y} = \frac{\left| \sum_{m=1}^{M} S(m)_{x,y} \right|}{\sum_{m=1}^{M} \left| S(m)_{x,y} \right| + \varepsilon} \tag{4.40}$$

where the addition of a small factor ε again avoids division by zero and any potential result when values of S are very small. This gives a measure of phase congruency, but is certainly a bit of an ouch, especially as it still needs refinement.

Note that keywords re-occur within phase congruency: frequency domain, wavelets and convolution. By its nature, we are operating in the frequency domain and there is not enough room in this text, and it is inappropriate to the scope here, to expand further.

Despite this, the performance of phase congruency certainly encourages its consideration, especially if local illumination is likely to vary and if a range of features is to be considered. It is derived by an alternative conceptual basis, and this gives different insight, let alone performance. Even better, there is a Matlab implementation available, for application to images – allowing you to replicate its excellent results. There has been further research, noting especially its extension in ultrasound image analysis [Mulet-Parada00] and its extension to spatiotemporal form [Myerscough04].

4.4 Localised feature extraction

There are two main areas covered here. The traditional approaches aim to derive local features by measuring specific image properties. The main target has been to estimate curvature: peaks of local curvature are corners, and analysing an image by its corners is especially suited to image of man-made objects. The second area includes more modern approaches that improve performance by employing region or patch-based analysis. We shall start with the more established curvature-based operators, before moving to the patch- or region-based analysis.

4.4.1 Detecting image curvature (corner extraction)

4.4.1.1 Definition of curvature

Edges are perhaps the low-level image features that are most obvious to human vision. They preserve significant features, so we can usually recognise what an image contains from its edge detected version. However, there are other low-level features that can be used in computer vision. One important feature is *curvature*. Intuitively, we can consider curvature as the rate of change in edge direction. This rate of change characterises the points in a curve; points where the edge direction changes rapidly are *corners*, whereas points where there is little change in edge direction correspond to straight lines. Such extreme points are very useful for shape description and matching, since they represent significant information with reduced data.

Curvature is normally defined by considering a parametric form of a planar curve. The parametric contour $v(t) = x(t)U_x + y(t)U_y$ describes the points in a continuous curve as the end points of the position vector. Here, the values of t define an arbitrary parameterisation, the unit vectors are again $U_x = [1,0]$ and $U_y = [0,1]$. Changes in the position vector are given by the tangent vector function of the curve $v(t)$. That is, $\dot{v}(t) = \dot{x}(t)U_x + \dot{y}(t)U_y$. This vectorial expression has a simple intuitive meaning. If we think of the trace of the curve as the motion of a point and t is related to time, the tangent vector defines the instantaneous motion. At any moment, the point moves with a speed given by $|\dot{v}(t)| = \sqrt{\dot{x}^2(t) + \dot{y}^2(t)}$ in the direction $\phi(t) = tan^{-1}(\dot{y}(t)/\dot{x}(t))$. The curvature at a point $v(t)$ describes the changes in the direction $\phi(t)$ with respect to changes in arc length. That is,

$$\kappa(t) = \frac{d\phi(t)}{ds} \tag{4.41}$$

where s is arc length, along the edge itself. Here ϕ is the angle of the tangent to the curve. That is, $\phi = \theta \pm 90^\circ$, where θ is the gradient direction defined in Eq. (4.13). That is, if we apply an edge detector operator to an image, then we can compute ϕ to obtain a normal direction for each point in a curve. The tangent to a curve is given by an orthogonal vector. Curvature is given with respect to arc length because a curve parameterised by arc length maintains a constant speed of motion. Thus, curvature represents changes in direction for constant displacements along the curve. By considering the chain rule, we have

$$\kappa(t) = \frac{d\phi(t)}{dt}\frac{dt}{ds} \tag{4.42}$$

The differential ds/dt defines the change in arc length with respect to the parameter t. If we again consider the curve as the motion of a point, this differential defines the instantaneous change in distance with respect to time. That is, the instantaneous speed. Thus,

$$ds\,/\,dt = |\dot{v}(t)| = \sqrt{\dot{x}^2(t) + \dot{y}^2(t)} \tag{4.43}$$

and

$$dt\,/\,ds = 1\Big/\sqrt{\dot{x}^2(t) + \dot{y}^2(t)} \tag{4.44}$$

By considering that $\phi(t) = \tan^{-1}(\dot{y}(t)/\dot{x}(t))$, then the curvature at a point $v(t)$ in Eq. (4.42) is given by

$$\kappa(t) = \frac{\dot{x}(t)\ddot{y}(t) - \dot{y}(t)\ddot{x}(t)}{(\dot{x}^2(t) + \dot{y}^2(t))^{3/2}} \tag{4.45}$$

This relationship is called the *curvature function*, and it is the standard measure of curvature for *planar* curves [Apostol66]. An important feature of curvature is that it relates the derivative of a tangential vector to a normal vector. This can be explained by the simplified Serret–Frenet equations [Goetz70] as follows. We can express the tangential vector in polar form as

$$\dot{v}(t) = |\dot{v}(t)|(\cos(\phi(t)) + j\sin(\phi(t))) \tag{4.46}$$

If the curve is parameterised by arc length, then $|\dot{v}(t)|$ is constant. Thus, the derivative of a tangential vector is simply given by

$$\ddot{v}(t) = |\dot{v}(t)|(-\sin(\phi(t)) + j\cos(\phi(t)))\frac{d\phi(t)}{dt} \tag{4.47}$$

Since we are using a normal parameterisation, then $d\phi(t)/dt = d\phi(t)/ds$. Thus, the tangential vector can be written as

$$\ddot{v}(t) = \kappa(t)\mathbf{n}(t) \tag{4.48}$$

where $\mathbf{n}(t) = |\dot{v}(t)|(-\sin(\phi(t)) + j\cos(\phi(t)))$ defines the direction of $\ddot{v}(t)$, whilst the curvature $\kappa(t)$ defines its modulus. The derivative of the normal vector is given by $\dot{\mathbf{n}}(t) = |\dot{\upsilon}(t)|(-\cos(\phi(t)) - j\sin(\phi(t)))\frac{d\phi(t)}{ds}$ and can be written as

$$\dot{\mathbf{n}}(t) = -\kappa(t)\dot{\upsilon}(t) \tag{4.49}$$

Clearly $\mathbf{n}(t)$ is normal to $\dot{\upsilon}(t)$. Therefore, for each point in the curve, there is a pair of orthogonal vectors $\dot{\upsilon}(t)$ and $\mathbf{n}(t)$ whose moduli are proportionally related by the curvature.

Generally, the curvature of a parametric curve is computed by evaluating Eq. (4.45). For a straight line, for example, the second derivatives $\ddot{x}(t)$ and $\ddot{y}(t)$ are zero, so the curvature function is nil. For a circle of radius r, we have that $\dot{x}(t) = r\cos(t)$ and $\dot{y}(t) = -r\sin(t)$. Thus, $\ddot{x}(t) = -r\sin(t)$, $\ddot{y}(t) = -r\cos(t)$ and $\kappa(t) = 1/r$. However, for curves in digital images, the derivatives must be computed from discrete data. This can be done in four main ways. The most obvious approach is to calculate curvature by directly computing the difference between angular direction of successive edge pixels in a curve. A second approach is to derive a measure of curvature from changes in image intensity. Finally, a measure of curvature can be obtained by correlation.

4.4.1.2 Computing differences in edge direction

Perhaps the easier way to compute curvature in digital images is to measure the *angular change* along the curve's path. This approach was considered in early corner detection techniques [Bennett75, Groan78, Kitchen82], and it merely computes the difference in edge direction between connected pixels forming a discrete curve. That is, it approximates the derivative in Eq. (4.41) as the difference between neighbouring pixels. As such, curvature is simply given by

$$k(t) = \phi_{t+1} - \phi_{t-1} \tag{4.50}$$

where the sequence $\ldots\phi_{t-1}, \phi_t, \phi_{t+1}, \phi_{t+2}\ldots$ represents the gradient direction of a sequence of pixels defining a curve segment. Gradient direction can be obtained as the angle given by an edge detector operator. Alternatively, it can be computed by considering the positions of pixels in the sequence. That is, by defining $\phi_t = (y_{t-1} - y_{t+1})/(x_{t-1} - x_{t+1})$ where (x_t, y_t) denotes pixel t in the sequence. Since edge points are only defined at discrete points, this angle can only take eight values, so the computed curvature is very ragged. This can be smoothed by considering the difference in mean angular direction of n pixels on the leading and trailing curve segment. That is,

$$k_n(t) = \frac{1}{n}\sum_{i=1}^{n}\phi_{t+i} - \frac{1}{n}\sum_{i=-n}^{-1}\phi_{t+i} \tag{4.51}$$

The average also gives some immunity to noise, and it can be replaced by a weighted average if Gaussian smoothing is required. The number of pixels considered, the value of n, defines a compromise between accuracy and noise sensitivity. Notice that filtering techniques may also be used to reduce the quantisation effect when angles are obtained

```
for x,y in itertools.product(range(0, width), range(0, height)):
    # Edge
    if magnitude[y,x] > 0:
        # Consider neighbor edges
        edgesNeigbor = [ ]
        for wx,wy in itertools.product(range(-windowDelta, windowDelta+1),        \
                                       range(-windowDelta, windowDelta+1)):
            if magnitude[y+wy, x+wx] > 0 :
                edgesNeigbor.append( (y+wy,x+wx) )

        # Use dot product to measure angle difference
        np = len(edgesNeigbor)
        for p in range(0, np):
            y1 = (edgesNeigbor[p])[0]
            x1 = (edgesNeigbor[p])[1]
            curvature[y,x] += 1.0-(cos(angle[y1,x1]) * cos(angle[y,x])          \
                                  + sin(angle[y1,x1]) * sin(angle[y,x]))
        if np > 0:
            curvature[y,x] /= np
```

CODE 4.9 Detecting curvature by angle differences.

by an edge detection operator. As we have already discussed, the level of filtering is related to the size of the template (as in Section 3.4.3).

In order to compute angular differences, we need to determine connected edges. Code 4.9 uses the data in the arrays `magnitude` and `angle` that contain the magnitude and angle of edges computed with the Canny edge operator. For each edge (i.e. a pixel with magnitude greater than one), the code fills the list `edgeNeigbours` with all the close edges. The curvature is computed by the average of the difference between the angle between the edge and the edges in its neighbour. The angle difference is computed by using the dot product of the vectors defining the edge direction.

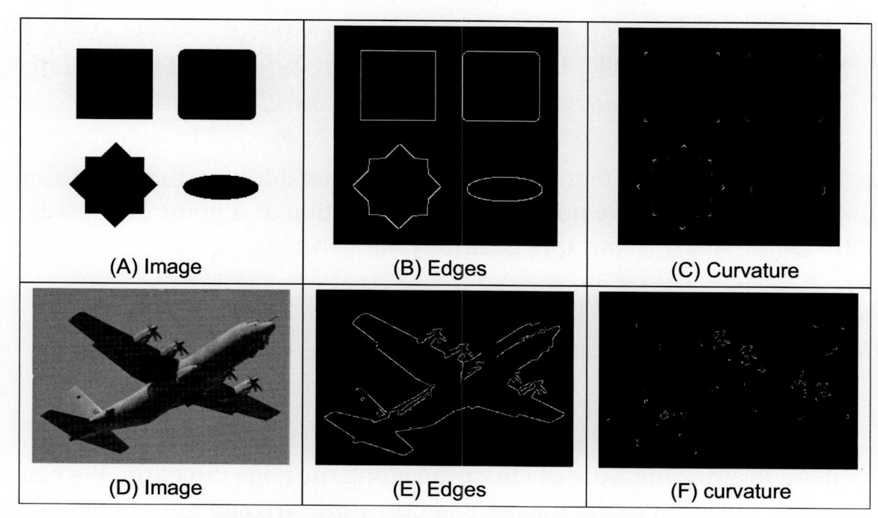

FIGURE 4.38 Curvature detection by angle differences.

The result of applying this type of curvature detection is shown in Fig. 4.38. Here Fig. 4.38A shows an image with regions whose borders have different curvature. Fig. 4.38D shows an image of a real of object. The edges computed by the Canny edge detector are shown in Figs. 4.38B and E. Figs. 4.38C and F show the curvature obtained by computing the rate of change of edge direction. In these figures, curvature is defined only at the edge points. Here, by its formulation the measurement of curvature κ gives just a thin line of differences in edge direction which can be seen to track the perimeter points of the shapes (at points where there is measured curvature). The brightest points are those with greatest curvature. In order to show the results, we have scaled the curvature values to use 256 intensity values. The estimates of corner points could be obtained by a uniformly thresholded version of Fig. 4.38F, well in theory anyway!

Unfortunately, as can be seen, this approach does not provide reliable results. It is essentially a reformulation of a first-order edge detection process and presupposes that the corner information lies within the threshold data (and uses no corner structure in detection). One of the major difficulties with this approach is that measurements of angle can be severely affected by quantisation error and accuracy is limited [Bennett75], a factor which will return to plague us later when we study methods for describing shapes.

4.4.1.3 Measuring curvature by changes in intensity (differentiation)

As an alternative way of measuring curvature, we can derive the curvature as a function of changes in image intensity. This derivation can be based on the measure of angular changes in the discrete image. We can represent the direction at each image point as the function $\phi'(x,y)$. Thus, according to the definition of curvature, we should compute the change in these direction values normal to the image edge (i.e. along the curves in an image). The curve at an edge can be locally approximated by the points given by the parametric line defined by $x(t) = x + t\,cos(\phi'(x,y))$ and $y(t) = y + t\,sin(\phi'(x,y))$. Thus, the curvature is given by the change in the function $\phi'(x,y)$ with respect to t. That is,

$$\kappa_{\phi'}(x,y) = \frac{\partial \phi'(x,y)}{\partial t} = \frac{\partial \phi'(x,y)}{\partial x}\frac{\partial x(t)}{\partial t} + \frac{\partial \phi'(x,y)}{\partial y}\frac{\partial y(t)}{\partial t} \tag{4.52}$$

where $\partial x(t)/\partial t = \cos(\phi')$ and $\partial y(t)/\partial t = \sin(\phi')$. By considering the definition of the gradient angle, we have that the normal tangent direction at a point in a line is given by $\phi'(x,y) = \tan^{-1}(Mx/(-My))$. From this geometry we can observe that

$$\cos(\phi') = -My\Big/\sqrt{Mx^2 + My^2} \quad \text{and} \quad \sin(\phi') = Mx\Big/\sqrt{Mx^2 + My^2} \tag{4.53}$$

By differentiation of $\phi'(x,y)$ and by considering these definitions we obtain

$$\kappa_{\phi'}(x,y) = \frac{1}{(Mx^2 + My^2)^{\frac{3}{2}}}\left\{My^2\frac{\partial Mx}{\partial x} - MxMy\frac{\partial My}{\partial x} + Mx^2\frac{\partial My}{\partial y} - MxMy\frac{\partial Mx}{\partial y}\right\} \tag{4.54}$$

This defines a forward measure of curvature along the edge direction. We can actually use an alternative direction to the measure of curvature. We can differentiate backwards (in the direction of $-\phi'(x,y)$) which gives $\kappa_{-\phi'}(x,y)$. In this case, we consider that the curve is given by $x(t) = x + t\,cos(-\phi'(x,y))$ and $y(t) = y + t\,sin(-\phi'(x,y))$. Thus,

$$\kappa_{-\phi'}(x,y) = \frac{1}{(Mx^2 + My^2)^{\frac{3}{2}}}\left\{ My^2 \frac{\partial Mx}{\partial x} - MxMy \frac{\partial My}{\partial x} - Mx^2 \frac{\partial My}{\partial y} + MxMy \frac{\partial Mx}{\partial y} \right\} \tag{4.55}$$

Two further measures can be obtained by considering the forward and a backward differential along the normal. These differentials cannot be related to the actual definition of curvature, but can be explained intuitively. If we consider that curves are more than one pixel wide, differentiation along the edge will measure the difference between the gradient angle between interior and exterior borders of a wide curve. In theory, the tangent angle should be the same. However, in discrete images there is a change due to the measures in a window. If the curve is a straight line, then the interior and exterior borders are the same. Thus, gradient direction normal to the edge does not change locally. As we bend a straight line, we increase the difference between the curves defining the interior and exterior borders. Thus, we expect the measure of gradient direction to change. That is, if we differentiate along the normal direction, we maximise detection of gross curvature. The value $\kappa_{\perp\phi'}(x,y)$ is obtained when $x(t) = x + t\,sin(\phi'(x,y))$ and $y(t) = y + t\,cos(\phi'(x,y))$. In this case,

$$\kappa_{\perp\phi'}(x,y) = \frac{1}{(Mx^2 + My^2)^{\frac{3}{2}}}\left\{ Mx^2 \frac{\partial My}{\partial x} - MxMy \frac{\partial My}{\partial x} - MxMy \frac{\partial My}{\partial y} + My^2 \frac{\partial Mx}{\partial y} \right\} \tag{4.56}$$

In a backward formulation along a normal direction to the edge, we obtain:

$$\kappa_{-\perp\phi'}(x,y) = \frac{1}{(Mx^2 + My^2)^{\frac{3}{2}}}\left\{ -Mx^2 \frac{\partial My}{\partial x} + MxMy \frac{\partial Mx}{\partial x} - MxMy \frac{\partial My}{\partial y} + My^2 \frac{\partial Mx}{\partial y} \right\} \tag{4.57}$$

This was originally used by Kass [Kass88] as a means to detect *line terminations*, as part of a feature extraction scheme called snakes (active contours) which are covered in Chapter 6. Code 4.10 shows an implementation of the four measures of curvature. The arrays `mX` and `mY` store the gradient obtained by the convolutions of the original image with Sobel kernels in horizontal and vertical directions. The arrays `mXx`, `mXy`, `mYx` and `mYy` contain the convolutions of `mX` and `mY` with Sobel kernels. Fig. 4.39 shows the form of the combined gradients where each combination detects changes in a different direction in the image. Code 4.10 combines the first- and second-order gradients according to *backward* and *forward* formulations along the normal and edge direction. The result is computed according to the selection of parameter `op`. The curvature value is only computed at edge pixels.

Fig. 4.40 shows the result for each operation for the synthetic image in Fig. 4.38A. We can see that the gradients locate edges and corners in different directions. That is, white and black alternates in each definition. However, all operations obtain maxima (or minima) where there is high curvature, so any of them can be used for curvature detection.

Fig. 4.41 shows the curvature detected for the images shown in Fig. 4.38. Curvature is obtained by the absolute value. In the figure, points where the curvature is large are highlighted. All functions obtain similar results and highlight features in the boundary,

```
for x,y in itertools.product(range(0, width), range(0, height)):
    # If it is an edge
    if magnitude[y,x] > 0:
        Mx2,My2,MxMy = mX[y,x]*mX[y,x], mY[y,x]*mY[y,x], mX[y,x]*mY[y,x]

        if Mx2 + My2 !=0.0:
            p = 1.0/ pow((Mx2 + My2), 1.5)

            if op == "T":
                curvature[y,x] = p * (My2 * mXx[y,x] - MxMy * mYx[y,x] +  \
                                      Mx2 * mYy[y,x] - MxMy * mXy[y,x])
            if op == "TI":
                curvature[y,x] = p * (-My2 * mXx[y,x] + MxMy * mYx[y,x] - \
                                      Mx2 * mYy[y,x] + MxMy * mXy[y,x])
            if op == "N":
                curvature[y,x] = p * (Mx2  * mYx[y,x] - MxMy * mYx[y,x] - \
                                      MxMy * mYy[y,x] + My2  * mXy[y,x])
            if op == "NI":
                curvature[y,x] = p * (-Mx2 *  mYx[y,x] + MxMy * mXx[y,x] + \
                                      MxMy * mYy[y,x] - My2 *  mXy[y,x])

            curvature[y,x] = fabs(curvature[y,x])
```

CODE 4.10 Curvature by measuring changes in intensity.

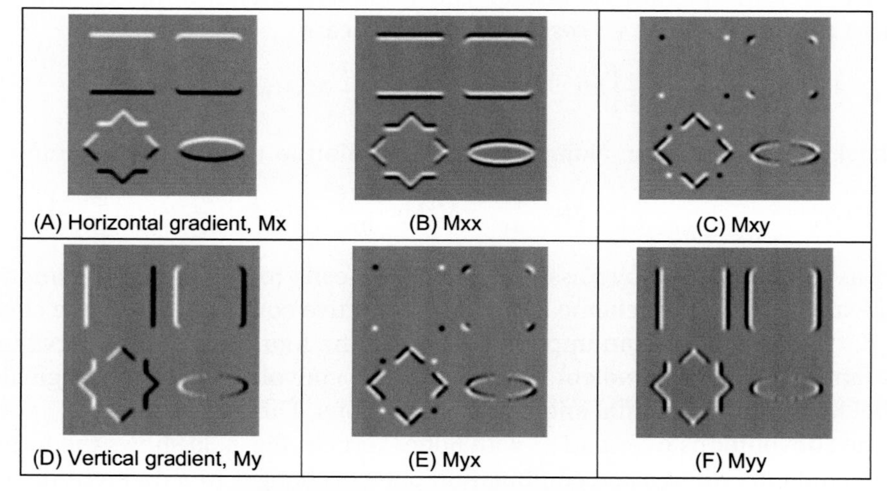

(A) Horizontal gradient, Mx (B) Mxx (C) Mxy (D) Vertical gradient, My (E) Myx (F) Myy

FIGURE 4.39 First- and second-order gradients.

In general, we expect that the computation based on regions obtains better edges than when using angle differences (Fig. 4.39) since convolution provides some filtering to the edges though there is little discernible performance. As the results in Fig. 4.41 suggest, detecting curvature directly from an image is not totally reliable and further analysis shows that the computed values are just rough estimates of the actual curvature; however, the results also show that these measures can effectively give strong evidence about the location of corners. The results are also very dependent on the size of the window used to compute the gradients and the size of the corners.

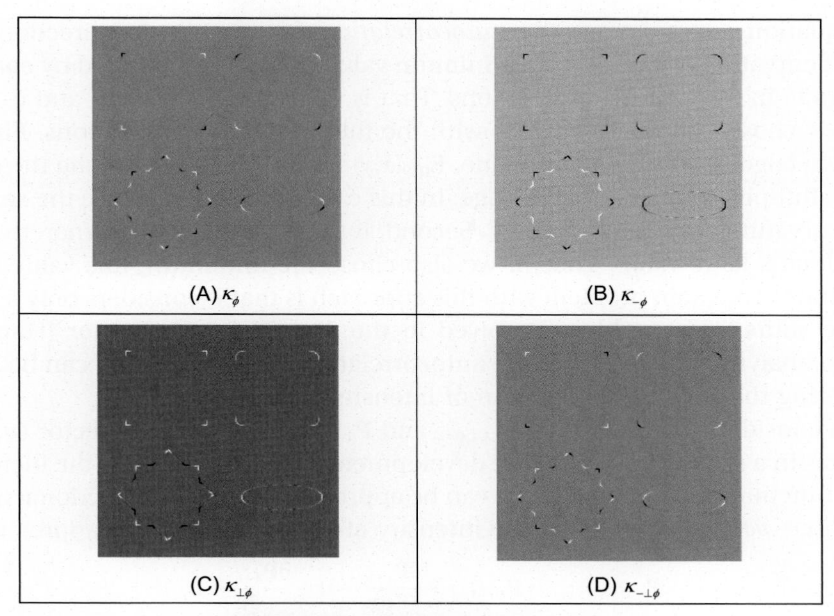

FIGURE 4.40 Comparing image curvature.

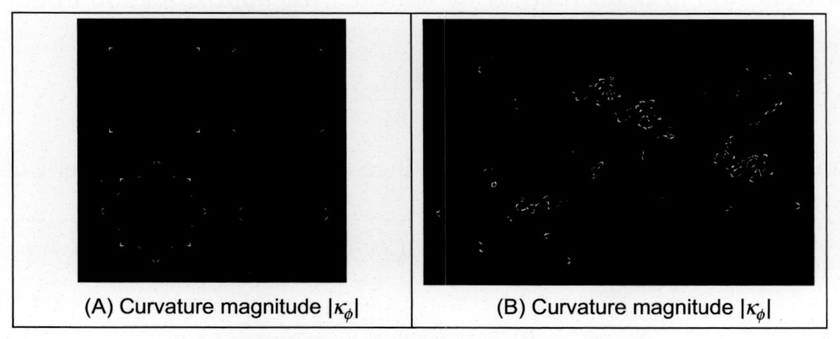

FIGURE 4.41 Curvature detection operators.

4.4.1.4 Moravec and Harris detectors

In the previous section, we measured curvature as the derivative of the function $\phi(x,y)$ along the normal and edge directions. Alternatively, a measure of curvature can be obtained by considering changes along alternative directions in the image **P** itself. This is the basic idea of *Moravec's corner detection operator*. This operator computes the average change in image intensity when a window is shifted in several directions. That is, for a pixel with co-ordinates (x,y), and a window size of $2w+1$ we have that

$$\mathbf{E}_{u,v}(x,y) = \sum_{i=-w}^{w} \sum_{j=-w}^{w} [\mathbf{P}_{x+i,y+j} - \mathbf{P}_{x+i+u,y+j+v}]^2 \tag{4.58}$$

This equation approximates the *autocorrelation function* in the direction (u,v). A measure of curvature is given by the minimum value of $\mathbf{E}_{u,v}(x,y)$ obtained by considering the shifts (u,v) in the four main directions. That is, by (1,0), (0,−1), (0,1) and (−1,0). The minimum is chosen because it agrees with the following two observations. First, if the pixel is in an edge defining a straight line, $\mathbf{E}_{u,v}(x,y)$ is small for a shift along the edge and large for a shift perpendicular to the edge. In this case, we should choose the small value since the curvature of the edge is small. Second, if the edge defines a corner, then all the shifts produce a large value. Thus, if we also chose the minimum, this value indicates high curvature. The main problem with this approach is that it considers only a small set of possible shifts. This problem is solved in the *Harris corner detector* [Harris88] by defining an analytic expression for the autocorrelation. This expression can be obtained by considering the local approximation of intensity changes.

We can consider that the points $\mathbf{P}_{x+i,y+j}$ and $\mathbf{P}_{x+i+u,y+j+v}$, define a vector (u,v) in the image. Thus, in a similar fashion to the development given in Eq. (4.58), the increment in the image function between the points can be approximated by the directional derivative $u\partial\mathbf{P}_{x+i,y+j}/\partial x + v\partial\mathbf{P}_{x+i,y+j}/\partial y$. Thus, the intensity at $\mathbf{P}_{x+i+u,y+j+v}$ can be approximated as

$$\mathbf{P}_{x+i+u,y+j+v} = \mathbf{P}_{x+i,y+j} + \frac{\partial\mathbf{P}_{x+i,y+j}}{\partial x}u + \frac{\partial\mathbf{P}_{x+i,y+j}}{\partial y}v \tag{4.59}$$

This expression corresponds to the three first terms of the Taylor expansion around $\mathbf{P}_{x+i,y+j}$ (an expansion to first-order). If we consider the approximation in Eq. (4.58), we have that

$$\mathbf{E}_{u,v}(x,y) = \sum_{i=-w}^{w}\sum_{j=-w}^{w}\left[\frac{\partial\mathbf{P}_{x+i,y+j}}{\partial x}u + \frac{\partial\mathbf{P}_{x+i,y+j}}{\partial y}v\right]^2 \tag{4.60}$$

By expansion of the squared term (and since u and v are independent of the summations), we obtain,

$$\mathbf{E}_{u,v}(x,y) = A(x,y)u^2 + 2C(x,y)uv + B(x,y)v^2 \tag{4.61}$$

where

$$\begin{aligned} A(x,y) &= \sum_{i=-w}^{w}\sum_{j=-w}^{w}\left(\frac{\partial\mathbf{P}_{x+i,y+j}}{\partial x}\right)^2 \quad B(x,y) = \sum_{i=-w}^{w}\sum_{j=-w}^{w}\left(\frac{\partial\mathbf{P}_{x+i,y+j}}{\partial y}\right)^2 \\ C(x,y) &= \sum_{i=-w}^{w}\sum_{j=-w}^{w}\left(\frac{\partial\mathbf{P}_{x+i,y+j}}{\partial x}\right)\left(\frac{\partial\mathbf{P}_{x+i,y+j}}{\partial y}\right) \end{aligned} \tag{4.62}$$

That is, the summation of the squared components of the gradient direction for all the pixels in the window. In practice, this average can be weighted by a Gaussian function to make the measure less sensitive to noise (i.e. by filtering the image data). In order to measure the curvature at a point (x,y), it is necessary to find the vector (u,v) that minimises $\mathbf{E}_{u,v}(x,y)$ given in Eq. (4.61). In a basic approach, we can recall that the minimum is obtained when the window is displaced in the direction of the edge. Thus, we can consider that $u = \cos(\phi(x,y))$ and $v = \sin(\phi(x,y))$. These values were defined in Eq. (4.53). Accordingly, the minima values that define curvature are given by

$$\kappa_{u,v}(x,y) = \min \mathbf{E}_{u,v}(x,y) = \frac{A(x,y)M_y^2 + 2C(x,y)M_xM_y + B(x,y)M_x^2}{M_x^2 + M_y^2} \tag{4.63}$$

In a more sophisticated approach, we can consider the form of the function $\mathbf{E}_{u,v}(x,y)$. We can observe that this is a quadratic function, so it has two principal axes. We can rotate the function such that its axes have the same direction that the axes of the coordinate system. That is, we rotate the function $\mathbf{E}_{u,v}(x,y)$ to obtain

$$\mathbf{F}_{u,v}(x,y) = \alpha(x,y)^2 u^2 + \beta(x,y)^2 v^2 \tag{4.64}$$

The values of α and β are proportional to the autocorrelation function along the principal axes. Accordingly, if the point (x,y) is in a region of constant intensity, we will have that both values are small. If the point defines a straight border in the image, then one value is large and the other is small. If the point defines an edge with high curvature, both values are large. Based on these observations a measure of curvature is defined as

$$\kappa_k(x,y) = \alpha\beta - k(\alpha + \beta)^2 \tag{4.65}$$

The first term in this equation makes the measure large when the values of α and β increase. The second term is included to decrease the values in flat borders. The parameter k must be selected to control the sensitivity of the detector. The higher the value, the computed curvature will be more sensitive to changes in the image (and therefore to noise).

In practice, in order to compute $\kappa_k(x,y)$, it is not necessary to compute explicitly the values of α and β, but the curvature can be measured from the coefficient of the quadratic expression in Eq. (4.61). This can be derived by considering the matrix forms of Eqs. (4.61) and (4.64). If we define the vector $\mathbf{D}^T = [u,v]$, then Eqs. (4.61) and (4.64) can be written as,

$$\mathbf{E}_{u,v}(x,y) = \mathbf{D}^T\mathbf{M}\mathbf{D} \quad \text{and} \quad \mathbf{F}_{u,v}(x,y) = \mathbf{D}^T\mathbf{Q}\mathbf{D} \tag{4.66}$$

where T denotes the transpose and where

$$\mathbf{M} = \begin{bmatrix} A(x,y) & C(x,y) \\ C(x,y) & B(x,y) \end{bmatrix} \quad \text{and} \quad \mathbf{Q} = \begin{bmatrix} \alpha & 0 \\ 0 & \beta \end{bmatrix} \tag{4.67}$$

In order to relate Eqs. (4.61) and (4.64), we consider that $\mathbf{F}_{u,v}(x,y)$ is obtained by rotating $\mathbf{E}_{u,v}(x,y)$ by a transformation $\mathbf{R}$ that rotates the axis defined by $\mathbf{D}$. That is,

$$\mathbf{F}_{u,v}(x,y) = (\mathbf{R}\mathbf{D})^T\mathbf{M}\mathbf{R}\mathbf{D} \tag{4.68}$$

This can be arranged as

$$\mathbf{F}_{u,v}(x,y) = \mathbf{D}^T\mathbf{R}^T\mathbf{M}\mathbf{R}\mathbf{D} \tag{4.69}$$

By comparison with Eq. (4.66), we have that

$$\mathbf{Q} = \mathbf{R}^T\mathbf{M}\mathbf{R} \tag{4.70}$$

This defines a well-known equation of linear algebra, and it means that $\mathbf{Q}$ is an orthogonal decomposition of $\mathbf{M}$. The diagonal elements of $\mathbf{Q}$ are called the eigenvalues. We can use Eq. (4.70) to obtain the value of $\alpha\beta$ which defines the first term in Eq. (4.65) by considering the determinant of the matrices. That is, $\det(\mathbf{Q}) = \det(\mathbf{R}^T)\det(\mathbf{M})\det(\mathbf{R})$. Since $\mathbf{R}$ is a rotation matrix $\det(\mathbf{R}^T)\det(\mathbf{R}) = 1$, thus

$$\alpha\beta = A(x,y)B(x,y) - C(x,y)^2 \tag{4.71}$$

which defines the first term in Eq. (4.65). The second term can be obtained by taking the trace of the matrices on each side of this equation. Thus, we have that

$$\alpha + \beta = A(x,y) + B(x,y) \tag{4.72}$$

We can also use Eq. (4.70) to obtain the value of $\alpha+\beta$ which defines the first term in Eq. (4.65). By taking the trace of the matrices in each side of this equation, we have that

$$\kappa_k(x,y) = A(x,y)B(x,y) - C(x,y)^2 - k(A(x,y) + B(x,y))^2 \tag{4.73}$$

Code 4.11 shows an implementation for Eqs. (4.64) and (4.73). The equation to be used is selected by the `op` parameter. Curvature is only computed at edge points. That is, at pixels whose edge magnitude is different from zero after applying nonmaximum suppression. The first part of the code computes the coefficients of the matrix $\mathbf{M}$. Then, these values are used in the curvature computation.

Fig. 4.42 shows the results of computing curvature using this implementation. The results are capable of showing the different curvature values in the border. We can observe that the Harris operator produces more contrast between lines with low and high curvature than when curvature is computed by the evaluating the minimum

```
for x,y in itertools.product(range(0, width), range(0, height)):
    # If it is an edge
    if magnitude[y,x] > 0:
        A, B, C = 0.0, 0.0, 0.0
        for wx,wy in itertools.product(range(0, kernelSize), range(0, kernelSize)):
            posY = y + wy - kernelCentre
            posX = x + wx - kernelCentre

            if posY > -1 and posY <  height and posX > -1 and posX <  width:
                A += mX[posY,posX] * mX[posY,posX]
                B += mY[posY,posX] * mY[posY,posX]
                C += mX[posY,posX] * mY[posY,posX]

        if op == "H":
                curvature[y,x] = (A * B) - (C * C) - (k * ((A+B) * (A+B)))
        if op == "M":
                d = mX[y,x] * mX[y,x] + mY[y,x] * mY[y,x]
                if d != 0.0:
                    curvature[y,x] = (A * mY[y,x] * mY[y,x] -                    \
                                      2.0 * C * mX[y,x] * mY[y,x] +              \
                                      B * mX[y,x] * mX[y,x]) / d
```

CODE 4.11 Harris corner detector.

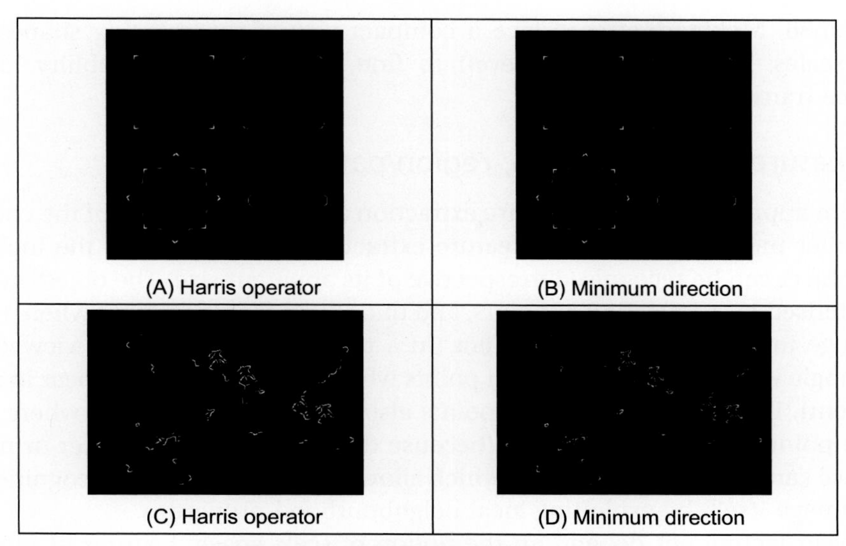

FIGURE 4.42 Curvature via the Harris operator.

direction. The reason is the inclusion of the second term in Eq. (4.73). In general, the measure of correlation is not only useful for computing curvature, but this technique has much wider application in finding points when matching pairs of images.

4.4.1.5 Further reading on curvature

Many of the arguments earlier advanced on extensions to edge detection in Section 4.2 apply to corner detection as well, so the same advice applies. There is much less attention paid by established textbooks to corner detection, though [Davies05] devotes a chapter to the topic. Van Otterloo's fine book on shape analysis [VanOtterloo91] contains a detailed analysis of measurement of (planar) curvature.

There are other important issues in corner detection. It has been suggested that corner extraction can be augmented by local knowledge to improve performance [Rosin96]. There are actually many other corner detection schemes, each offering different attributes though with differing penalties. Important work has focused on characterising shapes using corners. In a scheme analogous to the primal sketch introduced earlier, there is a *curvature primal sketch* [Asada86], which includes a set of primitive parameterised curvature discontinuities (such as termination and joining points). There are many other approaches: one (natural) suggestion is to define a corner as the intersection between two lines, this requires a process to find the lines; other techniques use methods that describe shape variation to find corners. We commented that filtering techniques can be included to improve the detection process; however, filtering can also be used to obtain a representation with multiple details. This representation is very useful to shape characterisation. A *curvature scale space* was developed

[Mokhtarian86, Mokhtarian03] to give a compact way of representing shapes, and at different scales, from coarse (low-level) to fine (detail) and with ability to handle appearance transformations.

4.4.2 Feature point detection; region/patch analysis

The modern approaches to local feature extraction aim to relieve some of the constraints on the earlier methods of localised feature extraction. This allows for the inclusion of scale: an object can be recognised irrespective of its apparent size. The object might also be characterised by a collection of points, and this allows for recognition where there has been change in the viewing arrangement (in a planar image an object viewed from a different angle will appear different, but points which represent it still appear in a similar arrangement). Using arrangements of points also allows for recognition where some of the image points have been obscured (because the image contains clutter or noise). In this way, we can achieve a description which allows for object or scene recognition direct from the image itself, by exploiting local neighbourhood properties.

The newer techniques depend on the notion of scale space: features of interest are those which persist over selected scales. The scale space is defined by images which are successively smoothed by the Gaussian filter, as in Eq. (3.26), and then subsampled to form an *image pyramid* at different scales, illustrated in Fig. 4.43 for three levels of resolution. There are approaches which exploit structure within the scale space to improve speed, as we shall find.

4.4.2.1 Scale invariant feature transform

The *scale invariant feature transform* (*SIFT*) [Lowe99, Lowe04] aims to resolve many of the practical problems in low-level feature extraction and their use in matching images. The earlier Harris operator is sensitive to changes in image scale and as such is unsuited to matching images of differing size. The SIFT transform actually involves two stages: feature extraction and description. The description stage concerns use of the low-level features in object matching, and this will be considered later. Low-level feature extraction within the SIFT approach selects salient features in a manner invariant to image

FIGURE 4.43 Illustrating scale space.

scale (feature size), and rotation and with partially invariance to change in illumination. Further, the formulation reduces the probability of poor extraction due to occlusion clutter and noise. Further, it shows how many of the techniques considered previously can be combined and capitalised on, to good effect.

First, the difference of Gaussians operator is applied to an image to identify features of potential interest. The formulation aims to ensure that feature selection does not depend on feature size (scale) or orientation. The features are then analysed to determine location and scale before the orientation is determined by local gradient direction. Finally, the features are transformed into a representation that can handle variation in illumination and local shape distortion. Essentially, the operator uses local information to refine the information delivered by standard operators. The detail of the operations is best left to the source material [Lowe99, Lowe04] for it is beyond the level or purpose here. As such, we shall concentrate on principle only.

Some features detected for an image are illustrated in Fig. 4.44. Here, the major features detected are shown by white lines where the length reflects magnitude, and the direction reflects the feature's orientation. These are the major features which include the head of the lizard and some leaves. The minor features are the smaller white lines: the ones shown here are concentrated around background features. In the full set of features detected at all scales in this image, there are many more of the minor features, concentrated particularly in the textured regions of the image (Fig. 4.45). Later we shall see how this can be used within shape extraction, but our purpose here is the basic low-level features.

In the first stage, the difference of Gaussians for an image $\mathbf{P}$ is computed in the manner of Eq. (4.28) as

$$\begin{aligned} D(x,y,\sigma) &= (g(x,y,k\sigma) - g(x,y,\sigma)) * \mathbf{P} \\ &= L(x,y,k\sigma) - L(x,y,k) \end{aligned} \tag{4.74}$$

The function L is actually a scale space function which can be used to define smoothed images at different scales. Rather than any difficulty in locating zero-crossing points, the features are the maxima and minima of the function. Candidate keypoints are then determined by comparing each point in the function with its immediate neighbours. The process then proceeds to analysis between the levels of scale, given

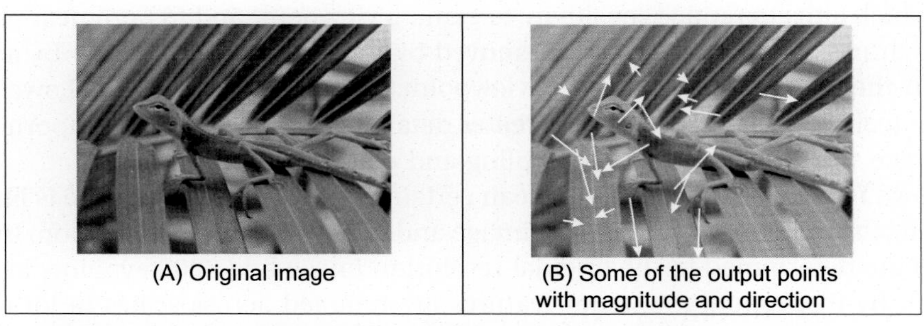

(A) Original image

(B) Some of the output points with magnitude and direction

FIGURE 4.44 Detecting features with the scale invariant feature transform operator.

FIGURE 4.45 Scale invariant feature transform feature detection at different scales.

appropriate sampling of the scale space. This then implies comparing a point with its eight neighbours at that scale and with the nine neighbours in each of the adjacent scales, to determine whether it is a minimum or maximum, as well as image resampling to ensure comparison between the different scales.

In order to filter the candidate points to reject those which are the result of low local contrast (low edge strength) or which are poorly localised along an edge, a function is derived by local curve fitting which indicates local edge strength and stability as well as location. Uniform thresholding then removes the keypoints with low contrast. Those that have poor localisation, i.e. their position is likely to be influenced by noise, can be filtered by considering the ratio of curvature along an edge to that perpendicular to it, in a manner following the Harris operator in Section 4.4.1.4, by thresholding the ratio of Eqs. (4.71) and (4.72).

In order to characterise the filtered keypoint features at each scale, the gradient magnitude is calculated in exactly the manner of Eqs. (4.12) and (4.13) as

$$M_{SIFT}(x,y) = \sqrt{(L(x+1,y) - L(x-1,y))^2 + (L(x,y+1) - L(x,y-1))^2} \tag{4.75}$$

$$\theta_{SIFT}(x,y) = \tan^{-1}\left(\frac{L(x,y+1) - L(x,y-1)}{(L(x+1,y) - L(x-1,y))}\right) \tag{4.76}$$

The peak of the histogram of the orientations around a keypoint is then selected as the local direction of the feature. This can be used to derive a canonical orientation, so that the resulting descriptors are invariant with rotation. As such, this contributes to the process which aims to reduce sensitivity to camera viewpoint and to nonlinear change in image brightness (linear changes are removed by the gradient operations) by analysing regions in the locality of the selected viewpoint. The main description [Lowe04] considers the technique's basis in much greater detail and outlines factors important to its performance such as the need for sampling and performance in noise.

As shown in Fig. 4.45, the technique can certainly operate well, and scale is illustrated by applying the operator to the original image and to one at half the resolution. In all, 601 keypoints are determined in the original resolution image and 320 keypoints at half the resolution. By inspection, the major features are retained across scales (a lot of minor regions in the leaves disappear at lower resolution), as expected. Alternatively the features can of course be filtered further by magnitude, or even direction (if appropriate). If you want more than results to convince you, implementations are available for Windows and Linux (https://www.cs.ubc.ca/~lowe/keypoints/ and some of the software sites noted in Table 1.2) – a feast for any developer. These images were derived by using `siftWin32`, version 4.

Note that description is inherent in the process – the standard SIFT keypoint descriptor is created by sampling the magnitudes and orientations of the image gradient in the region of the keypoint. An array of histograms, each with orientation bins, captures the rough spatial structure of the patch. This results in a vector which was later compressed by using *Principal Component Analysis (PCA)* [Ke04] to determine the most salient features. Clearly this allows for faster matching than the original SIFT formulation, but the improvement in performance was later doubted [Mikolajczyk05].

4.4.2.2 Speeded up robust features

The central property exploited within SIFT is the use of difference of Gaussians to determine local features. In a relationship similar to the one between first- and second-order edge detection, the *speeded up robust features (SURF)* approach [Bay06, Bay08] employs approximations to second-order edge detection, at different scales. The basis of the SURF operator is to use the integral image approach of Section 2.7.3.2 to provide an efficient means to compute approximations of second-order differencing, shown in Fig. 4.46. These are the approximations for a Laplacian of Gaussian operator with $\sigma = 1.2$ and represent the finest scale in the SURF operator. Other approximations can be derived for larger scales, since the operator – like SIFT – considers features which persist over scale space. The scale space can be derived by upscaling the approximations (wavelets) using larger templates which gives for faster execution than the use of smoothing and resampling in an image to form a pyramidal structure of different scales, which is more usual in scale space approaches.

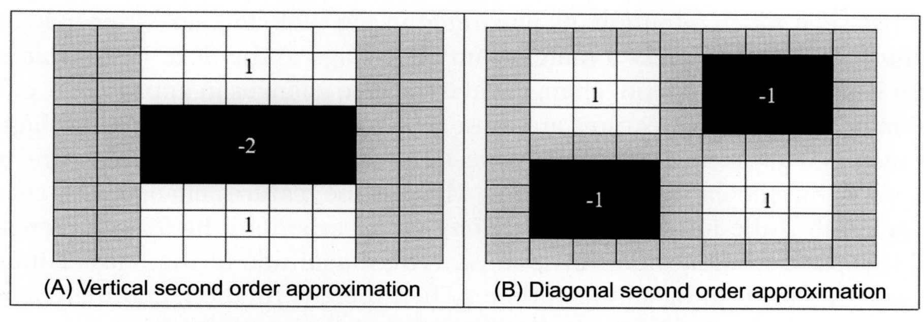

FIGURE 4.46 Basis of speeded up robust features feature detection.

By the Taylor expansion of the image brightness (Eq. (4.59)), we can form a (Hessian) matrix **M** (Eq. (4.67)) from which the maxima are used to derive the features. This is

$$\det(\mathbf{M}) = \begin{bmatrix} L_{xx} & L_{xy} \\ L_{xy} & L_{yy} \end{bmatrix} = L_{xx}L_{yy} - w \cdot L_{xy}^2 \tag{4.77}$$

where the terms in **M** arise from the convolution of a second-order derivative of Gaussian with the image information as

$$L_{xx} = \frac{\partial^2(g(x,y,\sigma))}{\partial x^2} * \mathbf{P}_{x,y} \quad L_{xy} = \frac{\partial^2(g(x,y,\sigma))}{\partial x \partial y} * \mathbf{P}_{x,y} \quad L_{yy} = \frac{\partial^2(g(x,y,\sigma))}{\partial y^2} * \mathbf{P}_{x,y} \tag{4.78}$$

and where w is carefully chosen to balance the components of the equation. To localise interest points in the image and over scales, nonmaximum suppression is applied in a $3 \times 3 \times 3$ neighbourhood. The maxima of the determinant of the Hessian matrix are then interpolated in scale space and in image space and described by orientations derived using the vertical and horizontal Haar wavelets described earlier (Section 2.7.3.2). Note that there is an emphasis on speed of execution, as well as on performance attributes, and so the generation of the templates to achieve scale space, the factor w, the interpolation operation to derive features and then their description are achieved using optimised processes. The developers have provided downloads for evaluation of SURF from www.vision.ee.ethz.ch/~surf/. The performance of the operator is illustrated in Fig. 4.47 showing the positions of the detected points for SIFT and for SURF. This shows that SURF can deliver fewer features, and which persist (and hence can be faster), whereas SIFT can provide more features (and be slower). As ever, choice depends on application – both techniques are available for evaluation and there are public domain implementations. The *Binary Robust Independent Elementary Features (BRIEF)* approach simply uses intensity comparison as a detector [Calonder10], which is innately simple though with proven capability, especially speed as it is very fast.

4.4.2.3 FAST, ORB, FREAK, LOCKY and other keypoint detectors

The need for fast interest point detection is manifested in the application of computer vision in *content-based image retrieval* (*CBIR*) in robots and autonomous driving, and so the area has seen much attention. As illustrated in Fig. 4.48, the aim is for matching: in autonomous driving one seeks a match from one image to the next; in face biometrics the target is points which do not change when the face changes in appearance, either by expression or by pose. The features are those which describe the underlying shape, and can be matched to each other. One basic tenet is whether the features are points-corners, or blobs (shown in Fig. 4.49), and whether the features change with change in the image itself. If the image is moved (along either axis) and the features remain the same, this represents translation invariance. (The magnitude of the Fourier transform was previously shown to be shift invariant.) Then there is rotation, and then change in scale in the two axis directions. If an operator is invariant to change in translation, rotation and scale, it is termed affine invariant, and these points are termed keypoints.

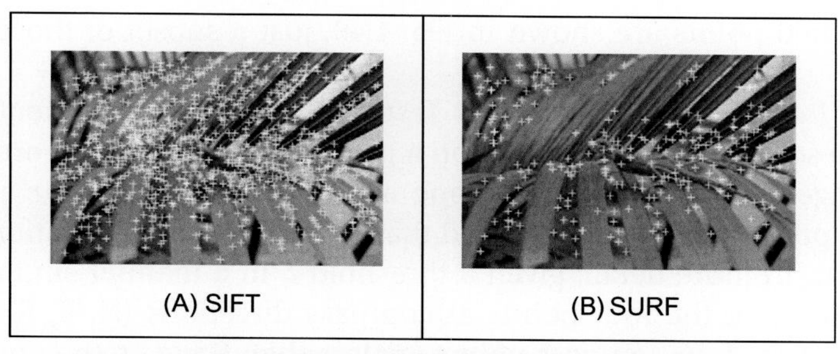

FIGURE 4.47 Comparing features detected by SIFT and SURF.

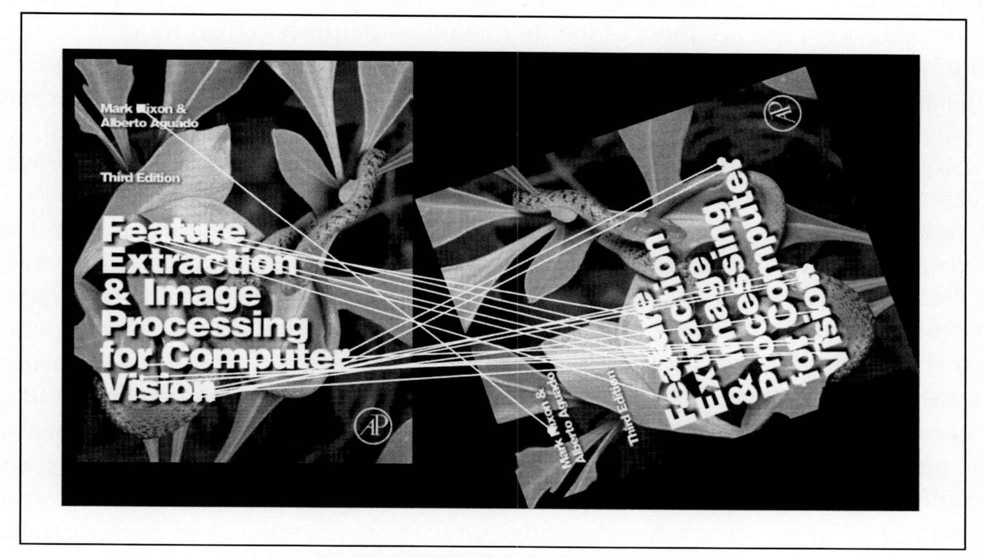

FIGURE 4.48 Matching by keypoint detection.

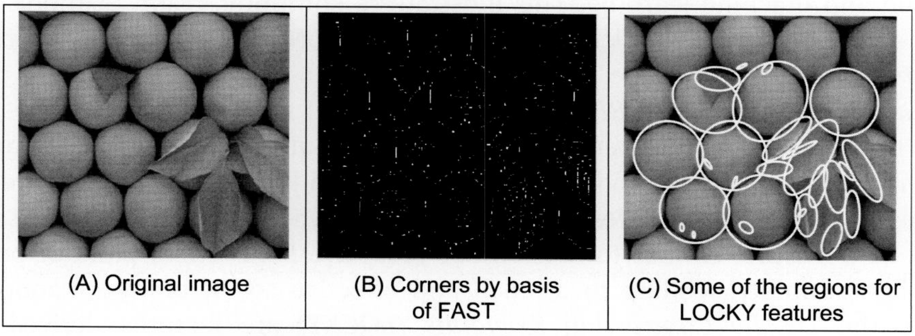

FIGURE 4.49 Detecting features by FAST and LOCKY.

Not all the matched points are shown in Fig. 4.49, just a subset of those automatically selected.

The *Features from Accelerated Segment Test* (*FAST*) approach [Rosten06] is based on simple tests on a set of 16 points centred on a pixel of interest with co-ordinates x,y. The points are arranged to be contiguous along a (discrete) circle and in principle if the brightness of all points on the circle exceed that of $\mathbf{I}(x,y)$, then the location x,y is labelled as a feature point. In more detail, given a threshold t, in a manner similar to hysteresis thresholding if three of the four points at compass directions (N, E, S and W) exceed $\mathbf{I}(x,y)+t$ or three of the four compass points are less than $\mathbf{I}(x,y)-t$, the point is possibly a feature point and the remaining 12 points are tested to determine if their brightness exceeds the centre point. Conversely, if three of the four compass points do not exceed $\mathbf{I}(x,y)+t$ nor are three of the four compass points less than $\mathbf{I}(x,y)-t$, the point cannot be a feature point and the test is not conducted. The basis of the technique is fast by its use of comparisons. As can be observed in Fig. 4.49B, it offers good performance but relies on choice of a threshold and lacks robustness in noise and capability for extension to larger templates, and so machine learning was deployed to improve its performance.

A potential limitation of the FAST operator (when used for matching) is that it tests for existence and does not include orientation – unlike the SURF and SIFT operators. This limitation was alleviated by the *ORB* operator [Rublee11] (where the acronym derives from *Oriented FAST and Rotated BRIEF*, the latter being a descriptive operator) which thus includes rotation invariance. Since FAST does not produce a measure of cornerness, and can have large responses along edges, as to be seen in Fig. 4.49B, potential responses are filtered by shape measures. The basis of the filter is shape measures called moments, and these will be covered in Chapter 7. The extension of ORB to include descriptive capability is to be found in Chapter 5. In general, the approaches are known as binary descriptors since a binary string results from a sequence of comparisons. In ORB, pairs of points are learnt to build the final descriptor.

Both FAST and ORB illustrate the nature of advanced operators, which employ many of the basic techniques used in computer vision, which are in shape extraction, description and machine learning. This illustrates a computer vision textbook author's difficulty since one writes a book to be read with linear progression, so one resorts (as we do) to forward references where necessary.

The *Fast Retina Keypoint* (*FREAK*) operator [Alahi12] was inspired by analysis of the retina in the human visual system. The descriptor is built using intensity comparisons between regions which are smoothed using a Gaussian kernel. The regions are large at the periphery of a point of interest and much smaller when closer to it (a coarse-to-fine strategy), in a manner similar to the retina's receptive field. Then, pairs of points are selected by variability, leading to a small and effective set of points. A more recent approach, the *Locally Contrasting Keypoints (LOCKY)* are features derived from a brightness clustering transform [Lomeli16] and can be thought as a coarse-to-fine search through scale spaces for the true derivative of the image. The brightness clustering uses a set of randomly positioned and (binary) sized rectangles which accumulate brightness using the integral image. The parameters to be chosen are the size of the rectangles and the number of votes to be accumulated. After thresholding the accumulated points the resulting image is thresholded and the LOCKY features are derived from the shapes of the connected components.

There are many more operators, each with particular advantage. For example, the *Binary Robust Invariant Scalable Keypoints* (*BRISK*) operator [Leutenegger11] uses a corner detector and then detects keypoints in scale space, *GIST* [Oliva06] employs Gabor wavelets aiming to describe scenes, and *STAR* [Agrawal08] uses a form of Haar wavelets via an integral image. By virtue for the need to find and match objects in images, this research is unlikely to cease with an optimum operator. Now, much research focusses on *convolutional neural networks* [Zheng18], and this will be considered later in Chapter 12.

The Oxford affine-covariant regions dataset [Mikolajczyk05] is an established dataset for evaluating feature detection. It is made up from eight sequences which comprise six images, each with increasing image transformations including change in illumination, perspective, blurring, (JPEG) compression and a combination of scale and rotation. A measure of repeatability is formed by projecting the detected features onto the same basis as the reference image (say, the first image of the sequence) using a homography matrix. The repeatability measure is one of how well the features detected on the images overlap, and it is preferable to achieve high repeatability. Using the correspondences with 40% overlap, Fig. 4.50 shows the reduction in repeatability for change in image appearance (the index). Comparison has been chosen to show no particular advantage; each technique has proponents (and antagonists!). As LOCKY is nondeterministic, it is shown with error bars (which are always welcome in any evaluation). One might prefer the consistency of SURF, or the performance of BRISK. LOCKY appears to be as fast as the STAR operator and faster than other approaches. But this is just one image, one series of (mainly OpenCV) implementations, and one

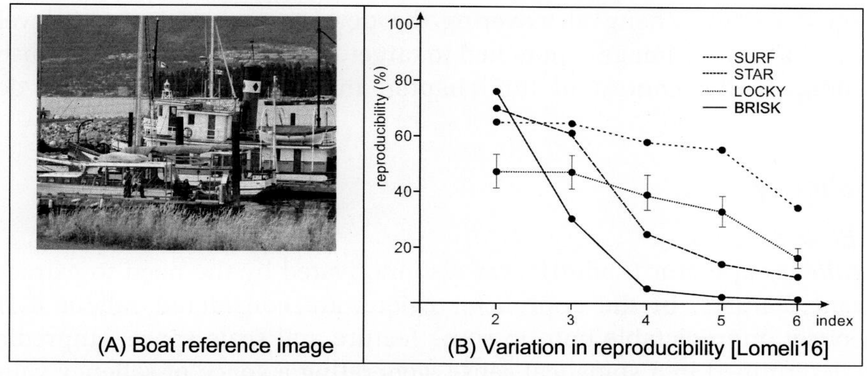

(A) Boat reference image (B) Variation in reproducibility [Lomeli16]

FIGURE 4.50 On the performance of interest point detectors [Lomeli16].

evaluation methodology: there are many variations to this theme. Another comparison [Mukherjee15] highlights the all-round performance of ORB, SIFT and BRIEF and is a good place to look. As ever, there is no panacea: techniques fit applications and not the other way round.

4.4.2.4 Other techniques and performance issues

There was a comprehensive *performance review* [Mikolajczyk05], comparing basic operators. The techniques which were compared included SIFT; differential derivatives by differentiation; cross-correlation for matching and a gradient location and orientation-based histogram (an extension to SIFT, which performed well). The criterion used for evaluation concerned the number of correct matches, and the number of false matches, between feature points selected by the techniques. The matching process was between an original image and one of the same scene when subject to one of the six image transformations. The image transformations covered practical effects that can change image appearance and were rotation; scale change; viewpoint change; image blur; JPEG compression and illumination. For some of these there were two scene types available, which allowed for separation of understanding of scene type and transformation. The study observed that, within its analysis, 'the SIFT-based descriptors perform best', but it is of course a complex topic and selection of technique is often application dependent. Note that there is further interest in performance evaluation, and in invariance to higher order changes in viewing geometry, such as invariance to affine and projective transformation. There are other comparisons available, either with new operators or in new applications, and there (inevitably) are faster implementations too. A later survey covered the field in more detail [Tuytelaars07], concerning principle and performance analysis. More recently, there has been much interest including deep learning for speed and accuracy. Given the continuing interest in CBIR, attention has turned to that. Note that CBIR includes detection and description, and the descriptions are covered in the next chapter. Chapter 12 covers deep learning in particular, and it is worth noting here that there has been a recent survey [Zheng18], covering the development of instance-level image retrieval (where a query image is matched to target images) and of its relationship with deep learning. In the context of this chapter, this concerns SIFT-based detection methods.

4.4.3 Saliency

4.4.3.1 Basic saliency

An early *saliency* operator [Kadir01] was also motivated by the need to extract robust and relevant features. In the approach, regions are considered salient if they are simultaneously unpredictable both in some feature and scale space. Unpredictability (rarity) is determined in a statistical sense, generating a space of saliency values over position and scale, as a basis for later understanding. The technique aims to be a generic approach to scale and saliency compared to conventional methods because both are defined independent of a particular basis morphology – meaning that it is not based on a particular geometric feature like a blob, edge or corner. The technique operates by determining the entropy (a measure of rarity) within patches at scales of interest, and the saliency is a weighted summation of where the entropy peaks. The method has practical capability in that it can be made invariant to rotation, translation, nonuniform scaling and uniform intensity variations and robust to small changes in viewpoint. An example result of processing the image in Fig. 4.51A is shown in Fig. 4.51B where the 200 most salient points are shown circled, and the radius of the circle is indicative of the scale. Many of the points are around the walking subject and others highlight significant features in the background, such as the waste bins, the tree or the time index. An example use of saliency was within an approach to learn and recognise object class models (such as faces, cars, or animals) from unlabelled and unsegmented cluttered scenes, irrespective of their overall size [Fergus03]. For further study and application, descriptions and Matlab binaries are available from Kadir's website (http://www.robots.ox.ac.uk/~timork/).

4.4.3.2 Context aware saliency

There has been quite a surge of interest in saliency detection since the early works. The *context aware saliency* is grounded in psychology [Goferman12] (learning from human vision is invariably a good idea). The approach uses colour images, and the colour representation is the CIE Lab (to be covered later in Chapter 11) as it is known to be the closest system to human colour vision. The operator generates maps of saliency. In its basis, the operator uses distance which is of a cue for saliency in human vision. A point in the background of an image is likely to have similarity to points which are both near and far away. In contrast, a point in the foreground, or a point of interest, is likely to

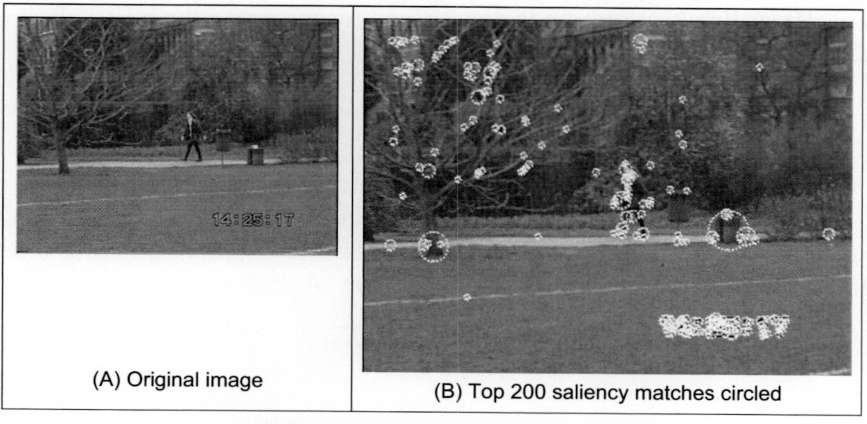

FIGURE 4.51 Detecting features by saliency.

be near another point of interest. Noting that a selection of distance measures is covered later in Chapter 12, the Euclidian distance d_p between the positions of two points p and q is

$$d_p(p,q) = \sqrt{(x(p) - x(q))^2 + (y(p) - y(q))^2} \tag{4.79}$$

which is normalised by the image dimensions. Similarly, in terms of colour, a point is likely to be salient when the difference in colour is large. The Euclidean distance in colour d_c between the two points is

$$d_c(p,q) = \sqrt{\sum_{cp=1}^{N_p} (plane_{cp}(p) - plane_{cp}(q))^2} \tag{4.80}$$

where N_p is the number of colour planes (usually 3, as in RGB). This is normalised to the range [0,1] by division by the maximum colour distance. The dissimilarity between a pair of points is then proportional to the colour distance and inversely proportional to the spatial distance

$$diss(p,q) = \frac{d_c(p,q)}{1 + g \cdot d_p(p,q)} \tag{4.81}$$

where g is a constant chosen by experiment (in the original $g = 3$, and one can experiment). When the dissimilarity is largest, the points are most salient. The operator is actually patch based (in a manner similar to the nonlocal means operator), and p and q are the centre co-ordinates of an $N \times N$ patch. A pixel a is considered to be salient if the appearance of the patch centred at the pixel a is distinctive with respect to all other image patches. The colour distance is then evaluated for two patches centred at a and b

$$d_{patch}(a,b) = \sum_{x(b) \in N} \sum_{y(b) \in N} diss(a,b) \tag{4.82}$$

Rather than use all the distances between patches, the operator uses the best K dissimilarities (the ones with the largest values). Again, the value for K can be chosen by experiment. The saliency at point a is determined by averaging the best K dissimilarities over patches b as

$$S(a) = 1 - e^{-\frac{\sum_{k=1}^{K} d_{patch}(a,b)}{K}} \tag{4.83}$$

and has a low value when the point is similar to the other image points and is closer to 1.0 when it is dissimilar. This can be viewed as an operation at a chosen scale. If the image is resampled, or the operator arranged to process points at different intervals (or the image is iteratively smoothed) then the saliency at scale s is

$$S(a,s) = 1 - e^{-\frac{\sum_{k=1}^{K} d_{patch}(a,b,s)}{K}} \tag{4.84}$$

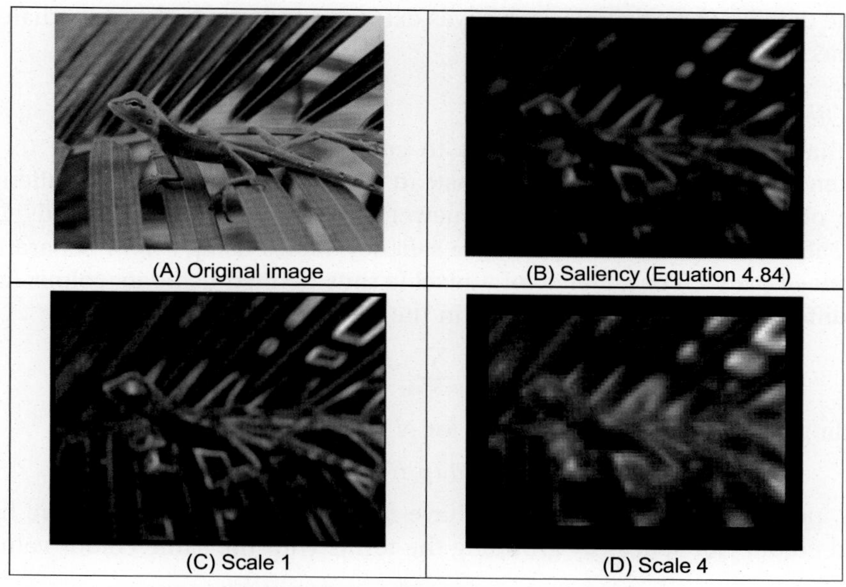

FIGURE 4.52 Detecting features by context aware saliency.

The overall saliency is then the average of the saliency over the number of scales NS

$$S(a) = \frac{1}{NS}(S(a,s)) \qquad s \in 1, NS \tag{4.85}$$

The process is illustrated in Fig. 4.52 for settings $K = 64$, $g = 3$ and $NS = 4$. Fig. 4.52 shows the original image (in printed versions a colour version of the original is to be found later) and the saliency at scales 1 and 4 (Eq. (4.84)) and the overall saliency over the four scales (Eq. (4.85)). Note that the eye features prominently as do some of the leaves (but not all). These are to be expected. There is also a region near the lizard's front left foot, which on closer inspection stands out, but is less apparent to human vision when looking at the whole image: one does not see a combination of colour and spatial difference, as exemplified by the context aware saliency operator.

This is neither the whole story nor the full one. Given the difficulty of exact implementation of any technique, one should consult Goferman's original version [Goferman12], and later any variants. Potential differences include the nature of the spatial operator and the normalisation procedures. There is also a question of windowing, and the version here used a basis similar to that of the nonlocal means smoothing operator (Section 3.5.3) and here the patch size was 7×7 and the search region 13×13 (a limitation of larger search size is that the inverse relationship with distance makes a large search infeasible as well as slow). One can of course analyse the result of processing the same images as in the original version, and the differences are more in the details. The original version was extended to include the immediate context and that has not been included here.

4.4.3.3 Other saliency operators

Methods that use local contrast, similar to context aware saliency, tend to produce higher saliency values near edge points instead of uniformly highlighting salient objects as can be observed in Fig. 4.52B. The newer *histogram contrast* method [Cheng15] measures saliency by evaluating pixelwise saliency values using *colour* separation from all other image pixels. The saliency of a pixel is thus defined using its colour (again the CIE Lab) difference from all other pixels in the image

$$S(p) = \sum_{q \in \text{Image}} d_c(p,q) \tag{4.86}$$

Expanding this as a list of differences for N image points

$$S(p) = d_c(p, I_1) + d_c(p, I_2) + \ldots + d_c(p, I_N) \tag{4.87}$$

By this, points with the same colour have the same saliency value as we have only considered colour not space. By grouping the terms with the same colour value

$$S(p) = S(c_l) = \sum_{i=1}^{NC} f_i d_c(c_l, c_i) \tag{4.88}$$

where c_l is the colour of point p, NC is the number of colours and f_i is the probability of pixel colour c_i. By comparing each point with every other point, Eq. (4.86), the computation is $O(N^2)$, whereas by Eq. (4.88) the computational complexity is $O(N + NC^2)$. So to speed up the operator, one needs to compress the colour space, to reduce NC. It is not the time to dwell on colour here, and this is achieved by colour quantisation and smoothing. The extension to include spatial awareness, called the region contrast operator, employs colour region segmentation and contrast with distance regions attracting low weight (as in contrast aware saliency).

As shown in Fig. 4.53, there is a variety of operators for saliency. Given the image of the gnome in Fig. 4.53A, there are two objects behind it and the gnome has eyes and a hat. One operator detects the objects (Fig. 4.53B), one the eyes, the edges and the objects (Fig. 4.53C), just the gnome's head and beard (in sections) (Fig. 4.53D), and the objects and the (sectioned) gnome (Fig. 4.53E). The latter operator is the region contrast refined

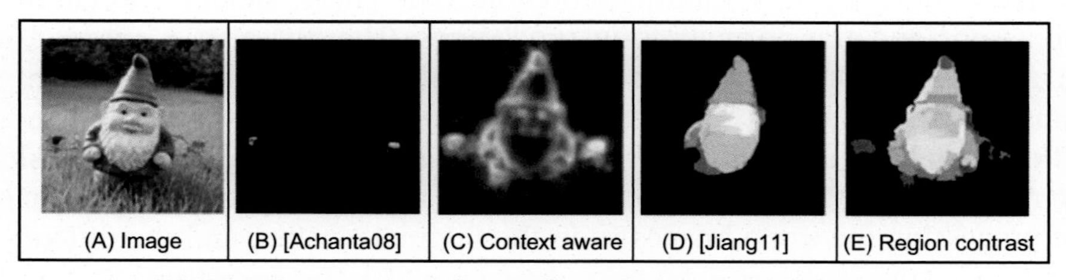

FIGURE 4.53 Comparison of state of art saliency methods [Cheng15].

version of the histogram contrast method described in Eq. (4.88). Clearly, saliency can be suck and see, as are many computer vision operators, and there is a rich selection of diverse techniques by which a version can be obtained. After all, what indeed is saliency? None of the approaches includes shape, implicitly and intentionally, and shape comes in the next chapter.

There has been a series of benchmarking studies for the performance (accuracy and speed) of the saliency operators. The most recent [Borji15] noted the continuing progress improving both factors, and that operators designed specifically for saliency outperformed those which were derived in other areas. There has been interest in using *deep learning* which aims for better performance and speed, and this has motivated *fast* analysis of *saliency* [Wang18]. Another study uses autoencoders [Li18] (see Chapter 12) and also introduces a dataset for video saliency analysis. Perhaps this is the way to achieve saliency at video rate. A, perhaps unwelcome, recent development is to refer to saliency as salient object detection and thus by the acronym SOD. Though it will allow native speakers of English to vent their frustration, we avoided the temptation to use that acronym here.

4.5 Describing image motion

We have looked at the main low-level features that we can extract from a single image. In the case of motion, we must consider more than one image. If we have two images obtained at different times, the simplest way in which we can detect *motion* is by image *differencing*. That is, changes or motion can be located by subtracting the intensity values; when there is no motion, the subtraction will give a zero value and when an object in the image moves their pixel's intensity changes, so the subtraction will give a value different from zero. There are links in this section, which determines detection of movement, to later material in Chapter 9 which concerns detecting the *moving object* and *tracking* its movement.

In order to denote a sequence of images, we include a time index in our previous notation. That is, $\mathbf{P}(t)_{x,y}$. Thus, the image at the origin of our time is $\mathbf{P}(0)_{x,y}$ and the next image is $\mathbf{P}(1)_{x,y}$. As such the image differencing operation which delivered the difference image $\mathbf{D}$ is given by

$$\mathbf{D}(t) = \mathbf{P}(t) - \mathbf{P}(t-1) \tag{4.89}$$

Fig. 4.54 shows an example of this operation. The image in Fig. 4.54A is the result of subtracting the image in Fig. 4.54B from the one in Fig. 4.54C. Naturally, this shows rather more than just the bits that are moving; we have not just highlighted the moving subject, we have also highlighted bits above the subject's head and around his feet. This is due mainly to change in the lighting (the shadows around the feet are to do with the subject's interaction with the lighting). However, perceived change can also be due to motion of the camera and to the motion of other objects in the field of view. In addition to these inaccuracies, perhaps the most important limitation of differencing is the lack of

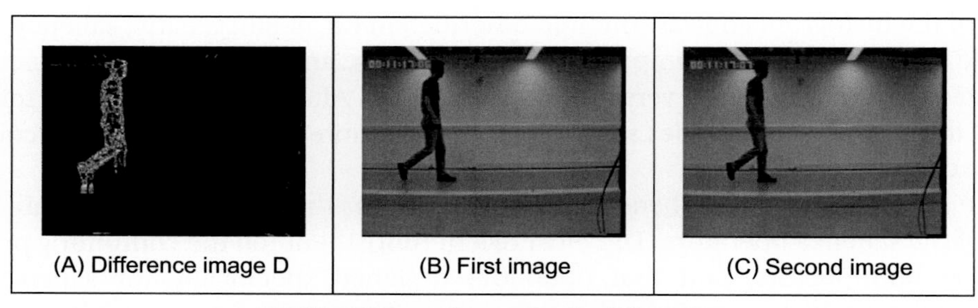

FIGURE 4.54 Detecting motion by differencing.

information about the movement itself. That is, we cannot see exactly how the image points have moved. In order to describe the way the points in an image actually move, we should study how the pixels' position changes in each image frame.

4.5.1 Area-based approach

When a scene is captured at different times, 3D elements are mapped into corresponding pixels in the images. Thus, if image features are not occluded, they can be related to each other and motion can be characterised as a collection of displacements in the image plane. The displacement corresponds to the projection of movement of the objects in the scene, and it is referred to as the *optical flow*. If you were to take an image, and its optical flow, you should be able to construct the next frame in the image sequence. So optical flow is like a measurement of movement in pixels/unit of time, or more simply pixels/frame. Optical flow can be determined by looking for corresponding features in images. We can consider alternative features such as points, pixels, curves or complex descriptions of objects.

The problem of finding correspondences in images has motivated the development of many techniques that can be distinguished by the features, the constraints imposed and by the optimisation or search strategy [Dhond89]. When features are pixels, the correspondence can be found by observing the similarities between intensities in image regions (local neighbourhood). This approach is known as area-based matching, and it is one of the most common techniques used in computer vision [Barnard87]. In general, pixels in nonoccluded regions can be related to each other by means of a general transformation of the form by

$$\mathbf{P}(t+1)_{x+\delta x, y+\delta y} = \mathbf{P}(t)_{x,y} + \mathbf{H}(t)_{x,y} \tag{4.90}$$

where the function $\mathbf{H}(t)_{x,y}$ compensates for intensity differences between the images, and $(\delta x, \delta y)$ defines the displacement vector of the pixel at time $t+1$. That is, the intensity of the pixel in the frame at time $t+1$ is equal to the intensity of the pixel at the position (x,y) in the previous frame plus some small change due to physical factors and temporal differences that induce the photometric changes in images. These factors can be due, for example, to shadows, specular reflections, differences in illumination or to changes in observation angle. In a general case, it is extremely difficult to account for the photometric differences, thus the model in Eq. (4.90) is generally simplified by assuming that:

1. the brightness of a point in an image is constant and
2. the neighbouring points move with similar velocity.

According to the first assumption, $\mathbf{H}(x)\approx 0$. Thus,

$$\mathbf{P}(t+1)_{x+\delta x,y+\delta y} = \mathbf{P}(t)_{x,y} \tag{4.91}$$

Many techniques have used this relationship to express the matching process as an optimisation or variational problem [Jordan92]. The objective is to find the vector $(\delta x,\delta y)$ that minimises the error given by

$$e_{x,y} = S\left(\mathbf{P}(t+1)_{x+\delta x,y+\delta y}, \mathbf{P}(t)_{x,y}\right) \tag{4.92}$$

where $S(\,)$ represents a function that measures the similarity between pixels. As such, the optimum is given by the displacements that minimises the image differences. There are alternative measures to using similarity to define the matching cost [Jordan92]. For example, we can measure the difference by taking the absolute value of the arithmetic difference. Alternatively, we can consider the correlation or the squared values of the difference or an equivalent normalised form. In practice, it is difficult to try to establish a conclusive advantage of a particular measure, since they will perform differently depending on the kind of image, the kind of noise and the nature of the motion we are observing. As such, one is free to use any measure as long as it can be justified based on particular practical or theoretical observations. The correlation and the squared difference will be explained in more detail in the next chapter when we consider how a template can be located in an image. We shall see that if we want to make the estimation problem in Eq. (4.92) equivalent to maximum likelihood estimation, then we should minimise the squared error. That is,

$$e_{x,y} = \left(\mathbf{P}(t+1)_{x+\delta x,y+\delta y}, \mathbf{P}(t)_{x,y}\right)^2 \tag{4.93}$$

In practice, the implementation of the minimisation is extremely prone to error since the displacement is obtained by comparing intensities of single pixels; it is very likely that the intensity changes or that a pixel can be confused with other pixels. In order to improve the performance, the optimisation includes the second assumption presented above. If neighbouring points move with similar velocity, we can determine the displacement by considering not just a single pixel, but pixels in a neighbourhood. Thus,

$$e_{x,y} = \sum_{(x',y')\in W} \left(\mathbf{P}(t+1)_{x'+\delta x,y'+\delta y}, \mathbf{P}(t)_{x',y'}\right)^2 \tag{4.94}$$

That is the error in the pixel at position (x,y) is measured by comparing all the pixels (x',y') within a window W. This makes the measure more stable by introducing an implicit smoothing factor. The size of the window is a compromise between noise and

```
# Compute Motion in sampled points
for x,y in itertools.product(range(2 * step, width-2*step, step),                  \
                             range(2 * step, height-2*step,step)):

    minDiference, nextDiference = float("inf"),  float("inf")
    mDisp = [0,0]
    for dx,dy in itertools.product(range(-maxDisp, maxDisp),                       \
                                   range(-maxDisp, maxDisp)):
        if dx != 0 or dy != 0:
            differenceMatching = 0
            for wx,wy in itertools.product(range(0, kernelSize),                   \
                                           range(0, kernelSize)):
                y1, x1 = y + wy - kernelCentre, x + wx - kernelCentre
                y2, x2 = y1 + dy, x1 + dx
                if y1 > -1 and y1 <  height and  x1 > -1 and x1 <  width and       \
                   y2 > -1 and y2 <  height and  x2 > -1 and x2 <  width:
                    differenceMatching += abs(float(inputImage1[y1,x1]) -          \
                                              float(inputImage2[y2,x2]))
            # Keep the most similar
            if differenceMatching < minDiference:
                nextDiference = minDiference
                minDiference = differenceMatching
                mDisp = [dy,dx]
            else:
                if differenceMatching < nextDiference:
                    nextDiference = differenceMatching
    # Set motion only if we find a good match
    if minDiference != nextDiference:
        motionMagnitude[y,x] = math.sqrt(mDisp[0]*mDisp[0]+mDisp[1]*mDisp[1])
        motionDirection[y,x] = math.atan2(mDisp[0],-mDisp[1])
        motionWeight[y,x] = nextDiference - minDiference
```

CODE 4.12 Implementation of area-based motion computation.

accuracy. Naturally, the automatic selection of the window parameter has attracted some interest [Kanade94]. Another important problem is the amount of computation involved in the minimisation when the displacement between frames is large. This has motivated the development of hierarchical implementations. Other extensions have considered more elaborate assumptions about the speed of neighbouring pixels.

A straightforward implementation of the minimisation of the squared error is presented in the Code 4.12. This implementation uses three parameters that define the maximum displacement, the window size and a step that is used to select the pixel locations where the motion is computed. That is, the implementation only evaluates the motion at some regular samples in the image. For each pixel, the implementation finds the two displacements that give the minimum error. The difference between the two values is used to define a weight that determines the confidence of the displacement. The resulting motion magnitude, the motion direction and the weights are stored in the arrays `motionMagnitude`, `motionDirection` and `motionWeight`. In a second step, the motion is averaged by considering the weight. The average corrects problems at the borders and reduces the irregularities produced by noise in the image. In general, implementations include other strategies to deal with the border, occlusions and noise. Also it is common to use multiple image resolutions to deal with the large number of computations required. In a more complex implementation, it is possible to obtain displacements with

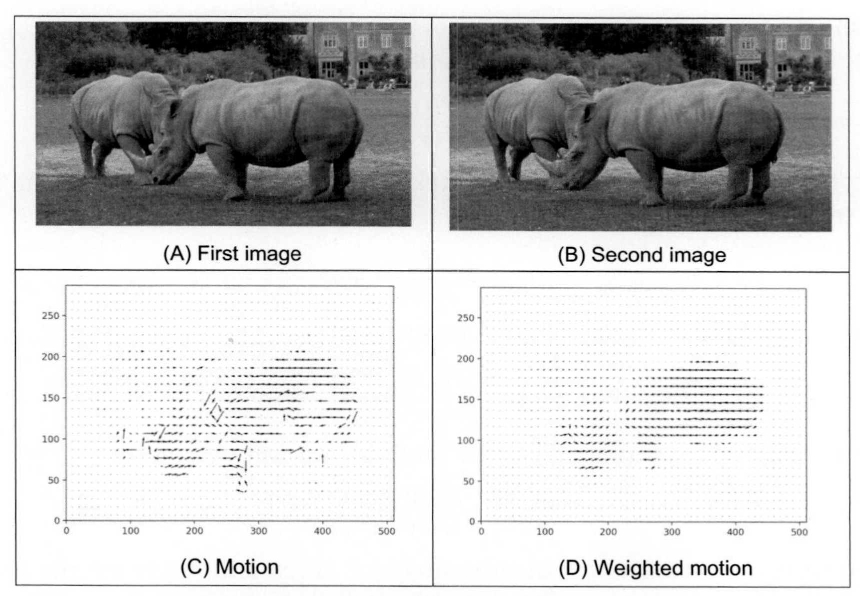

FIGURE 4.55 Example of area-based motion computation.

subpixel accuracy [Lawton83]. This is normally achieved by a post-processing step based on subpixel interpolation or by matching surfaces obtained by fitting the data at the integer positions.

Fig. 4.55 shows an example of the motion estimated with Code 4.12. Figs. 4.55A and B show two frames used to compute the motion. Fig. 4.55C shows the motion obtained by considering only the best displacement. We can see that the result has noise close to the borders due to occlusions and it has noise in regions with similar textures. In general, noise can be reduced by increasing the size of the window used in the comparison, but this also reduces the motion detail. Fig. 4.55D shows the result of estimating the motion using a weighted average. In this case, pixels determine the motion from pixels that contain better features for the estimation thus the motion is more uniform.

4.5.2 Differential approach

Another popular way to estimate motion focusses on the observation of the differential changes in the pixel values. There are actually many ways of calculating the optical flow by this approach [Nagel87], Barron[94]. We shall discuss one of the more popular techniques, the *differential approach* [Horn81]. We start by considering the intensity equivalence in Eq. (4.91). According to this, the brightness at the point in the new position should be the same as the brightness at the old position. Like Eq. (4.5), we can expand $\mathbf{P}(t+\delta t)_{x+\delta x,y+\delta y}$ by using a Taylor series as

$$\mathbf{P}(t+\delta t)_{x+\delta x,y+\delta y} = \mathbf{P}(t)_{x,y} + \delta x \frac{\partial \mathbf{P}(t)_{x,y}}{\partial x} + \delta y \frac{\partial \mathbf{P}(t)_{x,y}}{\partial y} + \delta t \frac{\partial \mathbf{P}(t)_{x,y}}{\partial t} + \xi \tag{4.95}$$

where ξ contains higher order terms. If we take the limit as $\delta t \to 0$ then we can ignore ξ as it also tends to zero which leaves

$$\mathbf{P}(t+\delta t)_{x+\delta x,y+\delta y} = \mathbf{P}(t)_{x,y} + \delta x \frac{\partial \mathbf{P}(t)_{x,y}}{\partial x} + \delta y \frac{\partial \mathbf{P}(t)_{x,y}}{\partial y} + \delta t \frac{\partial \mathbf{P}(t)_{x,y}}{\partial t} \tag{4.96}$$

Now by Eq. (4.91), we can substitute for $\mathbf{P}(t+\delta t)_{x+\delta x,y+\delta y}$ to give

$$\mathbf{P}(t)_{x,y} = \mathbf{P}(t)_{x,y} + \delta x \frac{\partial \mathbf{P}(t)_{x,y}}{\partial x} + \delta y \frac{\partial \mathbf{P}(t)_{x,y}}{\partial y} + \delta t \frac{\partial \mathbf{P}(t)_{x,y}}{\partial t} \tag{4.97}$$

which with some rearrangement gives the motion constraint equation

$$\frac{\delta x}{\delta t}\frac{\partial \mathbf{P}}{\partial x} + \frac{\delta y}{\delta t}\frac{\partial \mathbf{P}}{\partial y} = -\frac{\partial \mathbf{P}}{\partial t} \tag{4.98}$$

We can recognise some terms in this equation. $\partial\mathbf{P}/\partial x$ and $\partial\mathbf{P}/\partial y$ are the first-order differentials of the image intensity along the two image axes. $\partial\mathbf{P}/\partial t$ is the rate of change of image intensity with time. The other two factors are the ones concerned with optical flow, as they describe movement along the two image axes. Let us call

$$u = \frac{\delta x}{\delta t} \quad \text{and} \quad v = \frac{\delta y}{\delta t}$$

These are the optical flow components: u is the *horizontal optical flow* and v is the *vertical optical flow*. We can write these into our equation to give

$$u\frac{\partial \mathbf{P}}{\partial x} + v\frac{\partial \mathbf{P}}{\partial y} = -\frac{\partial \mathbf{P}}{\partial t} \tag{4.99}$$

This equation suggests that the optical flow and the spatial rate of intensity change together describe how an image changes with time. The equation can actually be expressed more simply in vector form in terms of the intensity change $\nabla\mathbf{P} = [\nabla x \quad \nabla y] = [\partial\mathbf{P}/\partial x \quad \partial\mathbf{P}/\partial y]$ and the optical flow $\mathbf{v} = [u \quad v]^{\mathrm{T}}$, as the dot product

$$\nabla\mathbf{P} \cdot \mathbf{v} = -\dot{\mathbf{P}} \tag{4.100}$$

We already have operators that can estimate the spatial intensity change, $\nabla x = \partial\mathbf{P}/\partial x$ and $\nabla y = \partial\mathbf{P}/\partial y$, by using one of the edge detection operators described earlier. We also have an operator which can estimate the rate of change of image intensity, $\nabla t = \partial\mathbf{P}/\partial t$, as given by Eq. (4.89). Unfortunately, we cannot determine the optical flow components from Eq. (4.99) since we have one equation in two unknowns (there are many possible pairs of values for u and v that satisfy the equation). This is actually called the *aperture problem* and makes the problem ill-posed. Essentially, we seek estimates of u and v that minimise the error in Eq. (4.102) over the entire image. By expressing Eq. (4.99) as,

$$u\nabla x + v\nabla y + \nabla t = 0 \tag{4.101}$$

we then seek estimates of u and v that minimise the error ec for all the pixels in an image

$$ec = \iint (u\nabla x + v\nabla y + \nabla t)^2 \, dxdy \tag{4.102}$$

We can approach the solution (equations to determine u and v) by considering the second assumption we made earlier, namely that neighbouring points move with similar velocity. This is actually called the *smoothness constraint* as it suggests that the velocity field of the brightness varies in a smooth manner without abrupt change (or discontinuity). If we add this in to the formulation, we turn a problem that is ill-posed, without unique solution, to one that is well-posed. Properly, we define the smoothness constraint as an integral over the area of interest, as in Eq. (4.102). Since we want to maximise smoothness, we seek to minimise the rate of change of the optical flow. Accordingly, we seek to minimise an integral of the rate of change of flow along both axes. This is an error es as

$$es = \iint \left(\left(\frac{\partial u}{\partial x}\right)^2 + \left(\frac{\partial u}{\partial y}\right)^2 + \left(\frac{\partial v}{\partial x}\right)^2 + \left(\frac{\partial v}{\partial y}\right)^2 \right) dxdy \tag{4.103}$$

The total error is the compromise between the importance of the assumption of constant brightness and the assumption of smooth velocity. If this compromise is controlled by a *regularisation* parameter λ, then the total error e is

$$\begin{aligned} e &= \lambda \times ec + es \\ &= \iint \left(\lambda \times \left(u\frac{\partial \mathbf{P}}{\partial x} + v\frac{\partial \mathbf{P}}{\partial y} + \frac{\partial \mathbf{P}}{\partial t} \right)^2 + \left(\left(\frac{\partial u}{\partial x}\right)^2 + \left(\frac{\partial u}{\partial y}\right)^2 + \left(\frac{\partial v}{\partial x}\right)^2 + \left(\frac{\partial v}{\partial y}\right)^2 \right) \right) dxdy \end{aligned} \tag{4.104}$$

There is a number of ways to approach the solution [Horn86], but the most appealing is perhaps also the most direct. We are concerned with providing estimates of optical flow at image points. So we are actually interested in computing the values for $u_{x,y}$ and $v_{x,y}$. We can form the error at image points, like $es_{x,y}$. Since we are concerned with image points, then we can form $es_{x,y}$ by using first-order differences, just like Eq. (4.1) at the start of this chapter. Eq. (4.103) can be implemented in discrete form as

$$es_{x,y} = \sum_x \sum_y \frac{1}{4} \left((u_{x+1,y} - u_{x,y})^2 + (u_{x,y+1} - u_{x,y})^2 + (v_{x+1,y} - v_{x,y})^2 + (v_{x,y+1} - v_{x,y})^2 \right) \tag{4.105}$$

The discrete form of the smoothness constraint is then that the average rate of change of flow should be minimised. To obtain the discrete form of Eq. (4.104), we then add in the discrete form of ec (the discrete form of Eq. (4.102)) to give

$$ec_{x,y} = \sum_x \sum_y \left(u_{x,y} \nabla x_{x,y} + v_{x,y} \nabla y_{x,y} + \nabla t_{x,y} \right)^2 \tag{4.106}$$

where $\nabla x_{x,y} = \partial \mathbf{P}_{x,y}/\partial x$, $\nabla y_{x,y} = \partial \mathbf{P}_{x,y}/\partial y$ and $\nabla t_{x,y} = \partial \mathbf{P}_{x,y}/\partial t$ are local estimates, at the point with co-ordinates x,y, of the rate of change of the picture with horizontal direction, vertical direction and time, respectively. Accordingly, we seek values for $u_{x,y}$ and $v_{x,y}$ that minimise the total error e as given by

$$\begin{aligned} e_{x,y} &= \sum_x \sum_y (\lambda \times ec_{x,y} + es_{x,y}) \\ &= \sum_x \sum_y \left(\begin{array}{l} \lambda \times \left(u_{x,y}\nabla x_{x,y} + v_{x,y}\nabla y_{x,y} + \nabla t_{x,y}\right)^2 + \\ \frac{1}{4}\left((u_{x+1,y} - u_{x,y})^2 + (u_{x,y+1} - u_{x,y})^2 + (v_{x+1,y} - v_{x,y})^2 + (v_{x,y+1} - v_{x,y})^2\right) \end{array} \right) \end{aligned} \tag{4.107}$$

Since we seek to minimise this equation with respect to $u_{x,y}$ and $v_{x,y}$, then we differentiate it separately, with respect to the two parameters of interest, and the resulting equations when equated to zero should yield the equations we seek. As such

$$\frac{\partial e_{x,y}}{\partial u_{x,y}} = \left(\lambda \times 2\left(u_{x,y}\nabla x_{x,y} + v_{x,y}\nabla y_{x,y} + \nabla t_{x,y}\right)\nabla x_{x,y} + 2\left(u_{x,y} - \overline{u}_{x,y}\right)\right) = 0 \tag{4.108}$$

and

$$\frac{\partial e_{x,y}}{\partial v_{x,y}} = \left(\lambda \times 2\left(u_{x,y}\nabla x_{x,y} + v_{x,y}\nabla y_{x,y} + \nabla t_{x,y}\right)\nabla y_{x,y} + 2\left(v_{x,y} - \overline{v}_{x,y}\right)\right) = 0 \tag{4.109}$$

This gives a pair of equations in $u_{x,y}$ and $v_{x,y}$

$$\begin{aligned} \left(1 + \lambda(\nabla x_{x,y})^2\right)u_{x,y} + \lambda \nabla x_{x,y}\nabla y_{x,y}v_{x,y} &= \overline{u}_{x,y} - \lambda \nabla x_{x,y}\nabla t_{x,y} \\ \lambda \nabla x_{x,y}\nabla y_{x,y}u_{x,y} + \left(1 + \lambda(\nabla y_{x,y})^2\right)v_{x,y} &= \overline{v}_{x,y} - \lambda \nabla x_{x,y}\nabla t_{x,y} \end{aligned} \tag{4.110}$$

This is a pair of equations in u and v with solution

$$\begin{aligned} \left(1 + \lambda\left((\nabla x_{x,y})^2 + (\nabla y_{x,y})^2\right)\right)u_{x,y} &= \left(1 + \lambda(\nabla x_{x,y})^2\right)\overline{u}_{x,y} - \lambda \nabla x_{x,y}\nabla y_{x,y}\overline{v}_{x,y} - \lambda \nabla x_{x,y}\nabla t_{x,y} \\ \left(1 + \lambda\left((\nabla x_{x,y})^2 + (\nabla y_{x,y})^2\right)\right)v_{x,y} &= -\lambda \nabla x_{x,y}\nabla y_{x,y}\overline{u}_{x,y} + \left(1 + \lambda(\nabla x_{x,y})^2\right)\overline{v}_{x,y} - \lambda \nabla y_{x,y}\nabla t_{x,y} \end{aligned} \tag{4.111}$$

The solution to these equations is in iterative form where we shall denote the estimate of u at iteration n as $u^{<n>}$, so each iteration calculates new values for the flow at each point according to

$$\begin{aligned} u_{x,y}^{<n+1>} &= \overline{u}_{x,y}^{<n>} - \lambda\left(\frac{\nabla x_{x,y}\overline{u}_{x,y} + \nabla y_{x,y}\overline{v}_{x,y} + \nabla t_{x,y}}{\left(1 + \lambda\left(\nabla x_{x,y}^2 + \nabla y_{x,y}^2\right)\right)}\right)(\nabla x_{x,y}) \\ v_{x,y}^{<n+1>} &= \overline{v}_{x,y}^{<n>} - \lambda\left(\frac{\nabla x_{x,y}\overline{u}_{x,y} + \nabla y_{x,y}\overline{v}_{x,y} + \nabla t_{x,y}}{\left(1 + \lambda\left(\nabla x_{x,y}^2 + \nabla y_{x,y}^2\right)\right)}\right)(\nabla y_{x,y}) \end{aligned} \tag{4.112}$$

Now we have it, the pair of equations gives iterative means for calculating the images of optical flow based on differentials. In order to estimate the first-order differentials, rather than use our earlier equations, we can consider neighbouring points in quadrants in successive images. This gives approximate estimates of the gradient based on the two frames. That is,

$$\nabla x_{x,y} = \frac{\begin{array}{c}\left(\mathbf{P}(0)_{x+1,y} + \mathbf{P}(1)_{x+1,y} + \mathbf{P}(0)_{x+1,y+1} + \mathbf{P}(1)_{x+1,y+1}\right) - \\ \left(\mathbf{P}(0)_{x,y} + \mathbf{P}(1)_{x,y} + \mathbf{P}(0)_{x,y+1} + \mathbf{P}(1)_{x,y+1}\right)\end{array}}{8}$$

$$\nabla y_{x,y} = \frac{\begin{array}{c}\left(\mathbf{P}(0)_{x,y+1} + \mathbf{P}(1)_{x,y+1} + \mathbf{P}(0)_{x+1,y+1} + \mathbf{P}(1)_{x+1,y+1}\right) - \\ \left(\mathbf{P}(0)_{x,y} + \mathbf{P}(1)_{x,y} + \mathbf{P}(0)_{x+1,y} + \mathbf{P}(1)_{x+1,y}\right)\end{array}}{8} \tag{4.113}$$

In fact, in a later reflection [Horn93] on the earlier presentation, Horn noted with rancour that some difficulty experienced with the original technique had actually been caused by use of simpler methods of edge detection which are not appropriate here, as the simpler versions do not deliver a correctly positioned result between two images. The time differential is given by the difference between the two pixels along the two faces of the cube, as

$$\nabla t_{x,y} = \frac{\begin{array}{c}\left(\mathbf{P}(1)_{x,y} + \mathbf{P}(1)_{x+1,y} + \mathbf{P}(1)_{x,y+1} + \mathbf{P}(1)_{x+1,y+1}\right) - \\ \left(\mathbf{P}(0)_{x,y} + \mathbf{P}(0)_{x+1,y} + \mathbf{P}(0)_{x,y+1} + \mathbf{P}(0)_{x+1,y+1}\right)\end{array}}{8} \tag{4.114}$$

Note that if the spacing between the images is other than one unit, this will change the denominator in Eqs. (4.113) and (4.114), but this is a constant scale factor. We also need means to calculate the averages. These can be computed as

$$\begin{aligned}\overline{u}_{x,y} &= \frac{u_{x-1,y} + u_{x,y-1} + u_{x+1,y} + u_{x,y+1}}{2} + \frac{u_{x-1,y-1} + u_{x-1,y+1} + u_{x+1,y-1} + u_{x+1,y+1}}{4} \\ \overline{v}_{x,y} &= \frac{v_{x-1,y} + v_{x,y-1} + v_{x+1,y} + v_{x,y+1}}{2} + \frac{v_{x-1,y-1} + v_{x-1,y+1} + v_{x+1,y-1} + v_{x+1,y+1}}{4}\end{aligned} \tag{4.115}$$

The implementation of the computation of optical flow by the iterative solution in Eq. (4.112) is presented in Code 4.13. Similar to the previous implementation, this implementation only computes the motion at some locations in the image. In this case, this is performed by reducing the image resolution. The original image is filtered by a Gaussian kernel and then is sampled at equal sized intervals. In gradient-based estimation, it is very important to filter and sample the image at low resolution not only to reduce noise but also to make sure that the displacements are not very large. Gradient is computed at a pixel distance, so the motion has similar short magnitudes. Generally, gradient algorithms are implemented with a hierarchical structure at different resolutions and combined into a final full resolution image. This will enable the computation of displacements larger than one pixel. Code 4.13 only shows the estimation in a single-resolution image. This implementation has two parameters that define the smoothing parameter and the number of iterations. Derivatives and averages are computed by using simplified forms of Eqs. (4.113)–(4.115). In a more elaborate implementation, it is

```
# Compute motion in the reduced image
for k in range(0,numIterations):
    for x,y in itertools.product(range(1, widthSmall-1), range(1, heightSmall-1)):

        # Derivatives
        gX = (float(image1Small[y,x+1]) - float(image1Small[y,x]) +          \
              float(image2Small[y,x+1]) - float(image2Small[y,x]) +          \
              float(image1Small[y+1,x+1]) - float(image1Small[y+1,x]) +      \
              float(image2Small[y+1,x+1]) - float(image2Small[y+1,x])) / 8.0

        gY = (float(image1Small[y+1,x]) - float(image1Small[y,x]) +          \
              float(image2Small[y+1,x]) - float(image2Small[y,x]) +          \
              float(image1Small[y+1,x+1]) - float(image1Small[y,x+1]) +      \
              float(image2Small[y+1,x+1]) - float(image2Small[y,x+1])) / 8.0

        gT = (float(image2Small[y,x]) - float(image1Small[y,x]) +            \
              float(image2Small[y+1,x]) - float(image1Small[y+1,x]) +        \
              float(image2Small[y,x+1]) - float(image1Small[y,x+1]) +        \
              float(image2Small[y+1,x+1]) - float(image1Small[y+1,x+1])) / 8.0

        # Average, but not use borders since the motion in borders is not defined
        average =[0.0, 0.0]
        n = 0.0
        for wx,wy in itertools.product(range(-1, 2), range(-1, 2)):
            posY, posX = y + wy, x + wx
            if posY > 0 and posY <  heightSmall-1 and posX > 0 and           \
                                                   posX <  widthSmall-1:
                average[0] += motion[posY,posX,0]
                average[1] += motion[posY,posX,1]
                n += 1.0

        if n != 0:
            average[0],  average[1] =  average[0]/ n, average[1] / n

        # Solve equation to update estimates
        A = float(gX * average[0] + gY * average[1] + gT)
        B = float(1.0 + smoothing * (gX*gX + gY*gY))
        motionTemp[y,x,0] = average[0] - (gX * smoothing * A / B)
        motionTemp[y,x,1] = average[1] - (gY * smoothing * A / B)

    # Update motion for next iteration
    for x,y in itertools.product(range(1, widthSmall-1), range(1, heightSmall-1)):
        motion[y,x,0] = motionTemp[y,x,0]
        motion[y,x,1] = motionTemp[y,x,1]
```

CODE 4.13 Implementation of gradient-based motion.

convenient to include averages as we discussed in the case of single image feature operators. This will improve the accuracy and will reduce noise.

Fig. 4.56 shows some examples of optical flow computation. In these examples, we used the same images as in Fig. 4.55. The first row in the figure shows three results obtained by different numbers of iterations and fixed smoothing parameter λ. In this case, the estimates converged quite quickly. Note that at the start, the estimates of flow in are quite noisy, but they quickly improve; as the algorithm progresses the results are refined and a smoother and accurate motion is obtained. The second row in Fig. 4.56 shows the results for a fixed number of iterations and a variable smoothing parameter. The regularisation parameter controls the compromise between the detail and the

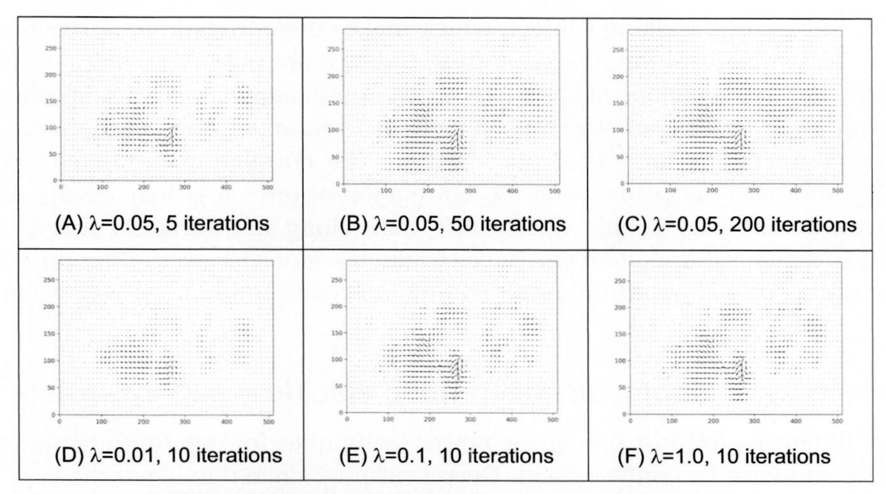

(A) λ=0.05, 5 iterations (B) λ=0.05, 50 iterations (C) λ=0.05, 200 iterations

(D) λ=0.01, 10 iterations (E) λ=0.1, 10 iterations (F) λ=1.0, 10 iterations

FIGURE 4.56 Example of differential-based motion computation.

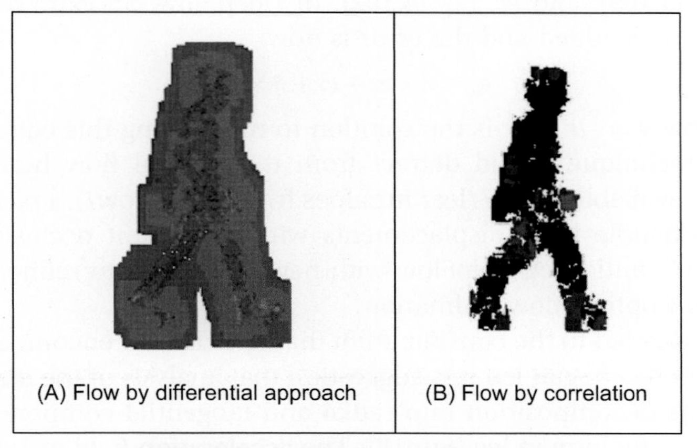

(A) Flow by differential approach (B) Flow by correlation

FIGURE 4.57 Optical flow of walking subject.

smoothness. A large value of λ will enforce the smoothness constraint, whereas a small value will make the brightness constraint dominate the result. In the results we can observe that the largest vectors point in the expected direction, upwards, whilst some of the smaller vectors are not exactly correct. This is because there are occlusions and some regions have similar textures. Clearly, we could select the brightest of these points by thresholding according to magnitude. That would leave the largest vectors (the ones which point in exactly the right direction).

Optical flow has been used in automatic gait recognition [Huang99, Little98], amongst other applications, partly because the displacements can be large between successive images of a walking subject, which makes the correlation approach suitable (note that fast versions of area-based correspondence are possible [Zabir94]). Fig. 4.57 shows the result for a walking subject where brightness depicts magnitude (direction is not shown). Fig. 4.57A shows the result for the differential approach, where the flow is clearly more uncertain than that produced by the correlation approach shown in Fig. 4.57B. Another reason for using the correlation approach is that we are not concerned with rotation as people (generally!) walk along flat surfaces. If 360 degrees rotation is to be considered, then you have to match regions for every rotation value and this can make the correlation-based techniques computationally very demanding indeed.

4.5.3 Recent developments: deep flow, epic flow and extensions

DeepFlow [Weinzaepfel13] is one of the newer techniques for determining optical flow. The Deep should not be confused with Deep Learning, since that is not the case ('deep' has meanings other than deep learning!). In Section 4.5.2, the optic flow was given as the solution to the minimisation of a function, e, Eq. (4.104), which was composed of two functions es, Eq. (4.103), and ec, Eq. (4.102). In DeepFlow, an extra term representing deep matching, em, is added and the error is now

$$e_{df} = \lambda \times ec + es + \beta \times em \tag{4.116}$$

The optical flow $\mathbf{v} = [u \quad v]^{\mathrm{T}}$ is the solution to minimising this equation. The development of this technique would detract from the general flow here, and there are implementations available (http://lear.inrialpes.fr/src/deepflow/). *EpicFlow* [Revaud15] was designed to handle large displacements with significant occlusions, and a later approach [Bailer15] initialised EpicFlow with new flow fields to refine performance on large displacement optical flow estimation.

An interest in gait, led to the consideration that optical flow encompasses many types of motion. The interest in gait led to a suggestion that analysis of the *acceleration* can be used, especially its decomposition into radial and tangential components, to differentiate the motion of the human leg [Sun18]. The acceleration field $\mathbf{a}(t)$ can be estimated by the temporal derivative of the optical flow between the motion from frames $t-1$ to t, $\mathbf{v}(t)$ and the motion from frames t to $t+1$, $\mathbf{v}(t+1)$, as

$$\mathbf{a}(t) = \mathbf{v}(t+1) - (-\mathbf{v}(t)) \tag{4.117}$$

The formulation differs from straight subtraction to ensure that the reference of motion is the current frame t. The inclination θ of the acceleration is

$$\theta = \cos^{-1}\frac{\mathbf{a} \cdot \mathbf{v}}{|\mathbf{a}||\mathbf{v}|} \tag{4.118}$$

which can be resolved as radial and tangential components. This is illustrated for radial acceleration in Fig. 4.58 (in the printed version, colour versions of these images are found later) which shows a subject walking in a laboratory (where illumination and background

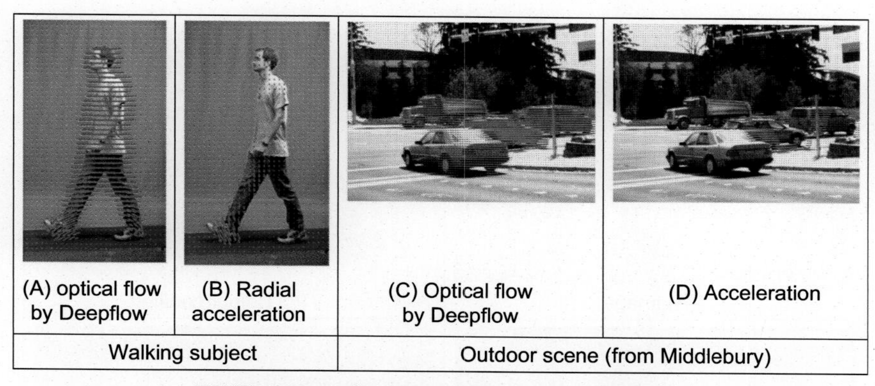

FIGURE 4.58 Analysing optical flow and acceleration.

were intentionally controlled) and the most radial acceleration is detected around the foot (Fig. 4.58B) in contrast with optical flow which selects the whole body, Fig. 4.58A. This was expected, as the foot moves the fastest of any body part when walking. Some radial acceleration was also detected for the thorax, and this is consistent with its inverted pendular nature. When applied to outdoor scenes, the optical flow selects all moving objects in Fig. 4.58C. By way of contrast, Fig. 4.58D acceleration allows for extraction of only the accelerating objects, and the new approach allows for the motion to be resolved into its different components.

By evaluation and by technique, especially that to be covered in Chapter 9, determining motion is not a complete topic. As vision moves more to analysing spatiotemporal data, especially in analysis of human movements and gesture, there is no doubt that techniques will continue to advance from their firm and longstanding basis and we shall look forward to this.

4.5.4 Analysis of optical flow

Determining optical flow does not get much of a mention in the established textbooks, even though it is a major low-level feature description. Rather naturally, it is to be found in depth in one of its early proponent's textbooks [Horn86]. Some surveys of the approaches to optical flow include the many facets of this task and its evaluation [Sun14, Fortun15] with depth that far exceeds the introductory treatment that can be achieved in a textbook. It is also worth noting the consideration of evaluation: how does one compare the performances of the different approaches. Note there are many variables, not only in the data but also in implementation, that might lead to preference for a particular technique. Clearly, there are many impediments to the successful calculation of optical flow such as change in illumination or occlusion (and by other moving objects). A major study [Baker11] has an extensive performance analysis (with succinct descriptions of the main approaches) and contributed four types of data to test different

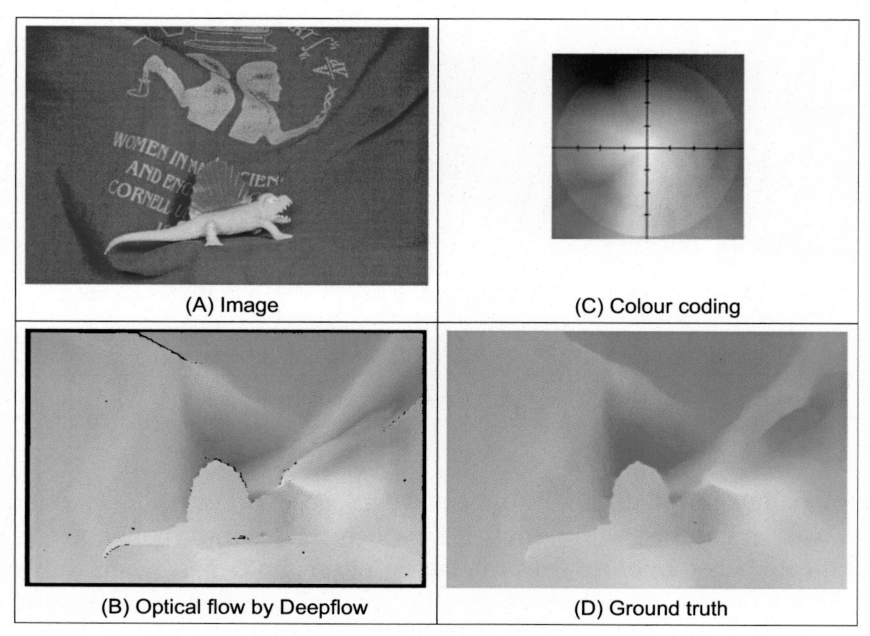

FIGURE 4.59 Evaluating optical flow [Baker11].

aspects of optical flow algorithms together with the ground truth evaluation. This is illustrated on Fig. 4.59 where Fig. 4.59A is the image of a toy chameleon which is shifted within the image sequence. (Only one image is shown as the toy moves only by a small amount.) This leads to optical flow between two of the frames which can be measured by DeepFlow in Fig. 4.59B. The colour coding of the result is shown in Fig. 4.59C wherein the direction is shown by colour and the magnitude by intensity. The result in Fig. 4.59B can be compared with the ground truth in Fig. 4.59D, and DeepFlow clearly performs very well in this case. There is a website associated with the work to which developers can submit their work and where its performance is evaluated. In Fig. 4.59, the analysis is visual and a better analysis is to use error metrics derived from multiple sequences. One conclusion on optical flow is that none of the methods was a clear winner on all of the datasets evaluated, though the overall aim of the study was to stimulate further development of technique, as well as performance analysis. Clearly, the *Middlebury* website (http://vision.middlebury.edu/flow/) is an important port of call for any developer or user of optical flow algorithms. Naturally, some of the more recent works have followed the deep learning revolution [Dosovitskiy15,Ilg17], and this will be described later in Chapter 12.

4.6 Further reading

This chapter has covered the main ways to extract low-level feature information. There has been an enormous amount of work in low-level features since this is a primary feature extraction task in computer vision and image processing. In some cases, this can prove sufficient for understanding the image. Often though, the function of low-level feature extraction is to provide information for later higher level analysis. This can be achieved in a variety of ways, with advantages and disadvantages and quickly or at a lower speed (or requiring a faster processor/more memory!). The range of techniques presented here has certainly proved sufficient for the majority of applications. There are other, more minor techniques, but the main approaches to boundary, corner, feature and motion extraction have proved sufficiently robust and with requisite performance that they shall endure for some time. Given depth and range, the further reading for each low-level operation is to be found at the end of each section. We shall collect the most recent work on deep learning in Chapter 12 and shall find that the techniques from this chapter are important in the new architectures for image analysis.

We now move on to using this information at a higher level. This means collecting the information so as to find shapes and objects, the next stage in understanding the image's content.

References

[Alahi12] Alahi, A., Ortiz, R., and Vandergheynst, P., Freak: Fast Retina Keypoint, *Proceedings of CVPR*, pp 510-517, 2012.

[Achanta08] Achanta, R., Estrada, F., Wils, P., and Süsstrunk, S., Salient Region Detection and Segmentation, *International Conference on Computer Vision Systems*, pp 66-75, 2008.

[Adelson85] Adelson, E. H., and Bergen, J. R., Spatiotemporal Energy Models for the Perception of Motion, *Journal of the Optical Society of America, A2*(2), pp 284-299, 1985.

[Agrawal08] Agrawal, M., Konolige, K., and Blas, M. R., Censure: Center Surround Extremas for Realtime Feature Detection and Matching, *Proceedings of ECCV*, pp 102-115, 2008.

[Apostol66] Apostol, T. M., *Calculus*, 2nd Edition, vol. 1, Xerox College Publishing, Waltham, 1966.

[Asada86] Asada, H., and Brady, M., The Curvature Primal Sketch, *IEEE Transactions on PAMI, 8*(1), pp 2-14, 1986.

[Bailer15] Bailer, C., Taetz, B., and Stricker, D., Flow Fields: Dense Correspondence Fields for Highly Accurate Large Displacement Optical Flow Estimation, *Proceedings of CVPR*, 2015.

[Baker11] Baker, S., Scharstein, D., Lewis, J.P., Roth, S., Black, M.J., and Szeliski, R., A Database and Evaluation Methodology for Optical Flow, *International Journal of Computer Vision, 92*(1), pp 1-31, 2011.

[Barnard87] Barnard, S. T., and Fichler, M. A., Stereo Vision, in *Encyclopedia of Artificial Intelligence*, New York: John Wiley, pp 1083-2090, 1987.

[Bay06] Bay, H., Tuytelaars, T., and Van Gool, L., SURF: Speeded up Robust Features, *Proceedings of ECCV 2006*, pp 404-417, 2006.

[Bay08] Bay, H., Eas, A., Tuytelaars, T., and Van Gool, L., Speeded-Up Robust Features (SURF), *Computer Vision and Image Understanding, 110*(3), pp 346-359, 2008.

[Bennet75] Bennet, J. R., and MacDonald, J. S., On the Measurement of Curvature in a Quantised Environment, *IEEE Transactions on Computers, C-24*(8), pp 803-820, 1975.

[Bergholm87] Bergholm, F., Edge Focussing, *IEEE Transactions on PAMI, 9*(6), pp 726-741, 1987.

[Borji15] Borji, A., Cheng, M.M., Jiang, H., and Li, J., Salient Object Detection: A Benchmark, *IEEE Transactions on IP, 24*(12), pp 5706-5722, 2015.

[Bovik87] Bovik, A. C., Huang, T. S., and Munson, D. C., The Effect of Median Filtering on Edge Estimation and Detection, *IEEE Transactions on PAMI, 9*(2), pp 181-194, 1987.

[Calonder10] Calonder, M., Lepetit, V., Strecha, C., and Fua, P., BRIEF: Binary Robust Independent Elementary Features, *Proceedings of ECCV*, pp 778-792, 2010.

[Canny86] Canny, J., A Computational Approach to Edge Detection, *IEEE Transactions on PAMI, 8*(6), pp 679-698, 1986.

[Cheng15] Cheng, M. M., Mitra, N. J., Huang, X., Torr, P. H., and Hu, S.M., Global Contrast Based Salient Region Detection, *IEEE Transactions on PAMI, 37*(3), pp 569-582, 2015.

[Clark89] Clark, J. J., Authenticating Edges Produced by Zero-Crossing Algorithms, *IEEE Transactions on PAMI, 11*(1), pp 43-57, 1989.

[Davies05] Davies, E. R., *Machine Vision: Theory, Algorithms and Practicalities*, 3rd Edition, Morgan Kaufmann (Elsevier), 2005.

[Deriche87] Deriche, R., Using Canny's Criteria to Derive a Recursively Implemented Optimal Edge Detector, *International Journal of Computer Vision, 1*, pp 167-187, 1987.

[Dhond89] Dhond, U. R., and Aggarwal J. K., Structure from Stereo- a Review, *IEEE Transactions on Systems, Man and Cybernetics, 19*(6), pp 1489-1510, 1989.

[Dollár15] Dollár, P., and Zitnick, C. L., Fast Edge Detection Using Structured Forests, *IEEE Transactions on PAMI, 37*(8), pp 1558-1570, 2015.

[Dosovitskiy15] Dosovitskiy, A., Fischer, P., Ilg, E., Hausser, P., Hazirbas, C., Golkov, V., Van Der Smagt, P., Cremers, D., and Brox, T., Flownet: Learning Optical Flow with Convolutional Networks, *Proceedings of ICCV*, pp 2758-2766, 2015.

[Fergus03] Fergus, R., Perona, P., and Zisserman, A., Object Class Recognition by Unsupervised Scale-Invariant Learning, *Proceedings of CVPR 2003, II*, pp 264-271, 2003.

[Fleet90] Fleet, D. J., and Jepson, A. D., Computation of Component Image Velocity from Local Phase Information, *International Journal of Computer Vision, 5*(1), pp 77-104, 1990.

[Forshaw88] Forshaw, M. R. B., Speeding up the Marr-Hildreth Edge Operator, *CVGIP, 41*, pp 172-185, 1988.

[Fortun15] Fortun, D., Bouthemy, P., and Kervrann, C., Optical Flow Modeling and Computation: a Survey, *Computer Vision and Image Understanding, 134*, pp 1-21, 2015.

[Goetz70] Goetz, A., *Introduction to Differential Geometry*, Addison-Wesley, Reading, MA, USA, 1970.

[Goferman12] Goferman, S., Zelnik-Manor, L., and Tal, A., Context-aware Saliency Detection, *IEEE Transactions on PAMI, 34*(10), pp 1915-1926, 2012.

[Grimson85] Grimson, W. E. L., and Hildreth, E. C., Comments on "Digital Step Edges from Zero Crossings of Second Directional Derivatives, *IEEE Transactions on PAMI, 7*(1), pp 121-127, 1985.

[Groan78] Groan, F., and Verbeek, P., Freeman-code Probabilities of Object Boundary Quantized Contours, *Computer Vision, Graphics, Image Processing, 7,* pp 391-402, 1978.

[Gunn99] Gunn, S. R., On the Discrete Representation of the Laplacian of Gaussian, *Pattern Recognition, 32*(8), pp 1463-1472, 1999.

[Haddon88] Haddon, J. F., Generalised Threshold Selection for Edge Detection, *Pattern Recognition, 21*(3), pp 195-203, 1988.

[Harris88] Harris, C., and Stephens, M., A Combined Corner and Edge Detector, *Proceedings of Fourth Alvey Vision Conference,* pp 147-151, 1988.

[Haralick84] Haralick, R. M., Digital Step Edges from Zero-Crossings of Second Directional Derivatives, *IEEE Transactions on PAMI, 6*(1), pp 58-68, 1984.

[Haralick85] Haralick, R. M., Author's Reply, *IEEE Transactions on PAMI, 7*(1), pp 127-129, 1985.

[Heath97] Heath, M. D., Sarkar, S., Sanocki, T., and Bowyer, K. W., A Robust Visual Method of Assessing the Relative Performance of Edge Detection Algorithms, *IEEE Transactions on PAMI, 19*(12), pp 1338-1359, 1997.

[Horn81] Horn, B. K. P., and Schunk, B. G., Determining Optical Flow, *Artificial Intelligence, 17,* pp 185-203, 1981.

[Horn86] Horn, B. K. P., *Robot Vision,* MIT Press, Cambridge, 1986.

[Horn93] Horn, B. K. P., and Schunk, B. G., Determining Optical Flow: a Retrospective, *Artificial Intelligence, 59,* pp 81-87, 1993.

[Huang99] Huang, P. S., Harris, C. J., and Nixon, M. S., Human Gait Recognition in Canonical Space Using Temporal Templates, *IEE Proceedings Vision Image and Signal Processing, 146*(2), pp 93-100, 1999.

[Huertas86] Huertas, A., and Medioni, G., Detection of Intensity Changes with Subpixel Accuracy Using Laplacian-Gaussian Masks, *IEEE Transactions on PAMI, 8*(1), pp 651-664, 1986.

[Ilg17] Ilg, E., Mayer, N., Saikia, T., Keuper, M., Dosovitskiy, A., and Brox, T., Flownet 2.0: Evolution of Optical Flow Estimation with Deep Networks, *Proceedings of CVPR,* 2017.

[Jia95] Jia, X., and Nixon, M. S., Extending the Feature Vector for Automatic Face Recognition, *IEEE Transactions on PAMI, 17*(12), pp 1167-1176, 1995.

[Jiang11] Jiang, H., Wang, J., Yuan, Z., Liu, T., Zheng, N., and Li, S., Automatic Salient Object Segmentation Based on Context and Shape Prior, in *Proceedings of BMVC,* 2011.

[Jordan92] Jordan III, J. R., and Bovik A. C., M. S., Using Chromatic Information in Dense Stereo Correspondence, *Pattern Recognition, 25,* pp 367-383, 1992.

[Kadir01] Kadir, T., and Brady, M., Scale, Saliency and Image Description, *International Journal of Computer Vision 45*(2), pp 83-105, 2001.

[Kanade94] Kanade, T., and Okutomi, M., A Stereo Matching Algorithm with an Adaptive Window: Theory and Experiment, *IEEE Transactions on PAMI, 16,* pp 920-932, 1994.

[Kass88] Kass, M., Witkin, A., and Terzopoulos, D., Snakes: Active Contour Models, *International Journal of Computer Vision, 1*(4), pp 321-331, 1988.

[Ke04] Y. Ke and R. Sukthankar. PCA-sift: A More Distinctive Representation for Local Image Descriptors, *Proceedings of CVPR, II,* pp 506–513, 2004.

[Kimia18] Kimia, B. B., Li, X., Guo, Y., and Tamrakar, A., Differential Geometry in Edge Detection: Accurate Estimation of Position, Orientation and Curvature, *IEEE Transactions on PAMI,* DOI 10.1109/TPAMI.2018.2846268, 2018.

[Kitchen82] Kitchen, L., and Rosenfeld, A., Gray-level Corner Detection, *Pattern Recognition Letter, 1*(2), pp 95-102, 1982.

[Korn88] Korn, A. F., Toward a Symbolic Representation of Intensity Changes in Images, *IEEE Transactions on PAMI, 10*(5), pp 610-625, 1988.

[Kovesi99] Kovesi, P., Image Features from Phase Congruency, *Videre: Journal of Computer Vision Research, 1*(3), pp 1–27, 1999.

[Lawton83] Lawton, D. T., Processing Translational Motion Sequences, *Computer Vision, Graphics and Image Processing, 22,* pp 116-144, 1983.

[LeCun15] LeCun, Y., Bengio, Y., and Hinton, G., Deep Learning, *Nature, 521*(7553), pp 437-444, 2015.

[Lee93] Lee, C. K., Haralick, M., Deguchi, K., Estimation of Curvature from Sampled Noisy Data, *ICVPR'93,* pp 536-541, 1993.

[Leutenegger11] Leutenegger, S., Chli, M., and Siegwart, R.Y., 2011, BRISK: Binary Robust Invariant Scalable Keypoints, *Proceedings of ICCV,* pp 2548-2555, 2011.

[Li 18] Li, J., Xia, C., and Chen, X., A Benchmark Dataset and Saliency-Guided Stacked Autoencoders for Video-Based Salient Object Detection, *IEEE Transactions on IP, 27*(1), pp 349-364, 2018.

[Lindeberg94] Lindeberg, T., Scale-Space Theory: a Basic Tool for Analysing Structures at Different Scales, *Journal of Applied Statistics, 21*(2), pp 224-270, 1994.

[Little98] Little, J. J., and Boyd, J. E., Recognizing People by Their Gait: The Shape of Motion, *Videre, 1*(2), pp 2-32, 1998, online at http://mitpress.mit.edu/e-journals/VIDE/001/v12.html.

[Lomeli16] Lomeli-R, J., and Nixon, M. S., An Extension to the Brightness Clustering Transform and Locally Contrasting Keypoints, *Machine Vision and Applications, 27*(8) pp 1187-1196, 2016.

[Lowe99] Lowe, D. G., Object Recognition from Local Scale-Invariant Features, *Proceedings of ICCV,* pp 1150-1157, 1999.

[Lowe04] Lowe, D. G., Distinctive Image Features from Scale-Invariant Key Points, *International Journal of Computer Vision, 60*(2), pp 91-110, 2004.

[Lucas81] Lucas, B., and Kanade, T., An Iterative Image Registration Technique with an Application to Stereo Vision, *Proceedings of DARPA Image Understanding Workshop,* pp 121-130, 1981.

[Marr80] Marr, D. C., and Hildreth, E., Theory of Edge Detection, *Proceedings of Royal Society of London, B207,* pp 187-217, 1980.

[Marr82] Marr, D., *Vision,* W. H. Freeman and Co., N.Y. USA, 1982.

[Mikolajczyk05] Mikolajczyk, K., and Schmid, C., A Performance Evaluation of Local Descriptors, *IEEE Transactions on PAMI, 27*(10), pp 1615- 1630, 2005.

[Mokhtarian86] Mokhtarian F., and Mackworth, A. K., Scale-Space Description and Recognition of Planar Curves and Two-Dimensional Shapes, *IEEE Transactions on PAMI, 8*(1), pp 34-43, 1986.

[Mokhtarian03] Mokhtarian F., and Bober, M., *Curvature Scale Space Representation: Theory, Applications and MPEG-7 Standardization,* Kluwer Academic Publishers, 2003.

[Morrone87] Morrone, M. C., and Owens, R. A., Feature Detection from Local Energy, *Pattern Recognition Letters, 6*, pp 303–313, 1987.

[Morrone88] Morrone M. C., and Burr, D. C., Feature Detection in Human Vision: a Phase-dependent Energy Model, *Proceedings of the Royal Society of London, Series B, Biological Sciences, 235*(1280), pp 221–245, 1988.

[Mukherjee15] Mukherjee, D., Wu, Q. J., and Wang, G., A Comparative Experimental Study of Image Feature Detectors and Descriptors, *Machine Vision and Applications, 26*(4), pp 443-466, 2015.

[Mulet-Parada00] Mulet-Parada, M., and Noble, J. A., 2D+T Acoustic Boundary Detection in Echocardiography, *Medical Image Analysis, 4*, pp 21–30, 2000.

[Myerscough04] Myerscough, P. J., and Nixon, M. S. Temporal Phase Congruency, *Proceedings of IEEE Southwest Symposium on Image Analysis and Interpretation SSIAI '04*, pp 76-79, 2004.

[Nagel87] Nagel, H. H., On the Estimation of Optical Flow: Relations between DifferentApproaches and Some New Results, *Artificial Intelligence, 33*, pp 299-324, 1987.

[Oliva06] Oliva, A., and Torralba, A., Building the Gist of a Scene: The Role of Global Image Features in Recognition, *Progress in Brain Research, 155*, pp 23-36, 2006.

[Otterloo91] van Otterloo, P. J., *A Contour-Oriented Approach to Shape Analysis*, Prentice Hall International (UK) Ltd., Hemel Hempstead, UK, 1991.

[Petrou91] Petrou, M., and Kittler, J., Optimal Edge Detectors for Ramp Edges, *IEEE Transactions on PAMI, 13*(5), pp 483-491, 1991.

[Petrou94] Petrou, M., The Differentiating Filter Approach to Edge Detection, *Advances in Electronics and Electron Physics, 88*, pp 297-345, 1994.

[Prewitt66] Prewitt, J. M. S., and Mendelsohn, M. L., The Analysis of Cell Images, *Annals of New York Academy of Sciences, 128*, pp 1035-1053, 1966.

[Revaud15] Revaud, J., Weinzaepfel, P., Harchaoui, Z., and Schmid, C., Epicflow: Edge-Preserving Interpolation of Correspondences for Optical Flow, *Proceedings of CVPR*, 2015.

[Roberts65] Roberts, L. G., *Machine Perception of Three-Dimensional Solids, Optical and Electro-Optical Information Processing*, MIT Press, pp 159-197, 1965.

[Rosin96] Rosin, P. L., Augmenting Corner Descriptors, *Graphical Models and Image Processing, 58*(3), pp 286-294, 1996.

[Rosten06] Rosten, E., and Drummond, T., Machine Learning for High-Speed Corner Detection, *Proceedings of ECCV*, pp 430-443, 2006.

[Rublee11] Rublee, E., Rabaud, V., Konolige, K., and Bradski, G., ORB: An Efficient Alternative to SIFT or SURF, *Proceedings of ICCV*, pp 2564-2571, 2011.

[Smith97] Smith, S. M., and Brady, J. M., SUSAN - A New Approach to Low Level Image Processing, *International Journal of Computer Vision, 23*(1), pp 45-78, May 1997.

[Sobel70] Sobel, I. E., *Camera Models and Machine Perception*, PhD Thesis, Stanford Univ., 1970.

[Spacek86] Spacek, L. A., Edge Detection and Motion Detection, *Image and Vision Computing, 4*(1), pp 43-56, 1986.

[Sun14] Sun, D., Roth, S., and Black, M. J., A Quantitative Analysis of Current Practices in Optical Flow Estimation and the Principles behind Them, *International Journal of Computer Vision, 106*(2), pp 115-137, 2014.

[Sun18] Sun, Y., Hare, J. S., and Nixon, M. S., Detecting Heel Strikes for Gait Analysis through Acceleration Flow, *IET Computer Vision, 12*(5), pp 686-692, 2018.

[Torre86] Torre, V., and Poggio, T. A., On Edge Detection, *IEEE Transactions on PAMI, 8*(2), pp 147-163, 1986.

[Tuytelaars07] Tuytelaars, T., and Mikolajczyk, K., Local Invariant Feature Detectors: A Survey, *Foundations and Trends in Computer Graphics and Vision, 3*(3), pp 177–280, 2007.

[Ulupinar90] Ulupinar, F., and Medioni, G., Refining Edges Detected by a LoG Operator, *CVGIP, 51*, pp 275-298, 1990.

[Venkatesh89] Venkatesh, S., and Owens, R. A. An Energy Feature Detection Scheme, *Proceedings of Of an International Conference on Image Processing*, pp 553–557, Singapore, 1989.

[Venkatesh95] Venkatesh, S, and Rosin, P. L., Dynamic Threshold Determination by Local and Global Edge Evaluation, *Graphical Models and Image Processing, 57*(2), pp146-160, 1995.

[Vliet89] Vliet, L. J., and Young, I. T., A Nonlinear Laplacian Operator as Edge Detector in Noisy Images, *CVGIP, 45*, pp 167-195, 1989.

[Wang18] Wang, W., Shen, J., and Shao, L., Video Salient Object Detection via Fully Convolutional Networks, *IEEE Transactions on IP, 27*(1), pp 38-49, 2018.

[Weinzaepfel13] Weinzaepfel, P., Revaud, J., Harchaoui, Z., and Schmid, C., DeepFlow: Large Displacement Optical Flow with Deep Matching, *Proceedings of ICCV*, pp 1385-1392, 2013.

[Yitzhaky03] Yitzhaky, Y., and Peli, E., A Method for Objective Edge Detection Evaluation and Detector Parameter Selection, *IEEE Transactions on TPAMI, 25*(8), pp 1027-1033, 2003.

[Zabir94] Zabir, R., and Woodfill, J., Non-parametric Local Transforms for Computing Visual Correspondence, *Proceedings of ECCV*, pp 151-158,1994.

[Zheng04] Zheng, Y., Nixon, M. S., and Allen R., Automatic Segmentation of Lumbar Vertebrae in Digital Videofluoroscopic Imaging, *IEEE Transactions on Medical Imaging, 23*(1), pp 45-52 2004.

[Zheng18] Zheng, L., Yang, Y., and Tian, Q., SIFT Meets CNN: A Decade Survey of Instance Retrieval, *IEEE Transactions on PAMI, 40*(5), pp 1224-1244, 2018.

5

High-level feature extraction: fixed shape matching

5.1 Overview

High-level *feature extraction* concerns finding shapes and objects in computer images. To be able to recognise human faces automatically, for example, one approach is to extract the component features. This requires extraction of, say, the eyes, the ears and the nose, which are the major face features. To find them, we can use their shape: the white part of the eyes is ellipsoidal; the mouth can appear as two lines, as do the eyebrows. Alternatively, we can view them as objects and use the low-level features to define collections of points, which define the eyes, nose and mouth, or even the whole face. This feature extraction process can be viewed as similar to the way we perceive the world: many books for babies describe basic geometric shapes such as triangles, circles and squares. More complex pictures can be decomposed into a structure of simple shapes. In many applications, analysis can be guided by the way the shapes are arranged. For the example of face image analysis, we expect to find the eyes above (and either side of) the nose and we expect to find the mouth below the nose.

In feature extraction, we generally seek *invariance* properties so that the extraction result does not vary according to chosen (or specified) conditions. This implies finding objects, whatever their position, their orientation or their size. That is, techniques should find shapes reliably and robustly whatever the value of any parameter that can control the appearance of a shape. As a basic invariant, we seek immunity to changes in the illumination level: we seek to find a shape whether it is light or dark. In principle, as long as there is contrast between a shape and its background, the shape can be said to exist, and can then be detected. (Clearly, any computer vision technique will fail in extreme lighting conditions; you cannot see anything when it is completely dark.) Following illumination, the next most important parameter is position: we seek to find a shape wherever it appears. This is usually called *position-*, *location-* or *translation-invariance.* Then, we often seek to find a shape irrespective of its rotation (assuming that the object or the camera has an unknown orientation): this is usually called *rotation-* or *orientation-invariance.* Then, we might seek to determine the object at whatever size it appears, which might be due to physical change, or to how close the object has been placed to the camera. This requires *size-* or *scale-invariance.* These are the main invariance properties we shall seek from our shape extraction techniques. However, nature (as usual) tends to roll balls under our feet: there is always noise in images. Also

Feature Extraction and Image Processing for Computer Vision. https://doi.org/10.1016/B978-0-12-814976-8.00005-1

since we are concerned with shapes, note that there might be more than one in the image. If one is on top of the other it will occlude, or hide, the other, so not all the shape of one object will be visible.

But before we can develop image analysis techniques, we need techniques to extract the shapes and objects. Extraction is more complex than detection, since extraction implies that we have a description of a shape, such as its position and size, whereas detection of a shape merely implies knowledge of its existence within an image. This chapter concerns shapes that are fixed in shape (such as a segment of bone in a medical image); the following chapter concerns shapes, which can deform (like the shape of a walking person).

The techniques presented in this chapter are outlined in Table 5.1. We first consider whether we can detect objects by thresholding. This is only likely to provide a solution when illumination and lighting can be controlled, so we then consider two main approaches: one is to extract constituent parts; the other is to extract constituent shapes. We can actually collect and describe low-level features described earlier. In this, wavelets can provide object descriptions, as can Scale-Invariant Feature Transform (SIFT) and distributions of low-level features. In this way we represent objects as a collection of interest points, rather than using shape analysis. Conversely, we can investigate the use of shape: template matching is a model-based approach in which the shape is extracted by searching for the best correlation between a known model and the pixels in an image. There are alternative ways to compute the correlation between the template and the image. Correlation can be implemented by considering the image or frequency domains, and the template can be defined by considering intensity values or a binary shape. The Hough transform defines an efficient implementation of template matching for binary templates.

Table 5.1 Overview of this chapter.

Main topic	**Subtopics**	**Main points**
Pixel operations	How we detect features at a pixel level. What are the limitations and advantages of this approach. Need for shape information.	*Thresholding. Differencing.*
Template matching	Shape extraction by matching. Advantages and disadvantages. Need for efficient implementation.	*Template matching*. Direct and Fourier implementations. Noise and occlusion.
Low-level features	Collecting low-level features for object extraction and their descriptional bases. Frequency-based and parts-based approaches. Detecting distributions of measures.	*Wavelets* and *Haar* wavelets. *SIFT, SURF, BRIEF* and *ORB* descriptions and *histogram of oriented gradients*.
Hough transform	Feature extraction by matching. Hough transforms for conic sections. Hough transform for arbitrary shapes. Invariant formulations. Advantages in speed and efficacy.	Feature extraction by evidence gathering. *Hough transforms* for lines, circles and ellipses. *Generalised* and *invariant Hough transforms*.

This technique is capable of extracting simple shapes such as lines and quadratic forms as well as arbitrary shapes. In any case, the complexity of the implementation can be reduced by considering invariant features of the shapes.

5.2 Thresholding and subtraction

Thresholding is a simple shape extraction technique, as illustrated in Section 3.3.4, where the images could be viewed as the result of trying to separate the eye from the background. If it can be assumed that the shape to be extracted is defined by its brightness, then thresholding an image at that brightness level should find the shape. Thresholding is clearly sensitive to change in illumination: if the image illumination changes then so will the perceived brightness of the target shape. Unless the threshold level can be arranged to adapt to the change in brightness level, any thresholding technique will fail. Its attraction is simplicity: thresholding does not require much computational effort. If the illumination level changes in a linear fashion, using histogram equalisation will result in an image that does not vary. Unfortunately, the result of histogram equalisation is sensitive to noise, shadows and variant illumination: noise can affect the resulting image quite dramatically and this will again render a thresholding technique useless. Let us illustrate this by considering Fig. 5.1, and let us consider trying to find either the ball, or the player, or both in Fig. 5.1A. Superficially, these are the brightest objects, so one value of the threshold, Fig. 5.1B, finds the player's top, shorts and socks, and the ball – but it also finds the text in the advertising and the goalmouth. When we increase the threshold, Fig. 5.1C, we lose the advertising, parts of the player, but still find the goalmouth. Clearly we need to include more knowledge, or to process the image more.

Thresholding after intensity normalisation (Section 3.3.2) is less sensitive to noise, since the noise is stretched with the original image, and cannot affect the stretching process by much. It is, however, still sensitive to shadows and variant illumination. Again, it can only find application where the illumination can be carefully controlled. This requirement is germane to any application that uses basic thresholding. If the overall illumination level cannot be controlled, it is possible to threshold edge magnitude data since this is insensitive to overall brightness level, by virtue of the implicit

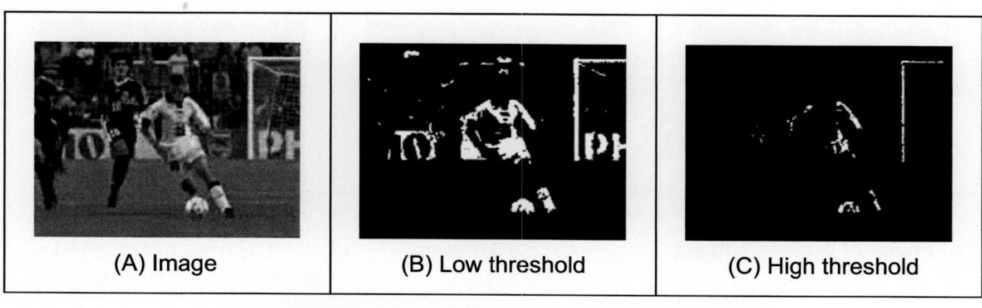

FIGURE 5.1 Extraction by thresholding.

differencing process. However, edge data is rarely continuous and there can be gaps in the detected perimeter of a shape. Another major difficulty, which applies to thresholding the brightness data as well, is that there are often more shapes than one. If the shapes are on top of each other, one occludes the other and the shapes need to be separated.

An alternative approach is to subtract an image from a known background before thresholding. This assumes that the background is known precisely, otherwise many more details than just the target feature will appear in the resulting image; clearly the subtraction will be unfeasible if there is noise on either image, and especially on both. In this approach, there is no implicit shape description, but if the thresholding process is sufficient, it is simple to estimate basic shape parameters, such as position.

The subtraction approach is illustrated in Fig. 5.2. Here, we seek to separate or extract a walking subject from their background. When we subtract the background of Fig. 5.2B from the image itself, we obtain most of the subject with some extra background just behind the subject's head (this is due to the effect of the moving subject on lighting). Also, removing the background removes some of the subject: the horizontal bars in the background have been removed from the subject by the subtraction process. These aspects are highlighted in the thresholded image, Fig. 5.2C. It is not a particularly poor way of separating the subject from the background (we have the subject but we have chopped through his midriff), but it is not especially good either. So it does provide an estimate of the object, but an estimate that is only likely to be reliable when the lighting is highly controlled. (A more detailed study of separation of moving objects from their static background, including estimation of the background itself, is to be found in Chapter 9.)

Even though thresholding and subtraction are attractive (because of simplicity and hence their speed), the performance of both techniques is sensitive to partial shape data, noise, variation in illumination and occlusion of the target shape by other objects. Accordingly, many approaches to image interpretation use higher level information in shape extraction, namely how the pixels are connected. This can resolve these factors.

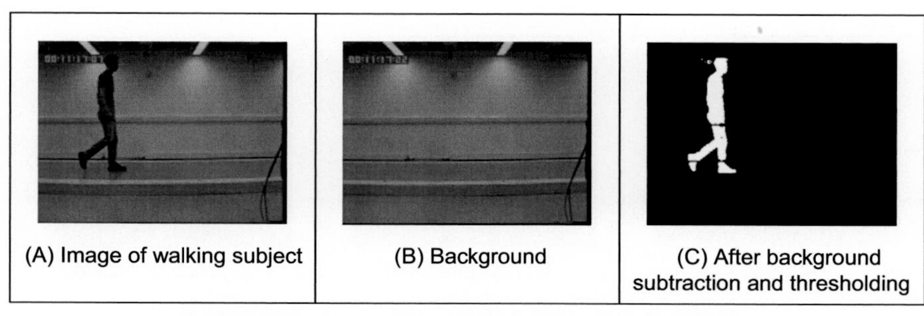

(A) Image of walking subject
(B) Background
(C) After background subtraction and thresholding

FIGURE 5.2 Shape extraction by subtraction and thresholding.

5.3 Template matching

5.3.1 Definition

Template matching is conceptually a simple process. We need to match a template to an image, where the template is a subimage that contains the shape we are trying to find. Accordingly, we centre the template on an image point and count how many points in the template matched those in the image. The procedure is repeated for the entire image and the point which led to the best match, the maximum count, is deemed to be the point where the shape (given by the template) lies within the image.

Consider that we want to find the template of Fig. 5.3B in the image of Fig. 5.3A. The template is first positioned at the origin and then matched with the image to give a count that reflects how well the template matched that part of the image at that position. The count of matching pixels is increased by one for each point where the brightness of the template matches the brightness of the image. This is similar to the process of template convolution, illustrated earlier in Fig. 3.11. The difference here is that points in the image are matched with those in the template, and the sum is the number of matching points as opposed to the weighted sum of image data. The best match which gives the maximum number of matching points is when the template is placed at the position where the target shape is matched to itself. Obviously, this process can be generalised to find, for example, templates of different size or orientation. In these cases, we have to try all the templates (at expected rotation and size) to determine the best match.

Formally, template matching can be defined as a method of parameter estimation. The parameters define the position (and pose) of the template. We can define a template as a discrete function $\mathbf{T}_{x,y}$. This function takes values in a window. That is, the co-ordinates of the points $(x, y) \in \mathbf{W}$. For example, for a 2×2 template, we have the set of points $\mathbf{W} = \{(0, 0), (0, 1), (1, 0), (1, 1)\}$. In general, a template can be defined by

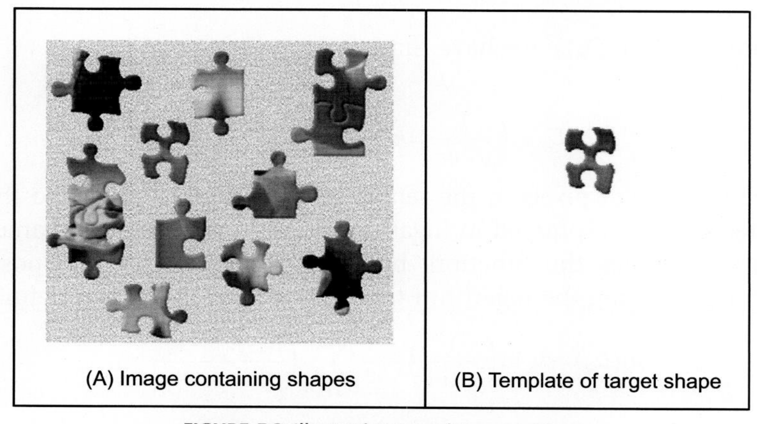

FIGURE 5.3 Illustrating template matching.

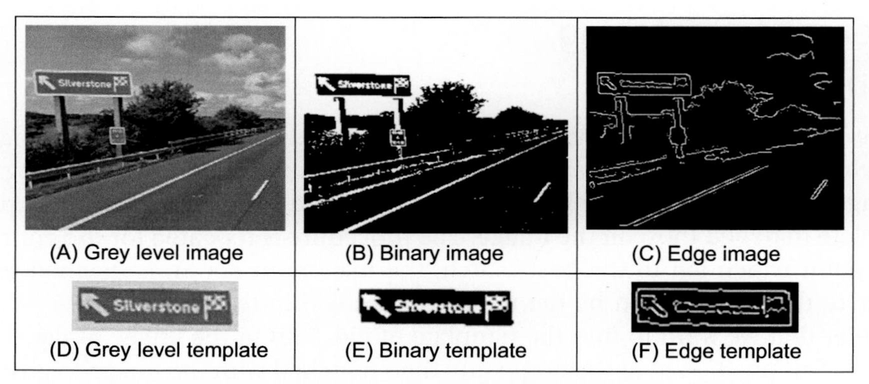

(A) Grey level image (B) Binary image (C) Edge image
(D) Grey level template (E) Binary template (F) Edge template

FIGURE 5.4 Examples of grey level, binary and edge template matching.

considering any property from an image. The example in Fig. 5.4 shows templates defined by grey values, binary values and image edges. Other templates can also define colours or multispectral data.

Let us consider that each pixel in the image $\mathbf{I}_{x,y}$ is corrupted by additive Gaussian noise. The noise has a mean value of zero, and the (unknown) standard deviation is σ. Thus, the probability that a point in the template placed at co-ordinates (i, j) matches the corresponding pixel at position $(x, y) \in \mathbf{W}$ is given by the normal distribution

$$p_{i,j}(x,y) = \frac{1}{\sqrt{2\pi}\sigma} e^{-\frac{1}{2}\left(\frac{\mathbf{I}_{x+i,y+j}-\mathbf{T}_{x,y}}{\sigma}\right)^2} \tag{5.1}$$

Since the noise affecting each pixel is independent, then the probability that the template is at position (i, j) is the combined probability of each pixel that the template covers. That is,

$$L_{i,j} = \prod_{(x,y)\in\mathbf{W}} p_{i,j}(x,y) \tag{5.2}$$

By substitution of Eq. (5.1), we have that

$$L_{i,j} = \left(\frac{1}{\sqrt{2\pi}\sigma}\right)^n e^{-\frac{1}{2}\sum_{(x,y)\in\mathbf{W}}\left(\frac{\mathbf{I}_{x+i,y+j}-\mathbf{T}_{x,y}}{\sigma}\right)^2} \tag{5.3}$$

where n is the number of pixels in the template. This function is called the *likelihood* function. Generally, it is expressed in logarithmic form to simplify the analysis. Notice that the logarithm scales the function, but it does not change the position of the maximum. Thus, by taking the logarithm the likelihood function is redefined as

$$\ln(L_{i,j}) = n\ \ln\left(\frac{1}{\sqrt{2\pi}\sigma}\right) - \frac{1}{2}\sum_{(x,y)\in\mathbf{W}}\left(\frac{\mathbf{I}_{x+i,y+j}-\mathbf{T}_{x,y}}{\sigma}\right)^2 \tag{5.4}$$

In *maximum likelihood estimation*, we have to choose the parameter that maximises the likelihood function. That is, the positions that minimise the rate of change of the objective function

$$\frac{\partial \ln(L_{i,j})}{\partial i}=0 \quad \text{and} \quad \frac{\partial \ln(L_{i,j})}{\partial j}=0 \tag{5.5}$$

That is,

$$\begin{aligned}
&\sum_{(x,y)\in\mathbf{W}}(\mathbf{I}_{x+i,y+j}-\mathbf{T}_{x,y})\frac{\partial \mathbf{I}_{x+i,y+j}}{\partial i}=0\\
&\sum_{(x,y)\in\mathbf{W}}(\mathbf{I}_{x+i,y+j}-\mathbf{T}_{x,y})\frac{\partial \mathbf{I}_{x+i,y+j}}{\partial j}=0
\end{aligned} \tag{5.6}$$

We can observe that these equations are also the solution of the minimisation problem given by

$$\min \quad e=\sum_{(x,y)\in\mathbf{W}}(\mathbf{I}_{x+i,y+j}-\mathbf{T}_{x,y})^2 \tag{5.7}$$

That is, maximum likelihood estimation is equivalent to choosing the template position that minimises the squared error (the squared values of the differences between the template points and the corresponding image points). The position where the template best matches the image is the estimated position of the template within the image. Thus, if you measure the match using the squared error criterion, then you will be choosing the *maximum likelihood* solution. This implies that the result achieved by template matching is optimal for images corrupted by Gaussian noise. (Note that the *central limit theorem* suggests that noise experienced practically can be assumed to be Gaussian distributed, though many images appear to contradict this assumption.) Of course you can use other error criteria such as the absolute difference rather than the squared difference or, if you feel more adventurous, you might consider robust measures such as M-estimators.

We can derive alternative forms of the squared error criterion by considering that Eq. (5.7) can be written as

$$\min \quad e=\sum_{(x,y)\in\mathbf{W}}\left(\mathbf{I}^2_{x+i,y+j}-2\mathbf{I}_{x+i,y+j}\mathbf{T}_{x,y}+\mathbf{T}^2_{x,y}\right) \tag{5.8}$$

The last term does not depend on the template position (i, j). As such, it is constant and cannot be minimised. Thus, the optimum in this equation can be obtained by minimising

$$\min \quad e=\sum_{(x,y)\in\mathbf{W}}\left(\mathbf{I}^2_{x+i,y+j}-2\sum_{(x,y)\in\mathbf{W}}\mathbf{I}_{x+i,y+j}\mathbf{T}_{x,y}\right) \tag{5.9}$$

If the first term

$$\sum_{(x,y)\in\mathbf{W}}\mathbf{I}^2_{x+i,y+j} \tag{5.10}$$

is approximately constant, then the remaining term gives a measure of the similarity between the image and the template. That is, we can maximise the cross-correlation between the template and the image. Thus, the best position can be computed by

$$\max \quad e = \sum_{(x,y)\in \mathbf{W}} \mathbf{I}_{x+i,y+j}\mathbf{T}_{x,y} \tag{5.11}$$

However, the squared term in Eq. (5.10) can vary with position, so the match defined by Eq. (5.11) can be poor. Additionally, the range of the cross-correlation is dependent on the size of the template, and it is noninvariant to changes in image lighting conditions. Thus, in an implementation it is more convenient to use either Eq. (5.7) or Eq. (5.9) (in spite of being computationally more demanding than the cross-correlation in Eq. (5.11). Alternatively, cross-correlation can be normalised as follows. We can rewrite Eq. (5.9) as

$$\min \quad e = 1 - 2\frac{\sum_{(x,y)\in \mathbf{W}} \mathbf{I}_{x+i,y+j}\mathbf{T}_{x,y}}{\sum_{(x,y)\in \mathbf{W}} \mathbf{I}^2_{x+i,y+j}} \tag{5.12}$$

Here the first term is constant and thus, the optimum value can be obtained by

$$\max \quad e = \frac{\sum_{(x,y)\in \mathbf{W}} \mathbf{I}_{x+i,y+j}\mathbf{T}_{x,y}}{\sum_{(x,y)\in \mathbf{W}} \mathbf{I}^2_{x+i,y+j}} \tag{5.13}$$

In general, it is convenient to normalise the grey level of each image window under the template. That is,

$$\max \quad e = \frac{\sum_{(x,y)\in \mathbf{W}} \left(\mathbf{I}_{x+i,y+j} - \bar{\mathbf{I}}_{i,j}\right)\left(\mathbf{T}_{x,y} - \bar{\mathbf{T}}\right)}{\sum_{(x,y)\in \mathbf{W}} \left(\mathbf{I}_{x+i,y+j} - \bar{\mathbf{I}}_{i,j}\right)^2} \tag{5.14}$$

where $\bar{\mathbf{I}}_{i,j}$ is the mean of the pixels $\mathbf{I}_{x+i,y+j}$ for points within the window (i.e. $(x, y) \in \mathbf{W}$) and $\bar{\mathbf{T}}$ is the mean of the pixels of the template. An alternative form to Eq. (5.14) is given by normalising the cross-correlation. This does not change the position of the optimum and gives an interpretation as the normalisation of the cross-correlation vector. That is, the cross-correlation is divided by its modulus. Thus,

$$\max \quad e = \frac{\sum_{(x,y)\in \mathbf{W}} \left(\mathbf{I}_{x+i,y+j} - \bar{\mathbf{I}}_{i,j}\right)\left(\mathbf{T}_{x,y} - \bar{\mathbf{T}}\right)}{\sqrt{\sum_{(x,y)\in \mathbf{W}} \left(\mathbf{I}_{x+i,y+j} - \bar{\mathbf{I}}_{i,j}\right)^2\left(\mathbf{T}_{x,y} - \bar{\mathbf{T}}\right)^2}} \tag{5.15}$$

However, this equation has a similar computational complexity to the original formulation in Eq. (5.7).

A particular implementation of template matching is when the image and the template are binary. In this case, the binary image can represent regions in the image or it can contain the edges. These two cases are illustrated in the example in Fig. 5.4. The advantage of using binary images is that the amount of computation can be reduced. That is, each term in Eq. (5.7) will take only two values: it will be one when $\mathbf{I}_{x+i,y+j} = \mathbf{T}_{x,y}$ and zero otherwise. Thus, Eq. (5.7) can be implemented as

$$\max \quad e = \sum_{(x,y) \in \mathbf{W}} \overline{\mathbf{I}_{x+i,y+j} \oplus \mathbf{T}_{x,y}} \tag{5.16}$$

where the symbol $\overline{\oplus}$ denotes the exclusive NOR operator. This equation can be easily implemented and requires significantly less resources than the original matching function.

Template matching develops an *accumulator space* that stores the match of the template to the image at different locations; this corresponds to an implementation of Eq. (5.7). It is called an accumulator since the match is accumulated during application. Essentially, the accumulator is a two-dimensional array that holds the difference between the template and the image at different positions. The position in the image gives the same position of match in the accumulator. Alternatively, Eq. (5.11) suggests that the peaks in the accumulator resulting from template correlation give the location of the template in an image: the co-ordinates of the point of best match. Accordingly, template correlation and template matching can be viewed as similar processes. The location of a template can be determined by either process. The binary implementation of template matching, Eq. (5.16), usually is concerned with thresholded edge data. This equation will be reconsidered in the definition of the Hough transform, the topic of Section 5.5.

Code 5.1 shows the implementation of template matching. The code uses an accumulator array, `accumulator` and the position of the template is given by its centre. The accumulator elements are incremented according to Eq. (5.7), and the match for each position is stored in the array. The implementation inverts the value of the difference in Eq. (5.7), so the best match can be shown as a peak in the accumulator. As such, after computing all the matches, the maximum element in the array defines the position where most pixels in the template matched those in the image. It is possible to implement a version of template matching without the accumulator array, by only storing the location of the minimum. This will give the same result, and it requires less storage. However, this implementation will provide a result that cannot support later image interpretation and that might require knowledge of more than just the best match.

The results of applying the template matching procedure are illustrated in Fig. 5.5. This figure shows the accumulators as images and as histograms. The height of the histogram corresponds to the value in the accumulator. This example shows the accumulator arrays for matching the images shown in Fig. 5.4 with their respective templates. The white points in each image are at the co-ordinates of the origin of the position where the template best matched the image (the maxima). Note that there is a border where the template has not been matched to the image data. At these border points, the template extended beyond the image data, so no matching has been performed. This is the same border as experienced with template convolution, Section 3.4.1. We can observe that a clearer maximum is obtained, Fig. 5.5C, from the edge images in Fig. 5.4. This is because

```
function image = template_match(image,template)
%get image dimensions
[rows,cols]=size(image);
%get template dimensions
[trows,tcols]=size(template);
%half of template rows is
tr=floor(trows/2);
%half of template cols is
tc=floor(tcols/2);

%set an output as black
accum(1:rows,1:cols)=0;

%then convolve the template
for x = tc+1:cols-tc %address all columns except border
    for y = tr+1:rows-tr %address all rows except border
        sum=0; %initialise the sum
        for iwin=1:tcols %address all points in the template
            for jwin=1:trows
                sum=sum+image(y+jwin-tr-1,x+iwin-tc-1)*...
                            template(jwin,iwin);
            end
        end
        accum(y,x)=sum;
    end
end

%find the maximum
biggest_vote=max(max(accum));
```

CODE 5.1 Implementing template matching.

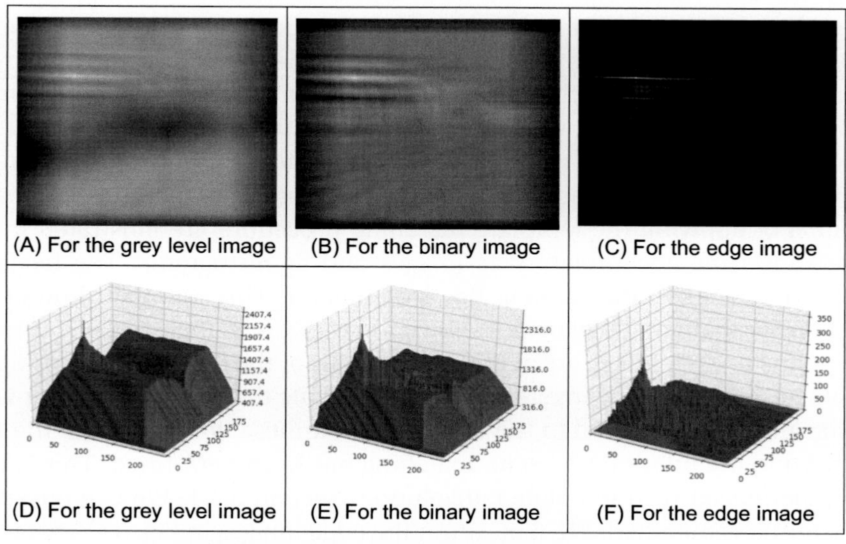

FIGURE 5.5 Accumulator arrays from template matching.

for grey level and binary images, there is some match when the template is not exactly in the best position. In the case of edges, the count of matching pixels is less.

Most applications require further degrees of freedom such as rotation (orientation), scale (size) or perspective deformations. Rotation can be handled by rotating the template, or by using polar co-ordinates; scale invariance can be achieved using templates of differing size. Having more parameters of interest implies that the accumulator space becomes larger; its dimensions increase by one for each extra parameter of interest. Position-invariant template matching, as considered here, implies a 2D parameter space, whereas the extension to scale and position invariant template matching requires a 3D parameter space.

The computational cost of template matching is large. If the template is square and of size $m \times m$ and is matched to an image of size $N \times N$, since the m^2 pixels are matched at all image points (except for the border), the computational cost is $O(N^2 m^2)$. This is the cost for position invariant template matching. Any further parameters of interest increase the computational cost in proportion to the number of values of the extra parameters. This is clearly a large penalty and so a direct digital implementation of template matching is slow. Accordingly, this guarantees interest in techniques that can deliver the same result, but faster, such as using a Fourier implementation based on fast transform calculus.

The main advantages of template matching are its insensitivity to *noise* and *occlusion*. Noise can occur in any image, on any signal – just like on a telephone line. In digital photographs, the noise might appear low, but in computer vision it is made worse by edge detection by virtue of the differencing (differentiation) processes. Likewise, shapes can easily be occluded or hidden: a person can walk behind a lamp post or illumination can also cause occlusion. The averaging inherent in template matching reduces the susceptibility to noise; the maximisation process reduces susceptibility to occlusion.

These advantages are shown in Fig. 5.6 which illustrates detection in the presence of increasing noise. Here, we will use template matching to locate the region containing the vertical rectangle near the top of the image (so we are matching a binary template of a black template on a white background to the binary image). The lowest noise level is in

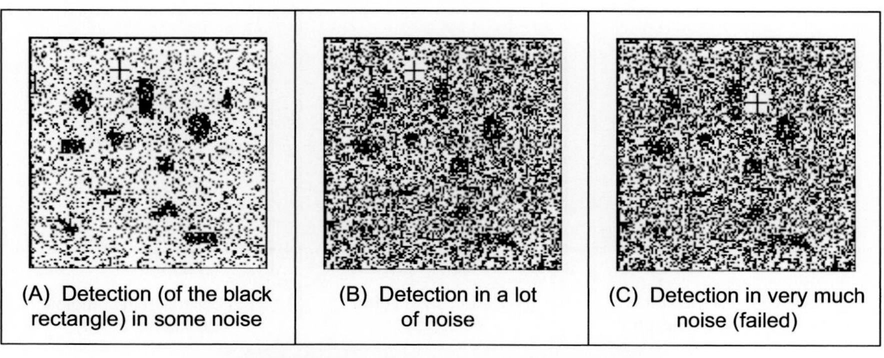

(A) Detection (of the black rectangle) in some noise

(B) Detection in a lot of noise

(C) Detection in very much noise (failed)

FIGURE 5.6 Template matching in noisy images.

Fig. 5.6A and the highest is in Fig. 5.6C; the position of the origin of the detected rectangle is shown as a black cross in a white square. The position of the origin of the region containing the rectangle is detected correctly in Figs. 5.6A and B but incorrectly in the noisiest image, Fig. 5.6C. Clearly, template matching can handle quite high noise corruption. (Admittedly this is somewhat artificial: the noise would usually be filtered out by one of the techniques described in Chapter 3, but we are illustrating basic properties here.) The ability to handle noise is shown by correct determination of the position of the target shape, until the noise becomes too much and there are more points due to noise than there are due to the shape itself. When this occurs, the votes resulting from the noise exceed those occurring from the shape, and so the maximum is not found where the shape exists.

Occlusion is shown by placing a grey bar across the image; in Fig. 5.7A, the bar does not occlude (or hide) the target rectangle, whereas in Fig. 5.7C, the rectangle is completely obscured. As with performance in the presence of noise, detection of the shape fails when the votes occurring from the shape exceed those from the rest of the image (the nonshape points), and the cross indicating the position of the origin of the region containing the rectangle is drawn in completely the wrong place. This is what happens when the rectangle is completely obscured in Fig. 5.7C.

So it can operate well, with practical advantage. We can include edge detection to concentrate on a shape's borders. Its main problem is still speed: a direct implementation is slow, especially when handling shapes that are rotated or scaled (and there are other implementation difficulties too). Recalling that from Section 3.4.4 that template convolution can be speeded up by using the Fourier transform, let us see if that can be used here too.

5.3.2 Fourier transform implementation

We can implement template matching via the Fourier transform by using the duality between *convolution* and multiplication, which was discussed earlier in Section 3.4.4. This duality establishes that a multiplication in the space domain corresponds to a

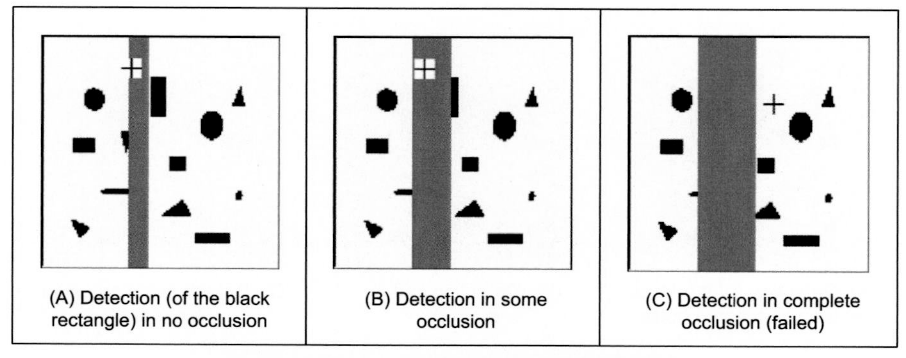

(A) Detection (of the black rectangle) in no occlusion
(B) Detection in some occlusion
(C) Detection in complete occlusion (failed)

FIGURE 5.7 Template matching in occluded images.

convolution in the frequency domain and vice versa. This can be exploited for faster computation by using the frequency domain, given the Fast Fourier Transform algorithm. Thus, in order to find a shape we can compute the cross-correlation as a multiplication in the frequency domain. However, the matching process in Eq. (5.11) is actually *correlation* (Section 2.3), not convolution. Thus, we need to express the correlation in terms of a convolution. This can be done as follows. First, we can rewrite the correlation (denoted by ⊗) in Eq. (5.11) as

$$\mathbf{I} \otimes \mathbf{T} = \sum_{(x,y)\in W} \mathbf{I}_{x',y'} \mathbf{T}_{x'-i,y'-j} \tag{5.17}$$

where $x' = x + i$ and $y' = y + j$. Convolution (denoted by $*$) is defined as

$$\mathbf{I} * \mathbf{T} = \sum_{(x,y)\in W} \mathbf{I}_{x',y'} \mathbf{T}_{i-x',j-y'} \tag{5.18}$$

Thus, in order to implement template matching in the frequency domain, we need to express Eq. (5.17) in terms of Eq. (5.18). This can be achieved by considering that the correlation

$$\mathbf{I} \otimes \mathbf{T} = \mathbf{I} * \mathbf{T}' = \sum_{(x,y)\in W} \mathbf{I}_{x',y'} \mathbf{T}'_{i-x',j-y'} \tag{5.19}$$

where

$$\mathbf{T}' = \mathbf{T}_{-x,-y} \tag{5.20}$$

That is, correlation is equivalent to convolution when the template is changed according to Eq. (5.20). This equation reverses the co-ordinate axes, and it corresponds to a horizontal and a vertical flip.

In the frequency domain, convolution corresponds to multiplication. As such, we have that Eq. (5.19) can be implemented by

$$\mathbf{I} \otimes \mathbf{T} = \mathbf{I} * \mathbf{T}' = \Im^{-1}(\Im(\mathbf{I}) \times \Im(\mathbf{T}')) \tag{5.21}$$

where $\Im$ denotes Fourier transformation as in Chapter 2 (and calculated by the fast Fourier transform (FFT)) and $\Im^{-1}$ denotes the inverse FFT. Note that the multiplication operator actually operates point by point, so each point is the product of the pixels at the same position in each image (in Matlab® the operation is `.*`). This is computationally faster than its direct implementation, given the speed advantage of the FFT. There are two ways to implement this equation. In the first approach, we can compute $\mathbf{T}'$ by flipping the template and then computing its Fourier transform $\Im(\mathbf{T}')$. In the second approach, we compute the transform of $\Im(\mathbf{T})$ and then we compute its complex conjugate. That is,

$$\Im(\mathbf{T}') = [\Im(\mathbf{T})]^* \tag{5.22}$$

where [ ]* denotes the complex conjugate of the transform data (yes, we agree it's an unfortunate symbol clash with convolution, but they are both standard symbols). So conjugation of the transform of the template implies that the product of the two transforms leads to correlation. (Since this product is point by point the two images/ matrices need to be of the same size.) That is,

$$\mathbf{I} \otimes \mathbf{T} = \mathbf{I} * \mathbf{T}' = \Im^{-1}(\Im(\mathbf{I}) \times [\Im(\mathbf{T})]^{*}) \tag{5.23}$$

For both implementations, Eqs. (5.21) and (5.23) will evaluate the match and, more quickly for large templates than by direct implementation of template matching (as per Section 3.4). Note that one assumption is that the transforms are of the same size, even though the template's shape is usually much smaller than the image. There is actually a selection of approaches; a simple solution is to include extra zero values (*zero-padding*) to make the image of the template the same size as the image.

Code 5.2 illustrates the implementation of template matching by convolution in the image domain. In this implementation, the input image is padded to include the size of the template. Fig. 5.8A shows the padding pixels in black. Padding is not necessary when computing convolution in the image domain, but it is included so the results can be compared with the computation of the convolution in the frequency domain in Code 5.3. The main loop in Code 5.2 computes the error criterion in Eq. (5.8). The code separates the computation of the correlation terms and those terms which are squared. The term which is squared is computed separately so it can be used later in Code 5.3. An example of the result of the template matching by convolution in the image domain is shown in Fig. 5.8D. The white point in the image defines the maximum value and indicates the position of the template. The peak is more evident in Fig. 5.8G where the accumulator is shown as a histogram.

Code 5.3 illustrates the computation of template matching by convolution in the frequency domain. Similar to Code 5.2, the input image is padded. In this case, the template is also transformed and padded according to Eq. (5.19). Fig. 5.8B shows the transformed and padded template. The implementation in Code 5.3 computes the Fourier coefficients of the image and of the template, and it stores them in the arrays `imageCoeff` and `templateCoeff`. These coefficients are then used to compute the

```
# Pad input
inputPad = createImageF(widthPad, heightPad)
for x,y in itertools.product(range(0, width), range(0, height)):
    inputPad[y,x] = inputImage[y,x]

# Compute correlation in image domain sum of square differences
squaredTerm = createImageF(widthPad, heightPad)
corrImage = createImageF(widthPad, heightPad)
for x,y in itertools.product(range(0, widthPad), range(0, heightPad)):
    for w,h in itertools.product(range(-widthTemplate+1,1),                 \
                                 range(-heightTemplate+1,1)):
        p, q = x+w, y+h
        if p >=0 and q>=  0 and p < width and q < height:
            squaredTerm[y,x] += inputPad[q,p] * inputPad[q,p]
            corrImage[y,x] += 2.0 * templatePad[h+heightTemplate,w+widthTemplate] \
                              * inputPad[q,p]
```

CODE 5.2 Implementing convolution in the image domain.

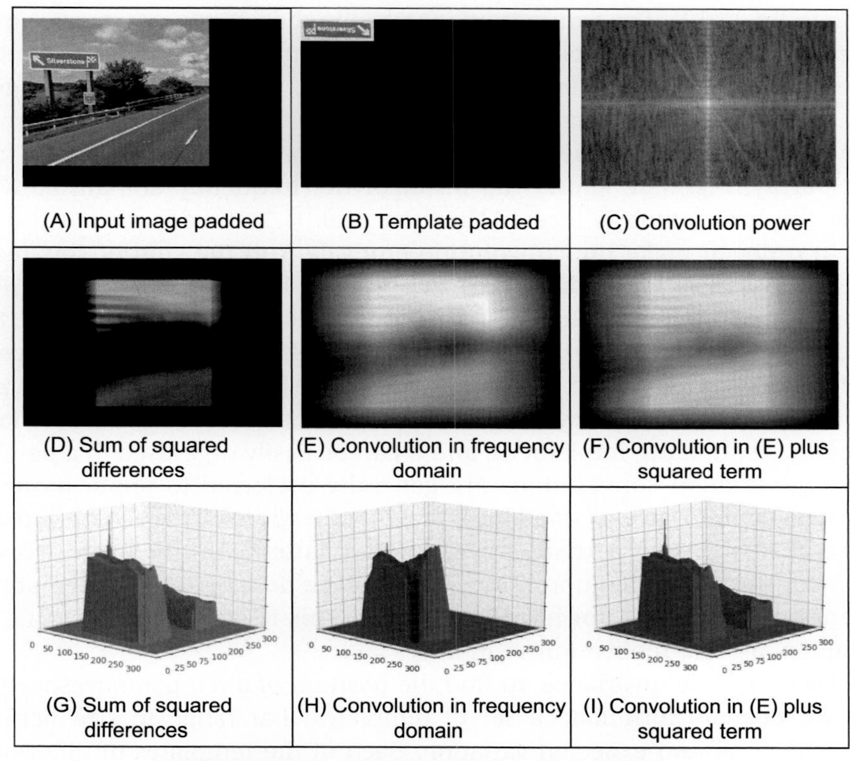

(A) Input image padded
(B) Template padded
(C) Convolution power
(D) Sum of squared differences
(E) Convolution in frequency domain
(F) Convolution in (E) plus squared term
(G) Sum of squared differences
(H) Convolution in frequency domain
(I) Convolution in (E) plus squared term

FIGURE 5.8 Template matching by Fourier transformation.

```
# Pad and invert template
templatePadFlip = createImageF(widthPad, heightPad)
for x,y in itertools.product(range(0, widthTemplate), range(0, heightTemplate)):
    templatePadFlip[y,x] = templateImage[heightTemplate-y-1, widthTemplate-x-1]

# Compute Fourier coefficients
imageCoeff, maxFrequencyW, maxFrequencyH = computeCoefficients(inputPad)
templateCoeff, _, _ = computeCoefficients(templatePadFlip)

# Frequency domain multiplication defines convolution is space domain
resultCoeff = createImageF(1 + 2 * maxFrequencyW ,1 + 2 * maxFrequencyH , 2)
for kw,kh in itertools.product(range(-maxFrequencyW, maxFrequencyW + 1),         \
                               range(-maxFrequencyH, maxFrequencyH + 1)):
    w = kw + maxFrequencyW
    h = kh + maxFrequencyH
    resultCoeff[h,w][0] = (imageCoeff[h,w][0] * templateCoeff[h,w][0] -          \
                           imageCoeff[h,w][1] * templateCoeff[h,w][1])
    resultCoeff[h,w][1] = (imageCoeff[h,w][1] * templateCoeff[h,w][0] +          \
                           imageCoeff[h,w][0] * templateCoeff[h,w][1])
# Inverse Fourier transform
reconstructedResult = reconstruction(resultCoeff)

# Add square term to define an operator equivalent to SSD
for x,y in itertools.product(range(0, widthPad), range(0, heightPad)):
    reconstructedResult[y,x] = -squaredTerm[y,x] + 2.0 * reconstructedResult[y,x]
```

CODE 5.3 Implementing convolution by the frequency domain.

summation in Eq. (5.19). The summation is stored in the `resultCoeff` array. Notice that the summation computes the convolution since the template has been rotated. The power spectrum of the convolution is shown in Fig. 5.8C. This corresponds to the frequency representation of the convolution. The function `reconstruction` obtains the image representation of the convolution by reconstructing the image from the `resultCoeff` array. Fig. 5.8E shows the result of the frequency domain convolution. Notice that the best match is located, but the peak is less evident than the peak in Fig. 5.8D. In order to make the convolution equivalent to the sum of squared differences, the code adds the quadratic term computed in Code 5.2. The result of the summation is shown in Figs. 5.8F and I. When the quadratic term is included, then the results are equivalent to the results in Figs. 5.8A and B. The only difference is how the convolution is computed (i.e. in the image or in the frequency domain). In practice, the computation in the frequency domain is more expensive and the summation in the image domain is simpler to implement, and it can be easily organised in a parallel way, thus the image domain convolutions are generally preferred in applications. Notice that the results contain several small local maxima (in white). This can be explained by the fact that the shape can partially match several patterns in the image. Also we can see that, in contrast to the computation in the image domain, the implementation in the frequency domain does not have any border. This is due to the fact that Fourier theory assumes picture replication to infinity.

Should we seek scale invariance, to find the position of a template irrespective of its size, then we need to formulate a set of templates that range in size between the maximum and minimum expected variation. Each of the templates of differing size is then matched by frequency domain multiplication. The maximum frequency domain value, for all sizes of template, indicates the position of the template and, naturally, gives a value for its size. This can of course be a rather lengthy procedure when the template ranges considerably in size.

There are several further difficulties in using the transform domain for template matching in discrete images. If we seek rotation invariance, then an image can be expressed in terms of its polar co-ordinates. Discretisation gives further difficulty since the points in a rotated discrete shape can map imperfectly to the original shape. This problem is better manifested when an image is scaled in size to become larger. In such a case, the spacing between points will increase in the enlarged image. The difficulty is how to allocate values for pixels in the enlarged image that are not defined in the enlargement process. There are several interpolation approaches, but it can often appear prudent to reformulate the original approach. Further difficulties can include the influence of the image borders: Fourier theory assumes that an image replicates spatially to infinity. Such difficulty can be reduced by using window operators, such as the Hamming or the Hanning windows. These difficulties do not obtain for optical Fourier transforms and so using the Fourier transform for position-invariant template matching is often confined to optical implementations.

5.3.3 Discussion of template matching

The advantages associated with template matching are mainly theoretical since it can be very difficult to develop a template matching technique that operates satisfactorily. The results presented here have been for position invariance only. This can cause difficulty if invariance to rotation and scale is also required. This is because the template is stored as a discrete set of points. When these are rotated, gaps can appear due to the discrete nature of the co-ordinate system. If the template is increased in size then again there will be missing points in the scaled-up version. Again, there is a frequency domain version that can handle variation in size, since scale invariant template matching can be achieved using the *Mellin transform* [Bracewell86]. This avoids using many templates to accommodate the variation in size by evaluating the scale-invariant match in a single pass. The Mellin transform essentially scales the spatial co-ordinates of the image using an exponential function. A point is then moved to a position given by a logarithmic function of its original co-ordinates. The transform of the scaled image is then multiplied by the transform of the template. The maximum again indicates the best match between the transform and the image. This can be considered to be equivalent to a change of variable. The logarithmic mapping ensures that scaling (multiplication) becomes addition. By the logarithmic mapping, the problem of scale invariance becomes a problem of finding the position of a match.

The Mellin transform only provides scale-invariant matching. For scale and position invariance, the Mellin transform is combined with the Fourier transform, to give the *Fourier–Mellin* transform. The Fourier–Mellin transform has many disadvantages in a digital implementation due to the problems in spatial resolution though there are approaches to reduce these problems [Altmann84], as well as the difficulties with discrete images experienced in Fourier transform approaches.

Again, the Mellin transform appears to be much better suited to an optical implementation [Casasent77], where continuous functions are available, rather than to discrete image analysis. A further difficulty with the Mellin transform is that its result is independent of the form factor of the template. Accordingly, a rectangle and a square appear to be the same to this transform. This implies a loss of information since the form factor can indicate that an object has been imaged from an oblique angle. There has been some interest in *log-polar mappings* for image analysis (e.g. [Zokai05]).

So there are innate difficulties with template matching whether it is implemented directly, or by transform operations. For these reasons, and because many shape extraction techniques require more than just edge or brightness data, direct digital implementations of feature extraction are usually preferred. This is perhaps also influenced by the speed advantage that one popular technique can confer over template matching. This is the Hough transform, which is covered in Section 5.5. Before that, we shall consider techniques which consider object extraction by collections of low-level features. These can avoid the computational requirements of template matching by treating shapes as collections of features.

5.4 Feature extraction by low-level features

There have been many approaches to feature extraction which combine a variety of features. It is possible to characterise objects by measures that we have already developed, by low-level features local features (such edges and corners), and by global features (such as colour). Later we shall find these can be grouped to give structure or shape (in this chapter and the next), and appearance (called texture, Chapter 8). The drivers for the earlier approaches which combine low-level features are the need to be able to search databases for particular images. This is known as image retrieval (Section 4.4.2), and in content-based retrieval that uses techniques from image processing and computer vision, there are approaches that combine a selection of features [Smeulders00]. Alternative search strategies include using text or sketches, and these are not of interest in the domain of this book. One approach is to develop features which include and target human descriptions and use techniques from machine intelligence [Datta08], which also implies understanding of semantics (how people describe images) as compared with the results of automated image analysis.

There is also interest in recognising objects, and hence images, by collecting descriptors for local features [Mikolajczyk05]. These can find application not just in image retrieval but also in stereo computer vision, navigating robots by computer vision and when stitching together multiple images to build a much larger panorama image. Much of this material relates to whole applications and therefore can rely not just on collecting local features, on shape, on texture and on classification. In these respects in this chapter we shall provide coverage of some of the basic ways to combine low-level feature descriptions. Essentially, these approaches show how techniques that have already been covered can be combined in such a way as to achieve a description by which an object can be recognised. The approaches tend to rely on the use of machine learning approaches to determine the relevant data (to filter it so as to understand its structure) so the approaches are described in basis only here and the classification approaches are described later, in Chapter 12.

5.4.1 Appearance-based approaches

5.4.1.1 Object detection by templates

The *Viola Jones approach* essentially uses the form of Haar wavelets defined earlier in Section 2.7.3.2 as a basis for object detection [Viola01] which was later extended to be one of the most popular techniques for detecting human faces in images [Viola04]. Using rectangles to detect image features is an approximation, as there are features which can describe curved structure (derived using Gabor wavelets, for example). It is, however, a fast approximation, since the features can be detected using the integral image approach. If we are to consider the face image in Fig. 5.9A, then the eyes are darker than the cheeks which are immediately below them, and the eyes are also darker than the bridge of the nose. As such, if we match the template in Fig. 5.9B (this is the inverted

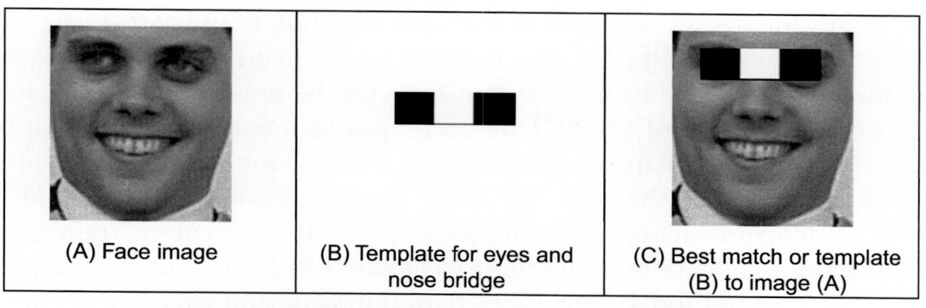

FIGURE 5.9 Object extraction by Haar Wavelet-based features.

form of the template in Fig. 2.32C), then superimposing this template on the image at the position where it best matches the face leads to the image of Fig. 5.9C. The result is not too surprising since it finds two dark parts between which there is a light part, and only the eyes and the bridge of the nose fit this description. (We could of course have a nostril template but (1) you might be eating your dinner and (2) when you look closely, quite a lot of the image fits the description 'two small dark blobs with a light bit in the middle' – we can successfully find the eyes since they are a large structure fitting the template well.)

In this way, we can define a series of templates (those in Fig. 2.29) and match them to the image. In this way we can find the underlying shape. We need to sort the results to determine which are the most important and which collection best describes the face. That is where the approach advances to machine learning, which comes later in Chapter 12. For now, we rank the filters as to their importance and then find shapes by using a collection of these low-level features. The original technique was phrased around detecting objects [Viola01] and later phrased around finding human faces in particular [Viola04], and it has now become one of the stock approaches to detecting faces automatically within image data.

There are limitations to this approach, naturally. The use of rectangular features allows fast calculation, but does not match well structures that have a smoother contour. There are very many features possible in templates of any reasonable size, and so the set of features must be pruned so that the best are selected, and that is where the machine learning processes are necessary. In turn this implies that the feature extraction process needs training (in features and in data) – and that is similar indeed to human vision. There are demonstration versions of the technique, and improvements include the use of rotated Haar features [Lienhart03] as well as inspiring many of the later approaches that collect parts for recognition. Should you be interested in more recent approaches to face detection, [Zafeiriou15] is well worth a look.

5.4.1.2 Object detection by combinations of parts

There have been many approaches which apply wavelets, and ones which are more complex than Haar wavelets, to detect objects by combinations of parts. These approaches allow for greater flexibility in the representation of the part since the wavelet can capture frequency, orientation and position (thus incurring the cost of computational complexity). A major advantage is that scale can be used, and objects can exist at, or persist over, a selection of scales. One such approach used wavelets as a basis for detecting people and cars [Schneiderman04] and even a door handle, thus emphasising generality of the approach. As with the Viola–Jones approach, this method requires deployment of machine learning techniques which then involves training. In this method, the training occurs over different viewpoints to factor out the subject's – or object's – pose. The method groups input data into sets, and each set is a part. For a human face, the parts include the eyes, nose and mouth and some unnamed, but classified face regions, and these parts are (statistically) interdependent in most natural objects. Then machine learning techniques are used to maximise the likelihood of finding the parts correctly. Highly impressive results have been provided, though again the performance of the technique depends on training as well as on other factors. The main point of the technique here, is that wavelets can allow for greater freedom when representing an object as a collection of parts.

In our own research, we have used Gabor wavelets in ear biometrics, where we can recognise a person's identity by analysis of the appearance of the ear [Hurley08]. It might be the ugliest biometric, but it also appears the most immune to effects of aging (except to enlarge): ears are fully formed at birth and change little throughout life, unlike the human face which changes rapidly as children grow teeth and then the general decline includes wrinkles and a few sags (unless a surgeon's expertise intervenes). In a way, ears are like fingerprints, but the features are less clear. In our own research in biometrics, we have used Gabor wavelets to capture the ear's features [Arbab-Zavar11] in particular those relating to smooth curves. To achieve rotational invariance (in case a subject's head was tilted when the image was acquired), a radial scan was taken based on an ear's centre point, Fig. 5.10A, deriving the two transformed regions in Figs. 5.10B and D, which are the same region for different images of the same ear. Then, these regions are transformed using a Gabor wavelet approach for which the real parts of the transform at two scales are shown in Figs. 5.10C and E. Here, the detail is preserved at the short wavelength, and the larger structures are detected at longer wavelengths. In both cases the prominent smooth structures are captured by the technique, leading to successful recognition of the subjects.

5.4.2 Distribution-based descriptors

5.4.2.1 Description by interest points (SIFT, SURF, BRIEF)

Lowe's *scale invariant feature transform (SIFT)* [Lowe04], Section 4.4.2.1, actually combines a scale invariant region detector with a descriptor which is based on the gradient distribution in the detected regions. The approach not only detects interest points but also provides a description for recognition purposes. The descriptor is represented by a 3D histogram of gradient locations and orientations and is created by first computing the

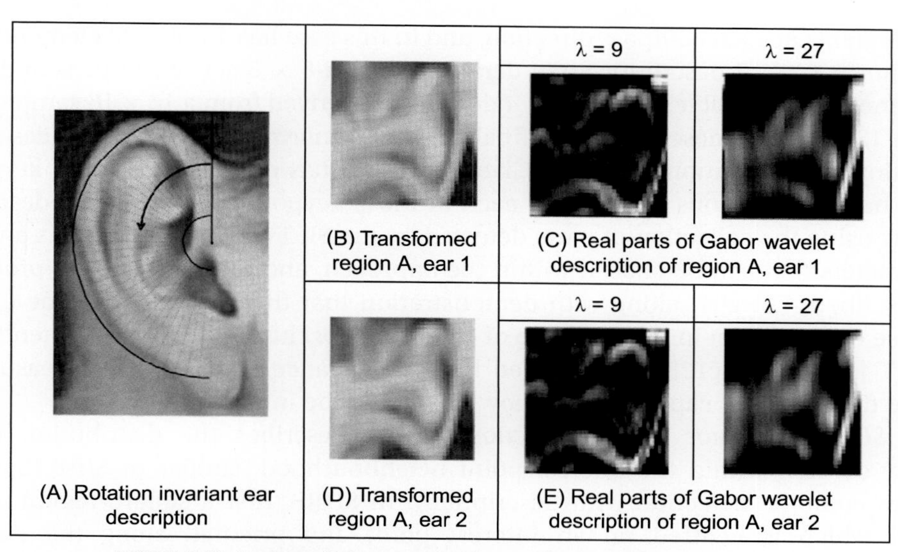

FIGURE 5.10 Applying Gabor wavelets in ear biometrics [Arbab-Zavar11].

gradient magnitude and orientation at each image point within the 8×8 region around the keypoint location, as shown in Fig. 5.11. These values are weighted by a Gaussian windowing function, indicated by the overlaid circle in Fig. 5.11A wherein the standard deviation is chosen according to the number of samples in the region (its width). This avoids fluctuation in the description with differing values of the keypoint's location and emphasises less the gradients that are far from the centre. These samples are then accumulated into orientation histograms summarising the contents of the four 4×4 subregions, as shown in Fig. 5.11B, with the length of each arrow corresponding to the sum of the gradient magnitudes near that direction within the region. This involves a binning procedure as the histogram is quantised into a smaller number of levels (here eight compass directions are shown). The descriptor is then a vector of the magnitudes

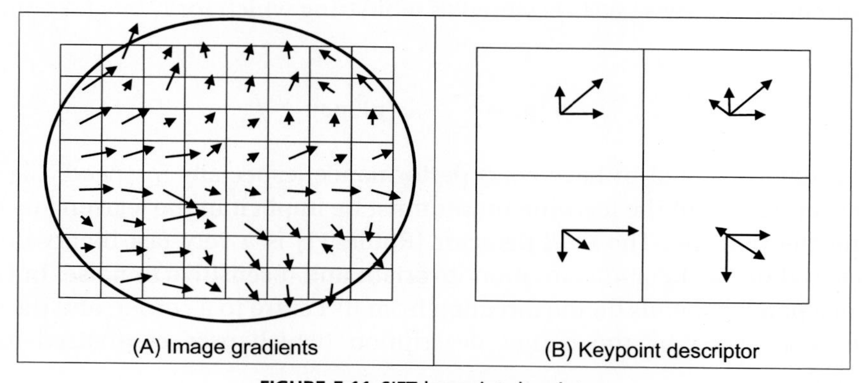

FIGURE 5.11 SIFT keypoint descriptor.

of the elements at each compass direction, and in this case has $4 \times 8 = 32$ elements. This figure shows a 2×2 descriptor array derived from an 8×8 set of samples, and other arrangements are possible, such as 4×4 descriptors derived from a 16×16 sample array giving a 128 element descriptor. The final stage is to normalise the magnitudes so the description is illumination invariant. Given that SIFT has detected the set of keypoints and we have descriptions attached to each of those keypoints, we can then describe a shape by using the collection of parts detected by the SIFT technique. There is a variety of parameters that can be chosen within the approach, and the optimisation process is ably described [Lowe04] along with demonstration that the technique can be used to recognise objects, even in the presence of clutter and occlusion. An improvement called *RootSIFT* [Arandjelović12] later changed the way distance/similarity was measured to improve descriptional capability and now appears to be in routine use.

The *SURF descriptor* [Bay08], Section 4.4.2.2, describes the distribution of the intensity content within the interest point neighbourhood, similar to SIFT (both approaches combine detection with description). In SURF, first a square region is constructed which is centred on an interest point and oriented along the detected orientation (detected via the Haar wavelets). Then, the description is derived from the Haar wavelet responses within the subwindows, and the approach argues the approach 'reduces the time for feature computation and matching, and has proven to simultaneously increase the robustness'.

The SIFT and SURF descriptors are large being vectors of 128 and 64 elements, respectively, and this can require much storage when millions of interest points are to be considered. The descriptors in *BRIEF* (Section 4.4.3) are longer but in number but comprise only bits, and the length is a natural compromise between speed and storage [Calonder10]. The bits are derived by pairwise intensity comparisons between smoothed patches thus predicating a need for sampling strategy and for smoothing (to reduce response to noise) where the comparison between intensities is

$$\tau(\mathbf{p}1, \mathbf{p}2) = \left| \begin{array}{ll} 1 & \mathbf{P}_{x1,y1} < \mathbf{P}_{x2,y2} \\ 0 & otherwise \end{array} \right. \tag{5.24}$$

The sequence of pairwise tests is stored as a bitstring which for N bits for comparison purposes

$$f_N(\mathbf{p}) = \sum_{i=1}^{N} 2^{i-1} \tau(\mathbf{p}1, \mathbf{p}2) \tag{5.25}$$

This was demonstrated to have good performance, especially in speed. Clearly it is very simple, and some of the learning power must be implicit in the learning techniques used within the pipeline. The *ORB* detector [Rublee11] is a very fast binary descriptor since it is based on BRIEF and is rotation invariant and insensitive to noise. In ORB, the direction of a patch depends on the direction from its centre to a corner, and the rotation invariance is achieved by the corner description (which uses centralised moments (Section 7.3.2).

A major performance evaluation [Mikolajczyk05] compared the performance of descriptors computed for local interest regions and studied a number of operators, concerning in particular the effects of geometric and affine transformations, for matching and recognition of the same object or scene. The operators included a form of Gabor wavelets and SIFT and introduced the *gradient location and orientation histogram* (GLOH) which is an extension of the SIFT descriptor, and which appeared to offer better performance. The survey predated SURF and BRIEF and so they was not included. SIFT also performed well, and there have been many applications of the SIFT approach for recognising objects in images, and the applications of SURF are burgeoning. One approach aimed to determine those key frames and shots of a video containing a particular object with ease and convenience of the Google search engine [Sivic03]. In this approach, elliptical regions are represented by a 128-dimensional vector using the SIFT descriptor which was chosen by virtue of superior performance, especially when the object's positions could vary by small amounts. From this, descriptions are constructed using machine learning techniques. A more recent comparison [Mukherjee15] highlights the all-round performance of ORB, SIFT and BRIEF, and is a good place to look.

In common with other object recognition approaches, we have deployed SIFT for ear biometrics [Arbab-Zavar11, Bustard10] to capture the description of an individual's ear by a constellation of ear parts, again confirming that people appear unique by their ear. Here, the points detected are those that are significant across scales, and thus provide an alternative characterisation (to the earlier Gabor wavelet analysis in Section 5.4.1.2) of the ear's appearance. Fig. 5.12A shows the SIFT points detected within a human ear, and Figs. 5.12B and C show the same point (the crus of helix, no less) being detected in two different ears and Fig. 5.12D shows the domains of the SIFT points dominant in the ear biometrics procedure. Note that these points do not include the outer perimeter of the ear, which was described by Gabor wavelets. Recognition by the SIFT features was complemented by the Gabor features, as we derive descriptions of different regions, leading to the successful identification of the subjects by their ears. An extended discussion of how ears can be used as a biometric and the range of techniques that can be used for recognition is available [Hurley08].

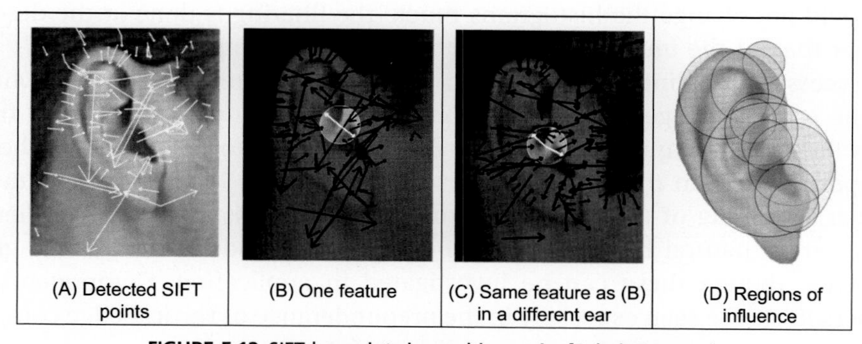

FIGURE 5.12 SIFT keypoints in ear biometrics [Arbab-Zavar11].

As such we have concerned a topical area which continues to be of major current interest: CBIR is a common application of computer vision techniques. A recent study notes the prevalence now of deep learning, ‘In recent years, the popularity of SIFT-based models seems to be overtaken by the convolutional neural network’ citing performance issues [Zheng18]. However, there are now many studies deploying interest point techniques for image matching, which show considerable performance capability. It is likely that the performance will be improved by technique refinement and analysis and therefore performance comparison and abilities will continue to develop.

5.4.2.2 Characterising object appearance and shape

There has long been an interest in detecting pedestrians within scenes, more for automated surveillance analysis than for biometric purposes. The techniques have included use of Haar features and SIFT description. An approach called the *histogram of oriented gradients (HoG)* [Dalal05] has received much interest. This captures edge or gradient structure that is very characteristic of local shape in a way which is relatively unaffected by appearance changes. Essentially, it forms a template and deploys machine learning approaches to expedite recognition, in an effective way. In this way it is an extension to describing objects by a histogram of the edge gradients.

First, edges are detected by the improved first-order detector shown in Fig. 4.4, and an edge image is created. Then, a vote is determined from a pixel’s edge magnitude and direction and stored in a histogram. The direction is ‘binned’ in that votes are cast into roughly quantised histogram ranges and these votes are derived from cells, which group neighbourhoods of pixels. One implementation is to use 8×8 image cells and to group these into 20 degrees ranges (thus nine ranges within 180 degrees of unsigned edge direction). Local contrast normalisation is used to handle variation in gradient magnitude due to change in illumination and contrast with the background, and this was determined to be an important stage. This normalisation is applied in blocks, eventually leading to the person’s description which can then be learnt by using machine learning approaches. Naturally there is a gamut of choices to be made, such as the choice of edge detection operator, inclusion of operator, cell size, the number of bins in the histogram and use of full 360 degrees edge direction. Robustness is achieved in that noise or other effects should not change the histograms much: the filtering is done at the description stage rather than at the image stage (as with wavelet-based approaches).

The process of building the HoG description is illustrated in Fig. 5.13 where Fig. 5.13A is the original image; Fig. 5.13B is the gradient magnitude constructed from the absolute values of the improved first order difference operator; Fig. 5.13C is the grid of 8×8, superimposed on the edge direction image and Fig. 5.13D illustrates the 3×3 (rectangular) grouping of the cells, superimposed on the histograms of gradient data. There is a rather natural balance between the grid size and the size of the grouping arrangements, though these can be investigated in application. Components of the walking person can be seen especially in the preponderance of vertical edge components

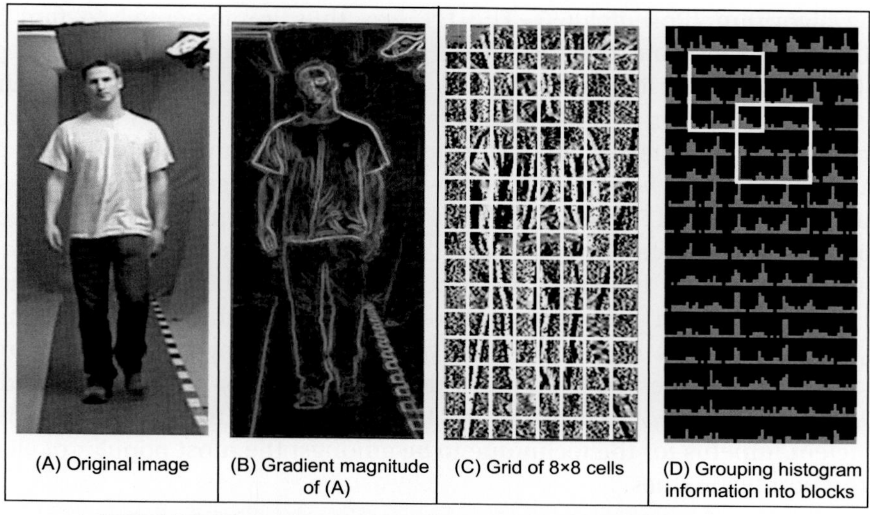

FIGURE 5.13 Illustrating the histogram of oriented gradients description.

in the legs and thorax. The grouping and normalisation of these data lead to the descriptor which can be deployed so as to detect humans/pedestrians in static images.

The approach is not restricted to detecting pedestrians since it can be trained to detect different shapes, and it has been applied elsewhere. Given there is much interest in speed of computation, rather unexpectedly a fast HoG was to appear soon after the original HoG [Zhu06] and which claims 30 fps capability. An alternative approach, and one which confers greater generality – especially with humans – is to include the possibility of deformation, as will be covered in Section 6.2.

Essentially, these approaches can achieve fast extraction by decomposing a shape into its constituent parts. Clearly one detraction of the techniques is that if you are to change implementation – or to detect other objects – then this requires construction of the necessary models and parts, and that can be quite demanding. In fact, it can be less demanding to include shape, and as template matching can give a guaranteed result, another class of approaches is to reformulate template matching so as to improve speed. That is the Hough transform, coming next.

5.5 Hough transform

5.5.1 Overview

The *Hough transform* (HT) [Hough62] is a technique that locates shapes in images. In particular, it has been used to extract lines, circles and ellipses (or conic sections). In the case of lines, its mathematical definition is equivalent to the Radon transform [Deans81]. The HT was introduced by Hough [Hough62], and then used to find bubble tracks rather than shapes in images. However, Rosenfeld noted its potential advantages as an image processing algorithm [Rosenfeld69]. The HT was thus implemented to find lines in images [Duda72], and it has been extended greatly, since it has many advantages and many potential routes for improvement. Its prime advantage is that it can deliver the same result as that for template matching, but faster [Princen92, Sklansky78, Stockman77]. This is achieved by a reformulation of the template matching process, based on an *evidence gathering* approach where the evidence is the votes cast in an accumulator array. The HT implementation defines a mapping from the image points into an accumulator space (Hough space). The mapping is achieved in a computationally efficient manner, based on the function that describes the target shape. This mapping requires much less computational resources than template matching. However, it still requires significant storage and high computational requirements. These problems are addressed later, since they give focus for the continuing development of the HT. However, the fact that the HT is equivalent to template matching has given sufficient impetus for the technique to be amongst the most popular of all existing shape extraction techniques.

5.5.2 Lines

We will first consider finding lines in an image. In a Cartesian parameterisation, collinear points in an image with co-ordinates (x, y) are related by their slope m and an intercept c according to

$$y = mx + c \tag{5.26}$$

This equation can be written in homogeneous form as

$$Ay + Bx + 1 = 0 \tag{5.27}$$

where $A = -1/c$ and $B = m/c$. Thus, a line is defined by giving a pair of values (A, B). However, we can observe a symmetry in the definition in Eq. (5.27). This equation is symmetric since a pair of co-ordinates (x, y) also defines a line in the space with parameters (A, B). That is, Eq. (5.27) can be seen as the equation of a line for fixed co-ordinates (x, y) or as the equation of a line for fixed parameters (A, B). Thus, pairs can be used to define points and lines simultaneously [Aguado00a]. The HT gathers evidence of the point (A, B) by considering that all the points (x, y) define the same line in the space (A, B). That is, if the set of collinear points $\{(x_i, y_i)\}$ defines the line (A, B), then

$$Ay_i + Bx_i + 1 = 0 \tag{5.28}$$

This equation can be seen as a system of equations, and it can simply be rewritten in terms of the Cartesian parameterisation as

$$c = -x_i m + y_i \tag{5.29}$$

Thus, to determine the line we must find the values of the parameters (m, c) (or (A, B) in homogeneous form) that satisfy Eq. (5.29) (or Eq. (5.28), respectively). However, we must notice that the system is generally over-determined. That is, we have more equations than unknowns. Thus, we must find the solution that comes close to satisfying all the equations simultaneously. This kind of problem can be solved, for example, using linear least-squares techniques. The HT uses an evidence gathering approach to provide the solution. Notice that if x is zero in Eq. (5.29), then $y_i = c$. That is, c is the intersection of the line with the y axis.

The relationship between a point (x_i, y_i) in an image and the line given in Eq. (5.29) is illustrated in Fig. 5.14. The points (x_i, y_i) and (x_j, y_j) in Fig. 5.14A define the lines U_i and U_j in Fig. 5.14B, respectively. All the collinear elements in an image will define dual lines with the same concurrent point (A, B). This is independent of the line parameterisation used. The HT solves it in an efficient way by simply counting the potential solutions in an accumulator array that stores the evidence, or votes. The count is made by tracing all the dual lines for each point (x_i, y_i). Each point in the trace increments an element in the array, thus the problem of line extraction is transformed to the problem of locating a maximum in the accumulator space. This strategy is robust and has demonstrated to be able to handle noise and occlusion.

The axes in the dual space represent the parameters of the line. In the case of the Cartesian parameterisation, m can actually take an infinite range of values, since lines can vary from horizontal to vertical. Since votes are gathered in a discrete array, then this will produce bias errors. It is possible to consider a range of votes in the accumulator space that cover all possible values. This corresponds to techniques of antialiasing and can improve the gathering strategy [Brown83, Kiryati91].

The implementation of the HT for lines is given in Code 5.4. The implementation gathers evidence for each point (x, y) by drawing a line obtained by iterating over the parameter m. Thus, the iteration generates points (m, c) in the accumulator. It is important to observe that Eq. (5.29) is not suitable for implementation since the parameter c can take an infinite range of values. In order to avoid this, the implementation uses two accumulator arrays. One accumulator is used to gather lines with slopes between $-45°$ and $45°$ and another accumulator for lines with slopes between $45°$ and $135°$. The main loop in the implementation iterates over a range from $0°$ to $90°$. Thus, each accumulator has $90°$ range and together both accumulators consider the full

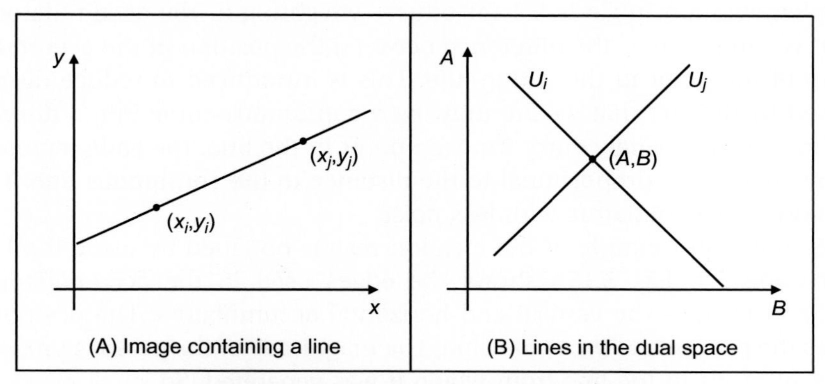

FIGURE 5.14 Illustrating the Hough transform for lines.

```
# Gather evidence
for x,y in itertools.product(range(0, width), range(0, height)):
    if magnitude[y,x] != 0:
        for m in range(0,90):

            # Lines between -45 and 45 degrees
            angle = ((-45 + m) * math.pi) / 180.0
            c = y - math.tan(angle) * x
            bucket = int(c)
            if bucket> 0 and bucket < 2*height - 1:
                weight = c - int(c)
                accHorizontal[m, bucket] += (1.0 - weight)
                accHorizontal[m, bucket+1] += weight

            # Lines between 45 and 135 degrees
            angle = ((45.0 + m) * math.pi) / 180.0
            c = x - y / math.tan(angle)
            bucket = int(c)
            if bucket> 0 and bucket < 2*width - 1:
                weight = c - int(c)
                accVertical[m, bucket] += (1.0 - weight)
                accVertical[m, bucket+1] += weight
```

CODE 5.4 Implementing the Hough transform for lines.

180°. For the first accumulator lines are horizontal, so we can compute the intercept c according to Eq. (5.29). In this case, the value c is the intersection of the line with the y axis. Notice that the size of the intercept is defined as twice the image size since the intercept of lines in images is not limited by the height of the image. In the second case, the lines are vertical, so the code computes the intersection with the x axis. As such, the line is then defined as $x = y/m + c$. Notice that when the tangent of m is computed in the code, m is limited to values between $-45°$ and $45°$.

The implementation in Code 5.4 introduces weighting in the accumulator process. This weight is computed as the difference between the position of the accumulator and the position of the point in the voting line. This is introduced to reduce discretisation errors caused by the fact that we are drawing a continuous curve into a discrete array. Instead of increasing a single entry for each point in the line, the code increments two positions by an amount proportional to the distance to the continuous line. The use of weights produces accumulators with less noise.

Fig. 5.15 shows an example of the location results obtained by using the HT implemented in Code 5.4. Fig. 5.15A shows the edges used in the accumulator process. Figs. 5.15C and D show the vertical and horizontal accumulators. The position of each peak defines the parameters (m, c) of a line. The magnitude of the peaks is proportional to the number of pixels in the line from which it was generated. So small peaks represent

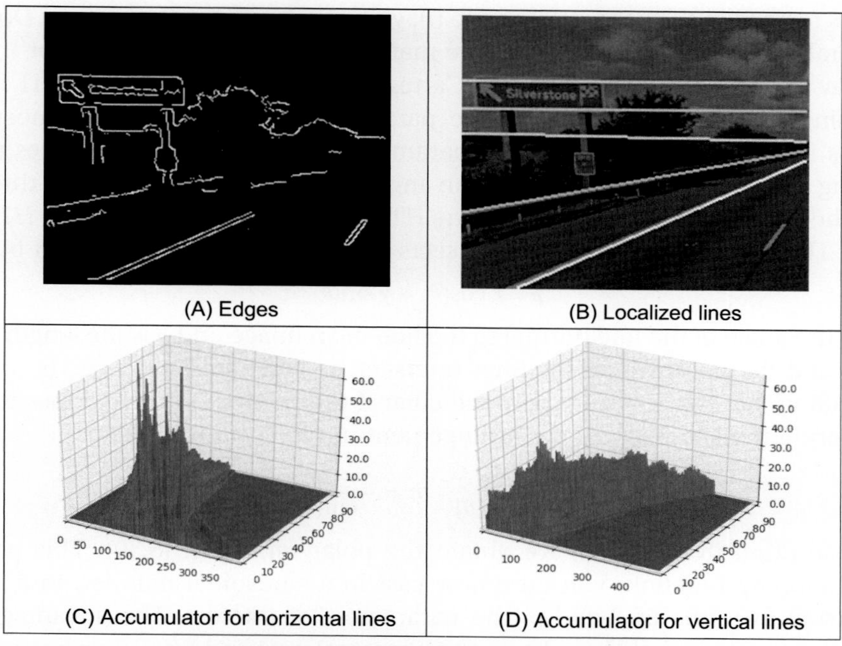

(A) Edges

(B) Localized lines

(C) Accumulator for horizontal lines

(D) Accumulator for vertical lines

FIGURE 5.15 Applying the Hough transform for lines.

small lines in the image. Fig. 5.15B shows the lines represented by the maxima in the accumulators. These lines were drawn by iterating the values (x, y) for a peak (m, c) in the accumulator. Here, we can see that the parameters describing the lines have been extracted well. Note that the end points of the lines are not delivered by the HT, only the parameters that describe them. You have to go back to the image to obtain the line length.

We can see that the HT delivers a correct response, correct estimates of the parameters used to specify the line, so long as the number of collinear points along that line exceeds the number of collinear points on any other line in the image. As such, the Hough transform has the same properties in respect of noise and occlusion, as with template matching. However, the nonlinearity of the parameters and the discretisation produce noisy accumulators. A major problem in implementing the basic HT for lines is the definition of an appropriate accumulator space. In application, *Bresenham*'s line drawing algorithm [Bresenham65] can be used to draw the lines of votes in the accumulator space. This ensures that lines of connected votes are drawn as opposed to use of Eq. (5.29) that can lead to gaps in the drawn line. Also, *backmapping* [Gerig86] can be used to determine exactly which edge points contributed to a particular peak. Backmapping is an inverse mapping from the accumulator space to the edge data and can allow for shape analysis of the image by removal of the edge points which contributed to particular peaks, and then by re-accumulation using the HT. Note that the computational cost of the HT depends on the number of edge points (n_e) and the length of the lines formed in the parameter space (l), giving a computational cost of $O(n_e l)$. This is considerably less than that for template matching, given earlier as $O(N^2m^2)$.

One way to avoid the problems of the Cartesian parameterisation in the HT is to base the mapping function on an alternative parameterisation. One of the most proven techniques is called the *foot-of-normal* parameterisation. This parameterises a line by considering a point (x, y) as a function of an angle normal to the line, passing through the origin of the image. This gives a form of the HT for lines known as the *polar HT for lines* [Duda72]. The point where this line intersects the line in the image is given by

$$\rho = x\cos(\theta) + y\sin(\theta) \tag{5.30}$$

where θ is the angle of the line normal to the line in an image and ρ is the length between the origin and the point where the lines intersect, as illustrated in Fig. 5.16.

By recalling that two lines are perpendicular if the product of their slopes is -1, and by considering the geometry of the arrangement in Fig. 5.16, we obtain

$$c = \frac{\rho}{\sin(\theta)} \quad m = -\frac{1}{\tan(\theta)} \tag{5.31}$$

By substitution in Eq. (5.26) we obtain the polar form, Eq. (5.30). This provides a different mapping function: votes are now cast in a sinusoidal manner, in a 2D accumulator array in terms of θ and ρ, the parameters of interest. The advantage of this alternative mapping is that the values of the parameters θ and ρ are now bounded to lie within a specific range. The range for θ is within 180 degrees; the possible values of ρ are given by the image size, since the maximum length of the line is $\sqrt{2} \times N$, where N is the (square) image size. The range of possible values is now fixed, so the technique is practicable.

As the voting function has now changed, we shall draw different loci in the accumulator space. In the conventional HT for lines, a straight line mapped to a straight line as in Fig. 5.17. In the polar HT for lines, points map to curves in the accumulator space.

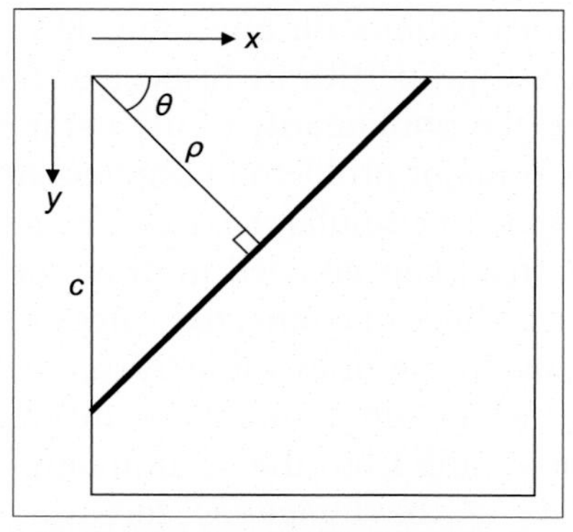

FIGURE 5.16 Polar consideration of a line.

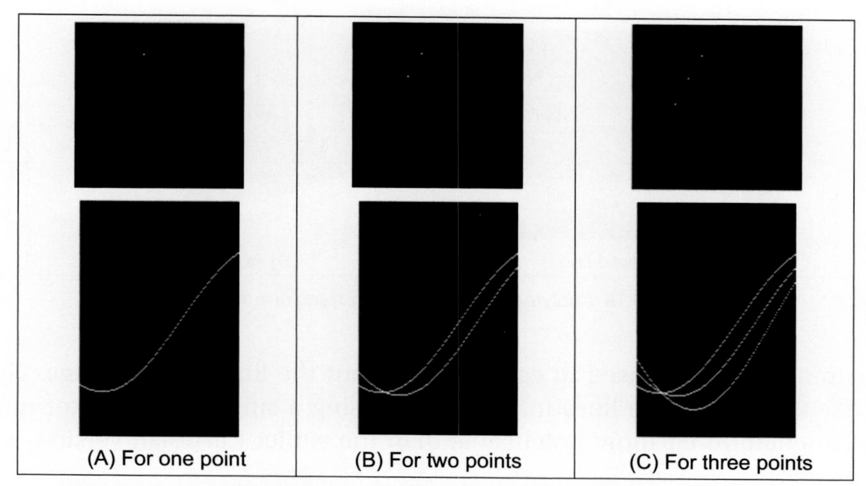

FIGURE 5.17 Images and the accumulator space of the polar Hough transform.

This is illustrated in Fig. 5.17 which shows the polar HT accumulator spaces for Fig. 5.17A one, Fig. 5.17B two and Fig. 5.17C three points, respectively. For a single point in the upper row of Fig. 5.17A, we obtain a single curve shown in the lower row of Fig. 5.17A. For two points we obtain two curves, which intersect at a position which describes the parameters of the line joining them, Fig. 5.17B. An additional curve obtains for the third point, and there is now a peak in the accumulator array containing three votes, Fig. 5.17C.

The implementation of the polar HT for lines is presented in Code 5.5. The accumulator array is a set of 360 bins for value of θ in the range $0°-180$ degrees, and for values of ρ in the range 0 to $\sqrt{N^2+M^2}$, where $N \times M$ is the picture size. Then, for image (edge) points greater than a chosen threshold, the angle relating to the bin size is evaluated (as radians in the range 0 to π) and then the value of ρ is evaluated using Eq. (5.30), and the appropriate accumulator cell is incremented so long as the parameters are within the range. Similar to the HT for lines, a weight is used to decrease the noise caused by the discretisation of the accumulator. The accumulator array obtained by applying this implementation to the image in Fig. 5.4 is shown in Fig. 5.18, and it shows a

```
# Gather evidence
for x,y in itertools.product(range(0, width), range(0, height)):
    if magnitude[y,x] != 0:
        for m in range(0,360):
            angle = (m * math.pi) / 180.0
            r = (x-cx) * math.cos(angle) + (y-cy) * math.sin(angle)
            bucket = int(r)
            if bucket> 0 and bucket < maxLenght - 1:
                weight = r - int(r)
                accumulator[m, bucket] += (1.0 - weight)
                accumulator[m, bucket+1] += weight
```

CODE 5.5 Implementation of the polar Hough transform for lines.

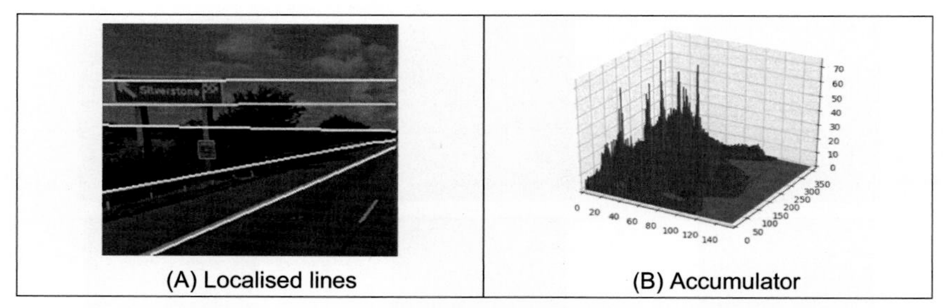

FIGURE 5.18 Applying the polar Hough transform for lines.

single accumulator that is used to gather data about the lines in the image. Fig. 5.18B shows peaks that define the lines in Fig. 5.18A. Using a single accumulator makes the polar implementation far more practicable than the earlier Cartesian version.

5.5.3 HT for circles

The HT can be extended by replacing the equation of the curve in the detection process. The equation of the curve can be given in explicit or parametric form. In explicit form, the HT can be defined by considering the equation for a circle given by

$$(x - x_0)^2 + (y - y_0)^2 = r^2 \tag{5.32}$$

This equation defines a locus of points (x, y) centred on an origin (x_0, y_0) and with radius r. This equation can again be visualised in two dual ways: as a locus of points (x, y) in an image, or as a locus of points (x_0, y_0) centred on (x, y) with radius r.

Fig. 5.19 illustrates this dual definition. Each edge point in Fig. 5.19A defines a set of circles in the accumulator space. These circles are defined by all possible values of the radius, and they are centred on the co-ordinates of the edge point. Fig. 5.19B shows three circles defined by three edge points. These circles are defined for a given radius value. Actually, each edge point defines circles for the other values of the radius. This implies that the accumulator space is three dimensional (for the three parameters of interest) and that edge points map to a cone of votes in the accumulator space. Fig. 5.19C illustrates this accumulator. After gathering evidence of all the edge points, the maximum in the accumulator space again corresponds to the parameters of the circle in the original image. The procedure of evidence gathering is the same as that for the HT for lines, but votes are generated in cones, according to Eq. (5.32).

Eq. (5.32) can be defined in parametric form as

$$x = x_0 + r\cos(\theta) \quad y = y_0 + r\sin(\theta) \tag{5.33}$$

The advantage of this representation is that it allows us to solve for the parameters. Thus, the HT mapping is defined by

$$x_0 = x - r\cos(\theta) \quad y_0 = y - r\sin(\theta) \tag{5.34}$$

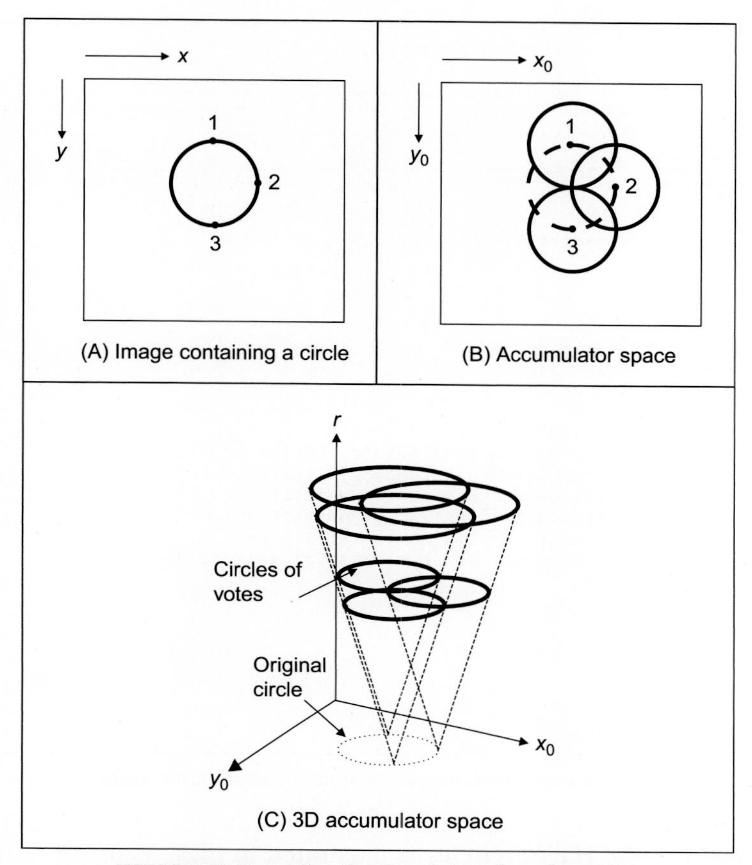

FIGURE 5.19 Illustrating the Hough transform for circles.

These equations define the points in the accumulator space (Fig. 5.19B) dependent on the radius r. Note that θ is not a free parameter, but defines the trace of the curve. The trace of the curve (or surface) is commonly referred to as the *point spread function*.

The implementation of the HT for circles is shown in Code 5.6. This is similar to the HT for lines, except that the voting function corresponds to that in Eq. (5.34) and the accumulator space is actually 3D, in terms of the centre parameters and the radius. The implementation the parameter `maxr` defines the maximum radius size. A circle of votes is generated by varying `theta` (Python and Matlab do not allow Greek symbols!) from 0 to 360 degrees. The discretisation of `theta` controls the granularity of voting, too small increments give very fine coverage of the parameter space, if it is too large then it produces a sparse coverage. The accumulator space, `accumulator` (initially zero), is incremented only for points whose co-ordinates lie within the specified range (in this case the centre cannot lie outside the original image).

```
function accum = circle_hough(image, maxr)

%get dimensions
[rows,cols]=size(image);

%set a start radius
startr=10;

%set the output image to black (0)
accum(1:rows,1:cols,1:(maxr-startr+1))=0;

%and an output image
accum(1:rows,1:cols)=0;

for x = 1:cols %address all columns
  for y = 1:rows %address all rows
      for rad = startr:maxr
          if image(y,x)>80
              for theta=1:360
                  xdash=round(rad*cos(theta*pi/180));
                  ydash=round(rad*sin(theta*pi/180));
                  if (((x+xdash)<cols)&&((x+xdash)>0)&&...
                      ((y+ydash)<rows)&&((y+ydash)>0))
                      accum(y+ydash,x+xdash,rad-startr+1)=...
                          accum(y+ydash,x+xdash,rad-startr+1)+1;
                  end
              end
          end
      end
  end
end

parameters=get_max(accum);
```

CODE 5.6 Implementation of the Hough transform for circles.

The application of the HT for circles is illustrated in Figs. 5.20. Fig. 5.20A shows an image of an eye. Fig. 5.20B shows the edges computed from the image. The edges are well defined, and there are many edges produced by noise (as ever). The result of the HT process is shown in Fig. 5.20C aimed to, and succeeding to, detect the border of the pupil. The peak of the accumulator space represents the centre of the circle, though it only just exists as a peak in this noisy image. Many votes exist away from the circle's centre, though these background votes are less than the actual peak. Fig. 5.20D shows the detected circle defined by the parameters with the maximum in the accumulator. The HT will detect the circle (provide the right result) as long as more points are in a circular locus described by the parameters of the target circle than there are on any other circle. This is exactly the same performance as for the HT for lines, as expected, and is consistent with the result of template matching. Note that the HT merely finds the circle with the maximum number of points (in Fig. 5.20D, a small range of radii was given to detect the perimeter of the pupil); it is possible to include other constraints to control the circle selection process, such as gradient direction for objects with known illumination profile. In the case of the human eye, the (circular) iris is usually darker than its white surroundings.

In application code, *Bresenham's algorithm* for discrete circles [Bresenham77] can be used to draw the circle of votes, rather than use the polar implementation of Eq. (5.34). This ensures that the complete locus of points is drawn and avoids the need to choose a value for increase in the angle used to trace the circle. Bresenham's algorithm can be used to generate the points in one octant, since the remaining points can be obtained by reflection. Again, backmapping can be used to determine which points contributed to the extracted circle.

Fig. 5.20 also shows some of the difficulties with the HT, namely that it is essentially an implementation of template matching, and does not use some of the richer stock of information available in an image. For example, we might know constraints on size: the largest size an iris or pupil would be in the image. Also, we know some of the topology: the eye region contains two ellipsoidal structures with a circle in the middle. We might also know brightness information: the pupil is darker than the surrounding iris. These factors can be formulated as constraints on whether edge points can vote within the accumulator array. A simple modification is to make the votes proportional to edge magnitude, in this manner, points with high contrast will generate more votes and hence have more significance in the voting process. In this way, the feature extracted by the HT can be arranged to suit a particular application.

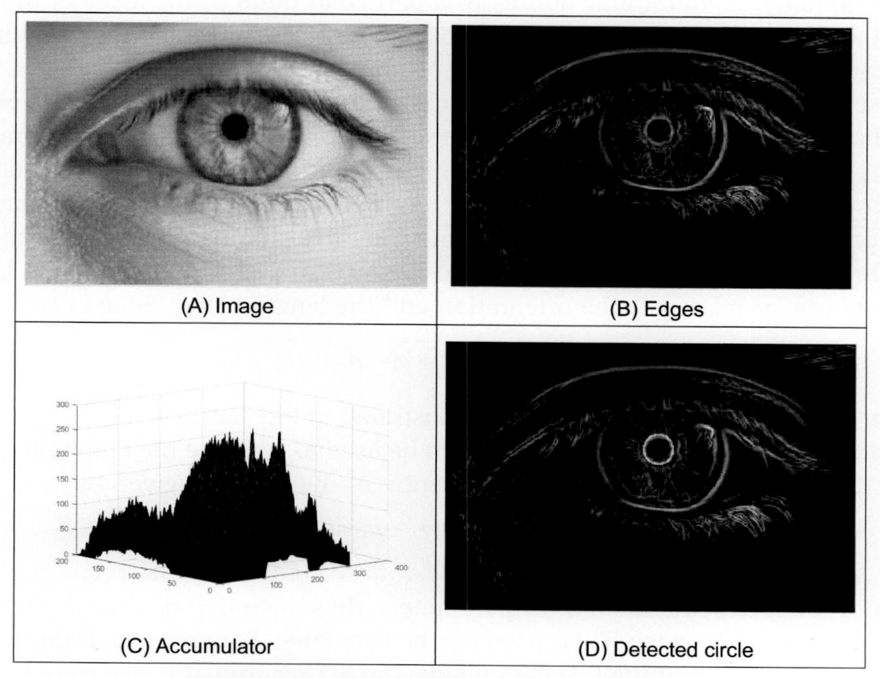

FIGURE 5.20 Applying the Hough transform for circles.

5.5.4 HT for ellipses

Circles are very important in shape detection since many objects have a circular shape. However, because of the camera's viewpoint, circles do not always look like circles in images. Images are formed by mapping a shape in 3D space into a plane (the image plane). This mapping performs a perspective transformation. In this process, a circle is deformed to look like an ellipse. We can define the mapping between the circle and an ellipse by a similarity transformation. That is,

$$\begin{bmatrix} x \\ y \end{bmatrix} = \begin{bmatrix} \cos(\rho) & \sin(\rho) \\ -\sin(\rho) & \cos(\rho) \end{bmatrix} \begin{bmatrix} S_x \\ S_y \end{bmatrix} \begin{bmatrix} x' \\ y' \end{bmatrix} + \begin{bmatrix} t_x \\ t_y \end{bmatrix} \tag{5.35}$$

where (x', y') define the co-ordinates of the circle in Eq. (5.33), ρ represents the orientation, (S_x, S_y) a scale factor and (t_x, t_y) a translation. If we define

$$\begin{aligned} a_0 &= t_x \quad a_x = S_x\cos(\rho) \quad b_x = S_y\sin(\rho) \\ b_0 &= t_y \quad a_y = -S_x\sin(\rho) \quad b_y = S_y\cos(\rho) \end{aligned} \tag{5.36}$$

then the circle is deformed into

$$\begin{aligned} x &= a_0 + a_x\cos(\theta) + b_x\sin(\theta) \\ y &= b_0 + a_y\cos(\theta) + b_y\sin(\theta) \end{aligned} \tag{5.37}$$

This equation corresponds to the polar representation of an ellipse. This polar form contains six parameters $(a_0, b_0, a_x, b_x, a_y, b_y)$ that characterise the shape of the ellipse. θ is not a free parameter, and it only addresses a particular point in the locus of the ellipse (just as it was used to trace the circle in Eq. (5.34)). However, one parameter is redundant since it can be computed by considering the orthogonality (independence) of the axes of the ellipse (the product $a_xb_x + a_yb_y = 0$ which is one of the known properties of an ellipse). Thus, an ellipse is defined by its centre (a_0, b_0) and three of the axis parameters (a_x, b_x, a_y, b_y). This gives five parameters which is intuitively correct since an ellipse is defined by its centre (two parameters), it size along both axes (two more parameters) and its rotation (one parameter). In total, this states that five parameters describe an ellipse, so our three axis parameters must jointly describe size and rotation. In fact, the axis parameters can be related to the orientation and the length along the axes by

$$\tan(\rho) = \frac{a_y}{a_x} \quad a = \sqrt{a_x^2 + a_y^2} \quad b = \sqrt{b_x^2 + b_y^2} \tag{5.38}$$

where (a, b) are the axes of the ellipse, as illustrated in Fig. 5.21.

In a similar way to Eq. (5.33), Eq. (5.36) can be used to generate the mapping function in the HT. In this case, the location of the centre of the ellipse is given by

$$\begin{aligned} a_0 &= x - a_x\cos(\theta) + b_x\sin(\theta) \\ b_0 &= y - a_y\cos(\theta) + b_y\sin(\theta) \end{aligned} \tag{5.39}$$

The location is dependent on three parameters, thus the mapping defines the trace of a hypersurface in a 5D space. This space can be very large. For example, if there are 100 possible values for each of the five parameters, the 5D accumulator space contains 10^{10}

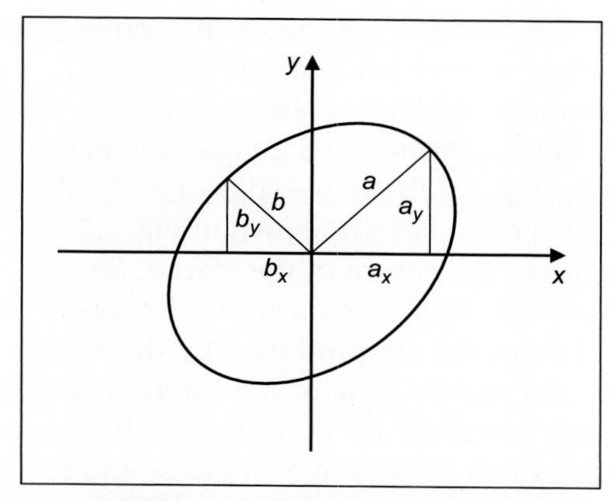

FIGURE 5.21 Definition of ellipse axes.

values. This is 10 GB of storage, which is of course tiny nowadays (at least, when someone else pays!). Accordingly there has been much interest in ellipse detection techniques which use much less space and operate much faster than direct implementation of Eq. (5.38).

Code 5.7 shows the implementation of the HT mapping for ellipses. A 5D accumulator imposes significant computational cost, thus the technique is only useful if it considers a small range for the parameters. In the code, the parameters `majorAxisRange`, `minorAxisRange` and `angleRange` determine the possible values for the axis and rotation

```
# Gather evidence
for x,y in itertools.product(range(0, width), range(0, height)):
    if magnitude[y,x] != 0:
        for majAxis, minAxis in itertools.product(range(0, majorAxisSize),          \
                                                  range(0, minorAxisSize)):
            a = majAxis + majorAxisRange[0]
            b = minAxis + minorAxisRange[0]
            for rot in range(0,angleSize):
                rotAngle = ((rot + angleRange[0]) * pi) / 180.0
                for m in range(0,360):
                    angle = (m * pi) / 180.0

                    x0 = x+ a*cos(angle)*cos(rotAngle) - b*sin(angle)*sin(rotAngle)
                    y0 = y+ a*cos(angle)*sin(rotAngle) + b*sin(angle)*cos(rotAngle)
                    bX0 = int(x0)
                    bY0 = int(y0)

                    if bX0>0 and bX0<width-1 and bY0>0 and bY0<height-1:
                        wX = x0 - bX0
                        wY = y0 - bY0
                        accumulator[bY0,bX0,majAxis,minAxis,rot] += (1.0-wX)+(1.0-wY)
                        accumulator[bY0+1,bX0,majAxis,minAxis,rot] += wX + (1.0-wY)
                        accumulator[bY0,bX0+1,majAxis,minAxis,rot] += (1.0-wX) + wY
                        accumulator[bY0+1,bX0+1,majAxis,minAxis,rot] +=  wX + wY
```

CODE 5.7 Implementation of the Hough transform for ellipses.

angles. The main loop in the function computes the centre parameters defined in Eq. (5.39) for an ellipse according to rotation and axis lengths.

Fig. 5.22 shows an example of the application of the ellipse extraction process described in the Code 5.7. Fig. 5.22A shows an image with an evident ellipse created from an oblique view of a circle. Fig. 5.22B shows edges obtained with the Canny edge detector. A 2D slice of the 5D accumulator is shown in Fig. 5.22C. The array shows a peak whose position corresponds to the centre of the ellipse. We can observe that the accumulator shows close peaks near the ellipse location, so there is more than one ellipse to be located in the figure. The peaks are produced by the double edge of the ellipse so different possible ellipses can match parts of the internal or external edges. Fig. 5.22D shows the ellipses that are obtained by considering the parameters defined by the maxima peaks. The rotation of all ellipses appears close to zero. However, the positions of different ellipses shift by a few pixels and the axis values vary slightly. This matches different segments of the interior and exterior ellipse's edges. Thus, as with the earlier examples for line and circle extraction, it is necessary to interpret the accumulator space in order to discover which structures produce particular parameter combinations.

5.5.5 Parameter space decomposition

The HT gives the same (optimal) result as template matching and even though it is faster, it still requires significant computational resources. In the previous sections, we saw that as we increase the complexity of the curve under detection, the computational requirements increase in exponential way. Thus, the HT becomes less practical. For this

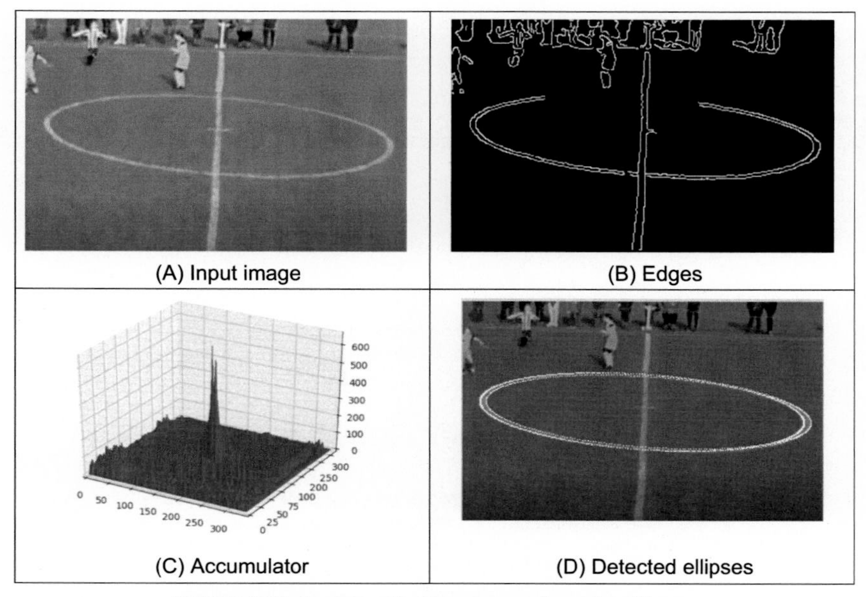

FIGURE 5.22 Applying the Hough transform for ellipses.

reason, most of the research in the HT has focused on the development of techniques aimed to reduce its computational complexity [Illingworth88, Leavers93]. One important way to reduce the computation has been the use of geometric properties of shapes to decompose the parameter space. Several techniques have used different geometric properties. These geometric properties are generally defined by the relationship between points and derivatives.

5.5.5.1 Parameter space reduction for lines

For a line, the accumulator space can be reduced from 2D to 1D by considering that we can compute the slope from the information of the image. The slope can be computed either by using the gradient direction at a point or by considering a pair of points. That is

$$m = \varphi \quad \text{or} \quad m = \frac{y_2 - y_1}{x_2 - x_1} \tag{5.40}$$

where φ is the gradient direction at the point. In the case of two points, by considering Eq. (5.26) we have that,

$$c = \frac{x_2 y_1 - x_1 y_2}{x_2 - x_1} \tag{5.41}$$

Thus, according to Eq. (5.30), we have that one of the parameters of the polar representation for lines, θ, is now given by

$$\theta = -\tan^{-1}\left[\frac{1}{\varphi}\right] \quad \text{or} \quad \theta = \tan^{-1}\left[\frac{x_1 - x_2}{y_2 - y_1}\right] \tag{5.42}$$

These equations do not depend on the other parameter ρ, and they provide alternative mappings to gather evidence. That is, they decompose the parametric space, such that the two parameters θ and ρ are now independent. The use of edge direction information constitutes the base of the line extraction method presented by O'Gorman and Clowes [O'Gorman76]. The use of pairs of points can be related to the definition of the randomised Hough transform [Xu90]. Obviously, the number of feature points considered corresponds to all the combinations of points that form pairs. By using statistical techniques, it is possible to reduce the space of points in order to consider a representative sample of the elements. That is, a subset which provides enough information to obtain the parameters with predefined and small estimation errors.

Code 5.8 shows the implementation of the parameter space decomposition for the HT for lines. In this implementation, the slope of the lines is computed by considering a pair of points. Pairs of points are restricted to a neighbourhood given by the parameter `deltaPointRange`. This defines the minimum and maximum distance between points in a pair. In general, we do not want to have points that are close to each other since the gradient will not be accurate due to the image discretisation. However, we do not want points too far apart since they may not belong to the same object in the image, and they will only generate noise. As such, the range should be chosen by considering the noise, the image resolution and the size of the lines.

```
# Gather evidence for a point x,y
for x,y in itertools.product(range(0, width), range(0, height)):
    if magnitude[y,x] != 0:
        # Look for points at this distance
        for dx,dy in itertools.product(range(-deltaPtRange[1],deltaPtRange[1]+1),    \
                                       range(-deltaPtRange[1],deltaPtRange[1]+1)):

            if abs(dx) > deltaPtRange[0] or abs(dy) > deltaPtRange[0]:
                wx,wy = x+dx, y+dy
                if wx > 0 and wy > 0 and wx < width and wy < height                  \
                          and magnitude[wy, wx] !=0:
                    pointAngle = math.atan2(-float(wx-x), float(wy-y)) + math.pi

                    # If r is negative, the line is in the other side of the centre
                    r = (x-cx) * math.cos(pointAngle) + (y-cy) * math.sin(pointAnge)
                    if r < 0:
                        if pointAngle > math.pi: pointAngle -= math.pi
                        else:                    pointAngle += math.pi

                    # Accumulator entries depend on the distance to the second point
                    deltaDistance = math.sqrt(dx*dx + dy*dy)
                    incAngle = int(math.atan(1.0/deltaDistance) * 180.0 /  math.pi)

                    buketAngleBase = int((pointAngle * 180.0) / math.pi)

                    # More buckets if the points are close
                    for deltaBucket in range(-incAngle, +incAngle+1):
                        bucket = buketAngleBase + deltaBucket
                        if bucket < 0:
                            bucket = 360 + bucket
                        if bucket >= 360:
                            bucket = bucket-360

                        w = (incAngle - math.fabs(deltaBucket)) / float(incAngle)
                        accM[bucket] += w
```

CODE 5.8 Implementation of the parameter space reduction for the Hough transform for lines. Angle accumulator.

In Code 5.8, the implementation of Eq. (5.42) is performed by using the function `atan2` that returns an angle between −180 degrees and 180 degrees. Since our accumulators only can store positive values, then we add 180 degrees to all values. The angle defined by two points is stored in the variable `pointAngle`. Notice that the centre point of the line (intersection of ρ with the line) can be out of the image, so in order to consider all possible lines we have to consider that θ has a 360 degrees range. The angle computed from the points is used, according to Eq. (5.42), to compute ρ. Notice that to gather evidence we need to consider that the distance between points defines a discrete set of possible angles. For example, for points that are a single pixel apart, there are only nine possible angles. Accordingly, the gathering process in the code increments the accumulator by a delta interval that is obtained according to the distance between the points.

Fig. 5.23 shows the accumulators for the two parameters θ and ρ as obtained by the implementation of Code 5.8. The accumulators are now one dimensional as in Figs. 5.23C and D and show clear peaks. The peaks in the first accumulator represent the value of θ, whilst the peaks in the second accumulator represent the value of ρ. Notice that when

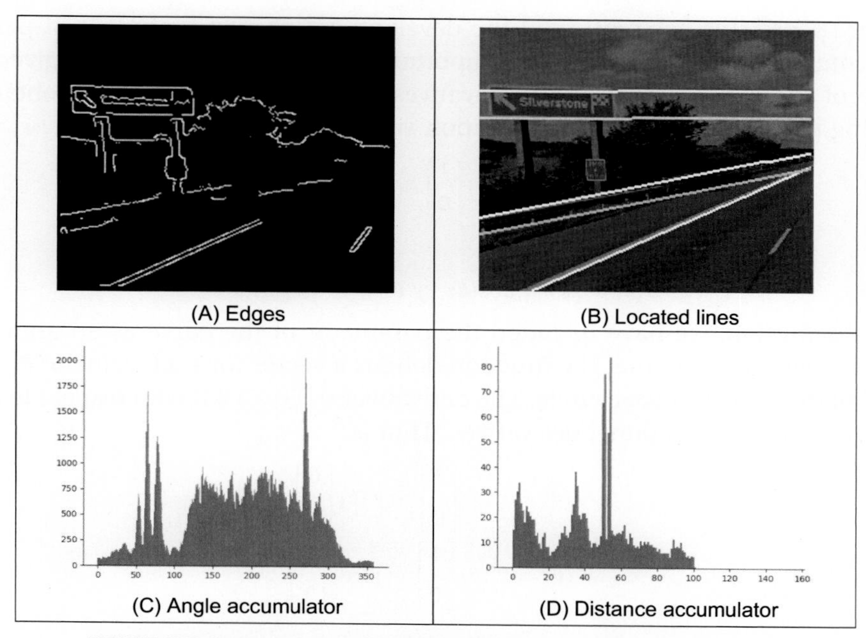

FIGURE 5.23 Parameter space reduction for the Hough transform for lines.

implementing the parameter space decomposition, it is necessary to follow a two-step process. First, it is necessary to gather data in one accumulator and search for the maximum. Second, the location of the maximum value is used as parameter value to gather data of the remaining accumulator. Thus, we first compute the accumulator θ and then for each peak (line), we generate an accumulator for ρ. That is, we have a single accumulator for the angle and as many accumulators for ρ as lines detected in the image. We can see that most of the peaks in the first accumulator are close to 60 degrees, so with similar slopes. The peaks define the lines in Fig. 5.23B. It is important to mention that in general parameter space decomposition produces accumulators with more noise than when gathering evidence in the full dimensional accumulator. So it is important to include strategies to select good candidate points. In this implementation we considered pairs of points within a selected distance, but other selection criteria like points with similar gradient direction or similar colours can help to reduce the noise in the accumulators.

5.5.5.2 Parameter space reduction for circles

In the case of lines the relationship between local information computed from an image and the inclusion of a group of points (pairs) is in an alternative analytical description that can readily be established. For more complex primitives, it is possible to include several geometric relationships. These relationships are not defined for an arbitrary set of points but include angular constraints that define relative positions between them. In general, we can consider different geometric properties of the circle to decompose the parameter space. This has motivated the development of many methods of parameter space decomposition [Aguado96b]. An important geometric relationship is given by the geometry of the second directional derivatives. This relationship can be obtained by considering that Eq. (5.33) defines a position vector function. That is,

$$\upsilon(\theta) = x(\theta)\begin{bmatrix}1\\0\end{bmatrix} + y(\theta)\begin{bmatrix}0\\1\end{bmatrix} \tag{5.43}$$

where

$$x(\theta) = x_0 + r\cos(\theta) \quad y(\theta) = y_0 + r\sin(\theta) \tag{5.44}$$

In this definition, we have included the parameter of the curve as an argument in order to highlight the fact that the function defines a vector for each value of θ. The end points of all the vectors trace a circle. The derivatives of Eq. (5.43) with respect to θ define the first and second directional derivatives. That is,

$$\begin{aligned}\upsilon'(\theta) &= x'(\theta)\begin{bmatrix}1\\0\end{bmatrix} + y'(\theta)\begin{bmatrix}0\\1\end{bmatrix}\\ \upsilon''(\theta) &= x''(\theta)\begin{bmatrix}1\\0\end{bmatrix} + y''(\theta)\begin{bmatrix}0\\1\end{bmatrix}\end{aligned} \tag{5.45}$$

where

$$\begin{aligned}x'(\theta) &= -r\sin(\theta) \quad y'(\theta) = r\cos(\theta)\\ x''(\theta) &= -r\cos(\theta) \quad y''(\theta) = -r\sin(\theta)\end{aligned} \tag{5.46}$$

Fig. 5.24 illustrates the definition of the first and second directional derivatives. The first derivative defines a tangential vector while the second one is similar to the vector function, but it has reverse direction. In fact, that the edge direction measured for circles can be arranged so as to point towards the centre was actually the basis of one of the early approaches to reducing the computational load of the HT for circles [Kimme75].

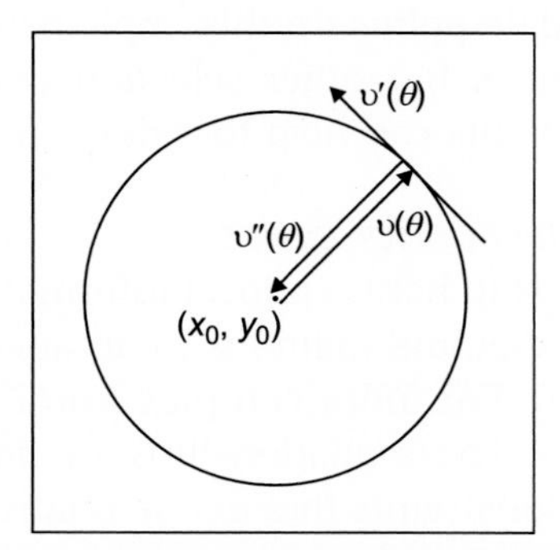

FIGURE 5.24 Definition of the first and second directional derivatives for a circle.

According to Eqs. (5.44) and (5.46), we observe that the tangent of the angle of the first directional derivative denoted as $\phi'(\theta)$ is given by

$$\phi'(\theta) = \frac{y'(\theta)}{x'(\theta)} = -\frac{1}{\tan(\theta)} \tag{5.47}$$

Angles will be denoted by using the symbol^. That is,

$$\hat{\phi}'(\theta) = \tan^{-1}(\phi'(\theta)) \tag{5.48}$$

Similarly, for the tangent of the second directional derivative we have that,

$$\phi''(\theta) = \frac{y''(\theta)}{x''(\theta)} = \tan(\theta) \quad \text{and} \quad \hat{\phi}''(\theta) = \tan^{-1}(\phi''(\theta)) \tag{5.49}$$

By observing the definition of $\phi''(\theta)$, we have

$$\phi''(\theta) = \frac{y''(\theta)}{x''(\theta)} = \frac{y(\theta) - y_0}{x(\theta) - x_0} \tag{5.50}$$

This equation defines a straight line passing through the points $(x(\theta), y(\theta))$ and (x_0, y_0), and it is perhaps the most important relation in parameter space decomposition. The definition of the line is more evident by rearranging terms. That is,

$$y(\theta) = \phi''(\theta)(x(\theta) - x_0) + y_0 \tag{5.51}$$

This equation is independent of the radius parameter. Thus, it can be used to gather evidence of the location of the shape in a 2D accumulator. The HT mapping is defined by the dual form given by

$$y_0 = \phi''(\theta)(x_0 - x(\theta)) + y(\theta) \tag{5.52}$$

That is, given an image point $(x(\theta), y(\theta))$ and the value of $\phi''(\theta)$, we can generate a line of votes in the 2D accumulator (x_0, y_0). Once the centre of the circle is known, then a 1D accumulator can be used to locate the radius. The key aspect of the parameter space decomposition is the method used to obtain the value of $\phi''(\theta)$ from image data. We will consider two alternative ways. First, we will show that $\phi''(\theta)$ can be obtained by edge direction information. Second, how it can be obtained from the information of a pair of points.

In order to obtain $\phi''(\theta)$, we can use the definition in Eqs. (5.47) and (5.49). According to these equations, the tangents $\phi''(\theta)$ and $\phi'(\theta)$ are perpendicular. Thus,

$$\phi''(\theta) = -\frac{1}{\phi'(\theta)} \tag{5.53}$$

Thus, the HT mapping in Eq. (5.52) can be written in terms of gradient direction $\phi'(\theta)$ as

$$y_0 = y(\theta) + \frac{x(\theta) - x_0}{\phi'(\theta)} \tag{5.54}$$

This equation has a simple geometric interpretation illustrated in Fig. 5.25A. We can see that the line of votes passes through the points $(x(\theta), y(\theta))$ and (x_0, y_0). The slope of the line is perpendicular to the direction of gradient direction.

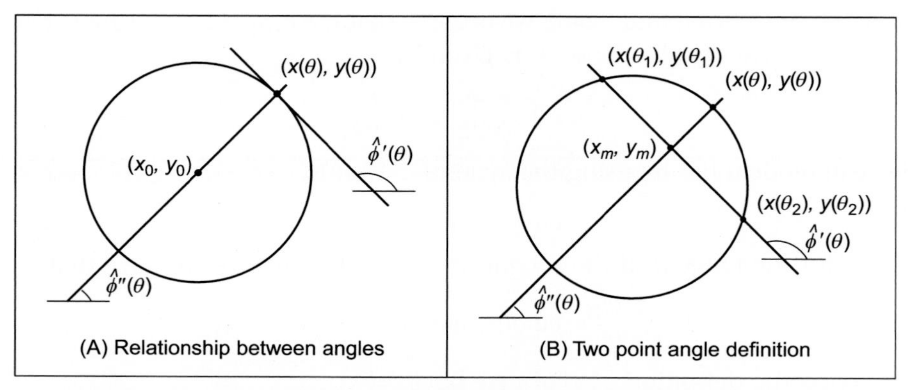

FIGURE 5.25 Geometry of the angle of the first and second directional derivatives.

An alternative decomposition can be obtained by considering the geometry shown in Fig. 5.25B. In the figure, we can see that if we take a pair of points (x_1, y_1) and (x_2, y_2), where $x_i = x(\theta_i)$, then the line that passes through the points has the same slope as the line at a point $(x(\theta), y(\theta))$. Accordingly,

$$\phi'(\theta) = \frac{y_2 - y_1}{x_2 - x_1} \tag{5.55}$$

where

$$\theta = \frac{1}{2}(\theta_1 + \theta_2) \tag{5.56}$$

Based on Eq. (5.55) we have that

$$\phi''(\theta) = -\frac{x_2 - x_1}{y_2 - y_1} \tag{5.57}$$

The problem with using a pair of points is that by Eq. (5.56) we cannot know the location of the point $(x(\theta), y(\theta))$. Fortunately, the voting line also passes through the midpoint of the line between the two selected points. Let us define this point as

$$x_m = \frac{1}{2}(x_1 + x_2) \quad y_m = \frac{1}{2}(y_1 + y_2) \tag{5.58}$$

Thus, by substitution of Eq. (5.55) in (5.54) and by replacing the point $(x(\theta), y(\theta))$ by (x_m, y_m), we have that the HT mapping can be expressed as

$$y_0 = y_m + \frac{(x_m - x_0)(x_2 - x_1)}{(y_2 - y_1)} \tag{5.59}$$

This equation does not use gradient direction information, but it is based on pairs of points. This is analogous to the parameter space decomposition of the line presented in Eq. (5.42). In that case, the slope can be computed by using gradient direction or, alternatively, by taking a pair of points. In the case of the circle, the tangent (and therefore the angle of the second directional derivative) can be computed by the gradient direction (i.e. Eq. 5.53) or by a pair of points (i.e. Eq. 5.57). However, it is important to notice that there are some other combinations of parameter space decomposition [Aguado96a].

Code 5.9 shows the implementation of the parameter space decomposition for the HT for circles. The implementation only detects the position of the circle, and it gathers evidence by using the mapping in Eq. (5.59). Similar to the implementation of lines, in this case points are selected from a neighbourhood defined by the parameter `deltaPointRange`. As such, we avoid using pixels that are close to each other since they do not produce accurate votes, and we also avoid using pixels that are far away from each other. In order to trace the line in Eq. (5.59), we use two equations: one for horizontal and one for vertical lines. As in previous implementations, it is important to include weighting to reduce discretisation errors.

Fig. 5.26 shows an example of the results obtained by the implementation in Code 5.9. The example shows the input edges obtained by the Canny edge detector for the eye image in Fig. 5.20. We can see that both accumulators show a clear peak that represents the location of the circle. Small peaks in the background of the accumulator in Fig. 5.26B correspond to circles with only a few points. In general, there is a compromise between

```
# Gather evidence for the circle location by using two points
accumulator = createImageF(width, height)
for x1,y1 in itertools.product(range(0, width), range(0, height)):
    if magnitude[y1,x1] != 0:
        # Look for points at this distance
        for dx,dy in itertools.product(range(0,deltaPointRange[1]+1),          \
                                       range(0,deltaPointRange[1]+1)):

            if (dx!=0 or dy!=0) and (abs(dx) > deltaPointRange[0] or           \
                                     abs(dy) > deltaPointRange[0]):
                x2, y2 = x1+dx, y1+dy
                if x2 > 0 and y2 > 0 and x2 < width and y2 < height and        \
                                             magnitude[y2, x2] !=0:
                    xm, ym = (x1 + x2) / 2.0, (y1 + y2) / 2.0
                    if abs(dx) < abs(dy):
                        m = float(dx) / float(-dy)
                        for x in range(0, width):
                            y = m *(x - xm) + ym
                            intY = int(y)
                            if intY > 0 and intY < height -1:
                                weight = y - intY
                                accumulator[ intY,   x] += (1.0 - weight)
                                accumulator[ intY+1, x] += weight
                    else:
                        m = float(-dy) / float(dx)
                        for y in range(0, height):
                            x = m *(y - ym) + xm
                            intX = int(x)
                            if intX > 0 and intX < width -1:
                                weight = x - intX
                                accumulator[ y, intX] += (1.0 - weight)
                                accumulator[ y, intX+1] += weight
```

CODE 5.9 Parameter space reduction for the Hough transform for circles.

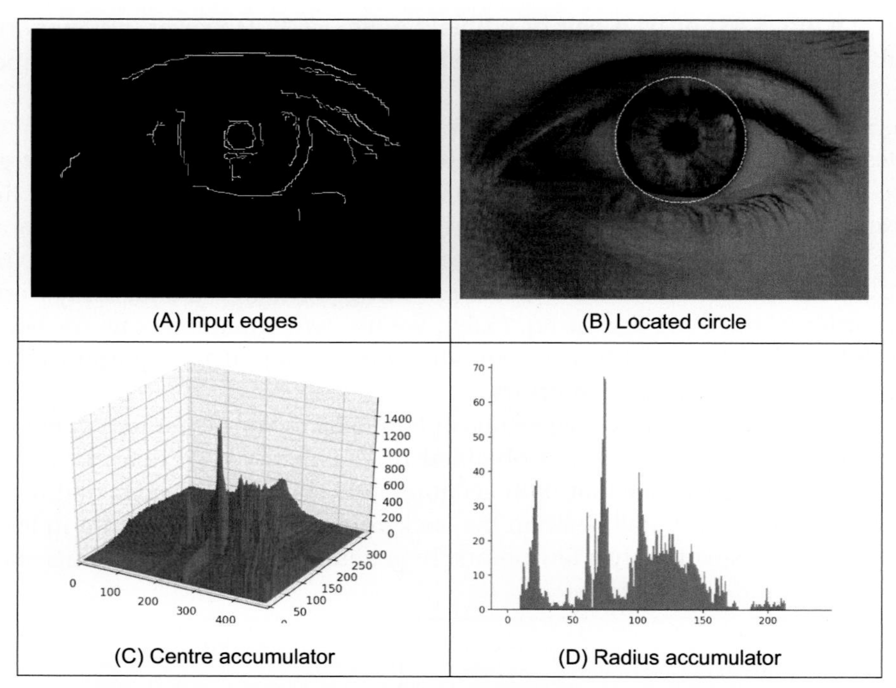

FIGURE 5.26 Parameter space reduction for the Hough transform for circles.

the width of the peak and the noise in the accumulator. The peak can be made narrower by considering pairs of points that are more widely spaced. However, this can also increase the level of background noise. Background noise can be reduced by taking points that are closer together, but this makes the peak wider. The accumulator in Fig. 5.26D shows the evidence gathered for the circle radius. This accumulator is obtained by selecting the location parameters as the maximum in the accumulator in Fig. 5.26C and then computing the gather evidence for the radius for each image point according to Eq. (5.32).

5.5.5.3 Parameter space reduction for ellipses

Part of the simplicity in the parameter decomposition for circles comes from the fact that circles are (naturally) isotropic. Ellipses have more free parameters and are geometrically more complex. Thus, geometrical properties involve more complex relationships between points, tangents and angles. However, they maintain the geometric relationship defined by the angle of the second derivative. According to Eqs. (5.43) and (5.45), the vector position and directional derivatives of an ellipse in Eq. (5.37) have the components

$$\begin{aligned} x'(\theta) &= -a_x \sin(\theta) + b_x \cos(\theta) \quad & y'(\theta) &= -a_y \sin(\theta) + b_y \cos(\theta) \\ x''(\theta) &= -a_x \cos(\theta) - b_x \sin(\theta) \quad & y''(\theta) &= -a_y \cos(\theta) - b_y \sin(\theta) \end{aligned} \tag{5.60}$$

The tangent of angle of the first and second directional derivatives are given by

$$\begin{aligned}\phi'(\theta) &= \frac{y'(\theta)}{x'(\theta)} = \frac{-a_y \sin(\theta) + b_y \cos(\theta)}{-a_x \sin(\theta) + b_x \cos(\theta)} \\ \phi''(\theta) &= \frac{y''(\theta)}{x''(\theta)} = \frac{-a_y \cos(\theta) - b_y \sin(\theta)}{-a_x \cos(\theta) - b_x \sin(\theta)}\end{aligned} \tag{5.61}$$

By considering Eq. (5.59), we have that Eq. (5.49) is also valid for an ellipse. That is,

$$\frac{y(\theta) - y_0}{x(\theta) - x_0} = \phi''(\theta) \tag{5.62}$$

The geometry of the definition in this equation is illustrated in Fig. 5.27A. As in the case of circles, this equation defines a line that passes through the points $(x(\theta), y(\theta))$ and (x_0, y_0). However, in the case of the ellipse, the angles $\hat{\phi}'(\theta)$ and $\hat{\phi}''(\theta)$ are not orthogonal. This makes the computation of $\phi''(\theta)$ more complex. In order to obtain $\phi''(\theta)$, we can extend the geometry presented in Fig. 5.25B. That is, we take a pair of points to define a line whose slope defines the value of $\phi'(\theta)$ at another point. This is illustrated in Fig. 5.27B. The line in Eq. (5.62) passes through the middle point (x_m, y_m). However, it is not orthogonal to the tangent line. In order to obtain an expression of the HT mapping, we will first show that the relationship in Eq. (5.56) is also valid for ellipses. Then we will use this equation to obtain $\phi''(\theta)$.

The relationships in Fig. 5.27B do not depend on the orientation or position of the ellipse. Thus, we have that three points can be defined by

$$\begin{aligned}x_1 &= a_x \cos(\theta_1) \quad x_2 = a_x \cos(\theta_2) \quad x(\theta) = a_x \cos(\theta) \\ y_1 &= b_x \sin(\theta_1) \quad y_2 = b_x \sin(\theta_2) \quad y(\theta) = b_x \sin(\theta)\end{aligned} \tag{5.63}$$

The point $(x(\theta), y(\theta))$ is given by the intersection of the line in Eq. (5.62) with the ellipse. That is,

$$\frac{y(\theta) - y_0}{x(\theta) - x_0} = \frac{a_x}{b_y} \frac{y_m}{x_m} \tag{5.64}$$

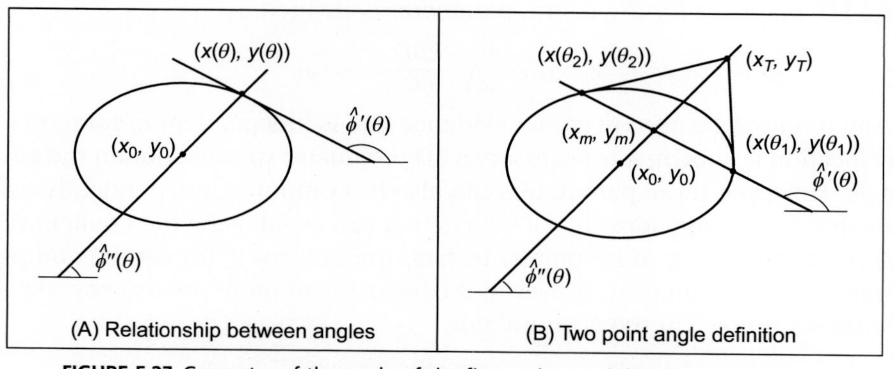

FIGURE 5.27 Geometry of the angle of the first and second directional derivatives.

By substitution of the values of (x_m, y_m) defined as the average of the co-ordinates of the points (x_1, y_1) and (x_2, y_2) in Eq. (5.58), we have that

$$\tan(\theta) = \frac{a_x}{b_y} \frac{b_y \sin(\theta_1) + b_y \sin(\theta_2)}{a_x \cos(\theta_1) + a_x \cos(\theta_2)} \tag{5.65}$$

Thus,

$$\tan(\theta) = \tan\left(\frac{1}{2}(\theta_1 + \theta_2)\right) \tag{5.66}$$

From this equation, it is evident that the relationship in Eq. (5.56) is also valid for ellipses. Based on this result, the tangent angle of the second directional derivative can be defined as

$$\phi''(\theta) = \frac{b_y}{a_x} \tan(\theta) \tag{5.67}$$

By substitution in Eq. (5.64) we have that

$$\phi''(\theta) = \frac{y_m}{x_m} \tag{5.68}$$

This equation is valid when the ellipse is not translated. If the ellipse is translated then the tangent of the angle can be written in terms of the points (x_m, y_m) and (x_T, y_T) as

$$\phi''(\theta) = \frac{y_T - y_m}{x_T - x_m} \tag{5.69}$$

By considering that the point (x_T, y_T) is the intersection point of the tangent lines at (x_1, y_1) and (x_2, y_2), we obtain

$$\phi''(\theta) = \frac{AC + 2BD}{2A + BC} \tag{5.70}$$

where

$$\begin{aligned} A &= y_1 - y_2 \quad & B &= x_1 - x_2 \\ C &= \phi_1 + \phi_2 \quad & D &= \phi_1 \cdot \phi_2 \end{aligned} \tag{5.71}$$

and ϕ_1, ϕ_2 are the slopes of the tangent line to the points. Finally, by considering Eq. (5.62), the HT mapping for the centre parameter is defined as

$$y_0 = y_m + \frac{AC + 2BD}{2A + BC}(x_0 - x_m) \tag{5.72}$$

This equation can be used to gather evidence that is independent of rotation or scale. Once the location is known, it is necessary a 3D parameter space to obtain the remaining parameters. However, these parameters can also be computed independently using two 2D parameter spaces [Aguado96b]. Of course that can avoid using the gradient direction in Eq. (5.70) by including more points. In fact, the tangent $\phi''(\theta)$ can be computed by taking four points [Aguado96a]. However, the inclusion of more points generally leads to more background noise in the accumulator.

Code 5.10 shows the implementation of the ellipse location by the mapping in Eq. (5.59). As in the case of the circle, pairs of points need to be restricted. However, in this implementation, we show a different approach to select pair of points. Instead of simply consider a distance range, we create curve segments by considering the neighbour pixels. In general, we expect that pixels in segments belong to the same primitive, so pair of pixels should provide better evidence than only selecting pixels in an image region. The segments are stored in the `segments` array. Pairs of points are formed by selecting random points in the segments. The implementation rejects pairs of points that have similar gradients since they produce a polar point that tends to infinity. Consequently, points with similar slope do not provide accurate evidence. We should notice that as the eccentricity of the ellipse increases, close points tend to have similar gradients making the detection process more difficult. Also notice that the gradient is noisy and not very accurate, so the resulting peak is generally quite wide. Again, the selection of the distance between points is a compromise between the level of background noise and the width of the peak. A relevant aspect of the implementation is that it is necessary to consider that evidence is actually gathered by tracing a line in the accumulator. Thus, as in the previous implementation, it is important to consider the slope of the line during the accumulation process. For horizontal lines, `x` is the independent variable, whilst for vertical lines, we use `y`.

Fig. 5.28 shows an example of the accumulators obtained by the implementation of Code 5.10 The peak in Fig. 5.28C represents the location of the ellipses. In general, there is noise, and the accumulator peak is spread out. This is for two main reasons. First, when the gradient direction is not accurate, then the line of votes does not pass precisely over the centre of the ellipse. This forces the peak to become wider with less height. Second, in order to avoid numerical instabilities, we need to select points that are well separated. However, this increases the probability that the points do not belong to the same ellipse, thus generating background noise in the accumulator. The accumulator in Fig. 5.28D shows the accumulator for the axis and rotation parameters. The figure shows a 2D slice of the 3D accumulator at the maximum point.

5.5.6 Generalised Hough transform

Many shapes are far more complex than lines, circles or ellipses. It is often possible to partition a complex shape into several geometric primitives, but this can lead to a highly complex data structure. In general, it is more convenient to extract the whole shape. This has motivated the development of techniques that can find arbitrary shapes using the evidence-gathering procedure of the HT. These techniques again give results equivalent to those delivered by matched template filtering, but with the computational advantage of the evidence gathering approach. An early approach offered only limited capability only for arbitrary shapes [Merlin75]. The full mapping is called the *generalised HT (GHT)* [Ballard81] and can be used to locate arbitrary shapes with unknown position, size and orientation. The GHT can be formally defined by considering the duality of a curve. One

```
# Gather evidence for the ellipse location on the valid points
accumulator = createImageF(width, height)
numPoints = len(segments)

# For a pair p1 = (x1,y1), p2=(x2,y2)
for p1 in range(0, numPoints):
    for p in range(0,pairsPerPoint):
        p2 = randint(0, numPoints-1)

        y1,x1 = (segments[p1])[0], (segments[p1])[1]
        y2,x2 = (segments[p2])[0], (segments[p2])[1]
        d = sqrt((x1-x2)*(x1-x2)+(y1-y2)*(y1-y2))
        if d > deltaPointRange[0]:
            angle1, angle2 = -angle[y1,x1], -angle[y2,x2]

            # To void parallel edge directions
            w = cos(angle1)*cos(angle2) + sin(angle1)*sin(angle2)
            if w < 0.9:
                xm, ym = (x1 + x2) / 2.0, (y1 + y2) / 2.0
                m1, m2 = tan(angle1), tan(angle2)
                A,B = y1-y2, x2-x1
                C,D = m1+m2, m1*m2
                M,N = A*C+2*B*D, 2*A+B*C

                norm = sqrt(M*M+N*N)
                M,N = M/norm, N/norm
                # Draw horizontal or vertical lines
                if abs(M) < abs(N):
                    m = float(M) / float(N)
                    b1, b2 = y1-m1*x1, y2-m2*x2
                    xIntersect = (b2-b1)/ (m1-m2)
                    if xIntersect < xm:
                        xi,xf = int(xm), min(int(xm + axisRange[1]), width-1)
                    else:
                        xi,xf = max(1,int(xm - axisRange[1])), int(xm)
                    for x in range(xi,xf):
                        y = m *(x - xm) + ym
                        d1 = sqrt((x-x1)*(x-x1)+(y-y1)*(y-y1))
                        if d1 > axisRange[0] and d1 < axisRange[1]:
                            yInt = int(y)
                            if yInt > 0 and yInt < height -1:
                                weight = y - yInt
                                accumulator[yInt,   x] += (1.0 - weight)
                                accumulator[yInt+1, x] += weight

                else:
                    m = float(N) / float(M)
                    b1, b2 = x1-m1*y1, x2-m2*y2
                    yIntersect = (b2-b1) / (m1-m2)
                    if yIntersect < ym:
                        yi,yf = int(ym), min(int(ym + axisRange[1]), height-1)
                    else:
                        yi,yf = max(1,int(ym - axisRange[1])), int(ym)
                    for y in range(yi,yf):
                        x = m *(y - ym) + xm
                        d1 = sqrt((x-x1)*(x-x1)+(y-y1)*(y-y1))
                        if d1 > axisRange[0] and d1 < axisRange[1]:
                            xInt = int(x)
                            if xInt > 0 and xInt < width -1:
                                weight = x - xInt
                                accumulator[y, xInt] += (1.0 - weight)
                                accumulator[y, xInt+1] += weight
```

CODE 5.10 Implementation of the parameter space reduction for the Hough transform for ellipses.

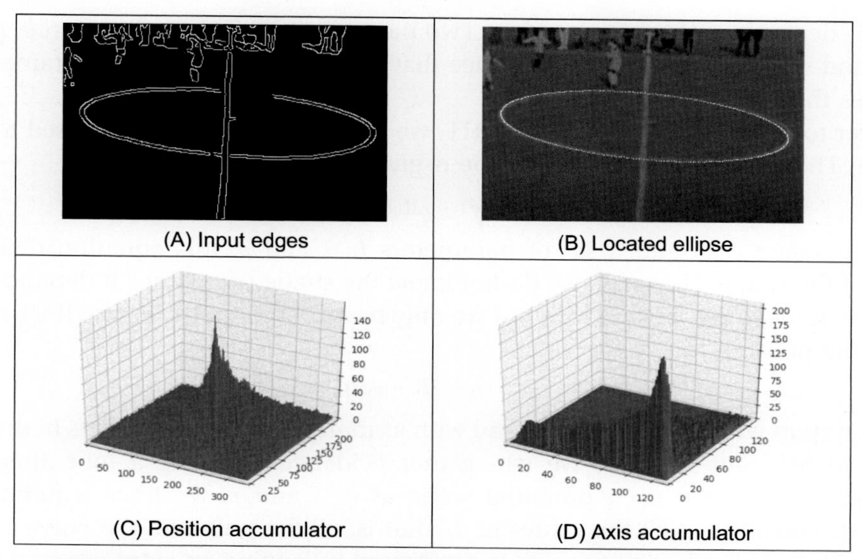

FIGURE 5.28 Parameter space reduction for the Hough transform for ellipses.

possible implementation can be based on the discrete representation given by tabular functions. These two aspects are explained in the following two sections.

5.5.6.1 *Formal definition of the GHT*

The formal analysis of the HT provides the route for generalising it to arbitrary shapes. We can start by generalising the definitions in Eq. (5.43). In this way a model shape can be defined by a curve

$$\upsilon(\theta) = x(\theta)\begin{bmatrix}1\\0\end{bmatrix} + y(\theta)\begin{bmatrix}0\\1\end{bmatrix} \tag{5.73}$$

For a circle, for example, we have that $x(\theta) = r\cos(\theta)$ and $y(\theta) = r\sin(\theta)$. Any shape can be represented by following a more complex definition of $x(\theta)$ and $y(\theta)$.

In general, we are interested in matching the model shape against a shape in an image. However, the shape in the image has a different location, orientation and scale. Originally the GHT defined a scale parameter in the x and y directions, but due to computational complexity and practical relevance, the use of a single scale has become much more popular. Analogous to Eq. (5.35), we can define the image shape by considering translation, rotation and change of scale. Thus, the shape in the image can be defined as

$$\omega(\theta, b, \lambda, \rho) = b + \lambda \mathbf{R}(\rho)\upsilon(\theta) \tag{5.74}$$

where $b = (x_0, y_0)$ is the translation vector, λ is a scale factor and $\mathbf{R}(\rho)$ is a rotation matrix (as in Eq. (5.33)). Here we have included explicitly the parameters of the transformation as arguments, but to simplify the notation they will be omitted later. The shape of

$\omega(\theta, b, \lambda, \rho)$ depends on four parameters. Two parameters define the location b, plus the rotation and scale. It is important to notice that θ does not define a free parameter, and only traces the curve.

In order to define a mapping for the HT, we can follow the approach used to obtain Eq. (5.37). Thus, the location of the shape is given by

$$b = \omega(\theta) - \lambda \mathbf{R}(\rho) \upsilon(\theta) \tag{5.75}$$

Given a shape $\omega(\theta)$ and a set of parameters b, λ and ρ, this equation defines the location of the shape. However, we do not know the shape $\omega(\theta)$ (since it depends on the parameters that we are looking for), but we only have a point in the curve. If we call $\omega_i = (\omega_{xi}, \omega_{yi})$ the point in the image, then

$$b = \omega_i - \lambda \mathbf{R}(\rho) \upsilon(\theta) \tag{5.76}$$

defines a system with four unknowns and with as many equations as points in the image. In order to find the solution, we can gather evidence by using a four-dimensional accumulator space. For each potential value of b, λ and ρ, we trace a point spread function by considering all the values of θ. That is, all the points in the curve $\upsilon(\theta)$.

In the GHT, the gathering process is performed by adding an extra constraint to the system that allows us to match points in the image with points in the model shape. This constraint is based on gradient direction information and can be explained as follows. We said that ideally, we would like to use Eq. (5.75) to gather evidence. For that we need to know the shape $\omega(\theta)$ and the model $\upsilon(\theta)$, but we only know the discrete points ω_i and we have supposed that these are the same as the shape, i.e. that $\omega(\theta) = \omega_i$. Based on this assumption, we then consider all the potential points in the model shape, $\upsilon(\theta)$. However, this is not necessary since we only need the point in the model, $\upsilon(\theta)$, that corresponds to the point in the shape, $\omega(\theta)$. We cannot know the point in the shape, $\upsilon(\theta)$, but we can compute some properties from the model and from the image. Then, we can check whether these properties are similar at the point in the model and at a point in the image. If they are indeed similar, the points might correspond: if they do we can gather evidence of the parameters of the shape. The GHT considers the gradient direction at the point as a feature. We can generalise Eqs. (5.47) and (5.48) to define the gradient direction at a point in the arbitrary model. Thus,

$$\phi'(\theta) = \frac{y'(\theta)}{x'(\theta)} \quad \text{and} \quad \widehat{\phi}'(\theta) = \tan^{-1}(\phi'(\theta)) \tag{5.77}$$

Thus Eq. (5.75) is true only if the gradient direction at a point in the image matches the rotated gradient direction at a point in the (rotated) model, that is

$$\phi'_i = \widehat{\phi}'(\theta) - \rho \tag{5.78}$$

where $\hat{\phi}'(\theta)$ is the angle at the point ω_i. Note that according to this equation, gradient direction is independent of scale (in theory at least), and it changes in the same ratio as rotation. We can constrain Eq. (5.76) to consider only the points $\upsilon(\theta)$ for which

$$\phi'_i - \widehat{\phi}'(\theta) + \rho = 0 \tag{5.79}$$

That is, a point spread function for a given edge point ω_i is obtained by selecting a subset of points in $\upsilon(\theta)$ such that the edge direction at the image point rotated by ρ equals the gradient direction at the model point. For each point ω_i and selected point in $\upsilon(\theta)$ the point spread function is defined by the HT mapping in Eq. (5.76).

5.5.6.2 *Polar definition*

Eq. (5.76) defines the mapping of the HT in Cartesian form. That is, it defines the votes in the parameter space as a pair of co-ordinates (x, y). There is an alternative definition in polar form. The polar implementation is more common than the Cartesian form [Hecker94, Sonka94]. The advantage of the polar form is that it is easy to implement since changes in rotation and scale correspond to addition in the angle–magnitude representation. However, ensuring that the polar vector has the correct direction incurs more complexity.

Eq. (5.76) can be written in a form that combines rotation and scale as

$$b=\omega(\theta)-\gamma(\lambda,\rho) \tag{5.80}$$

where $\gamma^{\mathrm{T}}(\lambda,\rho)=\left[\gamma_x(\lambda,\rho)\ \ \gamma_y(\lambda,\rho)\right]$ and where the combined rotation and scale is

$$\begin{aligned}\gamma_x(\lambda,\rho)&=\lambda(x(\theta)\cos(\rho)-y(\theta)\sin(\rho))\\ \gamma_y(\lambda,\rho)&=\lambda(x(\theta)\sin(\rho)+y(\theta)\cos(\rho))\end{aligned} \tag{5.81}$$

This combination of rotation and scale defines a vector, $\gamma(\lambda,\rho)$, whose tangent angle and magnitude are given by

$$\tan(\alpha)=\frac{\gamma_y(\lambda,\rho)}{\gamma_x(\lambda,\rho)}\qquad r=\sqrt{\gamma_x^2(\lambda,\rho)+\gamma_y^2(\lambda,\rho)} \tag{5.82}$$

The main idea here is that if we know the values for α and r, then we can gather evidence by considering Eq. (5.80) in polar form. That is,

$$b=\omega(\theta)-re^{j\alpha} \tag{5.83}$$

Thus, we should focus on computing values for α and r. After some algebraic manipulation, we have that

$$\alpha=\phi(\theta)+\rho\qquad r=\lambda\Gamma(\theta) \tag{5.84}$$

where

$$\phi(\theta)=\tan^{-1}\left(\frac{y(\theta)}{x(\theta)}\right)\qquad \Gamma(\theta)=\sqrt{x^2(\theta)+y^2(\theta)} \tag{5.85}$$

In this definition, we must include the constraint defined in Eq. (5.79). That is, we gather evidence only when the gradient direction is the same. Notice that the square root in the definition of the magnitude in Eq. (5.85) can have positive and negative values. The sign must be selected in a way that the vector has the correct direction.

5.5.6.3 *The GHT technique*

Eqs. (5.76) and (5.83) define an HT mapping function for arbitrary shapes. The geometry of these equations is shown in Fig. 5.29. Given an image point ω_i, we have to find a

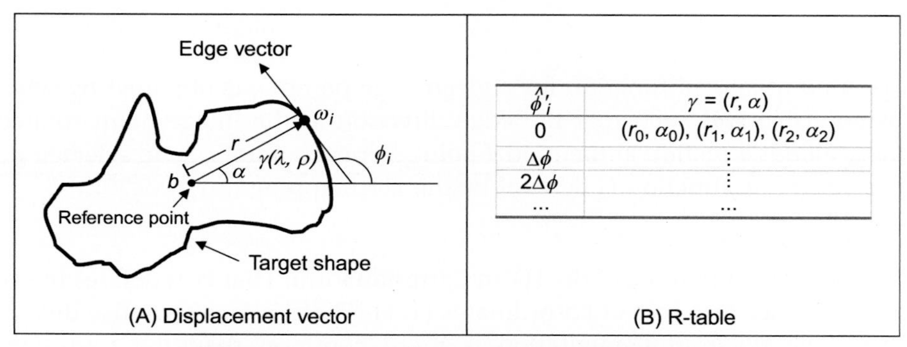

$\hat{\phi}'_i$	$\gamma = (r, \alpha)$
0	$(r_0, \alpha_0), (r_1, \alpha_1), (r_2, \alpha_2)$
$\Delta\phi$	⋮
$2\Delta\phi$	⋮
...	...

FIGURE 5.29 Geometry of the generalised Hough transform.

displacement vector $\gamma(\lambda, \rho)$. When the vector is placed at ω_i, then its end is at the point b. In the GHT jargon, this point is called the reference point. The vector $\gamma(\lambda, \rho)$ can be easily obtained as $\lambda R(\rho)\upsilon(\theta)$ or alternative as re^{α}. However, in order to evaluate these equations, we need to know the point $\upsilon(\theta)$. This is the crucial step in the evidence gathering process. Notice the interesting similarity between Fig. 5.25A, Fig 5.27A and Fig. 5.29A. This is not a coincidence, but Eq. (5.62) is a particular case of Eq. (5.75).

The process of determining $\upsilon(\theta)$ centres on solving Eq. (5.78). According to this equation, since we know $\hat{\phi}'_i$, then we need to find the point $\upsilon(\theta)$ whose gradient direction is $\widehat{\phi}'_i + \rho = 0$. Then we must use $\upsilon(\theta)$ to obtain the displacement vector $\gamma(\lambda, \rho)$. The GHT pre-computes the solution of this problem and stores it in an array called the *R-table.* The R-table stores for each value of $\hat{\phi}'_i$ the vector $\gamma(\lambda, \rho)$ for $\rho = 0$ and $\lambda = 1$. In polar form, the vectors are stored as a magnitude direction pair and in Cartesian form as a co-ordinate pair.

The possible range for $\hat{\phi}'_i$ is between $-\pi/2$ and $\pi/2$ radians. This range is split into N equi-spaced slots or bins. These slots become rows of data in the R-table. The edge direction at each border point determines the appropriate row in the R-table. The length, r, and direction, α, from the reference point is entered into a new column element, at that row, for each border point in the shape. In this manner, the N rows of the R-table have elements related to the border information, elements for which there is no information contain null vectors. The length of each row is given by the number of edge points that have the edge direction corresponding to that row; the total number of elements in the R-table equals the number of edge points above a chosen threshold. The structure of the R-table for N edge direction bins and m template border points is illustrated in Fig. 5.29B.

The process of building the R-table is illustrated in Code 5.11. In this code, we implement the Cartesian definition given in Eq. (5.76). According to this equation the displacement vector is given by

$$\gamma(r, \alpha) = w(\theta) + b \tag{5.86}$$

```
# Compute reference point in the template
refPoint = [0,0]
edgePoints = []
for x,y in itertools.product(range(0, widthTemplate), range(0, heightTemplate)):
    if magnitudeTemplate[y,x] != 0:
        refPoint[0] += y
        refPoint[1] += x
        edgePoints.append((y,x))
numPts = len(edgePoints)
refPoint = [int(refPoint[0]/numPts),int(refPoint[1]/numPts)]

# Build Rtable as a list of lists
rTable = [[] for entryIndex in range(numEntries)]
deltaAngle = 2.0 * pi / (numEntries - 1.0)
for p in range(0, numPts):
    y, x = (edgePoints[p])[0], (edgePoints[p])[1]

    # The angle is in the interval -pi,+pi
    ang = angleTemplate[y,x] + pi
    entryIndex = int(ang/deltaAngle)
    entry = rTable[entryIndex]
    entry.append((y-refPoint[0], x-refPoint[1]))
```

CODE 5.11 Constructing the R-Table.

The code stores the reference point b in the variable `refPoint`. The edge points are stored in the `edgePoints` list that is created by iterating over all the pixels in the template image. The list `rTable` is built for the number of entries defined by the parameter `numEntries`. Each entry covers an angle range defined in the variable `deltaAngle`. Each edge point is added as an entry in the table according to the angle stored in `angleTemplate`. This angle is the direction of the edge and was obtained when edges are detected by the Canny operator.

Code 5.12 shows the implementation of the gathering process of the GHT by using the Cartesian definition in Eq. (5.76). We apply the Canny edge detection operator to the input image, and the result is stored in the arrays `magnitude` and `angle`. The `magnitude` value is used to determine if a pixel is an edge, and the `angle` is used to locate an entry in the R-Table. The `entryIndex` defines the index on the table, and the `row` variable is a list that contains the table's entry. Each entry in the row increases a cell in the accumulator. The maximum number of votes occurs at the location of the original reference point. After all edge points have been inspected, the location of the shape is given by the maximum of the accumulator array.

Note that if we want to try other values for rotation and scale, then it is necessary to compute a table $\gamma(\lambda,\rho)$ for all potential values. However, this can be avoided by considering that $\gamma(\lambda,\rho)$ can be computed from $\gamma(1,0)$. That is, if we want to accumulate evidence for $\gamma(\lambda,\rho)$, then we use the entry indexed by $\widehat{\phi}'_i+\rho$ and we rotate and scale the vector $\gamma(1,0)$. That is,

```
# Gather evidence of the template in the image
accumulator = createImageF(width, height)
maxSegmentLenght = 0
for x,y in itertools.product(range(0, width), range(0, height)):
    if magnitude[y,x] != 0:
        # The angle is in the interval -pi,+pi
        ang = angle[y,x] + pi
        entryIndex = int(ang/deltaAngle)
        row = rTable[entryIndex]
        numPts = len(row)
        for p in range(0, numPts):
            x0, y0 = x - (row[p])[1], y - (row[p])[0]
            if y0>0 and x0>0 and y0<height and x0<width:
                accumulator[y0][x0] += 1
```

CODE 5.12 Implementing the generalised Hough transform.

$$\begin{aligned}\gamma_x(\lambda,\rho) &= \lambda\big(\gamma_x(1,0)\cos(\rho) - \gamma_y(1,0)\sin(\rho)\big)\\ \gamma_y(\lambda,\rho) &= \lambda\big(\gamma_x(1,0)\sin(\rho) + \gamma_y(1,0)\cos(\rho)\big)\end{aligned} \tag{5.87}$$

In the case of the polar form, the angle and magnitude need to be defined according to Eq. (5.84).

The application of the GHT to detect an arbitrary shape with unknown translation is illustrated in Fig. 5.30. We constructed an R-table from the template shown in Fig. 5.30A. The table contains 180 rows. The accumulator in Fig. 5.30D was obtained by applying the GHT to the image in Fig. 5.30B. Since the table was obtained from a shape with the same scale and rotation than the primitive in the image, then the GHT produces an

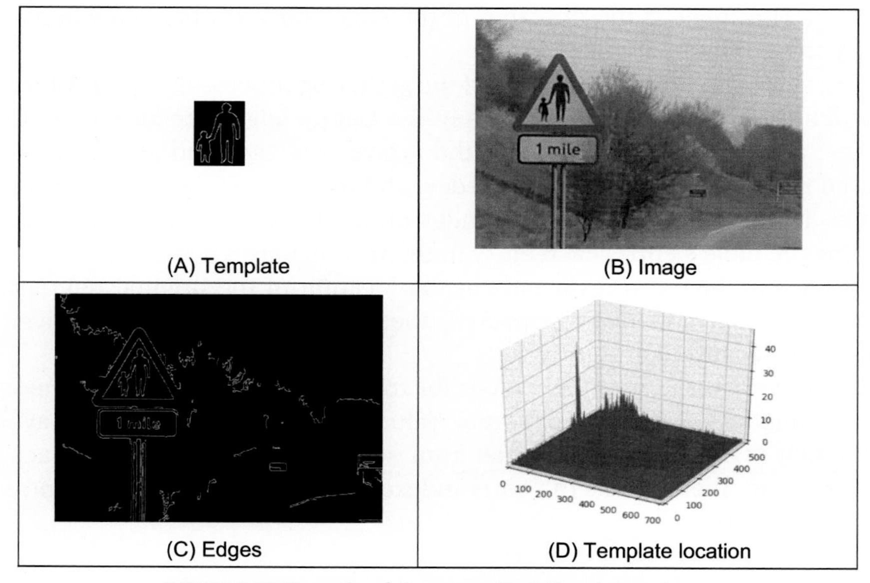

FIGURE 5.30 Example of the generalised Hough transform.

accumulator with a clear peak at the centre of mass of the shape. The edges used to gather evidence are shown in Fig. 5.30C.

Although the example in Fig. 5.30 shows that the GHT is an effective method for shape extraction, there are several inherent difficulties in its formulation [Aguado00b, Grimson90]. The most evident problem is that the table does not provide an accurate representation when objects are scaled and translated. This is because the table implicitly assumes that the curve is represented in discrete form. Thus, the GHT maps a discrete form into a discrete parameter space. Additionally, the transformation of scale and rotation can induce other discretisation errors. This is because when discrete images are mapped to be larger, or when they are rotated, loci which are unbroken sets of points rarely map to unbroken sets in the new image. Another important problem is the excessive computations required by the four-dimensional parameter space. This makes the technique impractical. Also, the GHT is clearly dependent on the accuracy of directional information. By these factors, the results provided by the GHT can become less reliable. A solution is to use an analytic form instead of a table [Aguado98]. This avoids discretisation errors and makes the technique more reliable. This also allows the extension to affine or other transformations. However, this technique requires solving for the point $\upsilon(\theta)$ in an analytic way increasing the computational load. A solution is to reduce the number of points by considering characteristics points defined as points of high curvature. However, this still requires the use of a four-dimensional accumulator. An alternative to reduce this computational load is to include the concept of invariance in the GHT mapping.

5.5.6.4 *Invariant GHT*

The problem with the GHT (and other extensions of the HT) is that they are very general. That is, the HT gathers evidence for a single point in the image. However, a point on its own provides little information. Thus, it is necessary to consider a large parameter space to cover all the potential shapes defined by a given image point. The GHT improves evidence gathering by considering a point and its gradient direction. However, since gradient direction changes with rotation, then the evidence gathering is improved in terms of noise handling, but little is done about computational complexity.

In order to reduce computational complexity of the GHT, we can consider replacing the gradient direction by another feature. That is, by a feature that is not affected by rotation. Let us explain this idea in more detail. The main aim of the constraint in Eq. (5.79) is to include gradient direction to reduce the number of votes in the accumulator by identifying a point $\upsilon(\theta)$. Once this point is known, then we obtain the displacement vector $\gamma(\lambda,\rho)$. However, for each value of rotation, we have a different point in $\upsilon(\theta)$. Now let us replace that constraint in Eq. (5.78) by a constraint of the form

$$Q(\omega_i)=Q(\upsilon(\theta)) \tag{5.88}$$

The function Q is said to be invariant, and it computes a feature at the point. This feature can be, for example, the colour of the point, or any other property that does not change in the model and in the image. By considering Eq. (5.88), Eq. (5.79) is redefined as

$$Q(\omega_i) - Q(\upsilon(\theta)) = 0 \tag{5.89}$$

That is, instead of searching for a point with the same gradient direction, we will search for the point with the same invariant feature. The advantage is that this feature will not change with rotation or scale, so we only require a 2D space to locate the shape. The definition of Q depends on the application and the type of transformation. The most general invariant properties can be obtained by considering geometric definitions. In the case of rotation and scale changes (i.e. similarity transformations), the fundamental invariant property is given by the concept of angle.

An angle is defined by three points and its value remains unchanged when it is rotated and scaled. Thus, if we associate to each edge point ω_i, a set of other two points $\{\omega_j, \omega_T\}$, we can compute a geometric feature that is invariant to similarity transformations. That is,

$$Q(\omega_i) = \frac{\omega_{xj}\omega_{yi} - \omega_{xi}\omega_{yj}}{\omega_{xi}\omega_{xj} + \omega_{yi}\omega_{yj}} \tag{5.90}$$

where ω_{xn} and ω_{yn} are the x and the y coordinates of point n. Eq. (5.90) defines the tangent of the angle at the point ω_T. In general, we can define the points $\{\omega_j, \omega_T\}$ in different ways. An alternative geometric arrangement is shown in Fig. 5.31A. Given the points ω_i and a fixed angle ϑ, then we determine the point ω_j such that the angle between the tangent line at ω_i and the line that joins the points is ϑ. The third point is defined by the intersection of the tangent lines at ω_i and ω_j. The tangent of the angle β is defined by Eq. (5.90). This can be expressed in terms of the points and its gradient directions as

$$\mathrm{Q}(\omega_i) = \frac{\phi'_i - \phi'_j}{1 + \phi'_i \phi'_j} \tag{5.91}$$

We can replace the gradient angle in the R-table, by the angle β whose tangent is defined by Eq. (5.91). The form of the new invariant table is shown in Fig. 5.31C. Since the angle β does not change with rotation or change of scale, then we do not need to

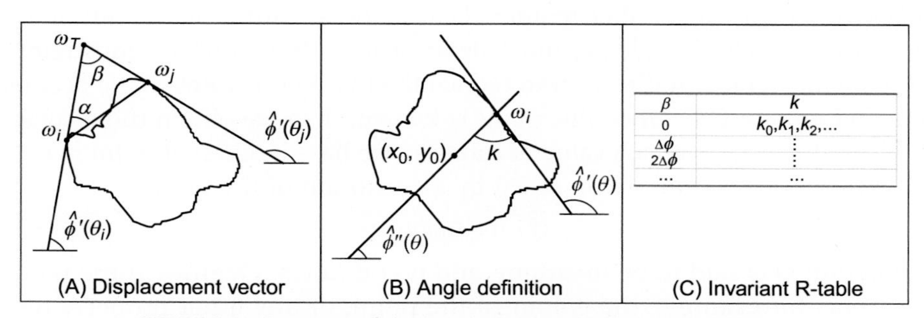

FIGURE 5.31 Geometry of the invariant generalised Hough transform.

change the index for each potential rotation and scale. However, the displacement vectors change according to rotation and scale (i.e. Eq. (5.87)). Thus, if we want an invariant formulation, we must also change the definition of the position vector.

In order to locate the reference point b from an entry on the table, we can generalise the ideas presented in Figs 5.27A and 5.29A. Fig. 5.31B shows this generalisation. As in the case of the circle and ellipse, we can locate the centre of a shape by considering a line of votes that passes through the centre point b. This line was determined for the circle and ellipse by the angle ϕ_i''. In order to use it in general shapes, we will need to do two things. First, we will find an invariant definition of this value. Second, we will need to include it on the GHT table.

We can develop Eq. (5.75) as

$$\begin{bmatrix} x_0 \\ y_0 \end{bmatrix} = \begin{bmatrix} \omega_{xi} \\ \omega_{yi} \end{bmatrix} + \lambda \begin{bmatrix} \cos(\rho) & \sin(\rho) \\ -\sin(\rho) & \cos(\rho) \end{bmatrix} \begin{bmatrix} x(\theta) \\ y(\theta) \end{bmatrix} \tag{5.92}$$

Thus, Eq. (5.62) generalises to

$$\phi_i'' = \frac{\omega_{yi} - y_0}{\omega_{xi} - x_0} = \frac{[-\sin(\rho) \quad \cos(\rho)]y(\theta)}{[\cos(\rho) \quad \sin(\rho)]x(\theta)} \tag{5.93}$$

By some algebraic manipulation, we have that

$$\phi_i'' = \tan(\xi - \rho) \tag{5.94}$$

where

$$\xi = \frac{y(\theta)}{x(\theta)} \tag{5.95}$$

In order to define ϕ_i'', we can consider the tangent angle at the point ω_i. By considering the derivative of Eq. (5.74) we have that

$$\phi_i' = \frac{[-\sin(\rho) \quad \cos(\rho)]y'(\theta)}{[\cos(\rho) \quad \sin(\rho)]x'(\theta)} \tag{5.96}$$

Thus,

$$\phi_i' = \tan(\phi - \rho) \tag{5.97}$$

where

$$\phi = \frac{y'(\theta)}{x'(\theta)} \tag{5.98}$$

By considering Eqs. (5.94) and (5.96) we define

$$\widehat{\phi}_i'' = k + \widehat{\phi}_i'' \tag{5.99}$$

The important point in this definition is that the value of k is invariant to rotation. Thus, if we use this value in combination with the tangent at a point, we can have an invariant characterisation. In order to see that k is invariant, we solve it for Eq. (5.99). That is,

$$k = \widehat{\phi}_i' - \widehat{\phi}_i'' \tag{5.100}$$

Thus,

$$k = \xi - \rho - (\phi - \rho) \tag{5.101}$$

That is,

$$k = \xi - \phi \tag{5.102}$$

That is independent of rotation. The definition of k has a simple geometric interpretation illustrated in Fig. 5.25.

In order to obtain an invariant GHT, it is necessary to know for each point ω_i, the corresponding point $\upsilon(\theta)$ and then compute the value of ϕ_i''. Then evidence can be gathered by the line in Eq. (5.93). That is,

$$y_0 = \phi_i''(x_0 - \omega_{xi}) + \omega_{yi} \tag{5.103}$$

In order to compute ϕ_i'', we can obtain k and then use Eq. (5.101). In the standard tabular form the value of k can be pre-computed and stored as function of the angle β.

Code 5.13 illustrates the implementation for obtaining the invariant R-Table. This code searches for two points along the line defined by the value of α. In the code, `alpha` is set to $\pi/2$. Each element of the table stores a single value computed according to Eq. (5.100). The more cumbersome part of the code is to search for the point ω_j. We search in two directions from ω_i, and we stop once an edge point has been located. This search is performed by tracing a line. The trace is dependent on the slope. When the slope is between -1 and $+1$, we then determine a value of y for each value of x, otherwise we determine a value of x for each value of y. The table is constructed by considering each pair of points. The value `beta` is obtained according to Eq. (5.89). The value k by following Eq. (5.102). The scale c is simply the ratio between the distance of the first point to the reference point and the distance between the points. The value `beta` is then used to find the index in the table where to insert the pair (k, c).

Code 5.14 illustrates the evidence gathering process according to Eq. (5.103). The first part of the process is to find for each edge point (x_1, y_1) all the points along the line defined by Eq. (5.94). This process is similar to the first part of Code 5.13 and the results are stored in the list `secondPoints`. Each point (x_1, y_1) is paired with each point in the `secondPoints` list to define the pairs (x_1, y_1), (x_2, y_2). For each pair, we can compute a value `beta` according to Eq. (5.91). This defines an entry on the table. The data (k, c) are recovered from the table, and they are used to compute the slope of the angle defined in Eq. (5.99). The slope of the line is obtained from k and the distance between the point, and the centre is determined by c. The accumulator is then incremented by a small segment of three pixels in the location of the reference point. We use a three-pixel segment to account for errors in the computation of the gradient, the discretisation of the table and the discretisation of the accumulator. We should expect the location of the centre to be close but not exactly at the position obtained from the table values. The increase in the accumulator includes a weighting obtained by the distance to the expected reference point position.

```
# Find the pairs of points in the template according to alpha angle
pairPoints = []
numPts = len(edgePoints)
for p in range(0, numPts):
    y1, x1 = (edgePoints[p])[0], (edgePoints[p])[1]
    # We are looking for two points along the line with slope m
    m = tan(angleTemplate[y1,x1] - alpha)
    if m>-1 and m<1:
        if x1 < refPoint[1]: xi, xf, step = x1 + minimaDistPoints,widthTemplate, 1
        else: xi, xf, step = x1 - minimaDistPoints, 0, -1
        for x2 in range(xi, xf, step):
            y2 = int(y1 - m * (x2 - x1))
            if y2 > 0 and y2 < heightTemplate and magnitudeTemplate[y2,x2] != 0:
                pairPoints.append((y2,x2,y1,x1))
                break
    else:
        m = 1.0/m
        if y1 < refPoint[0]: yi, yf, step = y1 + minimaDistPoints,heightTemplate, 1
        else: yi, yf, step = y1 - minimaDistPoints, 0, -1
        for y2 in range(yi, yf, step):
            x2 = int(x1 - m * (y2 - y1))
            if x2 > 0 and x2 < widthTemplate and magnitudeTemplate[y2,x2] != 0:
                pairPoints.append((y2,x2,y1,x1))
                break

# Build table (k,c) from each pair of points
rTable = [[] for entryIndex in range(numEntries)]
deltaAngle = pi / (numEntries - 1.0)
numPairs = len(pairPoints)
for pair in range(0, numPairs):
    y2, x2 = (pairPoints[pair])[0], (pairPoints[pair])[1]
    y1, x1 = (pairPoints[pair])[2], (pairPoints[pair])[3]
    # Compute beta
    phi1, phi2 = tan(-angleTemplate[y1,x1]), tan(-angleTemplate[y2,x2])

    if 1.0+phi1*phi2 != 0: beta = atan((phi1-phi2)/(1.0+phi1*phi2))
    else:                  beta=1.57

    # Compute k
    if x1- refPoint[1] !=0: m = atan(-float(y1-refPoint[0])/(x1-refPoint[1]))
    else:                   m =1.57

    k = angleTemplate[y1,x1] - m
    # Scale
    distCentre = sqrt((y1-refPoint[0])*(y1-refPoint[0]) +                    \
                      (x1-refPoint[1])*(x1-refPoint[1]))
    distPoints = sqrt((y2-y1)*(y2-y1) + (x2-x1)*(x2-x1))
    c = distCentre/distPoints
    # Insert in the table. The angle is in the interval -pi/2 to pi/2
    entryIndex = int((beta+(pi/2.0))/deltaAngle)
    entry = rTable[entryIndex]
    entry.append((k,c))
```

CODE 5.13 Constructing the invariant R-Table.

Fig. 5.32 shows an example of the accumulator obtained by the implementation of Code 5.13. Fig. 5.32A shows the template used in this example. This template was used to construct the R-Table in Code 5.13. The R-Table was used to accumulate evidence when searching for the template in the image in Fig. 5.32B. Fig. 5.32D shows the result of the evidence gathering process. We can observe a peak in the location of the object.

```
# Gather evidence
numPts = len(secondPoints) > 0
for ptIndex in range(0, numPts):
    secondPoint = secondPoints[ptIndex]
    y2, x2 = secondPoint[0], secondPoint[1]
    distPoints = sqrt((y2-y1)*(y2-y1) + (x2-x1)*(x2-x1))

    # Compute beta
    phi1, phi2 = tan(-angle[y1,x1]), tan(-angle[y2,x2])
    if 1.0+phi1*phi2 != 0:
        beta = atan((phi1-phi2)/(1.0+phi1*phi2))
    else:
        beta=1.57
    # Find entry in table
    entryIndex = int((beta+(pi/2.0))/deltaAngle)

    row = rTable[entryIndex]
    numEntriesinRow = len(row)

    for kIndex in range(0, numEntriesinRow):
        k, c = (row[kIndex])[0], (row[kIndex])[1]
        distCentre = c * distPoints
        m = tan(angle[y1,x1] - k)
        if m>-1 and m<1:
            for x in range(0, width):
                y = int(y1 - m * (x - x1))
                d = sqrt((x-x1)*(x-x1)+(y-y1)*(y-y1))
                if y > 0 and y < height and abs(d-distCentre) < 3:
                    accumulator[y,x] += 3.0 - abs(d-distCentre)
        else:
            m = 1.0/m
            for y in range(0, height):
                x = int(x1 - m * (y - y1))
                d = sqrt((x-x1)*(x-x1)+(y-y1)*(y-y1))
                if x > 0 and x < width and abs(d-distCentre) < 3:
                    accumulator[y,x] += 3.0 - abs(d-distCentre)
```

CODE 5.14 Implementation of the invariant generalised Hough transform.

However, this accumulator contains some noise. The noise is produced since rotation and scale change the value of the computed gradient. Thus, the line of votes is only approximated. Another problem is that pairs of points ω_i and ω_j might not be found in an image, thus the technique is more sensitive to occlusion and noise than the GHT.

5.5.7 Other extensions to the HT

The motivation for extending the HT is clear: keep the performance, but improve the speed. There are other approaches to reduce the computational load of the HT. These approaches aim to improve speed and reduce memory focusing on smaller regions of the accumulator space. These approaches have included: the *fast HT* [Li86] which successively splits the accumulator space into quadrants and continues to study the quadrant with most evidence; the *adaptive HT* [Illingworth87] which uses a fixed accumulator size to iteratively focus onto potential maxima in the accumulator space; the *randomised HT*

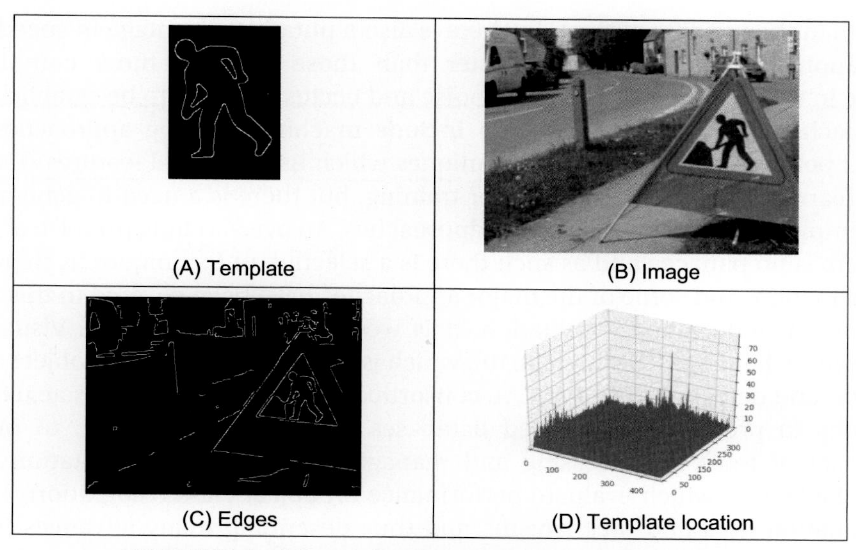

FIGURE 5.32 Applying the invariant generalised Hough transform.

[Xu90] and the *probabilistic HT* [Kälviäinen95] which use a random search of the accumulator space; and other pyramidal techniques. One main problem with techniques which do not search the full accumulator space, but a reduced version to save speed, is that the wrong shape can be extracted [Princen89], a problem known as *phantom shape location*. These approaches can also be used (with some variation) to improve speed of performance in template matching. There have been many approaches aimed to improve performance of the HT and of the GHT.

There has been a comparative study on the GHT (including efficiency) [Kassim99] and alternative approaches to the GHT include two *fuzzy* HTs: [Philip91] which [Sonka94] includes uncertainty of the perimeter points within a GHT structure, and [Han94] which approximately fits a shape but which requires application-specific specification of a fuzzy membership function. There have been two major reviews of the state of research in the HT [Illingworth88, Leavers93] (but they are rather dated now) and a textbook [Leavers92] which covers many of these topics. The analytic approaches to improving the HTs' performance use mathematical analysis to reduce size, and more importantly dimensionality, of the accumulator space. This concurrently improves speed. A review of HT-based techniques for circle extraction [Yuen90] covered some of the most popular techniques available at the time.

5.6 Further reading

It is worth noting that research has focussed on shape extraction by combination of low-level features, Section 5.4, rather than on HT-based approaches. The advantages of the low-level feature approach are simplicity, in that the features exposed are generally less complex than the variants of the HT. There is also a putative advantage in speed, in that simpler approaches are invariably faster than those that are more complex. Any advantage in respect of performance in noise and occlusion is yet to be established. The HT approaches do not (or do not yet) include machine learning approaches whose potency is perhaps achieved by the techniques which use low level features. The use of machine learning also implies a need for training, but there is a need to generate some form of template for the HT or template approaches. An over-arching premise of this text is that there is no panacea and as such there is a selection of techniques as there are for feature extraction, and some of the major approaches have been covered in this chapter.

In terms of performance evaluation, it is worth noting the PASCAL Visual Object Classes (VOC) Challenge [Everingham10], which is a benchmark in visual object category recognition and detection. The PASCAL consortium (http://host.robots.ox.ac.uk/pascal/VOC/) aims to provide standardised databases for object recognition; to provide a common set of tools for accessing and managing the database annotations and to conduct challenges, which evaluate performance on object class recognition. This provides evaluation data and mechanisms and thus describing many advances in recognising objects from a number of visual object classes in realistic scenes.

The majority of further reading in finding shapes concerns papers, many of which have already been referenced, especially in the newer techniques. An excellent survey of the techniques used for feature extraction (including template matching, deformable templates, etc.) can be found in [Trier96]. A recent survey of the HT techniques can be found in [Mukhopadhyay15]. Few of the textbooks devote much space to shape extraction except *Shape Classification and Analysis* [Costa09] and *Template Matching Techniques in Computer Vision* [Brunelli09], sometimes dismissing it in a couple of pages. This rather contrasts with the volume of research there has been in this area, and the Hough transform finds increasing application as computational power continues to increase (and storage cost reduces). Other techniques use a similar evidence gathering process to the HT. These techniques are referred to as Geometric Hashing and Clustering Techniques [Lamdan88, Stockman87]. In contrast with the HT, these techniques do not define an analytic mapping, but they gather evidence by grouping a set of features computed from the image and from the model.

There are deep learning replacing interest point detectors [Zheng18] and deep learning-based object detectors [Redmon16, Ren15]. There are also newer approaches that perform segmentation based on evidence gathering, e.g. Hough–CNN [Milletari117], which perhaps can handle better noise in medical images. Time will tell on these new approaches, and some are described in Chapter 12. Essentially, this chapter has focussed on shapes which can in some form have a fixed appearance, whether it is exposed by a template, a set of keypoints or by a description of local properties. In order to extend the approaches to shapes with a less constrained description, and rather than describe such shapes by constructing a library of their possible appearances, we require techniques for deformable shape analysis, as we shall find in the next chapter.

References

[Aguado96a] Aguado, A. S., *Primitive Extraction via Gathering Evidence of Global Parameterised Models*, PhD Thesis, University of Southampton, 1996.

[Aguado96b] Aguado, A. S., Montiel, E., and Nixon, M. S., On Using Directional Information for Parameter Space Decomposition in Ellipse Detection, *Pattern Recognition*, **28**(3), pp 369-381, 1996.

[Aguado98] Aguado, A. S., Nixon, M. S., and Montiel, M. E., Parameterising Arbitrary Shapes via Fourier Descriptors for Evidence-Gathering Extraction, *Computer Vision and Image Understanding*, **69**(2), pp 202-221, 1998.

[Aguado00a] Aguado, A. S., Montiel, E., and Nixon, M. S., On the Intimate Relationship between the Principle of Duality and the Hough Transform, *Proceedings of the Royal Society A*, **456**, pp 503-526, 2000.

[Aguado00b] Aguado, A.S., Montiel, E., and Nixon, M.S., Bias Error Analysis of the Generalised Hough Transform, *Journal of Mathematical Imaging and Vision*, **12**, pp 25—42, 2000

[Altman84] Altman, J., and Reitbock, H. J. P., A Fast Correlation Method for Scale- and Translation-Invariant Pattern Recognition, *IEEE Transactions on PAMI*, **6**(1), pp 46-57, 1984.

[Arandjelović12] Arandjelović, R., and Zisserman, A., Three Things Everyone Should Know to Improve Object Retrieval. *Proceedings of IEEE CVPR*, pp 2911-2918, 2012.

[Arbab-Zavar11] Arbab-Zavar, B., and Nixon, M. S., On Guided Model-Based Analysis for Ear Biometrics, *Computer Vision and Image Understanding*, **115**, pp 487—502, 2011.

[Ballard81] Ballard, D. H., Generalising the Hough Transform to Find Arbitrary Shapes, *CVGIP*, **13**, pp111-122, 1981.

[Bay08] Bay, H., Eas, A., Tuytelaars, T., and Van Gool, L., Speeded-Up Robust Features *Computer Vision and Image Understanding*, **110**(3), pp 346-359, 2008.

[Bracewell86] Bracewell, R. N., *The Fourier Transform and its Applications*, 2nd Edition, McGraw-Hill Book Co, Singapore, 1986.

[Bresenham65] Bresenham, J. E., Algorithm for Computer Control of a Digital Plotter, *IBM Systems Journal*, **4**(1), pp 25-30, 1965.

[Bresenham77] Bresenham, J. E., A Linear Algorithm for Incremental Digital Display of Circular Arcs, *Communications of the ACM*, **20**(2), pp 750-752, 1977.

[Brown83] Brown, C. M., Inherent Bias and Noise in the Hough Transform, *IEEE Transactions on PAMI*, **5**, pp 493-505, 1983.

[Brunnelli09] Brunelli, R., *Template Matching Techniques in Computer Vision*, Wiley, Chichester, UK, 2009.

[Bustard10] Bustard, J. D., and Nixon, M. S., Toward Unconstrained Ear Recognition from Two-Dimensional Images, *IEEE Transactions on SMC(A)*, **40**(3), pp 486-494, 2010.

[Calonder10] Calonder, M., Lepetit, V., Strecha, C., and Fua, P., BRIEF: Binary Robust Independent Elementary Features. *Proceedings of ECCV*, pp. 778-792, 2010.

[Casasent77] Casasent, D., and Psaltis, D., New Optical Transforms for Pattern Recognition, *Proceedings of the IEEE*, **65**(1), pp 77-83, 1977.

[Costa09] Costa, L. F., and Cesar, L. M., *Shape Classification and Analysis*, 2nd Edition, CRC Press (Taylor & Francis), Boca Raton, FL, USA, 2009.

[Dalal05] Dalal, N., and Triggs, B., Histograms of Oriented Gradients for Human Detection, *Proceeding of IEEE Conference on Computer Vision and Pattern Recognition*, **2**, pp 886-893, 2005.

[Datta 08] Datta, R., Joshi, D., Li, J., and Wang, J. Z., Image Retrieval: Ideas, Influences, and Trends of the New Age. *ACM Computing Surveys*, **40**(2), 2008.

[Deans81] Deans, S. R., Hough Transform from the Radon Transform, *IEEE Transactions on PAMI*, **13**, pp 185-188, 1981.

[Duda72] Duda, R. O., and Hart, P. E., Use of the Hough Transform to Detect Lines and Curves in Pictures, *Communications of the ACM*, **15**, pp 11-15, 1972.

[Everingham10] Everingham, M., Van Gool, L., Williams, C. K. I., Winn, J., and Zisserman, A., The PASCAL Visual Object Classes (VOC) Challenge, *International Journal of Computer Vision*, **88**(2), pp 303-338, 2010.

[Gerig86] Gerig, G., and Klein, F., Fast Contour Identification through Efficient Hough Transform and Simplified Interpretation Strategy, *Proceedings of 8th International Conference on Pattern Recognition*, pp 498-500, 1986.

[Grimson90] Grimson, W. E. L., and Huttenglocher, D. P., On the Sensitivity of the Hough Transform for Object Recognition, *IEEE Transactions on PAMI*, **12**, pp 255-275, 1990.

[Han94] Han, J. H., Koczy, L. T., and Poston, T., Fuzzy Hough Transform, *Pattern Recognition Letters*, **15**, pp 649-659, 1994.

[Hecker94] Hecker, Y. C., and Bolle, R. M., On Geometric Hashing and the Generalized Hough Transform, *IEEE Transactions on Systems, Man and Cybernetics*, **24**, pp 1328-1338, 1994.

[Hough62] Hough, P. V. C., *Method and Means for Recognising Complex Patterns*, US Patent 3069654, 1962.

[Hurley08] Hurley D. J., Arbab-Zavar, B., and Nixon, M. S., The Ear as a Biometric, In A. Jain, P. Flynn and A. Ross Eds.: *Handbook of Biometrics*, pp 131-150, 2008.

[Illingworth87] Illingworth, J., and Kittler, J., The Adaptive Hough Transform, *IEEE Transactions on PAMI*, **9**(5), pp 690-697, 1987.

[Illingworth88] Illingworth, J., and Kittler, J., A Survey of the Hough Transform, *CVGIP*, **48**, pp 87-116, 1988.

[Kälviäinen95] Kälviäinen, H., Hirvonen, P., Xu, L., and Oja, E., Probabilistic and Non-probabilistic Hough Transforms: Overview and Comparisons, *Image and Vision Computing*, **13**(4), pp 239-252, 1995.

[Kassim99] Kassim, A. A., Tan, T., Tan K. H., A Comparative Study of Efficient Generalised Hough Transform Techniques, *Image and Vision Computing*, **17**(10), pp. 737-748, 1999.

[Kimme75] Kimme, C., Ballard, D., and Sklansky, J., Finding Circles by an Array of Accumulators, *Communications of the ACM*, **18**(2), pp 120-1222, 1975.

[Kiryati91] Kiryati, N., and Bruckstein, A. M., Antialiasing the Hough Transform, *CVGIP: Graphical Models and Image Processing*, **53**, pp 213-222, 1991.

[Lamdan88] Lamdan, Y., Schawatz, J., and Wolfon, H., Object Recognition by Affine Invariant Matching, *Proceedings of IEEE Conference on Computer Vision and Pattern Recognition*, pp 335-344, 1988.

[Leavers92] Leavers, V., *Shape Detection in Computer Vision Using the Hough Transform*, Springer-Verlag, London, 1992.

[Leavers93] Leavers, V., Which Hough Transform, *CVGIP: Image Understanding*, **58**, pp 250-264, 1993.

[Li86] Li, H., and Lavin, M. A., Fast Hough Transform: a Hierarchical Approach, *CVGIP*, **36**, pp 139-161, 1986.

[Lienhart03] Lienhart, R., Kuranov, A., and Pisarevsky, V., Empirical Analysis of Detection Cascades of Boosted Classifiers for Rapid Object Detection, *LNCS* **2781**, pp. 297–304, 2003.

[Lowe04] Lowe, D. G., Distinctive Image Features from Scale-Invariant Key Points, *International Journal of Computer Vision*, **60**(2), pp 91-110, 2004.

[Merlin75] Merlin, P. M., and Farber, D. J., A Parallel Mechanism for Detecting Curves in Pictures, *IEEE Transactions on Computers*, **24**, pp 96-98, 1975.

[Mikolajczyk05] Mikolajczyk, K., and Schmid, C., A Performance Evaluation of Local Descriptors, *IEEE Transactions on PAMI*, **27**(10), pp 1615- 1630, 2005.

[Milletari117] Milletari, F., Ahmadi, S.A., Kroll, C., Plate, A., Rozanski, V., Maiostre, J., Levin, J., Dietrich, O., Ertl-Wagner, B., Bötzel, K., and Navab, N., Hough-Cnn: Deep Learning for Segmentation of Deep Brain Regions in MRI and Ultrasound. *Computer Vision and Image Understanding*, **164**, pp 92-102, 2017.

[Mukherjee15] Mukherjee, D., Wu, Q. J., and Wang, G., A Comparative Experimental Study of Image Feature Detectors and Descriptors. *Machine Vision and Applications*, **26**(4), pp.443-466, 2015.

[Mukhopadhyay15] Mukhopadhyay, P., and Chaudhuri, B. B., A Survey of Hough Transform. *Pattern Recognition*, **48**(3), pp.993-1010, 2015.

[O'Gorman76] O'Gorman, F., and Clowes, M. B., Finding Picture Edges through Collinearity of Feature Points, *IEEE Transactions on Computers*, **25**(4), pp 449-456, 1976.

[Philip91] Philip, K. P., *Automatic Detection of Myocardial Contours in Cine Computed Tomographic Images*, PhD Thesis, Univ. Iowa USA, 1991.

[Princen89] Princen, J., Yuen, H. K., Illingworth, J., and Kittler, J., Properties of the Adaptive Hough Transform, In Proc. 6th Scandinavian Conf. On Image Analysis, Oulu Finland, June, 1992.

[Princen92] Princen, J., Illingworth, J., and Kittler, J., A Formal Definition of the Hough Transform: Properties and Relationships, *Journal of Mathematical Imaging and Vision*, **1**, pp153-168, 1992.

[Redmon16] Redmon, J., Divvala, S., Girshick, R., and Farhadi, A., You Only Look once: Unified, Real-Time Object Detection. *Proceedings of IEEE CVPR*, pp 779-788, 2016.

[Ren15] Ren, S., He, K., Girshick, R., and Sun, J., Faster r-cnn: Towards Real-Time Object Detection with Region Proposal Networks. *Proceedings of Advances in Neural Information Processing Systems* pp 91-99, 2015.

[Rosenfeld69] Rosenfeld, A., *Picture Processing by Computer*, Academic Press, London UK, 1969.

[Rublee11] Rublee, E., Rabaud, V., Konolige, K., and Bradski, G., ORB: An Efficient Alternative to SIFT or SURF, *Proceedings of ICCV*, pp 2564-2571, 2011.

[Schneiderman04] Schneiderman, H., and Kanade, T., Object Detection Using the Statistics of Parts, *International Journal of Computer Vision*, **56**(3), pp 151–177, 2004.

[Sivic03] Sivic, J., Zisserman, A., Video Google: A Text Retrieval Approach to Object Matching in Videos, *Proceedings of IEEE ICCV'03*, **2**, p.1470-1477, 2003.

[Sklansky78] Sklansky, J., On the Hough Technique for Curve Detection, *IEEE Transactions on Computers*, **27**, pp 923-926, 1978.

[Smeulders00] Smeulders, A. W. M., Worring, M., Santini, S., Gupta, A., and Jain, R., Content-Based Image Retrieval at the End of the Early Years, *IEEE Transactions on PAMI*, **22**(12), pp 1349-1378, 2000.

[Sonka94] Sonka, M., Hllavac, V., and Boyle, R, *Image Processing, Analysis and Computer Vision*, Chapman Hall, London, UK, 1994.

[Stockman77] Stockman, G. C., and Agrawala, A. K., Equivalence of Hough Curve Detection to Template Matching, *Communications of the ACM*, **20**, pp 820-822, 1977.

[Stockman87] Stockman, G., Object Recognition and Localization via Pose Clustering, *CVGIP*, **40**, pp361-387, 1987.

[Trier96] Trier, O. D., Jain, A. K., and Taxt, T., Feature Extraction Methods for Character Recognition – A Survey, *Pattern Recognition*, **29**(4), pp 641-662, 1996.

[Tuytelaars07] Tuytelaars, T., and Mikolajczyk, K., Local Invariant Feature Detectors: A Survey, *Foundations and Trends in Computer Graphics and Vision*, **3**(3), pp 177–280, 2007.

[Viola01] Viola, P., and Jones, M., Rapid Object Detection Using a Boosted Cascade of Simple Features, *Proceedings of IEEE Conference on Computer Vision and Pattern Recognition*, **1**, pp 511-519, 2001.

[Viola04] Viola, P., and Jones, M. J., Robust Real-Time Face Detection, *International Journal of Computer Vision*, **57**(2), 137–154, 2004.

[Yuen90] Yuen, H. K., Princen, J., Illingworth, J., and Kittler, J., Comparative Study of Hough Transform Methods for Circle Finding, *Image and Vision Computing*, **8**(1), pp 71-77, 1990.

[Xu90] Xu, L., Oja, E., and Kultanen, P., A New Curve Detection Method: Randomised Hough Transform, *Pattern Recognition Letters*, **11**, pp 331-338, 1990.

[Zhu06] Zhu, Q., Avidan, S., Yeh, M-C., and Cheng, K-T., Fast Human Detection Using a Cascade of Histograms of Oriented Gradients, *Proceedings of IEEE Conference on Computer Vision and Pattern Recognition*, **2**, pp 1491-1498, 2006.

[Zafeiriou15] Zafeiriou, S., Zhang, C., and Zhang, Z., A Survey on Face Detection in the Wild: Past, Present and Future. *CVIU*, **138**, pp 1-24, 2015.

[Zokai05] Zokai, S., and Wolberg G., Image Registration Using Log-Polar Mappings for Recovery of Large-Scale Similarity and Projective Transformations, *IEEE Transactions on IP*, **14**, pp 1422-1434, October 2005.

[Zheng18] Zheng, L., Yang, Y., and Tian, Q., SIFT Meets CNN: A Decade Survey of Instance Retrieval. *IEEE Transactions on PAMI*, **40**(5), pp.1224-1244, 2018.

6

High-level feature extraction: deformable shape analysis

6.1 Overview

The previous chapter covered finding shapes by matching. This implies knowledge of a model (mathematical or template) of the target shape (feature). The shape is fixed in that it is flexible only in terms of the parameters that define the shape, or the parameters that define a template's appearance. Sometimes, however, it is not possible to model a shape with sufficient accuracy, or to provide a template of the target as needed for the Generalised Hough Transform. It might be that the exact shape is unknown or it might be that the perturbation of that shape is impossible to parameterise. In this case, we seek techniques that can evolve to the target solution, or adapt their result to the data. This implies the use of flexible shape formulations. This chapter presents four techniques that can be used to find flexible shapes in images. These are summarised in Table 6.1 and can be distinguished by the matching functional used to indicate the extent of match between image data and a shape. If the shape is flexible or deformable, so as to match the image data, we have a *deformable template*. This is where we shall start. Later, we shall move to techniques that are called *snakes* because of their movement. We shall explain

Table 6.1 Overview of this chapter.

Main topic	Subtopics	Main points
Deformable templates	Template matching for deformable shapes. Defining a way to analyse the best match.	Energy maximisation, computational considerations, optimisation. *Parts-based* shape analysis.
Active contours and snakes	Finding shapes by evolving contours. Discrete and continuous formulations. Operational considerations and newer active contour approaches.	Energy minimisation for curve evolution. *Greedy* algorithm. *Kass snake*. Parameterisation; initialisation and performance. *Gradient Vector Field* and *Level Set* approaches.
Shape skeletonisation	Notions of distance, skeletons and symmetry and its measurement. Application of symmetry detection by evidence gathering. Performance factors.	*Distance transform* and shape skeleton; *medial axis transform. Discrete symmetry operator*. Accumulating evidence of symmetrical point arrangements. Performance: speed and noise.
Active shape models	Expressing shape variation by statistics. Capturing shape variation within feature extraction.	*Active shape model. Active appearance* model. *Principal component* analysis.

Feature Extraction and Image Processing for Computer Vision. https://doi.org/10.1016/B978-0-12-814976-8.00006-3

two different implementations of the snake model. The first one is based on discrete minimisation, and the second one on finite element analysis. We shall also look at determining a shape's skeleton, by *distance* analysis and by the *symmetry* of their appearance. This technique finds any symmetric shape by gathering evidence by considering features between pairs of points. Finally, we shall consider approaches that use of the statistics of a shape's possible appearance to control selection of the final shape, called *active shape models.*

6.2 Deformable shape analysis

6.2.1 Deformable templates

One of the earlier approaches to deformable template analysis [Yuille91] was aimed to find facial features for purposes of recognition. The approach considered an eye to be comprised of an iris which sits within the sclera and which can be modelled as a combination of a circle that lies within a parabola. Clearly, the circle and a version of the parabola can be extracted by using Hough transform techniques, but this cannot be achieved in combination. When we combine the two shapes and allow them to change in size and orientation, whilst retaining their spatial relationship (that the iris or circle should reside within the sclera or parabola), then we have a deformable template.

The parabola is a shape described by a set of points (x,y) related by

$$y = a - \frac{a}{b^2}x^2 \tag{6.1}$$

where, as illustrated in Fig. 6.1A, a is the height of the parabola and b is its radius. As such, the maximum height is a and the minimum height is zero. A similar equation describes the lower parabola, it terms of b and c. The 'centre' of both parabolae is $\mathbf{c}_p$. The circle is as defined earlier, with centre co-ordinates $\mathbf{c}_c$ and radius r. We then seek values of the parameters which give a best match of this template to the image data. Clearly, one match we would like to make concerns matching the edge data to that of the

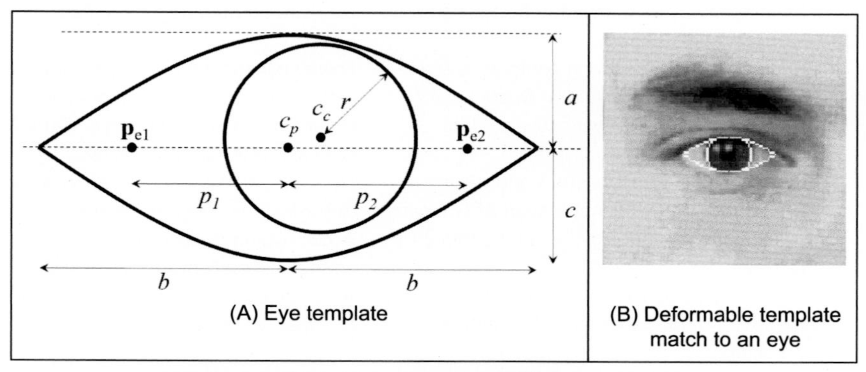

FIGURE 6.1 Finding an eye with a deformable template.

template, like in the Hough transform. The set of values for the parameters which give a template which matches the most edge points (since edge points are found at the boundaries of features) could then be deemed to be the best set of parameters describing the eye in an image. We then seek values of parameters that maximise

$$\{\mathbf{c}_p, a, b, c, \mathbf{c}_c, r\} = \max\left(\sum_{x,y \in \text{circle.perimeter,parabolae.perimeter}} \mathbf{E}_{x,y}\right) \tag{6.2}$$

Naturally, this would prefer the larger shape to the smaller ones, so we could divide the contribution of the circle and the parabolae by their perimeter to give an edge energy contribution E_e

$$E_e = \sum_{x,y \in \text{circle.perimeter}} \mathbf{E}_{x,y} \Big/ \text{circle.perimeter} + \sum_{x,y \in \text{parabolae.perimeter}} \mathbf{E}_{x,y} \Big/ \text{parabolae.perimeter} \tag{6.3}$$

and we seek a combination of values for the parameters $\{\mathbf{c}_p, a, b, c, \mathbf{c}_c, r\}$ which maximise this energy. This, however, implies little knowledge of the structure of the eye. Since we know that the sclera is white (usually ...) and the iris is darker than it, then we could build this information into the process. We can form an energy E_v functional for the circular region which averages the brightness over the circle area as

$$E_v = -\sum_{x,y \in \text{circle}} \mathbf{P}_{x,y} \Big/ \text{circle.area} \tag{6.4}$$

This is formed in the negative, since maximising its value gives the best set of parameters. Similarly, we can form an energy functional for the light regions where the eye is white as E_p

$$E_p = \sum_{x,y \in \text{parabolae}-\text{circle}} \mathbf{P}_{x,y} \Big/ \text{parabolae} - \text{circle.area} \tag{6.5}$$

where parabolae-circle implies points within the parabolae but not within the circle. We can then choose a set of parameters which maximise the combined energy functional formed by adding each energy when weighted by some chosen factors as

$$E = c_e \cdot E_e + c_v \cdot E_v + c_p \cdot E_p \tag{6.6}$$

where c_e, c_v and c_p are the weighting factors. In this way, we are choosing values for the parameters which simultaneously maximise the chance that the edges of the circle and the perimeter coincide with the image edges, that the inside of the circle is dark and that the inside of the parabolae is light. The value chosen for each of the weighting factors controls the influence of that factor on the eventual result.

The energy fields are shown in Fig. 6.2 when computed over the entire image [Benn99]. Naturally, the valley image shows up regions with low image intensity and the peak image shows regions of high image intensity, like the whites of the eyes. In its

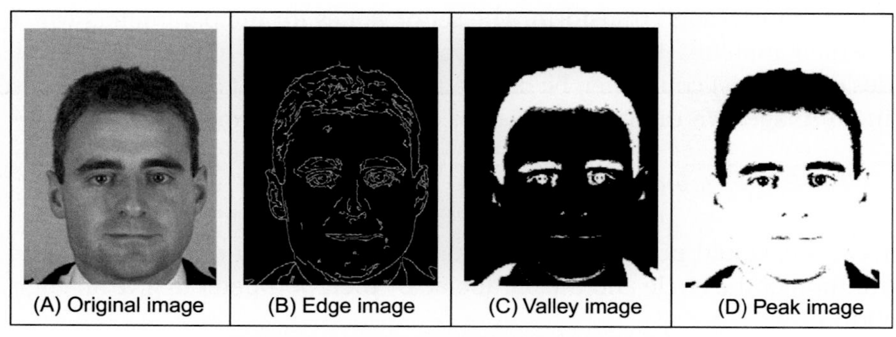

FIGURE 6.2 Energy fields over whole face image.

original formulation, this approach actually had five energy terms, and the extra two are associated with the points $\mathbf{p}_{e1}$ and $\mathbf{p}_{e2}$ on either side of the iris in Fig. 6.1A.

This is where the problem starts, as we now have 11 parameters (eight for the shapes and three for the weighting coefficients). We could of course simply cycle through every possible value. Given, say, 100 possible values for each parameter, we then have to search 10^{22} combinations of parameters which would be no problem given multithread computers with Terra Hz processing speed achieved via optical interconnect, but computers like that are not ready yet (on our budgets at least). Naturally, we can reduce the number of combinations by introducing constraints on the relative size and position of the shapes, e.g. the circle should lie wholly within the parabolae, but this will not reduce the number of combinations much. We can seek two alternatives: one is to use *optimisation* techniques. The original approach [Yuille91] favoured the use of gradient descent techniques; currently, the *genetic algorithm* approach [Goldberg88] seems to be the most favoured in many approaches which use optimisation, and this was shown to good effect for deformable template eye extraction on a database of 1000 faces [Benn99] (this is the source of the images shown here).

6.2.2 Parts-based shape analysis

A more advanced class of approaches is called '*parts-based*' object analysis: rather than characterising an object by a single feature (as in the previous chapter) objects are represented as a collection of parts arranged in a deformable structure. This follows an approach which predates the previous template approach [Fischler73]. Essentially, objects can be modelled as a network of masses which are connected by springs. This is illustrated in Fig. 6.3A where, for a face, the two upper masses could represent the eyes and the lower mass could represent the mouth. The springs then constrain the mouth to be beneath and between the eyes. The springs add context to the position of the shape; the springs control the relationships between the objects and allow the object parts to move relative to one another. The extraction of the representation is then a compromise between the match of the features (the masses) to the image and the inter-relationships

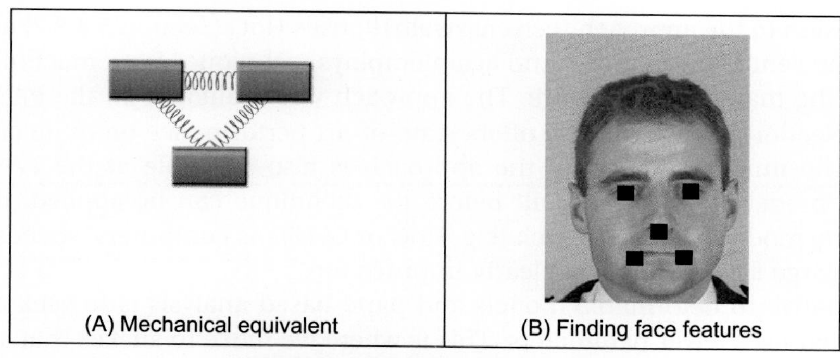

FIGURE 6.3 Parts-based shape model.

(the springs) between the locations of the features. A result by a later technique is shown in Fig. 6.3B which shows that the three mass models of face features can be extended to one with five parts (in a star arrangement), and the image shows the best fit of this arrangement to an image containing a face.

Let us suggest that we have n parts (in Fig. 6.3 $n=3$) and $m_i(l_i)$ represents the difference from the image data when each feature f_i (f_1, f_2 and f_3 in Fig. 6.3) is placed at location l_i. The features can differ in relative position, and so a measure of the misplacement within the configuration (by how much the springs extend) can be a function $d_{ij}(l_i,l_j)$ which measures the degree of deformation when features f_i and f_j are placed at location l_i and l_j, respectively. The best match L^* of the model to the image is then

$$L^* = \arg\left[\min\left(\sum_{i=1}^{N} m_i(l_i) + \sum_{f_i,f_j \in \Re} d_{ij}(l_i,l_j)\right)\right] \tag{6.7}$$

These components can be weighted, thus the optimisation is the form of Eq. (6.6). The parameters thus derived are those which are the best compromise between the positions of the parts and the deformation. Determining these parameters is computationally very challenging, as it was for deformable templates. In the earliest approach, the optimisation strategy was dynamic programming (the Viterbi algorithm). (It's fantastic that they even tried. In 1973, computers had the computational power of a modern doorbell, and perhaps the same amount of memory – in the paper the resulting images are by character printing!) Minimisation has been phrased as a statistical problem, and the solution requires structure to be imposed on the models in order that an efficient solution is achieved [Felzenszwalb05]. In this way, machine learning approaches are used to learn – or train – from examples of the target structures, and these models are then applied in an efficient manner by these methods. The method was demonstrated in its earliest forms capable of determining facial features in images, as shown in Fig. 6.3B, and of locating the human body by representing it as a set of interconnected parts.

An extension to the approach [Felzenszwalb10] uses HoG (Section 5.4.2.2) at different scales to represent spatial models and again employs techniques from machine learning to improve the matching procedure. The approach was evaluated on the PASCAL VOC Challenge (Section 5.6) and clearly offers state-of-art performance on quite challenging data sets. The implementation of the approach is also available at the PASCAL site. Arguably, a model needs to be built before the technique can be applied, but that is central to any model-based approach (e.g. HoG or GHT). As computers' speeds increase, training on large sets of data will clearly improve too.

An alternative to deformable models and parts-based analysis is to seek a different technique that uses fewer parameters. This is where we move to snakes that are a more popular approach. These snakes evolve a set of points (a contour) to match the image data, rather than evolving a shape.

6.3 Active contours (snakes)

6.3.1 Basics

Active contours or *snakes* [Kass88] are a completely different approach to feature extraction. An active contour is a set of points which aims to enclose a target feature, the feature to be extracted. It is a bit like using a balloon to 'find' a shape: the balloon is placed outside the shape, enclosing it. Then by taking air out of the balloon, making it smaller, the shape is found when the balloon stops shrinking, when it fits the target shape. By this manner, active contours arrange a set of points so as to describe a target feature, by enclosing it. Snakes' original formulation was as an interactive extraction process, though they are now usually deployed for automatic feature extraction.

An initial contour is placed outside the target feature and is then evolved so as to enclose it. The process is illustrated in Fig. 6.4 where the target feature is the perimeter of the iris. First, an initial contour is placed outside the iris, Fig. 6.4A. The contour is then minimised to find a new contour which shrinks so as to be closer to the iris, Fig. 6.4B. After a number of iterations, the contour points can be seen to match the iris perimeter well, Fig. 6.4D.

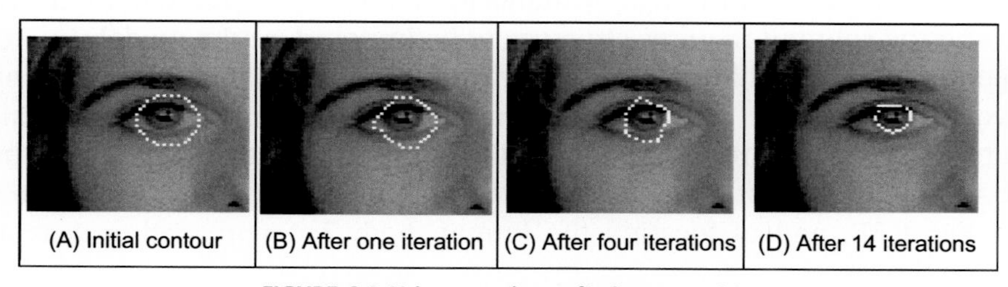
(A) Initial contour (B) After one iteration (C) After four iterations (D) After 14 iterations

FIGURE 6.4 Using a snake to find an eye's iris.

Active contours are actually expressed as an energy minimisation process. The target feature is a minimum of a suitably formulated energy functional. This energy functional includes more than just edge information: it includes properties that control the way the contour can stretch and curve. In this way, a snake represents a compromise between its own properties (like its ability to bend and stretch) and image properties (like the edge magnitude). Accordingly, the energy functional is the addition of a function of the contour's internal energy, its constraint energy, and the image energy: these are denoted E_{int}, E_{con} and E_{image}, respectively. These are functions of the set of points which make up a snake, $\mathbf{v}(s)$, which is the set of x and y coordinates of the points in the snake. The energy functional is the integral of these functions of the snake, given $s \in [0,1)$ is the normalised length around the snake. The energy functional E_{snake} is then

$$E_{snake} = \int_{s=0}^{1} E_{\text{int}}(\mathbf{v}(s)) + E_{image}(\mathbf{v}(s)) + E_{con}(\mathbf{v}(s))ds \tag{6.8}$$

In this equation: the internal energy, E_{int}, controls the natural behaviour of the snake and hence the arrangement of the snake points; the image energy, E_{image}, attracts the snake to chosen low-level features (such as edge points) and the constraint energy, E_{con}, allows higher level information to control the snake's evolution. The aim of the snake is to evolve by minimising Eq. (6.8). New snake contours are those with lower energy and are a better match to the target feature (according to the values of E_{int}, E_{image} and E_{con}) than the original set of points from which the active contour has evolved. In this manner, we seek to choose a set of points $\mathbf{v}(s)$ such that

$$\frac{dE_{snake}}{d\mathbf{v}(s)} = 0 \tag{6.9}$$

This can of course select a maximum rather than a minimum, and a second order derivative can be used to discriminate between a maximum and a minimum. However, this is not usually necessary as a minimum is usually the only stable solution (on reaching a maximum, it would then be likely to pass over the top to then minimise the energy). Prior to investigating how we can minimise Eq. (6.8), let us first consider the parameters which can control a snake's behaviour.

The energy functionals are expressed in terms of functions of the snake, and of the image. These functions contribute to the snake energy according to values chosen for respective weighting coefficients. In this manner, the internal image energy is defined to be a weighted summation of first- and second-order derivatives around the contour.

$$E_{int} = \alpha(s)\left|\frac{d\mathbf{v}(s)}{ds}\right|^2 + \beta(s)\left|\frac{d^2\mathbf{v}(s)}{ds^2}\right|^2 \tag{6.10}$$

The first-order differential, $d\mathbf{v}(s)/ds$, measures the energy due to stretching which is the elastic energy since high values of this differential imply a high rate of change in that region of the contour. The second-order differential, $d^2\mathbf{v}(s)/ds^2$, measures the energy due to bending, the curvature energy. The first-order differential is weighted by $\alpha(s)$ which controls the contribution of the elastic energy due to point spacing; the second-order differential is weighted by $\beta(s)$ which controls the contribution of the curvature energy due to point variation. Choice of the values of α and β controls the shape the snake aims to attain. Low values for α imply the points can change in spacing greatly, whereas higher values imply that the snake aims to attain evenly spaced contour points. Low values for β imply that curvature is not minimised and the contour can form corners in its perimeter, whereas high values predispose the snake to smooth contours. These are the properties of the contour itself, which is just part of a snake's compromise between its own properties and measured features in an image.

The image energy attracts the snake to low-level features, such as brightness or edge data, aiming to select those with least contribution. The original formulation suggested that lines, edges and terminations could contribute to the energy function. Their energy is denoted E_{line}, E_{edge} and E_{term}, respectively, and are controlled by weighting coefficients w_{line}, w_{edge} and w_{term}, respectively. The image energy is then

$$E_{image} = w_{line}E_{line} + w_{edge}E_{edge} + w_{term}E_{term} \tag{6.11}$$

The line energy can be set to the image intensity at a particular point. If black has a lower value than white, then the snake will be extracted to dark features. Altering the sign of w_{line} will attract the snake to brighter features. The edge energy can be that computed by application of an edge detection operator, the magnitude, say, of the output of the Sobel edge detection operator. The termination energy, E_{term} as measured by Eq. (4.52), can include the curvature of level image contours (as opposed to the curvature of the snake, controlled by $\beta(s)$), but this is rarely used. It is most common to use the edge energy, though the line energy can find application.

6.3.2 The Greedy Algorithm for snakes

The implementation of a snake, to evolve a set of points to minimise Eq. (6.8), can use finite elements, or finite differences, which is complicated and follows later. It is easier to start with the *Greedy algorithm* [Williams92] which implements the energy minimisation process as a purely discrete algorithm, illustrated in Fig. 6.5. The process starts by specifying an initial contour. Earlier, Fig. 6.4A used points along the perimeter of a circle. Alternatively, these can be specified interactively. The Greedy algorithm then evolves the snake in an iterative manner by local neighbourhood search around contour points to select new ones which have lower snake energy. The process is called Greedy by virtue of the way the search propagates around the contour. At each iteration, all contour points are evolved and the process is actually repeated for the first contour point. The index to snake points is computed modulo S (the number of snake points).

For a set of snake points $\mathbf{v}_s, \quad \forall s \in 0, S-1$, the energy functional minimised for each snake point is

$$E_{snake}(s) = E_{int}(\mathbf{v}_s) + E_{image}(\mathbf{v}_s) \tag{6.12}$$

This is expressed as

$$E_{snake}(s) = \alpha(s)\left|\frac{d\mathbf{v}_s}{ds}\right|^2 + \beta(s)\left|\frac{d^2\mathbf{v}_s}{ds^2}\right|^2 + \gamma(s)E_{edge} \tag{6.13}$$

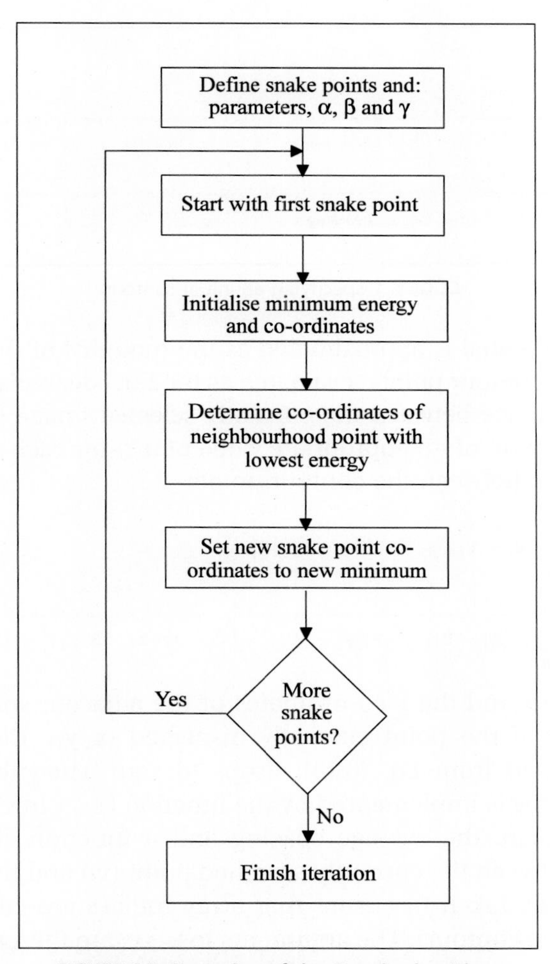

FIGURE 6.5 Operation of the Greedy algorithm.

where the first-order and second-order differentials are approximated for each point searched in the local neighbourhood of the currently selected contour point. The weighting parameters, α, β and γ are all functions of the contour. Accordingly, each contour point has associated values for α, β and γ. An implementation of the specification of an initial contour by a function `points` is given in Code 6.1. In this implementation, the contour is stored as a matrix of vectors, in a cell array (allowing different types of data). Each vector has five elements: two are the x and y co-ordinates of the contour point, the remaining three parameters are the values of α, β and γ for that contour point, all set here to 0.5. The `no` contour points are arranged to be in a circle, radius `rad` and centre `(xc,yc)`. As such, a vector is returned for each snake point, `contour`, where `contour{s,1}`, `contour{s,2}`, `contour{s,3}`, `contour{s,4}`, `contour{s,5}` are the x co-ordinate, the y co-ordinate and α, β and γ for the particular snake point s: $\mathbf{x}_s$, $\mathbf{y}_s$, α_s, β_s, and γ_s, respectively.

```
function contour = points(rad,no,xc,yc)

for s = 1:no %address all points
    x=floor(xc+rad*cos(s*2*pi/no)+0.5);
    y=floor(yc+rad*sin(s*2*pi/no)+0.5);
    alpha=0.5;
    beta=0.5;
    gamma=0.5;
    contour(s,1:5)={x,y,alpha,beta,gamma};
end
```

CODE 6.1 Specifying an initial contour.

The first-order differential is approximated as the modulus of the difference between the average spacing of contour points (evaluated as the Euclidean distance between them) and the Euclidean distance between the currently selected image point $\mathbf{v}_s$ and the next contour point. By selection of an appropriate value of $\alpha(s)$ for each contour point $\mathbf{v}_s$, this can control the spacing between the contour points

$$\begin{aligned}\left|\frac{d\mathbf{v}_s}{ds}\right|^2 &= \left|\sum_{i=0}^{S-1}\|\mathbf{v}_i-\mathbf{v}_{i+1}\|/S-\|\mathbf{v}_s-\mathbf{v}_{s+1}\|\right| \\ &= \left|\sum_{i=0}^{S-1}\sqrt{(\mathbf{x}_i-\mathbf{x}_{i+1})^2+(\mathbf{y}_i-\mathbf{y}_{i+1})^2}\Big/S-\sqrt{(\mathbf{x}_s-\mathbf{x}_{s+1})^2+(\mathbf{y}_s-\mathbf{y}_{s+1})^2}\right|\end{aligned} \tag{6.14}$$

as evaluated from the x and the y co-ordinates of the adjacent snake point ($\mathbf{x}_{s+1}$, $\mathbf{y}_{s+1}$) and the co-ordinates of the point currently inspected ($\mathbf{x}_s$,$\mathbf{y}_s$). Clearly, the first-order differential, as evaluated from Eq. (6.14), drops to zero when the contour is evenly spaced, as required. This is implemented by the function `Econt` in Code 6.2 which uses a function `dist` to evaluate the average spacing and a function `dist2` to evaluate the Euclidean distance between the currently searched point ($\mathbf{v}_s$) and the next contour point ($\mathbf{v}_{s+1}$) (care needs to be taken to ensure that array indices are computed modulo the number of points in the contour). The arguments to `Econt` are the x and y co-ordinates of the point currently being inspected, `x` and `y`, the index of the contour point currently under consideration, `s`, and the contour itself, `contour`.

```
function dist = dist(s,contour)
dist=sqrt((contour{s,1}-contour{s2,1})^2+(contour{s,2}-contour{s2,2})^2);

function dist2 = dist2(x,y,s,contour)
dist2=sqrt((x-contour{s2,1})^2+(y-contour{s2,2})^2);

function contour_energy= Econt(x,y,s,contour)
[rowsc,colsc]=size(contour);
sum=0;
for i=1:rowsc
   sum=sum+dist(i,contour); %sum up distances
end
D=sum/rowsc; %normalise
contour_energy=abs(D-dist2(x,y,s,contour)); %and return difference
```

CODE 6.2 Evaluating the contour energy.

```
function curvature_energy= Ecur(x,y,s,contour)

curvature_energy=(contour{s1,1}-2*x+contour{s2,1})^2+...
                 (contour{s1,2}-2*y+contour{s2,2})^2; %and return
```

CODE 6.3 Evaluating the contour curvature.

The second-order differential can be implemented as an estimate of the curvature between the next and previous contour points, $\mathbf{v}_{s+1}$ and $\mathbf{v}_{s-1}$, respectively, and the point in the local neighbourhood of the currently inspected snake point $\mathbf{v}_s$

$$\begin{aligned} \left|\frac{d^2\mathbf{v}_s}{ds^2}\right|^2 &= |(\mathbf{v}_{s+1} - 2\mathbf{v}_s + \mathbf{v}_{s-1})|^2 \\ &= (\mathbf{x}_{s+1} - 2\mathbf{x}_s + \mathbf{x}_{s-1})^2 + (\mathbf{y}_{s+1} - 2\mathbf{y}_s + \mathbf{y}_{s-1})^2 \end{aligned} \tag{6.15}$$

This is implemented by a function `Ecur` in Code 6.3, whose arguments again are the x and y co-ordinates of the point currently being inspected, `x` and `y`, the index of the contour point currently under consideration, `s`, and the contour itself, `contour`.

E_{edge} can be implemented as the magnitude of the Sobel edge operator at point x,y. This is normalised to ensure that its value lies between zero and unity. This is also performed for the elastic and curvature energies in the current region of interest. This is achieved by normalisation using Eq. (3.2) arranged to provide an output ranging between 0 and 1. The edge image could also be normalised within the current window of interest, but this makes it more possible that the result is influenced by noise. Since the snake is arranged to be a minimisation process, the edge image is inverted so that the points with highest edge strength are given the lowest edge value (0), whereas the areas where the image is constant are given a high value (1). Accordingly, the snake will be attracted to the edge points with greatest magnitude. The normalisation process ensures that the contour energy and curvature and the edge strength are balanced forces and eases appropriate selection of values for α, β and γ. This is achieved by a balancing function (`balanceforces`) that normalises the contour and curvature energy within the window of interest.

The Greedy algorithm then uses these energy functionals to minimise the composite energy functional, Eq. (6.13), given in the function `grdy` in Code 6.4. This gives a single iteration in the evolution of a contour wherein all snake points are searched. The energy for each snake point is first determined and is stored as the point with minimum energy. This ensures that if any other point is found to have equally small energy, then the contour point will remain in the same position. Then, the local 3×3 neighbourhood is searched to determine whether any other point has a lower energy than the current contour point. If it does, that point is returned as the new contour point.

A verbatim implementation of the Greedy algorithm would include three thresholds. One is a threshold on tangential direction and another on edge magnitude. If an edge point were adjudged to be of direction above the chosen threshold, and with magnitude above its corresponding threshold, then β can be set to zero for that point to allow corners to form. This has not been included in Code 6.4, in part because there is mutual dependence between α and β. Also, the original presentation of the Greedy algorithm

```
function contour= grdy(edg,contour)

[rowsc,colsc]=size(contour);
[rows,cols]=size(edg);
for s=1:rowsc %consider all points
    xmin=contour{s,1}; %initialise minimum values
    ymin=contour{s,2};
    forces=balanceforces(xmin,ymin,edg,s,contour); %balance all forces
    %evaluate intitial minimum
    Emin=contour{s,3}*Econt(xmin,ymin,s,contour)+...
         contour{s,4}*Ecur(xmin,ymin,s,contour)+...
         contour{s,5}*edg(ymin,xmin);
    for x=contour{s,1}-1:contour{s,1}+1 %look around current contour point
        for y=contour{s,2}-1:contour{s,2}+1
            if ((x<cols+1)&&(x>1))&&((y<rows+1)&&(y>1))
                xx=x-contour{s,1}+2; %need to start from 1
                yy=y-contour{s,2}+2; %since local energies are [1:3,1:3]
                %now evaluate energy
                Ej=contour{s,3}*forces(yy,xx,1)+...
                   contour{s,4}*forces(yy,xx,2)+...
                   contour{s,5}*edg(y,x);
                if Ej<Emin %is it a new minimum?
                    Emin=Ej; %store it
                    xmin=x;
                    ymin=y;
                end
            end
        end
    end
    %store minimum as new contour point
    contour(s,1:5)={xmin,ymin,contour{s,3},contour{s,4},contour{s,5}};
end
```

CODE 6.4 The Greedy algorithm.

proposed to continue evolving the snake until it becomes static, when the number of contour points moved in a single iteration is below the third threshold value. This can lead to instability since it can lead to a situation where contour points merely oscillate between two solutions and the process would appear not to converge. Again, this has not been controlled here.

The effect of varying α and β is shown in Figs 6.6 and 6.7. Lower values of α reduce the influence of spacing on the contour points' arrangement. In this manner, the points will become to be unevenly spaced, Fig. 6.6B, and eventually can be placed on top of each other. Reducing the control by spacing can be desirable for features that have high localised curvature. Low values of α can allow for bunching of points in such regions, giving a better feature description.

Lower values of β reduce the influence of curvature on the contour points' arrangement, allowing corners to form in the contour, as illustrated in Fig. 6.7. This is manifested in the first iteration, Fig. 6.7B, and since with β set to zero for the whole contour, each contour point can become a corner with high curvature, Fig. 6.7C, leading to the rather ridiculous result in Fig. 6.7D. Reducing the control by curvature can clearly be desirable for features that have high localised curvature. This illustrates the mutual dependence between α and β, since low values of α can accompany low values of β in regions of high localised curvature. Setting γ to zero would force the snake to ignore image data and evolve under its own forces. This would be rather farcical. The influence

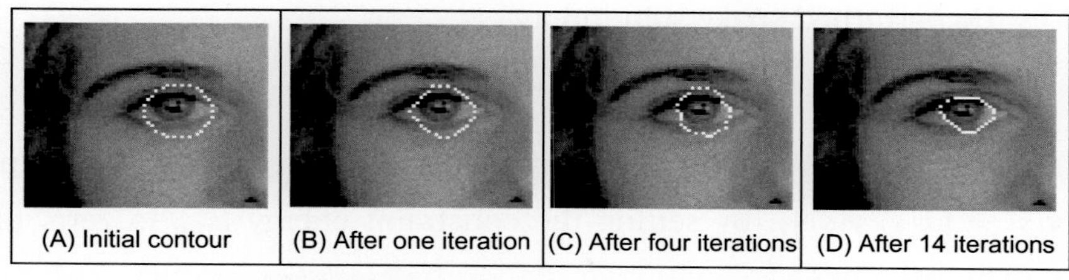

FIGURE6.6 Effect of removing control by spacing.

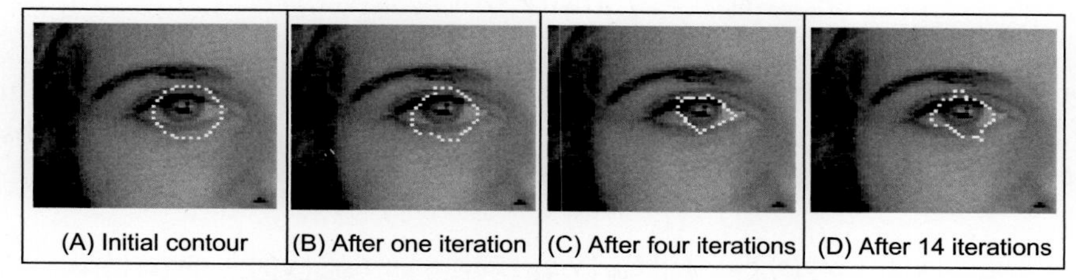

FIGURE 6.7 Effect of removing low curvature control.

of γ is reduced in applications where the image data used are known to be noisy. Note that one fundamental problem with a discrete version is that the final solution can oscillate when it swaps between two sets of points which are both with equally low energy. This can be prevented by detecting the occurrence of oscillation. A further difficulty is that as the contour becomes smaller, the number of contour points actually constrains the result as they cannot be compressed into too small a space. The only solution to this is to resample the contour.

6.3.3 Complete (Kass) Snake implementation

The Greedy method iterates around the snake to find local minimum energy at snake points. This is an approximation, since it does not necessarily determine the 'best' local minimum in the region of the snake points, by virtue of iteration. A *complete snake implementation,* or *Kass snake,* solves for all snake points in one step to ensure that the snake moves to the best local energy minimum. We seek to choose snake points ($\mathbf{v}(s)=(\mathbf{x}(s),\mathbf{y}(s))$) in such a manner that the energy is minimised, Eq. (6.9). Calculus of variations shows how the solution to Eq. (6.8) reduces to a pair of differential equations that can be solved by finite difference analysis [Waite90]. This results in a set of equations that iteratively provide new sets of contour points. By calculus of variation, we shall consider an admissible solution $\hat{\mathbf{v}}(s)$ perturbed by a small amount, $\varepsilon\delta\mathbf{v}(s)$, which achieves minimum energy, as

$$\frac{dE_{snake}\left(\hat{\mathbf{v}}(s)+\varepsilon\delta\mathbf{v}(s)\right)}{d\varepsilon}=0 \tag{6.16}$$

where the perturbation is spatial, affecting the x and y co-ordinates of a snake point

$$\delta\mathbf{v}(s)=(\delta_x(s),\delta_y(s)) \tag{6.17}$$

This gives the perturbed snake solution as

$$\hat{\mathbf{v}}(s)+\varepsilon\delta\mathbf{v}(s)=\left(\hat{x}(s)+\varepsilon\delta_x(s),\hat{y}(s)+\varepsilon\delta_y(s)\right) \tag{6.18}$$

where $\hat{x}(s)$ and $\hat{y}(s)$ are the x and y co-ordinates, respectively, of the snake points at the solution ($\hat{\mathbf{v}}(s)=\left(\hat{x}(s),\hat{y}(s)\right)$). By setting the constraint energy E_{con} to zero, the snake energy, Eq. (6.8), becomes

$$E_{snake}(\mathbf{v}(s))=\int_{s=0}^{1}\{E_{int}(\mathbf{v}(s))+E_{image}(\mathbf{v}(s))\}ds \tag{6.19}$$

Edge magnitude information is often used (so that snakes are attracted to edges found by an edge detection operator), so we shall replace E_{image} by E_{edge}. By substitution for the perturbed snake points, we obtain

$$E_{snake}\left(\hat{\mathbf{v}}(s)+\varepsilon\delta\mathbf{v}(s)\right)=\int_{s=0}^{1}\left\{E_{int}\left(\hat{\mathbf{v}}(s)+\varepsilon\delta\mathbf{v}(s)\right)+E_{edge}\left(\hat{\mathbf{v}}(s)+\varepsilon\delta\mathbf{v}(s)\right)\right\}ds \tag{6.20}$$

By substitution from Eq. (6.10), we obtain

$$E_{snake}\left(\hat{\mathbf{v}}(s)+\varepsilon\delta\mathbf{v}(s)\right)=$$
$$\int_{s=0}^{s=1}\left\{\alpha(s)\left|\frac{d\left(\hat{\mathbf{v}}(s)+\varepsilon\delta\mathbf{v}(s)\right)}{ds}\right|^2+\beta(s)\left|\frac{d^2\left(\hat{\mathbf{v}}(s)+\varepsilon\delta\mathbf{v}(s)\right)}{ds^2}\right|^2+E_{edge}\left(\hat{\mathbf{v}}(s)+\varepsilon\delta\mathbf{v}(s)\right)\right\}ds \tag{6.21}$$

By substitution from Eq. (6.18),

$$E_{snake}(\hat{\mathbf{v}}(s)+\varepsilon\delta\mathbf{v}(s))=$$
$$\int_{s=0}^{s=1}\left\{\begin{array}{l}\alpha(s)\left\{\begin{array}{l}\left(\frac{d\hat{x}(s)}{ds}\right)^2+2\varepsilon\frac{d\hat{x}(s)}{ds}\frac{d\delta_x(s)}{ds}+\left(\varepsilon\frac{d\delta_x(s)}{ds}\right)^2+\\ \left(\frac{d\hat{y}(s)}{ds}\right)^2+2\varepsilon\frac{d\hat{y}(s)}{ds}\frac{d\delta_y(s)}{ds}+\left(\varepsilon\frac{d\delta_y(s)}{ds}\right)^2\end{array}\right\}+\\ \beta(s)\left\{\begin{array}{l}\left(\frac{d^2\hat{x}(s)}{ds^2}\right)^2+2\varepsilon\frac{d^2\hat{x}(s)}{ds^2}\frac{d^2\delta_x(s)}{ds^2}+\left(\varepsilon\frac{d^2\delta_x(s)}{ds^2}\right)^2+\\ \left(\frac{d^2\hat{y}(s)}{ds^2}\right)^2+2\varepsilon\frac{d^2\hat{y}(s)}{ds^2}\frac{d^2\delta_y(s)}{ds^2}+\left(\varepsilon\frac{d^2\delta_y(s)}{ds^2}\right)^2\end{array}\right\}\\ +E_{edge}(\hat{\mathbf{v}}(s)+\varepsilon\delta\mathbf{v}(s))\end{array}\right\}ds \tag{6.22}$$

By expanding E_{edge} at the perturbed solution by Taylor series, we obtain

$$\begin{aligned} E_{edge}\left(\hat{\mathbf{v}}(s)+\varepsilon\delta\mathbf{v}(s)\right) &= E_{edge}\left(\hat{x}(s)+\varepsilon\delta_x(s),\hat{y}(s)+\varepsilon\delta_y(s)\right) \\ &= E_{edge}\left(\hat{x}(s),\hat{y}(s)\right)+\varepsilon\delta_x(s)\left.\frac{\partial E_{edge}}{\partial x}\right|_{\hat{x},\hat{y}}+\varepsilon\delta_y(s)\left.\frac{\partial E_{edge}}{\partial y}\right|_{\hat{x},\hat{y}}+O(\varepsilon^2) \end{aligned} \tag{6.23}$$

This implies that the image information must be twice differentiable which holds for edge information, but not for some other forms of image energy. Ignoring higher order terms in ε (since ε is small), by reformulation, Eq. (6.22) becomes

$$\begin{aligned} &E_{snake}\left(\hat{\mathbf{v}}(s)+\varepsilon\delta\mathbf{v}(s)\right)=E_{snake}\left(\hat{\mathbf{v}}(s)\right)+ \\ &2\varepsilon\int_{s=0}^{s=1}\alpha(s)\frac{d\hat{x}(s)}{ds}\frac{d\delta_x(s)}{ds}+\beta(s)\frac{d^2\hat{x}(s)}{ds^2}\frac{d^2\delta_x(s)}{ds^2}+\frac{\delta_x(s)}{2}\left.\frac{\partial E_{edge}}{\partial x}\right|_{\hat{x},\hat{y}}ds+ \\ &2\varepsilon\int_{s=0}^{s=1}\alpha(s)\frac{d\hat{y}(s)}{ds}\frac{d\delta_y(s)}{ds}+\beta(s)\frac{d^2\hat{y}(s)}{ds^2}\frac{d^2\delta_y(s)}{ds^2}+\frac{\delta_y(s)}{2}\left.\frac{\partial E_{edge}}{\partial y}\right|_{\hat{x},\hat{y}}ds \end{aligned} \tag{6.24}$$

Since the perturbed solution is at a minimum, the integration terms in Eq. (6.24) must be identically zero

$$\int_{s=0}^{s=1}\alpha(s)\frac{d\hat{x}(s)}{ds}\frac{d\delta_x(s)}{ds}+\beta(s)\frac{d^2\hat{x}(s)}{ds^2}\frac{d^2\delta_x(s)}{ds^2}+\frac{\delta_x(s)}{2}\left.\frac{\partial E_{edge}}{\partial x}\right|_{\hat{x},\hat{y}}ds=0 \tag{6.25}$$

$$\int_{s=0}^{s=1}\alpha(s)\frac{d\hat{y}(s)}{ds}\frac{d\delta_y(s)}{ds}+\beta(s)\frac{d^2\hat{y}(s)}{ds^2}\frac{d^2\delta_y(s)}{ds^2}+\frac{\delta_y(s)}{2}\left.\frac{\partial E_{edge}}{\partial y}\right|_{\hat{x},\hat{y}}ds=0 \tag{6.26}$$

By integration we obtain

$$\begin{aligned} &\left[\alpha(s)\frac{d\hat{x}(s)}{ds}\delta_x(s)\right]_{s=0}^{1}-\int_{s=0}^{s=1}\frac{d}{ds}\left\{\alpha(s)\frac{d\hat{x}(s)}{ds}\right\}\delta_x(s)ds \\ &\left[\beta(s)\frac{d^2\hat{x}(s)}{ds^2}\frac{d\delta_x(s)}{ds}\right]_{s=0}^{1}-\left[\frac{d}{ds}\left\{\beta(s)\frac{d^2\hat{x}(s)}{ds^2}\right\}\delta_x(s)\right]_{s=0}^{1} \\ &+\int_{s=0}^{s=1}\frac{d^2}{ds^2}\left\{\beta(s)\frac{d^2\hat{x}(s)}{ds^2}\right\}\delta_x(s)ds+\frac{1}{2}\int_{s=0}^{1}\left.\frac{\partial E_{edge}}{\partial x}\right|_{\hat{x},\hat{y}}\delta_x(s)ds=0 \end{aligned} \tag{6.27}$$

Since the first, third and fourth terms are zero (since for a closed contour, $\delta_x(1)-\delta_x(0)=0$ and $\delta_y(1)-\delta_y(0)=0$), this reduces to

$$\int_{s=0}^{s=1}\left\{-\frac{d}{ds}\left\{\alpha(s)\frac{d\hat{x}(s)}{ds}\right\}+\frac{d^2}{ds^2}\left\{\beta(s)\frac{d^2\hat{x}(s)}{ds^2}\right\}+\frac{1}{2}\left.\frac{\partial E_{edge}}{\partial x}\right|_{\hat{x},\hat{y}}\right\}\delta_x(s)ds=0 \tag{6.28}$$

Since this equation holds for all $\delta_x(s)$, then,

$$-\frac{d}{ds}\left\{\alpha(s)\frac{d\hat{x}(s)}{ds}\right\}+\frac{d^2}{ds^2}\left\{\beta(s)\frac{d^2\hat{x}(s)}{ds^2}\right\}+\frac{1}{2}\frac{\partial E_{edge}}{\partial x}\bigg|_{\hat{x},\hat{y}}=0 \tag{6.29}$$

Similarly, by a similar development of Eq. (6.26), we obtain

$$-\frac{d}{ds}\left\{\alpha(s)\frac{d\hat{y}(s)}{ds}\right\}+\frac{d^2}{ds^2}\left\{\beta(s)\frac{d^2\hat{y}(s)}{ds^2}\right\}+\frac{1}{2}\frac{\partial E_{edge}}{\partial y}\bigg|_{\hat{x},\hat{y}}=0 \tag{6.30}$$

This has re-formulated the original energy minimisation framework, Eq. (6.8), into a pair of differential equations. To implement a complete snake, we seek the solution to Eqs. (6.29) and (6.30). By the method of finite differences, we substitute for $d\mathbf{x}(s)/ds \cong \mathbf{x}_{s+1}-\mathbf{x}_s$, the first-order difference, and the second-order difference is $d^2\mathbf{x}(s)/ds^2 \cong \mathbf{x}_{s+1}-2\mathbf{x}_s+\mathbf{x}_{s-1}$ (as in Eq. (6.13)), which by substitution into Eq. (6.29), for a contour discretised into S points equally spaced by an arc length h (remembering that the indices $s\in[1,S)$ to snake points are computed modulo S) gives

$$\begin{gathered}-\frac{1}{h}\left\{\alpha_{s+1}\frac{(\mathbf{x}_{s+1}-\mathbf{x}_s)}{h}-\alpha_s\frac{(\mathbf{x}_s-\mathbf{x}_{s-1})}{h}\right\}+\\ \frac{1}{h^2}\left\{\beta_{s+1}\frac{(\mathbf{x}_{s+2}-2\mathbf{x}_{s+1}+\mathbf{x}_s)}{h^2}-2\beta_s\frac{(\mathbf{x}_{s+1}-2\mathbf{x}_s+\mathbf{x}_{s-1})}{h^2}+\beta_{s-1}\frac{(\mathbf{x}_s-2\mathbf{x}_{s-1}+\mathbf{x}_{s-2})}{h^2}\right\}\\ +\frac{1}{2}\frac{\partial E_{edge}}{\partial x}\bigg|_{\mathbf{x}_s,\mathbf{y}_s}=0\end{gathered} \tag{6.31}$$

By collecting the coefficients of different points, Eq. (6.31) can be expressed as

$$f_s=a_s\mathbf{x}_{s-2}+b_s\mathbf{x}_{s-1}+c_s\mathbf{x}_s+d_s\mathbf{x}_{s+1}+e_s\mathbf{x}_{s+2} \tag{6.32}$$

where

$$f_s=-\frac{1}{2}\frac{\partial E_{edge}}{\partial x}\bigg|_{\mathbf{x}_s,\mathbf{y}_s}$$

$$a_s=\frac{\beta_{s-1}}{h^4}$$

$$b_s=-\frac{2(\beta_s+\beta_{s-1})}{h^4}-\frac{\alpha_s}{h^2}$$

$$c_s=\frac{\beta_{s+1}+4\beta_s+\beta_{s-1}}{h^4}+\frac{\alpha_{s+1}+\alpha_s}{h^2}$$

$$d_s=-\frac{2(\beta_{s+1}+\beta_s)}{h^4}-\frac{\alpha_{s+1}}{h^2}$$

$$e_s=\frac{\beta_{s+1}}{h^4}$$

This is now in the form of a linear (matrix) equation

$$\mathbf{Ax} = fx(\mathbf{x}, \mathbf{y}) \tag{6.33}$$

where $fx(\mathbf{x},\mathbf{y})$ is the first-order differential of the edge magnitude along the x axis and where

$$\mathbf{A} = \begin{bmatrix} c_1 & d_1 & e_1 & 0 & \ldots & a_1 & b_1 \\ b_2 & c_2 & d_2 & e_2 & 0 & \ldots & a_2 \\ a_3 & b_3 & c_3 & d_3 & e_3 & 0 & \\ \ldots & \ldots & \ldots & \ldots & \ldots & & \\ & & & & & & \\ e_{S-1} & 0 & \ldots & a_{S-1} & b_{S-1} & c_{S-1} & d_{S-1} \\ d_S & e_S & 0 & \ldots & a_S & b_S & c_S \end{bmatrix}$$

Similarly, by analysis of Eq. (6.30) we obtain

$$\mathbf{Ay} = fy(\mathbf{x}, \mathbf{y}) \tag{6.34}$$

where $fy(\mathbf{x},\mathbf{y})$ is the first-order difference of the edge magnitude along the y axis. These equations can be solved iteratively to provide a new vector $\mathbf{v}^{<i+1>}$ from an initial vector $\mathbf{v}^{<i>}$ where i is an evolution index. The iterative solution is

$$\frac{(\mathbf{x}^{<i+1>} - \mathbf{x}^{<i>})}{\Delta} + \mathbf{Ax}^{<i+1>} = fx(\mathbf{x}^{<i>}, \mathbf{y}^{<i>}) \tag{6.35}$$

where the control factor Δ is a scalar chosen to control convergence. The control factor, Δ, actually controls the rate of evolution of the snake: large values make the snake move quickly, small values make for slow movement. As usual, fast movement implies that the snake can pass over features of interest without noticing them, whereas slow movement can be rather tedious. So the appropriate choice for Δ is again a compromise, this time between selectivity and time. The formulation for the vector of y co-ordinates is

$$\frac{(\mathbf{y}^{<i+1>} - \mathbf{y}^{<i>})}{\Delta} + \mathbf{Ay}^{<i+1>} = fy(\mathbf{x}^{<i>}, \mathbf{y}^{<i>}) \tag{6.36}$$

By rearrangement, this gives the final pair of equations that can be used to iteratively evolve a contour; the complete snake solution is then

$$\mathbf{x}^{<i+1>} = \left(\mathbf{A} + \frac{1}{\Delta}\mathbf{I}\right)^{-1} \left(\frac{1}{\Delta}\mathbf{x}^{<i>} + fx(\mathbf{x}^{<i>}, \mathbf{y}^{<i>})\right) \tag{6.37}$$

where $\mathbf{I}$ is the identity matrix. This implies that the new set of x co-ordinates is a weighted sum of the initial set of contour points and the image information. The fraction is calculated according to specified snake properties, the values chosen for α and β. For the y co-ordinates, we have

$$\mathbf{y}^{<i+1>} = \left(\mathbf{A} + \frac{1}{\Delta}\mathbf{I}\right)^{-1} \left(\frac{1}{\Delta}\mathbf{y}^{<i>} + fy(\mathbf{x}^{<i>}, \mathbf{y}^{<i>})\right) \tag{6.38}$$

The new set of contour points then become the starting set for the next iteration. Note that this is a continuous formulation, as opposed to the discrete (Greedy) implementation. One penalty is the need for matrix inversion, affecting speed. Clearly, the benefits are that co-ordinates are calculated as real functions and the complete set of new contour points is provided at each iteration. The result of implementing the complete solution is illustrated in Fig. 6.8. The initialisation, Fig. 6.8A, is the same as for the Greedy algorithm, but with 32 contour points. At the first iteration, Fig. 6.8B, the contour begins to shrink, and move towards the eye's iris. By the sixth iteration, Fig. 6.8C, some of the contour points have snagged on strong edge data, particularly in the upper part of the contour. At this point, however, the excessive curvature becomes inadmissible, and the contour releases these points to achieve a smooth contour again, one which is better matched to the edge data and the chosen snake features. Finally, Fig. 6.8E is where the contour ceases to move. Part of the contour has been snagged on strong edge data in the eyebrow, whereas the remainder of the contour matches the chosen feature well.

Clearly, a different solution could be obtained by using different values for the snake parameters; in application the choice of values for α, β and Δ must be made very carefully. In fact, this is part of the difficulty in using snakes for practical feature extraction; a further difficulty is that the result depends on where the initial contour is placed. These difficulties are called parameterisation and initialisation, respectively. These problems have motivated much research and development.

6.3.4 Other Snake approaches

There are many further considerations to implementing snakes, and there is a great wealth of material. One consideration is that we have only considered closed contours. There are, naturally, *open contours*. These require slight difference in formulation for the Kass snake [Waite90] and only minor modification for implementation in the Greedy algorithm. One difficulty with the Greedy algorithm is its sensitivity to noise due to its local neighbourhood action. Also, the Greedy algorithm can end up in an oscillatory position where the final contour simply jumps between two equally attractive energy minima. One solution [Lai94] resolved this difficulty by increase in the size of the snake neighbourhood, but this incurs much greater complexity. In order to allow snakes to expand, as opposed to contracting, a *normal force* can be included which inflates a snake and pushes it over unattractive features [Cohen91, Cohen93]. The force is implemented by addition of

$$F_{normal} = \rho \mathbf{n}(s) \tag{6.39}$$

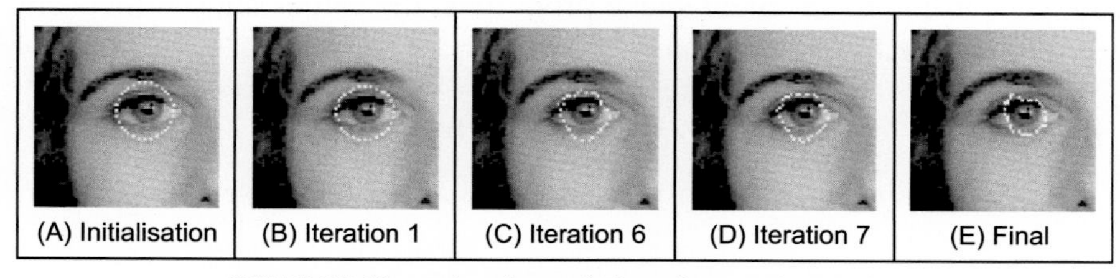

(A) Initialisation (B) Iteration 1 (C) Iteration 6 (D) Iteration 7 (E) Final

FIGURE 6.8 Illustrating the evolution of a complete snake.

to the evolution equation, where $\mathbf{n}(s)$ is the normal force and ρ weights its effect. This is inherently sensitive to the magnitude of the normal force that, if too large, can force the contour to pass over features of interest. Another way to allow expansion is to modify the elasticity constraint [Berger91] so that the internal energy becomes

$$E_{int} = \alpha(s)\left(\left|\frac{d\mathbf{v}(s)}{ds}\right|^2 - (L+\varepsilon)\right)^2 + \beta(s)\left|\frac{d^2\mathbf{v}(s)}{ds^2}\right|^2 \tag{6.40}$$

where the length adjustment ε, when positive, $\varepsilon > 0$, and added to the contour length L, causes the contour to expand. When negative, $\varepsilon < 0$, this causes the length to reduce, and so the contour contracts. To avoid imbalance due to the contraction force, the technique can be modified to remove it (by changing the continuity and curvature constraints) without losing the controlling properties of the internal forces [Xu94] (and which, incidentally, allowed corners to form in the snake). This gives a contour no prejudice to expansion or contraction as required. The technique allowed for integration of prior shape knowledge; methods have also been developed to allow local shape to influence contour evolution [Berger91, Williams92].

Some snake approaches have included factors that attract contours to regions using statistical models [Ronfard94] or texture [Ivins95], to complement operators that combine edge detection with region-growing. Also, the snake model can be generalised to higher dimensions, and there are 3D snake surfaces [Cohen92, Wang92]. Finally, a later approach has introduced shapes for moving objects, by including velocity [Peterfreund99].

6.3.5 Further Snake developments

Snakes have been formulated not only to include local shape but also phrased in terms of *regularisation* [Lai95] where a single parameter controls snake evolution, emphasising a snake's natural compromise between its own forces and the image forces. Regularisation involves using a single parameter to control the balance between the external and the internal forces. Given a regularisation parameter λ, the snake energy of Eq. (6.37) can be given as

$$E_{snake}(\mathbf{v}(s)) = \int_{s=0}^{1} \{\lambda E_{\text{int}}(\mathbf{v}(s)) + (1-\lambda)E_{image}(\mathbf{v}(s))\}ds \tag{6.41}$$

Clearly, if $\lambda = 1$, then the snake will use the internal energy only, whereas if $\lambda = 0$, the snake will be attracted to the selected image function only. Usually, regularisation concerns selecting a value in between zero and one guided, say, by knowledge of the likely confidence in the edge information. In fact, Lai's approach calculates the regularisation parameter at contour points as

$$\lambda_i = \frac{\sigma_\eta^2}{\sigma_i^2 + \sigma_\eta^2} \tag{6.42}$$

where σ_i^2 appears to be the variance of the point i and σ_η^2 is the variance of the noise at the point (even digging into Lai's PhD thesis provided no explicit clues here, say that 'these parameters may be learned from training samples' – if this is impossible a procedure can be invoked). As before, λ_i lies between zero and one, and where the variances are bounded as

$$\frac{1}{\sigma_i^2}+\frac{1}{\sigma_\eta^2}=1 \tag{6.43}$$

This does actually link these generalised active contour models to an approach we shall meet later, where the target shape is extracted conditionally upon its expected variation. Lai's approach also addressed initialisation and showed how a GHT could be used to initialise an active contour and built into the extraction process. A major development of new external force model is called the *Gradient Vector Flow (GVF)* [Xu98]. The GVF is computed as a diffusion of the gradient vectors of an edge map. There is, however, natural limitation on using a single contour for extraction, since it is never known precisely where to stop.

In fact, many of the problems with initialisation with active contours can be resolved by using a dual contour approach [Gunn97] that also includes local shape and regularisation. This approach aims to enclose the target shape within an inner and an outer contour. The outer contour contracts, whilst the inner contour expands. A balance is struck between the two contours to allow them to allow the target shape to be extracted. Gunn showed how shapes could be extracted successfully, even when the target contour was far from the two initial contours. Further, the technique was shown to provide better immunity to initialisation, in comparison with the results of a Kass snake, and Xu's approach.

Later, the dual approach was extended to a discrete space [Gunn98], using an established search algorithm. The search algorithm used dynamic programming which has already been used within active contours to find a global solution [Lai95] in matching and tracking contours [Geiger95]. This new approach was used within an enormous study (using a database of over 20,000 images no less) on automated cell segmentation for cervical cancer screening [Bamford98], achieving more than 99% accurate segmentation. The approach was formulated as a discrete search using a dual contour approach, illustrated in Fig. 6.9. The inner and the outer contour aim to be inside and outside the target shape, respectively. The space between the inner and the outer contours is divided into lines (like the spokes on the wheel of a bicycle), and M points are taken along each of the N lines. We then have a grid of $M \times N$ points, in which the target contour (shape) is expected to lie. The full lattice of points is shown in Fig. 6.10A. Should we need higher resolution, then we can choose large values of M and of N, but this in turn implies more computational effort. One can envisage strategies which allow for linearisation of the coverage of the space in between the two contours, but these can make implementation much more complex.

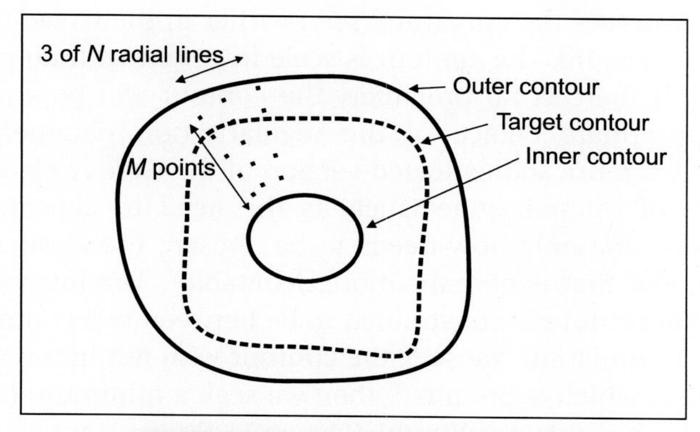

FIGURE 6.9 Discrete dual contour search.

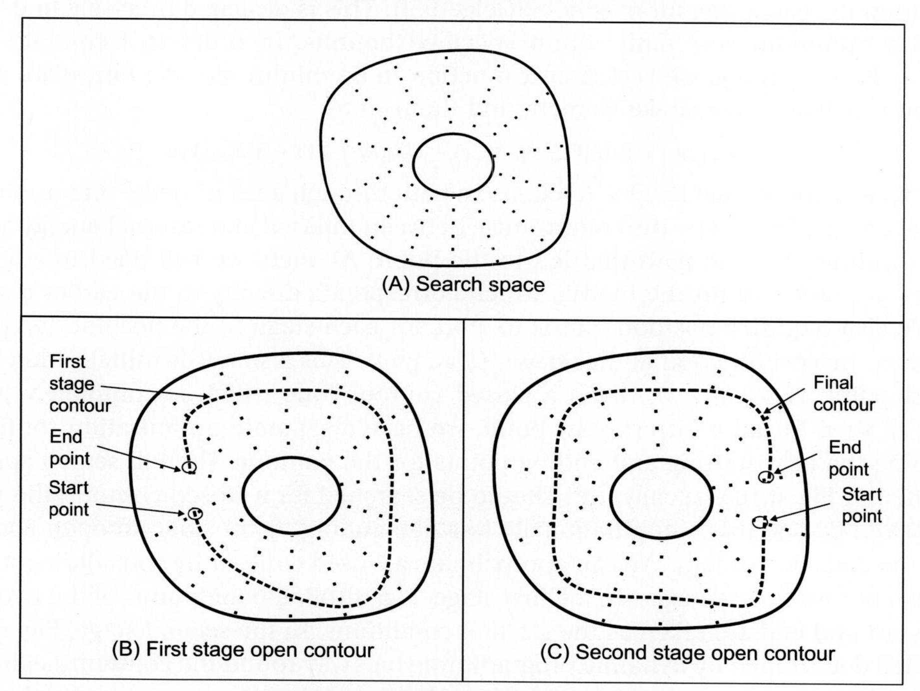

FIGURE 6.10 Discrete dual contour point space.

The approach again uses regularisation, where the snake energy is a discrete form to Eq. (6.41), so the energy at a snake point (unlike earlier formulations, e.g. Eq. (6.12)) is

$$E(\mathbf{v}_i) = \lambda E_{int}(\mathbf{v}_i) + (1-\lambda)E_{ext}(\mathbf{v}_i) \tag{6.44}$$

where the internal energy is formulated as

$$E_{int}(\mathbf{v}_i) = \left(\frac{|\mathbf{v}_{i+1} - 2\mathbf{v}_i + \mathbf{v}_{i-1}|}{|\mathbf{v}_{i+1} - \mathbf{v}_{i-1}|}\right)^2 \tag{6.45}$$

The numerator expresses the curvature, seen earlier in the Greedy formulation. It is scaled by a factor that ensures the contour is scale invariant with no prejudice as to the size of the contour. If there is no prejudice, the contour will be attracted to smooth contours, given appropriate choice of the regularisation parameter. As such, the formulation is simply a more sophisticated version of the Greedy algorithm, dispensing with several factors of limited value (such as the need to choose values for three weighting parameters: one only now needs to be chosen; the elasticity constraint has also been removed, and that is perhaps more debatable). The interest here is that the search for the optimal contour is constrained to be between two contours, as in Fig. 6.9. By way of a snake's formulation, we seek the contour with minimum energy. When this is applied to a contour which is bounded, then we seek a minimum cost path. This is a natural target for the well-known Viterbi (Dynamic Programming) algorithm (for its application in vision, see, for example, [Geiger95]). This is designed precisely to do this: to find a minimum cost path within specified bounds. In order to formulate it by Dynamic Programming, we seek a cost function to be minimised. We formulate a cost function C between one snake element and the next as

$$C_i(\mathbf{v}_{i+1}, \mathbf{v}_i) = \min[C_{i-1}(\mathbf{v}_i, \mathbf{v}_{i-1}) + \lambda E_{int}(\mathbf{v}_i) + (1-\lambda)E_{ext}(\mathbf{v}_i)] \tag{6.46}$$

In this way, we should be able to choose a path through a set of snake that minimises the total energy, formed by the compromise between internal and external energy at that point, together with the path that led to the point. As such, we will need to store the energies at points within the matrix, which corresponds directly to the earlier tessellation. We also require a position matrix to store for each stage (i) the position ($\mathbf{v}_{i-1}$) that minimises the cost function at that stage ($C_i(\mathbf{v}_{i+1},\mathbf{v}_i)$). This also needs initialisation to set the first point, $C_1(\mathbf{v}_1,\mathbf{v}_0) = 0$. Given a closed contour (one which is completely joined together), then for an arbitrary start point, we have a separate optimisation routine to determine the best starting and ending points for the contour. The full search space is illustrated in Fig. 6.10A. Ideally, this should be searched for a closed contour, the target contour of Fig. 6.9. It is computationally less demanding to consider an open contour, where the ends do not join. We can approximate a closed contour by considering it to be an open contour in two stages. In the first stage, Fig. 6.10B, the midpoints of the two lines at the start and end are taken as the starting conditions. In the second stage, Fig. 6.10C, the points determined by dynamic programming half way round the contour (i.e. for two lines at $N/2$) are taken as the start and the end points for a new open-contour dynamic programming search, which then optimises the contour from these points. The premise is that the points half way round the contour will be at, or close to, their optimal position after the first stage, and it is the points at, or near, the starting points in the first stage that require refinement. This reduces the computational requirement by a factor of M^2.

The technique was originally demonstrated to extract the face boundary, for feature extraction within automatic face recognition, as illustrated in Fig. 6.11. The outer boundary (Fig. 6.11A) was extracted using a convex hull which in turn initialised an inner

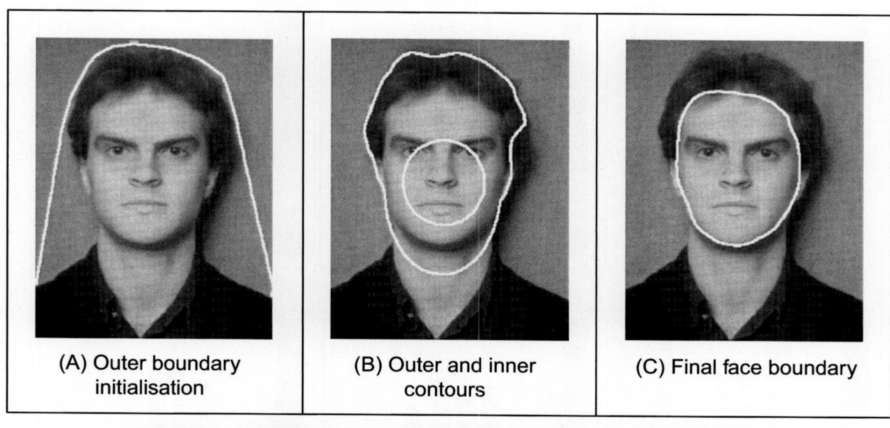

FIGURE 6.11 Extracting the face outline by a discrete dual contour.

and an outer contour (Fig. 6.11B). The final extraction by the dual discrete contour is the boundary of facial skin, Fig. 6.11C. The number of points in the mesh naturally limits the accuracy with which the final contour is extracted, but application could naturally be followed by use of a continuous Kass snake to improve final resolution. In fact, it was shown that human faces could be discriminated by the contour extracted by this technique, though the study highlighted potential difficult with facial organs and illumination. As already mentioned, it was later deployed in cell analysis where the inner and the outer contour were derived by analysis of the stained-cell image.

6.3.6 Geometric active contours (Level Set-Based Approaches)

Problems discussed so far with active contours include initialisation and poor convergence to concave regions. Also, parametric active contours (the snakes discussed previously) can have difficulty in segmenting multiple objects simultaneously because of the explicit representation of curve. *Geometric Active Contour* models have been introduced to solve this problem, where the curve is represented implicitly in a *level set function*. Essentially, the main argument is that by changing the representation, we can improve the result, and there have indeed been some very impressive results presented. Consider, for example, the result in Fig. 6.12, where we are extracting the boundary of the hand, by using the initialisation shown in Fig. 6.12A. This would be hard to achieve by the active contour models discussed so far: there are concavities, sharp corners and background contamination which it is difficult for parametric techniques to handle. It is not perfect, but it is clearly much better (there are techniques to improve on this result, but this is far enough for the moment). On the other hand, there are no panaceas in engineering, and we should not expect them to exist. The new techniques can be found to be complex to implement, even to understand, though by virtue of their impressive results there are new approaches aimed to speed application and to ease implementation. As yet, the techniques do not find routine deployment (certainly not in real-time

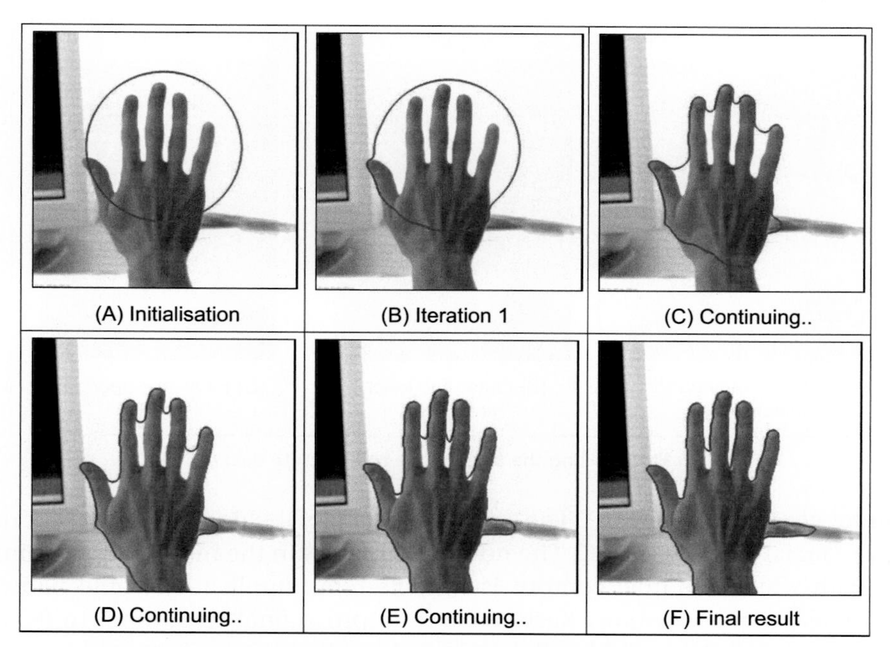

FIGURE 6.12 Extraction by curve evolution (a diffusion snake) [Cremers02].

applications), but this is part of the evolution of any technique. The complexity and scope of this book mandate a short description of these new approaches here, but as usual we shall provide pointers to more in-depth source material.

Level set methods [Osher88] essentially find the shape without parameterising it, so the curve description is implicit rather than explicit, by finding it as the zero level set of a function [Osher03, Sethian99]. The zero level set is the interface between two regions in an image. This can be visualised as taking slices through a surface shown in Fig. 6.13A. As we take slices at different levels (as the surface evolves) then the shape can split, Fig. 6.13B. This would be difficult to parameterize (we would have to detect when it splits), but it can be handled within a level set approach by considering the underlying surface. At a lower level, Fig. 6.13C, we have a single composite shape. As such, we have an extraction which evolves with time (to change the level). The initialisation is a closed curve and we shall formulate how we want the curve to move in a way analogous to minimising its energy.

The level set function is the signed distance to the contour. This distance is arranged to be negative inside the contour and positive outside it. The contour itself, the target shape, is where the distance is zero – the interface between the two regions. Accordingly, we store values for each pixel representing this distance. We then determine new values for this surface, say by expansion. As we evolve the surface, the level sets evolve accordingly, equivalent to moving the surface where the slices are taken, in Fig. 6.13.

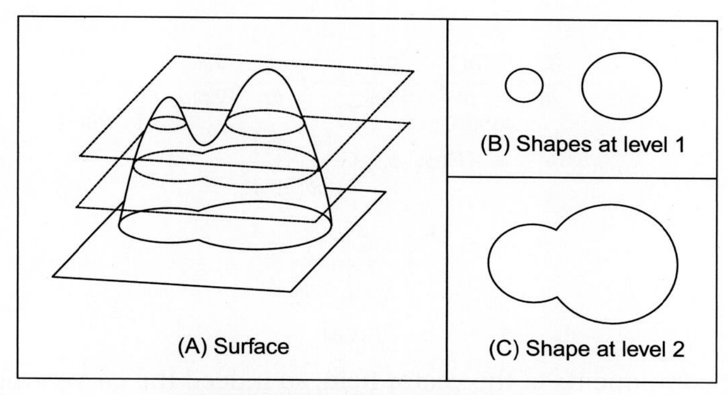

FIGURE 6.13 Surfaces and level sets.

Since the distance map needs renormalisation after each iteration, it can make the technique slow in operation (or need a fast computer).

Let us assume that the interface C is controlled to change in a constant manner and evolves with time t by propagating along its normal direction with speed F (where F is a function of, say, curvature (Eq. (4.61)) and speed) according to

$$\frac{\partial C}{\partial t} = F \cdot \frac{\nabla \phi}{|\nabla \phi|} \tag{6.47}$$

Here, the term $\frac{\nabla \phi}{|\nabla \phi|}$ is a vector pointing in the direction normal to the surface – previously discussed in Section 4.4.1, Eq. (4.52). (The curvature at a point is measured perpendicular to the level set function at that point.) The curve is then evolving in a normal direction, controlled by the curvature. At all times, the interface C is the zero level set

$$\phi(C(t), t) = 0 \tag{6.48}$$

The level set function ϕ is positive outside of the region and negative when it is inside and it is zero on the boundary of the shape. As such by differentiation, we get

$$\frac{\partial \phi(C(t), t)}{\partial t} = 0 \tag{6.49}$$

and by the chain rule we obtain

$$\frac{\partial \phi}{\partial C}\frac{\partial C}{\partial t} + \frac{\partial \phi}{\partial t} = 0 \tag{6.50}$$

By rearrangement and substitution from Eq. (6.47) we obtain

$$\frac{\partial \phi}{\partial t} = -F\frac{\partial \phi}{\partial C} \cdot \frac{\nabla \phi}{|\nabla \phi|} = -F|\nabla \phi| \tag{6.51}$$

which suggests that the propagation of a curve depends on its gradient. The analysis is actually a bit more complex since F is a scalar and C is a vector in (x,y), we have that

$$\frac{\partial \phi}{\partial t} = -\frac{\partial C}{\partial t}F \cdot \frac{\nabla \phi}{|\nabla \phi|} = -F\frac{\partial C}{\partial t} \cdot \frac{\nabla \phi}{|\nabla \phi|}$$
$$= -F(\phi_x, \phi_y) \cdot \frac{(\phi_x, \phi_y)}{\sqrt{\phi_x^2 + \phi_y^2}}$$
$$= -F\frac{\phi_x^2 + \phi_y^2}{\sqrt{\phi_x^2 + \phi_y^2}}$$
$$= -F|\nabla \phi|$$

where (ϕ_x,ϕ_y) are components of the vector field, so indeed the curve evolution depends on gradient. In fact, we can include a (multiplicative) stopping function of the form

$$S = \frac{1}{1 + |\nabla \mathbf{P}|^n} \tag{6.52}$$

where $\nabla\mathbf{P}$ is the magnitude of the image gradient giving a stopping function (like the one in anisotropic diffusion in Eq. (3.51)) which is zero at edge points (hence stopping evolution) and near unity when there is no edge data (allowing movement). This is in fact a form of the Hamilton–Jacobi equation which is a partial differential equation that needs to be solved so as to obtain our solution. One way to achieve this is by finite differences (as earlier approximating the differential operation) and a spatial grid (the image itself). We then obtain a solution which differences the contour at iterations $<n+1>$ and $<n>$ (separated by an interval Δt) as

$$\frac{\phi(i,j,\Delta t)^{<n+1>} - \phi(i,j,\Delta t)^{<n>}}{\Delta t} = -F\left|\nabla_{ij}\phi(i,j)^{<n>}\right| \tag{6.53}$$

where $\nabla_{ij}\phi$ represents a spatial derivative, leading to the solution

$$\phi(i,j,\Delta t)^{<n+1>} = \phi(i,j,\Delta t)^{<n>} - \Delta t\left(F\left|\nabla_{ij}\phi(i,j)^{<n>}\right|\right) \tag{6.54}$$

and we then have the required formulation for iterative operation.

This is only an introductory view, rather simplifying a complex scenario, and much greater detail is to be found in the two major texts in this area [Osher03, Sethian99]. The real poser is how to solve it all. We shall concentrate on some of the major techniques, but not go into their details. Caselles et al. [Caselles93] and Malladi et al. [Malladi95] were the first to propose geometric active contour models, which use gradient-based information for segmentation. The gradient-based geometric active contour can detect multiple objects simultaneously, but it has other important problems, which are boundary leakage, noise sensitivity, computational inefficiency, and difficulty of implementation. There have been formulations [Caselles97, Siddiqi98, Xie04] introduced to solve these problems; however, they can just increase the tolerance rather than achieve an exact solution. Several numerical schemes have also been proposed to improve computational efficiency of the level set method, including *narrow band* [Adalsteinsson95] (to find the solution within a constrained distance, i.e. to compute the level set only near the contour), *fast marching methods* [Sethian99] (to constrain movement) and *additive operator splitting* [Weickert98]. Despite substantial improvements in efficiency, they can be difficult to implement and can be slow (we seek the zero level set only, but solve the whole thing). These approaches show excellent results, but they are not for the less than brave – though there are numerous tutorials and implementations available on the web. Clearly there is a need for unified presentation, and some claim this – e.g. [Caselles97] (and linkage to parametric active contour models).

The technique which many people compare the result of their own new approach with is a GAC called the *active contour without edges*, introduced by Chan and Vese [Chan95] which is based on the Mumford–Shah functional [Mumford89]. Their model uses regional statistics for segmentation and as such is a region-based level set model. The overall premise is to avoid using gradient (edge) information since this can lead to boundary leakage and cause the contour to collapse. A further advantage is that it can find objects when boundary data are weak or diffuse. The main strategy is to minimise energy, as in an active contour. To illustrate the model, let us presume we have a bimodal image **P** which contains an object and a background. The object has pixels of intensity $\mathbf{P}^i$ within its boundary and the intensity of the background is $\mathbf{P}^o$, outside of the boundary. We can then measure a fit of a contour, or curve, C to the image as

$$F^i(C) + F^o(C) = \int_{inside(C)} |\mathbf{P}(x,y) - c^i|^2 \mathrm{d}x\mathrm{d}y + \int_{outside(C)} |\mathbf{P}(x,y) - c^o|^2 \mathrm{d}x\mathrm{d}y \tag{6.55}$$

where the constant c^i is the average brightness inside the curve, depending on the curve, and c^o is the brightness outside of it. The boundary of the object C_O is the curve which minimises the fit derived by expressing the regions inside and outside the curve as

$$C_O = \min_C (F^i(C) + F^o(C)) \tag{6.56}$$

(Note that the original description was excellent, though Chan and Vese are from a maths department, which makes the presentation a bit terse. Also, the strict version of minimisation is actually the infimum or greatest lower bound; inf(X) is the biggest real number that is smaller than or equal to every number in X.) The minimum is when

$$F^i(C_O) + F^o(C_O) \approx 0 \tag{6.57}$$

when the curve is at the boundary of the object. When the curve C is inside the object $F^i(C) \approx 0$ and $F^o(C) > 0$; conversely when the curve is outside the object $F^i(C) > 0$ and $F^o(C) \approx 0$. When the curves straddles the two and is both inside and outside the object, then $F^i(C) > 0$ and $F^o(C) > 0$; the function is zero when C is placed on the boundary of the object. By using regions, we are avoiding using edges and the process depends finding the best separation between the regions (and by the averaging operation in the region, we have better noise immunity). If we constrain this process by introducing terms which depend on the length of the contour and the area of the contour, we extend the energy functional from Eq. (6.55) as

$$F(c^i, c^o, C) = \mu \cdot length(C) + \upsilon \cdot area(C) + \lambda_1 \cdot \int_{inside(C)} |\mathbf{P}(x,y) - c^i|^2 \mathrm{d}x\mathrm{d}y$$
$$+ \lambda_2 \cdot \int_{outside(C)} |\mathbf{P}(x,y) - c^o|^2 \mathrm{d}x\mathrm{d}y \tag{6.58}$$

where μ, υ, λ_1 and λ_2 are parameters controlling selectivity. The contour is then, for a fixed set of parameters, chosen by minimisation of the energy functional as

$$C_O = \min_{c^i, c^o, C} (F(c^i, c^o, C)) \tag{6.59}$$

A level set formulation is then used wherein an approximation to the unit step function (the Heaviside function) is defined to control the influence of points within and without (outside) the contour, which by differentiation gives an approximation to an impulse (the Dirac function), and with a solution to a form of Eq. (6.51) (in discrete form) is used to update the level set.

The active contour without edges model can address problems with initialisation, noise and boundary leakage (since it uses regions, not gradients) but still suffers from computational inefficiency and difficulty in implementation because of the level set method. An example result is shown in Fig. 6.14 where the target aim is to extract the hippo – the active contour without edges aims to split the image into the extracted object (the hippo) and its background (the grass). In order to do this, we need to specify an initialisation which we shall choose to be within a small circle inside the hippo, as shown in Fig. 6.14A. The result of extraction is shown in Fig. 6.14B and we can see that the technique has detected much of the hippo, but the result is not perfect. The values used for the parameters here were $\lambda_1 = \lambda_2 = 1.0$; $\upsilon = 0$ (i.e. area was not used to control evolution); $\mu = 0.1 \times 255^2$ (the length parameter was controlled according to the image resolution) and some internal parameters were $h = 1$ (a one pixel step space); $\Delta t = 0.1$ (a small time spacing) and $\varepsilon = 1$ (a parameter within the step, and hence the impulse functions). Alternative choices are possible and can affect the result achieved. The result here has been selected to show performance attributes, the earlier result (Fig. 6.12) was selected to demonstrate finesse.

The regions with intensity and appearance that are most similar to the selected initialisation have been identified in the result: this is much of the hippo, including the left ear and the region around the left eye, but omitting some of the upper body. There are some small potential problems too: there are some birds extracted on the top of the hippo and a small region underneath it (was this hippo's breakfast we wonder?). Note that by virtue of the regional level set formulation the image is treated in its entirety and multiple shapes are detected, some well away from the target shape. By and large, the result looks encouraging as much of the hippo is extracted in the result and the largest shape contains much of the target; if we were to seek to get an exact match then we would need to use an exact model such as the GHT, or impose a model on the extraction, such as a statistical shape prior. That the technique can operate best when the image is

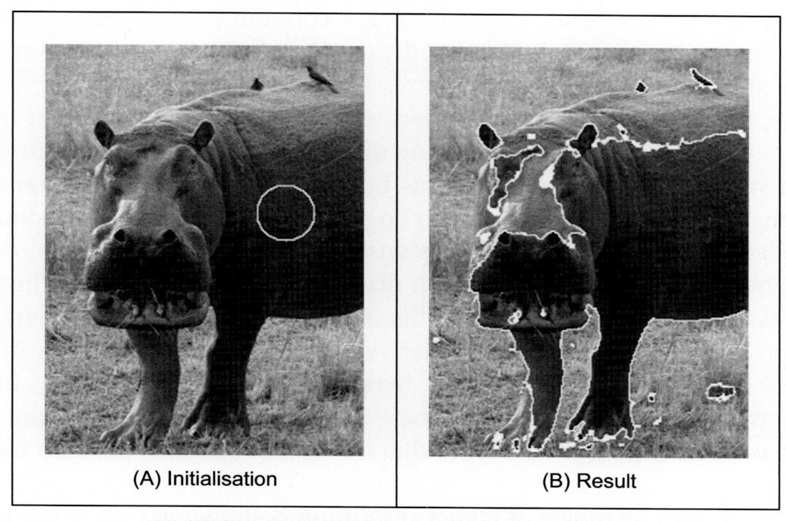

FIGURE 6.14 Extraction by a level set-based approach.

bimodal is reflected in that extraction is most successful when there is a clear difference between the target and the background, such as in the lower body. An alternative interpretation is that the technique clearly can handle situations where the edge data are weak and diffuse, such as in the upper body.

Techniques have moved on, and one can include statistical priors to guide shape extraction [Cremers07]. One study showed the relationship between parametric and geometric active contours [Xu00]. Of the more recent developments, many are guided by application domains, and one [Niu17] was designed specifically to handle noise. There are as yet few deep learning approaches and [Rupprecht16] used a convolutional network to predict potential target points on the target contour forming a vector field used for evolution. More recently, [Marcos18] combined the expressiveness of deep learning with the versatility of active contour models, showing how boundaries, edges and corners could be used to effect better segmentation of building footprints. We shall now move to determining skeletons and symmetry which can describe shapes by their basis and with high invariance capability, respectively.

6.4 Shape Skeletonisation

6.4.1 Distance transforms

It is possible to describe a shape not just by its perimeter, or its area, but also by its *skeleton*. Here we do not mean an anatomical skeleton, more a central axis to a shape. This is then the axis which is equidistant from the borders of a shape and can be determined by a *distance transform*. In this way, we have a representation that has the same topology, the same size and orientation, but contains just the essence of the shape. As such, we are again in morphology, and there has been interest for some while in binary shape analysis [Borgefors86].

Essentially, the distance transform shows the distance from each point in an image shape to its central axis. (We are measuring distance here by difference in co-ordinate values, other measures of distance such as Euclidean are considered later in Chapter 12.) Intuitively, the distance transform can be achieved by successive erosion, and each pixel is labelled with the number of erosions before it disappeared. Accordingly, the pixels at the border of a shape will have a distance transform of unity, those adjacent inside will have a value of two, et. seq. This is illustrated in Fig. 6.15 where Fig. 6.15A shows the analysed shape (a rectangle derived by, say, thresholding an image – the superimposed pixel values are arbitrary here as it is simply a binary image), and Fig. 6.15B shows the distance transform where the pixel values are the distance. Here the central axis has a value of three as it takes that number of erosions to reach it from either side.

The application to a rectangle at higher resolution is shown in Figs. 6.16A and B. Here we can see that the central axis is quite clear and actually includes parts that reach towards the corners (and the central axis can be detected [Niblack92] from the transform data). The application to a more irregular shape is shown applied to that of a card suit in Figs. 6.16C and D.

The natural difficulty is of course the effect of noise. This can change the resulting, as shown in Fig. 6.17. This can certainly be ameliorated by using the earlier morphological operators (Section 3.6) to clean the image, but this can obscure the shape when the noise is severe. The major point is that this noise shows that the effect of a small change in the

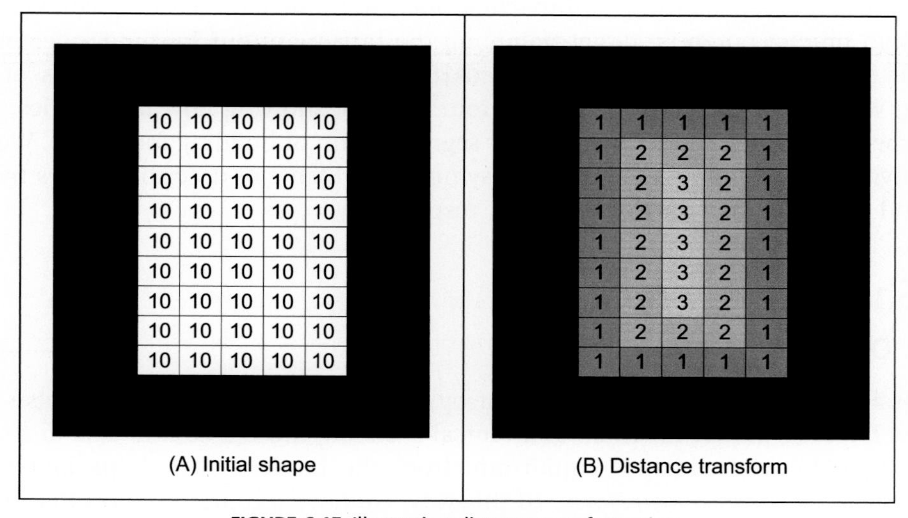

FIGURE 6.15 Illustrating distance transformation.

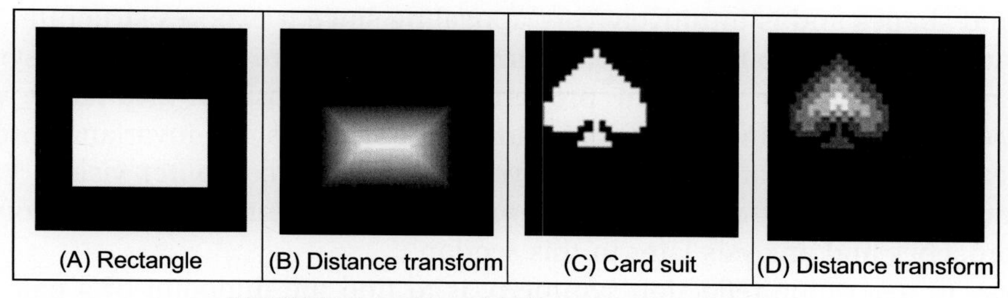

FIGURE 6.16 Applying the distance transformation.

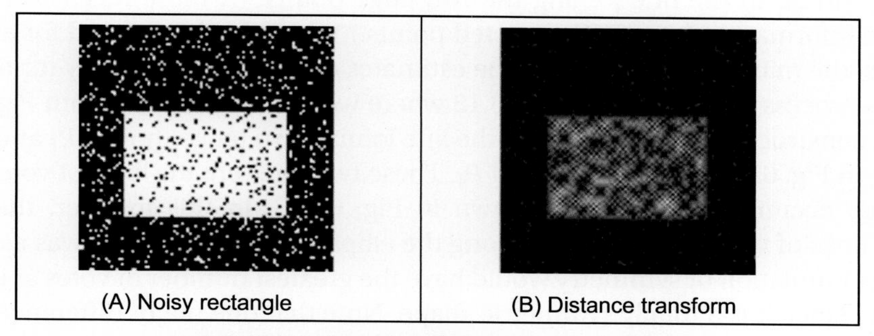

FIGURE 6.17 Distance transformation on noisy images.

object can be quite severe on the resulting distance transform. As such, it has little tolerance of occlusion or in change to its perimeter.

The natural extension from distance transforms is to the *medial axis transform* [Blum67] which determines the skeleton that consists of the locus of all the centres of maximum disks in the analysed region/shape. This has found use in feature extraction and description, so naturally approaches have considered improvement in speed [Lee82]. One study [Katz03] noted the practical difficulty experienced in noisy imagery: 'It is well documented how a tiny change to an object's boundary can cause a large change in its Medial Axis Transform'. To handle this, and hierarchical shape decomposition, the approach 'provides a natural parts-hierarchy while eliminating instabilities due to small boundary changes'. In fact, there is a more authoritative study available on medial representations [Siddiqi08] which describes formulations and properties of medial axis and distance transformations, together with applications. An alternative is to seek an approach which is designed implicitly to handle noise, say by averaging, and we shall consider this type of approach next.

6.4.2 Symmetry

Symmetry is a natural property, and there have been some proposed links with human perception of beauty. Rather than rely on finding the border of a shape, or its shape, we can locate features according to their symmetrical properties. So it is a totally different basis to find shapes and is intuitively very appealing since it exposes structure. (An old joke is that 'symmetry' should be a palindrome, fail!) There are many types of symmetry that are typified by their invariant properties such as position-invariance, *circular symmetry* (which is invariant to rotation) and reflection. Thus, the invariance properties of symmetry make it an attractive high-level operation in computer vision. We shall concentrate here on *bilateral reflection symmetry* (mirror-symmetry), giving pointers to other approaches and analysis later in this section.

One way to determine reflection symmetry is to find the midpoint of a pair of edge points and to then draw a line of votes in an accumulator wherein the gradient of the line of votes is normal to the line joining the two edge points. (A more recent version is to accumulate information from SIFT detected points.) When this is repeated for all pairs of edge points, the maxima should define the estimates of maximal symmetry for the largest shape. This process is illustrated in Fig. 6.18 where we have an ellipse. From Fig. 6.18A, a line can be constructed that is normal to the line joining two (edge) points P_1 and P_2 and a similar line in Fig. 6.18B for points P_3 and P_4. These two lines are the lines of votes that are drawn in an accumulator space as shown in Fig. 6.18C. In this manner, the greatest number of lines of votes will be drawn along the ellipse axes. If the shape was a circle, the resulting accumulation of symmetry would have the greatest number of votes at the centre of the circle, since it is a totally symmetric shape. Note that one major difference between the symmetry operator and a medial axis transform is that the symmetry operator will find the two axes, whereas the medial transform will find the largest.

This is shown in Fig. 6.19B which is the accumulator for the ellipse in Fig. 6.19A. The resulting lines in the accumulator are indeed the two axes of symmetry of the ellipse. This procedure might work well in this case but lacks the selectivity of a practical operator and will be sensitive to noise and occlusion. This is illustrated for the accumulation for the shapes in Fig. 6.19C. The result in Fig. 6.19D shows the axes of symmetry for the two ellipsoidal shapes and the point at the centre of the circle. It also shows a great deal of noise (the mush in the image) and this renders this approach useless. (Some of the noise in Figs. 6.19B and D is due to implementation, but do not let that distract you.) Basically, the technique needs greater selectivity.

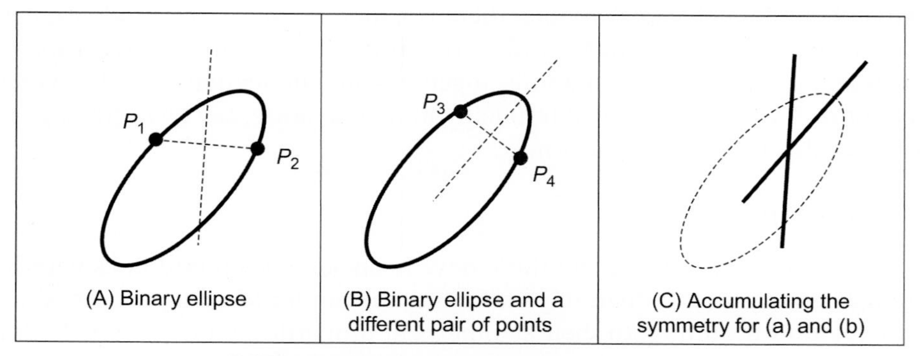

FIGURE 6.18 Primitive symmetry operator – basis.

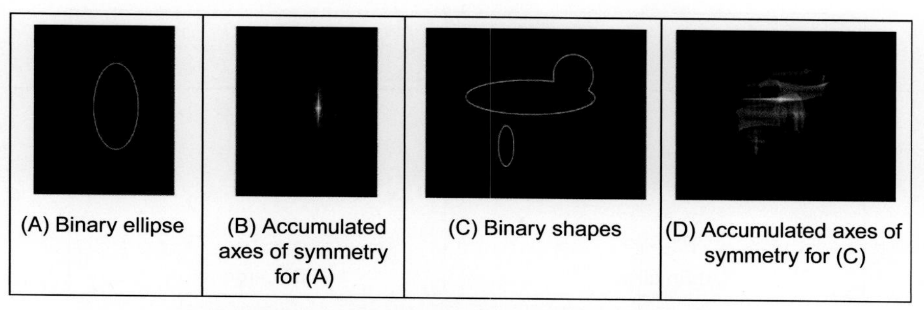

(A) Binary ellipse
(B) Accumulated axes of symmetry for (A)
(C) Binary shapes
(D) Accumulated axes of symmetry for (C)

FIGURE 6.19 Application of a primitive symmetry operator.

To achieve selectivity, we can use edge direction to filter the pairs of points. If the pair of points does not satisfy specified conditions on gradient magnitude and direction, then they will not contribute to the symmetry estimate. This is achieved in the *discrete symmetry operator* [Reisfeld95] which essentially forms an accumulator of points that are measures of symmetry between image points. Pairs of image points are attributed symmetry values that are derived from a distance weighting function, a phase weighting function and the edge magnitude at each of the pair of points. The distance weighting function controls the scope of the function, to control whether points which are more distant contribute in a similar manner to those which are close together. The phase weighting function shows when edge vectors at the pair of points point to each other and is arranged to be zero when the edges are pointing in the same direction (were that to be the case, they could not belong to the same shape – by symmetry). The symmetry accumulation is at the centre of each pair of points. In this way, the accumulator measures the degree of symmetry between image points, controlled by the edge strength. The distance weighting function D is

$$D(i,j,\sigma)=\frac{1}{\sqrt{2\pi\sigma}}e^{-\frac{|\mathbf{P}_i-\mathbf{P}_j|}{2\sigma}} \tag{6.60}$$

where i and j are the indices to two image points $\mathbf{P}_i$ and $\mathbf{P}_j$ and the deviation σ controls the scope of the function, by scaling the contribution of the distance between the points in the exponential function. A small value for the deviation σ implies local operation and detection of local symmetry. Larger values of σ imply that points that are further apart contribute to the accumulation process, as well as ones that are close together. In, say, application to the image of a face, large and small values of σ will aim for the whole face or the eyes, respectively.

The effect of the value of σ on the scalar distance weighting function expressed as Eq. (6.61) is illustrated in Fig. 6.20.

$$Di(j,\sigma)=\frac{1}{\sqrt{2\pi\sigma}}e^{-\frac{j}{\sqrt{2\sigma}}} \tag{6.61}$$

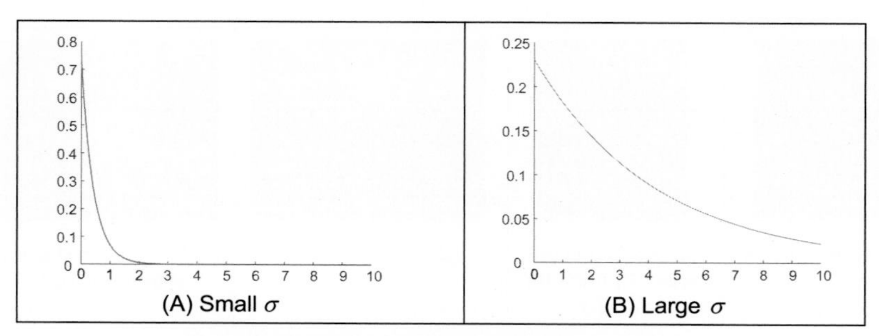

FIGURE 6.20 Effect of σ on distance weighting.

Fig. 6.20A shows the effect of a small value for the deviation, $\sigma = 0.6$, and shows that the weighting is greatest for closely spaced points and drops rapidly for points with larger spacing. Larger values of σ imply that the distance weight drops less rapidly for points that are more widely spaced, as in Fig. 6.20B where $\sigma = 5$, allowing points which are spaced further apart to contribute to the measured symmetry. The phase weighting function P is

$$P(i,j) = (1 - \cos(\theta_i + \theta_j - 2\alpha_{ij})) \times (1 - \cos(\theta_i - \theta_j)) \tag{6.62}$$

where θ is the edge direction at the two points and α_{ij} measures the direction of a line joining the two points

$$\alpha_{ij} = \tan^{-1}\left(\frac{y(\mathbf{P}_j) - y(\mathbf{P}_i)}{x(\mathbf{P}_j) - x(\mathbf{P}_i)}\right) \tag{6.63}$$

where $x(\mathbf{P}_i)$ and $y(\mathbf{P}_i)$ are the x and y co-ordinates of the point $\mathbf{P}_i$, respectively. This function is minimum when the edge direction at two points is in the same direction ($\theta_j = \theta_i$), and is a maximum when the edge direction is away from each other ($\theta_i = \theta_j + \pi$), along the line joining the two points ($\theta_j = \alpha_{ij}$).

The effect of relative edge direction on phase weighting is illustrated in Fig. 6.21 where Fig. 6.21A concerns two edge points that point towards each other and describes the effect on the phase weighting function by varying α_{ij}. This shows how the phase weight is maximum when the edge direction at the two points is along the line joining them, in this case when $\alpha_{ij} = 0$ and $\theta_i = 0$. Fig. 6.21B concerns one point with edge direction along the line joining two points, where the edge direction at the second point is varied. The phase weighting function is maximum when the edge direction at each point is towards each other, in this case when $|\theta_j| = \pi$. Naturally, it is more complex than this, and Fig. 6.21C shows the surface of the phase weighting function for $\alpha_{ij} = 0$, with its four maxima.

The symmetry relation between two points is then defined as

$$C(i,j,\sigma) = D(i,j,\sigma) \times P(i,j) \times E(i) \times E(j) \tag{6.64}$$

where E is the edge magnitude expressed in logarithmic form as

$$E(i) = \log(1 + M(i)) \tag{6.65}$$

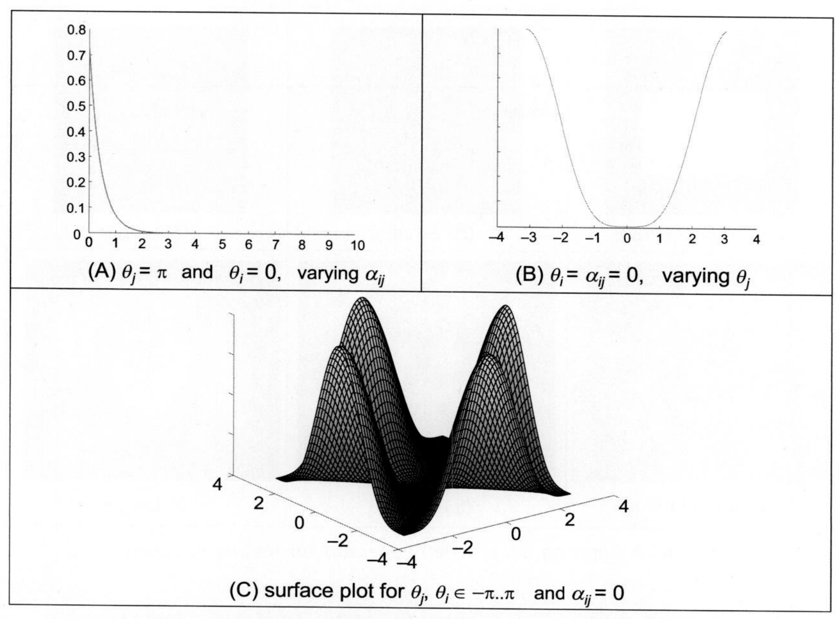

(A) $\theta_j = \pi$ and $\theta_i = 0$, varying α_{ij}
(B) $\theta_i = \alpha_{ij} = 0$, varying θ_j
(C) surface plot for θ_j, $\theta_i \in -\pi..\pi$ and $\alpha_{ij} = 0$

FIGURE 6.21 Effect of relative edge direction on phase weighting.

where M is the edge magnitude derived by application of an edge detection operator. The symmetry contribution of two points is accumulated at the midpoint of the line joining the two points. The total symmetry $S_{\mathbf{P}_m}$ at point $\mathbf{P}_m$ is the sum of the measured symmetry for all pairs of points which have their midpoint at $\mathbf{P}_m$, i.e. those points $\Gamma(\mathbf{P}_m)$ given by

$$\Gamma(\mathbf{P}_m) = \left[(i,j) \middle| \frac{\mathbf{P}_i + \mathbf{P}_j}{2} = \mathbf{P}_m \quad \forall \quad i \neq j \right] \tag{6.66}$$

and the accumulated symmetry is then

$$S_{\mathbf{P}_m}(\sigma) = \sum_{i,j \in \Gamma(\mathbf{P}_m)} C(i,j,\sigma) \tag{6.67}$$

The result of applying the symmetry operator to two images is shown in Fig. 6.22, for small and large values of σ. Figs. 6.22A and D show the image of a rectangle and the image of the face (with colours varied - in the pdf version - to highlight face features), respectively, to which the symmetry operator was applied, Figs. 6.22B and E for the symmetry operator with a low value for the deviation parameter, showing detection of areas with high localised symmetry; Figs. 6.22C and F are for a large value of the deviation parameter which detects overall symmetry and places a peak near the centres. In Figs. 6.22B and E the symmetry operator acts as a corner detector where the edge direction is discontinuous. (Note that the rectangle is one of the synthetic images we can

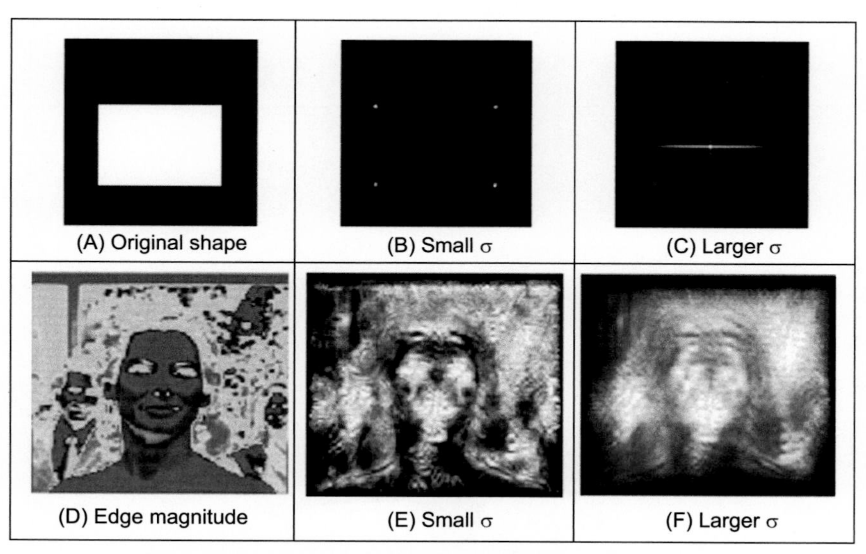

FIGURE 6.22 Applying the symmetry operator for feature extraction.

use to test techniques, since we can understand its output easily. We also tested the operator on the image of a circle, since the circle is completely symmetric its symmetry plot is a single point, at the centre of the circle.) In Fig. 6.22E, the discrete symmetry operator provides a peak close to the position of the accumulator space peak in the GHT. Note that if the reference point specified in the GHT is the centre of symmetry, the results of the discrete symmetry operator and the GHT would be the same for large values of deviation.

We have been considering a discrete operator, a *continuous symmetry operator* has been developed [Zabrodsky95], and a later clarification [Kanatani97] was aimed to address potential practical difficulty associated with hierarchy of symmetry (namely that symmetrical shapes have subsets of regions, also with symmetry). More advanced work includes symmetry between pairs of (SIFT) points and its extension to constellations [Loy06] thereby imposing structure on the symmetry extraction; and analysis of local image symmetry to expose structure via derivative of Gaussian filters [Griffin10], thereby accruing the advantages of a frequency domain approach. There have also been sophisticated approaches to detection of *skewed symmetry*, [Gross94] and [Cham95], with later extension to detection in *orthographic projection* [VanGool95]. Another generalisation addresses the problem of scale [Reisfeld96] and extracts points of symmetry, together with scale. There is also *glide symmetry* which can detect the curved axis of bilateral symmetry [Lee12] (again via SIFT). One result from this operator is shown in Fig. 6.23B. A rather extended application is shown in Fig. 6.23C which as derived by combining LoG with Sobel and then with Gaussian smoothing and hysteresis thresholding of the accumulated symmetry result. The glide symmetry operator is clearly much

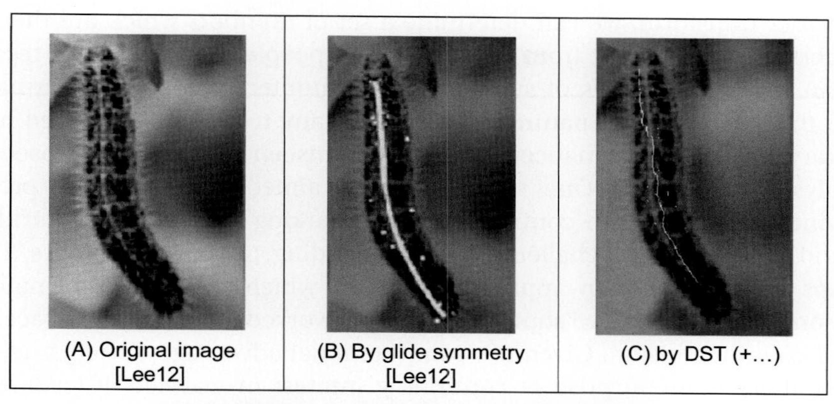

FIGURE 6.23 Results from different symmetry operators.

smoother and better placed than the approximation by the DST. This demonstrates not only that there are more sophisticated operators than the DST, but also, as ever, that it is possible to combine operators to achieve desired effects.

A *focussing* ability was added to the discrete symmetry operator by reformulating the distance weighting function [Parsons99], and we were to deploy this when using symmetry to in an approach which recognises people by their gait (the way they walk) [Hayfron-Acquah03]. Why symmetry was chosen for this task is illustrated in Fig. 6.24: this shows the main axes of symmetry of the walking subject, Fig. 6.24B, which exist within the body, largely defining the skeleton. There is another axis of symmetry, between the legs. When the symmetry operator is applied to a sequence of images, this axis grows and retracts. By agglomerating the sequence and describing it by a (low-pass

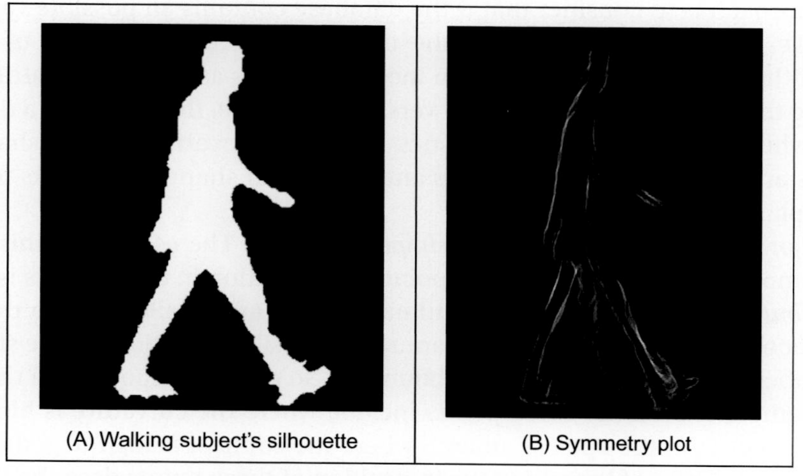

FIGURE 6.24 Applying the symmetry operator for recognition by gait.

filtered) Fourier transform, we can determine a set of numbers which are the same for the same person and different from those for other people, thus achieving recognition.

The main issues in analysis of symmetry by computer vision are performance and speed (OK, that tends to be a natural concern with any technique described herein). A contemporary issue is performance in previously unseen images, as opposed to optimised analysis of datasets. One study [Funk17] aimed 'to gauge the progress in computational symmetry with continuous benchmarking of both new algorithms and datasets' and was based on a challenge format including spatial and 3D data. The study was perhaps motivated by an approach [Funk16] which included information from human vision (derived by crowd sourcing) and thus worked on the key interface between human and computer vision. Given the computational advantage of frequency domain approaches, there is no surprise at continuing interest in wavelets [Cicconet17], and partly by links with convolution one can image progress in deep learning. In fact there was indeed one early study. Given the attractiveness and complexity of symmetry operators, this was a welcome development indeed.

6.5 Flexible shape models — active shape and active appearance

So far, our approaches to analysing shape have concerned a match to image data. This has concerned usually a match between a model (either a template that can deform, or a shape that can evolve) and a single image. An active contour is flexible, but its evolution is essentially controlled by local properties, such as the local curvature or edge strength. The chosen value for, or the likely range of, the parameters to weight these functionals may have been learnt by extensive testing on a database of images of similar type to the one used in application, or selected by experience. A completely different approach is to consider that if the database contains all possible variations of a shape, like its appearance or pose, the database can form a model of the likely variation of that shape. As such, if we can incorporate this as a global constraint, whilst also guiding the match to the most likely version of a shape, then we have a deformable approach which is guided by the statistics of the likely variation in a shape. These approaches are termed *flexible templates* and use global shape constraints formulated from exemplars in training data.

This major approach is called *active shape modelling*. The essence of this approach concerns a model of a shape made up of points: the variation in these points is called the *point distribution model*. The chosen landmark points are labelled on the training images. The set of training images aims to capture all possible variations of the shape. Each point describes a particular point on the boundary, so order is important in the labelling process. Example choices for these points include where the curvature is high (e.g. the corner of an eye) or at the apex of an arch where the contrast is high (e.g. the top of an eyebrow). The statistics of the variations in position of these points describe the ways in which a shape can appear. Example applications include finding the human face in images, for purposes say of automatic face recognition. The only part of the face for which a distinct model is available is the round circle in the iris – and this can be small except at very high resolution. The rest of the face is made of unknown shapes and these can change with change in face expression. As such, they are well suited to a technique which combines shape with distributions since we have a known set of shapes and a fixed inter-relationship, but some of the detail can change. The variation in detail is what is captured in an active shape model.

Naturally, there are a lot of data. If we choose lots of points and we have lots of training images, we shall end up with an enormous number of points. That is where *principal component analysis* comes in as it can compress data into the most significant items. Principal component analysis is an established mathematical tool: help is available on the web and in the literature *Numerical Recipes* [Press92]. Essentially, it rotates a co-ordinate system so as to achieve maximal discriminatory capability: we might not be able to see something if we view it from two distinct points, but if we view it from some point in between then it is quite clear. That is what is done here: the co-ordinate system is rotated so as to work out the most significant variations in the morass of data. Given a set of N training examples where each example is a set of n points, for the ith training example $\mathbf{x}_i$ we have

$$\mathbf{x}_i = (x_{1i}, x_{2i}, \ldots x_{ni}) \quad i \in 1, N \tag{6.68}$$

where x_{ki} is the kth variable in the ith training example. When this is applied to shapes, each element is the two co-ordinates of each point. The average is then computed over the whole set of training examples as

$$\overline{\mathbf{x}} = \frac{1}{N}\sum_{i=1}^{N}\mathbf{x}_i \tag{6.69}$$

The deviation of each example from the mean $\delta\mathbf{x}_i$ is then

$$\delta\mathbf{x}_i = \mathbf{x}_i - \overline{\mathbf{x}} \tag{6.70}$$

This difference reflects how far each example is from the mean at a point. The $2n \times 2n$ covariance matrix $\mathbf{S}$ shows how far all the differences are from the mean as

$$\mathbf{S} = \frac{1}{N}\sum_{i=1}^{N}\delta\mathbf{x}_i\delta\mathbf{x}_i^{\text{T}} \tag{6.71}$$

Principal component analysis of this covariance matrix shows by how much these examples, and hence a shape, can change. In fact, any of the exemplars of the shape can be approximated as

$$\mathbf{x}_i = \overline{\mathbf{x}} + \mathbf{P}\mathbf{w} \tag{6.72}$$

where $\mathbf{P} = (\mathbf{p}_1, \mathbf{p}_2 \ldots \mathbf{p}_t)$ is a matrix of the first t eigenvectors, and $\mathbf{w} = (w_1, w_2 \ldots w_t)^{\text{T}}$ is a corresponding vector of weights where each weight value controls the contribution of a particular eigenvector. Different values in $\mathbf{w}$ give different occurrences of the model, or shape. Given that these changes are within specified limits, then the new model or shape will be similar to the basic (mean) shape. This is because the modes of variation are described by the (unit) eigenvectors of **S**, as

$$\mathbf{S}\mathbf{p}_k = \lambda_k \mathbf{p}_k \tag{6.73}$$

where λ_k denotes the eigenvalues and the eigenvectors obey orthogonality such that

$$\mathbf{p}_k \mathbf{p}_k^{\mathrm{T}} = 1 \tag{6.74}$$

and where the eigenvalues are rank ordered such that $\lambda_k \geq \lambda_{k+1}$. Here, the largest eigenvalues correspond to the most significant modes of variation in the data. The proportion of the variance in the training data, corresponding to each eigenvector, is proportional to the corresponding eigenvalue. As such, a limited number of eigenvalues (and eigenvectors) can be used to encompass the majority of the data. The remaining eigenvalues (and eigenvectors) correspond to modes of variation that are hardly present in the data (like the proportion of very high frequency contribution of an image; we can reconstruct an image mainly from the low-frequency components, as used in image coding). Note that in order to examine the statistics of the labelled landmark points over the training set applied to a new shape, the points need to be aligned, and established procedures are available [Cootes95].

The process of application (to find instances of the modelled shape) involves an iterative approach to bring about increasing match between the points in the model and the image. This is achieved by examining regions around model points to determine the best nearby match. This provides estimates of the appropriate translation, scale rotation and eigenvectors to best fit the model to the data. This is repeated until the model converges to the data, when there is little change to the parameters. Since the models only change to better fit the data, and are controlled by the expected appearance of the shape, they were called active shape models. The application of an active shape model to find the face features of one of the technique's inventors (yes, that's Tim behind the target shapes) is shown in Fig. 6.25 where the initial position is shown in Fig. 6.25A, the result after five iterations in Fig. 6.25B and the final result in Fig. 6.25C. The technique can operate in a coarse-to-fine manner, working at low resolution initially (and making relatively fast moves) whilst slowing to work at finer resolution before the techniques result improves no further, at convergence. Clearly, the technique has not been misled either by the spectacles, or by the presence of other features in the background. This can be used either for enrolment (finding the face, automatically), or for automatic face recognition (finding and describing the features). Naturally, the technique cannot handle initialisation which is too poor – though clearly by Fig. 6.25A the initialisation need not to be too close either.

Active Shape Models (ASM) have been applied in face recognition [Lanitis97], medical image analysis [Cootes94] (including 3D analysis [Hill94]) and industrial inspection [Cootes95]. A similar theory has been used to develop a new approach that incorporates texture, called *Active Appearance Models (AAMs)* [Cootes98]. This approach again

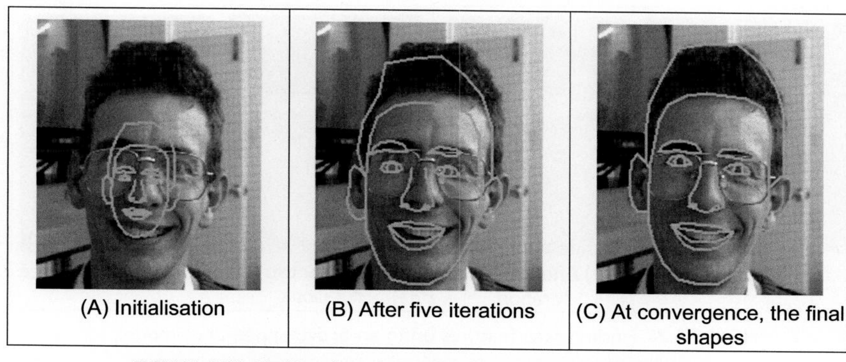

FIGURE 6.25 Finding face features using an active shape model.

represents a shape as a set of landmark points and uses a set of training data to establish the potential range of variation in the shape. One major difference is that AAMs explicitly include texture and updates model parameters to move landmark points closer to image points by matching texture in an iterative search process. The essential differences between ASMs and AAMs include the following:

1. ASMs use texture information local to a point, whereas AAMs use texture information in a whole region;
2. ASMs seek to minimise the distance between model points and the corresponding image points, whereas AAMs seek to minimise distance between a synthesised model and a target image and
3. ASMs search around the current position – typically along profiles normal to the boundary, whereas AAMs consider the image only at the current position.

One comparison [Cootes99] has shown that although ASMs can be faster in implementation than AAMs, the AAMs can require fewer landmark points and can converge to a better result, especially in terms of texture (wherein the AAM was formulated). We await with interest further developments in these approaches to flexible shape modelling. An example result by an AAM for face feature finding is shown in Fig. 6.26. Clearly, this cannot demonstrate computational advantage, but we can see the inclusion of hair in the eyebrows has improved segmentation there. Inevitably, interest has concerned improving computational requirements, in one case by an efficient fitting algorithm based on the inverse compositional image alignment algorithm [Matthews04]. There has been concern about ability to handle occlusion [Gross06], as occurring either by changing (3D) orientation or by gesture. There is much interest in detecting and tracking face points, and as shown by the examples here there is natural interest. This can be used for (automatic) face recognition, emotional state analysis and, rather inevitably in current society, marketing. Face recognition can make life much easier when you can be identified

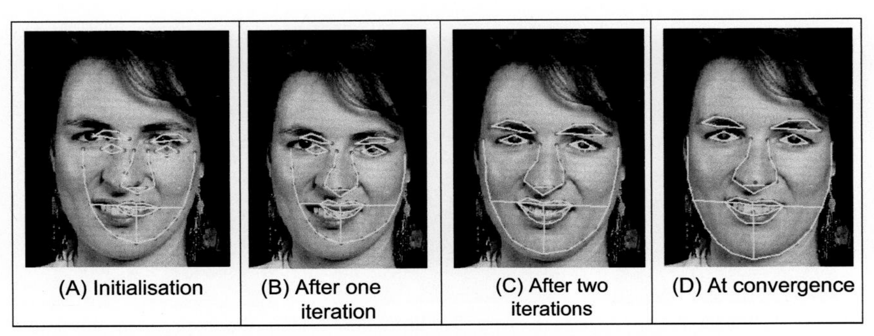

FIGURE 6.26 Finding face features using an active appearance model.

by who you are (biometrics) rather than by what you carry (identity card, etc). One approach (of many) jointly addresses the tasks of face detection, pose estimation, and landmark estimation [Zhu12] and state of the art approaches include deep learning and can estimate gender too [Ranjan2019]. The current state of the art can be found in competitions, and for faces this concerns images collected from natural scenes [Shen15].

6.6 Further reading

The majority of further reading in finding shapes concerns papers, many of which have already been referenced. An excellent survey of the techniques used for feature extraction (including template matching, deformable templates, etc.) can be found in [Trier96], whilst a broader view was taken later [Jain98]. A comprehensive survey of flexible extractions from medical imagery [McInerney96] reinforces the dominance of snakes in medical image analysis, to which they are particularly suited given a target of smooth shapes. (An excellent survey of history and progress of medical image analysis is available [Duncan00].) Few of the textbooks devote much space to shape extraction and snakes, especially level set methods. One text alone is dedicated to shape analysis [VanOtterloo91] and contains many discussions on symmetry and there is a text on distance and medial axis transformation [Siddiqi08]. A visit to Prof. Cootes' (personal) web pages https://personalpages.manchester.ac.uk/staff/timothy.f.cootes/ reveals a lengthy report on flexible shape modelling and a lot of support material (including Windows and Linux code) for active shape modelling. Alternatively, a textbook from the same team is available [Davies08]. For a review of work on level set methods for image segmentation, see [Cremers07] and [Mitiche10]. As in the previous chapters, we have mentioned deep learning at the end of each section, and this will be collected in Chapter 12 (not that there is much deep learning for deformable shape analysis).

References

[Adalsteinsson95] Adalsteinsson, D., and Sethian, J., A Fast Level Set Method for Propagating Interfaces, *Journal of Computational Physics,* **118**(2), pp 269-277, 1995.

[Bamford98] Bamford, P., and Lovell, B., Unsupervised Cell Nucleus Segmentation with Active Contours, *Signal Processing,* **71**, pp 203-213, 1998.

[Berger91] Berger, M. O., Towards Dynamic Adaption of Snake Contours, *Proc. 6th Int. Conf. On Image Analysis and Processing,* Como, Italy, pp 47-54, 1991.

[Benn99] Benn, D. E., Nixon, M. S., and Carter, J. N., Extending Concentricity Analysis by Deformable Templates for Improved Eye Extraction. *Proc. Of the 2nd Int. Conf. on Audio- and Video-Based Biometric Person Authentication AVBPA99,* pp 1-6, 1999.

[Blum67] Blum, H., A Transformation for Extracting New Descriptors of Shape, in Wathen-Dunn, W., Ed.: *Models for the Perception of Speech and Visual Form,* MIT Press, Cambridge, MA, USA, 1967.

[Borgefors86] Borgefors, G., Distance Transformations in Digital Images, *Computer Vision, Graphics, and Image Processing,* **34**(3), pp 344-371, 1986.

[Caselles93] Caselles, V., Catte, F., Coll, T., and Dibos, F., A Geometric Model for Active Contours. *Numerische Mathematic,* **66**, pp 1-31, 1993.

[Caselles97] Caselles, V., Kimmel, R., and Sapiro, G., Geodesic Active Contours, *International Journal of Computer Vision,* **22**(1), pp 61-79, 1997.

[Cham95] Cham, T. J., and Cipolla, R., Symmetry Detection through Local Skewed Symmetries, *Image and Vision Computing,* **13**(5), pp 439-450, 1995.

[Chan95] Chan, T. F., and Vese, L. A., Active Contours without Edges, *IEEE Transactions on IP,* **10**(2), pp 266-277, 2001.

[Cicconet17] Cicconet, M., Birodkar, V., Lund, M., Werman, M., and Geiger, D., A Convolutional Approach to Reflection Symmetry. *Pattern Recognition Letters,* **95**, pp 44-50, 2017.

[Cohen91] Cohen, L. D., NOTE: On Active Contour Models and Balloons, *CVGIP: Image Understanding,* **53**(2), pp 211-218, 1991.

[Cohen92] Cohen, I., Cohen, L. D., and Ayache, N., Using Deformable Surfaces to Segment 3D Images and Inter Differential Structures, *CVGIP: Image Understanding,* **56**(2), pp 242-263, 1992.

[Cohen93] Cohen L. D., and Cohen I., Finite-Element Methods for Active Contour Models and Balloons for 2D and 3D Images, *IEEE Transactions on PAMI,* **15**(11), pp 1131-1147, 1993.

[Cootes94] Cootes, T. F., Hill, A., Taylor, C. J., and Haslam, J., The Use of Active Shape Models for Locating Structures in Medical Images, *Image and Vision Computing,* **12**(6), pp 355-366, 1994.

[Cootes95] Cootes, T. F., Taylor, C. J., Cooper, D. H., and Graham, J., Active Shape Models – Their Training and Application, *CVIU,* **61**(1), pp 38-59, 1995.

[Cootes98] Cootes, T. F., Edwards, G. J., and Taylor, C. J, A Comparative Evaluation of Active Appearance Model Algorithms, In: Lewis, P. H., and Nixon, M. S. Eds., *Proc British Machine Vision Conference 1998 BMVC98,* **vol. 2,** pp 680-689, 1998.

[Cootes98] Cootes, T., Edwards, G. J., and Taylor, C. J, Active Appearance Models, In: Burkhardt, H., and Neumann, B., Eds., *Proc. ECCV,* **vol. 98, 2**, pp 484-498, 1998.

[Cootes99] Cootes, T. F., Edwards, G. J., and Taylor, C. J., Comparing Active Shape Models with Active Appearance Models, In: Pridmore, T., and Elliman, D. Eds., *Proc British Machine Vision Conference 1999 BMVC99,* **vol. 1,** pp 173-182, 1999.

[Cremers02] Cremers, D., Tischhäuser, F., Weickert, J., and Schnörr, C., Diffusion Snakes: Introducing Statistical Shape Knowledge into the Mumford-Shah Functional, *International Journal of Computer Vision,* **50**(3), pp 295-313, 2002.

[Cremers 07] Cremers, D., Rousson, M., and Deriche, R., A Review of Statistical Approaches to Level Set Segmentation: Integrating Color, Texture, Motion and Shape, *International Journal of Computer Vision,* **72**(2), pp 195–215, 2007.

[Davies08] Davies, R., Twining, C., and Taylor, C. J., *Statistical Models of Shape: Optimisation and Evaluation,* Springer, 2008.

[Duncan00] Duncan, J. S., and Ayache, N., Medical Image Analysis: Progress over Two Decades and the Challenges Ahead, *IEEE Transactions on PAMI,* **22**(1), pp 85-106, 2000.

[Felzenszwalb05] Felzenszwalb, P. F., and Huttenlocher, D. P., Pictorial Structures for Object Recognition, *International Journal of Computer Vision,* **61**(1), pp 55-79, 2005.

[Felzenszwalb10] Felzenszwalb, P. F., Girshick, R. B., McAllester, D., and Ramanan, D., Object Detection with Discriminatively Trained Part Based Models, *Transactions on PAMI,* **32**(9), pp 1627-1645, 2010.

[Fischler73] Fischler, M. A., and Elschlager, R. A., The Representation and Matching of Pictorial Structures, *IEEE Transactions on Computers,* **C-22**(1), pp 67 – 92, 1973.

[Funk16] Funk, C., and Liu, Y., Symmetry Recaptcha. *Proc. IEEE Conference on Computer Vision and Pattern Recognition,* pp 5165-5174, 2016.

[Funk17] Funk, C., Lee, S., Oswald, M. R., Tsogkas, S., Shen, W., Cohen, A., Dickinson, S., and Liu, Y., ICCV Challenge: Detecting Symmetry in the Wild. *Proceedings of IEEE International Conference on Computer Vision Workshop (ICCVW),* pp 1692-1701, 2017.

[Geiger95] Geiger, D., Gupta, A., Costa, L. A., and Vlontsos, J., Dynamical Programming for Detecting, Tracking and Matching Deformable Contours, *IEEE Transactions on PAMI,* **17**(3), pp 294-302, 1995.

[Goldberg88] Goldberg, D., *Genetic Algorithms in Search, Optimisation and Machine Learning,* Addison-Wesley, 1988.

[Griffin10] Griffin, L. D., and Lillholm, M., Symmetry Sensitivities of Derivative-Of-Gaussian Filters, *IEEE Transactions on PAMI,* **32**(6), pp 1072-1083, 2010.

[Gross94] Gross A. D., and Boult, T. E., Analysing Skewed Symmetries, *International Journal of Computer Vision,* **13**(1), pp 91-111, 1994.

[Gross06] Gross, R., Matthews I., and Baker S., Active Appearance Models with Occlusion. *Image and Vision Computing,* **24**(6), pp 593-604, 2006.

[Gunn97] Gunn, S. R., and Nixon M. S., A Robust Snake Implementation; a Dual Active Contour, *IEEE Transactions on PAMI,* **19**(1), pp 63-68, 1997.

[Gunn98] Gunn, S. R., and Nixon, M. S., Global and Local Active Contours for Head Boundary Extraction, *International Journal of Computer Vision,* **30**(1), pp 43-54, 1998.

[Hayfron-Acquah03] Hayfron-Acquah, J. B., Nixon, M. S., and Carter, J. N., Automatic Gait Recognition by Symmetry Analysis, *Pattern Recognition Letters,* **24**(13), pp 2175-2183, 2003.

[Hill94] Hill, A., Cootes, T. F., Taylor, C. J., and Lindley, K., Medical Image Interpretation: a Generic Approach Using Deformable Templates, *Journal of Medical Informatics*, **19**(1), pp 47-59, 1994.

[Jain98] Jain, A. K., Zhong, Y., and Dubuisson-Jolly, M-P., Deformable Template Models: a Review, *Signal Processing*, **71**, pp 109-129, 1998.

[Ivins95] Ivins, J., and Porrill, J., Active Region Models for Segmenting Textures and Colours, *Image and Vision Computing*, **13**(5), pp 431-437, 1995.

[Kanatani97] Kanatani, K., Comments on "Symmetry as a Continuous Feature", *IEEE Transactions on PAMI*, **19**(3), pp 246-247, 1997.

[Kass88] Kass, M., Witkin, A., and Terzopoulos, D., Snakes: Active Contour Models, *International Journal of Computer Vision*, **1**(4), pp 321-331, 1988.

[Katz03] Katz, R. A., and Pizer, S. M., Untangling the Blum Medial Axis Transform, *International Journal of Computer Vision*, **55**(2-3), pp 139-153, 2003.

[Lai94] Lai, K. F., and Chin, R. T., On Regularisation, Extraction and Initialisation of the Active Contour Model (Snakes), *Proc. 1st Asian Conference on Computer Vision*, pp 542-545, 1994.

[Lai95] Lai, K. F., and Chin, R. T., Deformable Contours - Modelling and Extraction, *IEEE Transactions on PAMI*, **17**(11), pp 1084-1090, 1995.

[Lanitis97] Lanitis, A., Taylor, C. J., and Cootes, T., Automatic Interpretation and Coding of Face Images Using Flexible Models, *IEEE Transactions on PAMI*, **19**(7), pp 743-755, 1997.

[Lee82] Lee, D. T., Medial Axis Transformation of a Planar Shape, *IEEE Transactions on PAMI*, **4**, pp 363-369. 1982.

[Lee12] Lee, S., and Liu, Y., Curved Glide-Reflection Symmetry Detection. *IEEE Transactions on PAMI*, **34**(2), pp 266-278, 2012.

[Loy06] Loy, G., and Eklundh, J-O., Detecting Symmetry and Symmetric Constellations of Features, *Proc. ECCV 2006, Part II, LNCS 3952*, pp. 508–521, 2006.

[Malladi95] Malladi, R., Sethian, J. A., and Vemuri, B. C., Shape Modeling with Front Propagation: A Level Set Approach, *IEEE Transactions on PAMI*, **17**(2), pp 158-175, 1995.

[Marcos18] Marcos, D., Tuia, D., Kellenberger, B., Zhang, L., Bai, M., Liao, R., and Urtasun, R. , Learning Deep Structured Active Contours End-To-End. In *Proceedings of the IEEE Conference on Computer Vision and Pattern Recognition*, pp. 8877-8885, 2018.

[Matthews04] Matthews I., and Baker S., Active Appearance Models Revisited,*International Journal of Computer Vision*, **60**(2), pp 135 – 164, 2004.

[McInerney96] McInerney, T., and Terzopolous, D., Deformable Models in Medical Image Analysis, a Survey, *Medical Image Analysis*, **1**(2), pp 91-108, 1996.

[Mitiche10] Mitiche, A., and Ayed, I. B., *Variational and Level Set Methods in Image Segmentation*, Springer Science & Business Media, Heidelberg Germany, 2010.

[Mumford89] Mumford, D., and Shah, J., Optimal Approximation by Piecewise Smooth Functions and Associated Variational Problems, *Communications on Pure and Applied Mathematics*, **42**, pp 577-685, 1989.

[Niblack92] Niblack, C. W., Gibbons, P. B., and Capson, D. W., Generating Skeletons and Centerlines from the Distance Transform, *CVGIP: Graphical Models and Image Processing*, **54**(5), pp 420 – 437, 1992.

[Niu17] Niu, S., Chen, Q., De Sisternes, L., Ji, Z., Zhou, Z., and Rubin, D. L., Robust Noise Region-Based Active Contour Model via Local Similarity Factor for Image Segmentation. *Pattern Recognition*, **61**, pp 104-119, 2017.

[Osher03] Osher, S. J., and Paragios, N., Eds., *Geometric Level Set Methods in Imaging, Vision and Graphics*, Springer (NY), 2003.

[Osher88] Osher, S. J., and Sethian, J., Eds., Fronts Propagating with Curvature Dependent Speed: Algorithms Based on the Hamilton-Jacobi Formulation, *Journal of Computational Physics*, **79**, pp 12-49, 1988.

[Parsons99] Parsons, C. J., and Nixon, M. S., Introducing Focus in the Generalised Symmetry Operator, *IEEE Signal Processing Letters*, **6**(1), pp 49-51, 1999.

[Peterfreund99] Peterfreund, N., Robust Tracking of Position and Velocity, *IEEE Transactions on PAMI*, **21**(6), pp 564-569, 1999.

[Ranjan2019] Ranjan, R., Patel, V.M., and Chellappa, R., Hyperface: A Deep Multi-Task Learning Framework for Face Detection, Landmark Localization, Pose Estimation, and Gender Recognition. *IEEE Transactions on PAMI*, **41**(1), pp 121-135, 2019.

[Siddiqi08] Siddiqi, K., and Pizer. S., Eds: *Medial Representations: Mathematics, Algorithms and Applications (Computational Imaging and Vision)*, Springer, 2008.

[Press92] Press, W. H., Teukolsky, S. A., Vettering, W. T., and Flannery, B. P., *Numerical Recipes in C - the Art of Scientific Computing*, 2nd Edition, Cambridge University Press, Cambridge UK, 1992.

[Reisfeld95] Reisfeld, D., Wolfson, H., and Yeshurun, Y., Context-Free Attentional Operators: the Generalised Symmetry Transform, *International Journal of Computer Vision*, **14**, pp 119-130, 1995.

[Reisfeld96] Reisfeld D., The Constrained Phase Congruency Feature Detector: Simultaneous Localization, Classification and Scale Determination, *Pattern Recognition Letters*, **17**(11), pp 1161-1169, 1996.

[Ronfard94] Ronfard, R., Region-based Strategies for Active Contour Models, *International Journal of Computer Vision*, **13**(2), pp 229-251, 1994.

[Rupprecht16] Rupprecht, C., Huaroc, E., Baust, M., and Navab, N., *Deep Active Contours*, arXiv preprint arXiv:1607.05074, 2016.

[Sethian99] Sethian, J., *Level Set Methods: Evolving Interfaces in Computational Geometry, Fluid Mechanics, Computer Vision, and Materials Science*, Cambridge Univ. Press, New York, 1999.

[Shen15] Shen, J., Zafeiriou, S., Chrysos, G. G., Kossaifi, J., Tzimiropoulos, G., and Pantic, M., The First Facial Landmark Tracking In-The-Wild Challenge: Benchmark and Results. *Proceedings of IEEE International Conference on Computer Vision Workshops* pp. 50-58, 2015.

[Siddiqi98] Siddiqi, K., Lauziere, Y., Tannenbaum, A., and Zucker S., Area and Length Minimizing Flows for Shape Segmentation, *IEEE Transactions on IP*, **7**(3), pp 433-443, 1998.

[Trier96] Trier, O. D., Jain, A. K., and Taxt, T., Feature Extraction Methods for Character Recognition – A Survey, *Pattern Recognition*, **29**(4), pp 641-662, 1996.

[VanGool95] Van Gool, L., Moons T., Ungureanu D., and Oosterlinck A., The Characterisation and Detection of Skewed Symmetry, *Computer Vision and Image Understanding*, **61**(1), pp 138-150, 1995.

[VanOtterloo91] Van Otterloo, P. J., *A Contour-Oriented Approach to Shape Analysis*, Prentice Hall International (UK) Ltd., Hemel Hempstead, 1991.

[Waite90] Waite, J. B., and Welsh, W. J., Head Boundary Location Using Snakes, *British Telecom Journal*, **8**(3), pp 127-136, 1990.

[Wang92] Wang, Y. F., and J. F. Wang, Surface Reconstruction Using Deformable Models with Interior and Boundary Constraints, *IEEE Transactions on PAMI*, **14**(5), pp 572-579, 1992.

[Weickert98] Weickert, J., Ter Haar Romeny, B. M., and Viergever, M. A., Efficient and Reliable Schemes for Nonlinear Diffusion Filtering, *IEEE Transactions on IP*, **7**(3), pp 398-410, March 1998.

[Williams92] Williams, D. J., and Shah, M., A Fast Algorithm for Active Contours and Curvature Estimation, *CVGIP: Image Understanding*, **55**(1), pp 14-26, 1992.

[Xie04] Xie, X., and Mirmehdi, M., RAGS: Region-Aided Geometric Snake, *IEEE Transactions on IP*, **13**(5), pp 640-652, 2004.

[Xu94] Xu, G., Segawa, E., and Tsuji, S., Robust Active Contours with Insensitive Parameters, *Pattern Recognition.*, **27**(7), pp 879-884, 1994.

[Xu98] Xu, C., and Prince, J. L., Snakes, Shapes, and Gradient Vector Flow, *IEEE Transactions on IP*, **7**(3), pp 359-369, 1998.

[Xu00] Xu, C., Yezzi, A., and Prince, J. L., On the Relationship between Parametric and Geometric Active Contours and its Applications, *Proc. 34th Asimolar Conf. On Sig.* Sys Comp., Pacific Grove CA, pp 483-489, 2000.

[Yuille91] Yuille, A. L., Deformable Templates for Face Recognition, *Journal of Cognitive Neuroscience*, **3**(1), pp 59-70, 1991.

[Zabrodsky95] Zabrodsky, H., Peleg, S., and Avnir, D., Symmetry as a Continuous Feature, *IEEE Transactions on PAMI*, **17**(12), pp 1154-1166, 1995.

[Zhu12] Zhu, X., and Ramanan, D., Face Detection, Pose Estimation, and Landmark Localization in the Wild. *Proceedingsof IEEE CVPR*, pp. 2879-2886, 2012.

7 Object description

7.1 Overview and invariance requirements

Objects are represented as a collection of pixels in an image. Thus, for purposes of recognition, we need to describe the properties of groups of pixels. The description is often just a set of numbers – the object's *descriptors*. From these, we can compare and recognise objects by simply matching the descriptors of objects in an image against the descriptors of known objects. However, in order to be useful for recognition, descriptors should have four important properties. First, they should define a *complete set*. That is, two objects must have the same descriptors if and only if they have the same shape. Secondly, they should be *congruent*. As such, we should be able to recognise similar objects when they have similar descriptors. Thirdly, it is convenient that they have invariant properties. For example, rotation invariant descriptors will be useful for recognising objects whatever their orientation. Other important invariance properties naturally include scale and position and also invariance to affine and perspective changes. These last two properties are very important when recognising objects observed from different viewpoints. In addition to these three properties, the descriptors should be a compact set. Namely, a descriptor should represent the essence of an object in an efficient way. That is, it should only contain information about what makes an object unique, or different from the other objects. The quantity of information used to describe this characterisation should be less than the information necessary to have a complete description of the object itself. Unfortunately, there is no set of complete and compact descriptors to characterise general objects. Thus, the best recognition performance is obtained by carefully selected properties. As such, the process of recognition is strongly related to each particular application with a particular type of object.

In this chapter, we present the characterisation of objects by two forms of descriptors. These descriptors are summarised in Table 7.1. Region and shape descriptors characterise an arrangement of pixels within the area and the arrangement of pixels in the perimeter or boundary, respectively. This region versus perimeter representation is common in image analysis. For example, edges can be located by region growing (to label area) or by differentiation (to label perimeter), as covered in Chapter 4. There are actually many techniques that can be used to obtain descriptors of an object's boundary. Here, we shall just concentrate on three forms of descriptors: *chain codes* and two forms based on *Fourier characterisation*. For region descriptors we shall distinguish between basic descriptors and statistical descriptors defined by moments.

Feature Extraction and Image Processing for Computer Vision. https://doi.org/10.1016/B978-0-12-814976-8.00007-5

Table 7.1 Overview of this chapter.

Main topic	**Subtopics**	**Main points**
Boundary descriptions	How to determine the boundary and the region it encloses. How to form a description of the boundary and necessary properties in that description. How we describe a curve/boundary by Fourier approaches.	Basic approach: *chain codes*. *Start point* and *rotation* invariance. *Fourier descriptors*: discrete approximations; cumulative angular function and *elliptic Fourier descriptors*.
Region descriptors	How we describe the area of a shape. Basic shape measures: heuristics and properties. Describing area by statistical moments: need for invariance and more sophisticated descriptions. What do the moments describe, and reconstruction from the moments.	Basic *shape measures*: area; perimeter; *compactness*; *irregularity*, and dispersion. *Moments*: basic; *centralised*; *invariant*; *Zernike*. *Krawtchouk*. Properties and reconstruction.

7.2 Boundary descriptions

7.2.1 Boundary and region

A region usually describes *contents* (or interior points) which are surrounded by a *boundary* (or perimeter) which is often called the region's *contour*. The form of the contour is generally referred to as its *shape*. A point can be defined to be on the boundary (contour) if it is part of the region and there is at least one pixel in its neighbourhood that is not part of the region. The boundary itself is usually found by contour following: we first find one point on the contour and then progress round the contour either in a clockwise direction, or anticlockwise, finding the nearest (or next) contour point.

In order to define the interior points in a region and the points in the boundary, we need to consider neighbouring relationships between pixels. These relationships are described by means of *connectivity* rules. There are two common ways of defining connectivity: *4-way* (or 4-neighbourhood) where only immediate neighbours are analysed for connectivity; or *8-way* (or 8-neighbourhood) where all the eight pixels surrounding a chosen pixel are analysed for connectivity. These two types of connectivity are illustrated in Fig. 7.1. In this figure, the pixel is shown in light grey and its neighbours in dark grey. In 4-way connectivity, Fig. 7.1A, a pixel has four neighbours in the directions: North, East, South and West, its immediate neighbours. The four extra neighbours in 8-way connectivity, Fig. 7.1B, are those in the directions: North East, South East, South West and North West, the points at the corners.

A boundary and a region can be defined using both types of connectivity and they are always complementary. That is, if the boundary pixels are connected in 4-way, the region pixels will be connected in 8-way and vice versa. This relationship can be seen in the example shown in Fig. 7.2. In the example in this figure, the boundary is shown in dark grey and the region in light grey. We can observe that for a diagonal boundary, the 4-way

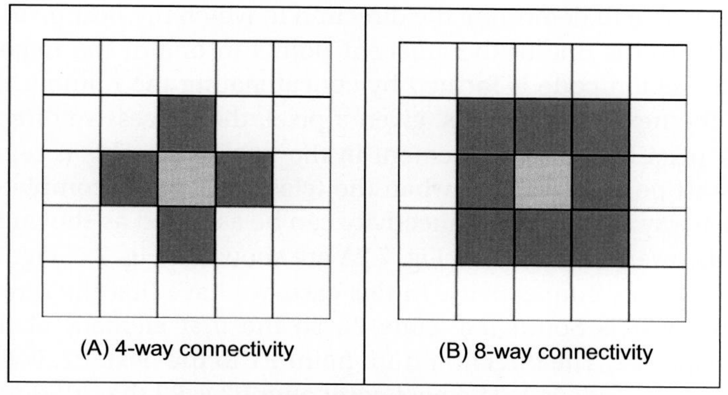

FIGURE 7.1 Main types of connectivity analysis.

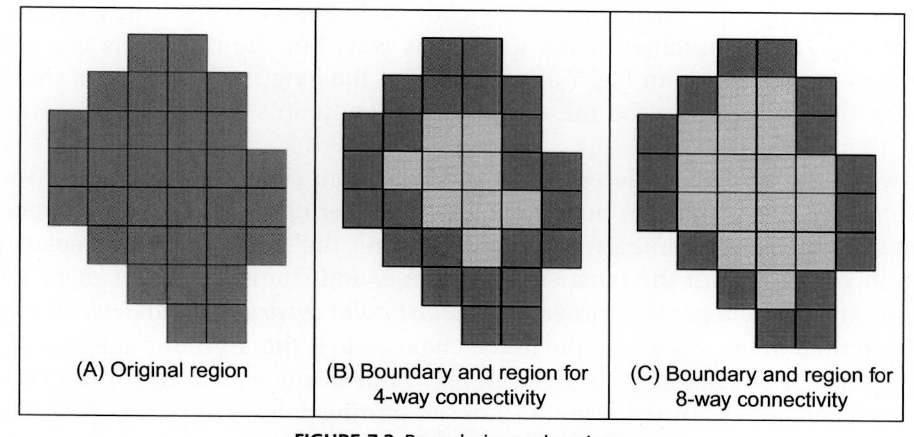

FIGURE 7.2 Boundaries and regions.

connectivity gives a staircase boundary, whereas 8-way connectivity gives a diagonal line formed from the points at the corners of the neighbourhood. Notice that all the pixels that form the region in Fig. 7.2B have 4-way connectivity, whilst the pixels in Fig. 7.2C have 8-way connectivity. This is complementary to the pixels in the border.

7.2.2 Chain codes

In order to obtain a representation of a contour, we can simply store the co-ordinates of a sequence of pixels in the image. Alternatively, we can just store the relative position between consecutive pixels. This is the basic idea behind *chain codes*. Chain codes are actually one of the oldest techniques in computer vision originally introduced in the 1960s [Freeman61] (an excellent review came later [Freeman74]). Essentially, the set of pixels in the border of a shape is translated into a set of connections between them. Given a complete border, one that is a set of connected points, then starting from one pixel we need to be able to determine the direction in which the next pixel is to be found. Namely, the next pixel is one of the adjacent points in one of the major compass directions. Thus, the chain code is formed by concatenating the number that designates the direction of the next pixel. That is, given a pixel, the successive direction from one pixel to the next pixel becomes an element in the final code. This is repeated for each point until the start point is reached when the (closed) shape is completely analysed.

Directions in 4-way and 8-way connectivity can be assigned as shown in Fig. 7.3. The chain codes for the example region in Fig. 7.2A are shown in Fig. 7.4. Fig. 7.4A shows the chain code for the 4-way connectivity. In this case, we have that the direction from the start point to the next is South (i.e. code 2), so the first element of the chain code describing the shape is 2. The direction from point P1 to the next, P2, is East (code 1) so the next element of the code is 1. The next point after P2 is P3 that is South giving a code 2. This coding is repeated until P23 that is connected eastwards to the starting point, so the last element (the 12th element) of the code is 1. The code for 8-way connectivity shown in Fig. 7.4B is obtained in an analogous way, but the directions are assigned according to the definition in Fig. 7.3B. Notice that the length of the code is shorter for this connectivity, given that the number of boundary points is smaller for 8-way connectivity than it is for 4-way.

Clearly this code will be different when the start point changes. Accordingly, we need *start point invariance.* This can be achieved by considering the elements of the code to constitute the digits in an integer. Then, we can shift the digits *cyclically* (replacing the least significant digit with the most significant one, and shifting all other digits left one place). The smallest integer is returned as the *start point invariant chain code description.* This is illustrated in Fig. 7.5 where the initial chain code is that from the shape in Fig. 7.4. Here the result of the first shift is given in Fig. 7.5B, this is equivalent to the code that would have been derived by using point P1 as the starting point. The result of two shifts, in Fig. 7.5C, is the chain code equivalent to starting at point P2, but this is not a code corresponding to the minimum integer. The minimum integer code, as in Fig. 7.5D, is the

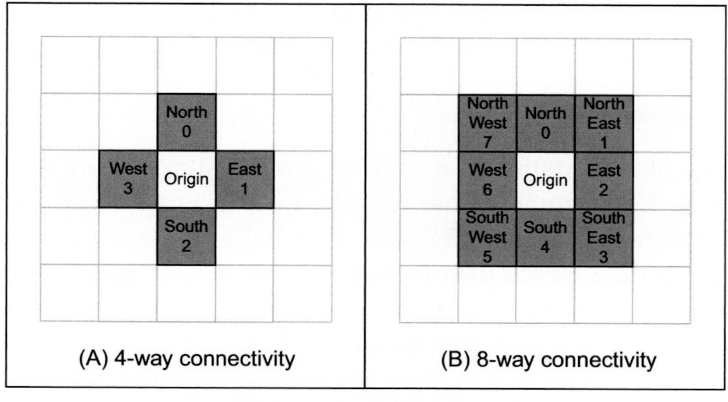

FIGURE 7.3 Connectivity in chain codes.

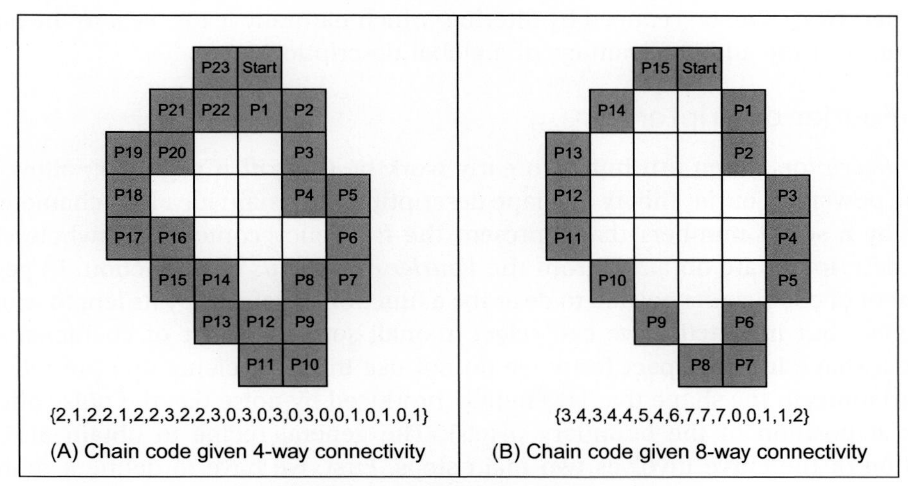

FIGURE 7.4 Chain codes by different connectivity.

Code = {3,4,3,4,4,5,4,6,7,7,7,0,0,1,1,2} (A) Initial chain code	Code = {4,3,4,4,5,4,6,7,7,7,0,0,1,1,2,3} (B) Result of one shift
Code = {3,4,4,5,4,6,7,7,7,0,0,1,1,2,3,4} (C) Result of two shifts	Code = {0,0,1,1,2,3,4,3,4,4,5,4,6,7,7,7} (D) Minimum integer chain code

FIGURE 7.5 Start point invariance in chain codes.

minimum of all the possible shifts and is actually the chain code which would have been derived by starting at point P11. That fact could not be used in application since we would need to find P11, naturally, it is much easier to shift to achieve a minimum integer.

In addition to starting point invariance, we can also obtain a code that does not change with *rotation*. This can be achieved by expressing the code as a difference of chain code: relative descriptions remove rotation dependence. Change of *scale* can complicate matters greatly, since we can end up with a set of points which is of different size to the original set. As such, the boundary needs to be resampled before coding. This is a tricky issue. Furthermore, noise can have drastic effects. If salt and pepper noise were to remove, or to add, some points the code would change. Clearly, such problems can lead to great difficulty with chain codes. However, their main virtue is their simplicity and as such they remain a popular technique for shape description. Further developments of chain codes have found application with corner detectors [Seeger94] and [Liu90]. However, the need to be able to handle noise, the requirement of connectedness and the local nature of description naturally motivates alternative approaches. Noise can be reduced by filtering, which naturally leads back to the Fourier transform, with the added advantage of a global description.

7.2.3 Fourier descriptors

Fourier descriptors, often attributed to early work by Cosgriff [Cosgriff60], allow us to bring the power of Fourier theory to shape description. The main idea is to characterise a contour by a set of numbers that represent the frequency content of a whole shape. Fourier descriptors are obtained from the *Fourier coefficients* of a function. In general, the number of coefficients needed to describe a function is defined by its length (number of samples), but in practice we can select a small set of number of coefficients that describe a shape in a compact form; we do not use the coefficients that are related to small variations in the shape that is generally produced by noise (i.e. the noise affecting the spatial position of the boundary pixels). The general recipe to obtain a Fourier description of the curve involves two main steps. First, we have to define a representation of a curve. Secondly, we expand it using Fourier theory. We can obtain alternative flavours by combining different curve representations and different Fourier expansions. Here, we shall consider Fourier descriptors of angular and complex contour representations. However, Fourier expansions can be developed for other curve representations [Persoon77, VanOtterloo91].

In addition to the curve's definition, a factor that influences the development and properties of the description is the choice of Fourier expansion. If we consider that the trace of a curve defines a periodic function, we can opt to use a Fourier series expansion. However, we could also consider that the description is not periodic. Thus, we could develop a representation based on the Fourier transform. In this case, we could use alternative Fourier integral definitions. Here, we will develop the presentation based on expansion in Fourier series. This is the common way used to describe shapes in pattern recognition.

It is important to notice that although a curve in an image is composed of discrete pixels, Fourier descriptors are developed for continuous curves. This is convenient since it leads to a discrete set of Fourier descriptors. Additionally, we should remember that the pixels in the image are actually the sampled points of a continuous curve in the scene. However, the formulation leads to the definition of the integral of a continuous curve. In practice, we do not have a continuous curve, but a sampled version. Thus, the expansion is actually approximated by means of numerical integration.

7.2.3.1 Basis of Fourier descriptors

In the most basic form, the co-ordinates of boundary pixels are x and y point co-ordinates. A Fourier description of these essentially gives the set of spatial frequencies that fit the boundary points. The first element of the Fourier components (the d.c. component), is simply the average value of the x and y co-ordinates, giving the co-ordinates of the centre point of the boundary, expressed in complex form. The second component essentially gives the radius of the circle that best fits the points. Accordingly, a circle can be described by its zero- and first-order components (the d.c. component and first harmonic). The higher-order components increasingly describe detail, as they are associated with higher frequencies.

This is illustrated in Fig. 7.6. Here, the Fourier description of the ellipse in Fig. 7.6A is the frequency components in Fig. 7.6B, depicted in logarithmic form for purposes of display. The Fourier description has been obtained by using the ellipse boundary points' co-ordinates. Here we can see that the low-order components dominate the description, as to be expected for such a smooth shape. In this way, we can derive a set a numbers that can be used to recognise the boundary of a shape: a similar ellipse should give a similar set of numbers, whereas a completely different shape will result in a completely different set of numbers.

We do, however, need to check the result. One way is to take the descriptors of a circle, since the first harmonic should be the circle's radius. A better way though is to reconstruct the shape from its descriptors, if the reconstruction matches the original shape then the description would appear correct. Naturally, we can reconstruct a shape from this Fourier description since the descriptors are regenerative. The zero-order component gives the position (or origin) of a shape. The ellipse can be reconstructed by adding in all spatial components, to extend and compact the shape along the x and y axes, respectively. By this inversion, we return to the original ellipse. When we include the zero (d.c.) and the first descriptor, then we reconstruct a circle, as expected, shown in Fig. 7.7B. When we include all Fourier descriptors the reconstruction, Fig. 7.7C is very close to the original Fig. 7.7A with slight difference due to discretisation effects.

But this is only an outline of the basis to Fourier descriptors, since we have yet to consider descriptors which give the same description whatever an object's position, scale and rotation. Here we have just considered an object's description that is achieved in a manner that allows for reconstruction. In order to develop practically useful descriptors, we shall need to consider more basic properties. As such, we first turn to the use of Fourier theory for shape description.

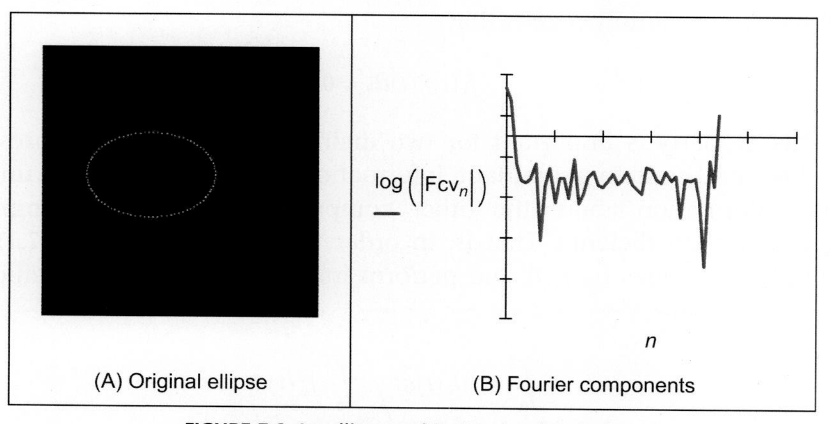

FIGURE 7.6 An ellipse and its Fourier description.

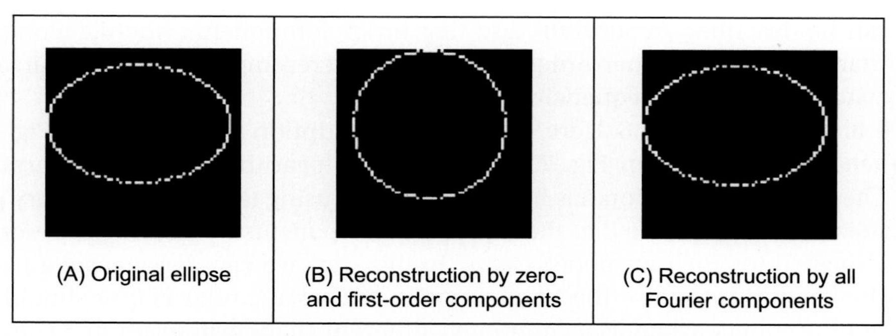

(A) Original ellipse

(B) Reconstruction by zero- and first-order components

(C) Reconstruction by all Fourier components

FIGURE 7.7 Reconstructing an ellipse from a Fourier description.

7.2.3.2 Fourier expansion

In order to define a Fourier expansion, we can start by considering that a continuous curve $c(t)$ can be expressed as a summation of the form

$$c(t) = \sum_k c_k f_k(t) \tag{7.1}$$

where c_k defines the coefficients of the expansion and the collection of functions $f_k(t)$ define the basis functions. The expansion problem centres on finding the coefficients given a set of basis functions. This equation is very general and different basis functions can also be used. For example, $f_k(t)$ can be chosen such that the expansion defines a polynomial. Other bases define splines, Lagrange and Newton interpolation functions. A Fourier expansion represents periodic functions by a basis defined as a set of infinite complex exponentials. That is,

$$c(t) = \sum_{k=-\infty}^{\infty} c_k e^{jk\omega t} \tag{7.2}$$

Here, ω defines the fundamental frequency, and it is equal to $2\pi/T$ where T is the period of the function. The main feature of the Fourier expansion is that it defines an orthogonal basis. This simply means that

$$\int_0^T f_k(t) f_j(t) dt = 0 \tag{7.3}$$

for $k \neq j$. This property is important for two main reasons. First, it ensures that the expansion does not contain redundant information (each coefficient is unique and contains no information about the other components). Second, it simplifies the computation of the coefficients. That is, in order to solve for c_k in Eq. (7.1), we can simply multiply both sides by $f_k(t)$ and perform integration. Thus, the coefficients are given by

$$c_k = \int_0^T c(t) f_k(t) dt \bigg/ \int_0^T f_k^2(t) dt \tag{7.4}$$

By considering the definition in Eq. (7.2) we have that

$$c_k = \frac{1}{T}\int_0^T c(t)e^{-jkwt}dt \tag{7.5}$$

In addition to the exponential form given in Eq. (7.2), the Fourier expansion can also be expressed in trigonometric form. This form shows that the Fourier expansion corresponds to the summation of trigonometric functions that increase in frequency. It can be obtained by considering that

$$c(t) = c_0 + \sum_{k=1}^{\infty}\left(c_k e^{jk\omega t} + c_{-k}e^{-jk\omega t}\right) \tag{7.6}$$

In this equation the values of $e^{jk\omega t}$ and $e^{-jk\omega t}$ define a pairs of complex conjugate vectors. Thus c_k and c_{-k} describe a complex number and its conjugate. Let us define these numbers as

$$c_k = c_{k,1} - jc_{k,2} \quad \text{and} \quad c_{-k} = c_{k,1} + jc_{k,2} \tag{7.7}$$

By substitution of this definition in Eq. (7.6) we obtain

$$c(t) = c_0 + 2\sum_{k=1}^{\infty}\left(c_{k,1}\left(\frac{e^{jk\omega t} + e^{-jk\omega t}}{2}\right) + jc_{k,2}\left(\frac{-e^{jk\omega t} + e^{-jk\omega t}}{2}\right)\right) \tag{7.8}$$

That is,

$$c(t) = c_0 + 2\sum_{k=1}^{\infty}\left(c_{k,1}\cos(k\omega t) + c_{k,2}\sin(k\omega t)\right) \tag{7.9}$$

If we define

$$a_k = 2c_{k,1} \quad \text{and} \quad b_k = 2c_{k,2} \tag{7.10}$$

we obtain the standard trigonometric form given by

$$c(t) = \frac{a_0}{2} + \sum_{k=1}^{\infty}\left(a_k\cos(k\omega t) + b_k\sin(k\omega t)\right) \tag{7.11}$$

The coefficients of this expansion, a_k and b_k are known as the *Fourier descriptors*. These descriptors control the amount of each frequency that contributes to make up the curve. Accordingly, these descriptors can be said to describe the curve since they do not have the same values for different curves. Notice that according to Eqs. (7.7) and (7.10), the coefficients of the trigonometric and exponential form are related by

$$c_k = \frac{a_k - jb_k}{2} \quad \text{and} \quad c_{-k} = \frac{a_k + jb_k}{2} \tag{7.12}$$

The coefficients in Eq. (7.11) can be obtained by considering the orthogonal property in Eq. (7.3). Thus, one way to compute values for the descriptors is

$$a_k = \frac{2}{T}\int_0^T c(t)\cos(k\omega t)dt \quad \text{and} \quad b_k = \frac{2}{T}\int_0^T c(t)\sin(k\omega t)dt \tag{7.13}$$

In order to obtain the Fourier descriptors, a curve can be represented by the complex exponential form of Eq. (7.2) or by the sin and cos relationship of Eq. (7.11). The descriptors obtained by using either of the two definitions are equivalent, and they can be related by the definitions of Eq. (7.12). Generally, Eq. (7.13) is used to compute the coefficients since it has a more intuitive form. However, some works have considered the complex form (e.g. [Granlund72]). The complex form provides an elegant development of rotation analysis.

7.2.3.3 Shift invariance

Chain codes required special attention to give start point invariance. Let us see if that is required here. The main question is whether the descriptors will change when the curve is shifted. In addition to Eqs. (7.2) and (7.11), a Fourier expansion can be written in another sinusoidal form. If we consider that

$$|c_k| = \sqrt{a_k^2 + b_k^2} \quad \text{and} \quad \varphi_k = a\tan^{-1}(b_k / a_k) \tag{7.14}$$

then the Fourier expansion can be written as

$$c(t) = \frac{a_0}{2} + \sum_{k=0}^{\infty} |c_k| \cos(k\omega t + \varphi_k) \tag{7.15}$$

Here $|c_k|$ is the amplitude and φ_k is the phase of the Fourier coefficient. An important property of the Fourier expansion is that $|c_k|$ does not change when the function $c(t)$ is shifted (i.e. translated), as in Section 2.6.1. This can be observed by considering the definition of Eq. (7.13) for a shifted curve $c(t+\alpha)$. Here, α represents the shift value. Thus,

$$a'_k = \frac{2}{T}\int_0^T c(t'+\alpha)\cos(k\omega t')dt \quad \text{and} \quad b'_k = \frac{2}{T}\int_0^T c(t'+\alpha)\sin(k\omega t')dt \tag{7.16}$$

By defining a change of variable by $t = t' + \alpha$, we have

$$a'_k = \frac{2}{T}\int_0^T c(t)\cos(k\omega t - k\omega\alpha)dt \quad \text{and} \quad b'_k = \frac{2}{T}\int_0^T c(t)\sin(k\omega t - k\omega\alpha)dt \tag{7.17}$$

After some algebraic manipulation we obtain

$$a'_k = a_k\cos(k\omega\alpha) + b_k\sin(k\omega\alpha) \quad \text{and} \quad b'_k = b_k\cos(k\omega\alpha) - a_k\sin(k\omega\alpha) \tag{7.18}$$

The amplitude $|c'_k|$ is given by

$$|c'_k| = \sqrt{(a_k\cos(k\omega\alpha) + b_k\sin(k\omega\alpha))^2 + (b_k\cos(k\omega\alpha) - a_k\sin(k\omega\alpha))^2} \tag{7.19}$$

That is,

$$|c'_k| = \sqrt{a_k^2 + b_k^2} \tag{7.20}$$

Thus, the amplitude is independent of the shift α. Although shift invariance could be incorrectly related to translation invariance, actually, as we shall see, this property is related to rotation invariance in shape description.

7.2.3.4 Discrete computation

Before defining Fourier descriptors, we must consider the numerical procedure necessary to obtain the Fourier coefficients of a curve. The problem is that Eqs. (7.11) and (7.13) are defined for a continuous curve. However, given the discrete nature of the image, the curve $c(t)$ will be described by a collection of points. This discretisation has two important effects. First, it limits the number of frequencies in the expansion. Second, it forces numerical approximation to the integral defining the coefficients.

Fig. 7.8 shows an example of a discrete approximation of a curve. Fig. 7.8A shows a continuous curve in a period, or interval, T. Fig. 7.8B shows the approximation of the curve by a set of discrete points. If we try to obtain the curve from the sampled points, we will find that the sampling process reduces the amount of detail. According to the *Nyquist theorem*, the maximum frequency f_c in a function is related to the sample period τ by

$$\tau = \frac{1}{2f_c} \tag{7.21}$$

Thus, if we have m sampling points, then the sampling period is equal to $\tau = T/m$. Accordingly, the maximum frequency in the approximation is given by

$$f_c = \frac{m}{2T} \tag{7.22}$$

Each term in Eq. (7.11) defines a trigonometric function at frequency $f_k = k/T$. By comparing this frequency with the relationship in Eq. (7.15), we have that the maximum frequency is obtained when

$$k = \frac{m}{2} \tag{7.23}$$

Thus, in order to define a curve that passes through the m sampled points, we need to consider only $m/2$ coefficients. The other coefficients define frequencies higher than the maximum frequency. Accordingly, the Fourier expansion can be redefined as

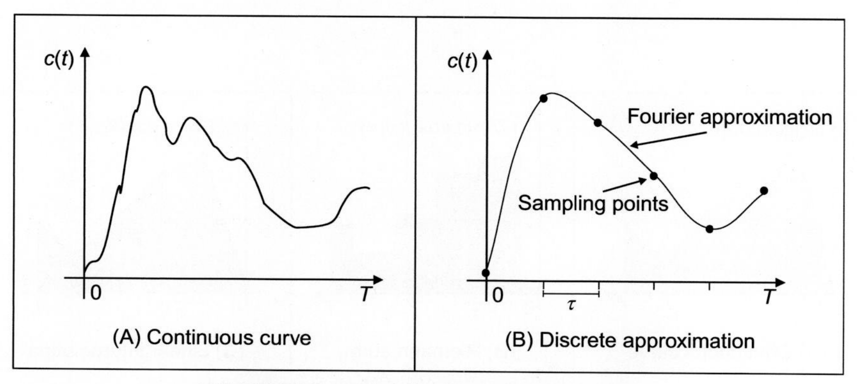

FIGURE 7.8 Example of a discrete approximation.

$$c(t) = \frac{a_0}{2} + \sum_{k=1}^{m/2} (a_k \cos(k\omega t) + b_k \sin(k\omega t)) \tag{7.24}$$

In practice, Fourier descriptors are computed for fewer coefficients than the limit of $m/2$. This is because the low-frequency components provide most of the features of a shape. High frequencies are easily affected by noise and only represent detail that is of little value to recognition. We can interpret Eq. (7.22) the other way around: if we know the maximum frequency in the curve, then we can determine the appropriate number of samples. However, the fact that we consider $c(t)$ to define a continuous curve implies that in order to obtain the coefficients in Eq. (7.13), we need to evaluate an integral of a continuous curve. The approximation of the integral is improved by increasing the number of sampling points. Thus, as a practical rule, in order to improve accuracy, we must try to have a large number of samples even if it is theoretically limited by the Nyquist theorem.

Our curve is only a set of discrete points. We want to maintain a continuous curve analysis in order to obtain a set of discrete coefficients. Thus, the only alternative is to approximate the coefficients by approximating the value of the integrals in Eq. (7.13). We can approximate the value of the integral in several ways. The most straightforward approach is to use a Riemann sum. Fig. 7.9 illustrates this approach. In Fig. 7.9B, the integral is approximated as the summation of the rectangular areas. The middle point of each rectangle corresponds to each sampling point. Sampling points are defined at the points whose parameter is $t = i\tau$ where i is an integer between 1 and m. We consider that c_i defines the value of the function at the sampling point i. That is,

$$c_i = c(i\tau) \tag{7.25}$$

Thus, the height of the rectangle for each pair of coefficients is given by $c_i \cos(k\omega i\tau)$ and $c_i \sin(k\omega i\tau)$. Each interval has a length $\tau = T/m$. Thus,

$$\int_0^T c(t)\cos(k\omega t)dt \approx \sum_{i=1}^{m} \frac{T}{m} c_i \cos(k\omega i\tau) \quad \text{and} \quad \int_0^T c(t)\sin(k\omega t)dt \approx \sum_{i=1}^{m} \frac{T}{m} c_i \sin(k\omega i\tau) \tag{7.26}$$

Accordingly, the Fourier coefficients are given by

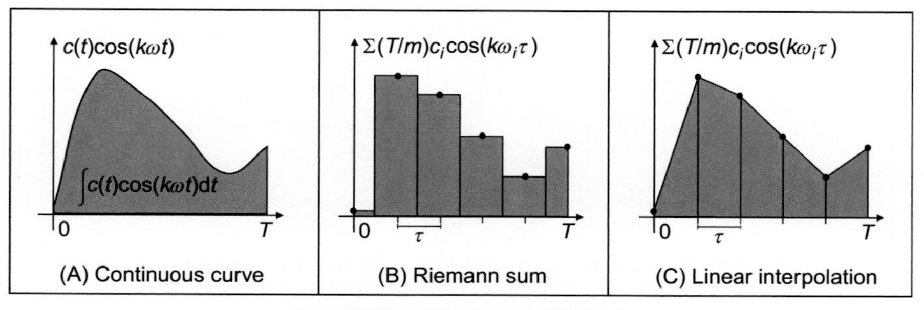

FIGURE 7.9 Integral approximation.

$$a_k = \frac{2}{m}\sum_{i=1}^{m} c_i \cos(k\omega i\tau) \quad \text{and} \quad b_k = \frac{2}{m}\sum_{i=1}^{m} c_i \sin(k\omega i\tau) \tag{7.27}$$

Here, the error due to the discrete computation will be reduced with increase in the number of points used to approximate the curve. These equations actually correspond to a linear approximation to the integral. This approximation is shown in Fig. 7.9C. In this case, the integral is given by the summation of the trapezoidal areas. The sum of these areas leads to Eq. (7.26). Notice that b_0 is zero and a_0 is twice the average of the c_i values. Thus, the first term in Eq. (7.24) is the average (or centre of gravity) of the curve.

7.2.3.5 Cumulative angular function

Fourier descriptors can be obtained by using many boundary representations. In a straightforward approach we could consider, for example, that t and $c(t)$ define the angle and modulus of a polar parameterisation of the boundary. However, this representation is not very general. For some curves, the polar form does not define a single valued curve, and thus we cannot apply Fourier expansions. A more general description of curves can be obtained by using the angular function parameterisation. This function was already defined in Chapter 4 in the discussion about curvature.

The angular function $\varphi(s)$ measures the angular direction of the tangent line as a function of arc length. Fig. 7.10 illustrates the angular direction at a point in a curve. In [Cosgriff60], this angular function was used to obtain a set of Fourier descriptors. However, this first approach to Fourier characterisation has some undesirable properties. The main problem is that the angular function has discontinuities even for smooth curves. This is because the angular direction is bounded from zero to 2π. Thus, the function has discontinuities when the angular direction increases to a value of more than 2π or decreases to be less than zero (since it will change abruptly to remain within bounds). In Zahn and Roskies' approach [Zahn72], this problem is eliminated by considering a normalised form of the cumulative angular function.

The *cumulative angular function* at a point in the curve is defined as the amount of angular change from the starting point. It is called cumulative, since it represents the

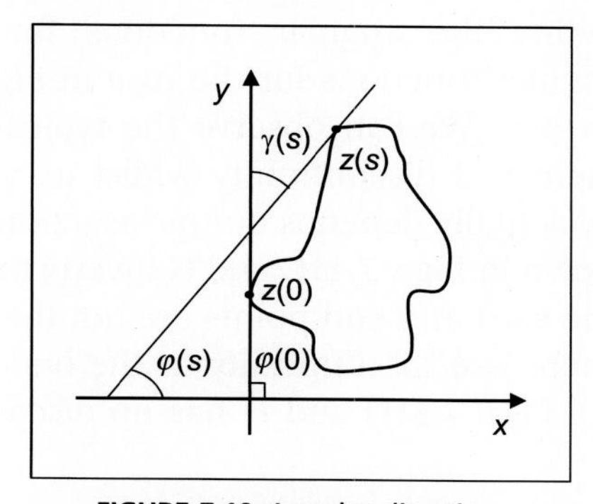

FIGURE 7.10 Angular direction.

summation of the angular change to each point. Angular change is given by the derivative of the angular function $\varphi(s)$. We discussed in Chapter 4 that this derivative corresponds to the curvature $\kappa(s)$. Thus, the cumulative angular function at the point given by s can be defined as

$$\gamma(s) = \int_0^s \kappa(r)dr - \kappa(0) \tag{7.28}$$

Here, the parameter s takes values from zero to L (i.e. the length of the curve). Thus, the initial and final values of the function are $\gamma(0) = 0$ and $\gamma(L) = -2\pi$, respectively. It is important to notice that in order to obtain the final value of -2π, the curve must be traced in a clockwise direction. Fig. 7.10 illustrates the relation between the angular function and the cumulative angular function. In the figure, $z(0)$ defines the initial point in the curve. The value of $\gamma(s)$ is given by the angle formed by the inclination of the tangent to $z(0)$ and that of the tangent to the point $z(s)$. If we move the point $z(s)$ along the curve, this angle will change until it reaches the value of -2π. In Eq. (7.28), the cumulative angle is obtained by adding the small angular increments for each point.

The cumulative angular function avoids the discontinuities of the angular function. However, it still has two problems. First, it has a discontinuity at the end. Second, its value depends on the length of curve analysed. These problems can be solved by defining the normalised function $\gamma^*(t)$ where

$$\gamma^*(t) = \gamma\left(\frac{L}{2\pi}t\right) + t \tag{7.29}$$

Here t takes values from 0 to 2π. The factor $L/2\pi$ normalises the angular function such that it does not change when the curve is scaled. That is, when $t = 2\pi$, the function evaluates the final point of the function $\gamma(s)$. The term t is included to avoid discontinuities at the end of the function (remember that the function is periodic). That is, it makes that $\gamma^*(0) = \gamma^*(2\pi) = 0$. Additionally, it causes the cumulative angle for a circle to be zero. This is consistent as a circle is generally considered the simplest curve and, intuitively, simple curves will have simple representations.

Fig. 7.11 illustrates the definitions of the cumulative angular function with two examples. Figs. 7.11B–D define the angular functions for a circle in Fig. 7.11A. Figs. 7.11F–H define the angular functions for the rose in Fig. 7.11E. Figs. 7.11B and F define the angular function $\varphi(s)$. We can observe the typical toroidal form. Once the curve is greater than 2π there is a discontinuity whilst its value returns to zero. The position of the discontinuity actually depends on the selection of the starting point. The cumulative function $\gamma(s)$ shown in Figs. 7.11C and G inverts the function and eliminates discontinuities. However, the start and end points are not the same. If we consider that this function is periodic, there is a discontinuity at the end of each period. The normalised form $\gamma^*(t)$ shown in Figs. 7.11D and H has no discontinuity and the period is normalised to 2π.

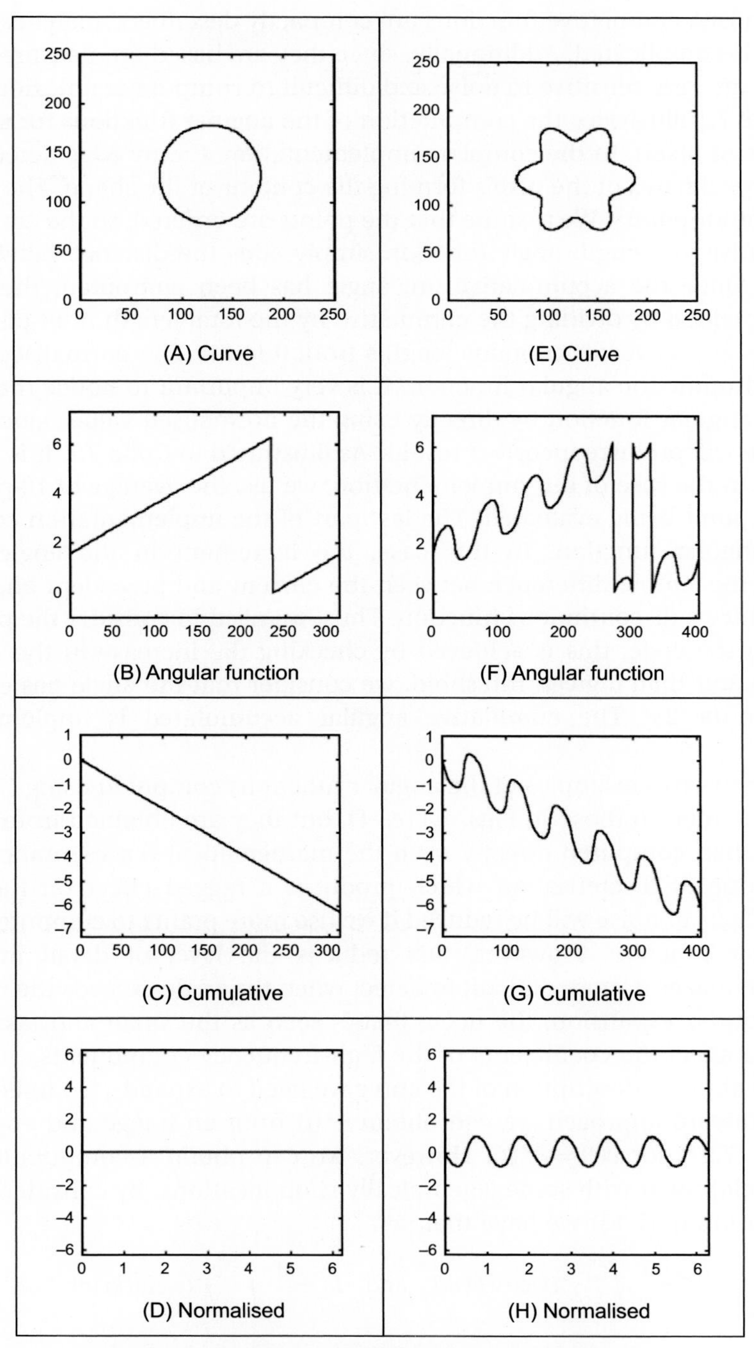

FIGURE 7.11 Angular function and cumulative angular function.

The normalised cumulative functions are compactly described, analytically, but their computation is complicated. Additionally, since they are based on measures of changes in angle, they are very sensitive to noise and difficult to compute at inflexion points (e.g. corners). Code 7.1 illustrates the computation of the angular functions for a curve given by a sequence of pixels. In the complete implementation, Canny edge detection is used to find the co-ordinates of the pixels forming the contour of the shape. The vector `shape` stores the contour points. We assume that the points are ordered, so the computation of the accumulative arc length angle function simply adds the distance between consecutive points. Once the accumulative arc angle has been computed, the normalised lengths are obtained by dividing the cumulative by the total length multiplied by 2π. As such, the `normLengths` vector contains lengths from 0 to 2π. The normalised arc lengths are used to compute the angular function. It is very important to notice that we cannot compute the angular function by directly using the normalised values since discretisation and noise will produce incorrect results. As illustrated in Code 7.1, it is necessary to use averages. In the case of our implementation, we use the average of 10 points before and after the point being evaluated. The last part of the implementation computes the cumulative angular function. In this case, the increment in the angle cannot be computed as the simple difference between the current and precedent angular values. This will produce a discontinuous function. Thus, we need to consider the periodicity of the angles. In the code, this is achieved by checking the increase in the angle. If the increase is greater than a given threshold, we consider that the angle has exceeded the limits of zero or 2π. The cumulative angular accumulated is implemented from Eq. (7.29).

Fig. 7.12 shows two examples of the angular functions computed using Code 7.1. The examples are similar to those in Figs. 7.11A–D, but they are obtained from pixels in an image rather than computed directly from the mathematical representation of curves. Noise arises due to discretisation which produces a ragged effect on the computed values. The effects of noise will be reduced if we use more points to compute the average in the angular function. However, this reduces the level of detail in the curve. Additionally, it makes it more difficult to detect when the angle exceeds the limits of zero or 2π. In a Fourier expansion, the noise that is seen as the small and fast changes in Fig. 7.12D will affect the coefficients of the high-frequency components.

In order to obtain a description of the curve we need to expand $\gamma^*(t)$ in Fourier series. In a straightforward approach we can obtain $\gamma^*(t)$ from an image and apply the definition in Eq. (7.27) for $c(t) = \gamma^*(t)$. However, we can obtain a computationally more attractive development with some algebraically simplifications. By considering the form of the integral in Eq. (7.13) we have that

$$a_k^* = \frac{1}{\pi}\int_0^{2\pi} \gamma^*(t)\cos(kt)dt \quad \text{and} \quad b_k^* = \frac{1}{\pi}\int_0^{2\pi} \gamma^*(t)\sin(kt)dt \tag{7.30}$$

```
# Compute the accumulative arc lengths
numPoints = len(shape[0])
sumLenghts = []
y0, x0 = shape[0, numPoints-1], shape[1, numPoints-1]
shapeLenght = 0.0
for p in range(0, numPoints):
    y,x = shape[0,p], shape[1,p]
    shapeLenght += sqrt((y-y0)*(y-y0) + (x-x0)*(x-x0))
    sumLenghts.append(shapeLenght)
    y0,x0 = y,x

# Normalised arc lengths
normLenghts = []
for p in range(0, numPoints):
    normLenghts.append((2.0*pi*sumLenghts[p])/shapeLenght);

# Compute angular function by an average window
windowSize = [1,10]
d = float(windowSize[1] -windowSize[0])
angularFunc = [ ]
for p in range(0, numPoints):
    x1,x2,y1,y2 = 0.0, 0.0, 0.0, 0.0
    # Average change
    for q in range(windowSize[0], windowSize[1]):
        pa,pb = p-q,p+q
        if pa<0:           pa += numPoints
        if pb>=numPoints:  pb -= numPoints

        ya,xa = shape[0,pa], shape[1,pa]
        yb,xb = shape[0,pb], shape[1,pb]

        x1,y1 = x1+xa, y1+ya
        x2,y2 = x2+xb, y2+yb
    dx, dy = (x2-x1)/d, (y2-y1)/d
    angle = atan2(dy, dx)
    angularFunc.append(angle)

# Compute cumulative angular function
cumulativeFunc = [ ]
angle0 = angularFunc[numPoints-1]
sumAngle = 0.0
for p in range(0, numPoints):
    angle = angularFunc[p]
    if abs(angle-angle0) < pi:
        sumAngle += angle-angle0
    else:
        sumAngle += angle-(angle0 + 2.0 *pi)
    cumulativeFunc.append(sumAngle)
    angle0 = angle

# Compute cumulative angular accumulated
cumNormFunc = [ ]
for p in range(0, numPoints):
    cumNormFunc.append(cumulativeFunc[p]+normLenghts[p])
```

CODE 7.1 Angular functions.

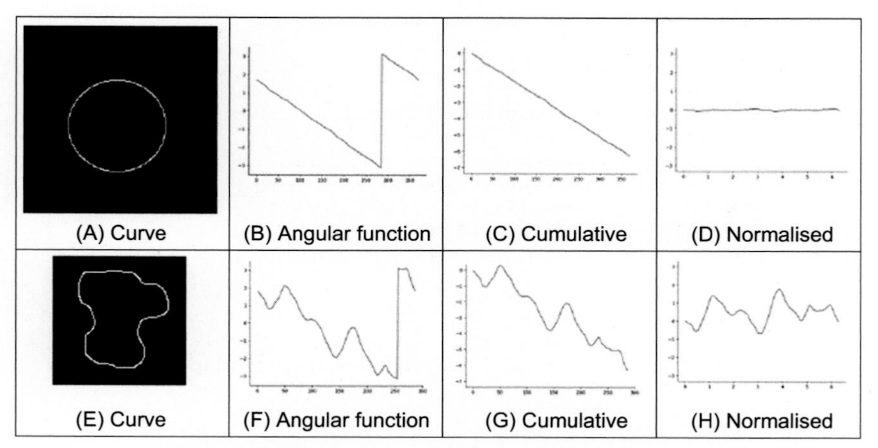

FIGURE 7.12 Discrete computation of the angular functions.

By substitution of Eq. (7.29) we obtain

$$\begin{aligned} a_0^* &= \frac{1}{\pi}\int_0^{2\pi} \gamma((L/2\pi)t)dt + \frac{1}{\pi}\int_0^{2\pi} tdt \\ a_k^* &= \frac{1}{\pi}\int_0^{2\pi} \gamma((L/2\pi)t)\cos(kt)dt + \frac{1}{\pi}\int_0^{2\pi} t\cos(kt)dt \\ b_k^* &= \frac{1}{\pi}\int_0^{2\pi} \gamma((L/2\pi)t)\sin(kt)dt + \frac{1}{\pi}\int_0^{2\pi} t\sin(kt)dt \end{aligned} \tag{7.31}$$

By computing the second integrals of each coefficient, we obtain a simpler form as

$$\begin{aligned} a_0^* &= 2\pi + \frac{1}{\pi}\int_0^{2\pi} \gamma((L/2\pi)t)dt \\ a_k^* &= \frac{1}{\pi}\int_0^{2\pi} \gamma((L/2\pi)t)\cos(kt)dt \\ b_k^* &= -\frac{2}{k} + \frac{1}{\pi}\int_0^{2\pi} \gamma((L/2\pi)t)\sin(kt)dt \end{aligned} \tag{7.32}$$

In an image, we measure distances, thus it is better to express these equations in arc-length form. For that, we know that $s = (L/2\pi)t$. Thus,

$$dt = \frac{2\pi}{L}ds \tag{7.33}$$

Accordingly, the coefficients in Eq. (7.32) can be rewritten as,

$$\begin{aligned} a_0^* &= 2\pi + \frac{2}{L}\int_0^{L} \gamma(s)ds \\ a_k^* &= \frac{2}{L}\int_0^{L} \gamma(s)\cos\left(\frac{2\pi k}{L}s\right)ds \\ b_k^* &= -\frac{2}{k} + \frac{2}{L}\int_0^{L} \gamma(s)\sin\left(\frac{2\pi k}{L}s\right)ds \end{aligned} \tag{7.34}$$

In a similar way to Eq. (7.26), the Fourier descriptors can be computed by approximating the integral as a summation of rectangular areas. This is illustrated in Fig. 7.13. Here, the discrete approximation is formed by rectangles of length τ_i and height γ_i. Thus,

$$\begin{aligned} a_0^* &= 2\pi + \frac{2}{L}\sum_{i=1}^{m}\gamma_i\tau_i \\ a_k^* &= \frac{2}{L}\sum_{i=1}^{m}\gamma_i\tau_i\cos\left(\frac{2\pi k}{L}s_i\right) \\ b_k^* &= -\frac{2}{k}+\frac{2}{L}\sum_{i=1}^{m}\gamma_i\tau_i\sin\left(\frac{2\pi k}{L}s_i\right) \end{aligned} \tag{7.35}$$

where s_i is the arc-length at the ith point. Note that

$$s_i = \sum_{r=1}^{i}\tau_r \tag{7.36}$$

It is important to observe that although the definitions in Eq. (7.35) only use the discrete values of $\gamma(t)$, they obtain a Fourier expansion of $\gamma^*(t)$. In the original formulation [Zahn72], an alternative form of the summations is obtained by rewriting the coefficients in terms of the increments of the angular function. In this case, the integrals in Eq. (7.34) are evaluated for each interval. Thus, the coefficients are represented as a summation of integrals of constant values as,

$$\begin{aligned} a_0^* &= 2\pi + \frac{2}{L}\sum_{i=1}^{m}\int_{s_{i-1}}^{s_i}\gamma_i ds \\ a_k^* &= \frac{2}{L}\sum_{i=1}^{m}\int_{s_{i-1}}^{s_i}\gamma_i\cos\left(\frac{2\pi k}{L}s\right)ds \\ b_k^* &= -\frac{2}{k}+\frac{2}{L}\sum_{i=1}^{m}\int_{s_{i-1}}^{s_i}\gamma_i\sin\left(\frac{2\pi k}{L}s\right)ds \end{aligned} \tag{7.37}$$

By evaluating the integral we obtain

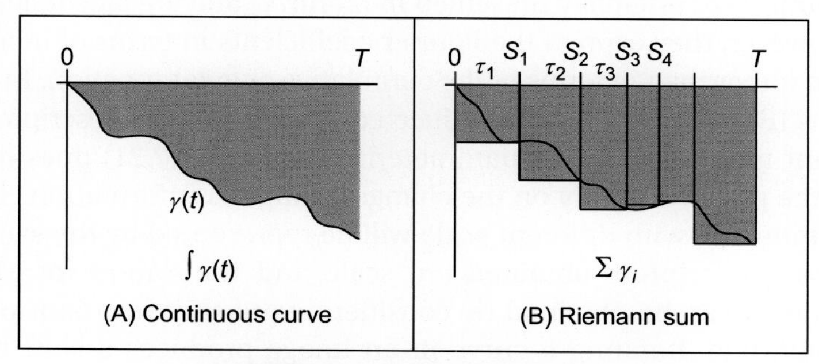

FIGURE 7.13 Integral approximations.

$$
\begin{aligned}
a_0^* &= 2\pi + \frac{2}{L}\sum\nolimits_{i=1}^{m} \gamma_i (s_i - s_{i-1}) \\
a_k^* &= \frac{1}{\pi k}\sum\nolimits_{i=1}^{m} \gamma_i \left(\sin\left(\frac{2\pi k}{L} s_i\right) - \sin\left(\frac{2\pi k}{L} s_{i-1}\right)\right) \\
b_k^* &= -\frac{2}{k} + \frac{1}{\pi k}\sum\nolimits_{i=1}^{m} \gamma_i \left(\cos\left(\frac{2\pi k}{L} s_i\right) - \cos\left(\frac{2\pi k}{L} s_{i-1}\right)\right)
\end{aligned} \tag{7.38}
$$

A further simplification can be obtained by considering that Eq. (7.28) can be expressed in discrete form as

$$
\gamma_i = \sum_{r=1}^{i} \kappa_r \tau_r - \kappa_0 \tag{7.39}
$$

where κ_r is the curvature (i.e. the difference of the angular function) at the rth point. Thus,

$$
\begin{aligned}
a_0^* &= -2\pi - \frac{2}{L}\sum\nolimits_{i=1}^{m} \kappa_i s_{i-1} \\
a_k^* &= -\frac{1}{\pi k}\sum\nolimits_{i=1}^{m} \kappa_i \tau_i \sin\left(\frac{2\pi k}{L} s_{i-1}\right) \\
b_k^* &= -\frac{2}{k} - \frac{1}{\pi k}\sum\nolimits_{i=1}^{m} \kappa_i \tau_i \cos\left(\frac{2\pi k}{L} s_{i-1}\right) + \frac{1}{\pi k}\sum\nolimits_{i=1}^{m} \kappa_i \tau_i
\end{aligned} \tag{7.40}
$$

Since

$$
\sum\nolimits_{i=1}^{m} \kappa_i \tau_i = 2\pi \tag{7.41}
$$

thus,

$$
\begin{aligned}
a_0^* &= -2\pi - \frac{2}{L}\sum\nolimits_{i=1}^{m} \kappa_i s_{i-1} \\
a_k^* &= -\frac{1}{\pi k}\sum\nolimits_{i=1}^{m} \kappa_i \tau_i \sin\left(\frac{2\pi k}{L} s_{i-1}\right) \\
b_k^* &= -\frac{1}{\pi k}\sum\nolimits_{i=1}^{m} \kappa_i \tau_i \cos\left(\frac{2\pi k}{L} s_{i-1}\right)
\end{aligned} \tag{7.42}
$$

These equations were originally presented in [Zahn72] and are algebraically equivalent to Eq. (7.35). However, they express the Fourier coefficients in terms of increments in the angular function rather than in terms of the cumulative angular function. In practice, both implementations (Eqs. 7.35 and 7.40) produce equivalent Fourier descriptors.

It is important to notice that the parameterisation in Eq. (7.21) does not depend on the position of the pixels, but only on the change in angular information. That is, shapes in different position and with different scale will be represented by the same curve $\gamma^*(t)$. Thus, the Fourier descriptors obtained are scale and translation invariant. Rotation invariant descriptors can be obtained by considering the shift invariant property of the coefficients' amplitude. Rotating a curve in an image produces a shift in the angular function. This is because the rotation changes the starting point in the curve description. Thus, according to Section 7.2.3.2, the values

$$|c_k^*| = \sqrt{(a_k^*)^2 + (b_k^*)^2} \tag{7.43}$$

provide a rotation, scale and translation invariant description.

Code 7.2 computes the Fourier descriptors in this equation by using the definitions in Eqs. (7.35) and (7.43). The code uses the angular functions computed in Code 7.1, and they are stored in the `cumulativeFunc` array. The coefficients are stored in the `coefficients` array. Each element in the array has two values that represent the pairs (a,b). The `descriptors` array contains the Fourier descriptors defined in Eq. (7.43).

Fig. 7.14 shows three examples of the results obtained using the Code 7.2. In each example, we show the curve, the angular function, the cumulative normalised angular function and the Fourier descriptors. The curves in Figs. 7.14A and E represent the same object (the contour of an F-14 fighter), but the curve in Fig. 7.14E was scaled and rotated. We can see that the angular function changes significantly, whilst the normalised function is very similar but with a remarkable shift due to the rotation. The Fourier descriptors shown in Figs. 7.14D and H are quite similar since they characterise the same object. We can see a clear difference between the normalised angular function for the object presented in Fig. 7.14I (the contour of a different plane, a B1 bomber). These examples show that Fourier coefficients are indeed invariant to scale and rotation, and that they can be used to characterise different objects.

```
# If number descriptors is 0 use the maximum according to the length
if numDescriptors == 0:
    numDescriptors = 1 + numEdges /2

# Compute coefficients
coefficients = createImageF(numDescriptors, 2)
lenghtNorm = 2.0 * pi / shapeLenght
for k in range(1, numDescriptors):
    arcLenght = 0
    for p in range(0, numEdges):
        coefficients[0, k] += cumulativeFunc[p] * (sumArcLenghts[p] - arcLenght)   \
                              * cos(k * sumArcLenghts[p] * lenghtNorm)
        coefficients[1, k] += cumulativeFunc[p] * (sumArcLenghts[p] - arcLenght)   \
                              * sin(k * sumArcLenghts[p] * lenghtNorm)
        arcLenght = sumArcLenghts[p]

    coefficients[0, k] = coefficients[0, k] *(2.0 / shapeLenght)
    coefficients[1, k] = coefficients[1, k] *(2.0 / shapeLenght) - (2.0/k)

# Rotation invariant descriptors
descriptors = createVectorF(numDescriptors)
for k in range(0, numDescriptors):
    descriptors[k] = sqrt(coefficients[0, k]*coefficients[0, k] +                 \
                          coefficients[1, k]*coefficients[1, k])
```

CODE 7.2 Angular Fourier descriptors.

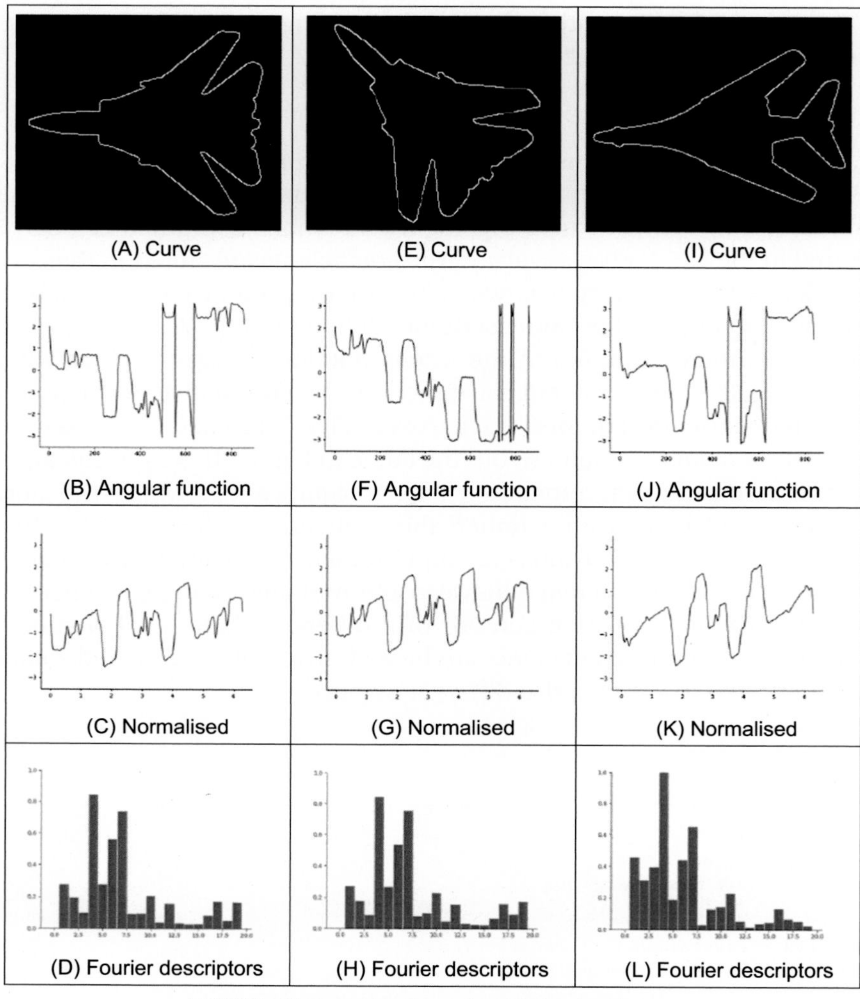

FIGURE 7.14 Example of angular Fourier descriptors.

7.2.3.6 Elliptic Fourier descriptors

The cumulative angular function transforms the two-dimensional description of a curve into a one-dimensional periodic function suitable for Fourier analysis. In contrast, *elliptic Fourier descriptors* maintain the description of the curve in a two-dimensional space [Granlund72]. This is achieved by considering that the image space defines the complex plane. That is, each pixel is represented by a complex number. The first co-ordinate represents the real part, whilst the second co-ordinate represents the imaginary part. Thus, a curve is defined as

$$c(t) = x(t) + jy(t) \tag{7.44}$$

Here we will consider that the parameter t is given by the arc-length parameterisation. Fig. 7.15 shows an example of the complex representation of a curve. This example illustrates two periods of each component of the curve. Generally, $T = 2\pi$, thus the fundamental frequency is $\omega = 1$. It is important to notice that this representation can be used to describe open curves. In this case, the curve is traced twice in opposite directions. In fact, this representation is very general and can be extended to obtain the elliptic Fourier description of irregular curves (i.e. those without derivative information) [Montiel96, Montiel97].

In order to obtain the elliptic Fourier descriptors of a curve, we need to obtain the Fourier expansion of the curve in Eq. (7.44). The Fourier expansion can be performed by using the complex or trigonometric form. In the original work in [Granlund72], the expansion is expressed in the complex form. However, other works have used the trigonometric representation [Kuhl82]. Here, we will pass from the complex form to the trigonometric representation. The trigonometric representation is more intuitive and easier to implement.

According to Eq. (7.5) we have that the elliptic coefficients are defined by

$$c_k = c_{xk} + jc_{yk} \tag{7.45}$$

where

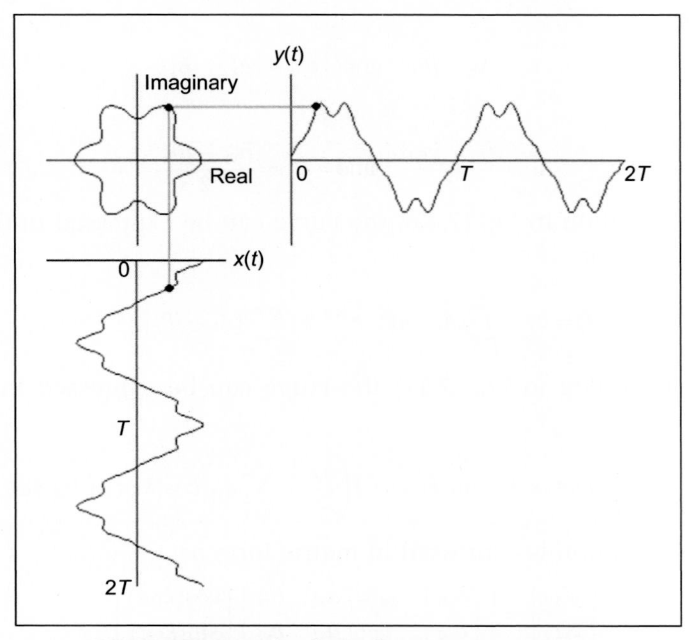

FIGURE 7.15 Example of complex curve representation.

$$c_{xk} = \frac{1}{T}\int_0^T x(t)e^{-jk\omega t}dt \quad \text{and} \quad c_{yk} = \frac{1}{T}\int_0^T y(t)e^{-jk\omega t}dt \tag{7.46}$$

By following Eq. (7.12), we notice that each term in this expression can be defined by a pair of coefficients. That is,

$$\begin{aligned} c_{xk} &= \frac{a_{xk} - jb_{xk}}{2} \quad c_{yk} = \frac{a_{yk} - jb_{yk}}{2} \\ c_{x-k} &= \frac{a_{xk} + jb_{xk}}{2} \quad c_{y-k} = \frac{a_{yk} + jb_{yk}}{2} \end{aligned} \tag{7.47}$$

Based on Eq. (7.13) the trigonometric coefficients are defined as

$$\begin{aligned} a_{xk} &= \frac{2}{T}\int_0^T x(t)\cos(k\omega t)dt \quad \text{and} \quad b_{xk} = \frac{2}{T}\int_0^T x(t)\sin(k\omega t)dt \\ a_{yk} &= \frac{2}{T}\int_0^T y(t)\cos(k\omega t)dt \quad \text{and} \quad b_{yk} = \frac{2}{T}\int_0^T y(t)\sin(k\omega t)dt \end{aligned} \tag{7.48}$$

According to Eq. (7.27) can be computed by the discrete approximation given by

$$\begin{aligned} a_{xk} &= \frac{2}{m}\sum_{i=1}^{m} x_i \cos(k\omega i\tau) \quad \text{and} \quad b_{xk} = \frac{2}{m}\sum_{i=1}^{m} x_i \sin(k\omega i\tau) \\ a_{yk} &= \frac{2}{m}\sum_{i=1}^{m} y_i \cos(k\omega i\tau) \quad \text{and} \quad b_{yk} = \frac{2}{m}\sum_{i=1}^{m} y_i \sin(k\omega i\tau) \end{aligned} \tag{7.49}$$

where x_i and y_i define the value of the functions $x(t)$ and $y(t)$ at the sampling point i. By considering Eqs. (7.45) and (7.47), we can express c_k as the sum of a pair of complex numbers. That is,

$$c_k = A_k - jB_k \quad \text{and} \quad c_{-k} = A_k + jB_k \tag{7.50}$$

where

$$A_k = \frac{a_{xk} + ja_{yk}}{2} \quad \text{and} \quad B_k = \frac{b_{xk} + jb_{yk}}{2} \tag{7.51}$$

Based on the definition in Eq. (7.45), the curve can be expressed in the exponential form given in Eq. (7.6) as

$$c(t) = c_0 + \sum_{k=1}^{\infty}(A_k - jB_k)e^{jk\omega t} + \sum_{k=-\infty}^{-1}(A_k + jB_k)e^{jk\omega t} \tag{7.52}$$

Alternatively, according to Eq. (7.11) the curve can be expressed in trigonometric form as

$$c(t) = \frac{a_{x0}}{2} + \sum_{k=1}^{\infty}\left(a_{xk}\cos(k\omega t) + b_{xk}\sin(k\omega t) + j\left(\frac{a_{y0}}{2} + \sum_{k=1}^{\infty} a_{yk}\cos(k\omega t) + b_{yk}\sin(k\omega t)\right)\right) \tag{7.53}$$

Generally, this Equation is expressed in matrix form as

$$\begin{bmatrix} x(t) \\ y(t) \end{bmatrix} = \frac{1}{2}\begin{bmatrix} a_{x0} \\ a_{y0} \end{bmatrix} + \sum_{k=1}^{\infty}\begin{bmatrix} a_{xk} & b_{xk} \\ a_{yk} & b_{yk} \end{bmatrix}\begin{bmatrix} \cos(k\omega t) \\ \sin(k\omega t) \end{bmatrix} \tag{7.54}$$

Each term in this equation has an interesting geometric interpretation as an elliptic phasor (a rotating vector). That is, for a fixed value of k, the trigonometric summation defines the locus of an ellipse in the complex plane. We can imagine that as we change the parameter t the point traces ellipses moving at a speed proportional to the harmonic number k. This number indicates how many cycles (i.e. turns) give the point in the time interval from zero to T. Fig. 7.16A illustrates this concept. Here, a point in the curve is given as the summation of three vectors that define three terms in Eq. (7.54). As the parameter t changes, each vector defines an elliptic curve. In this interpretation, the values of $a_{x0}/2$ and $a_{y0}/2$ define the start point of the first vector (i.e. the location of the curve). The major axes of each ellipse are given by the values of $|A_k|$ and $|B_k|$. The definition of the ellipse locus for a frequency is determined by the coefficients as shown in Fig. 7.16B.

7.2.3.7 Invariance

As in the case of angular Fourier descriptors, elliptic Fourier descriptors can be defined such that they remain *invariant* to geometric transformations. In order to show these definitions we must first study how geometric changes in a shape modify the form of the Fourier coefficients. Transformations can be formulated by using both the exponential or trigonometric form. We will consider changes in translation, rotation and scale using the trigonometric definition in Eq. (7.54).

Let us denote $c'(t) = x'(t) + jy'(t)$ as the transformed contour. This contour is defined as,

$$\begin{bmatrix} x'(t) \\ y'(t) \end{bmatrix} = \frac{1}{2}\begin{bmatrix} a'_{x0} \\ a'_{y0} \end{bmatrix} + \sum_{k=1}^{\infty}\begin{bmatrix} a'_{xk} & b'_{xk} \\ a'_{yk} & b'_{yk} \end{bmatrix}\begin{bmatrix} \cos(k\omega t) \\ \sin(k\omega t) \end{bmatrix} \tag{7.55}$$

If the contour is translated by t_x and t_y along the real and the imaginary axes, respectively, we have that

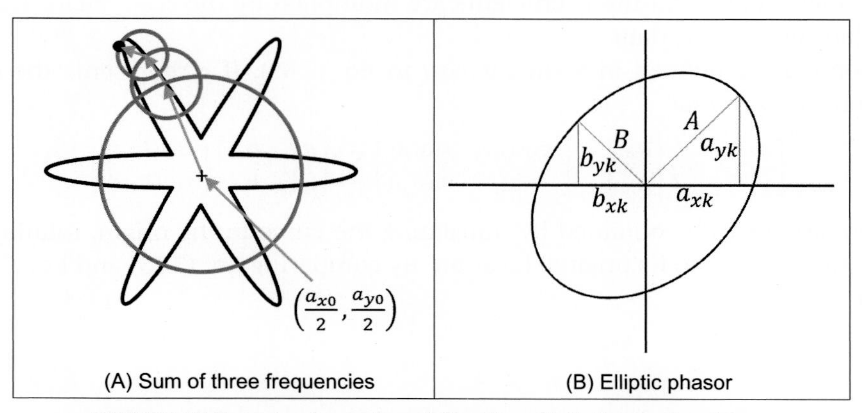

FIGURE 7.16 Example of a contour defined by elliptic Fourier descriptors.

$$\begin{bmatrix} x'(t) \\ y'(t) \end{bmatrix} = \frac{1}{2}\begin{bmatrix} a_{x0} \\ a_{y0} \end{bmatrix} + \sum_{k=1}^{\infty}\begin{bmatrix} a_{xk} & b_{xk} \\ a_{yk} & b_{yk} \end{bmatrix}\begin{bmatrix} \cos(k\omega t) \\ \sin(k\omega t) \end{bmatrix} + \begin{bmatrix} t_x \\ t_y \end{bmatrix} \tag{7.56}$$

That is,

$$\begin{bmatrix} x'(t) \\ y'(t) \end{bmatrix} = \frac{1}{2}\begin{bmatrix} a_{x0} + 2t_x \\ a_{y0} + 2t_y \end{bmatrix} + \sum_{k=1}^{\infty}\begin{bmatrix} a_{xk} & b_{xk} \\ a_{yk} & b_{yk} \end{bmatrix}\begin{bmatrix} \cos(k\omega t) \\ \sin(k\omega t) \end{bmatrix} \tag{7.57}$$

Thus, by comparing Eq. (7.55) and Eq. (7.57), we have that the relationship between the coefficients of the transformed and original curves is given by

$$\begin{aligned} &a'_{xk} = a_{xk} \quad b'_{xk} = b_{xk} \quad a'_{yk} = a_{yk} \quad b'_{yk} = b_{yk} \quad \text{for } k \neq 0 \\ &a'_{x0} = a_{x0} + 2t_x \quad a'_{y0} = a_{y0} + 2t_y \end{aligned} \tag{7.58}$$

Accordingly, all the coefficients remain invariant under translation except a_{x0} and a_{y0}. This result can be intuitively derived by considering that these two coefficients represent the position of the centre of gravity of the contour of the shape and translation changes only the position of the curve.

The change in scale of a contour $c(t)$ can be modelled as the dilation from its centre of gravity. That is, we need to translate the curve to the origin, scale it and then return it back to its original location. If s represents the scale factor, then these transformations define the curve as,

$$\begin{bmatrix} x'(t) \\ y'(t) \end{bmatrix} = \frac{1}{2}\begin{bmatrix} a_{x0} \\ a_{y0} \end{bmatrix} + s\sum_{k=1}^{\infty}\begin{bmatrix} a_{xk} & b_{xk} \\ a_{yk} & b_{yk} \end{bmatrix}\begin{bmatrix} \cos(k\omega t) \\ \sin(k\omega t) \end{bmatrix} \tag{7.59}$$

Notice that in this equation the scale factor does not modify the coefficients a_{x0} and a_{y0} since the curve is expanded with respect to its centre. In order to define the relationships between the curve and its scaled version, we compare Eq. (7.55) and Eq. (7.59). Thus,

$$\begin{aligned} &a'_{xk} = sa_{xk} \quad b'_{xk} = sb_{xk} \quad a'_{yk} = sa_{yk} \quad b'_{yk} = sb_{yk} \quad \text{for } k \neq 0 \\ &a'_{xk} = a_{x0} \quad a'_{y0} = a_{y0} \end{aligned} \tag{7.60}$$

That is, under dilation, all the coefficients are multiplied by the scale factor except a_{x0} and a_{y0} that remain invariant.

Rotation can be defined in a similar way to Eq. (7.59). If ρ represents the rotation angle, then we have that

$$\begin{bmatrix} x'(t) \\ y'(t) \end{bmatrix} = \frac{1}{2}\begin{bmatrix} a_{x0} \\ a_{y0} \end{bmatrix} + \begin{bmatrix} \cos(\rho) & \sin(\rho) \\ -\sin(\rho) & \cos(\rho) \end{bmatrix}\sum_{k=1}^{\infty}\begin{bmatrix} a_{xk} & b_{xk} \\ a_{yk} & b_{yk} \end{bmatrix}\begin{bmatrix} \cos(k\omega t) \\ \sin(k\omega t) \end{bmatrix} \tag{7.61}$$

This equation can be obtained by translating the curve to the origin, rotating it and then returning it back to its original location. By comparing Eq. (7.55) and Eq. (7.61), we have that

$$\begin{aligned} a'_{xk} &= a_{xk}\cos(\rho) + a_{yk}\sin(\rho) & b'_{xk} &= b_{xk}\cos(\rho) + b_{yk}\sin(\rho) \\ a'_{yk} &= -a_{xk}\sin(\rho) + a_{yk}\cos(\rho) & b'_{yk} &= -b_{xk}\sin(\rho) + b_{yk}\cos(\rho) \\ a'_{x0} &= a_{x0} \quad a'_{y0} = a_{y0} \end{aligned} \tag{7.62}$$

That is, under rotation the coefficients are defined by a linear combination dependent on the rotation angle, except for a_{x0} and a_{y0} that remain invariant. It is important to notice that rotation relationships are also applied for a change in the starting point of the curve.

Eqs. (7.58), (7.60) and (7.62) define how the elliptic Fourier coefficients change when the curve is translated, scaled or rotated, respectively. We can combine these results to define the changes when the curve undergoes the three transformations. In this case, transformations are applied in succession. Thus,

$$\begin{aligned} a'_{xk} &= s(a_{xk}\cos(\rho) + a_{yk}\sin(\rho)) & b'_{xk} &= s(b_{xk}\cos(\rho) + b_{yk}\sin(\rho)) \\ a'_{yk} &= s(-a_{xk}\sin(\rho) + a_{yk}\cos(\rho)) & b'_{yk} &= s(-b_{xk}\sin(\rho) + b_{yk}\cos(\rho)) \\ a'_{x0} &= a_{x0} + 2t_x \quad a'_{y0} = a_{y0} + 2t_y \end{aligned} \tag{7.63}$$

Based on this result we can define alternative invariant descriptors. In order to achieve invariance to translation, when defining the descriptors the coefficient for $k = 0$ is not used. In [Granlund72] invariant descriptors are defined based on the complex form of the coefficients. Alternatively, invariant descriptors can be simply defined as

$$\frac{|A_k|}{|A_1|} + \frac{|B_k|}{|B_1|} \tag{7.64}$$

The advantage of these descriptors with respect to the definition in [Granlund72] is that they do not involve negative frequencies and that we avoid multiplication by higher frequencies that are more prone to noise. By considering the definitions in Eqs. (7.51) and (7.63) we can prove that,

$$\frac{|A'_k|}{|A'_1|} = \frac{\sqrt{a_{xk}^2 + a_{yk}^2}}{\sqrt{a_{x1}^2 + a_{y1}^2}} \quad \text{and} \quad \frac{|B'_k|}{|B'_1|} = \frac{\sqrt{b_{xk}^2 + b_{yk}^2}}{\sqrt{b_{x1}^2 + b_{y1}^2}} \tag{7.65}$$

These equations contain neither the scale factor, s, nor the rotation, ρ. Thus, they are invariant. Notice that if the square roots are removed, invariance properties are still maintained. However, high-order frequencies can have undesirable effects.

Code 7.3 computes the elliptic Fourier descriptors of a curve. The code implements the summations defined in Eqs. (7.49) and (7.64). By default, the number of coefficients is half of the number of points that define the curve. However, the number of coefficients can be specified by the parameter `numDescriptors`. The number of coefficients used defines the level of detail of the characterisation. In order to illustrate this idea, we can consider the different curves that are obtained by using a different number of coefficients. Fig. 7.17 shows an example of the reconstruction of a contour. In Fig. 7.17A, we can observe that the first coefficient represents an ellipse. When the second coefficient is considered (Fig. 7.17B), then the ellipse changes into a triangular shape. When adding

```
# Compute coefficients. The vector a contains ax,ay and b contains bx,by
t = 2.0 * pi / numEdges
a = createImageF(numDescriptors, 2)
b = createImageF(numDescriptors, 2)
for k in range(1, numDescriptors):
    for p in range(0, numEdges):
        a[0, k] += x[p] * cos(k*t*p)
        a[1, k] += y[p] * cos(k*t*p)
        b[0, k] += x[p] * sin(k*t*p)
        b[1, k] += y[p] * sin(k*t*p)

for k in range(1, numDescriptors):
    a[0, k] *= (2.0/numEdges)
    a[1, k] *= (2.0/numEdges)
    b[0, k] *= (2.0/numEdges)
    b[1, k] *= (2.0/numEdges)

# Compute descriptors
normA = a[0, 1]*a[0, 1] + a[1, 1]*a[1, 1]
normB = b[0, 1]*b[0, 1] + b[1, 1]*b[1, 1]
descriptors = createVectorF(numDescriptors)
for k in range(0, numDescriptors):
    descriptors[k] = sqrt( (a[0, k]*a[0, k] + a[1, k]*a[1, k])/normA) + \
                     sqrt( (b[0, k]*b[0, k] + b[1, k]*b[1, k])/normB)
```

CODE 7.3 Elliptic Fourier descriptors.

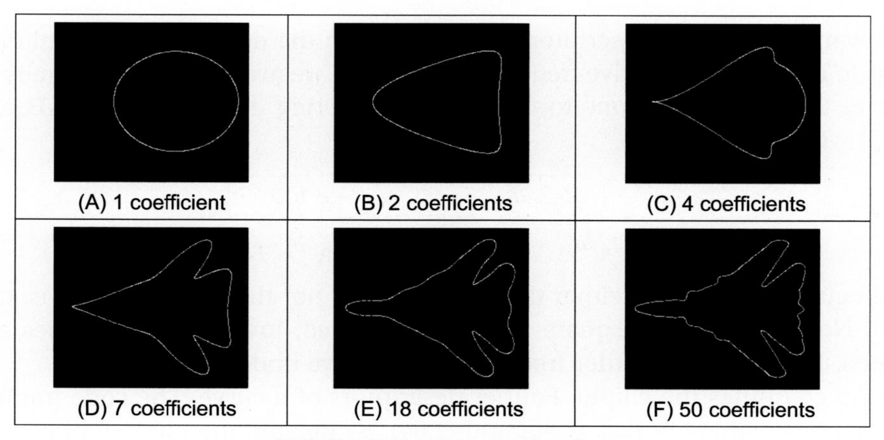

FIGURE 7.17 Fourier approximation.

more coefficients the contour is refined until the curve represents an accurate approximation of the original contour. In this example, the contour is represented by 100 points. Thus, the maximum number of coefficients is 50.

Fig. 7.18 shows three examples of the results obtained using Code 7.3. Each example shows the original curve, the x and y co-ordinate functions and the Fourier descriptors

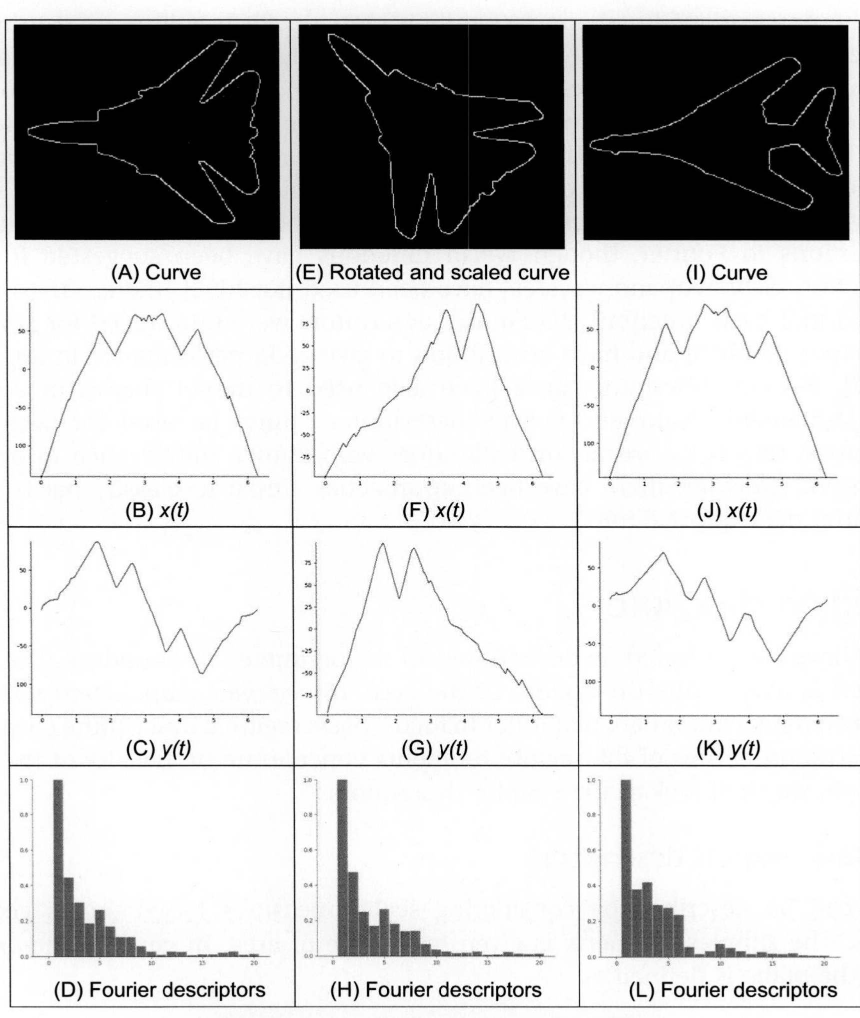

FIGURE 7.18 Example of elliptic Fourier descriptors.

defined in Eq. (7.64). The maximum in Eq. (7.64) is equal to two and is obtained when $k = 1$. In the figure we have scaled the Fourier descriptors to show the differences between higher order coefficients. In this example, we can see that the Fourier descriptors for the curves in Figs. 7.18A and E (F-14 fighter) are very similar. Small differences can be explained by discretisation errors. However, the coefficients remain similar with changes in location, orientation and scale. The descriptors of the curve in Fig. 7.18I (B1 bomber) are clearly different, showing that elliptic Fourier descriptors truly characterise the shape of an object.

Fourier descriptors are one of the most popular boundary descriptions. As such, they have attracted considerable attention, and there are many further aspects. Naturally, we can use the descriptions for shape recognition [Aguado98]. It is important to mention that some work has suggested that there is some ambiguity in the Fourier characterisation. Thus, an alternative set of descriptors has been designed specifically to reduce ambiguities [Crimmins82]. However, it is well known that Fourier expansions are unique. Thus, Fourier characterisation should uniquely represent a curve. Additionally, the mathematical opacity of the technique in [Crimmins82] does not lend itself to tutorial type presentation. Interestingly, there has not been much study on alternative decompositions to Fourier, though Walsh functions have been suggested for shape representation [Searle70] and wavelets have been used [Kashi96] (though these are not an orthonormal basis function). 3D Fourier descriptors were introduced for analysis of simple shapes [Staib92] and have been found to give good performance in application [Undrill97]. Fourier descriptors have been also used to model shapes in computer graphics [Aguado99]. Naturally, Fourier descriptors cannot be used for occluded or mixed shapes, relying on extraction techniques with known indifference to occlusion (the HT, say). However, there have been approaches aimed to classify partial shapes using Fourier descriptors [Lin87].

7.3 Region descriptors

So far, we have concentrated on descriptions of the perimeter, or boundary. The natural counterpart is to describe the region, or the area, by *regional shape descriptors*. Here, there are two main contenders that differ in focus: basic regional descriptors characterise the geometric properties of the region; moments concentrate on density of the region. First though, we shall look at the simpler descriptors.

7.3.1 Basic region descriptors

A region can be described by considering scalar measures based on its geometric properties. The simplest property is given by its size or area. In general, the *area* of a region in the plane is defined as

$$A(S) = \int_x \int_y \mathbf{P}_{x,y} dydx \tag{7.66}$$

where $\mathbf{P}_{x,y} = 1$ if the pixel is within a shape, $(x,y) \in S$, and 0 otherwise. In practice, integrals are approximated by summations. That is,

$$A(S) = \sum_x \sum_y \mathbf{P}_{x,y} \Delta A \tag{7.67}$$

where ΔA is the area of one pixel. Thus, if $\Delta A = 1$, then the area is measured in pixels. Area changes with changes in scale. However, it is invariant to image rotation. Small errors in the computation of the area will appear when applying a rotation transformation due to discretisation of the image.

Another simple property is defined by the *perimeter* of the region. If $x(t)$ and $y(t)$ denote the parametric co-ordinates of a curve enclosing a region S, then the perimeter of the region is defined as

$$P(S) = \int_t \sqrt{(x'(t))^2 + (y'(t))^2} dt \tag{7.68}$$

This equation corresponds to the sums all the infinitesimal arcs that define the curve. In the discrete case, $x(t)$ and $y(t)$ are defined by a set of pixels in the image. Thus, Eq. (7.68) is approximated by

$$P(S) = \sum_i \sqrt{(x_i - x_{i-1})^2 + (y_i - y_{i-1})^2} \tag{7.69}$$

where x_i and y_i represent the co-ordinates of the ith pixel forming the curve. Since pixels are organised in a square grid, then the terms in the summation can only take two values. When the pixels (x_i, y_i) and (x_{i-1}, y_{i-1}) are 4-neighbours (as shown in Fig. 7.1A), the summation term is unity. Otherwise, the summation term is equal to $\sqrt{2}$. Notice that the discrete approximation in Eq. (7.69) produces small errors in the measured perimeter. As such, it is unlikely that an exact value of $2\pi r$ will be achieved for the perimeter of a circular region of radius r.

Based on the perimeter and area, it is possible to characterise the compactness of a region. *Compactness* is an oft-expressed measure of shape given by the ratio of perimeter, P, to area, A. That is,

$$C(S) = \frac{4\pi A(s)}{P^2(s)} \tag{7.70}$$

In order to show the meaning of this equation, we can rewrite it as

$$C(S) = \frac{A(s)}{P^2(s)/4\pi} \tag{7.71}$$

Here, the denominator represents the area of a circle whose perimeter is $P(S)$. Thus, compactness measures the ratio between the area of the shape and the circle that can be traced with the same perimeter. That is, compactness measures the efficiency with which a boundary encloses area. In mathematics, it is known as the *isoperimetric quotient*, which smacks rather of grandiloquency. For a perfectly circular region (Fig. 7.19A)

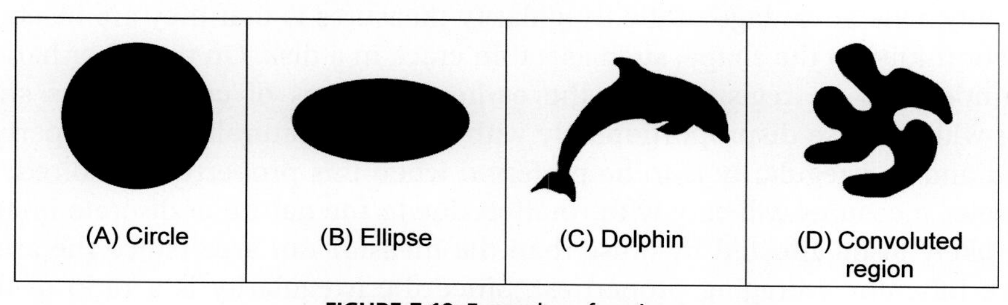

FIGURE 7.19 Examples of regions.

we have that $C(circle) = 1$ which represents the maximum compactness value: a circle is the most compact shape. Figs. 7.19B and C show two examples in which compactness is reduced. If we take the perimeter of these regions and draw a circle with the same perimeter, we can observe that the circle contains more area. This means that the shapes are not compact. A shape becomes more compact if we move region pixels far away from the centre of gravity of the shape to fill empty spaces closer to the of centre of gravity. For a perfectly square region, $C(\text{square}) = \pi/4$. Note that neither for a perfect square nor for a perfect circle, does the measure include size (the width and radius, respectively). In this way, compactness is a measure of shape only. Note that compactness alone is not a good discriminator of a region; low values of C are associated with convoluted regions such as the one in Fig. 7.19B and also with simple though highly elongated shapes. This ambiguity can be resolved by employing additional shape measures.

Another measure that can be used to characterise regions is *dispersion*. Dispersion (irregularity) has been measured as the ratio of major chord length to area [Chen95]. A simple version of this measure can be defined as *irregularity*

$$I(S) = \frac{\pi \max\left((x_i - \overline{x})^2 + (y_i - \overline{y})^2\right)}{A(S)} \tag{7.72}$$

where $(\overline{x}, \overline{y})$ represent the co-ordinates of the centre of mass of the region. Notice that the numerator defines the area of the maximum circle enclosing the region. Thus, this measure describes the density of the region. An alternative measure of dispersion can actually also be expressed as the ratio of the maximum to the minimum radius. That is an alternative form of the irregularity

$$IR(S) = \frac{\max\left(\sqrt{(x_i - \overline{x})^2 + (y_i - \overline{y})^2}\right)}{\min\left(\sqrt{(x_i - \overline{x})^2 + (y_i - \overline{y})^2}\right)} \tag{7.73}$$

This measure defines the ratio between the radius of the maximum circle enclosing the region and the maximum circle that can be contained in the region. Thus, the measure will increase as the region spreads. In this way, the irregularity of a circle is unity, $IR(circle) = 1$; the irregularity of a square is $IR(square) = \sqrt{2}$ which is larger. As such the measure increases for irregular shapes, whereas the compactness measure decreases. Again, for perfect shapes the measure is irrespective of size and is a measure of shape only. One advantage of the irregularity measures is that they are insensitive to slight discontinuity in the shape, such as a thin crack in a disk. On the other hand, these discontinuities will be registered by the earlier measures of compactness since the perimeter will increase disproportionately with the area. Naturally, this property might be desired and so irregularity is to be preferred when this property is required. In fact, the perimeter measures will vary with rotation due to the nature of discrete images and are more likely to be affected by noise than the measures of area (since the area measures have inherent averaging properties). Since the irregularity is a ratio of distance measures and compactness is a ratio of area to distance then intuitively it would appear that irregularity will vary less with noise and rotation. Such factors should be explored in application, to check that desired properties have indeed been achieved.

Code 7.4 shows the implementation for the region descriptors. The code is a straightforward implementation of Eqs. (7.67), (7.69), (7.70), (7.72) and (7.73). Notice that the area is directly computed from the image pixels and that the perimeter and other descriptions are computed from the border pixels in the vector `shape`. A comparison of these measures for the four regions in Fig. 7.19 is shown in Fig. 7.20. Clearly, for the circle the compactness and dispersion measures are close to unity. For the ellipse the compactness and dispersion increase. The convoluted region has the lowest compactness measure and a high dispersion value. The maxima dispersion is for the dolphin since it is not symmetrical and thus the border is close to the region's centre. Clearly, the

```
# Area. Pixels with value shapeGrayLevel define the shape
area = 0
for x,y in itertools.product(range(0, width), range(0, height)):
        if inputImage[y,x] == shapeGrayLevel:
            area += 1

# Obtain shape contour
shape, width, height = findLongesSegmentinImage(pathToDir + imageName,       \
                        gaussianKernelSize, sobelKernelSize, upperT, lowerT)

# Perimeter and mean. The mean is the centre. The perimeter is the arc length
numPoints = len(shape[0])
mean = [0,0]
perimeter = 0.0
y0, x0 = shape[0, numPoints-1], shape[1, numPoints-1]
for p in range(0, numPoints):
    y,x = shape[0,p], shape[1,p]
    mean[0], mean[1] =  mean[0]+x, mean[1]+y
    perimeter += sqrt((y-y0)*(y-y0) + (x-x0)*(x-x0))
    y0,x0 = y,x
mean[0],mean[1] = mean[0] / numPoints, mean[1] / numPoints

# Compactness
compactness = (4.0*pi*area) / (perimeter*perimeter);

# Dispersion
maxDist, minDist = 0, float('Inf')
for p in range(0, numPoints):
    y,x = shape[0,p], shape[1,p]
    d = sqrt((x-mean[0])**2 + (y-mean[1])**2)
    if d >maxDist:
        maxDist = d
    if d <minDist:
        minDist = d

dispersion = pi*maxDist*maxDist / area
dispertionRatio = sqrt(maxDist / minDist)
```

CODE 7.4 Evaluating basic region descriptors.

Area = 147899 Mean = 298.52, 271.51 Perimeter = 1391.50 Compactness = 0.96 Dispersion = 1.01 DispertionRatio = 1.00	Area = 96618 Mean = 294.70, 276.84 Perimeter = 1232.66 Compactness = 0.80 Dispersion = 2.08 DispertionRatio = 1.44	Area = 51673 Mean = 256.97, 258.67 Perimeter = 1665.23 Compactness = 0.23 Dispersion = 5.15 DispertionRatio = 4.05	Area = 105795 Mean = 303.15, 288.87 Perimeter = 2587.24 Compactness = 0.20 Dispersion = 1.89 DispertionRatio = 2.26
(A) Circle	(B) Ellipse	(C) Dolphin	(D) Convoluted region

FIGURE 7.20 Basic region descriptors.

basic region descriptors can be used to characterise, and hence discriminate between areas of differing shapes.

Other measures, rather than focus on the geometric properties, characterise the structure of a region. This is the case of the *Poincarré measure* and the *Euler number*. The Poincarré measure concerns the number of holes within a region. Alternatively, the Euler number is the difference of the number of connected regions from the number of holes in them. There are many more potential measures for shape description in terms of structure and geometry. A measure has been developed [Rosin05] that can discriminate *rectilinear* regions, e.g. for discriminating buildings from within remotely sensed images. We could evaluate global or local curvature (convexity and concavity) as a further measure of geometry; we could investigate proximity and disposition as a further measure of structure. However, these do not have the advantages of a unified structure. We are simply suggesting measures with descriptive ability but this ability is reduced by the correlation between different measures. We have already seen the link between the Poincarré measure and the Euler number; there is a natural link between circularity and irregularity. But the region descriptors we have considered so far lack structure and are largely heuristic – though clearly they may have sufficient descriptive ability for some applications. As such we shall now look at a unified basis for shape description which aims to reduce this correlation and provides a unified theoretical basis for region description, with some similarity to the advantages of the frequency selectivity in a Fourier transform description.

7.3.2 Moments

7.3.2.1 Definition and properties

Moments describe a shape's layout (the arrangement of its pixels), a bit like combining area, compactness, irregularity and higher-order descriptions together. Moments are a global description of a shape, accruing this same advantage as Fourier descriptors since there is selectivity which is an in-built ability to discern, and filter, noise. Further, in image analysis, they are *statistical moments*, as opposed to mechanical ones, but the two are analogous. For example, the mechanical moment of inertia describes the rate of change in momentum; the statistical second-order moment describes the rate of change in a shape's area (i.e. distribution of mass). In this way, statistical moments can be considered as a global region description. Moments for image analysis were again originally introduced in the 1960s [Hu62] (an exciting time for computer vision researchers too!) and an excellent review is available [Prokop92].

Moments are actually often associated more with statistical pattern recognition, than with model-based vision since a major assumption is that there is an unoccluded view of the target shape. Target images are often derived by thresholding, usually one of the optimal forms that can require a single object in the field of view. More complex applications, including handling occlusion, could presuppose feature extraction by some means, with a model to in-fill for the missing parts. However, moments do provide a global description with invariance properties and with the advantages of a compact description aimed to avoid the effects of noise. As such, they have proved popular and successful in many applications.

From a mathematical definition, moments are projections of a function into a basis. The general form of a linear projection of a two-dimensional function $I(x,y)$ can be defined as

$$m_{pq} = \iint_{-\infty}^{\infty} \mathbf{P}_{x,y}\, b_{pq}(x,y)dxdy \tag{7.74}$$

Here b defines the basis functions and m are the coefficients or weights. So a moment is a weighted sum of the pixels in the region $I(x,y)$. We can recall from the discussion of the Fourier basis than the basis functions can be combined to obtain the original function

$$I(x,y) = \iint_{-\infty}^{\infty} m_{pq}\, b_{pq}(x,y)dxdy \tag{7.75}$$

That is, the projection defines weights that can be used to reconstruct or approximate the function. This is the reason why the basis functions are also called blending or interpolation functions. By changing the value of b, we can obtain different projections with different properties. Properties include the mathematical properties, reconstruction properties, computation properties and description properties. A Fourier basis is a popular choice since it makes evident the detail (frequency content) in an image, but there are other basis aimed at representing the function locally or to give a simple form for interpolation. For object description, the coefficients m_{pq} are called moments and the basis is defined to describe the shape of an image region $I(x,y)$.

7.3.2.2 Geometric moments

The *two-dimensional Cartesian moments* are defined by considering as basis functions the polynomials of the form

$$b_{pq}(x,y) = x^p y^q \tag{7.76}$$

Thus, the moment of order p and q, m_{pq} of a function $I(x,y)$ is defined as

$$m_{pq} = \int_{-\infty}^{\infty}\int_{-\infty}^{\infty} x^p y^q \mathbf{P}_{x,y} dxdy \tag{7.77}$$

For discrete images, this equation is approximated by

$$m_{pq} = \sum_x \sum_y x^p y^q \mathbf{P}_{x,y} \Delta A \tag{7.78}$$

where Δa is the area of a pixel. These descriptors have a uniqueness which means that they uniquely determine the original function (they are different for different image regions). This property also implies that the region can be exactly reconstructed from the moments. The *zero-order moment* m_{00}, is

$$m_{00} = \sum_x \sum_y \mathbf{P}_{x,y} \Delta A \tag{7.79}$$

which represents the total mass of a function. Notice that this equation is equal to Eq. (7.67) when $\mathbf{P}_{x,y}$ takes values of zero and one. However, Eq. (7.76) is more general since the function $\mathbf{P}_{x,y}$ can take a range of values. In the definition of moments, these values are generally related to density. The two *first-order moments*, m_{01} and m_{10}, are given by

$$m_{10} = \sum_x \sum_y x \ \mathbf{P}_{x,y} \Delta A \quad m_{01} = \sum_x \sum_y y \ \mathbf{P}_{x,y} \Delta A \tag{7.80}$$

For binary images, these values are proportional to the shape's centre co-ordinates (the values merely require division by the shape's area). In general, the *centre of mass* $(\overline{x}, \overline{y})$ can be calculated from the ratio of the first-order to the zero-order components as

$$\overline{x} = \frac{m_{10}}{m_{00}} \quad \overline{y} = \frac{m_{01}}{m_{00}} \tag{7.81}$$

As an example, we can see the first 10 x-axis moments of an ellipse are shown in Fig. 7.21. The moments rise exponentially, so they are plotted in logarithmic form. Regions with different shapes will produce different moments. Thus, they can be used as a set of descriptors of the shape: measures that can be collected together to differentiate between different shapes.

Code 7.5 illustrates the computation of the moments for a region in an image. In this implementation, the vector `imageRegion` contains the pixels forming the region. The first two components define the co-ordinates of the pixels, and the third component defines the grey level value. Notice that the moments can be also computed directly from the image pixels by iterating the pixels in the image and including in the summation pixels that are labelled as belonging to the region.

Fig. 7.22 shows the moments for four example regions. The 3×3 matrix in the figure shows the logarithmic value of the moment m_{pq}. The top corner is the zero-order moment. We can see that moments distinguish different shapes. However, they are not invariant. That is, they will change if we apply a geometric transformation of the image. In a more general characterisation, we are interested on finding descriptors capable of characterising regions after they have been geometrically transformed. As we shall discuss in the next sections, this is achieved by changing the basis functions in the moments' definition.

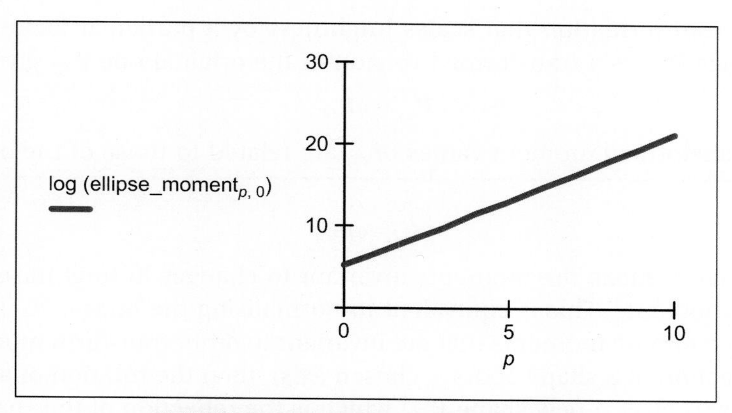

FIGURE 7.21 Horizontal axis ellipse moments.

```
numPoints = len(imageRegion)
M = createImageF(numMoments,numMoments)
for m,n in itertools.product(range(0, numMoments), range(0, numMoments)):
    for indexPixel in range(0, numPoints):
        y = (imageRegion[indexPixel])[0]
        x = (imageRegion[indexPixel])[1]
        v = (imageRegion[indexPixel])[2]
        M[n,m] += (x**n) * (y**m) * v
```

CODE 7.5 Computing geometric moments.

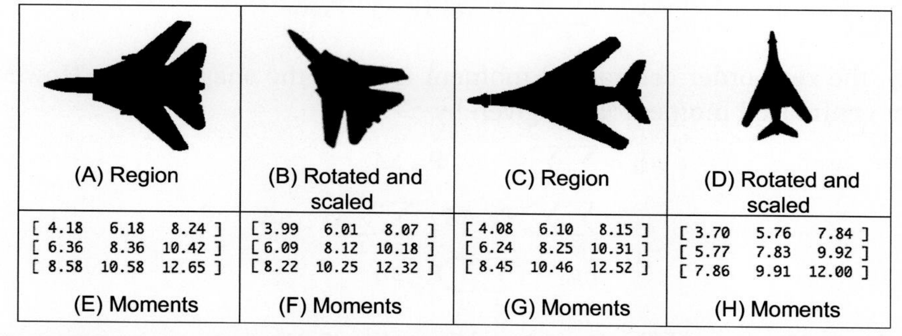

FIGURE 7.22 Examples of geometric moments. In (E) to (H), moment $m_{p,q}$ in row p and column q. Top row and first column $m_{0,0}$.

7.3.2.3 Geometric complex moments and centralised moments

The motivation of developing complex moments was to characterise image regions under different conditions. That is, to construct invariant descriptors. Invariance can have different forms depending on the transformation we consider. For example, if there is an intensity transformation that scales brightness by a particular factor, say α, such that a new image $\mathbf{P}'_{x,y}$ is a transformed version of the original one $\mathbf{P}_{x,y}$ given by

$$\mathbf{P}'_{x,y} = \alpha \mathbf{P}_{x,y} \tag{7.82}$$

Then the transformed moment values m'_{pq} are related to those of the original shape m_{pq} by

$$m'_{pq} = \alpha m_{pq} \tag{7.83}$$

Thus, in order to make the moments invariant to changes in brightness, we need to normalise the moments. This is equivalent to normalising the image.

We can also compute moments that are invariant to other transformations like *mirror symmetry* (reflection of a shape about a chosen axis), then the rotation of a shape about the, say, the x axis gives a new shape $\mathbf{P}'_{x,y}$ which is the reflection of the shape $\mathbf{P}_{x,y}$ given by

$$\mathbf{P}'_{x,y} = \mathbf{P}_{-x,y} \tag{7.84}$$

The transformed moment values can be given in terms of the original shape's moments as

$$m'_{pq} = (-1)^p m_{pq} \tag{7.85}$$

However, we are usually concerned with more basic invariants than mirror images, namely invariance to position, size and rotation. Given that we now have an estimate of a shape's centre (in fact, a reference point for that shape), the *centralised moments*, μ_{pq} which are invariant to translation, can be defined by

$$\mu_{pq} = \sum_x \sum_y (x - \overline{x})^p (y - \overline{y})^q \mathbf{P}_{x,y} \Delta A \tag{7.86}$$

Clearly, the zero-order centralised moment is again the shape's area. However, the first-order centralised moment μ_{01} is given by

$$\begin{aligned} \mu_{01} &= \sum_x \sum_y (y - \overline{y})^1 \mathbf{P}_{x,y} \Delta A \\ &= \sum_x \sum_y y \mathbf{P}_{x,y} \Delta A - \sum_x \sum_y \overline{y} \mathbf{P}_{x,y} \Delta A \\ &= m_{01} - \overline{y} \sum_x \sum_y \mathbf{P}_{x,y} \Delta A \end{aligned} \tag{7.87}$$

From Eq. (7.80), $m_{01} = \sum_x \sum_y y \mathbf{P}_{x,y} \Delta A$ and from Eq. (7.81), $\overline{y} = m_{01} / m_{00}$ so

$$\begin{aligned} \mu_{01} &= m_{01} - \frac{m_{01}}{m_{00}} m_{00} \\ &= 0 \\ &= \mu_{10} \end{aligned} \tag{7.88}$$

Clearly, neither of the first-order centralised moments has any description capability since they are both zero. Going to higher order, one of the second-order moments, μ_{20}, is

$$\mu_{20} = \sum_x\sum_y (x-\bar{x})^2 \mathbf{P}_{x,y}\Delta A$$
$$= \sum_x\sum_y (x^2 - 2x\bar{x} + \bar{x}^2)\mathbf{P}_{x,y}\Delta A \tag{7.89}$$
$$= \sum_x\sum_y x^2\mathbf{P}_{x,y}\Delta A - 2\bar{x}\sum_x\sum_y x\mathbf{P}_{x,y}\Delta A + \bar{x}^2\sum_x\sum_y \mathbf{P}_{x,y}\Delta A$$

since $m_{10} = \sum_x\sum_y x\mathbf{P}_{x,y}\Delta A$ and since $\bar{x} = m_{10}/m_{00}$

$$\mu_{20} = m_{20} - 2\frac{m_{10}}{m_{00}}m_{10} + \left(\frac{m_{10}}{m_{00}}\right)^2 m_{00}$$
$$= m_{20} - \frac{m_{10}^2}{m_{00}} \tag{7.90}$$

and this has descriptive capability. Code 7.6 implements the computation of centralised moments in Eq. (7.86). The centre (*cx, cy*) is computed from the geometric moments presented in the previous section.

The use of centralised moments to describe a shape is shown in Fig. 7.23. The matrix in this figure shows the logarithm of the centralised moments, except for the moments that are zero. The moments in Fig. 7.23E of the translated region in Fig. 7.23B are the same as those of the original region in Fig. 7.23A. In fact, these moments show that the greatest rate of change in mass is around the horizontal axis, as consistent with the shape. The second-order moments Fig. 7.23F of the shape when rotated by 90 degrees, Fig. 7.23C, are transposed, as expected: the rate of change of mass is now greatest around the vertical axis. This illustrates how centralised moments are invariant to translation, but not to rotation.

7.3.2.4 Rotation and scale invariant moments

Centralised moments are only translation invariant: they are constant only with change in position, and no other appearance transformation. In order to obtain scale invariance, we should observe how the moments change when the size of the region changes [Hu62]. Under the scale *s*, the co-ordinates (*x,y*) of the points in a region change to (*x′,y′*) for

```
xc,yc = M[1,0]/M[0,0], M[0,1]/M[0,0]
centMom = createImageF(numMoments,numMoments)
for m,n in itertools.product(range(0, numMoments), range(0, numMoments)):
    for indexPixel in range(0, numPoints):
        y = (imageRegion[indexPixel])[0]
        x = (imageRegion[indexPixel])[1]
        v = (imageRegion[indexPixel])[2]
        centMom[n,m] += ((x-xc)**n) * ((y-yc)**m) * v
```

CODE 7.6 Computing geometric central moments.

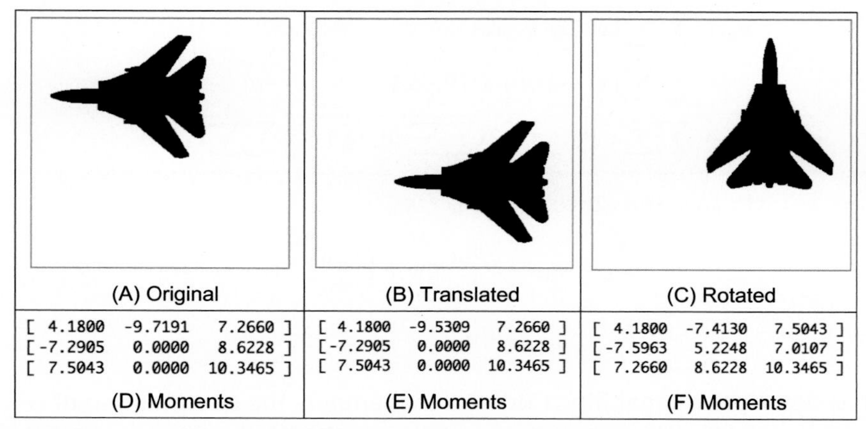

FIGURE 7.23 Describing a shape by centralised moments. In (D) to (F), moment $m_{p,q}$ in row p and column q. Top row and first column $m_{0,0}$.

$$x' = sx \quad y' = sy \tag{7.91}$$

The changes in positions of the points in the region also move the location of the centre $(\bar{x}, \bar{y})$ to

$$\bar{x}' = s\bar{x} \quad \bar{y}' = s\bar{y} \tag{7.92}$$

Accordingly, the central moments defined in Eq. (7.86) can be computed from a scaled image as

$$\eta_{pq} = \sum\sum \left(\frac{x'}{s} - \frac{\bar{x}'}{s}\right)^p \left(\frac{y'}{s} - \frac{\bar{y}'}{s}\right)^q \mathbf{P}_{\frac{x'}{s},\frac{y'}{s}} \Delta_x,\ \Delta_y \tag{7.93}$$

We call η_{pq}, the moment obtained from the scaled image. This equation includes the delta of area in each co-ordinate. This is because $\Delta = \Delta_x \Delta_y$. We can think of Δ as the area of the pixels and Δ_x, Δ_y the length of its sides. In order to obtain invariant descriptors, we should consider that

$$\Delta_{x'} = s\Delta_x \quad \Delta_{y'} = s\Delta_y \tag{7.94}$$

Thus,

$$\eta_{pq} = \frac{1}{s^p}\frac{1}{s^q}\frac{1}{s^2}\sum\sum (x' - \bar{x}')^p (y' - \bar{y}')^q \mathbf{P}_{x',y'} \Delta_{x'} \Delta_{y'} \tag{7.95}$$

That is,

$$\eta_{pq} = \frac{1}{s^{p+q+2}}\sum\sum (x - \bar{\bar{x}})^p (y - \bar{\bar{y}})^q \mathbf{P}_{x',y'} \Delta_{x'} \Delta_{y'} \tag{7.96}$$

or

$$\eta_{pq} = \frac{1}{s^{p+q+2}}\ \mu_{pq} \tag{7.97}$$

Thus, when a region is scaled by s, the momentum is scaled by s^{p+q+2}. To define invariance, we can eliminate the scale by normalising. If we define the scale for the zero order moment to be unity as

$$\eta_{00} = \mu_{00}/s^2 = 1 \tag{7.98}$$

then, we can define the normalisation scale as

$$s = \sqrt{\mu_{00}} \tag{7.99}$$

and according to Eq. (7.97)

$$\eta_{pq} = \frac{1}{\mu_{00}^{\left(\frac{p+q+2}{2}\right)}} \mu_{pq} \tag{7.100}$$

Accordingly, scale invariant moments can be defined as

$$\eta_{pq} = \frac{\mu_{pq}}{\mu_{00}^{\gamma}} \tag{7.101}$$

where

$$\gamma = \frac{p+q}{2} + 1 \quad \forall p+q \geq 2 \tag{7.102}$$

Rotation invariant moments can be computed by considering the transformation of the moments for a rotated image. In this, case we have that the co-ordinates (x,y) of the points in the region change to (x',y') for

$$x' = x\cos(\theta) + y\sin(\theta) \quad y' = -x\sin(\theta) + y\cos(\theta) \tag{7.103}$$

Here θ defines the rotation angle from the centre of the region. Rotation does not change the centre of the region, thus the moments of the rotated shape are

$$\rho_{pq} = \sum\sum ((x - \bar{x})\cos(\theta) + (y - \bar{y})\sin(\theta))^p \times (-(x - \bar{x})\sin(\theta) + (y - \bar{y})\cos(\theta))^q \mathbf{P}_{x,y}\Delta_x\Delta_y \tag{7.104}$$

Unfortunately, the algebraic development of invariance is complicated since the power function does not have simple rotation properties. The strategy in [Hu62] is to define a function system that eliminates rotations. For example, if we define

$$M_1 = \rho_{20} + \rho_{02} \tag{7.105}$$

That is,

$$M_1 = \sum\sum (x\cos(\theta) + y\sin(\theta))^2 + (-x\sin(\theta) + y\cos(\theta))^2 \mathbf{P}_{x,y}\Delta_x\Delta_y \tag{7.106}$$

In this equation, we have eliminated the centre of the region since rotation is independent of the centre and we just want to show the rotation property. By algebraic development we can simplify the previous equation as

$$M_1 = \sum\sum (x\cos(\theta) + y\sin(\theta)\ )^2 + (\ -x\sin(\theta) + y\cos(\theta))^2 \mathbf{P}_{x,y}\Delta_x\Delta_y \tag{7.107}$$

which can be reduced algebraically to

$$M_1 = \sum\sum (x^2(\cos^2(\theta) + \sin^2(\theta)\ ) + y^2(\cos^2(\theta) + \sin^2(\theta)\ ))\mathbf{P}_{x,y}\Delta_x\Delta_y \tag{7.108}$$

or simply as

$$M_1 = \sum\sum (x^2 + y^2)\mathbf{P}_{x,y}\Delta_x\Delta_y \tag{7.109}$$

That is invariant to rotation. Notice that in practice this value can be computed either by Eq. (7.107) or by Eq. (7.109). Similarly to the definition of M_1, the following invariants can be defined

$$\begin{aligned}
M1 &= \eta_{20} + \eta_{02} \\
M2 &= (\eta_{20} - \eta_{02})^2 + 4\eta_{11}^2 \\
M3 &= (\eta_{30} - 3\eta_{12})^2 + (3\eta_{21} - \eta_{03})^2 \\
M4 &= (\eta_{30} + \eta_{12})^2 + (\eta_{21} + \eta_{03})^2 \\
M5 &= (\eta_{30} - 3\eta_{12})(\eta_{30} + \eta_{12})\left((\eta_{30} + \eta_{12})^2 - 3(\eta_{21} - \eta_{03})^2\right) \\
&\quad +(3\eta_{21} - \eta_{03})(\eta_{21} + \eta_{03})\left(3(\eta_{30} + \eta_{12})^2 - (\eta_{21} + \eta_{03})^2\right) \\
M6 &= (\eta_{20} - \eta_{02})\left((\eta_{30} + \eta_{12})^2 - (\eta_{21} + \eta_{03})^2\right) + 4\eta_{11}(\eta_{30} + \eta_{12})(\eta_{21} + \eta_{03}) \\
M7 &= (3\eta_{21} - \eta_{03})(\eta_{30} + \eta_{12})\left((\eta_{30} + \eta_{12})^2 - 3(\eta_{21} + \eta_{03})^2\right) \\
&\quad +(3\eta_{12} - \eta_{30})(\eta_{21} + \eta_{03})\left(3(\eta_{12} + \eta_{30})^2 - (\eta_{21} + \eta_{03})^2\right)
\end{aligned} \tag{7.110}$$

The first of these, $M1$ and $M2$, are second-order moments — those for which $p+q=2$. Those remaining are third-order moments, since $p+q=3$. (The first-order moments are of no consequence since they are zero.) The last moment $M7$ is introduced as a skew invariant designed to distinguish mirror images.

A practical alternative to rotation invariants is to determine the angle and explicitly compute the moments by inverting the rotation. We have seen in Fig. 7.23 that moments are related to the axis of the region, thus if we can use the moments to determine the axis and thus the rotation, we can compute rotation-invariant centralised moments by rotating the points in the region by $-\theta$. That is,

$$\eta_{pq} = \sum\sum ((x - \overline{x})\cos(\theta) - (y - \overline{y})\sin(\theta)\ )^p \times ((x - \overline{x})\sin(\theta) + (y - \overline{y})\cos(\theta))^q \mathbf{P}_{x,y}\Delta_x\Delta_y \tag{7.111}$$

The rotation angle can be obtained by finding the principal axis of the region. This is achieved by noticing that the first and second moments define an ellipse. The equation of the ellipse is given by

$$[x \quad y]\begin{bmatrix} \mu_{20} & \mu_{11} \\ \mu_{11} & \mu_{02} \end{bmatrix}\begin{bmatrix} x \\ y \end{bmatrix} = 0 \tag{7.112}$$

This equation commonly appears in physics when describing the moments of inertia of a rigid body. We can consider that the angle θ defines a rotation matrix R that aligns the major axis of the ellipse with the x axis. In this case the rotation matrix diagonalises Eq. (7.112). That is, we want the equation to be transformed so that there are no quadratic terms. Paraphrasing, we want the previous equation to have the form

$$[x \quad y]\begin{bmatrix} \lambda_1 & 0 \\ 0 & \lambda_2 \end{bmatrix}\begin{bmatrix} x \\ y \end{bmatrix}=0 \tag{7.113}$$

To obtain the form in the equation above, we apply the rotation R. That is,

$$R^T\begin{bmatrix} \mu_{20} & \mu_{11} \\ \mu_{11} & \mu_{02} \end{bmatrix}R=\begin{bmatrix} \lambda_1 & 0 \\ 0 & \lambda_2 \end{bmatrix} \tag{7.114}$$

by algebraic manipulation we have that

$$\begin{bmatrix} \mu_{20} & \mu_{11} \\ \mu_{11} & \mu_{02} \end{bmatrix}R=R\begin{bmatrix} \lambda_1 & 0 \\ 0 & \lambda_2 \end{bmatrix} \tag{7.115}$$

or

$$\begin{bmatrix} \mu_{20} & \mu_{11} \\ \mu_{11} & \mu_{02} \end{bmatrix}\begin{bmatrix} \cos(\theta) & \sin(\theta) \\ -\sin(\theta) & \cos(\theta) \end{bmatrix}=\begin{bmatrix} \cos(\theta) & \sin(\theta) \\ -\sin(\theta) & \cos(\theta) \end{bmatrix}\begin{bmatrix} \lambda_1 & 0 \\ 0 & \lambda_2 \end{bmatrix} \tag{7.116}$$

By expansion we obtain two equations for the principal axis λ_1. That is,

$$\begin{aligned} (\mu_{20}-\lambda_1)\cos(\theta)+\mu_{11}\sin(\theta)=0 \\ \mu_{11}\cos(\theta)+(\mu_{02}-\lambda_2)\sin(\theta)=0 \end{aligned} \tag{7.117}$$

Eliminating λ_1 between the above two equations we have that

$$\tan(2\theta)=\frac{2\mu_{11}}{\mu_{20}-\mu_{02}} \tag{7.118}$$

This equation gives the angle of rotation of the region, and it can be used to compute the rotation invariant moments in Eq. (7.111).

Code 7.7 shows how invariant moments are computed from an image. The implementation computes the different moments presented in this section. The array `centMomNorm` defines scale invariant moments by the definition in Eq. (7.101). These moments are scale and translation invariant, but they change with rotation. For rotation invariance, the code computes the rotation angle according to Eq. (7.118). Notice that the rotation defines a ratio, so it is not defined for regions when the dominator is zero (i.e. a circle), but in this case the moments should be the same independent of the rotation. The rotation angle is used to obtain the translation and rotation invariant moments in Eq. (7.111). These are stored in the vector `vn`. The code also computes the invariant moments according to the definitions of M_1, M_2 and M_3 in Eq. (7.110). These are also invariant to changes in scale, translation and rotation.

Fig. 7.24 shows the computation of moments with Code 7.7. Figs. 7.24B and D correspond to the same shapes than in Figs. 7.24A and C, but with a change of scale and a rotation. The matrix shows the values of the moments in the `vn` array in logarithmic

```
# Scale normalised geometric central Moments
centMomNorm = createImageF(numMoments,numMoments)
for m,n in itertools.product(range(0, numMoments), range(0, numMoments)):
    c = 1 + ((n + m) / 2.0)
    centMomNorm[n,m] = centMom[n,m] / pow(centMom[0,0], c)

# Angle from central moments
if centMom[2,0] < centMom[0,2]:
    t = 0.5 * atan(2.0*centMom[1,1]/(centMom[2,0]-centMom[0,2])) + pi/2.0
else:
    t = 0.5 * atan(2.0*centMom[1,1]/(centMom[2,0]-centMom[0,2]))

# Opposite direction for rotation invariant
t = -t;

# Geometric invariant moments from image region
vn = createImageF(numMoments,numMoments)
for m,n in itertools.product(range(0, numMoments), range(0, numMoments)):
    for indexPixel in range(0, numPoints):
        y = (imageRegion[indexPixel])[0]
        x = (imageRegion[indexPixel])[1]
        val = (imageRegion[indexPixel])[2]
        vn[n,m] += ((x-xc)*cos(t) - (y-yc)*sin(t))**n *                    \
                   ((x-xc)*sin(t) + (y-yc)*cos(t))**m * val
    c = 1 + ((n + m) / 2.0)
    if vn[n,m] > 0: vn[n,m] = log10(vn[n,m] / pow(M[0,0],c))
    else:           vn[n,m] = 0

printImageRangeF(vn, [0,numMoments-1],[0,numMoments-1], "6.2f")

# Compute invariant moments from normalised central moments
m1 = centMomNorm[2,0] + centMomNorm[0,2]
m2 = (centMomNorm[2,0] - centMomNorm[0,2])**2 + 4*  (centMomNorm[1,1]**2)
m3 = (centMomNorm[3,0] - 3.0*centMomNorm[1,2])**2 + (3.0*centMomNorm[2,1]  \
                       - centMomNorm[0,3])**2
```

CODE 7.7 Invariant geometric moments.

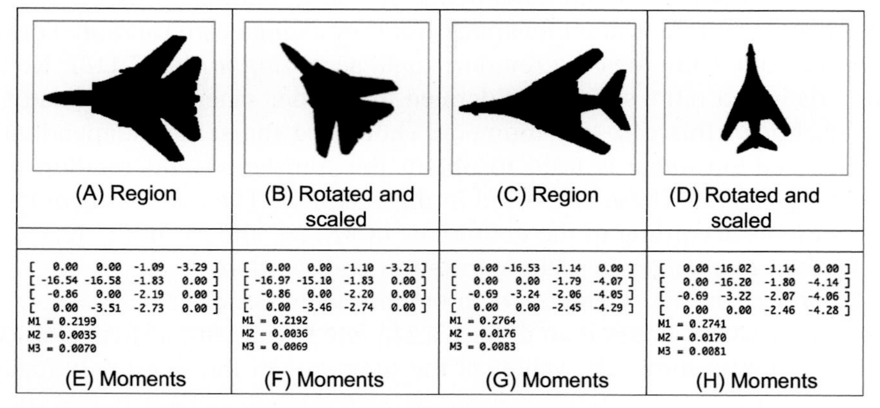

FIGURE 7.24 Examples of invariant geometric moments. In (E) to (H), moment $m_{p,q}$ in row p and column q. Top row and first column $m_{0,0}$.

form. The figure also show the values of M_1, M_2 and M_3. Notice that the invariant moments for the same shapes are very similar. In contrast, the invariant moments for the shapes in Figs. 7.24A and C differ. These invariant moments have the most important invariance properties. However, these moments are not orthogonal and produce highly correlated descriptors, as such there is potential for reducing the size of the set of moments required to describe a shape accurately.

7.3.2.5 Zernike moments

Invariance can be achieved by using *Zernike moments* [Teague80] that give an orthogonal set of rotation-invariant moments. These find greater deployment where invariant properties are required. Rotation invariance is achieved by using polar representation, as opposed to the Cartesian parameterisation for centralised moments. The complex Zernike moment, Z_{pq}, is

$$Z_{pq} = \frac{p+1}{\pi} \int_0^{2\pi} \int_0^{\infty} V_{pq}(r,\theta)^* f(r,\theta) r dr d\theta \tag{7.119}$$

where p is now the radial magnitude and q is the radial direction and where * again denotes the complex conjugate of a Zernike polynomial, V_{pq}, given by

$$V_{pq}(r,\theta) = R_{pq}(r) e^{jq\theta} \quad \text{where} \quad p-q \text{ is even and } 0 \le q \le |p| \tag{7.120}$$

where R_{pq} is a real-valued polynomial given by

$$R_{pq}(r) = \sum_{m=0}^{\frac{p-|q|}{2}} (-1)^m \frac{(p-m)!}{m! \left(\frac{p+|q|}{2} - m \right)! \left(\frac{p-|q|}{2} - m \right)!} r^{p-2m} \tag{7.121}$$

The order of the polynomial is denoted by p and the repetition by q. The repetition q can take negative values (since $q \le |p|$) so the radial polynomial uses its magnitude and thus the inverse relationship holds: $R_{p,q}(r) = R_{p,-q}(r)$ (changing the notation of the polynomial slightly by introducing a comma to make clear the moment just has the sign of q inverted). The polynomials of lower degree are

$$\begin{aligned} R_{00}(r) &= 1 \\ R_{11}(r) &= r \\ R_{22}(r) &= r^2 \\ R_{20}(r) &= r^2 - 1 \\ R_{31}(r) &= 3r^2 - 2r \\ R_{40}(r) &= 6r^4 - 6r^2 + 1 \end{aligned} \tag{7.122}$$

and some of these are plotted in Fig. 7.25. In Fig. 7.25A, we can see that the frequency components increase with the order p and the functions approach unity as $r \to 1$. The frequency content reflects the level of detail that can be captured by the particular polynomial. The change between the different polynomials shows how together they can capture different aspects of an underlying signal, across the various values of r. The

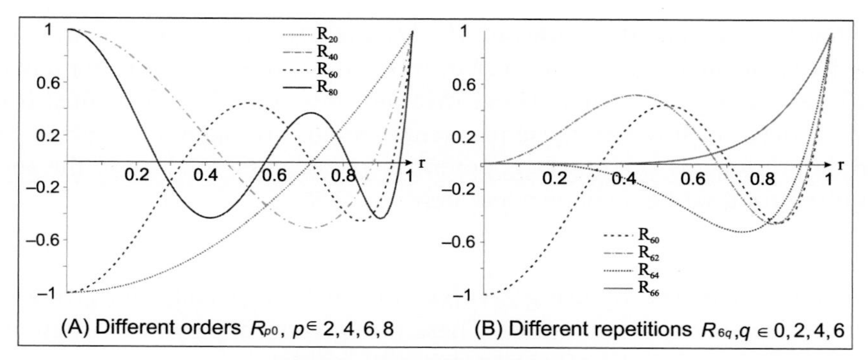

FIGURE 7.25 Zernike polynomials.

repetition controls the way in which the function approaches unity: the influence along the polynomial and the polynomials for different values of q are shown in Fig. 7.25B.

These polynomials are orthogonal within the unit circle, so the analysed shape (the area of interest) has to be re-mapped to be of this size before calculation of its moments. This naturally implies difficulty in mapping a unit circle to a Cartesian grid. As illustrated in Fig. 7.26: (A) the circle can be within the area of interest, losing corner information (but that is information rarely of interest) or (B) around (encompassing) the area of interest which then covers areas where there is no information, but ensures that all the information within the area of interest is included.

The orthogonality of these polynomials assures the reduction in the set of numbers used to describe a shape. More simply, the radial polynomials can be expressed as

$$R_{pq}(r) = \sum_{k=q}^{p} B_{pqk} r^k \tag{7.123}$$

where the Zernike coefficients are

$$B_{pqk} = (-1)^{\frac{p-k}{2}} \frac{((p+k)/2)!}{((p-k)/2)!((k+q)/2)!((k-q)/2)!} \tag{7.124}$$

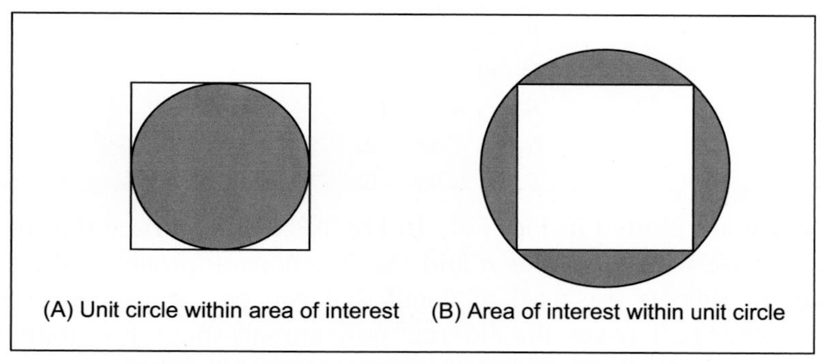

(A) Unit circle within area of interest
(B) Area of interest within unit circle

FIGURE 7.26 Mapping a unit circle to an area of interest.

for $p-k=$ even. The Zernike moments can actually be calculated from centralised moments as

$$Z_{pq}=\frac{p+1}{\pi}\sum_{k=q}^{p}\sum_{l=0}^{t}\sum_{m=0}^{q}(-j)^{m}\binom{t}{l}\binom{q}{m}B_{pqk}\mu_{(k-2l-q+m)(q+2l-m)} \tag{7.125}$$

where $t=(k-q)/2$ and where

$$\binom{t}{l}=\frac{t!}{l!(t-l)!} \tag{7.126}$$

A Zernike polynomial kernel is illustrated in Fig. 7.27. This shows that the kernel can capture differing levels of shape detail (and that multiple kernels are needed to give a shape's description). This kernel is computed in radial form, which is how it is deployed in shape analysis. Note that differing sets of parameters such as order and repetition control the level of detail that is analysed by application of this kernel to a shape. The plot shows the real part of the kernel; the imaginary part is similar, but rotated.

Analysis (and by Eq. (7.86)), assuming that x and y are constrained to the interval [-1,1], gives

$$\begin{aligned}
Z_{00} &= \frac{\mu_{00}}{\pi} \\
Z_{11} &= \frac{2}{\pi}(\mu_{01}-j\mu_{10})=0 \\
Z_{22} &= \frac{3}{\pi}(\mu_{02}-j2\mu_{11}-\mu_{20})
\end{aligned} \tag{7.127}$$

which can be extended further [Teague80], and with remarkable similarity to the Hu invariant moments (Eq. (7.110)).

The magnitude of these Zernike moments remains invariant to rotation which affects only the phase; the Zernike moments can be made scale invariant by normalisation. An

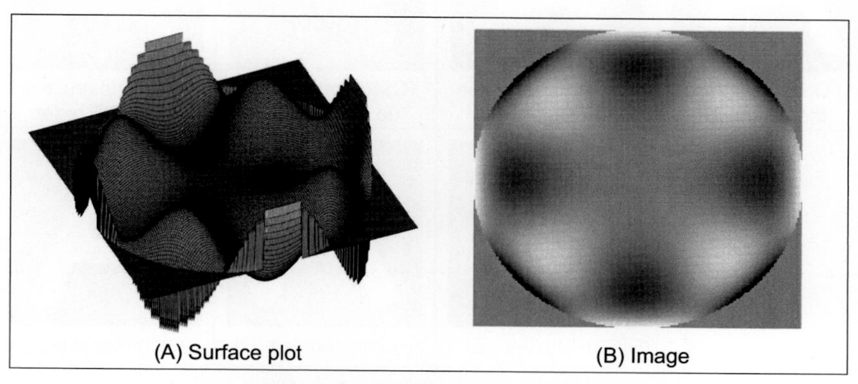

FIGURE 7.27 Zernike polynomial kernel.

additional advantage is that there is a *reconstruction* theorem. For Nm moments, the original shape f can be reconstructed from its moments and the Zernike polynomials as

$$f(x,y)\approx\sum_{p=0}^{Nm}\sum_{q}Z_{pq}V_{pq}(x,y) \tag{7.128}$$

This is illustrated in Fig. 7.28 for reconstructing a simple binary object, the letter A, from different numbers of moments [Prismall02]. When reconstructing this up to the 10th order of a Zernike moment description (this requires 66 moments) we achieve a grey level image, which contains much of the overall shape, shown in Fig. 7.28B. This can be thresholded to give a binary image, Fig. 7.28E which shows the overall shape, without any corners. When we use more moments, we increase the detail in the reconstruction: Fig. 7.28C is up to 15th order (136 moments), and Fig. 7.28D is 20th order (231 moments). The latter of these is much closer to the original image, especially in its thresholded form, Fig. 7.28D. This might sound like a lot of moments, but the compression from the original image is very high. Note also that even though we can achieve recognition from a smaller set of moments, these might not represent the hole in the shape which is not present at the 10th order which just shows the overall shape of the letter A. As such, reconstruction can give insight as to the shape contribution of selected moments: their significance can be assessed by this and other tests.

These Zernike descriptors have been shown to good effect in application by reconstructing a good approximation to a shape with only few descriptors [Boyce83] and in recognition [Khotanzad90]. As ever, fast computation has been of (continuing) interest [Mukundan95, Gu02].

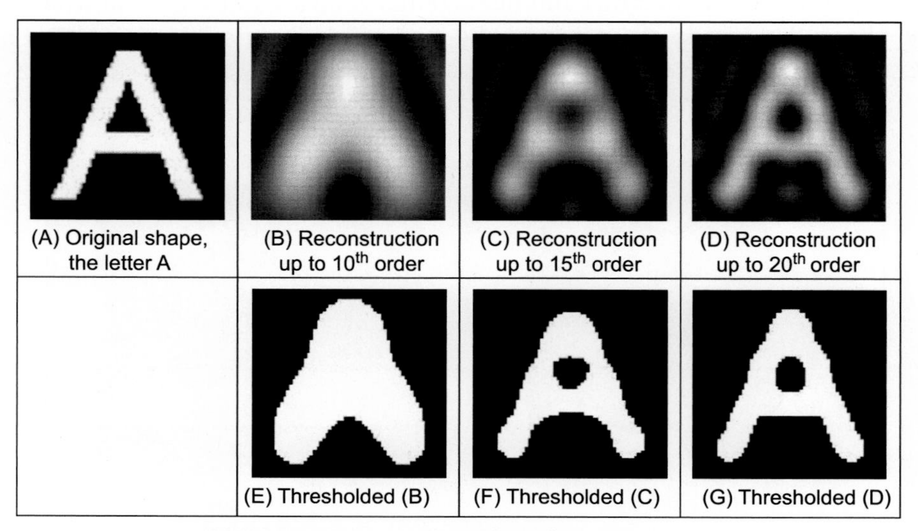

FIGURE 7.28 Reconstructing a shape from its moments.

7.3.2.6 Tchebichef moments

Since there is an infinite variety of functions that can be used as the basis function we also have Legendre [Teague80] and later *Tchebichef* (though this is sometimes spelt as *Chebyshev*) *moments* [Mukundan02]. There is no detailed comparison yet available, but there are advantages and disadvantages to the differing moments, often exposed by application.

7.3.2.7 Krawtchouk moments

Krawtchouk moments were presented in [Yap2003], and they are defined by using the Krawtchouk polynomials as basis functions $b_{pq}(x,y)$ in Eq. (7.74). Krawtchouk polynomials are orthogonal, thus, similar to the Zernike moments, they have minimal information redundancy and thus regions can be better characterised with few descriptors. Additionally, they are defined in the discrete domain and thus they reduce discretisation errors. Discretisation errors occur since moments are obtained by approximating an integral as a summation. Intuitively, one can see that the summation approximates the integral by adding parallelepipeds with a base defined by the pixel area. As the order of the moments increases, the flat tops of the parallelepipeds give just a very rough approximation of the shape of the functions. Thus, for high-order moments the error increases and the summation produces results that can be quite different from the value of the integral. As such, it is desirable to use polynomials that are defined in the discrete domain.

Krawtchouk polynomials have a discrete domain defined by a collection of points x in a range [0,N]. The polynomial n is defined as

$$K_n(x;p,N) = \sum_{i=0}^{N} a_{i,n,p}\, x^i \tag{7.129}$$

That is, the value at the point x in the interval [0,N] is the polynomial with N terms defined by the powers of the value of x. For a function with an interval [0,N], we can compute N+1 polynomials. That is, $x,n \in [0,N]$ are discrete values.

The parameter p defines a family of polynomials, and it has the effect of shifting the points of the function. As such, to compute the polynomials we need to select a value p and we need to define the range N where we will evaluate the function. Krawtchouk moments are defined for central polynomials with $p = .5$ and n is defined by the size of the image. The coefficients (or weights) $a_{i,n,p}$ in Eq. (7.129) do not have an explicit definition, but they are the result of developing a function that is obtained by considering discrete steps at each point in the domain. This function is defined as

$$\sum_{i=0}^{N} a_{i,n,p}\, x^i = \sum_{i=0}^{N} -1^i \binom{N-x}{n-i}\binom{x}{i}(p)^{n-i}(1-p)^i \tag{7.130}$$

Here, $\binom{r}{s}$ defines the combinations, and it is defined using a factorial as

$$\binom{r}{s} = \frac{r!}{s!(r-s)!} \tag{7.131}$$

As a solid example, we can develop three polynomials for $p = .5$ as

$$\begin{aligned} K_0(x;N) &= 1 \\ K_1(x;N) &= -\frac{N}{2} + x \\ K_2(x;N) &= \frac{N^2 - N}{8} - \frac{Nx}{2} + \frac{x^2}{2} \end{aligned} \tag{7.132}$$

We should note that there is an alternative definition of Eq. (7.130) that expresses the polynomial using the gamma function. Both definitions are equivalents; Eq. (7.130) is often used when discussing the polynomial as a step function and the gamma version is used when discussing recursive relationships.

In order to make the polynomials in Eq. (7.130) orthogonal, it is necessary to multiply them by a weighting function as

$$\overline{K_n}(x;p,N) = w(x,n)K_n(x;p,N) \quad \text{for} \quad w(x,n) = \sqrt{\frac{\sigma(x;p,N)}{\rho(n;p,N)}} \tag{7.133}$$

where

$$\sigma(x;p,N) = \binom{N}{x} p^x (1-p)^{N-x} \tag{7.134}$$

and

$$\rho(n;p,N) = (-1)^n \left(\frac{1-p}{p}\right)^n \left(\frac{n!}{\langle -N \rangle_n}\right) \tag{7.135}$$

Here $\langle -N \rangle_n$ defines the rising factorial function. Notice that $\sigma(x;p,N)$ defines a weight for each x in the interval $[0,N]$ independent of the polynomial order n. The function $\rho(n;p,N)$ defines a weight that is independent of the position x, but depends on the polynomial index n.

Code 7.8 shows the implementation of Eq. (7.133). The vector `sigma` stores the values defined in Eq. (7.134), and it is computed for each point x. The vector `ro` stores the weights in Eq. (7.135), and it is computed for each polynomial `n`. The matrix `K` stores the polynomials in Eq. (7.130). The results of the orthogonal normalised coefficients in Eq. (7.133) are stored in the matrix `Kweighted`. A main issue with the definition in Eq. (7.133) is that it requires evaluation of large factorials that involve larger numbers that cannot be represented in a computer (i.e. overflow). So the straightforward implementation of the equations cannot be used for a large domain N. In [Yap2003], this is resolved by including alternative relations that compute the weights and polynomials in a recursive fashion.

Fig. 7.29 shows the polynomials computed with Code 7.8 for `p` = .5 and `K` = 100. Thus, we can obtain 100 polynomials and each one evaluates 100 points. Fig. 7.29A shows all the polynomials forming a surface. One axis defines the points x and the other the

```
# Combination functions
def nCr(n, r):
    if n < 0 or r < 0 or n-r < 0: return 0
    return factorial(n) / (factorial(r) * factorial(n-r))

def risingFactorial(x, n):
    p = 1
    for k in range(0,n):
        p = p * (x + k)
    return p

# Coefficient size
N = width-1

# Weight. It can be replaced by recurrence relation
for x in range(0,width):
    sigma[x] = nCr(N, x) * pow(p,x) * pow(1-p,N-x)

# Scale factor. It can be replaced by recurrence relation
for n in range(0,width):
    ro[n] = pow(-1,n) * pow((1-p)/p,n)*(float(factorial(n)) / risingFactorial(-N,n))

# Krawtchouk matrix that store result of the polynomial
# Each row is a polynomial each column is the polynomial value for an x value
# Alternatively, we could have used the polynomial generating function
for n,x in itertools.product(range(0, width), range(0, width)):
    for i in range(0,width):
        K[n,x] += pow(-1,i) * nCr(N-x, n-i) * nCr(x,i) * pow(p,n-i) * pow(1.0-p,i)

# Normalize rows for stability
for n in range(0,width):
    scale = K[n,0]
    for x in range(0,width):
        K[n,x] /= scale

# Product defining the weighted
Kweighted = createImageF(width,width)
for n,x in itertools.product(range(0, width), range(0, width)):
    Kweighted[n,x] = K[n,x]*sqrt(sigma[x]/ro[n])
```

CODE 7.8 Krawtchouk polynomials.

polynomial n. The graphs in Figs. 7.29B–F correspond to columns in the surface. That is, each polynomial is a slice of the surface in Fig. 7.29A.

Krawtchouk polynomials define functions in one dimension; however, moments are computed on two-dimensional images. Thus, moments are defined by combining polynomials in the x and y directions. By using the definition in Eq. (7.74) with the Krawtchouk polynomials as projections, we obtain the definition of the Krawtchouk moments. In discrete from, these are given by

$$Q_{nm} = \sum_{x=0}^{N} \sum_{y=0}^{M} \overline{K_n}(x;p,N)\overline{K_m}(y;p,M)\mathbf{P}_{x,y}\Delta A \tag{7.136}$$

Here N, M define the size of the image. We can notice an intimate relationship between the Krawtchouk moments and the geometric moments by developing the above

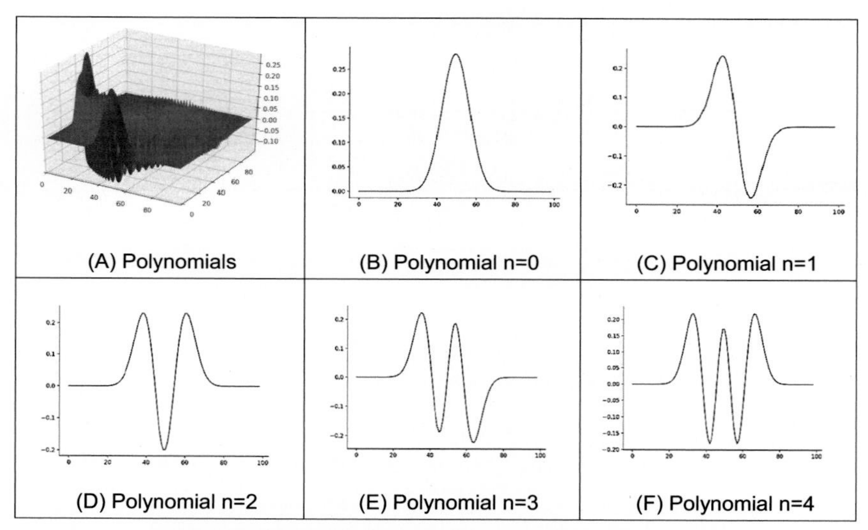

FIGURE 7.29 Krawtchouk polynomials for $p = .5$ and $K = 100$.

equation. By considering the definition in Eq. (7.129), the equation above can be written as

$$Q_{nm} = \sum_{x=0}^{N}\sum_{y=0}^{M}\left(w(x,n)\sum_{i=0}^{N}a_{i,n,p}\,x^{i}\right)\left(w(y,m)\sum_{j=0}^{M}b_{j,n,p}\,y^{j}\right)\mathbf{P}_{x,y}\Delta A \tag{7.137}$$

Here we use a and b to distinguish between the coefficient of the x and y directions, but if N equals M (i.e. a square image), then the coefficients are the same. By rearranging the terms we have

$$Q_{nm} = \sum_{i=0}^{N}\sum_{j=0}^{M}a_{i,n,p}\,b_{j,n,p}\sum_{x=0}^{N}\sum_{y=0}^{M}w(x,n)w(y,m)\;x^{i}y^{j}\mathbf{P}_{x,y}\Delta A \tag{7.138}$$

The weights $w(x,n)$ and $w(y,m)$ can be separated into their two components defined in Eq. (7.133). Thus,

$$Q_{nm} = \sum_{i=0}^{N}\sum_{j=0}^{M}\boldsymbol{H}_{nm}a_{i,n,p}b_{j,n,p}\sum_{x=0}^{N}\sum_{y=0}^{M}\boldsymbol{Z}_{xy}x^{i}y^{j}\mathbf{P}_{x,y}\Delta A \tag{7.139}$$

for

$$\boldsymbol{H}_{nm} = \frac{1}{\sqrt{\rho(n;p,N)\rho(m;p,M)}} \quad \textit{and} \quad \boldsymbol{H}_{xy} = \sqrt{\sigma(x;p,N)\sigma(y;p,M)} \tag{7.140}$$

If we compare the last two summations in Eq. (7.139) with Eq. (7.78), we can see that the summations define a weighted version of the geometric moments. As we indicated before, the weights normalise and produce orthonormal moments. As such, according to

Eq. (7.139), the Krawtchouk moments can be defined as the weighted combinations of the geometric moments,

$$Q_{nm} = \sum_{i=0}^{N} \sum_{j=0}^{M} \mathbf{H}_{nm} a_{i,n,p}\, b_{j,n,p} \overline{G}_{ij} \tag{7.141}$$

wherein $\overline{G}_{ij}$ are the weighted geometric moments

$$\overline{G}_{ij} = \sum_{x=0}^{N} \sum_{y=0}^{M} \mathbf{Z}_{xy} x^i y^j \mathbf{P}_{x,y} \Delta A \tag{7.142}$$

Code 7.9 illustrates the computation of the Krawtchouk moments. The image region is contained in the `shapeImage` array. This array contains a list of pixel co-ordinates x,y and the pixel value v. For simplicity, the code uses the same polynomials for the x and y co-ordinates. This is achieved by defining the domain as the maximum of the width and the height. That is, we are considering that the image is square. The function `weightedKrawtchoukPolynomials` computes the polynomials as explained in Code 7.8. The function returns arrays containing the non-normalised polynomials `kW` in Eq. (7.130) and the polynomial coefficients `aW` in Eq. (7.129). It also returns the weights; The arrays `sigma`, `ro` and `w` store the weights defined in Eqs. (7.134), (7.135) and (7.133), respectively. The implementation computes the moments in two alternative ways. First by using Eq. (7.136). The result is stored in the array `Q`. Second, from the weighted geometric moments according to Eq. (7.141). The results are stored in the array `Qs`. Both computations

```
# Polynomials, coefficients and weights for the Krawtchouk polynomials
# Considering that A*C = k. For a the coefficients and C the powers x, x^2, x^3,..
N = max(width, height)
kW, aW, sigma, ro, w = weightedKrawtchoukPolynomials(p, N)

# Krawtchouk moments of the shape by the standard definition
Q = createImageF(numMoments, numMoments)
for m,n in itertools.product(range(0, numMoments), range(0, numMoments)):
    for indexPixel in range(0, numPoints):
        y, x = (shapeImage[indexPixel])[0], (shapeImage[indexPixel])[1]
        v = (shapeImage[indexPixel])[2]
        Q[n,m] += w[x,m] * kW[x,m] * w[y,n] * kW[y,n] * v

# Krawtchouk moments from the geometric moments Gij = x**i , y**j.
G = createImageF(N, N)
for i,j in itertools.product(range(0, N), range(0, N)):
    for indexPixel in range(0, numPoints):
        y, x= (shapeImage[indexPixel])[0], (shapeImage[indexPixel])[1]
        v = (shapeImage[indexPixel])[2]
        G[j,i] +=  sqrt(sigma[x] * sigma[y]) * y**j * x**i * v

Qs = createImageF(numMoments, numMoments)
for m,n in itertools.product(range(0, numMoments), range(0, numMoments)):
    for i,j in itertools.product(range(0, N), range(0, N)):
        Qs[n,m] +=  aW[m,i] * aW[n,j] * G[j,i]

    Qs[n,m] *= (1.0 / sqrt(ro[n]*ro[m]))
```

CODE 7.9 Krawtchouk moments.

produce the same results, and it shows that effectively Krawtchouk moments are a weighted combination of geometric moments. The array `G` in the code stores the weighted geometric moments defined in Eq. (7.142).

Fig. 7.30 presents the results obtained from Code 7.9 for four different regions. The moments for the regions on the left are shown as the top matrix in the figures on the right. We can notice that the moments characterise the different regions. However, they are not invariant since geometric transformations of the regions produce different moments.

The Krawtchouk moments can be made invariant based on its relation to geometric moments. The basic idea is to replace the definition of the weighted geometric moments

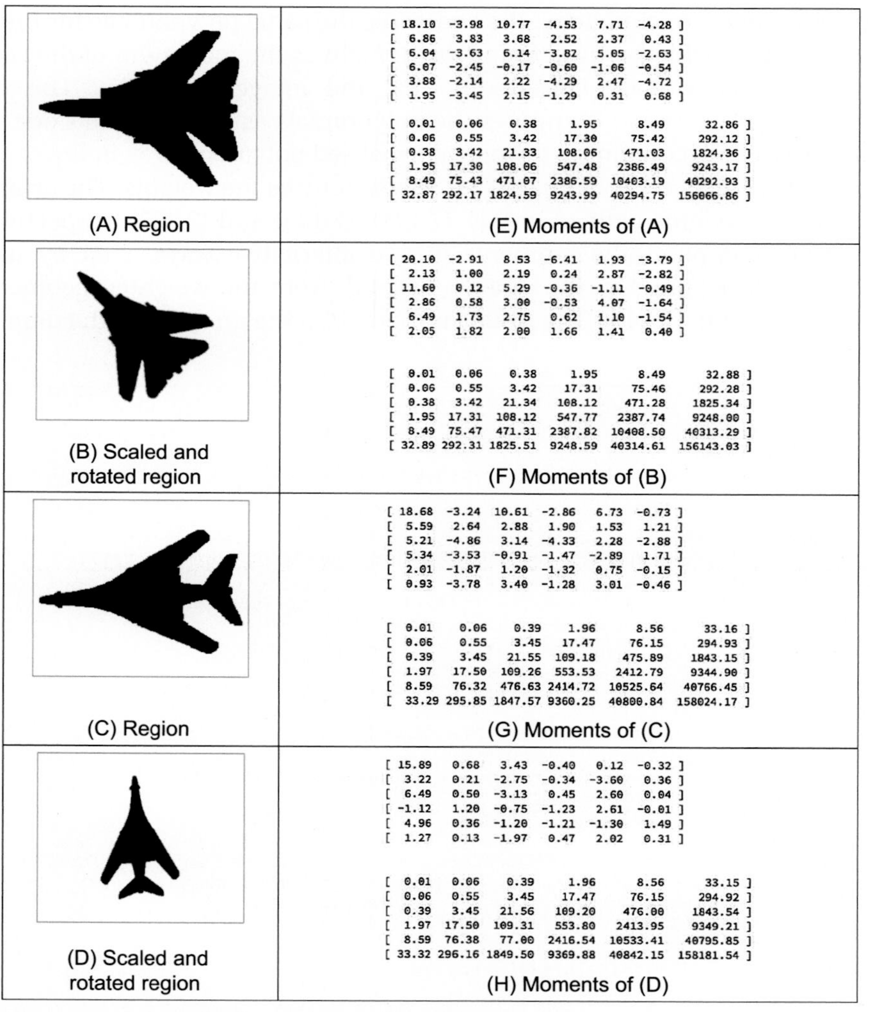

FIGURE 7.30 Examples of Krawtchouk moments. In (E) to (H), moment $Q_{n,m}$ in row n and column m. Top row and first column $Q_{0,0}$ moment. Top matrix in (E) to (H) Krawtchouk moments, bottom matrix invariant moments.

in Eq. (7.141) by a definition that includes weighted invariant geometric moments. We start by defining a map that transforms the co-ordinates x and y of the region as

$$\begin{aligned}\alpha &= (x - \bar{x})\sin(\theta) + (y - \bar{y})\cos(\theta)\\ \beta &= (x - \bar{x})\cos(\theta) - (y - \bar{y})\sin(\theta)\end{aligned} \tag{7.143}$$

The centre $(\bar{x},\bar{y})$ and the rotation angle θ are already defined in Eqs. (7.81) and (7.118), respectively, and they can be obtained from the geometric moments. The moments for (α,β) are rotation and translation invariant since the region has been translated to the origin and its rotation has been removed.

We can normalise the size by dividing by the total area of the region. Since the total area is M_{00} each component is normalised by $\sqrt{M_{00}}$. That is,

$$u = \frac{\alpha}{\sqrt{M_{00}}} \quad \text{and} \quad v = \frac{\beta}{\sqrt{M_{00}}} \tag{7.144}$$

Thus, the region defined by this equation is a region centred in the origin, without rotation and with a normalised area. However, we need the area to be defined in the Krawtchouk polynomial domain. That is, in the $N\times M$ image. Accordingly, we scale and translate the new region to fit the polynomial domain. That is,

$$u = \frac{N}{\sqrt{2M_{00}}}\alpha + \frac{N}{2} \quad \text{and} \quad v = \frac{N}{\sqrt{2M_{00}}}\beta + \frac{N}{2} \tag{7.145}$$

This definition maps the original region defined by the points (x,y) into a new region defined by the points (u,v) that is invariant and that fits the polynomial domain. Thus, we can now use this new region to compute the invariant moments following Eq. (7.142). That is,

$$\bar{\nu}_{ij} = \sum_{x=0}^{N}\sum_{y=0}^{M}\sqrt{\sigma(u;p,N)\sigma(v;p,N)}a^i b^j \mathbf{P}_{x,y}\Delta A \tag{7.146}$$

Then the invariant Krawtchouk moments are defined following Eq. (7.141) as

$$\overline{Q}_{nm} = \sum_{i=0}^{N}\sum_{j=0}^{M}\mathbf{H}_{nm}a_{i,n,p}\, b_{i,n,p}\bar{\nu}_{ij} \tag{7.147}$$

Code 7.10 illustrates the computation of invariant moments according to this equation. The geometric moments are used to compute the centre and rotation parameters. The matrix `Nu` stores the result of Eq. (7.146). The matrix `Qi` stores the result of Eq. (7.147). Notice that in the implementation, once the invariant moments are computed they are transformed by Eq. (7.100) since the region (α,β) is not scale invariant. We can also notice that although in theory the summations should be performed for all the image domain $N\times M$, in practice the weights σ and ρ tend to zero rapidly as we increase the values of x and n, so a good approximation can be obtained after few iterations.

Fig. 7.30 shows four examples of the computation of moments with the Code 7.10. The invariant moments for the regions on the left are shown as the lower matrix in the figures

```
# Invariant  Krawtchouk moments by using weighted invariant Geometric moments
G(j,i)
Qi = createImageF(numMoments, numMoments)
M = geometricMoments(shapeImage, 3)

xc,yc = M[1,0]/M[0,0], M[0,1]/M[0,0]
m11 = M[1,1]/M[0,0] - xc*yc
m20 = M[2,0]/M[0,0] - xc**2
m02 = M[0,2]/M[0,0] - yc**2

if m20 < m02:  t = -(0.5 * atan(2.0*m11/(m20-m02)) + pi/2.0)
else:          t = -(0.5 * atan(2.0*m11/(m20-m02)))

# Scale
q, n2 = (N*N/2.0)/M[0,0],  N / 2.0

Nu = createImageF(N, N)
for j,i in itertools.product(range(0, N), range(0, N)):
    for indexPixel in range(0, numPoints):
        y, x = (shapeImage[indexPixel])[0], (shapeImage[indexPixel])[1],
        val  = (shapeImage[indexPixel])[2]

        # Invariant moments
        a =  ((x-xc)*sin(t) + (y-yc) * cos(t))
        b =  ((x-xc)*cos(t) - (y-yc) * sin(t))

        # To NxN image
        u =  sqrt(q) * a + n2
        v =  sqrt(q) * b + n2

        if int(v) < N and int(u) < N:
            Nu[i,j] += a**i * b**j * val * sqrt(sigma[int(v)] * sigma[int(u)])

    c = 1.0 + ((i + j) / 2.0)
    Nu[i,j] = (Nu[i,j] / pow(M[0,0],c))

for m,n in itertools.product(range(0, numMoments), range(0, numMoments)):
    # Descriptors
    for j,i in itertools.product(range(0, N), range(0, N)):
        Qi[n,m] +=  Nu[i,j] * aW[m,i] * aW[n,j]

    Qi[n,m] *= (1.0 / sqrt(ro[n]*ro[m]))
```

CODE 7.10 Krawtchouk invariant moments.

on the right. We can observe that the same region under geometric transformations have similar moments, and they change when the shape of the region changes.

7.3.2.8 Other moments

There are *pseudo Zernike moments* [Teh88] aimed to relieve the restriction on normalisation to the unit circle. Also, there are *complex moments* [Abu-Mostafa85], again aimed to provide a simpler moment description with invariance properties.

Finally, there are *affine invariant moments* which do not change with position, rotation and different scales along the co-ordinate axes, as a result, say, of a camera not being normal to the object plane. Here, the earliest approach appears to be by Flusser and Suk [Flusser93]. One of the reviews [Teh88] concentrates on information content (redundancy), noise sensitivity and on representation ability, comparing the performance of several of the more popular moments in these respects. It is actually possible to explore the link between moments and Fourier theory [Mukundan98]. The discrete Fourier transform of an image, Eq. (2.22), can be written as

$$\mathbf{FP}_{u,v} = \frac{1}{N}\sum_{x=0}^{N-1}\sum_{y=0}^{N-1}\mathbf{P}_{x,y}e^{-j\frac{2\pi}{N}ux}e^{-j\frac{2\pi}{N}vy} \tag{7.148}$$

By using the Taylor expansion of the exponential function

$$e^{z} = \sum_{p=0}^{\infty}\frac{z^{p}}{p!} \tag{7.149}$$

we can substitute for the exponential functions as

$$\mathbf{FP}_{u,v} = \frac{1}{N}\sum_{x=0}^{N-1}\sum_{y=0}^{N-1}\mathbf{P}_{x,y}\sum_{p=0}^{\infty}\frac{\left(-j\frac{2\pi}{N}ux\right)^{p}}{p!}\sum_{q=0}^{\infty}\frac{\left(-j\frac{2\pi}{N}vy\right)^{q}}{q!} \tag{7.150}$$

which by collecting terms gives

$$\mathbf{FP}_{u,v} = \frac{1}{N}\sum_{x=0}^{N-1}\sum_{y=0}^{N-1}x^{p}y^{q}\mathbf{P}_{x,y}\sum_{p=0}^{\infty}\sum_{q=0}^{\infty}\frac{\left(-j\frac{2\pi}{N}\right)^{p+q}}{p!q!}u^{p}v^{q} \tag{7.151}$$

and by the definition of Cartesian moments, Eq. (7.74), we have

$$\mathbf{FP}_{u,v} = \frac{1}{N}\sum_{p=0}^{\infty}\sum_{q=0}^{\infty}\frac{\left(-j\frac{2\pi}{N}\right)^{p+q}}{p!q!}u^{p}v^{q}m_{pq} \tag{7.152}$$

This implies that the Fourier transform of an image can be derived from its moments. There is then a link between the Fourier decomposition and that by moments, showing the link between the two. But we can go further, since there is the inverse Fourier transform, Eq. (2.23),

$$\mathbf{P}_{x,y} = \sum_{u=0}^{N-1}\sum_{v=0}^{N-1}\mathbf{FP}_{u,v}e^{j\frac{2\pi}{N}ux}e^{j\frac{2\pi}{N}vy} \tag{7.153}$$

So the original image can be computed from the moments as

$$\mathbf{P}_{x,y} = \sum_{x=0}^{N-1}\sum_{y=0}^{N-1}e^{j\frac{2\pi}{N}ux}e^{j\frac{2\pi}{N}vy}\,\frac{1}{N}\sum_{p=0}^{\infty}\sum_{q=0}^{\infty}\frac{\left(-j\frac{2\pi}{N}\right)^{p+q}}{p!q!}u^{p}v^{q}m_{pq} \tag{7.154}$$

and this shows that we can get back to the image from our moment description, though care must be exercised in the choice of windows from which data are selected. This is *reconstruction*: we can reconstruct an image from its moment description. Potency is usually investigated in application by determining the best set of moment features to maximise recognition capability (and we shall turn to this later). Essentially, reconstruction from basic geometric (Cartesian) moments is impractical [Teague80] and the orthogonal bases functions such as the Zernike polynomials offer a simpler route to reconstruction, but these still require thresholding. Prismall [Prismall02] used (Zernike) moments for the reconstruction of moving objects. Frequency domain moment based analysis continues to be of interest (e.g. [Wang19]), especially in image reconstruction.

7.4 Further reading

This chapter has essentially been based on unified techniques for border and region description. There is actually much more to contour and region analysis than indicated at the starting of the chapter, for this is one the start points of morphological analysis. There is an extensive review available [Loncaric98] with many important references in this topic. The analysis neighbourhood can be extended to be larger [Marchand97] and there is consideration of appropriate distance metrics for this [Das88]. A much more detailed study of boundary-based representation and application can be found in Otterloo's fine text [VanOtterloo91]. Naturally, there are many other ways to describe features, though few have the unique attributes of moments and Fourier descriptors. Naturally, there is an inter-relation between boundary and region description: curvature can be computed from a chain code [Rosenfeld74]; Fourier descriptors can also be used to calculate region descriptions [Kiryati89]. There have been many approaches to boundary approximation by fitting curves to the data. Some of these use polynomial approximation, or there are many *spline-based* techniques. A spline is a local function used to model a feature in sections. There are quadratic and cubic forms (for a good review of spline theory, try [Ahlberg67] or [Dierckx95]); of interest, snakes are actually energy minimising splines. There are many methods for polygonal approximations to curves, and a measure has been applied to compare performance on a suitable curve of techniques based on dominant point analysis [Rosin97]. To go with the earlier-mentioned review [Prokop92], there is a book available on moment theory [Mukundan98] showing the whole moment picture. As in the previous chapter, the skeleton of a shape can be used for recognition. This is a natural target for *thinning* techniques that have not been covered here. An excellent survey of these techniques, as used in character description following extraction, can be found in [Trier96] – describing use of moments and Fourier descriptors.

References

[Abu-Mostafa85] Abu-Mostafa, Y. S., and Psaltis, D., Image Normalisation by Complex Moments, *IEEE Transactions on PAMI*, **7**, pp 46-55, 1985.

[Aguado98] Aguado, A. S., Nixon, M. S., and Montiel, E., Parameterising Arbitrary Shapes via Fourier Descriptors for Evidence-Gathering Extraction, *CVIU: Computer Vision and Image Understanding*, **69**(2), pp 202-221, 1998.

[Aguado99] Aguado, A. S., Montiel, E., Zaluska, E., Modelling Generalised Cylinders via Fourier Morphing, *ACM Transactions on Graphics*, **18**(4), pp 293 – 315, 1999.

[Ahlberg67] Ahlberg, J. H., Nilson, E. N., and Walsh, J. L., The Theory of Splines and Their Applications, Academic Press, N. Y., USA, 1967.

[Boyce83] Boyce, J. F., and Hossack, W. J., Moment Invariants for Pattern Recognition, *Patt. Recog. Lett.*, **1**, pp 451-456, 1983.

[Chen95] Chen, Y. Q., Nixon, M. S., and Thomas, D. W., Texture Classification Using Statistical Geometric Features, *Pattern Recog.*, **28**(4), pp 537-552, 1995.

[Cosgriff60] Cosgriff, R. L., Identification of Shape, Rep. 820-11, ASTIA AD 254792, Ohio State Univ. Research Foundation, Columbus, Ohio, USA, 1960.

[Crimmins82] Crimmins, T. R., A Complete Set of Fourier Descriptors for Two-Dimensional Shapes, *IEEE Transactions on SMC*, **12**(6), pp 848-855, 1982.

[Das88] Das, P. P., and Chatterji, B. N., Knight's Distances in Digital Geometry, *Pattern Recognition Letters*, **7**, pp 215-226, 1988.

[Dierckx95] Dierckx, P., Curve and Surface Fitting with Splines, Oxford University Press, Oxford, UK, 1995.

[Flusser93] Flusser, J., and Suk, T., Pattern-Recognition by Affine Moment Invariants, *Pattern Recognition*, **26**(1), pp 167-174, 1993.

[Freeman61] Freeman, H., On the Encoding of Arbitrary Geometric Configurations, *IRE Transactions*, **EC-10**(2), pp 260-268, 1961.

[Freeman74] Freeman, H., Computer Processing of Line Drawing Images, *Computing Surveys*, **6**(1), pp 57-95, 1974.

[Granlund72] Granlund, G. H., Fourier Preprocessing for Hand Print Character Recognition, *IEEE Transactions on Computers*, **21**, pp 195-201, 1972.

[Gu02] Gu, J., Shua, H. Z., Toumoulinb, C., and Luoa, L. M. A Novel Algorithm for Fast Computation of Zernike Moments, *Pattern Recognition*, **35**(12), pp 2905-2911, 2002.

[Hu62] Hu, M. K., Visual Pattern Recognition by Moment Invariants, *IRE Transactions on Information Theory*, **IT-8**, pp 179-187, 1962.

[Kashi96] Kashi, R. S., Bhoj-Kavde, P., Nowakowski, R. S., and Papathomas, T. V., 2-D Shape Representation and Averaging Using Normalised Wavelet Descriptors, *Simulation*, **66**(3), pp 164-178, 1996.

[Khotanzad90] Khotanzad, A., and Hong, Y. H., Invariant Image Recognition by Zernike Moments, *IEEE Transactions on PAMI*, **12**, pp 489-498, 1990.

[Kiryati89] Kiryati, N., and Maydan, D., Calculating Geometric Properties from Fourier Representation, *Pattern Recognition*, **22**(5), pp 469-475.

[Kuhl82] Kuhl, F. P., and Giardina, C. R., Elliptic Fourier Descriptors of a Closed Contour. *CVGIP*, **18**, pp 236-258, 1982.

[Lin87] Lin C. C., and Chellappa, R., Classification of Partial 2D Shapes Using Fourier Descriptors, *IEEE Transactions on PAMI*, **9**(5), pp 686-690, 1987.

[Liu90] Liu, H. C., and Srinath, M. D., Corner Detection from Chain-Coded Curves, *Pattern Recognition*, **23**(1), pp 51-68, 1990.

[Loncaric98] Loncaric, S., A Survey of Shape Analysis Techniques, *Pattern Recognition*, **31**(8), pp 983-1001, 1998.

[Marchand97] Marchand, S., and Sharaiha, Y. M., Discrete Convexity, Straightness and the 16-Neighbourhood, *Computer Vision and Image Understanding*, **66**(3), pp 416-329, 1997.

[Montiel96] Montiel, E., Aguado, A.S., and Zaluska, E., Topology in Fractals, *Chaos, Solitons and Fractals*, **7**(8), pp 1187-1207, 1996.

[Montiel97] Montiel, E., Aguado, A.S., and Zaluska, E., Fourier Series Expansion of Irregular Curves, *Fractals*, **5**(1), pp 105-199, 1997.

[Mukundan95] Mukundan, R., and Ramakrishnan, K. R., Fast Computation of Legendre and Zernike Moments. *Pattern Recognition*, **28**(9), pp 1433-1442, 1995.

[Mukundan98] Mukundan, R., Ramakrishnan, K. R., Moment Functions in Image Analysis: Theory and Applications, World Scientific Pte. Ltd., Singapore, 1998.

[Mukundan02] Mukundan, R., Image Analysis by Tchebichef Moments, *IEEE Transactions on IP*, **10**(9), pp 1357-1364, 2001.

[Persoon77] Persoon, E., and Fu, K-S, Shape Description Using Fourier Descriptors, *IEEE Transactions on SMC*, **3**, pp 170-179, 1977.

[Prismall02] Prismall, S. P., Nixon, M. S. and Carter, J. N., On Moving Object Reconstruction by Moments, *Proceedings of BMVC*, **2002**, pp 73-82, 2002.

[Prokop92] Prokop, R. J., and Reeves A. P., A Survey of Moment-Based Techniques for Unoccluded Object Representation and Recognition, *CVGIP: Graphical Models and Image Processing*, **54**(5), pp 438-460, 1992.

[Rosenfeld74] Rosenfeld, A., Digital Straight Line Segments, *IEEE Transactions on Computers*, **23**, pp 1264-1269, 1974.

[Rosin97] Rosin, P., Techniques for Assessing Polygonal Approximations to Curves, *IEEE Transactions on PAMI*, **19**(6), pp 659-666, 1997.

[Rosin05] Rosin, P., and Zunic, J., Measuring Rectilinearity, *Computer Vision and Image Understanding*, **99**(2), pp 175-188, 2005.

[Searle70] Searle, N. H., Shape Analysis by Use of Walsh Functions, In: Machine Intelligence 5, B. Meltzer and D. Mitchie Eds., Edinburgh University Press, 1970.

[Seeger94] Seeger, U., and Seeger, R., Fast Corner Detection in Gray-Level Images, *Pattern Recognition Letter*, **15**, pp 669-675, 1994.

[Staib92] Staib, L., and Duncan, J., Boundary Finding with Parametrically Deformable Models, *IEEE Transactions on PAMI*, **14**, pp 1061-1075, 1992.

[Teague80] Teague, M. R., Image Analysis by the General Theory of Moments, *Journal of the Optical Society of America*, **70**, pp 920-930, 1980.

[Teh88] Teh, C. H., and Chin, R. T., On Image Analysis by the Method of Moments, *IEEE Transactions on PAMI*, **10**, pp 496-513, 1988.

[Trier96] Trier, O. D., Jain, A. K., and Taxt, T., Feature Extraction Methods for Character Recognition – A Survey, *Pattern Recognition*, **29**(4), pp 641-662, 1996.

[Undrill97] Undrill, P. E., Delibasis, K., and Cameron, G. G., An Application of Genetic Algorithms to Geometric Model-Guided Interpretation of Brain Anatomy, *Pattern Recognition*, **30**(2), pp 217-227, 1997.

[VanOtterloo91] Van Otterloo, P. J., A Contour-Oriented Approach to Shape Analysis, Prentice Hall International (UK) Ltd., Hemel Hempstead, 1991.

[Yap03] Yap, P. T., Paramesran R., Ong, S. H., Image Analysis by Krawtchouk Moments, *IEEE Transactions on IP*, **12**(11), pp 1367-1377, 2003.

[Wang19] Wang, X. Y., Wang, Q., Wang, X. B., Yang, H. Y., Wu, Z. F. and Niu, P. P., Color image segmentation using proximal classifier and quaternion radial harmonic Fourier moments, *Pattern Analysis and Applications*, pp 1-20, 2019.

[Zahn72] Zahn, C. T., and Roskies, R. Z., Fourier Descriptors for Plane Closed Curves, *IEEE Transactions on Computers*, **C-21**(3), pp 269-281, 1972.

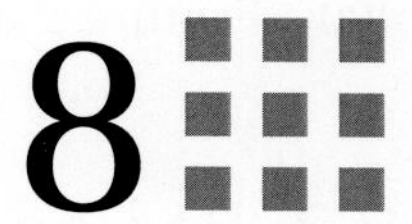

Region-based analysis

8.1 Overview

This chapter is concerned with how we can characterise regions in an image, often by their texture. We shall first consider some of the grouping techniques that have been developed to form regions within an image. These essentially change the image resolution from high to very low. We shall then consider what is meant by texture and then how we can use Fourier transform techniques, statistics and region measures to describe it. We shall then look at how the measurements provided by these techniques, the description of the texture, can be collected together to recognise it. Finally, we shall label an image according to the texture found within it, to give a segmentation into classes known to exist within the image (Table 8.1).

The description of objects requires identification of groups of pixels in images. In previous chapters, we have shown how simple techniques like thresholding and edge detection can be used to delineate regions that can represent objects or to find interesting parts in an image. In general, the process of partitioning the pixels in an image to form regions is known as image segmentation or pixel labelling. Image *segmentation* is a very important subject, and many approaches exist to segment an image. In this chapter, we illustrate the analysis of regions by considering techniques that group pixels according to their properties.

Table 8.1 Overview of this chapter.

Main topic	Subtopics	Main points
Region clustering	Use the properties of pixels and regions to form groups that delineate areas in an image. The regions facilitate the interpretation of an image.	*Watershed* transform: distance transform; gradient transform. *Maximally stable extremal regions*. *Superpixels*: *SLIC*.
Texture description	What is image texture and how do we determine sets of numbers that allow us to be able to recognise it.	Feature extraction: Fourier transform; *co-occurrence matrices*; and regions, *local binary patterns (LBP)* and *uniform LBP*. Feature *descriptions*: energy; entropy and inertia.
Texture segmentation	How do we find regions of texture within images.	Convolution; tiling; and thresholding.

Feature Extraction and Image Processing for Computer Vision. https://doi.org/10.1016/B978-0-12-814976-8.00008-7

8.2 Region-based analysis

We have discussed how a region in an image can be characterised by descriptors that can be computed from borders or by pixels' positions. This can be useful for recognition tasks but requires the pixels that form the region to be identified. Finding meaningful regions in images is a very challenging problem and there are many techniques that delineate regions guided by the properties computed from pixels or groups of pixels. This section presents several techniques that grow regions by following an iterative process that aggregates pixels according to measured local properties. This approach is very popular to create support regions that form primitives that can be used to segment meaningful structures in images.

8.2.1 Watershed transform

The *watershed* method derives from the morphological operations [Beucher93], and it partitions the image into multiple segments by growing regions from a set of initial seeds [Beniek00]. The main idea is to use labels to aggregate pixels in an iterative process. The pixels in each region have a different label. During each iteration, pixels that have not been aggregated into any region are labelled according to the labels of its neighbours. As such, connected components grow and edges that limit the regions can be delineated.

The growing process follows an analogy of flooding areas in hydrology where the image is considered as a topographic surface. This idea is shown in Fig. 8.1. Fig. 8.1A illustrates an image as a curve. The x axis defines pixels, and the y axis defines a distance property measured for all the pixels. Notice that the curve represents only a row in an image. To represent the whole 2D image, the curve should be visualised as a surface. However, we can describe the flooding analogy by visualising only a curve as a topographic surface. In this curve, the valleys have minimum points and we can observe catching basins that are limited by watersheds.

In Fig. 8.1, we can visualise a region growing process as a flooding of the topographic surface. The flooding starts with a flow level of zero, and it is uniformly increased at each iteration. As illustrated in Fig. 8.1B, at every iteration there are separated flooding areas that correspond to different regions in an image. During flooding, each region grows in

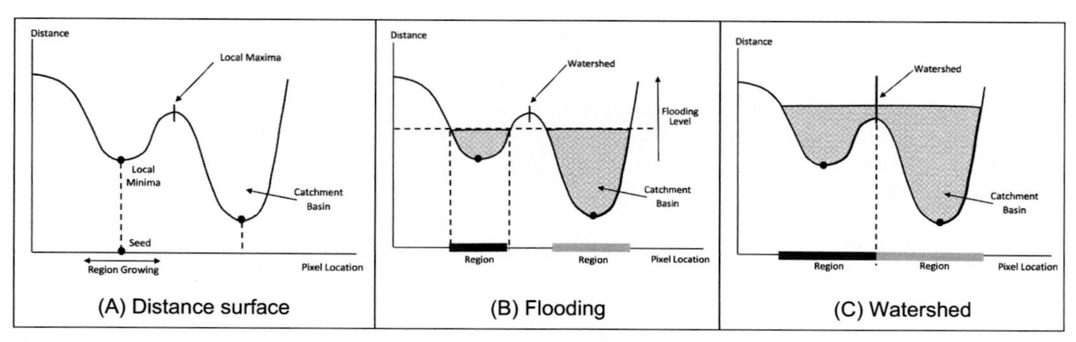

FIGURE 8.1 Watershed method.

its catchment basin from the minimal points (initial seeds). If we identify each minimum with a label, then we can label each pixel in the flooding area by keeping the label from which it started. As such, we can distinguish different regions. The interesting part of the flooding process occurs when the flooding level increases to the point in which two or more catchment basins merge (Fig. 8.1C). At this point, we can decide to merge the regions or to keep them separated by creating a dam to prevent merging. The dam corresponds to an edge, and it is called the watershed line.

According to the flooding analogy, the watershed process involves three main steps: (1) to compute a distance or property for each pixel, this property represents how pixels are organised in regions and it defines a topographic surface; (2) to find a local minima that represent initial regions; and (3) to flood the topographic surface by labelling pixels and delineating edges. Although these three steps are fixed, there are many ways in which they can be implemented, thus there are many algorithms that segment an image following the watershed process. Perhaps the most significant difference between algorithms is the way in which the flooding is implemented. For example, there are approaches that label pixels by scanning the image horizontally and vertically, whilst other implementations exploit analogies with rain falling to trace paths that label pixels. Some algorithms are implemented by using hierarchical data structures that make efficient the computation of the flooding process. Here, we will illustrate the watershed process by using a region growing approach.

Generally, the distance property is defined as the radial distance between pixel's positions and their closest edge. The main idea is to make the watersheds flood the image towards the edges. That is, pixels far away from edges are considered the centre of the regions (i.e. minima) and the flooding makes the regions grow until the region reaches the image edges (i.e. maxima). To compute the radial distances, it is necessary to identify edges and to find the closest edge to every pixel. Code 8.1 illustrates this process. Here, edges are first located and stored in the list `edgePixels`. The distance is stored in the `distanceImage` array that is filled by computing the minimum distance between the pixels and the pixels in the edge list.

Fig. 8.2B shows an example of the distance computed using Code 8.1 for the image in Fig. 8.2A. This example shows a binary image, so the edge list can be filled with pixels in

```
# Compute the radial distance to the edge
distanceImage = createImageF(width, height)
numEdges = len(edgePixels)
for indexPixel in range(0, numPoints):
    y, x = (shapeImage[indexPixel])[0], (shapeImage[indexPixel])[1]
    minEdgeDist = FLT_MAX
    for indexEdge in range(0, numEdges):
        edgeY, edgeX = (edgePixels[indexEdge])[0], (edgePixels[indexEdge])[1]
        minEdgeDist = min(minEdgeDist, sqrt((edgeX-x)**2+(edgeY-y)**2))
    distanceImage[y,x] = minEdgeDist
```

CODE 8.1 Distance to an edge list.

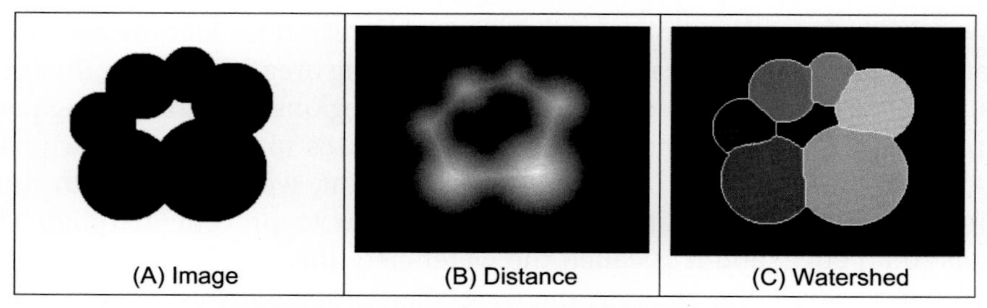

FIGURE 8.2 Watershed based on edge distance.

```
# Flooding
maxDistance, _ = imageMaxMin(distanceImage)
for floodValue in range(int(maxDistance), 0, -1):
    flooded = True
    while flooded:
        flooded = False
        newFloodRegion = [ ]
        growRegion = [ ]
        shuffle(floodRegion)
        for indexPixel in range(0, len(floodRegion)):
            y, x = (floodRegion[indexPixel])[0], (floodRegion[indexPixel])[1]

            # Points not flooded will be considered in following iterations
            if distanceImage[y,x] <= floodValue:
                newFloodRegion.append((y,x))
            else:
                n = [ ] #  List of neighbours
                for wx,wy in itertools.product(range(-1, 2), range(-1, 2)):
                    posX, posY = x + wx, y+ wy
                    if posY > -1 and posY < height and  posX > -1 and posX < width:
                        if watershed[posY, posX] != 0:
                            n.append(watershed[posY, posX])

                # No neighbours, so we cannot grow
                if(len(n) == 0):
                    newFloodRegion.append((y,x))
                else:
                    # Grow of only one type of region
                    if len(set(n)) == 1:
                        growRegion.append((y,x,n[0]))
                        flooded  = True

        for pixel in growRegion:
            y, x, idRegion = pixel[0] , pixel[1] , pixel[2]
            watershed[y, x] = idRegion

        floodRegion = newFloodRegion
```

CODE 8.2 Watershed flooding.

the background that have at least one neighbour from the foreground (object). Notice that Code 8.1 will obtain small values for pixels close to the edges and larger values for pixels far away. Consequently, the distance should be inverted or alternatively the initial regions should be located as local maxima and the flooding should be performed from highest to lower values.

For grey level images, the computation of the radial distance can be performed by using an edge detection operator. The example in Fig. 8.3C shows the result of computing the distance from the edge image in Fig. 8.3B. In this example, edges were obtained using the Canny edge detector. The resulting edges are added to the `edgePixels` list in Code 8.1. Notice that, as in the case of Fig. 8.2B, the distances values are maxima for pixels far away from the edges. A common alternative to compute the distance is to use the gradient. We shall recall that the gradient image represents the rate of change in pixel's intensity, so the gradient is high when the pixel is close to the edges. As such, the gradient gives a measure of proximity to edges, and it can be considered as the distance measured in the watershed process. Fig. 8.3F shows an example of the distance obtained from the gradient image in Fig. 8.3E. The gradient in Fig. 8.3E was computed using the Sobel operator, and it was smoothed using a Gaussian operator. Smoothing is necessary to spread the distance to all pixels in an image since the gradient is very localised at the edges. Additionally, the smoothing removes sharp changes in the edges producing soft region borders in the watershed.

In the watershed process, initial regions are found by looking for extreme values. In general, these values are determined by finding minima in a local neighbourhood. This process has to deal with two practical issues. First, the minima can be extended over large regions forming a plateau, and second, there may be small changes in the distance values due to noise. Thus, strategies for finding local minima require filtering as well as considering neighbours of different sizes. In the implementation of the flooding process shown in Code 8.2 initial regions were located in the distance image by using a peak

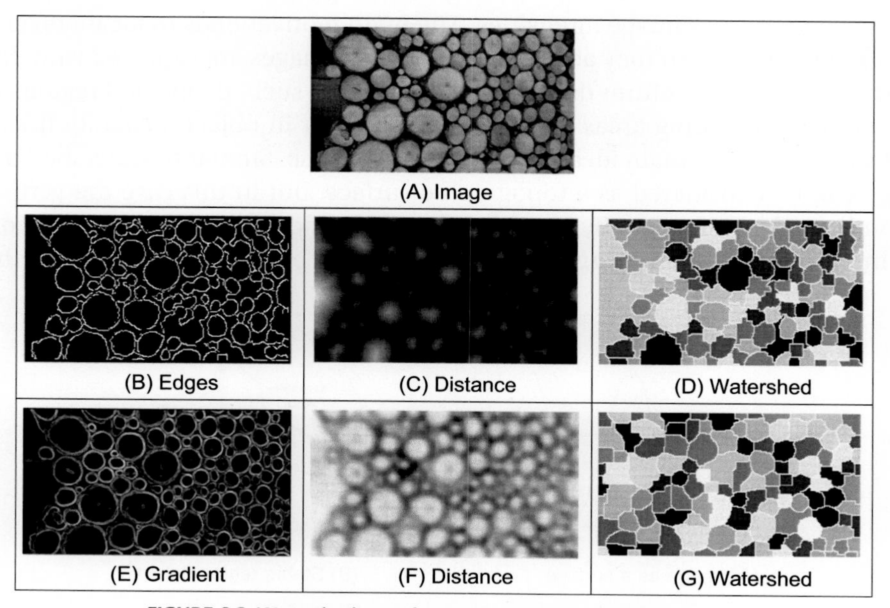

FIGURE 8.3 Watershed transform on gradient and edge images.

detector that takes as parameter the size of the neighbourhood. If a peak is found, the entire neighbourhood is labelled as a region. Every region has a different label, and it is stored in the image `watershed`. All the pixels that are not a seed are collected in the `floodRegion` list, and they indicate the locations that will be flooded. The flooding process in Code 8.2 repeatedly changes the flood value (i.e. `floodValue`) to increase the size of the regions. Each iteration selects the pixels in the `floodRegion` list that are under the `floodValue` (i.e. are being flooded). For those pixels, the implementation looks into the neighbours to determine if they are next to a region. If all the neighbours have the same label, then the pixel takes the same label (i.e. the region grows). This process will grow the regions without mixing pixels with different labels. At the end of the growing process, borders are identified as pixels that have not been labelled.

Fig. 8.2C shows the result of the flooding process for the distance in Fig. 8.2B. The grey level of each pixel in the figure corresponds to its label, and the watersheds are shown in white. Figs. 8.3D and G show the result of applying the watershed process to the distance images in Figs. 8.3C and F, respectively. Notice that the smoothing of the distance in Fig. 8.3F produces smoother region borders.

8.2.2 Maximally stable extremal regions

The previous section showed how region growing can be used to find image regions according to the radial distance between pixel positions and edges; in the watershed method, regions are grown towards edges, thus the segmentation contains regions delimited by significant changes in image intensities. *Maximal Stable Extremal Region (MSER)* [Matas2002] also follows a region growing approach, but instead of using the distance to edges, it uses image intensities. The main motivation is to locate regions that are uniform in intensity, so they are maintained when images are captured with different illumination conditions or from different viewpoints. As such, delineated regions can be used to find corresponding areas for stereo matching or in object recognition tasks.

Fig. 8.4 illustrates the main idea of the MSER technique. Similar to watershed process, the image can be considered as a topographic surface, but in this case the vertical axis corresponds to pixel intensity. By iteratively changing the flood level, image regions will change in size, either by growing inside the attraction basin or by merging with other

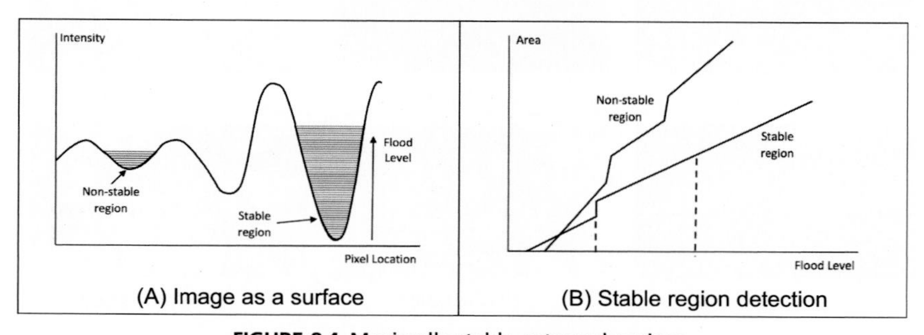

FIGURE 8.4 Maximally stable extremal regions.

regions. Since, the surface is defined from pixel's intensities, then the flood level is actually equivalent to an image threshold, and so the MSER can be seen as a region growing process or as a multi-thresholding method. In any case, the aim of the flooding (or thresholding) is to obtain a description of how the size of connected components changes as a function of the flooding level (or threshold). Fig. 8.4B visualises how the size of regions is used in MSER. In this figure, the vertical axis represents the area of the region (i.e. number of pixels) and the horizontal axis defines the flooding level (or threshold). As such, each curve in Fig. 8.4B describes the area of a region as a function of the flooding level.

Fig. 8.4B illustrates how the area of stable and non-stable regions changes as a function of the flood level. In general, the curve describing a region can have abrupt changes when regions are merged. Also, we have that the growth in area is inversely proportional to the slope of the catchment basin. That is, if the walls of the catching basin have a small slope then the area of the region will have a large increase when the flooding level is increased. We expect that stable regions will have a deep catchment basin, and they will not merge with other regions as the flood level is increased. Thus, on stable regions, the change in area as a function of flood level should produce a curve with a small slope. On the other hand, non-stable regions will change their size due to merging or because the slope of the catchment basins is low.

Based on the description of the size of the regions, we can determine if a region is stable or not. This can be achieved by specifying two criteria that define: (1) a growing rate that defines how much a region can grow per flooding level and; (2) for how long the region should be under that growing rate. For example, we can define as stable regions, those regions whose size does not increase more than 100 pixels during 20 flooding steps. With this criterion, we can analyse the regions during the flooding process and select the stable regions.

Although the description and motivation of the process of extracting stable regions is not complicated, the implementation is not simple since it has to determine the increment in size of each region when flooding. This requires to consider how regions merge as well as to identify new regions at each flooding iteration. A general implementation requires four main steps: (1) to grow existing regions and store their size increment, this can be implemented as a flooding process similar to the one discussed in the previous section; (2) to merge touching regions and to update the change in sizes accordingly, which requires deletion of all the regions but one wherein all the pixels are aggregated; (3) to find new regions when the flooding reaches a minimum and (4) to detect stable regions by recording the number of times the regions have grown under the growing criteria.

The implementation in Code 8.3 illustrates how the MSER algorithm detects stable regions. The full process performs the four steps mentioned in the previous paragraph, and it creates the dictionary `incSizeRegions` that provides the increase of size for each region. First, the size of the region is updated according to its increase in size. Afterwards, if the increment in size is under our growing criteria, it is increased in the

```
# Update times for regions
for idRegion in incSizeRegions:
    # Update the size
    incSize = incSizeRegions[idRegion]
    sizeRegions[idRegion] += incSize

    # Update  stable
    if incSize < incThreshold:
        timeRegions[idRegion] += 1
    else:
        timeRegions[idRegion] = 0

    # Stable region condition
    if timeRegions[idRegion]>timeThreshold and sizeRegions[idRegion]>minRegionSize:
        for x,y in itertools.product(range(0, width), range(0, height)):
            if regionsImage[y,x] == idRegion:
                resultImage[y,x] = 255
        timeRegions[idRegion] = 0
```

CODE 8.3 Update regions times for maximal stable extremal region.

counter that indicates how many iterations has the region been stable. If a region has been stable for `timeThreshold` iterations and the region is big enough, then the region pixels are used to draw a stable region in the resulting `resultImage`.

Fig. 8.5 shows two examples of applying MSER. The input images are 400 pixels wide, and the area of the stable regions was constrained to be larger than 50 pixels. This avoids small regions defined by bricks and noise or shadows. For this example, the stable regions criteria aim to detect regions whose size does not increase more than 20 pixels

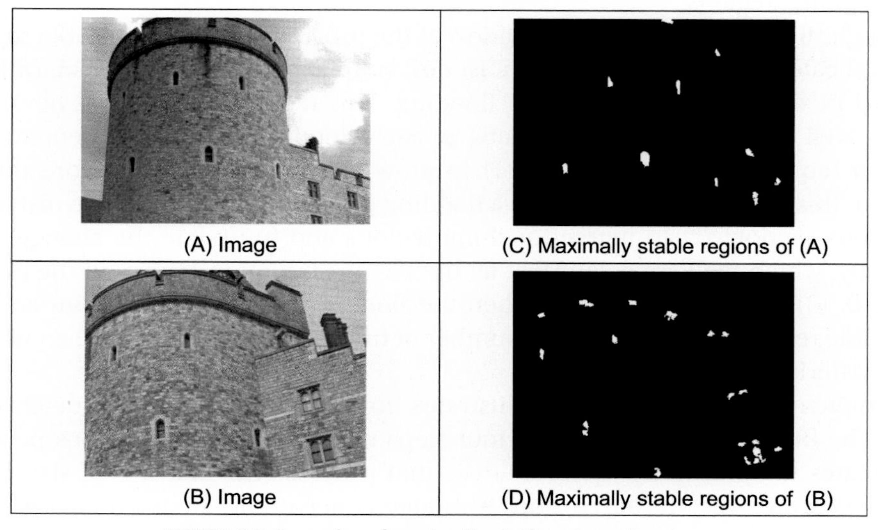

FIGURE 8.5 Examples of maximally stable extremal regions.

during 30 flooding steps. Each flooding step increases by two grey levels so that the measure of the increment in size is less sensitive to image noise. We can see that though the images have very significant changes in viewpoint and illumination, the regions represent similar objects. In general, dark regions are favoured since the flooding starts from black, so those regions appear as regions in the image during more iterations.

8.2.3 Superpixels

8.2.3.1 Basic techniques and normalised cuts

Superpixel techniques segment an image into regions by considering similarity measures defined using perceptual features. That is, different from watersheds and MSER, superpixel techniques create groups of pixels that look similar. The motivation is to obtain regions that represent meaningful descriptions with far less data than is the case when using all the pixels in an image. The premise is that by reducing the number of primitives, redundancy is reduced thus reducing the complexity of recognition tasks. In addition, superpixels replace the rigid pixel structure by delineating regions that maintain meaning in the image, so the regions provide information about the structure of the scene making other processing tasks simpler than using single image pixels. In general, superpixel techniques are based on measures that look for colour similarities and measures of the regions' shape. The segmentation process also incorporates edges or strong changes in intensity to delineate regions.

Superpixel techniques can be divided into two main approaches: (1) graph-based methods and (2) region growing or clustering methods. Graph-based methods create groups of pixels by formulating the segmentation problem as a graph partitioning problem [Shi00]. The main idea is to create a graph by considering that each pixel is a node. Edges are formed between pairs of nodes, and each edge has a weight that measures the similarity between the pixel pairs. A graph partition defines disjoint regions and is created by removing edges such that only the pixels in each region are interconnected. The similarity of a region is defined by the sum of the weights in the partition. As such, the segmentation looks for an optimal partition that obtains regions with maximal similarities. The partition is obtained by a recursive process that visits the nodes in the graph. In general, looking for the partition on a graph is complex, and it is difficult to incorporate control about uniformity and properties of the regions. *Clustering* approaches follow a simpler process that naturally includes the proximity of pixels in images. Similar to watersheds and MSER, the process iteratively aggregates pixels on a local window. However, whilst region growing aggregates pixels that have not been assigned to a region, clustering grows and reduces regions by changing the pixels' labels.

8.2.3.2 Simple linear iterative clustering

Perhaps the most popular superpixel method is the *Simple Linear Iterative Clustering (SLIC)* technique presented in [Achanta12]. This technique is simple and is a powerful tool for generating meaningful image regions. It uses clustering to create uniform size and compact superpixels that adequately describe the structure of objects in an image. In the SLIC technique, each pixel is characterised by a five-dimensional vector. Three components of the vector represent the colour and two components its position. The pixels' colour is represented using the CIELAB (Section 11.3.4) colour space that, as we shall discuss in Chapter 11, gives a good similarity measure for colour perception. However, the processing in the algorithm is very general and it can obtain plausible results by using alternative measures of similarity, so it can also accommodate greyscale images. What is important is that the vector components can effectively differentiate objects in an image. Similarity between pixels is defined as

$$D = d_c + m\frac{d_s}{s} \tag{8.1}$$

Here, d_c and d_s are the colour and spatial differences. Given two points with co-ordinates (x_i, y_i) and (x_j, y_j) with colour components (l_i, a_i, b_i) and (l_j, a_j, b_j), we have that

$$\begin{aligned} d_s(p_i, p_j) &= \sqrt{(x_j - x_i)^2 + (y_j - y_i)^2} \\ d_c(p_i, p_j) &= \sqrt{(l_j - l_i)^2 + (a_j - a_i)^2 + (b_j - b_i)^2} \end{aligned} \tag{8.2}$$

In Eq. (8.1), the constant s is used to normalise the distance d_s. In SLIC the initial centre of a region is defined in a regular grid with sides s. Thus the normalisation $\frac{d_s}{s}$ defines the distance in terms of number of interval lengths. If we decrease the grid size (i.e. we have more regions), then the distance contributes more to the similarity increasing the compactness. The constant m controls the compactness independent of the grid size. The greater the value of m the more special proximity is emphasised.

The SLIC algorithm creates regions by three main steps:

1. creates initial regions according to a parameter that defines the desired number of superpixels;
2. performs region clustering to aggregate pixels to the regions according to the similarity criteria and
3. reinforces connectivity.

The process of creating initial regions is illustrated in Code 8.4. The algorithm uses a parameter that defines the number of superpixels. This parameter is used to determine the length of the initial superpixels defined by a regular grid.

$$s = \sqrt{\frac{N}{K}} \tag{8.3}$$

Here N is the number of pixels in the input image and K is the number of superpixels. This value is used to define a grid with `regW` × `regH` superpixels. The initialisation code determines an initial location (p_x, p_y) for each superpixel by using constant distance increments. As such, initial regions define a regular grid. The problem with this distribution of regions is that centres may be placed at an image border and thus it can fail to obtain a good segmentation. Accordingly, the algorithm shifts the centres to the locations of the lowest gradient in a 3 × 3 neighbourhood. Once the final positions are determined, the code fills in the array `regionsID` that stores a label that identifies a region for each pixel. Code 8.4 also computes the average colour of each region in the array `regionColour`. Notice that region positions and colour arrays `regionColour` and `regionPos` have a size `regW` × `regH`. The label is for each pixel, so the `regionsID` array is of the size of the image.

The iterative region update process is illustrated in Code 8.5. Each iteration computes new region positions and average colours. The new region sizes are stored in the `newRegionSize` array. The array `regionsID` determines the superpixels position in the grid (r_x, r_y). This is used to find superpixels in a neighbourhood. The measure is used to determine the best match of, the similarity between, the pixel and the superpixels. The pixel's label is changed so it is assigned to the superpixel with the lowest distance (i.e. `minD`). After all pixels have been assigned to a region, the centres and region colours are update. Notice that this grouping approach corresponds to *k-means clustering* that partitions the data considering a grid structure on the image.

The compactness parameter m will ensure that pixels in close proximity belong to the same region. However, when there are many mixed colours in image, the resulting regions cannot be compact. Thus, the SLIC technique suggests post-processing the results to remove small unconnected fragments. Pre-processing such as smoothing can also help to create compact regions.

Fig. 8.6 shows some example results of the clustering in Code 8.5 (in the print edition of this book coloured versions can be found at the end). In general, more superpixels can delineate better the border of the objects but increases the oversegmentation (too many superpixels). The extension in [Zhang17] includes a boundary term to make the edges of

```
# Initial regions
regionsID = createImage2I(width, height)
for x,y in itertools.product(range(0, regW), range(0, regH)):
    ry, rx = y * regionSide, x * regionSide
    # Position
    py, px = int(ry + halfRegionSide), int(rx + halfRegionSide)
    regionPos[y,x] = [py, px]
    minGradient = FLT_MAX
    for wx,wy in itertools.product(range(px-1, px+2), range(py-1, py+2)):
        if (wy < height and wx < width):
            if gradient[wy,wx] < minGradient:
                minGradient = gradient[wy,wx]
                regionPos[y,x] = [wy, wx]
    # Colour
    colour = [0, 0, 0]
    npts = 0.0
    for wx,wy in itertools.product(range(rx, rx + regionSide),                    \
                                   range(ry, ry + regionSide)):
        if wy>=0 and wy<height and wx>=0 and wx<width:
            regionsID[wy, wx] = [y, x]
            colour += inputImage[wy,wx]
            npts += 1
        if npts > 0:
            regionColour[y,x] = [int(colour[0] / npts),                          \
                                 int(colour[1] / npts), int(colour[2] / npts)]
```

CODE 8.4 Initial regions for simple linear iterative clustering.

```
# Modify regions
for itr in range(0, numIter):
    # Values for new regions
    newRegionColour = createImageF(regW, regH,3)
    newRegionPos = createImageUV(regW, regH)
    newRegionSize = createImageF(regW, regH)

    # Per pixel
    for x,y in itertools.product(range(0, width), range(0, height)):
        ry, rx = regionsID[y,x]
        colour = [float(inputImage[y,x][0]), float(inputImage[y,x][1]),      \
                  float(inputImage[y,x][2])]
        minD = [FLT_MAX, ry, rx]
        for wx,wy in itertools.product(range(rx-2, rx + 3), range(ry-2, ry + 3)):
            if wy>=0 and wy<regH and wx>=0 and wx<regW:
                ds = sqrt((regionPos[wy,wx][0]- y)**2 +(regionPos[wy,wx][1]- x)**2)
                dc = sqrt((float(regionColour[wy,wx][0]) - colour[0])**2 +    \
                          (float(regionColour[wy,wx][1]) - colour[1])**2 +    \
                          (float(regionColour[wy,wx][2]) - colour[2])**2)
                D = dc/255.0 + (m / regionSide) * ds
                if D < minD[0]:
                    minD = [D, wy, wx]
        [_, minY, minX] = minD
        newRegionColour[minY, minX] += colour
        newRegionPos[minY, minX] += [y,x]
        newRegionSize[minY, minX] += 1
        regionsID[y, x] = [minY, minX]

    # Update regions
    for x,y in itertools.product(range(0, regW), range(0, regH)):
        if newRegionSize[y,x] > 0:
            regionPos[y,x] = newRegionPos[y,x] / newRegionSize[y,x]
            regionColour[y,x] = newRegionColour[y,x] / newRegionSize[y,x]
```

CODE 8.5 Region update for simple linear iterative clustering.

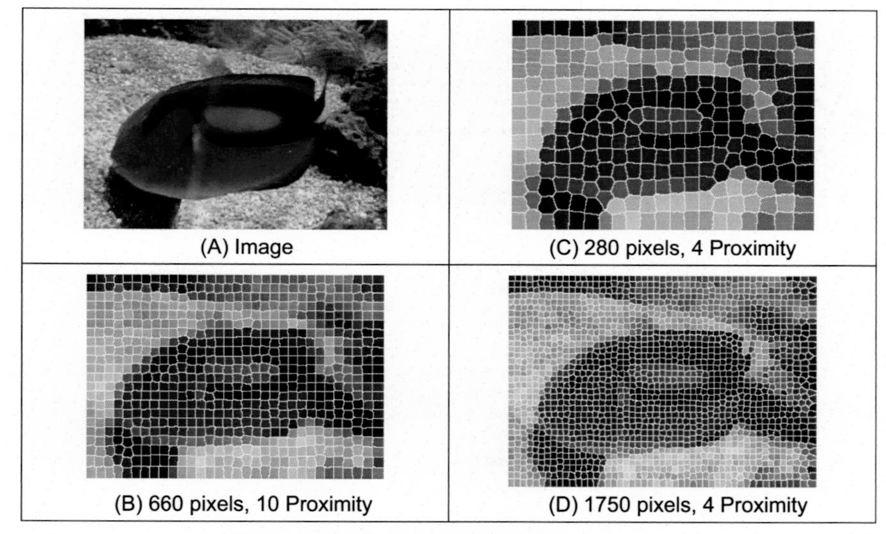

FIGURE 8.6 Simple linear interactive clustering.

superpixels consistent with image edges. So better delineation can be obtained with fewer superpixels. Like many computer vision approaches, research in superpixels is not finished. In one recent approach [Yongxia17] the approach seeks "a balance among boundary adherence, intensity homogeneity, and compactness", factors we have previously discussed in this book.

8.3 Texture description and analysis

8.3.1 What is texture?

Texture is actually a very nebulous concept, often attributed to human perception, as either the feel or the appearance of (woven) fabric. Everyone has their own interpretation as to the nature of texture; there is no mathematical definition for texture, it simply exists. By way of reference, let us consider one of the dictionary definitions [Oxford96]:

> *texture* n., & v.t. *1.* n. *arrangement of threads etc. in textile fabric. characteristic feel due to this; arrangement of small constituent parts, perceived structure,* (of *skin, rock, soil, organic tissue, literary work, etc.); representation of structure and detail of objects in art; ...*

That covers quite a lot. If we change 'threads' for 'pixels', the definition could apply to images (except for the bit about artwork). Essentially, texture can be what we define it to be. Why might we want to do this? By way of example, analysis of remotely sensed images is now a major application of image processing techniques. In such analysis, pixels are labelled according to the categories of a required application, such as whether the ground is farmed or urban in land-use analysis, or water for estimation of surface analysis. An example of remotely sensed image is given in Fig. 8.7A which is of an urban area (in the top left) and some farmland. Here, the image resolution is low and each pixel corresponds to a large area of the ground. Square groups of pixels have then been labelled either as urban, or as farmland, according to their texture properties as shown in Fig. 8.7B where

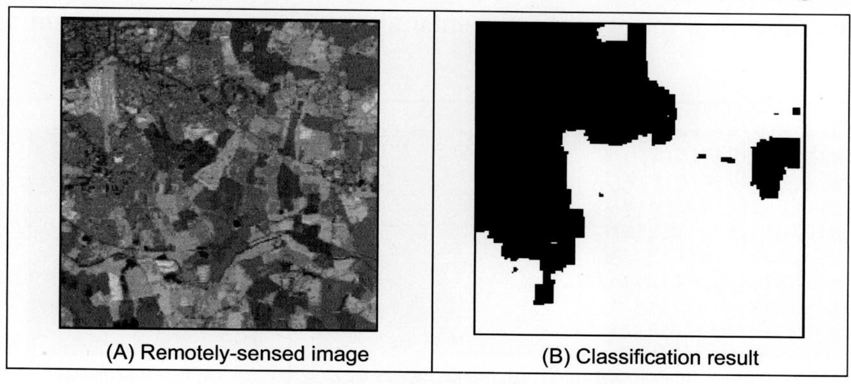

FIGURE 8.7 Example texture analysis.

black represents the area classified as urban and white is for the farmland. In this way, we can assess the amount of area that urban areas occupy. As such, we have used real textures to label pixels, the perceived textures of the urban and farming areas.

As an alternative definition of texture, we can consider it as being defined by the database of images that researchers use to test their algorithms. Many texture researchers have used a database of pictures of textures [Brodatz68], produced for artists and designers, rather than for digital image analysis. Parts of three of the *Brodatz* texture images are given in Fig. 8.8. Here, the French canvas (Brodatz index D20) in Fig. 8.8A is a detail of Fig. 8.8B (Brodatz index D21), taken at four times the magnification. The beach sand in Fig. 8.8C, Brodatz index D29, is clearly of a different texture to that of cloth. Given the diversity of texture, there are now many databases available on the web, at the sites given in Chapter 1 or at this book's website. Alternatively, we can define texture simply as a quantity for which texture extraction algorithms provide meaningful results. One study [Karru96] suggested

> *The answer to the question 'is there any texture in the image?' depends not only on the input image, but also on the goal for which the image texture is used and the textural features that are extracted from the image.*

As we shall find, texture analysis has a rich history in image processing and computer vision, and there are even books devoted to texture analysis [Petrou06]. Despite this, approaches which synthesise texture are relatively recent. This is of course motivated also by graphics, and the need to include texture to improve the quality of the rendered scenes [Heckbert86]. By way of example, one well-known approach to texture synthesis is to use a Markov random field [Efros99], but we shall not dwell on that here.

Essentially, there is no unique definition of texture and there are many ways to describe and extract it. It is a very large and exciting field of research and there continue to be many new developments.

Clearly, images will usually contain samples of more than one texture. Accordingly, we would like to be able to describe texture (*texture descriptions* are measurements which characterise a texture) and then to *classify* it (classification is attributing the correct class label to a set of measurements) and then, perhaps to segment an image

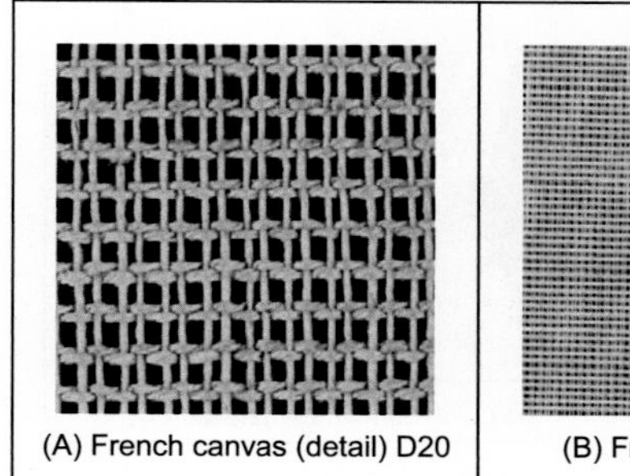

(A) French canvas (detail) D20

(B) French canvas D21

(C) Beach sand D29

FIGURE 8.8 Three Brodatz textures.

according to its texture content. We have used similar classification approaches to characterise the shape descriptions in the previous chapter. Actually, these are massive fields of research that move on to the broad subject of pattern recognition, and this is covered later in Chapter 12. Since texture itself is an enormous subject, you will find plenty of references to established approaches and to surveys of the field. First, we shall look at approaches to deriving the features (measurements) which can be used to describe textures. Broadly, these can be split into *structural* (transform-based), *statistical* and *combination* approaches. Clearly the frequency content of an image will reflect its texture; we shall start with Fourier. First though, we shall consider some of the required properties of the descriptions.

8.3.2 Performance requirements

The purpose of texture description is to derive some measurements that can be used to classify a particular texture. As such, there are invariance requirements on the measurements, as there were for shape description. Actually, the invariance requirements for feature extraction, namely invariance to position, scale and rotation, can apply equally to texture extraction. After all texture is a feature, albeit a rather nebulous one as opposed to the definition of a shape. Clearly we require position invariance: the measurements describing a texture should not vary with the position of the analysed section (of a larger image). Also, we require rotation invariance but this is not as strong a requirement as position invariance; the definition of texture does not imply knowledge of orientation, but could be presumed to. The least strong requirement is that of scale, for this depends primarily on application. Consider using texture to analyse forests in remotely sensed images. Scale invariance would imply that closely spaced young trees should give the same measure as widely spaced mature trees. This should be satisfactory if the purpose is only to analyse foliage cover. It would be unsatisfactory if the purpose was to measure age for purposes of replenishment, since a scale-invariant measure would be of little use as it could not, in principle, distinguish between young trees and old ones.

Unlike feature extraction, texture description rarely depends on edge extraction since one main purpose of edge extraction is to remove reliance on overall illumination level. The higher-order invariants, such as perspective invariance, are rarely applied to texture description. This is perhaps because many applications are like remotely sensed imagery, or are in constrained industrial application where the camera geometry can be controlled.

8.3.3 Structural approaches

The most basic approach to texture description is to generate the *Fourier transform* of the image and then to group the transform data in some way so as to obtain a set of measurements. Naturally, the size of the set of measurements is smaller than the size of the image's transform. In Chapter 2, we saw how the transform of a set of horizontal lines was a set of vertical spatial frequencies (since the point spacing varies along the vertical axis). Here, we must remember that for display we rearrange the Fourier transform so that the d.c. component (the zero-frequency component) is at the centre of the presented image.

The transforms of the three Brodatz textures of Fig. 8.8 are shown in Fig. 8.9. Fig. 8.9A shows a collection of frequency components which are then replicated with the same structure (consistent with the Fourier transform) in Fig. 8.9B (Figs. 8.9A and B also show the frequency scaling property of the Fourier transform: greater magnification reduces the high-frequency content.) Fig. 8.9C is clearly different in that the structure of the transform data is spread a different manner to that of Figs. 8.9A and B. Naturally, these images have been derived by application of the FFT which we shall denote as

$$\mathbf{FP} = \Im(\mathbf{P}) \tag{8.4}$$

where **FP** and **P** are the transform (spectral) and pixel data, respectively. One clear advantage of the Fourier transform is that it possesses shift invariance (Section 2.6.1): the transform of a bit of (large and uniform) cloth will be the same, whatever segment we inspect. This is consistent with the observation that phase is of little use in Fourier-based texture systems [Pratt92], so the modulus of the transform (its magnitude) is usually used. The transform is of the same size as the image, even though conjugate symmetry of the transform implies that we do not need to use all its components as measurements. As such we can filter the Fourier transform (Section 2.8) so as to select those frequency components deemed to be of interest to a particular application. Alternatively, it is convenient to collect the magnitude transform data in different ways to achieve a reduced set of measurements. First though, the transform data can be normalised by the sum of the squared values of each magnitude component (excepting the zero-frequency components, those for $u = 0$ and $v = 0$), so that the magnitude data are invariant to linear shifts in illumination to obtain normalised Fourier coefficients **NFP** as

$$\mathbf{NFP}_{u,v} = \frac{\left|\mathbf{FP}_{u,v}\right|}{\sqrt{\sum_{(u \neq 0) \wedge (v \neq 0)} \left|\mathbf{FP}_{u,v}\right|^2}} \tag{8.5}$$

The denominator is then a measure of total power, so the magnitude data become invariant to linear shifts. Alternatively, histogram equalisation (Section 3.3.3) can provide

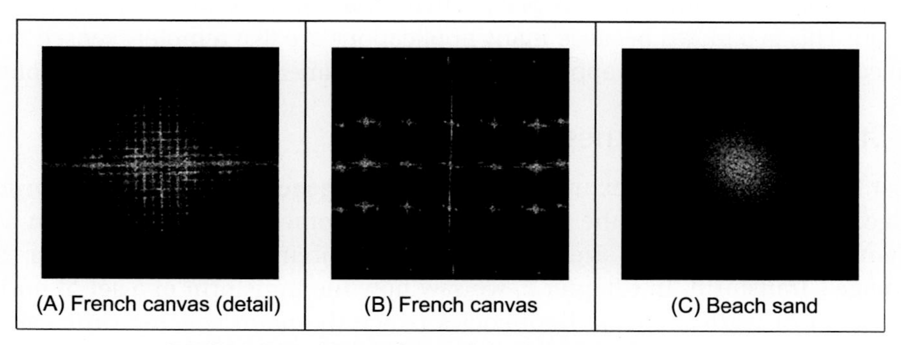

FIGURE 8.9 Fourier transforms of the three Brodatz textures.

such invariance but is more complicated than using Eq. (8.5). The spectral data can then be described by the *entropy, h,* as

$$h = \sum_{u=1}^{N}\sum_{v=1}^{N} \mathbf{NFP}_{u,v} \log(\mathbf{NFP}_{u,v}) \tag{8.6}$$

which gives compression weighted by a measure of the information content. A uniformly distributed image would have zero entropy, so the entropy measures by how much the image differs from a uniform distribution. Another measure is the *energy, e,* as

$$e = \sum_{u=1}^{N}\sum_{v=1}^{N} (\mathbf{NFP}_{u,v})^2 \tag{8.7}$$

which gives priority to larger items (by virtue of the squaring function). The measure is then appropriate when it is the larger values which are of interest; it will be of little use when the measure has a uniform distribution. Another measure is the *inertia, i,* defined as

$$i = \sum_{u=1}^{N}\sum_{v=1}^{N} (u-v)^2 \mathbf{NFP}_{u,v} \tag{8.8}$$

which emphasises components which have a large separation. As such, each measure describes a different facet of the underlying data. These measures are shown for the three Brodatz textures in Code 8.6. In a way, they are like the shape descriptions in the previous chapter: the measures should be the same for the same object and should differ for a different one. Here, the texture measures are actually different for each of the textures. Perhaps the detail in the French canvas, Code 8.6(A), could be made to give a closer measure to that of the full resolution, Code 8.6(B) by using the frequency scaling property of the Fourier transform, discussed in Section 2.6.3. The beach sand clearly gives a different set of measures from the other two, Code 8.6(C). In fact, the beach sand in Code 8.6(C) would appear to be more similar to the French canvas in Code 8.6(B), since the inertia and energy measures are much closer than those for Code 8.6(A) (only the entropy measure in Code 8.6(A) is closest to Code 8.6(B)). This is consistent with the images: each of the beach sand and French canvas has a large proportion of higher frequency information, since each is a finer texture than that of the detail in the French canvas.

By Fourier analysis, the measures are inherently position-invariant. Clearly, the entropy, inertia and energy are relatively immune to rotation, since order is not important in their calculation. Also, the measures can be made scale invariant, as a consequence of

entropy (FD20) = –253.11 inertia (FD20) = $5.55 \cdot 10^5$ energy (FD20) = 5.41	entropy (FD21) = –196.84 inertia (FD21) = $6.86 \cdot 10^5$ energy (FD21) = 7.49	entropy (FD29) = –310.61 inertia (FD29) = $6.38 \cdot 10^5$ energy (FD29) = 12.37
(A) French canvas (detail)	(B) French canvas	(C) Beach sand

CODE 8.6 Measures of the Fourier transforms of the three Brodatz textures.

the frequency scaling property of the Fourier transform. Finally, the measurements (by virtue of the normalisation process) are inherently invariant to linear changes in illumination. Naturally, the descriptions will be subject to noise. In order to handle large data sets we need a larger set of measurements (larger than the three given here) in order to better discriminate between different textures. Other measures can include:

1. the energy in the major peak;
2. the Laplacian of the major peak;
3. the largest horizontal frequency magnitude and
4. the largest vertical frequency magnitude.

Amongst others, these are elements of Liu's features [Liu90] chosen in a way aimed to give Fourier transform-based measurements good performance in noisy conditions.

Naturally, there are many other transforms, and these can confer different attributes in analysis. The wavelet transform is very popular since it allows for localisation in time and frequency [Laine93] and [Lu97]. Other approaches use the Gabor wavelet [Bovik90, Daugman93, Jain91], and [Riaz13] as introduced in Section 2.7.3. One comparison between Gabor wavelets and tree- and pyramidal-structured wavelets suggested that Gabor has the greater descriptional ability, at penalty of greater computational complexity [Pichler96, Grigorescu02]. There has also been interest in Markov random fields [Gimel'farb96] and [Wu96]. In fact, one survey [Randen00] includes use of Fourier, wavelet and discrete cosine transforms (Section 2.7.1) for texture characterisation. These approaches are structural in nature: an image is viewed in terms of a transform applied to a whole image as such exposing its structure. This is like the dictionary definition of an arrangement of parts. Another part of the dictionary definition concerned detail: this can of course be exposed by analysis of the high-frequency components, but these can be prone to noise. An alternative way to analyse the detail is to consider the statistics of an image.

8.3.4 Statistical approaches

8.3.4.1 Co-occurrence matrix

The most famous statistical approach is the *co-occurrence matrix*. This was the result of the first approach to describe, and then classify, image texture [Haralick73]. It remains popular today, by virtue of good performance. The co-occurrence matrix contains elements that are counts of the number of pixel pairs for specific brightness levels, when separated by some distance and at some relative inclination. For brightness levels $b1$ and $b2$ the co-occurrence matrix $\mathbf{C}$ is

$$\mathbf{C}_{b1,b2} = \sum_{x=1}^{N} \sum_{y=1}^{N} (\mathbf{P}_{x,y} = b1) \wedge (\mathbf{P}_{x',y'} = b2) \tag{8.9}$$

where $\wedge$ denotes the logical AND operation and the x co-ordinate x' is the offset given by the specified distance d and inclination θ by

$$x' = x + d\cos(\theta) \quad \forall \quad (d \in 1, \max(d)) \wedge (\theta \in 0, 2\pi) \tag{8.10}$$

and the y co-ordinate y' is

$$y' = y + d\sin(\theta) \quad \forall \quad (d \in 1, \max(d)) \wedge (\theta \in 0, 2\pi) \tag{8.11}$$

When Eq. (8.9) is applied to an image, we obtain a square, symmetric, matrix whose dimensions equal the number of grey levels in the picture. The co-occurrence matrices for the three Brodatz textures of Fig. 8.8 are shown in Fig. 8.10. In the co-occurrence matrix generation, the maximum distance was 1 pixel and the directions were set to select the four nearest neighbours of each point. Now the result for the two samples of French canvas, Figs. 8.10A and B, appear to be much more similar (especially in the dominance of the bottom right corner) and quite different to the co-occurrence matrix for sand, Fig. 8.10C. As such, the co-occurrence matrix looks like it can better expose the underlying nature of texture than can the Fourier description. This is because the co-occurrence measures spatial relationships between brightness, as opposed to frequency content. This clearly gives alternative results. To generate results faster, the number of grey levels can be reduced by brightness scaling of the whole image thus reducing the dimensions of the co-occurrence matrix, though this reduces discriminatory ability.

The subroutine `tex_cc`, Code 8.7, generates the co-occurrence matrix of an image given a maximum distance `dist` and a number of directions `dirs`. If `dist` and `dirs` are set to 1 and 4, respectively (as for the results in Fig. 8.10), then the co-occurrence will be evaluated from a point and its four nearest neighbours. First, the co-occurrence matrix is cleared. Then, for each point in the image and for each value of distance and relative inclination (and so long as the two points are within the image), then the element of the co-occurrence matrix indexed by the brightness of the two points is incremented. Finally, the completed co-occurrence matrix is returned. Note that even though the co-occurrence matrix is symmetric, this factor cannot be used to speed its production.

Again, we need measurements that describe these matrices. We shall use the measures of entropy, inertia and energy defined earlier. The results are shown in Code 8.8. Unlike visual analysis of the co-occurrence matrices, the difference between the measures of the three textures is less clear: classification from them will be discussed later.

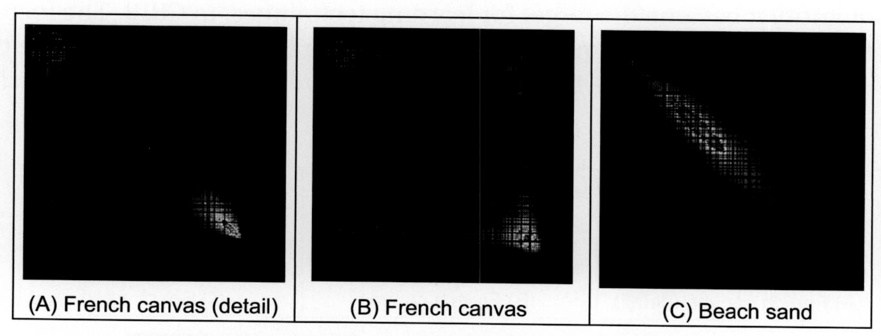

FIGURE 8.10 Co-occurrence matrices of the three Brodatz textures.

```
function coocc = tex_cc(image,dist,dirs)
%get dimensions
[rows,cols]=size(image);
%clear output
coocc(1:256,1:256)=0;

for x = 1:cols %address all columns
  for y = 1:rows %address all rows
    for r = 1:dist %and cover all radii
      for theta = 0:2*pi/dirs:2*pi*(1-1/dirs) %and angles in radians
        xc=round(x+r*cos(theta));
        yc=round(y+r*sin(theta));
        %check coordinates within image
        if yc>0&&yc<=rows&&xc>0&&xc<=cols
          %image brightness is 0..2^(N-1) so add 1 (for 1..2^N)
          coocc(image(y,x)+1,image(yc,xc)+1)=...
                      coocc(image(y,x)+1,image(yc,xc)+1)+1;
        end
      end
    end
  end
end
```

CODE 8.7 Co-occurrence matrix generation.

Clearly, the co-occurrence matrices have been reduced to only three different measures. In principle, these measurements are again invariant to linear shift in illumination (by virtue of brightness comparison). As with Fourier, scale can affect the structure of the co-occurrence matrix, but the description can be made scale invariant. Grey level difference statistics (a first order measure) were later added to improve descriptional capability [Weszka76]. Other statistical approaches include the Statistical Feature Matrix [Wu92] with the advantage of faster generation (Code 8.7).

8.3.4.2 Learning-based approaches

Julesz introduced the term *texton* for elementary units of texture perception [Julesz81], analogous to a phoneme in speech recognition, and this was used to determine an operational definition of textons and an algorithm for partitioning the image into disjoint regions of coherent brightness and texture [Malik01]. Then, given that texture is a nebulous quantity it became the target for learning techniques, in CBIR. The focus of this text is on feature extraction and not on learning though it is worth noting here that one approach used SIFT (Section 4.4.2) with variants to represent images as histograms

$\text{entropy}(\text{CCD20}) = 7.052 \cdot 10^5$	$\text{entropy}(\text{CCD21}) = 5.339 \cdot 10^5$	$\text{entropy}(\text{CCD29}) = 6.445 \cdot 10^5$
$\text{inertia}(\text{CCD20}) = 5.166 \cdot 10^8$	$\text{inertia}(\text{CCD21}) = 1.528 \cdot 10^9$	$\text{inertia}(\text{CCD29}) = 1.139 \cdot 10^8$
$\text{energy}(\text{CCD20}) = 5.16 \cdot 10^8$	$\text{energy}(\text{CCD21}) = 3.333 \cdot 10^7$	$\text{energy}(\text{CCD29}) = 5.315 \cdot 10^7$
(A) French canvas (detail)	(B) French canvas	(C) Beach sand

CODE 8.8 Measures of co-occurrence matrices of the three Brodatz textures.

which were compared using some of the distance measures described earlier (Earth Mover's Distance and the χ^2 distance, Section 12.3.1). Given with the trend for simpler descriptors previously observed with the BRIEF (Section 5.4.2) descriptor, one approach used extremely compact neighbourhoods together with extremely clever machine learning techniques to classify materials. Later in Chapter 12, and at the end of this chapter, we shall summarise some of the newer approaches in deep learning which has largely supplanted these approaches, primarily by performance.

8.3.5 Combination approaches

The previous approaches have assumed that we can represent textures by purely structural, or purely statistical description, combined in some appropriate manner. Since texture is not an exact quantity, and is more a nebulous one, there are naturally many alternative descriptions. One approach [Chen95] suggested that texture combines geometrical structures (as say in patterned cloth) with statistical ones (as say in carpet) and has been shown to give good performance in comparison with other techniques, and using the whole Brodatz data set. The technique is called *Statistical Geometric Features (SGF)*, reflecting the basis of its texture description. This is not a dominant texture characterisation: the interest here is that we shall now see the earlier shape measures in action, describing texture. Essentially, geometric features are derived from images, and then described by using statistics. The geometric quantities are actually derived from $NB - 1$ binary images **B** which are derived from the original image **P** (which has NB brightness levels). These binary images are given by

$$\mathbf{B}(\alpha)_{x,y} = \begin{vmatrix} 1 & \text{if} \quad \mathrm{P}_{\mathrm{x,y}} \geq \alpha \\ 0 & \text{otherwise} \end{vmatrix} \qquad \forall \alpha \in 1, NB \tag{8.12}$$

Then, the points in each binary region are connected into regions of 1s and 0s. Four geometrical measures are made on these data. First, in each binary plane, the number of regions of 1s and 0s (the number of connected sets of 1s and 0s) is counted to give $NOC1$ and $NOC0$. Then, in each plane, each of the connected regions is described by its irregularity which is a local shape measure of a region **R** of connected 1s giving irregularity $I1$ defined by

$$I1(\mathbf{R}) = \frac{1 + \sqrt{\pi}\,\max\limits_{i \in \mathbf{R}} \sqrt{(x_i - \bar{x})^2 + (y_i - \bar{y})^2}}{\sqrt{N(\mathbf{R})}} - 1 \tag{8.13}$$

where x_i and y_i are co-ordinates of points within the region, $\bar{x}$ and $\bar{y}$ are the region's centroid (its mean x and y co-ordinates), and N is the number of points within (i.e. the area of) the region. The irregularity of the connected 0s, $I0(\mathbf{R})$ is similarly defined. When this is applied to the regions of 1s and 0s it gives two further geometric measures, $IRGL1(i)$ and $IRGL0(i)$, respectively. To balance the contributions from different regions, the irregularity of the regions of 1s in a particular plane is formed as a weighted sum

$WI1(\alpha)$ as

$$WI1(\alpha) = \frac{\sum_{\mathbf{R} \in \mathbf{B}(\alpha)} N(\mathbf{R}) I(\mathbf{R})}{\sum_{\mathbf{R} \in \mathbf{P}} N(\mathbf{R})} \tag{8.14}$$

giving a single irregularity measure for each plane. Similarly, the weighted irregularity of the connected 0s is *WI*0. Together with the two counts of connected regions, *NOC*1 and *NOC*0, the weighted irregularities give the four geometric measures in SGF. The statistics are derived from these four measures. The derived statistics are the maximum value of each measure across all binary planes, *M*. Using $m(\alpha)$ to denote any of the four measures, the maximum is

$$M = \max_{\alpha i \in 1, NB} (m(\alpha)) \tag{8.15}$$

the average $\bar{m}$ is

$$\bar{m} = \frac{1}{255} \sum_{\alpha=1}^{NB} m(\alpha) \tag{8.16}$$

the sample mean $\bar{s}$ is

$$\bar{s} = \frac{1}{\sum_{\alpha=1}^{NB} m(\alpha)} \sum_{\alpha=1}^{NB} \alpha m(\alpha) \tag{8.17}$$

and the final statistic is the sample standard deviation *ssd* as

$$ssd = \sqrt{\frac{1}{\sum_{\alpha=1}^{NB} m(\alpha)} \sum_{\alpha=1}^{NB} (\alpha - \bar{s})^2 m(\alpha)} \tag{8.18}$$

The irregularity measure can be replaced by compactness (Section 7.3.1), but compactness varies with rotation, though this was not found to influence results much [Chen95].

In order to implement these measures, we need to derive the sets of connected 1s and 0s in each of the binary planes. This can be achieved by using a version of the connection routine in hysteresis thresholding (Section 4.2.1.5). The reformulation is necessary because the irregularity measures require a list of points in the connected region so that the centroid (and hence the maximum distance of a point from the centroid) can be calculated. The results for four of the measures (for the region of 1s, the maximum and average values of the number of connected regions and of the weighted irregularity) are shown in Code 8.9. Again, the set of measures is different for each texture. Of note the last measure, $\bar{m}$ (*WI*1), does not appear to offer much discriminatory capability here, whereas the measure *M*(*WI*1) appears to be a much more potent descriptor. Classification, or discrimination, is to select which class the measures refer to.

$M(NOC1) = 52.0$	$M(NOC1) = 178$	$M(NOC1) = 81$
$\bar{m}(NOC1) = 8.75$	$\bar{m}(NOC1) = 11.52$	$\bar{m}(NOC1) = 22.14$
$M(WI1) = 1.50$	$M(WI1) = 1.42$	$M(WI1) = 1.00$
$\bar{m}(WI1) = 0.40$	$\bar{m}(WI1) = 0.35$	$\bar{m}(WI1) = 0.37$
(A) French canvas (detail)	(B) French canvas	(C) Beach sand

CODE 8.9 Four of the statistical geometric features measures of the three Brodatz textures.

8.3.6 Local binary patterns

The *Local Binary Pattern (LBP)* texture description is a relatively recent approach, and it rapidly gained favour in the research community due to its attractive performance capabilities. There was an early approach [Ojala96] which gives the concept, and this was then refined over some time to give perhaps the most popular approach [Ojala02]. (It derives originally from the University of Oulu which must be the closest university to the Santa theme park – but that is mere digression.) We shall progress from where it started, the basic LBP to the current version since the advanced approaches would be rather a mind stretch without this. Essentially, for a 3 × 3 region the basic LBP is derived by comparing the centre point with its neighbours, to derive a code which is stored at the centre point. For points P and $\mathbf{P}_x$, the process depends on thresholding, which is the function

$$s(x) = \begin{vmatrix} 1 & \text{if} & \mathbf{P}_x > P \\ 0 & & \text{otherwise} \end{vmatrix} \tag{8.19}$$

The code is derived from binary weighting applied to result of thresholding (which is equivalent to thresholding the points neighbouring the centre point and then unwrapping the code as a binary code). So the code LBP for a point P with eight neighbours x is

$$LBP = \sum_{i \in 1,8} s(x) \times 2^{i-1} \tag{8.20}$$

This is illustrated in Fig. 8.11 where point LBP is the centre point and the eight values for i address its eight immediate neighbours. For the 3 × 3 patch in Fig. 8.11A the value of the centre point is exceeded three times, so there are three 1s in the resulting code in Fig. 8.11B. When this is unwrapped clockwise from the top left point (and the top middle

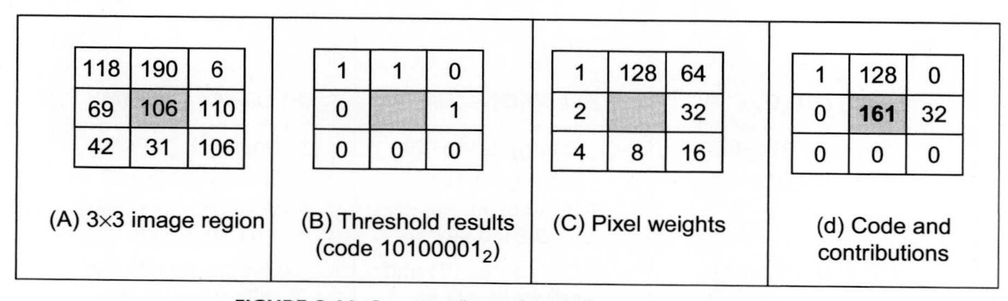

FIGURE 8.11 Constructing a local binary pattern code.

point is the most significant bit) the resulting code is $101{,}000{,}01_2$. When this is considered as a binary code, with weightings shown in Fig. 8.11C we arrive at a final value $LBP = 161$, Fig. 8.11D. Naturally, the thresholding process, the unwrapping and the weighting can be achieved in different ways, but it is essential that it is consistent across the whole image and between images for a meaningful comparison. The code P now encodes the local intensity structure: the local binary pattern.

The basic LBP code was complemented by two local measures: contrast and variance. The former of these was computed from the difference between points encoded as a '1' and those encoded as a '0'; the variance was computed from the four neighbour pixels aiming to reflect pattern correlation as well as contrast. Of these two complementary measures, contrast was found to add most to discriminatory capability.

The LBP approach then determines a histogram of the codes derived for an entire image and this histogram describes the texture. The approach is inherently *translation invariant* by its formulation: a texture which is shifted should achieve the same histogram of LBP codes. By virtue of its formulation, the basic process is not scale or rotation invariant, as in the case of rotation a different weighting will be applied to the point comparisons resulting in a different code value. The histogram of LBP values for the French canvas texture Fig. 8.12A is shown in Fig. 8.12D. Rather than show the histogram for the shifted French canvas Fig. 8.12B (as the visible difference is little) we show the differences between the LBP histograms of Figs. 8.12A and B, which shows little

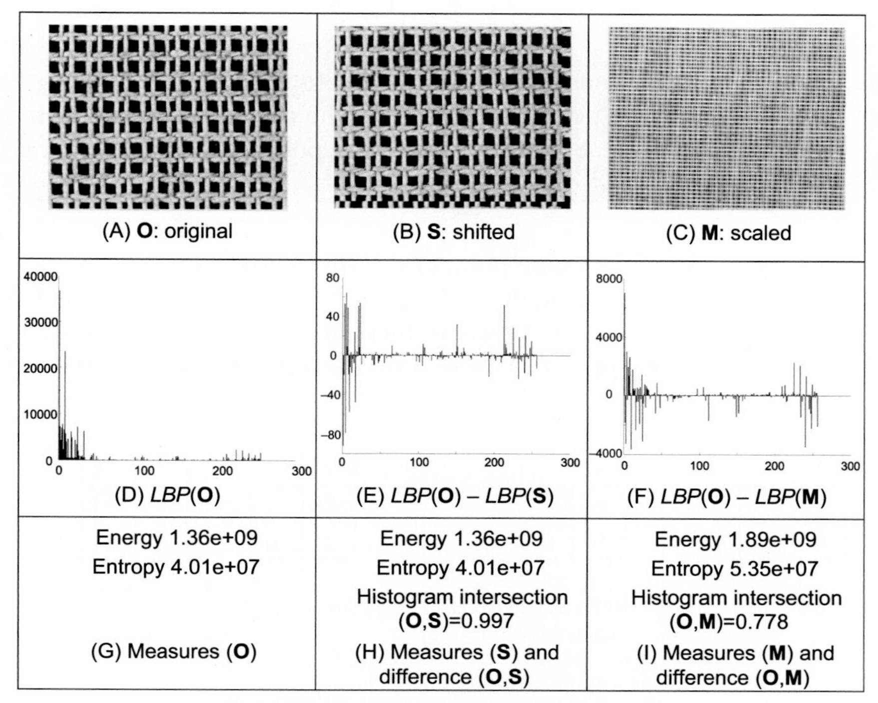

FIGURE 8.12 Local binary patterns and descriptions.

difference, Fig. 8.12C shows the (highly scaled) version of Fig. 8.12A, and the differences between the LBP histograms of Figs. 8.12A and C appear to be large. We also show the measures of energy and entropy, which behave as expected. The numbers are large so we shall also use the *histogram intersection* to measure the distance, with normalisation if necessary. This is described later in Section 12.3.1, and it is a measure which is 1.0 for histograms which are the same, and a smaller value when they differ, as to be seen here.

The next consideration is *scale invariance*. This requires consideration of points at a greater distance. If the space is sampled in a circular manner, and P points are derived at radius R, then the co-ordinate equations for $i \in (1, P)$ are

$$x(i) = \begin{bmatrix} x_0 + R\cos\left(\frac{2\pi}{P}i\right) \\ y_0 + R\sin\left(\frac{2\pi}{P}i\right) \end{bmatrix} \tag{8.21}$$

As in the Hough Transform for circles, Section 5.5.3, Bresenham's algorithm offers a more efficacious method for generating circle. As we can now have a different number of points within the code, the code generation becomes for a scale invariant LBP *LBP_S* is

$$LBP\_S(P,R) = \sum_{i \in 1,P} s(x(i))2^{i-1} \tag{8.22}$$

The patterns for radial sampling for different values of P and R are shown in Fig. 8.13 where Fig 8.13A is the sampling for a circle with 8 points radius 1 and is equivalent to the earlier 3 × 3 patch in Figs. 8.11A and Fig. 8.13B is for a radius 2 also with 8 points and Fig 8.13C is yet larger. All show the effect of discretisation on low-resolution generation of circular patterns, and it is more usual to use interpolation to determine point values, rather than the nearest pixel's value.

The *rotation invariant* arrangement then shifts the derived code so as to achieve a minimum integer, as in the rotation invariant chain code Section 7.2.2 (except the LBP is a pattern of ones and zeroes, not integers), and the rotation invariant LBP *LBP_R* is then

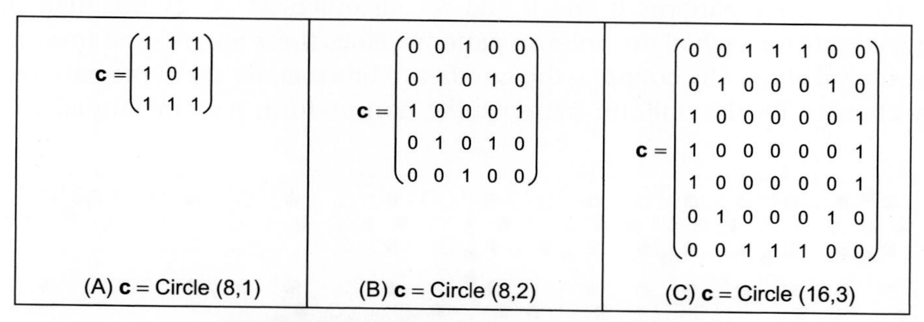

FIGURE 8.13 Sampling in a radial pattern for (P,R).

$$LBP\_R(P,R) = \min\left\{ ROR\left(\sum_{i \in 1,P} s(x(i))2^{i-1} \right) \right\} \tag{8.23}$$

where $ROR(\ )$ is the (circular) rotation operator. For the sampling arrangement of $LBP\_S(8,1)$, Fig. 8.13A, the approach was found to determine 36 individual patterns for which the occurrence frequencies varied greatly and, given the coarse angular measure used in that arrangement, the technique was found to lack discriminatory ability and so a more potent approach was required.

In order to achieve better discriminatory ability, it was noticed that some basic patterns dominated discriminatory ability and the occurrence of these patterns dominates texture description capability [Ojala02]. For the sampling arrangement of $LBP\_S(8, 1)$, Fig. 8.13A, and denoting the output of thresholding relative to the central point as black ('0') or white ('1'), then we achieve the arrangements given in Fig. 8.14. In these, patterns 0 to 8 correspond to basic features: pattern 0 represents the thresholding for a bright spot (all surrounding points have a lower value) and pattern 8 represents a dark spot (all points are brighter). Patterns 1 to 7 represent lines of varying degrees of curvature: pattern 1 represents the end of a line (a termination), pattern 2 a sharp point and pattern 4 represents an edge. These are called the *uniform binary patterns* and are characterised by having at most two transitions of '1' to '0' (or vice versa) when progressing around the circular pattern. The remaining patterns (those which have no label) have more than two transitions of '1' to '0' in a circular progression and are called non-uniform. There are more non-uniform patterns available than those shown in the second row of Fig. 8.14. These patterns can occur at any rotation, so the LBP can be arranged to detect them in a rotation invariant manner.

For the *uniform LBP* approach, first we need to detect whether the patterns are uniform or not. This is achieved using an operator U which counts the number of transitions of '1' to '0' (or vice versa)

$$U(LBP\_S(P,R)) = \left| s(x(0)) - s(x(P)) \right| + \sum_{i \in 1,P-1} \left| s(x(i)) - s(x(i+1)) \right| \tag{8.24}$$

For the arrangement $LBP\_S(8, 1)$ the patterns 0 to 8 thus have a maximum value of $U = 2$ ($U = 0$ for patterns 0 and 8 and for all others $U = 2$). We then need to determine a code for each of the uniform patterns. Since these are rotation invariant, this can be achieved simply by counting the number of bits that are set in the pattern. These are only counted for the uniform patterns; the non-uniform patterns are all set to the

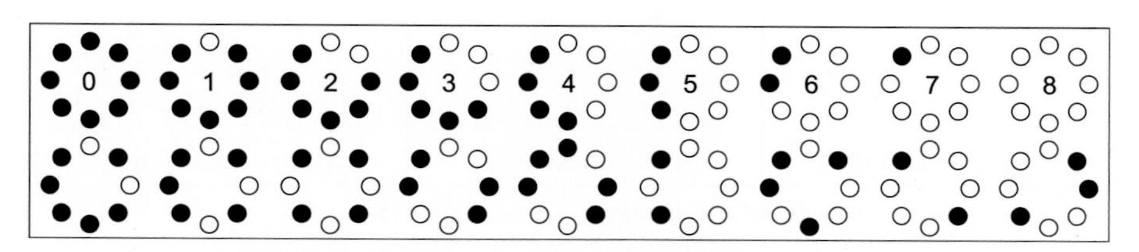

FIGURE 8.14 Rotation invariant binary patterns for *LBP_S*(8, 2).

same code value (the easiest value is to exceed by one the number of patterns to be expected for that sampling arrangement). For the patterns in Fig. 8.14, which are for the sampling arrangement *LBP_S*(8, 1), there are codes 0 to 8 so we can lump together the non-uniform patterns to a code value of 9. For *N* patterns ranging from 0 to *N* − 1, we can then define the rotation invariant code as

$$LBP\_U(P,R) = \left| \begin{array}{ll} \sum_{i \in 1,P} s(x(i)) & \text{if} \quad U \leq 2 \\ N & \text{otherwise} \end{array} \right. \tag{8.25}$$

We then derive a histogram of occurrence of these basic features, we characterise a texture by the frequency of occurrence of local basic structures and this has proved to be a very popular way for describing texture.

Applying the uniform LBP description implemented in Code 8.10 to the earlier texture D20 and its rotated and shifted version, we again achieve a similar histogram of code

```
function codes = uniform_lbp(image, dirs, rad)
%get dimensions
[rows,cols]=size(image);
%clear output
codes(1:rows,1:cols)=0;

for x = rad+1:cols-rad-1 %address all columns except border
    for y = rad+1:rows-rad-1 %address all rows except border
        counter=0; %initialise i
        code_p=0;  %and temporary summation
        for theta = 0:2*pi/dirs:2*pi*(1-1/dirs) %angles in radians
            xc=round(x+rad*cos(theta));
            yc=round(y+rad*sin(theta));
            if image(yc,xc)>image(y,x) %eq 8.19
                code_p(counter+1)=1; %generate points
            else
                code_p(counter+1)=0; %point 0
            end
            counter=counter+1; %increment i
        end
        zero_crossings=0; %eq 8.24
        for i=1:counter-1 %now count the zero crossings
            if code_p(i)~=code_p(i+1)
                zero_crossings=zero_crossings+1;
            end
        end %and check start to end transition
        if code_p(1)~=code_p(counter)
            zero_crossings=zero_crossings+1;
        end
        if zero_crossings<3 %eq 8.25
            codes(y,x)=0;
            for i=1:counter %sum up the set bits
                codes(y,x)=codes(y,x)+code_p(i);
            end
        else
            codes(y,x)=9; %defaults to no code
        end
    end
end
```

CODE 8.10 Uniform local binary patterns.

values. The implementation in Code 8.10 follows the description here and could easily be optimised further, e.g. some operations included for clarity like the `if code_p(i)~ = code_p(i+1)` structures could be replaced with arithmetic ones. In this histogram, the most popular codes are those for the line structures (code 4, remembering that the description is rotation invariant), which is entirely consistent with the image from which the histogram was derived. The results for a shifted and rotated version of texture D20 are shown in Fig. 8.15. Here, we see in Fig. 8.15A the original texture and Fig. 8.15C, its shifted and rotated version. The description of the original texture is given in Fig. 8.15B, and its shifted and rotated version is in Fig. 8.15D. Visually there is little difference between the histograms but there is actually some slight difference, of less than 100 count values, and the histogram intersection is 0.996 (they are very close indeed).

To apply the technique over different scales the histograms obtained at each scale can be concatenated. The LBP becomes multi-scaled since it can classify any texture pattern which is repeated within the one of the neighbourhoods. Two-dimensional similarity metrics are used to classify textures using this method because each texture class has a histogram for each scale. The preferred measure for the dissimilarity L, between the concatenated histograms of a sample S and a model M, is

$$L(S,M) = -\sum_{h=1}^{H}\sum_{n=1}^{N_h}\frac{T_{hs}S_{hn}}{\sum_h T_{hs}}\ln\frac{T_{hm}M_{hn}}{\sum_h T_{hm}} \tag{8.26}$$

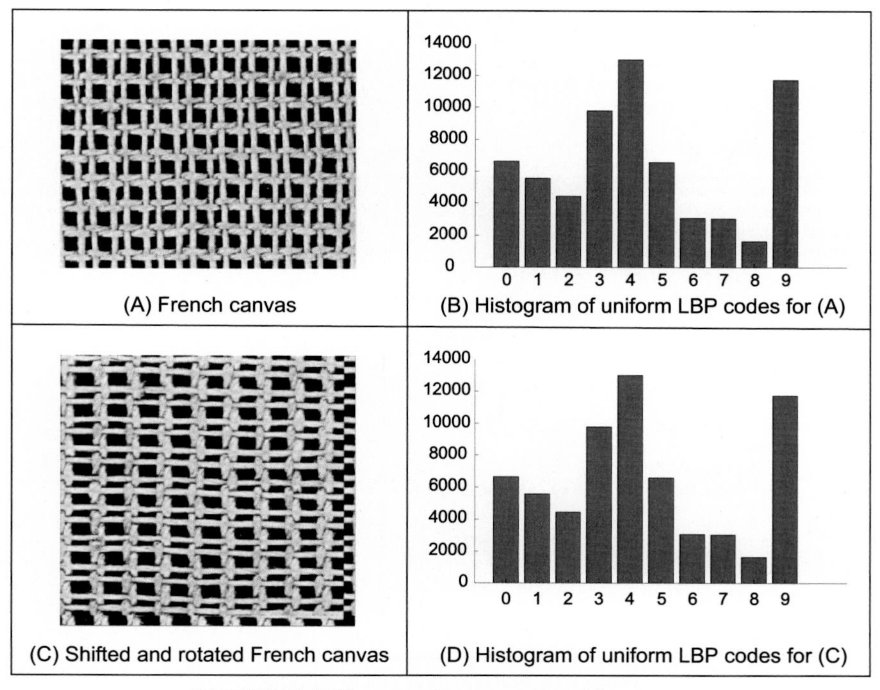

FIGURE 8.15 Uniform local binary pattern histograms.

where S_{hn} and M_{hn} are the probabilities of the nth bin in the hth sample and model histogram respectively, N_h is the number of patterns in the H histograms, and T_{hs} and T_{hm} are the total number of entries in the sample and model histograms.

The original presentation of the Uniform LBP technique [Ojala02] contains an extensive experimental evaluation on texture databases (including Brodatz), considers more of the ramifications of the representation and implementation of the Uniform LBP approach, and contains links to (Matlab®) code and data. There have been many extensions and applications of the local binary pattern technique. One particular use is in biometrics, in face detection and recognition, e.g. [Ahonen06]. There is also a book by its originators [Pietikäinen11], giving more complete treatment of the LBP approach and describing many of the variants now available, and there was a largely contemporaneous study [Nanni12]. There is also a recent survey, which sets LBP in the context of other descriptors (and history) [Liu18], and a systematic review of LBP techniques with performance evaluation [Liu17]. On particular variant LBP-TOP was designed for analysis and recognition of dynamic texture [Zhao07], and this has been demonstrated to be particularly effective to prevent face spoofing (to pretend to be someone else for fraudulent access in a situation with biometric security) [de Freitas Pereira14].

8.3.7 Other approaches

There have been many approaches to texture and we have so far concentrated on themes of approaches. Of other themes, one early approach was to develop (Gaussian) *random field models* [Cross83, Chellappa85]. In these, the approach was to determine a model to generate an example texture and to use the model parameters for classification – thus affording a way of texture synthesis. The approach was theoretically elegant, but computationally unattractive. Techniques have been extended to *dynamic textures* [Szummer96] which are those textures which exhibit temporal motion such as 'wavy water, rising steam and fire' like the random field models, these were described using a statistical model allowing for recognition and for synthesis, with impressive results. It is a large field though and there are many derivatives of these themes, and combinations. These are ably described elsewhere [Petrou06].

8.3.8 Segmentation by texture

In order to *segment* an image according to its texture, we can measure the texture in a chosen region and then classify it. This is equivalent to template convolution but where the result applied to pixels is the class to which they belong, as opposed to the usual result of template convolution. Here, we shall use a 7×7 template size: the texture measures will be derived from the 49 points within the template. First though, we need data from which we can make a classification decision, the training data. Naturally, this depends on a chosen application. Here we shall consider the problem of segmenting the eye image into regions of hair and skin.

This is a two class problem for which we need samples of each class, samples of skin and hair. We will take samples of each of the two classes. The texture measures are the energy, entropy and inertia of the co-occurrence matrix of the 7 × 7 region, so the feature space is three-dimensional. The training data are derived from regions of hair and from regions of skin, as shown in Figs. 8.16A and B, respectively. The first half of this data is the samples of hair, the other half is samples of the skin, as required for the *k*-nearest neighbour classifier of Chapter 12.

We can then segment the image by classifying each pixel according to the description obtained from its 7 × 7 region. Clearly, the training samples of each class should be classified correctly. The result is shown in Fig. 8.17A. Here, the top left corner is first (correctly) classified as hair, and the top row of the image is classified as hair until the skin commences (note that the border inherent in template convolution reappears). In fact, much of the image appears to be classified as expected. The eye region is classified as hair, but this is somewhat arbitrary decision, it is simply that hair is the closest texture feature. Also, some of the darker regions of skin are classified as hair, perhaps the result of training on regions of brighter skin.

Naturally, this is a computationally demanding process. An alternative approach is to simply classify regions as opposed to pixels. This is the tiled approach, with result shown in Fig. 8.17B. The resolution is clearly very poor: the image has effectively been reduced to a set of 7 × 7 regions, but it is much faster, requiring only 2% of the computation of the convolution approach.

A comparison with the result achieved by uniform thresholding is given, for comparison, in Fig. 8.17C. This is equivalent to pixel segmentation by brightness alone. Clearly, there are no regions where the hair and skin are mixed and in some ways the result appears superior. This is in part due to the simplicity in implementation of texture segmentation. But the result of thresholding depends on illumination level and on appropriate choice of the threshold value. The texture segmentation method is completely automatic and the measures are known to have invariance properties to illumination, as well as other factors. Also, in uniform thresholding there is no extension possible to separate more classes (except perhaps to threshold at differing brightness levels).

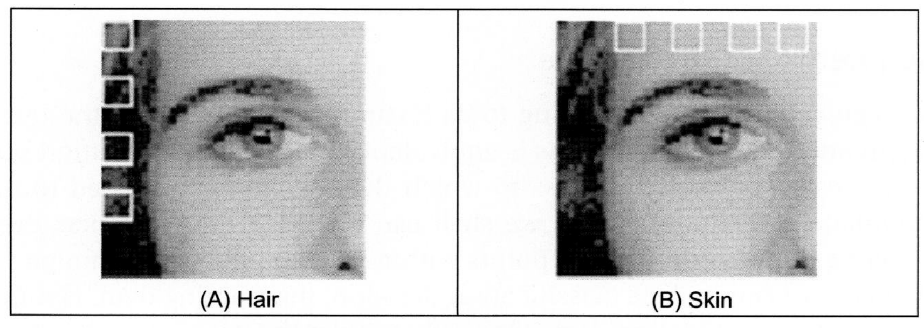

FIGURE 8.16 Training regions for classification.

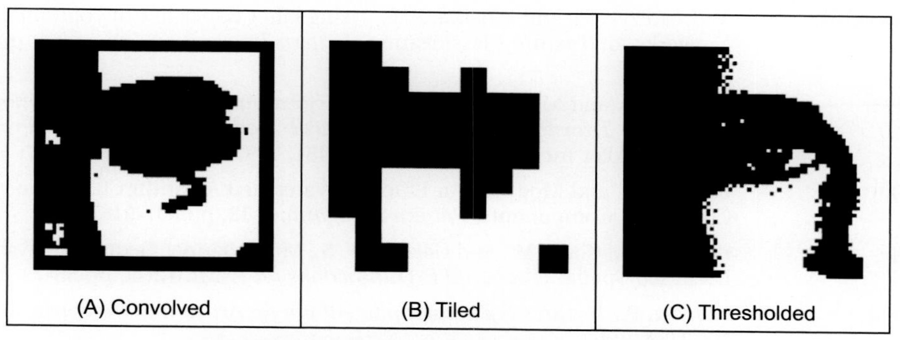

FIGURE 8.17 Segmenting the eye image into two classes.

8.4 Further reading

Clearly, there is much further reading in the area of texture description, classification and segmentation, as evidenced by the volume of published work in this area. The best place to start for texture is Maria Petrou's book [Petrou06]. There is one fairly comprehensive – but dated – survey [Reed93]. An updated review has a wide bibliography [Tuceryan98]. Another [Zhang02] offers review of the approaches which are invariant to rotation, translation, and affine or projective transforms, but texture is a large field of work to survey with many applications. Even though it is a large body of work, it is still only a subset of the field of pattern recognition. In fact, reviews of pattern recognition give many pointers to this fascinating and extensive field [e.g. Jain00]. There is a much newer survey on texture (covering research from 2000 onwards), and which describes the recent influence of deep learning [Liu18]. We shall briefly cover deep learning for texture, noting that in depth material on deep learning is covered in Chapter 12. The first study on using deep learning to handle detection of texture in images affected by noise revealed the early promise of the new techniques [Cimpoi15]. The popularity and capability of filter banks for texture analysis has been reflected in a deep learning approach where the layers can be considered as akin with filter banks [Andrearczyk16]. More recently with an 'end-to-end learning framework' (a complete one) the power of learning has shown greater discrimination [Zhang17], and there are CNNs for texture synthesis [Gatys15]. Given that texture is a nebulous and ubiquitous property, one expects that the deep learning literature in this area will only increase.

References

[Achanta12] Achanta, R., Shaji, A., Smith, K., Lucchi, A., Fua, P., and Susstrunk, S., SLIC Superpixels Compared to State-Of-The-Art Superpixel Methods, *IEEE Transactions on PAMI*, **34**(11), pp 2274-2282.

[Ahonen06] Ahonen, T., Hadid, A., and Pietikäinen, M., Face Description with Local Binary Patterns: Application to Face Recognition, *IEEE Transactions on PAMI*, **28**(12), pp 2037-2041, 2006.

[Andrearczyk16] Andrearczyk, V., and Whelan, P. F., Using Filter Banks in Convolutional Neural Networks for Texture Classification. *Pattern Recognition Letters*, **84**, pp 63-69, 2016.

[Beucher93] Beucher S., and Meyer F., *The Morphological Approach to Segmentation: The Watershed Transformation, Mathematical Morphology in Image Processing*, Marcel Dekker Inc., New York, pp 433-481, 1993.

[Bieniek00] Bieniek, A., and Moga A., An Efficient Watershed Algorithm Based on Connected Components, *Pattern Recognition*, **33**, pp 907-916, 2000.

[Bovik90] Bovik, A. C., Clark, M., and Geisler, W. S., Multichannel Texture Analysis Using Localised Spatial Filters, *IEEE Transactions on PAMI*, **12**(1), pp 55-73, 1990.

[Brodatz68] Brodatz, P., *Textures: A Photographic Album for Artists and Designers*, Reinhold, NY, USA, 1968.

[Chellappa85] Chellappa, R., and Chatterjee, S., Classification of Textures Using Gaussian Markov Random Fields, *IEEE Transactions on ASSP*, **33**(4), pp 959-963, 1985.

[Chen95] Chen, Y. Q., Nixon, M. S., and Thomas, D. W., Texture Classification Using Statistical Geometric Features, *Pattern Recognition*, **28**(4), pp 537-552, 1995.

[Cimpoi15] Cimpoi, M., Maji, S., and Vedaldi, A., Deep Filter Banks for Texture Recognition and Segmentation. *Proceedings of IEEE CVPR*, pp 3828-3836, 2015.

[Cross83] Cross, G. R., and Jain, A. K., Markov Random Field Texture Models, *IEEE Transactions on PAMI*, **5**(1), pp 25-39, 1983.

[Daugman93] Daugman, J., G., High Confidence Visual Recognition of Persons Using a Test of Statistical Independence, *IEEE Transactions on PAMI*, **18**(8), pp 1148-1161, 1993.

[Efros99] Efros, A., and Leung, T., Texture Synthesis by Non-parametric Sampling, *Proceedings of ICCV*, pp. 1033-1038, 1999.

[de Freitas Pereira14] de Freitas Pereira, T., Komulainen, J., Anjos, A., De Martino, J. M., Hadid, A., Pietikäinen, M. and Marcel, S., Face Liveness Detection Using Dynamic Texture. *EURASIP Journal on Image and Video Processing*, **2**, 2014.

[Gatys15] Gatys, L., Ecker, A. S. and Bethge, M., Texture Synthesis Using Convolutional Neural Networks. *Proceedings of Advances in Neural Information Processing Systems*, pp. 262-270, 2015.

[Gimel'farb96] Gimmel'farb, G. L., and Jain, A. K., On Retrieving Textured Images from an Image Database, *Pattern Recognition*, **28**(12), pp 1807-1817, 1996.

[Grigorescu02] Grigorescu, S.E., Petkov, N., and Kruizinga, P. Comparison of Texture Features Based on Gabor Filters, *IEEE Transactions on Image Processing*, **11**(10), pp 1160-1167, 2002.

[Haralick73] Haralick, R. M., Shanmugam, K., and Dinstein, I., Textural Features for Image Classification, *IEEE Transactions on Systems, Man and Cybernetics*, **2**, pp 610-621, 1973.

[Heckbert86] Heckbert, P. S., Survey of Texture Mapping, *IEEE Computer Graphics and Applications*, pp. 56-67, 1986.

[Jain91] Jain, A. K., and Farrokhnia, F., Unsupervised Texture Segmentation Using Gabor Filters, *Pattern Recognition*, **24**(12), pp 1186-1191, 1991.

[Jain00] Jain, A. K., Duin, R. P. W., and Mao, J., Statistical Pattern Recognition: a Review, *IEEE Transactions on PAMI*, **22**(1), pp 4-37, 2000.

[Julesz81] Julesz, B., Textons, the Elements of Texture Perception, and Their Interactions, *Nature* **290**, pp 91-97, 1981.

[Karru96] Karru, K., Jain, A. K., and Bolle, R., Is There Any Texture in an Image?, *Pattern Recognition*, **29**(9), pp 1437-1446, 1996.

[Laine93] Laine, A., and Fan, J., Texture Classification via Wavelet Pattern Signatures, *IEEE Transactions on PAMI*, **15**(11), pp 1186-1191, 1993.

[Liu90] Liu, S. S., and Jernigan, M. E., Texture Analysis and Discrimination in Additive Noise, *CVGIP*, **49**, pp 52-67, 1990.

[Liu17] Liu, L., Fieguth, P., Guo, Y., Wang, X. and Pietikäinen, M., Local binary features for texture classification: Taxonomy and experimental study. *Pattern Recognition*, 62, pp 135-160, 2017.

[Liu18] Liu, L., Chen, J., Fieguth, P., Zhao, G., Chellappa, R. and Pietikainen, M., *From BoW to CNN: Two Decades of Texture Representation for Texture Classification.* arXiv preprint arXiv:1801.10324, 3, 2018.

[Lu97] Lu, C. S., Chung, P. C., and Chen, C. F., Unsupervised Texture Segmentation via Wavelet Transform, *Pattern Recognition*, **30**(5), pp 729-742, 1997.

[Malik01] Malik, J., Belongie, S., Leung, T., and Shi, J., Textons, Contour and Texture Analysis for Image Segmentation, *International Journal of Computer Vision*, **43**(1), pp 7-27, 2001.

[Matas02] Matas, J., Chum, O., Urban, M., Pajdla, T., Robust Wide Baseline Stereo from Maximally Stable External Regions, *Proceedings of BMVC*, pp 384-396, 2002.

[Nanni12] Nanni, L., Lumini, A. and Brahnam, S., Survey on LBP Based Texture Descriptors for Image Classification, *Expert Systems with Applications*, **39**(3), pp 3634-3641, 2012.

[Ojala96] Ojala T., Pietikäinen M., and Harwood D., A Comparative Study of Texture Measures with Classification Based on Featured Distribution, *Pattern Recognition*, **29**(1), pp 51-59, 1996.

[Ojala02] Ojala, T., Pietikäinen, M., Mäenpää, T., Multiresolution Gray-Scale and Rotation Invariant Texture Classification with Local Binary Patterns. *IEEE Transactions on PAMI*, **24**(7), pp 971-987, 2002.

[Oxford96] The Concise English Dictionary of Current English, *Oxford University Press*, Oxford UK, 1996.

[Pietikäinen11] Pietikäinen, M., Hadid, A., Zhao, G., and, Ahonen, T., *Computer Vision Using Local Binary Patterns*, Springer, 2011.

[Petrou06] Petrou, M., and Sevilla, O. G., *Image Processing: Dealing with Texture*, Wiley, 2006.

[Pichler96] Pichler, O., Teuner, A., and Hosticka, B. J., A Comparison of Texture Feature Extraction Using Adaptive Gabor Filtering, Pyramidal and Tree Structured Wavelet Transforms, *Pattern Recognition*, **29**(5), pp 733-742, 1996.

[Pratt92] Pratt, W. K., *Digital Image Processing*, Wiley, 1992.

[Randen00] Randen, T., and Husoy, J. H., Filtering for Texture Classification: A Comparative Study, *IEEE Transactions on PAMI*, **21**(4), pp 291-310, 2000.

[Riaz13] Riaz, F., Hassan, A., Rehman, S. and Qamar, U., Texture Classification Using Rotation-And Scale-Invariant Gabor Texture Features. *IEEE Signal Processing Letters*, **20**(6), pp 607-610, 2013.

[Reed93] Reed, T. R., and du Buf, H., A Review of Recent Texture Segmentation and Feature Extraction Techniques, *CVGIP: Image Understanding*, **57**(3) pp 359-372, 1993.

[Shi00] Shi, J., Malik, J., Normalized Cuts and Image Segmentation, *IEEE Transactions on PAMI*, **22**(8) pp 888–905, 2000.

[Szummer96] Szummer, M., and Picard, R. W. Temporal Texture Modelling, *Proceedings of ICIP*, **3**, pp 823-826, 1999.

[Tuceryan98] Tuceryan, M., and Jain, A. K., Texture Analysis, In: C. H. Chen, L. F. Pau, and P. S. P. Wang (Eds.) *The Handbook of Pattern Recognition and Computer Vision* 2nd Edition, World Scientific Publishing Co., Singapore, pp 207-248, 1998.

[Varma09] Varma, M. and Zisserman, A., A Statistical Approach to Material Classification Using Image Patch Exemplars. *IEEE Transactions on PAMI*, **31**(11), pp 2032-2047, 2009.

[Weszka76] Weska, J. S., Dyer, C. R., and Rosenfeld, A., A Comparative Study of Texture Measures for Terrain Classification, *IEEE Transactions on SMC*, **SMC-6**(4), pp 269-285, 1976.

[Wu92] Wu, C. M., and Chen, Y. C., Statistical Feature Matrix for Texture Analysis, *CVGIP: Graphical Models and Image Processing*, **54,** pp 407-419, 1992.

[Wu96] Wu, W and Wei, S., Rotation and Gray-Scale Transform-Invariant Texture Classification Using Spiral Resampling, Subband Decomposition and Hidden Markov Model, *IEEE Transactions on Image Processing*, **5**(10), pp 1423-1434, 1996.

[Yongxia17] Yongxia, Z., Xuemei, L., Xifeng G., and Caiming Z., A Simple Algorithm of Superpixel Segmentation with Boundary Constraint, *IEEE Transactions on Circuits and Systems for Video Technology*, 27(7), pp 1502-1514, 2017.

[Zhang02] Zhang, J., and Tan T., Brief Review of Invariant Texture Analysis Methods, *Pattern Recognition*, **35**, pp 735–747, 2002.

[Zhang17] Zhang, H., Xue, J. and Dana, K., Deep Ten: Texture Encoding Network. *Proceedings of IEEE CVPR*, pp 708-717, 2017.

[Zhao07] Zhao, G. and Pietikainen, M., Dynamic Texture Recognition Using Local Binary Patterns with an Application to Facial Expressions. *IEEE Transactions on PAMI*, **29**(6), pp 915-928, 2007.

Moving object detection and description

9.1 Overview

This chapter is concerned with how we can find and describe moving objects. This implies that we do not have a single image, but a sequence of images (or video frames). The objects we seek to find and describe are those which move from place to place in one image to the next. We shall first describe methods which extract the moving objects, separating them from their background. We shall then consider ways to describe the trajectories made by these objects. We shall then consider ways to analyse the trajectories, using the motion of the shape and its trajectory for recognition purposes before moving to techniques for describing moving objects. This chapter is summarised in Table 9.1.

Table 9.1 Overview of this chapter.

Main topic	Subtopics	Main points
Moving object extraction	How do we separate moving objects from their background. Methods of estimating the background. Methods of adapting the background model. Using morphology to improve silhouette quality.	Averaging and median filter for estimation of *background* image; *background separation* by subtraction; improvement by *mixture of Gaussians* and *thresholding*. Problems: Colour, lighting and shadows. Using *erosion* and *dilation*; opening and closing. Connected component analysis.
Tracking moving objects	Tracking single and multiple objects; achieving temporal consistency in the tracking process; modelling linear system dynamics.	*Tracking* by local search; the *Lucas–Kanade* approach. Including movement in the tracking process; *Kalman filter*; multiple object tracking; the *Condensation* algorithm; feature point versus background subtraction; problems and solutions. *Camshift* and *Meanshift* approaches. Tracking with object detection.
Analysis	Moving shape analysis and description.	Describing motion and extracting moving shapes by *evidence gathering*. Adding velocity and movement into the shape description. Describing the moving object for *recognition* purposes.

Feature Extraction and Image Processing for Computer Vision. https://doi.org/10.1016/B978-0-12-814976-8.00009-9

The topic of moving object description and tracking is very large, and there are many examples. Many of these images are of people since analysing their motion is required by many applications; beyond the general computer-vision-based analysis of human movement [Gavrila99, Wang03a, Moeslund06], people are interested in computer-vision-based analysis of sport, and of automated analysis of surveillance images [Hu04], and of course moving objects in medical image analysis. Computers now have much more computing power than they did when computer vision started and memory is much cheaper, so interest has moved on to capitalise on and to exploit how we can find and describe moving objects in sequences of images. There is also a bit of bias here: Mark co-authored the first text on identifying people by the way they walk [Nixon05] since his team were amongst the earliest workers in gait biometrics. We shall start with basic techniques for background estimation since it can be used to determine the moving object in a scene, before moving on to the more modern approaches for foreground/background separation.

9.2 Moving object detection

One of the main problems in detecting moving objects is that the insertion of a moving object in a scene does not obey the principle of superposition. Since the moving object obscures the background, there is no linear (filtering) approach which can separate the moving object from its background. As such we are left with a variety of approaches to achieve this task, as ever ranging from simple to complex and with different performance attributes.

9.2.1 Basic approaches

9.2.1.1 Detection by subtracting the background

The basic way to separate a moving object from its background is to *subtract* the background from the image, leaving just the moving object (the foreground). This is illustrated in Fig. 9.1 where we subtract an estimate of the background, Fig. 9.1B, from an image in a sequence, Fig. 9.1A, to determine the moving object, Fig. 9.1C. The basic approaches to estimating the *background* to an image are actually an example of application of the statistical operators covered in Chapter 3. In principle, there are two

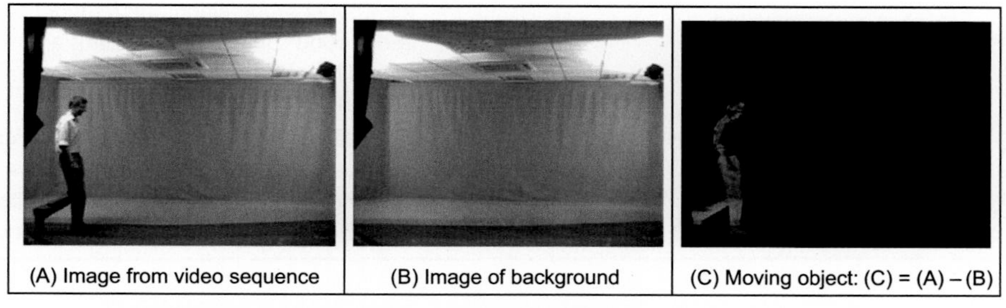

FIGURE 9.1 Detecting moving objects by differencing from the background.

ways to form the background image: the most obvious is to record images which contain only the background and then process them to reduce any variation within them. If no background images are available, then we need to determine the background from the images containing the moving object. We shall consider deriving an estimate of the background only in this section, from images which contain a moving subject. The approaches covered here in this subsection are equally applicable to processing sequences of images of the background (without a moving subject).

Say we have a sequence of images of a walking subject, and we want to be able to find the background, such as the sequence of images shown in Figs. 9.2A–E where a subject is walking from left to right. These images are part of the Southampton Gait Database [Shutler02] which is a collection of image sequences of subjects walking indoors and outdoors for evaluation of human gait as a biometric. The indoor laboratory had controlled illumination; in a complementary dataset collected outdoors, the illumination was uncontrolled. One way to determine the background is to average the images. If we form a *temporal average*, an image **TP** where each point is the average of the points in the same position in each of the five images, $\mathbf{P}_1$, $\mathbf{P}_2$ .... $\mathbf{P}_5$ (Eq. (9.1)), we achieve a result which shows the background though with a faint version of the walking subject, as in Fig. 9.2F. The faint version of the subject occurs since the walking subject's influence on image brightness is reduced by one-fifth, but it is still there. We could of course use more images, the ones in between the ones we have already used and then the presence of the subject would become much fainter.

$$\mathbf{TP}_{x,y} = \left(\mathbf{P}_{1_{x,y}} + \mathbf{P}_{2_{x,y}} + \mathbf{P}_{3_{x,y}} + \mathbf{P}_{4_{x,y}} + \mathbf{P}_{5_{x,y}}\right)/5 \tag{9.1}$$

We can also include 5×5 spatial averaging, as in Section 3.4, wherein the average is formed from the spatially averaged images using the 5×5 mean operator *mean5*( ) to further reduce the presence of the walking subject (Eq. (9.2)) as shown in Fig. 9.2G. This gives *spatiotemporal averaging*. For this, we have not required any more images, but the

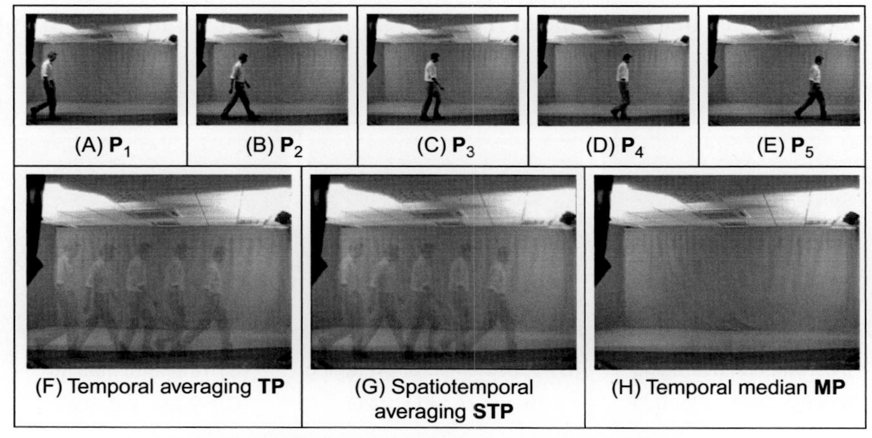

FIGURE 9.2 Background estimation by sequence filtering.

penalty paid for the improvement in the estimate of the background is lack of detail (and of course it took longer).

$$\mathbf{STP}_{x,y} = (mean5(\mathbf{P}_{1_{x,y}}) + mean5(\mathbf{P}_{2_{x,y}}) + mean5(\mathbf{P}_{3_{x,y}}) + mean5(\mathbf{P}_{4_{x,y}}) + mean5(\mathbf{P}_{5_{x,y}}))/5 \tag{9.2}$$

However, if we form the background image by taking the median of the five images, as in Section 3.5.1 (i.e. the median of the values of the points at the same position in each of the five images), a *temporal median* (Eq. (9.3)), then we obtain a much better estimate of the background as shown in Fig. 9.2H. A lot of the image detail is retained, whilst the walking subject disappears – all we appear to retain is the empty laboratory. In this case, for a sequence of images where the target walks in front of a static background, the median is the most appropriate operator. If we did not have a sequence of images, we could just average the single image with a large operator and that could provide some estimate (but a rather poor one) of the background.

$$\mathbf{MP}_{x,y} = median(\mathbf{P}_{1_{x,y}}, \mathbf{P}_{2_{x,y}}, \mathbf{P}_{3_{x,y}}, \mathbf{P}_{4_{x,y}}, \mathbf{P}_{5_{x,y}}) \tag{9.3}$$

Having formed an image of the background, we now subtract the background image from the images in the sequence, and then threshold the images, to show the objects moving within them as shown in Fig. 9.3, for the three estimates of the background. When this is applied to these laboratory-derived images, where the lighting was controlled, the operation can be quite successful: we find the moving object. By these results, the median filter is best (Fig. 9.3C) (but requires the most computational effort) whereas the temporal average works least best (Fig. 9.3A) (since the moving figure forms part of the background and appears in the final image). There are a few problems with the lighting which are shown by the shadow detected around the feet, but that is natural since objects will always interact with the lighting when moving (note that these effects are reduced – between the feet – with spatiotemporal averaging). Static objects are part of the background since they are not moving. Note that the front part of the shirt has not been detected in any of the images (and Mark definitely has a chest). The difference image has been thresholded, so altering the threshold (or the technique) will change performance. This has been optimised here and has a different value for each approach.

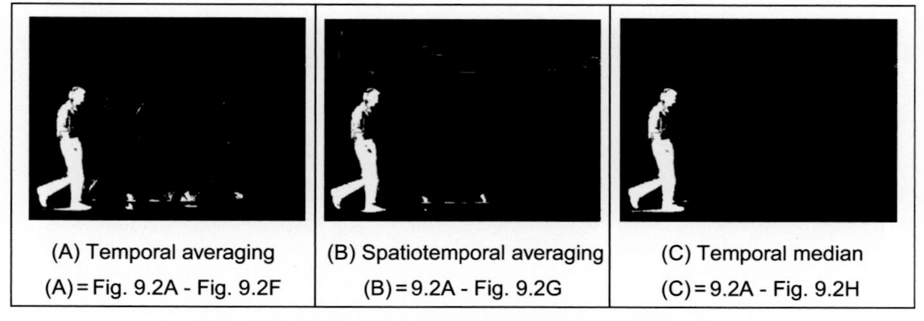

FIGURE 9.3 Detecting moving objects by mean and median filtering.

The original images are part of one of the databases freely available for evaluation of gait biometrics from the University of Southampton. The indoor data are derived from progressive scan digital video where subjects walked in front of a chromakey background. This was designed to show basic performance: a single subject moves in front of a static monochrome background. (The chromakey colour is green unlike the blue which is often used, largely because our students insisted on wearing blue clothes and disappeared into a blue background. No-one at Southampton wears bright green!) The outdoor data show the same subject walking outside where the lighting is uncontrolled: people and vehicles move in the background, and the weather caused the foliage to move (it even interrupted filming occasionally). This is a considerably more challenging environment for background extraction.

The approaches start to fall apart when we consider outdoor images. The same techniques (with the same parameter values) are now applied to a sequence of outdoor images, Figs. 9.4A–E. By Figs. 9.4I–K, we can see that we have again found the moving subject – the foreground to the image. The median approach is again the best (the averaging approaches continue to have the subject in the background), but doh! – there's a lot more which appears to move. This is true for each of the ways in which the

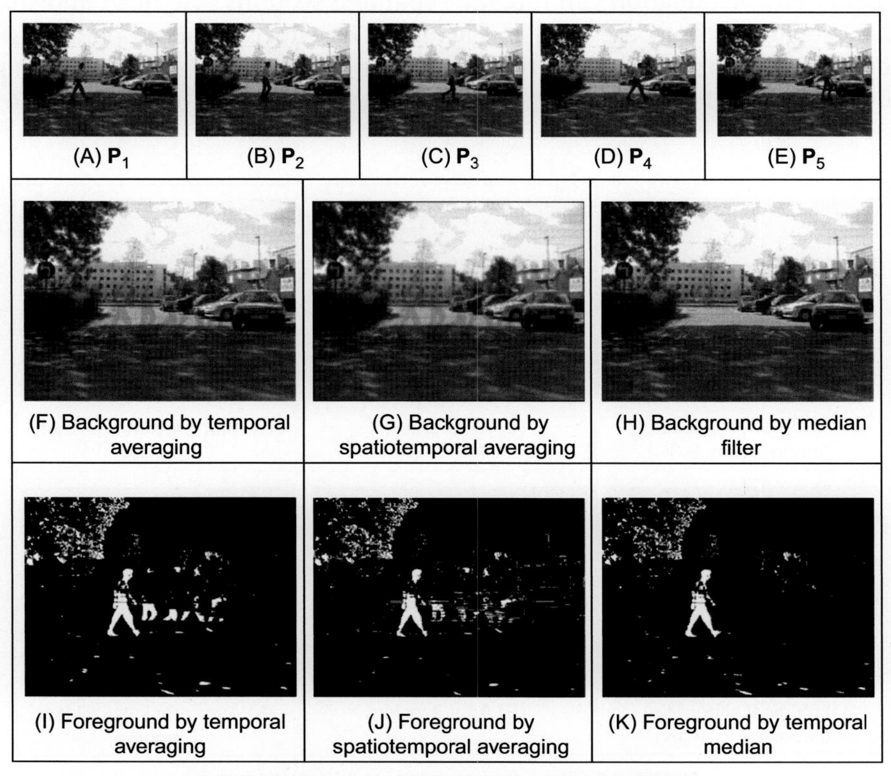

FIGURE 9.4 Detecting moving objects in outdoor images.

background is estimated, and that is to be expected. The lighting outdoors will change more than indoors (especially in the UK where we 'enjoy' winter, summer, autumn and spring all in the same day) and there can be shadows, as can be seen in the foreground. There is wind too, so the bushes and the tree will be moving. And we do not live in a vacuum, there are other objects moving in the background (there is another pedestrian walking directly behind). So we have made a good start, but that is all it is. We could optimise the values better (change the thresholds and extent of the averaging and median operator) and that would improve matters a bit, but not by much. One way to improve the quality of the extracted human silhouette is to filter the noise – all the small points. That uses morphology, coming next.

9.2.1.2 Improving quality by morphology

One of the main problems observed so far is the noise points contaminating the detected moving object and the image. Given that these points arise from motion, it is unlikely that the image can be smoothed sufficiently to remove them without obliterating the image detail. As such, it is common to use morphology (explained in Section 3.6) to remove them. This can be achieved either by removing the isolated white points, or by using erosion and dilation (opening and closing). Erosion removes noise whilst preserving shape. Putatively, dilation can link the separated sections (the head and shoulders are actually separated from the body in Fig. 9.4). The effect of these operations on the images derived by temporal median filtering on the indoor and the outdoor imagery, is shown in Fig. 9.5. In Figs. 9.5B and E, we can see that erosion removes some of the

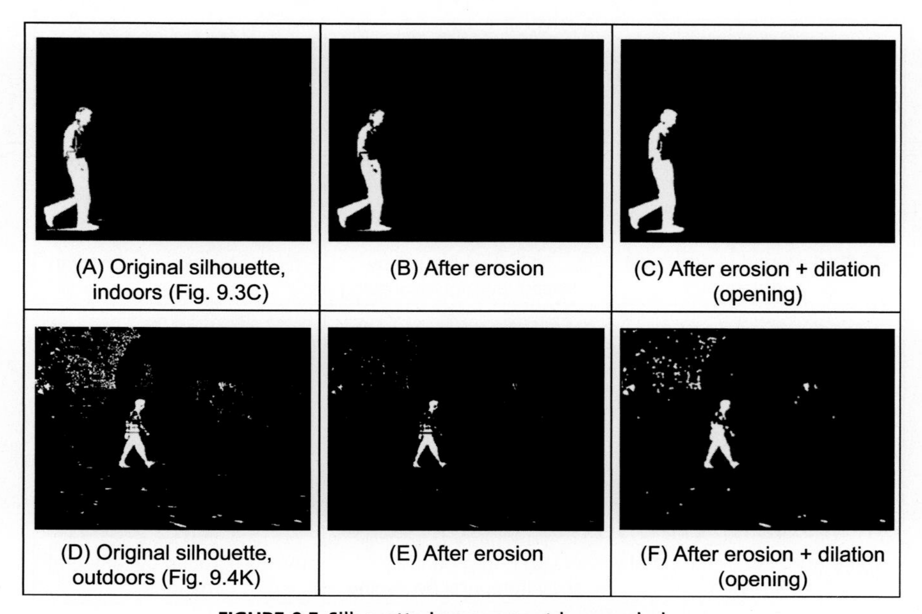

(A) Original silhouette, indoors (Fig. 9.3C)	(B) After erosion	(C) After erosion + dilation (opening)
(D) Original silhouette, outdoors (Fig. 9.4K)	(E) After erosion	(F) After erosion + dilation (opening)

FIGURE 9.5 Silhouette improvement by morphology.

shadow in the indoor imagery, and most of the effects of the tree in the outdoor imagery. Dilation then returns the silhouettes to be of the same size, in Figs. 9.5C and F.

Naturally the result depends on the degrees of erosion and dilation, and this is a natural compromise. If too much filtering is applied, then the features will be lost too. Here, we have applied erosion and dilation by a circular mask of radius 2. By Fig. 9.5C, the process has improved the quality of the silhouette, but there are still rather too many noise points in the final image in Fig. 9.5F. As such, the last stage is to find the largest shape wherein white points are connected (the largest connected-component) and this but shown for the indoor and outdoor silhouettes in Fig. 9.6 – this is fine for the indoor silhouette and outdoors we have most of the body, but not the head and shoulders. We now have quite a few parameters that can be changed to suit a particular application or a particular imaging scenario, but the technique is not yet as sophisticated as it can be. We can detect a moving object, and the process can be optimised for a particular scene, but the quality is unlikely to be sufficient for general application.

9.2.2 Modelling and adapting to the (static) background

The need to achieve fast and accurate background extraction has spawned many approaches. We have already seen many of the problems in the previous section – what happens when a subject's clothing is similar to the background, the effects of shadows, fragmentary shape detection, etc. The techniques so far process a set of images so as to estimate an image of the background, and this implies need for storage. We can of course, have an estimate which is updated for each new image

$$\mathbf{NTP}_{x,y}^{<i+1>} = \alpha\mathbf{NTP}_{x,y}^{<i>} + (1-\alpha)\mathbf{P}_{i_{x,y}} \tag{9.4}$$

given $\mathbf{NTP}^{<0>} = \mathbf{0}$ and α is the learning rate ($0 < \alpha \leq 1$). In this way a fraction of the new image is added to the background image and so we only need to store a single background image. By this process, if a person is to walk into a scene and then stop, they will be detected as they walk in, and afterwards will cease to be detected (at a time dictated by the learning rate) since when stopped they will become part of the background. As such it is indeed possible for people to blend in with the background. In an extension, as new objects appear in the image they can be labelled as either background (in which

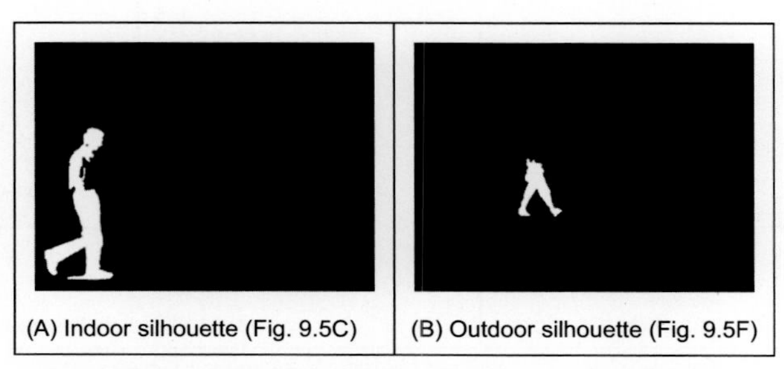

FIGURE 9.6 Finding the largest connected-component shape.

case they add to the background image) or as foreground (and then not contribute to the background image). Further, this can include analysis of the variance of the pixel distribution at each point, and this leads to techniques which can accommodate changes in the background. Our next two approaches were developed during the DARPA VSAM sponsored project and are two of the most popular background subtraction techniques. The first approach was developed by Stauffer and Grimson at MIT [Stauffer99, Stauffer00] and is now one of the most popular techniques for separating a moving object from its background.

Naturally, we can *model* the background as a system wherein each pixel has a probability distribution. In the indoor images, Fig. 9.2, the probability distribution will peak due to the large and uniform background. A subject's clothing should deviate from this, and so they can be detected. Naturally, a background model arises from more factors, so we can model it as a *mixture* of probability distributions. Each pixel in the background is then described by the chance that they are due to the uniform background, to the ceiling, or to other factors. This is illustrated in Fig. 9.7, wherein Fig. 9.7A shows the distribution from a single Gaussian distribution (this is probably suitable for the pixels in the large uniform background) which is rather simple in contrast with Fig. 9.7B which shows three Gaussian distributions (as dotted lines) and the probability distribution arising from their addition (the solid line). Clearly, the distribution arising from multiple distributions has better capability to model more complex backgrounds: the three distributions could be the uniform background, the track the subject is walking on and the ceiling, since there is a good chance that a pixel in the background will fall into one of these three categories.

A centred Gaussian distribution g (an extended version of Eq. (3.26)) for a single variable x is a function of mean μ, and standard deviation σ

$$g(x, \mu, \sigma) = \frac{1}{\sqrt{2\pi\sigma^2}} e^{\frac{-(x-\mu)^2}{2\sigma^2}} \tag{9.5}$$

Given that we have colour, we then need a multidimensional space (colour models are covered in Chapter 11). Here, we shall first assume that each image in the sequence is

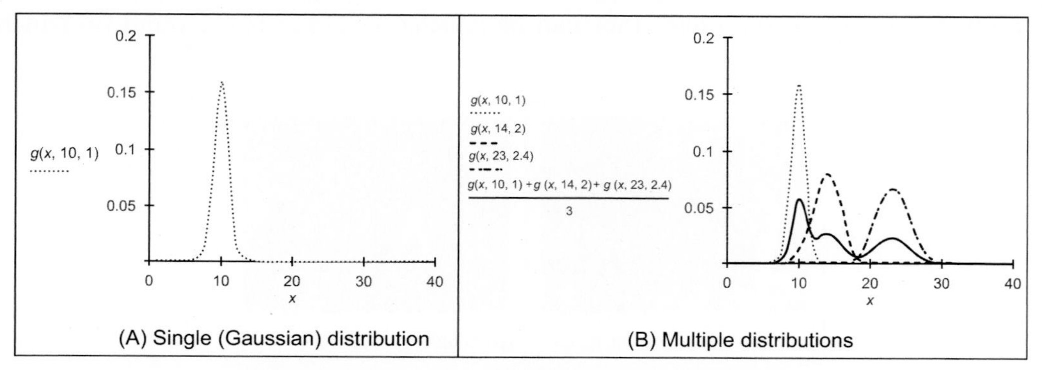

FIGURE 9.7 Distribution for Gaussian and for mixture of Gaussians.

RGB, stored in the three colour planes. For d dimensions, the *multivariate Gaussian distribution G* is denoted by

$$G\left(\mathbf{x},\boldsymbol{\mu},\sum\right)=\frac{1}{(2\pi)^{d/2}\left|\sum\right|^{1/2}}e^{\frac{-(\mathbf{x}-\boldsymbol{\mu})^{T}\Sigma^{-1}(\mathbf{x}-\boldsymbol{\mu})}{2\sigma^{2}}} \tag{9.6}$$

where d is the number of variables in the multidimensional quantity $\mathbf{x}$, $\boldsymbol{\mu}$ is the means of the variables and $\sum$ is the $d \times d$ covariance matrix. Given that one assumption is that the covariance matrix reduces to a diagonal (given independent variables wherein the off-diagonal elements – those which expose correlation – are zero) then the multivariate Gaussian simplifies to

$$GS(\mathbf{x},\boldsymbol{\mu}_j,\sigma_j)=\frac{1}{\left(2\pi\sigma_j^2\right)^{d/2}}e^{\frac{-\left\|\mathbf{x}-\boldsymbol{\mu}_j\right\|^2}{2\sigma_j^2}} \tag{9.7}$$

where $d=3$ for a thee-axis colour model (e.g. red/green/blue RGB, noting the colour models exposed in Chapter 11). The addition of k Gaussian multivariate distributions is

$$p(x)=\sum_{j=1}^{k}w_j GS(\mathbf{x},\boldsymbol{\mu}_j,\sigma_j) \tag{9.8}$$

where w_j is the weight, or significance, of the jth distribution. We then need a system which learns the mixture of Gaussian distributions – the differing values for w_j – which is appropriate for each pixel in the background image. Using a Gaussian distribution is attractive since it is characterised by mean and variance only and this reduces computational requirements. There are distributions which are associated with the background and with the foreground, where the foreground is the moving object. A pixel is compared with its existing k distributions. If the value of the pixel is within $2.5 \times \sigma_j$ of the jth distribution (which makes the probability of it belonging to this distribution 99%) then it is deemed to belong to that distribution. If the pixel matches any of the background distributions, it is deemed to be a background pixel. The background model is formed from B distributions which in rank order satisfy

$$\sum_{j=1}^{B}w_j > T \tag{9.9}$$

where the value of the threshold T controls the number of distributions for the background model. Reducing the value of T increases the chance that distributions can form part of the background model. A larger value of T is more restrictive, and hence more selective, allowing the background model to accommodate bimodal distributions.

There is a ranking procedure with the distributions, to indicate which is most likely. This is achieved by using a ratio of weight to variance (w_j/σ_j). By this, the most probable distributions are those with high weight and low variance, whereas the least probable have the lowest weight and highest variance. If the pixel matches no distribution, then it is considered to be a new distribution, replacing the distribution with the lowest confidence (the value for w_j/σ_j) and the mean of the new distribution is set to the value of the current pixel and the variance to a high value. If the pixel matches a foreground distribution, or none of the background ones, it is deemed to be a foreground pixel, belonging to the moving object.

We have yet to determine how the weights are calculated. Initially, they are set to low values, with high values for the variance of each distribution. Then a pixel comparison is made, and at the first iteration the pixel matches no distribution and so becomes a new one. At the second and later iterations, the values of the weights of the k distributions are updated to become $w_{j,t}$ (where $w_{j,t-1}$ is their previous value) by

$$w_{j,t} = (1-\alpha)w_{j,t-1} + \alpha M_{j,t} \tag{9.10}$$

where the value of α controls the learning rate, the speed at which the approach accommodates change in the background data, and where $M_{j,t} = 1$ for a matching distribution and $M_{j,t} = 0$ for the remaining distributions. The weights are normalised after this process, to sum to unity. The values of mean $\mu_{j,t}$ and variance $\sigma_{j,t}^2$ are then updated for the matching distribution as

$$\mu_{j,t} = (1-\rho)\mu_{j,t-1} + \rho\mathbf{x}_t \tag{9.11}$$

$$\sigma_{j,t}^2 = (1-\alpha)\sigma_{j,t-1}^2 + \rho\left(\mathbf{x}_t - \mu_{j,t}\right)^T\left(\mathbf{x}_t - \mu_{j,t}\right) \tag{9.12}$$

where

$$\rho = \alpha GS\left(\mathbf{x}_t, \mu_{j,t-1}, \sigma_{j,t-1}\right) \tag{9.13}$$

After pixels have been labelled as foreground and background, a connected component analysis can be used to remove noise pixels. The result of moving-object detection applied to images from an indoor sequence, and from an outdoor sequence (described in Section 9.2.1.1), is shown in Fig. 9.8. Note that these images have only had slight application of morphology, aiming to show performance (but without the distractions of noise) and can be improved beyond the results here. Clearly, there is improvement in segmentation of the moving object, over extractions achieved by the basic approaches. What is not shown here are the images that arise whilst the approach is converging to the background. When a pure background image sequence (one without moving objects) is available, then the technique can converge to the background before detecting moving objects. If one is not available, then the quality of moving-object detection is impaired whilst the process adapts to the background. The technique was designed for video rate implementation and this can be achieved, so it can be deployed and then adapt to the background, before moving objects are detected. Given that the process adapts the background model, moving objects which become stationary will become part of the background model, until they move again. Note that in the outdoor image, there is a subject walking in the background who then appears in the foreground extraction, as do some artefacts (the wind caused the thin trees to wave). The shadow has been handled quite nicely and does not affect the outdoor segmented image much. This is achieved by

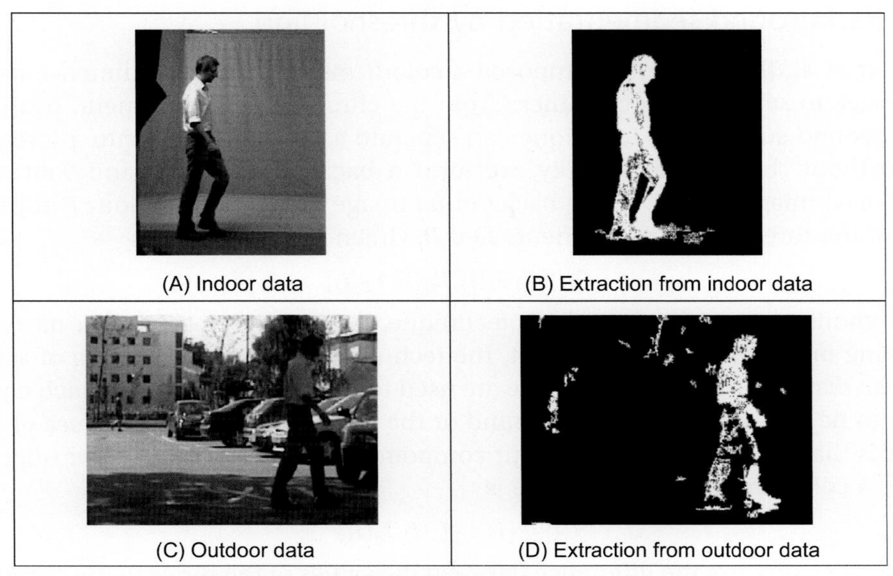

FIGURE 9.8 Moving object extraction by mixture of Gaussians.

a colour space transformation (in shadow, the colour is maintained whilst the saturation/intensity reduces) [Kaewtrakulpong01].

Several parameters can affect performance. First, there is the learning rate α which controls the number of iterations taken to adapt to the background. Then there is the threshold T, $0 < T \leq 1$, and the larger values of T make it better able to accommodate multimodal backgrounds. Then there is the number of Gaussian distributions per mixture and the values selected for the initial variance. Naturally a smaller number of Gaussians is attractive computationally, but complex backgrounds will suit a larger number. If the initial variance is too large, this increases the chance that a moving object with colour similar to the background might be labelled as background. This will be the case until the estimate of variance converges, and with a large value this can require more iterations.

Given its popularity, there have naturally been approaches aimed to improve performance. An obvious change is to use a different colour space: using Hue Saturation Intensity/Value (HSI/HSV) rather than RGB colour should be less prone to the effects of shadows (since a shaded background will retain the same colour only changing in intensity), and that is indeed the case [Harville01]. One approach aimed to detect (adapt to and remove) shadows, whilst improving speed of convergence [Kaewtrakulpong01] (as used here), and another was directed to improving speed of convergence in particular [Lee05], with an adaptive learning rate. Another approach aimed specifically to avoid fragmentation of the detected moving objects [Tian05]. As such, there are many ways to improve the performance of the basic technique still further.

9.2.3 Background segmentation by thresholding

Horprasert et al. [Horprasert99] proposed a colour model in a three-dimensional RGB colour space to separate the brightness from the chromaticity component. In this way the background subtraction technique can separate a moving object into a foreground image, without shadows. Essentially, we form a background image and subtract the current (new) image from it. In the background image the expected colour E at pixel i is formed of the three colour components Red R, Green G and Blue B as

$$E(i) = \{E_R(i), E_G(i), E_B(i)\} \tag{9.14}$$

Throughout the presentation of this technique, the notation looks rather nasty as we are working in 3D colour space. In fact, the technique becomes a neat use of statistics derived via distance functions and these are used to derive thresholds by which a pixel is ascribed to be a member of the foreground or the background image. The use of colour just means that we have the three colour components instead of a scalar for brightness. The pixel's colour in the current image is

$$I(i) = \{I_R(i), I_G(i), I_B(i)\} \tag{9.15}$$

and we seek to measure the difference between the values of the pixels in the current and the background image. This is the difference between the point in the current image and the line from the origin passing though the point E. This line represents the brightness of the point in the background image which is its brightness scaled by a factor α. If α exceeds 1 then the point is brighter, and if it is less than 1 it is darker, so α is a measure of the brightness difference. The brightness distortion BD is the value of α which brings the observed colour closest to the line

$$BD(\alpha(i)) = \min(I(i) - \alpha(i)E(i))^2 \tag{9.16}$$

If we measure the distance as the Euclidean distance (Section 12.3.1) then we obtain the chrominance distortion CD as the distance of $I(i)$ from $\alpha(i)E(i)$.

$$CD(i) = \|I(i) - \alpha(i)E(i)\| \tag{9.17}$$

This is illustrated in RGB space in Fig. 9.9 where the chrominance distortion (the difference in colour) is the length along the line normal to line from the origin to E.

The algorithm initially uses N frames to form the background model. From these frames, the mean and the standard deviation are computed for each colour band (R, G, B) in each pixel. The expected colour E is then the average over these N frames

$$E(i) = \{\mu_R(i), \mu_G(i), \mu_B(i)\} \tag{9.18}$$

and the variance

$$s(i) = \{\sigma_R(i), \sigma_G(i), \sigma_B(i)\} \tag{9.19}$$

The value of α is that which minimises

$$\min\left(\left(\frac{I_R(i) - \alpha(i)\mu_R(i)}{\sigma_R(i)}\right)^2 + \left(\frac{I_G(i) - \alpha(i)\mu_G(i)}{\sigma_G(i)}\right)^2 + \left(\frac{I_B(i) - \alpha(i)\mu_B(i)}{\sigma_B(i)}\right)^2\right) \tag{9.20}$$

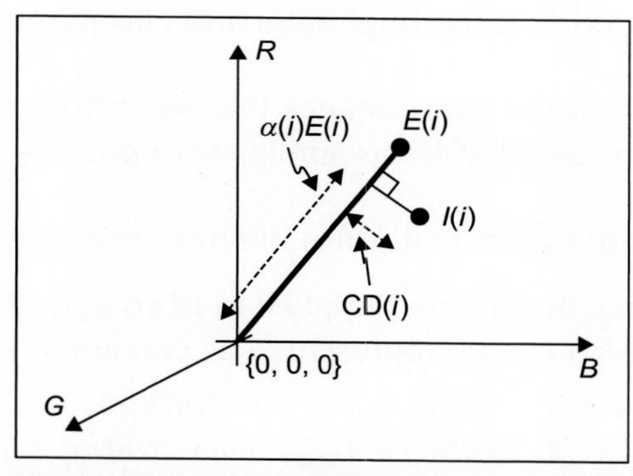

FIGURE 9.9 Difference between background and current image components.

giving

$$BD(i) = \alpha(i) = \frac{\frac{I_R(i)\mu_R(i)}{\sigma_R^2(i)} + \frac{I_G(i)\mu_G(i)}{\sigma_G^2(i)} + \frac{I_B(i)\mu_B(i)}{\sigma_B^2(i)}}{\left(\frac{\mu_R(i)}{\sigma_R(i)}\right)^2 + \left(\frac{\mu_G(i)}{\sigma_G(i)}\right)^2 + \left(\frac{\mu_B(i)}{\sigma_B(i)}\right)^2} = \frac{\sum_{C\in\{R,G,B\}} \left(\frac{I_C(i)\mu_C(i)}{\sigma_C^2(i)}\right)}{\sum_{C\in\{R,G,B\}} \left(\frac{\mu_C(i)}{\sigma_C(i)}\right)^2} \tag{9.21}$$

and

$$CD(i) = \sqrt{\sum_{C\in\{R,G,B\}} \left(\frac{I_C(i) - \alpha(i)\mu_C(i)}{\sigma_C(i)}\right)^2} \tag{9.22}$$

Different pixels exhibit different distributions, of brightness and of chrominance distortion, and these need to be used so that we can learn appropriate thresholds. The variation of the brightness distortion is given by

$$a(i) = RMS(BD(i)) = \sqrt{\frac{\sum_{i=0}^{N-1} (\alpha(i) - 1)^2}{N}} \tag{9.23}$$

and the variation of the chrominance distortion as

$$b(i) = RMS(CD(i)) = \sqrt{\frac{\sum_{i=0}^{N-1} (CD(i))^2}{N}} \tag{9.24}$$

The values of $BD(i)$ and $CD(i)$ are then normalised to be in the same range as $a(i)$ and $b(i)$ as $NBD(i) = (BD(i) - 1)/a(i)$ and $NCD(i) = CD(i)/b(i)$. The background image is stored as

$$B(i) = \{E(i), s(i), a(i), b(i)\} \quad C\in\{R,G,B\} \tag{9.25}$$

By analysing the chrominance and brightness, the pixels in the current image can be classified as one of four categories:

1. the (original) background B: if the brightness and chrominance are similar to those of the original image;
2. the shadow S: if it has similar chrominance but lower brightness;
3. the highlighted background H: if it has similar chrominance and higher brightness and
4. the moving (foreground) object F: if it has different chrominance.

This is achieved by using thresholds T applied to $BD(i)$ and $CD(i)$. Our resulting image is then a set of labels (which can be represented as colours or shades) as

$$M(i) = \begin{vmatrix} F & \text{if} & NCD(i) > T_{CD} \quad \text{or} \quad NBD(i) < T_{BD\min} \\ B & \text{if} & NBD(i) < T_{BDlow} \quad \text{and} \quad NBD(i) > T_{BDhigh} \\ S & \text{if} & NBD(i) < 0 \\ H & & \text{otherwise} \end{vmatrix} \tag{9.26}$$

The foreground condition F avoids misclassifying dark pixels as shadow by including a brightness constraint. We now have a technique which splits an image into four categories, given a current image, a set of background images, and a few equations. As such, it is an alternative premise to the mixture of Gaussians approach, and one which was originally designed to handle shadows. An example of the technique's original application is given in Fig. 9.10 where the moving person has been separated from their static background, as has their shadow (beneath them).

9.2.4 Problems and advances

Many of the problems have been covered previously in that there are problems with shadows, changes in illumination, background motion, object fragmentation and practical concerns such as speed of operation, speed of adaption and memory requirements. There was one early survey on background estimation [Piccardi04], though it could be more comprehensive. There again, it covers the major techniques and aspects of practical concern – the inevitable compromise between speed and performance. There is a more recent review [Bouwmans14] which is much more complete. Since the problem is

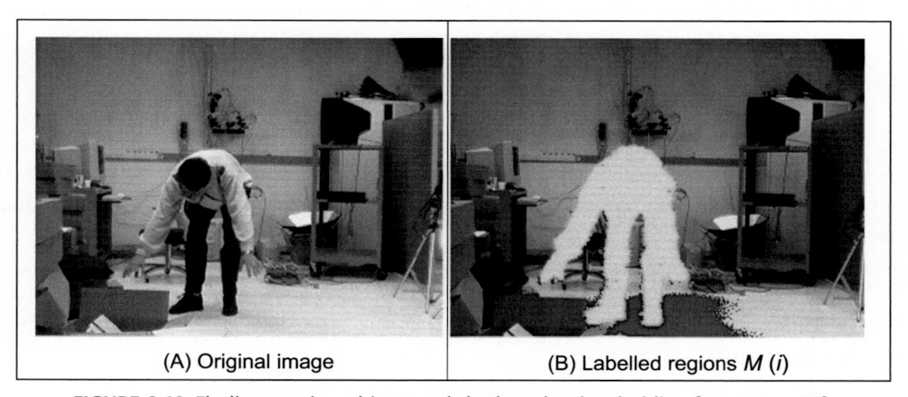

(A) Original image (B) Labelled regions $M(i)$

FIGURE 9.10 Finding moving objects and shadows by thresholding [Horprasert99].

germane to the analysis and detection of moving objects, there are many more approaches, e.g. [Ivanov00, Elgammal02]. The techniques can deliver an estimate of an object's silhouette, but problems remain which can only be sorted at a higher level. The first of these is to determine the track of the silhouette, the position of the object in successive image frames. Performance is the key here, and there have naturally been analyses of performance, concentrating especially on the data used for evaluation [Brutzer11, Sobral14].

9.3 Tracking moving features

9.3.1 Tracking moving objects

So far we have extracted moving objects from their background. To analyse movement, it is necessary to link the appearance of the object in successive frames, to determine the motion trajectory of the moving shape. This is called object *tracking*. This can be used for recognising moving objects (this can allow automated surveillance of urban areas e.g. to find subjects behaving suspiciously, or just for traffic analysis), to enable us to interact with computers (as in gesture recognition), to give facility for analysing video streams as in vehicle navigation (and for autonomous vehicles). It is actually wider than this, since air–ship traffic systems use radars and moving ships and aeroplanes are tracked as well.

We could simply aim to derive the trajectories by determining the nearest object in a successive frame. This assumes there has been little motion between the successive frames and that another moving object has not appeared close to the object of interest. It also assumes that the initial position of the object is known. We can constrain the procedure by using texture or appearance (e.g. colour), but this presumes in turn that the illumination does not change significantly between image frames. Clearly, this is a complex problem, since objects move and change in appearance and we want to determine which track was, or is being, taken. This is illustrated in Fig. 9.11 which shows the result of tracking a person walking in a sequence of video images, of which four are shown here. A black rectangle has been drawn around the walking subject in each frame and the parameters of this rectangle are delivered by the tracking algorithm. As the subject walks, the position of the rectangle is centred on the walking subject and the

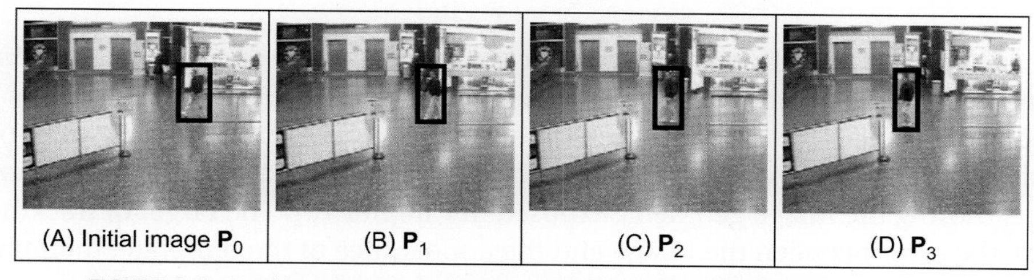

(A) Initial image $\mathbf{P}_0$ (B) $\mathbf{P}_1$ (C) $\mathbf{P}_2$ (D) $\mathbf{P}_3$

FIGURE 9.11 Tracking a walking subject (detected subject within black rectangle).

width of the rectangle changes as the subject's legs swing when walking. From this, we can then analyse the person and their motion.

One strategy is to determine the moving object, by background removal, and to then track points in the moving object. Another strategy is to determine interest points, such as corners, and to then track the appearance of these points in successive frames (and there is natural debate on which features to track [Shi94]). There has been an enormous effort in computer vision and many, very sophisticated, approaches have been made [Yilmaz06, Lepetit05]. We shall start with a basic approach before moving on to some of the more sophisticated approaches that are now available. We shall use the basic approach as a vehicle to emphasise performance requirement and then concentrate on the aspects of feature extraction and description consistent with the other approaches, rather than detail the tracking operations themselves since that is beyond the scope of this text and is left to the other literature in this field.

9.3.2 Tracking by local search

The *Lucas–Kanade* approach [Lucas81] is one of the original approaches to tracking. It is in fact a way of determining temporal alignment: if we can determine alignment then we can determine movement, so it is also a method for determining optical flow (Section 4.5). We shall follow a reflective analysis of the Lucas–Kanade approach [Baker04], to expose its iterative basis. Their analysis unifies the presentation of the approach and reformulates the technique, with computational advantage (and Matlab® code is available), though we shall concentrate on the basic approach only. (One rather nice touch is the use of an image of Takeo Kanade to illustrate the eponymous approach.) Though a simpler solution is available for optical flow, we are concerned here with tracking, and this implies arbitrary movement in the image. Essentially, we are concerned with determining the motion of an image template, or patch, from one frame to the next: we seek to align a template $\mathbf{T}(\mathbf{x})$ to an image $\mathbf{P}(\mathbf{x})$ where $\mathbf{x} = [x \quad y]^T$ is a vector of the pixel co-ordinates. The aim of tracking is to determine the motion from one image to the next. This motion is the *warp* (or projection) $\mathbf{W}(\mathbf{x}, \mathbf{p})$ which takes a template point to the image point. Different choices for the parameters $\mathbf{p}$ give different warps, and the point moves to a different place in a different way. If the position of a patch is to move within the image, a translation, then

$$\mathbf{W}(\mathbf{x}, \mathbf{p}) = \begin{bmatrix} x + p_1 \\ y + p_2 \end{bmatrix} \tag{9.27}$$

The warp is the mapping and the parameters p_1 and p_2 are the optical flow. As such there are links between tracking and between optical flow (Section 4.5): this is to be expected since optical flow is movement and tracking concerns estimating the position to which points have moved. The presentation here is general and maps to more dimensions (noting the image geometry exposed in Chapter 10). The target of tracking is to minimise the error between the image and the appearance of the template, then tracking has been achieved. This is expressed as minimising the difference between the image when warped to the template and the template itself. We then seek to minimise

$$\min \sum_{\mathbf{x}} (\mathbf{P}(\mathbf{W}(\mathbf{x},\mathbf{p})) - \mathbf{T}(\mathbf{x}))^2 \tag{9.28}$$

which minimises (for all values of the point co-ordinates $\mathbf{x}$) the sum of the differences squared between the projection of the image and the template. This is a new version of Eq. (4.93) which describes the error in estimating optical flow. The projection of the image is the warping of the image $\mathbf{P}$ via the warp factor $\mathbf{W}$ which is governed by the values for the parameters $\mathbf{p}$. We then need to determine the values of the parameters which minimise the summation. We then seek to add a small value $\Delta\mathbf{p}$ to the parameters and we shall iteratively seek new values for $\Delta\mathbf{p}$, forming at each iteration i the new values for the parameters $\mathbf{p}^{<i+1>} = \mathbf{p}^{<i>} + \Delta\mathbf{p}$ until the changes become small, $\Delta\mathbf{p} \to 0$. The first step is to perform a Taylor expansion on the projection to the new parameter values

$$\mathbf{P}(\mathbf{W}(\mathbf{x},\mathbf{p}+\Delta\mathbf{p})) = \mathbf{P}(\mathbf{W}(\mathbf{x},\mathbf{p})) + \nabla\mathbf{P}\frac{\partial \mathbf{W}}{\partial \mathbf{p}}\Delta\mathbf{p} \tag{9.29}$$

which ignores terms in $\Delta\mathbf{p}^2$ and higher (since $\Delta\mathbf{p}$ is small, higher-order terms become vanishingly small). This is then a different version of Eq. (4.96) used to calculate optical flow. In this, the term $\nabla\mathbf{P}$ is the gradient of the image $\mathbf{P}$, $\nabla\mathbf{P} = (\partial\mathbf{P}/\partial x \quad \partial\mathbf{P}/\partial y)$, computed from the image and then warped back into the template using the current value of $\mathbf{W}$. The differential term is actually called a Jacobian since it is a differential with respect to each of the parameters and then linearises the expression around these values as

$$\frac{\partial \mathbf{W}}{\partial \mathbf{p}} = \begin{bmatrix} \partial W_x/\partial p_1 & \partial W_x/\partial p_2 & \dots & \partial W_x/\partial p_n \\ \partial W_y/\partial p_1 & \partial W_y/\partial p_2 & \dots & \partial W_y/\partial p_n \end{bmatrix} \tag{9.30}$$

We can now substitute Eq. (9.29) into Eq. (9.28), and we seek to minimise

$$\min_{\Delta\mathbf{p}} \sum_{\mathbf{x}} \left(\mathbf{P}(\mathbf{W}(\mathbf{x},\mathbf{p})) + \nabla\mathbf{P}\frac{\partial \mathbf{W}}{\partial \mathbf{p}}\Delta\mathbf{p} - \mathbf{T}(\mathbf{x}) \right)^2 \tag{9.31}$$

By differentiation, the minimum is when the differential is zero, so by this

$$2\sum_{\mathbf{x}} \left(\nabla\mathbf{P}\frac{\partial \mathbf{W}}{\partial \mathbf{p}} \right)^T \left(\mathbf{P}(\mathbf{W}(\mathbf{x},\mathbf{p})) + \nabla\mathbf{P}\frac{\partial \mathbf{W}}{\partial \mathbf{p}}\Delta\mathbf{p} - \mathbf{T}(\mathbf{x}) \right) = 0 \tag{9.32}$$

which gives a solution for the parameter updates

$$\Delta\mathbf{p} = \mathbf{H}^{-1} \sum_{\mathbf{x}} \left(\nabla\mathbf{P}\frac{\partial \mathbf{W}}{\partial \mathbf{p}} \right)^T (\mathbf{T}(\mathbf{x}) - \mathbf{P}(\mathbf{W}(\mathbf{x},\mathbf{p}))) \tag{9.33}$$

where $\mathbf{H}$ is an approximation to the Hessian matrix

$$\mathbf{H} = \sum_{\mathbf{x}} \left(\nabla\mathbf{P}\frac{\partial \mathbf{W}}{\partial \mathbf{p}} \right)^T \left(\nabla\mathbf{P}\frac{\partial \mathbf{W}}{\partial \mathbf{p}} \right) \tag{9.34}$$

The updates are actually computed by steepest descent, we are forming the gradient of the change in a function with respect to parameters, and seeking the minimum of the function in that way. (Imagine a concave surface – like a bowl – and then bounce a ball downwards in direction of the surface normal, the ball will eventually locate the lowest point. With extreme luck it will get there in a single bounce, but it usually takes more.)

The stages of the algorithm are shown in Fig. 9.12. Essentially, the procedure aims to calculate values for the parameter updates, which are used in the next iteration of the algorithm, until the values for the updates are less than a chosen threshold. As with any algorithm, the devil tends to be in the detail. In the first stage, to project **P** to compute **P**(**W**(**x**,**p**)) requires interpolating the image **P** at sub pixel locations. Later, the gradient image **∇P** is computed from the image and then warped back into the template using the current value of **W**. To compute the Jacobian **∂W/∂p** the warps **W** need to be differentiable with respect to the parameters. In the case of simple projections, such as translation, the Jacobians are constant, but not for more complex cases. Further, we need to calculate the Hessian matrix **H** at each iteration (since it also depends on the current value of the parameters). The total cost of these operations is $O(n^2N^2 + n^3)$ for n parameters and an $N \times N$ image **P**. This can be reduced by later formulations [Baker04], thus leading to faster execution, and which also lead to reduced tracking error.

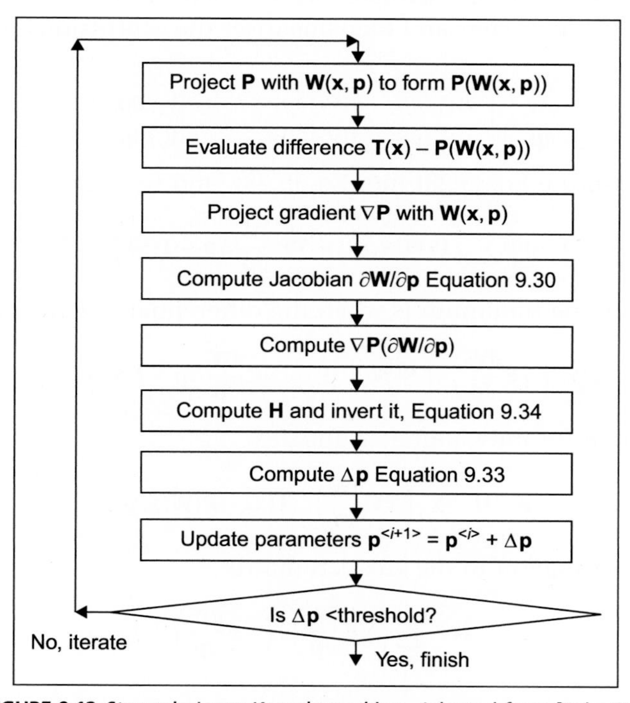

FIGURE 9.12 Stages in Lucas Kanade tracking. *Adapted from [Baker04].*

9.3.3 Problems in tracking

There are of course inherent problems which will be found with many approaches (and thence approaches which solve the problems). First there is initialisation – how do we start? After all, we are tracking from one frame to the next. Next – what about appearance? The object might move and rotate. In the Lucas–Kanade approach is one template enough for the appearance change, or can the template be modified or updated? Then there is illumination – the object will appear to change under varying illumination conditions (as in background subtraction). In the Lucas–Kanade approach, this means that the contribution by gradient information will change. There might also be a difficulty with conditioning – do the assumptions of the algorithm fit the chosen application? In Lucas–Kanade there has been a further assumption that we can ignore second-order terms since our first approximation is quite close, and there is an assumption that errors are of a normal distribution in the minimum least squares approach. Then – what happens under occlusion? The object might disappear from view for a few frames and the tracker needs either to re-initialise, or to continue tracking uninterrupted. Finally, there might be multiple objects in the same scene, with similar appearance properties and that can naturally confuse any tracking algorithm. These are part of the central difficulty in computer vision: there are some jobs which human vision can accomplish with ease, but which are much more complex in an automated analysis scenario.

9.3.4 Approaches to tracking

There is a rich selection of approaches to tracking and many depend on techniques which have been presented earlier. First, there is what precisely is tracked: this can be *points* or neighbourhoods, *kernels* or shapes, or tracking can be based on the object's *silhouette* or its perimeter.

In *point tracking*, we represent the object to be tracked as a set of points, or neighbourhoods. The earliest form of points used were low-level feature extraction such as edges (as such were available), colour, corners derived by the Harris operator or optical flow. Now the selection of operators extends to localised features. To determine an object's track, we seek to link points in one frame to points in the next, based on the previous object state which can include object position and motion. Naturally, allowing free motion makes the tracking problem very difficult, so it is usual to impose constraints on the tracking procedure, such as constraints on consistency (how fast can an object move), proximity (how much change in direction is likely) and rigidity (by how much an object can change shape) and in some formulations these are expressed as uncertainty, whereas they can also be fixed parameters. Points are tracked by solving for the correspondence deterministically, or by using a statistical approach. One early approach [Sethi87] solved for the *correspondence* by using a greedy approach constrained by proximity and rigidity. Later, this was extended [Veenman01] by enforcing a consistency on points that derive from the same object. Another of the earliest approaches [Broida86] used a statistical framework, the *Kalman filter*, to track points in noisy images. The Kalman filter is a recursive predictor–corrector framework based on the state space framework and which assumes that the noise is of a Gaussian distribution. Modelling an object's dynamics in this way can improve consistency in the tracking procedure. The limitation of the assumption of Gaussian noise can be alleviated using a *particle filter*, and there is an excellent textbook available which describes this [Blake98] though it is rather dated (in mitigation, full text can be downloaded and principles do not change). This develops the *condensation* (*Con*ditional *Dens*ity Propag*ation*) algorithm [Isard98] which can track objects through highly cluttered scenes. Multiple objects can be handled within the condensation approach and by proximity or consistency in *multiple hypothesis tracking* [Reid79] (which emphasises the link to radar analysis) for which an efficient implementation is available [Cox96]. The results of foreground/background segmentation (specifically the approach in Section 9.2.2) were tracked using Kalman filters [Stauffer00] for which multiple models were available within a multiple hypotheses tracking algorithm based on linear prediction, to achieve a real-time system.

In *kernel tracking*, a *template* is used to determine the position to which the object has moved. The template can be a simple shape, such as a circle, or more complex. Then, the matching procedure can be achieved by using Eq. (5.14) for a range of anticipated template positions (the vicinity within which the template is expected to move). Edge information found early use [Birchfield98] when using an ellipse to model a moving subject's head; others used 'dispersedness' to categorise objects which were tracked using templates [Lipton98]. Naturally consideration must be made for appearance change as the object moves within the image sequence: one approach is to adapt the template during the sequence. In the W^4 real-time approach (the name derives from Who? What? Where? When?) [Haritaoglu00], background detection was combined with shape analysis and tracking to locate people and their parts and to create models of their appearance to achieve tracking through interactions such as occlusions (and in groups). The mean-shift tracker [Comaniciu00, Comaniciu03] iteratively maximises the appearance similarity iteratively by comparing the histograms of the object and the window around the hypothesised object location, aiming to increase (histogram) similarity. The approaches can be used to detect and track shapes or silhouettes in multiple appearances by adaptation or by prediction.

9.3.5 MeanShift and Camshift

Camshift (*Continuously Adaptive Mean Shift*) is a kernel-based technique for object tracking [Bradsky98] that is widely used in applications like photography (i.e. face tracking), video surveillance and modern user interfaces. It is based on the *mean-shift* technique [Comaniciu00] and uses a histogram to represent a tracked object. The position of an object is computed by looking for the image location that maximises the similarity between the tracked object's histogram and the local image histogram. The maximisation process is formulated based on *non-parametric density estimation* and *gradient optimisation.*

9.3.5.1 Kernel-based density estimation

An object in an image can be characterised by considering that pixel values define a random variable. That is, by taking an image of an object, we obtain a sequence of numbers that describe the probability of obtaining particular pixel values when the object is located in an image. The characterisation can use raw pixel values that give features like grey level values or colours, but it is also possible to consider more complex characterisations of objects. In general, there is no rule for selecting the best features, but they are dependent on the application, the object and the background; simple features like grey level values can be useful in some applications, whilst complex features sometimes cannot disambiguate objects in complex scenes. Thus, to determine which features are useful in an application, it is necessary to evaluate how much they change from frame to frame and their capability of distinguishing objects form the background. For simplicity, in the examples in this section, we will illustrate the concepts by characterising objects using two-dimensional colour histograms. The presented formulation is very general and features can describe data in any dimension.

Since pixels can have a finite number of values, then they define a probability function $q_{\mathbf{s}}(\mathbf{y})$. In this notation, the symbol $\mathbf{s}$ represents the position of a fixed-size region where the probability is computed. A value of the function $q_{\mathbf{s}}(\mathbf{y})$ will be denoted as $q_{\mathbf{s}}(\mathbf{y}_u)$ and it gives the likelihood of obtaining a pixel with value $\mathbf{y}_u$. The feature obtained from a pixel $\mathbf{x}_i$ will be denoted as $\mathbf{y}_u = b(\mathbf{x}_i)$. Notice that $\mathbf{y}_u$ is a vector. For example, when using colour features, $\mathbf{y}_u$ can be a two-dimensional or a three-dimensional vector containing colour components. Thus, in a face tracking application, $q_{\mathbf{s}}(\mathbf{y}_u)$ can represent the probability that a given colour $\mathbf{y}_u$ can be found in the pixels representing a face, whilst in a sport tracking application $q_{\mathbf{s}}(\mathbf{y}_u)$ can define probabilities that characterise the players on the pitch.

In order to define a probability function, $q_{\mathbf{s}}(\mathbf{y})$ should be normalised. Thus, if n denotes the number of possible features, then

$$\sum_{u=1}^{n} q_{\mathbf{s}}(\mathbf{y}_u) = 1 \tag{9.35}$$

$q_{\mathbf{s}}(\mathbf{y})$ is generally called the density function since it is considered to be an approximation of a continuous function. However, in practice it is defined by a discrete set of values, so it can be formulated using a probability function.

In a parametric approach, the form of $q_{\mathbf{s}}(\mathbf{y})$ is known or assumed. Thus, pixel values are used to estimate the parameters of the probability function. For example, we could assume that $q_{\mathbf{s}}(\mathbf{y})$ is approximately normal, thus an object is described by estimating the mean and standard deviation. In a non-parametric approach, the function is not related to a particular density form, but the estimation computes probabilities for each of the values of the distribution. That is, it is necessary to estimate each value of $q_{\mathbf{s}}(\mathbf{y}_u)$.

A non-parametric estimate of $q_{\mathbf{s}}(\mathbf{y})$ is obtained by computing a normalised histogram. That is, by counting the value of each feature found in an image and by dividing each entry by the total number of features. That is,

$$q_{\mathbf{s}}(\mathbf{y}_u) = \frac{\sum\limits_{\mathbf{x}_i \in R_{\mathbf{s}} \wedge b(\mathbf{x}_i) = \mathbf{y}_u} K(\mathbf{s}, \mathbf{x}_i)}{m} \tag{9.36}$$

In this equation, m is the total number of features obtained from the image region $R_{\mathbf{s}}$, so the histogram is normalised. The summation is evaluated for each pixel $\mathbf{x}_i$ in the region $R_{\mathbf{s}}$ whose feature is $\mathbf{y}_u$. That is, if $K(\mathbf{s}, \mathbf{x}_i) = 1$, then this equation defines how many of the m features are equal to the feature $\mathbf{y}_u$. The function $K(\mathbf{s}, \mathbf{x}_i)$ is called the kernel, and Eq. (9.36) is called the kernel density estimator [Wand95].

Eq. (9.36) can also be written by using the delta function. That is,

$$q_{\mathbf{s}}(\mathbf{y}_u) = \frac{\sum\limits_{\mathbf{x}_i \in R_{\mathbf{s}}} K(\mathbf{s}, \mathbf{x}_i)\delta(b(\mathbf{x}_i) - \mathbf{y}_u)}{m} \tag{9.37}$$

Here, $\delta(b(\mathbf{x}_i) - \mathbf{y}_u)$ will be one if $b(\mathbf{x}_i) = \mathbf{y}_u$ and zero otherwise. In the Meanshift tracking technique, the kernel is selected such that it gives more importance to points closer to the centre of the region R_s than to the borders. This is convenient since the border of the region generally contains background values that do not belong to the object being tracked, but most importantly it makes the histogram smooth and biased towards the centre of the region. Thus, techniques based on gradient maximisation can effectively locate the tracked object. Two popular kernels are defined by the Gaussian and the Epanechnikov functions. The Gaussian kernel is defined by

$$K(\mathbf{s}, \mathbf{x}_i) = \frac{1}{2\pi h^2} e^{-\frac{\|\mathbf{s}-\mathbf{x}_i\|^2}{2h^2}} \tag{9.38}$$

The Epanechnikov kernel is defined by

$$K(\mathbf{s}, \mathbf{x}_i) = \begin{cases} \frac{3}{2}\left(1 - \left\|\frac{\mathbf{s} - \mathbf{x}_i}{h}\right\|^2\right) & \frac{\|\mathbf{s} - \mathbf{x}_i\|}{h} \leq 1 \\ 0 & \textit{otherwise} \end{cases} \tag{9.39}$$

These kernels are defined in two dimensions since they depend on pixel positions. However, they can be defined in any dimension. These equations use the same parameter h to indicate the size of the kernel. In practice, the value of h can be determined by empirical performance evaluations on test images. For the Gaussian kernel, the density defined in Eq. (9.36) is given by

$$q_{\mathbf{s}}(\mathbf{y}_u) = \frac{1}{2m\pi h^2} \sum_{\mathbf{x}_i \in R_{\mathbf{s}} \wedge b(\mathbf{x}_i) = \mathbf{y}_u} e^{-\frac{\|\mathbf{s}-\mathbf{x}_i\|^2}{2h^2}} \tag{9.40}$$

Since the kernel is applied to a limited region in an image, then it actually defines a truncated Gaussian. Thus, its area is not correctly normalised in Eq. (9.40). However, for simplicity in the presentation we will consider that the error is insignificant.

For the Epanechnikov kernel, the density in Eq. (9.36) is given by

$$q_{\mathbf{s}}(\mathbf{y}_u) = \frac{3}{2m} \sum_{\mathbf{x}_i \in R_{\mathbf{s}} \wedge b(\mathbf{x}_i) = \mathbf{y}_u \wedge \|\mathbf{s}-\mathbf{x}_i\| \le h} \left(1 - \left\| \frac{\mathbf{s}-\mathbf{x}_i}{h} \right\|^2\right) \tag{9.41}$$

In practice, both kernels are useful for object tracking. However, the Epanechnikov function is sometimes preferred since it produces simpler computations during the gradient optimisation (as we will see in the next section). The Gaussian kernel is also attractive since it has well-known properties.

Code 9.1 illustrates the implementation of Eq. (9.40). The function parameters are the image, the location of the tracking region, the region size and the kernel size h. The function uses as features the colour components C_b and C_r defined in Chapter 11. Thus, the entries $\mathbf{y}_u$ correspond to two-dimensional colour features, and image regions are characterised using a two-dimensional histogram. In the example code, the histogram is defined by the parameter `histSize`. The `colourScale` is the scale used to map 256 colour values to the histogram size. In applications, the size of the histogram should be determined by considering factors such as quantisation, noise, computational load and discrimination capability. In general, small histograms are good to avoid sparse distributions, are smooth and can handle changes in features created as the object moves. However, small histograms have less features, so have less ability to characterise or discriminate between similar objects.

Fig. 9.13 shows an example of the histograms obtained by using Code 9.1. The image in Fig. 9.13A shows a frame of a video sequence. The black square indicates the region to be tracked. The detail of this region is shown in Fig. 9.13B. The region has a size of 12x18 pixels. Figs. 9.13C–E show the histograms obtained by considering values of h. This

```
# Quantization scale
colourScale = 256.0 / histSize

# Create region image and histogram
histogram = createImageF(histSize, histSize)
sumValue = 0
for deltaX, deltaY in itertools.product(range(-regionRadius[0],regionRadius[0]),    \
                                        range(-regionRadius[1], regionRadius[1])):
    x, y  = position[0] + deltaX, position[1] + deltaY
    px,py = deltaX+regionRadius[0], deltaY+regionRadius[1]

    if x>0 and y>0 and x<width and y<height:
        w = exp(-(deltaX*deltaX + deltaY*deltaY)/(2*sigma*sigma))

        rgb = inputImage[y,x] / 256.0
        Cb = int((128 - 37.79*rgb[0] - 74.203*rgb[1] +    112*rgb[2])/colourScale)
        Cr = int((128 +    112*rgb[0] - 93.786*rgb[1] - 18.214*rgb[2])/colourScale)

        histogram[Cr,Cb] += w
        sumValue += w

for r,b in itertools.product(range(0, histSize), range(0, histSize)):
    histogram[r,b] /= sumValue
```

CODE 9.1 Density estimation.

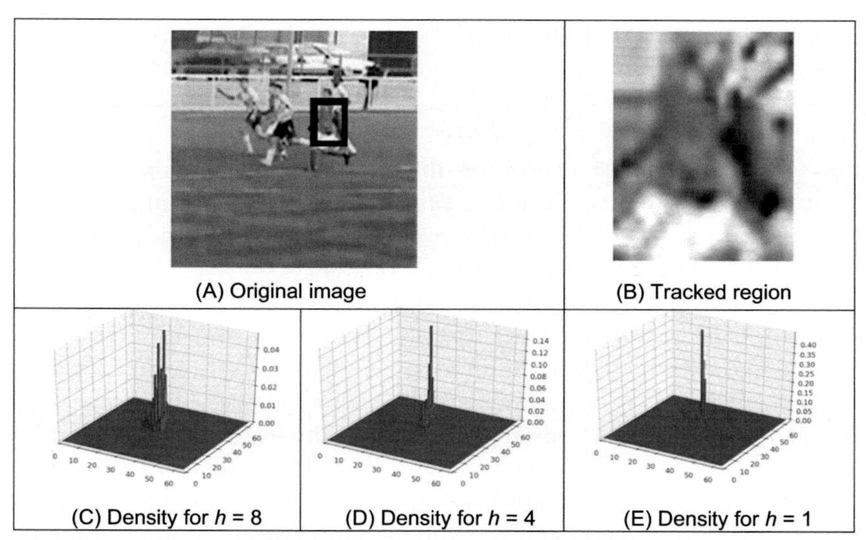
(A) Original image (B) Tracked region
(C) Density for $h = 8$ (D) Density for $h = 4$ (E) Density for $h = 1$

FIGURE 9.13 Example density estimation.

value is the standard deviation of the Gaussian function and it is given in pixels. As the value of h increases, the histograms have a smoother appearance and are less sparse. However, the region is characterised by less colours. In general, it is difficult to find an optimal value that provides a good convergence for tracking and that gives a good object characterisation in the feature space [Comaniciu03].

9.3.5.2 MeanShift tracking

9.3.5.2.1 Similarity function

The location of a region in an image sequence can be determined by searching for the position that maximises the similarity between the region's density and the image density. The search can be simplified by considering that the speed of the object and the frame rate of the sequence are such that the region's location does not change much. Thus, a neighbourhood close to the current target's positions gives a collection of target candidates $q_{\mathbf{s}}(\mathbf{y})$. In this section, we will use the symbol $\widehat{q}(\mathbf{y})$ to indicate the density characterising the tracking region. This density is obtained by considering the first frame of a sequence. Thus, it does not change during the tracking and consequently it does not depend on $\mathbf{s}$. As such, in order to determine the position of the tracked object, we can look for the position $\mathbf{s}$ that maximises the similarity between $\widehat{q}(\mathbf{y})$ and $q_{\mathbf{s}}(\mathbf{y})$. The similarity between densities can be measured by using the *Bhattacharyya coefficient*. According to this coefficient, the similarity at location $\mathbf{s}$ is defined as

$$r(\mathbf{s}) = \sum_{u=1}^{n} \sqrt{\widehat{q}(\mathbf{y}_u)\, q_{\mathbf{s}}(\mathbf{y}_u)} \tag{9.42}$$

Note that since the distributions are normalised, then this equation computes a dot product. That is,

$$r(\mathbf{s}) = \left[\sqrt{\widehat{q}(\mathbf{y}_1)}, \sqrt{\widehat{q}(\mathbf{y}_2)} \ldots, \sqrt{\widehat{q}(\mathbf{y}_n)}\right] \left[\sqrt{q_s(\mathbf{y}_1)}, \sqrt{q_s(\mathbf{y}_2)} \ldots, \sqrt{q_s(\mathbf{y}_n)}\right] \tag{9.43}$$

Since the dot product is equal to the cosine of the angle between the two vectors, then the coefficient will be one if the two distributions are equal and zero when they are completely different (i.e. orthogonal). The reason of using the square root of the values rather than the histogram entries is because the square root defines unitary vectors. That is, since the densities are normalised, then we have that the modulus of the vectors in Eq. (9.43) is unity. For example, for $q_{\mathbf{s}}(\mathbf{y})$ we have that

$$\sqrt{\left(\sqrt{q_{\mathbf{s}}(\mathbf{y}_1)}\right)^2 + \left(\sqrt{q_{\mathbf{s}}(\mathbf{y}_2)}\right)^2 + \ldots + \left(\sqrt{q_{\mathbf{s}}(\mathbf{y}_n)}\right)^2} = 1 \tag{9.44}$$

As such, a simple approach for tracking a region consists on finding the maximum by evaluating Eq. (9.42) for potential target locations. Unfortunately, this process is too intensive to be practical in applications. Thus, a more practical solution is to use gradient information to look for the local maximum. This can be implemented by approximating the function by using a Taylor series. That is, if we consider that the position of the object in the current frame defines the origin of $r(\mathbf{s})$, then a close value can be approximated by

$$r(\mathbf{s}) \approx r(\mathbf{s}_0) + \frac{dr(\mathbf{s}_0)}{d\mathbf{s}} \Delta_s \tag{9.45}$$

Here, $\mathbf{s}_0$ denotes the position in the current frame. Thus, the similarity value is approximated as the value in the origin plus a value in the direction of gradient. By developing Eq. (9.45) we have

$$r(\mathbf{s}) \approx \sum_{u=1}^{n} \sqrt{\widehat{q}(\mathbf{y}_u)\, q_{\mathbf{s}_0}(\mathbf{y}_u)} + \sum_{u=1}^{n} \frac{d\sqrt{\widehat{q}(\mathbf{y}_u)}\sqrt{q_{\mathbf{s}_0}(\mathbf{y}_u)}}{d\mathbf{s}} \Delta_s \tag{9.46}$$

By considering the derivate of the product in the second term,

$$\begin{aligned} r(\mathbf{s}) \approx & \sum_{u=1}^{n} \sqrt{\widehat{q}(\mathbf{y}_u)\, q_{\mathbf{s}_0}(\mathbf{y}_u)} + \frac{1}{2} \sum_{u=1}^{n} \sqrt{\frac{\widehat{q}(\mathbf{y}_u)}{q_{\mathbf{s}_0}(\mathbf{y}_u)}} \Delta_s \frac{dq_{\mathbf{s}_0}(\mathbf{y}_u)}{ds} + \\ & + \frac{1}{2} \sum_{u=1}^{n} \sqrt{\frac{q_{\mathbf{s}_0}(\mathbf{y}_u)}{\widehat{q}(\mathbf{y}_u)}} \Delta_s \frac{d\widehat{q}(\mathbf{y}_u)}{ds} \end{aligned} \tag{9.47}$$

The last term evaluates the derivative of a constant. Thus,

$$r(\mathbf{s}) \approx \sum_{u=1}^{n} \sqrt{\widehat{q}(\mathbf{y}_u) q_{\mathbf{s}_0}(\mathbf{y}_u)} + \frac{1}{2} \sum_{u=1}^{n} \sqrt{\frac{\widehat{q}(\mathbf{y}_u)}{q_{\mathbf{s}_0}(\mathbf{y}_u)}} \Delta_s \frac{dq_{\mathbf{s}_0}(\mathbf{y}_u)}{ds} \tag{9.48}$$

Since Δ_s is small, then the derivative can be approximated by $q_s - q_{s_0}$. Since q_{s_0} is constant, then the maximum can be found by

$$r(\mathbf{s}) \approx \sum_{u=1}^{n} \sqrt{\widehat{q}(\mathbf{y}_u) q_{\mathbf{s}_0}(\mathbf{y}_u)} + \frac{1}{2} \sum_{u=1}^{n} q_{\mathbf{s}}(\mathbf{y}_u) \sqrt{\frac{\widehat{q}(\mathbf{y}_u)}{q_{\mathbf{s}_0}(\mathbf{y}_u)}} \tag{9.49}$$

The summation in the first term of this equation is independent of **s**, thus the maximum can be obtained by only considering the second term. This term will be denoted as $\widehat{r}(\mathbf{s})$. Thus, the best location is obtained by finding the maximum of

$$\widehat{r}(\mathbf{s}) = \frac{1}{2} \sum_{u=1}^{n} q_{\mathbf{s}}(\mathbf{y}_u) \sqrt{\frac{\widehat{q}(\mathbf{y}_u)}{q_{\mathbf{s}_0}(\mathbf{y}_u)}} \tag{9.50}$$

By using the definition in Eq. (9.37), this equation can be rewritten as

$$\widehat{r}(\mathbf{s}) = \frac{1}{2m} \sum_{u=1}^{n} \sum_{\mathbf{x}_i \in R_{\mathbf{s}}} K(\mathbf{s}, \mathbf{x}_i) \delta(b(\mathbf{x}_i) - \mathbf{y}_u) \sqrt{\frac{\widehat{q}(\mathbf{y}_u)}{q_{\mathbf{s}_0}(\mathbf{y}_u)}} \tag{9.51}$$

This equation provides an estimate of the similarity of a region at position **s** given the initial distribution of the region (i.e. $\widehat{q}(\mathbf{y}_u)$) and the distribution of the region at the current tracking position (i.e. $q_{\mathbf{s}_0}(\mathbf{x})$). Eq. (9.51) can be re-arranged as

$$\widehat{r}(\mathbf{s}) = \frac{1}{2m} \sum_{\mathbf{x}_i \in R_{\mathbf{s}}} K(\mathbf{s}, \mathbf{x}_i) \sum_{u=1}^{n} \delta(b(\mathbf{x}_i) - \mathbf{y}_u) \sqrt{\frac{\widehat{q}(\mathbf{y}_u)}{q_{\mathbf{s}_0}(\mathbf{y}_u)}} \tag{9.52}$$

That is,

$$\widehat{r}(\mathbf{s}) = \frac{1}{2m} \sum_{\mathbf{x}_i \in R_{\mathbf{s}}} W_{\mathbf{s}_0}(\mathbf{x}_i) \; K(\mathbf{s}, \mathbf{x}_i) \tag{9.53}$$

for

$$W_{\mathbf{s}_0}(\mathbf{x}_i) = \sum_{u=1}^{n} \delta(b(\mathbf{x}_i) - \mathbf{y}_u) \sqrt{\frac{\widehat{q}(\mathbf{y}_u)}{q_{\mathbf{s}_0}(\mathbf{y}_u)}} \tag{9.54}$$

As such, the problem of finding the maximum of Eq. (9.42) can be solved by finding the maximum of Eq. (9.53). Notice that the approximation assumes that $r(\mathbf{s})$ is smooth at the region close to the current solution, so the function can be approximated by a second-order Taylor series. The maximum of Eq. (9.53) can be found by gradient optimisation that is formulated using the concepts of *kernel profiles* and *shadow kernels.*

9.3.5.2.2 Kernel profiles and shadow kernels

In gradient optimisation techniques, kernels are differentiated to obtain the direction of the maxima or the minima of a function. In some cases, this process can be simplified by a re-parameterisation of the kernel such that the kernel, and thus the optimisation problem, can be solved in a lower dimension. The new parameterisation is called the profile of the kernel and for the kernels in Eqs. (9.38) and (9.39) defined by

$$K(\mathbf{s}, \mathbf{x}_i) = k\left(\left\|\frac{\mathbf{s} - \mathbf{x}_i}{h}\right\|^2\right) \tag{9.55}$$

Note that k and K are the same function but with a change of variable. We will denote the new variable as

$$a = \left\| \frac{\mathbf{s} - \mathbf{x}_i}{h} \right\|^2 \tag{9.56}$$

As such, for the Gaussian kernel in Eq. (9.38), we have

$$k(a) = \frac{1}{2\pi h^2} e^{-\frac{1}{2}a} \tag{9.57}$$

For the kernel in Eq. (9.39), we have

$$k(a) = \begin{cases} \frac{3}{2}(1-a) & \sqrt{a} \leq 1 \\ 0 & otherwise \end{cases} \tag{9.58}$$

Thus, the differential of the kernel can be expressed using the profile kernel as

$$\frac{dK(\mathbf{s}, \mathbf{x}_i)}{d\mathbf{x}} = \frac{dk(a)}{da} \frac{da}{d\mathbf{x}} \tag{9.59}$$

That is,

$$\frac{dK(\mathbf{s}, \mathbf{x}_i)}{d\mathbf{x}} = \frac{2}{h}(\mathbf{s} - \mathbf{x}_i)\ k'\left(\left\| \frac{\mathbf{s} - \mathbf{x}_i}{h} \right\|^2 \right) \tag{9.60}$$

This equation can be rewritten as

$$\frac{dK(\mathbf{s}, \mathbf{x}_i)}{d\mathbf{x}} = \frac{2}{h}(\mathbf{x}_i - \mathbf{s})\ g\left(\left\| \frac{\mathbf{s} - \mathbf{x}_i}{h} \right\|^2 \right) \tag{9.61}$$

for

$$g\left(\left\| \frac{\mathbf{s} - \mathbf{x}_i}{h} \right\|^2 \right) = -k'\left(\left\| \frac{\mathbf{s} - \mathbf{x}_i}{h} \right\|^2 \right) \tag{9.62}$$

The function g is called the *shadow kernel*. According to this definition, the shadow kernel for the Gaussian kernel in Eq. (9.57) is

$$g(a) = \frac{1}{4\pi h^2} e^{-\frac{1}{2}a} \tag{9.63}$$

That is, the Gaussian kernel and its shadow kernel are the same. For the Epanechnikov kernel in Eq. (9.58), we have that

$$k(a) = \begin{cases} 3/2 & \sqrt{a} \leq 1 \\ 0 & otherwise \end{cases} \tag{9.64}$$

That is, the shadow kernel is defined by a flat kernel. Since the computations of a flat kernel are simple, then the Epanechnikov kernel is very attractive for gradient optimisation implementations.

9.3.5.2.3 Gradient maximisation

The maxima of Eq. (9.53) can be obtained by an iterative procedure that looks for a path along the direction of the derivative. The direction is defined by the gradient of the function. Thus, a step ascent in the similarity function in Eq. (9.53) is given by

$$\mathbf{s}_{+1} = \mathbf{s} + \nabla\hat{r}(\mathbf{s})\Delta_s \tag{9.65}$$

Here $\mathbf{s}_{+1}$ is a new position obtained from the current position $\mathbf{s}$ by moving into the direction of the gradient with a step Δ_s. In an iterative process, the new position becomes the current position, and Eq. (9.65) is re-evaluated until the solution converges. According to Eq. (9.53), the gradient in Eq. (9.65) is given by

$$\nabla\hat{r}(\mathbf{s}) = \frac{1}{2m}\sum_{\mathbf{x}_i \in R_\mathbf{s}} W_{\mathbf{s}_0}(\mathbf{x}_i)\,\frac{dK(\mathbf{s},\mathbf{x}_i)}{d\mathbf{x}} \tag{9.66}$$

By considering Eq. (9.61), we can rewrite this equation using the shadow kernel. That is,

$$\nabla\hat{r}(\mathbf{s}) = \frac{2}{2mh}\sum_{\mathbf{x}_i \in R_\mathbf{s}} (\mathbf{x}_i - \mathbf{s})W_{\mathbf{s}_0}(\mathbf{x}_i)g\left(\left\|\frac{\mathbf{s}-\mathbf{x}_i}{h}\right\|^2\right) \tag{9.67}$$

By developing the multiplication terms in this equation we have that

$$\nabla\hat{r}(\mathbf{s}) = \frac{2}{2mh}\sum_{\mathbf{x}_i \in R_\mathbf{s}} \mathbf{x}_i W_{\mathbf{s}_0}(\mathbf{x}_i)\, g\left(\left\|\frac{\mathbf{s}-\mathbf{x}_i}{h}\right\|^2\right) - \frac{2}{2mh}\mathbf{s}\sum_{\mathbf{x}_i \in R_\mathbf{s}} W_{\mathbf{s}_0}(\mathbf{x}_i)\, g\left(\left\|\frac{\mathbf{s}-\mathbf{x}_i}{h}\right\|^2\right) \tag{9.68}$$

By dividing both sides by the last summation we have that

$$\frac{\nabla\hat{r}(\mathbf{s})}{p(\mathbf{s})} = \frac{\sum_{\mathbf{x}_i \in R_\mathbf{s}} \mathbf{x}_i W_{\mathbf{s}_0}(\mathbf{x}_i)\, g\left(\left\|\frac{\mathbf{s}-\mathbf{x}_i}{h}\right\|^2\right)}{p(\mathbf{s})} - \mathbf{s} \tag{9.69}$$

for

$$p(\mathbf{s}) = \frac{2}{2mh}\sum_{\mathbf{x}_i \in R_\mathbf{s}} W_{\mathbf{s}_0}(\mathbf{x}_i)\, g\left(\left\|\frac{\mathbf{s}-\mathbf{x}_i}{h}\right\|^2\right) \tag{9.70}$$

Eq. (9.69) defines the *mean shift*, and it corresponds to a step in the direction of the maximum (i.e. the gradient). If we consider that $\nabla\hat{r}(\mathbf{s})\frac{1}{p(\mathbf{s})} = \nabla\hat{r}(\mathbf{s})\Delta_s$, then the magnitude of the step is inversely proportional to the distance to the maximum. By substituting Eq. (9.69) into Eq. (9.65), we have

$$\mathbf{s}_{+1} = \mathbf{s} + \frac{\sum_{\mathbf{x}_i \in R_\mathbf{s}} \mathbf{x}_i W_{\mathbf{s}_0}(\mathbf{x}_i)\, g\left(\left\|\frac{\mathbf{s}-\mathbf{x}_i}{h}\right\|^2\right)}{p(\mathbf{s})} - \mathbf{s} \tag{9.71}$$

That is, a position in the maximum direction is determined by

$$\mathbf{s}_{+1} = \frac{\sum_{\mathbf{x}_i \in R_\mathbf{s}} \mathbf{x}_i W_{\mathbf{s}_0}(\mathbf{x}_i)\, g\left(\left\| \frac{\mathbf{s} - \mathbf{x}_i}{h} \right\|^2\right)}{p(\mathbf{s})} \tag{9.72}$$

This equation is simply defining the weighted mean of the positions in the region. Thus, the position is moved towards the current local estimation of the mean. Successive steps will lead to the local maxima of the function.

Code 9.2 illustrates an implementation of Eq. (9.72). The main loop computes the position of the tracking region for each frame. A new position `newPos` is obtained from the original density `q` of the region with size `sizeReg`. The array `q` is computed according to Code 9.1 for frame 0. To obtain the position in a frame, the code first computes the density `qs` from the frame image and the current position. The densities `q` and `qs` are used to obtain the values defined in Eq. (9.54). The result is stored in the array `weights`. Finally, the summations in Eq. (9.72) are evaluated and the new position is estimated. The new position in a frame is refined using the updated region position until there is no change in the region's position. Fig. 9.14 shows the results obtained by using the implementation in Code 9.2 for tracking a region in six frames.

9.3.5.3 Camshift technique

One of the problems of the Meanshift technique is that since size of a tracking object in an image depends on the distance between the object and the camera, then the tracking can fail when the same region size is maintained in all image frames. The *Camshift* technique [Bradski98] is an adaptation of the Meanshift method that re-computes the region distribution at each frame by considering changes in region size. The sizes of the regions are determined by using moments on the *back-projection* image.

The back-projection image is obtained by setting the value of each pixel to be equal to the entry in the region's histogram. That is, the value in a pixel $\mathbf{x}_i$ is given by

$$p(\mathbf{x}_i) = q_\mathbf{s}(b(\mathbf{x}_i)) \tag{9.73}$$

Thus, the image value $p(\mathbf{x}_i)$ defines the probability that the pixel $\mathbf{x}_i$ belongs to the image from where the histogram was computed. Code 9.3 illustrates the implementation of the process described by Eq. (9.73). The implementation assigns the histogram value to the pixel value. Notice that in practice, the Camshift method only requires computation of the back projection for pixels close to the tracking region; however, for simplicity and illustration purposes, Code 9.3 computes the probabilities for all the image.

Fig. 9.15 shows an example of a result obtained by using Code 9.3. This image was obtained by computing a histogram from the region in Fig. 9.14A. This histogram is then back projected in the image. In the result image, white values represent pixels that are probably part of the tracking region. It is important to mention that in order to reduce the influence of pixels in the background, the histogram can be computed by using a weighting as described in Eq. (9.36). For example, for the region in Fig. 9.14A, the green

```
# Process frames
numImages = len(imageNames)
for frameNum in range(1, numImages):

    inputImage, _, _ = imageReadRGB(pathToDir + imageNames[frameNum])

    currPos = [0, 0]
    newPos = positions[frameNum-1]
    while(currPos != newPos):
        currPos = newPos
        qs = densityHistogram(inputImage, currPos, sizeReg, sigma, histoSize)

        # Weights
        for deltaX, deltaY in itertools.product(range(-sizeReg[0],sizeReg[0]),    \
                                                range(-sizeReg[1], sizeReg[1])):
            # Position of the pixel in the image and in the weight array
            x, y = currPos[0] + deltaX, currPos[1] + deltaY
            px, py = deltaX+sizeReg[0], deltaY+sizeReg[1]

            # Features
            Cb, Cr= colourFeature(inputImage[y,x], colourScale)

            # Update
            if qs[Cr, Cb] == 0:
                qs[Cr, Cb] = epsilon
            weights[py, px] = sqrt(q[Cr, Cb] / qs[Cr, Cb])

        # Compute mean shift sums
        meanSum = [0, 0]
        kernelSum = 0
        for deltaX, deltaY in itertools.product(range(-sizeReg[0], sizeReg[0]),   \
                                                range(-sizeReg[1], sizeReg[1])):
            # Position of the pixel in the image
            x, y  = currPos[0] + deltaX, currPos[1] + deltaY

            # Kernel parameter
            w = exp(-(deltaX*deltaX + deltaY*deltaY)/(2*sigma*sigma));

            # Weight index
            px, py = deltaX+sizeReg[0], deltaY+sizeReg[1]

            # Mean sum
            meanSum[0] += w * weights[py, px] * x
            meanSum[1] += w * weights[py, px] * y

            # Kernel sum
            kernelSum += w * weights[py, px]

        # Mean shift
        newPos = [int(meanSum[0] / kernelSum), int(meanSum[1] / kernelSum)]

    positions.append(newPos);
```

CODE 9.2 Meanshift.

values in the background (i.e. the grass) should not have a significant contribution in the histogram. Otherwise, the back-projection image will have probabilities that can make the tracking region increase in size at each iteration.

As illustrated in Fig. 9.15, the back-projection image gives a hint of the position and size of the tracked region. The Camshift technique is developed on this observation; it

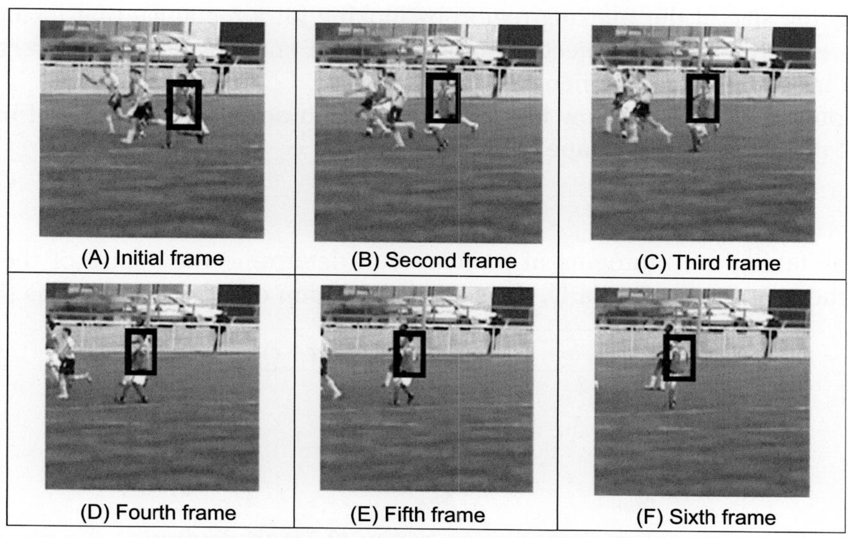

FIGURE 9.14 Example results of the Meanshift technique.

```
projection = createImageF(width, height)
for x, y in itertools.product(range(0,width), range(0, height)):
    Cb,Cr = colourFeature(image[y,x], colourScale)
    projection [y,x] = q[Cr,Cb]
```

CODE 9.3 Back-projection.

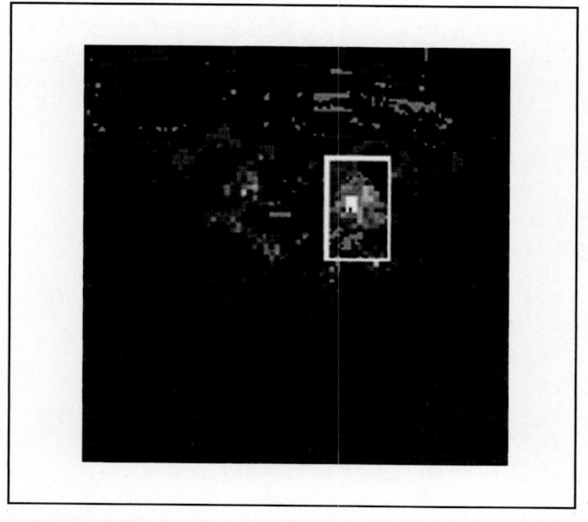

FIGURE 9.15 Back-projection of the first frame in the image.

determines the size of the tracking region by looking for a rectangle that includes high values close to the current object position. The size and position of the rectangle is computed by using image moments.

In Chapter 7, we showed how image moments can describe the shape of image regions, and the centre of the shape is determined by

$$x_c = \frac{M_{10}}{M_{00}} \qquad y_c = \frac{M_{01}}{M_{10}} \tag{9.74}$$

Thus, by taking the moments of $p(\mathbf{x}_i)$ we can determine the centre of the tracked region in the next frame. Similarly, the size of the region can be computed as [Horn86].

$$S_x = \sqrt{\frac{(a+c)+\sqrt{b^2+(a-c)}}{2}} \qquad S_y = \sqrt{\frac{(a+c)-\sqrt{b^2+(a-c)}}{2}} \tag{9.75}$$

for

$$a = \frac{M_{20}}{M_{00}} - x_c^2 \qquad b = 2\frac{M_{11}}{M_{00}} - x_c y_c \qquad c = \frac{M_{02}}{M_{00}} - y_c^2 \tag{9.76}$$

Code 9.4 illustrates an implementation of Eq. (9.75) to determine the position and size of the tracking regions. In this example code, there are computed the moments of two projected images that represent the previous and current frames. These are stored in

```
ps, pt = positions[0], positions[1]
sizeSearch = [int(sizeReg[0] *1.5), int(sizeReg[1] *1.5)]
for deltaX, deltaY in itertools.product(range(-sizeSearch[0], sizeSearch[0]),    \
                                        range(-sizeSearch[1], sizeSearch[1])):
    xs, ys  = ps[0] + deltaX, ps[1] + deltaY
    xt, yt  = pt[0] + deltaX, pt[1] + deltaY
    for m,n in itertools.product(range(0, 3), range(0, 3)):
        momS[n,m] += (xs**n) * (ys**m) * projectionSource[y,x]
        momT[n,m] += (xt**n) * (yt**m) * projectionTarget[y,x]

# Compute sxS, syS, the size of the projection in previous frame
xc,yc = momS[1,0]/momS[0,0], momS[0,1]/momS[0,0]
a = momS[2,0]/momS[0,0] - xc*xc;
b = 2*(momS[1,1]/momS[0,0] - xc * yc);
c = momS[0,2]/momS[0,0]- yc*yc;
sxS = int(sqrt((a+c-sqrt(b*b+(a-c)*(a-c))/2)));
syS = int(sqrt((a+c+sqrt(b*b+(a-c)*(a-c))/2)));

# Compute sx, sy, the size of the projection in current frame
xc,yc = momT[1,0]/momT[0,0], momT[0,1]/momT[0,0]
a = momT[2,0]/momT[0,0] - xc*xc;
b = 2*(momT[1,1]/momT[0,0] - xc * yc);
c = momT[0,2]/momT[0,0]- yc*yc;
sx = int(sqrt((a+c-sqrt(b*b+(a-c)*(a-c))/2)));
sy = int(sqrt((a+c+sqrt(b*b+(a-c)*(a-c))/2)));

#Determine size of the region in current frame
sy = sy * sizeReg[1] /  syS
sx = sx * sizeReg[0] /  sxS
```

CODE 9.4 Region size computation.

the momS and momT arrays. The ps and pt variables store the positions of the previous frame and the new position obtained by using the MeanShift for the current frame. The computation of the new size combines the sizes given by the moments and the size of the tracked region in the previous frame. The idea is to change the size of the tracking region in proportion of the change of the region defined by the moments. That is, it computes the size by observing a relationship between the size of the moments and the size of the tracked region.

Code 9.5 shows the use of projection and region size computation in CamShift. First, the density used for the tracking and the back projection of the first frame are computed. Then, for each frame, the code obtains a new position newPos by using the MeanShift technique. The back-projection of the current frame and the position computed by MeanShift are then used to update the size and position of the tracked region according to the computations described in Code 9.4. That is, by using the moments of the projections of current and previous frames.

Fig. 9.16 shows an example of the tracking obtained by using the region estimation in Code 9.5. In this example, although the tracked objects are moving without large change in the camera and object distances, Camshift obtains regions that change in vertical and horizontal size due to the change in position of the players.

9.3.6 Other approaches

Tracking is attractive since it is required by many applications though it is naturally a difficult task and there are problems with occlusion, especially in indoor scenes; lighting, especially in outdoor scenes; clutter; and occlusion, by indoor or street furniture. An allied field concerns target tracking in, say, radar imagery – as used in air traffic control.

```
# Density and back projection of the region to track
q = densityHistogram(inputImage, positions[0], sizeReg, sigma, histoSize)
backProjImage = backProjectionImage(inputImage, q, histoSize)

# Process frames
numImages = len(imageNames)
for frameNum in range(1, numImages):

    currentImage, _, _ = imageReadRGB(pathToDir + imageNames[frameNum])
    newPos = meanShift(currentImage,q,sizeReg,sigma,histoSize,positions[frameNum-1])

    # Back project
    newBackProjImage = backProjectionImage(currentImage, q, histoSize)
    pos,newSize = regionSize(backProjImage, newBackProjImage,                    \
                             positions[frameNum-1], newPos, sizeReg)
    positions.append(pos)
    sizes.append(newSize)

    # Update density and image
    inputImage = currentImage
    sizeReg = newSize
    backProjImage = newBackProjImage
```

CODE 9.5 CamShift tracking.

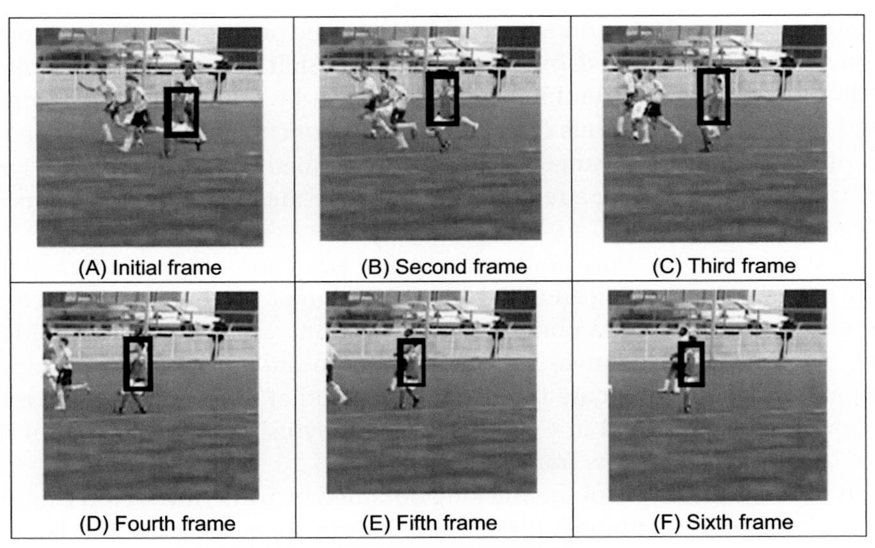

FIGURE 9.16 Example results of the Camshift technique.

We shall explore some of the newer approaches and newer data, but the interested reader must note that it is a field which continues to progress and satisfy more challenging application requirements.

The more advanced approaches couple object detection with tracking [Leibe08] which can reconcile difficulty with large changes in background and when the camera itself might be moved, unlike the classic (static) background subtraction methods. The procedure also aims to avoid drift in the estimates of position, which can be inherent in such scenarios. One approach [Leibe08] employed an object detection framework was a probabilistic extension of the Generalised Hough Transform, using learning (though HoG could equally have been used). Tracking can add a temporal context to the detections and can be used to predict future locations. The best set of trajectories were selected from those which by homologising the positions of the detected objects with the hypothetical trajectories from a simple (first-order) dynamical model. The task is to determine the object location given constraints that two objects can neither be in the same place at the same time nor account for the same pixels simultaneously. The process uses automatically derived scene geometry to reconcile the object detection and tracking processes (should two objects appear in the same place in an image then the object furthest from the camera must be occluded by the nearest object), whilst implicitly handling multiple objects. This leads to a system demonstrated to be able to track cars and people, in data derived from moving cameras. Another approach [Huang08] considered ability to track within crowded scenes, where objects can have similar appearances. Arguing that approaches to object detection are insufficient and lead to missed detections, false alarms or error, the approach used a hierarchical process from short segments to longer tracks, including scene ingress and egress points, and shown capable of tracking people in two popular datasets. The *Tracking–Learning–Detection (TLD)* approach [Kalal10a, Kalal10b] is an algorithm that simultaneously tracks, learns and detects an unknown object in a video stream. TLD makes minimal assumptions about the object, the scene or the camera's motion. It requires only initialisation by a bounding box and operates in real-time, as has been shown on YouTube.

Aiming to increase robustness of object detection for tracking, Stalder introduced [Stalder10] *Cascaded Confidence Filtering (CCF)* which incorporates constraints on the size of the object, on the preponderance of the background and on the smoothness of trajectories to adapt a generic person detector to a specific scene. The approach was demonstrated to better enable tracking by detection on complex data derived from an industrial scene, as shown in Fig. 9.17. Here, the images are of workers assembling a car from parts, and the detections of the workers are shown [Stalder10]. Note the high level of occlusion and clutter within the viewed scene, and the moving people are identified successfully (except in one case in Fig. 9.17C – but also note the apparent similarity between the person and his background).

The approach achieves its success by incorporating many previously described approaches in stages and the example results of the result of each added stage are shown in Fig. 9.18 [Stalder10]. This is an image from a sequence of images (and detections) wherein the workers move parts to a welding station. First, the object detector is HoG, and this is reconciled with scene geometry to give a geometric filter, with best result of detecting a single subject in Fig. 9.18A. A background filter derived from mixture of Gaussians can increase the ability to differentiate a subject from their background, allowing detection of the previously undetected workers, Fig. 9.18B. The trajectory filter allows for temporal consistency allowing for detection of other workers who would have been visible in previous (or successive) image frames, Fig. 9.18C. A particle filter is used in post-processing to enhance possible structures which might be (missed) trajectories.

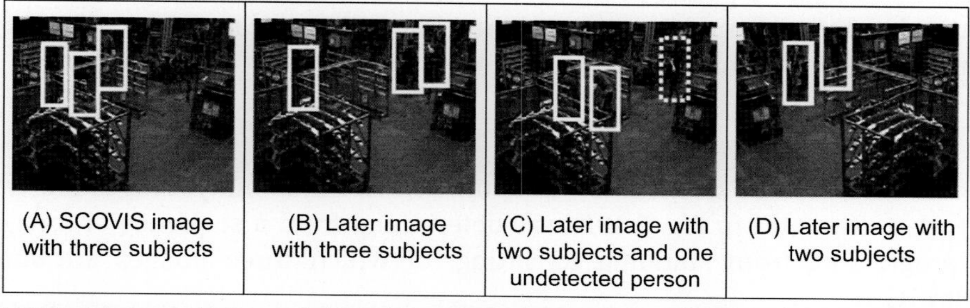

(A) SCOVIS image with three subjects
(B) Later image with three subjects
(C) Later image with two subjects and one undetected person
(D) Later image with two subjects

FIGURE 9.17 Tracking people in an industrial scene (detected subjects within white rectangles; undetected subjects within dotted rectangle).

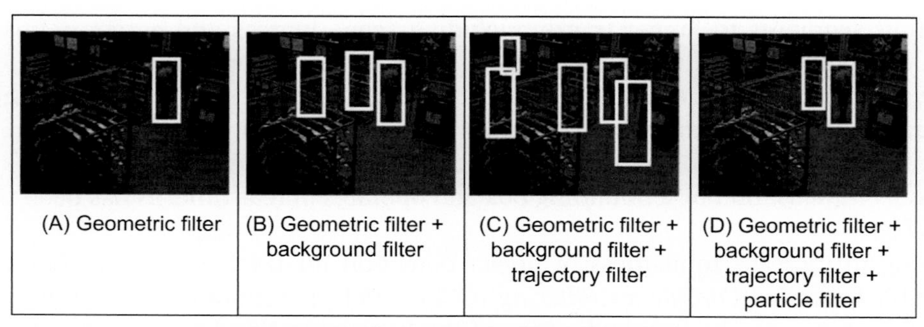

FIGURE 9.18 Including detection approaches in tracking.

9.4 Moving feature extraction and description

9.4.1 Moving (biological) shape analysis

If we are to find and recognise moving shapes the approach depends on their basic nature. If the shape is that of a man-made object, then we can deploy the object detection approaches of Section 9.2 and the tracking approaches of Section 9.3 so as to derive a trajectory from which the motion can be determined. Certainly these techniques can operate at high speed, especially when compared with later approaches but can lack an explicit model of the tracked object. The tracking procedure does depend on appearance, and viewpoint invariant approaches are those which can recognise an object irrespective of the pose of the object relative to the direction of view of a camera. Alternatively, we may seek to find and recognise biological shapes which deform as the subject moves.

One of the first approaches to representing movement for recognition purposes aimed to recognise motion alone. The motion can be described by a *Motion Energy Image (MEI)* which shows where motion has occurred (over the whole sequence) and a *Motion History Image (MHI)* which shows how recent the motion was. The MHI values occur at the positions of points in the MHI image, and the distinction between the two was used to increase discriminatory capability. The MEI was calculated as a function of the temporal extent of movement (τ) as

$$\text{MEI}(\tau)_{t_{x,y}} = \bigcup_{t=0}^{\tau-1} \mathbf{P}_{t-1_{x,y}} \tag{9.77}$$

and the value of τ can be determined to optimise discriminability. This is illustrated in Fig. 9.19 where the MEI in Fig. 9.19D was determined from a sequence of images, of a subject progressing from standing to sitting, of which three images are shown in Figs. 9.19A–C.

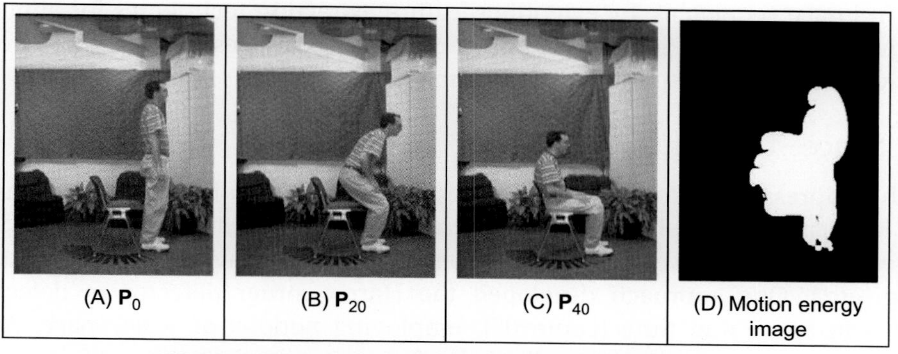

FIGURE 9.19 Determining a motion energy image [Bobick01].

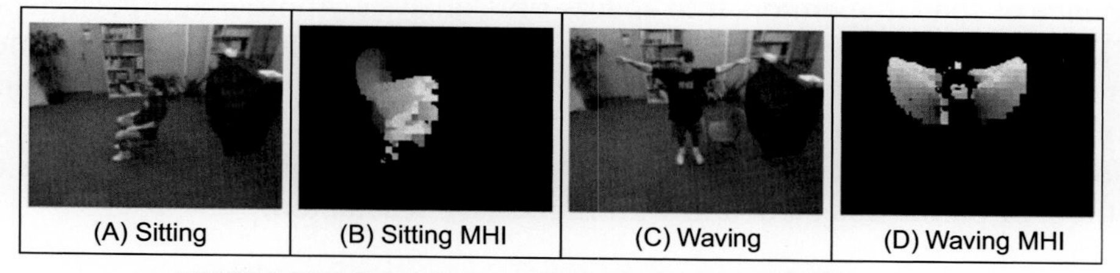

FIGURE 9.20 Determining a motion history image (MHI) [Bobick01].

The MHI, illustrated in Fig. 9.20, was calculated as

$$\text{MHI}(\tau)_{t_{x,y}} = \begin{vmatrix} \tau & \mathbf{P}_{t_{x,y}} = 1 \\ \max\left(0, \text{MHI}(\tau)_{t-1_{x,y}} - 1\right) & \mathbf{P}_{t_{x,y}} \neq 1 \end{vmatrix} \tag{9.78}$$

Hu invariant moments were used to describe the MEI and MHI images, and the Mahalanobis distance was calculated between the moment descriptions. Thus, multiple video sequences were recorded of separate actions at different view angles. The Hu moments were observed to smooth the description of movement and the actions could be recognised/discriminated successfully.

There has been considerable (and continuing) research in (human) action recognition [Poppe10], and this has been accompanied by development of standardised datasets and evaluations. In motion analysis and recognition, the recovery of human poses and motion from image sequences can be viewed as a regression/tracking problem, whereas recognition of action is a classification problem. In global representations of human motion, the action is described as a whole and obtained by background subtraction/tracking approaches. An alternative is to use local features, which generally employ learning approaches. By the data used, actions are often pre-segmented, though there are emergent approaches to action detection. As such, the approaches have less focus on feature extraction and description by computer vision which we shall move to in this section. We shall consider approaches which aim to segment and describe moving objects in image sequences, by extending feature extraction techniques for application to a sequence of images (largely, thereby, accruing advantages of correlation between successive images in the spatiotemporal domain).

9.4.2 Space–time interest points

Given the impressive performance of interest point detectors in CBIR, there has been natural interest in developing *spatio temporal interest point* detectors. These have been employed in particular to discriminate between different behaviours (walking, running, skipping, etc.). One approach developed the Harris corner detector to detect local structures in space and time [Laptev05], employing notions of scale space. Another approach aimed to extract and describe behaviour using spatio-temporal feature points [Dollár05] showing that carefully designed 3D detectors can transfer the established performance of spatial operators into space–time analysis. Another approach deployed the SIFT descriptor in 3D to encode the information 'local in both space and time in a manner which allows for robustness to orientations and noise' [Scovanner07], which are issues of central importance to any detector. As with their spatial counterparts, the aim is to use local invariant structures and then to deploy machine learning approaches to sift the plethora of points detected, and with impressive results too.

9.4.3 Detecting moving shapes by shape matching in image sequences

Section 9.2 described approaches which can extract moving objects. In general, this was achieved by modelling the background and then removing it to find the moving shape. An alternative approach is to model the moving shape so as to be able to separate it from the background. To extract the moving object by shape matching, one approach is to determine the moving shape in each separate image and then the collated results can be used to estimate the shape's motion. Alternatively, there is the *velocity Hough transform* for detecting moving shapes [Nash97]. This parameterises shapes together with their motion, thus allowing a collective description of the motion between frames. To deploy this, we need to develop a model of the moving shape under consideration, as was performed in Section 5.5 for static shapes. For a circle moving with (linear) velocity, v_x and v_y along the x and y directions, respectively, we have point co-ordinates which are a function of time t as

$$\begin{aligned} x(t) &= c_x + v_x t + r\cos\theta \\ y(t) &= c_y + v_y t + r\sin\theta \end{aligned} \tag{9.79}$$

where c_x, c_y are the co-ordinates of the circle's centre, r is the circle's radius and θ allows us to draw the locus of the circle at time t. We then construct a five-dimensional accumulator array in terms of the unknown parameters c_x, c_y, v_x, v_y, r and then vote for each image of the sequence (after edge detection and thresholding) in this accumulator array. By voting in a five-dimensional space, the technique is clearly computationally more demanding than other approaches, but retains and exact description of the object under consideration. Naturally, by grouping the information across a sequence the technique was shown to be more reliable in occlusion than by extracting a single circle for each frame and determining the track as the locus of centres of the extracted circles.

The approach can be extended to determine shapes with pulsatile motion. This requires a model of pulsation which can be achieved by changing the (fixed) radius of the circle to that of a pulsating circle r_p. This radius, subject to a pulsatile motion of amplitude a, pulse width w, period T and phase ϕ, is given by

$$r_p = r - a\sin\left(\frac{t - iT - \phi}{w}\right) \qquad i = 0, 1...; \phi < t < \phi + w \tag{9.80}$$

Fig. 9.21 shows the result of deploying the velocity HT, using the circle generating function of Eq. (9.79) (with $v_x = v_y = 0$) and the pulsatile radius function of Eq. (9.80), to a sequence of ultrasound images of an artery (and the detected artery is highlighted in black) [Nash97]. The artery pulsates as blood is pumped around the body by the heart; the images are of the carotid artery which is in the neck and is of prime interest in studies of atherosclerosis (stroke). Here, the noise level is clearly very high and the motion is such that the pulsatile velocity HT is the only conceivable approach to accurately determining the pulsating artery in the sequence.

The velocity HT was extended to a technique for finding moving lines as in the motion of the human thigh in the first model-based approach for recognising people by the way they walk [Cunado03]. It is to be noted that human walking is periodic in that the pattern of motion exists with a period defined by the time at which a foot makes contact with the floor and the time at which the same foot next makes contact with the floor. The model concentrated of the motion of the upper parts of the human leg, the thighs. Here, the model needed to account not only for the lateral displacement of the walking human, and the change in inclination of the human thigh. The model first considered the horizontal displacement of the human hips, which was derived as the motion of a centre point with co-ordinates c_x, c_y

$$\begin{aligned} c_x(t) &= -\frac{\beta}{\omega_0} + \left(v_x t + \frac{\alpha}{\omega_0}\sin(\omega_0 t) + \frac{\beta}{\omega_0}\cos(\omega_0 t)\right) \\ c_y(t) &= -\frac{\beta}{\omega_0} + \left(v_y t + \frac{\alpha}{\omega_0}\sin(\omega_0 t) + \frac{\beta}{\omega_0}\cos(\omega_0 t)\right) \end{aligned} \tag{9.81}$$

where v_x is the average velocity along the x axis and v_y is that for the y direction, ω_0 is the angular velocity of the gait cycle and α and β are determined by modelling the pelvis

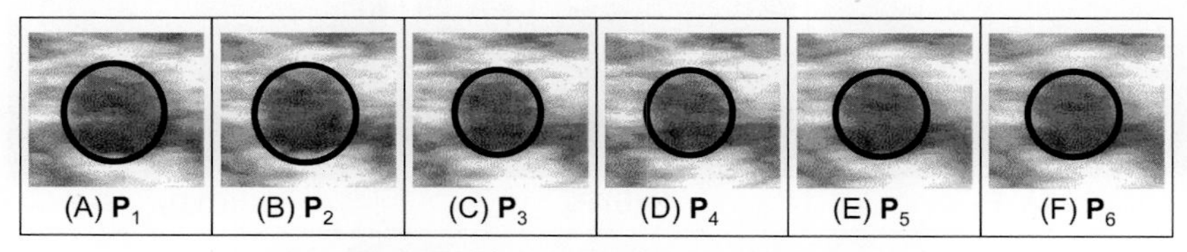

FIGURE 9.21 Detecting pulsating artery [Nash97].

motion. This is used as a basis for the model of the thigh, as

$$\begin{aligned} r_x &= c_{x0} + c_x(t) - \lambda \sin(\phi(t)) \\ r_y &= c_{y0} + c_y(t) - \lambda \cos(\phi(t)) \end{aligned} \tag{9.82}$$

where c_{x0} and c_{y0} are the initial position of the hip and λ can take any real value representing points from the hip to the knee. For a constant walking speed, the hip rotation $\phi(t)$ is a periodic function with period T. A Fourier series can represent any periodic signal with fundamental frequency $\omega_0 = 2\pi/T$. For a real periodic signal, the Fourier series representation can have the form

$$x(t) = a_0 + \sum_{k=1}^{N} \Re\left(a_k e^{j\omega_0 kt}\right) \tag{9.83}$$

and the function $\phi(t)$ can be represented by Eq. (9.83). As such, the inclination of the thigh is represented by a series of harmonics, as consistent with observations from earlier medical studies and the earlier model-based approaches to gait description. Essentially, by this and other techniques, the extracted sets of numbers which describe walking gait appear to be unique to, and repeatable for, each individual. Gait as a biometric easily precedes computer vision: in *The Tempest* Shakespeare wrote (and Ceres observed) in Act 4 that 'Great Juno comes, I do know her by her gait' and some other examples confirm Shakespeare knew (or used) this well. Detailed material on gait biometrics is not our issue here and can be found elsewhere [Nixon05].

The analysis by this model is illustrated in Fig. 9.22 which shows frames of a walking subject on which are superimposed a line showing the extracted position and orientation of the (moving) human thigh [Cunado03].

The velocity HT was also used in a generalised HT for *moving* shapes [Grant02] which imposed a motion trajectory on the GHT extraction. The shape was extracted from the image of a subject and constituted the silhouette profile of the upper body and the head. For an arbitrary shape which simply translates, the arbitrary shape can be described by Fourier descriptors as in Section 7.2.3. Given a moving (non-deforming) shape s with initial scale and rotation $\mathbf{a}_s = [l_g\ \rho_g]$ described by FDs $\overline{FD_x}$ and $\overline{FD_y}$ converted to vectors (along x- and y-axis) from the origin to a point on the curve, the scaled and rotated shape itself can be described as

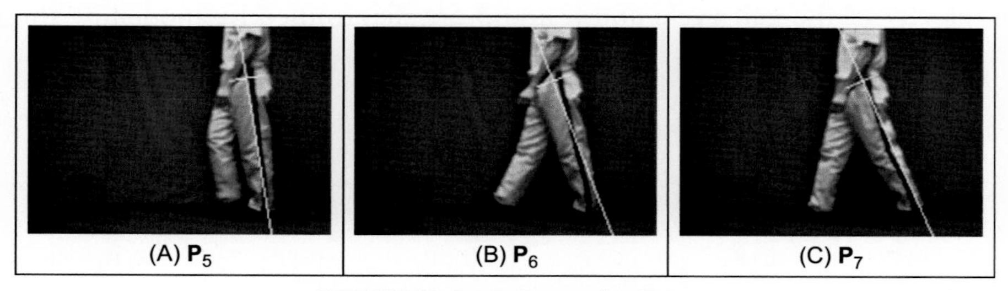

FIGURE 9.22 Detecting moving lines.

$$
\begin{aligned}
R_x(s, a_s) &= l_g u_x\left(s, \overline{FD_x}\right)\cos(\rho_g) - l_g u_y\left(s, \overline{FD_y}\right)\sin(\rho_g) \\
R_y(s, a_s) &= l_g u_x\left(s, \overline{FD_x}\right)\sin(\rho_g) + l_g u_y\left(s, \overline{FD_y}\right)\cos(\rho_g)
\end{aligned} \tag{9.84}
$$

Then the curves **w** which vote for the reference point (in this case the centre of the shape) are

$$\mathbf{w}(s, i, l, \rho, v_x, v_y) = R_x(s, l, \rho)U_x + R_y(s, l, \rho)U_y + iv_x U_x + iv_y U_y \tag{9.85}$$

where i is the image number within the sequence, v_x and v_y are the x centre and y centre velocity parameters, respectively, and U_x and U_y are two orthogonal (unit) vectors defining the x- and y-axis, respectively.

$$\mathbf{A}(\mathbf{b}, l, \rho, v_x, v_y) = \sum_{i \in D_i} \sum_{t \in D_t} \sum_{s \in D_s} M(\mathbf{b}, \boldsymbol{\lambda}(t, i) - \mathbf{w}(s, i, l, \rho, v_x, v_y)) \tag{9.86}$$

where **b** is the translation vector; a matching function $M(a,b) = 1$ if $a = b$; D_i, D_t, D_s are the domains of the sequence, the image and the shape, respectively; and $\boldsymbol{\lambda}(t, i)$ is a parametric function that defines the points in the image sequence for image i. This expression gives an accumulation strategy for finding moving arbitrary shapes. For each edge pixel in a frame, a locus of votes is calculated from the Fourier description of the template shape s and entered into the accumulator **A**. The co-ordinates of the loci are adjusted to allow for the predicted motion of the shape, dependent on the frame index, as in the velocity HT. This gives a generalised HT for finding an arbitrary shape moving with constant velocity (and acceleration could also be modelled). This is illustrated in Fig. 9.23 where the booster of the space shuttle is the target shape (highlighted in white), and the above technique is used to determine its position within a sequence of images of a shuttle's launch.

In human motion, body parts move up and down as the legs are vertical (in the stance phase) and when the legs are extended (at heel strike). Thus, the movement of a human body requires incorporation of a motion template [Grant02]. The expected (quasi-sinusoidal) trajectory is highlighted and the position of the centre of mass depicted in each frame. In frame 24 (Fig. 9.24A) the template is at its highest position and drops in the succeeding frames (Figs. 9.24B and C). The motion trajectory can then be imposed within an evidence gathering framework, thus allowing the successful extraction of the template's position in each frame of the sequence.

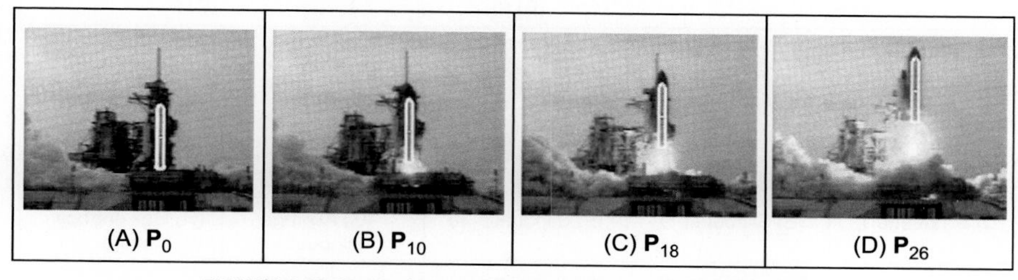

FIGURE 9.23 Detecting a moving arbitrary shape [Grant02].

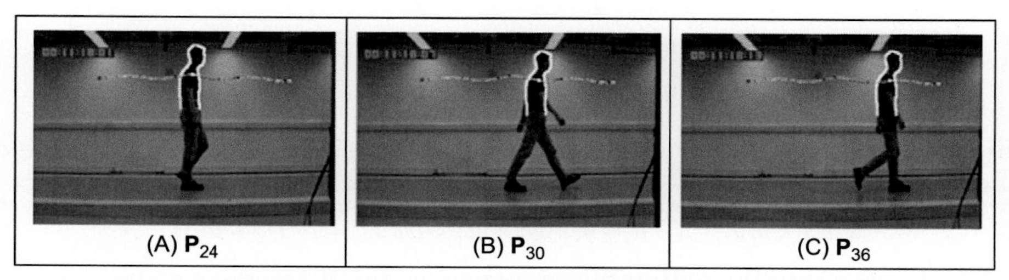

FIGURE 9.24 Detecting moving people by a generalised HT [Grant02].

Later a GHT was developed which can extract deforming moving shapes [Mowbray04] (articulated ones) which have a cyclic deformation. This used Fourier descriptors within an evidence gathering framework and successfully extracted pedestrians in sequences of images derived outdoors (as in Fig. 9.8).

9.4.4 Moving shape description

Essentially, we are considering how to determine sets of numbers which can describe uniquely moving shapes. Since we are aiming for a unique description, we can then recognise the moving shape. When the object is biological, we can determine numbers which represent the shape and its deformation. When the object is a person we can then recognise them by their body shape and their movement, this is recognition by their gait.

The most basic description of an object is its silhouette, which is an image. The simplest image to form from a sequence of silhouettes is the average silhouette, which is the image formed by averaging the silhouette images $\mathbf{P}_i$ (computed from silhouettes cropped in the manner of Figs. 9.25D–F) within an image sequence [Zongyi04, Veres04]. Thus

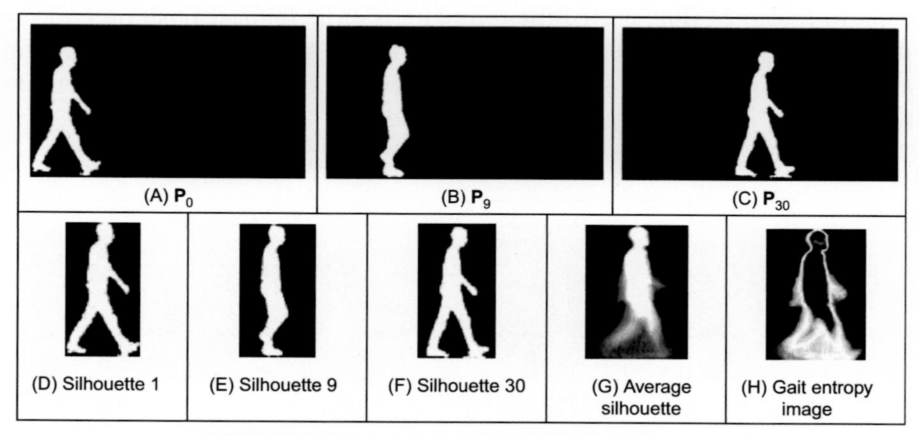

FIGURE 9.25 Processing a walking subject's silhouettes.

$$average\_silhouette_{x,y} = \frac{1}{N}\sum_{i=1}^{N}\mathbf{P}_{i_{x,y}} \tag{9.87}$$

This is illustrated in Figs. 9.25A–C which show three frames from a sequence of 30 frames comprising the full period of the subject's walking cycle (which is from the time when one foot strikes the ground until the frame when the same foot again strikes the ground). These silhouettes were derived from a sequence of images recorded in the laboratory conditions of Fig. 9.2. The quality is higher than the silhouettes shown earlier in Fig. 9.8 reflecting use of morphological operations and connected component analysis (as in Fig. 9.6). The silhouettes are then extracted from these images using a fixed bonding box, Figs. 9.25D–F. The average silhouette resulting from applying Eq. (9.87) to a sequence of such silhouettes is shown in Fig. 9.25G and the subject's thorax and its inclination can be seen very clearly; the legs and arms are quite blurred according to the subject's movement and the effects of the small errors/shadows due to the subject's interaction with the illumination have been reduced by the averaging process. The subject in Fig. 9.25G is clearly different to the subject in Figs. 9.25A–F by virtue of a different shape of head and thorax inclination when walking. The average silhouette, also known as the gait energy image [Han06] (thus showing its relation with the Motion Energy Image in Section 9.4.1 but here the walking motion is periodic), can be used for recognition purposes and has proved the most simple and a quite effective method for subject recognition by gait. Another form of the average silhouette is the gait entropy image [Khalid10], again computed from silhouettes cropped in the manner of Figs. 9.25D–F, is

$$gait\_entropy_{x,y} = \frac{1}{N}\sum_{i=1}^{N}\mathbf{P}_{i_{x,y}}\ln\left(\mathbf{P}_{i_{x,y}}\right) \tag{9.88}$$

and shown in Fig. 9.25H. This shows more clearly the subject's contour and the points affected most by walking.

These descriptions are images, and they can be used directly, or compressed using subspace analysis such as PCA to extract the most important parts of the silhouette and to reduce the effects of noise. As such we can use either an image of points or a compressed version as the set of numbers used for recognition purposes. An alternative representation of the silhouette is to use its symmetry, as in Section 6.4.2. There, an image was formed which reflected not only the symmetry with a human's shape, but the symmetry of their motion was determined (particularly in the region between the legs. This represents walking differently and provides a different means to describe moving biological shapes by their shape and motion.

One approach [Wang03b] used the perimeter of the silhouette, to reduce computational requirements. The 2D silhouettes were transformed into a sequence of 1D signals by storing the distance from the centroid to the silhouette perimeter. The silhouette was unwrapped in an anticlockwise manner, Fig. 9.26A, to determine a signal which changed with the position along the perimeter of a subject's silhouette. The vertical axis is the

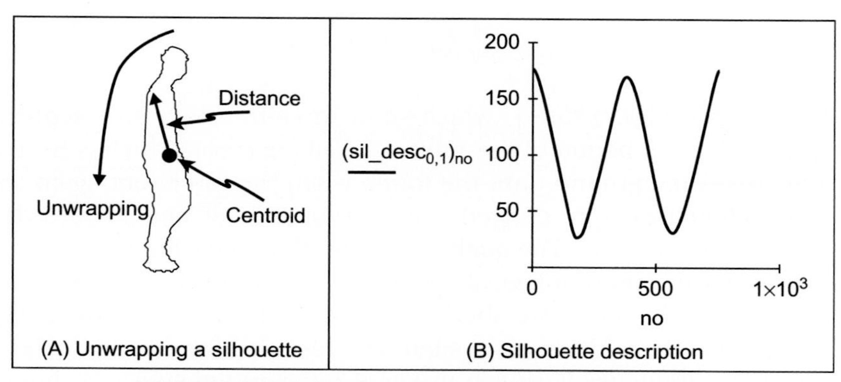

FIGURE 9.26 Analysing the perimeter of a subject's silhouette.

distance of a perimeter point from the centroid, and the horizontal axis is an index to all points in the perimeter of the walking figure. To enable comparison between subjects, the distances were normalised for magnitude and resampled so as to become a vector of fixed size. This is then the description of the moving subject and by its formulation using perimeter, provides an alternative to the gait energy/average silhouette approach.

As an extension of a standard approach to feature description, Shutler [Shutler06] developed *velocity moments* which can be used to recognise moving objects over a sequence of images, such as those in Figs. 9.25A–C, applied to recognising people by their gait. The moments are derived from a complete cycle since human gait is periodic and a single cycle suffices to derive the measures that are used for recognition.

The velocity moments vm sum over a sequence of I images as

$$vm_{pq\alpha\gamma} = N\sum_{i=2}^{I}\sum_{x\in\mathbf{P}}\sum_{y\in\mathbf{P}} U(i,\alpha,\gamma)S(i,p,q)\mathbf{P}_{i_{x,y}} \tag{9.89}$$

where N is a scaling coefficient, $\mathbf{P}_{i_{x,y}}$ is the ith image in the sequence, S are the moments describing a shape's structure (and can be Cartesian or Zernike). For centralised moments

$$S(i,p,q) = (x-\overline{x}_i)^p(y-\overline{y}_i)^p \tag{9.90}$$

where $\overline{x}_i$ is the current centre in the x direction, and similarly for y. The components U are moments which describe the movement of the shape's centre of mass between frames.

$$U(i,\alpha,\gamma) = (\overline{x}_i-\overline{x}_{i-1})^{\alpha}(\overline{y}_i-\overline{y}_{i-1})^{\gamma} \tag{9.91}$$

where $\overline{x}_{i-1}$ is the previous centre of mass in the x direction, and similarly for y. Rotation was not included; the technique was shown capable of use to recognise walking subjects, not gymnasts. For a database in which each of 10 subjects walked in front of the camera four times, and for each a period of their silhouettes was extracted. The moments were then calculated and three of the moments are depicted in Fig. 9.27 (the moments are the axes in 3D space).

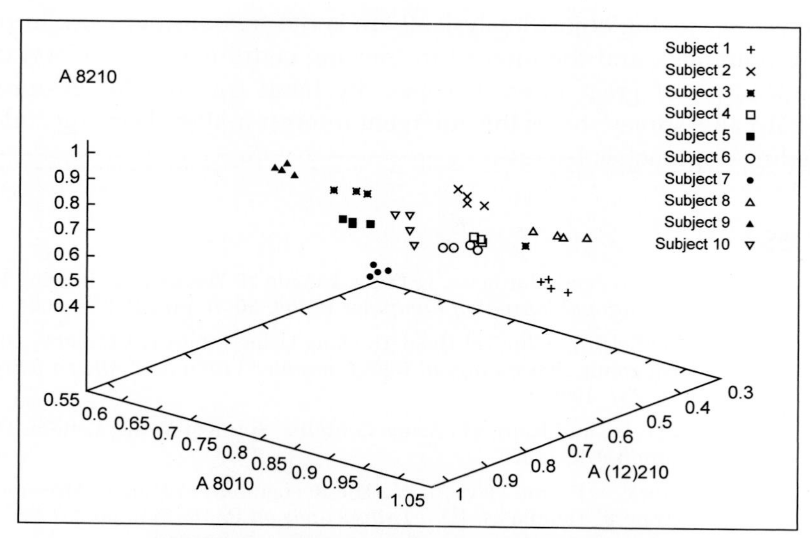

FIGURE 9.27 Velocity moments for ten walking subjects.

Once the description has been achieved, then it is used for classification purposes. The feature vectors can be compressed using PCA or transformed for classification purposes: the distance measures (Section 12.3.1) allow us to determine how different the moving subjects are; classification (Section 12.3.2) concerns how well we can discriminate between subjects and machine learning approaches (Section 12.4) can be used to better enable this task. If subjects can indeed be discriminated/recognised by the way they walk, and the velocity moments are sufficient to achieve this, then the measures should cluster, forming 10 groups of clusters of four points. This is what happens in Fig. 9.27, though by this viewpoint, the cluster for Subject 4 appears to be close to Subject 6 (but there are many more moments and more views of this data). This reflects not just the fact the people can be recognised by the way they walk, but also that by moving object extraction and description, computer vision is well up to this task.

9.5 Further reading

As has been mentioned throughout, there are many more works on moving object detection, tracking and description than have been cited here. As interest moves towards analysing sequences of images, these techniques are bound to continue to develop.

In this text, the general paradigm is to extract features that describe the target and then to classify it for purposes of recognition. In vision-based systems such approaches are used in biometrics: ways to recognise a person's identity by some innate human properties. The biometrics of major interest are fingerprint, iris and face, and others include hand geometry, ears and gait. The main text on biometrics [Jain07] surveys all major biometric approaches, many of which use computer vision approaches. Of the massive interest in moving object analysis, there is the (reassuring) work in pedestrian detection [Geronimo09], and the interest in tracking continues [Smeulders14]. Human activity [Poppe10] is of great interest, especially hand tracking for gesture analysis [Rautaray15]. An able survey shows the emergent interest in deep learning and contrasts it with preceding approaches [Herath17].

References

[Baker04] Baker, S., and Matthews, I., Lucas-kanade 20 Years on: a Unifying Framework, *International Journal of Computer Vision*, **56**(3), pp 221-255, 2004.

[Birchfield98] Birchfield, S., Elliptical Head Tracking Using Intensity Gradients and Color Histograms. *Proceedings of IEEE Computer Vision and Pattern Recognition*, pp 232—237, 1998.

[Blake98] Blake, A., and Isard, M., *Active Contours*, Springer-Verlag London Limited, London, UK, 1998.

[Bobick01] Bobick, A. F., and Davis, J. W., The Recognition of Human Movement Using Temporal Templates, *IEEE Transactions on PAMI*, **3**(3), pp 257-267, 2001.

[Bouwmans14] Bouwmans, T., Traditional and Recent Approaches in Background Modeling for Foreground Detection: An Overview. *Computer Science Review*, **11**, pp 31-66, 2014.

[Bradski98] Bradski, G. R., Computer Vision Face Tracking for Use in a Perceptual User Interface, *Intel Technology Journal*, **Q2**, 1998.

[Broida86] Broida, T. J., and Chellappa, R., Estimation of Object Motion Parameters from Noisy Images. *IEEE Transactions on PAMI*, **8**(1), pp 90—99, 1986.

[Brutzer11] Brutzer, S., Höferlin, B., and Heidemann, G., Evaluation of Background Subtraction Techniques for Video Surveillance. *Proceedings of IEEE CVPR*, pp 1937-1944, 2011.

[Comaniciu00] ComaniciuV. RameshP. MeerReal-time Tracking of Non-rigid Objects Using Mean Shift, *Proceedings of IEEE Computer Vision and Pattern Recognition* **2**, pp 142-149, 2000.

[Comaniciu03] Comaniciu, D., Rames, V., and Meer, P., Kernel-based Object Tracking. *IEEE Transactions on PAMI*, **25**(5), 564—575. 2003.

[Cox96] Cox, I. J., and Hingorani, S. L., An Efficient Implementation of Reid's Multiple Hypothesis Tracking Algorithm and its Application to Visual Tracking, *IEEE Transactions on PAMI*, **18**(2), pp 138-150, 1996.

[Cunado03] Cunado, D., Nixon, M. S., and Carter, J. N., Automatic Extraction and Description of Human Gait Models for Recognition Purposes, *Computer Vision and Image Understanding*, **90**(1), pp 1-41, 2003.

[Dollár05] Dollár, P., Rabaud, V., Cottrell, G. and Belongie, S., Behavior Recognition via Sparse Spatio-Temporal Features. *Proceeding of IEEE International Workshop on Visual Surveillance and Performance Evaluation of Tracking and Surveillance*, **2005**, pp 65-72, 2005.

[Elgammal02] Elgammal, A. M., Duraiswami, R., Harwood, D., Davis, L. S., Background and Foreground Modelling Using Nonparametric Kernel Density Estimation for Visual Surveillance, *Proceedings of the IEEE*, **90**, pp 1151-1163, 2002.

[Gavrila99] Gavrila, D. M., The Visual Analysis of Human Movement: a Survey. *Computer Vision and Image Understanding*, **73**(1), pp 82-98, 1999.

[Geronimo09] Geronimo, D., Lopez, A.M., Sappa, A.D. and Graf, T., Survey of Pedestrian Detection for Advanced Driver Assistance Systems. *IEEE Transactions on PAMI*, (7), pp 1239-1258, 2009.

[Grant02] Grant, M. G., Nixon, M. S., and Lewis, P. H., Extracting Moving Shapes by Evidence Gathering, *Pattern Recognition*, **35**, pp 1099–1114, 2002.

[Han06] Han, J., Bhanu, B., Individual Recognition Using Gait Energy Image, *IEEE Transactions on PAMI*, **28**(2), pp 316-322, 2006.

[Haritaoglu00] Haritaoglu, I., Harwood, D., Davis, L. S., W4: Real-Time Surveillance of People and Their Activities, *IEEE Transactions on PAMI*, **22**(8), pp 809-830, 2000.

[Harville01] Harville, M., Gordon, G., Woodfill, J., Foreground Segmentation Using Adaptive Mixture Models in Color and Depth, *Proceedings of IEEE Workshop on Detection and Recognition of Events in Video*, pp 3-11, 2001.

[Herath17] Herath, S., Harandi, M. and Porikli, F., Going Deeper into Action Recognition: A Survey. *Image and Vision Computing*, **60**, pp 4-21, 2017.

[Horn86] Horn, B. K. P., *Robot Vision*, MIT Press, 1986.

[Horprasert99] Horprasert, T., Harwood, D., and Davis, L. S., A Statistical Approach for Real-Time Robust Background Subtraction and Shadow Detection, *Proc. IEEE ICCV'99 Frame-Rate Workshop, Corfu, Greece*, September 1999.

[Hu04] Hu, W. M., Tan, T. N., Wang, L. A., and Maybank, S., A Survey on Visual Surveillance of Object Motion and Behaviors, *IEEE Transactions on SMC(A)*, **34**(3), pp 334-352, 2004.

[Huang08] Huang, C., Wu, B., Nevatia, R., Robust Object Tracking by Hierarchical Association of Detection Responses. *Proceedings of ECCV (2008)*, pp 788–801, 2008.

[Isaard98] Isaard, M., and Blake, A., CONDENSATION - Conditional Density Propagation for Visual Tracking, *International Journal of Computer Vision*, **29**(1), pp 5–28, 1998.

[Ivanov00] Ivanov, Y., Bobick, A., and Liu, J., Fast Lighting Independent Background Subtraction, *International Journal of Computer Vision*, **37**(2), pp 199–207, 2000.

[Jain07] Jain, A. K., Flynn, P., and Ross, A., Eds.: Handbook of Biometrics, Springer, 2007.

[KaewTraKulPong01] Kaewtrakulpong P., and Bowden, R., An Improved Adaptive Background Mixture Model for Realtime Tracking with Shadow Detection, *Proceedings of 2nd European Workshop on Advanced Video Based Surveillance Systems*, 2001.

[Kalal10a] Kalal, Z., Mikolajczyk, K., and Matas, J., Face-Tld: Tracking-Learning-Detection Applied to Faces, *Proceedings of International Conference on Image Processing*, 2010.

[Kalal10b] Kalal, Z., Matas, J., and Mikolajczyk, K., P-N Learning: Bootstrapping Binary Classifiers by Structural Constraints, *Proceedings of IEEE Computer Vision and Pattern Recognition*, 2010.

[Khalid10] Khalid, K., Xiang, T., and Gong, S., Gait Recognition without Subject Cooperation, *Pattern Recognition Letters*, **31**(13), pp 2052-2060, 2010.

[Laptev05] Laptev, I., On Space-Time Interest Points. *International Journal of Computer Vision*, **64**(2-3), pp 107-123, 2005.

[Lee05] Lee, D-S., Effective Gaussian Mixture Learning for Video Background Subtraction, *IEEE Transactions on PAMI*, **27**(5), pp 827-832, 2005.

[Leibe08] Leibe, B., Schindler, K., Cornelis, N., and van Gool, L., Coupled Object Detection and Tracking from Static Cameras and Moving Vehicles, *IEEE Transactions on PAMI*, **30**(10), pp 1683-1698, 2008.

[Lepetit05] Lepetit, V., and Fua, P., Monocular Model-Based 3D Tracking of Rigid Objects: a Survey, *Foundations and Trends in Computer Graphics and Vision*, **1**(1), pp 1–89, 2005.

[Lipton98] Lipton, A., Fujiyoshi, H. and Patil, H., Moving Target Detection and Classification from Real-Time Video, *Proceedings of IEEE Workshop Applications of Computer Vision*, 1998.

[Lucas81] Lucas B., and Kanade, T., An Iterative Image Registration Technique with an Application to Stereo Vision. *Proceedings of the International Joint Conference on Artificial Intelligence*, pp 674–679, 1981.

[Moeslund06] Moeslund, T. B., Hilton, A., Krüger, V., A Survey of Advances in Vision-Based Human Motion Capture and Analysis, *Computer Vision and Image Understanding*, **104**(2-3), pp 90-126, 2006.

[Mowbray04] Mowbray, S. D., and Nixon, M. S., Extraction and Recognition of Periodically Deforming Objects by Continuous, Spatio-Temporal Shape Description, *Proceedings of IEEE Computer Vision and Pattern Recognition*, **2**, pp 895-901, 2004.

[Nash97] Nash, J. M., Carter, J. N., and Nixon, M. S., Dynamic feature extraction via the velocity Hough transform, Pattern Recognition Letters, 18(10), pp 1035-1047, 1997

[Nixon05] Nixon, M. S., Tan T. N., and Chellappa, R., *Human Identification Based on Gait, Springer, International Series on Biometrics* (A. K. Jain and D. Zhang Eds.) 2005.

[Piccardi04] Piccardi, M., Background Subtraction Techniques: a Review, *Proceedings of of IEEE SMC 2004 International Conference on Systems, Man and Cybernetics*, 2004.

[Poppe10] Poppe, R., A Survey on Vision-Based Human Action Recognition, *Image and Vision Computing*, **28**, pp 976–990, 2010.

[Rautaray15] Rautaray, S.S. and Agrawal, A., Vision Based Hand Gesture Recognition for Human Computer Interaction: a Survey. *Artificial Intelligence Review*, **43**(1), pp 1-54, 2015.

[Reid79] Reid, D. B., An Algorithm for Tracking Multiple Targets. *IEEE Transactions on Automatic Control* **24**(6), pp 843–854, 1979.

[Scovanner07] Scovanner, P., Ali, S. and Shah, M., A 3-dimensional Sift Descriptor and its Application to Action Recognition. *Proceedings of 15th ACM International Conference on Multimedia*, pp 357-360, 2007.

[Sethi87] Sethi, I., and Jain R., Finding Trajectories of Feature Points in a Monocular Image Sequence. *IEEE Transactions on PAMI*, **9**(1), 56–73, 1987.

[Shi94] Shi, J., and Tomasi, C., Good Features to Track, *Proceedings of IEEE Computer Vision and Pattern Recognition*, pp 593-600, 1994.

[Shutler02] Shutler, J. D., Grant, M. G., Nixon, M. S. and Carter, J. N., On a Large Sequence-Based Human Gait Database, *Proceedings of 4th International Conference on Recent Advances in Soft Computing, Nottingham (UK)*, pp 66-71, 2002.

[Shutler06] Shutler, J. D., and Nixon, M. S., Zernike Velocity Moments for Sequence-Based Description of Moving Features, *Image and Vision Computing*, **24**(4), pp 343-356, 2006.

[Smeulders14] Smeulders, A.W., Chu, D.M., Cucchiara, R., Calderara, S., Dehghan, A. and Shah, M., Visual Tracking: An Experimental Survey. *IEEE Transactions on PAMI*, **36**(7), pp 1442-1468, 2014.

[Sobral14] Sobral, A. and Vacavant, A., A Comprehensive Review of Background Subtraction Algorithms Evaluated with Synthetic and Real Videos. *Computer Vision and Image Understanding*, **122**, pp 4-21, 2014.

[Stalder10] Stalder, S., Grabner, H., and Van Gool, L., Cascaded Confidence Filtering for Improved Tracking-By-Detection, *Proceedings of European Conference on Computer Vision (ECCV)*, 2010.

[Stauffer99] Stauffer, C., and Grimson, W. E. L., Adaptive Background Mixture Models for Real-Time Tracking, *Proceedings of IEEE Computer Vision and Pattern Recognition*, pp 246-252, 1999.

[Stauffer00] Stauffer, C., and Grimson, W. E. L., Learning Patterns of Activity Using Real-Time Tracking, *IEEE Transactions on PAMI*, **22**(8), pp 747-757, 2000.

[Tian05] Tian, Y-L. Lu, M., and Hampapur, A. Robust and Efficient Foreground Analysis for Real-Time Video Surveillance, *Proceedings of IEEE Computer Vision and Pattern Recognition 2005*, **1**, pp 1182-1187, 2005.

[Veenman01] Veenman, C., Reinders, M., and Backer, E., Resolving Motion Correspondence for Densely Moving Points. *IEEE Transactions on PAMI*, **23**(1), pp 54–72, 2001.

[Veres04] Veres, G. V., Gordon, L., Carter, J. N., and Nixon M. S., What Image Information Is Important in Silhouette-Based Gait Recognition? *Proceedings of IEEE Computer Vision and Pattern Recognition*, **2**, pp 776-782, 2004.

[Wand95] Wand, M. P., and Jones MC, Kernel Smoothing, Monographs on Statistics and Applied Probability, Chapman & Hall, 1995.

[Wang03a] Wang, L. A., Hu, W. M., and Tan, T. N. Recent Developments in Human Motion Analysis, *Pattern Recognition*, **36**(3), pp 585-601, 2003.

[Wang03b] Wang, L., Tan, T., Ning, H. Z., and Hu, W. M., Silhouette Analysis-Based Gait Recognition for Human Identification, *IEEE Transactions on PAMI*, **25**(12), pp 1505-2528, 2003.

[Yilmaz06] Yilmaz, A., Javed, O., and Shah, M., Object Tracking: A Survey. *ACM Computing Surveys* **38**(4), 45 pp, 2006.

[Zongyi04] Zongyi L., and Sarkar, S., Simplest Representation yet for Gait Recognition: Averaged Silhouette, *Proceedings of ICPR*, **4**, pp 211-214, 2004.

10 Camera geometry fundamentals

10.1 Overview

This chapter is concerned with the geometry that describes how objects in the 3D world are captured as 2D pixels. These descriptions are mathematical models that define a mapping between 3D objects (generally points) in the world and 2D objects in a plane that represents an image. The final aim is to be able to obtain 3D information from the 2D position of pixels. The techniques of 3D analysis such as reconstruction or photogrammetry are studied in computer vision [Trucco98, Hartley01]. This chapter does not cover computer vision techniques, but gives an introduction to the fundamental concepts of the geometry of computer vision. It aims to complement the concepts in Chapter 1 by increasing the background knowledge of how camera geometry is mathematically modelled. This chapter explains basic aspects of common camera geometry models.

Although the mapping between 3D points and pixels can be defined using functions in Euclidean co-ordinates, the notation and development is better expressed by using matrix operations in the projective space. As such, we start this chapter by introducing the space defined by *homogenous co-ordinates* and by considering how transformations can be defined using a matrix notation. We will see that there are different models that can be used to represent alternative image capture technologies or that approximate the image capture by using different complexity. A model defines a general type of image formation process, whilst particular models for specific cameras are defined by values given to the camera parameters. Different models can be used according to the capture technology and according to the type of objects in the scene. For example, an affine model can be a good approximation of a projective model when objects are far away or placed in a plane with similar alignment than the camera plane (i.e. images with little or no perspective). The chapter is summarised in Table 10.1.

10.2 Projective space

You should be familiar with the concept of the Euclidean space as the conventional way to represent points, lines, panes and other geometric objects. Euclidean geometry is algebraically represented by the *Cartesian co-ordinate system* in which points are defined by tuples of numbers. Each number is related to one axis, and a set of axes determines the space's dimensions. This representation is a natural way to describe 3D objects in the world, and it is very useful in image processing to describe pixels in 2D images. Cartesian

Feature Extraction and Image Processing for Computer Vision. https://doi.org/10.1016/B978-0-12-814976-8.00010-5

Table 10.1 Overview of this chapter.

Main topic	Subtopics	Main points
Projective space	What is the projective space and what are homogenous co-ordinates.	Transforming *Euclidean co-ordinates* to *homogeneous co-ordinates. Homogenous matrix* transformations. *Similarity* and *affine* transformations. *Homography*. How to obtain a homography.
Perspective camera	A general description of how 3D points are mapped into an image plane. How we define a model for the perspective projection.	Image *projection, principal point, focus length* and *camera parameters*. Parameters of the *perspective camera* model. *Projections*.
Affine camera	Affine as a simplification of the perspective camera.	*Affine projection*. Affine *camera model, linear* camera. Affine camera *parameters*.
Weak perspective	Weak perspective camera model.	Relationship between *weak perspective* and *perspective models. Weak perspective camera parameters*.

co-ordinates are convenient to describe angles and lengths, and they are simply transformed by matrix algebra to represent translations, rotations and changes of scale. However, the relationship defined by projections cannot be described with the same algebraic simplicity (it can be done but it is cumbersome). For example, it is difficult to express that parallel lines in the 3D world actually have an intersection point when considered in a projection or it is difficult to write that the projection of a point is defined as a line. The best way to express the relationship defined by projections is to use projective geometry. Projective geometry replaces the Cartesian system with homogenous co-ordinates. In a similar way to how Cartesian co-ordinates define the Euclidean space, homogenous co-ordinates define the projective space. This section explains the fundamental concepts of projective geometry.

10.2.1 Homogeneous co-ordinates and projective geometry

Projective geometry is algebraically represented by the homogeneous co-ordinate system. This representation is a natural way to formulate how we relate camera co-ordinates to *real-world* co-ordinates: the relation between image and physical space. Its major advantages are that image transformations like rotations, change of scale and projections become matrix multiplications. Projections provide perspective that corresponds to the distance of objects that affects their size in the image.

It is possible to map points from Cartesian co-ordinates into homogeneous co-ordinates. The 2D point with Cartesian co-ordinates

$$\mathbf{x}_c = [x \quad y]^{\mathrm{T}} \tag{10.1}$$

is mapped into homogeneous co-ordinates to the point

$$\mathbf{x}_h = [wx \quad wy \quad w]^{\mathrm{T}} \tag{10.2}$$

where w is an arbitrary scalar. Note that a point in Cartesian co-ordinates is mapped into several points in homogeneous co-ordinates; one point for any value of w. This is why homogeneous co-ordinates are also called redundant co-ordinates. We can use the definition on Eq. (10.2) to obtain a mapping from homogeneous co-ordinates to Cartesian co-ordinates. That is,

$$x_c = \frac{w_x}{w} \text{ and } y_c = \frac{w_y}{w} \tag{10.3}$$

The homogeneous representation can be extended to any dimension. For example, a 3D point in Cartesian co-ordinates

$$\mathbf{x}_c = [x \quad y \quad z]^T \tag{10.4}$$

is mapped into homogeneous form as

$$\mathbf{x}_h = [wx \quad wy \quad wz \quad w]^T \tag{10.5}$$

This point is mapped back to Cartesian co-ordinates by

$$x_c = \frac{w_x}{w}, y_c = \frac{w_y}{w} \text{ and } z_c = \frac{w_z}{w} \tag{10.6}$$

Although it is possible to map points from Cartesian co-ordinates to homogeneous co-ordinates and vice versa, points in both systems define different geometric spaces. Cartesian co-ordinates define the Euclidean space and the points in homogeneous co-ordinates define the projective space. The projective space distinguishes a particular class of points defined when the last co-ordinate is zero. These are known as *ideal points* and to understand them, we need to understand how a line is represented in projective space. This is related to the concept of *duality*.

10.2.2 Representation of a line, duality and ideal points

The homogeneous representation of points has a very interesting idea that relates points and lines. Let us consider the equation of a 2D line in Cartesian co-ordinates,

$$Ax + By + C = 0 \tag{10.7}$$

The same equation in homogeneous co-ordinates becomes

$$Ax + By + Cz = 0 \tag{10.8}$$

It is interesting to notice that in this definition, points and lines are indistinguishable. Both a point $[x \quad y \quad z]^T$ and a line $[A \quad B \quad C]^T$ are represented by triplets, and they can be interchanged in the homogeneous equation of a line. This concept can be generalised and points are indistinguishable to planes for the 3D projective space. This symmetry is known as the *duality of the projective space* that can be combined with the concept of concurrence and incidence to derive the principle of duality [Aguado00]. The principle of duality constitutes an important concept for understanding the geometric relationship in the projective space; the definition of the line can be used to derive the concept of ideal points.

We can use the algebra of homogeneous co-ordinates to find the intersection of parallel lines, planes and hyper-planes. For simplicity, let us consider lines in the 2D plane. In the Cartesian co-ordinates in Eq. (10.7), two lines are parallel when their slopes $y' = -A/B$ are the same. Thus, in order to find the intersection between two parallel lines in the homogeneous form in Eq. (10.8), we need to solve the following system of equations

$$\begin{aligned} A_1x + B_1y + C_1z &= 0 \\ A_2x + B_2y + C_2z &= 0 \end{aligned} \tag{10.9}$$

for $A_1/B_1 = A_2/B_2$. By dividing the first equation by B_1, the second equation by B_2 and by subtracting the second equation to the first, we have that

$$(C_2 - C_1)z = 0 \tag{10.10}$$

Since we are considering different lines, then $C_2 \neq C_1$ and consequently $z = 0$. That is, the intersection of parallel lines is defined by points of the form

$$\mathbf{x}_h = [x \quad y \quad 0]^{\mathrm{T}} \tag{10.11}$$

Similarly, in 3D, the intersection of parallel planes is defined by the points given by

$$\mathbf{x}_h = [x \quad y \quad z \quad 0]^{\mathrm{T}} \tag{10.12}$$

Since parallel lines are assumed to intersect at infinity, then points with the last co-ordinate equal to zero are called points at infinity. They are also called ideal points, and these points plus all the other homogeneous points form the projective space.

The points in the projective space can be visualised by extending the Euclidean space as shown in Fig. 10.1. This figure illustrates the 2D projective space as a set of points in the 3D Euclidean space. According to Eq. (10.3), points in the homogeneous space are mapped into the Euclidean space when $z = 1$. In the figure, this plane is called the

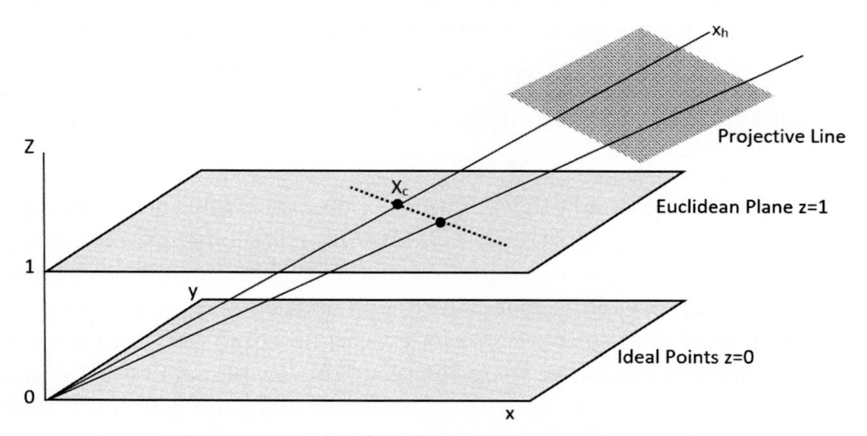

FIGURE 10.1 Model of the 2D projective space (ray space).

Euclidean plane. Fig. 10.1 shows two points in the Euclidean plane. These points define a line that is shown as a dotted line and it extends to infinity in the plane. In homogeneous co-ordinates, points in the Euclidean plane become rays from the origin in the projective space. Each point in the ray is given by a different value of z. The homogeneous co-ordinates of the line in the Euclidean plane define the plane between the two rays in the projective space. When two lines intersect in the Euclidean plane, they define a ray that passes through the intersection point in the Euclidean plane. However, if the lines are parallel, then they define an ideal point. That is a point in the plane $z = 0$.

Note that the origin $[0 \quad 0 \quad 0]^{\mathrm{T}}$ is ambiguous since it can define any point in homogeneous co-ordinates or an ideal point. To avoid this ambiguity, this point is not considered to be part of the projective space. Also remember that the concept of point and line are indistinguishable, so it is possible to draw a dual diagram, where points become lines and vice versa.

10.2.3 Transformations in the projective space

Perhaps the most practical aspect of homogeneous co-ordinates is the way transformations are represented algebraically. This section shows how different types of transformations in Cartesian co-ordinates can be written in a simple form by using homogenous co-ordinates. This is because the Euclidean plane is included in the projective space, so Euclidean transformations are special cases of projective transformations. We start with similarity or rigid transformations. These transformations do not change the angle values in any geometric shape and they define rotations, changes in scale and translations (i.e. position). Similarity transformations are algebraically represented by matrix multiplications and additions. A 2D point $p = (x, y)$ is transformed into a point $p'=(x', y')$ by a similarity transformation as,

$$\begin{bmatrix} x' \\ y' \end{bmatrix} = \begin{bmatrix} \cos(\theta) & \sin(\theta) \\ -\sin(\theta) & \cos(\theta) \end{bmatrix} \begin{bmatrix} s_x \\ s_y \end{bmatrix} \begin{bmatrix} x \\ y \end{bmatrix} + \begin{bmatrix} t_x \\ t_y \end{bmatrix} \tag{10.13}$$

where θ is a rotation angle, $\mathbf{S} = [s_x, s_y]^T$ defines the scale and $\mathbf{T} = [t_x, t_y]^T$ the translation along each axis. This transformation can be generalised to any dimension and it is written in short form as

$$\boldsymbol{x}' = \mathbf{RS}\boldsymbol{x} + \mathbf{T} \tag{10.14}$$

Notice that $\mathbf{R}$ is an orthogonal matrix. That is, its transpose is equal to its inverse or $\mathbf{R}^T = \mathbf{R}^{-1}$.

There is a more general type of transformations known as *affine transformations* where the matrix $\mathbf{R}$ is replaced by a matrix $\mathbf{A}$ that is not necessarily orthogonal. That is,

$$\boldsymbol{x}' = \mathbf{AS}\boldsymbol{x} + \mathbf{T} \tag{10.15}$$

Affine transformations do not preserve the value of angles, but they preserve parallel lines. The principles and theorems studied under similarities define Euclidean geometry, and the principles and theorems under affine transformations define the affine geometry.

In the projective space, transformations are called *homographies*. They are more general than similarity and affine transformations; they only preserve collinearities and cross ratios. That is, points forming a straight line are transformed into points forming another straight line and the distance ratio computed from four points is maintained. Image homographies are defined in homogeneous co-ordinates. A 2D point is transformed as,

$$\begin{bmatrix} x' \\ y' \\ w' \end{bmatrix} = \begin{bmatrix} h_{1,1} & h_{1,2} & h_{1,3} \\ h_{2,1} & h_{2,2} & h_{2,3} \\ h_{3,1} & h_{3,2} & h_{3,3} \end{bmatrix} \begin{bmatrix} x \\ y \\ w \end{bmatrix} \tag{10.16}$$

This transformation can be generalised to other dimensions and it is written in short form as

$$\boldsymbol{x}' = \mathbf{H}\boldsymbol{x} \tag{10.17}$$

A similarity transformation is a special case of an affine transformation, and that an affine transformation is a special case of a homography. That is, rigid and affine transformations can be expressed as homographies. For example, a rigid transformation for a 2D point can be defined as,

$$\begin{bmatrix} x' \\ y' \\ 1 \end{bmatrix} = \begin{bmatrix} s_x \cos(\theta) & s_x \sin(\theta) & t_x \\ -s_y \sin(\theta) & s_y \cos(\theta) & t_y \\ 0 & 0 & 1 \end{bmatrix} \begin{bmatrix} x \\ y \\ 1 \end{bmatrix} \tag{10.18}$$

Or in a more general form as

$$\boldsymbol{x}' = \begin{bmatrix} \mathbf{RS} & \mathbf{T} \\ 0 & 1 \end{bmatrix} \boldsymbol{x} \tag{10.19}$$

An affine transformation is defined as,

$$\boldsymbol{x}' = \begin{bmatrix} \mathbf{A} & \mathbf{T} \\ 0 & 1 \end{bmatrix} \boldsymbol{x} \tag{10.20}$$

The zeros in the last row are actually defining a transformation in a plane; the plane where $z = 1$. According to the discussion in Section 10.2.2, this plane defines the Euclidean plane. Thus these transformations are performed to Euclidean points.

Code 10.1 illustrates the definition of the transformations in Eqs. (10.17), (10.19) and (10.20). This code uses a transformation `T` that is defined according to the transformation type. The main iteration maps the pixels from an input image to an output image by performing the matrix multiplication. Note that the pixel positions are defined such that the centre of the image has the co-ordinates (0,0). Thus, the transformation includes the translations `centreX`, `centreY`. This permits definition of the rotation in the similarity transformation with respect to the centre of the image.

```
if transformationType  == "Similarity":
    # Similarity transformation
    s = [.4, 0.8, 0.8, 100.0, 0.0] # Angle, scaleXY, trahslationXY
    T = [[ s[1]*cos(s[0]), s[1]*sin(s[0]), s[3]],                              \
         [ -s[2]*sin(s[0]), s[2]*cos(s[0]), s[4]],                             \
         [0 ,0, 1]]
if transformationType  == "Affine":
    # Affine transformation
    T = [[ .8, .1, 100],                                                       \
         [ -.2, 1, 0],                                                         \
         [0 ,0, 1]]
if transformationType  == "Homography":
    # Homography
    T = [[ .8, 0, 100],                                                        \
         [ .2,1, 0],                                                           \
         [.0005 ,-0.0005 , 1.2]]

tImage = createImageRGB(width, height)
for y, x in itertools.product(range(0, height-1), range(0, width-1)):
    # Alpha and colour
    alpha = maskImage[y,x]/256.0
    if alpha == 0:
        continue
    rgb = (inputImage[y,x]/4.0   + inputImage[y+1,x+1]/4.0 +                  \
           inputImage[y+1,x]/4.0 + inputImage[y,x+1]/4.0) * alpha

    # Transform
    cx, cy = x - centreX, y - centreY
    p0z = T[2][0] * cx + T[2][1] * cy + T[2][2]
    p1z = T[2][0] * (cx+1) + T[2][1] * cy + T[2][2]
    p2z = T[2][0] * (cx+1) + T[2][1] * (cy+1) + T[2][2]

    if p0z != 0 and p1z != 0 and p2z !=0:
        p0x = int((T[0][0] * cx + T[0][1] * cy + T[0][2]) / p0z + centreX)
        p0y = int((T[1][0] * cx + T[1][1] * cy + T[1][2]) / p0z + centreY)
        p1x = int((T[0][0] * (cx+1) + T[0][1] * cy + T[0][2]) / p1z + centreX)
        p1y = int((T[1][0] * (cx+1) + T[1][1] * cy + T[1][2]) / p1z + centreY)
        p2x = int((T[0][0] * (cx+1) + T[0][1] * (cy+1) + T[0][2]) / p2z + centreX)
        p2y = int((T[1][0] * (cx+1) + T[1][1] * (cy+1) + T[1][2]) / p2z + centreY)

        # Fill output image
        v1,v2 = [p1x - p0x, p1y - p0y], [p2x - p0x, p2y - p0y]

        lv1 = max(.001,sqrt(v1[0]*v1[0] + v1[1]*v1[1]))
        lv2 = max(.001,sqrt(v2[0]*v2[0] + v2[1]*v2[1]))
        v1N = [v1[0]/lv1, v1[1]/lv1]
        v2N = [v2[0]/lv2, v2[1]/lv2]

        for dV1, dV2 in itertools.product(range(0, int(lv1)+1), range(0, int(lv2)+1)):
            a = int(p0x + dV1 * v1N[0] + dV2 * v2N[0])
            b = int(p0y + dV1 * v1N[1] + dV2 * v2N[1])
            if a>0 and a < width and b > 0 and b < height:
                tImage[b,a] = rgb
```

CODE 10.1 Apply a geometric transformation to an image.

The implementation in Code 10.1 includes a simple image *warping* process that transforms squares defined by four pixels in the input image into polygons (rhomboids) in the output image. The rhomboids are filled with the average colour of the pixels in the input. In a better implementation, the colours for the rhomboids can be determined by interpolation. Also a more accurate position of the rhomboids' vertices can be obtained by considering sub-pixel positions. The implementation includes a mask image, so only pixels in the region defined by the Rubik's cube are shown in the output image.

Fig. 10.2 shows an example of the image transformations obtained with Code 10.1. Notice how the similarity transformation preserves angles, the affine transformation preserves parallel lines and the homography preserves straight lines (collinearity). Each transformation can be used to model different changes on the object and the camera. Similarities can be used to find rigid changes in objects or to align images or for simple operations like change aspect ratio or zoom. Affine transformations can be used to correct geometric distortions. Homographies are mainly used for image alignment, and they are useful to obtain relative cameras' positions.

10.2.4 Computing a planar homography

Although applying a transformation to an image is important in some applications, the central problem in computer vision focuses on finding a transformation from image data. This is a parameter estimation problem, and there are many techniques aimed at dealing with problems like noise and occlusions. This section introduces the estimation concepts by considering how four points in corresponding images can be used to solve for **H** in the system of equations defined in Eq. (10.17).

According to Eq. (10.3), a point $\mathbf{p}=(x, y, 1)$ is mapped into $\mathbf{p}'=(x', y', 1)$ by

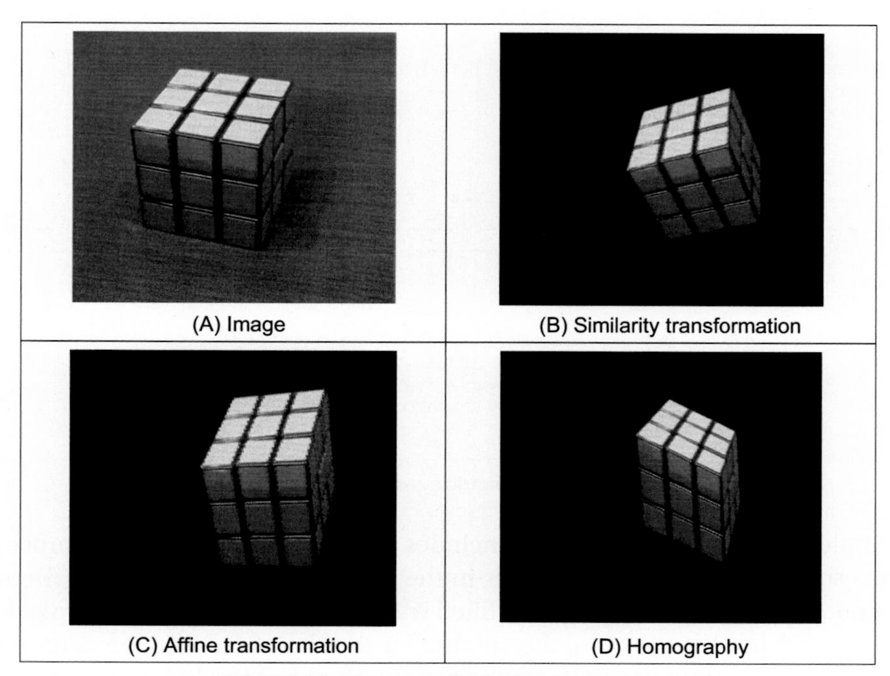

FIGURE 10.2 Image transformations and warping.

$$x' = \frac{xh_{1,1} + yh_{1,2} + zh_{1,3}}{xh_{3,1} + yh_{3,2} + zh_{3,3}} \text{ and } y_2' = \frac{x_1 h_{2,1} + y_1 h_{2,2} + z_1 h_{2,3}}{x_1 h_{3,1} + y_1 h_{3,2} + z_1 h_{3,3}} \tag{10.21}$$

Since the transform is in the Euclidean plane (i.e. 2D images), then $z = 1$. That is,

$$\begin{aligned} x'(xh_{3,1} + yh_{3,2} + h_{3,3}) &= xh_{1,1} + yh_{1,2} + h_{1,3} \\ y'(xh_{3,1} + yh_{3,2} + h_{3,3}) &= xh_{2,1} + yh_{2,2} + h_{2,3} \end{aligned} \tag{10.22}$$

By rearranging the terms in these equations, we have that

$$\begin{aligned} -xh_{1,1} - yh_{1,2} - h_{1,3} + x'xh_{3,1} + x'yh_{3,2} + x'h_{3,3} &= 0 \\ -xh_{2,1} - yh_{2,2} - h_{2,3} + y'xh_{3,1} + y'yh_{3,2} + y'h_{3,3} &= 0 \end{aligned} \tag{10.23}$$

This can be written in matrix form as

$$\begin{aligned} [\,-x \quad -y \quad -1 \quad 0 \quad 0 \quad 0 \quad x'x \quad x'y \quad x'\,]\,\mathbf{h}^{\mathrm{T}} &= 0 \\ [\,0 \quad 0 \quad 0 \quad -x \quad -y \quad -1 \quad y'x \quad y'y \quad y'\,]\,\mathbf{h}^{\mathrm{T}} &= 0 \end{aligned} \tag{10.24}$$

where $\mathbf{h}$ is the vector containing the coefficients of the homography. That is,

$$\mathbf{h} = [\, h_{1,1} \quad h_{1,2} \quad h_{1,3} \quad h_{2,1} \quad h_{2,2} \quad h_{2,3} \quad h_{3,1} \quad h_{3,2} \quad h_{3,3} \,] \tag{10.25}$$

As such, a pair of corresponding points $\mathbf{p}=(x, y, 1)$ and $\mathbf{p}'=(x', y', 1)$ define a pair of rows of a linear system of equations of rank nine. In order to make the system determined, we need four corresponding pairs. This defines eight rows in the equation system. To define the last row, we should notice that the system is homogenous. That is, any scalar product of $\mathbf{h}$ is solution of the system. Thus last row of the system can be defined by considering a scale value for the matrix. As such, by considering four corresponding pair of points $\mathbf{p}_i = (x_i, y_i, 1)$ and $\mathbf{p}_i' = (x_i', y_i', 1)$, we can form the system of equations

$$\begin{bmatrix} -x_1 & -y_1 & -1 & 0 & 0 & 0 & x_1'x_1 & x_1'y_1 & x_1' \\ 0 & 0 & 0 & -x_1 & -y_1 & -1 & y_1'x_1 & y_1'y_1 & y_1' \\ -x_2 & -y_2 & -1 & 0 & 0 & 0 & x_2'x_2 & x_2'y_2 & x_2' \\ 0 & 0 & 0 & -x_2 & -y_2 & -1 & y_2'x_2 & y_2'y_2 & y_2' \\ -x_3 & -y_3 & -1 & 0 & 0 & 0 & x_3'x_3 & x_3'y_3 & x_3' \\ 0 & 0 & 0 & -x_3 & -y_3 & -1 & y_3'x_3 & y_3'y_3 & y_3' \\ -x_4 & -y_4 & -1 & 0 & 0 & 0 & x_4'x_4 & x_4'y_4 & x_4' \\ 0 & 0 & 0 & -x_4 & -y_4 & -1 & y_4'x_4 & y_4'y_4 & y_4' \\ 1 & 1 & 1 & 1 & 1 & 1 & 1 & 1 & 1 \end{bmatrix} \mathbf{h}^{\mathrm{T}} = \begin{bmatrix} 0 \\ 0 \\ 0 \\ 0 \\ 0 \\ 0 \\ 0 \\ 0 \\ 1 \end{bmatrix} \tag{10.26}$$

Code 10.2 illustrates the use of this equation to compute a homography. The corresponding points are given in the lists `p` and `q`. The matrices `M` and `b` store the coefficients and constant terms of the system. After the system is solved, the function `imageTransform` is used to obtain an image of the transformation using warping as implemented in Code 10.1 Apply a geometric transformation to an image. Notice that in general we would like to include more points in the solution to increase accuracy and to deal with noise. Thus a better implementation should solve for an overdetermined system.

Fig. 10.3 shows an example of a homography computed with Code 10.2. The homography is computed by considering the corresponding points defined by the four

```
# Corresponding points
p = [[116-centreX,202-centreY],[352-centreX,234-centreY],                                    \
     [140-centreX,384-centreY],[344-centreX,422-centreY]]
q = [[118-centreX,168-centreY],[312-centreX,238-centreY],                                    \
     [146-centreX,352-centreY],[322-centreX,422-centreY]]

# Find transform
M = [[-p[0][0], -p[0][1], -1, 0, 0, 0,  p[0][0]*q[0][0], p[0][1]*q[0][0], q[0][0]], \
     [ 0, 0, 0, -p[0][0], -p[0][1], -1, p[0][0]*q[0][1], p[0][1]*q[0][1], q[0][1]], \
     [-p[1][0], -p[1][1], -1, 0, 0, 0,  p[1][0]*q[1][0], p[1][1]*q[1][0], q[1][0]], \
     [ 0, 0, 0, -p[1][0], -p[1][1], -1, p[1][0]*q[1][1], p[1][1]*q[1][1], q[1][1]], \
     [-p[2][0], -p[2][1], -1, 0, 0, 0,  p[2][0]*q[2][0], p[2][1]*q[2][0], q[2][0]], \
     [ 0, 0, 0, -p[2][0], -p[2][1], -1, p[2][0]*q[2][1], p[2][1]*q[2][1], q[2][1]], \
     [-p[3][0], -p[3][1], -1, 0, 0, 0,  p[3][0]*q[3][0], p[3][1]*q[3][0], q[3][0]], \
     [ 0, 0, 0, -p[3][0], -p[3][1], -1, p[3][0]*q[3][1], p[3][1]*q[3][1], q[3][1]], \
     [ 1, 1, 1,     1,         1,     1,        1,               1,            1  ]]

# Solves the equation A*x=b
b = [0,0,0,0,0,0,0,0,1]
h = solveSystem(M, b)

H = [[h[0], h[1], h[2]],    \
     [h[3], h[4], h[5]],    \
     [h[6], h[7], h[8]] ]

tImage = imageTransform(inputImage, maskImage, H)
```

CODE 10.2 Compute homography.

corners of the front face of the cube in the images in Figs. 10.3A and B (points shown as dots). Fig. 10.3C shows the result of applying the computed homography to the image in Fig. 10.3A. Notice that the cube's face defined by the corresponding points matches the face of the cube in the target image in Fig. 10.3B. However, other planes of the cube appear distorted. This occurs since a homography is a linear transformation that maps points in a planar surface. This is why this transformation is commonly called planar homography. Notice that we used four pairs of 2D image points to obtain the homography, but also three pairs of 3D world points can be used to solve the system in Eq. (10.3). Both approaches define the same homography. However, it is more evident

FIGURE 10.3 Computing a homography.

that three 3D points define a plane such that the mapping defines a transformation between two 3D planes.

Homographies are useful for several image processing operations like stitching and for creating transformations for far or planar objects. Perhaps the most important homography in computer vision is the one defined by the Epipolar geometry. Epipolar geometry defines a homography known as the fundamental matrix whose transformation aligns the rows of two images. The essential matrix is a particular form of the fundamental matrix, and it is used to find the relative position of two cameras from image correspondences [Hartley01]. The development of these homographies is based on the ideas of projections that describe the perspective camera.

10.3 The perspective camera

As discussed in Chapter 1, an image is formed by a complex process involving optics, electronics and mechanical devices. This process maps information in a 3D scene into pixels in an image. A camera model uses mathematical representations to describe the geometry in this process. Different models include different aspects of the image formation, and they are based on different assumptions or simplifications. The perspective camera is the most common model since it gives a good approximation of the geometrical optics in most cameras, and it can be considered a general model that includes other models as simplified cases.

Fig. 10.4 shows the model of the *perspective* camera. This model is also known as the *pinhole* camera since it describes the image formation process of a simple optical device with a small hole. This device is known as camera obscura, and it was developed in the 16th century as to aid artists to create the correct perspective in paintings. Light going

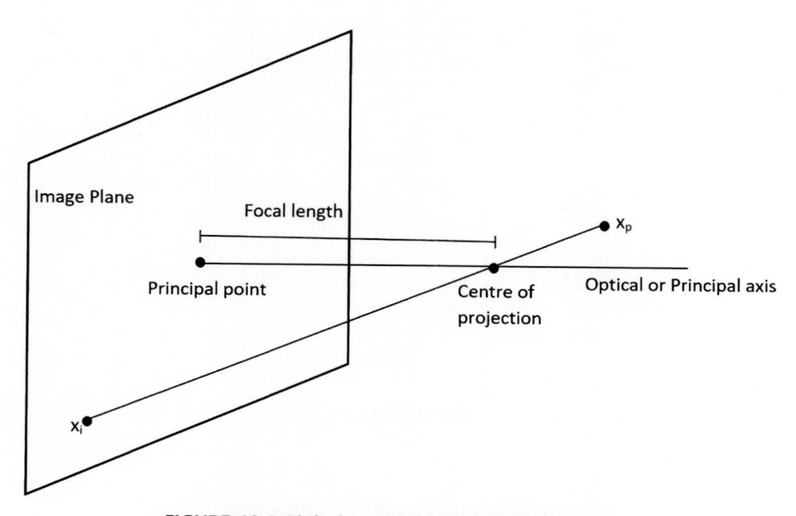

FIGURE 10.4 Pinhole model of perspective camera.

through a pinhole projects an image of a scene onto a back screen. The pinhole is called the centre of projection. Thus, a pixel is obtained by intersecting the image plane with the line between the 3D point and the centre of projection. In the projected image, parallel lines intersect at infinity giving a correct perspective.

Although based on an ancient device, this model represents an accurate description of modern cameras where light is focused in a single point by using lenses. In Fig. 10.1, the centre of projection corresponds to the pinhole. Light passes through the point and it is projected in the image plane. Fig. 10.5 illustrates an alternative configuration where light is focused back to the image plane. The models are equivalent: the image is formed by projecting points through the centre of projection; the point $\mathbf{x}_p$ is mapped into the point $\mathbf{x}_i$ in the image plane and the *focal length* determines the *zoom* distance.

The perspective camera model can be developed using algebraic functions, nevertheless the notation is greatly simplified by using matrix representations. In matrix form, points can be represented in Euclidean co-ordinates, yet a simpler notation is developed using *homogeneous co-ordinates.* Homogeneous co-ordinates represent the projection of points and planes as a simple multiplication.

10.3.1 Perspective camera model

The *perspective camera model* uses the algebra of the projective space to describe the way in which 3D space points are mapped into an image plane. By using homogeneous co-ordinates the geometry of image formation is simply defined by the projection of a 3D point into the plane by one special type of homography known as a projection. In a projection, the matrix $\mathbf{H}$ is not square, so a point in a higher dimension is mapped into a lower dimension. The perspective camera model is defined by the projection transformation,

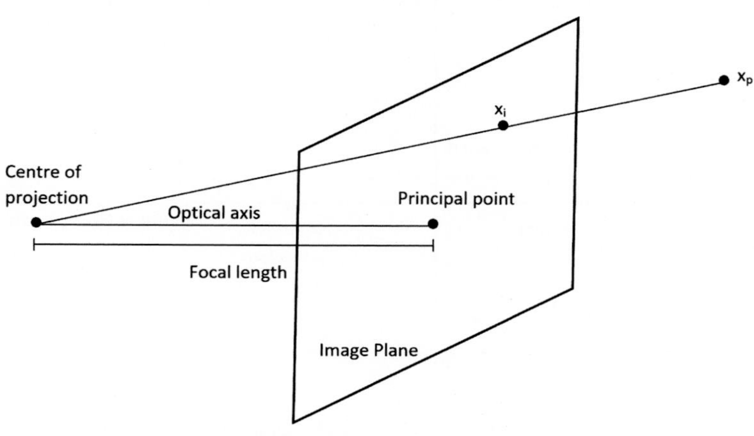

FIGURE 10.5 Perspective camera.

$$\begin{bmatrix} w_i x_i \\ w_i y_i \\ w_i \end{bmatrix} = \begin{bmatrix} p_{1,1} & p_{1,2} & p_{1,3} & p_{1,4} \\ p_{2,1} & p_{2,2} & p_{2,3} & p_{2,4} \\ p_{3,1} & p_{3,2} & p_{3,3} & p_{3,4} \end{bmatrix} \begin{bmatrix} x_p \\ y_p \\ z_p \\ 1 \end{bmatrix} \tag{10.27}$$

This equation can be written in short form as

$$\mathbf{x}_i = \mathbf{P}\mathbf{x}_p \tag{10.28}$$

Here, we have changed the elements from h to p to emphasise that we are using a projection. Also, we use $\mathbf{x}_i$ and $\mathbf{x}_p$ to denote the space and image points as introduced in Fig. 10.4. Notice that the point in the image is in homogeneous form, so the co-ordinates in the image are given by Eq. (10.3).

The matrix **P** is generally described by three geometric transformations as

$$\mathbf{P} = \mathbf{V}\,\mathbf{Q}\,\mathbf{M} \tag{10.29}$$

The matrix **M** transforms the 3D co-ordinates of $\mathbf{x}_p$ to make them relative to the camera system. That is, it transforms world co-ordinates into camera co-ordinates. That is, it transforms the co-ordinates of the point as if the camera were the origin of the co-ordinate system.

If the camera is posed in the world by a rotation and a translation, then the transformation between world and camera co-ordinates is given by the inverse of rotation and translation. We define this matrix as

$$\mathbf{M} = [\mathbf{R} \quad \mathbf{T}] \tag{10.30}$$

or more explicitly as

$$\mathbf{M} = \begin{bmatrix} r_{1,1} & r_{1,2} & r_{1,3} & t_x \\ r_{2,1} & r_{2,2} & r_{2,3} & t_y \\ r_{3,1} & r_{3,2} & r_{3,3} & t_z \end{bmatrix} \tag{10.31}$$

The matrix **R** defines a rotation matrix and **T** a translation vector. The rotation matrix is composed by rotations along each axis. If α, β and γ are the rotation angles, then

$$\mathbf{R} = \begin{bmatrix} \cos(\alpha) & -\sin(\alpha) & 0 \\ \sin(\alpha) & \cos(\alpha) & 0 \\ 1 & 0 & 1 \end{bmatrix} \begin{bmatrix} \cos(\beta) & 0 & -\sin(\beta) \\ 0 & 1 & 0 \\ \sin(\beta) & 0 & \cos(\beta) \end{bmatrix} \begin{bmatrix} 1 & 0 & 0 \\ 0 & \cos(\gamma) & -\sin(\gamma) \\ 0 & \sin(\gamma) & \cos(\gamma) \end{bmatrix} \tag{10.32}$$

Once the points are made relative to the camera frame, the transformation **Q** obtains the co-ordinates of the point projected into the image. As illustrated in Fig. 10.5, the focal length of a camera defines the distance between the centre of projection and the image plane. If f denotes the focal length of a camera, then

$$\mathbf{Q} = \begin{bmatrix} f & 0 & 0 \\ 0 & f & 0 \\ 0 & 0 & 1 \end{bmatrix} \tag{10.33}$$

To understand this projection, let us consider the way a point is mapped into the camera frame as shown in Fig. 10.6. This figure illustrates the side view of the camera; to the right is the depth z axis and to the top down is the y axis. The image plane is shown as a dotted line. The point $\mathbf{x}_p$ is projected into $\mathbf{x}_i$ in the image plane. The tangent of the angle between the line from the centre of projection to $\mathbf{x}_p$ and the principal axis is given by

$$\frac{y_i}{f} = \frac{y_p}{z_p} \tag{10.34}$$

That is

$$y_i = \frac{y_p}{z_p} f \tag{10.35}$$

Using a similar rationale, we can obtain the value

$$x_i = \frac{x_p}{z_p} f \tag{10.36}$$

That is, the projection is obtained by multiplying by the focal length and by dividing by the depth of the point. The transformation matrix in Eq. (10.33) multiplies each co-ordinate by the focal length and copies the depth value into the last co-ordinate of the point. However, since Eq. (10.28) is in homogeneous co-ordinates, the depth value is actually used as divisor when obtaining co-ordinates of the point according to Eq. (10.3). Thus projection can be simply defined by a matrix multiplication as defined in Eq. (10.33).

The factors **M** and **Q** define the co-ordinates of a point in the image plane. However, the co-ordinates in an image are given in pixels. Thus, the last factor **V** is used to change from image co-ordinates to pixels. This transformation also includes a skew deformation to account for misalignments that may occur in the camera system. The transformation **V** is defined as

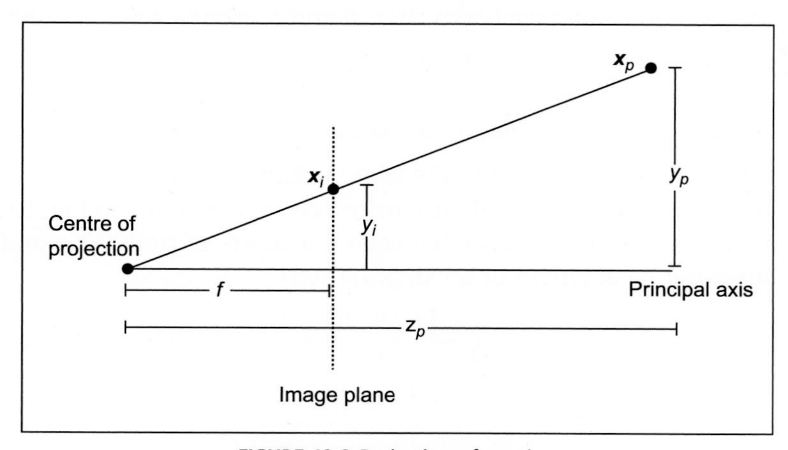

FIGURE 10.6 Projection of a point.

$$\mathbf{V} = \begin{bmatrix} k_u & k_u \cot(\varphi) & u_0 \\ 0 & k_v \sin(\varphi) & v_0 \\ 0 & 0 & 1 \end{bmatrix} \tag{10.37}$$

The constants k_u and k_v define the number of pixels in a world unit, the angle φ defines the skew angle and (u_0, v_0) is the position of the principal point in the image.

Fig. 10.7 illustrates the transformation in Eq. (10.37). The image plane is shown as a dotted rectangle, but it actually extends to infinity. The image is delineated by the axes u and v. A point (x_1, y_1) in the image plane has co-ordinates (u_1, v_1) in the image frame. As previously discussed in Fig. 10.1, the co-ordinates of (x_1, y_1) are relative to the principal point (u_0, v_0). As shown in Fig. 10.7, the skew displaces the point (u_0, v_0) by an amount given by,

$$a_1 = y_1 \cot(\varphi) \text{ and } c_1 = y_1/\sin(\varphi) \tag{10.38}$$

Thus, the new co-ordinates of the point after skew are

$$(\, x_1 + y_1 \cot(\varphi) \quad y_1/\sin(\varphi)\,) \tag{10.39}$$

To convert these co-ordinates to pixels, we need to multiply by the number of pixels that define a unit in the image plane and we also need to add the displacement (u_0, v_0) in pixels. That is,

$$u_1 = k_u x_1 + k_u y_1 \cot(\varphi) + u_0 \text{ and } v_1 = k_v y_1/\sin(\varphi) + v_0 \tag{10.40}$$

These algebraic equations are expressed in matrix form by Eq. (10.37).

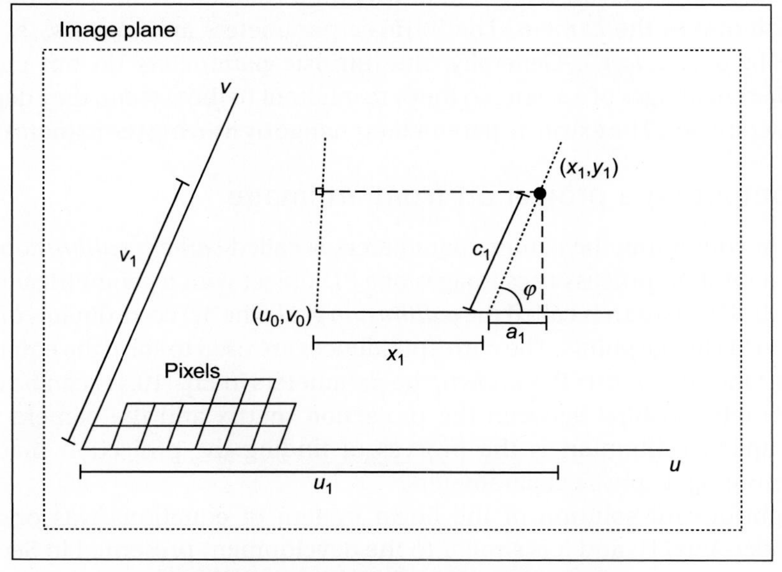

FIGURE 10.7 Image plane to pixels transformation.

10.3.2 Parameters of the perspective camera model

The perspective camera model in Eq. (10.27) has 12 elements. Thus, a particular camera model is completely defined by giving values to 12 unknowns. These unknowns are determined by the parameters of the transformations **M**, **Q** and **V**. The transformation **M** has three rotation angles (α, β, γ) and three translation parameters (t_x, t_y, t_z). The transformation **V** has a single parameter f, whilst the transformation **Q** has the two translation parameters (u_0, v_0), two scale parameters (k_u, k_v) and one skew parameter φ. Thus, 12 parameters of the transformation matrices define 12 elements of the projection model. However, one parameter can be eliminated by combining the matrices **V** and **Q**. That is, the projection matrix in Eq. (10.29) can be written as,

$$\mathbf{P} = \begin{bmatrix} k_u & k_u\cot(\varphi) & u_0 \\ 0 & k_v\sin(\varphi) & v_0 \\ 0 & 0 & 1 \end{bmatrix} \begin{bmatrix} f & 0 & 0 \\ 0 & f & 0 \\ 0 & 0 & 1 \end{bmatrix} \begin{bmatrix} r_{1,1} & r_{1,2} & r_{1,3} & t_x \\ r_{2,1} & r_{2,2} & r_{2,3} & t_y \\ r_{3,1} & r_{3,2} & r_{3,3} & t_z \end{bmatrix} \tag{10.41}$$

or

$$\mathbf{P} = \begin{bmatrix} s_u & s_u\cot(\varphi) & u_0 \\ 0 & s_v\sin(\varphi) & v_0 \\ 0 & 0 & 1 \end{bmatrix} \begin{bmatrix} r_{1,1} & r_{1,2} & r_{1,3} & t_x \\ r_{2,1} & r_{2,2} & r_{2,3} & t_y \\ r_{3,1} & r_{3,2} & r_{3,3} & t_z \end{bmatrix} \tag{10.42}$$

for

$$s_u = fk_u \text{ and } s_v = fk_v \tag{10.43}$$

Thus, the camera model is actually defined by the eleven camera parameters $(\alpha, \beta, \gamma, t_x, t_y, t_z, u_0, v_0, s_u, s_v, \varphi)$.

The camera parameters are divided into two groups to indicate the parameters that are internal or external to the camera. The intrinsic parameters are $(u_0, v_0, s_u, s_v, \varphi)$ and the extrinsic are $(\alpha, \beta, \gamma, t_x, t_y, t_z)$. Generally, the intrinsic parameters do not change when capturing different images of a scene, so they are inherent to the system; they depend on the camera characteristics. The extrinsic parameters change by moving the camera in the world.

10.3.3 Computing a projection from an image

The process of computing the camera parameters is called *camera calibration*. Generally, the camera calibration process uses images of a 3D object with a geometrical pattern (e.g. checker board). The pattern is called the *calibration grid*. The 3D co-ordinates of the pattern are matched to 2D image points. The correspondences are used to solve the equation system in Eq. (10.28). Once the matrix **P** is known, the parameters in Eq. (10.41) can be obtained by observing the relationships between the projection matrix and the camera parameters [Truco98]. Implicit calibration is the process of finding the projection matrix without explicitly computing its physical parameters.

The straightforward solution of the linear system of equations was originally presented in [Abdel-Aziz71], and it is similar to the development presented in Section 10.2.4.

The solution starts by observing that according to Eq. (10.28), a point $\mathbf{x}_p = (x_p, y_p, z_p)$ is mapped into $\mathbf{x}_i = (x_i, y_i)$ by

$$x_i = \frac{x_p p_{1,1} + y_p p_{1,2} + z_p p_{1,3} + p_{1,4}}{x_p p_{3,1} + y_p p_{3,2} + z_p p_{3,3} + p_{3,4}} \quad \text{and} \quad y_i = \frac{x_p p_{2,1} + y_p p_{2,2} + z_p p_{2,3} + p_{2,4}}{x_p p_{3,1} + y_p p_{3,2} + z_p p_{3,3} + p_{3,4}} \tag{10.44}$$

That is,

$$\begin{aligned} x_p p_{1,1} + y_p p_{1,2} + z_p p_{1,3} + p_{1,4} - x_i\left(x_p p_{3,1} + y_p p_{3,2} + z_p p_{3,3} + p_{3,4}\right) = 0 \\ x_p p_{2,1} + y_p p_{2,2} + z_p p_{2,3} + p_{2,4} - y_i\left(x_p p_{3,1} + y_p p_{3,2} + z_p p_{3,3} + p_{3,4}\right) = 0 \end{aligned} \tag{10.45}$$

This can be written in matrix form as

$$\begin{aligned} [\, x_p \;\; y_p \;\; z_p \;\; 1 \;\; 0 \;\; 0 \;\; 0 \;\; 0 \;\; -x_i x_p \;\; -x_i y_p \;\; -x_i z_p \;\; -x_i \,]\, \mathbf{p}^{\mathrm{T}} = 0 \\ [\, 0 \;\; 0 \;\; 0 \;\; 0 \;\; x_p \;\; y_p \;\; z_p \;\; 1 \;\; -y_i x_p \;\; -y_i y_p \;\; -y_i z_p \;\; -x_i \,]\, \mathbf{p}^{\mathrm{T}} = 0 \end{aligned} \tag{10.46}$$

where $\mathbf{p}$ is the vector containing the coefficients of the projection. That is,

$$\mathbf{p} = [\, p_{1,1} \;\; p_{1,2} \;\; p_{1,3} \;\; p_{1,4} \;\; p_{2,1} \;\; p_{2,2} \;\; p_{2,3} \;\; p_{2,4} \;\; p_{3,1} \;\; p_{3,2} \;\; p_{3,3} \;\; p_{3,4} \,] \tag{10.47}$$

Thus, a pair of corresponding points defines two rows of a system of equations with 12 unknowns. Six points will provide 12 rows so that the system is determined. More than 12 points define an overdetermined system that can be solved using least squares.

Code 10.3 illustrates the system of equations defined by Eq. (10.46) for six corresponding points. The lists `pts` and `q` store the corresponding image and 3D points, respectively. In this example, we define the unseen vertex of the cube as origin of the 3D world, and the axes are aligned with the cube edges. The x-axis is towards the right, the y-axis upwards and the z-axis is towards the image plane. The points are defined by the corners of the cube. The matrix in Eq. (10.46) is stored in the variable `M`, and it is filled by using an iteration that takes a pair of corresponding points and evaluates the relation in Eq. (10.46). The solution of the system is stored in the variable `p`. Notice that Eq. (10.46) defines a homogenous system, thus to avoid the trivial solution, we need to include a normalisation. In this case, we set the last value of the coefficient to one. In general, a better normalisation consists on including the constraint $p_{3,1}^2 + p_{3,2}^2 + p_{3,3}^2 = 1$ [Faugeras87].

In order to illustrate the projection, Code 10.3 uses the computed projection to map 100×100 points from the cube's faces into the image. The points in the image are stored in the list `xy`. Since four neighbour points in the face of the cube are mapped as a polygon in the image, then the warping process defined in Code 10.1 can be used to fill the image with a colour. Fig. 10.8 shows the result of this process. Fig. 10.8A shows the original image. Fig. 10.8B shows the filled polygons formed by the projected points. This example uses a different colour for each cube's face. We can see that the computed projection matrix provides a description of how 3D points are mapped into the image.

Code 10.4 illustrates the use of the projection to get a transformation of an image. Similar to the previous example, the implementation computes the projection by using the corners of the cube. Also, the projection is used to map 3D points from the cube's faces into the image. The function `projectionCubePoints` obtains the projection points in a similar fashion to the implementation in Code 10.3. The function `getPointColours`

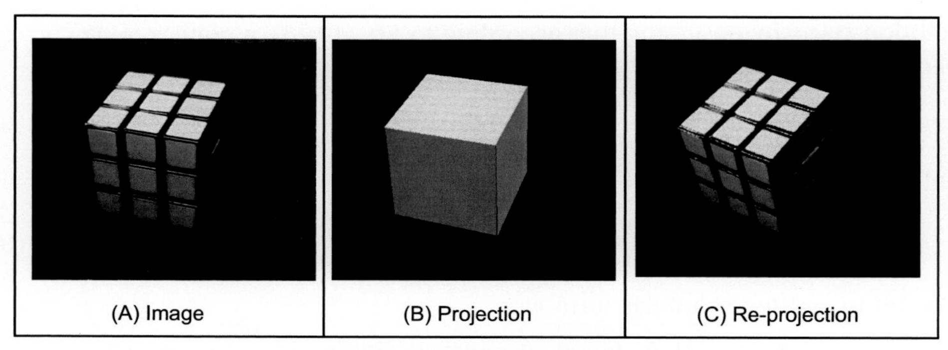

FIGURE 10.8 Image projections.

```
# Points in the cube image
pts = [[131-centreX,378-centreY],[110-centreX,188-centreY],
       [200-centreX,73-centreY],[412-centreX,100-centreY],
       [410-centreX,285-centreY],[349-centreX,418-centreY],
       [345-centreX,220-centreY]]

# Points in the 3D space
q = [[0,0,1],[0,1,1], [0,1,0],[1,1,0], [1,0,0],[1,0,1], [1,1,1]]

# Fill matrix
M = [ ]
for row in range(0,6):
    r1 = [ q[row][0],q[row][1], q[row][2],1,0,0,0,0,-pts[row][0]*q[row][0],   \
          -pts[row][0]*q[row][1],-pts[row][0]*q[row][2],-pts[row][0] ]
    r2 = [ 0,0,0,0,q[row][0],q[row][1], q[row][2],1,-pts[row][1]*q[row][0],   \
          -pts[row][1]*q[row][1],-pts[row][1]*q[row][2], -pts[row][1] ]
    M.append(r1)
    M.append(r2)

# Solves the equation M*p=r
r = [0,0,0,0,0,0,0,0,0,0,0,1]
p = solveSystem(M, r)
P = [[p[0], p[1], p[2], p[3]],     \
     [p[4], p[5], p[6], p[7]],     \
     [p[8], p[9], p[10], p[11]] ]

# Project world points into the image using the computed projection
npts = 100
origin, v1, v2 = [0,0,1], [1,0,0], [0,1,0]
xy = [ ]
for a in range(0, npts):
    rowxy = [ ]
    for b in range(0, npts):

        v1D = [a*v1[0]/float(npts-1), a*v1[1]/float(npts-1), a*v1[2]/float(npts-1)]
        v2D = [b*v2[0]/float(npts-1), b*v2[1]/float(npts-1), b*v2[2]/float(npts-1)]
        s = [origin[0]+v1D[0]+v2D[0], origin[1]+v1D[1]+v2D[1], origin[2]+v1D[2]+v2D[2]]

        sx = p[0]*s[0] + p[1]*s[1] + p[2]*s[2]  + p[3]
        sy = p[4]*s[0] + p[5]*s[1] + p[6]*s[2]  + p[7]
        sz = p[8]*s[0] + p[9]*s[1] + p[10]*s[2] + p[11]

        rowxy.append([int(sx/sz) + centreX, int(sy/sz) + centreY])

    xy.append(rowxy)
```

CODE 10.3 Compute projection.

```
# Obtain the projection
p = computeProjection(pts,q)

npts = 100
xy = projectionCubePoints(npts, p, centreX, centreY)
colours = getPointColours(xy, maskImage, inputImage)

# Transform points
qT = [ ]
angY = 0.3
angX = -0.2
for pointNum in range(0,len(q)):
    s = [q[pointNum][0]-.5, q[pointNum][1]-.5, q[pointNum][2]-.5]
    rx = .5 + cos(angY)*s[0] + sin(angY)*s[2]
    ry = .5 + sin(angX)*sin(angY)*s[0] + cos(angX)*s[1] - sin(angX)*cos(angY)*s[2]
    rz = .5 - cos(angX)*sin(angY)*s[0] + sin(angX)*s[1] + cos(angX)*cos(angY)*s[2]

    qT.append([rx,ry,rz])

p = computeProjection(pts,qT)
xy = projectionCubePoints(npts, p, centreX, centreY)

# Output image
tImage = createImageRGB(width, height)
fillImageColours(colours, xy, tImage)
showImageRGB(tImage)
```

CODE 10.4 Compute re-projection

obtains the colours of the projected points from the original image. That is, for each point in the cubes' face, it obtains the colour in the original image. A re-projection is obtained by projecting the 3D coloured points into another image to generate a new view. To explain this process, we should remember that according to Eq. (10.29) the projection is defined as

$$\mathbf{x}_i = \mathbf{VQMx}_p \tag{10.48}$$

Since **M** defines the rotation and translation, then we can define a new view by changing the projection as

$$\mathbf{x}_i = \mathbf{VQM'x}_p \tag{10.49}$$

If we define $\mathbf{M}' = \mathbf{ML}$,

$$\mathbf{x}_i = \mathbf{VQMLx}_p \text{ or } \boldsymbol{x}_i = \mathbf{PLx}_p \tag{10.50}$$

That is, a new view can be obtained by transforming the points $\mathbf{x}_p$ by a rigid transformation **L** and then using the matrix projection. Accordingly, the implementation in Code 10.4 first transforms the original points in the list `q` into the points in the list `qT` by a transformation **L** that, in this example, only rotates along the x and y axis. Afterwards, the transformed points are used to compute a new projection that maps the transformed points into the image projection. The projection is used to map the faces of the cube into the new image, and the result is used in the warping process with the colours obtained from the original projection. Fig. 10.8C shows the result of the whole process. Other views can be generated by changing the transformation **L**. The obtained view contains the geometry of the model and the textures of the original image.

10.4 Affine camera

Although the perspective camera model is probably the most common model used in computer vision, there are alternative models that are useful in particular situations. One alternative model of reduced complexity and that is useful in many applications is the *affine camera model*. This model is also called the *paraperspective* or *linear* model and it reduces the perspective model by setting the focal length f to infinity. Fig. 10.9 compares how the perspective and affine camera models map points into the image plane. The figure illustrates the projection of points from a side view, and it projects the corner points of a pair of objects represented by two rectangles. In the projective model, the projection produces changes of size in the objects according to their distance to the image plane; the far object is projected into a smaller area than the close object. The size

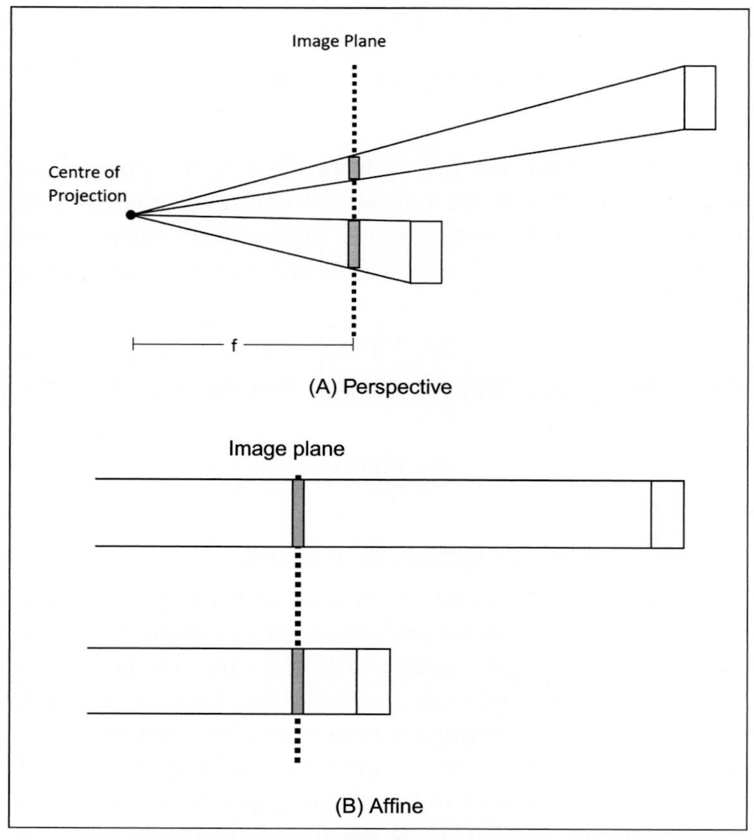

FIGURE 10.9 Perspective and affine camera models.

and distance relationship is determined by the focal length f. As we increase the focal length, projection lines decrease their slope and become horizontal. As illustrated in the figure, in the limit when the centre of projection is infinitely far away from the image plane, the lines do not intersect and the objects have the same projected area.

In spite of not accounting for changes in size due to distances, the affine camera provides a useful model when the depth position of objects in the scene with respect to the camera frame does not change significantly. This is the case in many indoor scenes and in many industrial applications where objects are aligned to a working plane. It is very useful to represent scenes on layers, that is, planes of objects with similar depth. Also affine models are simple and thus algorithms are more stable. Additionally, an affine camera is linear since it does not include the projection division.

10.4.1 Affine camera model

In the affine camera model, Eq. (10.27) is defined as

$$\begin{bmatrix} x_i \\ y_i \\ 1 \end{bmatrix} = \begin{bmatrix} p_{1,1} & p_{1,2} & p_{1,3} & p_{1,4} \\ p_{2,1} & p_{2,2} & p_{2,3} & p_{2,4} \\ 0 & 0 & 0 & 1 \end{bmatrix} \begin{bmatrix} x_p \\ y_p \\ z_p \\ 1 \end{bmatrix} \quad (10.51)$$

This equation can be written in short form as

$$\mathbf{x}_i = \mathbf{P_A x}_p \quad (10.52)$$

Here, we use the sub-index **A** to indicate that the affine camera transformation is given by a special form of the projection **P**. The last row in Eq. (10.39) can be omitted. It is only shown to emphasise that it is a special case of the perspective model. However, at difference of the perspective camera, points in the image plane are actually in Euclidean co-ordinates. That is, the affine camera maps points from the projective space to the Euclidean plane.

Similar to the projection transformation, the transformation **A** can be factorised in three factors that account for the camera's rigid transformation, the projection of points from space into the image plane and for the mapping of points on the image plane into image pixels.

$$\mathbf{A} = \mathbf{V}\,\mathbf{Q_A}\,\mathbf{M_A} \quad (10.53)$$

Here, the sub-index **A** indicates that these matrices are the affine versions of the transformations defined in Eq. (10.29). We start by a rigid transformation as defined in Eq. (10.31). As in the case of the perspective model, this transformation is defined by the position of the camera and makes the co-ordinates of a point in 3D space relative to the camera frame.

$$\mathbf{M_A} = \begin{bmatrix} r_{1,1} & r_{1,2} & r_{1,3} & t_x \\ r_{2,1} & r_{2,2} & r_{2,3} & t_y \\ r_{3,1} & r_{3,2} & r_{3,3} & t_z \\ 0 & 0 & 0 & 1 \end{bmatrix} \quad (10.54)$$

That is,

$$\mathbf{M_A} = \begin{bmatrix} \mathbf{R} & \mathbf{T} \\ 0 & 1 \end{bmatrix} \tag{10.55}$$

The last row is added so the transformation $\mathbf{Q_A}$ can have four rows. We need four rows in $\mathbf{Q_A}$ in order to define a parallel projection into the image plane. Similar to the transformation $\mathbf{Q}$, the transformation $\mathbf{Q_A}$ projects a point in the camera frame into the image plane. The difference is that in the affine model, points in space are orthographically projected into the image plane. This can be defined by

$$\mathbf{Q_A} = \begin{bmatrix} 1 & 0 & 0 & 0 \\ 0 & 1 & 0 & 0 \\ 0 & 0 & 0 & 1 \end{bmatrix} \tag{10.56}$$

This defines a projection when the focal length is set to infinity. Intuitively, you can see that when transforming a point $\mathbf{x}_p^T = [x_p \quad y_p \quad z_p \quad 1]$ by Eq. (10.56), the x and y co-ordinates are copied and the depth z_p value does not change the projection. Thus, Eqs. (10.34) and (10.35) for the affine camera become

$$x_i = x_p \text{ and } y_i = y_p \tag{10.57}$$

That is, the points in the camera frame are projected along the line $z_p = 0$. This is a line parallel to the image plane. The transformation $\mathbf{V}$ in Eq. (10.53) provides the pixel co-ordinates of points in the image plane. This process is exactly the same in the perspective and affine models and it is defined by Eq. (10.37).

10.4.2 Affine camera model and the perspective projection

It is possible to show that the affine model is a particular case of the perspective model by considering the alternative camera representation illustrated in Fig. 10.10. This figure is similar to Fig. 10.6. The difference is that in the previous model, the centre of the camera frame is in the centre of projection and in Fig. 10.10 it is considered to be the principal point (i.e. on the image plane). In general, the camera frame does not need to be located at a particular position in the camera, but it can be arbitrarily set. When set in the image plane, as illustrated in Fig. 10.10, the z camera co-ordinate of a point defines its depth in the image plane. Thus Eq. (10.34) is replaced by

$$\frac{y_i}{f} = \frac{h}{z_p} \tag{10.58}$$

From Fig. 10.10, we can see that $y_p = y_i + h$. Thus,

$$y_p = y_i + z_p \frac{y_i}{f} \tag{10.59}$$

Solving for y_i we have that

$$y_i = \frac{f\, y_p}{f + z_p} \tag{10.60}$$

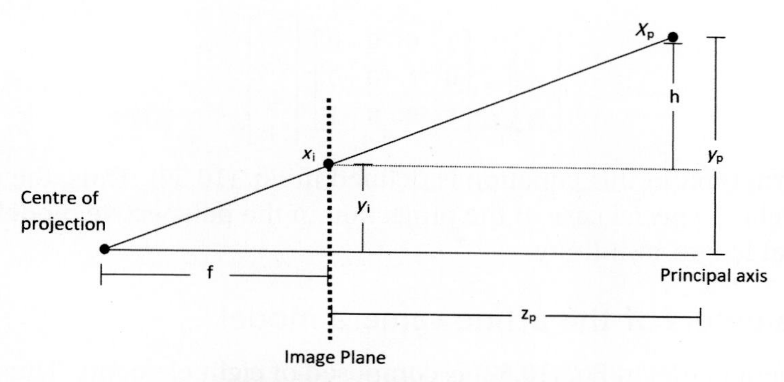

FIGURE 10.10 Projection of a point.

We can use a similar development to find the x_i co-ordinate. That is,

$$x_i = \frac{f\, x_p}{f + z_p} \tag{10.61}$$

Using homogeneous co-ordinates, Eqs. (10.60) and (10.61) can be written in matrix form as

$$\begin{bmatrix} x_i \\ y_i \\ z_i \end{bmatrix} = \begin{bmatrix} f & 0 & 0 & 0 \\ 0 & f & 0 & 0 \\ 0 & 0 & 1 & f \end{bmatrix} \begin{bmatrix} x_p \\ y_p \\ z_p \\ 1 \end{bmatrix} \tag{10.62}$$

This equation is an alternative to Eq. (10.33); it represents a perspective projection. The difference is that Eq. (10.62) assumes that the camera axis is the located at the principal point of a camera. Using Eq. (10.62), it is easy to see the projection in the affine camera model as a special case of projection in the perspective camera model. To show that Eq. (10.33) becomes an affine model when f is set to be infinite, we define $B = 1/f$. Thus, Eq. (10.60) can be rewritten as,

$$y_i = \frac{y_p}{1 + B\, z_p} \quad \text{and} \quad x_i = \frac{x_p}{1 + B z_p} \tag{10.63}$$

or

$$\begin{bmatrix} x_i \\ y_i \\ z_i \end{bmatrix} = \begin{bmatrix} 1 & 0 & 0 & 0 \\ 0 & 1 & 0 & 0 \\ 0 & 0 & B & 1 \end{bmatrix} \begin{bmatrix} x_p \\ y_p \\ z_p \\ 1 \end{bmatrix} \tag{10.64}$$

When f tends to infinity B tends to zero. Thus, the projection in Eq. (10.62) for an affine camera becomes

$$\begin{bmatrix} x_i \\ y_i \\ z_i \end{bmatrix} = \begin{bmatrix} 1 & 0 & 0 & 0 \\ 0 & 1 & 0 & 0 \\ 0 & 0 & 0 & 1 \end{bmatrix} \begin{bmatrix} x_p \\ y_p \\ z_p \\ 1 \end{bmatrix} \tag{10.65}$$

The transformation in this equation is defined in Eq. (10.56). Thus, the projection in the affine model is a special case of the projection in the perspective model obtained by setting the focal length to infinity.

10.4.3 Parameters of the affine camera model

The affine camera model in Eq. (10.52) is composed of eight elements. Thus, a particular camera model is completely defined by giving values to eight unknowns. These unknowns are determined by the 11 parameters $(\alpha, \beta, \gamma, t_x, t_y, t_z, u_0, v_0, k_u, k_v, \varphi)$ defined in the matrices in Eq. (10.53). However, since we are projecting points orthographically into the image plane, the translation in depth is lost. This can be seen by combining the matrices $\mathbf{Q_A}$ and $\mathbf{M_A}$ in Eq. (10.53). That is,

$$\mathbf{G} = \begin{bmatrix} 1 & 0 & 0 & 0 \\ 0 & 1 & 0 & 0 \\ 0 & 0 & 0 & 1 \end{bmatrix} \begin{bmatrix} r_{1,1} & r_{1,2} & r_{1,3} & t_x \\ r_{2,1} & r_{2,2} & r_{2,3} & t_y \\ r_{3,1} & r_{3,2} & r_{3,3} & t_z \\ 0 & 0 & 0 & 1 \end{bmatrix} \tag{10.66}$$

or

$$\mathbf{G_A} = \begin{bmatrix} r_{1,1} & r_{1,2} & r_{1,3} & t_x \\ r_{2,1} & r_{2,2} & r_{2,3} & t_y \\ 0 & 0 & 0 & 1 \end{bmatrix} \tag{10.67}$$

Thus Eq. (10.53) becomes

$$\mathbf{A} = \mathbf{V}\,\mathbf{G_A} \tag{10.68}$$

Similar to Eq. (10.55), the matrix $\mathbf{G_A}$ can be written as

$$\mathbf{G_A} = \begin{bmatrix} \mathbf{R_A} & \mathbf{T_A} \\ 0 & 1 \end{bmatrix} \tag{10.69}$$

and it defines the orthographic projection of the rigid transformation $\mathbf{M_A}$ into the image plane. According to Eq. (10.67), we have that the translation is,

$$\mathbf{T_A} = \begin{bmatrix} t_x \\ t_y \\ 1 \end{bmatrix} \tag{10.70}$$

Since we do not have the translation t_z, we cannot determine if objects are far away or close to the camera. The rotation is defined according to Eq. (10.66) as

$$\mathbf{R_A} = \begin{bmatrix} \cos(\alpha) & -\sin(\alpha) & 0 \\ \sin(\alpha) & \cos(\alpha) & 0 \\ 0 & 0 & 0 \end{bmatrix} \begin{bmatrix} \cos(\beta) & 0 & -\sin(\beta) \\ 0 & 1 & 0 \\ 0 & 0 & 0 \end{bmatrix} \begin{bmatrix} 1 & 0 & 0 \\ 0 & \cos(\gamma) & -\sin(\gamma) \\ 0 & 0 & 0 \end{bmatrix} \tag{10.71}$$

Thus, the eight elements of the affine camera projection matrix are determined by the intrinsic parameters $(u_0, v_0, s_u, s_v, \varphi)$ and the extrinsic parameters $(\alpha, \beta, \gamma, t_x, t_y)$.

10.5 Weak perspective model

The *weak perspective model* defines a geometric mapping that stands between the perspective and the affine models. This model considers the distance between points in the scene is small relative to the focal length. Thus, Eqs. (10.34) and (10.35) are approximated by

$$y_i = \frac{y_p}{\mu_z} f \text{ and } x_i = \frac{x_p}{\mu_z} f \tag{10.72}$$

for μ_z is the average z co-ordinate of all the points in a scene.

Fig. 10.11 illustrates two possible geometric interpretations for the relationships defined in Eq. (10.72). Fig. 10.11A, illustrates a two-step process wherein first all points are affine projected to a plane orthogonal to the image plane and at a distance μ_z. Points on this plane are then mapped into the image plane by a perspective projection. The projection on the plane $z = \mu_z$ simply replaces the z co-ordinates of the points by μ_z. Since points are assumed to be close, then this projection is a good approximation of the scene. Thus, the weak perspective model corresponds to a perspective model for scenes approximated by planes parallels to the image plane.

A second geometric interpretation of Eq. (10.72) is illustrated in Fig. 10.11B. In Eq. (10.72), we can combine the values f and μ_z into a single constant. Thus, Eq. (10.72) actually corresponds to a scaled version of Eq. (10.57). In Fig. 10.11B, objects in the scene are first mapped into the image plane by an affine projection and then the image is rescaled by a value f/μ_z. Thus, the affine model can be seen as a particular case of the weak perspective model when $f/\mu_z = 1$.

By following the two geometric interpretations discussed above, the weak perspective model can be formulated by changing the projection equations of the perspective or the affine models. For simplicity, we consider the weak perspective from the affine model. Thus, Eq. (10.56) should include a change in scale. That is,

$$\mathbf{Q_A} = \begin{bmatrix} f/\mu_z & 0 & 0 & 0 \\ 0 & f/\mu_z & 0 & 0 \\ 0 & 0 & 0 & 1 \end{bmatrix} \tag{10.73}$$

By considering the definition in Eq. (10.53), we can move the scale factor in this matrix to the matrix **V**. Thus the model for the weak-perspective model can be expressed as

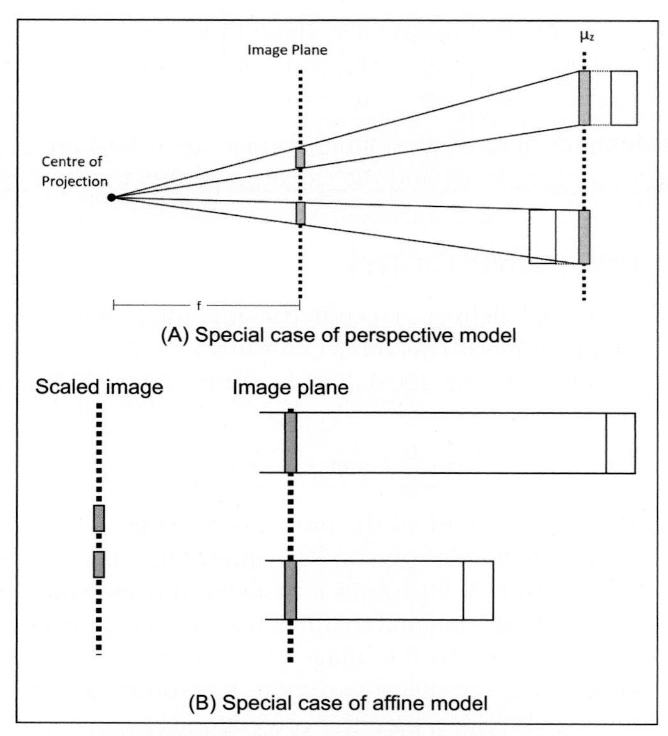

FIGURE 10.11 Weak perspective camera model.

$$\mathbf{P} = \begin{bmatrix} s_u & s_u\cot(\varphi) & u_0 \\ 0 & s_v\sin(\varphi) & v_0 \\ 0 & 0 & 1 \end{bmatrix} \begin{bmatrix} 1 & 0 & 0 & 0 \\ 0 & 1 & 0 & 0 \\ 0 & 0 & 0 & 1 \end{bmatrix} \begin{bmatrix} r_{1,1} & r_{1,2} & r_{1,3} & t_x \\ r_{2,1} & r_{2,2} & r_{2,3} & t_y \\ r_{3,1} & r_{3,2} & r_{3,3} & t_z \\ 0 & 0 & 0 & 1 \end{bmatrix} \tag{10.74}$$

for

$$s_u = fk_u/\mu_z \text{ and } s_v = fk_v/\mu_z \tag{10.75}$$

Thus the weak perspective is a scaled version of the affine model. The scale is a function of f that defines the distance of the centre of the camera to the image plane and the average distance μ_z.

10.6 Discussion

In this chapter, we have formulated the most common models of camera geometry. However, in addition to perspective and affine camera models there exist other models that consider different camera properties. For example, cameras built from a linear array of sensors can be modelled by particular versions of the perspective and affine models obtained by considering a 1D image plane. These 1D camera models can also be used to represent stripes of pixels obtained by cameras with 2D image planes, and they have found an important application in mosaic construction from video images.

Besides image plane dimensionality, perhaps the most evident extension of camera models is to consider lens distortions. Small geometric distortions are generally ignored or deal with as noise in computer vision techniques. Strong geometric distortions such as the ones produced by wide-angle or fish-eye lens can be modelled by considering a spherical image plane or by non-linear projections. Camera models can include linear or non-linear distortions. The model of wide-angle cameras has found applications in environment map capture and panoramic mosaics.

The formulation of camera models is the basis of two central problems in computer vision. The first problem is known as camera calibration, and it focuses on computing the camera parameters from image data. There are many camera calibration techniques based on the camera model and different types of data. In general, camera calibration techniques are grouped into two main classes. Strong camera calibration assumes knowledge of the 3D co-ordinates of image points. Weak calibration techniques do not know 3D co-ordinates, but they assume knowledge of the type of motion of a camera. Also, some techniques focus on intrinsic or extrinsic parameters. The second central problem in computer vision is called scene reconstruction and focuses on recovering the co-ordinates of points in the 3D scene from image data.

10.7 Further reading

The main source for further material on this topic is the main textbook [Hartley01]. One of the early texts [Trucco98] has endured for many years and another [Cyganek11] considers recovery of 3D surfaces from stereo images. A more recent textbook [Laga19] 'establishes links between solutions proposed by different communities that studied 3D shape, such as mathematics and statistics, medical imaging, computer vision, and computer graphics'. These textbooks use the camera models to develop computer vision techniques such as reconstruction and motion estimation. There are several papers that review and compare different calibration techniques. A discussion about calibration types is presented in [Salvi02] and [Remondino06]. A survey including camera models, acquisition technologies and computer vision techniques is presented in [Strum11]. Perhaps the most important camera model after the projective camera is the projection defined by an omnidirectional camera. An *omnidirectional camera* has a visual field that covers a hemisphere or (approximately) the entire sphere [Danillidis00]. These types of images cannot be described using the conventional pinhole model because of the very high distortion.

References

[Aguado00] Aguado, A. S., Montiel, E., and Nixon, M. S., On the Intimate Relationship between the Principle of Duality and the Hough Transform, *Proceedings of the Royal Society of London*, **456**, pp 503-526, 2000.

[Abdel-Aziz71] Abdel-Aziz, Y.I., and Karara, H.M., Direct Linear Transformation into Object Space Co-ordinates in Close-Range Photogrammetry. *Proceedings of Symposium on Close-Range Photogrammetry*, pp 1-18, 1971.

[Cyganek11] Cyganek, B., and Siebert, J. P., *An Introduction to 3D Computer Vision Techniques and Algorithms*, John Wiley & Sons, NJ, USA, 2011.

[Daniilidis00] Daniilidis K., Geyer C., Omnidirectional Vision: Theory and Algorithms, *Proceedings of 15th International Conference on Pattern Recognition*, 2000.

[Faugeras87] Faugeras, O. D., and Toscani, G., Camera Calibration for 3D Computer Vision. *Proceedings of International Workshop on Industrial Applications of Machine Vision and Machine Intelligence*, Silken, Japan, pp 240-247, 1987.

[Hartley01] Hartley, R., and Zisserman, A., *Multiple View Geometry in Computer Vision*, Cambridge University Press, Cambridge, UK, 2001.

[Laga19] Laga, H., Guo, Y., Tabia, H., Fisher, R. B., Bennamoun, M., *3D Shape Analysis: Fundamentals, Theory, and Applications*, John Wiley & Sons, NJ, USA, 2019.

[Remondino06] Remondino and C. Fraser. Digital Camera Calibration Methods: Considerations and Comparisons. *Proceedings of ISPRS Commission V Symposium*, **6**, pp 266-272, 2006.

[Salvi02] Salvi J., Armangu X., and Batlle J., A Comparative Review of Camera Calibrating Methods with Accuracy Evaluation, *Pattern Recognition*, **35**, pp 1617–1635, 2002.

[Strum11] Sturm P., Ramalingam S., Tardif J-P., Gasparini S., and Barreto J., Camera Models and Fundamental Concepts Used in Geometric Computer Vision. *Foundations and Trends in Computer Graphics and Vision*, **6**(1-2), pp 1-183, 2011.

[Trucco98] Trucco E., Verri, A., *Introductory Techniques for 3-D Computer Vision*, Prentice Hall, 1998.

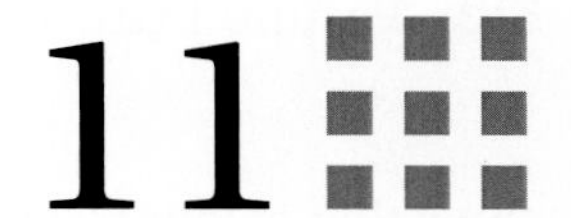

Colour images

11.1 Overview

Grey level images use a single value per pixel that it is called intensity or brightness. As presented in Chapter 2, the intensity represents the amount of light reflected or emitted by an object, and it is dependent on the object's material properties as well as on the sensitivity of the camera sensors. Historically, image processing and computer vision have mainly used grey level images since colour sensors were very expensive and the computer processing was very limited. Also, grey level images have less noise, so they are adequate for locating low-level features like edges and corners. However, as devices have increased processing power and with the development of inexpensive colour sensors of high quality, colour images are now ubiquitous. So image processing is now commonly used to process colour information and not only to develop algorithms for image understanding and scene representation, but also to create images that appeal to humans. Thus, colour image processing has become increasingly necessary, as seen in superpixels (Section 8.2.3). Besides, it is evident that some processes like the localisation and identification of objects can obtain clear advantage by incorporating colour information, as we have already seen in saliency detection. For example, colour is an important clue in traffic sign recognition.

In general, the processing of colour images is an extensive subject of study. This chapter only introduces the fundamental concepts that are used to represent and describe colours. We know that a camera creates a representation of colour according to sensor responses. When an image is displayed, the representation in the camera is transformed into electromagnetic waves that we perceive as colours. In this process, some information is lost and changed, so in general we do not perceive an image the same as a viewed scene. The aim of a colour model is to be able to represent colours such that an image is an accurate representation of the way we perceive the world, to be able to recreate colours or to create an adequate representation for particular processes such as video transmission. As such, colour models are not concerned much with the physical nature of electromagnetic waves (i.e. spectrometry) but the focus is on obtaining a description or catalogue that organises and depicts colour properties. Thus, colour models provide a numerical representation for a particular colour and they define the relationship of this colour with other colours, but the representation is not concerned with the electromagnetic spectrum.

In this chapter, we shall see how a description is obtained based on the *tristimulus theory* and how alternative colour models organise and describe the colours. We shall

Feature Extraction and Image Processing for Computer Vision. https://doi.org/10.1016/B978-0-12-814976-8.00011-7

show that colour models describe each colour as a set of components, so each colour can be stored digitally for processing and reproduction. Colour models are important since they permit analysis and study of the relationships and properties of colours.

In this chapter, we distinguish four types of colour models. The first type of model is based on perception. Perception models sort out colours according to the similarities we perceive, and they were developed by experiments aimed at establishing measurable links between colours. The second type of model describes colours according to the way they are used in reproduction systems (e.g. printing and displaying). The third type of model looks for separating the brightness from the hue (pigment). These models were created by the practical necessity of video transmission and have become very popular for video encoding. The last type of colour model creates a perceptual organisation by rearranging the colour of other models by using a colour transformation. The aim is to create an arrangement that is more intuitive and easy to interpret. The chapter is summarised in Table 11.1.

11.2 Colour image theory

11.2.1 Colour images

The representation of colour is based on the relationships between coloured light and perception. Light can be understood as an electromagnetic wave, and when these waves hit an object some light frequencies are absorbed whilst some others are reflected

Table 11.1 Overview of this chapter.

Main topic	Sub topics	Main points
Colour theory	What are colour images and what is the theory used to create colour images? What are colour components?	Visible *spectrum*. *Multispectral* images and *colour* images. *Tristimulus* theory. *Metamers*. Colour principles.
Colour models	How do we represent a colour?	*Geometric equation*, primaries, *Grassmann's* law. *Lumen*. *Luminous* efficiency.
Perception colour models	How do we represent colours according to the way we perceive them? Uniform colour models.	*CIE*, *RGB*, *XYZ*. *Colour matching function*. Chromaticity co-ordinates. *MacAdam* ellipses. *CIE LUV* and *CIE LAB*.
Additive colour models	Representation of colours for reproduction systems like printers and displays.	*Additive* and *subtractive* reproduction of colour. The colour cube. *RGB* and *CMY*. *Colour transformations*.
Luminance and chrominance colour models	Colour models based on brightness.	*Luma* and *chrominance*. *Hue* and *saturation*. *Gamma* correction. *Power* function. Component video. *Digital video*. *YUV*, *YIC* and *YCbCr*.
Transformations to create intuitive colour models	How more intuitive colour models are obtained by a colour transformation.	*HSV*, *HLS* and *HSI*. *Chroma*, shade and tone. The *hexagonal* model. The *triangular* model. *Saturation*.

towards our eye and thus creating what we perceive as colours. Similarly, when the reflected light hits a camera's sensor, it obtains a measure of intensity by adding energy on a range of frequencies. In general, *multi-spectral* images maintain information about the absorption characteristics of particular materials by maintaining the measured energy over several frequencies. This can be achieved by using filters on the top of the sensors, by using prisms to disperse the light or by including several sensors sensitive to particular frequencies on the electromagnetic spectrum. In any case, colour images are obtained by selecting different frequencies. Multi-spectral images which cover frequencies in the visible spectrum are called colour images. Other multi-spectral images covering other part of the spectrum capture the energy with wavelengths that cannot be perceived by the human eye.

Since colour cameras have several sensors per pixel over a specific frequency range, then colour images contain information about the luminance intensities over several frequencies. A colour model gives meaning to this information by organising colours in a way that can be related to the colours we perceive. In colour image processing, colours are not described by a frequency signature, but they are described and organised according to our perception. The description of how light is perceived by the human eye is based on the *tristimulus theory*.

11.2.2 Tristimulus theory

Electromagnetic waves have an infinite range of frequencies, but the human eye can only perceive the range of frequencies in the visible spectrum which ranges from about 400 to 700 nm. Each frequency defines a different colour as illustrated in Fig. 11.1. Generally, we refer to light as the electromagnetic waves that transfer energy in this part of the spectrum. Electromagnetic waves beyond the visual spectrum have special names like X-rays, gamma rays, microwaves, or ultraviolet light.

In the visible spectrum, each wavelength is perceived as a colour; the extreme values are perceived as violet and red and between them there are greens and yellows. However, not all the colours that we perceive are in the visible spectrum, but many colours are

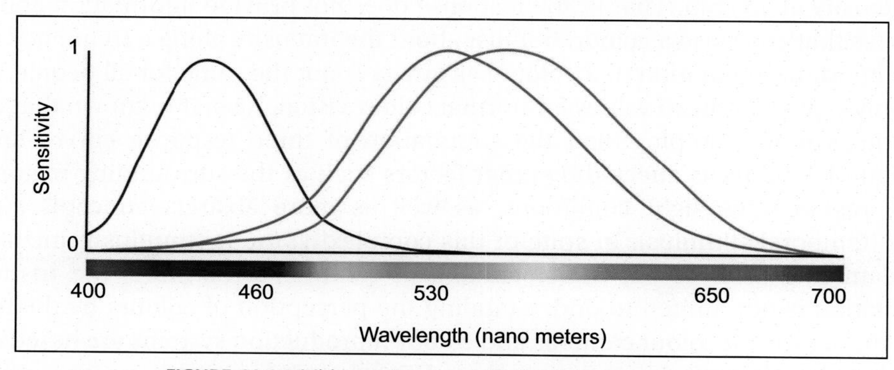

FIGURE 11.1 Visible spectrum and tristimulus response curves.

created when light with different wavelengths reaches our eye at the same time. For example, pink or white are perceived from a mix of light at different frequencies. In addition to new colours, mixtures of colours can produce colours that we cannot distinguish as new colours, but they may be perceived as a colour in the visible spectrum. That is, the light created by mixing the colours of the spectrum does not produce a stimulus that we can identify as unique. This is why applications such astronomy cannot identify composition elements from colour images, but they rely on spectrograms to measure the actual spectral content of light. *Metamers* are colours that we perceive as the same, but have a different mix of colours.

As explained in Section 1.3, our own representation of colour is created by three types of cell receptors in our eyes that are sensitive to a range of frequencies near blue, red and green. Thus, instead of describing colours by frequency content or radiometric properties, colours can be represented by three stimuli according to the way we perceive them. This way of organising colours is known as *trichromatic* or *tristimulus* representation. The tristimulus representation was widely used by artists in the 18th century and was experimentally developed by physicists. The theory was formally developed by Thomas Young and Hermann von Helmholtz [Sherman81] with two main principles:

1. all the colours we perceive can be represented by a mixture of three primary colours and
2. the colour space is linear. That is, the mixture is defined by summations and the addition of two colours is achieved by adding its primary components.

In addition to these principles, the tristimulus representation establishes how the primaries are defined by considering the sensitivity of each cell receptor to each frequency in the visual spectrum. Each receptor defines a tristimulus response curve as illustrated in Fig. 11.1. That is, the blue receptor will generate a high response for energy around 430 nm, the green and the red around 550 and 560 nm, respectively. The receptors integrate the values in all frequencies and provide a single value, thus the same response can be obtained by different stimulus. For example, the blue receptor will provide the same response for a light with a high value at 400 nm and for a light with lower intensity at 430 nm. That is, the response does not provide information about the frequencies that compose a colour, but just about the intensity along a frequency range.

It is important to mention that colour sensitivity is not the same for all people, so the curves only represent mean values for normal colour vision. Also, it is known that colour perception is more complex than the summation of three response curves and the perception of a colour is affected by other factors such as the surrounding regions (i.e. context), region sizes, light conditions, as well as more abstract concepts such as memory (temporal stimulus). In spite of this complexity, the tristimulus principles are the fundamental basis of our understanding of colour. Furthermore, the tristimulus representation is not limited to understanding the perception of colours by the human eye, but the sensors in colour cameras and colour reproduction systems are based on the same principles. That is, according to the tristimulus theory, these systems only use three values to capture and re-create all the visible colours. This does not imply that the theory describes the nature of light composition or the true perception of the human eye, and it only provides a mechanism to represent the perception of colours.

11.2.3 The colourimetric equation

According to the tristimulus theory, all the possible colours we perceive can be defined in a three-dimensional linear space. That is, if $[c_1\ c_2\ c_3]$ define *colour components* (or weights) and $[A_1\ A_2\ A_3]$ some *base colours* (or *primaries*), then a colour is defined by the colourimetric equation defined by

$$C = c_1A_1 + c_2A_2 + c_3A_3 \tag{11.1}$$

Here, superposition is expressed as an algebraic summation according to Grassmann's law of linearity. This law was developed empirically and establishes that colours are combined linearly. Thus, a colourimetric relationship of our perception is written as a linear algebraic equation. It is important to notice that the equality does not mean that the algebraic summation in the right side gives a numerical value C that can be used to represent or recreate the colour. The symbol C is not a value or a colour representation, but the equation expresses the idea that three stimuli are combined by superposition of lights recreate the perception of the colour C. The actual representation of the colour is given by the triplet $[c_1\ c_2\ c_3]$.

The base colours in Eq. (11.1) can be defined according to the visual system by considering the responses of the receptors in the human eye. That is, by considering as primaries the colours that we perceive as red, green and blue. However, there are other interpretations that give particular properties to the colour space and that define different *colour models*. For example, there are colour models that consider how colours are created on reproduction systems like printers, or models that rearrange colours such that special properties correspond to colour properties. In any case, all the colour models follow the tristimulus principles and they give a particular meaning to the values of $[c_1\ c_2\ c_3]$ and $[A_1\ A_2\ A_3]$ in Eq. (11.1).

A way to understand colour models is to consider them as created by geometric transformations. If you can imagine that you can arrange all the colours that you can see in an enclosed space, then a colour model will order those colours by picking up each colour and give it the co-ordinates $[c_1\ c_2\ c_3]$ in a space delineated by $[A_1\ A_2\ A_3]$. Sometimes the transformation is constrained to some colours, so not all the colour models contain all the visible colours. Also, although the space is linear, the transformation can organise the colours using nonlinear mappings. Independently of the way the space is defined, since there are three components per colour, then a colour space can be shown in a three-dimensional graph. However, since the interpretation of three-dimensional data is difficult, sometimes the data are shown using two-dimensional graphs.

As such, each colour model defines and represents colours that form a colour order system. Geometric properties of the space are related to colour properties making each model important for colour understanding, synthesis and processing. Therefore, many models have been developed. Historically, the first models were motivated by the scientific interest in colour perception, the need of colour representations in dye manufacture as well as to provide practical guidance and colour creation to painters. These models have created the fundamentals of colour representation [Kuehni03]. Some of them, like the colour sphere developed by Philipp Runge or the hexahedric model of Tobias Meyer, are close to the ideas of modern theory of colour, but perhaps the first model with strong significance in modern theory of colour is the CIE XYZ model. This model was developed from the CIE RGB model, and it has been used as basis of other modern colour representations. In order to explain these colour models it is important to have an understanding of the *luminosity function*.

11.2.4 Luminosity function

The expression in Eq. (11.1) provides a framework to develop colour models by adding three components. However, this expression is related to the *hue* of a colour, but not to its *brightness*. This can be seen by considering what happens to a colour when its components are multiplied by the same constant. Since multiplication does not change the colour wavelength and the equation is linear, we could expect to obtain a brighter (or darker) version of the colour proportional to the constant. However, since the human eye does not have the same sensitivity to all frequencies, then the resulting colour brightness actually depends on composition. For example, since the human eye is more sensitive to colours whose wavelength is close to green, then colours having a large green component will increase their intensity significantly when the components are increased. For the same increment in the components, blue colours will show less intensity. Colours composed of several frequencies can shift in hue according to the sensitivity to each frequency to the human eye.

The *luminosity* or *luminous efficiency function* is denoted as V_λ, and describes the average sensitivity of the human eye to a colour's wavelength [Sharpe05]. This function was determined experimentally by the following procedure. First, the frequency of a light of constant intensity was changed until observers perceived the maximum brightness. The maximum was obtained with a wavelength of 555 nm. Secondly, a different light's wavelength was chosen and the power was adjusted until the perceived intensity of the new wavelength was the same as the 555 nm. Thus, the luminous efficiency for the light at the chosen wavelength was defined as the ratio between the power at the maximum and the power at the wavelength. The experiments for several wavelengths produce the general form illustrated in Fig. 11.4. This figure represents the daytime efficiency (i.e. *photopic vision*). Under low light conditions (i.e. *scotopic vision*) the perception is mostly performed by the rods in the eye, so the curve is shifted to have a maximum efficiency around 500 nm. In intermediate light conditions (i.e. *mesopic vision*) the efficiency can be expressed as a function of photopic and scotopic functions [Sagawa86]. The luminosity function in Fig. 11.4 is normalised, thus it represents the relative intensity rather than the actual visible energy or power perceived by the human eye. The perceived power generally is expressed in *lumen*, and it is proportional to this curve. Bear in mind that the perceived intensity is related to the luminous flux of a source whilst the actual physical power is related to the radiant flux and it is generally measured in *Watts*.

In the description of colour models, the luminous efficiency is used to provide a reference for the perceived brightness. This is achieved by relating the colour components to the luminous efficiency via the *luminance coefficients* $[v_1\ v_2\ v_3]$. These coefficients define the contribution of each base colour to the brightness as

$$V = v_1 c_1 + v_2 c_2 + v_3 c_3 \tag{11.2}$$

For example, the luminance coefficients [1 4 2] indicate that the second component contributes four times more to the brightness than the first one. Thus, an increase in the second component will create a colour that is four times brighter than the colour created by increasing the first one the same amount. It is important to emphasise that this function describes our perception of brightness and not the actual radiated power.

In general, the luminance coefficients of a colour model can be computed by fitting the brightness to the luminosity function, i.e., by finding the values $\alpha,\ \beta, \gamma$ that minimise the summation

$$\sum_{\lambda} \left| V_\lambda - (\alpha c_{1,\lambda} + \beta c_{2,\lambda} + \gamma c_{3,\lambda}) \right| \tag{11.3}$$

where $c_{1,\lambda},\ c_{2,\lambda},\ c_{3,\lambda}$ are the components that generate the colour with a single wavelength λ, and | | defines a metric error. Colours formed by a single wavelength are referred to as *monochromatic*. Since the minimisation is for all wavelengths, then the best fit value only gives an approximation to our perception of brightness. However, in general, the approximation provides a good description of the perceived intensity and luminance coefficients are commonly used to define and study the properties of colour models.

11.3 Perception-based colour models: CIE RGB and CIE XYZ

Colours models define colour according to the colourimetric equation. The *CIE RGB* and *CIE XYZ* colour models were defined in 1931 by the *Commission Internationale de L'Eclairage (CIE)*. Both models provide a description of the colours according to human perception and they characterise the same colour's properties, nevertheless they use different base colours. Whilst the CIE RGB uses visible physical colours, the XYZ uses imaginary or inexistent colours that only provide a theoretical basis. That is, the CIE RGB is the physical model developed based on perception experiments, whilst the CIE XYZ is theoretically derived from the CIE RGB. The motivation to develop the CIE XYZ is to have a colour space with better descriptive properties. However, in order to achieve that description, the base colours are shifted out of the visible spectrum.

11.3.1 CIE RGB colour model: Wright–Guild data

The base of the CIE *RGB* colour space is denoted by the triplet $[R \quad G \quad B]$ and its components are denoted as $[r \quad g \quad b]$. Thus, the definition in Eq. (11.1) for this model is written as

$$\mathbf{C} = rR + gG + bB \tag{11.4}$$

This model is based on how colours are perceived by the human eye, and it was developed using colour matching experiments. The experiments were similar to previous experiments developed in the 19th century by Helmholtz and Maxwell. Those experiments were used to organise colours according to its primary compositions (i.e. the Maxwell triangle). In the CIE RGB colour model experiments, a person was presented with two colours; the first colour defines a target colour with a single known frequency wavelength and the second is produced by combining the light of three sources defined by the base colours. To determine the composition of the target colour, the intensity of the base colours is changed until the colour produced by the combination of lights matches the target colour. The intensities of the composed sources define the colour components of the target colour.

The experiments that defined the CIE RGB model were published by Wright and Guild [Wright29, Guild32] and the results are known as the Wright–Guild data. Wright experiments used seven observers and light colours created by monochromatic lights at 650, 530 and 460 nm. The experiments matched monochromatic colours from 380 to 780 nm at 5 nm intervals. Guild used 10 observers and primaries composed of several wavelengths. In order to use both the Guild and Wright experimental data, the CIE RGB results are expressed in a common colour base using colour lights at 700, 546.1 and 435.8 nm. These lights were the standard basis used by the National Physical Laboratory in London, and they were chosen since the last two are easily producible by a mercury vapour discharge and the 700 nm wavelength has the advantage of having a small perceptual change for different people. Therefore, small errors in the measure of the light intensity produce only small errors on the composed colour.

An important result of the colour matching experiments was the observation that many colours cannot be created by *addition* of the primary lights, but they can only be produced by *subtraction* of light values. In the experiments, subtraction does not mean using negative light intensities, but to add a base colour to the target colour. This process desaturates the colours and since the mix of colours is linear, then adding to the target is equal than subtracting from the light mixture that creates the second colour in the experiments. For example, to generate violet requires adding a green light to the target, thus generating a negative green value. In practice, this means that the base colours are not saturated enough (i.e. far away from white) to generate those colours. In fact, there is no colour basis that can generate all visible colours. However, it is possible to define theoretical basis that, although are too saturated to be visible, it can create all the colours. This is the basic rationale for creating the CIE XYZ model that is presented later.

11.3.2 CIE RGB colour matching functions

It is impractical to perform colour matching experiments to obtain the components of all the visible colours, but the experiments were limited to a finite set of colours. Thus, the colour description should provide a rule that can be used to infer the components of any possible colour according to the results obtained in the matching experiments. The mechanism that permits the determination of the components of any colour is based on the *colour matching functions.*

The colour matching functions are illustrated in Fig. 11.2 and they define the intensity values of the base colours that produce any monochromatic colour with a normalised intensity. The functions give three values that represent the components of the colour generated by a single wavelength and with unit intensity. For example, to create the same colour as a single light at 580 nm, we combine three base colours with intensities 0.24, 0.11 and −0.001.

It is important to mention that the colour matching functions do not correspond to the actual intensities measured in the colour matching experiments, but the values are manipulated to provide a normalised description that agrees with our colour perception and such that they are referenced with respect to the white colour. The definition of the colour matching functions involves four steps [Broadbent04]. First, a different scale factor for each base colour was defined such that the colour mixture agrees with our perceptions of colour. That is, yellow can be obtained by the same amount of red and green whilst the same amount of green and blue matched cyan (or the monochromatic light at 494 nm). Secondly, the data are normalised such that the sum of the components for any given colour is unity. That is, the colour is made independent of the colour luminous energy by dividing each measure by the total energy $r + g + b$. Thirdly, the

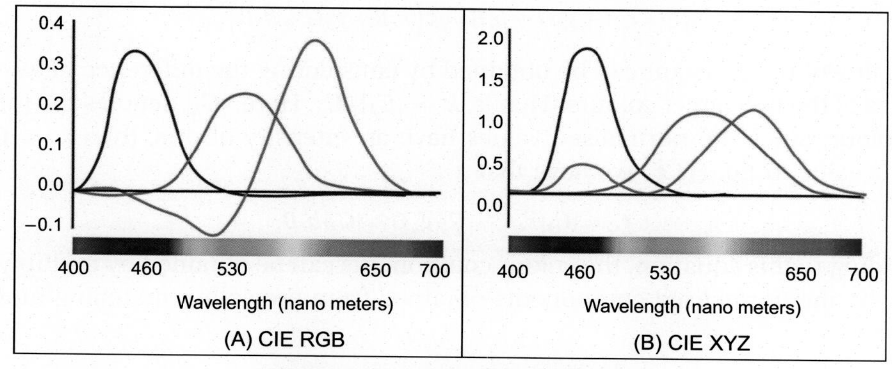

FIGURE 11.2 Colour matching functions.

colour is centred using as a reference for white. Finally, the colour is transformed to characterise colour using coloured lights at 700, 546.1 and 435.8 nm.

The normalisation of brightness and the centre around the reference point of the transformation are very important factors related to *chromatic adaptation*. Chromatic adaptation is a property of the human visual system that provides constant perceived colours under different illumination conditions. For example, we perceive an object as white when we see it in direct sunlight or illuminated by an incandescent bulb. However, since the colour of an object is actually produced by the light it reflects, then the measure of the colour is different when using different illumination. Therefore, normalisation and the use of a reference ensure that the measures are comparable and can be translated to different light conditions by observing the co-ordinates of the white colour. As such, having white as the reference can be used to describe colour under different illumination.

In order to centre the model basis on white, observers were also presented with a standard white colour to determine its components. There were large variations in each observer's measures, so the white colour was defined by taking an average. The white colour was defined by the values 0.243, 0.410 and 0.347. Thus, the results of the matching experiments were transformed such that the white colour has its three components equal to 0.333. The values centred on white are finally transformed to the basis defined by 700, 546.1 and 435.8 nm.

Once the matching functions are defined, then the components for colours with a single wavelength can be obtained by interpolating the data. Moreover, the colour matching functions can also be used to obtain the components of colours composed by mixtures of lights by considering the components of each wavelength in the mixture. To explain this, we consider that the components of a colour $\widehat{\mathbf{C}}_\lambda$ created by a light with a normalised intensity value of one and a single frequency with wavelength λ is denoted as $\left[\widehat{r}_\lambda \quad \widehat{g}_\lambda \quad \widehat{b}_\lambda\right]$. That is,

$$\widehat{\mathbf{C}}_\lambda = \widehat{r}_\lambda R + \widehat{g}_\lambda G + \widehat{b}_\lambda B \tag{11.5}$$

Since colours are linear, then a colour with an arbitrary intensity and same single frequency is

$$\mathbf{C}_\lambda = r_\lambda R + g_\lambda G + b_\lambda B = k\left(\widehat{r}_\lambda R + \widehat{g}_\lambda G + \widehat{b}_\lambda B\right) \tag{11.6}$$

The value of the constant can be obtained by considering the difference between the intensities of the two target colours. That is, $k = |\mathbf{C}_\lambda| / \widehat{\mathbf{C}}_\lambda$. Here, $|\mathbf{C}_\lambda|$ denotes the intensity of the colour. Since the normalised values have an intensity of one, then $k = |\mathbf{C}_\lambda|$. By using this value in Eq. (11.6) we have that

$$\mathbf{C}_\lambda = |\mathbf{C}_\lambda|\widehat{r}_\lambda R + |\mathbf{C}_\lambda|\widehat{g}_\lambda G + |\mathbf{C}_\lambda|\widehat{b}_\lambda B \tag{11.7}$$

According to this equation, the colour components can be obtained by multiplying its intensity by the normalised components obtained from the colour matching functions. That is,

$$r_\lambda = |\mathbf{C}_\lambda|\widehat{r}_\lambda \quad g_\lambda = |\mathbf{C}_\lambda|\widehat{g}_\lambda \quad b_\lambda = |\mathbf{C}_\lambda|\widehat{b}_\lambda \tag{11.8}$$

This approach can be generalised to obtain the components of colours composed of several frequencies. For example, for two colours containing two frequency components λ_1 and λ_2, we have that

$$\begin{aligned}\mathbf{C}_{\lambda_1} &= r_{\lambda_1}R + g_{\lambda_1}G + b_{\lambda_1}B \\ \mathbf{C}_{\lambda_2} &= r_{\lambda_2}R + g_{\lambda_2}G + b_{\lambda_2}B\end{aligned} \tag{11.9}$$

Since the colour space is linear, the colour containing both frequencies is given by

$$\mathbf{C}_{\lambda_1} + \mathbf{C}_{\lambda_2} = (r_{\lambda_1} + r_{\lambda_2})R + (g_{\lambda_1} + g_{\lambda_2})G + (b_{\lambda_1} + b_{\lambda_3})B \tag{11.10}$$

By using the definitions in Eq. (11.8), we have that the colour components can be obtained by adding the colour matching functions of each frequency. That is,

$$\begin{aligned}\mathbf{C}_{\lambda_1} + \mathbf{C}_{\lambda_2} = (|\mathbf{C}_{\lambda_1}|\widehat{r}_{\lambda 1} + |\mathbf{C}_{\lambda_2}|\widehat{r}_{\lambda_2})R + \left(|\mathbf{C}_{\lambda_1}|\widehat{g}_{\lambda_1} + |\mathbf{C}_{\lambda_2}|\widehat{g}_{\lambda_2}\right)G + \\ \left(|\mathbf{C}_{\lambda_1}|\widehat{b}_{\lambda_1} + |\mathbf{C}_{\lambda_2}|\widehat{b}_{\lambda_3}\right)B\end{aligned} \tag{11.11}$$

Therefore, the colour components are the sum of the colour matching functions multiplied by the intensity of each wavelength components. The summation can be generalised to include all the frequencies by considering infinite sums of all the wavelength components. That is,

$$\begin{aligned} r &= \int |\mathbf{C}_\lambda|\widehat{r}_\lambda d_\lambda \\ g &= \int |\mathbf{C}_\lambda|\widehat{g}_\lambda d_\lambda \\ b &= \int |\mathbf{C}_\lambda|\widehat{b}_\lambda d_\lambda \end{aligned} \tag{11.12}$$

As such, the colour components of any colour can be obtained by summing the colour matching functions weighted by its spectral power distribution. Since the colour matching functions are represented in tabular form, sometimes the integrals are expressed as a matrix multiplication of the form

$$\begin{bmatrix} r \\ g \\ b \end{bmatrix} = \begin{bmatrix} \widehat{r}_{\lambda_0} & \widehat{r}_{\lambda_1} & \cdots & \widehat{r}_{\lambda_{n-1}} & \widehat{r}_{\lambda_n} \\ \widehat{g}_{\lambda_0} & \widehat{g}_{\lambda_1} & \cdots & \widehat{g}_{\lambda_{n-1}} & \widehat{g}_{\lambda_n} \\ \widehat{b}_{\lambda_0} & \widehat{b}_{\lambda_1} & \cdots & \widehat{b}_{\lambda_{n-1}} & \widehat{b}_{\lambda_n} \end{bmatrix} \begin{bmatrix} |\mathbf{C}_{\lambda_0}| \\ |\mathbf{C}_{\lambda_1}| \\ \vdots \\ |\mathbf{C}_{\lambda_{n-1}}| \\ |\mathbf{C}_{\lambda_n}| \end{bmatrix} \tag{11.13}$$

The first matrix in the right side of this equation is given by the CIE RGB colour matching functions table, and it is generally given by discrete values at 5 nm intervals from 380 to 480 nm. However, it is also common to use tables that have been interpolated at 1 nm intervals [Wyszecki00]. The second matrix represents the power of the colour in a wavelength interval.

11.3.3 CIE RGB chromaticity diagram and chromaticity co-ordinates

The CIE RGB model characterises colours by three components, thus the graph of the full set of colours is a three-dimensional volume. The general shape of this volume is illustrated on the top left in Fig. 11.3. As colours increase in distance from the origin, their brightness increases and more colours become visible forming a conical shaped volume. In the figure, the base colours coincide with the corners of the triangle drawn with black dashed lines. Thus, the triangular pyramid defined by this triangle contains the colours that can be created by addition.

In general, the visualisation and interpretation of colours using three-dimensional representations is complicated, thus colour properties are sometimes visualised using two-dimensional graphs. The most common way to illustrate the CIE RGB colour space is to consider only the colour's *chromaticity*. That is, the *luminous energy* is eliminated by normalising against the total energy. The *chromaticity co-ordinates* are defined as

$$\overline{r}=\frac{r}{r+g+b} \quad \overline{g}=\frac{g}{r+g+b} \quad \overline{b}=\frac{b}{r+g+b} \tag{11.14}$$

Only two of the three normalised colours are independent and one value can be determined from the other two. For example, we can compute blue as

$$\overline{b}=1-\overline{r}-\overline{g} \tag{11.15}$$

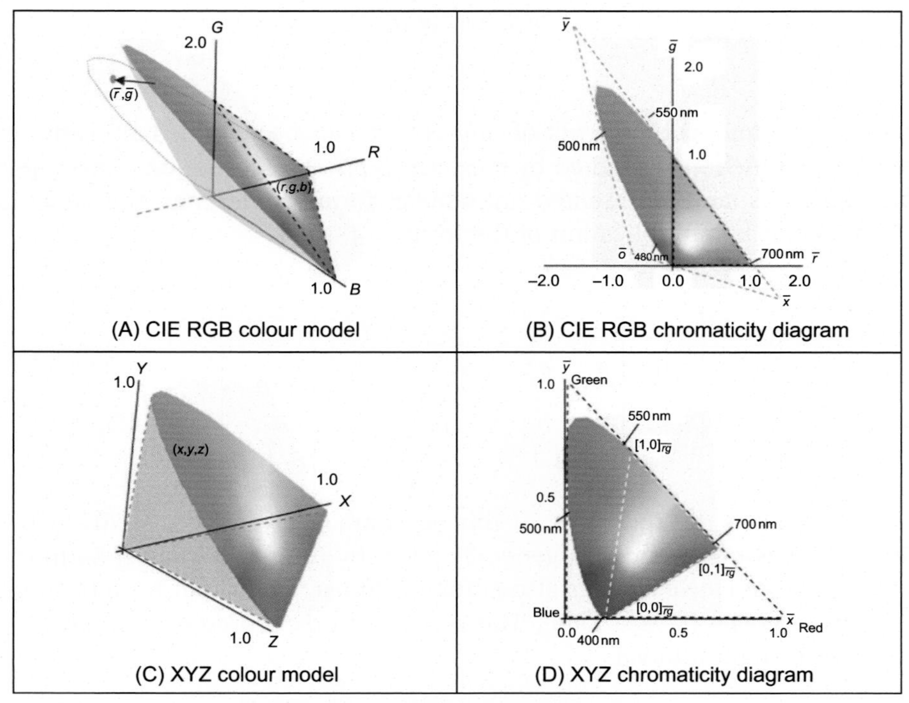

FIGURE 11.3 CIE RGB and XYZ colour models.

As such, only two colours can be used to characterise the chromaticity of the colour model and the visible colours can be visualised using a two-dimensional graph. The graph created by considering the colour's chromaticity is called the *chromaticity diagram*.

The geometrical interpretation of the transformation in Eq. (11.14) is illustrated in Fig. 11.3A. Any point in the colour space is mapped into the chromaticity diagram by two transformations. First, the central projection in Eq. (11.14) maps the colours into the plane that contains the coloured shape in the figure. That is, by tracing radial lines from the origin to the plane. Secondly, the points are orthogonally projected into the plane RG. That is, the $\bar{b}$ co-ordinate is eliminated or set to zero. In the figure, the border of the area resulting from the projection is shown by the dotted curve in the RG plane.

Fig. 11.3B shows the projected points into the RG plane, and this corresponds to the chromaticity diagram for the CIE RGB model. Notice from the transformation that any point in the same radial projection line will end up in the same point in the chromaticity diagram. That is, points in the chromaticity diagram characterise colours independent of their luminous energy. For example, the colours with chromaticity co-ordinates $[0.5 \quad 0.5 \quad 0.5]$ and $[1 \quad 1 \quad 1]$ are shown as the same point $[1/3 \quad 1/3]$ in the diagram. This point represents both white and grey since they have the same chromaticity, but the first one is a less bright version of the second one. Since the chromaticity cannot show white and grey for the same point, it is coloured by the normalised colour $[\bar{r} \quad \bar{g} \quad \bar{b}]$.

It is not possible to use the inverse of Eq. (11.14) to obtain the colour components from the chromaticity co-ordinates, but the inverse only defines a line passing through the origin and through colours with the same chromaticity. That is,

$$r = k\bar{r} \quad g = k\bar{g} \quad b = k\bar{b} \tag{11.16}$$

The value of k in this equation defines a normalisation constant that according to Eq. (11.14) is given by $k = r + g + b$.

As illustrated in Fig. 11.3B, the visible spectrum of colours outlines a horseshoe-shaped region in the chromaticity diagram. The red and green components of each colour are determined by the position of the colours in the axes in the graph whilst the amount of blue is determined according to Eq. (11.13). The top curved rim delineating the visible colours is formed by colours with a single-frequency component. This line is called the spectral line, and it represents lights from 400 to 700 nm. Single wavelength colours do not have a single component, but the diagram shows the amount of each component of the basis that is necessary to create the perception of the colour. The spectral line defines the border of the horseshoe-shaped region since these colours are the limit of the human eye's perception. The straight line of the horseshoe region is called the purple line and is not formed by single wavelength colours but each point in this line is formed by mixing the two monochromatic lights at 400 and 700 nm.

In addition to identifying colours, the chromaticity diagram can be used to develop a visual understanding of its properties and relationships. However, the interpretation of colours using chromaticity is generally performed in the XYZ colour space, so we will consider the properties of the chromaticity diagram later.

11.3.4 CIE XYZ colour model

The CIE RGB model has several undesirable properties. First, as illustrated in Fig. 11.2, its colour matching functions contain negative values. Negative colours do not fit well with the concept of producing colours by adding base colours and they introduce sign computations. This is important since at the time the CIE XYZ model was developed, the computations were done manually. Secondly, the colour components are not normalised, for example, a colour created by a light with a single frequency at 410 nm are $\begin{bmatrix} 0.03 & -0.007 & 0.22 \end{bmatrix}$. A better colour description should have the components bounded to range from zero to one. Finally, all the base colours have a contribution to the brightness of a colour. That is, the perceived brightness is changed by modifying any component. However, the distribution of cones and rods in the human eye has a different sensitivity for perception of brightness and colour. Thus, a more useful description should concentrate the brightness on a single component such that the perception of a colour can be related to the definition of chromaticity and brightness. The CIE XYZ model was developed to become a universal reference system that overcomes these unwanted properties.

The basis of the CIE XYZ model is denoted by the triplet $\begin{bmatrix} X & Y & Z \end{bmatrix}$ and its components are denoted as $\begin{bmatrix} x & y & z \end{bmatrix}$. Thus, the definition in Eq. (11.1) for this model is written as

$$\mathbf{C} = xX + yY + zZ \tag{11.17}$$

and the chromaticity co-ordinates are defined as

$$\overline{x} = \frac{x}{x+y+z} \quad \overline{y} = \frac{y}{x+y+z} \quad \overline{z} = \frac{z}{x+y+z} \tag{11.18}$$

Similar to Eq. (11.13), we have that

$$\overline{z} = 1 - \overline{x} - \overline{y} \tag{11.19}$$

Thus, according to Eq. (11.16), colours with the same chromaticity are defined by the inverse of Eq. (11.18). That is,

$$x = k\overline{x} \quad y = k\overline{y} \quad z = k\overline{z} \tag{11.20}$$

For the normalisation constant for $k = x + y + z$. At difference of the CIE RGB, the colour components in the XYZ colour model are not defined directly by matching colour experiments, but they are obtained from the components of the CIE RGB model by a linear transformation. That is,

$$\begin{bmatrix} x \\ y \\ z \end{bmatrix} = \mathbf{M} \begin{bmatrix} r \\ g \\ b \end{bmatrix} \tag{11.21}$$

Here, **M** is a nonsingular 3×3 matrix. Thus, the mapping from the XYZ colour model to the CIE RGB is given by

$$\begin{bmatrix} r \\ g \\ b \end{bmatrix} = \mathbf{M}^{-1} \begin{bmatrix} x \\ y \\ z \end{bmatrix} \tag{11.22}$$

The definition in Eq. (11.21) uses a linear transformation in order to define a one-to-one mapping that maintains collinearity. The one-to-one property ensures that the identity of colours is maintained, thus colours can be identified in both models without any ambiguity. Collinearity ensures that lines defined by colours with the same chromaticity are not changed. Thus, colours are not scrambled, but the transformation maps the colours without changing its chromaticity definition. Additionally, the transformation does not have any translation, so it actually rearranges the chromaticity lines defined from the origin by stretching the colours in the CIE RGB model. This produces a shift that translates the base colours into the invisible region.

Eq. (11.21) defines a system of three equations, thus the matrix can be determined by defining the mapping of three no coplanar points. That is, if we know the CIE RGB and XYZ components of three points, then we can substitute these values in Eq. (11.21) and solve for **M**. As such, in order to define the XYZ model, we just need to find three points. These points are defined by considering the criteria necessary to achieve desired properties in the chromaticity diagram [Fairman97].

Since **M** is defined by three points, then the development of the XYZ colour model can be reasoned as the mapping of a triangle. This idea is illustrated in Fig. 11.3. In this figure, the dashed triangle in the CIE RGB diagram in Fig. 11.3B is transformed into the dark dashed triangle in the XYZ diagram in Fig. 11.3D. In Fig. 11.3D, the sides of the triangles coincide with the axis of the XYZ model and the visible colours are constrained to the triangle defined in the unit positive quadrant. By aligning the triangle to the XYZ axes we are ensuring that the transformation maps the colour components to positive values. That is, since the triangle is at the right and top of the axis, then $\overline{x} > 0$ and $\overline{y} > 0$. The definition of the diagonal side ensures that the remaining component is positive. This can be seen by considering that according to the definition of chromaticity in Eq. (11.18), we have that

$$\overline{x} + \overline{y} = 1 - \overline{z} \tag{11.23}$$

Thus, in order for $\overline{z}$ to take values from zero to one it is necessary that

$$\overline{x} + \overline{y} \leq 1 \tag{11.24}$$

That is, the colours should be under the diagonal line. Once the triangle in the XYZ chromaticity diagram has been defined, the problem of determining the transformation

M in Eq. (11.21) consists of finding the corresponding triangle in the CIE RGB diagram. This can be achieved by considering the properties of the colours on the lines $\overline{ox}$, $\overline{oy}$ and $\overline{xy}$ (i.e. triangle sides) that define the triangle. In other words, we can establish criteria to look for the corresponding lines in both diagrams. The first criterion to be considered is to give the contribution of brightness to a single component.

Since the human eye is more sensitive to colours whose wavelength is close to green, then the contribution of brightness in the XYZ model is given by the Y component. That is, changes in the X and Z components of a colour produce insignificant changes of intensity, but small changes along the Y axis will produce a strong intensity variation. For this reason, the Y component is called the *colour intensity*. In the CIE RGB, all components have a contribution to the intensity of the colour according to the luminance coefficients of the base colours. That is, $[1 \quad 4.59 \quad 0.06]$. Thus, the luminosity function in Eq. (11.2) for the CIE RGB model is given by

$$V = r + 4.59g + 0.06b \tag{11.25}$$

Since in the XYZ colour model, the contribution to the intensity is only given by the Y component, then the colours for which $\overline{y} = 0$ should have $V = 0$. That is, if $\overline{y} = 0$ then

$$r + 4.59g + 0.06b = 0 \tag{11.26}$$

This equation defines a plane that passes through the origin in the three-dimensional CIE RGB colour space. A projection into the chromaticity diagram is obtained by considering Eq. (11.14). That is,

$$0.17\overline{r} + 0.81\overline{g} + .01 = 0 \tag{11.27}$$

This line goes through the points $\overline{o}$ and $\overline{x}$ shown in Fig. 11.3B, and it corresponds to the line $\overline{ox}$ in Fig. 11.3D. The colours in this line are called *alychne* or colours with zero luminance and these colours are formed by negative values of green or red. According to the definition of luminosity function, these colours do not produce any perceived intensity to the human eye and according to the locus of the line in the chromaticity diagram they are not visible. The closest sensation we can have about a colour that does not create any luminance is close to deep purple.

The definition of the line $\overline{xy}$ considers that the line passing through the points $[1 \quad 0]$ and $[0 \quad 1]$ in the CIE RGB chromaticity diagram can be a good mapping for the diagonal line in the XYZ chromaticity diagram. It is a good mapping since it maximises the coverage of the area defined by the visible colours, and it delineates the contour of the colour region that is tangential to the region defining the visible colours over a large wavelength range. However, this line does not encompass all the visible colours. This can be seen by considering that this line is defined by

$$\overline{r} + \overline{g} = 1 \tag{11.28}$$

Thus, the points on or below the line should satisfy the constraint given by

$$\overline{r} + \overline{g} \leq 1 \tag{11.29}$$

The blue colour can be used in this equation by considering that according to Eq. (11.19)

$$\overline{r} + \overline{g} = 1 - \overline{b} \tag{11.30}$$

Thus, the constraint in Eq. (11.29) can be true only if $\overline{b}$ is positive. However, the colour matching functions define small negative values between 546 and 600 nm. Consequently, some colours are above the line. To resolve this issue, the line that defines the XYZ model is obtained by slightly shifting the slope of the line in Eq. (11.28). The small change in the slope was calculated such that the line contains the colour obtained by the minimum blue component. Thus, the second line that defines the XYZ model is given by

$$\overline{r} + 0.99\overline{g} = 1 \tag{11.31}$$

This line is illustrated in Fig. 11.3B as the dotted line going through the points $\overline{x}$ and $\overline{y}$. The corresponding line in the XYZ chromaticity diagram can be seen in Fig. 11.3D.

The definition of the line $\overline{oy}$ in the CIE XYZ chromaticity diagram was chosen to maximise the area covering the visible colours. This was achieved by defining the line tangential to the point defining the 500 nm colour. The position of the line is illustrated by the points $\overline{o}$ and $\overline{y}$ in Fig. 11.3B. This line corresponds to the vertical axis of the XYZ diagram shown in the bottom right of the figure. The equation of the line in the CIE RGB chromaticity diagram is defined as

$$2.62\overline{r} + 0.99\overline{g} = -0.81 \tag{11.32}$$

Thus, the lines that define the triangle in the CIE RGB diagram are given by Eqs. (11.27), (11.31) and (11.32). The vertices of the triangle are obtained by computing the intersection of these lines and they are given by the points $[1.27 \quad -0.27]$, $[-1.74 \quad 2.76]$ and $[-0.74 \quad 0.14]$. In order to obtain the position of these points in the CIE RGB colour space, it is necessary to include the component $\overline{b}$. This is achieved by considering Eq. (11.15). Thus, the chromaticity co-ordinates of the points in the CIE RGB colour model are $[1.27 \quad -0.27 \quad 0.002]$, $[-1.74 \quad 2.76 \quad -0.02]$ and $[-0.74 \quad 0.14 \quad 1.6]$. Thus, we have that the colour components defined by these co-ordinates are given by the three points

$$\begin{gathered} \alpha[1.27 \quad -0.27 \quad 0.002] \\ \beta[-1.74 \quad 2.76 \quad -0.02] \\ \gamma[-1.74 \quad 0.14 \quad 1.6] \end{gathered} \tag{11.33}$$

The symbols α, β and γ denote the normalisation constants. In order to justify these constants, we should recall that points in the chromaticity diagram represent a line of points in the colour space. That is, for any values of α, β and γ we obtain the same three points of the form $[\overline{r} \quad \overline{g}]$. As such, for any value of the constants, the points in Eq. (11.33) have chromaticity co-ordinates that satisfy the criteria defined based on the chromaticity properties.

Since we define the triangle in the XYZ model to coincide with its axes, then Eq. (11.21) transforms the points in Eq. (11.33) to the points $[1 \quad 0 \quad 0]$, $[0 \quad 1 \quad 0]$ and

$[0 \quad 0 \quad 1]$. As such, the transformation **M** can be found by substitution of the three points defined in both spaces. However, this requires solving three systems of equations; each system gives a row of the matrix. A simpler approach consists of using Eq. (11.22) instead of Eq. (11.21). It is simpler to use Eq. (11.22) since the points in the XYZ system contain zeroes in two of its elements. Thus, the three systems of equations are reduced to equalities. That is, by substitution of the three points in Eq. (11.22), we obtain the three equations

$$\alpha\begin{bmatrix}1.27\\-0.27\\0.002\end{bmatrix}=\mathbf{M}^{-1}\begin{bmatrix}1\\0\\0\end{bmatrix},\quad \beta\begin{bmatrix}-1.74\\2.76\\-0.02\end{bmatrix}=\mathbf{M}^{-1}\begin{bmatrix}0\\1\\0\end{bmatrix},\quad \gamma\begin{bmatrix}-0.74\\0.14\\1.6\end{bmatrix}=\mathbf{M}^{-1}\begin{bmatrix}0\\0\\1\end{bmatrix} \tag{11.34}$$

The right side of the first equation gives the first column of $\mathbf{M}^{-1}$, the right side in the second equation the second column and the third equation the last column. That is,

$$\mathbf{M}^{-1}=\begin{bmatrix}1.27\alpha & -1.74\beta & -0.74\gamma\\ -0.27\alpha & 2.76\beta & 0.14\gamma\\ 0.002\alpha & -0.02\beta & 1.6\gamma\end{bmatrix} \tag{11.35}$$

We can rewrite this matrix as a product. That is,

$$\mathbf{M}^{-1}=\begin{bmatrix}1.27 & -1.74 & -0.74\\ -0.27 & 2.76 & 0.14\\ 0.002 & -0.02 & 1.6\end{bmatrix}\begin{bmatrix}\alpha & 0 & 0\\ 0 & \beta & 0\\ 0 & 0 & \gamma\end{bmatrix} \tag{11.36}$$

The normalisation constants are determined by considering that the chromaticity of the reference point (i.e. white) is the same in both models. However, instead of transforming the reference point by using Eq. (11.36), a simpler algebraic development can be obtained by considering the inverse of the matrix product. Thus, from Eq. (11.36)

$$\mathbf{M}=\begin{bmatrix}1/\alpha & 0 & 0\\ 0 & 1/\beta & 0\\ 0 & 0 & 1/\gamma\end{bmatrix}\begin{bmatrix}0.90 & 0.57 & 0.37\\ 0.09 & 0.41 & 0.005\\ -0.00002 & 0.006 & 0.62\end{bmatrix} \tag{11.37}$$

In the CIE RGB the co-ordinates of the reference white are $[0.33 \quad 0.33 \quad 0.33]$. By considering that this point is the same in the CIE RGB and in the XYZ colour models, then according to Eq. (11.21) we have that

$$\eta\begin{bmatrix}0.33\\0.33\\0.33\end{bmatrix}=\begin{bmatrix}1/\alpha & 0 & 0\\ 0 & 1/\beta & 0\\ 0 & 0 & 1/\gamma\end{bmatrix}\begin{bmatrix}0.90 & 0.57 & 0.37\\ 0.09 & 0.41 & 0.005\\ -0.00002 & 0.006 & 0.62\end{bmatrix}\begin{bmatrix}0.33\\0.33\\0.33\end{bmatrix} \tag{11.38}$$

This equation introduces the normalisation constant η. This is because the constraint establishes that the chromaticity co-ordinates of the white point should be the same, but not their colour components; by substitution in Eq. (11.14), it is easy to see that the colours $[0.33 \quad 0.33 \quad 0.33]$ and $\eta[0.33 \quad 0.33 \quad 0.33]$ have the same chromaticity values.

By developing Eq. (11.38) we have

$$\begin{bmatrix}\alpha\\\beta\\\gamma\end{bmatrix}=\frac{1}{\eta}\begin{bmatrix}1/0.33 & 0 & 0\\0 & 1/0.33 & 0\\0 & 0 & 1/0.33\end{bmatrix}\begin{bmatrix}0.90 & 0.57 & 0.37\\0.09 & 0.41 & 0.005\\-0.00002 & 0.006 & 0.62\end{bmatrix}\begin{bmatrix}0.33\\0.33\\0.33\end{bmatrix} \tag{11.39}$$

Thus,

$$\begin{bmatrix}\alpha\\\beta\\\gamma\end{bmatrix}=\frac{1}{\eta}\begin{bmatrix}1.84\\0.52\\0.62\end{bmatrix} \tag{11.40}$$

By using these values in Eqs. (11.35) and (11.37)

$$\mathbf{M}=\frac{1}{\eta}\begin{bmatrix}0.489 & 0.31 & 0.20\\0.17 & 0.81 & 0.01\\0.00 & 0.01 & 0.99\end{bmatrix},\quad \mathbf{M}^{-1}=\eta\begin{bmatrix}2.36 & -0.89 & -0.45\\-0.51 & 1.42 & -0.088\\-0.005 & -0.01 & 1.00\end{bmatrix} \tag{11.41}$$

To determine η, we consider the second row of the transformation. That is,

$$y=\frac{0.17r+0.81g+0.01b}{\eta} \tag{11.42}$$

This value corresponds to the perceived intensity, and it is given in Eq. (11.25). Thus,

$$r+4.59g+0.06b=\frac{0.17r+0.81g+0.01b}{\eta} \tag{11.43}$$

Consequently,

$$\eta=\frac{0.17r+0.81g+0.01b}{r+4.59g+0.06b}=0.17 \tag{11.44}$$

and

$$\mathbf{M}=\begin{bmatrix}2.76 & 1.75 & 1.13\\1.0 & 4.59 & 0.06\\0.00 & 0.05 & 5.59\end{bmatrix},\quad \mathbf{M}^{-1}=\begin{bmatrix}0.41 & -0.15 & -0.08\\-0.09 & 0.25 & -0.016\\0.0 & 0.0 & 0.17\end{bmatrix} \tag{11.45}$$

The second row in the first matrix defines γ by the luminance coefficients of the CIE RGB model. Thus, the γ component actually gives the colour's perceived brightness. Notice that since these equations were derived from the luminosity of the photopic vision, the maximum luminance is around 555 nm. However, alternative equations can be developed by considering other illumination and other definitions of the white colour.

11.3.5 CIE XYZ colour matching functions

The transformation defined in Eq. (11.21) can be used to obtain the colours in the XYZ model from the components of the CIE RGB model. However, a definition of the XYZ colour model cannot be given just by a transformation, but a practical definition of the colour model should provide a mechanism that permits obtaining the representation of colours without reference to other colour models. This mechanism is defined by the colour matching functions.

Similar to the definition of the CIE RGB, the colour components in the XYZ model can be defined by considering a sample of single colours. Subsequently, the components of any colour can be obtained by considering its spectral composition. This process can be described in a way analogous to Eq. (11.12). That is,

$$\begin{aligned} x &= \int |\mathbf{C}_\lambda| \widehat{x}_\lambda d_\lambda \\ y &= \int |\mathbf{C}_\lambda| \widehat{y}_\lambda d_\lambda \\ z &= \int |\mathbf{C}_\lambda| \widehat{z}_\lambda d_\lambda \end{aligned} \tag{11.46}$$

Here, the components $[x \quad y \quad z]$ of a colour are obtained from the intensity $\boldsymbol{C}_\lambda$ at wavelength λ and the colour matching functions $\widehat{x}_\lambda$, $\widehat{y}_\lambda$ and $\widehat{z}_\lambda$. These functions are defined by the XYZ components of monochromatic lights. Thus, the definition of the XYZ system uses the transformation in Eq. (11.21) to determine the values for single colours that define the XYZ colour matching functions. That is,

$$[\widehat{x}_\lambda \quad \widehat{y}_\lambda \quad \widehat{z}_\lambda]^T = \mathbf{M}\left[\widehat{r}_\lambda \quad \widehat{g}_\lambda \quad \widehat{b}_\lambda\right]^T \tag{11.47}$$

The problem with this equation is that the $\widehat{y}_\lambda$ values are related to the perceived intensity only in average terms. This can be seen by recalling that Eq. (11.25) only defines the perceived intensity that minimises the error over all wavelengths. Thus, the value of $\widehat{y}_\lambda$ will not be equal to the perceived intensity, but we can only expect that the average difference between these values for all wavelengths is small.

In order to make $\widehat{y}_\lambda$ equal to V_λ, the definition of the XYZ model considered a different value for the constant η for every wavelength. To justify this definition, it should be noticed that the selection of the value of the constant does not change the chromaticity properties of the model; the constant multiplies the three colour components, thus it does not change the values obtained in Eq. (11.14). Accordingly, by changing the constant of the transformation for each wavelength, then the criteria defined in the chromaticity diagram are maintained, and just the components (including the intensity) are rescaled. Thus, it is possible to define a scaling that satisfies the criteria and that makes the intensity equal to V_λ. As such, the scale that gives the value of the perceived intensity dependent of the wavelength λ is given by

$$\eta_\lambda = \frac{0.17\widehat{r}_\lambda + 0.81\widehat{g}_\lambda + 0.01\widehat{b}_\lambda}{V_\lambda} \tag{11.48}$$

Eq. (11.44) is a special form of this equation, but the constant is defined to obtain the best average intensity whilst this equation is defined per frequency. By considering the constant defined in Eq. (11.48) in Eq. (11.42) we have that

$$y = \frac{0.17r + 0.81g + 0.01b}{0.17\widehat{r}_\lambda + 0.81\widehat{g}_\lambda + 0.01\widehat{b}_\lambda} V_\lambda \tag{11.49}$$

Thus, if we are transforming the monochromatic colour $\widehat{x}_\lambda$, $\widehat{y}_\lambda$ and $\widehat{z}_\lambda$, the intensity y is equal to V_λ. This implies that there is a matrix for each wavelength. That is,

$$\mathbf{M}_\lambda = \frac{1}{\eta_\lambda}\begin{bmatrix} 0.489 & 0.31 & 0.20 \\ 0.17 & 0.81 & 0.01 \\ 0.00 & 0.01 & 0.99 \end{bmatrix} \tag{11.50}$$

This matrix was obtained by considering Eq. (11.41) for the definition in Eq. (11.48). Thus, the transformation in Eq. (11.47) is replaced by

$$[\widehat{x}_\lambda \quad \widehat{y}_\lambda \quad \widehat{z}_\lambda]^T = M_\lambda\left[\widehat{r}_\lambda \quad \widehat{g}_\lambda \quad \widehat{b}_\lambda\right]^T \tag{11.51}$$

This transformation defines the colour matching functions for the XYZ model. The general form of the curves is shown in Fig. 11.2. The $\widehat{y}_\lambda$ component illustrated as a green curve in the figure is equal to the intensity V_λ in Fig. 11.4. Thus, a single component in the XYZ model gives the maximum perceivable brightness.

Evidently, since Eq. (11.51) defines the colour matching functions, then the calculations of the colour components based on Eq. (11.21) are inaccurate. That is, the CIE RGB and the XYZ model are not related by a single matrix transformation; when computing a colour by using the transformation and the colour matching functions, we obtain different results since the colour matching functions are obtained from several scaled matrices. Additionally, when considering colours composed of several frequencies, the transformation will include inaccuracies given the complexity of the actual intensity resulting from the mixture of wavelengths. Nevertheless, Eq. (11.21) is approximately correct on average and in practice can be used to transform colours. Alternatively, there are standard tables for the colour matching functions of both models, so the representation of a colour can be obtained by considering Eq. (11.12) and Eq. (11.46).

Actually there is little practical interest in transforming colours between the CIE RGB and XYZ models. The actual importance of their relationship is to understand the

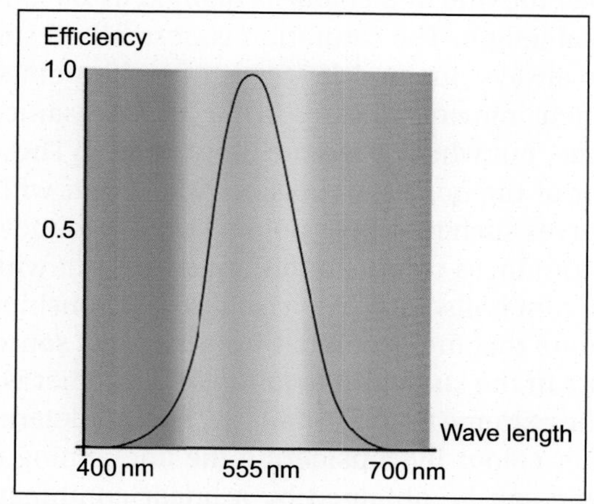

FIGURE 11.4 Luminous efficiency defined by the photopic luminosity function.

physical realisation of colour models and the theoretical criteria used to develop the XYZ model. The understanding of the physical realisation of a colour model describes perception or image capture. That is, how colours become numbers and what these numbers represent to our perception. The understanding of the XYZ criteria gives a justification to the creation of nonphysically realisable models to satisfy properties that are useful in understanding colours. In fact, there is always interest in using the properties of the XYZ model for other physical models; properties and colour relationships in practical models are commonly explained by allusion to properties of the XYZ model. These properties are generally described using the XYZ chromaticity diagram.

11.3.6 XYZ chromaticity diagram

The visible colours of the XYZ model delineate the pyramid-like volume illustrated in Fig. 11.3C. Each line from the origin defines colours with the same chromaticity. The chromaticity co-ordinates are defined according to Eqs. (11.18) and (11.19). The chromaticity diagram in Fig. 11.3 is obtained by considering these definitions.

The chromaticity diagram provides a visual understanding of the properties of colours. The origin of the diagram is labelled as blue and the end of the axis as red and green. This indicates how colours change along each axis. The $\bar{y}$ value represents the perceived brightness. Similar to the CIE RGB chromaticity diagram, the visible colours define a horseshoe-shaped region. The colours along the curved rim of this region are colours with a single frequency component. This line is called the spectral line. The straight line of the horseshoe region is called the purple line. Colours in this line are created by mixing the monochromatic lights at the extremes of the visual spectrum, at 400 and 700 nm.

In addition to showing the palette of colours in the visual spectrum, the chromaticity diagram is also useful for visualising *hue* and *saturation*. These properties are defined by expressing colours relative to white using polar co-ordinates. By taking the white point $[1/3 \quad 1/3]$ as a reference, the hue of a colour is defined as the angular component and its saturation as the radial length. The saturation is normalised such that the maximum value for a given hue is always one and it is given for the points in the border of the horseshoe region. As such, moving towards white on the same radial line produces colours with the same hue, but which are more de-saturated. These define the shades of the colour on the border of the horseshoe region. Any colour with small saturation becomes white. Tracing curves such that their points keep the same distance to the border of the horseshoe region produces colours of different hue, but with constant saturation.

The chromaticity diagram is also useful to visualise relationships between mixtures of colours. The mix of colours that are generated from any two source colours is found by considering all the points in the straight line joining them. That is, the colours obtained by linearly combining the extreme points. Similarly, we can determine how a colour can be obtained from another colour by considering the line joining two points in the diagram. Any point in a line can be obtained by a linear combination of any other two points in the same line. Thus, the chromaticity diagram can be used to show how to mix colours to create the same perceived colour (metamerism).

11.3.7 Uniform colour spaces: CIE LUV and CIE LAB

The XYZ model is very useful for visualising the colours we can perceive and their relationships. However, it lacks uniformity or perceptual linearity. That is, the perceived difference between two colours is not directly related to the distance of the colours as represented in the chromaticity diagram. In other words, the perceived difference between points at the same distance in chromaticity can be significantly dissimilar. In practice, uniformity and linearity are important properties if we are using the measure of colour differences as an indication of how similar are the colours for the visual system. For example, in image classification, if we measure a large difference between the colour of two pixels we may wrongly assume that they form part of a different class, but in fact these can be very similar to our eye. Another example of the importance of using uniform colour systems is when colour measures are used to determine the accuracy of colour reproduction systems. In this case, the quality of a system is given by how different the colours are actually perceived rather than how different are in the chromaticity diagram. Also linearity is desirable in reproduction systems since we do not want to spend resources storing different colours that look the same to the human eye.

The nonuniformity of the XYZ system is generally illustrated by using the MacAdam ellipses shown in Fig. 11.5A. These ellipses were obtained by experiments using matching colours [MacAdam42]. In the experiments, observers were asked to adjust the colour components of one colour until it matches a fixed colour from the chromaticity diagram. The results showed that the accuracy of matching depends on the test colour and that the matching colours obtained from different observers lie within ellipses with different orientations and sizes. The original experiments derived the 25 ellipses

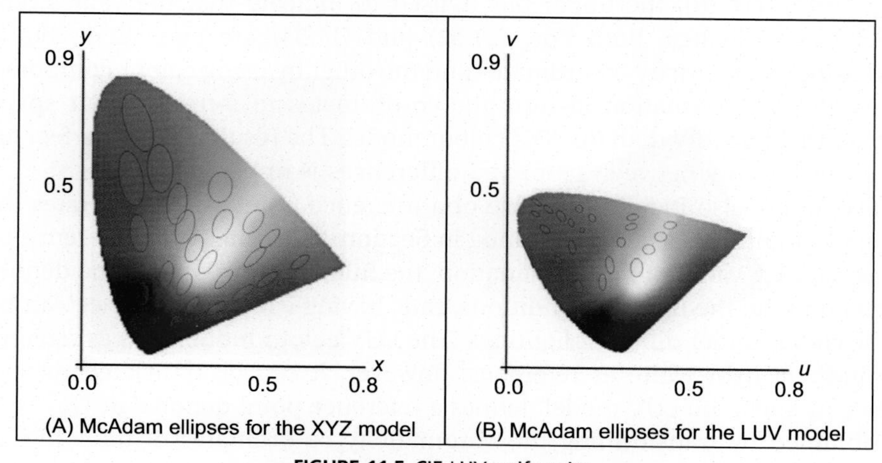

FIGURE 11.5 CIE LUV uniformity.

illustrated in Fig. 11.5A. The centre of the ellipse is given by the fixed colour and their area encompasses the matching colours by the observers.

The MacAdam experiments showed that our ability to distinguish between colours is not the same for all colours, thus distances in the chromaticity diagram are not a good measure of colour differences. Ideally, observed differences should be delineated by circles with the same radius such that a given distance between colours has the same meaning independent of the position in the diagram. The study of the nonuniformity of the XYZ colour model motivated several other models that look for better linearity. In 1976, the CIE provided two standards for these uniform spaces. They are known as the *CIE LUV* and the *CIE LAB* colour models. The basic concept of these models is to transform the colour components of the XYZ colours so that perceptual differences in the chromaticity diagram are more uniform.

The definition of the CIE LUV model is based on the following equation that transforms the colour components of the XYZ model.

$$u = \frac{4x}{x + 15y + 3z} \quad v = \frac{9y}{x + 15y + 3z} \tag{11.52}$$

This transformation was originally used as a simple way to improve perceptual linearity in earlier colour models [Judd35]. Later, the transformation was used to define the LUV colour model. This equation can also be expressed in terms of the colour components by considering the definitions in Eqs. (11.18) and (11.19). According to those definitions, we have that

$$x = \overline{x}(x + y + z) \quad y = (x + y + z) \quad \overline{z} = \frac{z}{(x + y + z)} = 1 - \overline{x} - \overline{y} \tag{11.53}$$

By substitution in Eq. (11.52) we have that

$$u = \frac{4\overline{x}}{-2\overline{x} + 12\overline{y} + 3} \quad v = \frac{9\overline{y}}{-2\overline{x} + 12\overline{y} + 3} \tag{11.54}$$

Similar to Eq. (11.18), the upper bar is used to indicate that the values represent chromaticity co-ordinates. Both Eqs. (11.52) and (11.54) are equivalent, but one is expressed using chromaticity co-ordinates and the other by using colour components. In both cases, the transformation distorts the co-ordinates to form a colour space with better perceptual linearity than the XYZ colour model. The result is not a perfect uniform space, but the linearity between perceived differences is improved.

The LUV model also includes the use of a reference point and it separates the normalisation of brightness. As we mentioned in Section 11.3.1 the white reference point is used to account for variations in illumination; the human eye adapts to the definition of white depending on the lighting conditions, thus having white as reference can be used to describe colour under different lightings. The LUV colour model uses as reference the standard indirect light white as reference; however, it can be translated to represent other lights. As such, the LUV model defines a reference point denoted as $[\,u_n \quad v_n\,]$. This point is obtained by transforming the chromaticity co-ordinates of the white colour.

That is, by considering the values $\overline{x}_n = 1/3$ and $\overline{y}_n = 1/3$ in Eq. (11.54). The transformation gives as result a reference point close to $[0.2 \quad 0.46]$. This point is used to define the colour components in the LUV model as

$$u^* = 13L^*(u - u_n) \quad v^* = 13L^*(v - v_n) \tag{11.55}$$

Here, $[u^* \quad v^*]$ are the colour components and the lightness L^* is given by

$$L* = \begin{Bmatrix} \left(\frac{29}{3}\right)^3 \left(\frac{y}{y_n}\right), & \frac{y}{y_n} \le \left(\frac{6}{29}\right)^3 \\ 116\left(\frac{y}{y_n}\right)^{1/3} - 16, & otherwise \end{Bmatrix} \tag{11.56}$$

Eqs. (11.55) and (11.56) transform colour components. However, equivalent equations can be developed to map chromaticity co-ordinates by following Eq. (11.54) instead of Eq. (11.52).

In addition to centring the transformation on the reference point, Eq. (11.55) introduces a brightness scale value L^*. Remember that the Y axis gives the perception of brightness, thus by dividing by y_n the colour is made relative to the brightness of the white colour and the linearisation is made dependent on the vertical distance to the reference point. When using the white colour as reference and since the XYZ is a normalised, then $y_n = 1$. However, other values may be used when using a different reference point.

Eq. (11.56) makes the perception of brightness more uniform and it has two parts that are defined by considering small and large intensity values. In most cases, the colour is normalised by the part containing the cubic root, thus the normalisation is exponentially decreased as y increases. That is, points closer to the $\overline{ox}$ axis in Fig. 11.5A have a larger scale than points far away from this axis. However, for small values the cube root function has a very large slope and as a consequence small differences in brightness produce very large values. Thus, the cubic root is replaced by a line that gives better scale values for small intensities. In addition to the cubic root, the normalisation includes constant factors that made the value to be in a range from 0 to 100. This was arbitrarily chosen as an appropriate range for describing colour brightness.

The constant values in Eq. (11.55) are chosen so that measured distances between systems can be compared. In particular, when the colour differences are computed by using the Euclidean distance, a distance of 13 in the XYZ model corresponds to the distance of one in the LUV colour model [Poyton03]. The constants produce a range of values between -134 and 220 for u^* and from -140 to 122 for v^*. However, these values can be normalised as illustrated in Fig. 11.5B. This diagram is known as the uniform chromaticity scale diagram. The figure illustrates the shape of the MacAdam ellipses in the LUV colour model with less eccentricity and more uniform size. However, they are not perfect circles. In practice, the approximation provides a useful model to measure perceived colour differences.

The CIE LAB colour model is an alternative to the LUV model. It uses a similar transformation for the brightness, but it changes the way colours are normalised with respect to the reference point. The definition of CIE LAB colour model is given by

$$L^* = 116f\left(\frac{y}{y_n}\right) - 16 \quad a^* = 500\left(f\left(\frac{x}{x_n}\right) - f\left(\frac{y}{y_n}\right)\right) \quad b^* = 200\left(f\left(\frac{y}{y_n}\right) - f\left(\frac{z}{z_n}\right)\right) \tag{11.57}$$

For

$$f(s) = \begin{cases} \frac{1}{3}\left(\frac{29}{6}\right)^2 s + \frac{16}{116}, & s \le (6/29)^3 \\ s^{1/3} & \textit{otherwise} \end{cases} \tag{11.58}$$

The definition of L^* is very similar to the LUV model. In fact, if we substitute Eq. (11.58) in the definition of L^* in Eq. (11.57), we obtain an equation that is almost identical to Eq. (11.56). The only difference is that the LUV model uses a line with zero intercept to replace the cubic root for small values whilst the LAB model uses a line with the same value and slope as the cubic part at the point $(6/29)^3$. In practice, the definition of L^* in both the LUV and LAB gives very similar values.

Although the definition of L^* is practically the same, the normalisation by using the reference point in the LUV and LAB colour models are different; the LUV colour model uses subtraction whilst the LAB divides the colour co-ordinates by the reference point. Additionally, in the LAB colour model, the co-ordinates are obtained by subtracting opposite colours. The use of opposite colours is motivated by the observation that most of the colours we normally perceive are not created by mixing opposites [Nida-Rümelin09]. That is, there is no reddish-green or yellowish-blue, but combinations of opposites have a tendency towards grey. Thus, the opposites provide natural axes for describing a colour. As such, the a^* and b^* values are called the red/green and the yellow/blue *chrominances*, and they have positive and negative values. These values do not have limits and they extend to colours not visible by the human eye; however, for digital representations, the range is limited by values between -127 and 127.

The a^*, b^* and the dark-bright luminosity define the axes of a three-dimensional diagram referred as the LAB chart and that is illustrated in Fig. 11.6. In this figure, the top/bottom axis of this graph represents the lightness L^* and it ranges from black to white. The other two axes represent the red/green and yellow/blue values. Negative values in a^* indicate green whilst positive values indicate magenta. Similarly, negative and positive values of b^* indicate yellow and blue colours. Since visualising three-dimensional data is difficult, generally the colours in the LAB model are shown as slices parallel to the a^* and b^* axes. Two of these slices are illustrated in Fig. 11.6.

In order to obtain an inverse mapping that obtains the components of a colour in the XYZ colour model from the LUV and LAB values, we can invert the equations defining the transformations. For example, the chromatic co-ordinates of a colour can be obtained from the LUV co-ordinates by inverting Eqs. (11.54) and (11.55). That is,

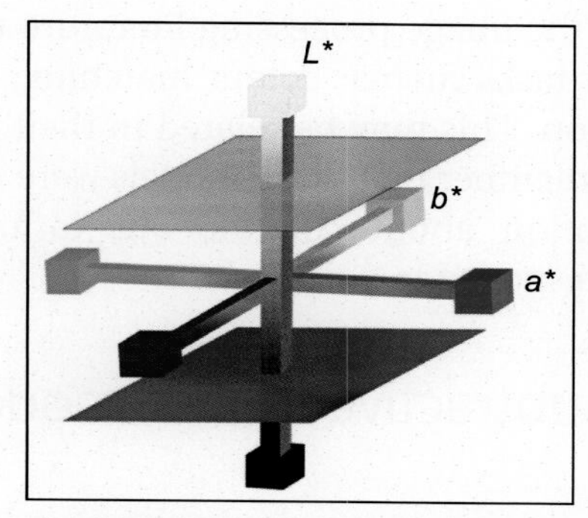

FIGURE 11.6 CIE LAB colour space.

$$\bar{x} = \frac{9u}{6u - 16v + 12} \quad \bar{y} = \frac{4v}{6u - 16v + 12} \tag{11.59}$$

and

$$u = \frac{u^*}{13L^*} + u_n \quad v = \frac{v^*}{13L^*} + v_n \tag{11.60}$$

For the LAB colour model, the co-ordinates in the XYZ space can be obtained by inverting Eqs. (11.57) and (11.58). That is,

$$y = y_n f^{-1}\left(\frac{L^* + 16}{116}\right) \quad x = x_n f^{-1}\left(\frac{L^* + 16}{116} + \frac{a^*}{500}\right) \quad b^* = y_n f^{-1}\left(\frac{L^* + 16}{116} + \frac{b^*}{200}\right) \tag{11.61}$$

For

$$f^{-1}(s) = \left\{ \begin{array}{cc} 3\left(\frac{6}{29}\right)^2\left(s - \frac{16}{116}\right), & s \leq 6/29 \\ s^3 & otherwise \end{array} \right\} \tag{11.62}$$

It is important to understand that the colours in the LUV, LAB, and XYZ models are the same and they represent the colours we can perceive. These transformations just define mappings between co-ordinates. That is, they change the way we name or locate each colour in a co-ordinate space. What is important is how co-ordinates of different colours are related to each other. That is, each colour model arranges or positions the colours differently in a co-ordinate space, so the special relationships between colours have specific properties.

As explained before, the XYZ provides a good understanding of colour properties and it is motivated by the way we match different colours using single frequency normalised components (i.e. colour matching functions). The LUV and LAB colour models provide an arrangement that approximates the way we perceive differences between colours. That is, they have better perceptual linearity, chromatic adaptation and they match better the human perception of lightness. This is important so, for example, to predict how observers will detect colour differences in graphic displays. Additionally, there is some experimental works in the image processing literature that have shown that these models can also be useful for tasks such as colour matching, detecting shadows, texture analysis and edge classification. This may be related to their better perceptual linearity; however, it is important to remember that these models were not designed to provide the best information or correlation about colours, but to model and give a special arrangement of the human response to colour data.

11.4 Additive and subtractive colour models

11.4.1 RGB and CMY

The CIE RGB and XYZ models represent all the colours that can be perceived by the human eye by combining three monochromatic lights (nonvisible for the XYZ model). Thus, although they have important theoretical significance, they are not adequate for modelling practical colour reproduction and capture systems such as photography, printers, scanners, cameras, and displays. In the case of reproduction systems, producing colours with a single frequency (e.g. lasers) with adequate intensity for generating visible colours with an adequate luminosity is very expensive. Similarly, sensors in cameras integrate the luminosity over a wide range of visible colours. Consequently, the base colours in capture and reproduction systems use visible colours composed of several electromagnetic frequencies. Thus, there is a need of device-dependent colour models that are determined by factors such as the amount of ink or video voltages. Fortunately, images rarely contain saturated colours, so a non-monochromatic base provides a good reproduction for most colours without compromising intensity.

The RGB colour models use base colours containing strong components close to the red, green and blue wavelengths. These models are used, for example, by LCD and plasma displays. The base colours in these models are denoted as $[R \quad G \quad B]$ and their components as $[r \quad g \quad b]$. Other reproduction systems, such as inkjet and laser printers use base colours close to the complementary of RGB. That is, cyan, yellow and magenta. These models are called *CMY* and their base colours and components are denoted as $[C \quad M \quad Y]$ and $[c \quad m \quad y]$, respectively. CIE RGB is a particular RGB model; however, the term RGB models is generally only used to refer colour models developed for practical reproduction systems. The motivation to have several RGB and CMY colour models is to characterise the physical properties of different reproduction systems.

The RGB and CMY colour models differ in the way in which the colours are created; RGB is an additive model whilst CMY is subtractive. The additive or subtractive nature of the models is determined by the physical mechanism used in the reproduction system. In the RGB, the base colours are generated by small light-emitting components such as fluorescent phosphors, diodes or semiconductors. These components are positioned very close to each other, so its light is combined and perceived as a single colour. Thus, the creation from colours stems from black and it adds the intensities of the base colours. In CMY, the base colours are colourants that are applied on a white surface. The colours act as filters between the white surface and the eye producing a change in our perception. That is, colours are subtracted from white. For example, to create green, we need to filter all the colours but green, thus we should apply the complementary or opposing colour to green: magenta.

CMY has been extended to CMYK model by adding black to the base colours. The use of black has two practical motivations. First, in a reproduction system, it is cheaper to include a black than use CMY to generate black. Secondly, using three different colours produces less detail and shade than using a single colour. This is particularly important if we consider that a great amount of printing material is in black and white.

Since RGB and CMY models are relevant for reproduction systems, in addition to the additive and subtractive properties, it is very important to determine which colours are included in the colour model. This is called the *gamut* and it is generally described using a triangle in the chromaticity diagram as illustrated in Fig. 11.7. In this figure, the triangles' vertices are defined by the base colours of typical RGB and CMY models. The triangle pointing upwards illustrates a typical RGB colour model whilst the upside down triangle illustrates a CMY model. Since colours are linearly combined, each triangle contains all the colours that can be obtained by the base colours. That is, the gamut. This can be seen by considering that any point between two of the base colours can be obtained by a linear combination between them. For example, any colour that can be obtained by combining R and G is in the line joining those points. Thus, the full trace of lines between a point in this line and B fill in the triangle covering all the colours that can be created with the base.

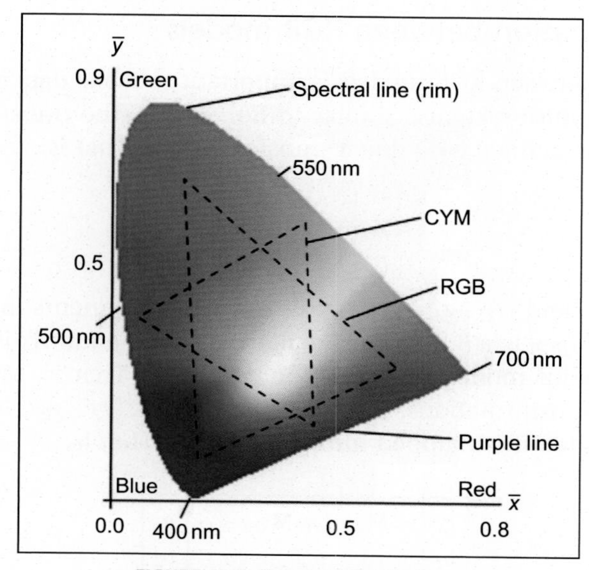

FIGURE 11.7 Chromaticity diagram.

In addition to visualising the model using the chromaticity diagram, sometimes the colours in the RGB and CMY models are shown using a three-dimensional cube where each axis defines one colour of the base. This is called the RGB colour cube and the range of possible values is generally normalised such that all colours are encompassed in a unit cube. The origin of the cube has co-ordinates $[0 \quad 0 \quad 0]$ and it defines black, whilst the diagonal opposite corner $[1 \quad 1 \quad 1]$ represents white. The vertices $[1 \quad 0 \quad 0]$, $[0 \quad 1 \quad 0]$ and $[0 \quad 0 \quad 1]$ represent the base colours red, green and blue, respectively, and the remaining three vertices represent the complementary colours yellow, cyan and magenta. In practice, the chromaticity diagram is used to visualise the possible range of colours of a reproduction system whilst the cube representation is useful to visualise the possible colour values.

Reproduction systems of the same type have similar base colours, but the exact spectral composition varies slightly. Thus, standards have been established to characterise different colour reproduction systems. For example, the *HDTV (High Definition Television)* uses points with chromaticity co-ordinates $R = [0.64 \quad 0.33]$, $G = [0.3 \quad 0.6]$ and $B = [0.15 \quad 0.06]$ whilst the *NTSC (National Television System Committee)* has the points $R = [0.67 \quad 0.33]$, $G = [0.21 \quad 0.71]$ and $B = [0.14 \quad 0.08]$. Other standards include the *PAL (Phase Alternate Line)* and the *ROMM (Reference Output Medium Metric)* developed by Kodak. In addition to standards, it is important to notice that since colour reproduction is generally done by using colours represented in digital form, often different colour models are also strongly related to the way the components are digitally stored. For example, *true colour* uses 8 bits per component whilst *high colour* uses 5 bits for red and blue and 6 bits for green. However, independently of the type of model and storage format, the colour representation uses the RGB and CMY colour models.

11.4.2 Transformation between RGB models

The *transformation* between RGB models is important to make data available to diverse reproduction and capture systems. Similar to Eq. (11.21), the transformation between RGB colour models is defined by a linear transformation. That is,

$$\begin{bmatrix} r_1 \\ g_1 \\ b_1 \end{bmatrix} = M_{RGB} \begin{bmatrix} r_2 \\ g_2 \\ b_2 \end{bmatrix} \tag{11.63}$$

Here, $[r_1 \quad g_1 \quad b_1]$ and $[r_2 \quad g_2 \quad b_2]$ are the colour components in two different RGB colour models, and $\mathbf{M}_{RGB}$ is a 3×3 nonsingular matrix. The matrix is generally derived by using the XYZ colour model as a common reference. That is, $\mathbf{M}_{RGB}$ is obtained by concatenating two transformations. First the component $[r_2 \quad g_2 \quad b_2]$ is mapped into the XYZ model and then it is mapped into $[r_1 \quad g_1 \quad b_1]$. That is,

$$\begin{bmatrix} r_1 \\ g_1 \\ b_1 \end{bmatrix} = \mathbf{M}_{RGB2,XYZ} \mathbf{M}_{XYZ,RGB1} \begin{bmatrix} r_2 \\ g_2 \\ b_2 \end{bmatrix} \tag{11.64}$$

The matrix $\mathbf{M}_{RGB2,XYZ}$ denotes the transformation from $[r_2 \quad g_2 \quad b_2]$ to $[x \quad y \quad z]$ and $\mathbf{M}_{XYZ,RGB1}$ denotes the transformation from $[x \quad y \quad z]$ to $[r_1 \quad g_1 \quad b_1]$.

In order to obtain $\mathbf{M}_{RGB2,XYZ}$, we can follow a similar development to the formulation presented in Section 11.3.4. However, in the RGB case, the co-ordinates of the points defining the colour model are known from the colour model standards. Thus, we only need to obtain the normalisation constants. For example, the definition of the NTSC RGB colour model gives the base colours with XYZ chromaticity co-ordinates $[0.67 \quad 0.33]$, $[0.21 \quad 0.71]$ and $[0.14 \quad 0.08]$. The definition also gives the white reference point $[0.31 \quad 0.316]$. The position of these points in the colour space is obtained by computing $\bar{z}$ according to Eq. (11.19) and by considering the mapping defined in Eq. (11.20). That is, the XYZ co-ordinates of the base colours for the NTSC model are given by

$$\begin{array}{c} \alpha[0.67 \quad 0.33 \quad 0.0] \\ \beta[0.21 \quad 0.71 \quad 0.08] \\ \gamma[0.14 \quad 0.08 \quad 0.78] \end{array} \tag{11.65}$$

This expression corresponds to Eq. (11.33) for the CIE RGB. However, in this case the points are co-ordinates in the XYZ colour space. Since these points are mapped into the points $[1 \quad 0 \quad 0]$, $[0 \quad 1 \quad 0]$ and $[0 \quad 0 \quad 1]$ in the NTSC colour space, we have that

$$\alpha\begin{bmatrix}0.67\\0.33\\0.0\end{bmatrix} = \mathbf{M}_{NTSC,XYZ}\begin{bmatrix}1\\0\\0\end{bmatrix}, \quad \beta\begin{bmatrix}0.21\\0.71\\0.08\end{bmatrix} = \mathbf{M}_{NTSC,XYZ}\begin{bmatrix}0\\1\\0\end{bmatrix}, \quad \gamma\begin{bmatrix}0.14\\0.08\\0.78\end{bmatrix} = \mathbf{M}_{NTSC,XYZ}\begin{bmatrix}0\\0\\1\end{bmatrix} \tag{11.66}$$

That is,

$$\mathbf{M}_{NTSC,XYZ} = \begin{bmatrix} 0.67\alpha & 0.21\beta & 0.14\gamma \\ 0.33\alpha & 0.71\beta & 0.08\gamma \\ 0.0\alpha & 0.08\beta & 0.78\gamma \end{bmatrix} \tag{11.67}$$

We can rewrite this matrix as

$$\mathbf{M}_{NTSC,XYZ} = \begin{bmatrix} 0.67 & 0.21 & 0.14 \\ 0.33 & 0.71 & 0.08 \\ 0.00 & 0.08 & 0.78 \end{bmatrix} \begin{bmatrix} \alpha & 0 & 0 \\ 0 & \beta & 0 \\ 0 & 0 & \gamma \end{bmatrix} \tag{11.68}$$

In order to compute the normalisation constants, we invert this matrix. That is

$$\mathbf{M}^{-1}_{NTSC,XYZ} = \begin{bmatrix} 1/\alpha & 0 & 0 \\ 0 & 1/\beta & 0 \\ 0 & 0 & 1/\gamma \end{bmatrix} \begin{bmatrix} 1.73 & -0.48 & -0.26 \\ -0.81 & 1.65 & -0.02 \\ 0.08 & -0.17 & 1.28 \end{bmatrix} \tag{11.69}$$

By using Eq. (11.19) and Eq. (11.20), we have that the XYZ co-ordinates of the NTSC reference point $[0.31 \quad 0.316]$ are $\eta[0.31 \quad 0.316 \quad 0.373]$ where η is a normalisation constant. By considering this point in the transformation defined in Eq. (11.69) we have that

$$\begin{bmatrix} 0.31 \\ 0.31 \\ 0.31 \end{bmatrix} = \eta \begin{bmatrix} 1/\alpha & 0 & 0 \\ 0 & 1/\beta & 0 \\ 0 & 0 & 1/\gamma \end{bmatrix} \begin{bmatrix} 1.73 & -0.48 & -0.26 \\ -0.81 & 1.65 & -0.02 \\ 0.08 & -0.17 & 1.28 \end{bmatrix} \begin{bmatrix} 0.310 \\ 0.316 \\ 0.373 \end{bmatrix} \tag{11.70}$$

By rearranging the terms in this equation

$$\begin{bmatrix} \alpha \\ \beta \\ \gamma \end{bmatrix} = \eta \begin{bmatrix} 1/0.31 & 0 & 0 \\ 0 & 1/0.31 & 0 \\ 0 & 0 & 1/0.31 \end{bmatrix} \begin{bmatrix} 1.73 & -0.48 & -0.26 \\ -0.81 & 1.65 & -0.02 \\ 0.08 & -0.17 & 1.28 \end{bmatrix} \begin{bmatrix} 0.310 \\ 0.316 \\ 0.373 \end{bmatrix} \tag{11.71}$$

Thus,

$$\begin{bmatrix} \alpha \\ \beta \\ \gamma \end{bmatrix} = \eta \begin{bmatrix} 0.92 \\ 0.84 \\ 1.45 \end{bmatrix} \tag{11.72}$$

By considering these values in Eq. (11.67),

$$M_{NTSC,XYZ} = \eta \begin{bmatrix} 0.62 & 0.18 & 0.20 \\ 0.30 & 0.59 & 0.11 \\ 0.00 & 0.07 & 1.13 \end{bmatrix} \tag{11.73}$$

The constant η is determined based on the perceived intensity. The brightest colour in the NTSC model is given by the point $[1 \quad 1 \quad 1]$. According to Eq. (11.73), the intensity value is $0.3 + 0.59 + 0.11$. Since the maxima intensity in the XYZ colour model is one, then we have that

$$\eta = \frac{1}{0.3 + 0.59 + 0.11} = 0.9805 \tag{11.74}$$

Thus,

$$\mathbf{M}^{-1}_{NTSC,XYZ} = \begin{bmatrix} 0.60 & 0.17 & 0.02 \\ 0.29 & 0.58 & 0.11 \\ 0.00 & 0.06 & 1.11 \end{bmatrix} \tag{11.75}$$

By considering Eq. (11.74) and Eq. (11.72) in Eq. (11.68), we have that

$$\mathbf{M}_{NTSC,XYZ} = \begin{bmatrix} 1.91 & -0.53 & -0.28 \\ -0.98 & 1.99 & -0.02 \\ 0.05 & -0.11 & 0.89 \end{bmatrix} \tag{11.76}$$

The transformation matrices for other RGB colour models can be obtained by following a similar procedure. For example, for the PAL RGB model the chromaticity coordinates of the base points are $[0.64 \quad 0.33]$, $[0.29 \quad 0.60]$ and $[0.15 \quad 0.06]$. The definition also gives the white reference point $[0.3127 \quad 0.3290]$. Thus,

$$\mathbf{M}_{PAL,XYZ} = \begin{bmatrix} 0.43 & 0.34 & 0.17 \\ 0.22 & 0.70 & 0.07 \\ 0.02 & 0.13 & 0.93 \end{bmatrix}, \quad \mathbf{M}^{-1}_{PAL,XYZ} = \begin{bmatrix} 3.06 & -1.39 & -0.47 \\ -0.96 & 1.87 & 0.04 \\ 0.06 & -0.22 & 1.06 \end{bmatrix} \tag{11.77}$$

According to Eq. (11.64), the transformation between the NTSC and PAL model can be obtained by considering that

$$\mathbf{M}_{PAL,NTSC} = \mathbf{M}_{PAL,XYZ}\mathbf{M}_{XYZ,NTSC} = \mathbf{M}_{PAL,XYZ}\mathbf{M}^{-1}_{NTSC,XYZ} \tag{11.78}$$

That is,

$$\mathbf{M}_{PAL,NTSC} = \begin{bmatrix} 0.35 & 0.28 & 0.23 \\ 0.33 & 0.44 & 0.15 \\ 0.05 & 0.13 & 1.04 \end{bmatrix} \tag{11.79}$$

Thus, the transformation between different colour models can be performed by considering the transformations using as reference the XYZ colour model. The advantage of using transformations for the XYZ model is that transformations between any colour model can be computed as a simple matrix multiplication. The transformations between different CMY models can be developed following a similar procedure. That is, by computing the normalisation constants according to three points and a reference white.

11.4.3 Transformation between RGB and CMY models

A very simple approach to transform between RGB and CMY colour models is to compute colours using the numerical complements of the co-ordinates. Thus, the transformation between RGB and CMY can be defined as

$$\begin{bmatrix} c \\ m \\ y \end{bmatrix} = \begin{bmatrix} -1 & 0 & 0 & 1 \\ 0 & -1 & 0 & 1 \\ 0 & 0 & -1 & 1 \end{bmatrix} \begin{bmatrix} r \\ g \\ b \\ 1 \end{bmatrix} \tag{11.80}$$

The problem with this definition is that it does not actually transform the co-ordinates between models. That is, instead of looking for corresponding colours in the XYZ model according the RGB and CMY base colours, it assumes that the base of the CMY are $[0\ \ 1\ \ 1]$, $[1\ \ 0\ \ 1]$ and $[1\ \ 1\ \ 0]$ in RGB co-ordinates. However, the base of the CMY model certainly does not match the RGB model. Additionally, colours in the CMY that are out of the RGB gamut are not used. Consequently, these types of transformations generally produce very different colours in both models.

A better way to convert between RGB and CMY colour models is to obtain a transformation by considering the base colours of the RGB and CMY in the XYZ reference. This approach is analogous to the transformation between models was development in the previous section. However, this approach also has the problem of mapping colours out of the gamut. As shown in Fig. 11.7, the triangles delineating the RGB and CMY models have large areas that do not overlap, thus some colours cannot be represented in both models. That is, a transformation based on the XYZ model will give co-ordinates of points outside the target gamut. Thus, for example, colours in a display will not be reproduced in a printed image. A solution to this problem is to replace colours mapped outside the target gamut by the closest colour in the gamut. However, this loses the colour gradients by saturating at the end of the gamut. Alternatively, the source colours can be scaled such that the gamut fits the target gamut. However, this reduces the colour tones.

Since there is no unique transformation between RGB and CMY models, then the change between colour models has been defined by using *colour management systems*. These are software systems that use *colour profiles* that describe the colour transformation for particular hardware and viewing characteristics. The format of colour profiles is standardised by the *ICC* (*International Colour Consortium*), and they define the transformation from the source to the XYZ or CIELAB. The transformation can be defined by parameters or by tables from where the intermediate colours can be interpolated. Since profiles use chromaticity co-ordinates, then they also contain the co-ordinates of the white reference point.

Many capture systems such as cameras and scanners use standard colour models. Thus, the profile for these systems is commonly defined. However, since there is no best way to transform between models, then every hardware device that captures or displays colour data can have several profiles. They are generally provided by hardware manufacturers and they are obtained by carefully measuring and matching colours in their systems. Generally, there are profiles that provide the closest possible colour matching as well as profiles that produce different colours, but use most part of the target gamut. Other profiles manipulate colours to highlight particular parts of the gamut and saturate others. These profiles are denoted as profiles for different *rendering intent*. The best profile depends on factors such as the colours on the image, colour relationships, desired lightness and saturation as well as subjective perception.

As we have already explained, corresponding chromaticity co-ordinates to the XYZ model and a white reference point can be used to compute normalisation constants that define the colour model transformations. Thus, colour management systems use colour profiles in a similar way to the colour transformation defined in Eq. (11.64). That is, they use the transformation of the source to convert to the reference frame and then the inverse of the target to obtain the final transformed data. If necessary, they will perform also transformations between the XYZ and CIELAB before transforming to the final colour model. For example, a transformation from RGB to CMY can be performed by two transformations as

$$\begin{bmatrix} c \\ m \\ y \end{bmatrix} = \mathbf{M}_{CMY,XYZ}^{-1}\mathbf{M}_{XYZ,RGB}\begin{bmatrix} r \\ g \\ b \end{bmatrix} \tag{11.81}$$

Here, the transformations are represented as matrices, but generally they are defined by tables. Thus, the implementation performs lookups and interpolations. In a typical case, the first transformation will be defined by the profile of a camera or scan, whilst the second is given by an output device such as a printer.

11.5 Luminance and chrominance colour models

The RGB colour models define base colours according to practical physical properties of reproduction systems. Thus, the brightness of each colour depends on all components. However, in some applications, like video transmission, it is more convenient to have a separate single component to represent the perceived brightness. From a historical perspective, perhaps the most relevant models that use a component to represent brightness are the YUV and YIQ. It is important to mention that sometimes the term YUV is used to denote any colour model that uses *luminance* and *chrominance* in different components; the Y component is called the *luma* and the remaining two components are referred to as the *chrominance*. However, YUV is actually a standard colour model that, like YIQ, was specifically developed for analogue television transmission.

In the early development of television systems, it was important to have the brightness in a single component for two main reasons. First, the system was compatible with the old black and white televisions that contained a single luminance component; the added colour data can be transmitted separately from the brightness. Secondly, the transmission bandwidth can be effectively reduced by dropping the bandwidth of the components having the chromaticity; since the human eye is more sensitive to luminance, the reduction in chromaticity produces less degradation in the images that when using the RGB model. Thus, transmission errors are less noticeable by the human eye. Currently, the data reduction achieved with this colour models is not only important for transmission and storing but also for video processing. For processing, a separate luminance can be used to apply techniques based on grey level values as well of techniques that are independent of the luminosity.

11.5.1 YUV, YIQ and YCbCr models

The YUV and YIQ colour models are specified by the NTSC and PAL television broadcasting standards. The difference between both colour models is that the YIQ has a rotation of 33° in the colour components. The rotation defines the I axis to have colours between orange and blue and the Q axis to have colours between purple and green. Since the human eye is more sensitive to changes in the I axis than to the colours in the Q component, then the signal transmission can use more bandwidth for I than for Q to create colours that are clearly distinguished. Unfortunately, the decoding of I and Q is very expensive and television sets did not achieve a full I and Q decoding. Nowadays, the NTSC and PAL standards are being replaced by digital standards such as the *ATSC (Advanced Television Systems Committee)*.

Video signals can be also transmitted without combining them into a single channel, but by using three independent signals. This is called component video and it is commonly used for wire video transmission such as analogue video cameras and DVD players. The colour model used in analogue component video is called YPbPr. The YCbCr is the corresponding standard for digital video. Since this standard separates luminance, then it is adequate for data reduction and thus it has been used for digital compression encoding formats like *MPEG (Moving Pictures Expert Group)* and *JPEG (Joint Photographic Expert Group)*. The data reduction in digital systems is implemented by having less samples of chrominance than luminance. Generally, the chrominance is only half or a quarter of the resolution of the luma component. There are other colour models such as YCC. This colour model was developed for digital photography, and it is commonly used in digital cameras.

There are applications that require converting between different luminance and chrominance models. For example, if processing increases the resolution of video images, then it will be necessary to change between the colour model used in standard definition and the colour model used in high definition. In these cases, the transformation can be developed in two steps by taking as reference RGB colour models. More often, conversions between RGB and YUV colour models are necessary when developing interfaces between transmission and reproduction systems. For example, when printing a digital image from a television signal or when using an RGB display to present video data. Conversion to the YUV colour model is also necessary when creating video data from data captured using RGB sensors, and it can also be motivated by processing reasons. For example, applications based on colour characterisations may benefit by using uniform spaces.

It is very important to notice that transformations between RGB colour models and luminance and chrominance models do not change the colour base, but they only rearrange the colours to give a different meaning to each component. Thus, the base colours of luminance and chrominance models are given by the RGB standards. For example, YIQ uses the NTSC RGB base colours. These are called the RGB base or primaries of the YIQ colour model. That means that the luminance and chrominance models are defined from RGB base colours, and this is the reason why sometimes luminance and chrominance are considered as a way of encoding RGB data rather than a colour model per se.

11.5.2 Luminance and gamma correction

The transformation from RGB to YUV is defined by considering the y component as the perceived intensity of the colour. The perceived intensity was defined by the luminosity function in Eq. (11.2). Certainly, this function depends on the composition of the base colours. For example, for the CIE RGB is defined by Eq. (11.25). Since the YUV and YIQ colour models were developed for television transmission, then perceived intensity was defined according to the properties of the *CRT (Cathode Ray Tube)* phosphorus used on early television sets. These are defined by the RGB NTSC base colours. If we consider the contribution that each component has to luminosity, then y will be approximately given by

$$y = 0.18r + 0.79g + 0.02b \tag{11.82}$$

This equation defines luminance. In the YUV and YIQ models, this equation is not directly used to represent brightness, but it is modified to incorporate a nonlinear transformation that minimises the perceived changes in intensity. The transformation minimises visible errors created by the necessary encoding of data using a limited bandwidth. Since the human eye distinguishes more clearly variations in intensity at low luminance than when the luminance is high, then an efficient coding of the brightness can be achieved if more bandwidth is used to represent dark values than bright values. Coding and decoding luminance is called *gamma encoding* or *gamma correction.*

The graph in Fig. 11.8A illustrates the form of the transformations used in gamma correction. The horizontal axis of the graph represents the luminance y and the vertical axis represents the luma. The luma is generally denoted as y', and it is the value used to represent brightness in the YUV and YIQ colour models. Accordingly, some texts use the notation Y'UV and YUV to distinguishing models using gamma corrected values. However, the transmission of analogue television always includes gamma corrected values. Curves representing gamma correction in Fig. 11.8 only illustrate an approximation of the transformation used to obtain the luma. In practice, the transformation is defined by two parts; a power function is used for most of the curve and a linear function is used for the smallest values. The linear part is introduced to avoid generating insignificant values when the slope of the power exponential is close to zero.

Fig. 11.8A illustrates the encoding power function that maps each luminance value into a point in the vertical axis. This mapping shrinks the intervals at low luminance and expands the intervals at high values. Thus, when y' is encoded, more bandwidth is given to the values where the human eye is more acute. The power function is

$$\Gamma(y) = y^{\left(\frac{1}{\gamma}\right)} \tag{11.83}$$

Here, $(1/\gamma)$ is called the gamma encoding value, and it was chosen by practical considerations for television sets. Since the CRT on television sets had a nonlinear

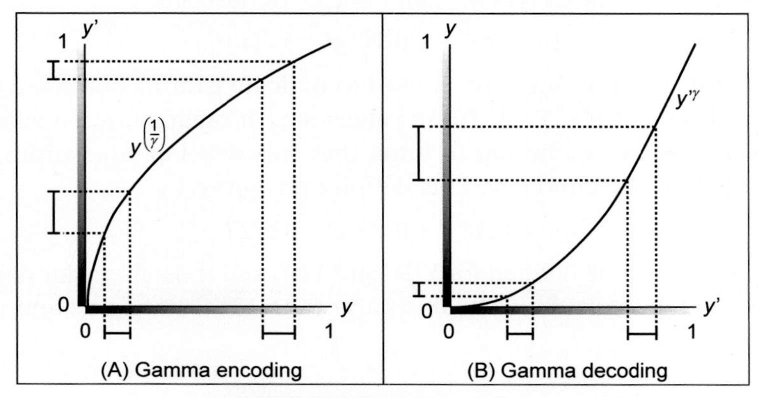

FIGURE 11.8 Gamma correction.

response that approximates the inverse of the transformation in Eq. (11.83), then the gamma value was choosing to match the inverse response. As such, there is no need for decoder hardware, but the CRT nonlinearity acts as a decoder and the intensity reaching the eye is linear. Thus, by using gamma correction, the transmission not only encoded the luminance efficiently, but at the same time it corrects for nonlinearity of the CRT. It is important to emphasise that the main aim of gamma encoding is not to correct the nonlinearity of CRT displays, but to improve the visual quality by efficiently encoding luminance. The gamma encoding of television transmission was carefully chosen such that the nonlinearity of the CRT was also corrected when the signal was displayed. However, gamma correction is important even when image data are not displayed on a CRT and video data are often gamma corrected. Consequently, to process the video data it is often necessary to have gamma decoding. After processing, if the results ought to be displayed on a screen, then it should be gamma encoded to match the screen gamma.

Fig. 11.8B illustrates the decoding gamma transformation. The function in this graph is a typical voltage/luminance response of a CRT and it corresponds to the inverse of Eq. (11.83). Thus, it expands the intervals at low luminance and shrinks the intervals at high luminance. Consequently, it will transform values that have been gamma encoded into linear luminance. Since the encoding occurs before the transmission of the signal, then limited bandwidth of the transmission produces larger errors at low luminance values than at high luminance values. Accordingly, the encoding effectively improves the perceived quality of the images; image artefacts such as banding and roping produced by quantisation are created at low intensities, so they are not evident to the human eye.

Evidently, the value of gamma varies depending on particular properties of the CRT, but for the YUV and YIQ standards it defines a value of $\gamma = 2.2$. That is, the gamma encoding for YUV, should transform the values in Eq. (11.82) by the power in Eq. (11.83) with encoding gamma of 0.45. Since the RGB components in television sets were produced by three independent electron beans, then the encoding cannot apply the transformation to combine luminance, but each component is separately gamma corrected. That is, the luma is defined as the sum of gamma corrected RGB components. Thus, by gamma correcting Eq. (11.82) for $\gamma = 2.2$ we have that

$$y' = 0.299\, r' + 0.587\, g' + 0.114\, b' \tag{11.84}$$

The prime symbol in this equation is used to indicate gamma corrected values. That is, $r' = \Gamma(r)$, $g' = \Gamma(g)$ and $b' = \Gamma(b)$. These values have a range between zero and one.

There is an alternative definition of luma that was developed according to current displays used for HDTV technology. This definition is given by

$$y' = 0.212\, r' + 0.715\, g' + 0.072\, b' \tag{11.85}$$

In practice, Eq. (11.84) is defined for YUV and YIQ, and it used for standard television resolutions (i.e. SDTV) whilst Eq. (11.85) is part of the ATSC standards and it is used for HDTV.

11.5.3 Chrominance

The U and V components represent the chrominance, and they are defined as the difference between the colour and the white colour at the same luminance. Given an RGB colour, the white at the same luminance is defined by Eq. (11.84). Thus, the chrominance is given by

$$\begin{aligned} u &= K_u(b' - y') \\ v &= K_v(r' - y') \end{aligned} \tag{11.86}$$

Only two components are necessary since for chromaticity one component is redundant according to the definition in Eq. (11.13). This definition uses gamma-encoded components and when a colour is between black and white (i.e. grey level values) the components have the same value. Thus, $y' = b' = r'$ and the chrominance becomes zero.

The constants K_u and K_v in Eq. (11.86) can be defined such that the values of u and v are within a predefined range. In television transmission, the colour components of YUV and YIQ are combined into a single composite signal that contains the luma plus a modulated chrominance. In this case, the composite transmission is constrained by the amplitude limits of the television signal. This requires that u being between ± 0.436 whilst the values of v must be between ± 0.611 [Poynton03].

The desired television transmission ranges for u and v are obtained by considering that the maximum and minimum of $b' - y'$ and $r' - y'$. The maximum of $b' - y$ is obtained when $r = g = 0$ and $b = 1$. That is, $1.0 - 0.114$. The minimum value is obtained when $r = g = 1$ and $b = 0$ That is, $0.0 - (0.299 + 0.587) = -(1.0 - 0.114)$. Similarly, for $b' - y$ we have that the maximum is obtained when $b = g = 0$ and $r = 1$ and the minimum when $b = g = 1$ and $r = 0$. That is, the extreme values are $\pm(1.0 - 0.299)$. Accordingly, the constants that bound the values to ± 0.436 and $\pm\ 0.613$ are

$$\begin{aligned} K_u &= 0.436/(1 - 0.114) \\ K_v &= 0.615/(1 - 0.299) \end{aligned} \tag{11.87}$$

That is,

$$\begin{aligned} u &= 0.493(b' - y') \\ v &= 0.877(r' - y') \end{aligned} \tag{11.88}$$

These constants are not related to perception or properties of the colours, but are defined such that signals are appropriate for composite transmission according to the NTSC and PAL standards. The same constants are used when the signal is transmitted over two channels (i.e. *S-Video*), but as we explain below they are different when the signal is transmitted over three channels.

11.5.4 Transformations between YUV, YIQ and RGB colour models

By considering the luma defined in Eq. (11.84) and by algebraically developing the chrominance defined in Eq. (11.88), we can be express the mapping from RGB colour model to YUV colour by using a 3×3 transformation matrix. That is,

$$\begin{bmatrix} y' \\ u \\ v \end{bmatrix} = \begin{bmatrix} 0.299 & 0.587 & 0.114 \\ -0.147 & -0.288 & 0.436 \\ 0.615 & -0.514 & -0.100 \end{bmatrix} \begin{bmatrix} r' \\ g' \\ b' \end{bmatrix} \tag{11.89}$$

A similar transformation for high definition video can be obtained by replacing the first row of the matrix according to Eq. (11.85). The transformation from YUV to RGB is defined by computing the inverse of the matrix in Eq. (11.89), That is,

$$\begin{bmatrix} r' \\ g' \\ b' \end{bmatrix} = \begin{bmatrix} 1.0 & 0.0 & 1.139 \\ 1.0 & -0.394 & -0.580 \\ 1.0 & 2.032 & 0.00 \end{bmatrix} \begin{bmatrix} y' \\ u \\ v \end{bmatrix} \tag{11.90}$$

In the case of the YIQ model, the luma and chrominance follows the same formulation, but the U and V components are rotated but 33 degrees. That is,

$$\begin{bmatrix} i \\ q \end{bmatrix} = \begin{bmatrix} \cos(33) & -\sin(33) \\ \sin(33) & \cos(33) \end{bmatrix} \begin{bmatrix} 0.877(r' - y') \\ 0.499(b' - y') \end{bmatrix} \tag{11.91}$$

By developing this matrix and by considering Eq. (11.82), we have that,

$$\begin{bmatrix} y' \\ i \\ q \end{bmatrix} = \begin{bmatrix} 0.299 & 0.587 & 0.114 \\ 0.596 & -0.275 & -0.321 \\ 0.212 & -0.523 & 0.311 \end{bmatrix} \begin{bmatrix} r' \\ g' \\ b' \end{bmatrix} \tag{11.92}$$

The transformation from YIQ to RGB is defined by taking the inverse of this matrix. That is,

$$\begin{bmatrix} r' \\ g' \\ b' \end{bmatrix} = \begin{bmatrix} 0.299 & 0.587 & 0.114 \\ 0.596 & -0.275 & -0.321 \\ 0.212 & -0.523 & 0.311 \end{bmatrix} \begin{bmatrix} y' \\ i \\ q \end{bmatrix} \tag{11.93}$$

11.5.5 Colour model for component video: YPbPr

The YPbPr colour model uses the definition of luma given in Eq. (11.84) and the chrominance is defined in an analogous way to Eq. (11.86). That is,

$$\begin{aligned} p_b &= K_b(b' - y') \\ p_r &= K_r(r' - y') \end{aligned} \tag{11.94}$$

The difference between this equation and Eq. (11.86) is that since YPbPr was developed for component video, then it assumes that signals are transmitted independently and consequently there are different constraints about the range of the transmission signals. For component video, the luma is transmitted using a 1 Volt signal, but this signal also contains sync tips, thus the actual luma has a 0–700 mV amplitude range. In order to bring the chrominance to the same range, the normalisation constants in Eq. (11.94) are defined such that the chrominance is limited to half the luma range (i.e. ± 0.5). Thus, signals are transmitted using a maximum amplitude of ± 0.350 mv that represent the same 700 mv range of the luma signal.

In a similar way to Eq. (11.87), in order to bound the chrominance values to ± 0.5, the normalisation constant are defined by multiplying by the desired range,

$$\begin{aligned} K_b &= 0.5/(1-0.114) \\ K_b &= 0.5/(1-0.299) \end{aligned} \tag{11.95}$$

By using these constants in Eq. (11.94), we have that

$$\begin{aligned} p_b &= 0.564(b'-y') \\ p_r &= 0.713(r'-y') \end{aligned} \tag{11.96}$$

As such, the transformation from the RGB colour model to the YUV colour model is given by

$$\begin{bmatrix} y' \\ p_b \\ p_r \end{bmatrix} = \begin{bmatrix} 0.299 & 0.587 & 0.114 \\ -0.169 & -0.331 & 0.500 \\ 0.500 & -0.419 & -0.081 \end{bmatrix} \begin{bmatrix} r' \\ g' \\ b' \end{bmatrix} \tag{11.97}$$

The inverse is then given by

$$\begin{bmatrix} r' \\ g' \\ b' \end{bmatrix} = \begin{bmatrix} 1.0 & 0.0 & 1.402 \\ 1.0 & -0.344 & -0.714 \\ 1.0 & 1.772 & 0.0 \end{bmatrix} \begin{bmatrix} y' \\ p_b \\ p_r \end{bmatrix} \tag{11.98}$$

The transformations for HDTV can be obtained by replacing the first row in Eq. (11.97) and Eq. (11.98) according to the definition of luma in Eq. (11.85).

11.5.6 Colour model for digital video: YCbCr

The YUV, YIQ and YPbPr colour models provide a representation of colours based on continuous values defined for the transmission of analogue signals. However, transmission and processing of data in digital technology requires a colour representation based on a finite set of values. The YCbCr colour model defines a digital representation of colour by digitally encoding the luma and chrominance components of the YPbPr model.

The YCbCr model encodes the values of YPbPr by using 8 bits per component, but there are extensions based on 10 bits. The luma byte represents an unsigned integer and its values range from 16 for black to 235 for white. Since chrominance values in the YPbPr model are positive and negative, then the chrominance bytes in YCbCr represent two's complement signed integers centred at 128. Also, the YCbCr standard defines that the maximum chrominance values should be limited to 240. The ranges of the components in the YCbCr model are called *YCbCr video levels* and they do not cover the maximum range that can be represented using 8 bits. The range is clipped to avoid having YCbCr colours that when mapped to the RGB can create saturate colours out of the RGB gamut. That is, the range of the YCbCr components is chosen to be a subset of the RGB gamut. The xvYCC colour model extends YCbCr representation by considering that modern displays and reproduction technologies can have a gamut that includes higher saturation values. Thus, the full 8-bit range is used. Also some applications, like JPEG encoding have considered more practical to use the full 8-bit range.

By considering the range of the components in the YCbCr model and by recalling that the luma in the YPbPr model ranges from zero to one whilst the chrominance takes values between ± 0.5, then the transformation that defines the YCbCr colour model is given by

$$y'_c = 16 + 219y' \quad C_b = 128 + 224p_b \quad C_r = 128 + 224p_r \tag{11.99}$$

Here we use y'_c to denote the luma component in the YCbCr colour model. For applications using the full range represented by 8 bits, we have the alternative definition given by

$$y'_c = 255y' \quad C_b = 128 + 256p_b \quad C_r = 128 + 256p_r \tag{11.100}$$

By developing Eq. (11.99) according to the definitions in Eq. (11.84) and Eq. (11.96) we have that the transformation from RGB to YCbCr can be written as

$$\begin{bmatrix} y'_c \\ C_b \\ C_r \end{bmatrix} = \begin{bmatrix} 65.481 & 128.553 & 24.966 \\ -37.797 & -74.203 & 112.0 \\ 112.0 & -93.786 & -18.214 \end{bmatrix} \begin{bmatrix} r' \\ g' \\ b' \end{bmatrix} + \begin{bmatrix} 16 \\ 128 \\ 128 \end{bmatrix} \tag{11.101}$$

By solving for r', g' and b', we have that the transformation from the YCbCr colour model to the RGB colour model is given by

$$\begin{bmatrix} r' \\ g' \\ b' \end{bmatrix} = \begin{bmatrix} 0.00456 & 0.0 & 0.00625 \\ 0.00456 & -0.00153 & -0.00318 \\ 0.00456 & 0.00791 & 0.0 \end{bmatrix} \begin{bmatrix} y' - 16 \\ p_b - 128 \\ p_r - 128 \end{bmatrix} \tag{11.102}$$

For high-definition data, the definition should use Eq. (11.85) instead of Eq. (11.84). Also when converting data considering full range defined by 8 bits, the transformation equations are developed from Eq. (11.100) instead of using Eq. (11.99). Also, since this representation is aimed at digital data, then there are formulae that approximate the transformation by using integers or bit manipulations.

Similar to colour models used for analogue transmission, the YCbCr encodes colours efficiently by using more data for the luma than for the chrominance. This is achieved by using different samplings for the image data. The notation 4:2:2 is used to indicate that images have been codified by sampling the chrominance half the frequency than the luma. That is, each pair of pixels in an image's row has 4 bytes that represent two luminance values and two chrominance values; there is a luma for each pixel, but the chrominance is the same for both pixels. The notation 4:1:1 is used to indicate that four pixels share the same chrominance values. In addition to these representations, some standards like MPEG support vertical and horizontal sampling. In this case, four pixels in two consecutive rows and two consecutive columns are represented by 6 bytes; four for luminance and two for chrominance.

11.6 Additive perceptual colour models

As mentioned in Section 11.4.1, RGB colour models are aimed at representing colours created in reproduction systems. Thus, the combination of RGB components can be not intuitive to human interpretation. That is, it is difficult to determine the precise values that should have colour components that create a particular colour. Even when using the visualisation of the RGB colour cube, the interpretation of colours is not simple since perceptual properties such as the colour brightness vary indistinctly along the RGB axes. Of course that the chromaticity diagram is very useful to visualise the relationships and properties of RGB colours. However, since this diagram is defined in the XYZ colour space, then it is difficult to relate colour's properties to RGB component values. Other colour models like YUV provide an intuitive representation of intensity, but chrominance only represents the difference to white at same luminance, thus the colour ranges are not very intuitive. *Perceptual colour models* are created by a transformation that re-arranges the colours defined by the RGB colour model such that their components are easy to interpret. This is achieved by relating components to colours' characteristics such as hue, brightness or saturation. Thus, tasks such as colour picking and colour adjustments can be performed using colour properties having an intuitive meaning.

11.6.1 The HSV and HLS colour models

There are many perceptual colour models, but perhaps the most common are the *HSV (Hue, Saturation, Value)* and the *HLS (Hue, Lightness, Saturation)*. The HSV is also referred to as *HSI* (*Hue, Saturation, Intensity*) or as the *HSB (Hue, Saturation, Brightness)*. HSV and HLS use two components to define the hue and saturation of a colour but they use different concepts to define the component that represents the brightness. It is important to make clear that the definition of hue and saturation used by these colour models does not correspond to the actual colour's properties defined in Section 11.3.6, but are ad hoc measures based on intuitive observations of the RGB colour cube. However, similar to the hue and saturation discussed in Section 11.3.6 and illustrated by using the chromaticity diagram in Fig. 11.3, the hue and saturation in the HLS and HSV colour models is defined by using polar co-ordinates relative to a reference grey or white point. The hue of a colour that provides a meaning to the colour family like, for example, red, yellow or green is defined by the angular component and the saturation that provides an intuitive meaning of colour sensation from white or grey is defined by the radial distance.

In order to compute hue and saturation according to the perception of the human eye, it is necessary to obtain the polar co-ordinates of the corresponding CIE RGB or XYZ colour's chromaticity co-ordinates. However, the development of the HSV and HLS colour models opts for a simpler method that omits the transformation between RGB and XYZ by computing the hue and saturation directly from the RGB co-ordinates [Smith78]. This simplicity in computation leads to three undesirable properties [Ford98]: first, as we discussed in Section 11.4.1, the RGB co-ordinates are device dependent. Thus, the colour description in these models will change depending on the reproduction or capture devices. That is, the same image used on television sets and on a digital camera will have different colour's properties. Secondly, RGB co-ordinates are not based on human perception, but are dependent on colour reproduction technology. Thus, the computations are not based on reference values that match our perception. As such, the colours' properties in HLS and HSV colour models give only rough approximations of perceived properties. Finally, since the colour's luminance is not actually correlated to definitions like the luminosity functions and the computations use approximations, the brightness component does not correspond to the actual perceived brightness. Consequently, changes in hue or saturation can be perceived as changes in brightness and vice versa. However, in spite of these drawbacks, the intuitive definition provided by the HLS and HSV colour models have demonstrated to be useful in developing tools for colour selection. In image processing, these models are useful for operations that categorise range of colours and automatic colour replacement since colour rules and conditionals can be simply specified based on intuitive concepts.

Since HSV and HLS are defined by ad hoc practical notions rather than by formal concepts, then there are several alternative transformations to compute the colours components. However, all transformations are special developments of the original hexagon and triangle geometries [Smith78]. The hexagon geometry defines the HSV and the triangle geometry the HLS. Both geometries define brightness by using planes with normal along the line defining grey. In the hexagonal model, planes are defined as projections of sub-cubes in the RGB colour cube whilst the triangle model planes are defined by three points in the RGB axes. In general, the hexagon model should be preferred because the transformations are simple to compute [Smith78]. However, there are implementations of the HLS transformations suitable for real-time processing in current hardware. Thus, other factors such as that the HLS model is more flexible about the definition of brightness and the better distribution of the colour make the HLS colour model more attractive for image processing applications.

11.6.2 The hexagonal model: HSV

Fig. 11.9 illustrates the derivation of the HSV colour model according to the hexagonal model. In this model, the RGB colour cube is organised by considering a collection of sub-cubes formed by changing the co-ordinates of the components from zero to the maxima possible co-ordinate value. The quantity defining the size of the sub-cubes is

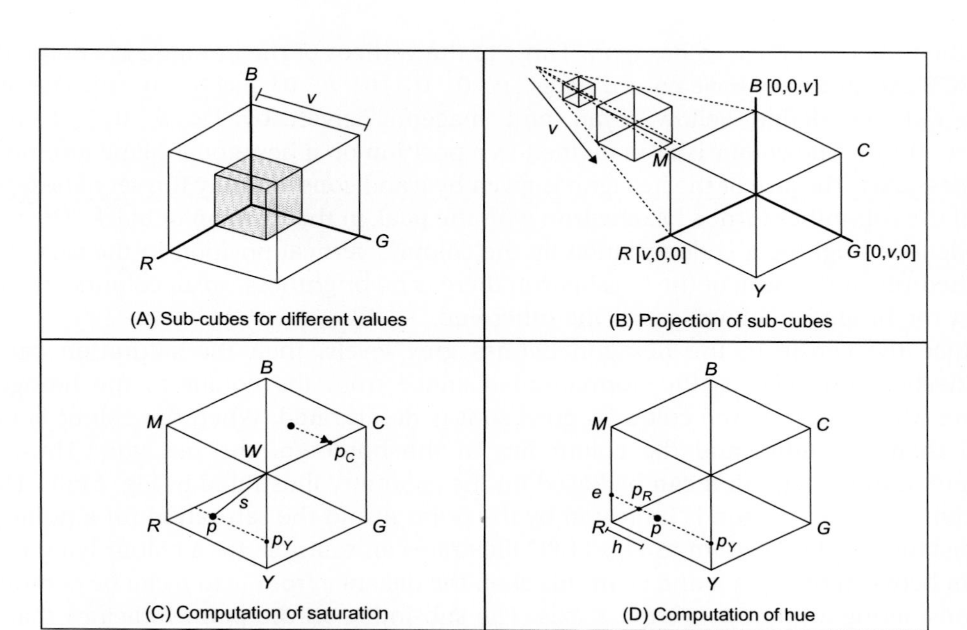

(A) Sub-cubes for different values (B) Projection of sub-cubes (C) Computation of saturation (D) Computation of hue

FIGURE 11.9 HSV colour model.

called the *value* which generally ranges from 0 to 1. A value of 0 defines a sub-cube enclosing a single colour (i.e. black) and a value of 1 encompasses the whole RGB cube. The sub-cubes do not contain all the colours they can enclose, but they only include the colours in the three faces that are visible from the point defining the white corner of the RGB colour cube and looking towards the origin. In Fig. 11.9A these are the shaded faces of the smaller sub-cube. As such, each colour in the RGB colour cube is uniquely included in a sub-cube and the value that defines the sub-cube for any chosen colour can be determined by computing the maxima of its co-ordinates. That is, a colour $[r \quad g \quad b]$ is included in the cube defined by a value given by

$$v = max(r, g, b) \tag{11.103}$$

According to this definition, the value in the HSV colour model is related to the distance from black. Fully saturated colours like red, green and yellow are in the same plane in the HSV colour space. Evidently, this is not in accordance to the perceived intensity as defined by the luminosity function in Fig. 11.4. However, this definition of blackness is useful to create user interfaces that permit the selection of colours given that hue is independent of brightness. In this method, the user can choose a desired hue or colour base and then add blackness to change its *shade*. Change in *tint* or whiteness is given by the saturation whilst tint and shade define the *tone* of the colour. In the HSV colour model saturation is sometimes referred as *chroma*.

Fig. 11.9B shows how the cubes are visualised as hexagons. In this figure, a 3D cube is projected into a plane. The cube is aligned with the points defining black and white such that the projection forms a hexagon. Three of the vertices of the hexagon are defined by the RGB axis and they have co-ordinates $[v \quad 0 \quad 0]$, $[0 \quad v \quad 0]$ and $[0 \quad 0 \quad v]$. The other three vertices define yellow, cyan and magenta, given by $[v \quad v \quad 0]$, $[0 \quad v \quad v]$ and$[v \quad 0 \quad v]$. The colour is then defined as a position on a hexagonal plane around the lightness axis. The size of the hexagon is given by v and consequently the set of hexagons for all the sub-cubes form a hexahedron with the peak in the location of black. The value that defines brightness is determined by the colour's vertical position in the axis of the hexahedron; at the peak of the hexahedron there is no brightness, so all colours are black whilst the brightest colours are at the other end.

Since the centre of the hexagon defines grey levels, then the saturation can be intuitively interpreted as the normalised distance from the colour to the hexagon's centre; when s is zero, the colour is grey, so it is desaturated. When the colour is saturated then s is unity and the colour lies in the border of the hexagon. Thus, the computation of saturation can be based on the geometry illustrated in Fig. 11.9C. Here, the centre of the hexagon is indicated by the point w and the saturation for a point p is the distance s. The diagram in Fig. 11.9C illustrates an example for a colour lying in the region between the axes R and G. In this case, the distance from w to p can be computed by considering a point p_Y on the Y axis. The sub-index on the point indicates that the point lies on a particular axis. Thus, p_M and p_C are the points on the C and M axes that are used for colours in the GB and BR regions, respectively. By considering the geometry in Fig. 11.9C, the saturation is defined by three equations that are applicable depending on the region where the point p lies. That is,

$$s=\frac{|wp_Y|}{|wy|}, \quad s=\frac{|wp_C|}{|wc|}, \quad s=\frac{|wp_M|}{|wm|} \tag{11.104}$$

The first equation defines saturation when p is in the RG regions and the two remaining equations when it is in the GB and BR regions. In these equations, the notation $|wy|$, $|wc|$ and $|wm|$ indicate the distances from the point w to the maxima point along the Y, C and M axis, respectively. Thus, the divisor normalises the distance to be between 0 and 1. In Fig. 11.9C, these distances correspond to the length of the sub-cube defining the hexagon given in Eq. (11.103). By considering the geometry in Fig. 11.9C, the distance for each point can be computed as

$$|wp_Y| = |wy| - |yp_Y|, \quad |wp_C| = |wc| - |wp_C|, \quad |wp_M| = |wm| - |wp_M| \tag{11.105}$$

Thus, by considering Eqs. (11.103) and (11.105) in Eq. (11.104),

$$s=\frac{v-|yp_Y|}{v}, \quad s=\frac{v-|yp_C|}{v}, \quad s=\frac{v-|yp_M|}{v} \tag{11.106}$$

We can also see in Fig. 11.9C that the distances in these equations correspond to the colour component in the direction of the axis where the point lies. That is,

$$s=\frac{v-b}{v}, \quad s=\frac{v-g}{v}, \quad s=\frac{v-r}{v} \tag{11.107}$$

In order to combine these three equations into a single relationship, it is necessary to observe how the $[r \quad g \quad b]$ co-ordinates of a colour determine its region in the hexagon. By observing the projection of the cube illustrated in Fig. 11.9, it can be seen that a colour is in the region RG only if the b component of the colour is lower than r and g. Similarly, the colour is in the GB region only if r is the smallest component and it is in the region BR only if g is the smallest component. Accordingly,

$$s = \frac{v - \min(r, g, b)}{v} \tag{11.108}$$

Similar to saturation, the hue of a colour is intuitively interpreted by considering the geometry of the hexagon obtained by the sub-cube's projection. As such, the hue is considered as the angular value taking as reference the centre of the hexagon; by changing the angle, we change the colour from red, yellow, green, cyan blue and magenta. Naturally, the computation of the hue is also dependent on the part of the hexagon where the colour lies.

Fig. 11.9D illustrates the geometry used to compute the angle for a point between the R and Y lines. The angular position of the point p is measured as a distance from the R line as

$$h = \frac{1}{6}\frac{|p_R p|}{|p_R p_Y|} \tag{11.109}$$

The divisor $|p_R p_Y|$ normalises the distance, thus the hue is independent of the saturation. According to this equation, the hue value is zero when the point is on the R line and it is 1/6 when it is on the Y line. This factor is included since we are measuring the distance in one sextant of the hexagon, thus the distance around all the hexagon is 1.

By considering the geometry in Fig. 11.9D, we have that Eq. (11.109) can be rewritten as.

$$h = \frac{|ep| - |ep_R|}{6 \cdot |wp_Y|} \tag{11.110}$$

The distance $|ep|$ is equal to the value given by the g component and by the similarity of the triangles in the figure, we have that $|ep_R|$ is equal to $|yp_Y|$. That is,

$$h = \frac{g - |yp_Y|}{6 \cdot |wp_Y|} \tag{11.111}$$

By considering Eq. (11.105), Eq. (11.111) can be rewritten as

$$h = \frac{g - |yp_Y|}{6 \cdot (|wy| - |yp_Y|)} \tag{11.112}$$

where $|wy|$ corresponds to the length of the sub-cube defining the hexagon given in Eq. (11.103). Thus,

$$h = \frac{g - |yp_Y|}{6 \cdot (v - |yp_Y|)} \tag{11.113}$$

According to Eqs. (11.106) and (11.107), the distance $|yp_Y|$ can be computed by the minimum value of the RGB components of the colour. Thus,

$$h = \frac{g - \min(r,g,b)}{6 \cdot (v - \min(r,g,b))} \tag{11.114}$$

This equation is generally algebraically manipulated to be expressed as

$$h = \frac{v - \min(r,g,b) - (v - g)}{6 \cdot (v - \min(r,g,b))} \tag{11.115}$$

As such, the hue is defined by

$$h = \frac{(1 - h_G)}{6} \tag{11.116}$$

where

$$h_G = \frac{(v - g)}{v - \min(r,g,b)} \tag{11.117}$$

In order to obtain the hue for any colour is necessary to consider all the regions in the hexagon. This leads to the following equations for each region

$$\begin{array}{ll} h = (1 - h_G)/6 \quad for\ RY & h = (1 + h_R)/6 \quad for\ YG \\ h = (3 - h_B)/6 \quad for\ GC & h = (3 + h_G)/6 \quad for\ CB \\ h = (5 - h_R)/6 \quad for\ BM & h = (5 - h_B)/6 \quad for\ MR \end{array} \tag{11.118}$$

In this notation, RY means when the colour is between the line R and Y in the hexagon and

$$h_R = \frac{(v - r)}{v - \min(r,g,b)}, \quad h_B = \frac{(v - b)}{v - \min(r,g,b)} \tag{11.119}$$

The definitions in Eq. (11.118) add the angular displacements of each sextant, such that 0 is obtained for the red colour, 1/6 for yellow, 2/6 for green, etc. That is, the value of h ranges from zero to one. In practical implementations, the h value is generally multiplied by 360 to represent degrees or by 255 so it can be stored in a single byte. Also, h is not defined when $r = g = b$, that is for desaturated colours. In these cases, implementations generally use the colours of neighbouring pixels to obtain a value for h or just use an arbitrary value.

The implementation of Eq. (11.118) requires determining in which sextant is a given colour. This is done by considering the maximum and minimum values of RGB. The colour will be in the regions RG, GB or GR when blue, red or green is the smallest value, respectively. Similarly, we can see in Fig. 11.9 that a colour will be in the regions MY, YC or CM when r, g or b are the maxima, respectively. Thus, by combining these conditions, we have that a colour will be in a particular sextant according to the following relationships,

$$\begin{array}{llll} RY & \text{if } r = \max RGB & \text{and} & b = \min RGB \\ YG & \text{if } g = \max RGB & \text{and} & b = \min RGB \\ GC & \text{if } g = \max RGB & \text{and} & r = \min RGB \\ CB & \text{if } b = \max RGB & \text{and} & r = \min RGB \\ BM & \text{if } b = \max RGB & \text{and} & g = \min RGB \\ MR & \text{if } r = \max RGB & \text{and} & g = \min RGB \end{array} \tag{11.120}$$

The maxima here can be substituted by v defined in Eq. (11.102).

The transformation from RGB to HSV colour models is defined by solving for r, g and b in Eqs. (11.103), (11.108) and (11.118). Since the transformations are defined for each sextant, then the inverse is also defined for each sextant. For the case of colours in the RY region, we can observe that according to Eq. (11.120), r is greater than the other two components, thus

$$r = v \tag{11.121}$$

Since in this sextant the minimum is b, then the saturation is given by the first relationship in Eq. (11.107). By using this relationship and Eq. (11.121) we have that

$$b = v(1 - s) \tag{11.122}$$

The green component can be obtained by considering Eq. (11.114). That is,

$$h = \frac{g - b}{6 \cdot (v - b)} \tag{11.123}$$

This equation was developed for the RY region wherein b is the minimum of the RGB components. The value of g expressed in terms of h, s and v can be obtained by substitution of Eq. (11.122) in Eq. (11.123). That is,

$$g = v(1 - s(1 - 6h)) \tag{11.124}$$

By performing similar developments for the six triangular regions on the hexahedron, the transformation from the HSV colour model to the RGB colour model is defined as

$$\begin{array}{llll} RY & r = v, & g = k, & b = m \\ YG & r = n, & g = v, & b = m \\ GC & r = m, & g = v, & b = k \\ CB & r = m, & g = n, & b = v \\ BM & r = k, & g = m, & b = v \\ MR & r = v, & g = m, & b = n \end{array} \tag{11.125}$$

For

$$\begin{aligned} m &= v(1 - s) \\ n &= \mathrm{v}(1 - s\,F) \\ k &= v(1 - s(1 - F)) \end{aligned} \tag{11.126}$$

The value of F in these equations is introduced since the equations use the displacement from the start of the interval defined by the region. That is,

$$F = 6h - floor(6h) \tag{11.127}$$

Thus, for the region RY the displacement is measured from the R axis, for the region YG is measured from the Y axis, etc. The development in Eqs. (11.122) and (11.124) uses $6h$ instead of F since both values are the same for the interval RY. In implementation of Eq. (11.125), the region in of the colour can be simply determined by considering the angle defined by h. The index of the region starting from zero for RY and ending with five for MR is $floor(6h)$.

11.6.3 The triangular model: HLS

Fig. 11.10 illustrates the definition of the triangular model. In this model, the colours in the RGB cube are organised by a set of triangles formed by three points on the RGB axes. Each triangle defines a plane that contains colours with the same lightness value. As the

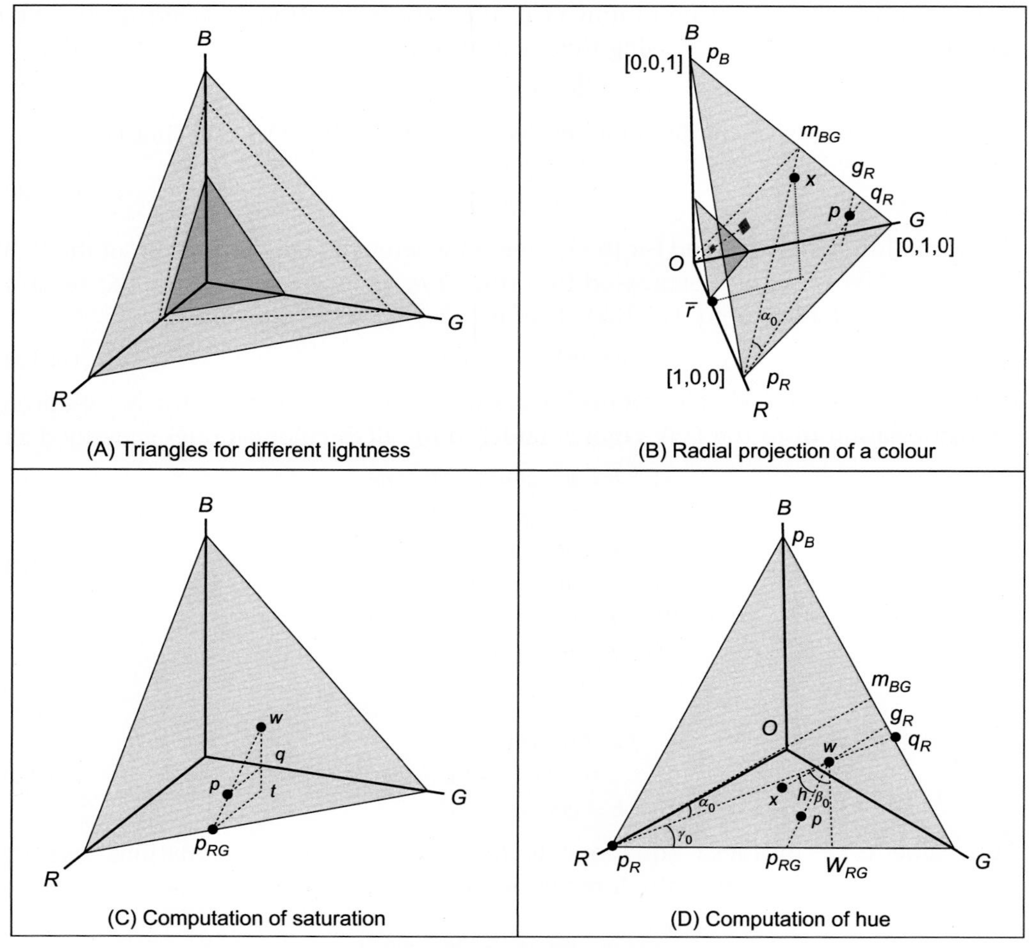

FIGURE 11.10 HLS colour model.

lightness increases, the triangle moves further away from the origin, thus it contains brighter colours. The lightness in this model is defined by the value given by

$$l = w_R r + w_G g + w_B b \tag{11.128}$$

The weights w_R, w_G and w_B are parameters of the colour model and they scale each of the axes. When the axes are scaled, the triangles' centre is biased towards a particular point. For example, if $w_R = 0.2$, $w_G = 0.4$ and $w_B = 0.4$, then the triangle intersects the R axis at the middle of the distance of the other axes, thus its centre will be biased towards the green and blue. This type of shift is illustrated by the dotted triangle in the diagram in Fig. 11.10A.

In the triangle model, a colour is normalised to be independent of brightness by division by l.

$$\overline{r} = w_r \frac{r}{l} \quad \overline{g} = w_g \frac{g}{l} \quad \overline{b} = w_b \frac{b}{l} \tag{11.129}$$

As such, a colour can be characterised by the lightness l and by its hue and saturation computed from normalised co-ordinates. The definition in Eq. (11.129) is similar to Eq. (11.14). This type of equation defines a central projection that maps the colours by tracing radial lines from the origin of the co-ordinate system. In the case of Eq. (11.129), the projection uses radial lines to map the colours into the normalised triangle defined by the points $[1 \quad 0 \quad 0]$, $[0 \quad 1 \quad 0]$ and $[0 \quad 0 \quad 1]$. Fig. 11.10B illustrates this mapping. In this figure, the square in the small triangle is mapped into the larger triangle. The dotted line in the figure corresponds to the radial axis of the projection. The hue and saturation of any triangle is computed by using normalised co-ordinates. That is, the hue and saturation of any colour are independent of its lightness, and they are computed by considering the geometric measures in the normalised triangle.

There are two cases of interest for the scale settings. The first case is called the *unbiased case,* and the second is called the *biased NTSC case.* The first considers that $w_R = w_G = w_B = 1/3$. That is, the grey points defined at the centres of the triangles are $[l/3 \quad l/3 \quad l/3]$. The white point is obtained for maxima lightness, $[1/3 \quad 1/3 \quad 1/3]$. According to Eq. (11.129), the lightness in the unbiased case is given by

$$l_{unbiased} = \frac{(r + g + b)}{3} \tag{11.130}$$

The problem with this definition is that the combination of luminance is poorly matched to the brightness perceived by the human eye. As shown in Fig. 11.4, the perceived brightness in the human eye is stronger for green colours than for red and blue. The *biased NTSC case* is aimed at giving a better correlation between lightness and the brightness perceived by the human eye by using the weights given by $w_R = 0.3$, $w_G = 0.59$ and $w_B = 0.11$. These weights shift the grey points to be at $[0.3l \quad 0.59l \quad 0.11l]$ and the white point is located at $[0.3 \quad 0.59 \quad 0.11]$. According to Eq. (11.129), the lightness in the biased NTSC case is given by

$$l_{NTSC} = 0.3r + 0.59g + 0.11b \tag{11.131}$$

This equation is the same as the definition in Eq. (11.84), thus it corresponds to the luma in the YUV and YIQ colour models. Accordingly, the lightness in this case should be well correlated to the human perception of luminance and it is compatible with analogue television. However, in order to be accurate, it is important that the RGB components to be gamma corrected. Another issue is that the weights values move the centre point to colours that do not match perceived grey colours. The grey values in the RGB colour models are generally defined for equal co-ordinates values, thus the hue and saturation are biased. It is also important to notice that although the triangle model uses the mapping in Eq. (11.14), it does not uses the chrominance diagram to define the co-ordinates, but the mapping is only used to obtain a radial projections. The chromaticity diagram is only defined for the CIE RGB and XYZ colour models since they are based on perception experiments.

The geometry used to define the saturation in the triangle colour model is illustrated in Fig. 11.10C. A colour is indicated by the point p and w denotes the white point. Both points are normalised according to Eq. (11.129), thus they lie on the plane defined by the normalised triangle. The location of the point w changes for biased and unbiased cases. In the figure, t is the projection of w on the plane $b = 0$ and q is on the line defined by the points w and t.

Saturation is defined as the difference of a colour from grey. That is, it can be intuitively interpreted as the normalised distance from p to w. When the distance is zero the point represents a grey colour and when it is one it represents one of the colours in the perimeter of the triangle. In order to formalise this concept, it is necessary to consider three different regions in the colour space. The regions are illustrated in Fig. 11.10D which shows the normalised triangle with the observer looking at the centre of the RGB colour cube. There are three triangles in this figure defining the regions RG, GB and BR. The geometry in Fig. 11.10C corresponds to a colour in the RG region. In this case, the distance should be normalised by dividing it by the distance to a point in the line joining the axes R and G. That is,

$$s_{RG} = \frac{|wp|}{|wp_{RG}|} \tag{11.132}$$

The sub-index on s indicates that this equation is valid only for colours in the region RG. If α is the angle formed by the lines $p_{RG}w$ and $p_{RG}t$, then according to the dotted triangles in Fig. 11.10C, we have the following two trigonometric identities.

$$\sin(\alpha) = \frac{|wq|}{|wp|}, \quad \sin(\alpha) = \frac{|wt|}{|wp_{RG}|} \tag{11.133}$$

By substitution of the values of $|wp|$ and $|wp_{RG}|$ from this equation into Eq. (11.132), we have

$$s_{RG} = \frac{|wq|}{|wt|} \tag{11.134}$$

By considering the definition of $|wq|$, we have that

$$s_{RG} = \frac{|wt| - |qt|}{|wt|} = 1 - |qt| \tag{11.135}$$

In the figure it can be observed that the distances $|qt|$ correspond to the blue component of the point p. This point is the projection of the colour according to Eq. (11.129). Thus,

$$s_{RG} = 1 - \frac{b}{l} \tag{11.136}$$

Similar developments can be performed for colours in the regions GB and BR. In these cases, the point t is the projection of w into the planes $r = 0$ and $g = 0$, respectively. This leads to the following equations that define the saturation on each region

$$s_{GB} = 1 - \frac{r}{l}, \quad s_{BR} = 1 - \frac{g}{l} \tag{11.137}$$

It is possible to combine Eqs. (11.136) and (11.137) into a single equation that defines the saturation for any colour by considering the way in which the $[r \quad g \quad b]$ components determine the region of the colour. By observing the projection of the colour in Fig. 11.10D, it can be seen that a colour is in the region RG only if b is the smallest component. It is in the GB region if r is the smallest component and it is in the region BR if g is the smallest component. Since the smallest component coincides with the colour component used to define the saturation in Eqs. (11.136) and (11.137), then

$$s = 1 - \frac{\min(r, g, b)}{l} \tag{11.138}$$

The hue of a colour is intuitively interpreted by considering the angular value in the normalised triangle by taking as reference the line joining the white point and the red colour. This is illustrated in Fig. 11.10D. Here, the hue for the colour represented by the point p corresponds to the angle defined between the lines wp_R and wp. In the example in this figure, the white point does not coincide with the centre of the co-ordinates; however, the same definitions and formulations are applicable for the unbiased case. In both cases, an angle of zero corresponds with the red colour.

By considering that the white point has the co-ordinates $[w_r \quad w_g \quad w_b]$ and the point p_R has the co-ordinates $[1 \quad 0 \quad 0]$, then the vector from w to p_R is given by

$$wp_R = [1 - w_r \quad -w_g \quad -w_b] \tag{11.139}$$

Since the co-ordinates of the point p are defined by Eq. (11.129), then the vector from w to p is given by

$$wp = \left[\frac{r}{l} - w_r \quad \frac{g}{l} - w_g \quad \frac{b}{l} - w_b\right] \tag{11.140}$$

The angle between the vectors in Eqs. (11.139) and (11.140) can be obtained by considering the dot product. That is,

$$wp_R \cdot wp = |wp_R||wp|cos(h) \tag{11.141}$$

By solving for h we have that

$$h = cos^{-1}\left(\frac{wp_R \cdot wp}{|wp_R||wp|}\right) \tag{11.142}$$

The dot product and the two modules can be computed for Eqs. (11.139) and (11.140). Thus,

$$h = cos^{-1}(k) \tag{11.143}$$

for

$$k = \frac{(1 - w_r)(r - w_r) - w_g(g - w_g) - w_b(b - w_b)}{\sqrt{(1 - w_r)^2 + w_g^2 + w_b^2 + (r - w_r)^2 + (g - w_g)^2 + (b - w_b)^2}} \tag{11.144}$$

The transformation in Eq. (11.143) is generally implemented by using an alternative expression that uses the arctangent function. That is, by using trigonometric identities, Eq. (11.143) becomes

$$h = \frac{\pi}{2} - tan^{-1}\left(\frac{k}{\sqrt{1 - k^2}}\right) \tag{11.145}$$

This equation will give the correct values only for angles between 0 and π. In this case, $b < g$. When the angle exceeds π, it is necessary to consider that the angle is negative (or measured clockwise). That is,

$$h = \begin{cases} \frac{\pi}{2} - tan^{-1}\left(\frac{k}{\sqrt{1 - k^2}}\right), & b < g \\ 2\pi - \frac{\pi}{2} - tan^{-1}\left(\frac{k}{\sqrt{1 - k^2}}\right), & otherwise \end{cases} \tag{11.146}$$

This equation gives a range of values from 0 to 2π. In an implementation, the value obtained is generally expressed on degrees so it can be represented by an integer number. Alternatively, the range can be quantised to be represented by a single byte.

11.6.4 Transformation between HLS and RGB

We have seen that the transformation from RGB to HLS is defined by Eqs. (11.130), (11.131), (11.138) and (11.146). Thus, the inverse transformation is obtained by solving for r, g and b in these equations. Naturally, the inverse depends on which region is the colour. This region can be determined by comparing the angle h against the angles formed between the red and green and between the green and blue axes. These angles are denoted by a_0 and a_1. For the unbiased case, the w point is at the centre of the triangle, thus $a_0 = a_1 = 120$ degrees. In the biased case, these angles are $a_0 = 156.8$ degrees and $a_1 = 115.68$ degrees. As such, the region of a colour is determined by

$$\begin{array}{ll} RG & if\ h < a_0 \\ GB & if\ a_0 \le h < a_0 + a_1 \\ BR & otherwise \end{array} \tag{11.147}$$

Once the region of a colour has been determined, a colour component can be obtained by considering Eqs. (11.136) or (11.137). For example, when the colour is in the RG region, we have that

$$b = l(1 - s) \tag{11.148}$$

Similarly, Eq. (11.137) can be used to find the red and green colours when the colour is in the GB or RB regions, respectively.

The computation of the remaining two colour components is based on the geometrical property of the normalised triangle, Fig. 11.10B. Consider the triangle in three-dimensional space that is formed by the points O, p_R and m_{BG}. Here, the point m_{BG} is the midpoint of the BG line, so the angle between $p_R m_{BG}$ and the line between the G and B axes is 90°. By following a similar development to the triangle relationships in Eq. (11.134), it is possible to relate the ratios between the distances along the OR axis and distances along the $p_R m_{BG}$ line. Thus, the distance for any colour represented by the point x on the line $p_R m_{BG}$ can be related to distances along the OR axis by the following expression

$$\frac{|O\overline{r}|}{|Op_R|} = \frac{|m_{BG}x|}{|m_{BG}p_R|} \tag{11.149}$$

However, the distance $|Op_R|$ is 1 and $|O\overline{r}|$ is the red co-ordinate of the point x. Thus, this equation can be simply written as

$$\overline{r} = \frac{|m_{BG}x|}{|m_{BG}p_R|} \tag{11.150}$$

That is, the red component of a colour is defined as a ratio in the diagonal line. Here we denote the red component as $\overline{r}$. This is because the point x is on the normalised triangle, thus the red component actually corresponds to the normalised value given in Eq. (11.129). Similar expressions can be obtained for other colour components. For example, for the blue component we have that

$$\overline{b} = \frac{|m_{GR}x|}{|m_{GR}p_B|} \tag{11.151}$$

Here m_{GR} is the middle point in the GR line, and x is a colour on the line $p_R m_{GR}$.

The relationship in Eq. (11.150) can be extended to lines that do not intersect BG at its middle point. For the point p on the line $p_R q_R$ in Fig. 11.10B, we have that the red value is given by

$$\overline{r} = \frac{|pg_R|}{|q_R p_R|\cos(\alpha_0)} \tag{11.152}$$

where

$$|pg_R| = |q_R p|\cos(\alpha_0) \tag{11.153}$$

Here, α_0 is the angle between the lines $p_R m_{BG}$ and $q_R p_R$. The cosine function is introduced such that distances are measured in the same direction that the midline. That is, the substitution of Eq. (11.153) in Eq. (11.152) leads to Eq. (11.150).

Fig. 11.10D illustrates how the definition in Eq. (11.152) can be used to obtain the red component for the colour represented by a point p. In the figure, the point x is the orthogonal projection of p on the line wg_R. Similar to Fig. 11.10B, this line has the same direction that the middle line $p_R m_{BG}$. The angle α_0 in the figure is defined by the location of the point w; for the unbiased case w is in the middle of the triangle, thus $\alpha_0 = 0$ and for the biased case the angle is $\alpha_0 = 21.60°$. From Fig. 11.10D

$$|xg_R| = |g_R w| + |wx| \tag{11.154}$$

That is,

$$|xg_R| = |q_R w|\cos(\alpha_0) + |wp|\cos(h - \alpha_0) \tag{11.155}$$

Here, the subtraction of the angles α_0 and h define the angle between the lines wx and wp. The subtraction is sometimes expressed as a summation by considering that α_0 is negative. By substitution of Eq. (11.155) in Eq. (11.152) we have

$$\bar{r} = \frac{|q_R w|\cos(\alpha_0) + |wp|\cos(\alpha_0 - h)}{|q_R p_R|\cos(\alpha_0)} \tag{11.156}$$

The first term in the right side of this equation defines the distance ratio for the point w. That is,

$$w_R = \frac{|q_R w|\cos(\alpha_0)}{|q_R p_R|\cos(\alpha_0)} \tag{11.157}$$

Thus,

$$\bar{r} = w_R + \frac{|wp|\cos(\alpha_0 - h)}{|q_R p_R|\cos(\alpha_0)} \tag{11.158}$$

By considering Eq. (11.132), this equation can be rewritten as

$$\bar{r} = w_R + \frac{s|wp_{RG}|\cos(\alpha_0 - h)}{|q_R p_R|\cos(\alpha_0)} \tag{11.159}$$

The distance $|wp_{RG}|$ can be obtained by considering the angle β_0 defined between the lines wp_{RG} and ww_{RG}. We can observe from Fig. 11.10D that

$$\cos(\beta_0 - h) = \frac{|ww_{RG}|}{|wp_{RG}|} \tag{11.160}$$

Thus,

$$|wp_{RG}| = \frac{|ww_{RG}|}{\cos(\beta_0 - h)} \tag{11.161}$$

The angle β_0 in this equation can be expressed in terms of α_0 by observing from the triangles in the figure that $\alpha_0 + \gamma_0 = 30°$ and $\alpha_0 + \beta_0 = 90°$. That is,

$$\beta_0 = \alpha_0 + 60° \tag{11.162}$$

By substitution of Eqs. (11.161) and (11.162) in Eq. (11.159) we have that

$$\bar{r} = w_R + s\frac{|ww_{RG}|cos(\alpha_0 - h)}{|q_R p_R|cos(\alpha_0)cos(60^\circ + \alpha_0 - h)} \tag{11.163}$$

By observing that the sides of the normalised triangle have the same length, we have that the middle distances are related by

$$|q_R p_R|\cos(\alpha_0) = |p_R m_{BG}| = |p_B m_{GR}| \tag{11.164}$$

That is,

$$\frac{|ww_{RG}|}{|q_R p_R|\cos(\alpha_0)} = \frac{|ww_{RG}|}{|p_B m_{GR}|} \tag{11.165}$$

The distances are measured in the same direction to the midline $|m_{GR} p_B|$. Thus, according to Eq. (11.151), the ratio in the left side in Eq. (11.165) defines the blue coordinate of the point. That is,

$$\frac{|ww_{RG}|}{|p_B m_{GR}|} = w_B \tag{11.166}$$

Thus, the equation for the red component is obtained by substitution of this relationship in Eq. (11.163). That is,

$$\bar{r} = w_R + sw_B\frac{cos(\alpha_0 - h)}{cos(60^\circ + \alpha_0 - h)} \tag{11.167}$$

This equation represents the red normalised component of a colour. The actual red component can be obtained by considering Eq. (11.129). That is,

$$r = l + sl\frac{w_B cos(\alpha_0 - h)}{w_R cos(60^\circ + \alpha_0 - h)} \tag{11.168}$$

As such, the r and b components of a colour can be computed using Eq. (11.148) and Eq. (11.168). The remaining component can be computed using Eq. (11.128). That is,

$$g = \frac{(l - w_R r - w_B b)}{w_G} \tag{11.169}$$

Similar developments can be performed for obtaining the RGB components of colours in the regions GB and BR. Therefore, the complete transformation from HLS to RGB according to the definitions in Eq. (11.147) is given by

$$\begin{aligned}
&\textit{if } h < a_0: \\
&\qquad b = l(1-s), \quad r = l + s\frac{w_B cos(A_0)}{w_R cos(60^\circ + A_0)}, \quad g = \frac{l - w_B b - w_R r}{w_G} \\
&\textit{if } a_0 \le h < a_0 + a_1: \\
&\qquad r = l(1-s), \quad g = l + s\frac{w_R cos(A_1)}{w_G cos(60^\circ + A_1)}, \quad b = \frac{l - w_R r - w_G g}{w_B} \\
&\textit{otherwise}: \\
&\qquad g = l(1-s), \quad b = l + s\frac{w_G cos(A_2)}{w_B cos(60^\circ + A_2)}, \quad r = \frac{l - w_G g - w_B b}{w_R}
\end{aligned} \tag{11.170}$$

for

$$\begin{aligned} A_0 &= \alpha_0 - h \\ A_1 &= \alpha_1 - h - a_0 \\ A_2 &= \alpha_2 - h - a_0 - a_1 \end{aligned} \tag{11.171}$$

These equations introduce the subtraction of the angles a_0 and a_1 so the computations are made relative to the first axis defining the region. In the unbiased model, the white point is at the centre of the triangle, so the constants are defined by

$$\begin{aligned} &w_R = 0.33, \quad w_G = 0.33, \quad w_B = 0.33 \\ &a_0 = 120^o, \quad a_1 = 120^o \\ &\alpha_0 = 0, \quad \alpha_1 = 0, \quad \alpha_2 = 0 \end{aligned} \tag{11.172}$$

For the biased model they are

$$\begin{aligned} &w_R = 0.30, \quad w_G = 0.59, \quad w_B = 0.11 \\ &a_0 = 156.58^o, \quad a_1 = 115.68^o \\ &\alpha_0 = 21.60^o, \quad \alpha_1 = -14.98^o, \quad \alpha_2 = -10.65^o \end{aligned} \tag{11.173}$$

The alpha sign is negative for the angles used in the GB and BR regions. This is because the lines defining those angles are in opposite direction to the direction of the angle α_0 used in the presented development.

11.7 More colour models

This chapter has discussed different types of colour spaces that have been created according to different motivations; there are colour spaces aimed to formalise and standardise our perception of colour whilst other models are developed for a more practical nature according to the way reproduction systems work or how data should be organised for particular process such as video signal transmission. In any case, the colour models are based on the tristimulus theory that formalised the sensations created by wavelengths in space. Thus, these models do not describe the physical spectral nature of colour, but they provide a way to specify, recreate and process our visual sensation of colour using a three dimensional space.

This chapter has considered the most common colour spaces; however, there are other important spaces that have similar motivations and properties, but they change the way colours are described. For example, the CIE LCH colour model uses the same transformations as the LAB, but it uses cylindrical co-ordinates instead of rectangular. This gives a uniform space with polar co-ordinates, so it can be related to hue and saturation. The saturation in this space is generally referred as *chroma* and it has the advantage of be more perceptually linear. Other example of an important colour description is the Munsell colour model. This colour model also uses cylindrical co-ordinates, it uses perceptual uniform saturation and it is based on measures of human perception. It is also important to mention that there exist other colour models that have focused on achieving a practical colour description. For example, the PANTONE colour system consists of a large catalogue of standardised colours.

In addition to many colour spaces, the literature has alternative transformations for the same colour space. Thus, in order to effectively use colour information in image processing, it is important to understand the exact meaning of the colour components in each colour model. As such, the importance of the transformations between models is not to define a recipe to convert colours, but to formalise the relationships defined by the particular concepts that define each colour space. Accordingly, the transformations presented in this chapter have been aimed at illustrating particular properties of the colour spaces to understand their strengths and weaknesses rather than to prescribe how colour spaces should be manipulated.

References

[Broadbent04] Broadbent, A. D., A Critical Review of the Development of the CIE1931 RGB Colour-Matching Function, *COLOUR Research and Application*, **29**(4), pp 267-272, 2004.

[Fairman97] Fairman, H. S., Brill, M. H., Hemmendinger, H., How the CIE 1931 Colour-Matching Functions Were Derived from Wright-Guild Data, *COLOUR Research and Application*, **22**(1), pp 11-23, 1997.

[Ford98] Ford, A., Roberts, A., *Colour Space Conversions*, August 1998 (http://www.poynton.com/PDFs/coloureq.pdf).

[Guild32] Guild, J., The Colourimetric Properties of the Spectrum, *Philosophical Transactions of the Royal Society London*, **A230**, pp149-187, 1932.

[Judd35] Judd, D. B., A Maxwell Triangle Yielding Uniform Chromaticity Scales, *Journal of the Optical Society of America*, **25**(1), pp 24-35, 1935.

[Kuehni03] Kuehni, R. G., *Colour Space and its Divisions: Colour Order from Antiquity to the Present*, John Wiley & Sons Inc., New Jersey, 2003.

[MacAdam42] MacAdam, D. L., Visual Sensitivities to Colour Differences in Daylight, *Journal of the Optical Society of America*, **32**(5), pp 247-274, 1942.

[Nida-Rümelin09] Nida-Rümelin, M., Suarez, J., Reddish Green: A Challenge for Modal Claims about Phenomenal Structure, *Philosophy and Phenomenological Research*, **78**(2), pp 346-391, 2009.

[Poynton03] Poynton, C. A., *Digital Video and HDTV: Algorithms and Interfaces*, Elsevier, San Francisco, 2003.

[Sagawa86] Sagawa, K., Takeichi, K., Spectral Luminous Efficiency Functions in the Mesopic Range, *Journal of the Optical Society of America*, **3**(1), pp 71-75, 1986.

[Sharpe05] Sharpe, L. T., Stockman, A., Jagla, W., Jägle, H., A Luminous Efficiency Function, $V^*(\lambda)$, for Daylight Adaptation, *Journal of Vision*, **5**(11), pp 948-968, 2005.

[Sherman81] Sherman, P. D., *Colour Vision in the Nineteenth Century: Young/Helmholtz/Maxwell Theory*, Adam Hilger Ltd, Bristol, 1981.

[Smith78] Smith, A. R., Colour Gamut Transform Pairs, *ACM SIGGRAPH Computer Graphics*, **12**(3), pp 12-19, 1978.

[Wright29] Wright, W. D., A Re-determination of the Trichromatic Coefficients of the Spectral Colours, *Transactions of the Optical Society*, **30**(4), pp 141-164, 1929.

[Wyszecki00] Wyszecki, G. W., Stiles, W. S., *Colour Science, Concept and Methods, Quantitative Data and Formulae*, John Wiley & Sons Inc., 2000.

12

Distance, classification and learning

12.1 Overview

This chapter is concerned with how we can characterise and recognise objects. This means we have to grasp the nettle here: a deep learning revolution has taken place in recent years and that affects computer vision very much. Naturally, a textbook is a time-controlled snapshot of its subject matter; by process, a textbook can be out of date when it is published. Bernard Shaw wrote that 'progress is impossible without change, and those who cannot change their minds cannot change anything,' so we shall consider deep learning as a new way for feature extraction and one which has demonstrated that it is an awesome cannon in the arsenal of techniques for machine learning. Arguably, in deep learning, the vast range of techniques that comprise computer vision are brought together, from low-level to high-level processing. We have previously considered it at the end of each section, and now we bring this material together. But the revolution continues, so we only offer a snapshot here and one taken in 2019. We shall start by describing how we can collect together measurements for purposes of recognition and subsequently introduce distance measures that describe how different features appear to be by their measurements (Table 12.1).

12.2 Basis of classification and learning

Machine learning is a different field from computer vision: vision extracts from, or transforms, spatial data, and machine learning derives information from it: we can learn from the data exposed using computer vision. In Fig. 12.1, we can use computer vision to derive positions of points on the face by using, say, SIFT (Chapter 4), the Hough transform (Chapter 5) or Active Shape Models (Chapter 6). Given measurements derived for different faces, machine learning can learn how to discriminate or recognise the different faces. With deep learning, the feature extraction and classification stages are combined, as in Fig. 12.1. We shall start by defining some of the terms that are used in classification and learning. When we learn, it is often by way of examples. In machine learning that is called *training*. Wherever we put knowledge into the system affects the result, so the question is how much training data exists. The number of shots describes the count of how many times a sample appears in the training data. So

1. *multi-shot* refers to situations where the sample occurs multiple times;
2. *single shot* is where the sample appears only once and
3. *zero shot* refers to where the sample does not appear in the training data.

Feature Extraction and Image Processing for Computer Vision. https://doi.org/10.1016/B978-0-12-814976-8.00012-9

Table 12.1 Overview of this chapter.

Main topic	Subtopics	Main points
Classification and learning	How do we learn from data? What do the terms mean? What is classification, and why are we doing this?	*Learning* and *deep learning*. *Training* and *testing*. *Classification*, *clustering* and *regression*.
Measuring distance	How different do features appear to be, from the measurements we have made. Different ways of measuring distance, and understanding dissimilarity, for points, sets, histograms and groups.	Distance metrics: *Manhattan* city block and *Euclidean* (L_1 and L_2 distances), *Mahalanobis*, *Bhattacharyya*, *cosine distance*, *histogram intersection*, *chi*^{2} (χ^2) and *earth mover's distance*. Construction, visualisation and the *confusion matrix*.
Classification	Classification and machine learning techniques for pattern classification.	The *k-nearest neighbour rule*, *support vector machines*, *neural architectures*.
Deep learning	Deep learning architectures, deep learning for feature detection and classification. How do these techniques work? How well does deep learning operate?	*Deep learning*, deep learning for *feature extraction*, deep learning for *classification*. Deep learning architectures: *Alexnet*, *VGG*, *Inception*, and *Resnet*. *Interpretability*. *Counterfactual reasoning*.

In terms of application, these cases reflect classifying the face of a subject from a set of face images, a single face image and from a live video feed, respectively. We need to apply it to application data, so data that are not contained in the training data are called the *test* data; the performance on test data assesses capability to *generalise* performance from that on training data. We can also learn by the degree of difference between the actual result and the expected result. In machine learning, this is called the *loss* function. In a training stage, the loss function can be used to change the model, or the approximation. In that way, the loss function reduces when the system converges to a reasonable model or approximation. Having trained a system we then apply it to the test data and find out how well it really works.

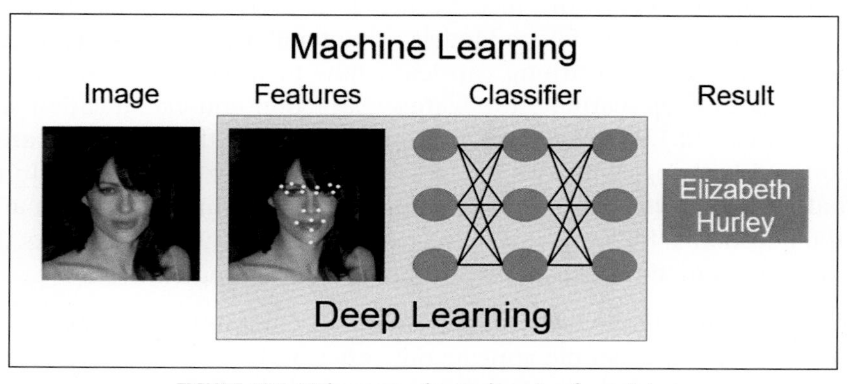

FIGURE 12.1 Main approaches to learning from data.

On the data usage:

1. *supervised* learning is based on data that have been previously labelled;
2. *unsupervised* learning uses data that have not been previously labelled and
3. *semi-supervised* learning uses an admixture of labelled and unlabelled data.

OK, there are (quite) a few more nuances, but we are at the start here and this is the 'what it says on the tin' stage. In applications, we have a sample and we want to find which sample (from a database) best matches it. If it is a face, we want to find out whom it belongs to; if it is a texture, we want to find which class it most closely resembles. What and how samples resemble data can be achieved in different ways:

1. *classification* is to associate the appropriate *class label* (type of sample) with a test sample by using the measurements that describe it;
2. *clustering* concerns partitioning samples into similar groups and
3. *regression* aims to determine the underlying model by dealing with continuous functions.

One way to achieve the classification (and clustering) is by finding the member of the class (e.g. the sample of a known texture) with measurements which differ by the least amount from the test sample's measurements. An example of classification is shown in Fig. 12.2 where the question was whether the gender of a subject can be determined from images of their body [Martinho-Corbishley19]. Rather than the conventional binary labels, here the labels reflect situations (as common in surveillance video) where it is not always possible to determine the gender with confidence. The data are split into five classes: the two conventional labels male and female; two that reflect uncertainty (possibly either) and one label that suggests it is difficult to determine gender. (The images actually derive from a standard database that includes binary ground truth labels of gender, and the results here rather question the confidence in those labels. For example, Fig. 12.2C has a ground truth label of male, by someone who has probably not visited China, but that is a different story.) Fig. 12.2 also demonstrates a form of clustering of the perception of gender in whole-body images.

So what exactly is deep learning? As in Fig. 12.1, if the approach used is traditional machine learning then features are derived from images and classes are learnt from these features. The classification process associates extracted features with data. This association can be achieved by some form of neural network on the premise that human brains operate in a manner similar to the architecture shown in Fig. 1.5. It is possible to apply a neural network directly to image data since they are matrices of numbers, just like the features. So if the features and classifier are combined, we have deep learning: classification and feature extraction is done in a single step, end to end. We shall find that the step is quite long and complicated, and requires much computer power. The classification of Fig. 12.2 is achieved in real time by deep learning applied to a video feed, after the system has been trained. We shall find similarity in the features detected by deep learning to those described earlier in the book, and that some of the deep neural

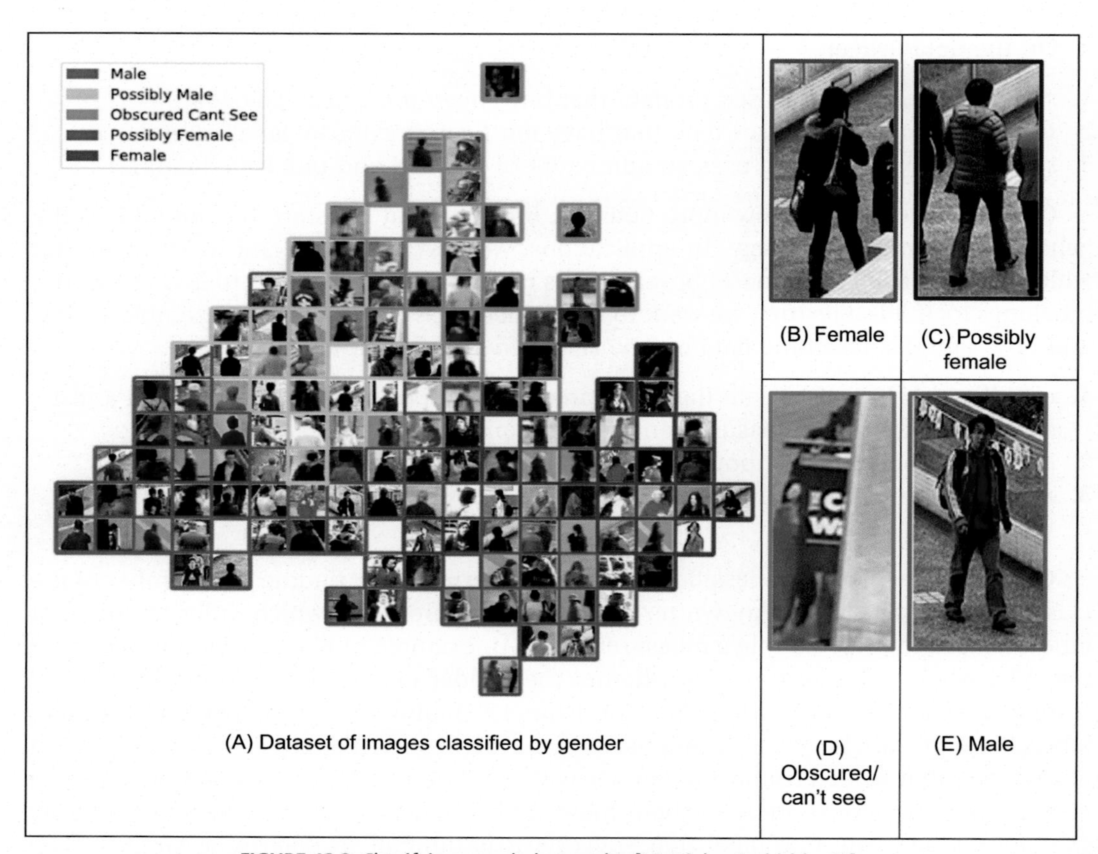

FIGURE 12.2 Classifying people by gender [Martinho-Corbishley19].

arrangements – or architectures – mimic processes we have previously observed to work well in image analysis, especially the convolution process.

As we are processing numbers, we assign a class by analysing distance. In Fig. 12.2, this can be the distance between the different images or even a class distance such as male versus female, or any other partition of the data. We shall therefore start by considering distance and classification, and later move to the newer approaches in deep learning.

12.3 Distance and classification

12.3.1 Distance measures

There is a selection of formulae to measure distance. This is reflected by the aphorism 'how long is a piece of string' which in colloquial English is used either to reflect uncertainty (or even just for sarcasm if the answer to a question cannot be known, just answer 'how long...'). It is an appropriate phrase here, since the measure of distance depends on what we want to achieve, and how we want to achieve it: there are many ways to measure the length of a piece of string.

We shall describe measures that often are used in image processing and computer vision. We have already used some of the measures in earlier techniques, as distance is a fundamental concept in applied science. In maths, the measure of distance extends to metric spaces and we shall not go there. We shall describe symmetric measures of distance (the distance between points a and b does not depend on which is the starting point: $dist(a,b) = dist(b,a)$) for individual points, sets of points, histograms of data and groups of points.

12.3.1.1 Manhattan and Euclidean L_n norms

Perhaps the most common measure of length is the distance between the endpoints, here equivalent to measuring the distance between two points using a ruler (perhaps the most common distance measure because Pythagoras' rule has a splendid graphical interpretation that is often demonstrated at junior school). For two points, this is illustrated in Fig. 12.3. In a two-dimensional plane, for a point $\mathbf{p1} = (\mathbf{p1}_x, \mathbf{p1}_y)$ and another point $\mathbf{p2} = (\mathbf{p2}_x, \mathbf{p2}_y)$, then

$$d_{\mathrm{E}}(\mathbf{p1},\mathbf{p2}) = \sqrt{(\mathbf{p1}_x - \mathbf{p2}_x)^2 + (\mathbf{p1}_y - \mathbf{p2}_y)^2} \tag{12.1}$$

This is the *Euclidean distance*, and for vector points the difference d between the N elements of $\mathbf{p1}$ and the elements of $\mathbf{p2}$ is

$$d_{\mathrm{E}}(\mathbf{p1},\mathbf{p2}) = \sqrt{\sum_{i=1}^{N} (\mathbf{p1}_i - \mathbf{p2}_i)^2} \tag{12.2}$$

which is also called the L_2 *norm* (or L_2 *distance*). The measure is invariant to rotation and translation. The distance that is measured rather depends on the nature of the property being measured, so there are alternative distance metrics. These include the L_1 *norm* which is the sum of the modulus of the differences between the measurements

$$d_{\mathrm{M}}(\mathbf{p1},\mathbf{p2}) = \|\mathbf{p1} - \mathbf{p2}\| = \sum_{i=1}^{N} |\mathbf{p1}_i - \mathbf{p2}_i| \tag{12.3}$$

It is invariant to translation only. This is also called the *Manhattan* distance or *taxicab* measure, by virtue of the analogy to distance in an urban neighbourhood. There, the distance travelled is along the streets since you cannot go through buildings. In a rectilinear urban system (i.e. an arrangement of perpendicular streets), then it does not matter which path you take (except in New York where you, or perhaps your taxi, can take Broadway which cuts across on a diagonal the North–South and East–West street system, and as such is like the Euclidean distance). So for the points $\mathbf{p1}$ and $\mathbf{p2}$ in a two-dimensional plane, the Manhattan distance is the distance along the x axis, added to the distance along the y axis, as illustrated in Fig. 12.3. (It is also called the L_1 *distance* or L_1 *norm*.)

$$d_{\mathrm{M}}(\mathbf{p1},\mathbf{p2}) = \|\mathbf{p1} - \mathbf{p2}\|_1 = |\mathbf{p1}_x - \mathbf{p2}_x| + |\mathbf{p1}_y - \mathbf{p2}_y| \tag{12.4}$$

These distance measures are illustrated for two points in a two-dimensional plane in Fig. 12.3. This is rather difficult to visualise for multidimensional data, so the

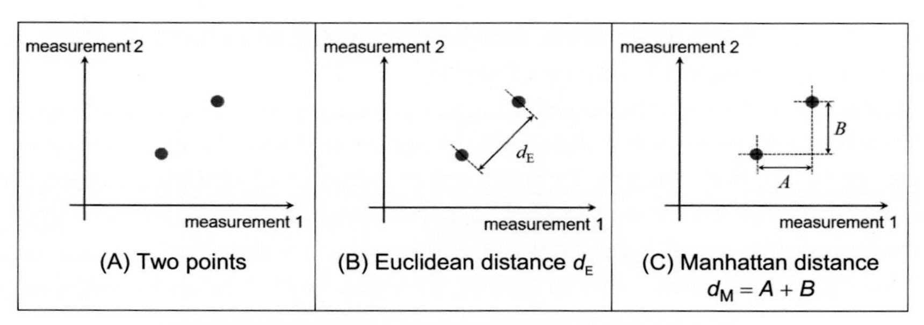

FIGURE 12.3 Distance measures in a two-dimensional plane.

multidimensional case is illustrated in Code 12.1 where the Euclidean distance is measured in a four-dimensional space.

12.3.1.2 Mahalanobis, Bhattacharrya and Matusita

For groups of points, we need to be able to handle sets of measurements. These can be derived, say, by applying the description process to a different image of the class of object. We then have multiple vectors of measurements, which we shall here store as a matrix, in Code 12.2. In this, there are two sets of measured feature vectors, `m1` and `m2`. Here two of the measures for `m2` appear different from those for `m1`, so these sets of measurements could be those taken from images of different textures (different classes of texture), or images of different people. These both have five sets of four different measurements. The Euclidean distance can then be the average distance over the sets of measurements. So we work out the Euclidean distance for each row and then average over these five values.

Naturally, the Euclidean distance between one set of points and itself is zero. The distance between set 1 and set 2 should be the same as the distance between set 2 and

```
function distance=dvE(vec1,vec2) %evaluate Euclidean distance
[rows,cols]=size(vec1);
distance=0;
for i=1:cols %for all vector elements
    distance=distance+(vec1(i)-vec2(i))*(vec1(i)-vec2(i));
end
distance=sqrt(distance);

pv1=[52,8.75,1.5,0.4];
pv2=[81,22.14,1.0,0.37];

>> dvE(pv1,pv2)
ans =
   31.9459
```

CODE 12.1 Illustrating the multidimensional Euclidean distance.

```
m1=[52  ,  8.75, 1.5 , 0.4 ;...
    51.9,  8.8 , 1.5 , 0.4 ;...
    52.2,  8.75, 1.49, 0.41;...
    52  ,  8.76, 1.51, 0.32;...
    51.5,  8.82, 1.46, 0.4 ];
```

```
m2=[81  , 22.14, 1.0 , 0.37;...
    80.5, 22.28, 1.1 , 0.39;...
    81.5, 22.16, 1.05, 0.41;...
    80.9, 22.18, 1.11, 0.32;...
    81  , 22.12, 1.16, 0.4 ];
```

```
function distance=averaged_dvE(mat1,mat2) %evaluate Euclidean distance
[rows,cols]=size(mat1);
distance=0;
for i=1:rows %for all vector elements
    distance=distance+dvE(mat1(i,:),mat2(i,:));
end
distance=distance/rows;
```

CODE 12.2 Illustrating the Euclidean distance for groups of points.

set 1. This is summarised as a *confusion matrix*, which shows the difference between the different sets of measurements. This is shown in Code 12.3, and the confusion matrix has zeroes on the leading diagonal and is symmetric, as expected.

Another way to estimate the distance is by using a matrix formulation. A more esoteric formulation is to use matrix norms. The advantages here are that there can be fast algorithms available for matrix computation. Another way to measure the distance would be to measure the distance between the means (the centres) of the clusters. As with the matrix formulations, that is a rather incomplete measure since it does not include the cluster spread. To obtain a distance measure between clusters, where the measure not only reflects the cluster spacing but also the cluster spread, we can use the *Mahalanobis distance* measure. This is illustrated in Fig. 12.4, where we have two sets of measures of vectors **P1** and **P2** (points denoted by + and ×, respectively). There are two different cases of the groups of data points: one which is tightly clustered (low variance), indicated by the solid line; and one which is spread out (high variance), indicated by the dotted line. If the variance in the second case was sufficiently high, the cluster for **P1** would intersect with the cluster for **P2** and so there would appear to be little difference between them (implying that the classes are the same). The Euclidean distance between the means will remain the same whatever the cluster spread, and so is not affected by this; conversely, the Euclidean distance only measures where the centre of mass is, and not the spread. The Mahalanobis distance includes the variance and so is a more

```
>> confusion=[averaged_dvE(m1,m1),averaged_dvE(m1,m2);...
              averaged_dvE(m2,m1),averaged_dvE(m2,m2)]

confusion =
          0   32.0039
    32.0039         0
```

CODE 12.3 Construction of a confusion matrix for two classes.

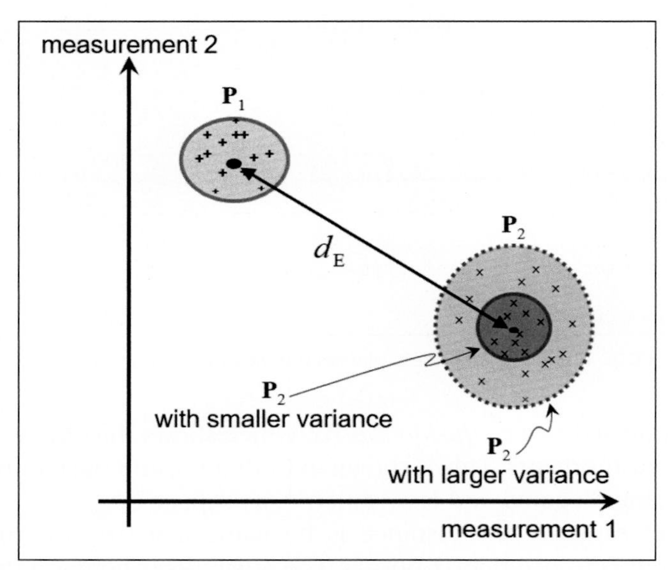

FIGURE 12.4 Illustrating the Mahalanobis distance measure.

perceptive measure of distance. The Mahalanobis distance between **P**1 and **P**2 would in this case change with the variance of **P**2.

For sets of vector points **P**1 where feature vectors are stored as rows of N elements $\mathbf{p}1_i = (\mathbf{p}1_{i,1}, \mathbf{p}1_{i,2}, \mathbf{p}1_{i,3}, \ldots \mathbf{p}1_{i,N})$, which have mean values $\boldsymbol{\mu}1_i = (\mu 1_{i,1}, \mu 1_{i,2}, \mu 1_{i,3}, \ldots \mu 1_{i,N})$ and covariance matrix $\sum$, the Mahalanobis distance is defined as

$$d_{MAH}(\mathbf{P}1, \mathbf{P}2) = \sqrt{(\mathbf{P}1 - \boldsymbol{\mu}1)\sum^{-1}(\mathbf{P}2 - \boldsymbol{\mu}2)^{\mathrm{T}}} \tag{12.5}$$

where the covariance matrix is formed of elements which express the variance as

$$\sum_{ij} = E[(\mathbf{P}_i - \boldsymbol{\mu}_i)^{\mathrm{T}}(\mathbf{P}_j - \boldsymbol{\mu}_j)] \tag{12.6}$$

where E denotes the expected value, in this case the mean value. Since our main consideration is the distance between two sets of feature vectors, we shall formulate this measure for feature vectors which are stored as rows (each sample is a row vector, each column contains the value of a particular measurement)

$$d_{MAH}(\mathbf{P}1, \mathbf{P}2) = \sqrt{(\mathbf{P}1 - \mathbf{P}2)\mathbf{C}^{-1}(\mathbf{P}1 - \mathbf{P}2)^{\mathrm{T}}} \tag{12.7}$$

where the covariance matrix **C** is

$$\mathbf{C} = \frac{\mathbf{C}1 + \mathbf{C}2}{2} \tag{12.8}$$

where the individual covariance matrices are calculated as

$$\mathbf{C}1 = \frac{1}{N}(\mathbf{P}1 - \boldsymbol{\mu}1)^{\mathrm{T}}(\mathbf{P}1 - \boldsymbol{\mu}1) \tag{12.9}$$

In this way, the distance is scaled by the variance. So the distance measure reflects the distributions of the data, which are ignored in the Euclidean distance formulation. The formulation does rather depend on the structure used for the data. The formulation here is consistent with the feature vectors delivered by texture and face extraction approaches (it can also be the same for feature vectors delivered by other applications, that is how general it is).

The calculation of the covariance matrix is illustrated for two classes (two sets of feature vectors) in Code 12.4. The mean for each column is subtracted from each column element in routine. The routine `covariance` implements Eq. (12.9). The final row shows the calculated covariance matrix for the two sets of measurements (`m1` and `m2`) given earlier. The diagonal elements reflect the variance in each measure; the off-diagonal measurements reflect the correlation between the different measurements. The properties of this matrix are that it is symmetric and positive definite. When assessing implementation, to test for symmetry when developing code check by subtracting the transpose (and the result should be zero). Positive definiteness can be assessed by an Eigenvector calculation, but it is simpler to submit an example to a mathematical package and check that Cholesky decomposition can be performed on it (if it cannot, then the matrix is not positive definite).

Determining the Mahalanobis distance is illustrated in Code 12.5 for the two classes, `m1` and `m2`. This is slightly different from Eq. (12.7). This is because Eq. (12.7) is the conventional expression. Here we are using vectors of measurements and we have

Remove mean:

```
function a_colmean=subtract_mean(matrix)
[rows,cols]=size(matrix);
a_colmean(1:cols,1:rows)=0;
for j=1:rows
    for i=1:cols
        a_colmean(j,i)=matrix(j,i)-mean(matrix(:,i));
    end
end
```

Evaluate covariance:

```
function cov=covariance(matrix)
[rows,cols]=size(matrix);
cov=1/rows*transpose(subtract_mean(matrix))*subtract_mean(matrix);
```

Evaluate mean covariance:

```
>> (covariance(m1)+covariance(m2))/2

ans =
    0.0776   -0.0090   -0.0013    0.0012
   -0.0090    0.0020   -0.0001    0.0001
   -0.0013   -0.0001    0.0016   -0.0002
    0.0012    0.0001   -0.0002    0.0011
```

CODE 12.4 Constructing the covariance matrix.

Operator:

```
function dist=d_Maha(mat1,mat2)
[rows,cols]=size(mat1);
cov=(covariance(mat1)+covariance(mat2))/2;
dist=1/rows*sqrt(trace((mat1-mat2)*inv(cov)*transpose(mat1-mat2)));
```

Result:

```
>> d_Maha(m1,m2)

ans =
  254.7758
```

CODE 12.5 The Mahalanobis distance between two classes.

multiple samples of these measurements. As such, the distance measure we are interested in is the sum of the values on the leading diagonal (the `trace` of the matrix). The implementation is the same in all other respects.

The confusion matrix derived by the Mahalanobis distance is little different from that derived by Euclidean distance, all that will change is that the values on the off-diagonal will be larger. To assess its effect, we need multiple samples of multiple classes and we need to evaluate the confusion matrix over these. This is shown in Code 12.6. Here we have five classes: `m1`; `m2`; `m3`; `m4` and `m5`. The confusion matrices are now 5×5, showing the confusion between each class and the other four. The leading diagonal is still zero, since each class is the same as itself. The off-diagonal elements show the difference between

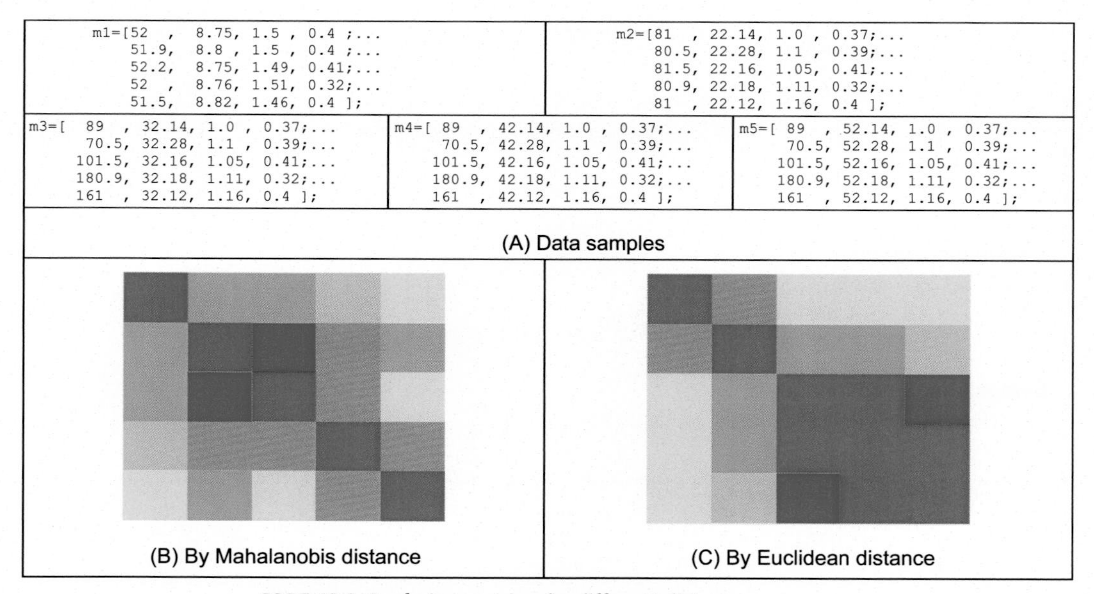

CODE 12.6 Confusion matrices by different distance measures.

the different classes. As the distance becomes larger, the cell becomes brighter. The confusion matrix by the Euclidean distance has more difficulty distinguishing between classes 3, 4 and 5 than that for the Mahalanobis distance, since the lower right-hand corner is largely dark, whereas in the Mahalanobis distance only the leading diagonal is dark. This is because the Mahalanobis distance uses the structure of the data (their variance) to determine distance.

There are many other distance measures. The *Bhattacharyya distance*

$$d_B(\mathbf{p1}, \mathbf{p2}) = -\ln \sum_{i=1}^{N} \sqrt{\mathbf{p1}_i \times \mathbf{p2}_i} \tag{12.10}$$

gives smaller precedence to larger distances by using the logarithm to compress them, but this appears to be used less, like other metrics such as the *Matusita difference*. There is a measure which emphasises relative direction rather than distance. This is the *cosine similarity* measure

$$d_C(\mathbf{p1}, \mathbf{p2}) = \cos(\theta) = \frac{\mathbf{p1} \cdot \mathbf{p2}}{|\mathbf{p1}||\mathbf{p2}|} \tag{12.11}$$

where '•' represents the scalar product of the two vectors $\mathbf{p1}$ and $\mathbf{p2}$ (the dot or inner product) and $||$ denotes the length of each vector. This measure is invariant to joint rotation of the two points (around the origin), by its basis. The angle θ is that between the two vectors to the points, as illustrated in Fig. 12.5. Note that in this case, similarity is when $\theta \rightarrow 0$ (so $d_C \rightarrow 1$) which is different for the other cases wherein similarity is reflected by a minimum of the distance measure.

12.3.1.3 Histogram intersection, Chi² (χ^2) and the Earth Mover's distance

How do we compare a pair of histograms? These could be sets of texture measures, or colour measures. One can rearrange the previous distance measures for histograms, but there are some more specific measures. The first of these is *histogram intersection* which is a measure that returns zero when the histograms differ completely, and unity when they are the same. The two histograms are vectors $\mathbf{h1}$ and $\mathbf{h2}$ with N elements; the measure uses normalised versions

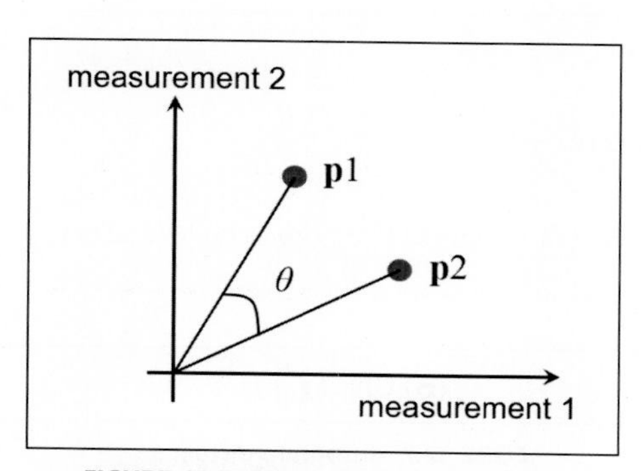

FIGURE 12.5 Cosine similarity measure.

$$\mathbf{h1}'_i = \frac{\mathbf{h1}_i}{\sum_{j=1}^{N} \mathbf{h1}_j} \tag{12.12}$$

Then the histogram intersection is

$$d_{\text{HI}}(\mathbf{h1}, \mathbf{h2}) = \sum_{j=1}^{N} \min\left(\mathbf{h1}'_j, \mathbf{h2}'_j\right) \tag{12.13}$$

and the measure is the same as the Manhattan distance of the normalised vectors. There is also the *chi*^{2} distance, mathematically denoted as χ^2, which compares histograms (or feature vectors) **h**1 and **h**2 given by

$$d_{\chi^2}(\mathbf{h1}, \mathbf{h2}) = \sum_{j=1}^{N} \frac{(\mathbf{h1}_j - \mathbf{h2}_j)^2}{(\mathbf{h1}_j + \mathbf{h2}_j)} \tag{12.14}$$

In the chi^2 distance, the numerator has Euclidean form and there is a denominator to ensure that small differences between small numbers are as significant as large differences between large numbers.

The operation of the histogram distance measures in Code 12.7 is shown in Fig. 12.6. Here, **h**3 is close in distribution to **h**1 (though the elements of **h**3 are about twice the value of those in **h**1) and different from **h**2. This is shown in a large value of histogram

```
function dist=histogram_intersection(vec1,vec2)
sum1=0;
sum2=0;
for k=1:cols
    sum1=sum1+vec1(k);
    sum2=sum2+vec2(k);
end
dist=0;
for k=1:cols
    dist=dist+min(vec1(k)/sum1, vec2(k)/sum2);
end
```

(A) Histogram intersection

```
function dist=chi2(vec1,vec2);
dist=0;
for k=1:cols
    if vec1(k)==0&&vec2(k)==0
        dist=dist+0;
    else
        dist=dist+((vec1(k)-vec2(k))^2/(vec1(k)+vec2(k)));
    end
end
```

(B) Chi^2 (χ^2)

CODE 12.7 Histogram distances.

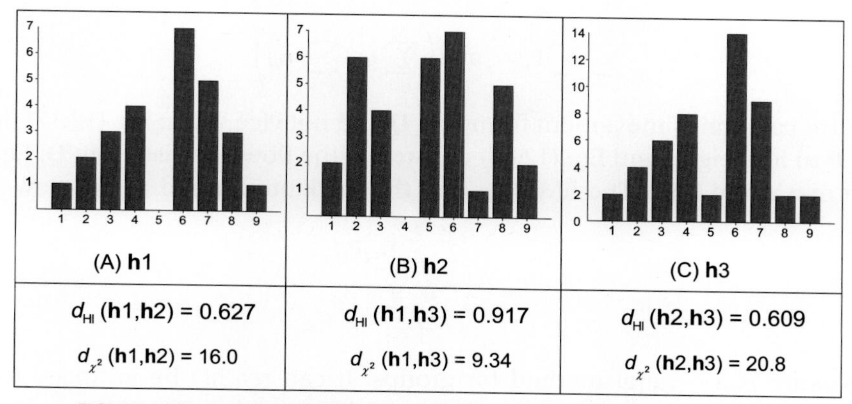

FIGURE 12.6 Histograms and their histogram intersections and χ^2 distances.

intersection for similar histograms and a smaller value of the χ^2 distance. Conversely if the histograms differ, the histogram intersection is smaller and the χ^2 distance is larger.

So we have looked at points, sets of points and histograms. Let us move on to groups. The *Earth Mover's Distance (EMD)* [Rubner00] was named at the start of the 21st century though it is actually a very old measure of dissimilarity dating back to the 18th century, since it is a solution to the transportation problem (how to match suppliers with consumers efficaciously...opportunity for a Brexit joke here—opportunity not taken, sic). Essentially, the distance is between distributions of elements and represents the cost of turning one group into another, by analogy it is the minimal cost of turning one pile of earth into another. As such we have one group **P** with M elements $\mathbf{P} = \{(\mathbf{p}_1, w_{\mathbf{p}1}), (\mathbf{p}_2, w_{\mathbf{p}2}), \ldots, (\mathbf{p}_M, w_{\mathbf{p}M})\}$ and another group **Q** has N elements $\mathbf{Q} = \{(\mathbf{q}_1, w_{\mathbf{q}1}), (\mathbf{q}_2, w_{\mathbf{q}2}), \ldots, (\mathbf{q}_M, w_{\mathbf{q}N})\}$. Each group has elements, say, $(\mathbf{p}_i, w_{\mathbf{p}i})$ where $\mathbf{p}_i$ is the data (say the mean of a cluster of feature vectors) and $w_{\mathbf{p}i}$ is the weight associated with that data (say the number of points in a group). **D** represents the distance between elements and $\mathbf{D}_{i,j}$ is the distance between $\mathbf{p}_i$ and $\mathbf{q}_j$. We seek to determine a flow **F** whose elements $\mathbf{F}_{i,j}$ describe the flow between the points $\mathbf{p}_i$ and $\mathbf{q}_j$ that minimises the overall cost (work). Work done is the product of distance and mass, so here we have

$$work(\mathbf{p}, \mathbf{q}, \mathbf{F}) = \sum_{i=1}^{M} \sum_{j=1}^{N} \mathbf{D}_{i,j}\mathbf{F}_{i,j} \tag{12.15}$$

and we seek a flow **F** to minimise this, subject to the constraints:

$$\mathbf{F}_{i,j} \geq 0 \quad 1 \leq i \leq M, 1 \leq j \leq N \tag{12.16}$$

$$\sum_{j=1}^{N} \mathbf{F}_{i,j} \leq w_{\mathbf{p}i} \quad 1 \leq i \leq M \tag{12.17}$$

$$\sum_{i=1}^{M} \mathbf{F}_{i,j} \leq w_{\mathbf{q}_j} \quad 1 \leq j \leq N \tag{12.18}$$

$$\sum_{i=1}^{M}\sum_{j=1}^{N}\mathbf{F}_{i,j} = \min\left(\sum_{i=1}^{M} w_{\mathbf{p}i}\sum_{j=1}^{N} w_{\mathbf{q}_j}\right) \tag{12.19}$$

Eq. (12.16) constrains movement from **P** to **Q** and not vice versa; Eq. (12.17) limits the flow from **P** to its weight, and Eq. (12.18) constrains the flow likewise from **Q**; Eq. (12.19) enforces a maximum flow. The EMD d_{EMD} is the work normalised by the flow

$$d_{\text{EMD}} = \frac{\sum_{i=1}^{M}\sum_{j=1}^{N}\mathbf{D}_{i,j}\mathbf{F}_{i,j}}{\sum_{i=1}^{M}\sum_{j=1}^{N}\mathbf{F}_{i,j}} \tag{12.20}$$

The measure is a general method for groups: it can readily be arranged to handle histograms and can be used to describe groups of different size. The measure is complex to implement as it needs minimisation and there are many techniques available: originally the Simplex method was used. There are public domain implementations available. As it is a minimisation problem it is (reputed to be) slow, so there exist ways to speed it up [Ling07]; it was noted in the original paper that 'it is important that the EMD can be computed efficiently'. One paper gives an excellent survey on distance measures [Cha02] as does the original EMD description [Rubner00].

We shall not delve further into distance measures: there is a rich selection and each has different properties. As ever, in engineering there is no panacea: we will not find a generic distance measure. One cannot develop an explicit formula that can be used to partition arbitrarily selected data. Essentially, the measure of distance depends on the technique used to make a measurement and the nature of the data itself. As ever, try a selection and use the one best suited to a particular application. We shall now move on to classification, since that is where we shall employ distance as a way to determine difference between classes.

12.3.2 The *k*-nearest neighbour for classification

We then need to use the distance measure to determine the class to be associated with the data points. If we have M measurements of N known classes and we have O samples of each, we have an M-dimensional *feature space* that contains the $N \times O$ points. If we select the point, in the feature space, which is closest to the current sample, then we have selected the sample's *nearest neighbour*. Fig. 12.7 shows a two-dimensional feature space produced by the two measures made on each sample, measure 1 and measure 2. Each sample gives different values for these measures, and the samples of different classes give rise to clusters in the feature space where each cluster is associated with a single class. In Fig. 12.7, we have seven samples of the two classes (which could describe faces or textures): Class A and Class B are depicted by $+$ and $\times$, respectively. We want to classify a test sample, depicted by *, as belonging either to Class A or to Class B (i.e. we assume that the training data contain representatives of all possible classes). Its nearest

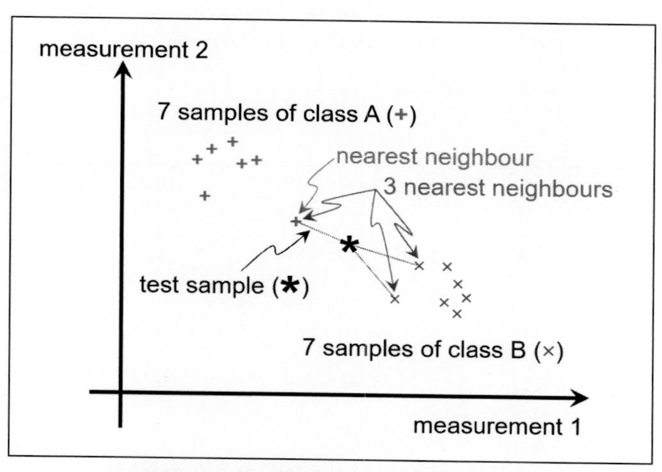

FIGURE 12.7 Feature space and classification.

neighbour, the sample with least distance, is one of the samples of Class A so we could then say that our test appears to be another sample of Class A (i.e. the class label associated with it is Class A). Clearly, the clusters will be far apart for measures that have good discriminatory ability, whereas the clusters will be overlapped for measures that have poor discriminatory ability. That is how we can choose measures for particular tasks. Before that, let us look at how best to associate a class label with our test sample.

Classifying a test sample as the training sample it is closest to in feature space is actually a specific case of a general classification rule known as the *k-nearest neighbour rule*. In this rule, the class selected is the mode class of the sample's nearest k neighbours. By the k-nearest neighbour rule, for $k=3$, we select the nearest three neighbours (those three with the least distance) and their mode class, the maximally represented class, is attributed to the sample. In Fig. 12.7, the 3-nearest neighbour is actually Class B since the three nearest samples contain one from Class A (its nearest neighbour) and two from Class B. Since there are two elements of Class B, then the sample is attributed to this class by the 3-nearest neighbour rule. As such, selection from more than one point introduces a form of feature space smoothing and allows the classification decision not to be affected by noisy *outlier* points. Clearly, this smoothing has greater effect for larger values of k. It is a relatively slow process since every sample has to be considered when classifying data. (Further details concerning of the k-nearest neighbour rule can be found in [Michie94].)

An implementation of the k-nearest neighbour rule is given in Code 12.8. The arguments are `test` (the vector of measurements of the test sample), `data` (the matrix of vectors of measurements of all samples), `value_k` (the value of k) and `no`. The parameter `no` dictates the structure of the presented data and is the number of classes within that data. The training data are presumed to have been arranged so that samples of each class

```
function test_class=knn(test, data, value_k, no)
[rows,cols]=size(data);
%use odd values of k and given data structure only
%first work out the distances from test to other classes
for i=1:rows
    dists(i)=dvE(test,data(i,:));
end
minim(1:value_k)=0; %now which are the k best matches
for s=1:value_k
    posmin=coord(min(dists),dists); %find the best
    minim(s)=posmin;  %and store its position
    dists(posmin)=max(dists)+1; %clear the best
end
fsp=rows/no; %size of classes in data
class(1:no)=0;
for i=1:value_k %look at all k minima
    for j=1:no %and all classes
        %check if within a class partition
        if ((minim(i)>=(j-1)*fsp+1)&&(minim(i)<(j*fsp+1)))
            class(j)=class(j)+1; %if so, increment class
        end
    end
end
[rowsc,colsc]=size(class);
no_unique_class=0; %check class label is unique
for i=1:colsc %look at all classes
    for j=i+1:colsc %upper half of matrix
        if (class(i)>0)&&(class(i)==class(j)) %check similarity
            no_unique_class=1; %if so, set flag
        end
    end
end
if no_unique_class %if two class labels same
    value_k= value_k-2;
    test_class=knn(test,data,value_k,no) %call knn with k=k-2
else
    test_class=coord(max(class),class); %return maximum class
end
```

CODE 12.8 Implementing the *k*-nearest neighbour rule.

are all stored together (as in the data in Code 12.9). Here, for two classes in the training data, `no` $= 2$, where each occupies one half. If `no` $= 3$, then there are three classes, each occupying one-third of the complete data set and the first third contains the first class, the second third contains samples of another class, whilst the remaining third contains samples of the final class. In application, first the distances between the current sample, `test`, and all other samples are evaluated by using Euclidean distance `dvE`. Then the *k*-nearest neighbours are selected to form a vector of distances `min`, these are the *k* neighbours which are closest (in the feature space) to the sample `test`. The number of feature space splits `fsp` is the spacing between the classes in the `data`. The class which occurs the most number of times in the set of `size` nearest neighbours is then returned as the *k*-nearest neighbour, by incrementing the class number to which each of the *k*

population1=[1.0, 2.0, 3.0;... 1.1, 2.0, 3.1;... 1.0, 2.1, 3.0;... 4.0, 6.0, 8.0;... 3.9, 6.1, 8.1;... 4.1, 5.9, 8.1;... 8.8, 6.1, 2.9;... 7.8, 5.0, 3.3;... 8.8, 6.4, 3.1]; (A) 3 classes, 3 samples, 3 features	population2=[2.0, 4.0, 6.0, 8.0;... 2.1, 3.9, 6.2, 7.8;... 2.3, 3.6, 5.8, 8.3;... 2.5, 4.5, 6.5, 8.5;... 3.4, 4.4, 6.6, 8.6;... 2.3, 4.6, 6.4, 8.5]; (E) 2 classes, 3 samples, 4 features
test_point1=[4,6,8]; (B) First test sample	test_point2=[2.5,3.8,6.4,8.5]; (F) Second test sample
>> a=knn(test_point1,population1,1,3) a = 2 (C) 1-nearest neighbour	>> a=knn(test_point2,population2,1,2) a = 1 (G) 1-nearest neighbour
>> a=knn(test_point1,population1,3,3) a = 2 (D) 3-nearest neighbour	>> a=knn(test_point2,population2,3,2) a = 2 (H) 3-nearest neighbour

CODE 12.9 Applying the *k*-nearest neighbour rule to synthetic data.

neighbours is associated. If no such decision is possible, i.e. there is no maximally represented class, the technique can be arranged recursively to return the class of the nearest neighbour for a smaller value of *k*. An alternative way is that the default class for *k*-NN is the 1-NN when all *k* classes are nearest neighbours.

The result of testing the *k*-nearest neighbour routine is illustrated on synthetic data in Code 12.9. Here there are two different data sets. The first, Code 12.9A, has three classes of which there are three samples (each sample is a row of data, so this totals nine rows) and each sample is made up of three measurements (the three columns). As this is synthetic data, it can be seen that each class is quite distinct: the first class is for measurements around [1,2,3]; the second class is around [4,6,8] and the third is around [8,6,3]. A small amount of noise has been added to the measurements. We then want to see the class associated with a test sample with measurements [4,6,8], Code 12.9B. Naturally, the 1-nearest nearest neighbour, Code 12.9C , associates it with the class with the closest measurements which is class 2 as the test sample's nearest neighbour is the fourth row of data. (The result is either class 1, class 2 or class 3.) The 3-nearest neighbour, Code 12.9D, is again class 2 as the nearest three neighbours are the fourth, fifth and sixth rows and each of these is from class 2.

The second data set, Code 12.9C, is two classes with three samples each made up of four measures. The test sample, Code 12.9F, is actually associated with class 1 by the 1-nearest neighbour, Code 12.9G, but with class 2 for the 3-nearest neighbour, Code 12.9H. This is because the test sample is actually closest to the sample in the third row. After the third row, the next two closest samples are in the fourth and sixth rows. As the nearest neighbour is in a different class (class 1) to that of the next two nearest neighbours (class

2), a different result has occurred when there is more smoothing in the feature space (when the value of k is increased).

When analysing sets of data, one can classify using *leave-one-out cross-validation* [Lachenbruch68]. Leave-one-out refers to the procedure where one of the samples is selected as the test sample, the others form the training data (this is the leave-one-out rule). Cross-validation is where the test is repeated for all samples: each sample becomes the test data once.

12.4 Neural networks and Support Vector Machines

As we have seen, classification is the process by which we assign class labels to sets of measurements. Clearly, classification depends on distance and structure. Essentially, this is the heart of pattern recognition: can we learn the structure of the data? Intuitively, there must be many approaches. These include statistical and structural approaches: an early review can be found in [Cherkassky98]. Some texts, such as [Forsyth02], [Szeliski11] and [Prince12], specifically include learning in computer vision and they offer great depth. And that is the position before the deep learning revolution.

One classic approach is to use a neural network which is a common alternative to using a classification rule. Essentially, modern approaches centre around using *multi-layer perceptrons (MLPs)* with *Artificial Neural Networks (ANNs)* in which the computing elements aim to mimic properties of neurons in the human brain. The input information is transformed to a classification decision via a *hidden layer* (described as hidden as its outputs are not the classification outputs). The universal approximation theorem states you need only one hidden layer to approximate an arbitrary continuous function but need an exponential number of neurons. As shown in Fig. 12.8, the function of the

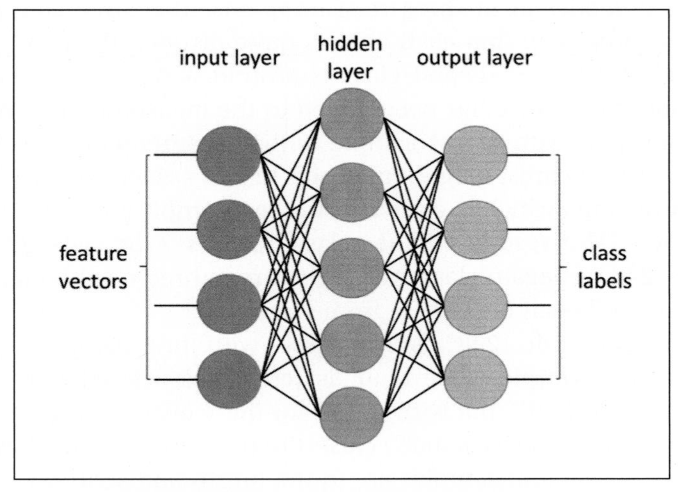

FIGURE 12.8 Basis of an artificial neural network.

artificial neural network is to learn the class labels from feature vectors using computational units. In basic form the neurons form a function z of the sum of the inputs $\mathbf{x}$ multiplied by their respective weights $\mathbf{w}$

$$z = f(\mathbf{w}_1 \times \mathbf{x}_1 + \mathbf{w}_2 \times \mathbf{x}_2 + \ldots + \mathbf{w}_N \times \mathbf{x}_N) \tag{12.21}$$

By changing the values of the weights, this can effect addition or subtraction or an input can be switched off, so as not to affect the output, by setting its weight to zero. The function can be chosen according to its required properties and a step like function is the *sigmoid* (which approximates thresholding)

$$f(t) = \frac{1}{1 + e^{-t}} \tag{12.22}$$

or there is the rather prosaically named *rectified linear unit* (*relu*, which is zero for $t < 0$) as

$$f(t) = \max(0, t) \tag{12.23}$$

The networks constructed from these neurons require training, typically by *error back-propagation*, aimed to minimise a loss function thereby minimising classification error on the training data. At this point, the network should have learnt how to recognise the test data (they aim to learn its structure): the output of a neural network can be arranged to be class labels. Neural networks are within a research field that has shown immense growth in the past two decades, further details may be found in [Michie94, Bishop96] (often a student favourite) and more targeted at vision in [Zhou92]. These are not deep neural networks, as depth concerns many more layers. Science gets nowhere by operating in a vacuum and these neural networks moved forwards, as the interest in machine learning continued to increase.

The learning can be achieved using *Stochastic Gradient Descent (SGD)* which aims to seek a minimum of a decision surface—one can formulate the difference between the current performance and the expected performance aiming to minimise the difference between the two. One of the distance measures described previously could form the loss function, although for tasks like classification one would use a loss such as cross-entropy to better control the optimisation. The minimisation can be achieved by changing operation in the way that maximised the rate at which the optimum is reached. This is *gradient descent*. Since a function which seeks to find a global minimum is likely to be sensitive to local minima (like rolling an Easter egg down a hill — a well-known English habit, not — only to get stuck in a walker's footprint). To avoid being stuck on the way down, one can shake things to escape a local minimum, and this is a stochastic function; in machine learning the term stochastic describes choosing one sample in each batch at random. The *learning rate* – or *step size* – describes the speed of approach to the minimum: too large and one can overshoot, whereas too small implies very slow operation.

Support Vector Machines (SVMs) [Vapnik95] are one of the more popular approaches to data modelling and classification. These are not actually machines, but a set of equations designed to give an optimal classification result in a repeatable and controlled manner. Originally, *linear SVMs* aimed to define a *hyperplane* that could separate classes. The best hyperplane was that which maximised the margin between the two classes, with *support vectors* positioned on the edges between the feature clusters. The fixed distinction between the two sets of features was relaxed in *soft margin SVMs* that introduced slack variables to describe and accommodate outlier data in the decision process. Interest naturally moved to using a more variable decision surface (a hypersurface) rather than a hyperplane. The *kernel trick* mapped data into a higher dimensional space where linear separation could be used, and there are many kernel methods [Shawe-Taylor04]. Their advantages include excellent *generalisation capability* which concerns the ability to classify correctly samples which are not within feature space used for training. Fig. 12.9 illustrates two classes of data (with samples ■ and ▲) and the decision boundary learnt by a kernel-based SVM. Some of the data samples have been learnt to be *outliers* and are beyond the complex classification boundary, appearing to reside within the area of the other class. This is an optimal result by this technique.

Interest has focused on combining different classifiers, and there are promising approaches to accommodate this [Kittler98a, Kittler98b]. There are methods aimed to improve classification capabilities by pruning the data to remove those which do not contribute to the classification decision. Guided ways which investigate the potency of measures for analysis are known as feature (subset) selection. *Principal component analysis* can reduce dimensionality, orthogonalise and remove redundant data. There is also *linear discriminant analysis* (also called *canonical analysis*) to improve class separability, whilst concurrently reducing cluster size (it is formulated to concurrently minimise the within-class distance and to maximise the between-class distance). There are also algorithms aimed at choosing a reduced set of features for classification: feature selection for improved discriminatory ability; a comparison can be found in [Jain97]. Alternatively, the basis functionals can be chosen in such a way as to improve classification capability. So until the deep learning revolution, feature extraction and learning from data were separate. Deep learning joined them together…it's nettle time.

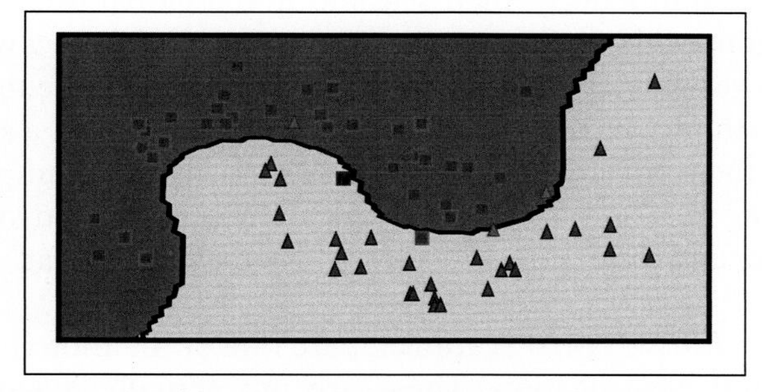

FIGURE 12.9 Classifying data by a kernel-based *support vector machine*.

12.5 Deep learning

12.5.1 Basis of deep learning

The origins of deep learning are some time ago now when it was shown that multilayer neural networks could achieve good results by gradient-based learning to minimise classification error (or loss) [LeCun98, LeCun15]. The training time was long, with many parameters and little data. Later the hardware advanced rapidly in terms of faster processing speeds (especially using graphics processing units (GPUs)) with cheaper and larger memory and so the networks could become larger. They were shown first to have excellent performance on an image classification problem and that is where the revolution started. Fig. 12.10 shows the basic architecture of a deep neural network. The input data are an image and the output is class labels. Feature extraction is performed within the network to achieve the classification decision. To do this, it needs more layers than the earlier ANN, thus it is a deep network. It is processing a rather small image too, and more pixels require more neurons so this network is much smaller than is usual, as we shall find.

So how do they work? Essentially, the neurons are computational units performing, say, the weighted addition of a number of inputs. If we arrange an architecture to detect horizontal, vertical and diagonal lines in a 2×2 image, we can use an architecture of the form shown in Fig. 12.11. The first layer is the input layer and the following layer evaluates the differencing functions. The points are added and subtracted in the orders that reflect the shapes to be detected, in the manner of edge detection, Section 4.2.1. This is followed by a form of thresholding to form the binary outputs using neurons, step up Brother Sigmoid, Eq. (12.22) (in a softmax operator no less). Given a database of images, we can train the network and learn the appropriate weights (as in Eq. (12.21), given here

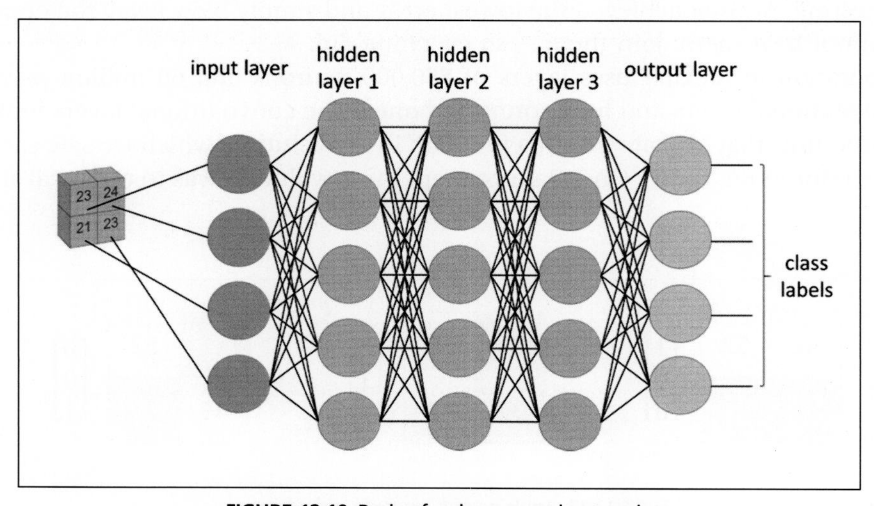

FIGURE 12.10 Basis of a deep neural network.

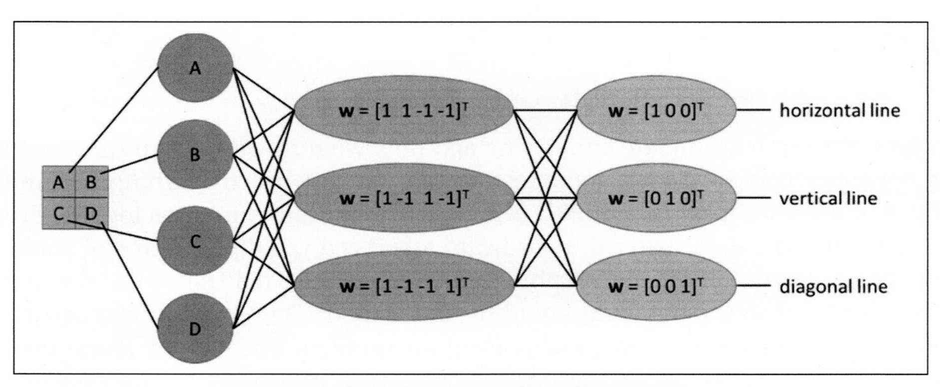

FIGURE 12.11 Trained example neural network.

as the target weights from top to bottom) to detect the given classes of shape in the database. Here we are combining feature detection and analysis with classification decisions.

Examples of the resulting outputs of this network are shown in Fig. 12.12 which shows the original images and to their right the class labels associated with each. Clearly it works, and it is also simple and fast. It is also of little use on its own (who needs to find a minus sign?) and could be arranged differently; it could naturally be part of a much larger network where the shapes detected could be segments of larger patterns.

Here we shall start at the beginning with *Alexnet* [Krizhevsky12] which largely started the deep learning revolution. It achieved markedly better performance than any other technique on a competition called the ImageNet Large-Scale Visual Recognition Challenge [Russakovsky15] that had labelled high-resolution images from around 1000 categories giving 1.2 million training images, 50,000 validation images and 150,000 images for testing. Alexnet achieved the lowest error and simply blew away the opposition. If you cannot beat them, join them – so everyone did.

Computation in Alexnet uses layers of 650,000 neurons and 60 million parameters with convolutional layers and fully connected ones. The convolutional layers implement neural structures that operate the area function in convolution, which we saw earlier as a group operator in Eq. (3.18). One main concept in convolution was to use local structure

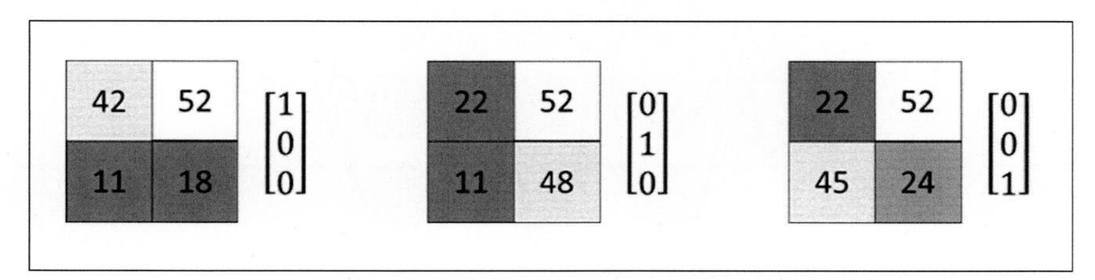

FIGURE 12.12 Applying the example neural network.

to ameliorate noise: that is the purpose here too. Some of the key concepts of the architectures are:

1. *locality*: local receptive fields are part of the first two layers of the human vision system and are thus attractive too in machine vision;
2. *convolutional*: local structures are described by the region in which they operate;
3. *stationarity*: small local patches are repeated across an image;
4. *multiscale* operators combine patches and these can be implemented by *downsampling* (reducing resolution) and *pooling* and
5. *fully connected* layers contain neurons which are all connected to all neurons in the previous layer.

The fully connected ANNs shown previously have many parameters to be learnt and are thus slow and can also respond to noise rather than accommodating it, which is called *overfitting*. Convolutional networks can learn structure and can accommodate noise, and so can be applied in many domains.

The architecture of Alexnet is shown in Fig. 12.13 where the main computational unit (the bit that does the 'heavy lifting') is the convolutional layers, conv1...conv5. These implement the convolution process using neurons and are depicted as blocks rather than draw masses of interconnected neurons. The convolution layers have a receptive field which we have hereto called the window size. These are arranged in series, to give depth. The dimensions of each layer, given underneath, show the numbers of neurons (number horizontally $\times$ number vertically $\times$ depth). The dimensions of the window sizes are also given from 11×11 in the first layer conv1 to 3×3 in later layers. Were the neurons in each layer to be fully connected as in Fig. 12.8, there would be parameters associated with all the links, and values would be needed to be learnt for all them. The freedom implies that values of many parameters need to be learnt. Instead, by

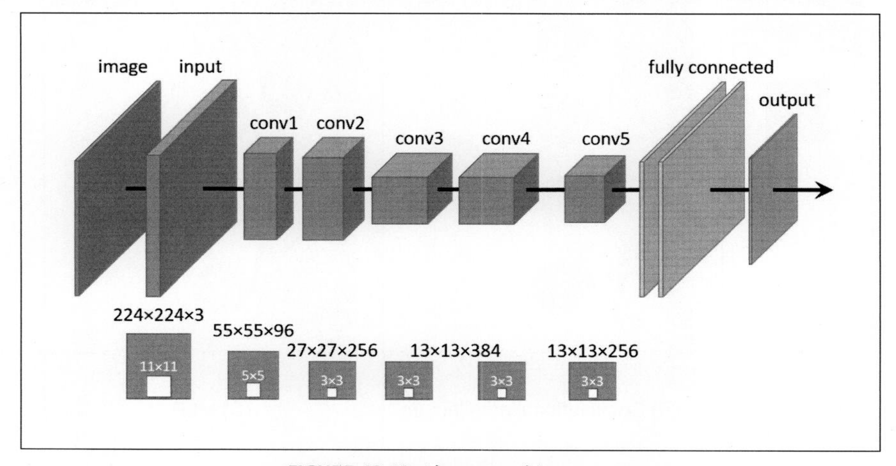

FIGURE 12.13 Alexnet architecture.

stationarity where regions are tiled and each shares the same weights in the convolution operation then the number of values to be learnt is fixed and is much smaller. This is especially suited to the low-level operators needed in image analysis. The architecture in Fig. 12.13 was originally implemented in two GPUs and is here shown for a single GPU, doubling the depth at each stage.

The difference between a convolutional layer and an MLP is shown in Fig. 12.14. Both are fed with an image, Fig. 12.14A, at the input layer, and apply a 2×2 template. The convolutional architecture considers local regions within an image, whereas the MLP looks at everything. (The architecture here is actually for a differencing operator to find vertical lines as in Fig. 12.11). There are many parameters to be learnt in the MLP, and comparatively many fewer in the convolutional network. The learning process is aimed to learn the weights for the connections, T_n. Note that the process is closer to correlation as there is no 'flipping' process, but also that the weights are learnt to achieve a desired outcome. The operation of the convolutional layer neurons at layer l is given by multiplying the weight **T** by the pixel **O** with the addition of the neuron's *bias*, *b*, as

$$(\mathbf{O} * \mathbf{T})_{i,j}^{l} = \sum_{ti=1}^{T_M} \sum_{tl=1}^{T_N} \mathbf{O}_{i+ti,j+tj}^{l-1} \mathbf{T}_{k,l}^{l} + b^{l} \tag{12.24}$$

The high-level reasoning in the neural network is achieved using the fully connected layers: these operate on the outputs of the convolutional layers to adjoin low-level structures to form high-level ones. Relu functions from Eq. (12.23) are applied after each convolutional and fully connected layer to set negative values to zero to admit the learning process. The pooling process downsamples an image, in the same manner as used in zero-crossing detection of the LoG operator, Section 4.2.2. Any reduction in size

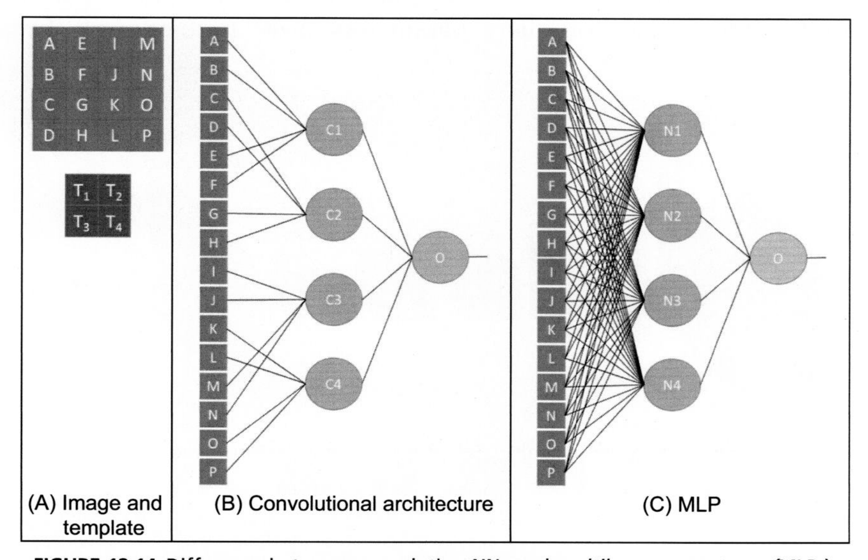

FIGURE 12.14 Difference between convolution NNs and *multilayer perceptrons* (MLPs).

of the computational footprint reduces the number of parameters required to be learnt, consistent with the use of smaller window sizes. *Max pooling* uses a maximum function to derive the output; *average pooling* derives the output from an average but has been found to offer diminished performance.

So this is all rather daunting as there are many computational units all requiring to be set, even with architectural choice aimed to reduce the computational load. The learning process was achieved by SGD and took 6 days. Once it is trained, it is fast and given that the performance was fantastic no one was concerned about a training time that allowed the excellent results to be achieved. Roll on Moore's law: if you develop something that is a bit slow now – wait a bit and it will be practicable later.

If the aim of recognition is to recognise squares in an image, then we can form an extended version of the network in Fig. 12.12, and collect together the features so as to signal the detection of a target object [de Freitas18]. A face is a more complex feature, and face recognition becomes ever present in modern society: one can forget passwords and key information but your face remains your face. Biometrics makes for a convenient lifestyle indeed. So given that we need to be able to recognise faces, and quickly, there is natural interest in using deep learning. Some of the features found in a data set of faces by a deep learning network are shown in Fig. 12.15. Fig. 12.15A shows some of the face images and the earliest features, Fig. 12.15B at the lowest level, are (coloured) blobs. In

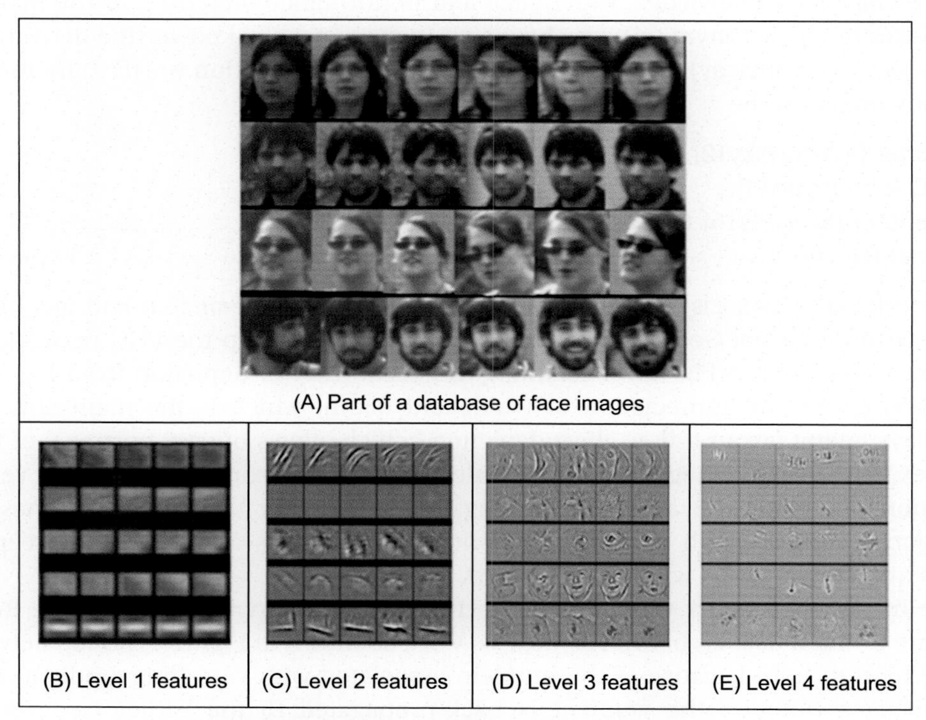

FIGURE 12.15 Features at different levels in deep learning.

the next layer (Fig. 12.15C) we find edges, these are collections of blobs. In the next layer (Fig. 12.15D) the edges are combined to give the shapes and in the last layer the context of the shapes is found. This is deep learning, and it is the way in which the results of Fig. 12.2 were determined. The manner of its operation is the order we have addressed image processing and computer vision throughout the book and is consistent with the operators that have previously been described.

12.5.2 Major deep learning architectures

Due to their innate complexity and the range of variation that is possible, there are many different architectures in deep learning. The main differences concern depth, width, and the use of different layers. A *shallow* network has few hidden layers, whereas a *deep* one has many. The width of a network describes the number of neurons in the layers, and width (as with depth) is often used as a comparative rather than an absolute description. The description that follows is by no means a definitive and absolute guide; our purpose at this stage is an introduction to deep learning architectures for feature extraction and computer vision. Increasing the depth and the width can improve classification performance until the increase leads to a number of parameters which is too large and stronger regularisation (inclusion of complexity in the minimisation function) is needed. There is no theory (yet?) to guide the selection of width and depth, and architectures are designed based on knowledge, experience and performance. Referring to the main architectures by the acronym or name by which they are usually known (the derivation is not always given anyway) the main architectures for classification (or flavours thereof) currently appear to be:

1. Alexnet [Krizhevsky12], as previously described;
2. *VGG* [Simonyan14];
3. *Inception* [Szegedy15] and
4. *Resnet* [He16].

The original Alexnet is now described as a shallow network since it had few hidden layers. Oxford's Visual Geometry Group went deeper to develop the VGG network. The network is depicted in Fig. 12.16 retaining the kebab-skewer depiction from Fig. 12.13 since this allows for appreciation of width and depth, which is the main aim here. Nowadays, many favour a flow chart depiction, which allows of easy portrayal of these complex networks. The network layers are described by horizontal resolution × vertical resolution × depth. There are (max) pooling layers as well as fully connected ones, and operation completes with a softmax function which allows association between the classes and the variables within the network.

The Inception network took the architecture deeper and wider whereas the Resnet structure is much deeper, but not as wide as VGG, as shown in Fig. 12.17. Deep networks can be hard to train because of the problem associated with vanishing gradient: when minimising a function the gradient is back-propagated to the earlier layers in the

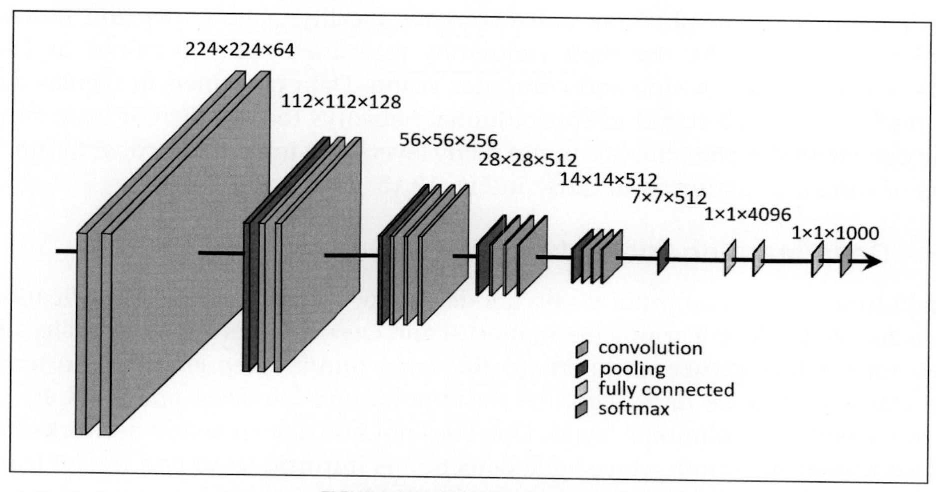

FIGURE 12.16 VGG architecture.

network, and the gradient can become very small (effectively vanishing). The version of Resnet shown here includes skip connections – or shortcuts – between the layers allowing the information to flow in many (different) ways and thus to maintain the integrity of the loss function within the network. The main architectures all contain fully connected layers at the output stage, whereas the All Convolutional Neural Network (All CNN) [Springenberg14], as by its name is all convolutional and lacks MLPs.

In the early days of deep learning, it was common for researchers to use a standard architecture which had been trained on similar data. The results in Fig. 12.2 were derived using a version of Resnet which had been pre-trained on the ILSVR2012 challenge data set and then applied and optimised on the new data set. As computational power increases, and as the techniques become better established with more support, a greater variety of architectures has started to abound. This is likely to increase.

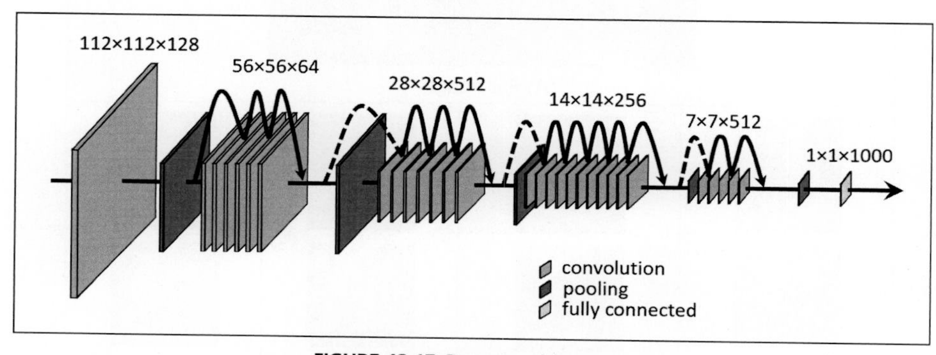

FIGURE 12.17 Resnet architecture.

It is evident that convolutional networks have locality, stationarity and multiscale properties. These are the invariant properties that are usually required in feature extraction in image processing and computer vision. Data presented in regular spatial structures is clearly well suited to convolutional networks too. As such, it is no surprise that the deep neural architectures contain many layers that implement convolution, with outputs of similar structure as to those in Fig. 12.15.

12.5.3 Deep learning for feature extraction

The main functions in computer vision are detection, localisation and classification, as can be achieved by deep learning [Sermanet13] and *Overfeat* offered a multiscale, sliding window approach (together with perhaps the worst pun in deep learning). In terms of feature extraction, as we have seen, the basic point and low-level operators are to be found in the early convolutional layers. One does not find a deep neural network offering edge detection as its output, since edge detection is intrinsic to an end to end learning process. We shall now pick out some new results via deep learning at many stages of feature extraction.

We shall start with the sensor: the micro-lens array in lightfield imaging (the sensor that includes depth perception, Section 1.4.1) can lead to low spatial resolution by sharing sensor functionality. This can be relieved by upsampling via a convolutional neural network [Gul18]. The architecture uses two convolutional layers of which 'the first layer extracts a high dimensional feature vector from the lenslet [image information] and the second convolution layer maps it onto another high-dimensional vector'. Fig. 12.18

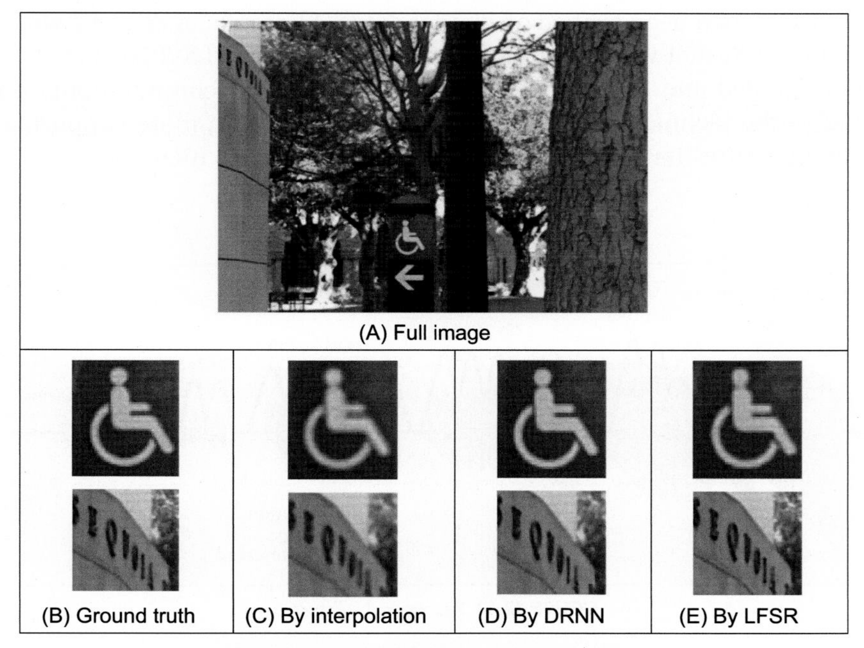

(A) Full image

(B) Ground truth (C) By interpolation (D) By DRNN (E) By LFSR

FIGURE 12.18 Lightfield image resizing [Gul18].

illustrates the result of applying the network (LFSR) in comparison with ground truth, a traditional method using interpolation, and another deep learning approach (DRNN). Clearly both deep learning results Figs. 12.18C–D approach the ground truth Fig. 12.18A, better than the traditional approach Fig. 12.18C.

The study in [Gul18] led to a method for image denoising. This has been a popular target for new deep learning approaches, since it is a standard problem as exposed in Section 3.5. [Zhang17] modified the VGG network [Simonyan14] for image denoising and set the depth of the network based on the patch sizes that had proved effective in state-of-art denoising methods, removing all pooling layers and using a residual learning formulation. In comparison with (traditional) transform-domain collaborative filtering applied to a noisy image Fig. 12.19A, both results have clearly improved clarity considerably, Figs. 12.19B–C. The differences between the areas of detail are perhaps best examined with a projector (or a microscope) though the signal-to-noise ratios on Figs. 12.19A–C are 14.8, 26.2, 26.9 dB, respectively. The advantage might appear small, but it could be crucial in some applications.

For object detection, one approach used convolutional networks [Girshick16] to propose regions which were then combined with CNNs thus bridging the gap between image classification and object detection. A sub issue was that the approach could handle a limited amount of training data, but that is a learning problem rather than a feature extraction one. The first stage generated region proposals from the input image, extracting a fixed-length feature vector from each proposal using a CNN, and then classified each region with category-specific linear SVMs. Anisotropic image scaling is used to compute a fixed-size CNN input from each region proposal. The approach used Alexnet and the first layers extracted edges and colour information, and these were grouped in later layers. The output of the final convolutional layer is shown in Fig. 12.20A together with the activation values which – amongst the top activations – shows units

(A) Image with added noise

(B) Denoising by transform domain

(C) Denoising by modified VGG

FIGURE 12.19 Image denoising [Zhang17].

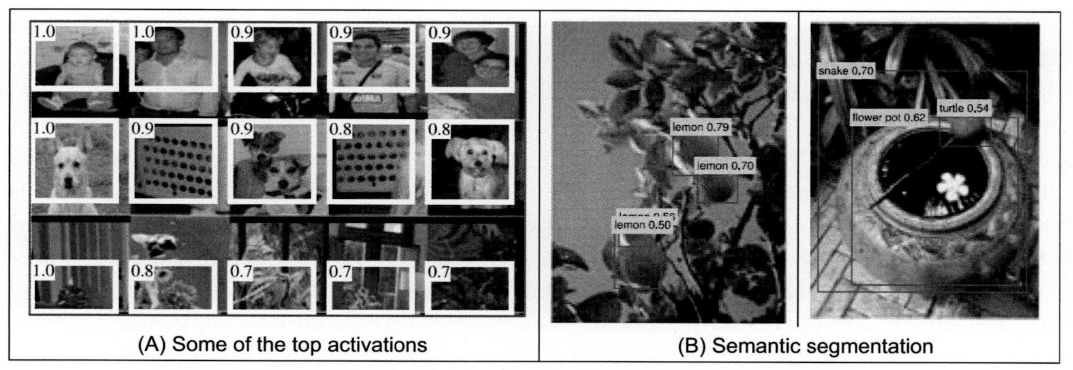

FIGURE 12.20 Object extraction by region-based convolutional networks [Girshick16].

detecting human faces, faces of dogs and red blobs. The final semantic segmentation is shown in Fig. 12.20B which shows the power of these new approaches.

Fig. 12.21 shows an example from the system previously shown in Fig. 12.2 which classes people by their gender and age [Martinho-Corbishley19]. Note that neither can be perceived directly in the image by human vision as the face is obscured (one of this book's authors is amongst the subjects and pleasingly – though erroneously – estimated to be 45 years old). The classification is achieved by soft biometric attributes (and many more than are shown here as the approach is aimed to identify people when their face and other conventional identifying attributes are obscured) that were originally derived by human vision then clarified by machine learning and classified by deep learning, via the Resnet architecture.

FIGURE 12.21 Classifying people by their gender and age.

There are many more examples of deep learning replicating and improving on feature extraction methods that have been described earlier, including active contours [Marcos18, Rupprecht16], and there are many usages in automatic face recognition, such as the excellent Hyperface system [Ranjan2019]. Given the power and speed, one expects this area to increase.

12.5.4 Deep learning performance evaluation

One advantage still enjoyed by traditional handcrafted measures is that it is possible and easy to find evidence of how and why techniques operate to success. With machine learning, this is clearly a more complicated task, as one can reasonably ask: precisely, what has the system learnt? This is a more complex task with deep learning, since the structures are massively more complex. There is natural interest in how any system works, as shown by investigations as to the performance of the layers in deep architectures, previously shown in Figs. 12.15 and 12.20. This might be critical in some domains such as finance and image domains such as medicine and security. For robust evidence we need to know the likely error to assess the significance of any result. That is basic science: results should have error bars. As one study notes 'these highly successful machine learning and artificial intelligence models are usually applied in a black box manner, i.e., no information is provided about what exactly makes them arrive at their predictions' [Samek17]. In another study we find 'deep neural networks obtain high discrimination power at the cost of a low interpretability of their black-box representations' [Zhang18]. It is more than just the significance of misclassification, there might be bias inherent in the processes used in system development. This is *interpretability*, and much needs to be done. One way is to visualise of image classification models say by saliency maps [Symonyan14] and another is to derive insight into the functionality of a network's layers and into the classifier's operation [Zeiler14]. One legal approach, motivated by the EU General Data Protection Regulation, argues that given 'a right to explanation that opens the 'black box' of algorithmic decision-making faces major legal and technical barriers' [Wachter17], then it is not actually necessary given that explanations which lead to decisions one can understand the basis on which they are made. This is not phrased in terms of deep learning but suggests that if the decisions are to be used, then it is more complex than simply training, testing and applying a technique. Given the enormous progress to date we look forward to the future advances in architecture, understanding and performance of deep learning.

12.6 Further reading

There is also a vast body of work on pattern classification and on deep learning, for this is the sphere of machine learning. Given that we are in the middle of a revolution and many people are working to develop new techniques, there will doubtless be many changes in the future. It is unlikely that the detected features will change, more that the range of the features detected in deep learning will extend to take advantage of invariant properties exposed earlier in this book. Beyond the texts already cited here, have a look for the Proceedings of the Neural Information Processing Conference: NeurIPS/NIPS or the International Conference on Learning Representations (ICLR). These are the top international conferences in machine learning, and you will find state-of-art papers there. For vision-based learning approaches, many of the conferences listed earlier in Section 1.6.1 have new papers in these fields.

This is the world of image processing and computer vision. Much of our life now depends on computer vision and thus on feature extraction. That is why this text has concentrated on feature extraction in image processing and computer vision, for no practical vision-based system can exist without it. The techniques might be buried in a network or explicit in the maths; they are still there. We finish here: we hope you enjoyed the book and will find it useful in your career or study. Certainly have a look at our website, https://www.southampton.ac.uk/~msn/book/, as you will find more material there. Do not hesitate to send us your comments or any suggestions. À bientôt! ¡Hasta pronto!

References

[Bishop96] Bishop, C. M., *Neural Networks for Pattern Recognition*, Oxford University Press, 1996.

[Cha02] Cha, S. H., and Srihari, S. N., On Measuring the Distance between Histograms, *Pattern Recognition*, **35**(6), pp 1355-1370, 2002.

[Cherkassky 98] Cherkassky, V., and Mulier, F., Learning from Data, Wiley, NY, 1998.

[Forsyth02] Forsyth, D., and Ponce, J., Computer Vision: A Modern Approach, Prentice Hall, NJ, USA, 2002.

[de Freitas18] de Freitas Pereira, T., Anjos, A., and Marcel, S., Heterogeneous Face Recognition Using Domain Specific Units, *IEEE Transactions on Information Forensics and Security*, **14**(7), pp 1803–1816, 2018.

[Girshick16] Girshick, R., Donahue, J., Darrell, T., and Malik, J., Region-based Convolutional Networks for Accurate Object Detection and Segmentation, *IEEE Transactions on PAMI*, **38**(1), pp 142–158, 2016.

[Gul18] Gul, M. S. K., and Gunturk, B. K., 2018, Spatial and Angular Resolution Enhancement of Light Fields Using Convolutional Neural Networks, *IEEE Transactions on IP*, **27**(5), pp 2146-2159.

[He16] He, K., Zhang, X., Ren, S., and Sun, J., Deep Residual Learning for Image Recognition, *Proceedings of IEEE CVPR*, pp 770-778, 2016.

[Jain97] Jain, A. K., and Zongker, D., Feature Selection: Evaluation, Application and Small Sample Performance, *IEEE Transactions on PAMI*, **19**(2), pp 153-158, 1997.

[Jain00] Jain, A. K., Duin, R. P. W., and Mao, J., Statistical Pattern Recognition: a Review, *IEEE Transactions on PAMI*, **22**(1), pp 4-37, 2000.

[Krizhevsky12] Krizhevsky, A., Sutskever, I., and Hinton, G.E., Imagenet Classification with Deep Convolutional Neural Networks, *Proceedings of Advances in Neural Information Processing Systems*, pp 1097-1105, 2012.

[Kim02] Kim, K. I., Jung K., Park, S. H., and Kim, H. J., Support Vector Machines for Texture Classification, *IEEE Transactions on PAMI*, **24**(11), pp 1542-1550, 2002.

[Kittler98a] Kittler, J., Hatef, M., Duin, R. P. W., and Matas, J., On Combining Classifiers, *IEEE Transactions on PAMI*, **20**(3), pp 226-239, 1998.

[Kittler98b] Kittler, J., Combining Classifiers: a Theoretical Framework, *Pattern Analysis & Applications*, **1**(1), pp 18-27, 1998.

[Lachenbruch68] Lachenbruch, P. A., and Mickey, M. R., Estimation of Error Rates in Discriminant Analysis, *Technometrics*, **10**, pp 1-11, 1968.

[LeCun98] LeCun, Y., Bottou, L., Bengio, Y., and Haffner, P., Gradient-based Learning Applied to Document Recognition, *Proceedings of the IEEE*, **86**(11), pp.2278-2324, 1998.

[LeCun15] LeCun, Y., Bengio, Y., and Hinton, G., Deep Learning, *Nature*, **521**(7553) pp 436–444, 2015.

[Ling07] Ling, H., and Okada, K., An Efficient Earth Mover's Distance Algorithm for Robust Histogram Comparison, *IEEE Transactions on PAMI*, **29**(5), pp 840-853, 2007.

[Marcos18] Marcos, D., Tuia, D., Kellenberger, B., Zhang, L., Bai, M., Liao, R., and Urtasun, R., Learning Deep Structured Active Contours End-To-End, In *Proceedings of the IEEE Conference on Computer Vision and Pattern Recognition* (pp. 8877-8885), 2018.

[Martinho-Corbishley19] Martinho-Corbishley, D., Nixon, M. S., and Carter, J. N., 2018, Super-fine Attributes with Crowd Prototyping, *IEEE Transactions on PAMI*, **41**(6), pp 1486-1500, 2019.

[Michie94] Michie, D., Spiegelhalter, D. J., and Taylor, C. C., Eds.: *Machine Learning, Neural and Statistical Classification*, Ellis Horwood, Hemel Hempstead UK, 1994.

[Prince12] Prince, S. J. D., *Computer Vision Models, Learning, and Inference*, Cambridge University Press, Cambridge, UK, 2012.

[Ranjan2019] Ranjan, R., Patel, V. M., and Chellappa, R., Hyperface: A Deep Multi-Task Learning Framework for Face Detection, Landmark Localization, Pose Estimation, and Gender Recognition, *IEEE Transactions on PAMI*, **41**(1), pp 121-135, 2019.

[Rubner00] Rubner, Y., Tomasi, C., and Guibas, L. J., The Earth Mover's Distance as a Metric for Image Retrieval, *International Journal of Computer Vision*, **40**(2), pp 99-121, 2000.

[Rupprecht16] Rupprecht, C., Huaroc, E., Baust, M., and Navab, N., *Deep Active Contours*, arXiv preprint arXiv:1607.05074, 2016.

[Russakovsky15] Russakovsky, O., Deng, J., Su, et al., Imagenet Large Scale Visual Recognition Challenge, *International Journal of Computer Vision*, **115**(3), pp 211–252, 2015.

[Samek17] Samek, W., Wiegand, T., and Müller, K. R., *Explainable Artificial Intelligence: Understanding, Visualizing and Interpreting Deep Learning Models*, arXiv preprint arXiv:1708.08296, 2017.

[Sermanet13] Sermanet, P., Eigen, D., Zhang, X., Mathieu, M., Fergus, R., and LeCun, Y., *Overfeat: Integrated Recognition, Localization and Detection Using Convolutional Networks*, arXiv preprint arXiv:1312.6229, 2013.

[Shawe-Taylor04] Shawe-Taylor, J., and Cristianini, N., *Kernel Methods for Pattern Analysis*, Cambridge University Press, 2004.

[Simonyan14] Simonyan, K., and Zisserman, A., *Very Deep Convolutional Networks for Large-Scale Image Recognition*, arXiv preprint arXiv:1409.1556, 2014.

[Symonyan14] Simonyan, K., Vedaldi, A., and Zisserman, A., *Deep inside Convolutional Networks: Visualising Image Classification Models and Saliency Maps*, arXiv preprint arXiv:1312.6034, 2013.

[Springenberg14] Springenberg, J. T., Dosovitskiy, A., Brox, T., and Riedmiller, M., *Striving for Simplicity: The All Convolutional Net*, arXiv preprint arXiv:1412.6806, 2014.

[Szegedy15] Szegedy, C., Liu, W., Jia, Y., Sermanet, P., Reed, S., Anguelov, D., Erhan, D., Vanhoucke, V., and Rabinovich, A., Going Deeper with Convolutions, *Proceedings of IEEE CVPR*, 2015.

[Szeliski11] Szeliski, R., *Computer Vision: Algorithms and Applications*, Springer Verlag, London UK, 2011.

[Vapnik95] Vapnik, V., *The Nature of Statistical Learning Theory*, Springer-Verlag, New York, 1995.

[Wachter17] Wachter, S., Mittelstadt, B., and Russell, C., Counterfactual Explanations without Opening the Black Box: Automated Decisions and the GDPR, *Harvard Journal of Law and Technology*, **31**(2), 52 pp, 2017.

[Zeiler14] Zeiler, M.D., and Fergus, R., Visualizing and Understanding Convolutional Networks, *Proceedings of ECCV*, pp 818-833, 2014.

[Zhang17] Zhang, K., Zuo, W., Chen, Y., Meng, D., and Zhang, L., Beyond a Gaussian Denoiser: Residual Learning of Deep CNN for Image Denoising, *IEEE Transactions on IP*, **26**(7), pp 3142-3155, 2017.

[Zhang18] Zhang, Q. S., and Zhu, S. C., Visual Interpretability for Deep Learning: a Survey, *Frontiers of Information Technology & Electronic Engineering*, **19**(1), pp.27-39, 2018.

[Zhou92] Zhou, Y-T, and Chellappa, R., *Artificial Neural Networks for Computer Vision*, Springer, NY, USA, 1992.

Index

'*Note:* Page numbers followed by "t" indicate tables and "f" indicate figures.'

C

E

H

I

M

N

Printed in the United States
By Bookmasters